D0142291

# COMPUTER GRAPHICS:

## THE PRINCIPLES BEHIND THE ART AND SCIENCE

CORNEL K. POKORNY
CALIFORNIA POLYTECHNIC STATE UNIVERSITY
SAN LUIS OBISPO

CURTIS F. GERALD
CALIFORNIA POLYTECHNIC STATE UNIVERSITY
SAN LUIS OBISPO

**Franklin, Beedle & Associates**
4521 Campus Drive, 327
Irvine, California 92715-9877
(714) 552-4155

Publisher: James F. Leisy, Jr.
Manuscript Editor: Sheryl Rose
Text Design: Cathy Rundell
Cover Design: Neo Nova
Composition: Graphic Typesetting Service
Project Coordination: Dan Tabata, Julia Wright



Franklin, Beedle & Associates
4521 Campus Drive, #327
Irvine, California 92715-9877

*Printed in the United States of America*
*by W. A. Krueger Company*

**Library of Congress Cataloging-in-Publication Data**

Pokorny, Cornel, 1941-
Computer graphics : the principles behind the art and science / Cornel Pokorny and Curtis Gerald.
p. cm.
Bibliography: p.
Includes index.
ISBN 0-938661-08-6
1. Computer graphics. I. Gerald, Curtis, 1915- . II. Title.
T385.P65 1988
006.6--dc19 88-30719
CIP

# Table of Contents

## 8

## OTHER CURVES & SURFACE PATCHES 258



## 9

## LIGHT and COLOR 299

# Preface

This book has been written for students majoring in computer science, engineering, or mathematics; and developers of computer graphics systems. It is intended to give users of graphics software the principles behind the art and science. Prerequisites for the material covered within include a working knowledge of both college level mathematics and a computer programming language.

Computer graphics is one of the most important applications of computers. Computer generated graphics are used in such diverse areas as displaying the results of engineering and scientific computations, producing television commercials, illuminating statistical data, generating the images for space movies, showing word processing documents as they will appear on paper, and computer-aided design. Consequently, the subject matter of this book is broad and combines elements of computer hardware and software, mathematics and numerical methods, art, and complex data structures.

The special features of this book are an emphasis on raster-scan technology rather than vector-scan techniques, completeness of coverage, full development of topics with comparison of alternative algorithms, and thorough review and explanation of the mathematics involved. Rather than discussing hardware as a separate topic, explanations of hardware are dispersed throughout the book where they are appropriate to the discussion of a graphics operation. Algorithms are initially implemented in Pascal and later in pseudocode.

Chapter 1 introduces computer graphics, gives an overview of the book, and reviews the mathematics required. Chapters 2 and 3 explain how lines, polygons, circles and ellipses can be drawn on a computer screen. Chapter 4 covers clipping of images to fit a window and algorithms for doing it. Transforming images is the subject of Chapter 5; Chapter 6 covers projections of three-dimensional objects on to the screen. In Chapters 7 and 8, curves and surfaces are discussed. Chapter 9 deals with color and color systems while Chapter 10 explains the fascinating topic of fractals. The more difficult subject of how a three-dimensional object can be shown realistically on a two-dimensional screen is developed in Chapters 11, 12, 13, 14, and 15. These chapters cover the topics of hidden line and hidden surface removal, reflections and shading, and surface mapping and ray tracing. Chapter 16 goes into techniques for animation.

The final chapter, Chapter 17, returns to a fuller description of the computer applications that were mentioned in Chapter 1. The emphasis in this concluding chapter is on the interaction between users and the graphics system. This interaction is especially dependent upon graphic standards (CORE, GKS, and PHIGS), so they are discussed here.

There is more in this book than can be covered in a one-term course. Depending on the intent of the instructor and the interests of the students, a judicious selection of topics to cover can be readily made. We suggest that it is essential to cover all of Chapter 2, most of Chapter 4, and all of Chapters 5 and 6.

We want to acknowledge the gracious support of our wives and families during the period when they lost us to this project. Jim Leisy was very helpful in the development of this project. Sheryl Rose did a superb job of editing the final manuscript. Work was contributed, particularly in the form of computer generated pictures, by Adrian Brandt, Hsueh-Mei Hsu and Ahmad Motiei, all from Cal Poly.

We thank the following people whose constructive reviews of the manuscript improved the book:

Edward Angel (University of New Mexico)
Brian Barsky (University of California, Berkeley)
Alfred Bork (University of California, Irvine)
Lorraine Callahan (Northern Arizona University)
Larre Egbert (Utah State University)
Morris Firebaugh (University of Wisconsin, Parkside)

Margaret Fitting (San Jose State University)
Lee Hill (Southern Oregon State University)
Nick Mousouris (California State University, Fullerton)
J. Denbigh Starkey (Montana State University)
Jim Wixom (Fort Lewis College)

C. K. P.
C. F. G.
San Luis Obispo
September, 1988

# Introduction

# 1

Each chapter of this book begins with a short overview to help prepare you for the material.

Chapter 1 tells why computer graphics is important, discusses a number of its applications, gives an overview of the book, and concludes with a summary of the mathematics knowledge that we expect you to have. The chapter is divided into four major sections.

**1.1 Importance of Computer Graphics** gives some reasons why you should know about computer graphics. The section discusses developments in computer systems that made it feasible to display information pictorially.

**1.2 Computer Graphics Applications** include paint systems, word processing, desktop publishing, business graphics, computer-aided design, and flight simulation. One of the earliest widespread applications was in computer games. The section ends with a definition of graphics primitives.

**1.3 Overview of the Book** lists the major topics of each chapter of the book to show the progression of ideas.

**1.4 Mathematics Background** is a summary of the variety of mathematical topics that we expect you to know. If you feel weak in any of these areas, check the appendix, which provides a tutorial.

# 1.1 IMPORTANCE OF COMPUTER GRAPHICS

Computer graphics—the art of creating pictures with a computer—is of great importance. Starting from tentative beginnings, it has continued to evolve until now it is widely used and available to nearly all computer users. Some decades ago, someone first had the idea of using a computer-controlled output device to produce something that resembled a picture; today, we can create elaborate, animated graphics, but that progress has been slow. Driven by the age-old desire to convey information through pictures, we are at last successful in building meaningful computer images. This has created a paraphrase of the adage: "A picture is worth more than a thousand words."

In the beginning, communication with the computer took place through decks of punched cards and by line-printer output—awkward at best and often time consuming. An improvement over this was the printing terminal. Up to this point communication accompanied by pictures was impossible, except by carefully arranging dots and asterisks. When the CRT replaced the slow printing terminal, the production of pictures was theoretically possible but seldom done, due to the need for a large amount of memory and data transfer. It took another major step—the development of the personal computer—for computer graphics to become popular.

One of the authors remembers the time, some 20 years past, when the decision about the university's mainframe rested on its ability to create graphic output on a vector CRT. Little did we know that using the device would require the dedication of the mainframe system. It just didn't have the power to do anything else when it was computing the graphics image. We thought, at that time, that 512K bytes was a large memory—it was certainly all we could afford!

The development of the personal computer was accompanied by drastically lower prices for hardware. With inexpensive memory, a low-cost but powerful processor, and cheap peripheral chips, the personal computer has given us more power than that mainframe. And it sits on a desktop! It has created a hardware environment that puts computer graphics within the reach of everyone. However, we still do not really know how to have the user interact effectively through a graphics interface, nor can users create pictures in a truly "friendly" way. In two-dimensional graphics, present-day paint systems are setting a de facto standard, but for three-dimensional work, everything is still rudimentary. It all rests with the development of graphics software. That is what this book is all about.

**Graphics Interfaces** The importance of pictorial information has long been recognized. We are visually oriented creatures; our visual perception is highly developed and extremely powerful. This makes a graphics interface attractive. It took hardware advances to make a graphics interface commonplace. No longer must we communicate with the computer by typing cryptic commands and receiving cryptic messages in return. The Apple Macintosh is possibly the most readily recognized example. Its windowing environment, drop-down menus and icons, and, significantly, its mouse-driven cursor have set the pattern for the two-dimensional graphics interface found in most present-day computers. Using the mouse implements a method of human-computer interaction that depends highly on optical feedback and on the visual perception of motion, and that operates in a fashion strikingly similar to the way a human hand grabs something. It is ergonomically far superior to text-oriented interaction.

## 1.2 COMPUTER GRAPHICS APPLICATIONS

Above all, computer graphics is applications oriented. From its beginnings, developers of computer graphics have used it to solve problems that require more than just words as output. The first application was in an area that may seem trivial but is not: a system that permits the user to draw on the screen. Ivan Sutherland's Sketchpad (SUTH63) showed that computers could be used interactively to produce graphic output on a CRT display. This early use of graphics to draw on the screen has grown into elaborate systems that permit all of us, amateurs as well as professionals, to become artists. The term we now use for such interactive programs is *paint system.*

**Paint Systems** The use of graphics interfaces is the hallmark of the new desktop computers, a major milestone in personal computing. But making the basic communication between human and computer more pictorial is just one example of the application of computer graphics. Another is the wide variety of paint systems available for the home computer. These are programs that allow the user to produce simple pictures that resemble but in many respects surpass the potential one has when drawing with pencil on paper. Such pictures are visible on the screen immediately, and can also be printed out on paper using the ubiquitous and inexpensive dot matrix printer.

MacPaint, running on the Apple Macintosh, was one of the early paint programs, soon followed by many others: Degas and Degas-Elite on the Atari ST, others for the Amiga and IBM-type PCs. Remarkably, these paint systems required no upgrade to the hardware; they ran on the computer literally as it came from the box. This was possible because the computers had enough memory to use a *bit-mapped* display method. (We will explain this term in Chapter 2.) The original IBM PC did not have such a large memory and its user interface is not graphic. As a consequence, it could accommodate a paint system only with added hardware. The newer IBM PS/2 units have an enlarged memory space and use bit-mapped graphics, joining the other brands in providing the hardware for excellent user-friendly graphics. This move by IBM underscores the importance of graphics capabilities.

**Word Processing** Word processing has long been an important use of computers, especially desktop machines. Here too, graphics has made a contribution, allowing the incorporation of pictures in the document. No longer must pictures be cut out and pasted into every new printout. The authors of this book have used such a system. These systems can be considered as something in between mere text word processors and the systems used for desktop publishing.

**Desktop Publishing** A desktop publishing system provides a complete way to produce printed information. What you see is what you get, meaning that the screen shows exactly what will appear in the printed output. (This is sometimes written as WYSIWYG). Such systems make much more thorough use of graphics principles and allow text and pictures to be changed in size as well as to be cut and pasted. These features make systems complex. They may require so much memory that even the latest desktop computers need some hardware upgrade to accommodate them. A difference between these systems and ordinary word processors with graphics capabilities is the way that hard copy is produced on dot matrix printers. Word processors use the text mode of the printer to print text, switching to graphics mode to print the pictures. A desktop publishing system prints everything, text included, in graphics mode. This is possible only through the use of a bit-mapped display, certainly the display method of the future. (An exception to this is the PostScript-compatible printer. When working with such a printer, the desktop publishing system sends character codes, not bit maps, for the text. These are transformed into bit maps by the printer's own highly sophisticated character generator.)

In Chapter 17 we will describe these popular applications of graphics in some detail. They are all interactive systems that give the user the benefit of pictorial expression without requiring him or her to have any knowledge about the underlying techniques and without requiring any programming. Every system strives to make the presentation, creation, and use of graphics as user friendly as possible. Of course, there are many views of "user friendliness"; this explains the differences in the user-to-computer interaction among the various systems.

**Business Graphics** Marketing is the key to success in business, and graphs, charts, and other displays of information are used increasingly to make the message forceful and emphatic. The presentation of complex ideas, especially those represented by lots of numbers, is facilitated by a well-designed bar chart, line graph, or pie chart. The use of color and three-dimensional forms makes these most attractive. Figure 1.1 shows two simple examples.

One graphic can combine several relationships, for example, showing sales by state as stacked bars superimposed on a map. The vertical bar can be subdivided into colors to show the relative importance for separate customer classes, giving a vivid visual impression of the classes that are most significant in each state. On a CRT display, animation can add impact, for example, calling attention to one slice of a pie chart by moving it in and out of the pie. At the same time, text can be displayed to provide further explanation of the idea that is being presented. Sound can be coordinated with the images. Color, motion, pictures, and sound all combine to get the message across.

Similar types of graphics applications are important in scientific presentations, in education, in publishing, in fact, whenever the need is to inform, teach, impress, or sell.

**Computer-Aided Design** One of the most important commercial applications of computer graphics is computer-aided design (CAD). CAD systems allow for speedy, easy design of buildings, mechanical systems, floor plans, or electronic circuit boards. Manpower savings are significant, especially when making revisions to the original design.

CAD has been a driving force in several computer hardware developments. But large-scale CAD requires expensive hardware and software. The underlying computer graphics theory is more complicated and of a different nature than that used in paint systems or desktop publishing systems because of the need to portray objects defined in three dimensions. A number of personal computer-based CAD systems have been developed that continue to approach large-scale CAD in capabilities, but as they grow in power, so do the mainframe-based systems, keeping a large gap between the two.

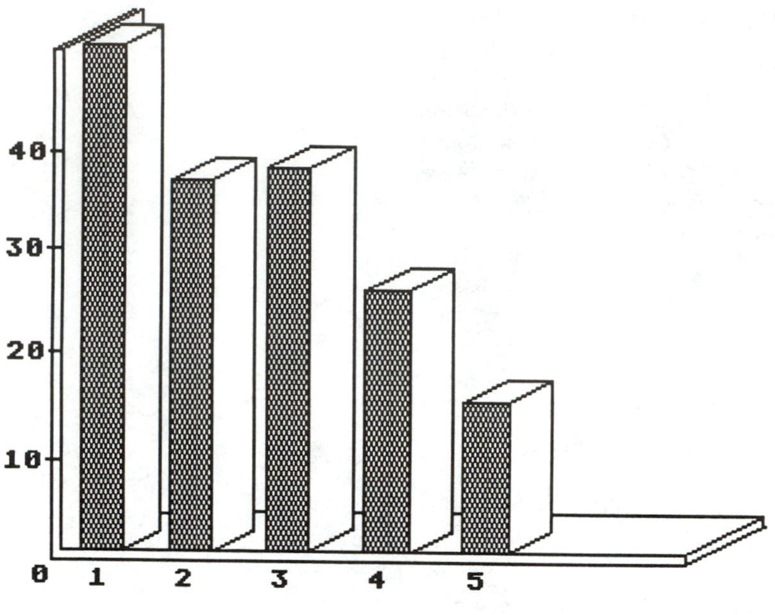


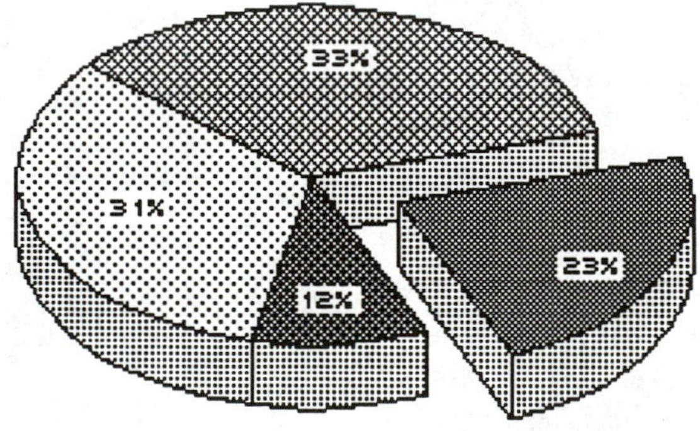


FIGURE 1.1

CAD systems try to be "user friendly"—one is not required to know the algorithms or to do any programming—but one still must have a thorough knowledge of the geometric and mathematical essentials that underly the design of the objects as well as the special commands that manipulate the drawing. The system's very power creates considerable complexity in the user interface itself; mastering a CAD system can only be accomplished after a long learning phase. The complexity of the underlying system, however, is even greater.

The development of CAD is a good example of the interplay between hardware and software development in computer graphics. The notion that a line is the basic element in creating pictures led to the early development of vector scan devices. These in turn led to algorithms for hidden line removal, still important for plotters, which are also vector devices. Vector scan technology was later surpassed by raster scan technology which is in many respects more powerful. Raster scanning permits solid modeling, which is becoming essential in CAD systems. This book will explain these algorithms and the hardware in detail.

**Flight Simulation** Another major application of computer graphics is for flight simulation. While flight simulation is of value only to a special class of users, it is so important for the training of pilots that a broad market is unnecessary. It affords great savings in fuel and aircraft, provides a safe learning environment, and can give the neophyte pilot experience in landing at many airports without leaving the ground. This application has led to the development of specialized hardware and software, with a strong emphasis on animation techniques. Custom electronic chips and highly parallel processing are employed to get the speeds needed for real-time simulation. But these systems are costly; prices are in the millions of dollars.

Even though much of the computations for flight simulation is done in hardware, the algorithmic principles are the same as those described in this book. Interestingly, quite realistic flight simulation is available for personal computers, though this application is more in the nature of a game. Figure 1.2 shows a simplified example; when presented in color and with changes of the landscape that simulate the actual approach of the plane to the runway, the result is most dramatic.

**Computer Games** Computer arcade games such as Pac-Man, Donkey-Kong, and others have contributed considerably to the popularity of computer graphics. The early ones produced only flat, two-dimensional graphics but later versions show excellent renditions of three-dimensional objects. Animation is a standard component. Custom-built hardware and sprites are used to achieve the speed necessary for their spectacular effects. Remarkably, these games don't use sophisticated graphics algorithms. They are interesting mainly from the standpoint of the digital electronic engineer. Almost all of them use color raster displays. Similar games that run on home computers are usually not as fast, because they lack the hardware support of the arcade games. But some of the newer home computers have programmable sprites which can speed up two-dimensional animation of certain kinds. We will discuss this in more detail later.

FIGURE 1.2

**"Pure" Computer Graphics** The area we call "pure" computer graphics is where this new science is being pushed to its limits. Algorithms and models are being developed to allow new rendering and shading techniques and new color effects. More challenging tasks are assumed and new hardware is designed and tested. Here, the concept of a "user" of the graphics system doesn't fit; the graphics artist must understand the mathematical background, master algorithmic details, be able to program everything to the last semicolon, cope with and understand the special hardware. There is no graphics package or system that can be purchased to help in the creation of the picture that resides in the mind of this advanced graphics artist.

This is the area in which the most beautiful and breathtaking displays are produced; the area in which complicated computations have to be performed and gigantic computers run for hours to produce a single frame; in which the graphics primitive is just a single pixel; where fractal landscapes of strange beauty are created or fragile looking-glass spheres float in space, penetrating and circling each other, reflecting and refracting the scene on their shiny surfaces. It is the area in which animated scenes are created that cannot be observed in reality—a medium that is a new art. But this area, too, has an application in the field of TV commercials and space movies. We will cover the most important aspects of such "pure" graphics.

Computer graphics has become such a diverse and complex discipline that it cannot be mastered in a short time, such as a quarter or a semester. Nor can this book cover the whole field, though it will provide a reasonably broad and thorough base of information and will give you many opportunities to practice the material.

This book will introduce you to the essentials of what you must know to be knowledgeable in computer graphics: mathematical background, a variety of algorithms, examples of programming, and some of the concepts behind the special hardware of graphics. A computer scientist is not expected just to use a graphics system. He or she must design the systems of the future.

**Graphics Primitives** Remarkably, this great variety of graphics applications does not mean that there is a similar great variety of elements with which to create them. In fact, everything is constructed from three basic "atoms" of computer graphics. We call these elemental structures *graphics primitives.* The most basic of all is the *pixel,* short for picture element. A pixel is a point of light on the computer's display screen, essentially a dot of very small size. Plotters and other output devices often do things differently, but they all can print or plot a dot.

The next important graphics primitive is the *line.* On a raster device, it is created by a sequence of closely spaced dots. A vector device draws a line continuously. In any case, a line is a primitive because we need to think of it and treat it as a unit, something not subdivisible into smaller pieces.

The third and last graphics primitive is the *polygon,* a plane figure of more than two sides. We will define the polygon in greater detail in Chapter 2, but it, too, is a primitive because of the need to treat it as a single entity.

From these three graphics primitives, single pixels, lines, and polygons, all the images that you see in computer graphics can be constructed. The only one that is strongly hardware based is the pixel. We will assume that the system has a command, probably at the lowest level of system design, that sets a pixel at a given location on the screen. The command that we will use to do this is:

```
SetPix(x,y);
```

where x and y are appropriate coordinates that specify the location on the screen.

# 1.3 OVERVIEW OF THE BOOK

In every scientific discipline, several solutions often exist for a particular problem and computer graphics is no exception. This is demonstrated by the fact that usually several different algorithms exist to produce a given graphic image. The various algorithms have different strengths and weaknesses. The circumstances of a particular problem may make one algorithm more efficient than another even when both can do the job.

In most of the chapters of this book, we present more than one method for the solution of a common problem. For example, in the chapters about scan conversion there are four procedures for drawing a straight line as well as four for doing circles and several more for ellipses and polygons. This can present a problem for you, the reader. You may wish to get an overview of them all and then choose to learn just one. But if you are willing to make the effort to learn all of them, you will acquire a more thorough understanding.

We have still made a selection from among the many algorithms that have been developed, choosing from among the most important of the established methods those that don't depend on difficult mathematics. Some that we have excluded because they are based on difficult mathematics include the Oslo algorithm used in ray tracing B-spline and other surfaces (Riesenfeld, Sweeney, Bartels), β-splines (Barsky), some of the newer shading and reflectance models (Blinn, Cook, Torrance, etc.), certain methods for fractal generation (Voss), scan line algorithms for curved surfaces (Blinn, Lane, Whitted, etc.).

While hardware is very important in computer graphics and some hardware items are constructed expressly for graphic output, you will not find a separate chapter on hardware. The reason for this is that hardware and software interact so strongly in computer graphics that neither can be considered alone. Whenever a knowledge of hardware is essential for the understanding of certain functions or algorithms, we will present the details in the context of the discussion, sometimes in sidebars.

Formal descriptions of algorithms, titled "coded algorithm," are done in Pascal. Sometimes a semiformal description in pseudocode is given instead or in addition, when the detailed formal description by itself might be confusing or when it doesn't illuminate the essentials. You are expected to have some familiarity with Pascal.

There are three ways in which this book differs from most other computer graphics texts. It gives a more complete survey of the field and covers some important modern topics that often are treated in less detail. It includes discussions of hardware on a "need to know" basis. And the treatment of required mathematical background does not assume that you are already knowledgeable about everything that we will discuss.

Each chapter starts with a description of its contents. Exercises at the end of all the chapters will expand and solidify your understanding. You should do most of them.

Chapter 1 contains general information and introduces the notion of a graphics primitive, the first and most basic thing to learn in computer graphics. The chapter summarizes the mathematics used later in the book.

Chapter 2 covers scan conversion for straight lines and polygons. Scan conversion is the process of converting the graphic image so it can be displayed on a raster display. It explains how two important graphics primitives—straight lines and polygons—are made visible on a raster CRT.

Chapter 3 continues the discussion of scan conversion to include circular and elliptical arcs. While most curved lines are drawn in computer graphics as a sequence of connected short straight lines, these curves are used frequently and are simple enough to be drawn directly.

Chapter 4 is about windowing and clipping, fundamental even for simple computer graphics. It introduces the concept of real-world or user coordinates versus absolute device coordinates, the transformations required to relate these, the concept of a window, and some algorithms that clip an image to fit a window.

Chapter 5 is an excursion into a more mathematically oriented area. This chapter explains the two- and three-dimensional transformations that display an object in an orientation different from its original description. Such transformations allow for changes in the location of the objects or in our viewing position. Here, for the first time, we work in three-dimensional space using vectors and matrices. Realizing that not every student has a strong mathematical background in vectors and matrices, we have given an introduction to this subject not only in this chapter but in the appendix as well. In addition, there is a summary/review below.

Chapter 6 deals with projections and three-dimensional windowing and clipping. Projections are essential for all three-dimensional objects because we must display all spatial objects on a medium that has only two dimensions. We have to create a picture, just as in every painting or drawing. A projection is basically the flattening of a volume into a two-dimensional plane, the display surface. It can be compared to the shadow that an object in space casts on a wall, except that we do not lose colors and other characteristics of the object. Three-dimensional windowing and clipping is included in this chapter because of its close relationship to projections.

Chapter 7 introduces a group of techniques for drawing plane curves. These are presented through parameterized equations. In this chapter we explain how splines can serve as a basis for drawing two-dimensional curves. There are several variations.

Chapter 8 continues the discussion of plane curves to cover Catmull-Rom curves and Bezier curves. In addition, the chapter explains the construction of curved surfaces by procedures based on the various types of plane curves.

Chapter 9 introduces the ideas of color and light. Up to now, all the topics we have discussed can be handled in monochrome on a black-and-white screen without color. This chapter adds color as a further element of displayed pictures. We explore the properties of light and present several color models.

Chapter 10 introduces fractals. These have become important in recent years in many fields besides computer graphics. In graphics they are useful to draw natural-looking scenes. We start with an easy introduction to the basic characteristics of fractals. We then develop the formalism to deal with them without using difficult mathematics. Finally, we give examples of ways to generate and render fractals.

Chapter 11 is the first of three that describe some techniques for hidden surface and hidden line removal. It introduces the data structure of the polygon mesh. Beginning with the simplest algorithm, backface removal, it moves to more complex ones that sort the polygons that make up surfaces into the order of their depth from the viewer.

Chapter 12 continues the explanation of procedures for finding which surfaces and parts of surfaces are hidden by other objects in a scene. We develop methods of more general application but more expensive to compute.

Chapter 13 concludes the discussion of methods for hidden line and surface removal by considering two special cases that have applications for displaying mathematical surfaces.

Chapter 14 explains some of the rendering techniques that have been developed in the quest for visual realism. The objective of rendering is to simulate as closely as possible what we perceive when we look at objects in the real world. There are many different models for rendering; we avoid those that have a difficult mathematical background. However, there are ingenious and simple models that give surprisingly good results. Phong shading, one of these, is widely used. This chapter discusses and compares Lambert and Gouraud to Phong shading and presents data structures useful in these methods.

Chapter 15 is also about rendering techniques. It covers methods for adding a pattern or a texture to a surface to make it a closer representation of the real world. We introduce ray tracing, important for showing objects that are transparent or that reflect other parts of the scene.

Chapter 16 covers animation. It explains why animation works and how it is done in computer graphics. It explains real-time animation and conventional animation done through a sequence of still pictures.

Chapter 17 describes interactive systems that either use a graphically oriented interface or are designed for the interactive production of graphics. Here we give the essentials behind graphical operating systems that are now so common, paint systems, desktop publishing, computer-aided-design, solid modeling, games, and flight simulation. A full description of any of these systems would take an entire book, so we cover only the underlying principles. Segmentation, which plays a vital role in interactive graphics, is treated in this chapter. We also include a discussion of the extremely important issue of standards and describe hard copy devices.

# 1.4 MATHEMATICS BACKGROUND

As we have said, we want to assure that your background in mathematics is sufficient. The mathematics used in computer graphics is not difficult; you have probably studied all that you need to know in previous courses. At the same time, it is easy to forget. The following summary will refresh your memory. In addition, we will point out below where the topic is useful to us. The appendix contains a tutorial on these same topics; refer to it if you need a fuller explanation.

**Coordinate Systems** We will normally use Cartesian coordinates to represent a point. The point (x,y) is at distances x and y from two perpendicular axes. The (x,y)-plane in which the coordinate axes lie can be divided into parts. The quarter between the two positive axes is the first quadrant. The first half of this is the first octant.

In three dimensions, the coordinates of (x,y,z) are measured from three mutually perpendicular axes. In 3-D, if the thumb, first, and middle fingers of the left hand can be aligned with the x-, y-, and z-axes, we have a left-handed system (LHS). When the z-axis points in the opposite direction, we have a right-handed system (RHS).

The distance between two points is:

$$d = ((x_2 - x_1) + (y_2 - y_1) + (z_2 - z_1))^{1/2}.$$

If we work in 2-D, we drop the z-terms.

Polar coordinates provide an alternative system: the point $(r,\Theta)$ is at a distance r from the origin; $\Theta$ is the angle from a reference axis to the ray to the point measured counterclockwise (ccw).

The use of coordinates of points is pervasive in computer graphics to describe the objects that we display as well as their images on the screen. In fact, the essential problem of computer graphics is to compute points on the screen that correspond to points on the real object.

One operation that we will want to do on points is to rotate them by a given angle about the origin. Rotating a point by the angle $\Phi$ is equivalent to rotating the axes by $-\Phi$. The coordinates of the point after rotation are:

$$x_r = x \cos \Phi - y \sin \Phi$$
$$y_r = x \sin \Phi + y \cos \Phi$$

**Analytical Geometry** A curve in the (x,y)-plane can be represented by a relation $y = f(x)$ and vice-versa. If the curve is a straight line, there are four forms in which the relation is conventionally expressed:

Two-point: $$\frac{y - y_1}{x - x_1} = \frac{y_2 - y_1}{x_2 - x_1}, \quad x_1 \neq x_2.$$

Point-slope: $$\frac{y - y_1}{x - x_1} = m, \text{ where m is the slope.}$$

Slope-intercept: $y = mx + b$, where b is the value of y at $x = 0$.
General: $Ax + By + C = 0$, where A and B are not both zero.

Two lines that are parallel have the same slope. If they are perpendicular, $m_1 = -1/m_2$.

The relation $y = f(x)$ can be put into parametric form:

$$x = X(u),\ y = Y(u), \text{ where u is the parameter.}$$

For a straight line between $(x_1,y_1)$ and $(x_2,y_2)$,

$$x = x_1 + u(x_2 - x_1), \qquad y = y_1 + u(y_2 - y_1).$$

As u varies from 0 to 1, (x,y) moves from end1 to end2 along the line.

A circle is described parametrically by:

$$x = r \cos \Theta,\ y = r \sin \Theta, \text{ where } \Theta \text{ is the parameter.}$$

The distance of the point $(x_1,y_1)$ from the line $Ax + By + C = 0$ is:

$$d = \frac{|C - Ax_1 - By_1|}{(A^2 + B^2)^{1/2}}$$ where the vertical bars mean absolute magnitude.

The general equation of a plane in space is:

$$Ax + By + Cz - D = 0.$$

The point $(x_1,y_1,z_1)$ is in the plane $A(x-x_1)+B(y-y_1)+C(z-z_1)=0$, and the equation is for a plane parallel to the above.

See also under matrices and vectors for more information on planes.

Conic sections are described by quadratic equations. In the general quadratic,

$$Ax^2 + Bxy + Cy^2 + Dx + Ey + F = 0,$$

the expression $B^2 - 4AC$ is called the discriminant. If

DISC $= 0$, the curve is a parabola
DISC $< 0$, the curve is an ellipse
DISC $> 0$, the curve is a hyperbola
(except for degenerate cases)

If the conic is rotated about the origin, the discriminant is invariant. The sum of A and B also does not change.

We will be most interested in points, lines, and planes as descriptors of objects to be displayed. The images will generally be formed from straight lines and polygons. Lines in parameterized form also are useful when computing projections.

**Algebra** We will solve quadratic equations by the formula:

$$x = \frac{-b \pm (b^2 - 4ac)^{1/2}}{2a} \qquad \text{when } ax^2 + bx + c = 0.$$

Newton's method solves equations iteratively. If $f(x) = 0$, an approximate solution can usually be obtained by repeating the computation:

$$x_{n+1} = x_n - \frac{f(x_n)}{f'(x_n)}, \qquad n = 0, 1, \ldots \text{ choosing } x_0 \text{ suitably.}$$

From linear algebra, we need the elimination method for solving a set of linear equations. The intersection of two lines is at the point (x,y) that satisfies both equations; the intersection of two planes is found similarly. Cramer's rule solves simultaneous equations using determinants.

**Vectors** A *vector* is an entity that has both magnitude and direction; this means that a vector can be represented by a directed line segment. Two vectors are equal if they have the same magnitude and direction, so the point (x,y) is equivalent to the vector in the (x,y)-plane from the origin to the point; x and y are called the components of the vector.

Vectors can be added and subtracted:

$$\mathbf{v}_1 + \mathbf{v}_2 = (x_1,y_1) + (x_2,y_2) = (x_1+x_2,\ y_1+y_2)$$
$$\mathbf{v}_1 - \mathbf{v}_2 = (x_1,y_1) - (x_2,y_2) = (x_1-x_2,\ y_1-y_2)$$

If a vector is multiplied by a scalar,

$$c\,\mathbf{v} = (cx,cy).$$

The magnitude of a vector is its length:

$$|\mathbf{v}| = (x^2 + y^2)^{1/2}.$$

A vector is normalized by dividing each component by the length, producing a vector of magnitude 1.

There are two kinds of products of vectors that we will use:

Dot product: $\mathbf{v}_1 \bullet \mathbf{v}_2 = x_1x_2 + y_1y_2 = |\mathbf{v}_1|\,|\mathbf{v}_2| \cos \Theta$.
Cross product: $\mathbf{v}_1 \times \mathbf{v}_2 = \mathbf{n}\,|\mathbf{v}_1|\,|\mathbf{v}_2| \sin \Theta$.

In the above, $\Theta$ is the angle between the two vectors when drawn from a common point. The *dot product* is a scalar quantity and the *cross product* is a vector. In the latter, the vector $\mathbf{n}$ is a unit vector perpendicular to the plane of $\mathbf{v}_1$ and $\mathbf{v}_2$. $\mathbf{v}_1$, $\mathbf{v}_2$, and $\mathbf{n}$ form an RHS system. The dot product is also called the *scalar product* and the cross product the *vector product.* When two vectors are perpendicular, their dot product is zero; when they are parallel, their cross product is zero. In 3-D, these all extend in an obvious way.

The cross product of two vectors that lie in a plane is the best way to describe the orientation of a plane because this defines a normal vector for the plane. By forming the cross product of vectors drawn through three points taken in ccw order, we define the positive side of the plane.

**Matrices** A *matrix* is a rectangular array of values where the position as well as the value is important. The size of a matrix is given by the number of rows and columns, $r \times c$. The elements of a matrix are often represented by a subscripted lowercase variable while the matrix itself is the same variable in bold uppercase or the general element enclosed in brackets:

$$\mathbf{A} = \begin{pmatrix} a_{11} & a_{12} & a_{13} \\ a_{21} & a_{22} & a_{23} \\ a_{31} & a_{32} & a_{33} \end{pmatrix} = [a_{ij}].$$

Two matrices of the same size may be added or subtracted:

$$\mathbf{C} = \mathbf{A} + \mathbf{B} = [a_{ij} + b_{ij}] = [c_{ij}],$$
$$\mathbf{D} = \mathbf{A} - \mathbf{B} = [a_{ij} - b_{ij}] = [d_{ij}].$$

Two matrices may be multiplied if the number of columns of the first equals the number of rows of the second. If **A** is r × c and **B** is c × t, then **E** = **A B** is r × t, and

$$e_{ij} = \sum_{k=1}^{c} a_{ik} b_{kj}, \quad i = 1..r, \quad j = 1..t.$$

The order of the factors cannot be reversed.

Multiplication by a scalar multiplies each element by the scalar:

$$\mathbf{F} = c\,\mathbf{A} = c[a_{ij}] = [ca_{ij}] = [f_{ij}].$$

A vector is a special case of a matrix. A matrix of only one row is a *row vector* and of one column, a *column vector.* Vectors are often written as a boldface, lower case letter. A column vector is often indicated by enclosing it in curly braces:

$$\mathbf{v} = (v_1\; v_2\; v_3); \quad \{\mathbf{w}\} = \begin{pmatrix} w_1 \\ w_2 \\ w_3 \end{pmatrix}$$

The dot product of two vectors is then **v** {**w**}.

A set of equations can be written in matrix form. If **A** is a square matrix of coefficients, {**x**} is the unknown vector, and {**b**} the right-hand sides,

$$\mathbf{A}\,\{\mathbf{x}\} = \{\mathbf{b}\}.$$

Solving a set of equations by elimination is equivalent to a succession of elementary row operations that makes the coefficient matrix upper-triangular (making all elements below the main diagonal equal to zero). The solution is then found by back substitutions.

Square matrices have special properties. A matrix with all diagonal elements equal to 1 and all others 0 is the identity matrix, and

$$\mathbf{I\,A} = \mathbf{A\,I} = \mathbf{A}.$$

If the product of two matrices is **I,** the matrices are inverses:

$$\mathbf{A\,A}^{-1} = \mathbf{I} = \mathbf{A}^{-1}\mathbf{A}.$$

A set of equations can be solved by multiplying by the inverse of the coefficient matrix, although this is usually less efficient than elimination:

$$\mathbf{A}^{-1}\mathbf{A\,x} = \mathbf{A}^{-1}\mathbf{b} = \mathbf{I\,x} = \mathbf{x}.$$

A square matrix has a determinant, represented by magnitude bars; the determinant can be expanded in terms of minors of any row or column. Expansion from row 1 of a 3 × 3 matrix gives:

$$|\mathbf{A}| = \det \mathbf{A} = a_{11}\begin{vmatrix} a_{22} & a_{23} \\ a_{32} & a_{33} \end{vmatrix} - a_{12}\begin{vmatrix} a_{21} & a_{23} \\ a_{31} & a_{33} \end{vmatrix} + a_{13}\begin{vmatrix} a_{21} & a_{22} \\ a_{31} & a_{32} \end{vmatrix}$$
$$= a_{11}(a_{22}a_{33} - a_{23}a_{32}) - a_{12}(a_{21}a_{33} - a_{23}a_{31}) + a_{13}(a_{21}a_{32} - a_{22}a_{31}).$$

If a matrix is triangular, its determinant is the product of its diagonal elements.

The equation of a line through points $(x_1,y_1)$ and $(x_2,y_2)$ is:

$$\begin{vmatrix} x & y & 1 \\ x_1 & y_1 & 1 \\ x_2 & y_2 & 1 \end{vmatrix} = 0.$$

The area of a triangle in the x-y plane can be computed as:

$$\text{area} = 1/2 \begin{vmatrix} x_1 & y_1 & 1 \\ x_2 & y_2 & 1 \\ x_3 & y_3 & 1 \end{vmatrix}$$

Matrices are widely used in graphics when an image is to be transformed: translated, scaled, or rotated.

**Derivatives** The following assumes $x = f(u)$ and uses the notation $dx/du = x'$. $dx/dx = 1$.

$$d(x+y)/du = x' + y'.$$
$$dy/dx = (dy/du)(du/dx) = (dy/du)/(dx/du) = y'/x'.$$
$$dx^n/du = nx^{n-1}x'.$$
$$d(\sin x)/du = (-\cos x)\, x'.$$
$$d(\cos x)/du = (\sin x)\, x'.$$

From the definition of $x'$ as a limit, the finite difference is an approximation:

$$(x_2 - x_1)/(u_2 - u_1) \approx x'.$$

If $\Delta u = u_2 - u_1$, $x' \approx \Delta x/\Delta u$.
A forward difference uses $u_2 = u_1 + \Delta u$ ($\Delta u$ is positive), $u_1$ being the point where the derivative applies. If the approximation applies at $u_2$, it is a backward difference. A central difference is usually more accurate. When the u's are equispaced,

$$x_1{}' \approx \frac{x_2 - x_0}{2\Delta u}.$$

Higher derivatives can also be approximated by finite differences.

Partial derivatives can be approximated by finite differences where the other variable is held constant.

Differential equations describe some important objects of computer graphics:

A line: dy/dx = constant.
A circle: dy/dx = $-x/y$ (center is at the origin).
An ellipse: dy/dx = $-(b^2/a^2)(x/y)$ (center is at the origin).

Derivatives are of value in expressing the slope of a curve. Since pixels are spaced a finite distance apart, finite difference approximations are frequently used. Equations for lines, circles, and ellipses can be expressed through their differential equations.

**Complex Numbers** Complex numbers are composed of a real part and an imaginary part, $z = a + ib$. Because they resemble two component vectors in their makeup, alternate representations are $z = (a,b)$ and as points in the complex plane, which has two perpendicular axes. Representing complex numbers as points in the complex plane is called an Argand diagram. A polar form is also useful, $z = (r,\Theta)$.

The operations of addition and subtraction are isomorphic to vectors. Multiplication and division are:

$$cz = (ca,cb).$$
$$(z_1)(z_2) = (a_1a_2 - b_1b_2) + i(a_1b_2 + a_2b_1).$$
$$(z_1)/(z_2) = ((a_1a_2 + b_1b_2) - i(a_1b_2 - a_2b_1))/(a_2^2 + b_2^2).$$

The magnitude of a complex number is:

$$|z| = (a^2 + b^2)^{1/2}.$$

We will use complex numbers in describing some fractals.

**Binary Numbers** Computer memories are composed of bistable elements so all values must be stored in binary. A binary number uses place values that are powers of 2. For example:

(1 0 1 1 0 1) as a base 2 number
$= 1(2^5) + 0(2^4) + 1(2^3) + 1(2^2) + 0(2^1) + 1(2^0)$
$= 32 + 0 + 8 + 4 + 0 + 1 = 45$ as a base 10 number.

The AND and OR of two binary numbers is computed by ANDing or ORing the corresponding bits, with each result given by:

| AND | 0 | 1 |
|---|---|---|
| 0 | 0 | 0 |
| 1 | 0 | 1 |

| OR | 0 | 1 |
|---|---|---|
| 0 | 0 | 1 |
| 1 | 1 | 1 |

Another operation is XOR:

| XOR | 0 | 1 |
|---|---|---|
| 0 | 0 | 1 |
| 1 | 1 | 0 |

**Random Numbers** Random numbers would result from drawing from an infinite pool of noncorrelated values, but computers must determine them by other means so they are really pseudorandom. In effect, a set of numbers is random if the value of any of them is not known in advance. We will use random numbers in computing some fractals.

**Data Structures** A set of values that are interrelated in some way can be stored within the computer in various ways. We will use arrays, records, and linked lists.

*Arrays:* The successive values of the set are referenced through a subscripted variable. For example, x[0], x[5], x[99] are the first, sixth, and one-hundredth members of the set. Double subscripts allow a table or matrix of values to be referenced. All elements of an array must be of the same type. In most computer languages, the size of the array must be predeclared.

*Records:* The members of the set are similar subsets of elements that are not necessarily alike (reals, integers, strings, etc. can be combined). Pascal permits great freedom in typing of variables and records.

*Linked lists:* Records can be linked together by including pointers to (addresses of) other records as elements of each record. The address of the first record of the list (head pointer) serves to enter the list and the end of the list is indicated by a null pointer in the last record.

We will use arrays and linked lists in storing information on the polygons that form the surfaces of most of our objects.

# EXERCISES FOR CHAPTER 1

1. Make a list of all the computer systems at your school or organization that have graphics capabilities. Which of these are accessible to you and which are restricted to a set of special users? Do all provide color displays or are some equipped only with monochrome displays? Are any what you would term "special purpose" installations?
2. In the card catalogue of your library, look up the titles of books under the heading Computer Graphics. How many are there? Make a list of those in some specialized field of interest to you.
3. Computer graphics probably began with an important study by Ivan Sutherland at Massachusetts Institute of Technology that developed Sketchpad. Do some literature research to find references to this system and write a brief report that summarizes its capabilities.
4. Most of today's so-called personal or desktop computers have graphics capabilities. Compare the features provided by two brands of small computers in a report that would help a prospective purchaser decide which would be the better choice.

# Straight Lines & Polygons

# 2

Straight lines and polygons, basic elements in computer graphics, form the subject matter of Chapter 2. There are four major sections.

**2.0 Introduction** explains why lines and polygons are important, how the spacing of pixels influences the problem of setting the proper pixels, and what criteria should be met by a good line-drawing algorithm. Since polygon edges are straight lines, these considerations apply to them as well.

**2.1 Straight Lines** can be developed in two different ways. A structural method determines which pixels should be set before drawing the line; a conditional method tests certain conditions to find which pixel should be set next.

**2.2 Polygons** are drawn with straight lines as their edges, but the problem of how the data that describe the polygon should be stored requires careful consideration. Once the edges have been drawn, one normally wants to fill the polygon. This problem is examined in some detail.

**2.3 Pattern Fills** are not much harder to obtain than a solid fill. We explain them in this section.

# 2.0 INTRODUCTION

Lines, especially straight lines, constitute an important building block of computer images. Examples of their use are in line graphs, bar and pie charts, two- and three-dimensional graphs of mathematical functions, engineering drawings, and architectural plans. Their importance becomes even clearer when we consider that curved lines are in most cases approximated by a sequence of short straight lines in computer graphics. You can see that it is worth considerable effort to develop efficient methods to draw straight lines. The concepts behind the algorithms that draw straight lines also extend to the drawing of curved lines such as circular and elliptical arcs. These are frequent enough and mathematically simple enough that we should consider special algorithms for them rather than always approximating them by short straight lines. This we will do in Chapter 3.

In computer graphics the straight line is so basic in creating an image that we call it a graphics primitive. When working on raster displays (see below) there is another basic building block, the pixel. This is just one tiny dot on the display. While the pixel certainly is a building block, to call it a graphics primitive is not entirely correct because it has no structure. But this is not really important. The third basic building block we consider to be a graphics primitive is the polygon; it will be introduced later in this chapter.

Actually, there is no generally accepted definition of a graphics primitive. Our definition, to be used throughout this book is: A primitive is a graphics object that is used so often that it is essential to the creation of images. Experience shows that these primitives, or building blocks, can be used to construct the most complex images.

When we use these primitives, we must specify certain parameters. With SetPix, which sets a single pixel, we give the coordinates of the pixel that is to be set. (With a color display, we add a third parameter for the color.) The straight line primitive requires that we specify the coordinates of the start and end of the line.

We have said that a pixel is the most basic graphic building block in pictures generated by computers on raster displays. In the next several pages we explain what pixels are and how we work with them. To do this, we must digress to explain the hardware for raster graphics. (In addition to the more common raster display, there are nonraster types of displays which we will describe later on. These other types of display are not as common and the scan conversion methods discussed in this chapter and the next are not significant for them.)

**The Cathode Ray Tube** The *CRT* (*cathode ray tube*) is the most important display device for computer graphics. Below is a description of the basic principle of the black-and-white CRT. This is used in black-and-white TVs as well as computer displays. Figure 2.1 shows a cross section.

At the narrow end of a sealed conical glass tube is an electron gun that emits a high-velocity, finely focused beam of electrons. The other end, the face of the CRT, is slightly curved and is coated inside with phosphor, which glows with a certain color when the electron beam strikes it. The energy of the beam can be controlled so as to vary the intensity of light output and, when necessary, to cut off the light altogether. The electron beam can be deflected by a system of electromagnetic coils mounted outside the tube at the base of the neck. It deflects the electron beam to different parts of the tube face. This system of coils is called the yoke.

The *phosphors* used in a graphic display are chosen for their color and persistence. The color is conventionally green but in newer tubes it is amber, or preferably white, particularly for applications where dark information appears on a light background. The persistence is measured as the time for the brightness to drop to one-tenth of its initial value after the electron beam stops exciting the phosphor. Ideally, it should last about 100 milliseconds or less, allowing refresh at 30 Hertz rates without noticeable lingering as the image is changed.

A picture is produced on the screen by tracing it out with the electron beam. There are two different methods of doing this. The most common one is the *raster scan*. In this scanning method the electron beam sweeps in a fixed path and with fixed speed over the entire screen surface. Two oscillators produce sawtoothlike curves of voltages which, after amplification, are applied to the deflector coils in the yoke. One of the oscillators deflects the beam left-right with a frequency between about 12 and 32 Khz, sometimes higher. The other deflects it up-down with a frequency of about 60 Hz. The movement to the left (*horizontal retrace*) is much faster than that to the right (*raster line*), see Figure 2.2. Similarly, the movement up (*vertical retrace*) is much faster than that down (*downward sweep*), see Figure 2.3.

The combination of these two oscillations makes the beam sweep the screen surface in parallel, almost horizontal lines. Figure 2.4 shows the path of the beam during a downward sweep and Figure 2.5 the path during a vertical retrace. A downward sweep is called a *field*. The covering of the whole screen surface with scan lines is called a *frame*. Obviously a field is identical to a frame.

**FIGURE 2.1**

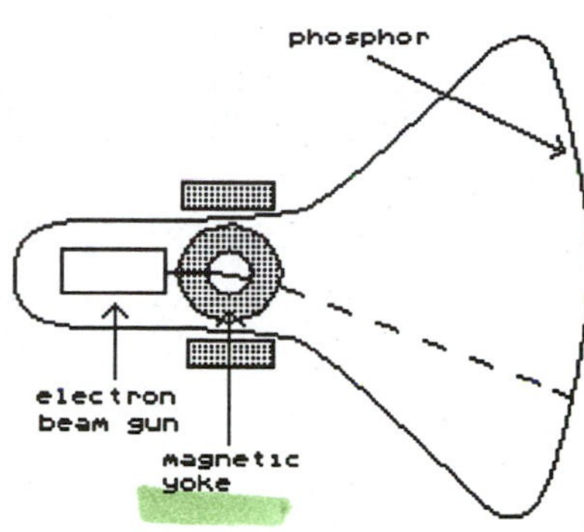


**FIGURE 2.2**

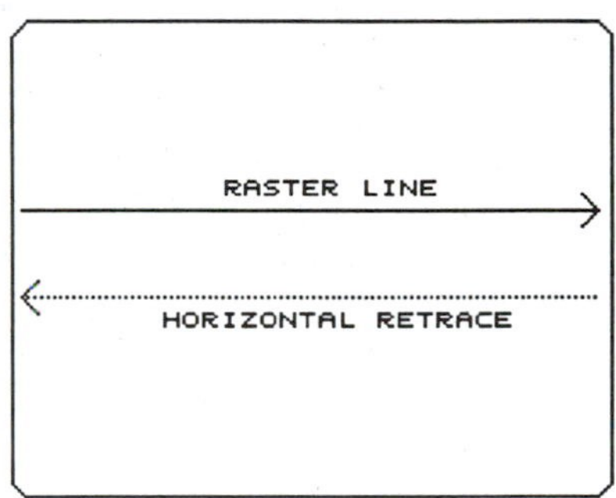


**FIGURE 2.3**

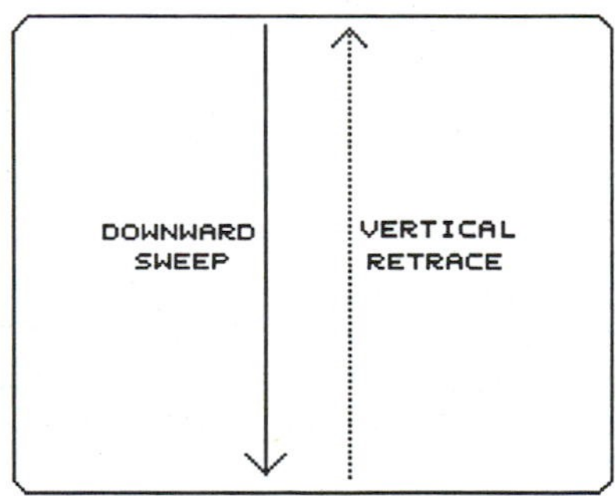

The heavy lines from left to right in Figure 2.4 are the only part of the path during which the beam can be turned on to a writing intensity. During the light lines the beam is always turned off. In practice there is a slight overscan on the left, right, and bottom which is not shown here. The lines are much denser, between 200 and 500 per sweep, sometimes up to 1000, depending on the tube model and driving circuitry. This makes the lines almost horizontal.

FIGURE 2.4

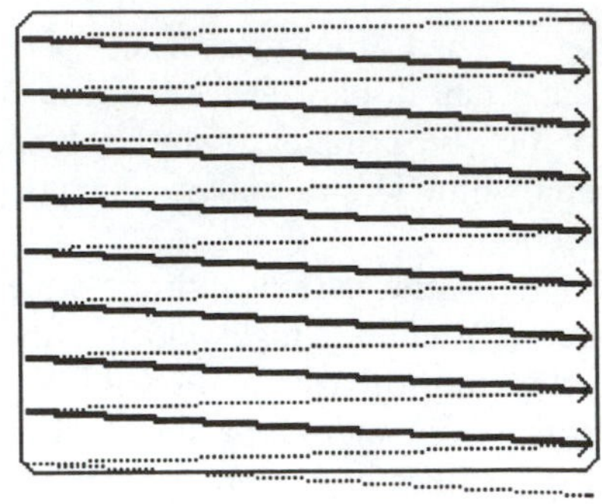

**Noninterlaced versus Interlaced Methods** Graphics CRT displays can work with as few as 200 and as many as 1000 scan lines. However, in our explanation of the difference between these two techniques, we assume a display of 400 scan lines.

If the horizontal frequency is about 400 cycles for each vertical cycle (vertical frequency 60 Hz), the beam will scan all 400 scan lines per field. Each field produces an entire frame. Our horizontal frequency needs to be approximately 24 Khz. We have to say "about 400" and "approximately 24 Khz" because some horizontal scans will be done during the vertical retrace and so will be lost for the count of scan lines, but these details are not important for your understanding of this simplified model. This straightforward scanning method is called *noninterlaced.* It corresponds directly to Figures 2.4 and 2.5. It is the highest quality CRT display method.

FIGURE 2.5

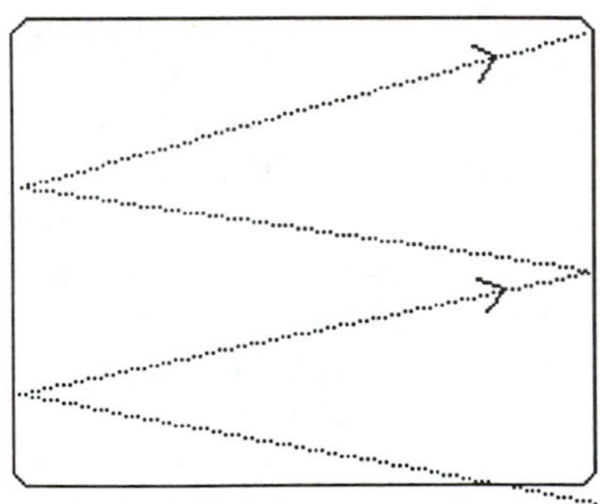

Usually the graphics CRT monitors (and other related hardware) cannot work with such a high horizontal frequency and apply the so-called *interlaced* display technique. This technique allows (in our example) the production of 400 scan lines on the screen while working with only half the horizontal frequency. With only 12 Khz, the left-right movement of the beam will be only half as fast. Conseqently only 200 horizontal lines will be drawn for one vertical sweep and they will be farther apart from each other. One field consists of only half the scan lines needed for a frame. How then do we get 400 scan lines? Through interlacing.

Interlacing results from making a slight change in the ratio between horizontal and vertical frequencies. This is chosen to give a nonintegral number of horizontal lines for each vertical retrace, say 200½ instead of 200 lines. The consequence is that the lowest scan line is drawn only half on the screen, as shown in Figure 2.6. In the next field, after the vertical retrace, the first scan line will be drawn only half on the screen. At the end of this field the last scan line will fit entirely on the screen; see Figure 2.7. Therefore, all scan lines of the second field will be drawn precisely in between the scan lines of the first field. We can verify this by superimposing these two figures.

FIGURE 2.6 Odd field.

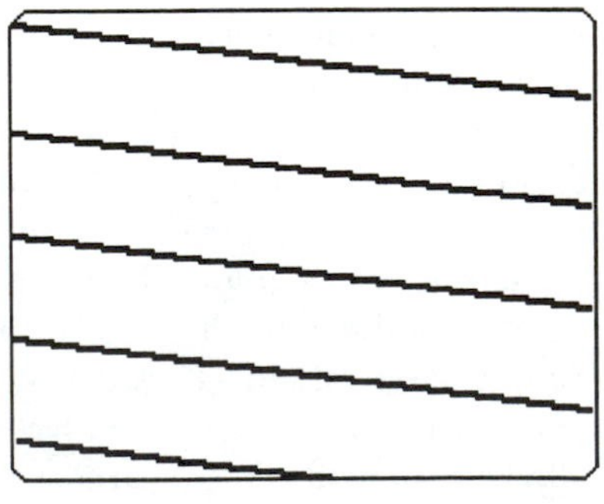

In the third field the first scan line will again fit entirely on the screen and so this field will be identical to the first. We get an alternation between two types of fields: an "odd" one and an "even" one. Two consecutive fields together put 400 scan lines on the screen, thereby producing one frame. But now a frame takes two vertical cycles and therefore 1/30 of a second. This technique is developed to perfection in TV monitors and is adopted in most CRT displays.

**FIGURE 2.7** Even field.

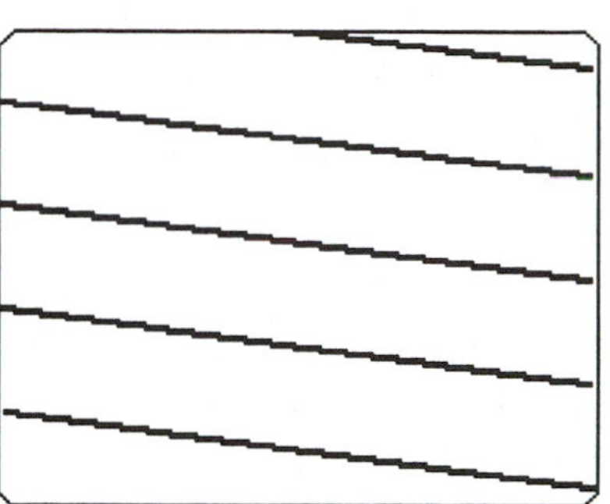

**Displaying a Picture** Displaying a picture is achieved by turning the beam on or off at certain points during its sweep over the screen. These points are called pixels. Each scan line can be seen as divided into a fixed number of pixels. How many pixels there are has nothing to do with the hardware of the CRT. It depends only on the frequency with which the beam can be switched on and off, or *pixel rate.*

The number of pixels per scan line is fixed for each display setup. Continuing with our example, we assume that a scan line has 640 pixels. Accordingly the whole screen is covered with a rectangular raster of $640 \times 400 = 256000$ pixels. The more pixels there are, the finer the resolution of the display. By turning on the proper pixels, we display pictures, but only within the limits of this finite resolution. The horizontal distance between pixel centers depends on the pixel rate; the vertical distance is identical to the scan line distance and depends on the horizontal frequency. Pixels therefore are not always square.

Figure 2.8 shows the raster display of a pie divided into six equal parts. The pie is very small in relation to the pixel raster to exaggerate the effects of this digitization. In reality, the pixel size is such that adjacent pixels touch or even overlap one another. This makes the picture a little smoother.

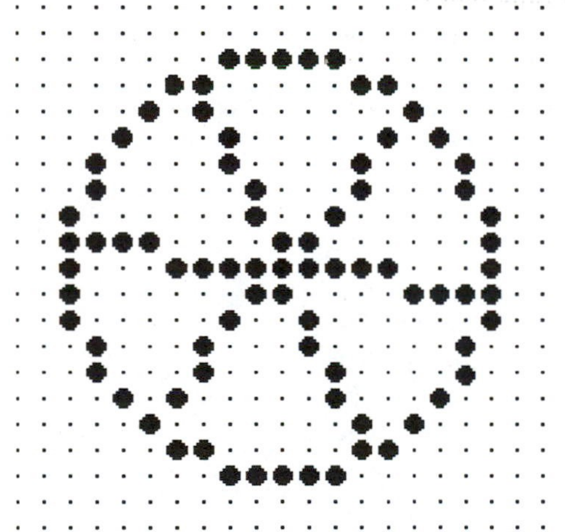

**FIGURE 2.8**

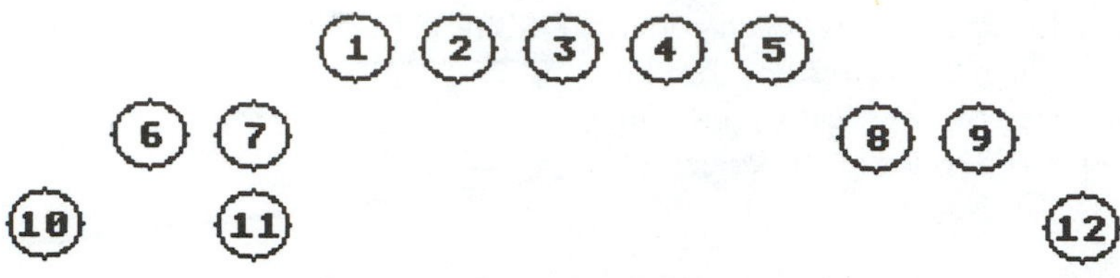


FIGURE 2.9

The movement of the beam is independent of the displayed picture; even if nothing is displayed, the beam still makes its sweep across the screen. As the beam travels through its scan lines, it is turned on or off at the proper positions. Figure 2.9 shows the uppermost three scan lines of the pie above and the sequence in which the beam hits the pixels to be turned on in noninterlaced display mode.

To produce a steady display the whole field has to be redrawn at least 30 times per second. The information as to which pixels are to be turned on is stored in the computer memory in what we call a *frame buffer.* For a simple black-and-white display, each pixel needs only one bit. In our example of 640 × 400 pixels, the frame buffer needs 32 Kbytes. A 1 bit means "pixel on" and a 0 bit means "pixel off." It is now the duty of the computer to read out the frame buffer information at precisely the same speed at which the monitor scans the screen and to send a "set" signal whenever it meets a 1 bit. This is usually done by a CRT controller.

**Operation of the CRT Controller** Every time the computer is booted up, the operating system prepares the CRT controller for its task by setting proper parameters for the display into its registers. The most important parameters are the number of bytes per scan line, the number of scan lines per field, interlaced or noninterlaced operation, and length of the horizontal and vertical retraces of the monitor.

To maintain a precise match of the speeds of these two processes (scanning of the screen by the electron beam and scanning of the frame buffer by the CRT controller), the CRT controller sends out horizontal and vertical synchronization signals. A horizontal sync is sent whenever the number of bytes corresponding to one scan line have been sent. A vertical sync is sent whenever the number of horizontal sync signals corresponding to one field have been sent. These sync signals are able to correct for moderate deviations in the speed of the monitor circuitry.

Here is an explanation of the process for the simple case of a black-and-white display without gray levels. One byte in the frame buffer contains information for eight consecutive pixels on the screen. When the CRT controller accesses the byte up for display, all its eight bits are moved in parallel into a shift register. From there they are shifted

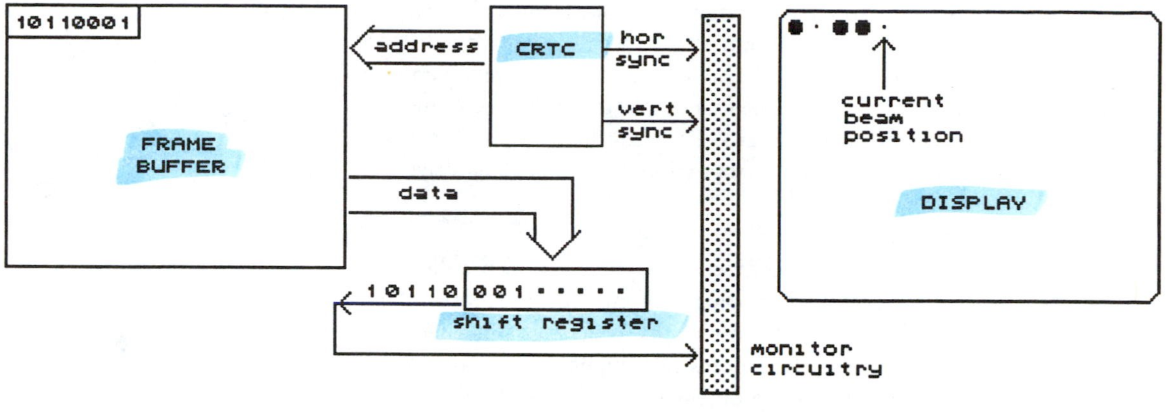


**FIGURE 2.10**

out serially to the monitor circuitry; see Figure 2.10. In that figure the byte containing the first eight bits in the first scan line has just been addressed and has moved into the shift register. The first five bits have been shifted out and are seen on the screen.

Here, the addressing mode is bytewise, the data bus has a width of eight, and the shift register holds eight bits. It shifts bits out at the pixel rate (approximately 15 Mhz for the noninterlaced display in our example). The frame buffer must be accessed once for eight pixels. This results in a contention for frame buffer accesses with the main processor that is setting the proper bits in the frame buffer to create pictures. If, for example, 256 bits could be shifted in parallel into a correspondingly long shift register, the contention problems would be reduced drastically. This has led to the development of so-called *video RAM chips*. These have long shift registers and are used for high-resolution graphic CRT displays (see, for example, the Texas Instruments TMS4161 description). The display technique in which each pixel is represented by one or more bits of memory is called *bit-mapping*.

**Gray Levels** The intensity of the electron beam can be not only on or off but also in intermediate states. The light emitted by the phosphor will then be of intermediate intensities. This is how gray levels can be achieved. To store the several possible gray levels of a pixel, we need more than one bit. With four bits we can store 16 different gray levels. The 640 × 400 pixel display then needs a frame buffer of 128 Kbytes.

We will not go into hardware details about the architecture of such frame buffers, reading the information, shifting it out, and so on. You will get some understanding of it by imagining that there are four of the above setups working in parallel, called *bit planes.* The addresses are the same for all four bit planes, and the data are shifted out in parallel. The four bits coming out of the four bit planes are taken together and fed into a D/A (*digital to analog*) converter. From there the analog intensity goes to the monitor. However, the luminosity of the pixels that are displayed is not exactly proportional to this voltage (see sidebar on gamma correction).

**Scan Conversion** Lines in computer graphics are also called *arcs.* The generation of arcs, whether straight or curved, is a problem on a raster display because it consists only of pixels arranged in a rectangular array. *Scan conversion* is the process of computing the pattern of dots that most closely matches the object to be displayed. In this chapter we will develop techniques for scan conversion of straight arcs and polygons; we will consider circular arcs and elliptical arcs in Chapter 3. While it is possible to build scan conversion algorithms for all sorts of algebraic curves, including parabolas and hyperbolas, they are not often needed; we will not develop algorithms for them. Another reason why these other curves can be ignored is that any algebraic curve can be so closely approximated by a sequence of short straight lines that it is impossible for a human observer to tell the difference. Finally, the raster of dots that are used to display everything forces an optical digitization; it follows that virtually everything on such a display is only an approximation of the precise real-world object.

**Pixel Ratio** The horizontal distance between pixel centers is not always the same as the vertical distance. How close they are to each other depends only on the characteristics of the display monitor and the setting of the CRT controller; this cannot normally be influenced by the programmer. Sometimes, especially on older CRTs, pixels are more closely spaced horizontally than vertically. We define the *pixel ratio* as the distance between the centers of two adjacent horizontal pixels divided by that of vertical pixels. This ratio must be considered in some of the line-generating algorithms. Pixels are not always round; they can also have the shape of an ellipse. The definition of a pixel on a color CRT is more complicated and will be discussed later.

**FIGURE 2.11**

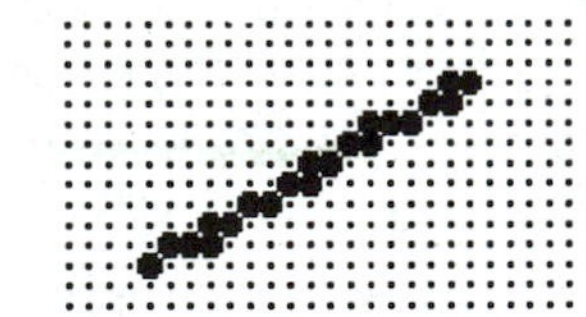

**Basic Problems** Several basic problems arise when a line is to be converted to pixels on a raster display. (A vector display has a different set of problems.) Circular arcs have the same problems as straight lines; we will only discuss the situation for straight lines.

To create the image of a line, certain pixels on the screen must be turned on. This set of pixels is often called a *digital arc* or *digital line.* For the same straight line, many different combinations of pixels can be set to give essentially the same impression; see Figures 2.11 and 2.12.

**FIGURE 2.12**

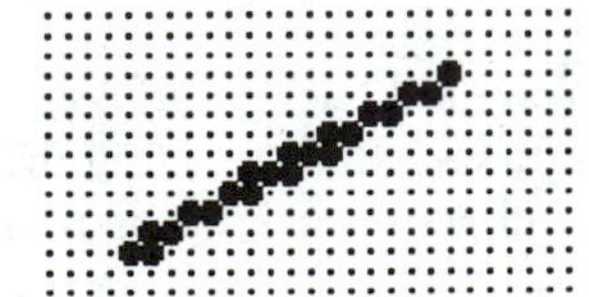

## GAMMA CORRECTION

A characteristic problem with CRT displays is the nonlinear relation of input to output. More precisely, the voltage applied to the CRT monitor to control the intensity of the electron beam is not linearly related to the intensity of the luminous output of the phosphors. For example, if we double the voltage of the input signal we do not get double the luminosity of pixels. The luminosity is less than expected at low voltages and more at higher voltages.

The input normally varies from 0 volt to about 5 volts but this varies widely from monitor to monitor. We can account for this variation by normalizing the range of the display signal inputs, considering its lowest value as 0 and its highest value as 1. Let us do the same for the luminosity output of the phosphors. Then the nonlinear relationship can be expressed approximately by the formula:

$$(\text{display signal input})^{\text{gamma}} = \text{luminous output}$$

in which gamma is not equal to 1. Figure 2.A shows a typical nonlinear relationship.

Even though monitors differ, the basic shape of this curve is about the same. The curve is well approximated by the above relation with gamma-values ranging from 2 to 2.8. While the gamma-values differ for different monitors, the international convention is to assume a gamma-value of 2.2. This means that applying 50 percent of full-scale input voltage will result in 22 percent of full-scale luminous output.

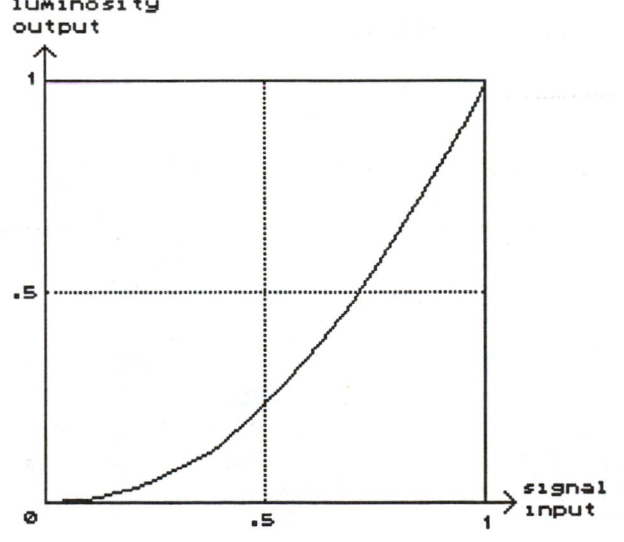


**FIGURE 2.A**

*(continued)*

### GAMMA CORRECTION (*continued*)

The nonlinearity of output versus input is fully described by the value of gamma. (A gamma-value of 1 would be a linear relation.) For television signals, the gamma nonlinearity is corrected at the source of the signal, the TV camera, by reversing the above relation. The signal output is raised to the power 1/2.2 = 0.454 by analog circuitry. The overall relation from source to CRT monitor will then be linear.

With a computer graphics monitor there are several ways to cope with this nonlinearity. One way is to have built-in analog circuitry that corrects the display signal generated by the D/A converter before it is applied to the monitor. Another way is to correct all intensity values by software. In case of a monochrome display with gray levels this can be done by correcting all intensities before entering them in the frame buffer. In case of a color display intensity values are stored in the lookup tables (see Chapter 9) and have to be corrected there for all three primaries. The correction consists of raising the fractional intensity value to the power 0.454.

For example, assume an intensity of 100 in a range of 0 to 255. The fractional value is 100/255 = 0.392. Since $0.392^{0.454} = 0.654$, the corresponding intensity of 167 ($0.654 * 255$) is entered instead of 100.

The designer of a graphics system must know whether or not the monitors that are to be used have built-in gamma correction so as to compensate if necessary. But sometimes we just ignore this and accept the nonlinearity as an inherent characteristic of the system.

Let us consider what criteria are appropriate for drawing a line by setting pixels on the screen.

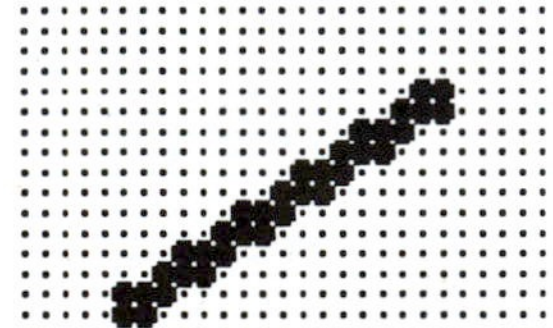

**FIGURE 2.13** 1. The line should not look too thick, as in Figure 2.13. Do not set more pixels than necessary for creating the impression of a line.

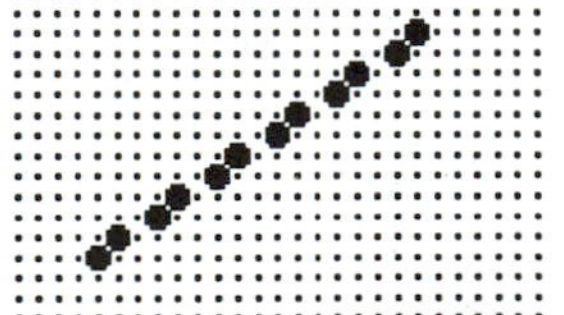

**FIGURE 2.14** 2. The line should not look too thin, as in Figure 2.14. Set enough pixels to have a coherent sequence of adjacent pixels. There should be no gaps.

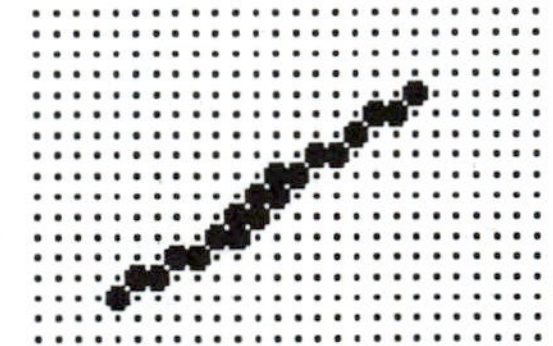

**FIGURE 2.15** 3. The line should have constant density—it should have equal thickness, not unevenness like the line in Figure 2.15.

We will not attempt to postulate a necessary minimum requirement for creating the impression of a straight line because this depends on many factors, including the user's judgment. For example: When are pixels adjacent? Here we could find a simple mathematical formula for our rectangular grid of pixels. We prefer not to give many mathematical definitions at this point because that would complicate our task. We will quantify some of these concepts later in this chapter.

As we have seen, the picture that appears on the screen is a representation of the contents of the frame buffer. Every pixel on the display corresponds to a certain location in the frame buffer. In order to set a certain pixel, the corresponding location in the frame buffer has to be set to a certain value. In the case of a simple black-and-white display, the corresponding location in the frame buffer consists of a single bit. This bit must be set to 1 if 1 expresses white and 0 expresses black (or the reverse if that is the way the hardware was designed). In the case of a color display the frame buffer locations that correspond to a pixel consist of several bits in order to express the particular color choice for this pixel. Regardless of the color to be shown, the task of the line-drawing algorithm is to determine the proper locations. This problem is identical with the geometrical problem of determining the pixels in the grid that best fit the theoretical line to be drawn.

Line-generating algorithms need to be fast because images are composed primarily of straight lines. It follows that they are usually written in machine language and are machine dependent. Special graphics chips are steadily becoming more popular; these perform such algorithms in hardware or microcode. The programs in Pascal show only the algorithmic principle. The compiled code will be machine dependent; a machine-independent line- or arc-drawing program is not feasible. This dependency relates to the hardware architecture of the bit map and how it is associated to the pixel grid, and in some cases to the pixel ratio mentioned above.

## 2.1 STRAIGHT LINES

All straight line-generating algorithms need only the starting and ending points in order to draw the line; they are the only parameters the algorithm requires. We will assume here that the start and end points lie exactly on pixel grid points. This is a modest restriction; it can be achieved by rounding the end point values if they are real numbers. Even so, the theoretical straight line that connects these two points usually does not go through other grid points. We also assume that the

## RECENT DEVELOPMENTS IN THIS AREA

Scan conversion algorithms are so important that several of them have already been implemented in hardware. In 1982 Nippon Electric Company and Intel produced a graphics coprocessor (NEC 7220 or Intel 82720) that could "hardware draw" straight lines in all directions, as well as circular arcs and rectangles, and also could fill rectangular areas with user-specified patterns. An even faster and much more advanced graphics coprocessor was released by Hitachi in 1985, with the modest name Advanced CRT Controller (HD63484-8).

These chips produce straight lines by executing line generators such as the Bresenham algorithm described below. This is not done by executing machine code stored in memory; instead it is achieved by executing microcode, thereby attaining very high speed. A further gain in speed with this approach is due to the fact that once a command for line drawing (or some other graphics primitive) is sent to the graphics coprocessor, the main processor is no longer involved—it can go on with other calculations. Both chips work for some time in parallel.

In order to generate a straight line on the NEC 7220 chip it is not enough to send just the address of the point to which the line should be drawn. The user has to calculate the many parameters the chip needs for drawing that line, and to distinguish among eight different drawing directions, depending on the octant of the drawing direction. There is quite a bit of complex calculation involved in getting the parameters of the line draw command. Sending them to the chip may require sending up to 10 bytes of information. Furthermore, the status of the chip must be checked regularly to avoid overflowing its input buffer. All this easily amounts to the time needed for 30 to 50 memory accesses by the main processor. This means that short lines can be performed faster by having the main processor directly execute a DDA algorithm (defined in Section 2.1.2) and set the appropriate pixels in the frame buffer. The break-even point is of the order of 20 to 30 pixels in line length (no precise analysis has yet been done). The relationship certainly depends on the architecture of the graphics frame buffer to which the coprocessor sends data.

Drawing with the Hitachi Advanced CRT Controller is much simpler. To draw a straight line, the user only has to send a command and the x- and y-coordinates of the point to which the line is to be drawn. Furthermore, the chip can perform a much greater number of graphics primitives. It has the capabilities of the NEC 7220, and in addition it can do relative move and draw, polygons and elliptic arcs, and other basic functions.

These devices are only the beginning of the development of dedicated graphics chips. More and more functions will be implemented in hardware and dedicated chips will play an increasingly important role in all computer graphics techniques.

two terminal points of the line have been translated to actual screen coordinates, so the pixel ratio is no problem for the straight line-generating algorithms given below.

## 2.1.1 Structural Methods

A *structural method* for drawing a line is one that generates all the pixel addresses of the line (its "structure") before any of the pixels are set. The whole structure is computed before the line is displayed. In contrast, another approach, the *conditional method,* can set each pixel before it is known where the next point will be. This alternate method is called conditional because the position of each pixel depends on conditions that are checked during the generation of the line. A structural method can be used to produce straight lines in a raster but it is still of more theoretical value.

As we discuss these algorithms, you will find precise definitions for *adjacent, digital line,* and *straightness.* The theory developed in connection with structural methods shows relations to number theory, linguistic methods, and automata theory. We will present two structural methods, Brons's method and the best-fit method.

**Chain Coding** To quantify the notions *coherent* and *adjacent,* we first explain the term *eight-connectedness:* Two pixels in a grid are eight-connected if they are vertically, horizontally, or diagonally adjacent. A pixel therefore has eight eight-connected neighbors (see Figure 2.16).

The *thinnest but still coherent line of pixels* in a grid is usually accepted as the representation of a line on a raster display. It can be expressed as a sequence of eight-connected pixels. For describing such a line, we can use Freeman's chain coding scheme (FREE70). Let the eight different directions of a pixel to its eight eight-connected neighbors be numbered as shown in Figure 2.17.

A *chain code* is a sequence of numbers that indicates the location of successive pixels on the screen. The Freeman chain can represent any digital arc by a string with elements 0, 1, 2, ..., 7, where the values show the relative direction to the next pixel. The word *arc* should be understood as any connected set of raster points. There is no implication that the arc is straight, circular, or any predefined pattern. We will, however, restrict ourselves to straight lines in the following discussion.

The chain code for the straight line from A to B in Figure 2.18 is 454545454.

**Straightness of a Digital Arc** One recent addition to the theory of digital arcs was discovered by Hung and Kasvand (HUKA84). They state that a digital arc represents a straight line if and only if the chain

**FIGURE 2.16**

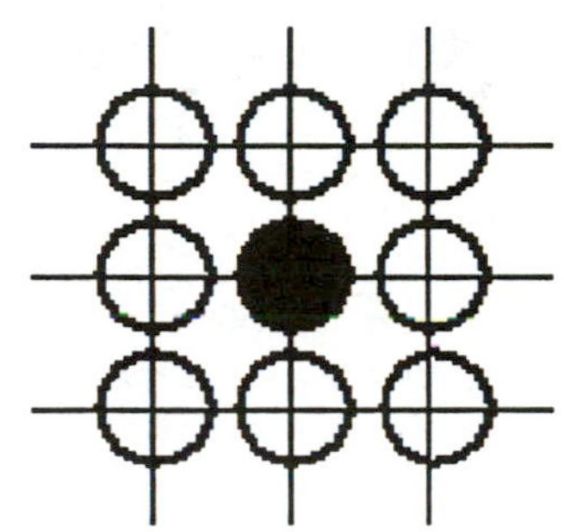

**FIGURE 2.17**

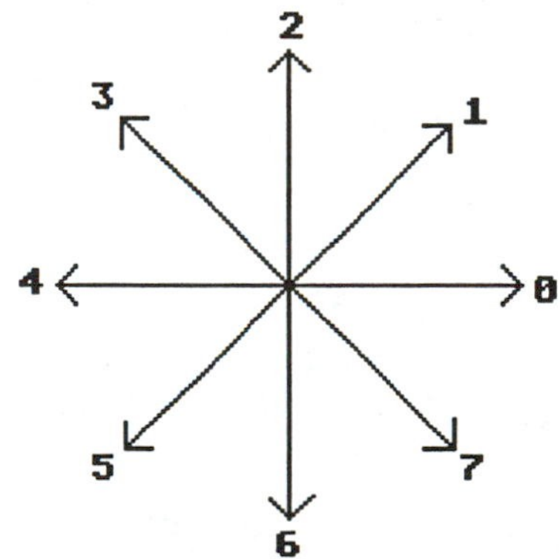

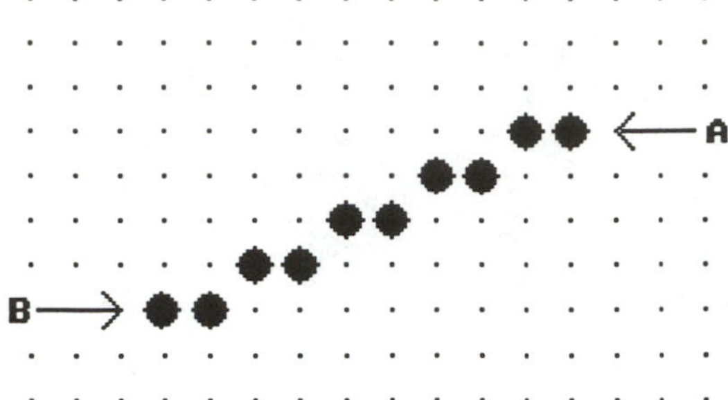


**FIGURE 2.18**

code of the digital arc contains no uneven substrings. (Two equally long substrings of a chain code are uneven if the sums of the values of the two substring elements differ by more than 1.) We list three interesting consequences without proof:

1. In the chain code, at most two different symbols can occur that differ by at most 1 modulo 8.
2. The less frequent symbol only occurs isolated.
3. The more frequent symbol occurs in runs that differ by at most 1 in length.

We can restrict ourselves to the consideration of straight lines with slopes between zero and 45 degrees. Every other straight line can be derived by symmetry. For such lines (they are in the first octant), the chain code is extremely simple—it consists only of 0's and 1's. (0 means that the next point lies to the right; 1 means that it lies above and to the right). A horizontal line will have a chain code of all 0's, a 45-degree line will have a chain code of all 1's (in a 1:1 pixel ratio). Lines with a slope between 0 and 1 have a mixture of 0's and 1's.

**Brons's Structural Method** This method was developed by R. Brons (BRON74, BRON85). It creates the chain code for a straight line with a rational slope (the slope = p/q where p and q are integers). Our assumption that the start and end points are exactly on grid points meets this assumption. This is precise enough for most graphics applications.

Some preparations are necessary before the algorithm can be explained. Every integer number can be decomposed into a sum of arbitrarily-many integer terms which differ only by 1 in size. For example: 37 can be decomposed into five terms: 7+7+7+8+8. The terms are found by dividing the first number by the desired number of terms: 37/5 = 7.4. The smaller term is 7 (integer part of 7.4) and the other term is 8. Another example: 37 can be decomposed into eight terms: 4+4+4+5+5+5+5+5.

In general, decomposing n into k terms consists of computing n/k. If n/k is an integer, then all n terms are equal to n/k. If n/k is not an integer, then the smaller terms are trunc(n/k) and the larger are trunc(n/k)+1. It follows that k * trunc(n/k) < n and k * (trunc(n/k) +1) > n. n − k * trunc(n/k) > 0 is the number of the larger terms; all the others are the smaller.

**Informal Description** We will demonstrate the structural method for creating a straight line with an example. We will construct a line from (0,0) to (41,25). (Note that the y-value of the end point is smaller than the x-value because of the restriction of the line to the first octant.) We need exactly 25 ones to get to the height 25, and 41 − 25 = 16 zeros to move 41 to the right. The first approximation of the straight line therefore is:

1111111111111111111111111 0000000000000000

(Although this is not essential, we will always write the more frequent symbol first.)

This digital arc is certainly not straight. We search for a proper distribution of the 1's and 0's to make the line as straight as possible. The problem now is to find the proper distribution.

The strategy consists of decomposing the bigger number (25) into a number of terms equal to the smaller number (16), with the terms differing by no more than 1 in size. Using the technique described above:

$$25 = 2+2+2+2+2+2+2+2+2+1+1+1+1+1+1+1$$
$$= 9*2 + 7*1$$

Now 16 groups must be built, nine of which must contain two elements and seven of which must contain one element. The more frequent symbol, the 1, which occurs 25 times, must be arranged into these 16 groups, exactly as the decomposition shows. We get nine groups of 11 and seven groups of 1. At the end of each such group of ones we append exactly one of the less frequent symbol, the 0. This will consume all of the zeros:

110 110 110 110 110 110 110 110 110 10 10 10 10 10 10 10

Writing this in a more concise notation gives:

$$(110)^9(10)^7$$

From now on the symbols to deal with are not 1's or 0's, but substrings. There are nine substrings of the form 110 and seven substrings of the

form 10. The more frequent substring occurs nine times and the less frequent one occurs seven times. The next decomposition therefore will consist of decomposing 9 into seven terms:

$$9 = 1+1+1+1+1+2+2 = 5*1 + 2*2$$

Now seven groups must be formed containing either one or two instances of the more frequent substring 110. The first five groups will each contain one such substring. The next two groups will each contain two instances of this substring. At the end of each group we append exactly one of the less frequent substring, which is 10.

$$(110)10\ (110)10\ (110)10\ (110)10\ (110)10\ (110)^2 10\ (110)^2 10$$

Writing this in a more concise notation gives:

$$(11010)^5((110)^2 10)^2$$

There are five substrings of the form 11010 and two substrings of the form $(110)^2 10$. The algorithm stops as soon as one of the substrings occurs only once, but this is not yet the case, so it continues. The more frequent substring occurs five times, and the less frequent substring two times. We have to decompose the bigger number, 5, into two terms:

$$5 = 3+2$$

Two groups must be formed, the first of which contains three instances of 11010 and the second of which contains two instances of 11010. At the end of each group we append the less frequent substring $(110)^2 10$. We get:

$$(11010)^3 (110)^2 10\ (11010)^2 (110)^2 10$$

Both of these newly formed substrings occur only once, therefore the algorithm stops. The resulting chain code is:

$$11010110101101011011010110101101011011010$$

Figure 2.19 shows the application of this chain code. It consists of first setting the pixel (0,0), then going diagonally for every 1 and horizontally for every 0 and setting the pixels at these raster points. This digitization starts at the pixel address (0,0) and leads to the pixel address (41,25). If we take a ruler and draw the true straight line from the first to the last pixel center, we see that the pixels in general lie above the line.

The digitization of the chain code shown above is not the best possible approximation of the line from (0,0) to (41,25). The digitization of the chain can be started at any arbitrary point within the chain, ending with the part of the chain to the left of the starting point. That is, it can be applied in a cyclic manner. We would like to have

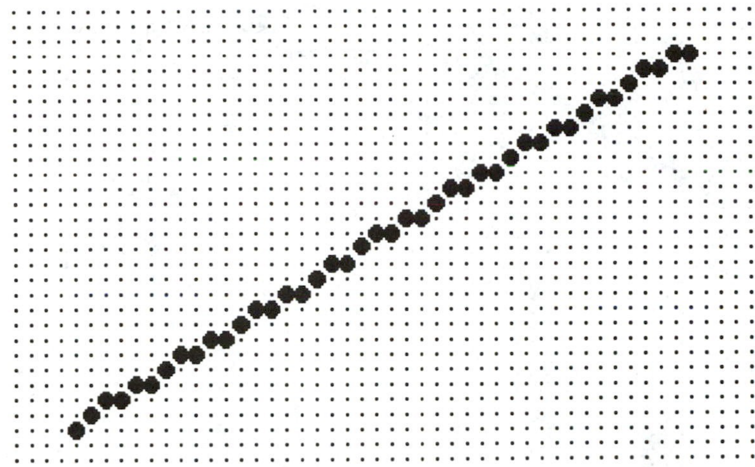

**FIGURE 2.19** Digitization of Brons's chain code.

the pixels centered more around the ideal line. This can easily be achieved if we observe that the reason that the pixels lie above the line is because of the two 1's with which the chain starts.

It follows that the less frequent element in a chain code for a straight line can occur only isolated, that is, in runs of length one. In our case only the symbol 1 can occur in longer runs. The digitization corresponding to such a chain will always lie above or below the true line if it is started at the end or beginning of a run of the more frequent element. A good (not necessarily the optimal) centering is obtained if the start is put approximately in the center of a long run. In our example the digitization starts with a run of length two of the symbol 1. It will be centered better by starting it with the second 1 and putting the first 1 at the end. The chain code then looks like this:

1010110101101011011010110101101011010101

Figure 2.20 shows this digitization. If we draw the straight line from the first to the last pixel, we see that it is well centered in this digitization.

**Coded Algorithm for Brons's Method** A Pascal procedure for Brons's chain code generation is given below. This procedure is of little practical value from the standpoint of speed and storage requirements, but it gives a formal description of the algorithm. Pascal does not allow us to declare a variable of type string of variable length. Such a variable would permit the string manipulations required to generate a chain code. (The C language perhaps would be better adapted for such a procedure.) Our procedure looks clumsy: it has to declare strings of

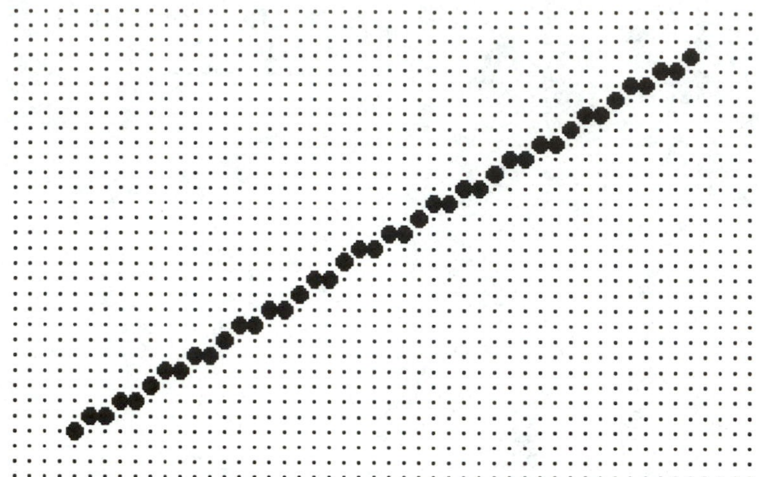

**FIGURE 2.20** Better centered digitization.

fixed maximal length for each of the substrings and keep track of the length in each case. The assignment of one string to another and concatenation must be done explicitly.

```
type    array200    =    array[1..200] of 0..1;

var     chain       :     array200;
        i,x,y       :     integer;

procedure brons(  x,y    :    integer;
             var chain   :    array200);

  {generates a chain code for a straight line
   from (0,0) to (x,y);
   the arguments have to fulfill: 0 < x, 0 ≤ y, y ≤ x;
   the procedure does not check this.
   the final chain code is generated on the parameter
   chain, maximal chain code length is 200}

type    array100    =    array[1..100] of 0..1;

var freq_symbol,rare_symbol,
    long_symbol,shrt_symbol,
    hold_symbol                          :    array100;
    freq_length,rare_length,
    long_length,shrt_length,
    hold_length,
    freq_count,rare_count,
```

```
    long_count,shrt_count,
    chain_length,term,i,j,k,n       :  integer;

procedure repeat_symbol(old_symbol  :  array100;
                        old_length  :  integer;
                        rep_factor  :  integer;
                    var new_symbol  :  array100;
                    var new_length  :  integer);
var  i,j,k  :  integer;

begin
  k := 0;
  for i := 1 to rep_factor do
    for j := 1 to old_length do begin
      k := k + 1;
      new_symbol[k] := old_symbol[j]
    end {for j,i};
  new_length := k
end {procedure repeat_symbol};

procedure add_symbol(first_symbol   :  array100;
                     first_length   :  integer;
                     second_symbol  :  array100;
                     second_length  :  integer;
                 var result_symbol  :  array100;
                 var result_length  :  integer);
var i   :   integer;

begin
  for i := 1 to first_length do
    result_symbol[i] := first_symbol[i];
  for i := 1 to second_length do begin
    result_symbol[first_length + i] := second_symbol[i]
  end;
  result_length := first_length + second_length
end {procedure add_symbol};

procedure assign_symbol(source_symbol1  :  array100;
                        source_length1  :  integer;
                    var dest_symbol1    :  array100;
                        source_symbol2  :  array100;
                        source_length2  :  integer;
                    var dest_symbol2    :  array100);
var    i    :  integer;

begin
  for i := 1 to source_length1 do
    dest_symbol1[i] := source_symbol1[i];
```

```
  for i := 1 to source_length2 do
    dest_symbol2[i] := source_symbol2[i]
end {procedure assign_symbol};

begin {procedure brons}
  freq_length := 1;
  rare_length := 1;
  long_length := 1;
  shrt_length := 1;
  if x-y > y
  then begin
    freq_symbol[1] := 0; rare_symbol[1] := 1;
    freq_count := x-y; rare_count := y
  end
  else begin
    freq_symbol[1] := 1; rare_symbol[1] := 0;
    freq_count := y; rare_count := x-y
  end;

  while (freq_count > 1) and (rare_count > 1) do begin
    term := freq_count div rare_count;

    {composition of the new long symbol}
    repeat_symbol(freq_symbol,freq_length,term+1,
                  hold_symbol,hold_length);
    add_symbol(hold_symbol,hold_length,rare_symbol,rare_length,
               long_symbol,long_length);
    long_count := freq_count - rare_count*term;

    {composition of the new short symbol}
    repeat_symbol(freq_symbol,freq_length,term,
                  hold_symbol,hold_length);
    add_symbol(hold_symbol,hold_length,rare_symbol,rare_length,
               shrt_symbol,shrt_length);
    shrt_count := rare_count - long_count;

    {assign new long and short symbols}
    if shrt_count > long_count
    then begin
      assign_symbol(shrt_symbol,shrt_length,freq_symbol,
                    long_symbol,long_length,rare_symbol);
      freq_count  := shrt_count;
      rare_count  := long_count;
      freq_length := shrt_length;
      rare_length := long_length
    end {then}
```

```
    else begin
      assign_symbol(long_symbol,long_length,freq_symbol,
                    shrt_symbol,shrt_length,rare_symbol);
      freq_count  := long_count;
      rare_count  := shrt_count;
      freq_length := long_length;
      rare_length := shrt_length
    end {else}
  end {while};

  repeat_symbol(freq_symbol,freq_length,freq_count,
                chain,chain_length);
  repeat_symbol(rare_symbol,rare_length,rare_count,
                hold_symbol,hold_length);
  add_symbol(chain,chain_length,hold_symbol,hold_length,
             chain,chain_length);

  end {procedure brons};
```

**The Best-Fit Method** The *best-fit method,* developed by Castle and Pitteway (CAPI85), uses Euclid's algorithm to generate the chain code for a straight line. Lines are restricted to the first octant; zero-degree and 45-degree lines must be excluded. (Amendments can be added to the algorithm to handle these cases.) This elegant method is conceptually much simpler than Brons's. It is interesting to observe that the generated chain code is identical to the Brons chain code but for a cyclic shift.

**Informal Description** We will demonstrate the generation of a chain code by the best-fit technique with an example. We need two substrings, sub1 and sub2, which are originally loaded with the primitive symbols 0 and 1. We also need the coordinates of the end point (x,y); the line is assumed to start at (0,0). The reverse of a string will be denoted by $(s)^{-1}$, so $(11101)^{-1} = 10111$, and concatenation will be denoted by +, so 1110+10 = 111010.

Here is the pseudocode to do it:

```
  x is assigned x-y
start:
  x is compared to y and, depending on the outcome:
    if x > y: then sub2 = sub1+(sub2)^-1 and
      y is subtracted from x
    if x = y: we are done and the final code is produced (see below)
    if x < y: then sub1 = sub2+(sub1)^-1 and
      x is subtracted from y
go to start.
```

**TABLE 2.1**

| x | y | sub1 | sub2 |
|---|---|---|---|
| 16 | 25 | 10 | 1 |
| 16 | 9 | 10 | 101 |
| 7 | 9 | 10101 | 101 |
| 7 | 2 | 10101 | 10101101 |
| 5 | 2 | 10101 | 1010110110101 |
| 3 | 2 | 10101 | 101011010110110101 |
| 1 | 2 | 10101101011011010110101 | 101011010110110101 |
| 1 | 1 | x = y so output final chain code: 10101101011011010110101101010110110101101 | |

Here are the successive values for a line from (0,0) to (41,25). Starting values are:

x = 16    y = 25    sub1 = 0    sub2 = 1

Table 2.1 shows how values develop.

The final chain code is obtained by concatenating sub1 + $(\text{sub2})^{-1}$ or sub2 + $(\text{sub1})^{-1}$ (these will be identical) and repeating the resulting string x or y times (x and y are equal at the conclusion). The ending values for x and y will be 1 unless the starting values have a common divisor. Observe that the resulting chain code is symmetric with respect to the center unless all the long runs are an odd number long. Even so, this method produces the best-fit line.

The best-fit method usually needs more steps than the Brons method. Consider the case of a line generated from (0,0) to (40,1). The first generated substring will be 01. With every step this substring will be reversed, a single 0 will be appended to the left of it, and x will be decremented by 1. The substring will grow in length by one only in every step and will assume the following values:

```
  01
  010
 0010
 00100
000100
0001000
  etc.
```

until it has the length 40. The continual reversing finally leads to the single 1 being in the middle of the whole string. Forty reversals of the substring are necessary, which makes the algorithm very slow. Brons's method doesn't have this problem.

### Coded Algorithm for the Best-Fit Structural Method

```
type   array200    =   array[1..200] of 0..1;

var    chain      :     array200;
       i,x,y      :     integer;

procedure bestfit(   x,y    :   integer;
               var chain    :   array200);
{x and y must fulfill: 0 < y < x <= 200,
 the procedure does not check this}
var symbol1,symbol2     :   array200;
    length1,length2,
       chain_length     :   integer;

procedure repeat_symbol(old_symbol    :    array200;
                        old_length    :    integer;
                        rep_factor    :    integer;
                    var new_symbol    :    array200;
                    var new_length    :    integer);
var   i,j,k    :   integer;

begin
  k := 0;
  for i := 1 to rep_factor do
    for j := 1 to old_length do begin
      k := k + 1;
      new_symbol[k] := old_symbol[j]
    end {for j,i};
    new_length := k
end {procedure repeat_symbol};

procedure add_symbol( first_symbol    :    array200;
                      first_length    :    integer;
                     second_symbol    :    array200;
                     second_length    :    integer;
                 var result_symbol    :    array200;
                 var result_length    :    integer);
var i    :   integer;

begin
  for i := 1 to first_length do
    result_symbol[i] := first_symbol[i];
  for i := 1 to second_length do begin
```

```
    result_symbol[first_length + i] := second_symbol[i]
  end;
  result_length := first_length + second_length
end {procedure add_symbol};

procedure invert_symbol(var symbol   :   array200;
                            length   :   integer);
var  help,i    :   integer;

begin
  for i := 1 to length div 2 do begin
    help := symbol[length-i+1];
    symbol[length-i+1] := symbol[i];
    symbol[i] := help
  end
end {procedure invert_symbol};

begin {procedure bestfit}
  length1 := 1;
  length2 := 1;
  symbol1[1] := 0;
  symbol2[1] := 1;
  x := x-y;

  repeat
    if x > y
    then begin
      invert_symbol(symbol2,length2);
      add_symbol(symbol1,length1,symbol2,length2,
                 symbol2,length2);
      x := x-y
    end;
    if x < y
    then begin
      invert_symbol(symbol1,length1);
      add_symbol(symbol2,length2,symbol1,length1,
                 symbol1,length1);
      y := y-x
    end
  until x = y;

  invert_symbol(symbol2,length2);
  add_symbol(symbol1,length1,symbol2,length2,
             chain,chain_length);
  repeat_symbol(chain,chain_length,x,chain,chain_length)

end {procedure bestfit};
```

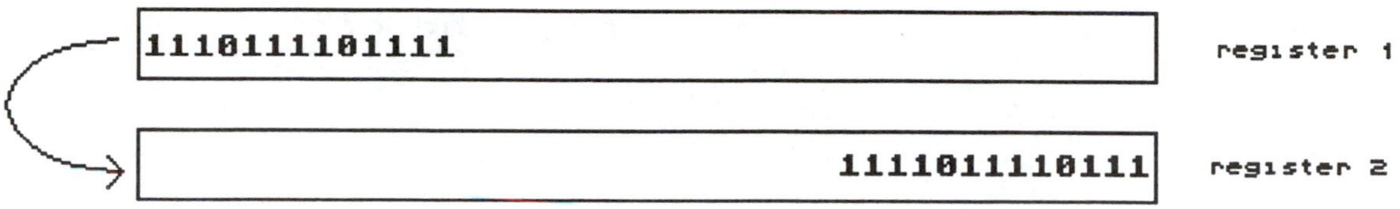

| 1110111101111 | register 1 |
|---|---|
| 1111011110111 | register 2 |

**FIGURE 2.21**

Structural methods are certainly worth considering even if the algorithms presented here are slow and look complicated compared to the conditional methods presented next. The string manipulations, which are so time consuming and awkward to perform in software, might easily be performed by hardware and then lead to very fast straight line generation. Only two kinds of symbols can occur, therefore a symbol could be represented by a single bit. It has been suggested that the concatenation and reversal of substrings could be done in long shift registers. A shift of one register into another can be used to implement a fast reversal of a string, as shown in Figure 2.21. Shifting register 1 into register 2 as indicated by the arrow performs the reversal of a string (CAPI85). We observe that the registers would have to be as long as the number of pixels horizontally on the screen. Very fast shifts can be achieved with so-called *barrel shifters,* a special hardware development used, for example, in video RAMs.

## 2.1.2 Conditional Methods

There are many different conditional methods for straight line generation. A conditional method can set each pixel without knowing where the next pixel will be, a significant difference from the structural methods. After one pixel has been set, certain conditions are checked to determine the position of the next. In this way a line is generated, stepping forward pixel by pixel until the end point is reached.

One possibility would be to calculate precisely the next grid point closest to the theoretical line and set a pixel there, but that would be very slow. As lines belong to the most used graphics primitives, it is essential that they be drawn very rapidly. We must therefore use only methods that require few computations. The incremental methods that we explain below are very fast. We introduce the topic with several examples.

**Incremental Methods** Suppose we want a line from the grid point (0,0) to the grid point (10,0). There is an increment of 10 in x

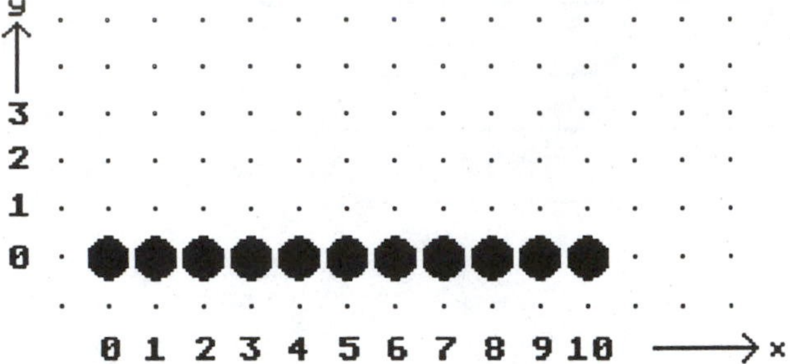


FIGURE 2.22

but no increment in y. We move from (0,0) to (10,0) by incrementing x at every step, never incrementing y, and setting all the pixels we come to. We stop as soon as we reach (10,0) (see Figure 2.22). Observe that the slope of the line is 0.

Now consider the case of a line from (0,0) to (10,10). Here, too, the incremental method is easy. We start at (0,0) and increment both x and y at each step, set all the pixels we come to, and stop as soon as the end point is reached (see Figure 2.23). Observe that the slope of the line is 1.

In the next example we create a straight line from (0,0) to (10,5). It is easy to see that y must be incremented half as often as x in order to reach the end point. This is realized by incrementing x at each step and y at each second step. The resulting line is shown in Figure 2.24. Observe that the slope of the line is 0.5.

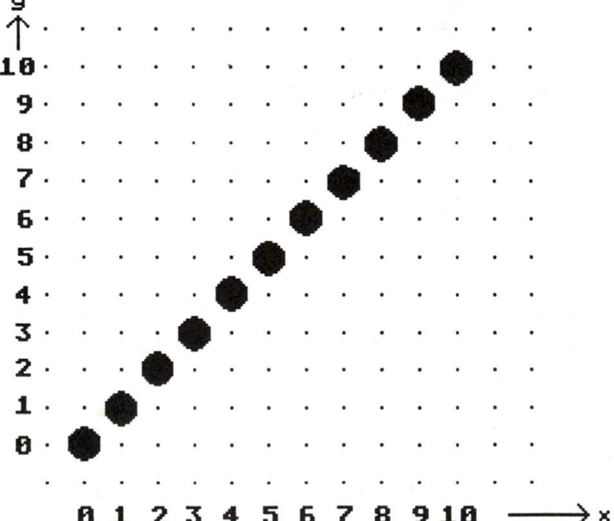


FIGURE 2.23

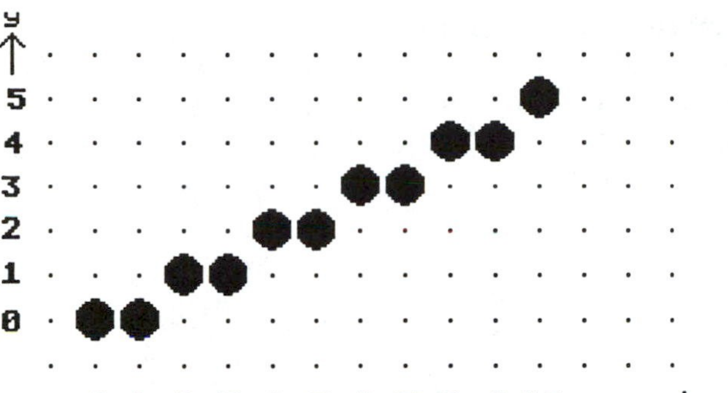


**FIGURE 2.24**

**DDA Algorithms** The above examples show that we increment y, relative to the incrementing of x, according to the slope of the line. Basically, incremental algorithms do only two things: they test and count. They test whether to increment a variable and they keep track of two counts. Before they start, these counts have to be determined using the start point and end point coordinates.

A *digital differential analyzer* (DDA) is such an incremental method. DDAs can be designed for circular arcs and other curves as well as straight lines. In fact, they can draw any curve whose differential equation is given. The differential equation of a straight line is:

$$dy/dx = c$$

where c is a constant. This relation remains true if we replace the derivative dy/dx by the quotient Dy/Dx where Dx and Dy are both finite differences. The quotient of the increments must be equal to the slope of the line (its derivative).

Given the start point and end point we can draw a line by doing the following: We calculate the derivative and choose incremental values Dx and Dy in the proper ratio. The start point is the first point on the line. We increment the x-value by Dx and the y-value by Dy. The result, in most cases, will not correspond to a pixel location, so we round it to the nearest integers, giving us the location of the closest grid point. We display a pixel at this location.

To get the next point, we must add Dx and Dy to the nonrounded results of the previous step. The nonrounded results will correspond exactly to points on the ideal line and the rounding process gives the closest grid point location for pixels. The internal iteration process is:

$$x_{n+1} = x_n + Dx$$
$$y_{n+1} = y_n + Dy$$
$$\text{SetPix}(\text{round}(x_{n+1}),\text{round}(y_{n+1}))$$

Each step is computed with just two floating point additions and two rounding operations.

The choice of values for Dx and Dy is important. If the values we choose are too small, then after rounding we could get the same pixel address again; this could happen several times before we really advance to a new pixel. If we set the incremental values too large, then we could jump over pixels that should be set. Figures 2.25 and 2.26 show these two situations. The arrows point to the actual pixels which are obtained by rounding the x- and y-values. In Figure 2.25 the incremental values are too small, so some pixels are computed and set several times. In Figure 2.26 the incremental values are too large and the line has gaps.

The proper choice of increments should lead to a new pixel at each step but should not be so large that the resulting pixel sequence is not eight-connected, as in Figure 2.14. This problem can be solved

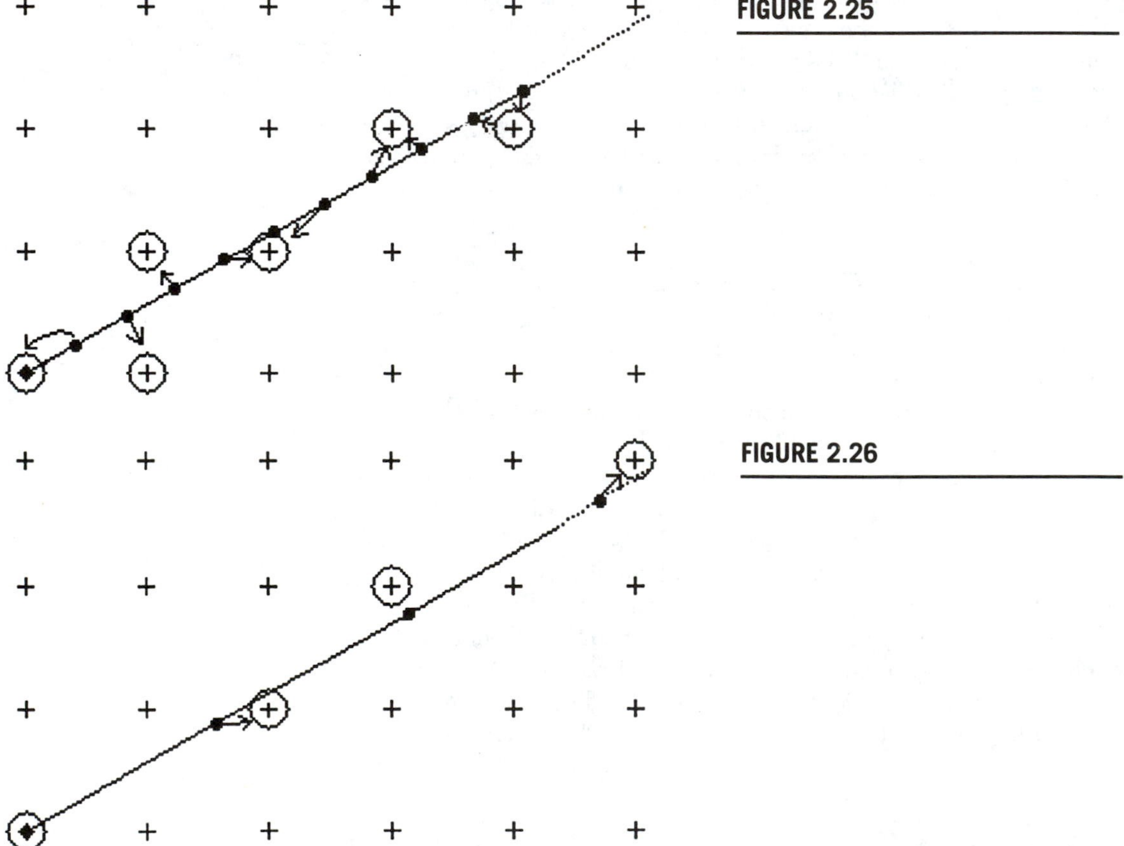

FIGURE 2.25

FIGURE 2.26

by computing the incrementation values so that the larger has magnitude 1. The simple straight line DDA presented below does exactly that.

#### 2.1.2.1 The Simple Straight Line DDA

This DDA first calculates the number of incrementing steps that are required. It sets distx = abs($x_{start} - x_{end}$) and disty = abs($y_{start} - y_{end}$) and computes:

$$\text{nstep} = \text{number of steps} = \max(\text{distx}, \text{disty}).$$

If we take Dx = distx/nstep and Dy = disty/nstep, it follows that either Dx or Dy equals 1. A true division is needed only to find the increment whose magnitude is less than 1. Comparing distx to disty can determine which one this is. We speed up the incrementing process by replacing one of the floating point adders by a simple counter. This algorithm draws exactly nstep pixels, one for each step.

The Pascal code below shows only the logic of this DDA. It does not implement all possibilities for further improvement. By considering whether Dx or Dy has magnitude 1 and their signs, each step needs only one rounding operation and one floating point addition. This should be considered when the algorithm is programmed in assembly; the floating point operations should be done by floating point hardware.

**Coded Algorithm**

```
Procedure SIMPDDA( xstart,ystart,
                       xend,yend   :  integer);
var      nstep,i    :   integer;
      x,y,Dx,Dy     :   real;

begin {procedure SIMPDDA}
   nstep := abs(xstart-xend);
   Dx := 0; Dy := 0;
   if abs(ystart-yend) > nstep then nstep := abs(ystart-yend);
   if nstep > 0
   then begin
      Dx := (xend-xstart)/nstep;
      Dy := (yend-ystart)/nstep
   end {then};
   x := xstart; y := ystart;
   for i := 0 to nstep do begin
      setpix(round(x),round(y));
      x := x+Dx;
      y := y+Dy
   end {for i}
end {procedure SIMPDDA};
```

### 2.1.2.2 Bresenham's Straight Line Algorithm

We will take a heuristic approach to explain Bresenham's straight line algorithm. We limit our consideration to lines from (0,0) to any point within the first octant; these lines are between zero and 45 degrees. Every other line is algorithmically identical except for simple symmetry considerations.

We will draw a line from (0,0) to (19,4). Imagine the precise straight line in the pixel grid from (0,0) to (19,4) as shown in Figure 2.27. The line intersects the vertical grid lines at 18 positions between the x-values of 0 and 19. In our given case (and also in general) these intersections are in between, not on, pixel locations. We set the pixel that is closer to the intersection. The start point and the end point of the line lie exactly on grid points. Figure 2.28 shows the beginning of the ideal line and the first few intersections.

The height at which the ideal line intersects the vertical grid line is 4/19 for the first intersection, 8/19 for the second, 12/19 for the third, and so on. Because the value for the first intersection is below 0.5, we choose the pixel at height 0, corresponding to a horizontal step. The second intersection also is below 0.5, so again the pixel at height 0 is chosen—another horizontal step. At the third intersection we have 12/19 which is greater than 0.5, so we choose the pixel at height 1, corresponding to a horizontal plus a vertical step. From now on the pixel at height 0 will never be chosen; the decision will be between the pixels at height 1 and height 2. The comparison will be to the number 1.5 instead of 0.5.

We can see that a horizontal step is always taken, and a vertical step is taken in addition to the horizontal step whenever the comparison shows the intersection to be above the halfway point. If the intersection is exactly at the halfway point, the pixel can be chosen arbitrarily.

**FIGURE 2.27**

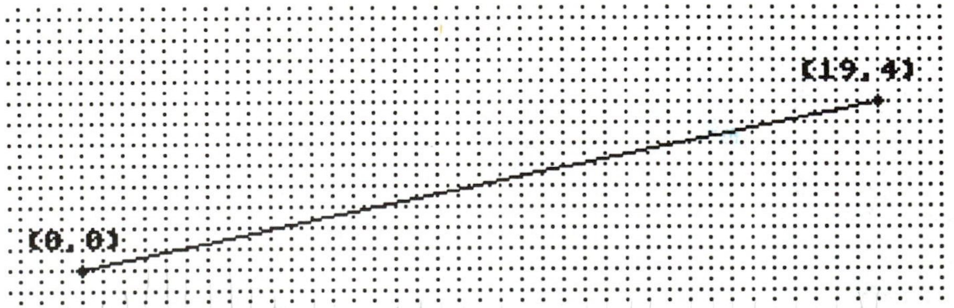

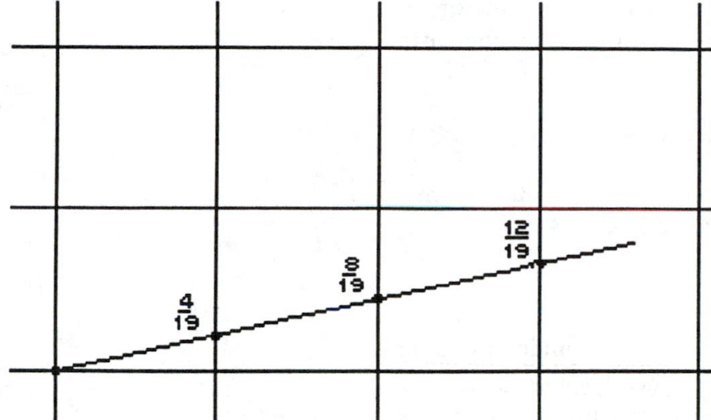


**FIGURE 2.28**

Perhaps we should summarize this, using some special terms: *elevation* is the value of the y-coordinate on the ideal line, *midpoint* is the value that we compare to in deciding whether to move vertically when setting a pixel. We set a pixel at (0,0) and make the elevation value 0. We then add 4/19 to it and compare it to a midpoint value of 0.5. If it is smaller, we make a horizontal step only; if greater, we make a horizontal and a vertical step. We repeat this for a total of 19 steps, adjusting the elevation and midpoint values as appropriate.

This algorithm can be demonstrated through a schematic in which we write the numbers themselves at the places where the pixels are to be set. The starting elevation is 0. It is increased by 4/19 with each step and a comparison is made to the midpoint of 0.5 = 9.5/19. As long as the elevation is smaller, we write it to the right of the current elevation value. If the elevation is larger than 9.5/19 we take a horizontal plus a vertical step; that is, we write the next number at 45 degrees above the last number. From now on the midpoint to compare to will be 1.5 = 28.5/19. The midpoint values to which we compare are shown at the left of the corresponding row. The schematic is not executed to completion; actually there will be 19 steps.

```
Midpoints                 Elevations

66.5/19 |                                                                    48/19 52/19 56/19 . . .
47.5/19 |                                                32/19 36/19 40/19 44/19
28.5/19 |                        12/19 16/19 20/19 24/19 28/19
 9.5/19 |  0/19  4/19  8/19
```

We can see that it is superfluous to carry the denominator 19 along in either the midpoints or the elevations. Below is the schematic without the denominator:

```
Midpoints                    Elevations

  66.5 |                                     48 52 56 ...
  47.5 |                         32 36 40 44
  28.5 |           12 16 20 24 28
   9.5 | 0  4  8
```

With denominators left out, the increase by one of the midpoint value appears as an increase by 19. The increase of the elevation is now by 4. Another change that will bring us closer to the final algorithm is that instead of increasing the midpoint values by 19 whenever a vertical step is taken, we can as well decrease the elevation by 19 and always compare to 9.5. This gives the following schematic:

```
                                                      -8  -4   0
                                  -9  -5  -1   3   7
                     -6  -2   2   6
      -7  -3   1   5   9
0  4  8
----------------------------------------------------------------
      -19             -19            -19             -19
```

Whenever the elevation becomes larger than 9.5 a vertical step is taken and 19 is subtracted. The $-19$ below the line indicates when this was done. It is no coincidence that we end up with 0 after 19 steps. Altogether we have added four 19 times and we have subtracted 19 four times. Therefore we must have exactly the starting elevation after doing the 19 horizontal steps. This will always be the case.

Two more major improvements can now be made. The first consists of working with all numbers doubled. This does not change the schematic and leads to pure integer arithmetic, not only in our example but in all cases. The reason is that the comparison to 9.5 resulted from the original comparison to 1/2, or 3/2, and so forth in finding the grid point to be set. This brought the denominator 2 into play. This denominator is eliminated when all numbers are doubled.

```
                                                        -16  -8   0
                                      -18 -10  -2   6  14
                         -12  -4   4  12
      -14  -6   2  10  18
0  8  16
------------------------------------------------------------------
      -38              -38             -38               -38
```

The number to add is now 8, the number to subtract is 38. The second improvement consists of comparing to 0 instead of to 19. This can easily be achieved: the schematic will not change if we start out with -19 instead of 0 and compare to 0 instead of 19. This will just decrease all numbers in the schematic by 19. Comparison to 0 is performed faster in machine code than comparison to any other number.

```
                                                                      -35 -27 -19
                                                  -37 -29 -21 -13  -5
                                  -31 -23 -15  -7
              -33 -25 -17  -9  -1
-19 -11  -3
```

This is Bresenham's straight line algorithm! Figure 2.29 shows the resulting line in the pixel grid.

**Coded Algorithm** We avoided strict mathematical reasoning in developing Bresenham's algorithm; the heuristic understanding is enough for our purposes. The code below reflects precisely the method we have explained above.

```
procedure bresline(xstart,ystart,xend,yend : integer);
var
         sum,
      Dx,Dy,
        x,y    :   integer;

begin
    sum := xstart-xend;
    Dx  := 2*(xend-xstart);
    Dy  := 2*(yend-ystart);
    x := xstart; y := ystart;
    for i := 0 to xend-xstart do begin
        setpix(x,y);
        x := x + 1;                  {horizontal step}
        sum := sum + Dy;
        if sum ≥ 0
        then begin
            y := y + 1;              {vertical step}
            sum := sum - Dx
        end {then}
    end {for i}
end {procedure bresline};
```

The above example and the code differ in that the code doesn't require the line to start at the point (0,0), but this implies no change in the algorithm. The coded algorithm is still restricted to lines in the

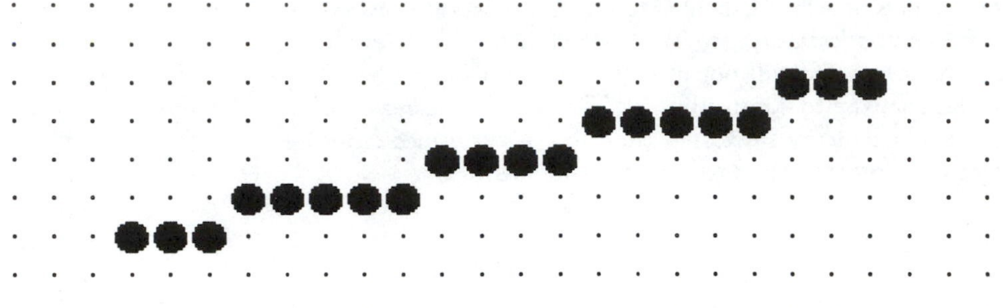

**FIGURE 2.29** Line drawn with Bresenham's algorithm.

first octant. The starting pixel is always set, so a line from a point to itself would result in setting just one pixel. It does no multiplications and no divisions—the multiplication by 2 cannot be considered as such, because it is only a left shift by one bit internally.

A full implementation of Bresenham's straight line algorithm requires testing for lines in other than the first octant. The logic can be derived by symmetry from the case presented. It is the fastest line-drawing algorithm and is well suited for implementation on raster graphics systems. Like the simple DDA above it never sets a pixel more than once.

# 2.2 POLYGONS

A polygon, even though generally constructed from straight lines, is also an important graphics primitive. We consider a polygon as a graphics primitive because we often want to handle it as a single entity. It is important because images of objects from the real world consist in large part of polygons.

We must understand polygons in a very broad sense. A *polygon* is any area of an image that is bounded by straight or curved lines and filled with one solid color. Since images are two-dimensional, a polygon is a closed planar figure. Accepting curved lines as boundaries poses no problem because of the ease of approximating a curved outline by a sequence of straight lines. When we do this, our image is no further from reality than if we used an outline defined by mathematical curves, because neither curves nor straight lines are real; both are abstractions in our mind. Our visual system readily merges straight line sequences to perceive them as a smooth curve. This justifies our including figures bounded by smooth outlines as polygons.

We will further broaden the definition by relaxing the requirement that the area be filled with one solid color when displayed on a color monitor. We consider areas in which gradual color changes occur as one polygon. Such color variations occur naturally due to differences in light reflection from surfaces. An abrupt color change indicates a boundary of the polygon. It is almost impossible to precisely define the degree of abruptness that defines a boundary, but such a definition is not needed. Nothing keeps us from specifically defining a polygon boundary wherever we desire. We will always decompose a scene from the real world into a collection of polygons of simple shapes.

Based on this general concept of a polygon, we can build every picture from filled polygons. Of course, what we get from this is only an approximation, but that is all we can hope to do. Actually, neither straight lines nor polygons precisely describe a real-world scene; such scenes actually seem to be of a fractal nature. We will study fractals in Chapter 10.

### 2.2.1 Internal Representation of Polygons

In the above paragraphs, the term polygon referred to one in two-dimensional space, the plane of the display screen where we create pictures. The external real-world objects that we model as pictures on the screen will be considered to have surfaces that are composed of polygons as well, but these are three-dimensional. This provides much simplification, but thinking of objects as being bounded by polygons is somewhat artificial; it has the same if not greater limitations as thinking of images as being composed only of polygons. For example, when a smooth curved surface of an object is represented by many flat polygons joined together, the result is not smooth. However, techniques have been developed to make the representation appear smoothly curved, with the joins between the polygons invisible.

The reason for using polygonal surfaces is that we must project every three-dimensional scene onto the two-dimensional display screen. So our three-dimensional polygons that compose surfaces are turned into two-dimensional polygons!

Implementing a polygon as a graphics primitive is natural and helpful. Even with our broad definition, a polygon consists of a finite ordered set of straight boundaries, called *edges*. Alternately, the polygon can be defined by an ordered sequence of *vertices*, the corners of the polygon. The edges of the polygon are then obtained by traversing the vertices in the given order; two consecutive vertices define one edge. We close the polygon by connecting the last vertex to the first.

If only the boundary of a polygon is needed, a sequence of line draw commands can produce it. Since a polygon is a graphics primitive, the system can distinguish between a sequence of unrelated line draw commands and a sequence of edges that belong to a polygon. This results from the data structure that is used. Polygons can be represented in a graphics system in various ways, depending on the types of data structures the programming language supports. One technique puts the sequence of edges into a linked list (see polygon meshes in Chapter 11). Another technique is to store the sequence of vertices in arrays that contain the x-, y-, and z-coordinates. The graphics system can use the stored polygon information to derive other information necessary for various algorithms. For example, it can find the plane in space in which a polygon lies, it can divide a polygon into smaller polygons for depth sorting, it can clip it against a given window, or it can fill the polygon.

Some of our polygon algorithms work only in three-dimensional space (such as finding the plane in which a polygon lies). Others, such as those that do clipping, apply in both two and three dimensions. Filling polygons has meaning only in two dimensions. It is a scan-converting process and, as such, is part of the production of the image. The scan conversion of a polygon is done in image space.

When we want to fill a polygon with color, the polygon must be stored in two arrays that contain the x- and y-coordinates of its vertices. If a spatial object bounded by polygons is to be displayed, then only the projections onto the screen of the bounding polygons are filled; therefore only two-dimensional polygon representations need be considered for filling. Because of this, the z-coordinates of three-dimensional polygons play no role.

Filling polygons can only be done on raster displays and on plotters because a vector display cannot show a filled polygon without flickering. The fill procedure is very closely related to the particular hardware used.

## 2.2.2 Polygon Filling

When in the same plane, an infinitely long horizontal line can intersect the boundaries of a polygon a certain number of times. This number can range from zero up to the number of polygon edges. For now, we restrict our consideration to horizontal lines because, when working on a raster display, the whole screen is filled by horizontal scan lines. These scan lines are a basis for the filling elements for a polygon. A polygon could also be filled with vertical or slanted lines but the limitations of hardware and display technology make this much slower. Filling with slanted lines would not work if solid filling is desired. (The reason for this is that slanted lines are stairstepped; if the lines are at other than 45°, this can leave holes in the fill when the stair steps do not match up.)

Figure 2.30 shows some possible situations when a horizontal line intersects the polygon boundaries. A little reflection makes it clear that an odd number of intersections can occur only if the line goes through a vertex. In all other cases the number of intersections must be even. This fact will be exploited to simplify the filling algorithm.

Filling the polygon is achieved by setting all pixels that are within or on the polygon boundary to the fill color. It is theoretically possible but not practical to decide individually for each pixel on the screen whether it is inside or outside a given polygon by using an inside-outside test. We do not define the notions "inside" and "outside" precisely. There is no need, since inside-outside tests are expensive to perform and we are able to avoid them.

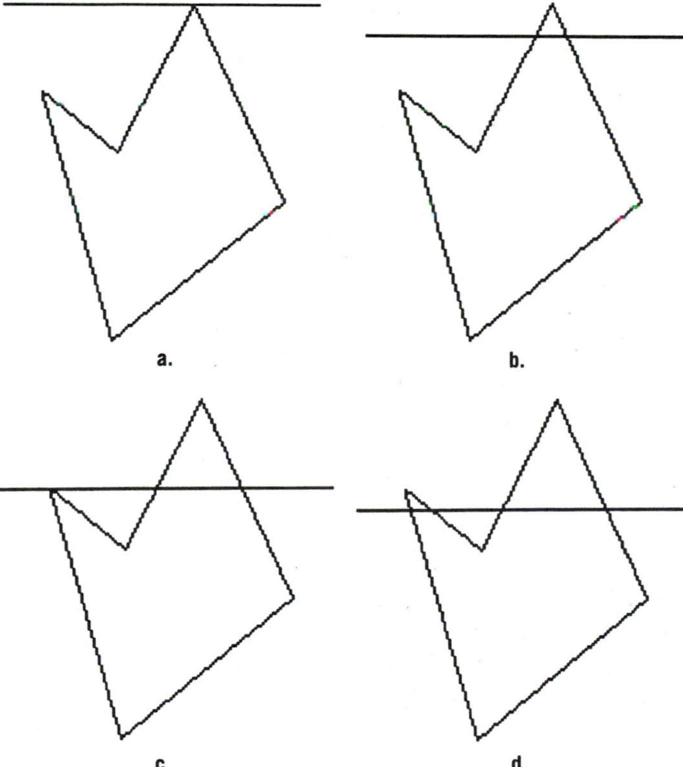


**FIGURE 2.30** Several positions of an intersecting line.

Recall that each pixel has a fixed location on the screen, arranged in scan lines. Scan lines will be used as the horizontal lines intersecting with the polygon.

Suppose we want to fill a polygon with a certain fill color. We could move down the whole screen starting with the uppermost scan line, traversing each scan line from left to right in steps of one pixel. When a step reaches or crosses a polygon boundary, we set the pixel and all following pixels to the fill color, stopping when we again reach or traverse a boundary. When this happens we leave the pixels in their unset state until we again reach or cross a boundary or until we reach the edge of the screen. Crossing polygon boundaries acts like a switch that determines if the pixels should be set or left alone.

Figure 2.31 shows two edges of a polygon and three scan lines with pixel positions. Scan lines are traversed in the direction of the arrow. The circles are set pixels; the dots are unchanged pixels. The solid lines are the precise polygon edges.

**FIGURE 2.31**

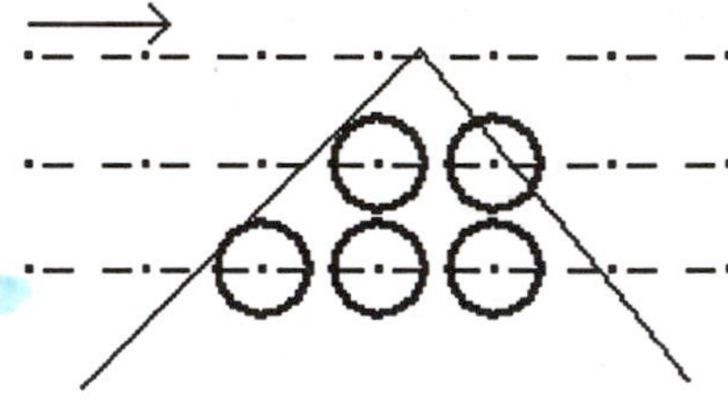

This method is simple. It works if the switch is always in the off position before we begin a scan and if no polygon extends beyond the screen boundaries. This requirement can be met by filling only polygons that have been *clipped,* meaning that parts beyond the screen are clipped off. A clipped polygon will always have an edge at the boundary of the screen, so the first and last pixel of a scan line will be either outside or on a polygon edge. Hitting a polygon vertex can be a problem. In such a case we don't necessarily cross an edge, as case a in Figure 2.30 shows. Visually, it is very easy to see when to switch, but in a computer program it is not so obvious. The fill algorithm we develop below will not run into this problem as we will avoid intersections with vertices.

We can make some improvements in this process. It is not necessary to traverse those scan lines that are above the highest vertex of the polygon nor those that are below the lowest vertex. Therefore we should find the highest y-coordinate and the lowest y-coordinate of all vertices and restrict the scanning process to scan lines within this range.

While traversing a scan line, we don't have to check for edges at the very first pixel and continue to test throughout the whole scan line. Instead, we can compute in advance all intersection points of the edges with this scan line. These intersections in general will not be integer values, so we round them to the closest integer values. This will always give us an even number of integer-valued intersections. They will be at most half a pixel off the true intersections; this is the best we can do. To perform the fill, we move to the leftmost intersection, draw horizontally to the next intersection, move to the next intersection, draw to the next, and so on until all intersection pairs are used up.

The above two paragraphs describe the essence of the polygon-filling algorithm. We will now implement it. The main implementation problem is to find an economical way of computing the intersection points for each scan line. This is discussed below.

As stated, we want to avoid encountering a vertex when we traverse along a scan line. We do this by replacing y-values at the vertices with trunc(y)+0.5. This distortion is smaller than half a pixel and generally cannot be perceived visually. The reason for doing this is that when we draw a horizontal fill line from one edge to the next, we round the intersections to the nearest pixel location. This makes the fill lines sometimes a little too long, sometimes a little too short. (This is unavoidable.) On average the fill lines will have the proper length. When we fill across a polygon from top to bottom, filling only along those scan lines that are below the highest and above the lowest true vertex value, the vertical extent of the filled area is always shorter than the total vertical extent of the polygon. No rounding effect takes place as it does at left and right edges. Distorting the y-coordinates produces something comparable to rounding in the vertical direction. We also get the best symmetry when the vertices are between two scan lines.

In Figure 2.32, only an even number of polygon edges intersect with a scan line. The polygon has six edges and five different scan lines are shown. Only those edges of the polygon whose greater y-value is above and whose smaller y-value is below the scan line value are cut.

| | |
|---|---|
| Scan line a intersects with two edges: | 4-5 and 5-6. |
| Scan line b intersects with four edges: | 4-5, 5-6, 6-1, and 1-2. |
| Scan line c intersects with six edges: | 4-5, 3-4, 2-3, 5-6, 6-1, and 1-2; |

and so on.

Edges 1-2, 6-1, 3-4, and 2-3 are not cut by scan line a.
Edges 5-6 and 6-1 are not cut by scan line d;

and so on.

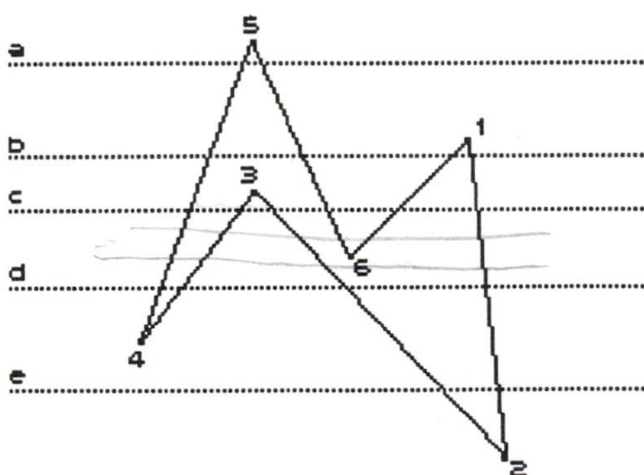


**FIGURE 2.32** Intersection of scan lines with polygon edges.

For a given scan line, we can go through all edges of the polygon and check the y-values of the two vertices that describe this edge. We call the larger y-coordinate ymax and the smaller y-coordinate ymin. (The case ymax = ymin is simple and will be explained later.) If ymin < scan < ymax, there is an intersection with the scan line and we compute it. As soon as we have all intersections, we draw horizontal lines between the intersection pairs as described above. This method would give correct results but it is not economical. For example, once the scan line gets lower than vertex 6 the two edges 5-6 and 6-1 can never be cut. It would be a waste to check all succeeding scan line values against ymin and ymax of these two edges.

**Informal Description of the Algorithm** We avoid the above inefficiency in this way: we use a data structure that contains only those edges that can be cut by the current scan line. We call these the *current edges.* For every new scan line value, the data structure is updated by excluding edges that have just been passed and including edges that have just been met. We will organize the data structure so that once an edge is excluded it will not be tested again for inclusion. This reduces the checking to a minimum.

The scan begins at the greatest y-value and continuously sweeps over the polygon from top to bottom, decreasing in steps of one at each scan. An edge is included in the data structure only if its ymax is greater than the current scan line, so only ymax values have to be checked for this purpose. An edge is excluded only if its ymin is greater than the current scan line, so only ymin values have to be checked. Furthermore, only the current edges have to be checked for exclusion. All this decreases considerably the amount of necessary checking.

If we provide a data structure that holds the edges of the polygon of Figure 2.32 after sorting on their ymax values, the arrangement would look like this:

4-5 5-6 6-1 1-2 3-4 2-3

The current edges can be indicated by two pointers—let's call them leftmost edge (lme) and rightmost edge (rme). The edges pointed to by lme and rme plus those between the pointers are considered current. For scan line a in Figure 2.32 we have:

```
4-5   5-6   6-1   1-2   3-4   2-3
 |     |
lme   rme
```

For scan line b we have:

```
4-5   5-6   6-1   1-2   3-4   2-3
 |                 |
lme               rme
```

And for the scan line c we have:

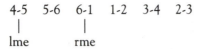

```
4-5   5-6   6-1   1-2   3-4   2-3
 |           |
lme         rme
```

Including new edges is done by testing whether scan is less than the ymax values of the edges to the right of rme. If the first comparison results in scan > ymax, there is no inclusion at all; no more comparisons are necessary because of the sorting on ymax values. Only if scan < ymax are further comparisons necessary. Inclusion is done by increasing rme to the most recently included edge.

Note that the edges between the lme and rme pointers are not necessarily arranged in a left-to-right order of the sequence of intersections. The algorithm must include a sorting among the current edges to obtain this; when that is done, the names for the pointers make sense.

Exclusion of edges is more complicated. We have to check the ymin values of all current edges against scan because an edge to be excluded can occur anywhere in the current edge list. If the edge to be excluded is not the leftmost current edge, we have to literally remove it from the data structure and shift the remaining edges to keep a coherent sequence of current edges.

Now that we know how to maintain a list of the current edges, we consider the computation of the intersection points. Not much computation is necessary because polygons are bounded by straight lines. Successive decreases of scan are in units of 1, therefore the intersection points of scan lines with a given edge will change by a constant amount for every successive change in scan (see Figure 2.33).

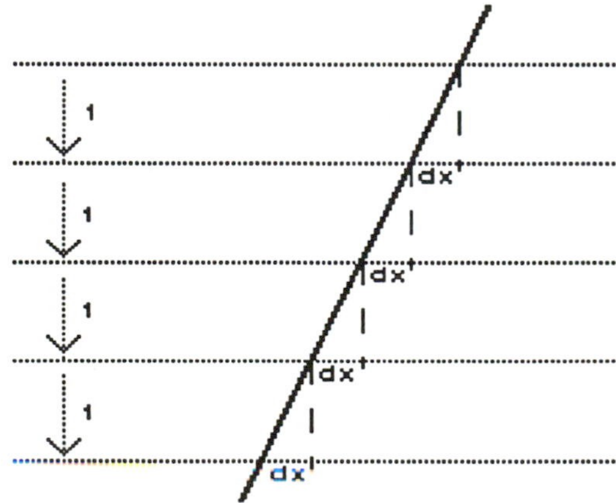


**FIGURE 2.33**

Figure 2.33 shows part of the edge 4-5 of the polygon of Figure 2.32 together with several successive scan lines. The x-value of the intersection point changes by the constant amount Dx for each new scan line. This quantity just has to be added to the old intersection value to get the new one. (Dx in this case is negative.) The constant Dx value for each edge will be computed before the scanning process begins and will be stored in the edge list for each edge.

For each edge, we also store the x-value of the intersection with the scan line. (See below on these values.) For each new scan line these values will be updated by going through all current edges and adding the Dx for each edge to its old intersection x-value.

We can now present the final data structure. It is a table with as many rows as there are edges and four entries for each edge. The four entries are:

the maximum y-coordinate of the edge, distorted : ymax
the minimum y-coordinate of the edge, distorted : ymin
the change in x-value for this edge per scan : Dx
the x-value of the intersection with the next scan : x

We will use a double-subscripted array for the table. Lme and rme are values of appropriate subscripts into this table. Ymax and ymin have already been explained. Dx is the negative inverse slope of the edge. Let $(x_1,y_1)$ and $(x_2,y_2)$ be the vertices of this edge. Then Dx is computed as:

$$Dx = -(x_1 - x_2)/(y_1 - y_2).$$

We know how to obtain the x-value for the next intersection from the previous one; we add Dx, but we need a value for x to initialize the table. Remembering that ymax is halfway between two scan lines, from ymax down to the next scan line is a distance of 0.5, so the first intersection x-value for a particular edge is the x-value corresponding to ymax plus Dx/2.

The algorithm will work best if the vertices are given in absolute screen units so that no more transformations except rounding are necessary and scan can decrease by 1 in screen units. The type of the variables in the table still has to be real because we must perform floating point arithmetic on x-values.

To show the initialization of the table and operation of the algorithm, consider the polygon in Figure 2.34.

A = (80.3, 58.8)
B = (101.6, 71.9)
C = (93.6, 25.2)
D = (147.7, 45.1)

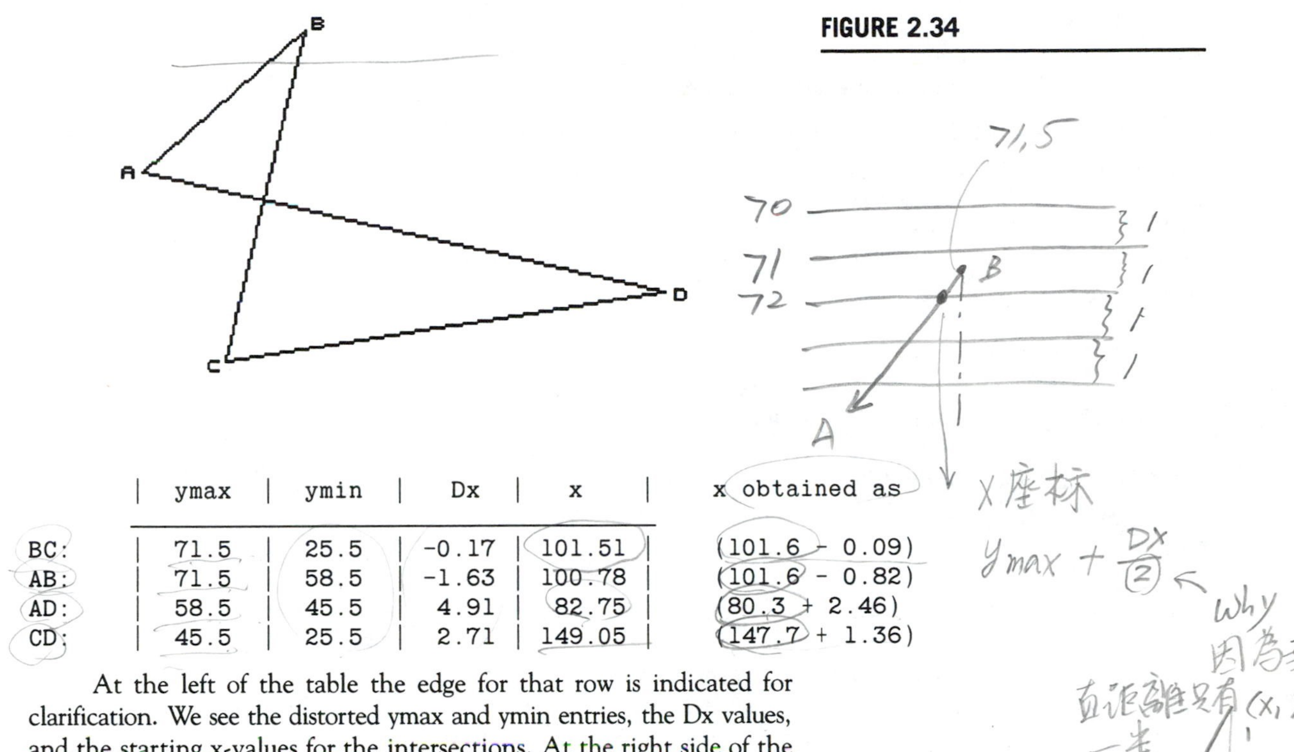


FIGURE 2.34

| | ymax | ymin | Dx | x | x obtained as |
|---|---|---|---|---|---|
| BC: | 71.5 | 25.5 | -0.17 | 101.51 | (101.6 - 0.09) |
| AB: | 71.5 | 58.5 | -1.63 | 100.78 | (101.6 - 0.82) |
| AD: | 58.5 | 45.5 | 4.91 | 82.75 | (80.3 + 2.46) |
| CD: | 45.5 | 25.5 | 2.71 | 149.05 | (147.7 + 1.36) |

At the left of the table the edge for that row is indicated for clarification. We see the distorted ymax and ymin entries, the Dx values, and the starting x-values for the intersections. At the right side of the table the expression shows how the starting x-value is obtained.

Scan will start with the value 71, which is the highest ymax in the table minus 0.5. This will lead to the inclusion of two edges, BC and AB, as their ymax is greater than scan. Lme will be 1 and rme will be 2. A horizontal fill line is drawn from round(100.78) to round(101.51) (from 101 to 102). The ordering of the x-values is achieved by sorting and will be explained later. The next scan value is 70. No inclusions or exclusions are required and the line is drawn from round(99.15) to round(101.34) (from 99 to 101). The line starts and ends sooner for every new scan value.

The first major change occurs when scan reaches the value 58. Then scan will be less than ymin of edge AB, so AB will be excluded; ymax of AD will be greater than scan, so AD will be included.

From now on the starting value of the fill line grows by 4.91 for every new scan line and soon the point will be reached where the two edges cross over. The starting value would then be greater than the terminating value. This shows that updating the x-values by adding the respective Dx's can change their order. We also saw that the starting entries in the table did not automatically put the x-values in increasing order. This ordering has to be obtained by sorting.

This means that we have to sort (on x) the current edges (but *not* the noncurrent edges!) after we update the x-values or after we include new edges; in short, for every new scan line value.

**Coded Algorithm** We now give the fill algorithm in detail. We require the polygon that we are to fill to be stored in two arrays of length 200, one for the x-coordinates and one for the y-coordinates. (Polygons with many vertices are needed for describing shapes with smooth outlines like pies, ellipses, etc.). These two arrays and the number of vertices of the polygon are the only global variables. They are declared as:

```
type array200 = array[0..200] of real;
var             px,py      :   array200 {the polygon};
     number_vertices      :   integer;
```

The table used by the filling algorithm consists of four arrays of the type array200. They are declared as local variables in the procedure polygon_fill as:

```
var  ymax, ymin, dx, x     :    array200 {the table};
```

All functions and procedures shown below are local within polygon_fill. For them the polygon arrays and the table are global. But it would not increase readability and in fact would decrease efficiency to have those six arrays as parameters in all calls. The procedures are presented in the order logically corresponding to the filling process.

The algorithm first initializes the table: it enters all edges of the polygon sorted on their ymax in descending order. The sorting can be done as the edges are entered, so sorting by insertion is used. When a ymax is entered into the table, the ymin (just the other y-coordinate of this edge) is also entered. Dx is computed for this edge and entered. The starting x-value is computed from the x belonging to ymax, using Dx, and is entered to complete the row. The following two routines do the initializing.

The actual entry of an edge into the table is done by procedure edgeinsert. It enters an edge in its proper place among the edges already entered. It also computes and enters the other items for this edge. The edge being entered is specified by two number pairs (xstart,ystart) and (xend,yend).

```
procedure edgeinsert(xstart,ystart,xend,yend    :    real;
                          number_entered_edges    :    integer);

var          j    :   integer;
     bigger_y     :   real
```

```
function max(x,y : real) : real;
begin {function max}
  if x > y
  then max := x
  else max := y;
end {function max};

begin {procedure edgeinsert}
  j := number_entered_edges;
  bigger_y := max(y1,y2);

  while (j <> 1) and (ymax[j-1] < bigger_y) do begin
    ymax[j] := ymax[j-1];
    ymin[j] := ymin[j-1];
    x[j]    := x[j-1];
    dx[j]   := dx[j-1];
    j       := j - 1;
  end {while};
  ymax[j] := bigger_y;
  dx[j]   := -(xend-xstart)/(yend-ystart);

  if bigger_y = ystart
  then begin
    ymin[j] := yend;
    x[j]    := xstart + dx[j]/2
  end {then}
  else begin
    ymin[j] := ystart;
    x[j]    := xend + dx[j]/2
  end {else}
end {procedure edgeinsert};
```

Edgeinsert is called by procedure loadtable. Loadtable requires that the polygon vertices be stored in correct order in two arrays x[1..n] and y[1..n], n being the number of vertices. It goes through these arrays, taking the two consecutive vertices that determine an edge. It checks if the edge is horizontal (ystart = yend). If it is, the edge is ignored. If the edge is not horizontal, edgeinsert is called to put the edge into the table.

```
procedure loadtable(     number_vertices     :  integer;
                     var number_entered_edges :  integer);

var              k    :   integer;
     xstart,ystart,
         xend,yend    :   real;
```

```
begin {procedure loadtable}
  xstart := x[number_vertices]; { begin with the last edge }
  ystart := trunc(y[number_vertice])+0.5;
  number_entered_edges := 0;
  for k := 1 to number_vertices do begin
    xend := x[k];
    yend := trunc(y[k])+0.5;
    if ystart = yend            {horizontal edges}
    then xstart := xend         {are not entered }
    else begin
      number_entered_edges := number_entered_edges + 1;
      edgeinsert(xstart,ystart,xend,yend,number_entered_edges);
      ystart := yend;
      xstart := xend
    end {else}
  end {for k}
end {procedure loadtable};
```

The following routines are for the actual filling process. For every new scan value we need to include all edges whose ymax is greater than scan. Only edges that are further down than rme have to be checked. This is done by procedure include.

```
procedure include(  left_most_edge    :  integer;
                var right_most_edge   :  integer;
                               scan,
               number_entered_edges   :  integer);

begin {procedure include}
  while (right_most_edge+1 <= number_entered_edges)
  and (ymax[right_most_edge+1] > scan) do
    right_most_edge := right_most_edge + 1;
end {procedure include};
```

We also need to exclude all edges whose ymin value is larger than scan. This is done by procedure exclude. All edges from left_most_edge to right_most_edge must be checked. When an edge is found for exclusion, all edges to the left of it must be shifted to the right to close this gap.

```
procedure exclude(var  left_most_edge    :   integer;
                       right_most_edge,
                                  scan   :   integer);
var   k,i    :   integer;

begin {procedure exclude}
```

```
for k := left_most_edge to right_most_edge do
  if ymin[k] > scan
  then begin
    left_most_edge := left_most_edge + 1;
    for i := k downto left_most_edge do begin
      ymin[i] := ymin[i-1];
      x[i]    := x[i-1];
      dx[i]   := dx[i-1]
    end {for i}
  end {if ymin[k] > scan}
end {procedure exclude};
```

We also need to update the x-values of all current edges. This is a very simple process, done by procedure updatex. The order in which updatex is listed here does not imply that it will be called in this order for every new scan line.

```
procedure updatex(left_most_edge,
                  right_most_edge    :    integer);
var  k    :   integer;

begin {procedure updatex}
  for k := left_most_edge to right_most_edge do
    x[k] := x[k] + dx[k];
end {procedure updatex};
```

We need to sort the current edges on the updated x-values before we can draw horizontal fill lines between the x pairs. The sorting is done by insertion by procedure sort_on_x. The x-value of the edge to the left of the current edges is assigned the smallest possible number, negative of maxint, in order to have a stop for the sorting process.

```
procedure sort_on_x(left_most_edge,
                    right_most_edge    :   integer);
var             helpx,
     helpdx,helpymin    :    real;
                i,j,k    :    integer;

begin {procedure sort_on_x}
x[left_most_edge-1] := -maxint;
for i := left_most_edge+1 to right_most_edge do begin
  helpx    := x[i];
  helpdx   := dx[i];
  helpymin := ymin[i];
  k := i-1;
  while x[k] > helpx do begin
```

```
    x[k+1]     := x[k];
    dx[k+1]    := dx[k];
    ymin[k+1] := ymin[k];
    k := k - 1
  end {while};
  x[k+1]     := helpx;
  dx[k+1]    := helpdx;
  ymin[k+1] := helpymin
end {for i}
end {procedure sort_on_x};
```

The fill lines are drawn by taking consecutive pairs of the x-values from among the current edges and drawing a horizontal line between each pair. This is done by procedure fillscan. The horizontal line should not be drawn by a general DDA algorithm because it is a very simple process and can be implemented much faster by a special machine-dependent implementation. Such a routine is called hline in this code. It needs only three arguments: start, end, and scan line height. The sidebar on drawing horizontal lines explains this.

```
procedure fillscan(left_most_edge,
                   right_most_edge   :  integer);
var  nx,j,i   :   integer;

begin {procedure fillscan}
  nx := (right_most_edge - left_most_edge + 1) div 2;
  j := left_most_edge;
  for i := 1 to nx do begin
    hline(round(x[j]),scan,round(x[j+1]));
    j := j + 2;
  end {for i}
end {procedure fillscan};
```

**Walk-Through of the Filling Process** With these routines we can start filling the polygon. For every new scan line value we first exclude edges that have been passed (if any). Then we update the x-values of the remaining edges. Only then do we include new edges (if any) because the x-values of newly included edges already have the proper start value, so they must not be changed. Then we sort on x and then we draw. All this must be repeated for scan decreasing in steps of 1 until the last edge in the table has been excluded; this is the case when left_most_edge is equal or greater than number_entered_edges (the number of edges in the table).

The entire filling process is done by procedure polygon_fill. It first calls loadtable to initialize the table. The pointers to the current edges are then initialized. As there are zero current edges at the begin-

## DRAWING HORIZONTAL LINES

A fill line is always horizontal and along a scan line of the raster display. Since the state of each pixel on the screen is determined by the values in that portion of memory that comprises the frame buffer or bit map, to draw any line requires accesses to corresponding memory cells. For a raster scan device, horizontally aligned pixels correspond to memory cells in adjacent memory locations. This means that the address-decoding logic of a linearly organized RAM, which associates each memory address with a group of eight bits (a byte) or, sometimes, 16 bits (a word), must only increment the address and fetch the byte or word. This can be done very rapidly by a dumb chip, perhaps a DMA chip, and does not have to involve the main processor. No computations are needed, in contrast to the many computations required for a general straight line. We do have to compute the start of each fill line and how many pixels should be set for each fill line, but that is all.

Keep in mind that the correspondence between bits in the bit map and pixels on the screen is determined by the way memory is organized. The exact relationship may vary but it is always true that it is simpler for horizontally adjacent pixels than for any other. This means that horizontal lines can always be drawn more rapidly than other lines. We shouldn't use a DDA algorithm to do filling. If not already available in hardware, a short machine-language segment will operate efficiently.

ning, it sets left_most_edge to 1 and right_most_edge to 0. By setting left_most_edge > right_most_edge, all loops that run from left_most_edge to right_most_edge are empty. To begin the loop logic, the starting value of scan will be the integer value just above ymax[1]. Scan is then decreased as described in the last paragraph and the loop runs until the last edge is excluded.

```
procedure polygon_fill(         var px,py   : array200;
                       number_of_vertices   :  integer);

var                   scan,
           left_most_edge,
          right_most_edge,
     number_entered_edges    :   integer;
           ymax,ymin,dx,x    :   array200;

{include here the declaration of the above procedures:
procedure edgeinsert();
```

```
procedure loadtable();
procedure include();
procedure exclude();
procedure updatex();
procedure sort_on_x();}

begin {procedure polygon_fill}
  if (number_vertices < 3) or (number_vertices > 200)
  then writeln('polygon size error')
  else begin
    loadtable(number_vertices,number_entered_edges)
    left_most_edge := 1; right_most_edge := 0;
    scan := round(ymax[1]+0.5);
    while left_most_edge < number_entered_edges do begin
      scan := scan - 1;
      exclude(left_most_edge,right_most_edge,scan)
             {can increase left_most_edge};
      updatex(left_most_edge,right_most_edge);
      include(left_most_edge,right_most_edge,scan,
              number_entered_edges)
             {can increase right_most_edge};
      sort_on_x(left_most_edge,right_most_edge);
      fillscan(left_most_edge,right_most_edge)
    end {while}
  end {else}
end {procedure polygon_fill};
```

**Applications of the Fill Algorithm** The basic purpose of this algorithm is to provide for traversing all pixels within a polygon that is defined by its vertices. In the form presented above it fills a polygon with only one solid color, but it can do much more than that. Several other algorithms need to traverse the pixels of a polygon in image space in order to do computations or to set individual pixel illuminations. These algorithms can use the scanning operation above but will not draw solid lines between x-value pairs.

We will utilize our routines when we discuss three-dimensional objects. In Z-buffer methods, a depth computation will be performed for each pixel within the polygon and a comparison with a given depth buffer will determine what color should be given to each pixel.

Shading methods do something similar. The illumination of each pixel within a polygon is computed individually depending on information derived from the three-dimensional polygon description, light source directions, and other factors.

We now consider two-dimensional applications of our routines. These are filling with certain patterns and crosshatching.

# 2.3 PATTERN FILLS

This section describes an adaptation of the algorithm that can fill a polygon with a predefined pattern. To do this effectively, we must pay particular attention to the specific hardware being used. Only one of our routines need be changed: the procedure fillscan. The step from filling with a solid color to filling with a pattern is an easy one.

The ideas and techniques of pattern fill stem from a time before bit-mapped graphics. Many devices then were provided with what we today call *semigraphics* or *character graphics*. Although raster displays were used, there was no frame buffer. Limited graphics can be displayed on the screen in the same way that text can be produced: through a character generator. Each character on the screen is a display of a sample that is stored only once as a bit map in the character generator ROM. The character generator can contain not only the letters of the alphabet but also certain simple shapes like a vertical bar, a horizontal bar, a right angle, and so on. Each such pattern can appear only at a limited number of positions on the screen, the positions where the characters in text display can appear. In fact, the patterns are only characters.

To fill a polygon with such a pattern consists of displaying these characters wherever they are totally inside the polygon. The place on the screen where such a character is to be displayed is represented only by a pointer to that pattern (text display is actually just that). Only the areas in which a partly cut-off pattern is to be displayed need more memory for representation. Most of the work is done during scanning. Some earlier devices accomplished polygon pattern fill in this and similar ingenious ways. We shall not discuss this further because it is an outdated technique. However, pattern filling as such has survived. Today we use bit-mapped displays and standard graphic techniques.

A predefined pattern is always stored in a rectangular sample, whose size depends on the graphics system. We will assume a pattern size of 8 × 8. Figure 2.35 shows a pattern and a polygon filled with it. If the frame buffer has a depth of eight, then each pixel in the pattern is represented by one byte. To develop an algorithm, we assume the pattern to be an 8 × 8 array of bytes. The fill algorithm will copy this little bit map into the polygon in such a way that row 0 of the pattern will always be put onto the rows 0 or 8 or 16, and so on, in the frame buffer. Row 1 of the pattern will go to rows 1 or 9 or 17, and so on. The same thing is done with the columns. This is easy to achieve through modulo arithmetic. To get the proper byte from the pattern matrix we need a row pointer and a column pointer. When a fill line is to be drawn from $x_1$ to $x_2$ at the scan height, scan, we compute the

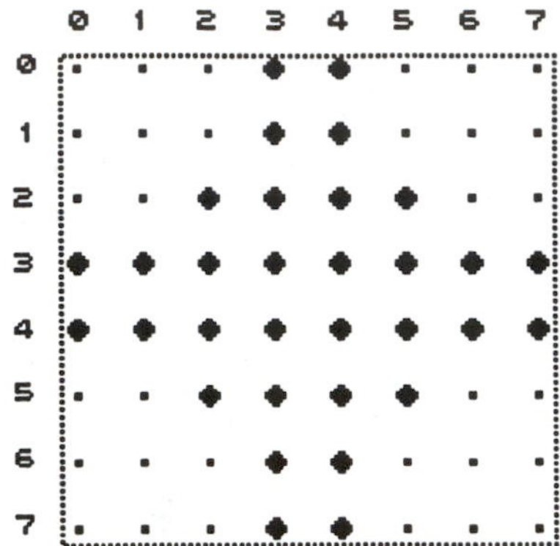


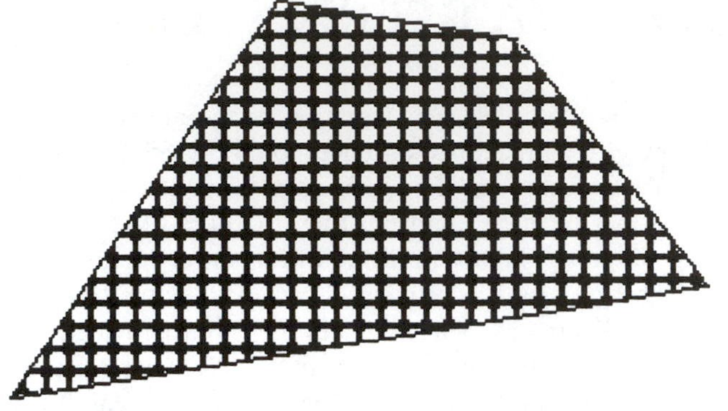

**FIGURE 2.35** Predefined pattern and pattern-filled polygon.

column pointer as $x_1$ mod 8 and the row pointer as scan mod 8. We add the following array to the variables of our fill algorithm; it can be set to represent any desired pattern:

var pattern : array[0..7,0..7] of byte;

We assume that there is a procedure SetPix for setting an individual pixel to a given value. The procedure fillscan is changed to:

```
procedure fillscan(left_most_edge,
                   right_most_edge   :   integer);
var     nx,j,i,k,
    row_pointer,
    col_pointer    :  integer;

begin {procedure fillscan}
  row_pointer := scan mod 8;
  nx := (right_most_edge - left_most_edge + 1) div 2;
  j := left_most_edge;
  for i := 1 to nx do begin
    for k := round(x[j]) to round(x[j+1]) do begin
      col_pointer := k mod 8;
      SetPix(k,scan,pattern[row_pointer,col_pointer])
    end {for k};
    j := j + 2
  end {for i}
end {procedure fillscan};
```

This Pascal code looks a little clumsy and would be somewhat slow; we present it only to demonstrate the idea of the algorithm. If programmed in assembly, there would be no subscript arithmetic and the modulo 8 arithmetic would be very easy. Col_pointer would be computed only once for each fill line piece; then it would be increased by 1 modulo 8. Row_pointer would be computed only once for the whole fill algorithm and would then be decreased by 1 modulo 8 for each row.

*Crosshatching* a polygon can be considered as filling it with a special crosshatch pattern. Two patterns are shown in Figure 2.36. Both would produce a crosshatch with only a slight difference in the way the lines cross. The resulting filled polygons would look almost identical. Our 8 × 8 matrix can only do crosshatches with a hatch line distance of 4 using this technique. For a different distance we would use a different size of pattern matrix and a different modulus in the arithmetic.

Another way of crosshatching a polygon in a raster display consists of computing only the positions where pixels are to be set and ignoring all other pixel positions. It is not dependent on the size of the pattern size and can have any desired distance between the hatch lines. The only procedure to be changed is fillscan. The code is a bit tricky. The position of the first pixel is computed and the pixel is set, then the step to the next pixel is computed. After this, the step size just varies between two values that depend on the scan.

The code below does a crosshatch with a hatch line distance of 6 pixels. It assumes the existence of procedure SetPix(x,y,color) for setting a pixel at (x,y) to a given color. To adjust the procedure to a different line distance the values 6 and 12 (two times 6) must be changed; the number 11 in the code, derived as $2*6-1$, must also be changed. As an exercise, you should rewrite this code for a variable line distance dist and test it.

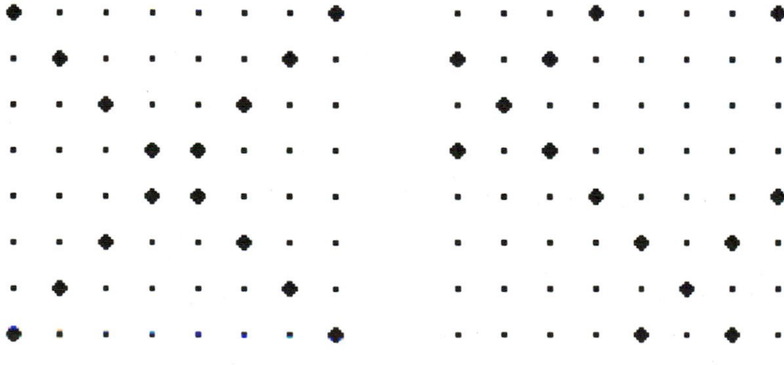

**FIGURE 2.36** Two crosshatch patterns.

```
procedure fillscan(left_most_edge,
                   right_most_edge    :    integer);
var     nx,j,i,si,
        htch,step,
        term,posn,
        xsrt,xend     :    integer;

begin {procedure fillscan}
  htch := 6 - abs(scan mod 12 - 6);
  nx := (right_most_edge - left_most_edge + 1) div 2;
  j := left_most_edge;
  for i := 1 to nx do begin
    xsrt := round(x[j]); xend := round(x[j+1]);
    term := (xrts-htch+11) div 12*12;
    si   := sign(xsrt-term+htch-0.5);
    posn := term + si*htch;
    step := 6 + si*(6-2*htch);
    while posn <= xend do begin
      SetPix(posn,scan,color);
      posn := posn + step;
      step :=  12  - step
    end {while};
    j := j + 2
  end {for i}
end {procedure fillscan};
```

# EXERCISES FOR CHAPTER 2

## Section 2.0

1. Try to determine the resolution (number of pixels on the screen) of the graphics monitor you are working on. You can do this by using a trial-and-error method. The only graphics primitive you need is the straight line with absolute screen coordinates as start and end points.
2. You might work on a graphics workstation that provides for a default user coordinate system that suggests a very high resolution like $4000 \times 3000$. Such a system will probably let you specify graphics primitives only within this coordinate system. Try to find out whether this user coordinate system really corresponds to the physical resolution of the monitor. *Hint:* draw a straight line, for example from (0,100) to (3500,101). You should obtain precisely one stair step in the middle of that line. If you don't, the physical resolution is lower.

3. How much memory is needed for the frame buffer to store a $640 \times 400$ display with 16 gray levels?
4. Consider a raster display with $1024 \times 1024$ pixels, noninterlaced display mode, and a screen width of 35 cm. Estimate the average speed of the point on the screen surface that is hit by the electron beam.
5. The horizontal oscillation frequency, also called scan rate, is expressed in Hertz (Hz), which is oscillations per second. Assume that the vertical retrace time is 10 percent of the vertical sweep time. Assume a $640 \times 400$ frame buffer and a refresh frequency of 60 frames per second. What scan rate is needed to display this frame buffer in noninterlaced mode?
6. Repeat Exercise 5 using an interlaced display.
7. Implement on your graphics device a graphics primitive called SetPix(x,y), which sets a single pixel at the absolute device address (x,y) (color or gray level is unimportant).
8. Distinguish between pixel ratio and the frequently encountered term *aspect ratio*. Aspect ratio is the physical height to width ratio of a display, for example, of a CRT. What is the aspect ratio of a 12 in $\times$ 16 in display?
9. CRTs give an actual luminosity that is nonlinear with respect to signal input (unless gamma corrected). At the same time, our eyes do not interpret a doubled luminosity as twice as bright, rather, doubling may give an apparent luminosity only about 1.5 times as much. Assuming this relation, how does the apparent luminosity vary with signal input if the CRT has a gamma of 2.2?

# Section 2.1.1

10. Draw the arc corresponding to the chain code 443443443344344.
11. Does the chain code 3233233223223323 represent a straight line? If not, why? Can this be seen directly from the chain code?
12. Write a program to test two chains for unevenness. The program should sum the symbols of all pairs of substrings of equal length and compare them.
13. Find a digital arc that looks almost straight but isn't. Find the two uneven substrings in its chain code.
14. One of the three consequences of Hung and Kasvand's straight line theorem is that the less frequent symbol only occurs isolated. Using an example, show that evenness is violated in a chain that does not fulfill this.
15. Start with the chain code 000000000000011111 (13 zeros and five ones), and proceed by hand as shown in the description of

Brons's method to arrive at the chain code for a straight line. Adjust the resulting chain code by cyclicly shifting it by half the length of the initial run.

16. Start with the same chain code as in Exercise 15. Proceed by hand as shown in the description of the best-fit method to arrive at the chain code for a straight line.
17. Shift Brons's chain code from Exercise 15 cyclically to make it equal to the best-fit code from Exercise 16.

# Section 2.1.2

18. Implement a straight line DDA according to the formula given in Section 2.1.2. Produce lines with very small and very big values for Dx and Dy. Observe how the line develops gaps when the steps are too big and becomes thicker when the steps are too small.
19. Use the graphics primitive SetPix from Exercise 7 to implement the simple straight line DDA in Pascal.
20. Increase the speed of the DDA algorithm of Exercise 18 by taking advantage of the fact that one of the increments always equals 1, so one of the additions can be done in integer arithmetic. Compare the speeds of the unimproved and the improved versions.
21. Modify the simple straight line DDA to draw either solid, dashed, or dotted lines.
22. Modify the simple straight line DDA to draw lines of three different widths: normal (thinnest eight-connected line), approximately two pixels thick, and approximately 3 pixels thick.
23. Execute Bresenham's straight line algorithm by hand as shown in the text to produce a line from (0,0) to (17,12).
24. Implement Bresenham's straight line algorithm in Pascal with case distinctions to enable the drawing of lines in *all* directions.
25. Compare the speed of Bresenham's straight line algorithm to the speeds of the DDA algorithms of Exercises 19 and 20.
26. Implement Bresenham's straight line algorithm in assembly language to achieve a fast execution time. For example, avoid calling the graphics primitive SetPix with the two arguments x and y, because each call involves complicated overhead.

# Section 2.2

27. If we don't distort the y-values of the polygon vertices by 0.5, we will have scan line values that go exactly through a vertex. So we end up intersecting an odd number of edges, unless we adopt a certain strategy about what we consider an edge intersection.

This would allow us to use all the other algorithmic principles as presented in the text. Explain and implement such a strategy.

# Section 2.3

28. The algorithm given in Section 2.3 crosshatches a polygon without using the pattern fill technique. It hatches with a line distance of six pixels. Write Pascal code that uses this technique to hatch with a general line distance of n.

*Crosshatching of polygons (information for Exercises 29 to 33).*

Crosshatching a polygon with the methods shown in the text will work only for raster displays. You cannot use these methods to crosshatch a polygon on a vector display or a line plotter. To do that you must crosshatch the polygon by literally drawing the crosshatch lines. We now explain a method to do this.

This method crosshatches a polygon with two sets of lines. The lines of one set are slanted at 45° and the lines of the other at −45°. The distance between the lines is enough to make them individually recognizable.

The basic setup of the algorithm, sorting the edges on ymax, drawing horizontal fill lines, and so on would have to undergo major changes if we really fill the given polygon with slanted lines. These complications can be avoided by doing the following. Instead of drawing slanted lines into the given polygon, rotate the polygon by −45° and compute the *horizontal* fill lines for that. These lines will have the proper position in relation to the polygon. Before we draw these lines we rotate them by 45°, so they will have the proper position in the unrotated polygon. The rotated polygon is never really drawn—we only need its vertices in memory. Therefore we can apply rotations just around the origin.

We rotate the point (x,y) by −45° into $(x_r,y_r)$ by transforming:

$$x_r = 0.707*(x+y)$$
$$y_r = 0.707*(-x+y).$$

We do this to all vertices of the given polygon, then we fill it with horizontal lines. Changes in the fill algorithm are the advancement of the scan line value and the change for the x-intersections. Let dist be the vertical distance between the crosshatch lines measured in pixels. We draw the first fill line at 0.5 below the highest ymax and therefore don't need to change the starting x-values. In procedure edgeinsert we change

```
dx[j] := -(xend-xstart)/(yend-ystart);
```

to

```
dx[j] := -dist*(xend-xstart)/(yend-ystart);
```

In procedure polygon_fill we change

```
scan := scan - 1;
```

to

```
scan := scan - dist;
```

The most significant change occurs in procedure fillscan. The end points of a horizontal fill line are (x[j],scan) and (x[j+1],scan). We have to rotate these points by 45° and then draw a straight line (not horizontal) between the rotated points. We replace

```
hline(round(x[j]),scan,round(x[j+1]))
```

with

```
xr := 0.707*(x[j]-scan);      yr := 0.707*(x[j]+scan);
move(round(xr),round(yr));
xr := 0.707*(x[j+1]-scan);  yr := 0.707*(x[j+1]+scan);
draw(round(xr),round(yr));
```

This gives us one set of hatch lines. The other set must be produced analogously.

29. Write a complete crosshatch algorithm for −45° and 45° hatch lines of distance dist.
30. Write an algorithm that hatches a polygon with one set of lines at an arbitrary angle $\alpha$ and a distance dist.
31. Why is polygon filling always done with horizontal lines? Can it be done with vertical lines?
32. Is filling with vertical lines slower than filling with horizontal lines?
33. Can a polygon be solidly filled with slanted lines? Why not? Show a counterexample. (An angle of 45° is an exception; explain why.)

# Circles and Ellipses

Circles and ellipses are important enough that we devote this chapter to methods for drawing them. There are three major sections in the chapter.

**3.0 Introduction** tells why you should know about methods that generate circular and elliptical figures.

**3.1 Circular Arcs** summarizes some useful properties of circles and describes three different ways for setting the pixels of the image of a circle. The most important are DDA methods that use equations for the slope to find which pixel should be set next.

**3.2 Elliptical Arcs** does the same for ellipses. The algorithms for drawing an ellipse are similar to those for circles because a circle is a special case of an ellipse.

# 3.0 INTRODUCTION

As mentioned in Chapter 2, curves in computer graphics are usually generated as sequences of many short straight lines. But some curves, in particular circles and ellipses, are so common that we should develop DDA and other specialized algorithms for them. Certainly, a specialized generator will be much faster than approximation by straight line segments. In applications where circles and ellipses or parts thereof are common, it makes sense to use these special algorithms.

# 3.1 CIRCULAR ARCS

Circles can be created by methods derived from differential equations. On most raster displays a regular polygon with 60 sides would look like a circle even though it consists only of a sequence of short straight lines that can be created by repeated invocations of a straight line DDA. Such a method is much slower than using a special circle-generating DDA that has been designed to attain speed. This section describes both DDA and non-DDA methods for circles, taking into consideration the pixel spacing ratio. However, before we describe the algorithms for generating circles, we cover some features of images of circular objects.

**Central Symmetry** As a first preliminary to circle generation, we consider how the symmetry of a circle can be used. If the center is at the origin and a pixel (x,y) lies on the circumference of the circle, then we can calculate seven more pixels on this circle trivially. Figure 3.1 shows the given pixel in black and the derived pixels as open circles.

The circle generators below first generate a circle with the origin at the center. The generation of a circle with a different center is no problem; it involves only the addition of the center coordinates to every generated pixel. The coded algorithms below therefore include this transformation.

The following procedure sets the eight symmetric pixels that correspond to a given point (x,y) on a circle. It works only for a display with a pixel ratio of 1. The coordinates of the center point are (xcenter,ycenter).

```
procedure EIGHT_OCTS(     x,y,
                     xcenter,
                     ycenter  :  integer);
```

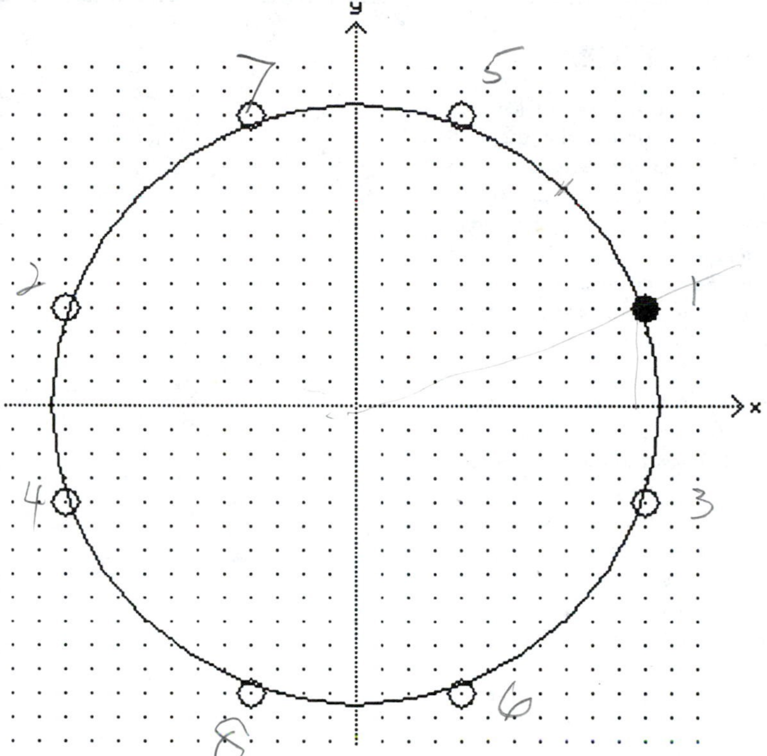


**FIGURE 3.1** Using symmetry in a circle.

```
begin
   SetPix( x+xcenter, y+ycenter);
   SetPix(-x+xcenter, y+ycenter);
   SetPix( x+xcenter,-y+ycenter);
   SetPix(-x+xcenter,-y+ycenter);
   SetPix( y+xcenter, x+ycenter);
   SetPix(-y+xcenter, x+ycenter);
   SetPix( y+xcenter,-x+ycenter);
   SetPix(-y+xcenter,-x+ycenter)
end {procedure EIGHT_OCTS};
```

**Correction for Pixel Ratio** Circle-drawing algorithms that don't allow for the pixel ratio will generate an ellipse whose major axis is in the direction of the larger pixel distance. To produce a circle on such a pixel ratio we can use one of two methods.

One method uses an ellipse generating algorithm that we discuss in Section 3.2. The second method simply corrects the output of the circle generator to the nonsquare pixel grid. The correction involves a

## THE LIQUID CRYSTAL DISPLAY (LCD)

Many substances can be in a state between crystallized and liquid. This means that the molecules have more freedom of motion than in the solid state but not as much as in a liquid, a condition called *mesostate.* It is a problem of chemistry to find substances that exhibit these properties at room temperature. Liquid crystal technology is an area of intensive research.

We distinguish among three types of liquid crystal substances. One is called *smectic.* In such a substance the molecules are arranged in layers with their long axes normal to the plane of the layers. Within a layer the molecules usually are regularly spaced with respect to each other but the layers can easily slide over each other.

Another type is called *nematic.* In this substance the molecules are arranged parallel to each other. They can move freely in all spatial directions but can rotate only around their own long axes so they stay parallel to each other.

The third type is called *cholesteric.* In this type, the molecules are arranged in thin parallel layers with their long axes parallel to the plane of the layer. The diameter of the thin layers is about one molecule. Several hundred thin layers make up a thick layer. The thin layers are not geometrically independent from each other. The direction of the long axis of a molecule in one thin layer is slightly and systematically rotated from the axis direction of molecules in the layers above and below. This results in a helical structure through one thick layer. Such substances have great optical activity because the diameter of the thick layers is about the wavelength of visible light.

The forces that maintain a certain order of the liquid crystal molecules in the mesostate are usually very weak. The order can easily be influenced, changed, or destroyed by electric or magnetic fields, by temperature, or by pressure. Figure 3.A shows unordered molecules in a liquid.

**FIGURE 3.A**

A single optical liquid crystal element basically consists of a liquid crystal substance in liquid crystal state that is enclosed between two transparent electrical conductors. If a voltage is applied between these two conductors, an electric field is created that changes the order of the molecules in between. Figure 3.B shows one possible arrangement of molecules in a smectic substance.

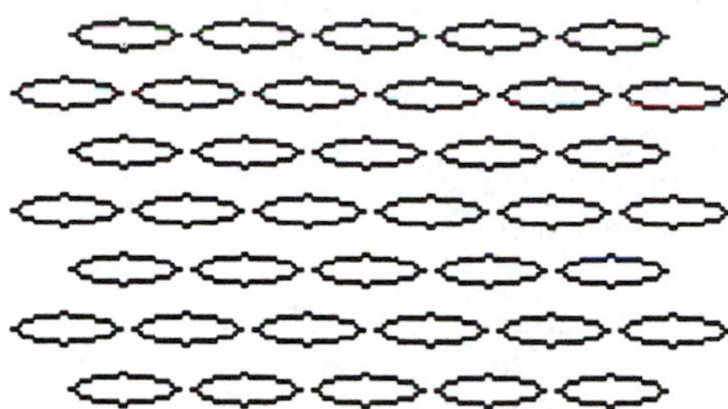

FIGURE 3.B

Figure 3.C shows the same substance with a different arrangement of molecules. When the electric field is switched off, the molecules return to their former arrangement.

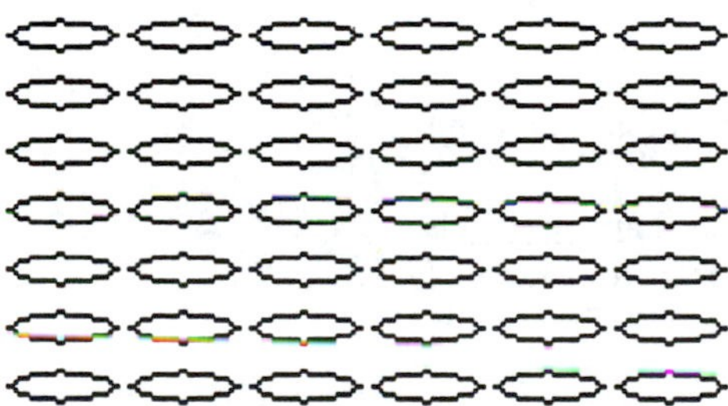

FIGURE 3.C

Simply stated, in one of the arrangements light can penetrate, while in the other it is blocked. Precisely how this works is complicated. Sometimes it is just the oscillating direction (polarization) of polarized light waves, which are rotated by passing through the helix of a cholesteric substance and are not rotated when the helix is disturbed by an electric field. A polarizing filter then blocks the rotated light and lets unrotated light pass. Sometimes dye molecules are mixed into the liquid crystal substance whose molecules force the dye molecules into certain arrangements. There are many different ways of using the optical activity of liquid crystal substances to switch individual LCD cells on and off.

Liquid crystals can even be used to store information. Certain smectic substances tend to align their molecules at one of two possible angles with the enclosing wall, say 45° or 135°. Interestingly, they then stay this way as if they were in a crystalline state. Applying a certain electric field can change the alignment angle; applying a different field changes it back. The arrangement can also be read out. This makes it possible to construct storage media with a density of $10^{12}$ bits per square inch (US patent 3,775,757).

The optical properties of liquid crystals are often used in displays for small calculators and for digital watches. Only a few coarsely shaped elements will form a few digits. To produce raster displays is a big technological challenge because the individual LCD pixels need to be very small and dense. Addressing the pixels individually in order to switch them requires a complicated wiring mechanism. Changing the arrangement of the molecules is often not as fast as desired. Research is directed toward finding fast switching substances. These difficulties are gradually being overcome by advancing manufacturing technology.

The energy needed to maintain the electric field and thus a certain arrangement of the molecules is very low because hardly any electricity is actually flowing. Their almost zero energy consumption is one of the big advantages of LCDs. The other is the essential flatness of the display. This makes liquid crystal raster displays more and more valuable for microcomputers. They may one day be used to provide a thin screen TV display.

multiplication and a division for each pixel but seven more pixels on the circle can then be derived trivially.

It is important that such corrections avoid the use of any divisions other than by powers of 2. If, for example, a correction to a ratio of 4/5 is necessary, it should be done by multiplying with 5/4. Practically all existing pixel ratios other than 1 have as one of their components a power of 2.

We can correct a distorted ellipse to a circle either by shrinking all x-coordinates by a certain factor or by multiplying all y-coordinates by the reciprocal factor. Depending on which is chosen, we must adjust the radius first.

We discuss this technique only because it is simple to program, easy to understand, and often done. However, it is not very efficient in terms of speed. It negates the purpose of a fast circle generator (for example, one that produces pixel addresses in integer arithmetic) if we then correct its output by applying multiplications and divisions to it. The above method should be used only if the circle generator calculates the pixels in floating point arithmetic. The coded algorithm below accepts two real-type arguments for a pixel and does the rounding operation after the correction to the pixel ratio.

Figure 3.2 shows a circle on a pixel ratio of 2/3. The black dots show the pixel positions obtained by rounding the x-values originally

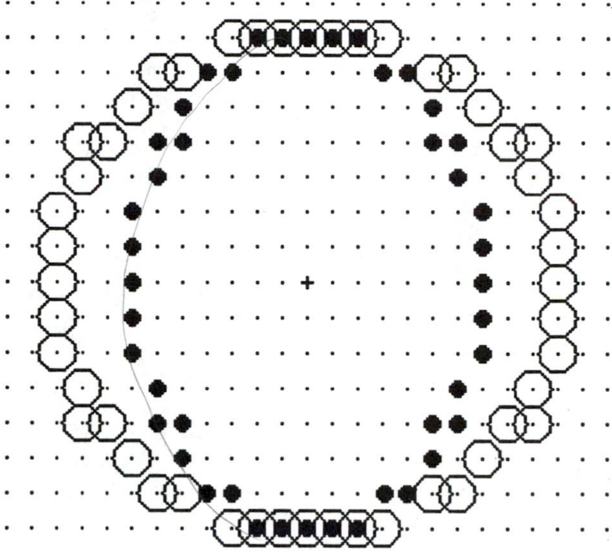

**FIGURE 3.2** Circle on a nonsquare pixel ratio.

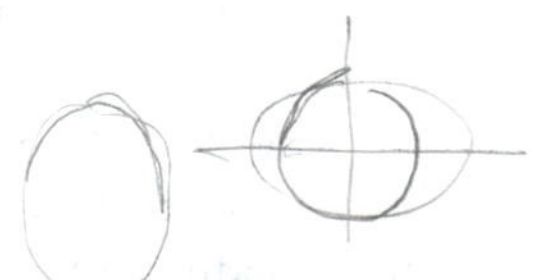

generated by the circle algorithm. The white circles show the corrected pixels obtained by multiplying the x-values by 3/2 *before* rounding. Both sets of pixels are generated with an algorithm that first produces pixel positions with floating point arithmetic and then rounds them to the grid. A small step size was used, so several of the pixels are set more than once. As the white pixels are obtained by multiplying by 3/2 *before* rounding, some x-values lead to the same black pixels but to different white pixels when corrected. This explains the different numbers of black and white pixels in the top and bottom rows and the gaps in the corrected circle.

The following procedure corrects the output of a real-type circle generator to a pixel ratio of 2/3 and simultaneously calculates trivially seven more pixels. For other pixel ratios, the adjustment of the algorithm is obvious. The calling routine needs one division to calculate the radius which is passed to the circle-generating algorithm. In the case of a 2/3 pixel ratio, if the radius of the circle is given as r in x-units, then the circle generation must be called with a radius of $r * 2/3$, which involves one division. (xr, yr) is a circumference point generated by some circle algorithm and (xcenter, ycenter) is the center of the circle. Rounding, multiplication by 3, and division by 2 are fast if they are programmed properly in machine code. The circle generator needs to produce the pixels for only one octant.

**Coded Algorithm**

```
procedure EIGHT_CORR(  xr,yr    :  real;
                       xcenter,
                       ycenter  :  integer);
var  xcorr,
     ycorr,
       x,y   :  integer;

begin
   x := round(xr); y := round(yr);
   xcorr := round(xr*3/2);
   ycorr := round(yr*3/2);
   setpix( xcorr+xcenter, y+ycenter);
   setpix( xcorr+xcenter,-y+ycenter);
   setpix(-xcorr+xcenter, y+ycenter);
   setpix(-xcorr+xcenter,-y+ycenter);
   setpix( ycorr+xcenter, x+ycenter);
   setpix( ycorr+xcenter,-x+ycenter);
   setpix(-ycorr+xcenter, x+ycenter);
   setpix(-ycorr+xcenter,-x+ycenter)
end {procedure EIGHT_CORR;};
```

With these preliminaries out of the way, we now discuss four circle generators. Two are non-DDA methods and two use DDA techniques.

## 3.1.1 Parameter Method

The first circle algorithm we discuss is not a DDA method. It consists of calculating:

$$x = r * \cos u \qquad y = r * \sin u$$

and increasing u in small steps from 0 to $2\pi$, which produces an entire circle around the origin with radius r. If we take advantage of the symmetry of the circle, u has to go only from 0 to $\pi/4$. The only variable in the above equations is the parameter u. It always produces the best possible circle, but it is slow because it involves the repeated evaluation of the sin and cos functions.

The x- and y-values from this calculation are real numbers that must be rounded to the nearest points in the pixel grid. This can be done by calling EIGHT_OCTS with the rounded pixel values, generating only one octant of the circle. To generate a circle for a pixel ratio not equal to 1 we call EIGHT_CORR or use $r_x$ and $r_y$ in the equations:

$$x = r_x * \cos u \qquad y = r_y * \sin u$$

with $r_x/r_y$ equal to the reciprocal of the pixel ratio.

## THE PLASMA DISPLAY

The main problems with the CRT as a display device are the very high voltages it requires, its bulkiness, and its weight. The plasma display solves some of these problems.

The principle of the plasma display is shown in Figure 3.D. There are two sheets of glass with thin, closely spaced gold electrodes attached to the inner faces and covered with a dielectric material. Each set of electrodes consists of a set of closely spaced parallel wires. The two sets of electrodes cross at a right angle. The two sheets of glass are spaced a few thousandths of a millimeter apart, and the intervening space is filled with a special gas and sealed. By applying voltages between the electrodes, we make the gas within the panel behave as if it were divided into tiny cells, each one independent of its neighbors. In other words, when a voltage is applied between two electrodes, an electric field is created at the place where the two electrodes are closest to each other. This electric field turns the gas in between into a plasma. *Plasma* is a gas in an electricity-conducting state. Plasmas usually also emit light.

Certain cells can be made to glow, thus generating a picture. A cell is made to glow by placing a firing voltage across it by means of the electrodes. The gas within begins to discharge, and this develops very rapidly into a glow. The glow can be sustained by maintaining a high-frequency alternating voltage across the cell. Furthermore, if the signal amplitude is chosen correctly, cells that have not been fired will not be affected. In other words, each cell has two stable states. We call an element with two stable states *bistable.*

Cells can be switched on by momentarily increasing the sustaining voltage. This can be done selectively by modifying the signal in the two conductors that intersect at the desired cell. Similarly, if the sustaining signal is lowered, the glow is removed. Thus the plasma panel allows both selective writing and selective erasing at speeds of about 20 microseconds per cell. This speed can be increased by writing or erasing several

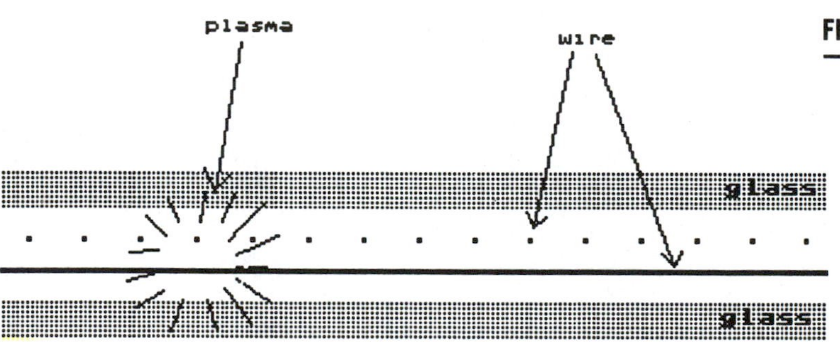


**FIGURE 3.D**

cells in parallel. A cell stays lit or unlit until changed, so the plasma display "remembers" the picture.

The plasma display produces a very steady image, totally free of flicker, and is a less bulky device than a CRT of comparable screen size. Its main disadvantages are its relatively poor resolution, about 60 dots per inch, and its complex addressing and wiring requirements. Its inherent memory is useful but is not as flexible as a frame buffer memory; besides, memory prices have come down quite a bit in recent years and will continue to do so. Plasma displays can be of value in portable microcomputers because of their flatness and low energy requirements.

## 3.1.2 Rotation Method

Another non-DDA method which generates an exact circle in a grid with a pixel ratio of 1 consists of using the equations for a two-dimensional rotation about the origin. We use the formula for rotation of a point about the origin:

$$x_{rot} = x * \cos u + y * \sin u$$
$$y_{rot} = -x * \sin u + y * \cos u$$

We compute a succession of rotated points, starting with $(x_0, y_0) = (r, 0)$:

$$x_{n+1} = x_n * \cos u + y_n * \sin u$$
$$y_{n+1} = -x_n * \sin u + y_n * \cos u$$

This generates points on a circle around the origin in a counterclockwise direction. We can choose u to be very small, so it is easy to compute sin u and cos u. Furthermore we can compute sin u and cos u only once and need not change them as we move around the circle. The size of u depends only on the circle radius. The larger the radius, the smaller the u that must be chosen. If we take $u \leqslant 1/r$, we get approximately one pixel increase with every step. This circle generation involves four multiplications by numbers that are not powers of 2 and two additions for every pixel, and therefore is slow.

The generated $x_n$ and $y_n$ values still must be rounded to the nearest pixel location. We call EIGHT_OCTS with the rounded pixel values and generate only one octant of the circle. The ending condition in the generating process would then be $x_n \leqslant y_n$. Generating a circle on a pixel ratio not equal to 1 is done by calling EIGHT_CORR.

## 3.1.3 DDA Algorithms

Because they are faster in execution, DDA methods are usually preferred for calculating which pixels are to be set to draw a circle. The differential equation for a circle centered at the origin is:

$$dy/dx = -x/y$$

where (x,y) is any point on the circle. The radius does not occur in this equation—it applies to all circles around the origin. The equation is true only when x and y have the same scale in Cartesian coordinates. dy/dx, of course, is the derivative, the slope of the tangent line at (x,y).

**The Spiral** We expect the relation to be close enough for practical purposes even if dy and dx in the above differential equation are replaced by small though not infinitesimal values. This gives:

$$Dy/Dx = -x_n/y_n$$

in which $(x_n,y_n)$ is the nth point that the DDA generates. It follows that there is some value $\epsilon$ such that $Dy = \epsilon \cdot x_n$ and $Dx = -\epsilon \cdot y_n$. This leads to a formula for calculating the n+1st point on the circle given the nth point:

$$x_{n+1} = x_n + Dx = x_n - \epsilon * y_n$$
$$y_{n+1} = y_n + Dy = y_n + \epsilon * x_n$$

We expect a deviation from the true circle because the continuously changing derivative has been replaced by a quotient which changes in steps as n increases. If (x,y) is a point in the iteration, the next point is $(x-\epsilon*y, y+\epsilon*x)$. The lengths of the vectors (radii to the two points) are not identical:

$$|(x-\epsilon * y, y+\epsilon * x)| = |(x,y)|\sqrt{1+\epsilon^2}.$$ *

This means that every consecutive point in the iteration is farther away from the origin by this constant factor. The deviation is such that the points lie on a curve that spirals outwards. The choice of a small epsilon makes the spiraling effect small and perhaps tolerable.

**The Ellipse** Modifying the iterations removes the continuing spiraling effect without increasing the number of operations. We use the already computed $x_{n+1}$ in the computation of $y_{n+1}$:

$$x_{n+1} = x_n - \epsilon * y_n$$
$$y_{n+1} = y_n + \epsilon * x_{n+1}$$

---

*You can verify the truth of this by expanding both sides. Recall that $|(x,y)| = \sqrt{x^2+y^2}$.

The reason this works is that the under- (over-) adjustments to the y-values in one octant are compensated by over- (under-) adjustments in the next. The curve so created still is not a circle. The proof is as follows. One iteration step can be expressed as a matrix multiplication:

$$(x_{n+1}, y_{n+1}) = (x_n, y_n) * \mathbf{A}$$

$$\text{where } \mathbf{A} = \begin{pmatrix} 1 & \epsilon \\ -\epsilon & 1-\epsilon^2 \end{pmatrix}$$

We should not be fooled, just because $\det(A) = 1$, into thinking that the length of $(x,y) * \mathbf{A}$ is the same as the length of $(x,y)$, and therefore all iterated points lie on a circle. They do not.† If any starting point (other than (0,0)) is taken, then the iterated points lie on an ellipse with center at (0,0), axes $2r/\sqrt{2+\epsilon}$ and $2r/\sqrt{2-\epsilon}$, and a tilt of 45°. The equation of this ellipse is:

$$x^2 - \epsilon xy + y^2 - 2r^2 = 0,$$

where r is a scaling factor depending on the starting point. An example of such an ellipse is shown in Figure 3.3. This method is just a special case ($\alpha = \beta = \epsilon$) of the general procedure for an ellipse given in Section 3.2.1.

The spiral and the ellipse methods both calculate the increments to $x_n$ and $y_n$ afresh in every step and produce a sequence of real number pairs that lie approximately on a circle. While these real values have to be kept internally for the next iteration, they are rounded to obtain the closest grid position and there a pixel is set.

We start the circle by choosing a starting point $(x_0, y_0)$ on the intended circumference and computing succeeding points $(x_n, y_n)$ until some terminating criterion is fulfilled. For example, with a starting point on the positive x-axis, the end could be when x becomes negative if we desire a quarter circle in the first quadrant. The end condition could be equality of x and y if only one octant is to be generated.

Both methods require two multiplications, two additions (or subtractions), and two rounding operations for every step. All these operations must be executed with real arithmetic. Because real arithmetic is more time consuming than simple integer arithmetic, much effort has been spent to design DDA algorithms that do everything in integer arithmetic (Bresenham's circle generation of Section 3.1.4 is an example).

---

*The length of $(x,y) * \mathbf{A}$, using Euclidean norms, is bounded only by $\|\mathbf{A}\|$ which is $\sqrt{L}$, where L is the largest eigenvalue of **ATA**. We find by direct calculation that $L = 1+\epsilon^4/2+\epsilon^2/2 * \sqrt{4+\epsilon^4} > 1$. It follows that $\|\mathbf{A}\| > 1$. So the vector $(x,y) * \mathbf{A}$ can be longer than $(x,y)$—indeed, taking (1,0) as the starting point, the next point is $(1,\epsilon)$ with $|(1,0)| = 1$ and $|(1,\epsilon)| > 1$. Therefore the interated points do not lie on a circle! Since the eigens of **A** are not real, they are not just stretched but are rotated as well.

FIGURE 3.3

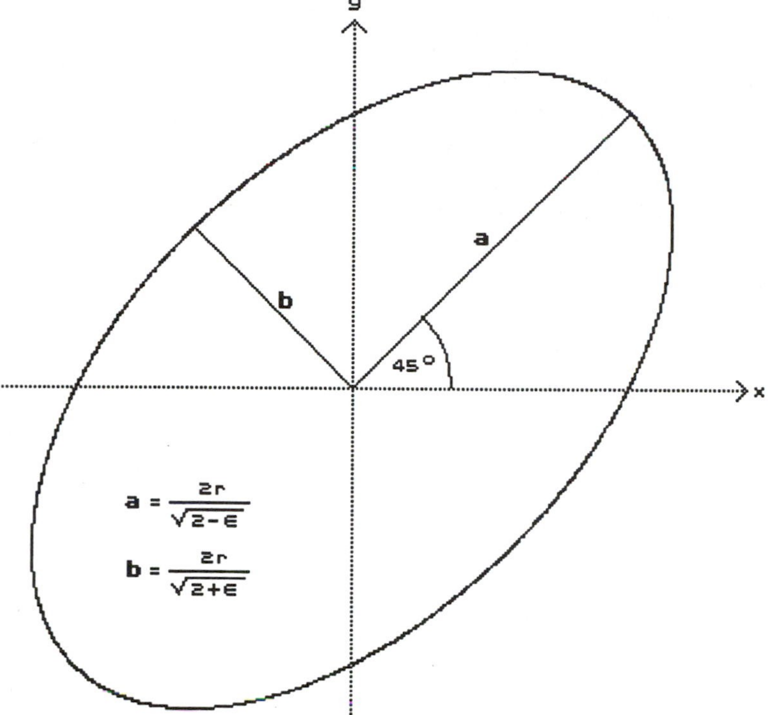


This situation is changing. Modern dedicated processors have floating point arithmetic built into their hardware and execute such arithmetic much faster than before. The tendency to put more and more into hardware will continue. Eventually floating point arithmetic may be almost as fast as integer arithmetic. Fast floating point hardware will reduce the advantage of the integer-arithmetic DDAs considerably, although these will always be faster if programmed properly. An advantage of the above two circle generators is that they have a straightforward code with no condition testing, as opposed to Bresenham's circle generator in which condition testing is an essential part. Although the condition there is very simple (just a sign flag test), it necessarily involves a conditional jump in the Bresenham assembly program, slowing it down.

When starting a circle of radius r on the positive x-axis at (r,0), $\epsilon$ could be chosen simply equal to 1/r. Because $\epsilon$ is a small number, a further improvement might be to choose a negative power of 2 for $\epsilon$. Then $\epsilon$ should equal $2^{-n}$ where $2^{-n-1} \leq r < 2^{-n}$. In this case the multiplications reduce to a subtraction in the exponent part of the real number representation of x or y, increasing the speed. This last improvement is normally insignificant.

We must also consider precision. Neither the spiral nor the ellipse method produce mathematically exact circles. How good are they for practical purposes? An answer to this can be found in the exercises.

In the code below the ellipse method is used. The generated $x_n$ and $y_n$ values are rounded to the nearest pixel location while calling EIGHT_OCTS. Only one octant of the circle is produced, so the ending condition to be met is $x_n \leq y_n$. Generating a circle on a pixel ratio not equal to one is done by calling EIGHT_CORR.

**Coded Algorithm—Ellipse Method**

```
procedure DDA_CIR(           radius   :  integer;
                    xcenter,ycenter   :  integer);
var
   epsilon,x,y    :   real;

begin {ellipse method}
  epsilon := 1/radius;
  x := radius; y := 0;
  while x > y do begin
    EIGHT_OCTS(round(x),round(y),xcenter,ycenter);
    x := x-epsilon*y;
    y := y+epsilon*x
  end
end {procedure DDA_CIR;};
```

## 3.1.4 Bresenham's Circle Generation

The main characteristic of this generator is that it does only integer arithmetic. This makes it considerably faster than any of the above methods if a processor has no hardware to perform floating point arithmetic. The original version of the algorithm (BRES77) was designed to create one quadrant (one-fourth) of a circle with an arbitrary center.

Our version creates only one octant (one-eighth) of the circle, e.g., the arc from 90° to 45° in a clockwise fashion (see Figure 3.4). The other seven octants of the circle are derived by symmetry. The circle is generated with the center at the origin and for an integer-valued radius r. The basic algorithmic idea is still the same as in the original version. The algorithm calculates one new pixel per step. From any point $(x_n, y_n)$ on the circle, the next point $(x_{n+1}, y_{n+1})$ must be one to the right or one to the right and one down from the current point because of the octant in which we are working. If $P_n$ with the coordinates $(x_n, y_n)$ is the current point, then the next point can be either A or B. Their coordinates are $(x_{n+1}, y_n)$ and $(x_{n+1}, y_{n-1})$ respectively. This is shown in Figure 3.5.

**FIGURE 3.4**

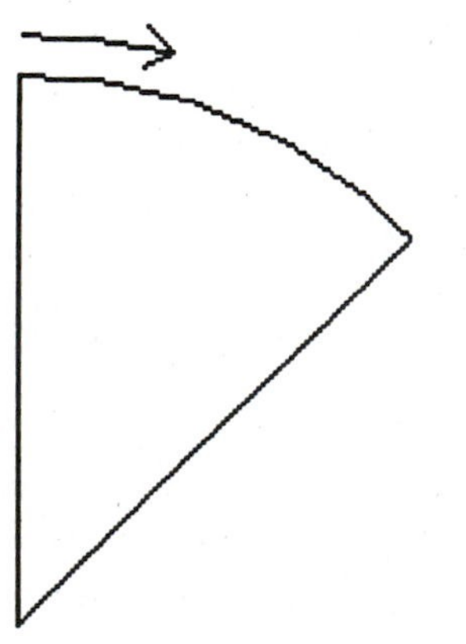

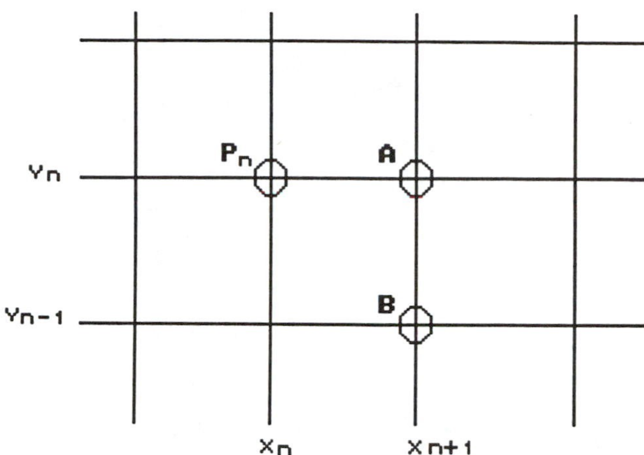

**FIGURE 3.5**

We choose one of these pixels based on a test. To do this, we observe that the function $f(x,y) = x^2 + y^2 - r^2$ determines a circle with radius r around the origin in the following way:

all points x,y for which $f(x,y) = 0$ lie on the circle
all points x,y for which $f(x,y) > 0$ lie outside the circle
all points x,y for which $f(x,y) < 0$ lie inside the circle

The sketches in Figure 3.6 show the point $P_n$, the two possible successors A and B, and five possible situations for the exact circular arc. In cases a, b, d, and e these are the only possible situations of the arc, but in case c the arc can as well pass below, through, or above $P_n$.

Functions that determine how the pixels A and B lie with respect to the circle are:

$$f(A) = (x_n + 1)^2 + {y_n}^2 - r^2$$
$$f(B) = (x_n + 1)^2 + (y_n - 1)^2 - r^2$$

Table 3.1 shows the signs of these expressions and the sign of their sum $s = f(A) + f(B)$ for the five possible positions of the true circle

**TABLE 3.1**

| | a | b | c | d | e |
|---|---|---|---|---|---|
| f(A) | – | 0 | + | + | + |
| f(B) | – | – | – | 0 | + |
| f(A)+f(B) (sum, s) | – | – | –,0,+ | + | + |

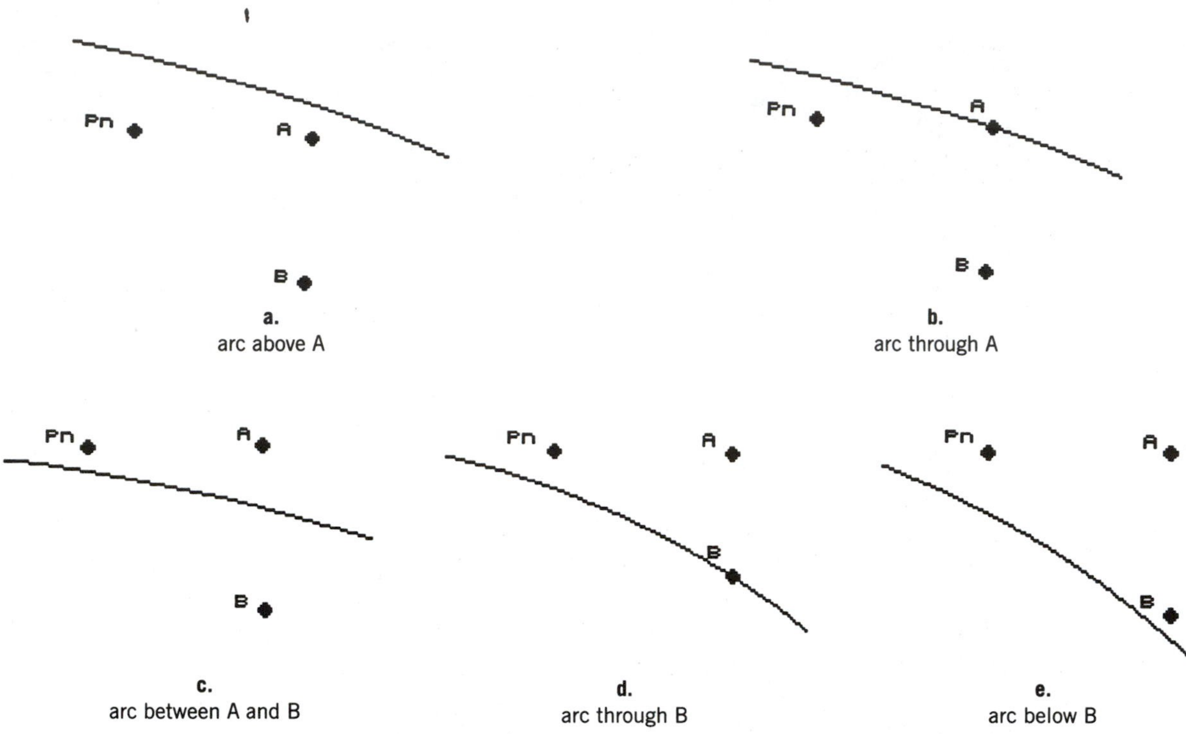


**FIGURE 3.6** The five possible cases of the circle arc.

relative to the points A and B. In case a, the pixels A and B both lie inside the circle. A is certainly closer to the circle and is chosen.

In case b, the pixel A lies precisely on the circle and is chosen.

In case c, the pixel A lies outside and the pixel B lies inside the circle. The sum f(A) + f(B) in this case always consists of a positive and a negative term. If it is negative or zero, then pixel A is closer to the circle (measured along a normal to the circle through the pixel center) and is chosen. If it is positive, then it is possible that pixel A is closer to the circle than pixel B. Even so, the algorithm in this case chooses pixel B because it is computationally expensive to calculate the actual distance. You can see that there is a slight tendency to choose the pixel inside the circle, but this does not significantly change the appearance of the resulting image. To find out which pixel is actually closer, it would be necessary to calculate:

$$dd = \mathrm{sqrt}((x+1)^2 + y^2) + \mathrm{sqrt}((x+1)^2 + (y-1)^2) - 2r \text{ and}$$

for dd $<$ 0 choose A
for dd $=$ 0 choose either
for dd $>$ 0 choose B

In case d, the pixel B lies precisely on the circle and is chosen.

In case e, the pixels A and B both lie outside the circle. B is certainly closer to the circle and is chosen.

In short, all that is needed to make a choice between pixels A and B is the sign of the sum f(A) + f(B). We now observe that it is not necessary to calculate both formulas and the sum for every step. The starting pixel $P_0$ is taken as $(x_0,y_0) = (0,r)$. We get:

$$f(A) = (0+1)^2 + r^2 - r^2 = 1$$
$$f(B) = (0+1)^2 + (r-1)^2 - r^2 = 2-2r$$

It follows that $s = 3 - 2r$.

Depending on s ($<0$, $=0$, $>0$) we choose A or B as the next pixel $P_1$. The next s needed to go from $P_1$ to $P_2$ can be expressed very simply in terms of the old s value.

We will show this for the general case $P_n$ with coordinates $(x_n,y_n)$. Consider how the next two pixels are chosen. The expression for s is:

$$s = (x_n+1)^2 + y_n^{\,2} - r^2 + (x_n+1)^2 + (y_n-1)^2 - r^2$$

For $s < 0$, we continue with pixel $P_{n+1}$ with coordinates $(x_n+1,y_n)$ as shown in Figure 3.7. (We consider $s = 0$ and $s > 0$ below.)

In order to go from here to the next pixel $P_{n+2}$ (which can be A or B in Figure 3.7), again the value of the sum must be computed. Let's call it $s_{new}$ and express it using the coordinates of $P_n$:

$$s_{new} = (x_n+2)^2 + y_n^{\,2} - r^2 + (x_n+2)^2 + (y_n-1)^2 - r^2$$

An algebraic transformation shows that:

$$s_{new} - s = 4x_n + 6, \text{ hence } s_{new} = s + 4x_n + 6.$$

FIGURE 3.7

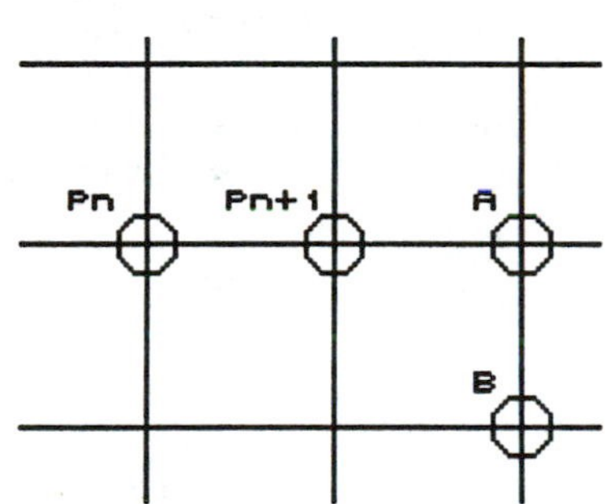


For $s >= 0$, we continue with pixel $P_{n+1}$ with coordinates $(x_{n+1},y_{n-1})$ as shown in Figure 3.8. In order to go from here to the next pixel $P_{n+2}$ (which can be A or B in Figure 3.8), again the value of the sum must be computed:

$$s_{new} = (x_n+2)^2 + (y_n-1)^2 - r^2 + (x_n+2)^2 + (y_n-2)^2 - r^2$$

An algebraic transformation shows that:

$$s_{new} - s = 4(x_n-y_n) + 10, \text{ hence } s_{new} = s + 4(x_n-y_n) + 10.$$

FIGURE 3.8

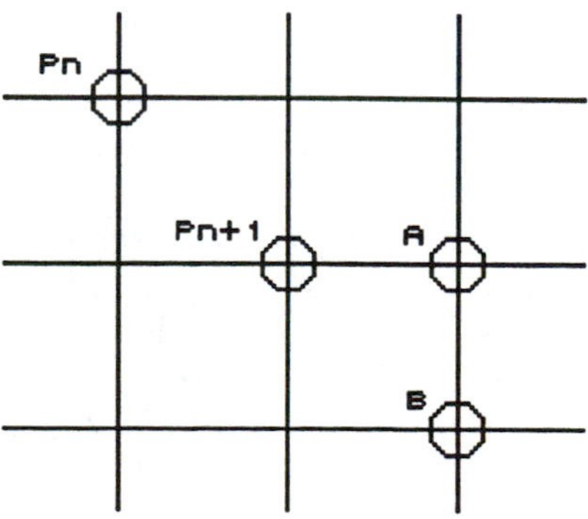


This shows that the calculation of $s_{new}$ from the former s is very simple in both cases. It uses only a multiplication by 4 (which is a left shift by two bits), an addition and sometimes a subtraction. Only the sign of s is used in making the decision about the next pixel.

### Coded Algorithm

```
procedure BRES_CIRCLE(          radius,
                     xcenter,ycenter  :  integer);
var   x,y,s  :  integer;

begin {start at 90 degrees}
  x := 0;
  y := radius;
  s := 3-2*radius;
  while x < y {stop at 45 degrees} do begin
    EIGHT_OCTS(x,y,xcenter,ycenter);
    if s ≤ 0
    then s :=s+4*x+6
    else begin
      s := s+4*(x-y)+10;
      y := y-1
    end {else};
    x := x+1
  end {while x < y};
  if x = y then EIGHT_OCTS(x,y,xcenter,ycenter)
end {procedure BRES_CIRCLE};
```

The above procedure generates an entire circle by calling EIGHT_OCTS. It works directly with the pixel addresses, performing integer arithmetic.

This works only for a pixel ratio of 1. Correcting this circle generator to a pixel ratio not equal to 1 can be done in the same way as for the other circle generators. However, this nullifies the advantage of the integer arithmetic and requires a type change of the pixel values from integer to real in order to call EIGHT_CORR.

## 3.2 ELLIPTIC ARCS

Algorithms for the generation of ellipses can also generate circles on raster displays with a pixel ratio other than 1. We draw an ellipse that turns out to be a circle by putting the major axis of the ellipse in the direction of the smaller pixel distance. For example, if the pixel ratio is 2/3 and we want a circle with a radius of r x-units, we can obtain it by drawing an ellipse with a half-diameter r in x-direction and a half-diameter r∗2/3 in y-direction.

KAPP_ELL and DDA_ELL are two ellipse generators described below. The calls

KAPP_ELL(r,r * 2/3,xcent,ycent)

or

DDA_ELL(r,r * 2/3,xcent,ycent)

would create circles on displays with a pixel ratio of 2/3.

**Symmetry in Ellipse Generation** For any point on the circumference of an ellipse parallel to the coordinate axes (except points *on* the coordinate axes), three more points can be derived by symmetry. The following procedure FOUR_QUADS makes use of this symmetry in the four quadrants around the center. The center point is also a parameter, permitting ellipses with arbitrary centers.

```
Procedure FOUR_QUADS(     x,y,
                      xcenter,
                      ycenter   : integer);
begin
   SetPix( x+xcenter, y+ycenter);
   SetPix(-x+xcenter, y+ycenter);
   SetPix(-x+xcenter,-y+ycenter);
   SetPix( x+xcenter,-y+ycenter)
end {procedure FOUR_QUADS};
```

## 3.2.1 A DDA Derived Ellipse Generator

We can produce an ellipse by choosing two small real numbers, $\alpha$ and $\beta$, with $0 < \alpha \cdot \beta < 4$, and a starting point $(x_0,y_0) \neq 0$. We perform the following iteration:

$$x_{n+1} = x_n - \alpha \cdot y_n$$
$$y_{n+1} = y_n + \beta \cdot x_{n+1}$$

To prove this assertion, express the iteration step as a matrix multiplication:

$$(x_{n+1},y_{n+1}) = (x_n,y_n) * \mathbf{A} \qquad \text{where } \mathbf{A} = \begin{pmatrix} 1 & \beta \\ -\alpha & 1-\alpha\beta \end{pmatrix}$$

The iteration process consists of a repeated multiplication of the starting vector (x,y) with the matrix **A**. This causes the point to rotate about the origin to create an ellipse.*

---

*The eigenvalues of A are $(2-\alpha\beta \pm \sqrt{\alpha\beta(\alpha\beta-4)})/2$. When $0 < \alpha\beta < 4$ the expression under the root is negative and yields complex eigenvalues. For such values of $\alpha\beta$, a real valued starting vector can never converge to an eigenvector of A by the repeated multiplications. In other words, such a starting vector will always be rotated around the origin; the multiplication cannot just stretch it without rotation. This is why the iteration works only for $0 < \alpha\beta < 4$.

Using this method gives a curve that looks like an ellipse with center (0,0), but we should prove that. To do this, we begin with the general equation for a conic with center at the origin:

$$ax^2 + 2bxy + cy^2 - 1 = 0$$

This equation is determined by the three coefficients: a, b, and c. The values of these constants can be found by solving the system of equations that results when coordinates (x,y) of three points through which the curve passes are substituted. (We solve the resulting system for the unknowns a, b, and c.)

We will do this with the initial point $\neq$ (0,0) and two iterated points. To make the calculation easy we start at (1,0), so the two following points are $(1,\beta)$ and $(1-\alpha\beta, 2\beta-\alpha\beta^2)$. The equations become:

$$\begin{aligned} a-1 &= 0 \text{ from which } a=1 \\ 2b\beta + c\beta^2 &= 0 \text{ giving } 2b=-c\beta \\ (1-\alpha\beta)^2 + 2b\beta(1-\alpha\beta)\,(2-\alpha\beta) - 2b\beta(2-\alpha\beta)^2 - 1 &= 0 \text{ giving } 2b=-\alpha \end{aligned}$$

We find the unknowns to be $a=1$, $2b=-\alpha$, and $c=\alpha/\beta$. Putting these into our general equation for a conic and multiplying with $\beta$ we get:

$$\beta x^2 - \alpha\beta xy + \alpha y^2 - \beta = 0$$

as the equation of the conic with a starting point of (1,0). As the constant term in the equation has only a scaling effect, we can replace it by r and thus get the general form of this conic through some starting point (q,0) and two succeeding points:

$$\beta x^2 - \alpha\beta xy + \alpha y^2 - r = 0$$

in which r depends on the starting point.

The discriminant equals $(\alpha\beta)^2 - 4(\alpha\beta) = 4(\alpha\beta(\alpha\beta/4-1))$. For $0 < \alpha\beta < 4$, this is negative; from analytical geometry, we know the figure must be an ellipse.

The above proves that the conic through the first three points is indeed an ellipse, but we should also prove that *all* points of the iteration lie on this ellipse. We have to show that for *any* point on the ellipse its successor from the iteration also lies on the ellipse.

If we start with a point (x,y) on the ellipse, it fulfills $\beta x^2 - \alpha\beta xy + \alpha y^2 - r = 0$. The successor point is $(x-\alpha y, \beta x + y - \alpha\beta y)$. If this point, when put into the equation, also makes it zero, then the assumption is proved to be correct. This is true but is left as an exercise.

For our ellipse, the slant angle of the major axis is $\delta$ where $\tan 2\delta$

$= \alpha\beta/(\alpha-\beta)$. For $\alpha/\beta > 1$, $-\pi/4 < \delta < \pi/4$ (ellipse is more horizontal); for $\alpha/\beta < 1$, $\pi/4 < \delta < 3\pi/4$ (ellipse is more vertical).*

Let $r_1$ and $r_2$ be the two axes of the ellipse. The ratio of their lengths is:

$$\frac{r_1}{r_2} = \frac{\sqrt{\beta\tan^2\delta - \alpha\beta\tan\delta + \alpha}}{\sqrt{\beta + \alpha\beta\tan\delta + \alpha\tan^2\delta}}$$

When $\alpha$ and $\beta$ both go to 0 with a constant ratio $\alpha/\beta \neq 1$, $\tan\delta$ goes to 0 with the same order as either $\alpha$ or $\beta$; the products go to 0 with a higher order than either $\alpha$ or $\beta$. The limit of the expression is then $\sqrt{\alpha}/\sqrt{\beta}$. As the axes are practically parallel to the coordinate axes, we can call them $r_x$ and $r_y$. The major axis will be in x-direction when $\alpha/\beta > 1$, and in y-direction if $\alpha/\beta < 1$. This is equivalent to:

$$\frac{r_x}{r_y} = \frac{\sqrt{\alpha}}{\sqrt{\beta}}$$

The iteration formula shows the changes for x and for y that occur in one step when the iteration is parallel to a coordinate axis. Either x or y is nearly 0 there. At the x-axis y is changed by $\beta \cdot x$ where x equals $r_x$; at the y-axis x is changed by $\alpha \cdot y$ where y equals $r_y$. From this, together with the length ratio for the axes, we find that the ratio of the step length in x-direction to the step length in y-direction equals $r_x/r_y$.

Figure 3.9 shows the ellipse corresponding to an iteration with $\alpha = 1.2$ and $\beta = 0.7$ and a starting point (2,0). Its major axis lies at an angle of 29.6°. The purpose of this figure is to make the development clearer. Do not get the impression that this method is used to create slanted ellipses. In practice, the method is used with very small values for $\alpha$ and $\beta$, so the ellipses will be practically parallel to the coordinate axes.

When we use this method we have to choose values for $\alpha$ and $\beta$ small enough so that adjacent pixels are set. If $r_x > r_y$ then the choice should be $\alpha = 1/r_y$ and $\beta = r_y/r_x^2$. If $r_y > r_x$ then the choice should be $\beta = 1/r_x$ and $\alpha = r_x/r_y^2$. This guarantees that the largest step will never exceed the distance between two pixels, but there will be times in the iteration where smaller steps are performed. This implies that

*The relation $\tan 2\delta = \alpha\beta/(\alpha-\beta)$ tells us which ellipse the iterated points approach in the limit, when $\alpha$ and $\beta$ both go to 0 with a constant ratio $\alpha/\beta \neq 1$. The product $\alpha\beta$ has a higher order approach to 0 than does $\alpha-\beta$; therefore $\alpha\beta/(\alpha-\beta)$ goes to 0. In the case $\alpha/\beta > 1$ the major axis is more horizontal, so the value of $\tan^{-1}(\alpha\beta/(\alpha-\beta))$ closest to 0 must be taken and it follows that $2\delta$ approaches 0. In other words, the smaller $\alpha$ and $\beta$, the closer to 0 the slant angle of the major axis will be. In the case of $\alpha/\beta < 1$ analogous reasoning shows that the slant angle of the major axis approaches $\pi/2$.

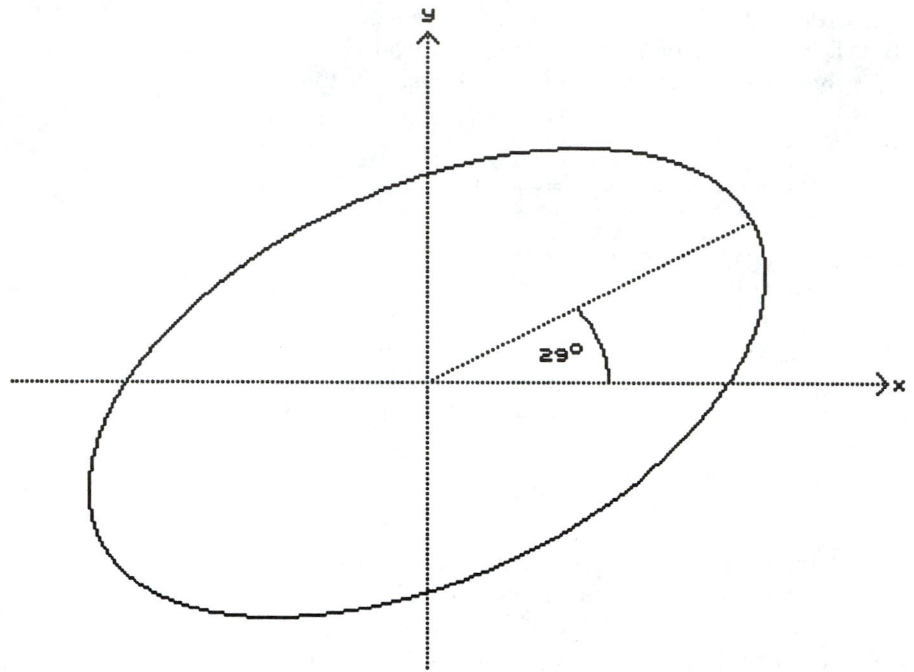


FIGURE 3.9

some superfluous pixels are set (some pixels are set twice). This effect becomes worse the more eccentric the ellipse is.

The method generates a sequence of real number pairs $x_i, y_i$ which must be rounded to the nearest location in the pixel grid. This is done automatically when we call FOUR_QUADS. Each iteration step requires two multiplications, two additions (or subtractions), and two rounding operations. If floating point arithmetic can be done in hardware, this method still is adequately fast. The algorithm is amazingly simple.

### Coded Algorithm

```
procedure DDA_ELL(  rx,ry   : real;
                   xcenter,
                   ycenter  : integer);
var  alfa,beta,
          x,y    :  real;

begin
  if rx > ry
  then begin
    alfa := 1/ry; beta := ry/(rx*rx)
```

```
    end
    else begin
      alfa := rx/(ry*ry); beta := 1/rx
    end;
    x := rx; y := 0;
    while x > 0 do begin
      FOUR_QUADS(round(x),round(y),xcenter,ycenter);
      x := x-alfa*y;
      y := y+beta*x
    end
  end {procedure DDA_ELL};
```

## 3.2.2 Kappel's Ellipse Generator

There are some close algorithmic analogies between Bresenham's circle and Kappel's ellipse generator (KAPP85), but the step from one to the other is not trivial. The basic difference is that Bresenham's circle algorithm, as we have presented it, evaluates the circle function at both points from which the choice is to be made, while Kappel's ellipse algorithm evaluates the ellipse function at only one point that lies between the two points from which we choose.

An ellipse around the origin can be expressed by the equation:

$$(x/r_1)^2 + (y/r_2)^2 - 1 = 0$$

in which $r_1$ and $r_2$ are the major and minor axes of the ellipse. Although this formula is strongly related to the circle formula, it is not true, as some authors assert, that Bresenham's algorithm can be modified to generate elliptical shapes by using the ellipse equation instead of the circle equation. If we were to parallel Bresenham's method, we would need a formula for the sum of the function values at the locations of the two pixels between which a decision is made. But this sum will contain a term involving the quotient ${r_2}^2/{r_1}^2$. To calculate the next sum value from the previous one involves multiplication with this quotient. We cannot use the simple integer arithmetic that is fundamental in Bresenham's circle algorithm.

We use a different approach to explain Kappel's ellipse generator: the function $f(x,y) = b^2x^2 + a^2y^2 - a^2b^2$ determines an ellipse in the following way:

all points x,y for which $f(x,y) = 0$ lie on the ellipse
all points x,y for which $f(x,y) > 0$ lie outside the ellipse
all points x,y for which $f(x,y) < 0$ lie inside the ellipse

This ellipse is centered at (0,0) and its major and minor axes are parallel to the coordinate axes. The ellipse intersects the x-axis at a and $-a$

and the y-axis at b and −b. In calculating the pixels that correspond to the ellipse we can restrict our consideration to the first quadrant. All other pixels of the ellipse can be obtained by symmetry around the origin. Ellipses not centered at the origin but with their axes parallel to the coordinate axes can be obtained with this algorithm by translating the results, requiring two additions per pixel. This algorithm cannot generate truly general ellipses whose axes are at an angle to the coordinate axes.

In the first quadrant the algorithm creates the pixels starting at the point (a,0) and moves in a counterclockwise direction along the curve. It will go through two different phases. As long as the slope of the ellipse is smaller than −1 the algorithm is in its first phase. It obtains the next pixel by always increasing y and possibly decreasing x. Here the essential work of the algorithm is to determine whether x must be decreased or not.

There is a point s on the ellipse where the slope is exactly −1 (see Figure 3.10). After crossing this point the algorithm enters the second phase. In this phase it obtains the next pixel by always decreasing x and possibly increasing y. Here the essential work of the algorithm is to determine whether y must be increased or not.

Kappel's algorithm uses the so-called *midpoint method.* This method was first employed by B. K. P. Horn (HORN76) to generate the raster points for a circle. At each step in the process a decision between two possible pixels must be made. The decision is based on the value of f(x,y) at the midpoint between the two possible pixels.

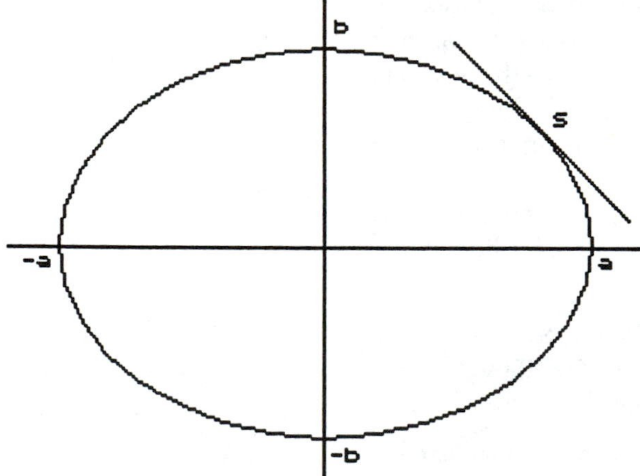


**FIGURE 3.10**

**First Phase** Until we reach point s, the decision will be made between two horizontally adjacent pixels A and B. This situation is shown in the figures below. The choice of pixel A or pixel B, is made according to the value of f(x,y) at the midpoint M1 which lies halfway between A and B. Only two cases need be considered. In the first case, shown in Figure 3.11, f(M1) < 0. The midpoint lies inside the ellipse, so A is closer to the curve and is chosen.

FIGURE 3.11

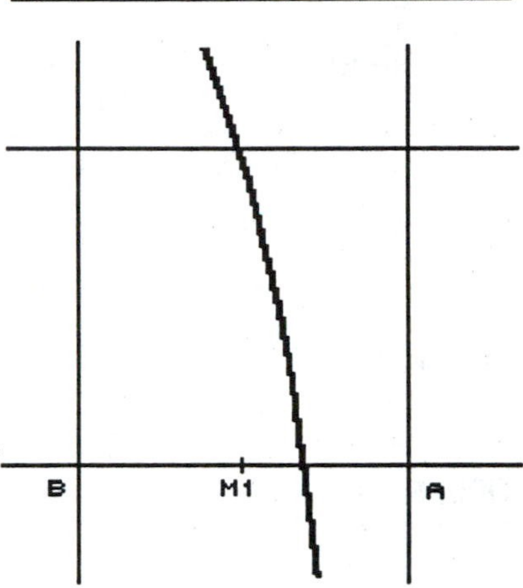


In the second case, shown in Figure 3.12, f(M1) > 0. The midpoint lies outside the ellipse, so B is closer to the curve and is chosen. When f(M1) = 0 either point can be chosen; it can be included in either of the above two cases.

The main novelty of the algorithm lies in the technique used to calculate the values of f(x,y) for the midpoints. We will now demonstrate this, again considering two cases.

Suppose pixel A was chosen. The next decision must be made between pixels C and D. (Bear in mind that the slope of the curve is smaller than −1.) If A has the coordinates (x,y) and B the coordinates (x−1,y), M1 = $(x-\frac{1}{2},y)$, and from this:

$$f(M1) = b^2(x-1/2)^2 + a^2y^2 - a^2b^2.$$

The next midpoint lies between C and D and has the coordinates M2 = (x+½,y+1) (see Figure 3.13). From this:

$$f(M2) = b^2(x-1/2)^2 + a^2(y+1)^2 - a^2b^2.$$

The difference between the function values at M1 and M2 is:

$$f(M2) - f(M1) = 2a^2y + a^2.$$

This value is not constant—it depends on y—but it is easy to calculate. At the starting point of the curve, where y is 0, this difference is just $a^2$, and then it becomes $2a^2+a^2$, $4a^2+a^2$, $6a^2+a^2$, and so on; it grows by $2a^2$ with every increase in y. The algorithm therefore uses a variable, yslope, which holds the value by which it grows. yslope starts at 0 and is increased by $2a^2$ for every increase in y. We can obtain the function value at the midpoint M2 by taking f(M1), adding the variable yslope, and adding the constant $a^2$ whenever the choice A is made:

$$f(M2) = f(M1) + yslope + a^2.$$

FIGURE 3.12

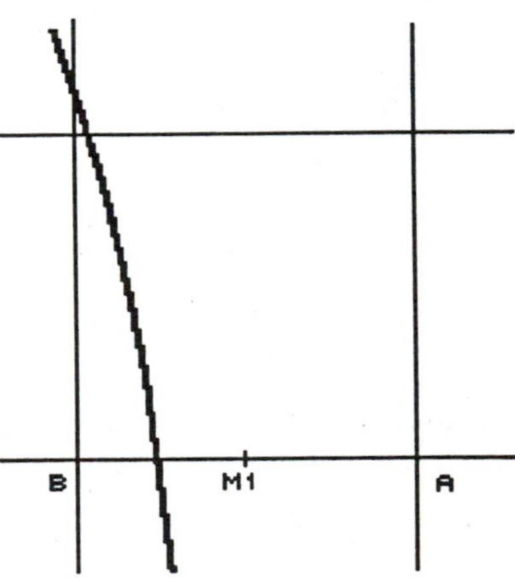


If pixel B is chosen, the next decision must be made between pixels C and E (see Figure 3.14). This is true even if the ellipse passes between pixels C and D (pixel D will not be considered because the x-coordinates of the pixels cannot increase). Assuming B has the coordinates (x,y) we get M1 = (x+½,y) and from this:

$$f(M1) = b^2(x+1/2)^2 + a^2y^2 - a^2b^2.$$

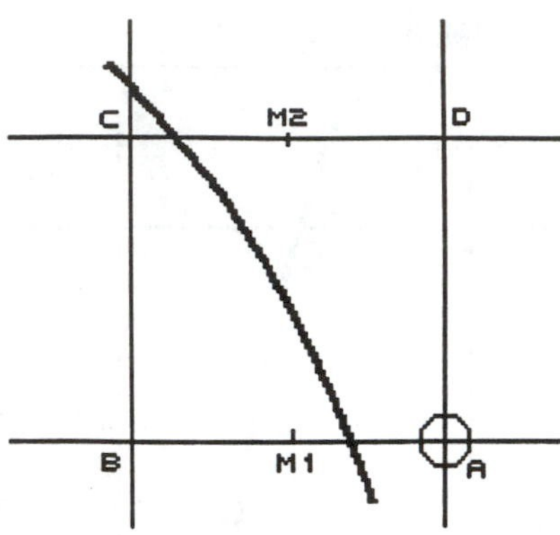


**FIGURE 3.13**

**FIGURE 3.14**

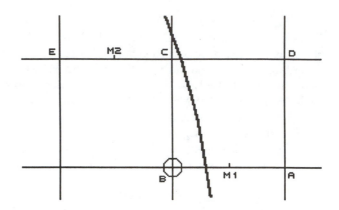

The midpoint between E and C has the coordinates $M2 = (x-½,y+1)$. From this we get:

$$f(M2) = b^2(x-½)^2 + a^2(y+1)^2 - a^2b^2.$$

The difference between the function values of M1 and M2 is:

$$f(M2) - f(M1) = -2b^2x + 2a^2y + a^2.$$

This difference depends on x and y but its calculation is easy. It increases by $2b^2$ whenever x is decreased and increases by $2a^2$ whenever y is increased. The algorithm therefore has another variable, xslope, which holds the value $2b^2x$. It starts with $2b^2a$ as the starting value for x is a, and is decreased by $2b^2$ with every decrease in x. We obtain the function value at the midpoint M2 by taking f(M1), subtracting the variable xslope, adding the variable yslope, and adding the constant $a^2$ whenever the choice B is made:

$$f(M2) = f(M1) - \text{xslope} + \text{yslope} + a^2.$$

This shows that in the first phase the function value of a midpoint can be obtained by simple additions from the function value of the former midpoint. The algorithm will use the variable fmid to hold this value; it is checked to decide between the two pixels.

Since x and y represent pixel addresses, they must be integers. As a is real, the starting value of x will be the nearest integer. The first pixel to be set will always be (round(a),0). The x coordinate of the first pixel depends on whether the rounding is up or down, but in either case, the algorithm will increase y and will make a choice between pixels (x−1,1) and (x,1) (see Figures 3.15 and 3.16).

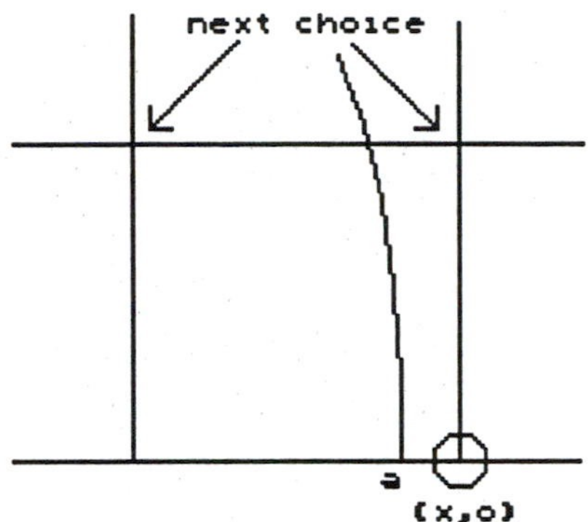


**FIGURE 3.15** Rounding up.

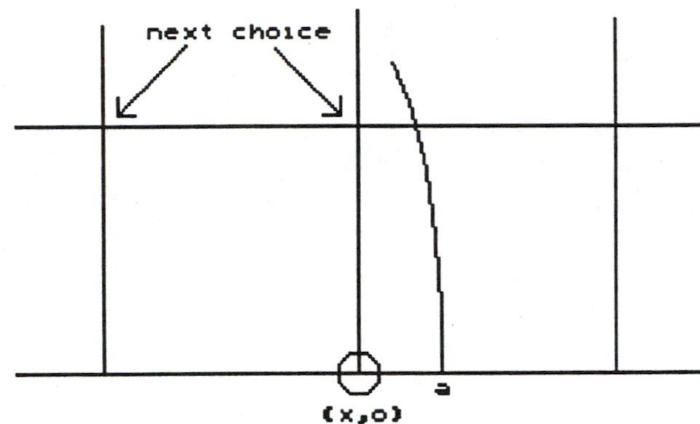


**FIGURE 3.16** Rounding down.

If rounding is down, the function value at the midpoint between pixels at $(x-\frac{1}{2},1)$ is needed. The starting value of fmid will therefore be:

$$\text{fmid} = b^2(x-½)^2 + a^2 - a^2b^2.$$

There was a good reason for naming the two variables xslope and yslope. The slope of a curve defined by $f(x,y) = 0$ is:

$$\frac{dy}{dx} = \frac{-f_x}{f_y},$$

where $f_x$ and $f_y$ are the partial derivatives of $f(x,y)$ with respect to x and y. We find that $-f_x = -2b^2x$ and $f_y = 2a^2y$, which are the values of the variables introduced above; that is why they have these names. The algorithm works in its first phase (below the point s), where the slope dy/dx is smaller than $-1$. The algorithm also checks the slope of the ellipse at every step in order to find if it is still in the first phase. However, the quotient $-2b^2x/2a^2y$ expresses the slope of the ellipse at the point (x,y) only if (x,y) lies precisely on the ellipse. During the algorithmic evaluation this is not the case. We use x- and y-values in the expression that are the coordinates of the last pixel set. What is checked is just a close approximation of the slope because this pixel is only close to the true curve. This fact gives rise to a potential error of one pixel for extremely narrow ellipses. (You can find a more detailed explanation in KAPP85.)

**Second Phase** As soon as $dy/dx \geqslant -1$, the algorithm enters its second phase in which x is always decreased with every new pixel calculation and y is possibly increased. In the second phase the midpoint is defined differently.

The choice is made between two vertically adjacent pixels A and B according to the function value at the midpoint M1 between these two. The situation is shown in Figures 3.17 and 3.18. When $f(M1) < 0$, the midpoint lies inside the ellipse, so A is closer to the curve and therefore is chosen (see Figure 3.17).

When $f(M1) > 0$, the midpoint lies outside the ellipse, so B is closer to the curve and therefore is chosen (see Figure 3.18). For the case $f(M1) = 0$, either A or B can be chosen; we can include it in either of the above two cases.

The following development is analogous to the first phase of the algorithm. If pixel B is chosen, the next decision must be made between pixels C and D (see Figure 3.19). (Bear in mind that the slope of the curve is greater than $-1$.) If A has the coordinates $(x,y+1)$ and B the coordinates $(x,y)$, we get $M1 = (x,y+½)$ and from this:

$$f(M1) = b^2x^2 + a^2(y+½)^2 - a^2b^2.$$

The midpoint between C and D has coordinates $M2 = (x-1,y+\frac{1}{2})$.

From this we get:

$$f(M2) = b^2(x-1)^2 + a^2(y+½)^2 - a^2b^2.$$

The difference between the function values at M1 and M2 is:

$$f(M2) - f(M1) = -2b^2x + b^2.$$

We obtain the function value at midpoint M2 by taking f(M1), subtracting xslope, and adding the constant $b^2$ whenever the choice B is made:

$$f(M2) = f(M1) - \text{xslope} + b^2.$$

If pixel A is chosen, the next decision must be made between pixels D and E (pixel C is not considered, because the y-coordinates of the pixels cannot decrease; (see Figure 3.20). If A has the coordinates $(x,y)$ and B the coordinates $(x,y-1)$, we get:

$$M1 = (x,y+½)$$

and from this,

$$f(M1) = b^2x^2 + a^2(y-½)^2 - a^2b^2.$$

The midpoint between the pixels D and E has the coordinates $M2 = (x-1,y+½)$, so:

$$f(M2) = b^2(x-1)^2+a^2(y+½)^2-a^2b^2.$$

The difference between the function values of M1 and M2 is:

$$f(M2) - f(M1) = -2bx^2 + 2a^2y + b^2.$$

**FIGURE 3.17**

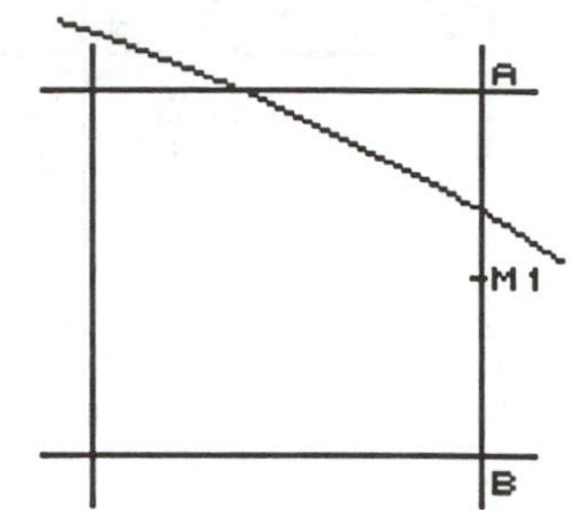


**FIGURE 3.18**

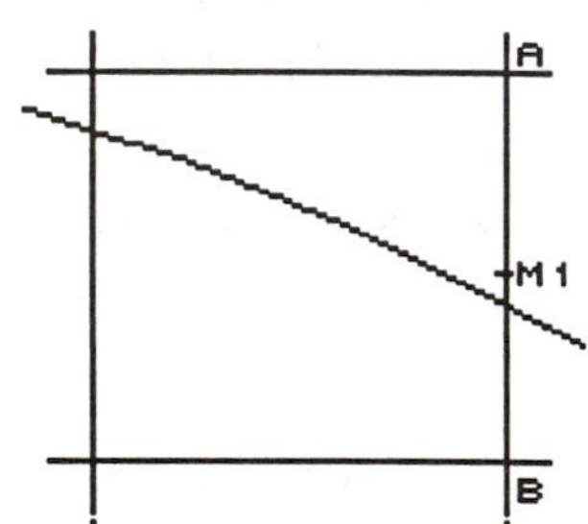


**FIGURE 3.19**

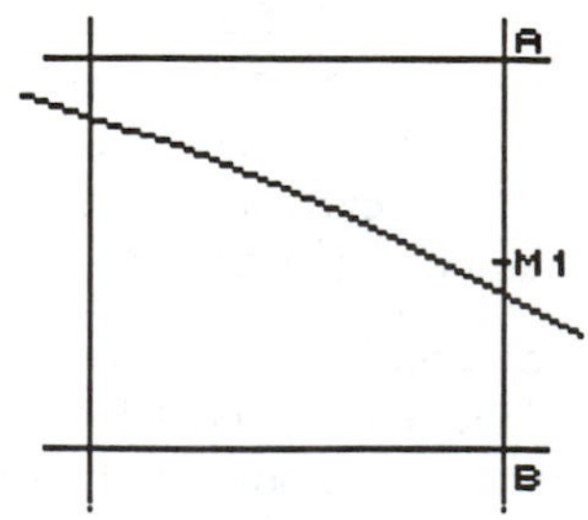

We obtain the function value at the midpoint M2 by taking f(M1), subtracting xslope, adding yslope, and adding the constant $b^2$:

$$f(M2) = f(M1) - \text{xslope} + \text{yslope} + b^2.$$

This shows that in the second phase, as in the first, the function value at a midpoint is easily derived from the function value at the previous midpoint. This value will be held in the variable fmid.

The starting value of fmid for the second phase is not equal to the value of fmid upon completion of the first phase. The first phase is left when xslope ≤ yslope. When this check is done, the algorithm has already calculated the new value of fmid as being between two horizontally adjacent pixels, as if it were still in the first phase. Since we have begun the second phase, the decision must be made between two vertically adjacent pixels, so fmid must be corrected. The new midpoint is always one-half pixel to the left and one-half pixel down from the old midpoint. Figure 3.21 shows the last chosen pixel, the projected midpoint M2 at the end of the first phase, the corrected midpoint Mc, and two possible positions of the ellipse.

The corrected fmid can be derived in the following way. The function value of the midpoint upon leaving the first phase (M2) is:

$$f(x - \tfrac{1}{2}, y + 1) = b^2(x^2 - x + \tfrac{1}{4}) + a^2(y^2 + 2y + 1) - a^2b^2.$$

The function value of the corrected midpoint (Mc) is:

$$f(x - 1, y + \tfrac{1}{2}) = b^2(x^2 - 2x + 1) + a^2(y^2 + y + \tfrac{1}{4}) - a^2b^2.$$

The difference between these two function values is:

$$b^2(-x + \frac{3}{4}) + a^2(-y - \frac{3}{4}).$$

This will be added to fmid as soon as the first phase is completed and will produce a proper starting value for the second phase. The second phase of the algorithm ends as soon as the first quadrant is filled, that is, as soon as x becomes negative.

**FIGURE 3.20**

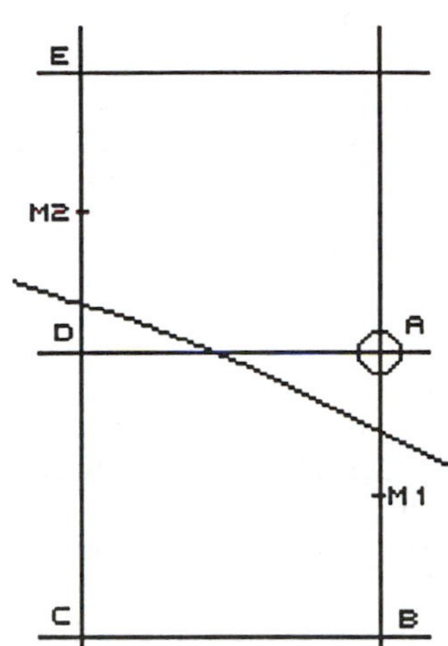


**FIGURE 3.21**

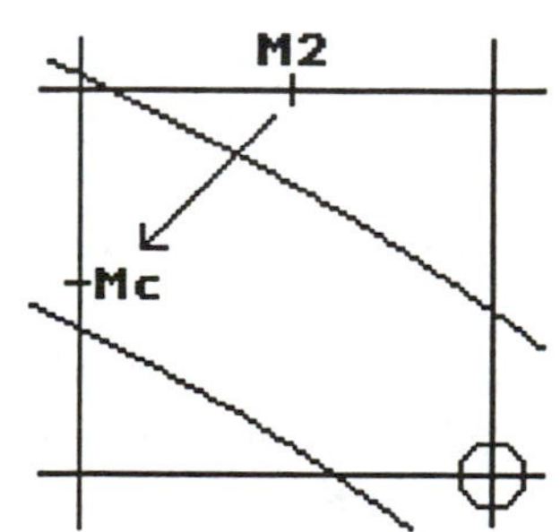


### Coded Algorithm

```
procedure KAPP_ELL(     a,b   : real;
                   xcenter,
                   ycenter   : integer);
var asquare,bsquare,
          a22,b22,
      xslope,yslope,
              fmid    :  real;
               x,y    :  integer;
```

```
begin
  x := round(a);
  y := 0;
  asquare := a*a;
  bsquare := b*b;
  a22 := asquare + asquare;
  b22 := bsquare + bsquare;
  xslope := b22*a;
  yslope := 0;

  {first phase}
  fmid := bsquare*(x*x-x+0.25) + asquare - asquare*bsquare;
  while xslope > yslope do begin
    FOUR_QUADS(x,y,xcenter,ycenter);
    y := y + 1;
    yslope := yslope + a22;
    if fmid < 0
    then fmid := fmid + yslope + asquare
    else begin
      x := x-1;
      xslope := xslope - b22;
      fmid := fmid - xslope + yslope + asquare
    end {else}
  end {while};

  {second phase}
  fmid := fmid - (yslope+xslope)/2 + 0.75*(bsquare-asquare);
  repeat
    FOUR_QUADS(x,y,xcenter,ycenter);
    x := x - 1;
    xslope := xslope - b22;
    if fmid > 0
    then fmid := fmid - xslope + bsquare
    else begin
      y := y + 1;
      yslope := yslope + a22;
      fmid := fmid - xslope + yslope + bsquare
    end {else}
  until x < 0
end {procedure KAPP_ELL};
```

**FIGURE 3.22** Elliptical arc.

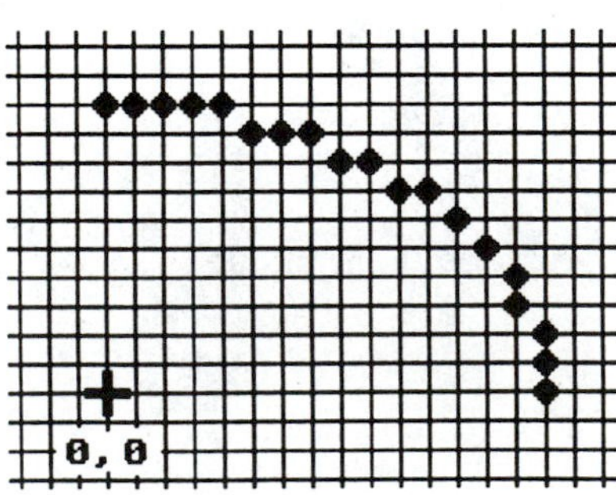


Figure 3.22 shows the first quadrant of an elliptical arc with a = 15 and b = 10, drawn by KAPP_ELL. The whole ellipse can be drawn using symmetry around the origin.

**Accuracy versus Speed** There is a version of this algorithm (explained in KAPP85) that uses only integer arithmetic. It requires integer values for the half-diameters (a and b). This integer version is essentially the same as the above. The only difference lies in the initial values for x and fmid. Since variables in the algorithm are integers, there are some round-off errors when fmid is initialized and when it is corrected at the transition from the first phase to the second.

The difference between integer-valued axes achieved by rounding from real values of the half-diameters is bounded by 0.5, corresponding to half a pixel. In raster displays with a fine resolution and small pixels this is negligible. It is likely that hardware developments in computer graphics will be in the direction of increasing the resolution of raster displays. At that time, it will be tolerable to sacrifice a negligible amount of exactness by applying an algorithm that is somewhat faster because of using integer arithmetic.

Actually, whether integer arithmetic is faster than real arithmetic depends on the way the arithmetic is performed. If the real arithmetic has to be emulated (executed step by step using integer arithmetic, shifts, etc.) then it is considerably slower than integer arithmetic. If it is executed in hardware, using a math coprocessor or some dedicated graphics chip, there may be no great difference in speed.

It is even likely that hardware being developed for computer graphics will provide dedicated chips that can generate straight lines, circles, and ellipses very rapidly. If that occurs, there will be no need for simplifying the algorithm to integer arithmetic. The real version of the algorithm will be preferred because it produces more accurate results.

**Error Considerations** It is certainly not possible that all pixels lie precisely on the ellipse—they can only be approximations to the path of the curve. How far off the true curve will they be in the worst case? The error of a pixel (its distance from the curve) can be defined in several ways. The following definition is the most natural one: The error of a pixel is defined to be the distance from its center to the nearest point on the ellipse (see Figure 3.23).

This distance must be measured along the line that is normal to the ellipse and that passes through the pixel center. However, it is time consuming to compute this distance. Therefore, the ellipse algorithm and practically all other curve generators don't use this error definition. Instead, the error at a pixel is defined to be the distance from the pixel center to the ellipse, measured in a direction parallel to the x-axis in phase 1 and parallel to the y-axis in phase 2 (see Figures 3.24 and 3.25).

Using this latter definition, the error at a pixel never exceeds 0.5. The line along which this distance is measured is generally not normal to the ellipse because it is parallel to either the x-axis or the y-axis. Note that the distance measured along a line normal to the ellipse through the same pixel center is not greater than this, so the error of a pixel with the first definition is also bounded by 0.5. However, the

**FIGURE 3.23**

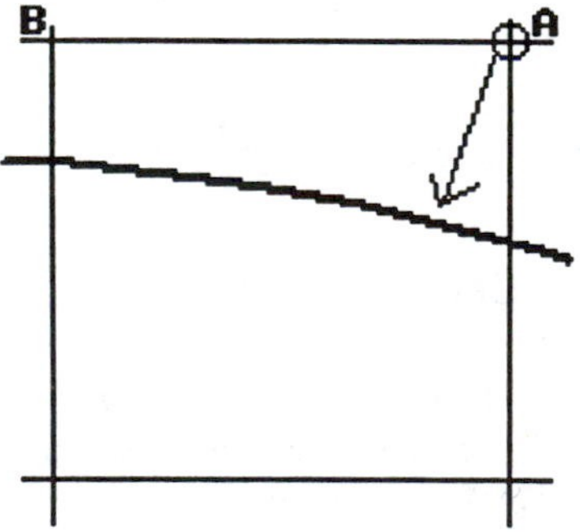

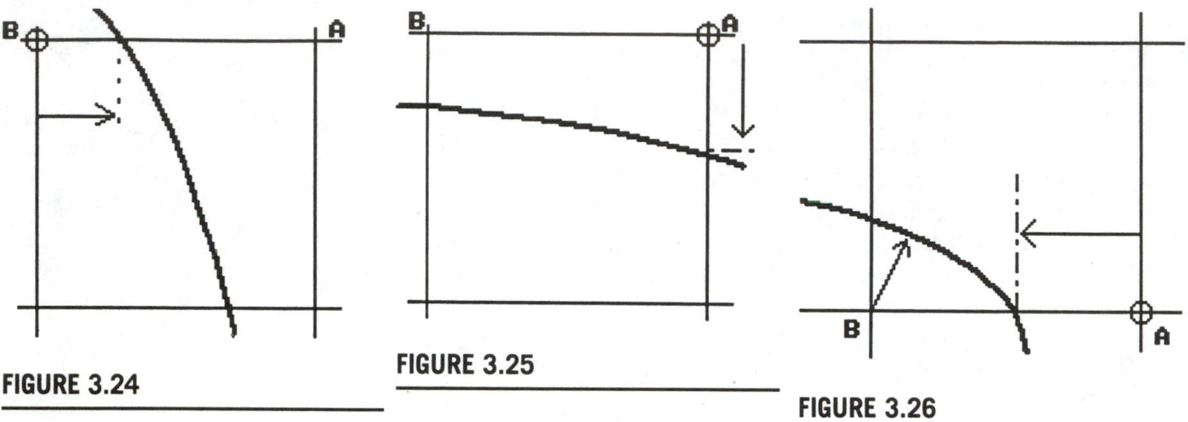


FIGURE 3.24

FIGURE 3.25

FIGURE 3.26

algorithm does not always choose the pixel closest to the curve according to the first definition. It can happen that a pixel is chosen even though there is a closer pixel—closer in terms of the first definition—adjacent to it. The errors of the pixels are bounded by 0.5 but are not optimal.

Figure 3.26 shows such a case. The true elliptical arc crosses the line between A and B somewhat closer to A and with a slope less than $-1$. The distance from the intersection point to A is less than 0.5, therefore A is chosen. But the arc then bends to the left enough so that point B is actually closer than A, according to the first error definition. B would have been a better choice. This may only occur at the transition point.

Many other curves can be produced with scan-converting techniques. These references describe some of them: hyperbolas, PITT67; conics in general, COHE69; other nonparametric curves, JOLH73. These methods are useful only in special cases; a specific algorithm can be faster than a general algorithm. It is not practical to have a special algorithm for each possible curve. It is enough to have very fast straight line, circle, and ellipse generators, approximating the wide variety of other curves with a sequence of short straight lines.

# EXERCISES FOR CHAPTER 3

## Section 3.0

1. List some advantages of a liquid crystal display over a CRT display.
2. List some advantages of a CRT display over an LCD.
3. What are the three main types of liquid crystals and what are their essential characteristics?

# Section 3.1

4. What advantage do LCD and plasma displays share over the CRT?
5. Implement the procedure EIGHT_CORR in Pascal for a pixel ratio 3/4, avoiding divisions by nonpowers of two.
6. Implement the parameter method for a circle. Assume that you have only the graphics primitive SetPix, that is, you cannot connect points on the circle perimeter by straight lines. Experiment with bigger and smaller step sizes for u.
7. Implement the choice of an optimal step size for u, that is, a step size small enough to set adjacent pixels but not smaller than necessary. *Hint:* For $u_0 = 0$ and radius $= r$ the first pixel to be set is $(r,0)$; r should not be too small. For the next parameter value, $u = u_1$, we want the pixel $(r,1)$ to be set, so we need $x = r \cdot \cos(u1) \approx r$ and $y = r \cdot \sin(u_1) \approx 1$, from which we see that $\sin(u_1) \approx 1/r$, therefore $u_1 \approx \arcsin(1/r)$.
8. If your system has a raster display with a nonsquare pixel ratio, implement the correction of the parameter method to your pixel ratio to obtain a "round" circle. You still want to set all pixels along the perimeter, even where they are closer together. Considering this, implement the choice of an optimal step size for u.
9. If your system has a square pixel ratio use the correction to obtain an ellipse from the parameter method.
10. Assuming you have the straight line graphics primitive, implement the parameter method for a circle by connecting points on the perimeter by straight lines. You can make much bigger steps than before with the parameter and still obtain reasonably smooth-looking circles. Here, too, the step size depends on the radius of the circle. Try to find a relation.

Exercises 11 through 13 assume that the computed points are connected by straight lines.

**FIGURE 3.27**

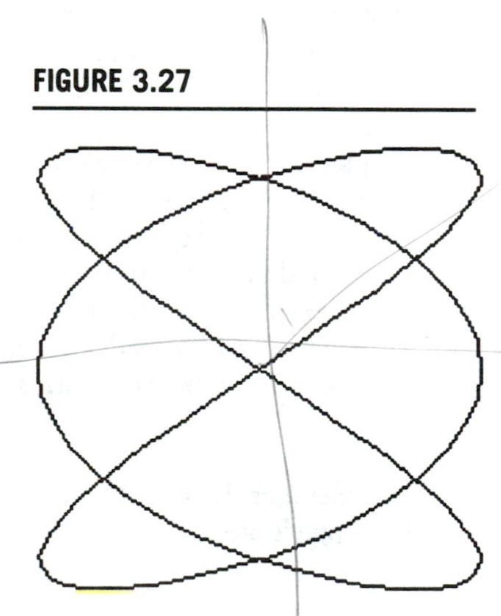

11. The method of Exercise 6 is the easiest circle generation to implement. By changing the expressions for x and y in the parameter equations, we can obtain all sorts of nice-looking curves, so-called Lissajous curves. For example:

$$x = r * \cos(3u)$$
$$y = r * \sin(2u)$$

gives the curve shown in Figure 3.27. Here the factors for the parameter inside the sin and cos expressions are still integers but are not equal. Experiment with other integer factors.

12. Another degree of variation consists of adding a certain constant to the parameter, as in:

$$x = r * \cos(3u+1)$$
$$y = r * \sin(2u)$$

This results in the curve shown in Figure 3.28. Experiment with other constants and integer factors.

**FIGURE 3.28**

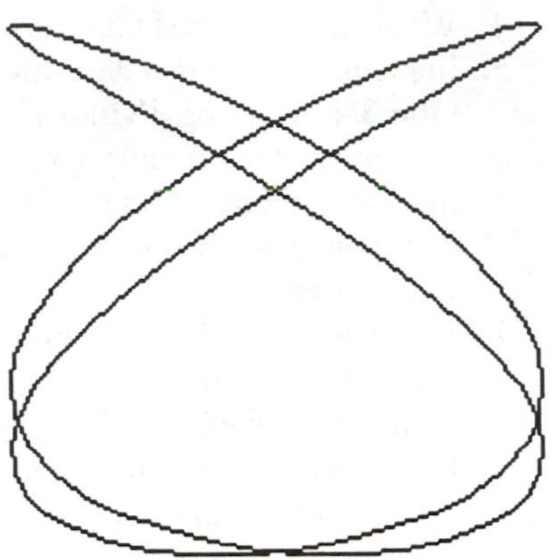

13. When multiplying the parameter with noninteger factors and letting it go from 0 to $2\pi$, we obtain a curve that does not close back to the starting point. A closed curve can be enforced by letting the parameter do several loops. If the equations are

$$x = r * \cos(3 * u) \qquad y = r * \sin(2.2 * u)$$

how many multiples of $2\pi$ does the parameter need to go through to obtain a closed curve? Draw this curve.

Exercises 14 through 17 deal with the spiral and the ellipse methods of generating circles. For these methods a small step size must be chosen, therefore the computed points are set as individual pixels and are not connected by straight lines. Choose $\epsilon$ to be $1/r$ as suggested in the text.

14. If the spiral method is used to generate one octant of a circle with a radius of 200 pixels, how much is the generated curve off the true circle in the worst case? *Hint:* For one octant $200 \cdot \pi/4 =$ 157 steps need to be done. With $\epsilon$ chosen to be 0.005, we get $1.0000124^{157} = 1.0019$ for the factor after 157 steps; this times the starting radius gives 200.38 pixels.
15. If the ellipse method is used to generate one octant of a circle starting at point (100,0), how much is the generated curve off the true circle? *Hint:* Point (100,0) lies on the ellipse, therefore from the ellipse equation we have $100^2 - 2r^2 = 0$, which gives $2r = 100\sqrt{2}$. The longer axis is $100\sqrt{2}/\sqrt{2-\epsilon}$. With $\epsilon$ chosen to be 0.01, this is 100.25. The biggest deviation from the circle is at 45°.
16. Implement the ellipse method without taking advantage of symmetry considerations and choose a rather big $\epsilon$, for example, $\epsilon =$ 0.5 or $\epsilon = 1$. Set only individual pixels, iterate for about 200 steps, and observe the resulting slanted ellipse.
17. The deviation from the true circle can be made arbitrarily small by choosing a very small $\epsilon$. What is the reason for not doing this? That is, why do we work with $\epsilon = 1/r$ and cope with the resulting error?

In Exercises 18 and 19 on Bresenham circle generation, only individual pixels are set.

18. Assume that the sum s in the BRES_CIRCLE procedure is exactly 0. Show that in this case pixel A is closer to the ideal circular arc than pixel B, with the distance measured along radials from the center to those pixels.
19. Assume that the sum s in the BRES_CIRCLE procedure is exactly 0. This does not imply that the ideal circular arc intersects the line between the two pixels at the midpoint. Show that the arc intersects at a point that is always a little closer to pixel A. *Hint:* s = 0. That is,

$$x^2 + y^2 - r^2 + x^2 + (y-1)^2 - r^2 = 0,$$

which can be compressed to:

I: $$x^2 + y^2 - y + \frac{1}{2} - r^2 = 0.$$

Also we have:

$$x^2 + (y-1+d)^2 - r^2 = 0,$$

which can be expanded to:

II: $x^2 + y^2 + d^2 + 1 + 2dy - 2d - 2y - r^2 = 0.$

Subtracting II from I gives a relation in d and y alone. Isolate d from that relation and show that the resulting expression in y is greater than 1/2 for every positive y-value.
20. Use the parameter method for a circle to implement a program that draws a pie chart. The program produces the pie chart interactively. It asks the user for the number of sections, n, then for the amounts of the sections. The amounts are converted by the program to percentages. The program then draws a circle and draws the sections by connecting the center to the proper points on the perimeter.

# Section 3.2

21. Given a raster with a pixel ratio of 2/3, a circle with radius 15 x-units can be produced by using a circle DDA with radius 10 y-units and multiplying all x-values by 3/2. This avoids the division by 3. Start the circle generator with the uppermost pixel of the circle and go clockwise for one-eighth of the circumference. Create the other circle points by symmetry. Implement this circle generator using the spiral method.
22. Given a raster with a pixel ratio of 2/3, a circle with radius 15 x-units can be produced by drawing an ellipse with half-diameter 15 in x-direction and half-diameter 10 in y-direction. Implement

the DDA ellipse generator to produce circles of a given radius on this pixel ratio.

23. Write a procedure

ellipse (a,b,xcenter,ycenter,type : integer);

that uses the parameter method for a circle with $r_x = a$ and $r_y = b$ to draw an ellipse with axes a and b, center at (xcenter,ycenter) and linetype specified by type: 1 = normal; 2 = dashed; 3 = dotted.

24. Draw one quadrant of a circle of given radius with the methods of Exercises 21 and 22 and find out if they differ in some pixels.

25. What is the value of r in the ellipse equation if the starting point is (c,0)?

26. When using the DDA ellipse generator we iterate a point $(x_n, y_n) \approx 0$ with $x_{n+1} = x_n - \alpha \cdot y_n$ and $y_{n+1} = y_n + \beta \cdot x_{n+1}$. Show that the points so iterated lie on the ellipse $\beta x^2 - \alpha\beta xy + \alpha y^2 - r = 0$. Show that if a point (x,y) fulfills the ellipse equation, the next point in the iteration: $x_1 = x - \alpha y$, and $y_1 = \beta x + y - \alpha\beta y$ also fulfills the equation. Insert $(x_1, y_1)$ into the equation, simplify, and use $\beta x^2 - \alpha\beta xy + \alpha y^2 - r = 0$.

27. Assume you have the straight line primitive. Implement an ellipse generation using the equation:

$$\frac{(x - xcenter)^2}{a^2} + \frac{(y - ycenter)^2}{b^2} = 1.$$

In this equation (xcenter,ycenter) is the center of the ellipse, a is the length of the horizontal axis, and b is the length of the vertical axis. Using this equation, compute points on the circumference and connect them by straight lines. Is this an efficient method? Why or why not?

28. Generate an ellipse slanted by $\alpha$ degrees. An ellipse with the center at the origin, slanted by $\alpha$ degrees, with axes a and b, is expressed parametrically by the formulas:

$$x = a * \cos(u) - b * \sin(u + \alpha) \quad y = b * \sin(u) + a * \cos(u + \alpha)$$

Generate an ellipse slanted by 15° with axes 50 and 30 in pixels. Compute points on the perimeter of the ellipse and connect them by straight lines.

29. Repeat Exercise 28 but don't use the straight line primitive; set only single pixels. You have to work with a very small step size. Find a good step size, small enough to set adjacent pixels, but not smaller than necessary.

Exercises 30 and 31 let you draw other curves. Use straight lines to connect individual points along the curves.

**30.** Draw the sin curve, expressed parametrically by:

$$x = u \qquad y = \sin(u)$$

**31.** Draw the curve:

$$x = u \qquad y = \sin(u) + \sin(2u) + \sin(3u)$$

# Windowing and Clipping

# 4

Chapter 4 defines the terms *window* and *viewport* as applied to computer graphics and describes how portions of a two-dimensional picture can be *clipped away* so as to fit within a window. There are three sections.

**4.0 Introduction** sets the background by defining window and clipping.

**4.1 The Two-Dimensional Window Concept** is a rectangular portion of the scene that is mapped onto a rectangular portion of the computer screen, the viewport. This mapping requires a transformation between coordinate systems.

**4.2 Clipping Algorithms** are systematic procedures for "not drawing" the parts of lines that lie outside the window. We describe three algorithms in detail. These are extended to the clipping of polygons. We also explain the different processes for clipping text.

# 4.0 INTRODUCTION

A window is a very familiar item. It is an opening through which we see a portion of the real world that exists outside. Its frame cuts off a portion of that outside world from view, but what we don't see still exists. In effect, we limit the view by an artificial device.

There doesn't have to be an actual window to achieve this limitation of what we want to see. We have all noticed photographers make a "window" with their hands in order to visualize what will appear in the final photograph. If we concentrate hard enough on a portion of the real world, we can mentally block out other details that are extraneous.

In computer graphics, the idea of a window is important. The word has a somewhat different meaning, however. This chapter first describes the general concept and purpose of a two-dimensional window in computer graphics. We follow this with descriptions of the problems that arise when we attempt to realize the concept.

We cannot limit what we see on the computer screen just by drawing a window frame. Instead, we must "not draw" those portions of the total image that lie outside the window, which we wish to suppress. Determining which portions to omit is called *clipping*. We will need to consider separately the clipping of lines, polygons, and text. We will discuss three different algorithms for clipping of lines, which differ in complexity and amount of computations required. Since clipping polygons is quite an involved process, we present only one algorithm for this procedure. Our treatment of text clipping will be less detailed.

Clipping images is important for three-dimensional objects also. Windowing and clipping in three dimensions are extensions of the two-dimensional concepts and the algorithms are basically the same. These topics are dealt with in Chapter 6.

# 4.1 THE TWO-DIMENSIONAL WINDOW CONCEPT

Most windows in the real world are rectangular. We can also think of a window as a rectangular frame that we imagine around some picture to limit what we see. In computer graphics, it is also most natural to have a rectangular window because the display areas are rectangular. The window that exists in the real world or in our imagination will be mapped onto a rectangular display. Such a window has to be associated with certain numbers that define it, or its *range*.

The range of a rectangular window can always be expressed by four numbers. Using a Cartesian coordinate system, we define the left boundary of the area with the smaller x-coordinate and the right boundary with the larger x-coordinate of the window. Similarly, we define the bottom boundary of the area with the smaller y-coordinate and the top boundary with the larger y-coordinate of the window. This implies that the x-coordinates grow from left to right and the y-coordinates from bottom to top. Such a window definition provides a coordinate system that overlies a rectangular portion of the real world or an imagined set of objects. Using these coordinates, we can describe each point within that area.

For many computer graphics applications this is a very important concept because objects can be described only by specifying numbers. For example, a house can be described in primitive terms by describing its outline, which consists of a pentagon. That in turn is described by specifying each of its vertices by a Cartesian number pair, as shown in Figure 4.1. Certainly this is a very inadequate and "unfriendly" way of describing or producing a picture, but in many systems it is the only way.

There are much more user-friendly graphic systems. For example, the user can move a graphics cursor on the screen by moving a mouse on the table, specifying certain points on the screen by clicking a button

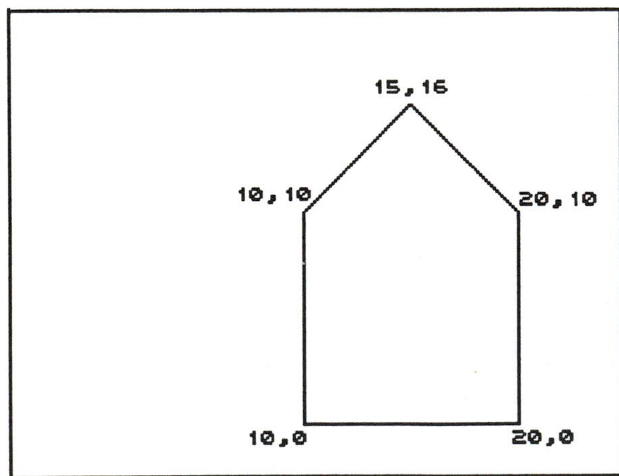


**FIGURE 4.1** A house described by Cartesian coordinates.

on the mouse. The points can be connected by straight lines ("rubber banding"), and other interactive operations can be performed. Using such methods, we can create a picture without ever having to think about a single number. Styluses, track balls, and light pens are other devices that make drawing an interactive process. Paint systems work without using windows.

Even so, objects often must be described by a set of numbers, since there are many times when we want the computer to create the picture for us. One example is drawing a complicated curve whose points must be calculated. In such a case, these numbers must be transformed into a picture. Another example is a picture originally created by a human that the computer is to transform in some way. The computer needs to have the picture described by numbers because it can only work with a numerical description. We are still decades away from true image processing by computers in the way that humans do it: without numbers, just by recognizing objects for what they are and transforming them in the way human brains do.

In short, for the computer to be able to do something with a picture besides merely displaying it, it needs a picture description that consists of a set of numbers in a certain logical arrangement. These numbers must refer to something. We will use the Cartesian number area, which is the window, as that reference.

Specifying a window by associating numbers with the window boundaries gives the user the additional advantage that the number range most suitable to the given drawing task can be employed. Therefore *window coordinates* are also called *user coordinates.* Another term that means the same thing is *world coordinates.*

Whenever a window is specified it is assumed that this window is displayed on the graphics output device (usually a CRT screen but it could be, for example, a plotter). In this chapter the term screen will also mean any appropriate display device.

While it is often assumed that the window is displayed on the whole screen, that is not essential. Often it is advantageous to use only a portion of the screen. In such cases, the rectangular part of the screen that is occupied by the window is called a *viewport.* If a viewport is not specified, we consider the entire screen to be the *default viewport.* In practically all graphics systems, the viewport is that area of the graphic output device onto which the window is mapped. The term "window" is sometimes misused. For example, the phrases "windowing environment" or "Microsoft windows" are really references to viewports.

The coordinates for specifying a viewport must be independent of the window coordinates. There are two different methods. One is to define the viewport in *absolute device coordinates;* the other is to use *normalized device coordinates.*

Using absolute device coordinates obviously depends on the device. Many personal computers run in different resolutions; they have different absolute coordinates for the same place on the screen.

The preferred method is to use normalized device coordinates. The display device is considered to have a coordinate range from 0 to 1 in x and from 0 to 1 in y no matter what the length-to-height ratio of the device really is. In this case the same graphics software can output to different graphics devices.

Figure 4.2 shows a window into a landscape. Figure 4.3 shows the representation of this window in a viewport on a display device.

Mapping a window onto a specified viewport is called the *window-to-viewport transformation.* When using a window, it is common practice to give the user the freedom to define the object in any way desired. The user then does not have to ensure that none of the points specifying the object lie outside the given window coordinate range, because only those parts of the object that lie within the window boundary will be displayed. The process of eliminating parts of the object that lie outside the window is called *clipping.* Figure 4.3 also shows the effect of clipping. The figure shows a border around the viewport. Such a border is not usually displayed; we use it so you can see the limits of the viewport.

It is a good exercise for the beginning student in computer graphics to first define an object by a set of points ((x,y)-values), place the object inside some rectangular area, and then find the window coordinates so that the given rectangular area just fits into the window. In the picture of the house in Figure 4.1 it turns out that the window boundaries have to be approximately $0 \leqslant x \leqslant 25$ and $-4 \leqslant y \leqslant 22$.

If we define a viewport in which to display the window of Figure 4.1, then we could get a display like that in Figure 4.4. (The border of the viewport is not displayed—we show it only for clarity.) The viewport boundaries on this display are approximately from 0.6 to 1.0 hor-

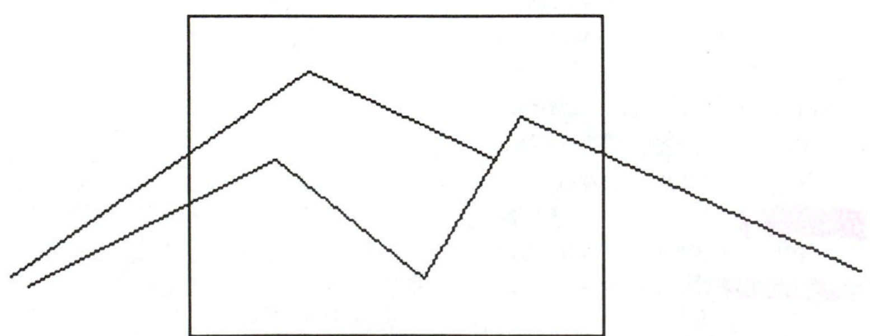

**FIGURE 4.2** Window into a landscape.

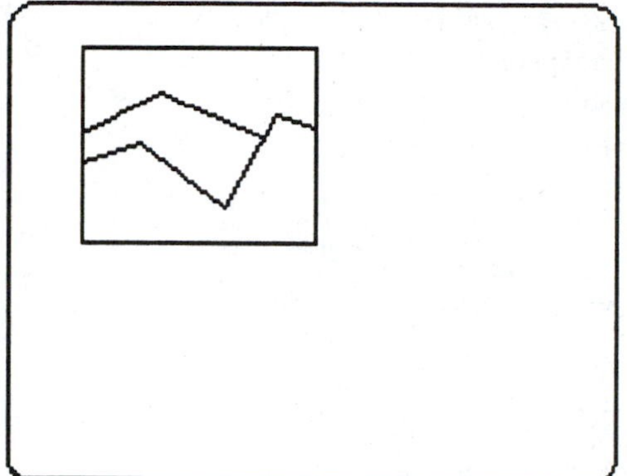

**FIGURE 4.3** Window with landscape mapped onto a viewport.

izontally and from 0.5 to 1.0 vertically. Notice that the house has been distorted slightly, because the height-to-width ratio of the window is not the same as that of the viewport.

Some interactive systems allow the user to specify windows and viewports without using any numbers. Such a definition, of course, is never very precise. There is a certain default window and default viewport to start with when you initialize the system. Selecting certain menu functions or pushing certain buttons can cause the window to become larger or smaller. In some systems, this appears as a zoom towards or away from the object being displayed. In other systems, changing the size of the window just reveals or hides part of the image. It is also possible to shift and drag the window up, down, left, or right, causing the objects to move around on the screen. In some systems, a command will display the current window coordinate range as numerical values.

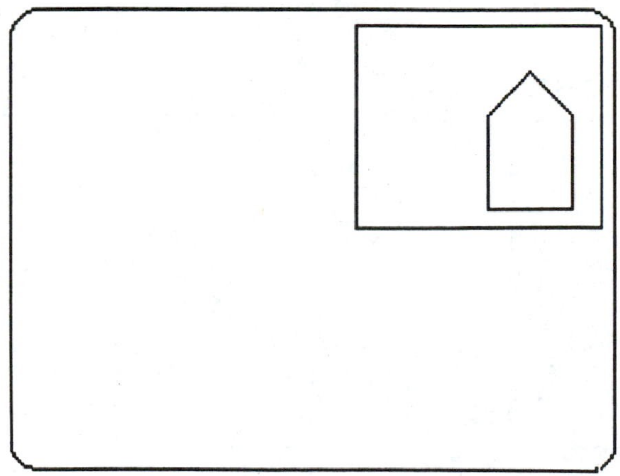

**FIGURE 4.4**

Another way to specify a window uses numbers. As we explained above, four numbers are necessary. The commands that specify a window and a viewport within an applications program will look like this:

```
window(wxl,wxh,wyl,wyh);
viewport(vxl,vxh,vyl,vyh);
```

The meaning of the abbreviations is explained below and shown in Figure 4.5:

wxl means window-x-low
wxh means window-x-high
vxl means viewport-x-low
vxh means viewport-x-high

wyl means window-y-low
wyh means window-y-high
vyl means viewport-y-low
vyh means viewport-y-high

The window and viewport definitions for the house in Figure 4.4 would be:

```
window(0,25,−4,22);
viewport (0.6,1.0,0.5,1.0);
```

Of course, real numbers can also be used in the window definition. Graphics systems are often configured in such a way that when no window and no viewport are specified, a default window and a default viewport are used. The user's moves, draws, and other commands are interpreted to be within these defaults. The default window is often

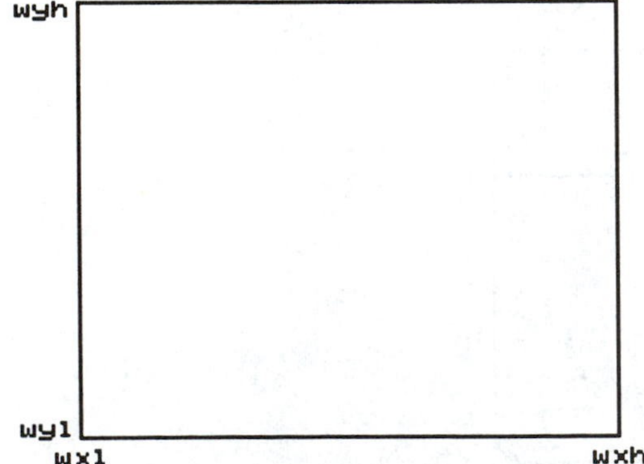


**FIGURE 4.5**

(0,1,0,1), but this varies from system to system. The default viewport is usually (0,1,0,1); in normalized device coordinates this is the whole screen.

When several small nonoverlapping viewports are specified on the screen, we can display several different objects side by side or the same object several times. We can also associate different windows with these different viewports, thus displaying different views of the same object on the screen using only a single definition of the object. Overlapping viewports can be specified and priorities can be associated with them, so that in the case of simultaneous display of several viewports, objects in higher priority viewports cover those in lower ones. You can imagine many strategies and combinations of strategies; some of these are implemented in graphics software.

When we specify the window and the viewport we want to use by:

```
window(0,25,−4,22);
viewport(0.6,1.0,0.5,1.0);
```

and then draw a house with the coordinates of Figure 4.1, we expect to get the picture of Figure 4.4. Where are the computations performed that eventually put a house of exactly this size at exactly this position? This is done by the *window-to-viewport transformation,* which we now explain.

Every line that is displayed must ultimately be drawn in absolute device coordinates. One might conclude from this that the window-to-viewport transformation has to transform the user coordinates into device coordinates, taking window and viewport definitions into account, and therefore must be device dependent. This is only partly correct. It is true that absolute device coordinates ultimately must be produced, but we can leave this task to a primitive low-ranking routine, practically as low as the DDA algorithm itself, which draws the line by calculating individual pixel positions and which, by its very nature, must be device dependent. When an image is specified in normalized device coordinates, the coordinates can be easily transformed into absolute device coordinates. The device dependency can thereby be reduced to the lowest level of the image-creating routines.

With this in mind, the viewing transformation consists of transforming the user coordinates into normalized device coordinates. The task is illustrated in Figure 4.6. According to our window and viewport specifications, the house with the five vertices (10,0), (10,10), (15,16), (20,10), and (20,0) will appear at the location within the display as shown. If we assume that the left lower corner of the display has the coordinates (0,0) and the right upper corner has the coordinates (1,1) (these are just the normalized device coordinates), what are the coor-

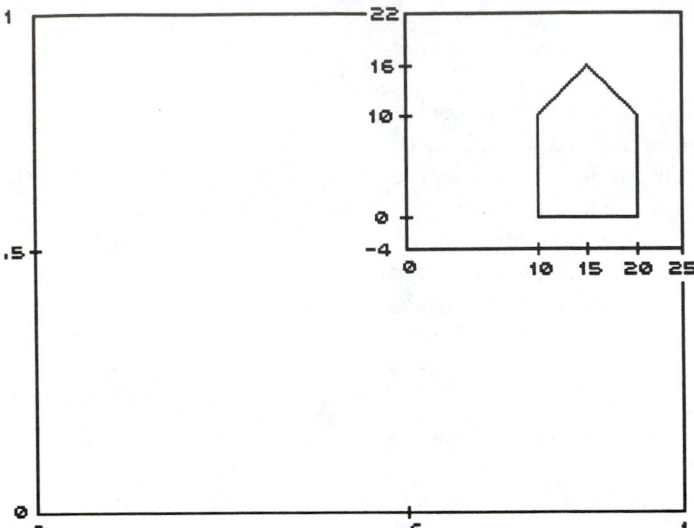


FIGURE 4.6

dinates of the five vertices of the house in that coordinate system? The task obviously consists of expressing the same points on the display in a different number system. We show below the formula that uses the values from the window and viewport definitions to transform any user-coordinate point $(x_{user}, y_{user})$ into a normalized-coordinate point $(x_{norm}, y_{norm})$. The formula is just a combination of simple translation and scaling transformations, so it is presented below without elaboration:

$$x_{norm} = (x_{user} - wxl)/(wxh - wxl) \cdot (vxh - vxl) + vxl$$
$$y_{norm} = (y_{user} - wyl)/(wyh - wyl) \cdot (vyh - vyl) + vyl$$

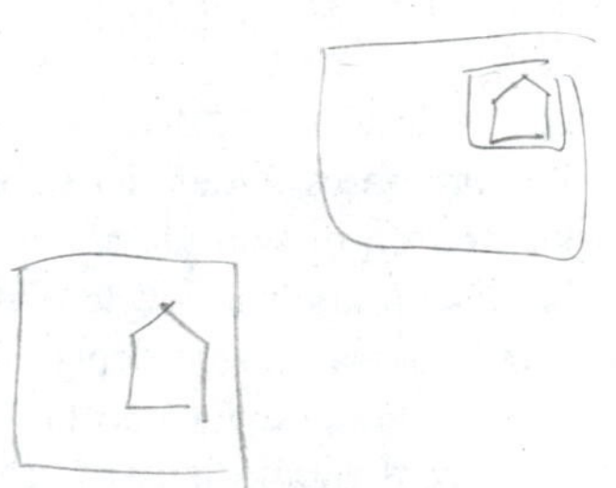

We see that this transformation is device independent. The device dependency is handled within the moving or drawing routines, which can easily handle the transformation of $(x_{norm}, y_{norm})$ to absolute device coordinates.

An important precaution: The viewing transformation does not check to see if a point is inside the given window. If it is called with a point outside the window, it produces a result outside the viewport and maybe even outside the display area. The primitive drawing and moving routines also don't check for this, so incorrect images can result. This means that the viewing transformation is to be called only with points inside the given window. Therefore, every window implementation should provide for clipping. (We discuss this in the next section.) When this is done, we are free to specify objects that are partially or totally outside the window; the clipping takes place before the viewing transformation.

# 4.2 CLIPPING ALGORITHMS

Clipping is easy for the human visual system, even with an imaginary window. We just don't see (or block out mentally) those parts of the world that lie outside the boundaries of the window. For a computer it's not so easy; in fact, it's complex. What needs to be done is clear enough: display in the viewport only those parts of the image that are inside the window boundary. Images may be lines, polygons, or text.

First, let's speculate a little about how clipping might be done. With bit-mapped graphics, so-called "low-level clipping" is feasible—something very closely related to the hardware of the particular system. Suppose we have a raster CRT, a window, and a viewport. As we have seen already, everything that is drawn on the screen must be written into the frame buffer with a pixel-by-pixel correspondence. The software that does this could be either a DDA algorithm, an algorithm that fills the interior of outlines, or possibly a microcode-implemented, fast line-drawing routine. The routines that set individual pixels in the frame buffer could check each pixel's address and just idle if this address is outside the window. The hardware that does the fast line drawing could do the same. This would certainly slow the drawing processes, but it would perform the clipping properly.

If clipping is not done, undesirable things may occur. Even when an address lies outside the frame buffer's absolute address range, the internal address decoding still produces a valid address because of binary modulo arithmetic. This causes the picture to wrap around; lines outside the screen area are drawn on the other side of the screen. This phenomenon will always be observed when no clipping software is present. If the viewport is smaller than the total display area, clipping is required, or else parts of the image will be drawn outside the viewport.

## 4.2.1 Line Clipping

The simplest form of clipping is to clip a straight line. Figure 4.7 shows several positions of a line in relation to the window.

### 4.2.1.1 Cohen-Sutherland Clipping

One well-known way to clip lines is by using the Cohen-Sutherland algorithm. This algorithm divides the whole 2-D plane into nine regions, as shown in Figure 4.8. Each region is assigned a "region-code." The innermost area in the diagram is the window.

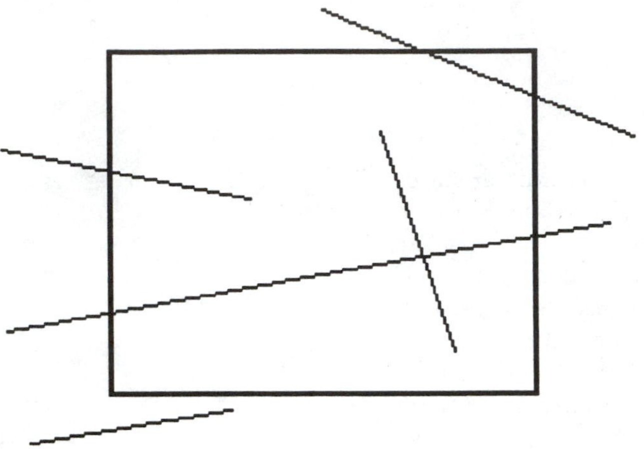

**FIGURE 4.7** Straight lines in relation to a window.

The region-code of a point in the 2-D plane is a four bit pattern. We number the bits in the order 3 2 1 0.

- Bit 3 indicates the left boundary and is 1 if the point is to the left of the left boundary.
- Bit 2 indicates the right boundary and is 1 if the point is to the right of the right boundary.
- Bit 1 indicates the bottom boundary and is 1 if the point is below the bottom boundary.
- Bit 0 indicates the top boundary and is 1 if the point is above the top boundary.
- Otherwise all bits are 0—the point is within the window. Note that this includes points precisely on the edges of the window.

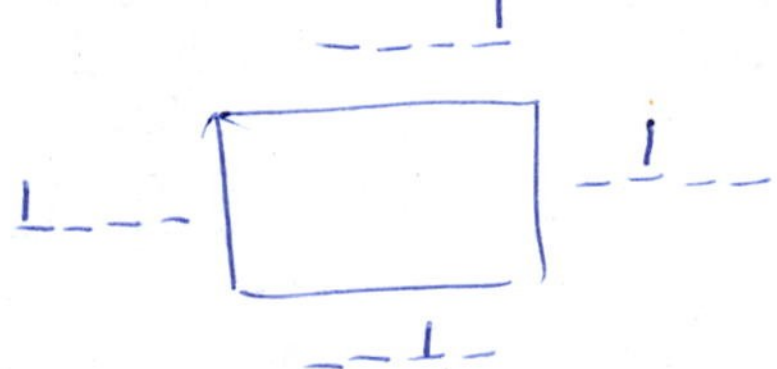

Clipping a line is as follows. The two end points of the line are each assigned their appropriate region-codes. Then the two region-codes are logically ORed. If the result is 0000, both end points lie within the window and no clipping is necessary; the line is trivially accepted.

If the first result is not 0000, the two region-codes are logically ANDed. If this result is not precisely 0000, that is, if it contains at least one 1, then the line lies totally outside the window. For example, if the ANDed result is 1000, bit 3 must be equal to 1 in both end point region-codes, implying that both end points of the line lie to the left of the left window boundary and therefore the line lies entirely to the left as well. A 1 in any other position implies a similar situation. Such a line does not need to be clipped because it will not be displayed at all. The line is trivially rejected.

**FIGURE 4.8**

| 1001 | 0001 | 0101 |
|---|---|---|
| 1000 | 0000 | 0100 |
| 1010 | 0010 | 0110 |

## NEWER GRAPHICS PROCESSORS

Some of the newer processors that emphasize graphics do clipping in microcode at the hardware level. The window boundaries are mapped internally to absolute device coordinates corresponding to the specified viewport and held in registers. A linear-to-xy address conversion routine is also implemented in hardware. Whenever an operation is performed that requires pixels to be set and a window has been specified, each SetPix command is preceded by a test of the xy-address against the window boundaries. If the address is outside, no pixel is set and, optionally, an interrupt can be generated. This permits an interrupt-servicing routine to cancel other pixel-setting operations that are invalid. If the processor is drawing a line, the algorithm can be terminated immediately. A good example of this is the TMS34010 processor (TEXA86).

Clipping by hardware is not just a recent phenomenon. For vector scan displays, very low-level (practically in hardware) clipping devices were developed many years ago. The first one was the "clipping divider" from Sproull and Sutherland (SPSU68). It is based on the midpoint subdivision algorithm described in this chapter in Section 4.2.1.2. Besides doing clipping, the hardware also performed the divisions for perspective transformations. More recently, J. H. Clark's "geometry processor" (CLAR80), implements the Cohen-Sutherland line-clipping algorithm (discussed in Section 4.2.1.1) against six clipping planes in space in floating point arithmetic, and includes 4 × 4 matrix multiplication and viewing transformations, all in hardware.

There now remain the nontrivial cases; still, the line may or may not cross the window. This can be found out only during the clipping process that we now explain through an example. The line we see in Figure 4.9 is neither rejected nor accepted trivially, therefore it must cross some boundary of the window. Both end points are not outside the same boundary and at least one of the region-codes contains 1-bits.

The algorithm will not know automatically which region-code this is. Therefore, it tests the region-code of any end point; if this is 0000, then it uses the other one. The region-code is tested bitwise in the order 3 2 1 0 for a bit that is 1. This tells the boundary outside of which the end point lies. The intersection of the line with that boundary is then computed with a simple mathematical formula. Then this particular end point will be replaced by the point of intersection.

Suppose that the algorithm first tests the region-code of point $P_1$. Testing the bits in the order 3 2 1 0, it finds that $P_1$ lies left of the left boundary. Therefore the intersection of the line with the left boundary is to be computed. Let the intersection point be called A. Point $P_1$ is

**FIGURE 4.9**

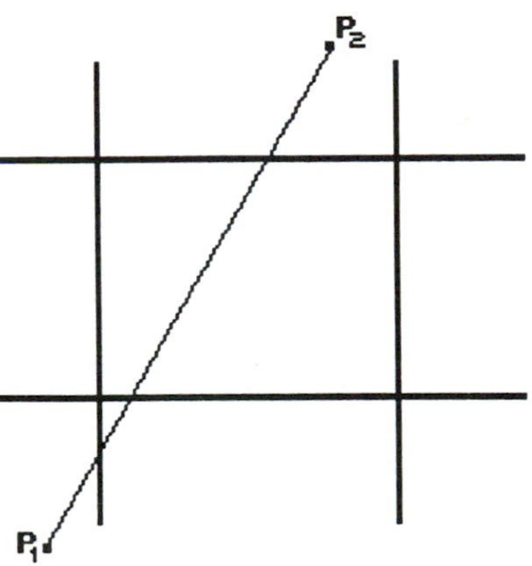

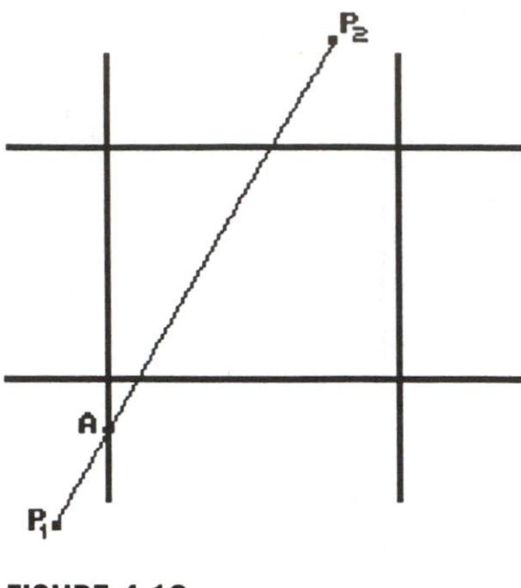

FIGURE 4.10

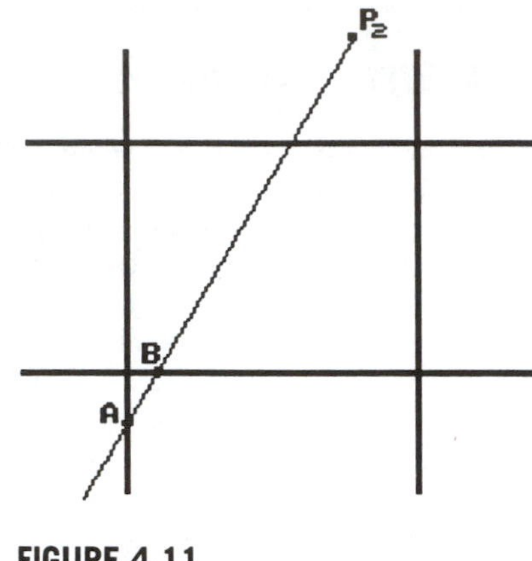

FIGURE 4.11

not interesting any more; it is clipped away. Point A is in some way closer to the window than $P_1$ (see Figure 4.10.)

Now the region-code of point A is calculated and the clipping process is repeated with the line from A to $P_2$. Again, the line $AP_2$ is not trivially accepted or rejected. Testing the bits of region-code A in the order 3 2 1 0 (left-right-bottom-top), the algorithm finds that A lies below the bottom boundary. Therefore it computes the intersection of the line with the bottom boundary, giving the intersection point B (see Figure 4.11).

Now the region-code of point B is calculated and the whole clipping process is repeated with the line from B to $P_2$. Again, the line is not trivially accepted or rejected. Testing the bits of region-code B in the order 3 2 1 0, the algorithm finds no 1-bits. Therefore points B and $P_2$ are swapped and region-code $P_2$ is tested. $P_2$ is found to lie above the top boundary, so the intersection of the line with the top boundary is calculated, giving the intersection point C in Figure 4.12.

FIGURE 4.12

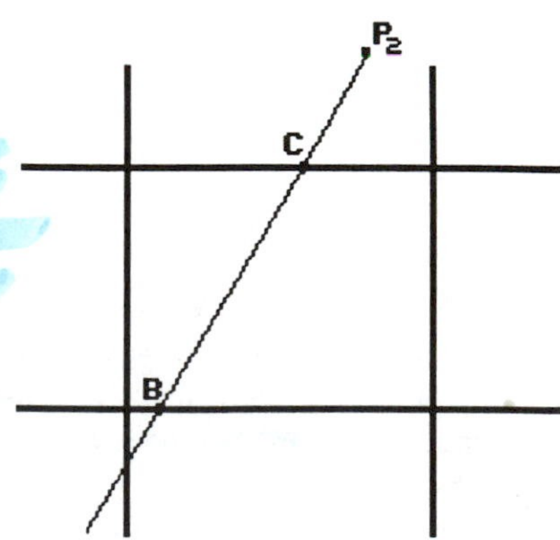


Now the region-code of point C is calculated, and the whole clipping process is repeated with the line from B to C. This time the line will be trivially accepted because both region-codes are 0000. In the worst case, the clipping process must be repeated four times. Which line constitutes the worst case depends on the order in which "out of bounds" is checked for a given point. For the checking order left-right-bottom-top, as in the above example, there are two worst-case lines, as shown in Figure 4.13.

**Coded Algorithm** The procedure CS_clip clips the line from (x1,y1) to (x2,y2) to its visible part against the window boundaries. If a visible part exists after clipping, this part is drawn by a call to a line-drawing procedure which we do not show. The end points of the line and the window boundaries are parameters of CS_clip. The meaning of the identifiers for the window boundaries is as in the text above.

Locally a type region_code is declared. The local procedure det_region determines the region-code of a point with respect to the window boundaries.

The procedure uses the internal label rejection to leave the while loop. Without a goto there are only complicated logical constructions for leaving the loop, which would decrease readability.

**FIGURE 4.13**

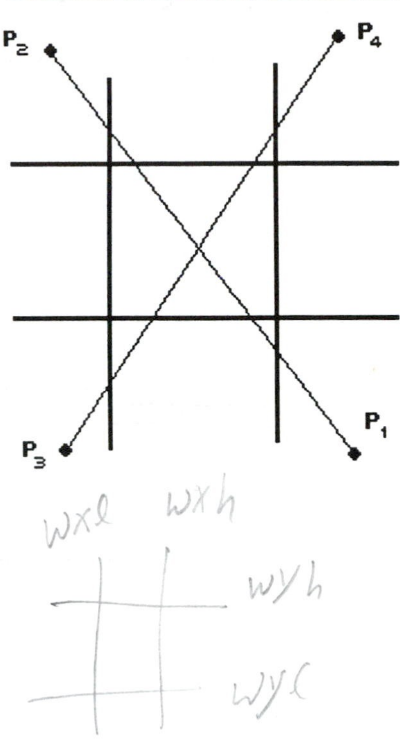


```
procedure CS_clip(     x1,y1,x2,y2,
                       wxl,wxh,wyl,wyh   :  real);
label rejection;

type boundaries    = (lef,rit,bot,top);
     region_code = set of boundaries;

procedure det_region(     x,y   :   real;
                     var region  :   region code);
{determines the region-code for point (x,y)}
begin
  region := [];
  if      x < wxl  then region := region+[lef]
  else if x > wxh  then region := region+[rit];
  if      y < wyl  then region := region+[bot]
  else if y > wyh  then region := region+[top]
end {procedure det_region};

var  region,
    region1,
    region2   :   region_code;
        x,y   :   real;

begin
  det_region(x1,y1,region1); det_region(x2,y2,region2);

  while (region1 <> []) or (region2 <> []) do begin
    if (region1 * region2) <> [] then goto rejection;
    region := region1;
    if region = [] then region := region2 {swap if necessary};
    if lef in region then begin
      {left boundary is crossed}
      x := wxl;
      y := y1+(y2-y1)*(wxl-x1)/(x2-x1)
    end
    else if rit in region then begin
      {right boundary is crossed}
```

```
      x := wxh;
      y := yl+(y2-yl)*(wxh-xl)/(x2-xl)
    end
    else if bot in region then begin
      {bottom boundary is crossed}
      x := xl+(x2-xl)*(wyl-yl)/(y2-yl);
      y := wyl
    end
    else if top in region then begin
      {top boundary is crossed}
      x := xl+(x2-xl)*(wyh-yl)/(y2-yl);
      y := wyh
    end;

    if region = regionl then begin
      xl := x; yl := y;          {point (xl,yl) is clipped off}
      det_region(xl,yl,regionl)  {region-code of intersection}
    end
    else begin
      x2 := x; y2 := y;          {point (x2,y2) is clipped off}
      det_region(x2,y2,region2)  {region-code of intersection}
    end
  end {while};

  {line is clipped or trivially accepted}
  drawline(xl,yl,x2,y2);

rejection:

end {procedure CS_clip};
```

If a worst-case line is clipped, the statements in the while loop are repeated four times. The formulas for finding the intersection points are obvious.

Be sure that you recognize that the region-code of a point on the window boundary is 0000; such a point is considered to be inside the window. Although this algorithm uses floating point arithmetic, it is very fast and efficient when it can be done in specialized hardware, like the VLSI-based floating point clipper described in CLAR80.

In languages that permit bit manipulation, such as C, the region-codes can be determined more readily by doing subtractions in registers and building the region-code from the sign bits:

x − wxl: sign bit gives bit 3 of region-code
wxh − x: sign bit gives bit 2
y − wyl: sign bit gives bit 1
wyh − y: sign bit gives bit 0

#### 4.2.1.2 Midpoint Subdivision

This algorithm is a variation of the Cohen-Sutherland straight line clipping algorithm above. The difference is that this method avoids the use of formulas that use floating point arithmetic to find the point of intersection of the line with a boundary in CS_clip. It uses a clever way to find the intersection point of a straight line with one of the window boundaries, a procedure that requires only integer arithmetic, so it may be faster.

The method of finding intersections with a window boundary is like a binary search. When the line is found to cross a window boundary, its midpoint is computed. This is very easy to do:

$$x_{mid} = (x1 + x2)/2 \qquad y_{mid} = (y1 + y2)/2$$

If the end points of the line are specified in absolute device coordinates (usually screen coordinates), all the values will be integers. The divisions by 2 are merely right shifts by one bit. The result $(x_{mid}, y_{mid})$ is obtained directly in screen coordinates. Once the midpoint of the line is found, its region-code is determined. Both halves of the line are then tested using the logic OR and logic AND of the region-codes of its end points. When one end of the line is already within the window, it is always true that one of the halves can be trivially rejected or accepted. In the first case we change the outer point to the midpoint; in the second case we change the inner point to the midpoint. The midpoint will converge to the intersection with the window.

Once the intersection is found, one of the original line end points is changed to the intersection and the shortened line will be put through the same process. This time it might be trivially accepted or rejected or again be shortened to another window intersection. Figures 4.14 to 4.17 show several stages of this process.

**FIGURE 4.14**

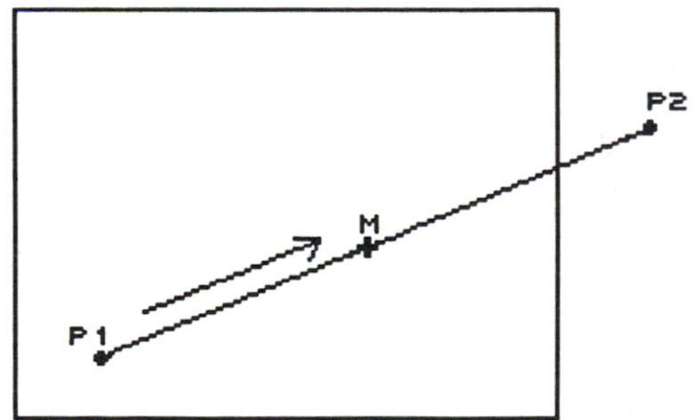


**FIGURE 4.15**

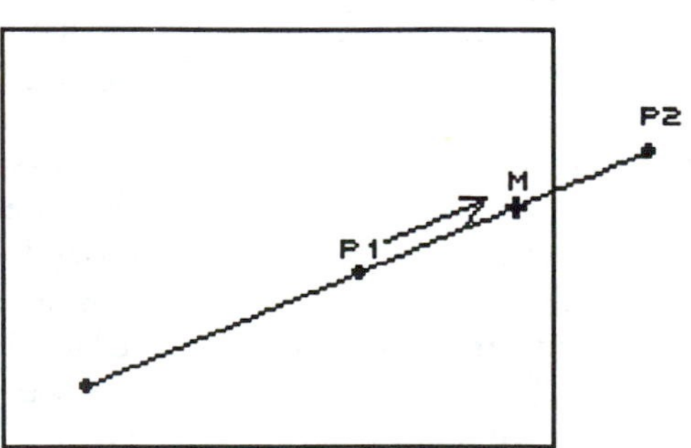

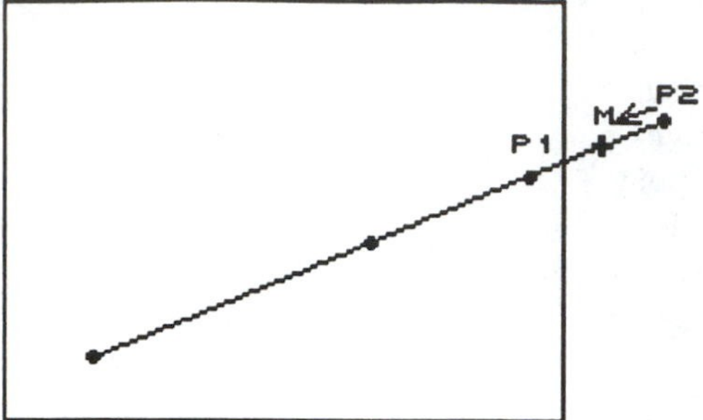

FIGURE 4.16

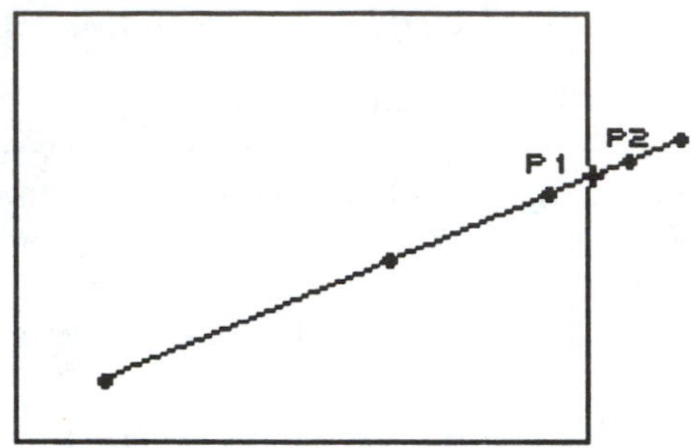


FIGURE 4.17

Finding the intersection with this method is basically an application of a binary search. Using integers for the line end points, for the midpoint, and for the window boundaries ensures that the iteration will stop after a relatively small number of steps. This method is a practical one only if all the parameters involved are given in absolute device coordinates (usually screen coordinates).

The maximum number of steps needed to find the intersection will be $\log_2 N$, where N is the longer of the horizontal or vertical lengths of the line, measured in absolute screen coordinates. If a screen with a good resolution is considered, a long line would have a horizontal or vertical length of no more than about 1000 screen units. The intersection would then be found in at most 10 iteration steps.

It can happen that the search loop for the intersection must run twice before finding the intersections with the window. This happens when both end points lie outside the window but in different regions and the line intersects with the window. In this case the midpoints will converge to the intersection closer to $P_1$ (see Figure 4.18). This is due to the order in which the checking and resetting of points is done in the algorithm below. This knowledge is the basis of the decision as to whether $P_1$ or $P_2$ is to be reset after the search loop.

A disadvantage of clipping by bisection is that it can be done only in absolute device coordinates. Many graphics routines store data about the objects (points, lines, etc.) as normalized coordinates and some algorithms need the result of clipping in normalized coordinates. With this method we would have to transform to screen coordinates first and then transform the result of clipping back into normalized coordinates.

Another point to consider is the fact that mathematical processors can do floating point arithmetic almost as fast as integer arithmetic. Considering that the midpoint method usually needs to do several iterations to find the intersection point, a speed gain from the midpoint method is questionable if the computer has a good floating point processor.

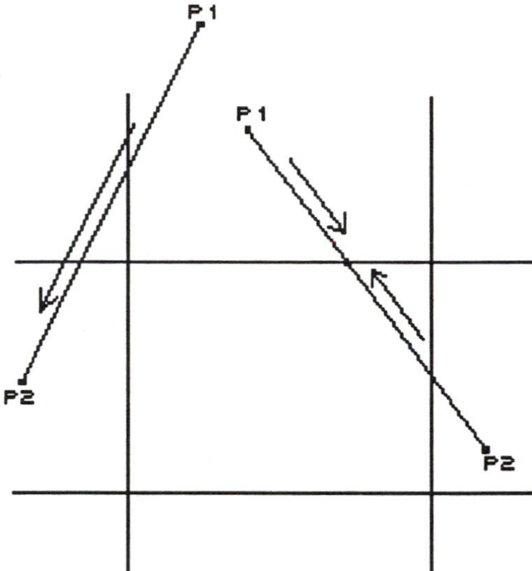


FIGURE 4.18

The midpoint method for finding intersections has been implemented through microcoded integer arithmetic in some graphics-oriented processors. With these, it turns out that approximately 11 iterations (consisting only of shifts and additions) can be done in less time than the four additions, one multiplication, and one division required by the analytical intersection scheme, even when the latter is done with a floating point processor!

**Description in Pseudocode** A fully coded clipping procedure by midpoint subdivision in Pascal looks unduly complicated because the many details of case distinctions and region code computations overwhelm the proper algorithmic idea. We therefore give only a description in pseudocode. The interesting feature of this algorithm is that it works with region codes alone and never checks against an individual window boundary. "Inside the window" includes all points on the boundary.

```
Set P1 and P2 to the line endpoints;
start:
  if P1 and P2 both inside window
  then begin
    draw(P1,P2);
    stop
  end;

  if P1 and P2 both outside window
  then stop;
```

```
in all other cases begin
  Hl := Pl;
  H2 := P2;
  {perform midpoint subdivision:}
sub:
  Mid := (Hl+H2)/2;
  if Hl and Mid both inside window
  or Hl and Mid both outside window
  then Hl := Mid
  else H2 := Mid;
  if Hl-H2 > 1
  then goto sub;
{Set CON to the convergence point}
if CON outside window
then stop
else begin
  {either Pl or P2 must be outside
  the window and adjoining CON}
  find which it is and
  change this point to CON;
  goto start
end.
```

#### 4.2.1.3 Liang-Barsky Line-Clipping Algorithm

The clipping method of Liang and Barsky (LIBA84), uses a parameterized representation of the line. Remember if $P_1 = (x_1,y_1)$ and $P_2 = (x_2,y_2)$ are two points in the plane, then a line from $P_1$ to $P_2$ can be expressed as two equations in the parameter t:

$$x = x_1 + (x_2 - x_1)t$$
$$y = y_1 + (y_2 - y_1)t$$

The coordinates x and y are both expressed as functions of the common parameter t, which is the only independent variable in these equations. As t goes from 0 to 1 the point (x,y) moves along the straight line from $P_1$ to $P_2$ (see Figure 4.19).

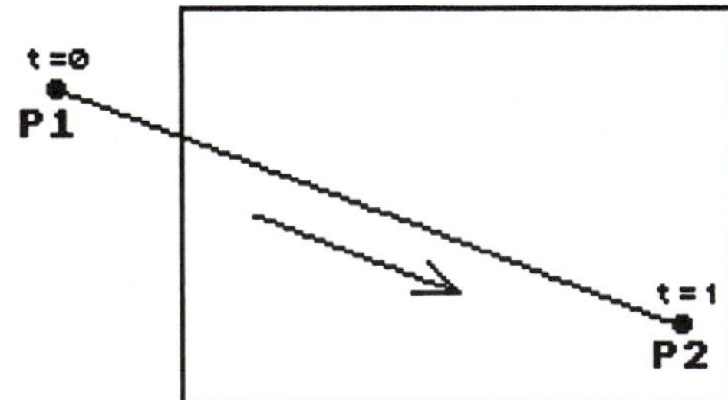


**FIGURE 4.19**

If we set $Dx = (x_2 - x_1)$ and $Dy = (y_2 - y_1)$, the equations are:

$$x = x_1 + Dx * t$$
$$y = y_1 + Dy * t$$

Any point (x,y) is inside the window if:

$$wxl \leqslant x \leqslant wxh \qquad \text{and} \qquad wyl \leqslant y \leqslant wyh$$

A point on the line is inside the window if the four inequalities

$$wxl \leqslant x_1 + Dx * t \leqslant wxh \qquad \text{and} \qquad wyl \leqslant y_1 + Dy * t \leqslant wyh$$

are fulfilled for a value of t between 0 and 1. If the inequalities can be fulfilled only for values of t outside the range from 0 to 1, then only the extension of the straight line passes through the window.

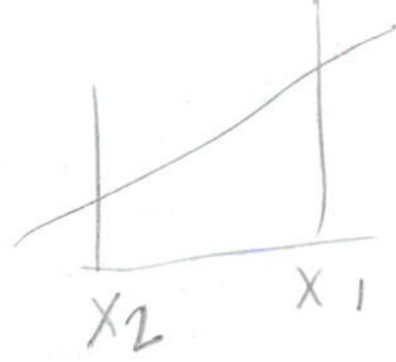

By writing the inequalities in a different way, we get:

$$-Dx * t \leqslant x_1 - wxl \qquad (1)$$
$$Dx * t \leqslant wxh - x_1 \qquad (2)$$
$$-Dy * t \leqslant y_1 - wyl \qquad (3)$$
$$Dv * t \leqslant wyh - y_1 \qquad (4)$$

Inequality (1) relates the line to the left window boundary in the following way. A value of t for which (1) is fulfilled specifies a point on the line which lies to the right of the left window boundary. The other inequalities relate to their respective window boundaries in analogous ways: (2) to the right, (3) to the bottom, and (4) to the top. We will put this into a more general notation by letting $C_k$ stand for the coefficients of t (the Dx's or Dy's) and letting $q_k$ stand for the right-hand sides, giving the general shorthand notation:

$$C_k * t \leqslant q_k \qquad \text{for } k = 1, \ldots, 4.$$

In other words:

$$C_1 = x_1 - x_2, \qquad q_1 = x_1 - wxl,$$
$$C_2 = x_2 - x_1, \qquad q_2 = wxh - x_1,$$
$$C_3 = y_1 - y_2, \qquad q_3 = y_1 - wyl,$$
$$C_4 = y_2 - y_1, \qquad q_4 = wyh - y_1.$$

We can think of k = 1,2 as relating to x-values (left, right) and k = 3,4 as relating to y-values (bottom, top). In the discussion below, "line" means the infinite extension of the line segment determined by $P_1$ and $P_2$; it is the line through these points.

If $C_k > 0$, the line goes from the inside to the outside with respect to that particular window boundary. This means that a point (x,y) that moves along the line as t increases crosses that particular boundary from its inside to its outside (but not necessarily from inside the window to outside the window). Consider the point $P_2$ and the line in Figure 4.20.

**FIGURE 4.20**

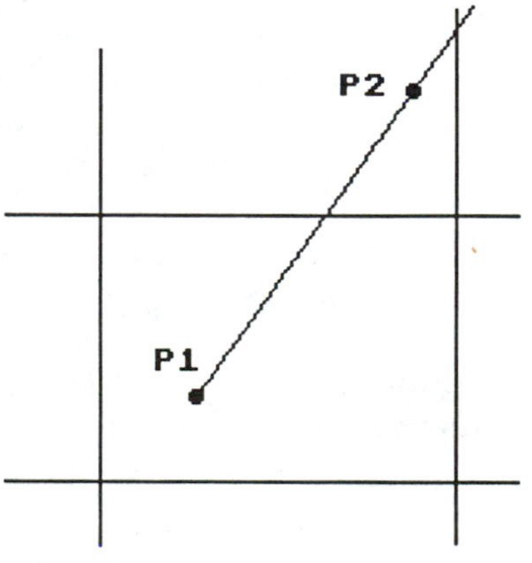

We have $x2 - x_1 = C_2 > 0$, therefore, as t increases, the corresponding point (x,y) on the line moves from left to right. With respect to the right window boundary, left is inside and right is outside, so the point moves from inside to outside. No statement is made about where the intersection with the boundary will take place; it may very well be outside the window and outside the finite line segment from $P_1$ to $P_2$, as in this case.

The meaning of inside and outside for all the other boundaries should be obvious. (For the left boundary outside is the area to its left and inside is the area to its right, and so on for all the others.) You should verify the statements given here about how the sign of $C_k$ tells how the point moves with respect to each boundary as t increases.

If $C_k < 0$ the line goes from the outside to the inside with respect to that window boundary. This case is symmetric to the case above.

$C_k = 0$ is a special case. The line does not cross that particular boundary; it is parallel to it. But the line can still go through the window if it is on the proper side of the boundary. It will not do so if the corresponding $q_k < 0$. If that is true, the line can be eliminated from further consideration.

The definition of $C_k$ shows that $C_1$ always equals $-C_2$ and $C_3$ always equals $-C_4$. In other words, for nonzero $C_k$ there is always a boundary for which the line goes from inside to out and another boundary for which it does the opposite.

For a nonzero $C_k$ the value of t corresponding to the intersection point is very simply:

$$t = q_k/C_k$$

From the value of t alone, the algorithm can derive information about the intersection without having to calculate the intersection point. This is an important advantage over the Cohen-Sutherland clipping method because it requires only one division and two subtractions to compute q and C. Computing the intersection points requires one division, one multiplication, two subtractions, and one addition. We discuss below the conditions under which a line is rejected.

In Figure 4.21, $C_3 < 0$, so the line crosses the bottom boundary from the outside as t increases. We can then say that the value of the parameter t that corresponds to the intersection point is an "entry value" for the line. If this value for t is calculated and found to be 1.3, this entry point of the line is already beyond the end point, P2. Whenever an entry value is greater than 1, the line is rejected.

Be sure to distinguish between an entry to a *boundary* from entry to the window itself. Also, remember that in this parameterized representation, the starting point of the line $P_1$ corresponds to $t = 0$ and

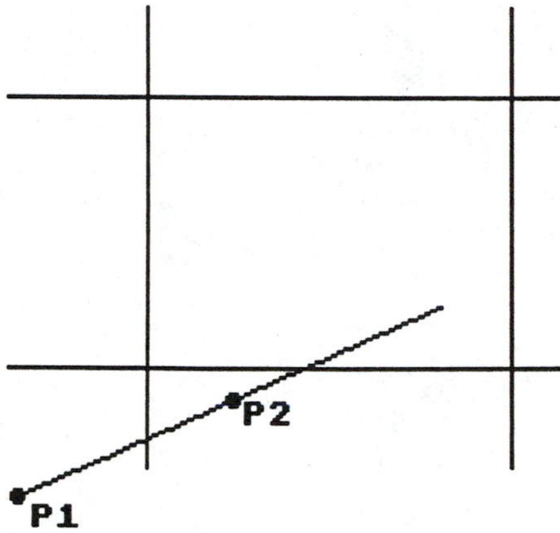


FIGURE 4.21

its end point $P_2$ corresponds to $t = 1$. This implies, in cases like this example, that the line is entirely outside the bottom boundary and therefore outside the window, so it will be rejected.

If $C_k > 0$ we calculate t values that can be interpreted as "exit values" of the line with respect to that boundary. If an exit value is smaller than 0 then the line segment is outside the window and will be rejected. Figure 4.22 shows such a case. In Figure 4.22, $C_4 > 0$ so the line crosses the top boundary from the inside out as t increases. We can say that the value of t that corresponds to the intersection is an exit value for the line. If this value is found to be $-0.1$ as in the figure, the exit point comes before the starting point of the segment, $P_1$. Whenever an exit value is less than 0, the line is rejected.

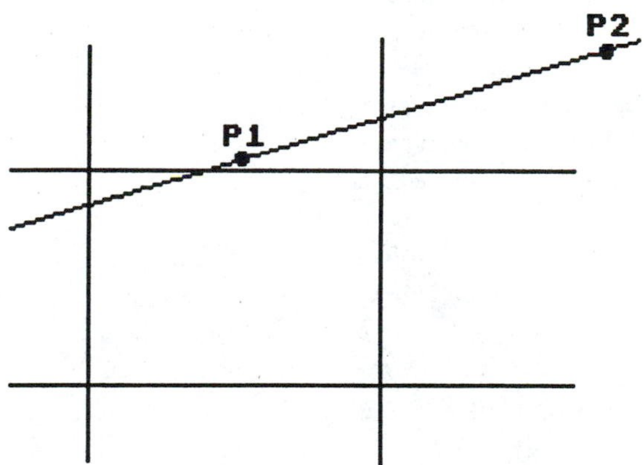


FIGURE 4.22

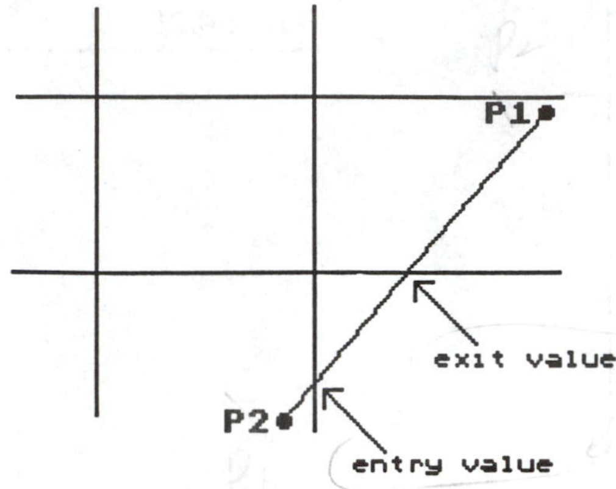


FIGURE 4.23

There is a third situation where a line will be rejected: when an entry value is greater than an exit value. Lines that miss the window but with both end points outside the same boundary are rejected in this case; see Figure 4.23.

Remember that the "line" is more than just the segment between the end points. The line may well cross two boundaries before it enters the window. In fact, it can happen that we calculate entry values for two different boundaries and still we do not know if the line actually goes into the window.

The algorithm will calculate at most two entry values and two exit values of t. (The line cannot cross more than two boundaries before it enters the window, nor can it cross more than two boundaries on leaving.) This will involve at most four divisions.

Consider now the portion (if any) of the line segment that is inside the window. Only nonnegative entry values make sense because points are not between $P_1$ and $P_2$ for negative t. By the same reasoning, the only exit values that make sense are $\leq 1$. Let us use the symbol t1 for the largest entry value from the set comprised of 0 and the two values of $q_k/C_k$ for negative $C_k$. We use t2 for the smallest exit value from the set comprised of 1 and the two values of $q_k/C_k$ for positive $C_k$. During its execution, the algorithm can stop and reject the line as soon as there is enough information to do so: entry value $> 1$ or exit value $< 0$ or entry value $>$ exit value. Intersection coordinates are calculated only if $t1 > 0$ or if $t2 < 1$.

It will help you to follow this reasoning if you look at some concrete examples. Table 4.1 gives six numerical examples. The window boundaries are kept fixed for all examples:

$$wxl = 10, \quad wxh = 20, \quad wyl = 3, \quad wyh = 11,$$

**TABLE 4.1**

| # | $x_1$ | $x_2$ | $y_1$ | $y_2$ | $C_1$ | $q_1$ | t | $C_2$ | $q_2$ | t | $C_3$ | $q_3$ | t | $C_4$ | $q_4$ | t | |
|---|---|---|---|---|---|---|---|---|---|---|---|---|---|---|---|---|---|
| 1 | 3 | 9 | 13.8 | 5.2 | -6 | -7 | $1.17_n$ | dis | | | | | | | | | |
| 2 | 21.2 | 27 | 4.1 | 14 | -5.8 | 11.2 | $-1.93_n$ | 5.8 | -1.2 | $-0.21_x$ | dis | | | | | | |
| 3 | 6.7 | 18 | -2.9 | 0 | -11.3 | -3.3 | $0.29_n$ | 11.3 | 13.3 | $1.18_x$ | -2.9 | -5.5 | $1.90_n$ | dis | | | |
| 4 | 16.6 | 12.4 | 12.5 | 22.2 | 4.2 | 6.6 | $1.57_x$ | -4.2 | 3.4 | $-.81_n$ | -9.7 | 9.5 | $-.98_n$ | 9.7 | -1.5 | $-0.15_x$ | dis |
| 5 | 26.5 | 16 | 7 | -3.4 | 10.5 | 16.5 | $1.57_x$ | -10.5 | -6.5 | $0.62_n$ | 10.4 | 4 | $0.38_x$ | dis | | | |
| 6 | 25 | 7.5 | 8.3 | 20.5 | 17.5 | 15 | $0.86_x$ | -17.5 | -5 | $0.28_n$ | -12.2 | 5.3 | $-0.43_n$ | 12.2 | 2.7 | $0.22_x$ | dis |

but the end points of the lines are varied as shown in the table. The algorithm starts by computing $C_1$, $q_1$ and $t = q_1/C_1$ and checks whether the line can be discarded. If not, it continues to compute $C_2$, $q_2$ and $t = q_2/C_2$, checks again, and so on. Each computed t-value is subscripted with n or x depending on whether it is an entry or an exit value. (If the corresponding C is $<0$ then t is an entry value; if it is $>0$, then t is an exit value.) All lines in these examples are discarded and the examples feature several different reasons for discarding. (See Figure 4.24 through 4.29.) (In Table 4.1, subscript n or x indicates an entry or exit value; dis indicates line is discarded.)

Reasons for discarding:

1. entry value $1.17 > 1$ after one step
2. exit value $-0.21 < 0$ after two steps
3. entry value $1.90 > 1$ after three steps

**FIGURE 4.24** Example 1.

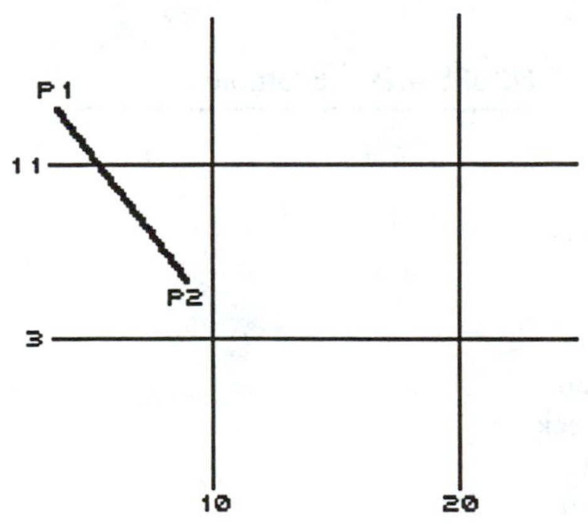


**FIGURE 4.25** Example 2.

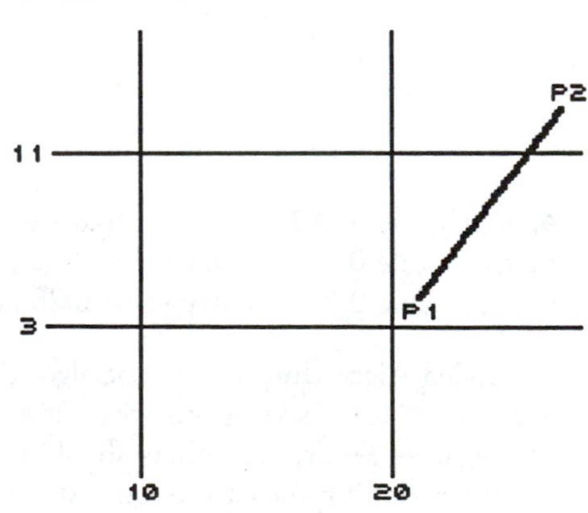

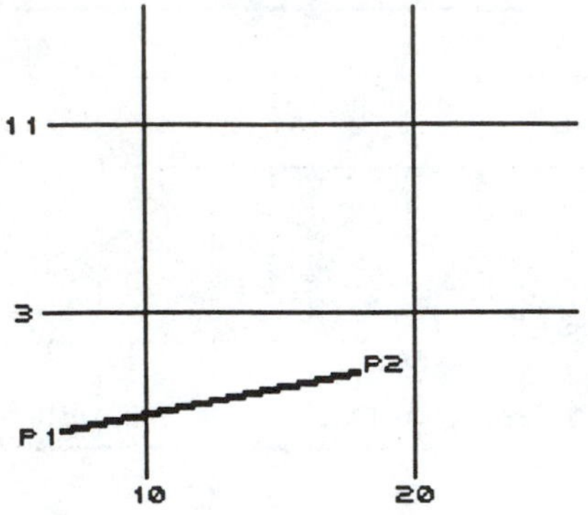


**FIGURE 4.26** Example 3.

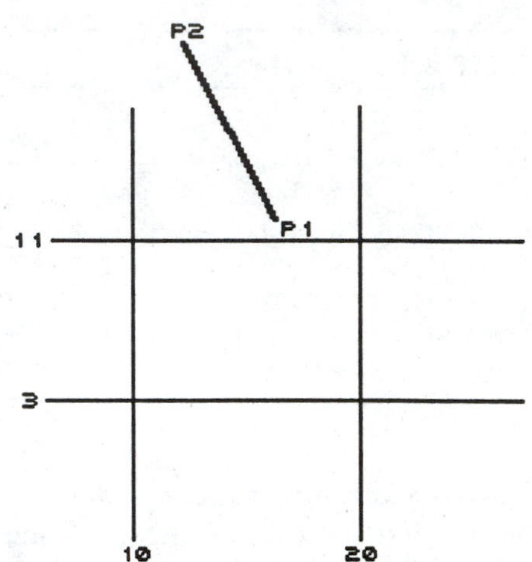


**FIGURE 4.27** Example 4.

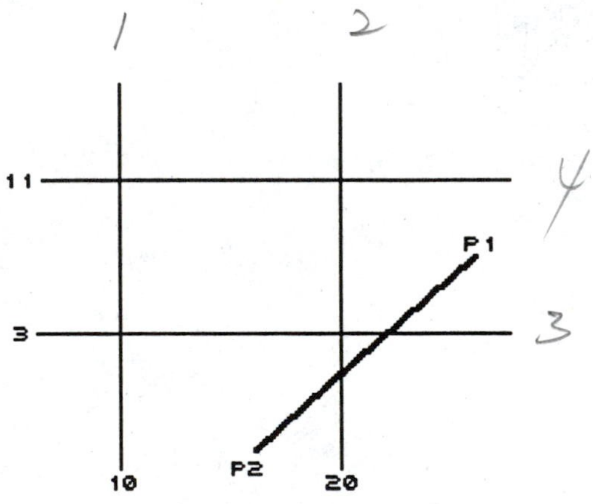


**FIGURE 4.28** Example 5.

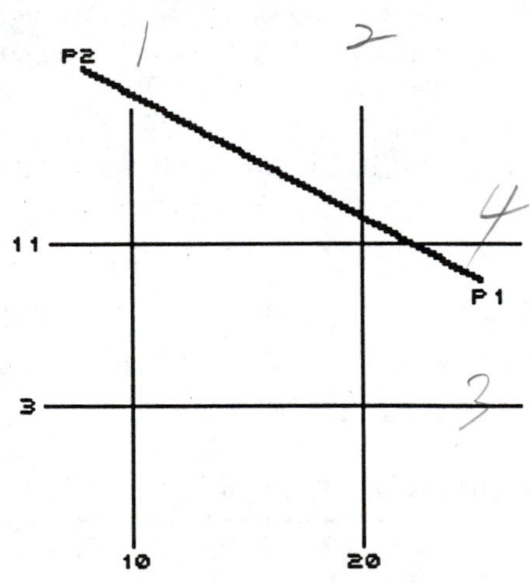


**FIGURE 4.29** Example 6.

4. exit value $-0.15 < 0$ after four steps
5. exit value $0.38 <$ entry value $0.62$ after three steps
6. exit value $0.22 <$ entry value $0.28$ after four steps

**Coded Algorithm** The basic algorithmic idea consists of at most four consecutive checks against the window boundaries. If one check has a negative result, the others should need not be performed. This leads to a code that either uses goto statements to leave the checking sequence or involves four nested if statements with ugly indentations as the price for goto-free code. We have chosen the goto-free solution.

```
procedure clip(var x1,y1,x2,y2
              wxl,wxh,wyl,wyh   :   real;
                   var reject   :   boolean);

{Clips the line from (x1,y1) to (x2,y2) to its
visible part against the window boundaries by
changing these coordinate values to correspond to
the clipped line segment. It does not draw the
visible part. If the line is outside the window, the
arguments are not changed but reject returns the
value true.}

var t1,t2, dx,dy : real;

procedure find_t(       p,q   :  real;
                var  t1,t2   :  real;
                var reject   :  boolean);
var r  :  real;

begin {procedure find_t}
  reject := false;
  if p < 0 then begin        {line from outside to inside  }
    r := q/p;                {with respect to that boundary}
    if r > t2 then           {intersection is past the     }
      reject := true         {end point of the line segment}
    else if r > t1 then      {intersection is past the}
      t1 := r                {start point of the line }
  end {if p < 0}
  else if p > 0 then begin   {line from inside to outside  }
    r := q/p;                {with respect to that boundary}
    if r < t1 then           {intersection is before the   }
      reject := true         {start point of the line segment}
    else if r < t2 then      {intersection is before the   }
      t2 := r                {end point of the line segment}
  end {if p > 0}
  else if q < 0 then         {p=0, line is parallel}
    reject := true           {to that boundary     }
end {procedure find_t};

begin {procedure clip}
  t1 := 0; t2 := 1;
  dx := x2 - x1;
  find_t(-dx,x1-wxl,t1,t2,reject);        {check left boundary}
  if not reject {continue checking}
  then begin
```

```
    find_t(dx,wxh-xl,tl,t2,reject);       {check right boundary}
    if not reject {continue checking}
    then begin
      dy := y2-yl;
      find_t(-dy,yl-wyl,tl,t2,reject);    {check bottom boundary}
      if not reject {continue checking}
      then begin
        find_t(dy,wyh,tl,t2,reject);      {check top boundary}
        if not reject {clip the line}
        then begin                      {the line or a part of}
          if tl > 0                     {it has survived all 4}
          then begin                    {rejection attempts    }
            xl := xl + tl*dx;           {calculate entry point}
            yl := yl + tl*dy
          end {if tl > 0};
          if t2 < 1
          then begin
            x2 := xl + t2*dx;           {calculate exit point}
            y2 := yl + t2*dy
          end {if t2 < 1}
        end
      end
    end
  end
end {procedure clip};
```

## 4.2.2 Polygon Clipping

The method presented here (see Figures 4.30 through 4.32) is based on the Sutherland-Hodgman basic clip, which is explained below. We cannot just use a line-clipping algorithm on each edge of the polygon because we must generate new edges along the window boundaries as well as clip the original edges. Clipping a polygon may produce a polygon with fewer vertices or one with more vertices than it had originally. It may even produce several nonconnected polygons.

A polygon consists of an ordered sequence of vertices. It is drawn by connecting each successive pair of consecutive vertices with straight lines, to produce its edges. The edges will be processed by the clipping algorithm in the order of the vertex pairs.

The clipping algorithm will be called once for each vertex of the polygon. For each call, the algorithm will return either no vertex at all, the original vertex without change, or one or more new vertices.

The algorithm can be best understood by imagining that it works by repeating what we will call a "basic clip." Such a basic clip does more

**FIGURE 4.30** Seven vertices before and three vertices after clipping.

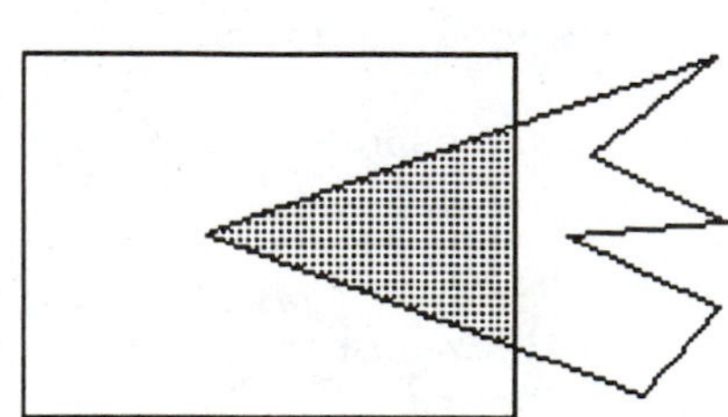

than just clip a line. Four possible cases have to be distinguished when describing a basic clip. These cases and the actions they take are demonstrated in Figures 4.33 through 4.36.

Be sure to note that the basic clip is in relation to a specific boundary of the window against which the polygon is to be clipped. Still, the four cases can be described in a general manner if we bear in mind that the notions "inside" and "outside" relate to a specific *boundary* of the window and not to the window itself. "Inside" for the left boundary is everything to the right of that boundary; "inside" for the right boundary is everything to the left of that boundary; "inside" for the bottom boundary is everything above that boundary; and "inside" for the top boundary is everything below that boundary even if it is not within the window.

The vertex where the edge begins is denoted by S and the vertex at which the edge terminates is denoted by P.

What we do in the basic clip is to generate a potential new vertex of the clipped polygon on a boundary. It will be an actual vertex if it lies within the window (including points on its border). If it does not lie in the window, further steps are required to generate an actual vertex.

To perform a basic clip requires knowing the vertices S and P and the boundary against which the edge is to be processed. An algorithm for the basic clip could be written whose arguments include this boundary, but it is better from the standpoint of clarity and ease of understanding to have four different algorithms, one for each boundary. We do this in the routine below.

The clipping algorithm for a specific edge of the polygon consists of putting the end point of this edge through these four basic clips. (It is just coincidence that there are four basic clips and four cases to consider.) Since the basic clip generates a potential vertex that may or may not belong to the final image, the output of the basic clip against one boundary is used as input for the basic clip against the next boundary until all four boundaries have been considered. Only then do we have an actual vertex of the final image.

The input to a basic clip is the end point of the edge. Since the beginning point of the edge is not input, it must be available to the basic clip by another mechanism. We do it via a global variable.

Each polygon vertex goes through these four basic clips as if it were going through a pipeline. In passing through the pipe, the vertex may be killed altogether, it may come out changed (clipped to a boundary), it may come out unchanged, or it may branch out into several different points (these will all be on the boundaries of the window).

The four basic clips are algorithmically almost identical. For each there is a global variable which remembers the point with which the basic clip was last called. The names of the basic clips reflect the bound-

**FIGURE 4.31** Four vertices before and 10 vertices after clipping.

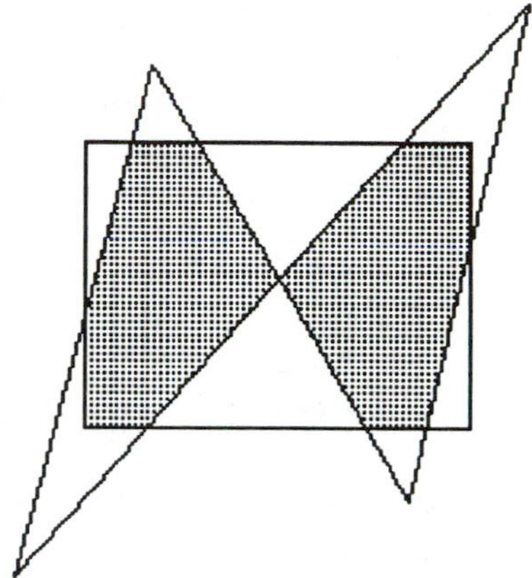

**FIGURE 4.32** Two nonconnected polygons after clipping.

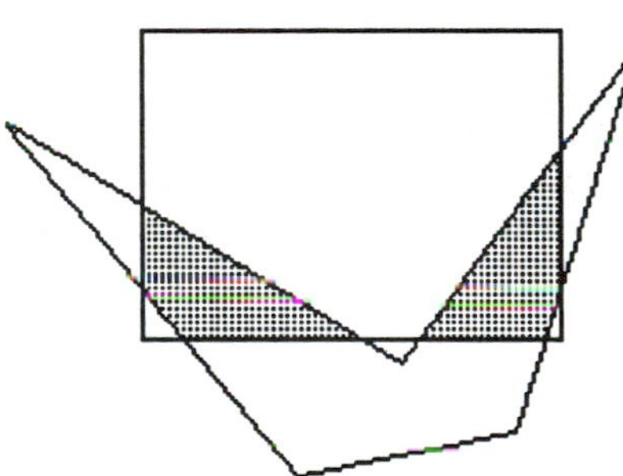

**FIGURE 4.33** S outside and O outside, no output.

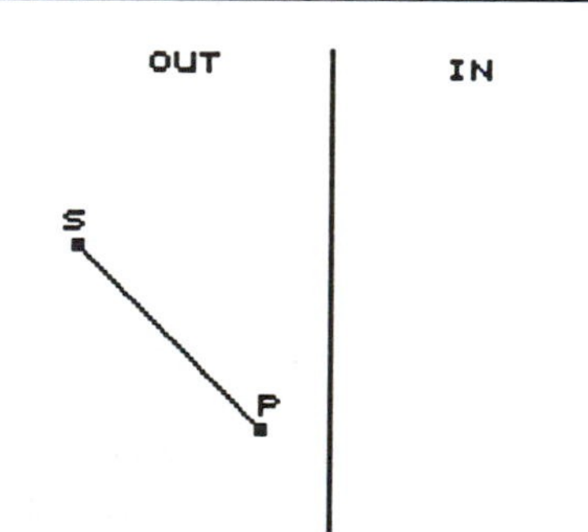

aries against which they process the vertex: clip_l, clip_r, clip_b, clip_t.

You will more easily understand the Pascal code if you first practice doing the "clipping pipe" by hand. This is not very difficult, and it will facilitate your understanding of the code.

In doing the basic clips by hand, you will need to keep track of several items. Here is a procedure for doing so as you pass vertices through the clipping pipe. It will help to keep these rules handy:

| *Case* | *Output* |
|---|---|
| S outside →P outside | None |
| S inside →P inside | P |
| S inside →P outside | Intersection |
| S outside →P inside | Intersection, plus P |

We first do a general example, then a specific one.

We write the four letters L R B T with some space between them. These represent the four basic clips in the order in which they are applied, left, right, bottom, top:

```
L        R        B        T
```

The vertices of the polygon are numbered from $P_1$ through $P_n$. Even though the basic clips have not been called before, we initialize the value for the last point with which the clip was called for all four clips with the value of $P_n$ (the last vertex of the definition of the original polygon). To help us remember the last point, we write it on a line above and to the left of the corresponding clip. Doing this, we have for the starting arrangement:

```
Pn       Pn       Pn       Pn
    L        R        B        T
```

We begin by putting the vertex $P_1$ into the left basic clip, L. This is indicated by writing it down at the left of the L:

```
Pn       Pn       Pn       Pn
P1  L        R        B        T
→
```

The arrow is to emphasize that $P_1$ is entering the pipe. We will not use it after this first example.

We now determine the output from L (with $P_n$ as the last point). The output from L could be nothing, or the point $P_1$, or a clipped point, or two points: a clipped point and $P_1$. If there is no output, then the

**FIGURE 4.34** S inside and P inside, output P.

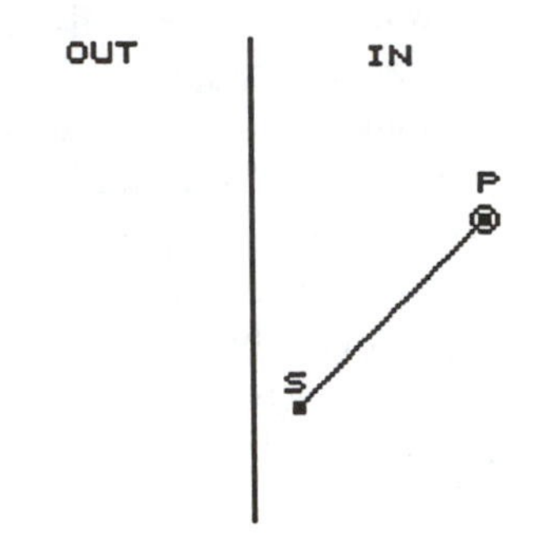


**FIGURE 4.35** S inside and P outside, output intersection of boundary with line from S to P.

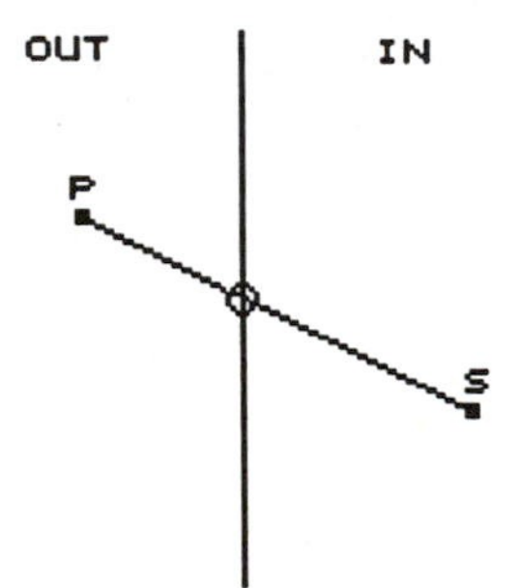


**FIGURE 4.36** S outside and P inside, output intersection of boundary with line from S to P and point P.

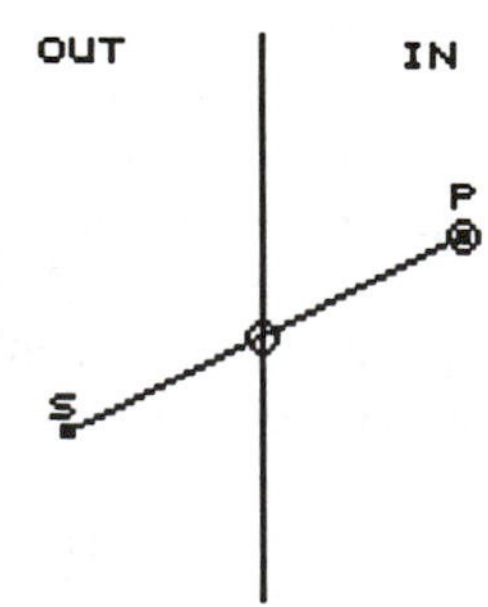

clipping of $P_1$ is over. If the output is one point, we write it between L and R, as input for the basic clip R. Here we assume that the output is a clipped point a:

```
Pn     Pn    Pn    Pn
P1  L  a  R     B     T
       →
```

If there are two outputs, the second output is written below the first, as a reminder that a branch in the pipe has occurred which must be processed as soon as the current branch is complete. When processing the second branch, we write the remaining basic clips as letters. Here we assume that the first branch of the pipe terminates with the output a from the top basic clip:

```
Pn     Pn    Pn    Pn
P1  L  a  R  a  B  a  T a
→      →     →     →
       P1  R     B     T
       →
```

We proceed in this way to send all vertices of the polygon through the pipe. For each vertex, we write a new pipe. As we write the new pipe, we update a drawing that shows the polygon being clipped.

Now for a specific example. We omit the arrows from now on. Given the polygon in Figure 4.37, L is called with $P_1$; its last point is $P_3$, so this is the case out-in. L will therefore produce two outputs to the next basic clip, the first with the intersection a, the next with $P_1$, so the pipe branches and we get:

```
P3   P3   P3   P3
P1 L a  R    B    T
     P1 R    B    T
```

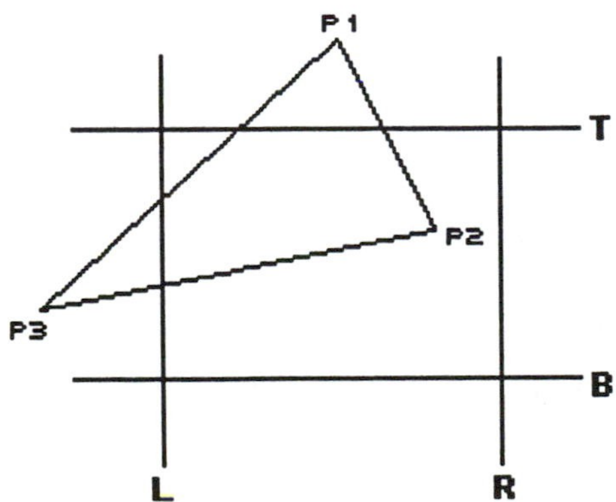


**FIGURE 4.37**

Following the upper branch, R is called with a; its last point is $P_3$. This is the case in-in, so R produces a and we get:

```
P3    P3    P3    P3
P1 L a  R a  B     T
      P1 R     B     T
```

B is called with a; its last point is $P_3$. From $P_3$ to a is the case in-in for B, so B produces a and we get:

```
P3    P3    P3    P3
P1 L a  R a  B a  T
      P1 R     B     T
```

T is called with a; its last point is $P_3$. From $P_3$ to a is the case in-in for T, so T produces a and we get:

```
P3    P3    P3    P3
P1 L a  R a  B a  T  a
      P1 R     B     T
```

The first pipe is finished. Now we must follow the lower branching. R is called with $P_1$; its last point is a, which can be seen in the line above. From a to $P_1$ is the case in-in for R, so R produces $P_1$ and we get:

```
P3    P3    P3    P3
P1 L a  R a  B a  T a
      P1 R P1 B     T
```

B is called with $P_1$; its last point is a. From a to $P_1$ is the case in-in for B, so B produces $P_1$ and we get:

```
P3    P3    P3    P3
P1 L a  R a  B a  T a
      P1 R P1 B P1 T
```

T is called with $P_1$ as shown in Figure 4.38. Its last point is a. From a to $P_1$ is the case in-out for T, so T produces the intersection point b and we get:

```
P3    P3    P3    P3
P1 L a  R a  B a  T a
      P1 R P1 B P1 T b
```

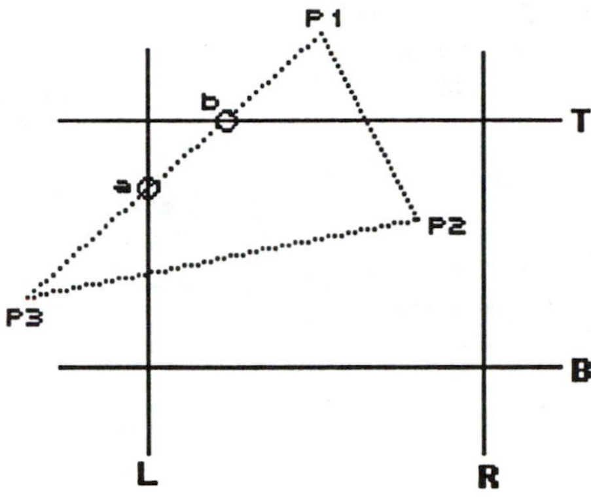


**FIGURE 4.38**

We have seen that putting the first point through the pipe gives two output points (a and b); both are intersections. We now continue the pipe with $P_2$:

```
P1   P1   P1   P1
P2 L    R    B    T
```

L is called with $P_2$; its last point is $P_1$, which can be seen in the last diagram above. From $P_1$ to $P_2$ is the case in-in for L, so L produces $P_2$ and we get:

```
P1   P1   P1   P1
P2 L P2 R    B    T
```

R is called with $P_2$; its last point is $P_1$. From $P_1$ to $P_2$ is the case in-in for R, so R produces $P_2$ and we get:

```
P1   P1   P1   P1
P2 L P2 R P2 B    T
```

B is called with $P_2$; its last point is $P_1$. From $P_1$ to $P_2$ is the case in-in for B, so B produces $P_2$ and we get:

```
P1   P1   P1   P1
P2 L P2 R P2 B P2 T
```

T is called with P2 as shown in Figure 4.39. Its last point is $P_1$ (the last point with which a basic clip is *called* is important, not the point it produces). From $P_1$ to $P_2$ is the case out-in for T, so T produces the intersection point c and the point $P_2$. The pipe branches and we get:

```
P1    P1    P1    P1
P2 L  P2 R  P2 B  P2 T  c
                        P2
```

This pipe also produces two points as output. Only one point is left to put through the pipe, $P_3$, so L is called with $P_3$; its last point is $P_2$. From $P_2$ to $P_3$ is the case in-out for L, so L produces the intersection point d and we get:

```
P2    P2     P2    P2
P3 L  d  R     B     T
```

which produces d. B and T produce d as well and we get:

```
P2    P2    P2    P2
P3 L  d  R  d  B  d  T  d
```

Now we have obtained all the vertices of the clipped polygon. They are a, b, c, $P_2$, and d (see Figure 4.40)

To summarize the example, we repeat the entire schematic here:

```
P3    P3    P3    P3
P1 L  a  R  a  B  a  T  a
      P1 R  P1 B  P1 T  b
P2 L  P2 R  P2 B  P2 T  c
                        P2
P3 L  d  R  d  B  d  T  d
```

The output is a, b, c, $P_2$, and d.

**FIGURE 4.39**

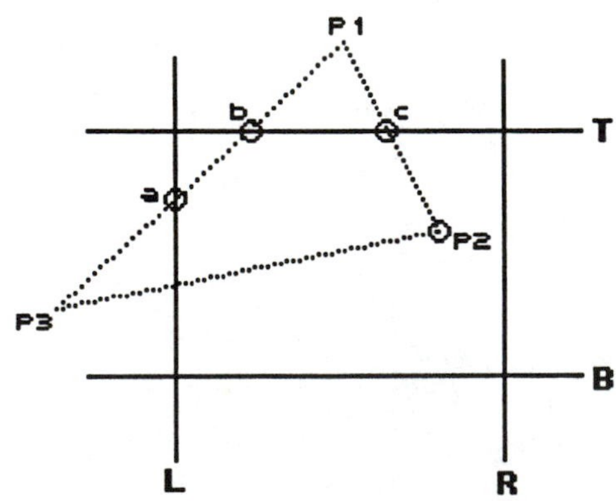


**FIGURE 4.40**

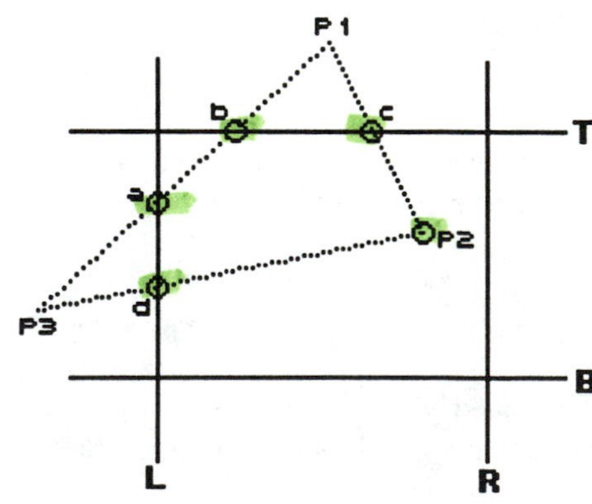

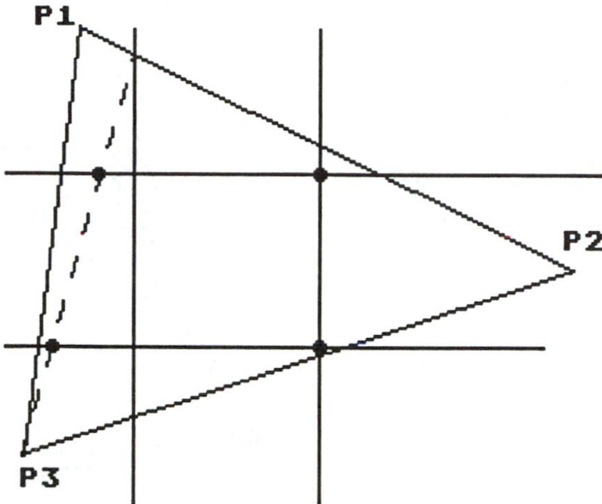


FIGURE 4.41

Unfortunately, not all cases are as simple as this example. When clipping the polygon shown in Figure 4.41, the algorithm produces the points indicated in the drawing. Two points are even outside the window. The result is wrong. The reason for this is the way we initialized the last points. When clip_b is called the first time (passing $P_1$ through the pipe) its last point is $P_3$ which is outside the window. This point could never actually be a last point resulting from a call to its preceding clipper, clip_r. The problem occurs from artificially setting the last points initially to $P_3$. Figure 4.42 through 4.45 show the possible ranges of the points with which the clippers can be called correctly.

FIGURE 4.42

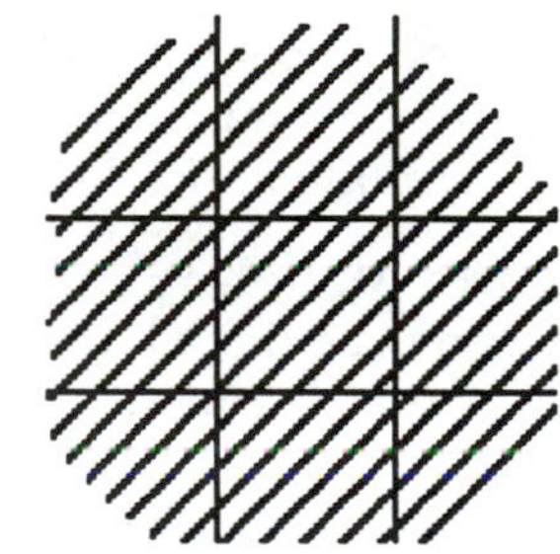

Clip_l can be called with any point, because it is the first to be called. Its last point, therefore, can also be any point. Clip_l is the first filter in the pipe (see Figure 4.42).

Clip_r is called only with points produced by clip_l, so points to the left of wxl are already clipped and cannot occur as arguments. Therefore they cannot be last points of clip_r. Clip_r is the second filter in the pipe (see Figure 4.43).

FIGURE 4.43

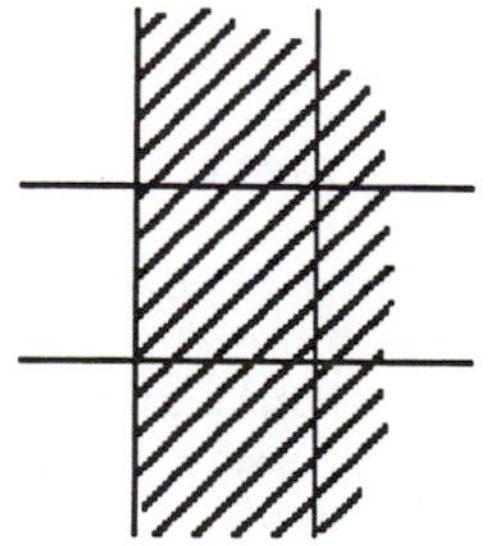

Clip_b is called only with points produced by clip_r, so points to the right of wxh are already clipped and cannot occur as arguments. Therefore they cannot be last points of clip_b. Clip_b is the third filter in the pipe (see Figure 4.44))

Clip_t is called only with points produced by clip_b, so points below wyl are already clipped and cannot occur as arguments. Therefore they cannot be last points of clip_t. Clip_t is the last filter in the pipe (see Figure 4.45).

This rule is obviously violated by the initialization of the last points with $P_n$. Initialization should be only with points that could be a result from a previous call. However, before we make any calls to the basic clippers, some initialization is necessary. This suggests that we can use a first pass of the vertices through the pipeline to generate a set of valid last points that we can use to initialize a second pass.

There is some freedom in how we initialize the last points. Only clip_l needs to be initialized with a last point that is an actual point on an edge of the polygon. For the other basic clips, using such points can result in intersection points outside the window, as we saw in the example. One safe way to initialize the other clips' last point is with any corner of the window. A window corner is "neutral" with respect to the clipping processes. If a basic clip is called with an argument that is inside, this argument will be passed on to the next basic clip; if it is called with an argument that is outside, no further basic clip is called with that outer point. Our coded algorithm just uses $P_n$ to initialize all the clips; this is both simple and effective.

In most cases a full run through the polygon to set up the last points is not necessary; a partial run is adequate. While it is possible to see in a hand computation how far we must go, this depends on the specific polygon. Introducing this into the algorithm would complicate it unduly. We therefore adopt this simple solution. First we perform a "fake" clip of the polygon and discard the output of the clipping pipe. This fake clip generates proper initial last points for the second real clip. The algorithm below reflects this idea precisely.

**FIGURE 4.44**

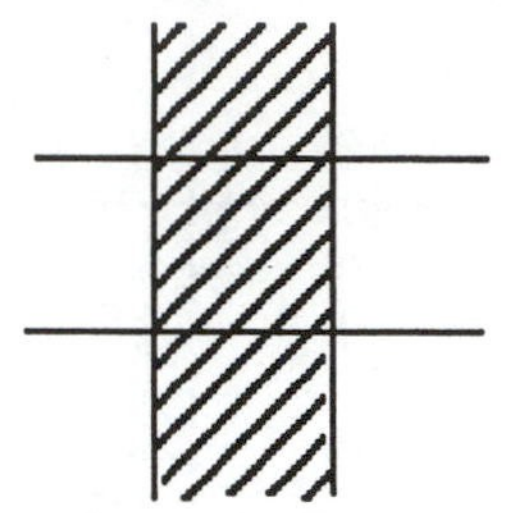

**FIGURE 4.45**

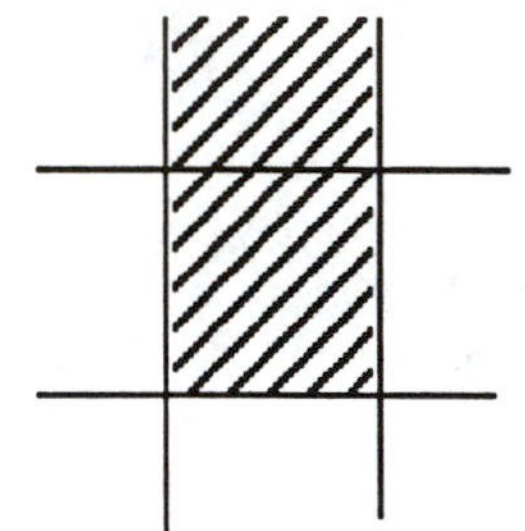

**Coded Algorithm** Parameters of the procedure polygon_clip are the polygon to be clipped, the resulting polygon, the polygon sizes, and the window to be clipped against. The individual basic clippers are called only with the end point of the edge they clip. The starting points of the edges, the so-called last points, must be kept outside as global variables, but they are still local within polygon_clip.

```
type      point    =   record x,y : real
                       end;
       vertices    =   array[1..50] of point;

procedure polygon_clip(var vxin,vxout      :  vertices;
                         var innum,outnum   :  integer;
                         wxl,wxh,wyl,wyh    :  real);
var  lastl,lastr,
     lastb,lastt    :    point

procedure store(x,y : real; var outnum : integer);
begin
  outnum := outnum + 1;
  vxout[outnum].x := x;
  vxout[outnum].y := y
end {procedure store};
```

```
procedure clip_t(x,y : real);
begin
  {if top boundary between last point and new point}
  if (y ≤ wyh) and (wyh < lastt.y) or (lastt.y < wyh) and (wyh ≤ y)
  then store((x-lastt.x)*(wyh-y)/(y-lastt.y)+x,wyh);
  lastt.x := x; lastt.y := y;  {save last point}
  if y < wyh    {case out-in}
  then store(x,y)
end {procedure clip_t};

procedure clip_b(x,y : real);
begin
  {if bottom boundary between last point and new point}
  if (lastb.y < wyl) and (wyl ≤ y) or (y ≤ wyl) and (wyl < lastb.y)
  then clip_b(wxh,(y-lastr.y)*(wxh-x)/(x-lastr.x)+y);
  lastr.x := x; lastr.y := y;  {save last point}
  if wyl < y    {case out-in}
  then clip_t(x,y)
end {procedure clip_b};

procedure clip_r(x,y : real);
begin
  {if right boundary between last point and new point}
  if (x ≤ wxh) and (wxh < lastr.x) or (lastr.x < wxh) and (wxh ≤ x)
  then clip_b(wxh,(y-lastr.y)•(wxh-x)/(x-lastr.x)+y);
  lastr.x := x; lastr.y := y;  {save last point}
  if x < wxh    {case out-in}
  then clip_b(x,y)
end {procedure clip_r};

procedure clip_l(x,y : real);
  begin
  {if left boundary between last point and new point}
  if (lastl.x < wxl) and (wxl ≤ x) or (x ≤ wxl) and (wxl < lastl.x)
  then clip_r(wxl,(y-lastl.y)*(wxl-x)/(x-lastl.x)+y);
  lastl.x := x; lastl.y := y;   {save last point}
  if wxl < x    {case out-in}
  then clip_r(x,y)
end {procedure clip_l};

begin {procedure polygon_clip}
  {Initializing the last points}
  lastl.x := vxin[innum].x; lastl.y := vxin[innum].y;
  lastr.x := wxl;           lastr.y := wyl;
  lastb.x := wxl;           lastb.y := wyl;
  lastt.x := wxl;           lastt.y := wyl;

  {fake run for setting the last points}
  outnum := 0;
  for i := 1 to innum do clip_l(vxin[i].x,vxin[i].y);
```

```
  {clipping the polygon}
  outnum := 0;
  for i := 1 to innum do clip_l(vxin[i].x,vxin[i].y);
end {procedure polygon_clip};
```

When the clipping of a polygon results in two disjoint parts, the resulting parts will be connected by two coincident lines, both along the window boundary. This represents a part of the polygon with area 0. A polygon that surrounds the window several times, with perhaps no edge ever penetrating into the window, may be clipped into multiple coincident lines along the whole window boundary, also representing a polygon of area 0. These degenerate clipped polygons usually pose no problems for other applications. Whether or not such polygons of area 0 are to be displayed when a polygon is filled is a matter of personal taste.

## 4.2.3 Text Clipping

When text is displayed within a window (remember that the entire screen can be a window), there are three levels of complexity to be considered. There are basically two different ways to generate characters. The method that is used to clip text to fit within the window depends on both of these factors.

We will first describe the three levels of complexity as applied to one method of generating characters, the *bit map character generator.*

**Bit Map Character Generator** A common way to produce characters on a graphics display consists of copying a bit map from a character generator (often in ROM) into the area where the character is to be displayed. The character generator contains one bit map for every possible character and the bit maps can be of different sizes. However, many character generators use the same size for all characters, such as nine pixels wide by 14 pixels high (some of the vertical space is for descenders, as on the letters p and y). If characters are produced this way, it is not possible to produce slanted characters because the bit maps are always rectangles parallel to the window boundaries.

FIGURE 4.46

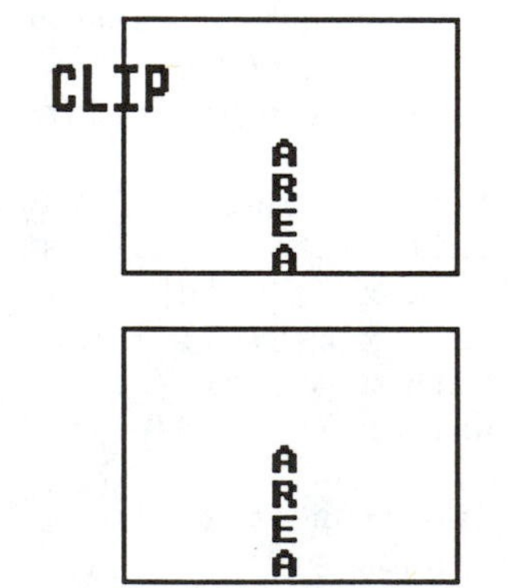


There are three strategies for clipping characters that are generated through bit maps. These differ depending on whether we clip individual characters or work with sets of characters, a string. *String* in this context means at most one line of text.

The first method is the "all-or-none string-clipping" strategy. The method consists of checking whether the entire text string is inside the window boundary. If it is not, we discard the whole string. The string is considered to cross a window boundary if any of the bit maps of the string cross it (see Figure 4.46). To carry this out, we must add all the widths of the bit maps of the characters composing this string. The height of the bit maps is usually the same for all characters. Using the sum of the widths and the height, we have a bounding rectangle for the string. This plus the starting position of the string tells us if the string would cross a window boundary. If so, the string is not displayed.

Another method is the "all-or-none character-clipping" strategy. It consists of displaying only those individual characters that fit entirely within the window. If a bit map is totally or partly outside a window boundary, that character will not be copied onto the screen. Figure 4.47 shows this. The checking must be done for each individual character bit map. The starting point together with the width and height of the individual bit map can tell us whether it crosses a window boundary. After checking one character, we must update the starting point by the width or height of that character, continuing this until the entire string is processed.

The third method is the "individual character-clipping" strategy. Characters whose bit maps are totally inside the window are copied onto the screen and those totally outside are ignored. Characters whose bit maps are partly within the window are partially displayed (see Figure 4.48). From the width and height of a bit map, we can calculate which pixels are within the window. Only these are displayed. This is a much more elaborate process than the other strategies.

**Vector Character Generator** In contrast to the bit map technique, characters can actually be drawn as a series of lines. This is called *vector character generation.* To accomplish this, each character is defined by a sequence of commands which define the start points and end points of straight lines (vectors) that will produce the character. Such character generators can easily produce slanted script or characters of different width and height. Vector character generation applies to plotters as well as to raster scan and vector scan CRTs because most plotters draw in vector mode.

The same three types of clipping strategies can be applied. First, we consider the "all-or-none string-clipping" strategy. We must compute the size of the rectangle that bounds the string and then check whether it lies totally inside the screen boundary. This involves knowing or computing the dimensions of bounding rectangles for each character. If the rectangle that bounds the entire string does not fall within the window, no part of the string will be displayed, as in Figure 4.49.

In the "all-or-none character-clipping" strategy, we must check each individual character for its fit into the window. This means that we must know or calculate the size of a rectangle that can just contain the vectors of the character being generated. If this rectangle is not totally inside the window, no part of the character is displayed. Figure 4.50 illustrates this.

**FIGURE 4.47**

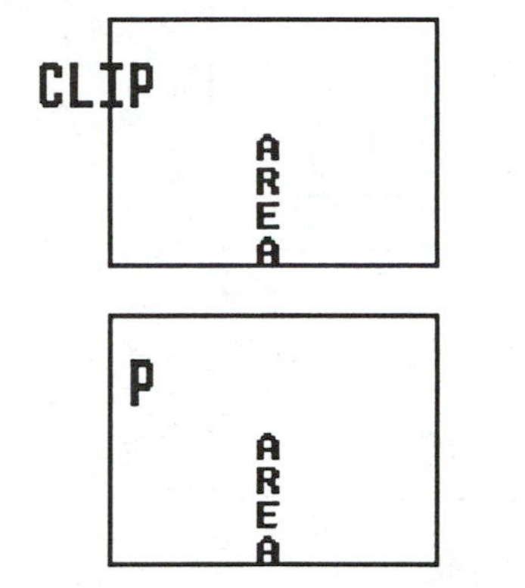


**FIGURE 4.48**

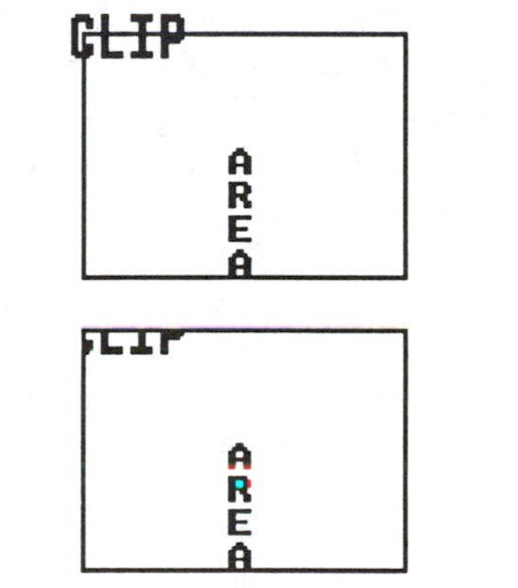


**FIGURE 4.49**

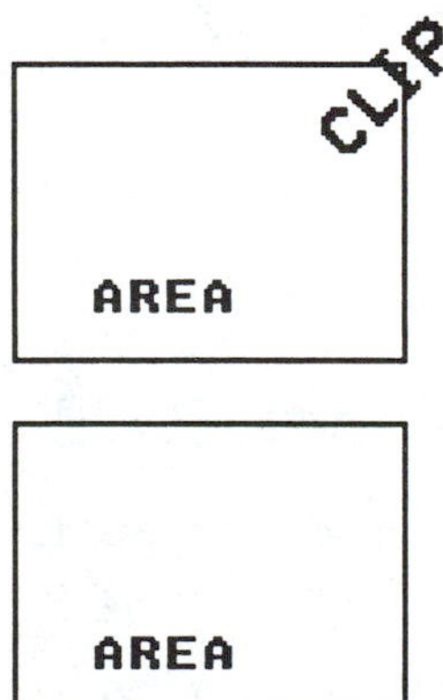

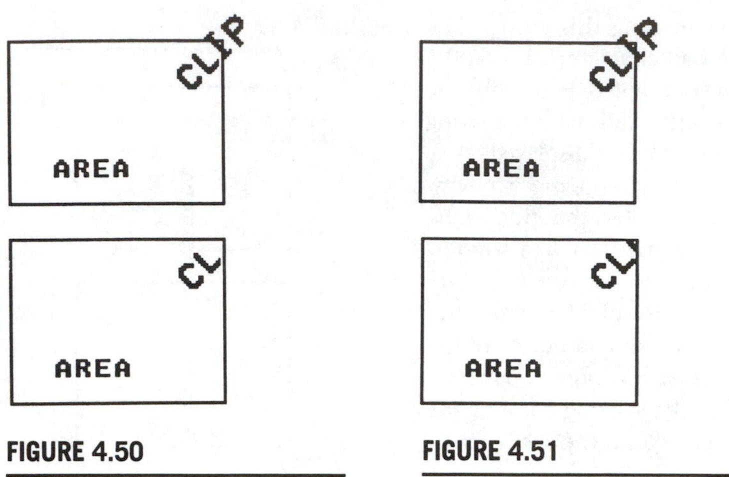


FIGURE 4.50

FIGURE 4.51

Using "individual character clipping" with vector-generated characters is more complicated than with a bit map character generator. To save computing time, it pays to first check the bounding rectangle for the character against the display boundaries. Information for such a containing rectangle can be derived from the description of the character. If the rectangle is totally inside or totally outside the display, no clipping is necessary; the character is either displayed in full or not. If the bounding rectangle crosses a window boundary, then a straight line-clipping algorithm such as Cohen-Sutherland or the midpoint method must be applied to each individual line of the character (see Figure 4.51).

# EXERCISES FOR CHAPTER 4

## Section 4.2.1.1

1. Draw two lines that cross a window in the worst case for the checking order left-top-right-bottom.
2. Repeat Exercise 1, but use the checking order right-top-bottom-left.

## Section 4.2.1.2

In all exercises below the starting values of $h_1$ and $h_2$ are the end points of the line.

3. Assume a line that has the endpoints $P_1$ and $P_2$ outside the window, but in different regions, and intersects with the window.

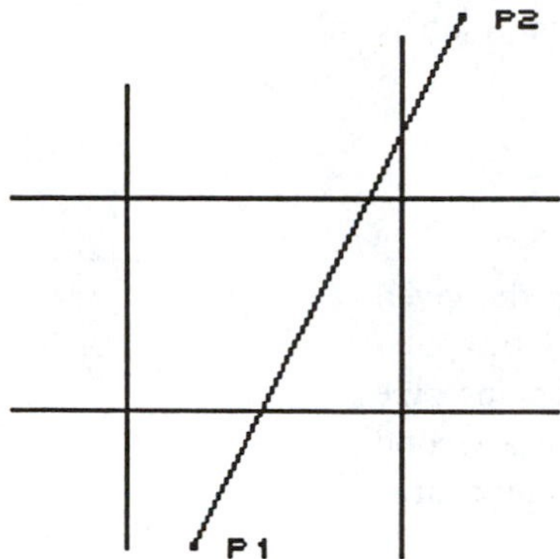


FIGURE 4.52

(See Figure 4.52). Explain how the logic of the code makes the midpoints converge to the intersection closer to $P_1$.

4. Using a copy of Figure 4.53, do five steps of the midpoint algorithm by hand and show where the midpoints, $h_1$, and $h_2$ are at the conclusion.
5. Using a copy of Figure 4.54, perform several steps of the midpoint method to show where the midpoints converge. Then repeat this, exchanging the starting points $h_1$ and $h_2$.

FIGURE 4.53

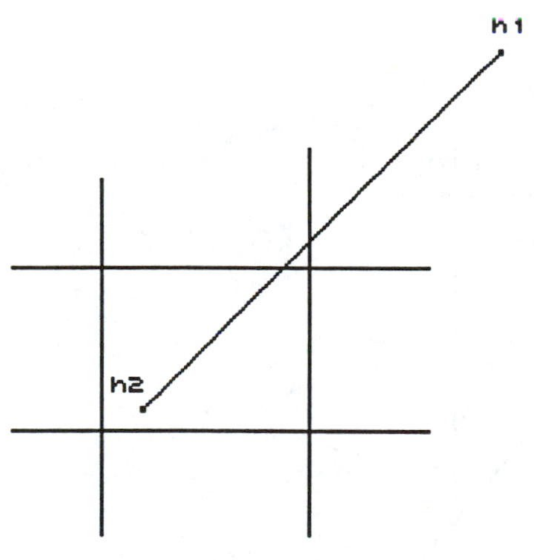


FIGURE 4.54

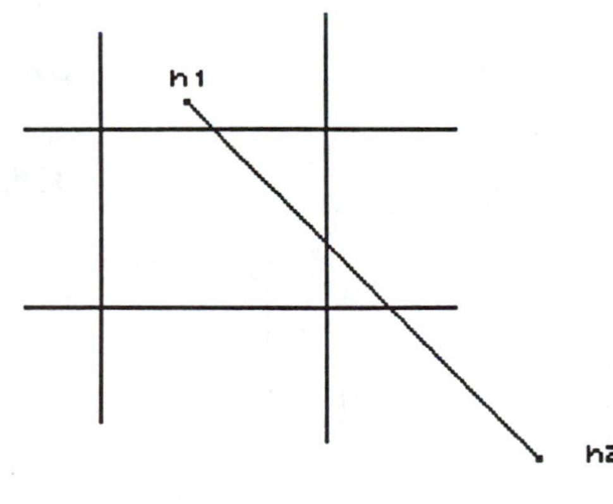


6. Assume a window with wxl = 0, wxh = 30, wyl = 0, wyh = 20. Perform the midpoint method according to the coded algorithm for the line from (0,29) to (29,2) (for a fraction of 0.5,

round up to the next integer). Observe how much the result is off the exact intersection.

## Section 4.2.2

In Exercises 7 through 12 (Figures 4.55 through 4.60) clip the given polygons against the window boundaries in the order L R B T by applying the clipping pipe as shown in the text. First run the clipping pipe and discard the output but keep the last points; then run it a second time. In simple cases two runs don't seem necessary, but in complicated cases a single run would not be enough.

**FIGURE 4.55** Exercise 7.

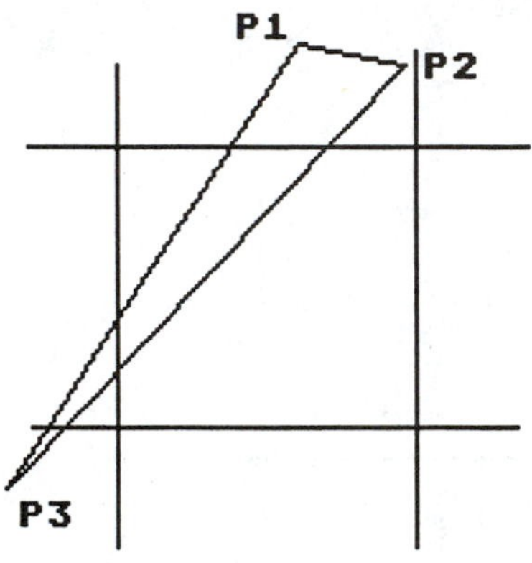


**FIGURE 4.56** Exercise 8.

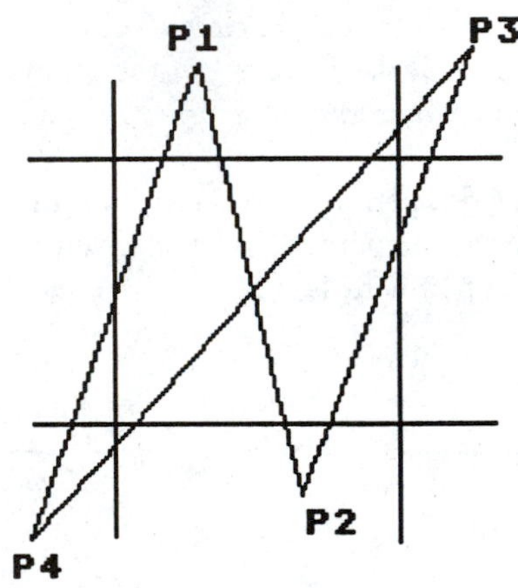


**FIGURE 4.57** Exercise 9.

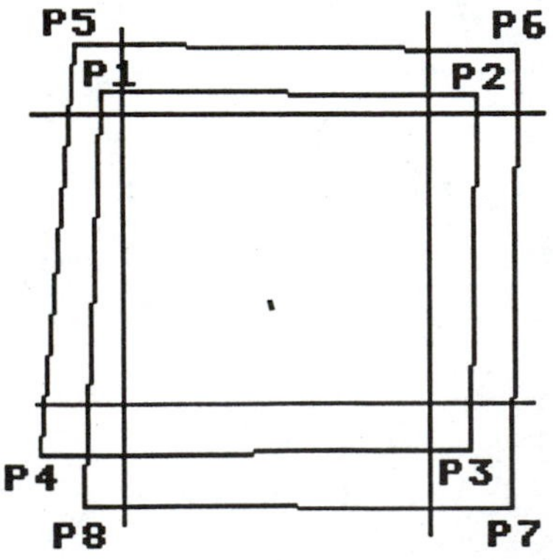


**FIGURE 4.58** Exercise 10.

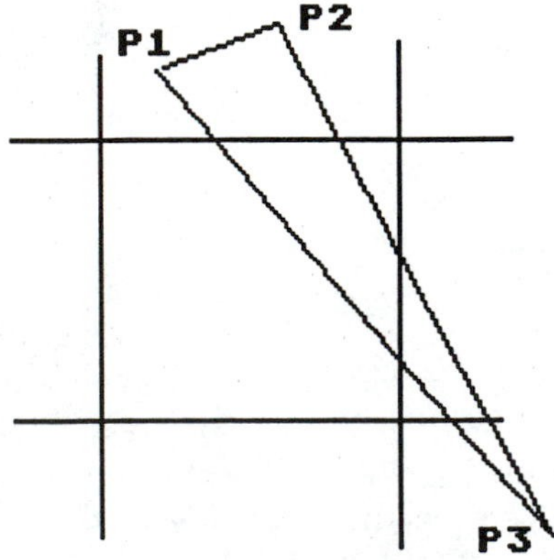

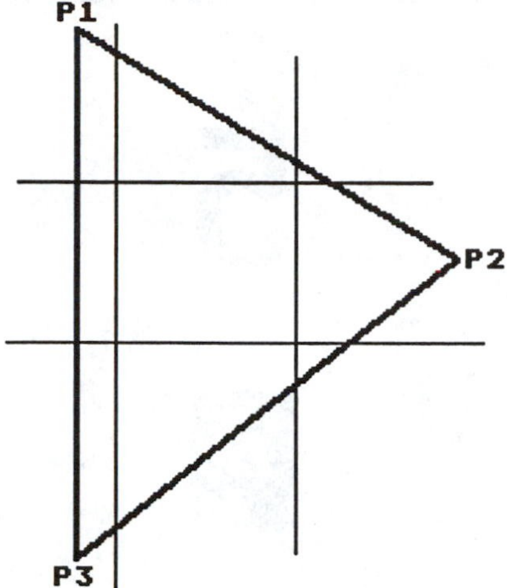


FIGURE 4.59 Exercise 11.

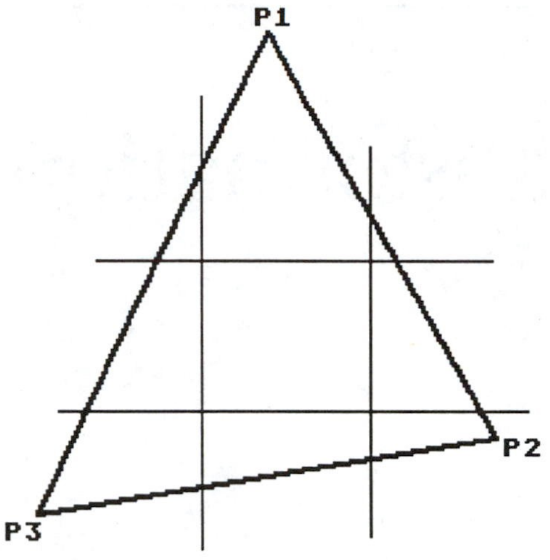


FIGURE 4.60 Exercise 12.

# Transformations

# 5

In Chapter 5 we study the mathematics required to change the size, location, or orientation of displayed objects. There are three sections.

**5.0 Introduction** describes the three separate transformations.

**5.1 Two-Dimensional Transformations** gives the mathematics behind translation, scaling, and rotation of two-dimensional objects, using homogeneous coordinates.

**5.2 Three-Dimensional Transformations** utilizes homogeneous coordinates to extend the formulas to the 3-D case. Rotating a point about an arbitrary axis involves first translating and rotating the axis line; this is followed by reversals of these processes.

## 5.0 INTRODUCTION

It is essential for a graphics system to allow the user to change the way objects appear. In the real world, we frequently rearrange objects or look at them from different angles. The computer should let us do the same with images on the screen. Objects in the real world move; our displays should be able to reflect such movement.

The effects that we desire include changing the size of an object, its position on the screen, or its orientation. When we define a two-dimensional object, we produce only one basic description of its shape. It is impractical to produce many different sizes or positions or orientations of the same object just because later we might want to view it differently. It is much more sensible to make changes later to the original basic description of the object. The implementation of such a change is called a *transformation.*

What display changes are we most likely to want? There are many different ones but only a few are really useful for effecting the changes an object may undergo in the real world. The two most obvious are *translation* (moving it) and *scaling* (changing its size). Equally important is *rotation* (turning it on an axis).

Translations occur constantly in the real world because objects move or we move, which makes objects appear translated in relation to us and other objects. Scaling is as common; as we approach an object or when it moves closer to us, it increases in size. The scaling done in computer graphics will actually allow for more than just increase or decrease in size. We can stretch an object in length or height in ways that do not correspond to natural phenomena. This is a consequence of the formalism that allows us to scale the two dimensions of an object independently. If we scale both dimensions by the same amount, we can achieve a simple size change. Figures 5.1 and 5.2 illustrate changing size and position. The original object is drawn in light lines and the transformed object in heavy lines. The screen frame serves as a refer-

**FIGURE 5.1**

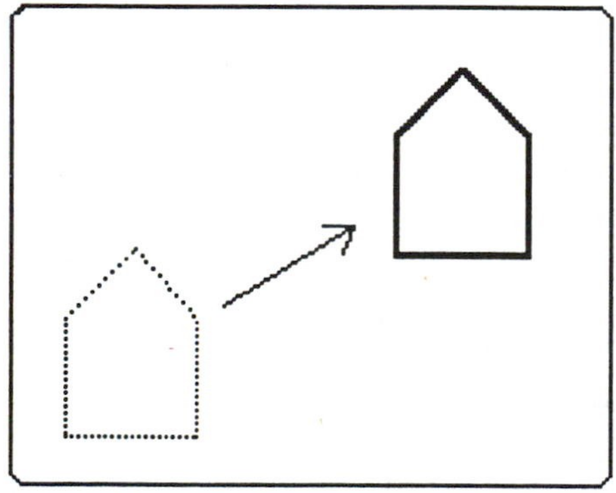

**FIGURE 5.2**

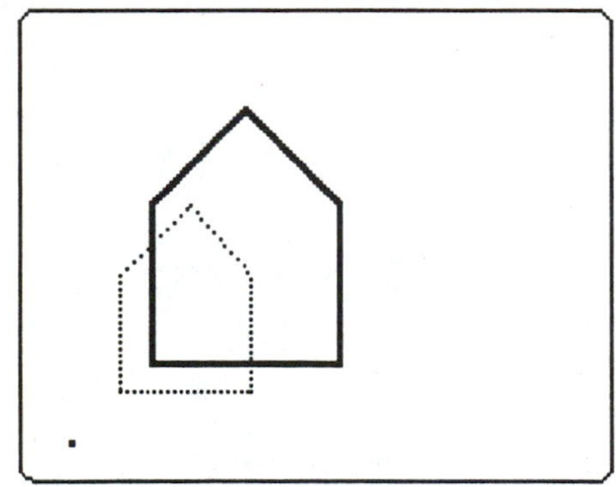

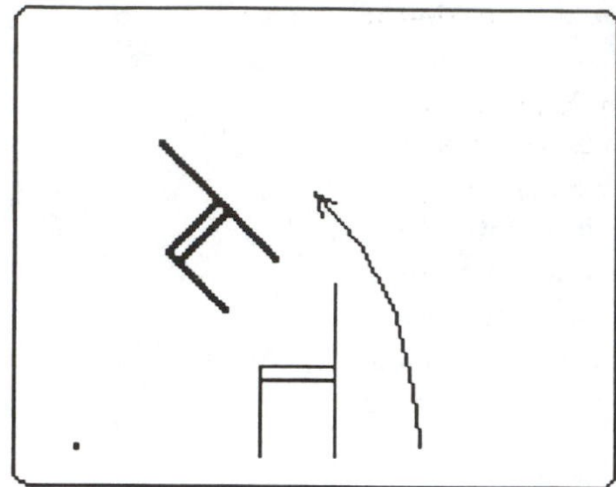

FIGURE 5.3

ence. Figure 5.1 shows a pure translation. The image is shifted to the right and upward. Size and orientation of the object are not changed; it remains parallel to itself. Figure 5.2 shows scaling. Both dimensions of the object (the x- and the y-dimension) are multiplied by the same factor of approximately 1.5. This results in a size change accompanied by a change of position. The orientation does not change; the object remains parallel to itself. We can see that the house is scaled relative to a point, which is indicated in the picture.

Figure 5.3 shows a rotation of a smaller object, a chair. We most often see small objects rotated in the real world. (Strictly speaking, houses and mountains also rotate when we tilt our heads to look at them. Since they are not rotated in relation to the surrounding environment, we don't have the feeling that the mountain rotates. Our view of it does, though.) Observe that the chair is rotated around a reference point in the lower left corner in the drawing.

Some other transformations are sometimes found in graphics packages, for example, several types of shears and reflections. These have no equivalent in reality and are not as useful as the three described above. They are mostly used for special effects. We will not deal with them at any length.

# 5.1 TWO-DIMENSIONAL TRANSFORMATIONS

We begin our discussion with transformations in the two-dimensional or (x,y)-plane. Later in the chapter we will cover their equivalents in three-dimensional space. These transformations are *linear,* meaning that straight lines are transformed into straight lines. It is then true that if an object is composed of vertices connected by straight lines, it can be transformed by transforming the vertices and connecting them by straight lines.

## 5.1.1 Translation

This transformation consists of a shift of the object parallel to itself in any direction in the (x,y)-plane. Any such shift can be accomplished by a shift in x-direction (horizontally) plus a shift in y-direction (vertically). The mathematical description is simple. We call the amount of x-shift $T_x$ and the amount of y-shift $T_y$. The translation of the point (x,y) into the point $(x_T, y_T)$ is expressed by the formulas:

$$x_T = x + T_x \text{ and } y_T = y + T_y.$$

Translation is the only transformation that is not in relation to a reference point. Its effect is independent of the original position of the object. As an example, consider the triangle defined by the vertices (10,0), (40,0), (30,30) being translated by 10 units to the right and 15 units upward ($T_x = 10$, $T_y = 15$). The formulas have to be applied to every vertex of the triangle. We get the translated vertices (20,15), (50,15), (40,45) (see Figure 5.4). Connecting these points yields the translated triangle.

**FIGURE 5.4** Translation example.

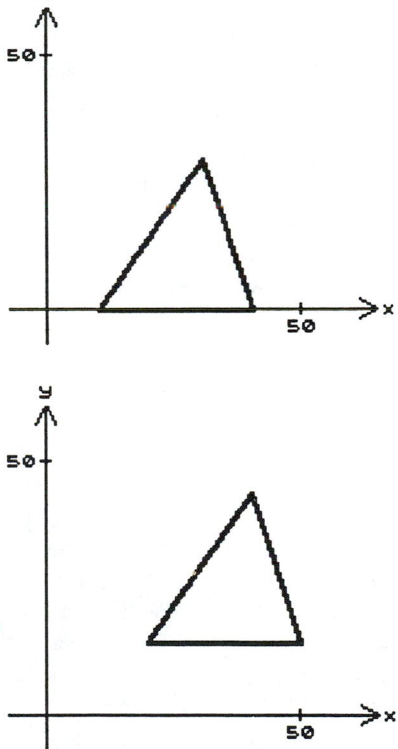


## 5.1.2 Scaling

Scaling consists of elongating or shrinking the object in the x-direction and in the y-direction by two independent factors, $S_x$ and $S_y$. If $S_x = S_y$, we have a simple size change of the object; otherwise we get an object elongated or shrunk in either the x- or y-direction. The scaling of the point (x,y) into the point $(x_S, y_S)$ is expressed by the formulas:

$$x_S = x * S_x \quad \text{and} \quad y_S = y * S_y.$$

As an example, take the same triangle as above and make it wider by a factor of 1.5 and taller by a factor of 1.2 ($S_x = 1.5$, $S_y = 1.2$). Applying the formulas to every vertex yields (15,0), (60,0), (45,36). Connecting these yields the scaled triangle (see Figure 5.5). We can see that all points move away from the origin. The enlargement is relative to (0,0). If the scale factor is less than 1.0, scaling shrinks the image. Scaling with negative numbers results in various types of reflections or mirror images. For example, scaling with $S_x = -1$, $S_y = 1$ produces a mirror image of the object with respect to the y-axis.

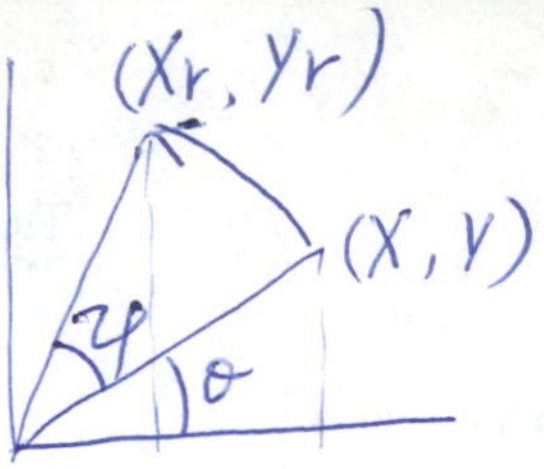

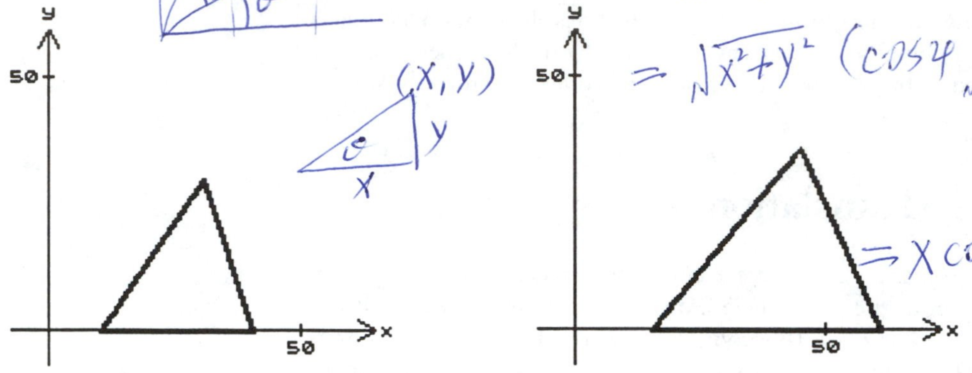

**FIGURE 5.5** Scaling example.

### 5.1.3 Rotation

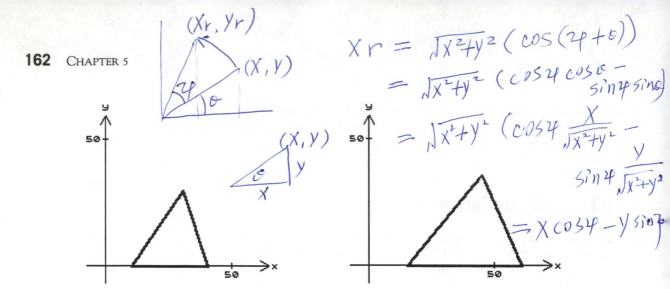

Rotation consists of rotating the object around the point (0,0). The points of a picture, when subjected to this transformation, rotate around (0,0) just as the stars in the sky rotate around the polar star. The rotation depends on only one number: the rotation angle $\Phi$. The rotation of the point (x,y) into the point ($x_R$,$y_R$) is expressed by the formulas:

$$x_R = x \cdot \cos\Phi - y \cdot \sin\Phi \quad \text{and} \quad y_R = x \cdot \sin\Phi + y \cdot \cos\Phi.$$

The rotation goes from the positive x-axis to the positive y-axis by an angle equal to $\Phi$. Observe that the rotation is counterclockwise (ccw). If we rotate the above triangle by 25°, the rotated vertices are at (9.06,4.22), (36.24,16.88), (14.52,39.84). We connect those points by straight lines (see Figure 5.6).

### 5.1.4 Concatenation of Transformations

The only transformation that was not in relation to a reference point was translation. The scaling and rotation done above were relative to the point (0,0). This is always true in the fundamental form of these transformations, but they can also be done relative to any other point in the plane. We now demonstrate how to scale and rotate relative to any arbitrary point. In both cases the same strategy is used. The object is translated along with the reference point so that the reference point is at (0,0). We next apply the fundamental transformation, then translate back the transformed image so that the reference point is restored

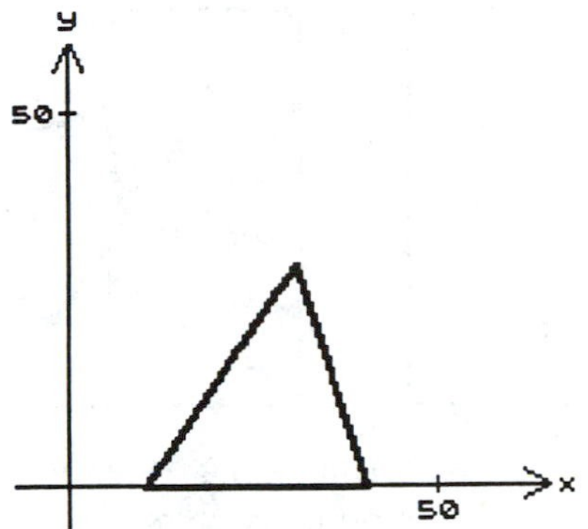


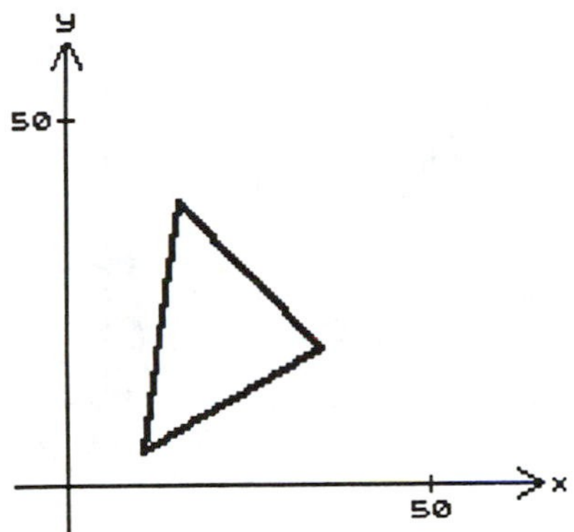


**FIGURE 5.6** Rotation example.

to its original position. If the arbitrary point is (x,y), the order of transformations will be:

translate ($T_{-x}$,$T_{-y}$)
rotate or scale
translate ($T_x$,$T_y$)

We show in Figures 5.7 and 5.8 the three stages of these generalized transformations. In both cases, the reference point is a point inside the house and the origin is near the lower left corner of the frame. The order in which successive transformations are done is not reversible—any other order will produce a different result. The example below has just two transformations, a rotation and a translation. Figures 5.9 and 5.10 show the different results when the same translation and the same rotation are applied in different order. The dot in the lower left corner of the screen is the origin.

**FIGURE 5.7** Scaling about an arbitrary point.

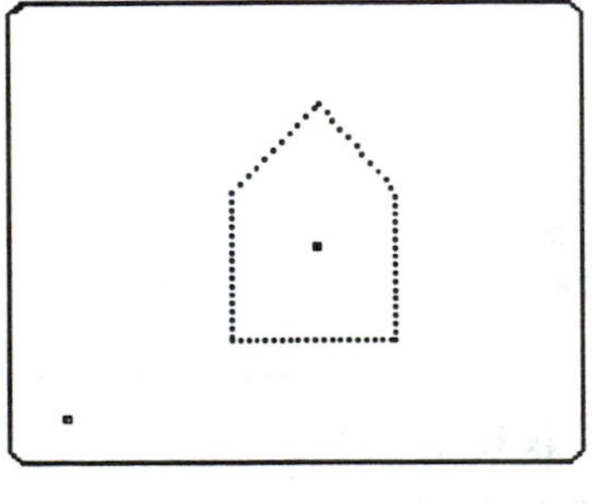

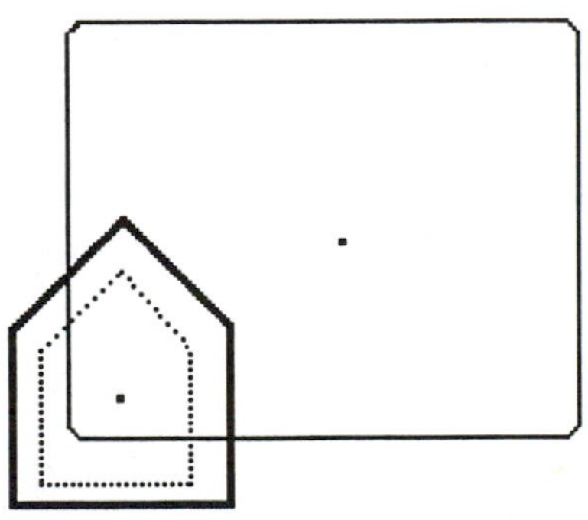

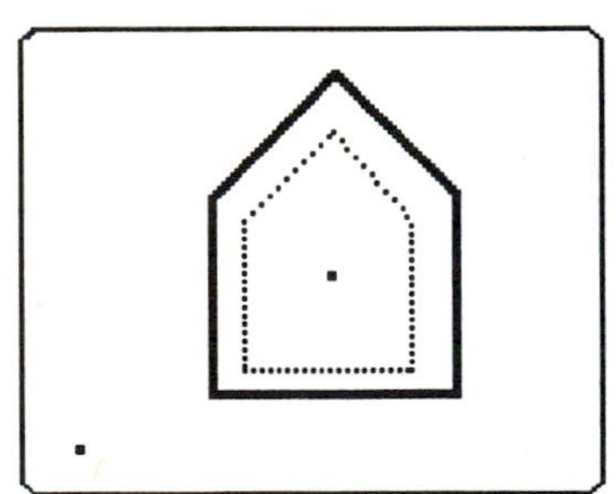

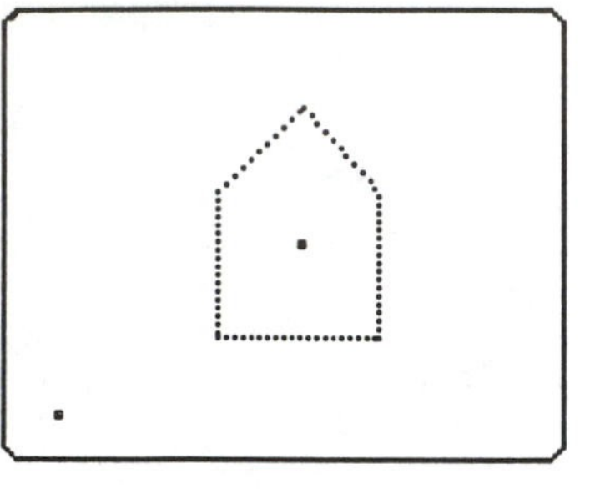

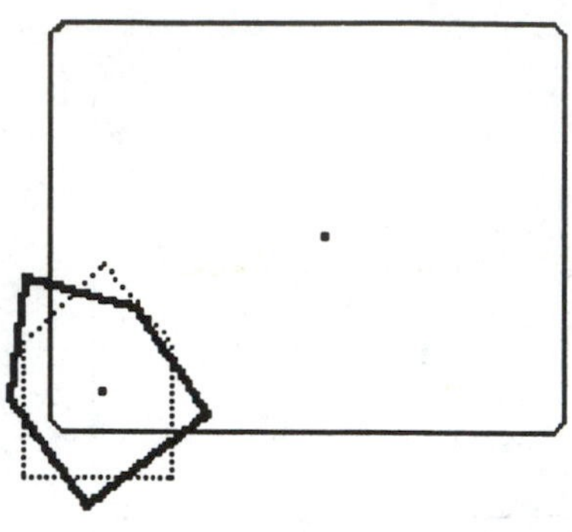

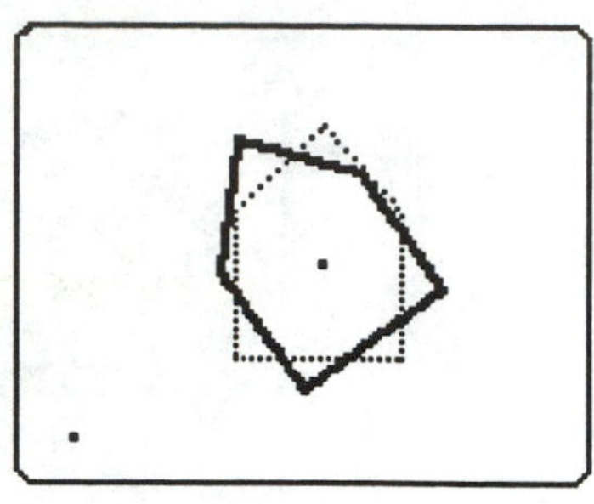

**FIGURE 5.8** Rotation about an arbitrary point.

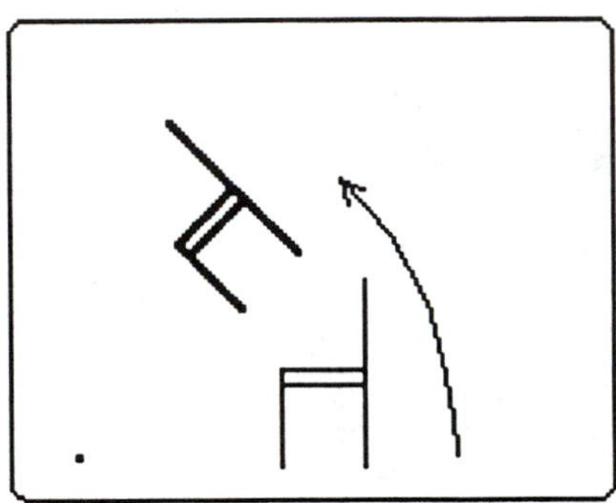

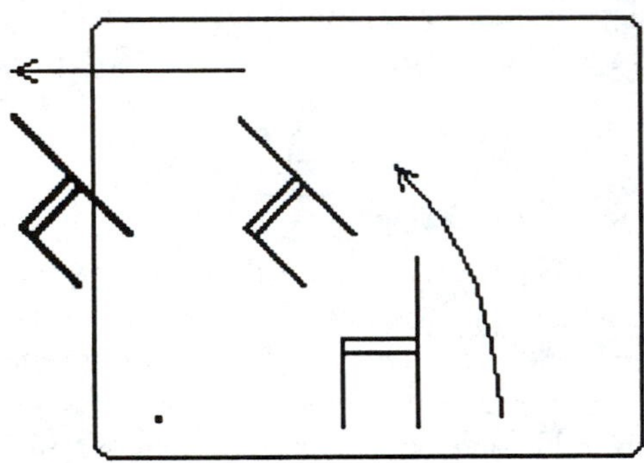

**FIGURE 5.9** First rotation, then translation.

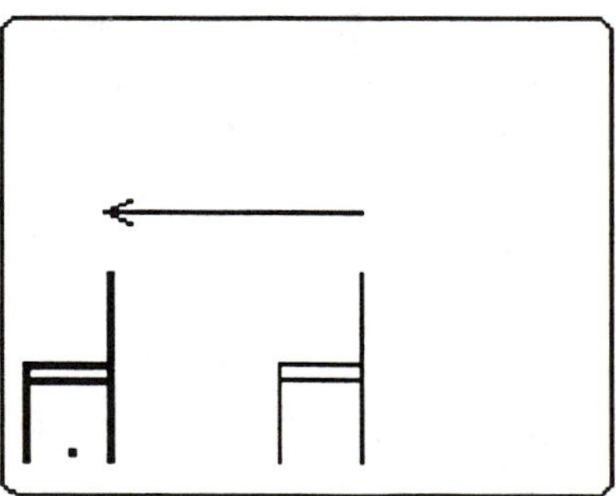

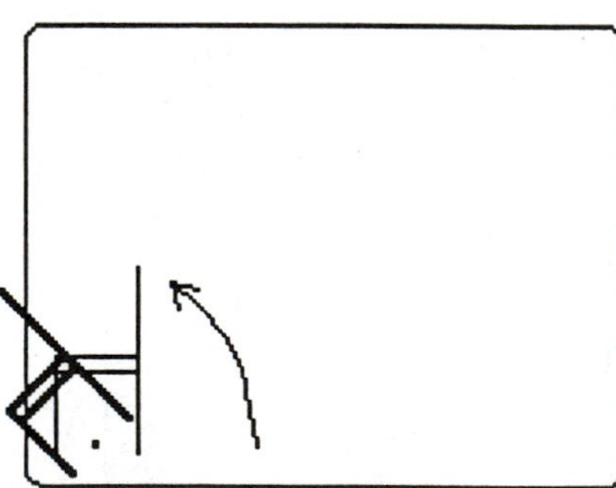

**FIGURE 5.10** First translation, then rotation.

More than two transformations are order dependent as well. There are exceptions in special cases, such as for combinations of transformations of the same kind.

### 5.1.5 Homogeneous Coordinates and Matrices

The above formulas for computing two-dimensional transformations can be represented in a uniform and most useful way by $3 \times 3$ matrices. Although they map two-dimensional space into two-dimensional space, $2 \times 2$ matrices cannot describe all three transformations; translation is impossible through a $2 \times 2$ matrix. We can get a uniform matrix formalism if we define so-called homogeneous coordinates.

We adopt the convention that the Cartesian description of a point (x,y) is equivalent to the normalized homogeneous description (x,y,1). (Note the 1 at the end.) The two expressions for the coordinates of the point are called *Cartesian coordinates* and *homogeneous coordinates*, respectively. Further, we consider all homogeneous coordinates $(w \cdot x, w \cdot y, w)$ for every value of $w \neq 0$ as identical to (x,y,1). (Note that this last vector has been normalized by dividing by w.) A particular advantage of homogeneous coordinates is that they are readily applied to three-dimensional transformations.

Using normalized homogeneous coordinates and matrices, the transformation equations become:

Translation by $(T_x, T_y)$:
$$(x_T, y_T, 1) = (x, y, 1)\begin{pmatrix} 1 & 0 & 0 \\ 0 & 1 & 0 \\ T_x & T_y & 1 \end{pmatrix}$$

Scaling by $(S_x, S_y)$:
$$(x_S, y_S, 1) = (x, y, 1)\begin{pmatrix} S_x & 0 & 0 \\ 0 & S_y & 0 \\ 0 & 0 & 1 \end{pmatrix}$$

Rotation by $\Phi$:
$$(x_R, y_R, 1) = (x, y, 1)\begin{pmatrix} \cos\Phi & \sin\Phi & 0 \\ -\sin\Phi & \cos\Phi & 0 \\ 0 & 0 & 1 \end{pmatrix}$$

Before performing the matrix multiplication we append a 1 at the end of the vector; we discard the 1 from the result. When multiplying a normalized homogeneous vector with any of the matrices shown, the result will always be a normalized homogeneous vector; that is, it will always have a 1 at the end.

Concatenating transformations is done by multiplying the corresponding matrices in the order in which the transformations are applied. The resulting matrix expresses the overall transformation. This formalism has one important advantage. No matter how many $3 \times 3$ matrices are multiplied with each other, the result is always a $3 \times 3$ matrix.

Suppose we have an object consisting of 200 vertices which is to be rotated around a point that is not the origin. We first translate the object, then rotate it, and finally translate it back. If we don't use our matrix formalism, we have to do 400 vertex translations and 200 vertex rotations. Using the matrix formalism, we first do two matrix multiplications to get the matrix corresponding to the overall transformation, and then apply this matrix to the 200 vertices of the object. Multiplying a vertex with the overall matrix takes roughly the same amount of computation as multiplying the vertex with any of the simple transformation matrices.

Our matrix formalism is very efficient. No matter how many matrices of the form

$$\begin{pmatrix} a & b & 0 \\ c & d & 0 \\ e & f & 1 \end{pmatrix}$$

we multiply, the resulting matrix will always have the vector $(0,0,1)^T$ in its rightmost column. To multiply a point $(x,y,1)$ with this matrix will at most require the computations:

$$x_T = ax + cy + e \quad \text{and} \quad y_T = bx + dy + f.$$

The lack of interchangeability of the order of transformations is analogous to the fact that matrix multiplication is not commutative.

## 5.2 THREE-DIMENSIONAL TRANSFORMATIONS

In this section we introduce for the first time a three-dimensional Cartesian coordinate system. It uses the three coordinate axes x, y, and z. In computer graphics we align the (x,y)-plane with the screen. Now it is important to recognize that there are two different orientations for the z-coordinate axis. A right-handed system (rhs) has the z-axis pointing toward the viewer. A left-handed system (lhs) has the z-axis pointing away from the viewer. In this book, if not explicitly stated otherwise, we will use lhs because it is more natural; it makes objects that are farther away have larger positive z-coordinates. (The few times that we depart from this will be made emphatically clear.) Other books do not always agree with us in using a left-handed system.

Figure 5.11 explains why a left-handed system is called by that name. You can orient your left hand as shown, but, try as you will, you cannot align the fingers of your right hand with the thumb pointing toward +x, your forefinger pointing toward +y, and your middle finger pointing towards +z. You can align in this order the thumb and fingers of your right hand only with a right-handed system.

FIGURE 5.11

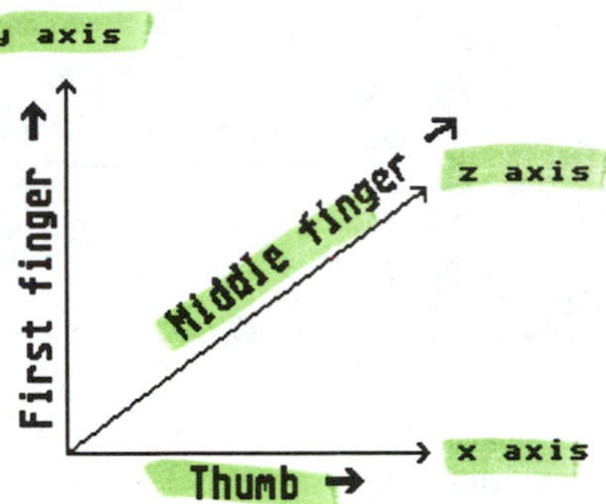


We consider five transformations of an object in space. The first two, translation and scaling, are simple extensions of the two-dimensional transformations into three dimensions. The other three transformations are rotations in space, one for each coordinate axis. They have no real counterpart in two dimensions, but they are not conceptually difficult. It is somewhat more difficult to combine these three rotations to obtain a rotation about an arbitrary axis in space.

The only object in space to which we shall apply transformations is a point. Of course, in most applications, entire objects are to be transformed. But if an object consists of points connected by straight lines (it then has a polygonal surface), it can be transformed by transforming all its vertices and connecting these transformed points by straight lines. The property that allows us to transform an object in this way is the linearity of the transformation. All the spatial transformations considered here are linear. Nonlinear transformations are not important in computer graphics.

## 5.2.1 Translation

Translation in space is similar to translation in the plane except that there is one more direction—parallel to the z-axis. The effect of the translation is to shift the point by any amount in space. Applied to an object, the effect is to shift the object parallel to itself by the given amount. The shift can be considered as a composite of a shift in the x-direction, plus a shift in the y-direction, plus a shift in the z-direction. We use $T_x$, $T_y$, and $T_z$ to represent these separate shifts. In all cases, a positive value for a shift represents a movement in the direction of the corresponding positive coordinate axis. The translation of the point (x,y,z) into the point $(x_T,y_T,z_T)$ is done by:

$$x_T = x + T_x \qquad y_T = y + T_y \qquad z_T = z + T_z$$

Translation is the only transformation that is not dependent on any reference point; its effect is the same no matter where the point is originally.

In matrix notation, using normalized homogeneous coordinates, this is performed by the matrix multiplication:

$$(x_T, y_T, z_T, 1) = (x, y, z, 1)\begin{pmatrix} 1 & 0 & 0 & 0 \\ 0 & 1 & 0 & 0 \\ 0 & 0 & 1 & 0 \\ T_x & T_y & T_z & 1 \end{pmatrix}$$

### 5.2.2 Scaling

Scaling in space is essentially identical to scaling in the plane; the formulas are the same with one more coordinate added. The scaling transformation relocates a point with relation to a reference point. When applied to the entire object, the result is a shrinking or enlarging of the object in its x-, y-, or z-dimension. (Of course, a change in size cannot be observed on a single point.) We use $S_x$, $S_y$, and $S_z$ to represent the scaling factors for the three dimensions. If $S_x = S_y = S_z$, there is a simple size change of the object. Factors $< 1$ shrink the object and factors $> 1$ enlarge it. A point (x,y,z) is scaled by computing:

$$x_S = x * S_x \qquad y_S = y * S_y \qquad z_S = z * S_z$$

Using matrix notation and homogeneous coordinates:

$$(x_S, y_S, z_S, 1) = (x, y, z, 1) * \begin{pmatrix} S_x & 0 & 0 & 0 \\ 0 & S_y & 0 & 0 \\ 0 & 0 & S_z & 0 \\ 0 & 0 & 0 & 1 \end{pmatrix}$$

Scaling is always relative to a reference point. The formulas above are for the simplest case in which the reference point is the origin. When an object is scaled, its distance from the origin is also changed by the same amount. For example, enlarging an object by a factor of 2 for all coordinates will also double its distance from the origin.

The most frequent application of scaling is to change the size of an object. In this case we scale with $S_x = S_y = S_z$. More importantly, we have to consider the reference point for scaling, otherwise the movement away from its original place may surprise us. What we normally think of as a size change is the enlarging or shrinking of the object about a point at its center. To do only a size change, we must compose it from three transformations: a translation that puts the object's center at the origin, then the scaling, and then a translation to relocate the center at its former location. The "center" of an object is hard to define formally, but we must specify it. What we mean by the center to which scaling is relative is a point in or on the object that does not move when the object grows or shrinks. After all, if an object changes in size,

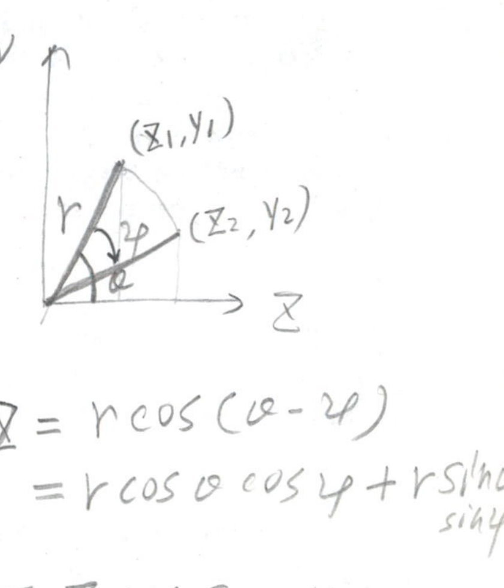

all points but one (the center) must move, and these moves are relative to that center. This idea will become more clear as the discussion continues.

If the center of the object is (cx,cy,cz), we perform a size change by performing the transformations in this order:

translate $(T_{-cx}, T_{-cy}, T_{-cz})$
scale$(S_x, S_y, S_z)$
translate $(T_{cx}, T_{cy}, T_{cz})$

### 5.2.3 Rotation

Rotation in space is essentially different from rotation in two dimensions. The main difference is that there are three cases of rotations. These are:

rotation about the x-axis
rotation about the y-axis
rotation about the z-axis

Each of these is independent of the others (which means that none of them can be expressed in terms of the others). However, we can combine these three to obtain rotation about any arbitrary line in space.

When we think of rotation, it is always about an axis and it can be in either of two directions—counterclockwise (ccw) or clockwise (cw). For rotation in the plane, the axis of rotation is an imaginary one, perpendicular to the plane and through the origin. This rotation axis could correspond to a z-axis that points toward us, giving a right-handed system (rhs), and the rotation, from positive x-axis to positive y-axis, would be ccw.

**Rotation about the x-axis** With our lhs convention, rotating a point clockwise (cw) by the angle Φ about the x-axis (looking along the positive x-axis toward the origin) will move a point on the positive y-axis in an arc toward the positive z-axis. For any point, the new coordinates become:

$$x_{Rx} = x$$
$$y_{Rx} = y \cdot \cos\Phi - z \cdot \sin\Phi$$
$$z_{Rx} = y \cdot \sin\Phi + z \cdot \cos\Phi$$

In matrix notation, with homogeneous coordinates:

$$(x_{Rx}, y_{Rx}, z_{Rx}, 1) = (x, y, z, 1) * \begin{pmatrix} 1 & 0 & 0 & 0 \\ 0 & \cos\Phi & \sin\Phi & 0 \\ 0 & -\sin\Phi & \cos\Phi & 0 \\ 0 & 0 & 0 & 1 \end{pmatrix}$$

**Rotation about the y-axis** Rotating a point on the positive x-axis ccw by the angle Φ about the y-axis (looking from the positive y-axis toward the origin) will move the point in an arc toward the positive z-axis. Note carefully that the sense of the rotation is different from the one we used for x-axis rotation, ccw instead of cw. For any point, the new coordinates become:

$$
\begin{aligned}
x_{Rx} &= x * \cos\Phi - z * \sin\Phi \\
y_{Rx} &= y \\
z_{Rx} &= x * \sin\Phi + z * \cos\Phi
\end{aligned}
$$

In matrix notation, with homogeneous coordinates:

$$
(x_{Ry}, y_{Ry}, z_{Ry}, 1) = (x, y, z, 1) \begin{pmatrix} \cos\Phi & 0 & \sin\Phi & 0 \\ 0 & 1 & 0 & 0 \\ -\sin\Phi & 0 & \cos\Phi & 0 \\ 0 & 0 & 0 & 1 \end{pmatrix}
$$

**Rotation about the z-axis** The cw rotation of a point on the positive x-axis by the angle Φ about the z-axis (when we look from the positive z-axis toward the origin) will move it in an arc toward the positive y-axis. (Remember that we are using a left-handed system!) For any point, the new coordinates become:

$$
\begin{aligned}
x_{Rx} &= x * \cos\Phi - y * \sin\Phi \\
y_{Rx} &= x * \sin\Phi + y * \cos\Phi \\
z_{Rx} &= z
\end{aligned}
$$

In matrix notation, with homogeneous coordinates:

$$
(x_{Rz}, y_{Rz}, z_{Rz}, 1) = (x, y, z, 1) * \begin{pmatrix} \cos\Phi & \sin\Phi & 0 & 0 \\ -\sin\Phi & \cos\Phi & 0 & 0 \\ 0 & 0 & 1 & 0 \\ 0 & 0 & 0 & 1 \end{pmatrix}
$$

If any of these rotations are done in the opposite sense—clockwise rather than counterclockwise, or vice versa—then the minus sign must be swapped between the sinΦ terms, from the lower left sinΦ to the upper right sinΦ. Also, if we were to specify the sense of the rotation while looking toward the origin from the *negative* end of the axis of rotation, then the meaning of cw and ccw reverses. Further, changing the *direction* of the z-axis to make the system right-handed also reverses the meaning of cw and ccw.

**A general rule for rotations in space** There is a general rule that is easy to remember and from which all the matrix rotation formulas can be deduced. According to the standard convention in geometry, we refer to the coordinate axes in the order x,y,z.

To define the three basic rotations in an unambiguous way, we require that a rotation of 90° will bring one positive axis into another positive axis without ever overcrossing the negative axis during the rotation. A rotation from the positive x-axis into the positive y-axis is then understood to be along the arrow indicated in Figure 5.12. The reason why we are so deliberate in stating that rotations must be from one positive axis to another positive axis without ever coinciding with the negative axis is that one could go from +x to +y by a 270° clockwise angle. This would violate our rule.

**FIGURE 5.12**

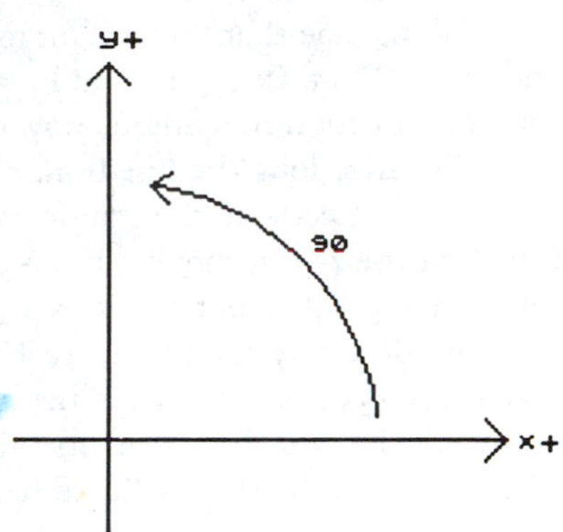


Using this direction rule, we can set up a general formula. A rotation from one +axis to the other +axis, in the order x,y,z around the remaining axis always has the schematic:

$$\begin{matrix} \cos\Phi & \sin\Phi \\ -\sin\Phi & \cos\Phi \end{matrix}$$

(the minus sign is at the lower left). The order x,y,z means that the "from"-axis is x or y, and the "to"-axis is y or z. More specifically, we mean $x \rightarrow y$, $y \rightarrow z$, and $x \rightarrow z$. This is not a cyclic permutation.

The rotation is expressed by a 4 × 4 matrix for homogeneous coordinates. In the matrix, the row and the column corresponding to the rotation axis contain all 0's except for a 1 where they cross. The fourth row and fourth column also contain 0's everywhere except for a 1 where they cross. The other two rows and columns are obtained by inserting the above schematic into the remaining places in the matrix.

For example, the rotation from $x_+$ to $z_+$ rotates about the y-axis, therefore the second row and second column as well as the fourth row and fourth column will contain all 0's but a 1 where they cross. The remaining four positions in the 4 × 4 matrix are occupied by the above schematic. We obtain the matrix:

$$\begin{bmatrix} \cos\Phi & 0 & \sin\Phi & 0 \\ 0 & 1 & 0 & 0 \\ -\sin\Phi & 0 & \cos\Phi & 0 \\ 0 & 0 & 0 & 1 \end{bmatrix}$$

This rule is independent of left-handed or right-handed systems, independent of clockwise or counterclockwise directions, and independent of the end from which we look along the rotation axis. All other rules can be derived from this one.

**Rotation about an arbitrary line** We now describe how to rotate a point (x,y,z) around an arbitrary line in space by the angle $\Phi$ to give the new point $(x_\Phi, y_\Phi, z_\Phi)$. Such a rotation is not commonly used directly in computer graphics, but it is important indirectly as an element in view-plane transformations and other viewing techniques.

We present it here to serve as a preparation for the view-plane transformation in Chapter 6.

We assume that the axis for rotation is the line given by the two end points $P_1 = (x_1,y_1,z_1)$ and $P_2 = (x_2,y_2,z_2)$. In order to define the rotation direction in a unique way, we specify that the direction is ccw when looking along the line from $P_1$ to $P_2$.

We first perform the transformations necessary to align the given line with the z-axis, moving the point to be rotated along with it. We rotate the point about the z-axis (which now plays the role of the axis for rotation), for which we have a formula. After the rotation about the z-axis, we transform the line back, together with the rotated point, so that the line is in its original position. The point will be where it would have been if we had rotated it about that line in the first place.

Actually, the transformation is applied only to the points (that is, all the points of an object) and not to the line. The line guides us so that we can find the necessary transformations. In the figures and explanations below, we will work with the given line.

First we compute the length, L, of the line:

$$a = x_2 - x_1,\ b = y_2 - y_1,\ c = z_2 - z_1,\ L = \sqrt{a^2 + b^2 + c^2}$$

Then we compute the length of the projection of the line onto the (y,z)-plane. We can visualize this projection by imagining light coming from the right parallel to the x-axis, with the (y,z)-plane acting as if it were a wall onto which the line casts a shadow (see Figure 5.13). The length of the projection is $p = \sqrt{b^2 + c^2}$.

Now we start with the transformations. We translate the line by the amount $(-x_1, -y_1, -z_1)$. This puts the endpoint $P_1$ at the origin with the line still parallel to itself, so the length of its projection onto the (y,z)-plane is not changed. The matrix that does this is:

$$\mathbf{T}_{-P1} = \begin{pmatrix} 1 & 0 & 0 & 0 \\ 0 & 1 & 0 & 0 \\ 0 & 0 & 1 & 0 \\ -x_1 & -y_1 & -z_1 & 1 \end{pmatrix}$$

Now we rotate the line cw around the x-axis until it is in the (x,z)-plane. Rotating the line will also rotate its projection on the (y,z)-plane but it will not change the length of the projection. When the line lies in the (x,z)-plane, its projection will lie on the z-axis. The figure tells us the angle by which we have to rotate. It is the angle that is swept by rotating the projection cw to the z-axis; call it $\alpha$. Actually, we don't need the angle itself, only the sine and cosine of the angle and

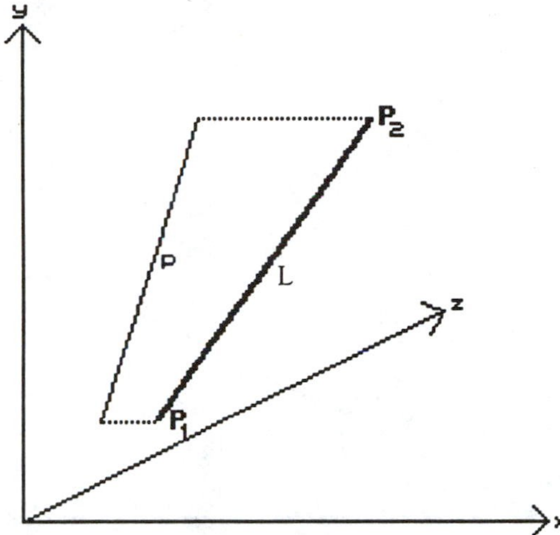


**FIGURE 5.13** The line $P_1P_2$ is projected onto the (y,z)-plane to give the line of length p.

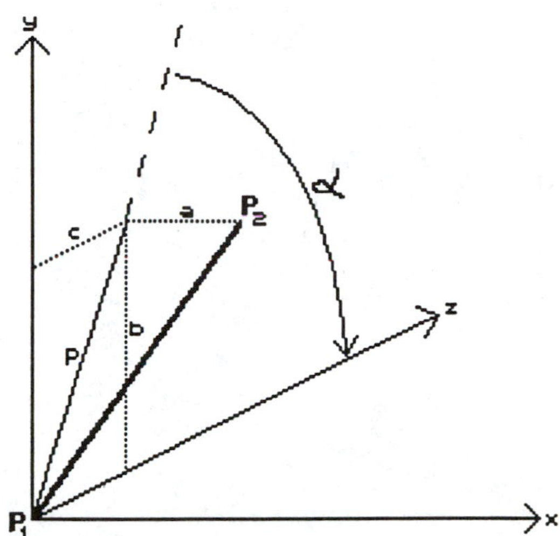


**FIGURE 5.14** The line $P_1P_2$ before the rotation by angle α about the x-axis.

these are readily available (see Figure 5.14). We have $\sin\alpha = b/p$, $\cos\alpha = c/p$. The matrix that does this rotation is:

$$\mathbf{R}_x = \begin{pmatrix} 1 & 0 & 0 & 0 \\ 0 & c/p & b/p & 0 \\ 0 & -b/p & c/p & 0 \\ 0 & 0 & 0 & 1 \end{pmatrix}$$

One more rotation is needed to put the line on the z-axis (see Figure 5.15). Although the coordinates of the end point $P_2$ are changed, the distance of $P_2$ from the (y,z)-plane is the same as it was after the translation, or a. There is a right triangle in the (x,z)-plane whose hypotenuse is L; its sides are p and a. The line $P_1P_2$ can now be aligned with the z-axis by rotating it ccw by the angle β around the y-axis. From the right triangle we can deduce: $\sin\beta = a/L$, and $\cos\beta = p/L$. The matrix that does this rotation is:

$$\mathbf{R}_y = \begin{pmatrix} p/L & 0 & a/L & 0 \\ 0 & 1 & 0 & 0 \\ -a/L & 0 & p/L & 0 \\ 0 & 0 & 0 & 1 \end{pmatrix}$$

Now we can perform the rotation about the line $P_1P_2$ by rotating about the z-axis (see Figure 5.16). We want to rotate in a ccw fashion

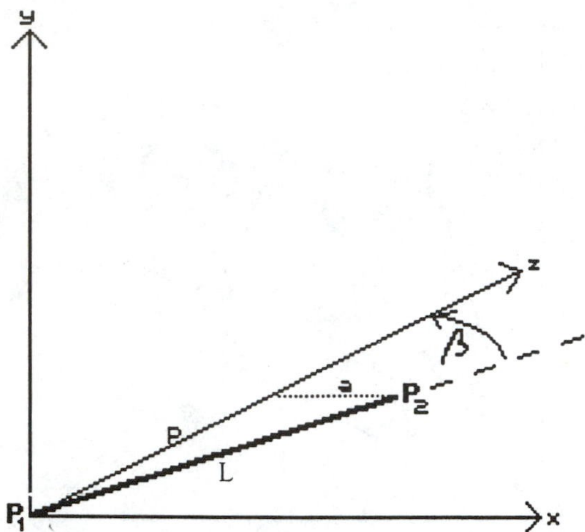


**FIGURE 5.15** The line $P_1P_2$ before the rotation by the angle β about the y-axis.

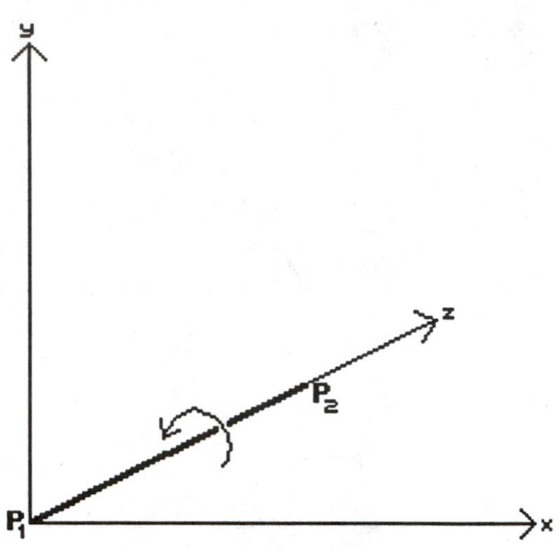


**FIGURE 5.16** The line $P_1P_2$ is now aligned with the z-axis.

because the point $P_1$ is at the origin and point $P_2$ is farther up the positive z-axis. Along the line from $P_1$ to $P_2$, a ccw direction rotates from x+ into y+ about the z-axis. So the matrix to perform this is:

$$\mathbf{R}_z = \begin{pmatrix} \cos\Phi & \sin\Phi & 0 & 0 \\ -\sin\Phi & \cos\Phi & 0 & 0 \\ 0 & 0 & 1 & 0 \\ 0 & 0 & 0 & 1 \end{pmatrix}$$

Now we must realign the line $P_1P_2$ into its former position. This is done by reversing all the transformation steps before the $R_z$ rotation. The order in which we do this is important.

The rotations are easily reversed by transferring the minus sign to the upper right sin in the matrices. The translation is reversed by changing the signs of the three translation parameters. We can now write down the whole transformation in one formula. We use homogeneous notation because translation matrices are involved:

$$(x_\Phi, y_\Phi, z_\Phi, 1) = (x,y,z,1)\,\mathbf{T}_{-P1}\,\mathbf{R}_x\,\mathbf{R}_y\,\mathbf{R}_z\,\mathbf{R}_{-y}\,\mathbf{R}_{-x}\,\mathbf{T}_{P1}$$

To carry out this operation, we first compute a, b, c, L (the length of the line), and p (the length of the projection), as shown above. We then compute the overall rotation matrix, which is the product of the above seven homogeneous matrices. The resulting matrix will be homo-

geneous as well. Multiplying every point of the object with the overall rotation matrix will give us the rotated vertices of the object with a considerable saving in computation time.

# EXERCISES FOR CHAPTER 5

## Section 5.1

1. Find the matrix that expresses a rotation by the angle $\Phi$ about the point $(c_x,c_y)$.
2. Find the matrix that expresses scaling by $(S_x,S_y)$ relative to the point $(c_x,c_y)$.
3. Find the matrix that magnifies the triangle A = (1,1), B = (2,2), C = (4, − 1) by the factor 2 while keeping the vertex B fixed.
4. Find the matrix for reflection about the x-axis.
5. Find the matrix for reflection about the y-axis.
6. Compose the reflection about an arbitrary line from translation, rotation, and reflection about the x-axis or y-axis. Let the arbitrary line have an angle $\Theta$ with the x-axis and intersect the y-axis at (0,b). *Hint:*

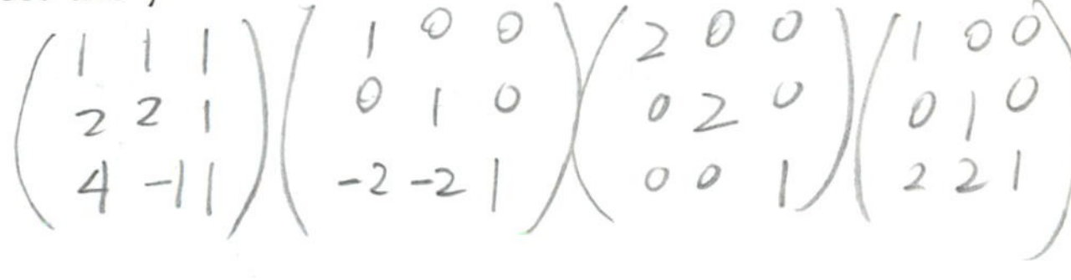

translate by $-b$
rotate about the origin by $-\Theta$
reflect about the x-axis
rotate about the origin by $\Theta$
translate by b

7. Find numerically (not in general form) the matrix for reflection about the line y = 0.8x + 2.
8. Show that the matrix that expresses the concatenation of rotation by $\alpha$ followed by a rotation by $\beta$ equals the matrix for the rotation by $\alpha+\beta$.
9. Prove that the transformation of the straight line from point $P_1$ to point $P_2$ is identical to the straight line between the transformations of $P_1$ and $P_2$.

In Exercises 10 through 16 use homogeneous matrices.

10. Compute the composite transformation matrix for the following transformations in the given order:

translate by $(-2,1)$
rotate by 70°
translate by (2,3)

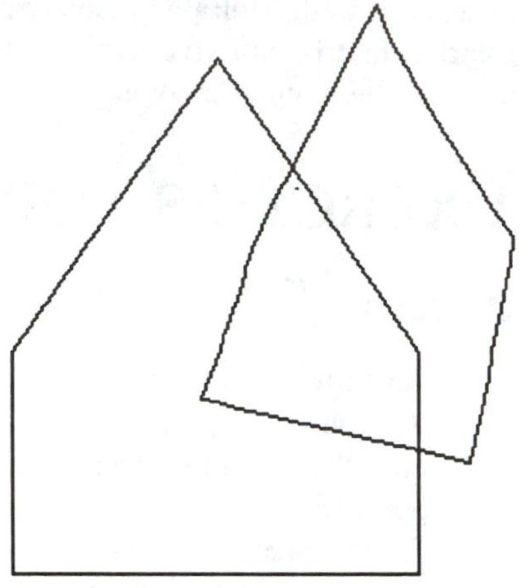

FIGURE 5.17

11. Write the procedures

```
acc_translate(tx,ty : real)
acc_rotate(alpha : real)
acc_scale(sx,sy : real)
```

that accumulate the specified two-dimensional transformations into TMATRIX, the corresponding global matrix.
12. Instead of performing each transformation separately, we compute a composite matrix and use that. What is the advantage?
13. Show analytically that translation followed by scaling is different from scaling followed by translation. Show it by multiplying a general scaling matrix and a general translation matrix in different orders to obtain different results.
14. Show analytically through matrix multiplication that when only translations are performed, their order is insignificant. Show it by multiplying two translation matrices.
15. Repeat Exercise 14 for scaling.
16. Repeat Exercise 14 for rotation.
17. The essential characteristic of a nonlinear transformation is that straight lines are not necessarily transformed into straight lines. Draw the house front specified by the following five points:

$$
\begin{array}{l}
(-0.40, -0.4) \\
(\ \ 0.70, -0.4) \\
(\ \ 0.70, \ \ 0.2) \\
(\ \ 0.70, \ \ 0.2) \\
(\ \ 0.15, \ \ 1.0) \\
(-0.40, \ \ 0.2)
\end{array}
$$

Then transform with:

$$x_t = x/2 + x*x/1.8 + y/5 + 0.3$$
$$y_t = y/2 + y*x/1.7 + 0.4$$

If we perform this transformation to the five vertices only and connect the transformed ones by straight lines, we do not obtain the correct transformation of the whole object. The lines connecting the vertices must be transformed individually by transforming as many individual points as possible on them and connecting them by straight lines. This certainly only approximates the transformation but we don't need to be more precise than the pixel resolution. The result of this transformation is shown in Figure 5.17. Write code that transforms and draws the given house.

## Section 5.2

18. Compute the composite transformation matrix for the following transformations in three dimensions:

    translate by (3,2,4)
    rotate about x by 60°
    scale by (1.5, −2,2)
    rotate about y by 25°

19. Write a procedure

```
acc_trafo(trafo:tra;  alpha,x,y,z : real)
```

    in Pascal that accumulates the specified three-dimensional transformation into a global matrix TMATRIX. The parameter trafo is of the type specified below:

```
type tra  =  (trans,scale,rotx,roty,rotz);
```

20. The five transformations presented in the text are linear. What is the practical consequence of this? *Hint:* to transform a straight line segment we have to transform only its end points.

# Three-Dimensional Viewing Techniques

# 6

The important and interesting problem of displaying a 3-D object on a 2-D screen is the subject of Chapter 6. There are four sections.

**6.0 Introduction** shows that we must project points of the object onto the screen and that there are several ways to do this.

**6.1 Projections** explains how we compute the new locations for points of the object after a parallel or perspective projection, or after a perspective depth transformation. There are variants of each of these procedures.

**6.2 View Plane Transformations** permit the display of a 3-D object as it would appear when viewed from any point in space. This requires the graphics system to do rotations before the projecting.

**6.3 Three-Dimensional Windowing and Clipping** extends the concepts of Chapter 4 to three dimensions. This permits the projection of a portion of a 3-D scene to fit a 2-D viewport. As you might expect, this is more complex.

# 6.0 INTRODUCTION

All graphic display media are two-dimensional: the screen of a CRT, the plot from a plotter, or the printout from a printer. We will base our explanations on a CRT, since there is really no difference in any of them. When we display a three-dimensional object, we have to *project* it. That means we have to flatten the three-dimensional representation onto the two-dimensional medium.

A projection can be compared to the shadow an object casts onto a wall. The mathematical model we use to calculate these projections is simpler than what actually happens with shadows. In computer graphics, both the "object" and the "wall" where it casts a shadow are imaginary. We calculate the projections of all points of the object, some of which would be invisible in the real shadow of the object. To some extent, we could consider this as surpassing nature, but removing these extraneous points will give us great trouble.

Let us distinguish between object space and image space. *Object space* is the three-dimensional space in which the object is defined; we can think of this space as the real world. *Image space* is a two-dimensional space onto which the object is projected; we could think of this space as the wall but it is better to think of it as the display screen.

Strictly speaking, an object is projected by projecting each of its points. As there are infinitely many points in the object, we cannot produce a projection in this way. But all projections that we will consider have the important property that straight lines are projected into straight lines. This has many beneficial consequences. The most important is that projecting a straight line can be done by projecting the two end points of the line in object space and then connecting the two projected points by a straight line in image space.

# 6.1 PROJECTIONS

We can do the projection in different ways: parallel or perspective. For a 3-D scene, we must also consider how to preserve the original depth information that is lost when points are projected onto the viewing screen. We will consider these three types of projections in turn.

## 6.1.1 Parallel Projection

*Parallel projection* simulates the shadow that is cast onto a flat wall by a light source that is infinitely far away, for example, the sun. The parallel projection of a point (x,y,z) in object space is obtained by drawing a line with a certain direction $(x_p,y_p,z_p)$ in space through this point. This line is called the *projection vector*. The point where this line intersects the plane $z = 0$ is the parallel projection of the given point with coordinates $(x_{pl},y_{pl},0)$. The angle of the projection vector within the coordinate system determines where the projection lies on the screen, which is the (x,y)-plane.

We represent the line (the projection vector) in parametric form:

$$x_u = x + u*x_p$$
$$y_u = y + u*y_p$$
$$z_u = z + u*z_p$$

In these equations, $(x_u,y_u,z_u)$ is any point on the projection vector, determined by the value of u. For $u = 0$ we get the point (x,y,z) itself, so the line does go through the point. All points in the (x,y)-plane have a z-coordinate of 0, so by setting $z_u$ equal to 0 we get $0 = z+u*z_p$. From this it follows that $u = -z/z_p$ at the intersection point. The coordinates of the intersection point are then:

$$x_{pl} = x - z/z_p*x_p$$
$$y_{pl} = y - z/z_p*y_p$$
$$z_{pl} = 0$$

These general formulas give the coordinates for projected points for any angle of the projection vector. When that angle is specified, we know $x_p$, $y_p$, and $z_p$ and we can solve for the unknown x- and y-coordinates of the projected point.

If the projection vector is normal to the projection plane, the projection is called *orthographic*. As we use the (x,y)-plane where $z = 0$ as the projection plane, the projection is orthographic if the projection vector is parallel to the z-axis. That means that the projection vector is $(0,0,-1)$; its x- and y-components are 0. The value for the z-coordinate means that it points towards us. The length is arbitrary, of course; here we let it be 1.

The formulas yield:

$$x_{ort} = x$$
$$y_{ort} = y$$
$$z_{ort} = 0$$

Formally, this projection is obtained by setting the z-coordinate to 0 so no calculations are necessary. This projection in many cases is a good approximation of the actual projections that the human visual system receives from the real world. It is most often used in engineering drawings to produce the front, side, and top views of an object. The front and side views are called *elevations;* the top view is called the *plan.*

Orthographic projections don't change the length of lines parallel to the projection plane. Other lines are projected with a reduced length. Figure 6.1 shows the orthographic projection of a house onto the plane $z = 0$, which is represented by the screen. Points in the object space with the same x- and y-coordinates are projected onto the same point on the screen. The projection lines are shown parallel to the z-axis.

If the projection vector is not parallel to the z-axis, we have an *oblique projection.* Examples of such a projection in nature are shadows cast on the ground by sunlight. This projection is used to draw shadows in pictures but it should not be used to display the objects themselves (except in special applications; see below), because it produces unnatural-looking distortions. Some distortions are not unnatural but this one is because it does not correspond to the way objects of the real world are projected into the human eye.

Formally, a parallel projection is oblique if the projection vector has nonzero x- and y-components. The above general formulas yield, for the projected point:

$$x_{obl} = x - z/z_p*x_p$$
$$y_{obl} = y - z/z_p*y_p$$
$$z_{obl} = 0$$

Two conditions must be specified before we know the direction of the projection vector. One is the angle it makes with the z-axis. The projection of a line parallel to the z-axis will be at some angle $\alpha$ with

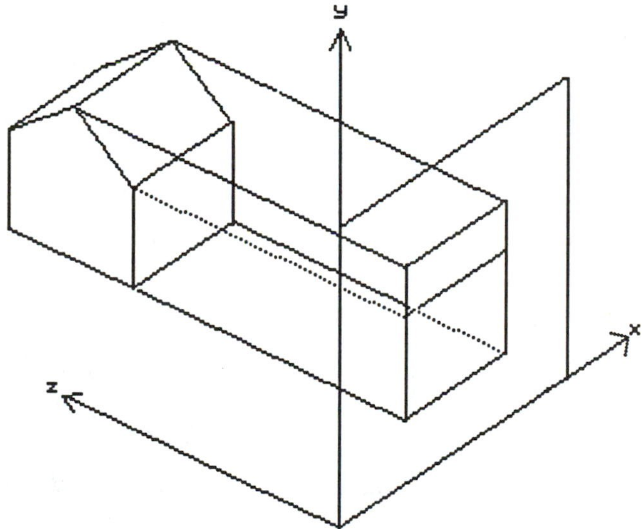


**FIGURE 6.1** Orthographic projection.

the horizontal on the projection plane. This can be determined from $\tan\alpha = y_p/x_p$. This angle is the second condition that we use to get the projection vector, as we will see below.

A special case of oblique projection is called *cavalier projection*. It is given when the projection vector forms an angle of 45° with the z-axis. This means that:

$$(x_p{}^2 + {}_yp^2)/z_p{}^2 = 1.$$

A cavalier projection projects lines parallel to the z-axis with unaltered length.

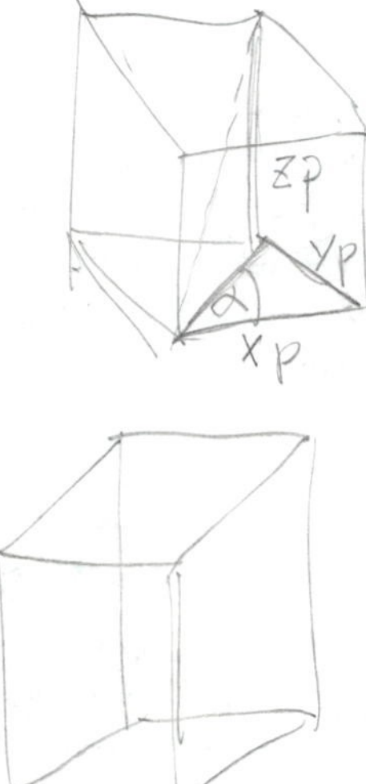

We still must use the second condition to specify fully the direction of the projection vector. As an example, let us find the projection vector for a cavalier projection of a cube so that the edges parallel to the z-axis result in lines at an angle of 45° with the horizontal. We set $z_p = -1$ arbitrarily. From $\tan 45° = 1$, it follows that $x_p = y_p$. We have $x_p{}^2 + y_p{}^2 = 1$, so we get $(.707, .707, -1)$ for the projection vector. The sketch at the left in Figure 6.2 shows the cube looking down the y-axis toward the origin in a left-handed system. The sketch at the right is its projection onto the plane $z = 0$ with this projection vector (hidden lines are not shown). We see that there is a distortion, which makes the cube look like an elongated parallelepiped.

Another special case is called *cabinet projection*. It uses a projection vector that forms an angle of approximately 26.6° with the z-axis, or:

$$(x_p{}^2 + y_p{}^2)/z_p{}^2 = 1/4.$$

A cabinet projection projects lines parallel to the z-axis with one-half their original length.

For the same cube as in the previous example, we will find the projection vector for a cabinet projection so that the edges parallel to

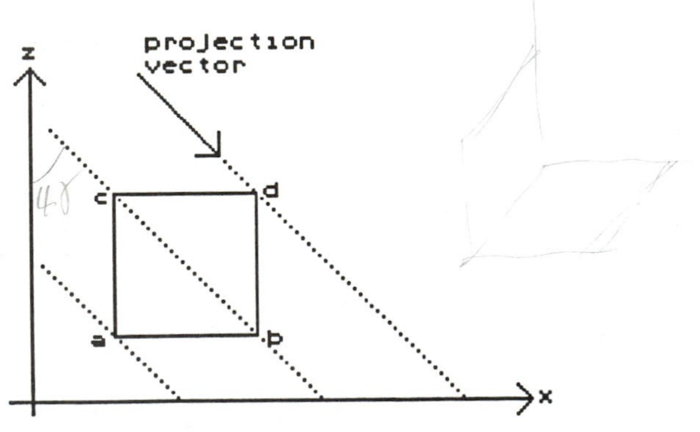


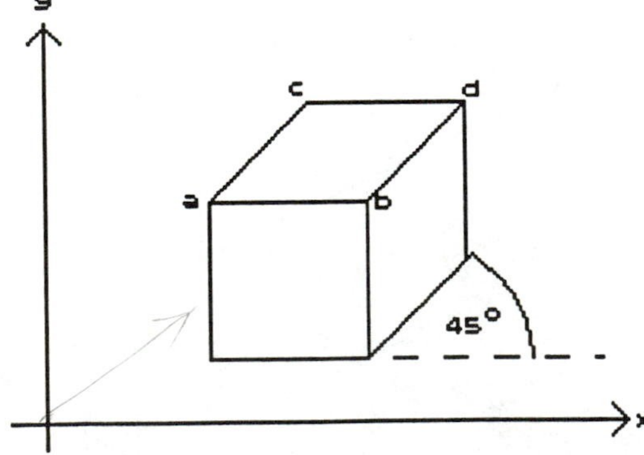


**FIGURE 6.2** Cavalier projection.

the z-axis result in lines at an angle of 30° with the horizontal. We set $z_p = -1$; we also have $\tan 30° = 0.577$. It follows that $0.577x_p = y_p$ or $0.333{x_p}^2 = {y_p}^2$, and we have ${x_p}^2 + {y_p}^2 = 1/4$, so $1.333{x_p}^2 = 0.25$. From this we get $x_p = 0.433$. The projection vector is $(.433, .25, -1)$.

The left drawing in Figure 6.3 shows our view of the cube as we look down the y-axis toward the origin in a left-handed system. On the right is its projection onto the plane $z = 0$ with this projection vector (hidden lines are not shown). This projection obviously produces a much more realistic-looking image than the cavalier projection.

## 6.1.2 Perspective Projection

*Perspective projection* is the preferred method since it comes closest to the way that real world objects are projected into the human eye. This projection technique is important not only in computer graphics but in most pictures and drawings. We all know that objects that are farther away appear smaller. This property is preserved by perspective projection. First, we need a center of projection. In the real world this center is the human eye. In computer graphics, it is basically the same.

In what follows, the word "center" stands for the center of projection. We compute the projection for some assumed position of the center. This assumed center is a point in front of the screen. It will be specified in the same coordinate system that we use in object space for the description of the object. It has no relation to the real physical distance of the user from the screen. The screen itself is assumed to be in the plane $z = 0$ of the coordinate system. The object will be described so that it is positioned behind the screen as seen by the user. Since we use a left-handed system, all z-coordinates of the object will be positive.

**FIGURE 6.3** Cabinet projection.

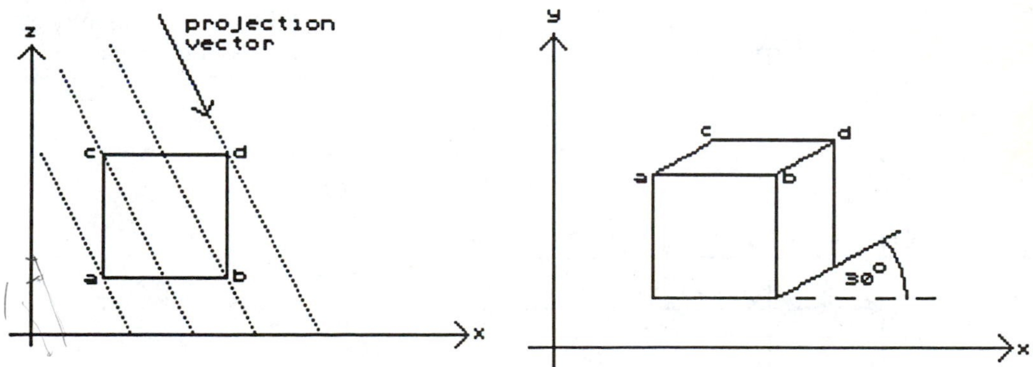

The distance of the center of projection from the plane $z = 0$ (the screen) is called d (and this will be given as a positive number). We assume that the coordinates of the center of projection are $(0,0,-d)$, that is, the center lies on the z-axis. With these assumptions the computations are simple.

The *projection* of a point is the intersection of the straight line from that point to the center with the plane $z = 0$. Figure 6.4 shows the side view of the projection of the point $(x,y,z)$ to give the point $(x_{ps}, y_{ps})$. Through similar triangles we get $y_{ps}/d = y/(d+z)$. We get $x_{ps}$ similarly. The coordinates of the projection are:

$$x_{ps} = d*x/(d+z)$$
$$y_{ps} = d*y/(d+z)$$
$$z_{ps} = 0$$

The assumptions that the center is on the z-axis and that the plane of projection is at $z = 0$ are not restricting, because the formulas for a perspective projection with another center and onto another plane can be obtained by adding a translation. View-plane transformations will always put the center of projection on the z-axis. It is essential, however, that the plane onto which we project be normal to the z-axis; this is necessary to give us simple formulas.

Figure 6.5 shows a prism as the object, the projection plane, the center, and the projection of the prism. This is a visual explanation of the process.

We consider the screen to be a part of the projection plane. That rectangular region of the screen within which we want to display an image is a viewport. If we want to know which part of the object space can be projected into the viewport, we have to draw lines from the center of projection through the four corners of the viewport. These lines will become the edges of the so-called *viewing pyramid*. The pro-

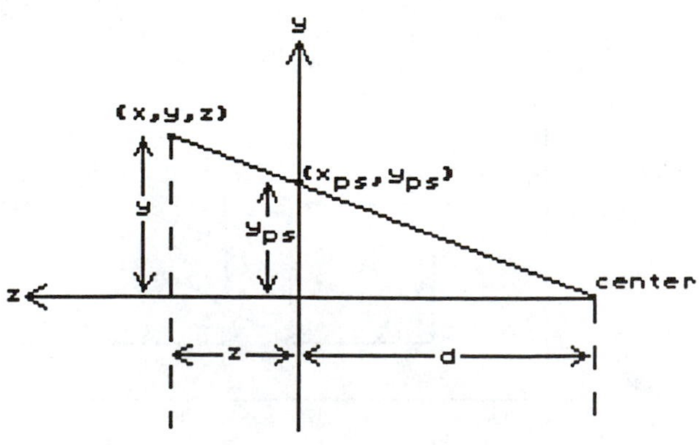


**FIGURE 6.4** Geometry of a perspective projection.

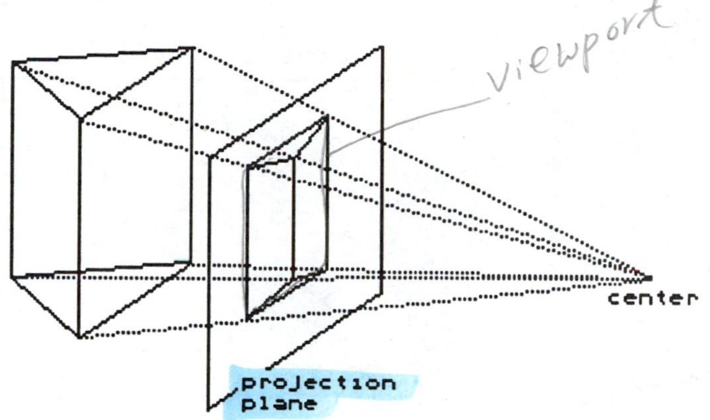


**FIGURE 6.5** Spatial view of a perspective projection.

jection center will be the top of this pyramid. Everything within the viewing pyramid will be visible (unless depth clipping is performed) and everything outside will be invisible. The viewing pyramid is also called the *view volume* in the case of a perspective projection. Figure 6.6 shows a viewing pyramid. The rectangle in the figure is the viewport (usually the screen). The coordinate origin is the center of the rectangle.

## 6.1.3 Perspective Depth Transformation

A *perspective depth transformation* does more than just compute a perspective projection. It transforms every point in object space into a point in image space, with image space now being understood as three-dimensional. This seems to be a contradiction in terms and there is really something artificial about this transformation. However, it is very useful for algorithms that need to know not only the projection of an object point but also its distance from the projection plane. Z-buffer and depth-sorting methods are two algorithms that use it.

In this projection, the image space is augmented to a three-dimensional space. The $x_{ps}$ and $y_{ps}$ coordinates of a transformed point specify the location of a perspective projection of this point into a two-dimensional image space exactly as above. The transformation also calculates a $z_{ps}$-coordinate; it is not set to 0. The interpretation of the $x_{ps}$- and $y_{ps}$-coordinates is not changed. The purpose of all this is to save the depth information of the original object point. The perspective projection of a point is then obtained by ignoring the $z_{ps}$ coordinate.

If we choose $x_{ps} = d*x/(d+z)$, $y_{ps} = d*y/(d+z)$, and simply $z_{ps} = z$ as suggested by some authors, we keep the depth information but this is a bad choice because such a transformation does not transform straight lines into straight lines. It is not a linear transformation.

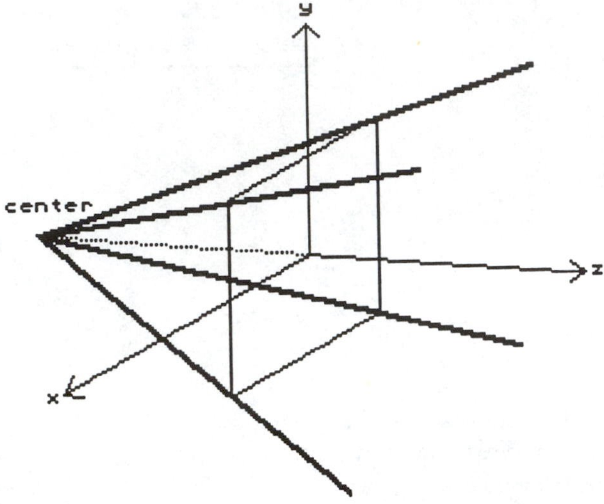


FIGURE 6.6 Viewing pyramid.

This has important consequences for algorithms that obtain their depth information from the image space—they will yield wrong results. Objects are usually described by vertices in space which are connected by straight lines or by planar polygons. A nonlinear transformation does not allow us to transform such an object by transforming all its vertices into image space and connecting the transformed vertices by straight lines or polygons. If (x,y) is a point on the object between two vertices, there is no depth information stored for it.

Figure 6.7 shows what can happen when $z_{ps}$ is just taken equal to z. A point or small object B is behind a planar surface which is shown in cross section; A and C are points in that surface. The transformed

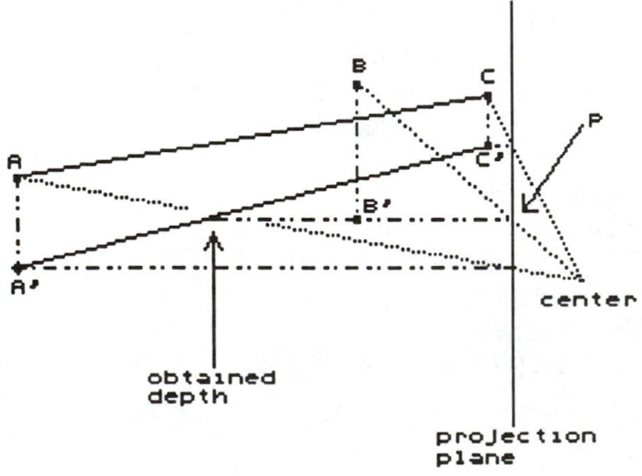


FIGURE 6.7 Effect of a nonlinear depth transformation.

points are A′, B′, and C′. To determine if B′ is in front or behind the surface A′C′, the algorithm computes the depth of the surface at the point (x,y) on the screen into which B is projected. Since it computes this depth as if A′C′ were a plane (which is not true), it gets a wrong value. Observe that the relative depths of the projected points puts B′ on the wrong side of the surface if the original z-values are used.

The explanation for the error is that the transformed surface A′C′ is not planar but curved. It actually passes between B′ and the projection plane, but this is not apparent from the original z-values.

The correct definition of $z_{ps}$ is $z_{ps} = z/(z+d)$ (for further analysis see NESP79, p.356). If ps(P) denotes the transformation of a point P, $\alpha$ and $\beta$ being constants, then $ps(\alpha P_1 + \beta P_2) \neq \alpha ps(P_1) + \beta ps(P_2)$. That is, we don't have linearity in the usual sense, yet straight lines are transformed into straight lines and planes into planes! To show this requires lengthy calculations and we will not do it. A hint of how to show it is given in the exercises.

A correct perspective depth transformation consists of:

$$x_{ps} = d*x/(d+z)$$
$$y_{ps} = d*y/(d+z)$$
$$z_{ps} = z/(d+z)$$

This preserves the relative depth of points in the object. By this we mean that even though the depth values in image and object space are not the same, their relative order will be preserved. This is easily shown. If $z_1 < z_2$, it follows that $z_1/(z_1+d) < z_2/(z_2+d)$. In other words, a point with larger z-coordinate in object space will have a larger z-coordinate in image space.

Let us look at some properties of this transformation. If we have a left-handed system and assume all objects to be "behind" the screen (in the area of positive z-coordinates), then the smallest z-coordinate of a transformed point can be 0 and the largest can approach 1. (It is possible to choose a different formula for obtaining $z_{ps}$ in order to give the $z_{ps}$-values a range different from 0-1, but this one is the most convenient.) All points in object space that lie on a ray emanating from the projection center are transformed onto a line that is parallel to the z-axis and bounded by 0 and 1, because of the definition of $z_{ps}$. It follows that the viewing pyramid behind the screen is transformed into a rectangular box, called the *view box,* which is bounded by the viewport on the projection plane and whose depth is 1 (see Figure 6.8). All objects in the viewing pyramid will be transformed into that box and their perspective projections can be obtained by performing an orthographic projection from the box onto the projection plane. This perspective depth transformation is often called a *normalized view box transformation* (normalized because of the 0-1 range of the $z_{ps}$ coordinate).

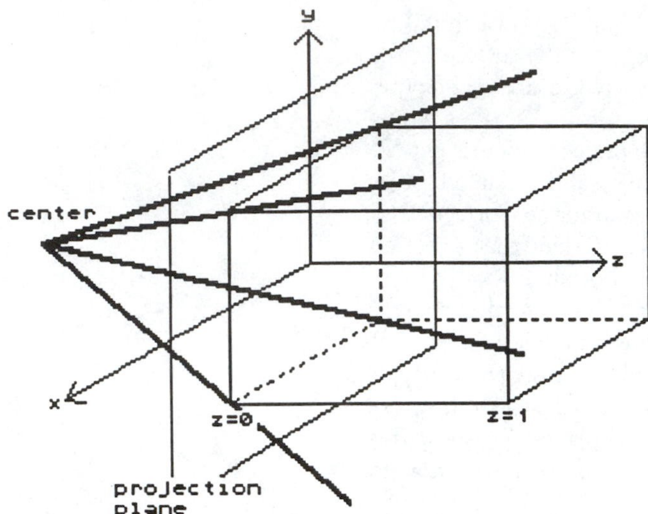


**FIGURE 6.8** The normalized view box transformation.

# 6.2 View Plane Transformations

Once an object has been been specified in its three dimensions, the graphics system should be able to produce any view of it. If we want to see it from the side or from behind, the system should be able to compute how the object would look from such a viewpoint and display the appropriate image. The mathematics necessary for these computations is explained in this section.

Let us see how we must interact with the system for such transformations. To see an object from the side we can rotate it around the y-axis by 90 degrees; this is easy to imagine. To see it from a point to the side and somewhat above the object, we can first rotate it about the y-axis by 90 degrees and then about the x-axis by a few degrees, or we could first rotate it around the z-axis by a few degrees and then around the y-axis by 90 degrees. In the latter case it is not as easy to specify the rotations needed for obtaining the view. In most cases they are hard to imagine. An additional requirement is to specify whether the rotation is ccw or cw.

Specifying a view by specifying the rotations about axes is not user friendly. How then should we tell the system what view of the object we want? The easiest and most natural way of specifying a view is to define the point in space from which the object should be viewed and have the system automatically derive all parameters for rotations and translations.

To specify the point in space from which we want to see the object, the *viewpoint,* we do not just use its Cartesian coordinates. Instead, we specify a direction vector N which points from that viewpoint to the object and the distance d from the viewpoint to the object. To do this, we must chose a point R, on or close to the object, as a reference point. R is the point onto which we focus our view.

Imagine that we place a screen at the viewpoint and aim it toward the object like a camera. We sit immediately behind this screen and look through it at the object. The distance of the screen from the reference point is d. The direction in which we look at the object is the vector N. The screen must be normal to the viewing direction (see Figure 6.9).

Imagine a coordinate system that has as its origin the viewpoint on the screen, its x-axis pointing to the right, its y-axis pointing up, and its z-axis identical with the viewing direction N. This coordinate system is called the *view plane system.* The (x,y)-plane of this system, where $z = 0$, is the view plane. The viewing direction N is called the *view plane normal* and d is called the *view distance.* We can think of the screen as being embedded in the view plane. From now on, we will talk of the view plane and not the screen.

The three items R, N, and d specify the viewpoint unambiguously. However, the view plane system itself is not yet adequately specified. Only the z-axis is fixed (the z-axis coincides with N). We need to fix one other axis to have an unambiguous specification of the view plane system. We will fix the y-axis to point upward by specifying a so-called *view-up direction.*

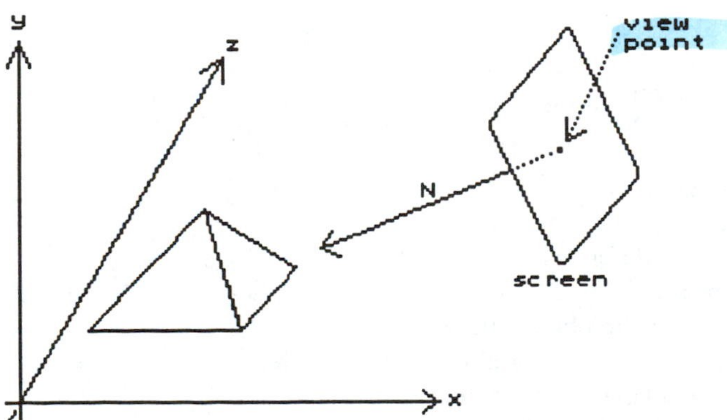


**FIGURE 6.9**

The user should not have to tell precisely the direction of the y-axis, because that would require specifying a vector normal to N. This would be difficult and not user friendly. We take a different approach.

The up direction is specified in relation to the object by a vector. This is easy to do. We then use the projection onto the view plane of this vector as the up direction in the view plane system. In other words, the direction of the y-axis of the view plane system is determined by this projection. This fixes the y-axis and with it the whole view plane system. The projection onto the view plane of this vector will be computed automatically and the y-axis of the view plane system will be aligned with it. If we don't tell the system what is "up" we could get a view of the object that shows it—although from the correct viewpoint—tilted or maybe even upside down.

There is one case in which this approach does not work—when we look straight down on the object. In this case the view-up vector points straight toward the view plane, that is, straight toward us, and it is parallel to N. Such a viewing situation does not make any sense. Seen from straight above through the view plane, the object has no up direction; all orientations are equal. The image on the screen will depend on how we position ourselves behind it. A projection of the view-up vector cannot be computed. In such a case we have to provide the view-up direction to the system in a different way. We will discuss more about this later.

Except for that special case, we can now compute, from the original coordinates of the object, the coordinates of the object in the view plane system. Using these, we can compute how to display it on the screen. The transformation from original coordinates to view plane coordinates is called the *view plane transformation.* The mathematics for this is explained below.

The user specifies the view reference point, the view plane normal, the view-up direction, and the view distance:

| | |
|---|---|
| $(R_x,R_y,R_z)$ | view reference point |
| $(N_x,N_y,N_z)$ | view plane normal |
| $(U_x,U_y,U_z)$ | view-up direction |
| $d$ | view distance |

Figure 6.10 is an example that identifies these vectors. The object is a solid pyramid. The view reference point is at the center of the base of the pyramid. The vector pointing to the view reference point is shown in full. The y-axis of the view plane system is indicated by yv.

What we need to do now is to reposition the object and with it the view plane system so that the viewpoint is at the origin of the object's coordinate system. We want the view plane normal coincident with the positive z-axis and the view plane y-axis coincident with the positive y-axis. To do this, we consider the object, the view-up vector,

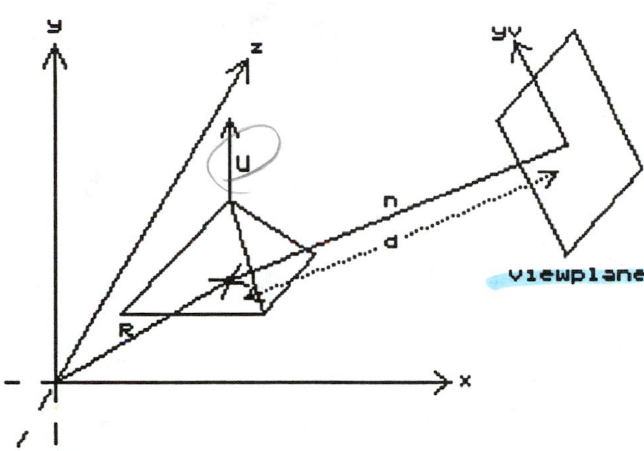


**FIGURE 6.10**

the view plane normal, and the view plane as one rigid unit which we shift around and rotate in space as an entity.

First some computations are necessary. The view plane normal as specified by the triple $(N_x,N_y,N_z)$ does not necessarily have the length d, so we adjust it to this length by computing:

$$L = \sqrt{N_x^2+N_y^2+N_z^2}$$
$$n_x = N_x*d/L$$
$$n_y = N_y*d/L$$
$$n_z = N_z*d/L \quad (1)$$

$(n_x,n_y,n_z)$ is the adjusted view plane normal. We then compute the length of its projection p on the (y,z)-plane:

$$p = \sqrt{n_y^2+n_z^2} \quad (2)$$

The first transformation is a translation by $(-R_x, -R_y, -R_z)$. This will move the view reference point to the origin (see Figure 6.11). The matrix that does this is:

$$\mathbf{T}_R = \begin{pmatrix} 1 & 0 & 0 & 0 \\ 0 & 1 & 0 & 0 \\ 0 & 0 & 1 & 0 \\ -R_x & -R_y & -R_z & 1 \end{pmatrix}$$

The next transformation is a translation by $(n_x,n_y,n_z)$. This will move the start point of the view plane normal into the origin (see Figure 6.12). The matrix that does this is:

$$\mathbf{T}_n = \begin{pmatrix} 1 & 0 & 0 & 0 \\ 0 & 1 & 0 & 0 \\ 0 & 0 & 1 & 0 \\ n_x & n_y & n_z & 1 \end{pmatrix}$$

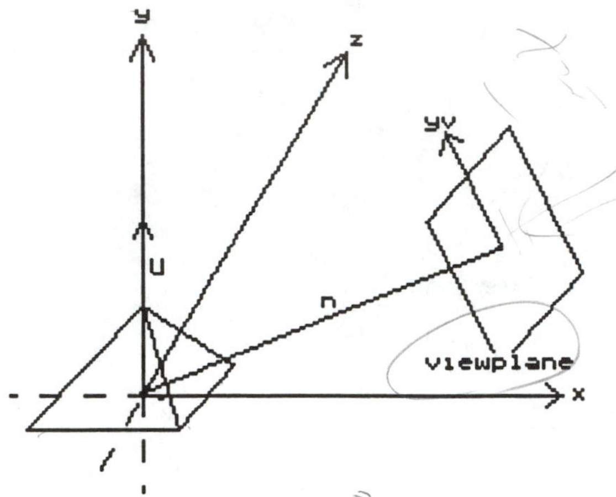


**FIGURE 6.11**

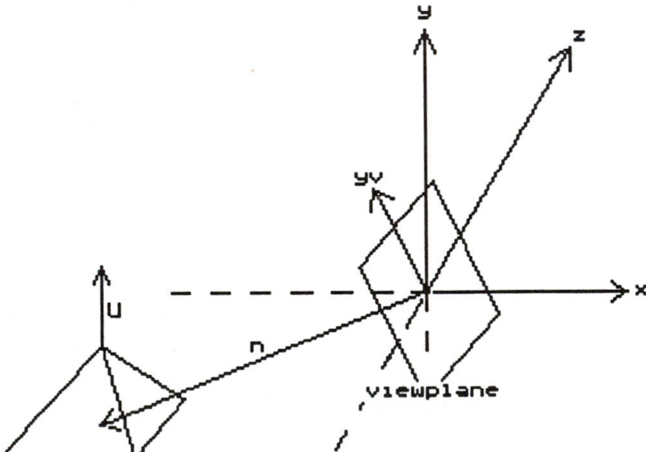


**FIGURE 6.12**

Next we rotate from y to z around the x-axis to put the view plane normal into the (x,z)-plane. Figure 6.13 shows the situation after this rotation. The matrix that does this is:

$$\mathbf{R}_x = \begin{pmatrix} 1 & 0 & 0 & 0 \\ 0 & n_z/p & n_y/p & 0 \\ 0 & -n_y/p & n_z/p & 0 \\ 0 & 0 & 0 & 1 \end{pmatrix}$$

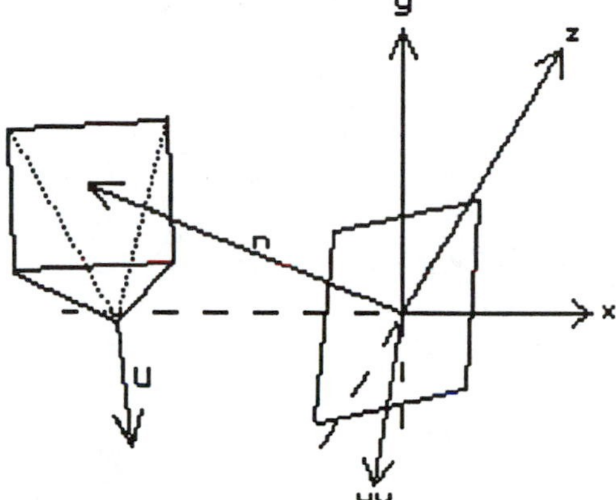


FIGURE 6.13

Now we rotate from x to z around the y-axis to put the view plane normal into the z-axis. Figure 6.14 shows the situation after this rotation. The matrix that does this is:

$$R_y = \begin{pmatrix} p/d & 0 & n_x/d & 0 \\ 0 & 1 & 0 & 0 \\ -n_x/d & 0 & p/d & 0 \\ 0 & 0 & 0 & 1 \end{pmatrix}$$

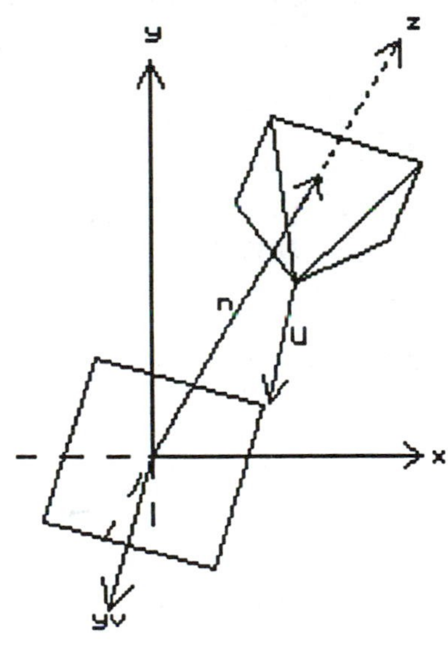


FIGURE 6.14

The view plane y-axis that pointed up in relation to the original object will not, after all these transformations, ordinarily point upward. That is, it will not be aligned with the original positive y-axis. It will point up relative to the object, in the sense that it was specified, because it was transformed together with the object, but it might now be tilted in any direction. If we project the object as it is now onto the screen, we get what is shown in Figure 6.15.

What is indicated as u is the projection of the view-up vector on the view plane. This projection points in the direction of the view plane's y-axis (recall that the direction of the view plane's y-axis is defined by this projection). We want this y-axis to coincide with the y-axis of the original coordinate system. This can be obtained through a rotation around the z-axis.

We have to find the angle for this rotation. The object has undergone certain transformations so far. We were also to transform the vector U. To know the coordinates of the transformed vector U, we apply the same transformations as we applied to the object. The first two transformations were translations; as U is a vector, it is not changed by a

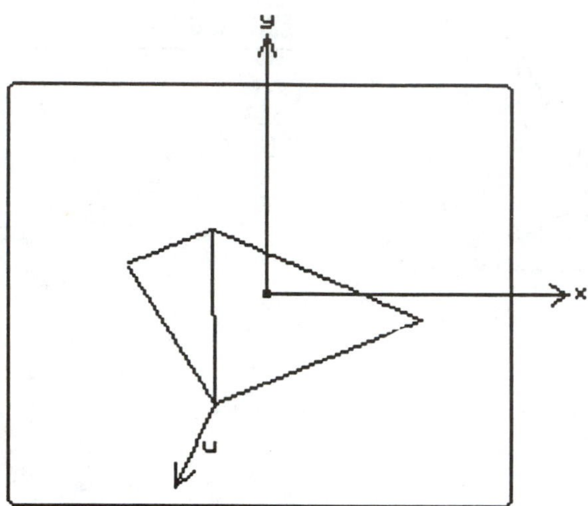


FIGURE 6.15

translation (see Figures 6.10 and 6.11). The two rotations do have to be performed, so we must multiply:

$$(U_x, U_y, U_z, 1)\begin{pmatrix} 1 & 0 & 0 & 0 \\ 0 & n_z/p & n_y/p & 0 \\ 0 & -n_y/p & n_z/p & 0 \\ 0 & 0 & 0 & 1 \end{pmatrix}\begin{pmatrix} p/d & 0 & n_x/d & 0 \\ 0 & 1 & 0 & 0 \\ -n_x/d & 0 & p/d & 0 \\ 0 & 0 & 0 & 1 \end{pmatrix}$$

Let the result be $(u_x, u_y, u_z, 1)$. The projection of this vector on the view plane is $(u_x, u_y)$. What we see in Figure 6.15 is actually this projection! An explicit expression for $u_x$ and $u_y$ is:

$$u_x = U_x\frac{p}{d} - \frac{n_x}{dp}(U_y n_y + U_z n_z) \qquad u_y = \frac{1}{p}(U_y n_z + U_z n_y) \tag{3}$$

The length of this projection is:

$$w = \sqrt{u_x^2 + u_y^2} \tag{4}$$

The sine and cosine of the angle between this projection and the positive y-axis are $u_x/w$ and $u_y/y$, as you can see in Figure 6.16. We therefore have to rotate the object around z in the direction from x to y, by multiplying with the matrix:

$$R_z = \begin{pmatrix} u_y/w & u_x/w & 0 & 0 \\ -u_x/w & u_y/w & 0 & 0 \\ 0 & 0 & 1 & 0 \\ 0 & 0 & 0 & 1 \end{pmatrix}$$

This final rotation will align the view plane y-axis with the original y-axis so both coordinate systems are now identical.

FIGURE 6.16

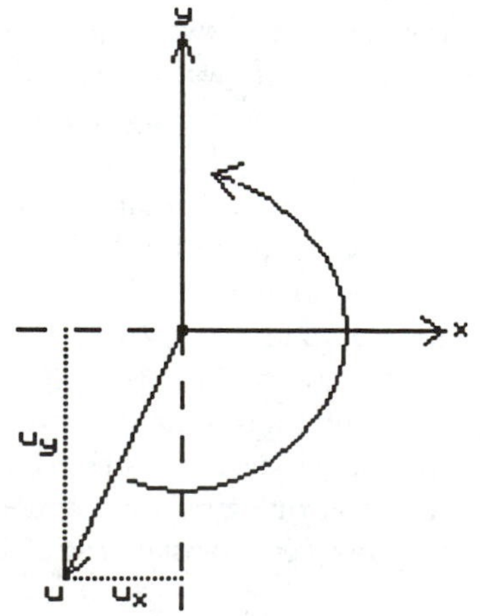

To summarize, the view plane transformation begins with four initial computations. We find $(n_x,n_y,n_z)$ from (1) and p from (2). We compute $(u_x,u_y)$ from (3) and w from (4). Following this, we transform every point (x,y,z) of the object to $(x_v,y_v,z_v)$ by performing the matrix multiplications below in the indicated order:

$$(x_v,y_v,z_v) = (x,y,z)\,\mathbf{T}_R\,\mathbf{T}_n\,\mathbf{R}_x\,\mathbf{R}_y\,\mathbf{R}_z.$$

These transformations change the coordinates of the object in its initial position within the original coordinate system into the new coordinates of its transformed position. This new position is precisely the view we want of the object. However, the object's position does not change in relation to the view plane system because we transform that system together with the object. Hence, the transformed coordinates of the object describe it not only in respect to the original system but also in the view plane system, as both systems now coincide.

As we mentioned above, there is a case in which the alignment of the view plane y-axis with the projected view-up vector U cannot be performed: when U is parallel to the view plane normal. In this case the projection of U on the view plane has the length 0, so we get w = 0 in (4). The sine and cosine for the rotation cannot be found. We have to consider this possibility in order to avoid a division by 0. The easiest solution, and it is as good as any other, is just not to perform the multiplication with $R^z$ in the case of w = 0. This means that the object will end up having an unpredictable orientation on the screen. But that is insignificant in this case. (Another possibility is to provide an arbitrary vector to align with if w = 0).

**Coded Algorithm** The procedure vpt_mat below computes the overall transformation matrix trafo for a view plane transformation. The user calls it with the arguments ref, normal, up, and d as specified in the procedure. The first three are declared as three-component vectors, called point in the type declaration, while d is a real number. Two checks are necessary to avoid divisions by zero: one to find whether the view plane normal is parallel to the x-axis, in which case no rotation around x is performed; the other to find whether w = 0, in which case no rotation around z is done.

The actual view plane transformation is done outside this procedure by performing a vector-matrix multiplication with trafo of the type shown in the previous development. This is done for all points of the object.

```
type point    =  record x,y,z : real
                 end;
     matrix   =  array[1..4,1..4] of real;
```

```
procedure vpt_mat(ref,normal,
                          up  :  point;
                           d  :  real;
                   var trafo  :  matrix);

var m            :     matrix;
    h,l,p,w      :     real;

pocedure idmat(var m : matrix);
{sets the matrix m to an identity matrix}
begin
  for i := 1 to 4 do
  for j := 1 to 4 do
    if i = j
    then m[i,j] := 1
    else m[i,j] := 0
end {procedure idmat};

procedure matmult(var trafo : matrix;
                          m : matrix);
{computes the product of trafo and m
 and puts it into trafo}
var h          :    matrix;
    i,j,k      :    integer;
    sum        :    real;

begin
  for i := 1 to 4 do
  for j := 1 to 4 do
    h[i,j] := trafo[i,j];
  for i := 1 to 4 do
  for j := 1 to 4 do begin
    sum := 0;
    for k := 1 to 4 do
      sum := sum + h[i,k]*m[k,j];
    trafo[i,j] := sum
  end
end {procedure matmult};

begin
  with normal do begin
    h := sqrt(x*x+y*y+z*z);
    x := x/h; y := y/h; z := z/h;
    p := sqrt(y*y+z*z)
  end;

  with up do begin {the z-coordinate is not needed}
    if p > 0.00001
```

```
    then begin
      x := x*p/d-normal.x/(d*p)*(y*normal.y+z*normal.z);
      y := (y*normal.z+z*normal.y)/p
    end
    else
      x := -z*normal.x/d;
    w := sqrt(x*x+y*y)
  end;

  idmat(trafo);
  trafo[4,1] := -ref.x+normal.x;
  trafo[4,2] := -ref.y+normal.y;
  trafo[4,3] := -ref.z+normal.z;

  if p > 0.00001
  then with normal do begin
    idmat(m);
    m[2,2] :=  z/p; m[2,3] := y/p;
    m[3,2] := -y/p; m[3,3] := z/p;
    matmult(trafo,m)
  end;

  idmat(m);
  m[1,1] :=  p/d;          m[1,3] := normal.x/d;
  m[3,1] := -normal.x/d; m[3,3] := p/d;
  matmult(trafo,m);

  if w > 0.00001
  then with up do begin
    idmat(m);
    m[1,1] :=  y/w; m[1,2] := x/w;
    m[2,1] := -x/w; m[2,2] := y/w;
    matmult(trafo,m)
  end
end {procedure vpt_mat};
```

# 6.3 THREE-DIMENSIONAL WINDOWING AND CLIPPING

A 3-D window is analogous to a 2-D window. Since the latter is a rectangular area of our visual perception of the real world, we extend this notion to three dimensions by defining a 3-D window as a rectangular box in space. This extension is not a very natural one because what we perceive from the real world is always a two-dimensional projection. Our visual system can add the feeling of depth through stereo vision and complicated internal processing but we don't think in 3-D windows.

Our perception of the real world is bounded at the left, right, bottom, and top—objects can be outside these areas but we don't see them. It is bounded at the front only by the physical presence of our perception mechanism—objects can be physically no closer than 0 from our eyes. An object that is behind us must be considered as being outside the left, right, bottom, or top boundary because we must turn our head to see it. Outside the front boundary is not physically possible.

Our perception of distant objects is unbounded. While distant objects may appear so small that we cannot make out details, still they are in our field of view. Hence, there exists no bounding of our perception from front to back in the same sense as it exists with left, right, bottom, and top.

For these reasons, a 3-D window is something artificial and is not a true generalization of the 2-D window concept. We will not call it a window; instead, we will call it a *view volume.* In some applications in computer graphics it is very useful to have such a view volume; for example, if we want to display only a part of a scene that has been defined in 3-D space.

### 6.3.1 Three-Dimensional Windows and View Volumes

The rectangular box in space that describes the view volume must be associated with numbers in certain ranges. We can consider the left-right range as the extent of the x-coordinates, the up-down range as the extent of the y-coordinates, and the front-back range as the extent of the z-coordinates. We require the front plane of this view volume to be parallel to the view plane, which normally coincides with the screen. The contents of the view volume will be projected onto the screen. (We will use the words screen and view plane interchangeably.) The projection of the view volume onto the screen acts like a 2-D window.

The different types of projections lead to different shapes of these view volumes. That is, 3-D windows may be of various shapes, not just rectangular boxes.

**Orthographic Projection** In this case the view volume is a rectangular box whose front plane is parallel to or coincident with the view plane. Objects within the box are visible when projected ortho-

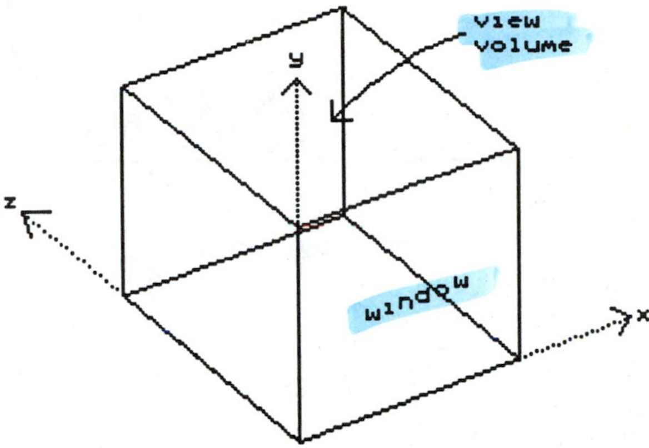


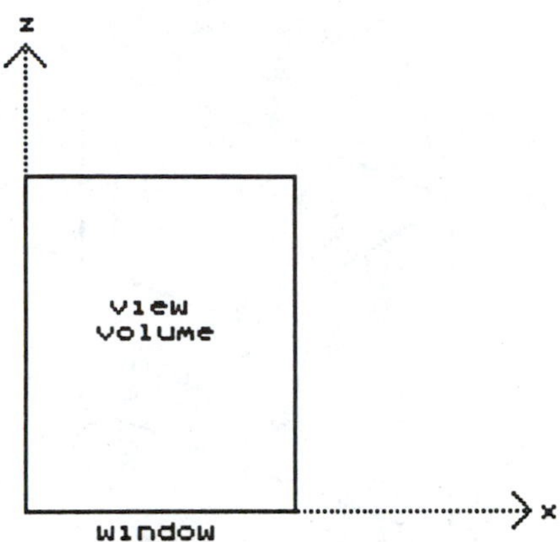


**FIGURE 6.17** Orthographic view volume.

graphically onto the view plane. Figure 6.17 shows an orthographic view volume in spatial view and top view.

**Oblique Projection** In this case, the view volume is a slanted parallelepiped. Objects within the view volume are visible when projected obliquely onto the view plane. Figure 6.18 shows an oblique view volume in spatial view and top view.

**Perspective Projection** In this case, the view volume is a truncated pyramid called a *frustrum.* The apex of the pyramid is the center of projection. Objects within the frustrum are visible when projected

**FIGURE 6.18** Oblique view volume.

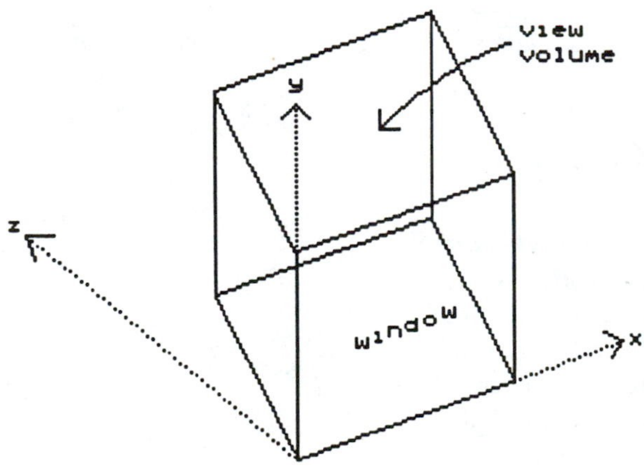


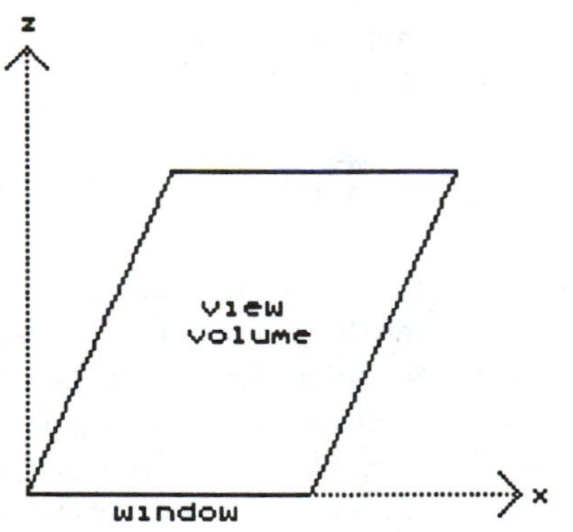

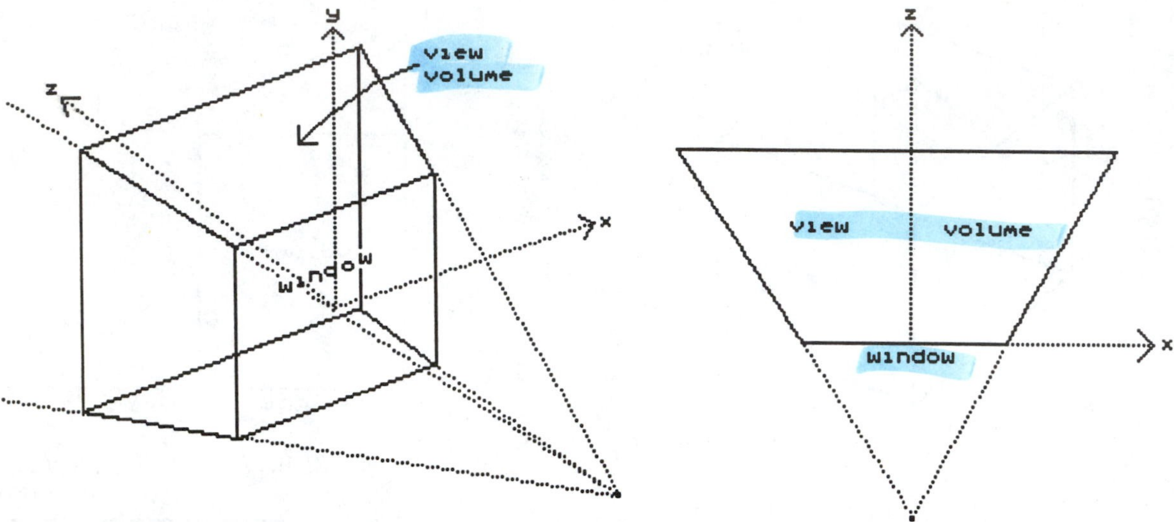


FIGURE 6.19 Perspective view volume.

perspectively onto the view plane. Figure 6.19 shows a perspective view volume in spatial view and top view.

The essential feature of these view volumes is that they are bounded from near to far (or front to back). In the figures above, the "near" plane is the view plane and the "far" plane is the other plane parallel to it. We can define *unbounded view volumes* in which unbounded applies in practical terms to the far plane only. The viewing pyramid of Figure 6.6 in this chapter is an example. We stated then that everything within this pyramid is visible—unless depth clipping is performed—and everything outside is not. Unbounded view volumes serve only as abstract models to visualize the various projection types; they are not useful for anything else.

## 6.3.2 Three-Dimensional Clipping

*Bounded view volumes* are used to perform *depth clipping*. This is a process that removes those parts of a three-dimensional scene that are closer than the near plane or farther than the far plane. (Actually, clipping is performed against all bounding planes of the volume and therefore is called 3-D clipping, but depth clipping is the "new" feature.) The bounded view volumes are often called *clipping volumes*. In the real world nothing can be closer than the near plane (the near plane being our eyes) but in computer graphics this is possible. Clipping such parts of a scene can be necessary because the projection algorithms do not distinguish between objects at greater and lesser depth and therefore project everything in the scene, even objects that are behind us. We don't see an object that is behind us, so that is a good reason for clipping it. Also, in perspective projection, an object in front of the near plane and very close to the center of projection would have a projection so large that it could obscure the whole picture.

Interesting effects can be obtained by depth clipping, interesting because they don't exist in the real world. We can, for example, walk through a scene, through houses, walls, and other objects. In walking forward we push the near and far planes forward also. When the near plane intersects an object, the part closer than the near plane is removed and we are able to see into the object or at least produce images of such an effect.

The sequence of Figure 6.20 shows a scene consisting of a wall with an open door and two objects: a table and a chair. On the left is a side view of the perspective view volume and on the right side the display. The wall and the objects are shown in heavy lines. A realistic display (solid model with removed hidden surfaces, etc.) shows only the front wall and the parts of the objects visible through the open door (see Figure 6.20a). When the view volume is moved forward the objects become larger, but the front wall is still not clipped (see Figure 6.20b). In Figure 6.20c the near plane has penetrated behind the front wall, the front wall is clipped, and the objects behind it become visible. If we did not clip the wall, it would still hide parts of the objects. Depth clipping is the most important aspect of 3-D windowing. It is performed by extended 2-D clipping algorithms that clip the objects against all six planes of the given view volume.

**FIGURE 6.20a** The wall obscures parts of the objects.

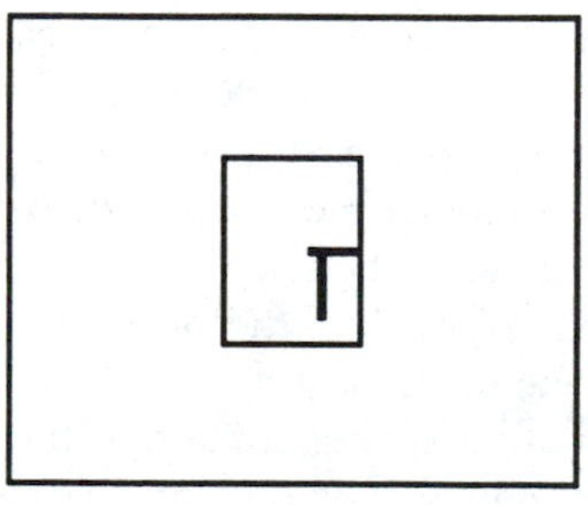

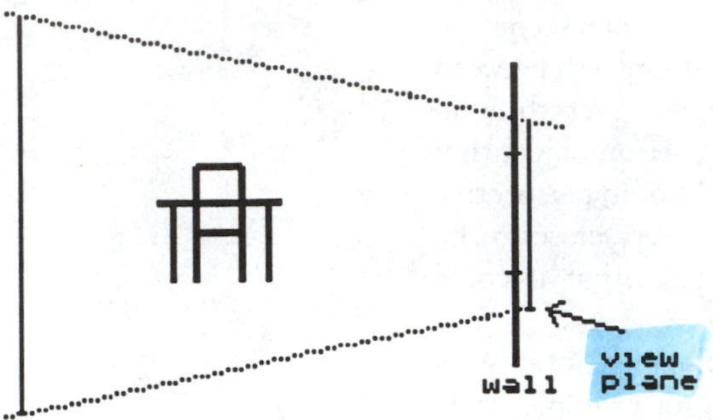


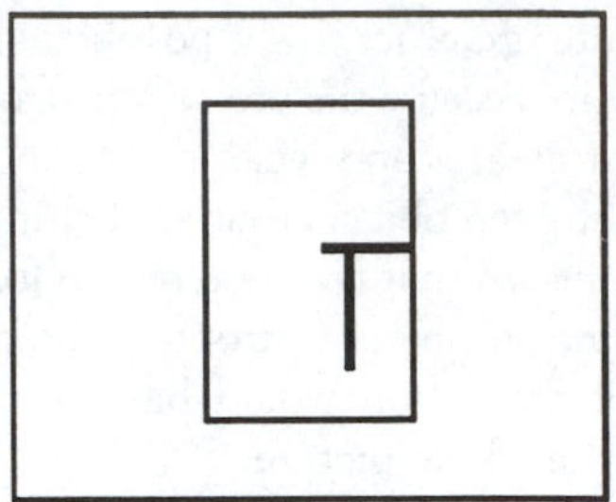

**FIGURE 6.20b** The near plane is closer to the wall.

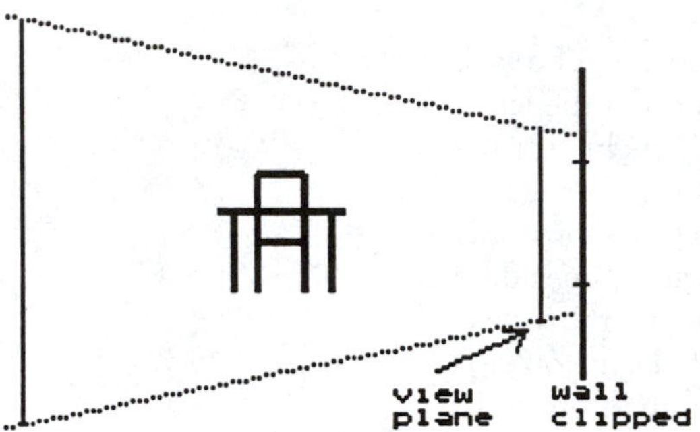


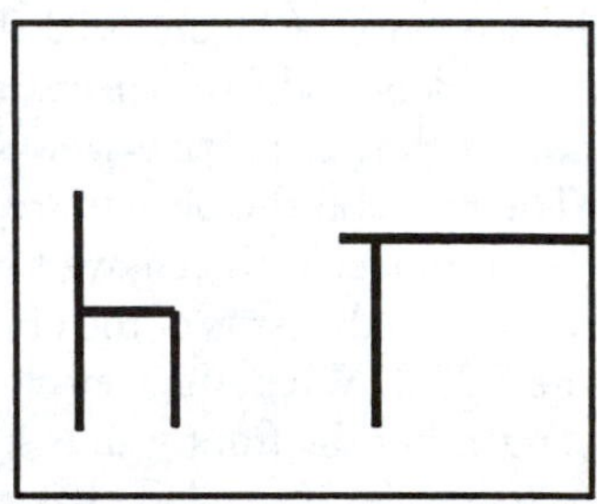

**FIGURE 6.20c** The wall is clipped against the near plane.

Depth clipping could be performed by clipping against the near and far planes only and ignoring the other planes. After projecting the depth-clipped objects onto the view plane, a 2-D clipping algorithm would be used to do the clipping against left, right, bottom, and top. In consequence, many parts of the scene would be projected only to be clipped away afterward. If we clip against all six planes in space before we project, then no superfluous projections will be performed. On the other hand, clipping in space is conceptually more difficult, although it does not require more intensive computations. It is hard to decide which approach is better.

Clipping against the near and far plane has to be done in any case, so one might as well perform the entire 3-D clipping through an extended 2-D clipping algorithm. In the 2-D plane we considered two types of clipping: clipping a single straight line and clipping a polygon.

The latter was more complicated because new edges and vertices had to be created. We have a similar situation here. We can either clip a single straight line or a polygon against all the six planes of the view volume. We first consider clipping a single straight line.

**Clipping a Single Straight Line** We will develop this only for an orthographic view volume; the more general polygon-clipping algorithm for a frustrum will be presented later. The extension of the 2-D Cohen-Sutherland algorithm to the 3-D case is straightforward for an orthographic view volume. The region code of a point (x,y,z) now consists of six bits. We number the bits in the order 5 4 3 2 1 0.

| | |
|---|---|
| bit 5 = 1 if $x <$ left | (= wxl) |
| bit 4 = 1 if $x >$ right | (= wxh) |
| bit 3 = 1 if $y <$ bottom | (= wyl) |
| bit 2 = 1 if $y >$ top | (= wyh) |
| bit 1 = 1 if $z <$ near | (= wzl) |
| bit 0 = 1 if $z >$ far | (= wzh) |
| otherwise all bits are zero | |

We compute the region codes of both end points of the line. Then we test. If the logic OR of the two codes is 0, the line is completely inside the view volume and is trivially accepted. If the logic AND of the two codes is $\neq 0$, the line is completely outside the volume and is trivially rejected. In all other cases there is at least one intersection of the line with a boundary. We compute the intersection and trim the line by replacing the proper end point with the intersection. So the line becomes shorter and shorter until it is totally contained in the volume. The algorithm is analogous to the two-dimensional case and is not repeated.

There is one major difference: we need the intersection of a line with a plane. The six numbers wxl, wxh, wyl, wyh, wzl, wzh are defined above. Let $P_1 = (x_1,y_1,z_1)$ and $P_2 = (x_2,y_2,z_2)$ be the end points of the line to be clipped.

The line through the two points is expressed parametrically by:

$$x = x_1 + s(x_2 - x_1)$$
$$y = y_1 + s(y_2 - y_1)$$
$$z = z_1 + s(z_2 - z_1)$$

To get the intersection with the near plane where $z = wzl$, we find the s value of the intersection point from $wzl = z_1 + s(z_2 - z_1)$, which gives:

$$s = \frac{wzl - z_1}{z_2 - z_1}$$

Inserting this into the above equations gives the intersection point:

$$x = x1 + \frac{wzl - z_1}{z_2 - z_1}(x_2 - x_1), \quad y = y_1 + \frac{wzl - z_1}{z_2 - z_1}(y_2 - y_1), z = wzl$$

We get all the other line-plane intersections as easily.

**Clipping a Polygon** We will extend the 2-D polygon-clipping algorithm to our 3-D case. When we we clipped a polygon against a rectangle, the result was another polygon. Clipping the triangle in Figure 6.21 against the upper right corner of the window resulted in a pentagon. We did not just clip the individual lines because that would have left the polygon open. We inserted vertices and edges to close the "wound."

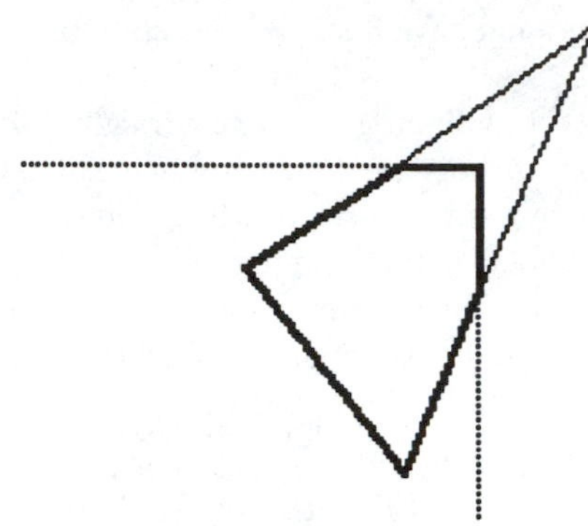

**FIGURE 6.21** The clipped triangle is shown in heavy lines.

What we must do now is to clip 3-D objects against a given view volume. When a volume is clipped against a volume, the result should be a volume. Three-dimensional clipping clips some solid object against the 3-D window—the view volume. This would be the true analogy to the two-dimensional polygon clipping. It is demonstrated in Figure 6.22.

Figure 6.22 shows 3-D clipping of a solid object. The front upper right corner of the view volume is shown in dotted lines. The object is a four sided prism. When clipped against the corner, the result would be similar to the drawing shown on the right. In that, the visible lines are heavy, the hidden lines are light. To achieve this result, not only do we clip off parts of the polygons that constitute this object, but we

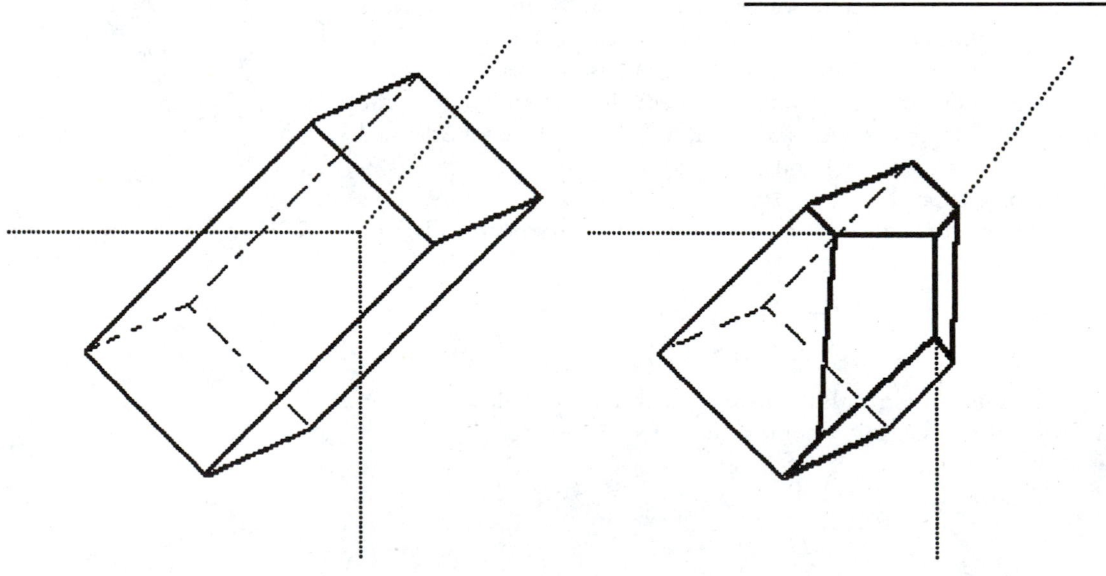

**FIGURE 6.22**

add new polygons to heal the wound. The algorithm can do this only if it has enough information about the object, that is, which vertices are adjacent to form polygons and which polygons are adjacent to form the surface. The analogy to the 2-D case is obvious. In that case, the algorithm needed information about the order of the vertices that formed the edges of the polygon. A polygon was more than just a set of edges or vertices.

We do not present such a general solid clipping algorithm—it would be very complicated. The explanation above was only to make the situation clear. Our algorithm is not a true extension of 2-D polygon clipping; it will clip individual polygons but it will clip them against a volume instead of a planar rectangle. This fact alone makes this algorithm somewhat demanding. But familiarity with 2-D polygon clipping will help you to understand it.

The volume we clip against is not necessarily rectangular. We will use the general case of a perspective frustrum. Clipping against a rectangular box is a simplification. We also consider only the clipping of a single planar polygon.

In clipping a single polygon, the analogy to the 2-D case is straightforward. We execute a clipping pipe in much the same way. We have four basic clips that are repeated by the six clippers. A basic clip acts exactly as explained in Section 4.2.2, only now it clips a line against a plane. The basic clip has to know the two end points of the line and the plane against which it is clipping. It will find out on which sides of the plane the end points lie. This is more complicated, because the planes are not necessarily parallel to the coordinate axes.

We explain the algorithm through an example without going into as much detail as in Section 4.2.2, but this should help you to understand the code. Our example clips a triangle whose vertices are all outside the view volume. Figure 6.23 shows a view only of the upper right far corner. Since the other planes of the view volume are not involved in this particular example, we avoid superfluous lines in the drawing. Hidden lines are removed to increase the spatial impression. The dotted line from e to b is the intersection line between the triangle plane and the right plane of the view volume. The other dotted lines are similar intersections.

While this spatial view serves to assist our imagination, it is not adequate for visualizing the process. For this we need two drawings that show edge-on views of all planes involved. These two drawings are Figures 6.24 and 6.25. No two planes in a frustrum necessarily intersect at right angles, but a view along the intersection line between two planes will show these two planes as lines. With a top view and a front view, we can position all points of the polygon and all generated inter-

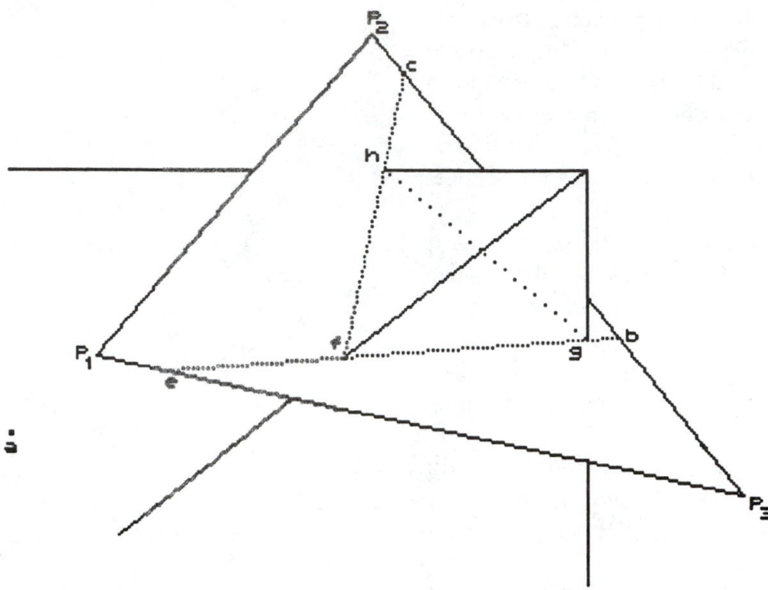


**FIGURE 6.23** Spatial view of the clipping process.

section points unmistakably in relation to the planes. With one spatial view this is not possible.

The clipping pipe is written down in the order:

**L**eft **R**ight **B**ottom **T**op **N**ear **F**ar

which indicates the six planes of the view volume. All clippers are initialized with the left lower near corner of the view volume, which we call O. If a clipper produces no output, a cross + is put behind it to indicate that the point died in the pipe. If a clipper produces two outputs, the second output is written in the next line under the first; the pipe branches. Whenever a point is produced, it must be entered in both edge-on views. In this example it is also entered in the spatial view to help visualize the process. The polygon must be put through the pipe twice. The first time the output serves only to get valid last points. Figure 6.24 is a front view. It shows the top plane and the right plane edge-on. Figure 6.25 is a top view. It shows the far plane and the right plane edge-on. The pipes are now executed:

| | | | | | | | | | | | | |
|---|---|---|---|---|---|---|---|---|---|---|---|---|
| 0 | | 0 | | 0 | | 0 | | 0 | | 0 | | |
| $P_1$ | **L** | $P_1$ | **R** | $P_1$ | **B** | $P_1$ | **T** | a | **N** | a | **F** | a |
| $P_2$ | **L** | $P_2$ | **R** | $P_2$ | **B** | $P_2$ | **T** | + | **N** | | **F** | |
| $P_3$ | **L** | $P_3$ | **R** | b | **B** | b | **T** | c | **N** | c | **F** | d |
| | | | | | | | | b | **N** | b | **F** | + |

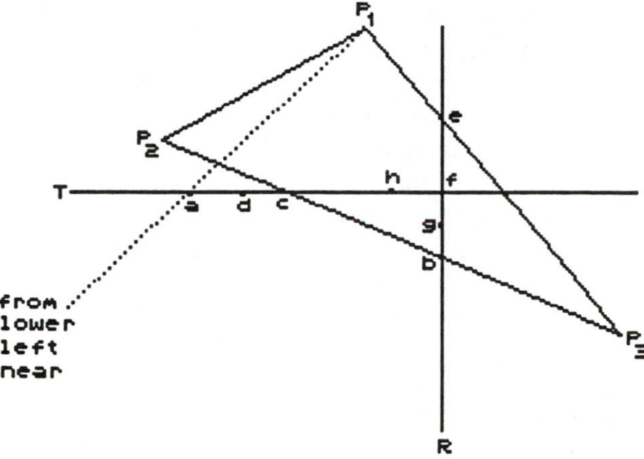


FIGURE 6.24

```
P1 L P1 R e  B e  T f N f F g
          P1 B P1 T +       f
P2 L P2 R P2 B P2 T + N   F
P3 L P3 R b  B b  T c N c F h
                    b N b F +
```

The whole clipping process is condensed in the two pipes. We also see that the second run produces the correct three vertices of the clipped triangle. A few explanations will be helpful.

First the left clipper is called with the line from O to $P_1$ so it produces $P_1$. The same occurs with the right and the bottom clipper. The top clipper then produces the intersection point a. Visually, we construct a from Figure 6.24 and also enter it in Figure 6.23 and 6.25

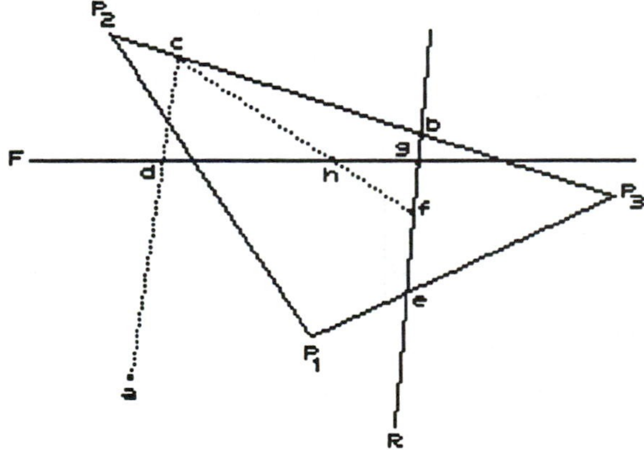


FIGURE 6.25

at the approximate prositions. The pipe outputs an a. Point $P_2$ dies in the pipe. Point $P_3$ will lead to an intersection b with the right plane, but that point is still outside the view volume. Visually, we construct it in Figure 6.24 and also enter it in the other drawings. This point will lead to a branch through the top clipper: we get c and b, constructed in Figure 6.24. The far clipper will produce point d which is the intersection of line ac with the far plane. The following reasoning is typical: As a and c lie in the top plane, d lies there also. As d lies in the far plane it must lie on the edge between top and far. Figure 6.23 does not show d—it is hidden below the triangle. Points a and d are the whole output of the first run.

In the second run $P_1$ leads to point e through the right clipper. It lies on the line from $P_3$ to $P_1$ and therefore in the triangle. It also lies in the right plane, so it lies on the intersection line of the triangle plane with the right plane, as does point b. The top clipper then produces point f where the line from b to e intersects the top plane. Point f therefore lies in the right plane and in the top plane and in the triangle plane. It is one of the intersection points of the triangle with the view volume. The far clipper produces the second intersection point, point g. Point $P_2$ dies in the pipe. Point $P_3$ leads to the third intersection point, point h.

**Mathematics of Three-Dimensional Clipping** We will develop the mathematics for a perspective view volume whose frustrum is shown in Figure 6.26. We make several assumptions. The coordinate system is left-handed; the center of projection is in the middle of the window at a distance of d from it; the window is in the plane $z = 0$ because most projections are done (and practically all can be done) to the plane

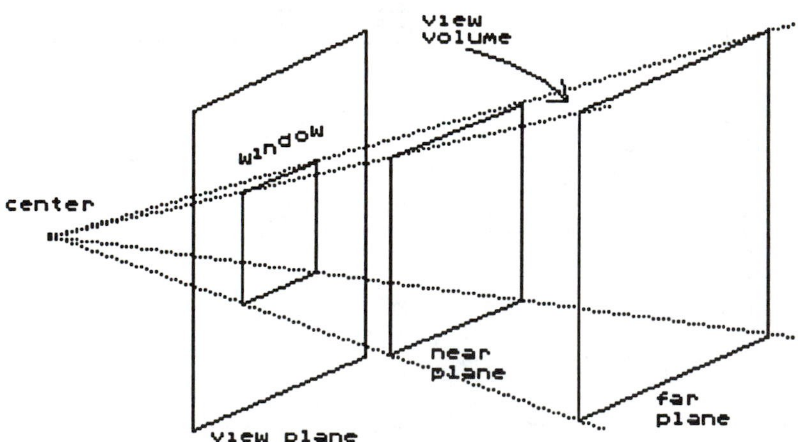


**FIGURE 6.26** General perspective view volume and window.

$z = 0$. The view plane is not coincident with the near plane. The near plane of the view volume is bounded by wxl, wxh, wyl, and wyh. When the perspective projection to the plane $z = 0$ is performed, after the 3-D clipping, everything will be projected into an area with the range wxl, wxh, wyl, and wyh.

These assumptions serve to keep the formulas from becoming too complex and to make the development easier to understand. There is no difficulty in adjusting the formulas to a different view volume position. Positions different from the one assumed are actually not necessary in computer graphics and usually are the result of a poor choice of the coordinate system and/or the center of projection.

We need four constants to express the equations of the four side planes. These are the slopes of the planes in relation to the z-axis. Figure 6.27 shows a vertical cross section through the frustrum and will help in determining the slopes for the top and bottom planes. A similar situation exists for the left and right planes.

slope of the right plane: $s_R = \frac{1}{2}(wxh - wxl)/(d + wzl)$
slope of the left plane: $s_L = -\frac{1}{2}(wxh - wxl)/(d + wzl)$
slope of the top plane: $s_T = \frac{1}{2}(wyh - wyl)/(d + wzl)$
slope of the bottom plane: $s_B = -\frac{1}{2}(wyh - wyl)/(d + wzl)$

With these constants the equations of the planes are:

$$
\begin{aligned}
L:&\ x = wxl + s_L(z - wzl)\\
R:&\ x = wxh + s_R(z - wzl)\\
B:&\ y = wyl + s_B(z - wzl)\\
T:&\ y = wyh + s_T(z - wzl)\\
N:&\ z = wzl\\
F:&\ z = wzh
\end{aligned}
$$

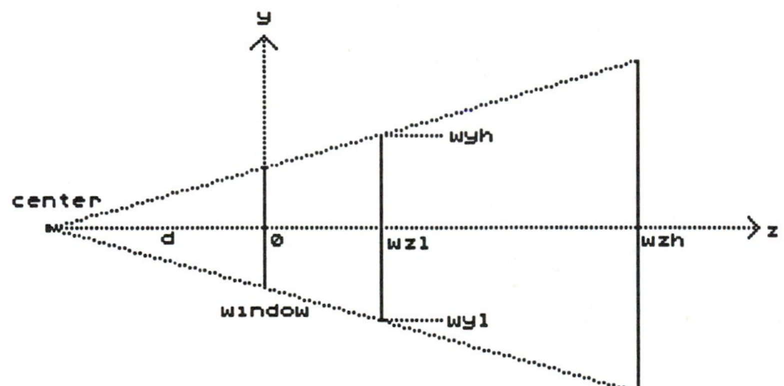


**FIGURE 6.27** Cross section through the view volume.

The near and far planes have especially simple equations. The others are simpler than general plane equations because they are parallel to either the x-axis or the y-axis.

The intersections of a line from $(x_1,y_1,z_1)$ to $(x_2,y_2,z_2)$ with these six planes are found as follows. For the six planes we compute the six t-values:

$$t_L = \frac{x_1 - wxl + s_L(wzl - z_1)}{x_1 - x_2 + s_L(z_2 - z_1)} \qquad t_R = \frac{x_1 - wxh + s_R(wzl - z_1)}{x_1 - z_2 + s_R(z_2 - z_1)}$$

$$t_B = \frac{y_1 - wyl + s_B(wzl - z_1)}{y_1 - y_2 + s_B(z_2 - z_1)} \qquad t_T = \frac{y_1 - wyh + s_T(wzl - z_1)}{y_1 - y_2 + s_T(z_2 - z_1)}$$

$$t_N = \frac{z_1 - wzl}{z_1 - z_2} \qquad t_F = \frac{z_1 - wzh}{z_1 - z_2}$$

The intersection point (x,y,z) with any of the planes is obtained by inserting the appropriate t-value into the parameterized line representation:

$$x = x_1 + t(x_2 - x_1)$$
$$y = y_1 + t(y_2 - y_1)$$
$$z = z_1 + t(z_2 - z_1)$$

A point (x,y,z) is inside the view volume in relation to any of these planes if the corresponding condition is true:

| | |
|---|---|
| for the left plane | $x \geqslant wxl + s_L(z - wzl)$ |
| for the right plane | $x \leqslant wxh + s_R(z - wzl)$ |
| for the bottom plane | $y \geqslant wyl + s_B(z - wzl)$ |
| for the top plane | $y \leqslant wyh + s_T(z - wzl)$ |
| for the near plane | $z \geqslant wzl$ |
| for the far plane | $z \leqslant wzh$ |

**Coded Algorithm** This code is an adaptation of the 2-D clipping code in Section 4.2.2. The variable names and types are kept the same as much as possible to stress the analogies and to make it easier to understand.

```
type    point       =    record x,y,x : real
                         end;
        vertices    =    array[1..10] of point;
var
   wxl,wxh,wyl,
   wyh,wzl,wzh,
             d      :    real;
```

```
procedure polyclip(var vxin,vxout    :  vertices;
                   var innum,outnum  :  integer);
var
  lastl,lastr,lastb,
  lastt,lastn,lastf    :   point;
  sl,sr,sb,st,t        :   real;
  i                    :   integer;

procedure store(x,y,z : real);
begin
  outnum := outnum + 1;
  vxout[outnum].x := x;
  vxout[outnum].y := y;
  vzout[outnum].z := z
end {procedure store};

procedure clip_f(x,y,z : real);
var prl,pr2 : real;
begin
  prl := wzh; pr2 := wzh;
  {if far plane between last point and new point}
  if (z ≤ prl) and (pr2 < lastf.z)
  or (lastf.z < pr2) and (prl ≤ z)
  then begin
    t := (lastf.z-wzh)/(lastf.z-z);
    store(lastf.x+t*(x-lastf.x),lastf.y+t*(y-lastf.y),wzh)
  end;
  lastf.x := x; lastf.y := y; lastf.z := z; {save last point}
  if z < prl     {case out-in}
  then store(x,y,z)
end {procedure clip_f};

procedure clip_n(x,y,z : real);
var prl,pr2 : real;
begin
  prl := wzl; pr2 := wzl;
  {if near plane between last point and new point}
  if (z ≤ prl) and (pr2 < lastn.z)
  or (lastn.z < pr2) and (prl ≤ z)
  then begin
    t := (lastn.z-wzl)/(lastn.z-z);
    clip_f(lastn.x+t*(x-lastn.x),lastn.y+t*(y-lastn.y),wzl)
  end;
  lastn.x := x; lastn.y := y; lastn.z := z; {save last point}
  if prl < z    {case out-in}
  then clip_f(x,y,z)
end {procedure clip_n};
```

```
procedure clip_t(x,y,z : real);
var pr1,pr2 : real;
begin
  pr1 := wyh+st*(z-wzl); pr2 := wyh+st*(lastt.z-wzl);
  {if top plane between last point and new point}
  if (y ≤ pr1) and (pr2 < lastt.y)
  or (lastt.y < pr2) and (pr1 ≤ y)
  then begin
    t := (lastt.y-wyh+st*(wxl-lastt.z))
         /(lastt.y-y+st*(z-lastt.z));
    clip_n(lastt.x+t*(x-lastt.x),lastt.y+t*(y-lastt.y),
                                 lastt.z+t*(z-lastt.z))
  end;
  lastt.x := x; lastt.y := y; lastt.z := z; {save last point}
  if y < pr1    {case out-in}
  then clip_n(x,y,z)
end {procedure clip_t};

procedure clip_b(x,y,z : real);
var pr1,pr2 : real;
begin
  pr1 := wyl+sb*(z-wzl); pr2 := wyl+sb*(lastb.z-wzl);
  {if bottom plane between last point and new point}
  if (lastb.y < pr2) and (pr1 ≤ y)
  or (y ≤ pr1) and (pr2 < lastb.y)
  then begin
    t := (lastb.y-wyl+sb*(wzl-lastb.z))
         /(lastb.y-y+sb*(z-lastb.z));
    clip_t(lastb.x+t*(x-lastb.x),lastb.y+t*(y-lastb.y),
                                 lastb.z+t*(z-lastb.z))
  end;
  lastb.x := x; lastb.y := y; lastb.z := z; {save last point}
  if pr1 < y    {case out-in}
  then clip_t(x,y,z)
end {procedure clip_b};

procedure clip_r(x,y,z : real);
var pr1,pr2 : real;
begin
  pr1 := wxh+sr*(z-wzl); pr2 := wxh+sr*(lastr.z-wzl);
  {if right plane between last point and new point}
  if (x ≤ pr1) and (pr2 < lastr.x)
  or (lastr.x < pr2) and (pr1 ≤ x)
  then begin
    t := (lastl.x-wxh+sr*(wzl-lastl.z)
         /(lastl.x-x+sr*(z-lastl.z);
    clip_b(lastr.x+t*(x-lastr.x),lastr.y+t*(y-lastr.y),
                                 lastr.z+t*(z-lastr.z))
```

```
  end;
  lastr.x := x; lastr.y := y; lastr.z := z;  {save last point}
  if x < prl    {case out-in}
  then clip_b(x,y,z)
end {procedure clip_r};

procedure clip_l(x,y,z : real);
var prl,pr2 : real;
begin
  prl := wxl+sl*(z-wzl); pr2 := wxl+sl*(lastl.z-wzl);
  {if left plane between last point and new point}
  if (lastl.x < pr2) and (prl ≤ x)
  or (x ≤ prl) and (pr2 < lastl.x)
  then begin
    t := (lastl.x-wxl+sl*(wzl-lastl.z))
         /(lastl.x-x+sl*(z2-lastl.z);
    clip_r(lastl.x+t*(x-lastl.x),lastl.y+t*(y-lastl.y),
                                 lastl.z+t*(z-lastl.z))
  end;
  lastl.x := x; lastl.y := y; lastl.z := z;  {save last point}
  if prl < x    {case out-in}
  then clip_r(x,y,z)
end {procedure clip_l};

begin {procedure polyclip}
  {initializing the last points}
  lastl.x := wxl; lastl.y := wyl; lastl.z := wzl;
  lastr.x := wxl; lastr.y := wyl; lastr.z := wzl;
  lastb.x := wxl; lastb.y := wyl; lastb.z := wzl;
  lastt.x := wxl; lastt.y := wyl; lastt.z := wzl;
  lastn.x := wxl; lastn.y := wyl; lastn.z := wzl;
  lastf.x := wxl; lastf.y := wyl; lastf.z := wzl;

  {computing the slopes}
  sl := (wxl-wxh)/(d+wzl)/2;
  sr := -sl;
  sb := (wyl-wyh)/(d+wzl)/2
  st := -sb;

  {fake run for setting the last points}
  outnum := 0;
  for i := 1 to innum do clip_l(vxin[i].x,vxin[i].y,vxin[i].z);

  {clipping the polygon}
  outnum := 0;
  for i := 1 to innum do clip_l(vxin[i].x,vxin[i].y,vxin[i].z);
end {procedure polyclip};
```

# EXERCISES FOR CHAPTER 6

1. Develop a procedure that computes the parallel projection of any given point (x,y,z) in a left-handed system for any given projection vector $(x_p,y_p,z_p)$.
2. Develop a procedure that computes the perspective projection of any given point (x,y,z) in a left-handed system for any given center of projection $(0,0,-d)$.
3. Let an object be defined in three-dimensional user coordinates. The left-right extent of the object is from $-1$ to $+1$ and the up-down extent from $+0.8$ to $-0.8$ in user coordinates. Assume absolute screen coordinates of $0 \leqslant x \leqslant 639$ and $0 \leqslant y \leqslant 399$. Define a procedure that computes the screen coordinates of the perspective projection of this object so that on the screen the left-right extent of the projection covers approximately 300 pixels. The center of the objects should be in the center of the screen.
4. In perspective depth transformation, a point (x,y,z) is transformed into ps(x,y,z) by:

$$
\begin{aligned}
x_{ps} &= xd/(z+d) \\
y_{ps} &= yd/(z+d) \\
z_{ps} &= z/(z+d)
\end{aligned}
$$

This transforms straight lines into straight lines. To show this, it suffices to show it for a two-dimensional line in (x,z)-coordinates only; the y-coordinates have the same transformation rule as the x-coordinates. A way of showing that the transformation of a straight line is a straight line is to express the transformation of the line as a parameterized straight line of the individual transformations. For the x-coordinate this is:

$$\frac{((x_1+t(x_2-x_1))d}{z_1+t(z_2-z_1)+d} = \frac{x_1d}{z_1+d} + \alpha_x\left(\frac{x_2d}{z_2+d} - \frac{x_1d}{z_1+d}\right)$$

For the z-coordinate this is:

$$\frac{z_1+t(z_2-z_1)}{z_1+t(z_2-z_1)d} = \frac{z_1}{z_1+d} + \alpha_z\left(\frac{z_2}{z_2+d} - \frac{z_1}{z_1+d}\right)$$

a. Show that from the first expression we get:

$$\alpha_x = t*\frac{d+z_2}{d+z_1+t(z_2-z_1)}$$

**b.** Show that from the second expression we get:

$$\alpha_z = t \cdot \frac{d+z_2}{d+z_1+t(z_2-z_1)}$$

**c.** What would we get for $\alpha_y$?

**d.** Why does this mean that the transform is a straight line?

**5.** The perspective depth transformation transforms planes into planes. If P is a plane in object space and ps(P) is its image (the set of all image points of points from P), then ps(P) also is a plane. Prove these assertions. *Hint:* assume first that ps(P) is not a plane. If so, we can find two points in it such that the straight line connecting them contains points that are not in ps(P). Take two such points $P_1$ and $P_2$. The originals of these points are $ps^{-1}(P_1)$ and $ps^{-1}(P_2)$. The straight line connecting the originals is all in P; ps of this straight line is itself a straight line and must be all in ps(P). The contradiction proves the assertion.

# Spline Curves

# 7

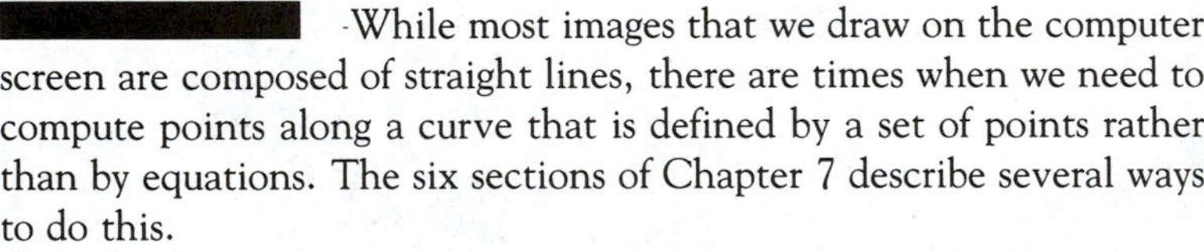

While most images that we draw on the computer screen are composed of straight lines, there are times when we need to compute points along a curve that is defined by a set of points rather than by equations. The six sections of Chapter 7 describe several ways to do this.

**7.0 Introduction** explains the application of curves in computer graphics, the value of parametric forms in the construction of curves, how interpolation differs from approximation, and introduces splines as a preferred type of curve.

**7.1 The Natural Cubic Spline** is widely used since it is often adequate for the job. These can be calculated either directly or by combining basic cubic splines.

**7.2 Uniform B-Splines** avoid the problem of global influence of the control points but are approximating curves rather than interpolating. Both cubic and quadratic forms of these are discussed.

**7.3 General B-Splines** are a superset of which the uniform B-splines are a special case. While the uniform curves are usually adequate for graphics applications, you may find a need for these more general curves.

**7.4 Interpolating B-Spline Curves** are a variation of general B-splines that interpolate rather than approximate to the control points, to form a natural cubic spline.

**7.5 Closed B-Spline Curves** tells how to force a B-spline curve to close on itself.

# 7.0 INTRODUCTION

Curves are important in many areas of computer graphics. One example is in animation. The animator draws key frames which must be linked together by many in-between frames, but these can be generated automatically by the computer. Points in these in-between frames that connect corresponding points of the key frames should not lie on a straight line, or else the motion of an object will be jerky and unnatural. What is wanted is a smooth curve that interpolates between the points on the key frames. The points of the in-between frames are created on that curve.

Another application of curves is to smooth an outline given approximately by a few points. In this case the curve itself is what we desire. It is usually created by an interactive process of specifying control points that shape the curve. If these control points can be interactively changed and if the resulting curve can be displayed rapidly, we can actually mold the curve to fit a desired outline. Such interactive modeling, done in real time on the screen, is easy and natural. This process is used in computer-aided design and manufacturing (CAD/CAM).

Still another application of curves is to create surfaces. This is usually achieved by specifying discrete points on the surface of an object which are then connected by interpolating or approximating surfaces. Curves are involved because all surfaces are ultimately derived from curves and exhibit the same characteristics of smoothness or roughness.

It is important to understand the concept of parametric representation before we discuss curves that are useful in computer graphics. We also need to understand the difference between interpolation and approximation. Once this has been explained, we will discuss the most important parametric curves, those for B-splines, Catmull-Rom curves, and Bezier curves.

The importance of parametric representation is that it allows us to derive curves for the 2-D plane; these can then be transferred without conceptual difficulties or any change in formalism to curves in three dimensions. A further conceptual step is necessary, however, to change from 3-D space curves to 3-D surfaces, as we will do in Chapter 8.

**Parametric Representations** A curve in the 2-D plane can be represented by the relationship between two variables. There are basically two ways to do this. We can write it with either y or x as the independent variable:

$$y = f(x) \quad \text{or} \quad x = g(y).$$

Such representations lead to difficulties when there are infinite slopes and where there are loops in the curve that give repeated points. There is lack of symmetry in such representations since one variable must be designated as independent and the other as dependent. Writing in parametric form avoids these difficulties. We use a single new independent variable, u, called the *parameter,* to write equations for both x and y:

$$x = X(u), \qquad y = Y(u)$$

The combination of $x = X(u)$ and $y = Y(u)$, for the same value of u, will be called the *combined curve* whenever confusion might result. Observe that there is now symmetry. The combined curve can loop and have infinite slopes in terms of x and y without having to have infinite slopes for the parametric equations. The slope of the combined curve is defined as the quotient of the derivatives written in terms of u:

$$dy/dx = (dy/du)/(dx/du)$$

It is easy to deal with only a finite portion of the curve by limiting the range of u. The examples of Figures 7.1a to 7.1c will help you visualize this. The two parameter curves are $x = \cos(u)$ and $y = \sin(u)$. The range of u is limited to $-\pi/4$ to $\pi/4$. The combined curve is the quarter-circle from $-45°$ to $45°$. The point (1,0) on the combined curve corresponds to $u = 0$; the quarter-circle has an infinite slope there.

An expression without a parameter would be $y = \pm\sqrt{1-x^2}$ with x limited to 0.707 to 1. Drawing the curve by a sequence of short straight lines from this expression is awkward because of the double sign. But this is a simpler case than most; in more complicated cases with a multitude of y-values for a given x-value, it is almost impossible.

Rendering curves is much easier using the parametric description rather than the functional one, so the parameter form is almost always used in computer graphics.

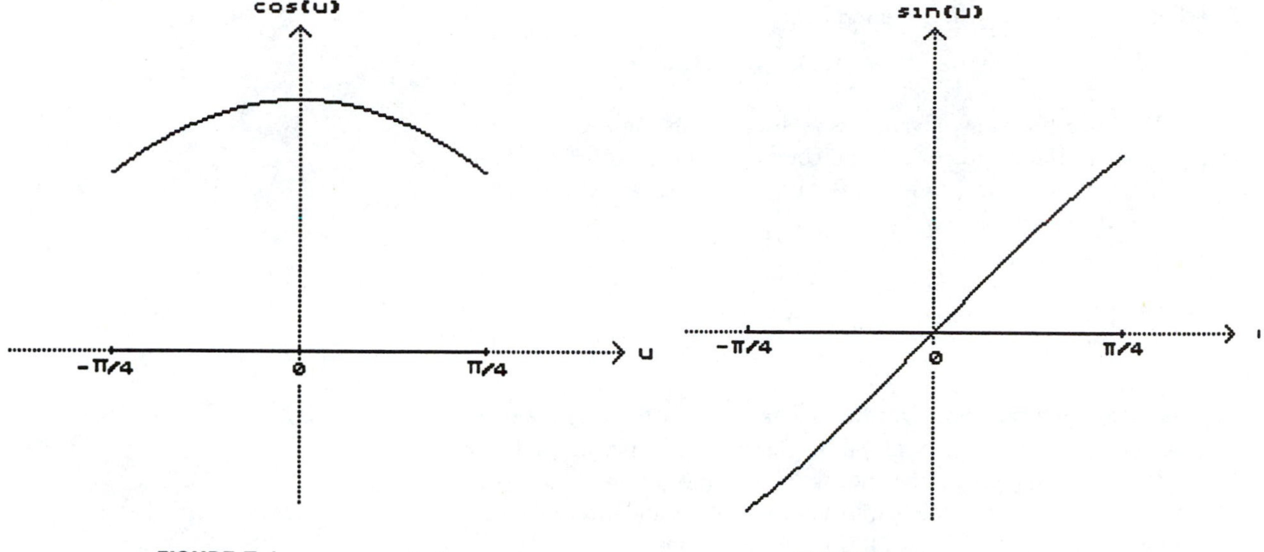


FIGURE 7.1a x = cos(u)

FIGURE 7.1b y = sin(u)

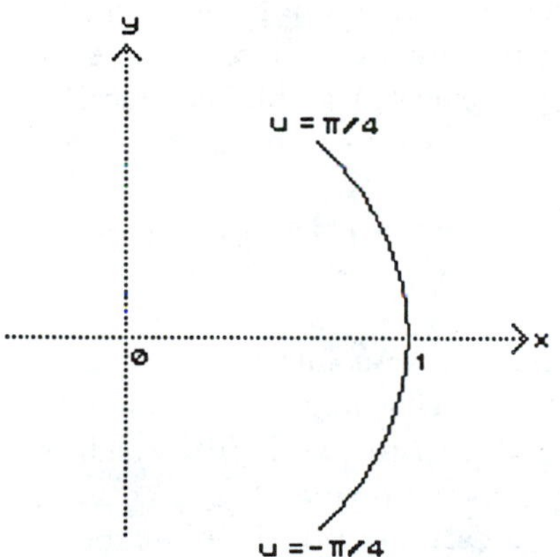


FIGURE 7.1c The combined curve is a quarter circle.

Everything we have said about 2-D curves in terms of x and y translates directly into 3-D space. We much prefer not to use two relations to define the curve:

$$y = f(x), \qquad z = g(x).$$

Rather, we should use the parametric form:

$$x = X(u), \qquad y = Y(u), \qquad z = Z(u).$$

We have the same advantages as discussed in the 2-D situation. The slopes of the projection of the combined curve onto one of the coordinate planes, the (x,y)-, (x,z)-, or (y,z)-plane, are the ratios of the derivatives with respect to u:

$$dy/dx = (dy/du)/(dx/du)$$
$$dx/dz = (dx/du)/(dz/du)$$
$$\text{etc.}$$

It is easy to deal with a finite segment of the curve by limiting the range of the parameter to a finite interval. In computer graphics we deal with bounded curve segments only; therefore, the range of u will always be limited. For reasons of simplicity, in approximations and interpolations, we usually work in the interval [0,n], where n is a natural number.

Given these advantages, we will henceforth consider only parametric representations of curves and surfaces. All the mathematical developments and the construction processes below will be done in a generic way. There is no need to consider whether it is the x-, y-, or z-coordinate that is being interpolated or approximated, as this is identical in all three cases. This must also be considered an advantage of parametric representations.

To go from the generic curve to the actual interpolating or approximating curve C(u) in two dimensions (in the plane), remember that the curve C(u) is defined by a parametric representation (there are two functions of the single parameter u), and that points $P_i$ are given as number pairs $(x_i,y_i)$. Whatever is shown below in a generic way is done first for the x-coordinates; this yields a first curve $C_x(u)$, which interpolates or approximates the $x_i$ values only. It must be done again for the y-coordinates; this yields a second curve, $C_y(u)$, that does the same for the $y_i$ values.

To go from the generic curve to an interpolating or approximating curve C(u) in three dimensions, think of this curve as being defined by a parametric representation (by three functions of a single parameter u), and that points $P_i$ are given as number triples $(x_i,y_i,z_i)$. Everything is analogous to the two-dimensional case.

From now on, $P_i$ will denote a point in the plane or in space, so $P_i$ will always stand for the number pair $(x_i,y_i)$ or for the number triple $(x_i,y_i,z_i)$, depending on the context. The lowercase $p_i$ denotes one of the coordinates, so it will stand for $x_i$, $y_i$, or $z_i$. The $P_i$ are also called *control points* because their positions control the course of the curve.

**Interpolation and Approximation** In areas more mathematically oriented than computer graphics, the problems of interpolation and approximation usually arise from the need to replace an analytically complicated function or one known only at certain points by a simple, well-defined curve. In computer graphics, we are primarily concerned with how the curve appears to a human observer and not with its mathematical properties. Our goal is not to replace one curve by another, worrying about error estimates and other matters, as is done in mathematics. Rather, we want to create a curve that has a smooth look and satisfies our visual sense. To this end, the interpolation and approximation methods developed mainly in numerical analysis have proven to be a good tool. The notions of interpolation and approximation may have a slightly different meaning in computer graphics. We will define these meanings precisely enough now to avoid confusion later on.

The usual graphics problem is to connect by a smooth curve a sequence of points in the plane or in space. There are two different ways to do this, interpolation and approximation.

In *interpolation,* the curve goes precisely through the points, as shown in Figure 7.2a. In approximation the curve does not necessarily go through the points; it goes near to, or approximates them (see Figure 7.2b). This is the terminology we will use from now on.

**Spline Curves** If we try to fit a curve to a given number of points by interpolation, we often find that doing so with a single polynomial of higher degree gives an unacceptable curve. This is because polynomials have a tendency that is called the Polynomial Wiggle Problem. If the points $P_0, \ldots, P_n$ do not already lie on a polynomial (and this is rare in computer graphics), then making a polynomial go through them may result in oscillations between some of the successive points. These oscillations (wiggles) become larger as the degree of the poly-

**FIGURE 7.2a** Interpolating curve.

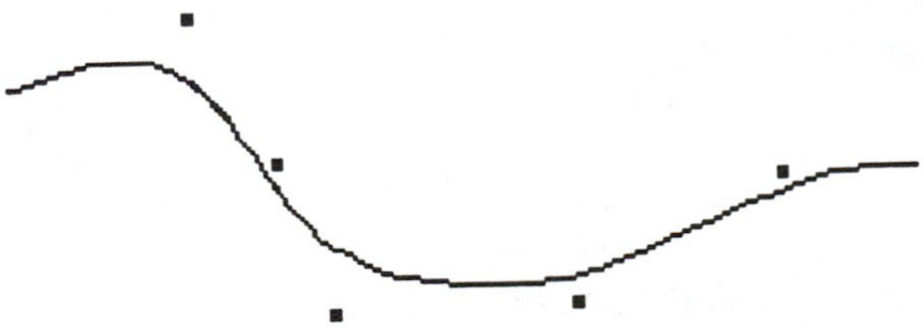

**FIGURE 7.2b** Approximating curve.

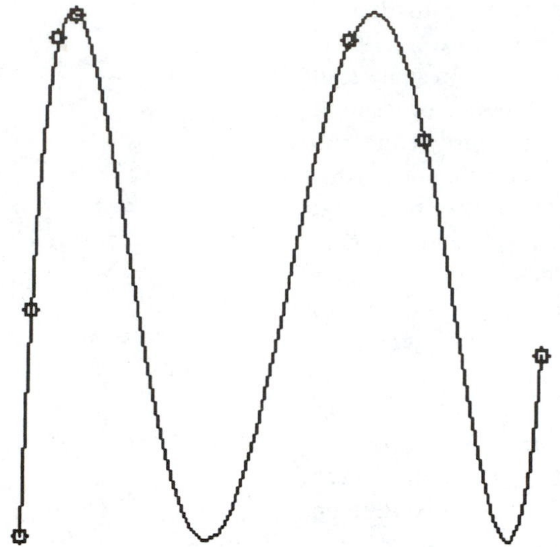

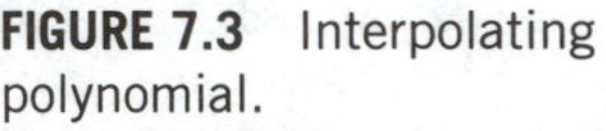

**FIGURE 7.3** Interpolating polynomial.

nomial is allowed to increase (MARO82, p. 203). Figure 7.3 shows a sixth degree polynomial fitted to the seven data points:

| x | 0 | .04 | .14 | .21 | 1.22 | 1.5 | 1.93 |
|---|---|---|---|---|---|---|---|
| y | −1 | −.151 | .894 | .986 | .895 | .5 | −.306 |

It develops strong wiggles in areas where the data points are sparse.

A high-degree polynomial that wiggles wildly, even though it matches all the data points, does not satisfy our desire for a smooth and "simplifying" curve. The best remedy is to use polynomials of low degree, but a single such low-degree polynomial cannot match the entire set. The solution is to separate the group of points into subsets and approximate the first three or four consecutive points by a low-degree polynomial, then the next three or four points by another polynomial, continuing like this until the whole group has been covered. It is also possible to use only a part of each of these polynomials and allow the subsets to overlap. There remains the problem of smoothing the joints where the separate polynomials meet. Several techniques have been developed to put these pieces of polynomials together so that the whole curve looks more or less smooth. The most popular of these techniques is a *spline curve.*

The term "spline" comes from the draftsman's spline, which is a flexible rod. By bending the flexible rod so that it fits at each of the given points, we can draw a smooth curve that interpolates the points. The main mathematical characteristic of splines is that they are not described by one single equation throughout their entire range of definition; they are certainly not a single polynomial. Instead they are "pieced together" from several other curves. Usually these individual pieces are themselves low-degree polynomials. The degree of the polynomials and other conditions that are imposed in the construction process determine the type of spline that results.

A more formal definition is that spline functions approximate or interpolate a set of points piecewise by polynomials of rather low degree, at the same time maintaining the continuity of the function values and one or more derivatives at the joints.

We will consider first the natural cubic spline, for reasons of completeness and because this spline is of historical importance. In computer graphics it is not used as much as other types of splines which we consider later. We also look at natural cubic splines to give a good understanding of the topic and to show why the newer developments are better suited for graphics purposes.

# 7.1 THE NATURAL CUBIC SPLINE

The *natural cubic spline* is an interpolating curve, called "natural" for several reasons. One is that it is a good compromise between flexibility, smoothness, and ease of computation. Flexibility here means how well the curve can bend to fit a certain outline. This concept is similar to how readily a natural elastic object can be bent to fit a certain outline without forcing or breaking; if the draftsman's spline is bent around pegs, it assumes a form that can be called natural. The natural cubic spline also resembles the actual elastic object in that it is a straight line outside the interpolation interval where there are no bending forces. Natural flexibility is given by using third-degree polynomials; this prevents the polynomials from making sharp bends. In computer graphics, the usual objective is not so much to make a curve go through the given points as to use the points to control the course of the curve. With degree three, the natural cubic spline is still flexible enough that it can be made to approximate a desired outline satisfactorily.

Figure 7.4 shows a natural cubic spline using the same control points as in Figure 7.3. The difference in behavior between this curve and the previous one is obvious. The flexibility of the spline can be increased by using polynomials of higher degree. The resulting curve will still look smooth and graceful but the amount of calculation to obtain the spline will be greater. All in all, the cubic spline seems to

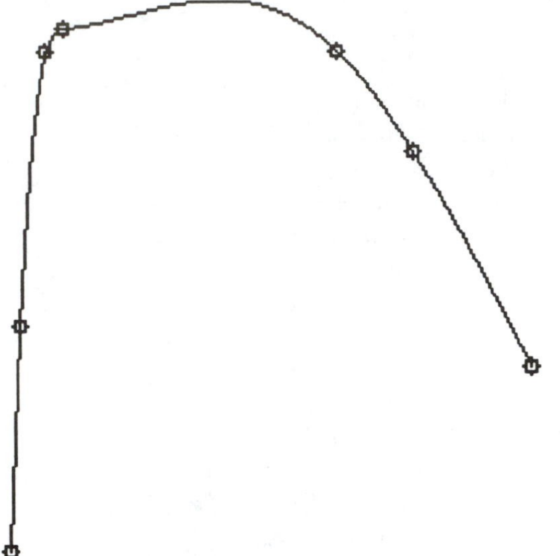

**FIGURE 7.4** Interpolating cubic spline.

be the best compromise to achieve a smooth, natural-looking interpolation of data points without too much calculation.

There is one property of splines that is undesirable in computer graphics: its global nature. By this we mean that it is not possible to change the course of the curve locally without affecting it in all other parts. Changing one of the points changes the curve throughout its length; more about this later.

## 7.1.1 Direct Calculation Method

We want to construct an interpolating natural cubic spline, given $n+1$ points $P_0, \ldots, P_n$. We need some notation. The interval $[0,n]$ is the range of the parameter u. We divide the interval into n subintervals of equal length. (Having equal lengths is not essential, but it makes the mathematical development simpler.) The n subintervals will be $[u_0,u_1], \ldots, [u_{n-1},u_n]$. We wish to interpolate the $n+1$ given points $P_i$ by a curve $C(u)$, which consists of a polynomial of degree three in each subinterval. Let the polynomial in $[u_{i-1},u_i]$ be called $q_i(u)$, then $C(u) = q_i(u)$ in the interval $[u_{i-1},u_i]$. The points $u_i$ are also called *knots*, because the polynomials are pieced together there to form the spline. It is required that:

$$
\begin{array}{ll}
q_i(u_{i-1}) = p_{i-1} \text{ and } q_i(u_i) = p_i & \text{for } i = 1, \ldots, n \\
q_i'(u_i) = q'_{i+1}(u_i) & \text{for } i = 1, \ldots, n-1 \\
q_i''(u_i) = q''_{i+1}(u_i) & \text{for } i = 1, \ldots, n-1 \\
q_1''(u_0) = 0 \text{ and } q''_n(u_n) = 0 &
\end{array}
$$

The first pair of conditions requires that the ends of each cubic fit to the two adjacent points. The next two say that the joints are smooth; both the first and second derivatives are the same where two cubics connect. The last two restrictions are so-called *end conditions,* because they define properties of the spline at the ends of the interpolation interval. The above end conditions define a natural cubic spline. There are many other conditions that can be used at the ends, for example, setting $q'(u_0) = c_0$ and $q'(u_n) = c_1$, where $c_0$ and $c_1$ are constants.

Above, the first line specifies 2n restrictions, the second and third lines specify $n-1$ each, and the fourth line specifies two. Altogether there are 4n restrictions. Each polynomial of degree three has four coefficients; there are n of these. We need 4n conditions and that is exactly how many there are. Hence we could set up a $4n \times 4n$ linear system from which we can obtain the 4n coefficients of the individual polynomials. Since the solution of a set of linear equations will change if any value in its array of coefficients (or right-hand sides) is changed, this implies that each point has a global influence. This conclusion becomes even clearer in the next section.

In practice it is not done this way. By rearranging the restrictions and preprocessing them in a certain way, we can arrive at an $(n-1) \times (n-1)$ linear system in which the system matrix is tridiagonal and well conditioned, making the system easy to solve. We do not explore this further because it would detract from our main goal: B-splines, Catmull-Rom curves, and Bezier curves. You should consult references such as MARO82 and GEWH84 for additional information.

## 7.1.2 Using Basic Global Splines

There is a completely different method for constructing an interpolating cubic spline. We build it from a set of basic splines combined as a linear sum. This is the approach used to get an interpolating polynomial in the Lagrange form (see GEWH84).

We start with $n+1$ points $P_0$ to $P_n$ defined through the parameter u on the interval [0,n]. We subdivide into n subintervals with $u_0 = 0$, $u_1 = 1, \ldots, u_n = n$. We construct $n+1$ basic spline functions $b_i(u)$ such that $b_i(u_i) = 1$ and $b_i(u_j) = 0$ for $j \neq i$. (This is a spline of degree three that is 0 at each knot except knot i where it is 1.) We take, without loss of generality, natural end conditions $b_i''(0) = 0$ and $b_i''(1) = 0$. Figure 7.5 shows the basic spline $b_2$ in an example where $n = 7$.

The interval [0,n] on which we define the basic splines has nothing to do with the domain in space or the plane in which the created curve will ultimately appear. It just represents the range of values for the parameter u as we move along the curve from $P_0$ to $P_n$, passing through the points in the plane or in space $P_i$, $i = 1, 2, \ldots, n$. It is sufficient to work only with this interval of parameter values.

**FIGURE 7.5** Basic cubic spline.

An arbitrary spline C(u) that interpolates through $p_0, \ldots, p_n$ is obtained by forming:

$$C(u) = \sum_{i=0}^{n} p_i * b_i(u)$$

It is helpful in considering a curve built from a linear sum of basic functions multiplied by the corresponding points, to think of these basic functions as weighting factors applied to the points and of the weighted sum as being the resulting curve.

It should be clear that the spline curve as defined above will pass through each of the given points. As all the $b_i$ are natural cubic splines, the linear combination will also be a natural cubic spline with the desired function values $C(u_i) = p_i$. The spline so obtained is identical to the one obtained as described above by solving a linear system of equations. Although it is possible to calculate a global spline this way it is not done in practical applications. We mention it here only to prepare you for the theory of B-splines.

Figure 7.5 showed that the $b_i$ oscillate from one knot to the next, the oscillations becoming smaller but never 0. The basic function $b_i$ represents the influence or control that the point $P_i$ has on the resulting interpolating curve. Its influence on the spline curve C at the point $P_i$ is total, as C goes through this point. At all the rest of the given points, it has no influence. In the intervals between these points it pulses in and out, weakening with growing distance. This shows that changing a single point $P_i$ influences the course of the whole spline. The influence of any of the points $P_i$ on the interpolating spline is not local but global.

**Toward Local Control** In computer graphics it is desirable, when constructing a curve through (or almost through) a series of given points, to ensure that the points exert only local control over the curve. Changing one of the points that determine the course of the curve should change the curve only in a limited neighborhood about this point and should not influence the curve outside this neighborhood. This is called *local control.*

How can we achieve such locality? We find the answer to this question by considering the above approach of using basic splines to construct a *global* interpolating spline. What made the influence of points global was that these basic splines are not zero between the knots. Suppose we could force each $b_i$ curve to be identical to zero outside a certain distance from the point $u_i$ (where it must equal 1). This would still make the curve C(u) go through the points $P_i$; the points retain full control over the curve at their specific locations but, at the same time, this control is limited to the region where the respective $b_i \neq 0$. With this in mind we postulate the following for the construction of the basic curves.

Given $n+1$ points $P_0$ to $P_n$, we again divide the parameter interval $[0,n]$ into n subintervals $[u_{i-1},u_i]$ with $u_i = i$. We want $n+1$ basic curves $b_i$ such that $b_i(u_i) = 1$ and $b_i(u_j) = 0$ for $j \neq i$. The $b_i$ also should have continuous first and second derivatives. Each $b_i$ should consist of four different polynomials of degree three in the four consecutive subintervals from $[u_{i-2},u_{i-1}]$ to $[u_{i+1},u_{i+2}]$; outside these subintervals it should be identical to the straight line $b_i(u) = 0$. Putting all these requirements together results in 18 conditions, which cannot be fulfilled by the 16 coefficients of the four polynomials; we have asked too much. The difficulty arises from the fact that $b_i$ must be identical to the line $b_i(u) = 0$ outside the interval $[u_{i-2},u_{i+2}]$ in order to achieve local control.

Does this mean that we cannot obtain the desirable locality of control of the points $P_i$? Yes and no. The locality can be obtained by dropping certain requirements, for example, the one that the curve goes through the points $P_i$. This leads to the cubic B-splines that we discuss below. Another way is to drop the requirement of second-order continuity as this implies only a slight change in the visual appearance of the resulting curve. This leads to the Catmull-Rom curves of Chapter 8.

# 7.2 UNIFORM B-SPLINES

The functions that later became known as B-splines were originally introduced by Curry and Schoenberg in 1947 (CUSC47). In 1967 Schoenberg called these functions B-splines (SCHO67). To make the approach to the B-spline methods easier, we will begin with uniform B-splines. After their properties and applications have been explained and you have become familiar with these, we will present the general B-splines.

The letter B in the word B-spline is derived from "basis." Therefore *B-splines* are often called *basic splines* or *bases*. They are spline functions that form a basis for the construction of curves from a set of control points. The construction is done by forming a linear combination of the basic splines.

Very often the curve obtained by the B-spline method is itself called a B-spline. We will not use this terminology; instead, using Schoenberg's terminology, the word B-spline will refer only to the basic splines from which the interpolating or approximating curve is obtained (DEBO78, p.114). This resulting curve is usually a spline, denoted by C, and will be called the *B-spline curve.* (Note carefully that the word "curve" is appended.) We used the word "usually" in the last sentence for the following reason: the curves in our applications are always obtained by parameterization. This introduces a further element into the process (which we do not investigate) but such parameterization can lead to properties of the combined curve that are not present in the parameter curve for a single component. Strictly speaking, the resulting combined curve may not be a spline.

B-splines can be defined for any degree. We will focus on the cubic and parabolic B-splines; for the others, we shall only make statements that point out certain properties or that give some broader overview.

In the previous section, we saw that it is desirable to construct a curve that is only locally controlled by the points it interpolates or approximates. We want the basic functions used in forming the curve to be nonzero on as small an interval as possible. This is exactly fulfilled by the B-spline functions: they are nonzero only in a finite interval.

## 7.2.1 Uniform Cubic B-Splines

We will introduce the properties that are most important for computer graphics for the case of the uniform cubic B-spline. (The term "periodic B-spline," which occurs often in the literature, means the same as uniform B-spline.) If we want to define a cubic spline on equally spaced knots that is nonzero on the smallest possible interval, it turns out that there is only one solution: the *uniform cubic B-spline.* The mathematical proof is beyond the scope of this book.

Our uniform cubic B-spline b stretches over five knots and is composed of cubic polynomials as described below. The distances between the knots are all taken as 1 and the point zero is put in the middle of the interval defined by these five knots in order to achieve symmetry in the formal description:

$$b(u) = 0 \qquad \text{if } u \leq -2$$

$$b(u) = 1/6(2+u)^3 \qquad \text{if } -2 \leq u \leq -1$$

$$
\begin{array}{llll}
b(u) = 1/6(2+u)^3 - 2/3(1+u)^3 & \text{if } -1 \leqslant u \leqslant 0 \\
b(u) = -2/3(1-u)^3 + 1/6(2-u)^3 & \text{if } \ 0 \leqslant u \leqslant 1 \\
b(u) = 1/6(2-u)^3 & \text{if } \ 1 \leqslant u \leqslant 2 \\
b(u) = 0 & \text{if } \ 2 \leqslant u
\end{array}
$$

At the knots $-2$ and $+2$ a polynomial is pieced together with the straight line $b(u) = 0$; at the knots $-1$, 0, 1, different polynomials are pieced together (see Figure 7.6). Some values are:

$$
\begin{array}{lll}
b(\pm 2) = 0 & b'(\pm 2) = 0 & b''(\pm 2) = 0 \\
b(\pm 1) = 1/6 & b'(-1) = 1/2 & \\
b(0) = 2/3 & b'(+1) = -1/2 &
\end{array}
$$

As before, it is helpful to think of these b-values as weighting factors that are applied to some of the given points.

If we need to draw a curve controlled by $n+1$ points $P_0$ to $P_n$, then we need $n+1$ uniform basic splines. Each of these is obtained by simply shifting the curve $b(u)$ by an integer amount to the right, which is done using the transformation:

$$b_i(u) = b(u-i) \qquad \text{for } i = 0, \ldots, n$$

We consider only those parts of the B-splines which are within the standard parameter interval [0,n], ignoring parts and knots of the B-splines outside the interval. A part of the interval from one knot value to the next is called a *subinterval.* The parameter values 0, 1, 2, . . . , n are knots shared by up to five of these B-splines.

**FIGURE 7.6** Uniform cubic B-spline.

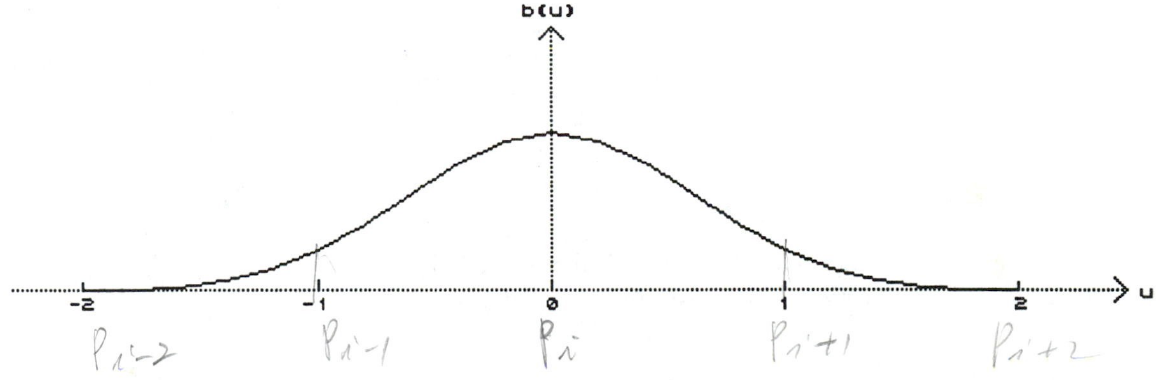

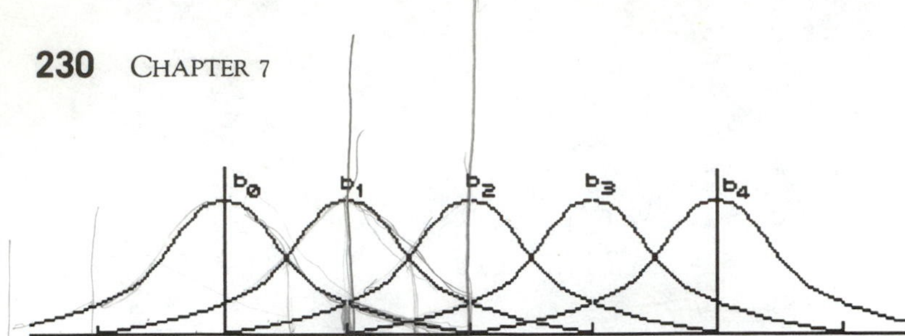


**FIGURE 7.7** Five uniform cubic B-splines.

As an example, the five uniform B-splines $b_0, \ldots, b_4$ on nine equidistant knots, $-2, -1, 0, \ldots, 6$, are shown in Figure 7.7 on the interval [0,4]. Only the knots 0, 1, 2, 3, and 4 lie within the interval. The function b and consequently all $b_i$ are continuous up to their second derivatives, which can easily be confirmed from the definition. Furthermore, these $n+1$ basic splines are linearly independent; they form a basis in an $n+1$ dimensional space; and the sum of the $b_i$ is identical to 1 at every place except in the first and last subinterval.

**Construction of a Uniform B-Spline Curve** Given $n+1$ points $P_0$ to $P_n$, we divide the parameter interval [0,n] into n subintervals $[u_i, u_i+1]$ with $u_0 = 0, u_1 = 1, \ldots, u_n = n$. Then we form the basis, consisting of $n+1$ uniform B-splines $b_i$ to the knots $u_i$, $i = 0, \ldots, n$ as described above. One way to construct the approximating curve is to form the linear combination:

$$C(u) = \sum_{i=0}^{n} p_i b_i(u)$$

$p_i$ stands for $x_i$ or $y_i$ or $z_i$ and represents in a generic way the coordinates of the control point $P_i$. From the graphs of the B-splines we can see that, for any given u, at most four of them are nonzero. Therefore, in each interval between two knots the sum is a linear combination of at most four B-splines $b_i$. As all $b_i$ in the sum are continuous to their second derivatives, the sum itself is also. It is interesting to investigate the properties of the curve C(u).

**Properties of the Curve** Some properties of the curve C result from certain properties of the B-splines; others result from the fact that C is a combined curve. The value of C(u) is always a weighted sum of the three or four closest control points. At the parameter value $u_i$, $C(u_i)$ is a weighted sum of the three immediately adjacent points $P_{i-1}$, $P_i$, and $P_{i+1}$. The weights are the values of $b_{i-1}(u)$, $b_i(u)$, and $b_{i+1}(u)$ at the knot $u_i$. These are 1/6, 2/3, and 1/6 respectively, so we have:

$$C(u_i) = 1/6p_{i-1} + 2/3p_i + 1/6p_{i+1}.$$

This shows that C(u) does not interpolate through the points $P_i$ but rather is an approximating curve. (If the three points are collinear and equispaced, the curve does pass through the middle point.) At a point on the curve corresponding to a parameter value u between $u_{i-1}$ and $u_i$, C(u) is a weighted sum of the four control points $P_{i-2}$, $P_{i-1}$, $P_i$, and $P_{i+1}$. It has a start point determined by the origin (0,0) and the first two control points and an end point determined by the origin and the last two control points.

The derivatives with respect to u at the end points of C are:

$$\frac{dC(0)}{du} = p_0 * \frac{db_0(0)}{du} + p_1 * \frac{db_1(0)}{du} = 1/2p_1$$

$$\frac{dC(n)}{du} = p_{n-1} * \frac{db_{n-1}(n)}{du} + p_n * \frac{db_n(n)}{du} = -1/2p_{n-1}$$

The slopes at the ends of the curve C are shown in Figure 7.8. They are computed by:

$$\frac{\frac{dC_y(0)}{du}}{\frac{dC_x(0)}{du}} = \frac{y_1}{x_1} \quad \text{and} \quad \frac{\frac{dC_y(n)}{du}}{\frac{dC_x(n)}{du}} = \frac{y_{n-1}}{x_{n-1}}$$

Geometrically, at the end corresponding to $P_0$ the slope of the curve will be parallel to the straight line from $P_1$ to the origin. At the other

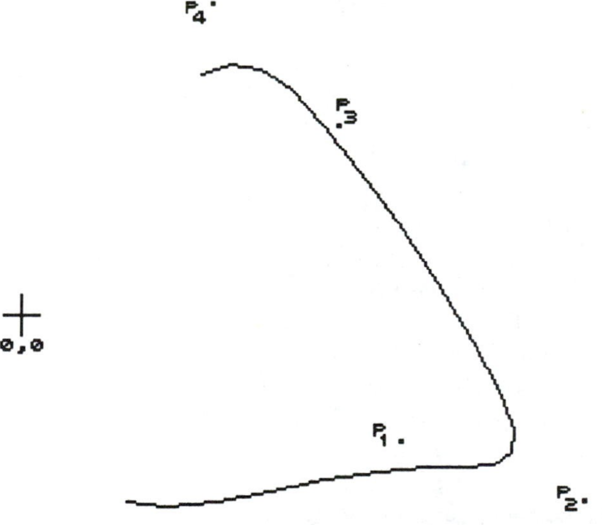


**FIGURE 7.8** B-spline curve to five control points.

end the slope will be parallel to the straight line from $P_{n-1}$ to the origin. All other points on the curve are not influenced by the origin. Figure 7.8 shows a curve drawn to five control points $P_0$ to $P_4$. The parameter u runs through the whole interval from 0 to 4.

**Double and Triple Control Points** The parametric representation of our curves allows us to specify the same control point two or three times and use a correspondingly increased number of B-splines and knots for the construction. Artificially using a control point more than once gives us extra control over the curve. We now explain the effect of this. First, some considerations about parametric curves are in order.

Assume that in a parametric representation of a curve all parameter functions $x = x(u)$, $y = y(u)$, $z = z(u)$ have derivatives equal to zero: $dx/du = 0$, $dy/du = 0$, and $dz/du = 0$ for u in $[u_i,u_i+1]$.

It follows that neither x(u) nor y(u) nor z(u) change as long as u is in this interval. In other words, the point $C_u = (x(u),y(u),z(u))$, which travels along the curve with growing u, halts at the place corresponding to $u_i$, stays there while u moves toward $u_{i+1}$, and then goes on as soon as u exceeds $u_{i+1}$. All parameter values in this interval designate the same point on the curve. A difference between parameter values does not imply a difference between the corresponding points on the curve! We can introduce many such *idle intervals* into the parameter functions simultaneously without affecting the curve that corresponds to parameter values outside these intervals.

If we specify a control point two or three times for adjacent knot values in the B-spline method, then we do something similar to introducing idle intervals into the individual parameter functions $C_x$, $C_y$, and $C_z$. The changes in the parameter functions become slower and an effect on the curve C can be observed. Genuine idle intervals would result if we repeat a control point more than three, say k, times. If we do this, the function $C_x(u)$ is identical to the coordinate $p_x$ of the control point between the second and the k-1st specification; $C_y$ and $C_z$ also equal the y- and z-coordinates. The curve C would be the same as with only three specifications of this control point! So we see that: two specifications produce a slight change in C, three specifications a stronger change, and four or more produce no further change in C. With B-splines of higher degree these numbers are correspondingly larger.

It is important to distinguish between having multiple control points and multiple knots. (Remember that control points are the $P_i$ values—the given points that can be artificially repeated—while knots are certain values of u in the parameter functions.) It is possible to specify multiple knots for the construction of a B-spline, but this leads away from the uniform B-splines to the general B-splines, which we briefly discuss later. Multiple knots must not be mistaken for multiple control points! The uniform cubic B-splines that form the basis for the construction of the cubic B-spline curves are always defined using different and equally spaced knots even in the case of multiply defined control points.

If there are $n+1$ control points $P_i$ at the knots $u_i$, $i = 0, \ldots, n$ and we specify the point $P_j$ twice, then we take a basis consisting of $n+2$ B-splines $b_i$, $i = 0, \ldots, n+1$ at $n+2$ knots

$$u_0 = 0,\ u_1 = 1,\ \ldots,\ u_{n+1} = n+1$$

and form the approximating curve as:

$$C(u) = p_0*b_0 + \ldots + p_j*b_j + p_j*b_{j+1} + \ldots p_n*b_{n+1}.$$

From the definition of the $b_i$ we see that:

$$C(u_j) = 1/6p_{j-1} + 5/6p_j \quad \text{and} \quad C(u_{j+1}) = 5/6p_j + 1/6p_{j+1}.$$

This shows the influence of the value $p_j$ on the points $C(u_j)$ and $C(u_{j+1})$ of the curve. The coordinates of these two curve points are both closer than usual to $P_j$ because $p_j$ is weighted more heavily than normal at these points. The visual effect is that the curve C is pulled in the direction of $P_j$ and makes a sharper turn there. Figure 7.9 shows the part of a curve that changes when a control point is specified twice. Both outlines are shown. For doubly specified $P_j$ the curve gets closer to $P_j$.

If a control point $P_j$ is specified three times, we have the following term in the sum for C(u):

$$\ldots + p_j*b_j(u) + p_j*b_{j+1}(u) + p_j*b_{j+2}(u) + \ldots$$

**FIGURE 7.9** Effect of doubly specified control point $P_j$.

For $u = u_{j+1}$, all $b_i(u)$ in the sum for $C(u)$ are 0 except for the above three which are 1/6, 2/3, and 1/6 respectively. It follows that:

$$C(u_{j+1}) = p_j*(1/6+2/3+1/6) = p_j.$$

The curve C is forced *through* the control point $P_j$. It is interesting to analyze what happens to C at this point. The calculation of the slope of C at $P_j$ is complicated in that it has two different slopes: one coming from point $P_{j-1}$ and one coming from point $P_{j+1}$. The calculation of the latter one is done below for the two-dimensional case.

Figure 7.10 shows two adjacent knots of a parameter subinterval. The knots correspond to the second and third specifications of $P_j$. The figure also shows the parts of the four basic B-splines that form C in this subinterval. In order to calculate $C'(u)$ in this interval we have to add the first derivatives of these basic splines weighted with the proper $p_i$. The values of the parameter are assumed to be 0 at the left and 1 at the right rather than i and i+1, just to make the calculation easier (this has no influence on the derivative). To get dy/dx we separately calculate $dC_y/du$ and $dC_x/du$ from their parameter representations.

| Equations of the polynomials multiplied with their weights: | Derivatives dCx/ds (of the equations at the left): |
|---|---|
| 1: $(1/6(1+u)^3 - 2/3u^3)x_j$ | $(1/2(1+u)^2 - 2u^2)x_j$ |
| 2: $(1/6u^3)x_{j+1}$ | $(1/2*u^2)x_{j+1}$ |
| 3: $(-2/3(1-u)^3 + 1/6(2-u)^3)x_j$ | $(2(1-u)^2 - 1/2(2-u)^2)x_j$ |
| 4: $(1/6(1-u)^3)x_j$ | $(-1/2(1-u)^2)x_j$ |
| sum | $(u^2/2)(x_{j+1} - x_j)$ |

Function 2 is the only one that is multiplied by $x_{j+1}$. When we sum up the derivatives most of the values cancel out. An analogous expression is obtained for the derivative dy/du. So we get:

$$dy/dx = (y_{j+1} - y_j)/(x_{j+1} - x_j)$$

which is independent of u. This is the slope of C with which it enters the point $P_j$ coming from $P_{j+1}$. In fact, there is a stretch on which C coincides with the straight line from $P_{j+1}$ to $P_j$. It starts at $P_j$ and ends at the point $5/6P_j + 1/6P_{j+1}$. Using symmetry, we get the direction of C with which it enters $P_j$, coming from $P_{j-1}$, as:

$$dy/dx = (y_{j-1} - y_j)/(x_{j-1} - x_j)$$

On the side of $P_j$ toward $P_{j-1}$ there is another stretch where C coincides with a straight line. Furthermore, the different left- and right-sided slopes mean that C has a sharp corner at the point $P_j$, in spite of the

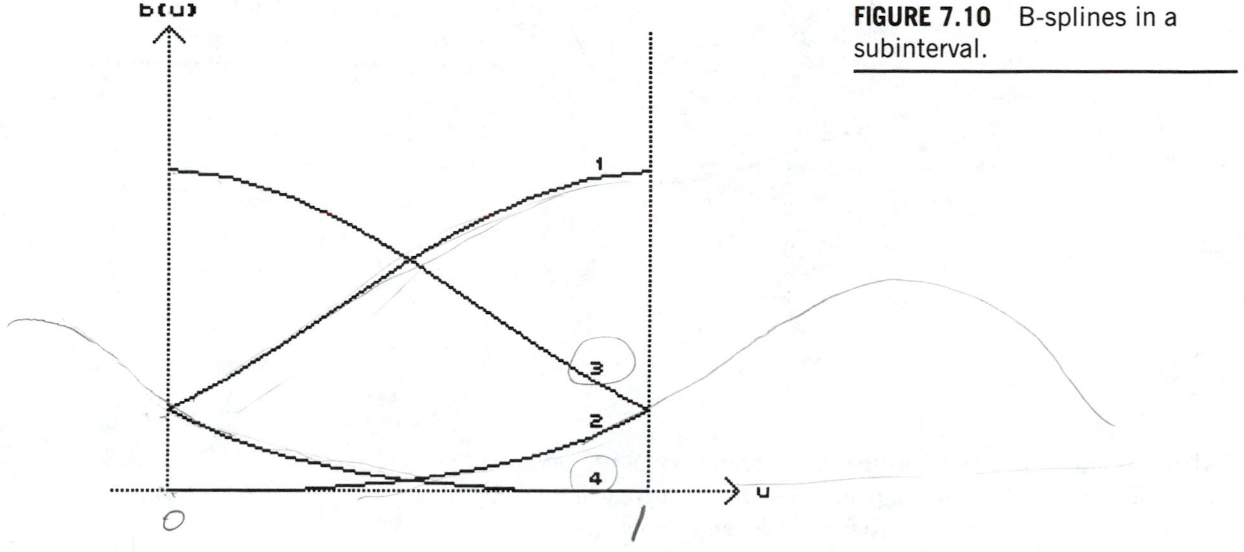


FIGURE 7.10 B-splines in a subinterval.

fact that all individual parameter curves $C_x(u)$, $C_y(u)$, $C_z(u)$ are perfectly smooth cubic splines. Figure 7.11 shows the part of a B-spline curve in which the point $P_j$ is specified three times.

**Specifying Triple Terminal Points** Specifying a control point two or three times is especially useful at the terminal points because it causes the curve to come closer or to attach to these points. The process is the same as the repeated specification of an interior point: a larger number of basic B-splines is used to form the resulting curve.

Consider the case of triple terminal points at each end. The basis has $n+5$ knots for the $n+1$ points $P_0$ to $P_n$. The knots $u_0$, $u_1$, and $u_2$ will all correspond to $P_0$; the knots $u_{n+3}$, $u_{n+4}$, and $u_{n+5}$ will all correspond to $P_n$. (These are not multiple knots; while the knots are

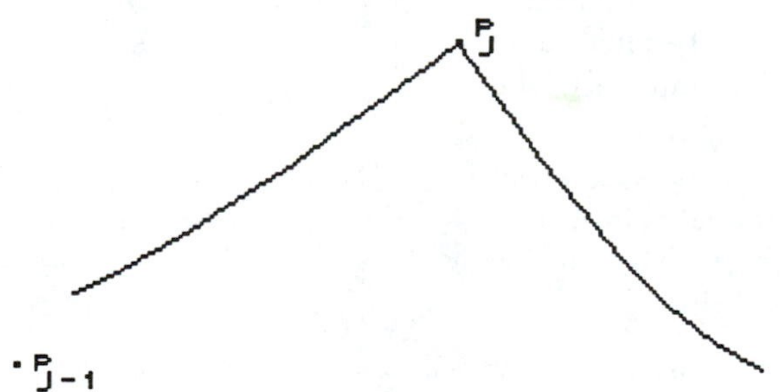


FIGURE 7.11 B-spline curve with corner at the triple point $P_j$.

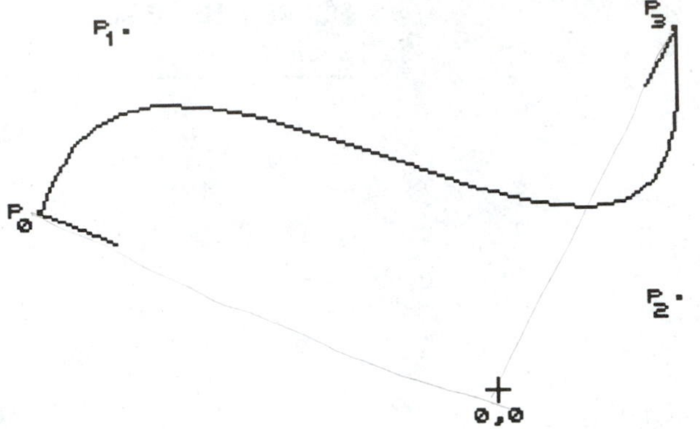


**FIGURE 7.12** Triple specification of terminal points.

all different, they correspond to the same control point.) In addition to being attached to the terminal points, near $P_0$ the curve will partially coincide with the straight line from $P_0$ to $P_1$ and similarly the other terminal point. Figure 7.12 shows such a curve.

It is of great value in interactive design to be able to attach the curve to two end points and still be able to mold it in between by changing other control points, adding some, deleting some, repeating some, and so forth, until it has the desired shape.

**Avoiding the Influence of the Origin** The B-spline curves we have constructed so far have the disadvantage that their terminal parts are strongly influenced by the origin: the slopes at the ends depend on the last two points and the origin. The ugliest manifestation of this can be seen in Figure 7.12 where two straight line pieces stick out toward the origin. This is because we use the uniform basic splines in the terminal subintervals as well as in the other subintervals. For the end subintervals, only three basic splines exist and these sum to less than 1. You will observe this for the subintervals [0,1] and [3,4] in Figure 7.7 (above). The influence of the origin can be avoided in two different ways. The easiest one is just not to draw the parts of the B-spline curve that correspond to parameter values in the terminal subintervals. The other way is to use general B-splines, which we discuss below.

If we draw the curve only between the knots $u_1$ and $u_{n+4}$, that is, in Figure 7.7, from 1 to 3 and, for triplicated terminal points, from 1 to $n+4$, then we get rid of the origin-influenced parts. The drawing algorithms presented below automatically take care of this.

**The Uniform Cubic B-Spline Formula** This formula is the most convenient way to draw the B-spline curve. We will present only the formula itself and no program, because the formula is much easier to understand and a corresponding program is trivial. We express the curve

$C(u)$ in a subinterval $[u_i, u_{i+1}]$ between two adjacent knots and take 0 as the left and 1 as the right knot value as in Figure 7.10. This makes the calculations easier and has no influence on the values of the basic splines there. As mentioned before, $p_i$ stands for $x_i$ or $y_i$ or $z_i$.

$$\begin{aligned} C(u) = & (1/6(1-u)^3)p_{i-1} \\ & + (-2/3(1-u)^3 + 1/6(2-u)^3)p_i \\ & + (1/6(1+u)^3 - 2/3u^3)p_{i+1} \\ & + (1/6u^3)p_{i+2} \end{aligned}$$

Combining terms in each power of u gives:

$$\begin{aligned} C(u) = & u^3(-1/6p_{i-1} + 1/2p_i - 1/2p_{+1} + 1/6p_{i+2}) \\ & + u^2(1/2p_{i-1} - 1p_i + 1/2p_{i+1}) \\ & + u^1(-1/2p_{i-1} + 1/2p_{i+1}) \\ & + (1/6p_{i-1} + 2/3p_i + 1/6p_{i+1}) \end{aligned}$$

This is conveniently written as a matrix expression:

$$C(u) = 1/6 * (u^3, u^2, u, 1) * \begin{pmatrix} -1 & 3 & -3 & 1 \\ 3 & -6 & 3 & 0 \\ -3 & 0 & 3 & 0 \\ 1 & 4 & 1 & 0 \end{pmatrix} * \begin{pmatrix} p_{i-1} \\ p_i \\ p_{i+1} \\ p_{i+2} \end{pmatrix}$$

We call this the *uniform cubic B-spline formula.* It expresses the value of C in any subinterval $[u_i, u_{i+1}]$ with $i \neq 0$ and $i \neq n-1$. There are always four basic splines that are nonzero in such a subinterval and these appear in the formula. Restricting these four B-splines to the subinterval gives what are called *blending functions.* If the subinterval goes from knot $u_i$ to knot $u_{i+1}$, there is at least the knot $u_{i-1}$ to its left and at least the knot $u_{i+2}$ to its right. The formula shows that drawing the curve from $P_i$ to $P_{i+1}$ requires the points $P_{i-1}$ and $P_{i+2}$.

As the parameter u is changed from 0 to 1, the formula gives the values of the curve from the point belonging to $P_i$ to the point belonging to $P_{i+1}$. After shifting the control points in the control point vector by 1, the parameter in the formula starts again with 0 and goes to 1. Although we originally had a parameter interval [0,n], now the parameter always goes from 0 to 1 for each subinterval. We obtained this formal simplification by expressing all four B-splines in the subinterval [0,1] and moving from one control point to the next instead of from one subinterval to the next. This allows the use of the same formula throughout the whole approximation.

To draw a smooth curve on the computer screen, we let the parameter u go from 0 to 1 in small steps for each control point vector and connect all curve values by straight lines. A curve not attached to the terminal control points is obtained by evaluating the formula for the following control point vectors:

$$\begin{pmatrix} p_0 \\ p_1 \\ p_2 \\ p_3 \end{pmatrix} \begin{pmatrix} p_1 \\ p_2 \\ p_3 \\ p_4 \end{pmatrix} \text{etc.} \ldots \begin{pmatrix} p_{n-3} \\ p_{n-2} \\ p_{n-1} \\ p_n \end{pmatrix}$$

This formula does not give the curve values in the leftmost or rightmost subinterval, since only three basic splines are nonzero there and only three points control the curve. A different matrix would be needed there. However, it is not desirable to draw these parts of the curve, as they are always influenced by the origin. It is better to start with the parameter at the second knot and stop one knot before the last. The uniform formula automatically achieves this. (Remember, don't confuse knots with control points!)

How far the curve extends at the ends depends on how often the terminal points are specified. Figure 7.13 shows the curve of the points $P_0$, $P_1$, $P_2$, etc. and shows that how it starts is according to the number of times $P_0$ is specified. The curve starts at $P_0$ for triple specification, at A for double, and at B for single. (The piece from $P_0$ to A is a straight line.)

The vectors of four control points that first enter the uniform formula are, for triple specification, $(p_0,p_0,p_0,p_1)^T$; for double specification, $(p_0,p_0,p_1,p_2)^T$, and for single specification, $(p_0,p_1,p_2,p_3)^T$.

**Hand-Drawing Rule** If we insert the parameter values $u = 0$ or $u = 1$ into the uniform B-spline formula we get:

$$C_x(0) = 1/6*(x_{i-1}+4x_i+x_{i+1}) \qquad C_x(1) = 1/6*(x_i+4x_{i+1}+x_{i+2})$$

$$C_y(0) = 1/6*(y_{i-1}+4y_i+y_{i+1}) \qquad C_y(1) = 1/6*(y_i+4y_{i+1}+y_{i+2})$$

For $u = 0$ the curve value depends only on the points $P_{i-1},P_i,P_{i+1}$ and for $u = 1$ only on the points $P_i,P_{i+1},P_{i+2}$. This last curve value is identical to the value for $u = 0$ when using the next set of four control points.

There is a geometrical construction for points on the curve that correspond to these values (see Figure 7.14). To get the curve point corresponding to any $P_i$ we connect the left and right neighbors of $P_i$ by a straight line. Then we connect the midpoint, M, of this line with $P_i$. We find the point on this connector that lies 1/3 away from $P_i$. The B-spine curve goes through this point. The slope of the curve at this point is parallel to the line that connects the two neighbors. This

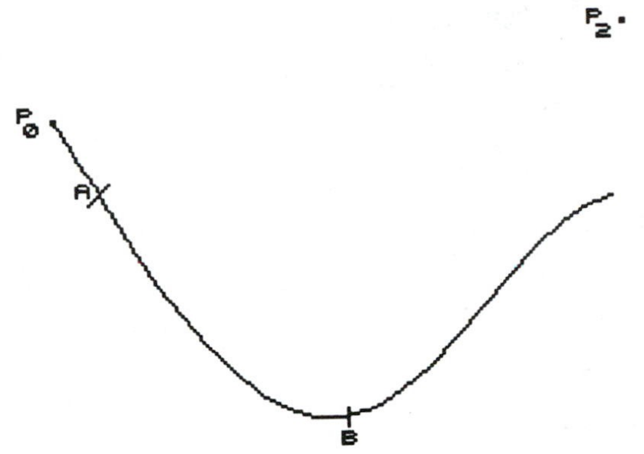

**FIGURE 7.13** Single, double, and triple specification of $P_0$.

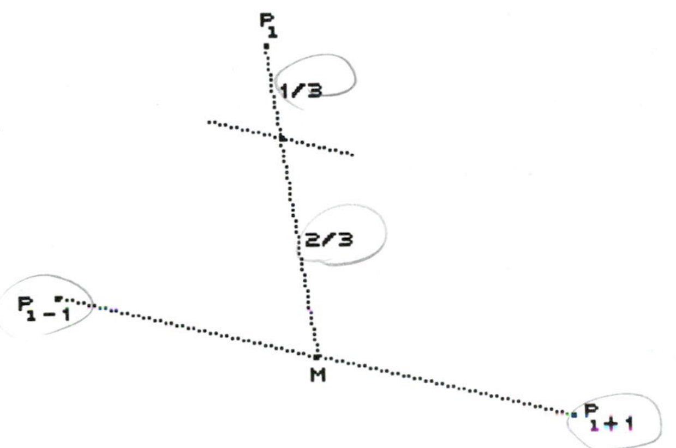


**FIGURE 7.14** Hand-drawing a cubic B-spline curve

drawing rule can also be used for doubled or tripled control points. We just assume that the two or three points are on top of each other.

## 7.2.2 Uniform Quadratic B-Splines

It is also possible to approximate a set of control points with *uniform quadratic B-splines,* also called *parabolic B-splines.* This curve stays closer to the points than the one obtained from cubic B-splines. We will describe the main properties of such curves shortly; the analogies to the cubic case are quite obvious.

The weighting factor b for the uniform quadratic B-spline stretches over four knots. We give a 0 value to the point that is centered within these in order to achieve symmetry in the formal description. The B-spline b is composed of polynomials of the second degree as follows:

$$
\begin{aligned}
b(u) &= 0 && \text{for} \quad u \leq -3/2 \\
b(u) &= 1/2(u+3/2)^2 && \text{for} \ -3/2 \leq u \leq -1/2 \\
b(u) &= -u^2+3/4 && \text{for} \ -1/2 \leq u \leq \ 1/2 \\
b(u) &= 1/2(u-3/2)^2 && \text{for} \quad 1/2 \leq u \leq \ 3/2 \\
b(u) &= 0 && \text{for} \quad 3/2 \leq u
\end{aligned}
$$

The values where the polynomials join are $-3/2$, $-1/2$, $+1/2$, and $+3/2$. Figure 7.15 shows the graph of b. If we want a curve controlled by $n+1$ points $P_0$ to $P_n$, we need $n+1$ canonical B-splines. They are obtained by simply shifting the curve b(u) by integer amounts to the right. These curves will constitute a basis in the standard parameter interval [0,n]. This is done using the transformation:

$$b_i(u) = b(u-i) \qquad \text{for } i = 0, \ldots, n$$

As an example, the graphs of the five uniform quadratic B-splines $b_0, \ldots, b_4$ with six equidistant knots $-3/2$, $-1/2$, ..., 11/2 are shown in Figure 7.16 for the interval [0,4]. Only the knots 1/2, 3/2, 5/2, and 7/2 are inside the interval. The approximating curve is formed (analogous to the cubic case) as:

$$C(u) = \sum_{i=0}^{n} b_i(u)p_i$$

The graph of the function C for five control points can be seen in Figure 7.17. This time we have not drawn the parts of the curve corresponding to terminal subintervals that are influenced by the origin. The curve starts precisely halfway between the first and second control points and stops between the next to last and last. The drawing algorithm presented below automatically omits these end intervals.

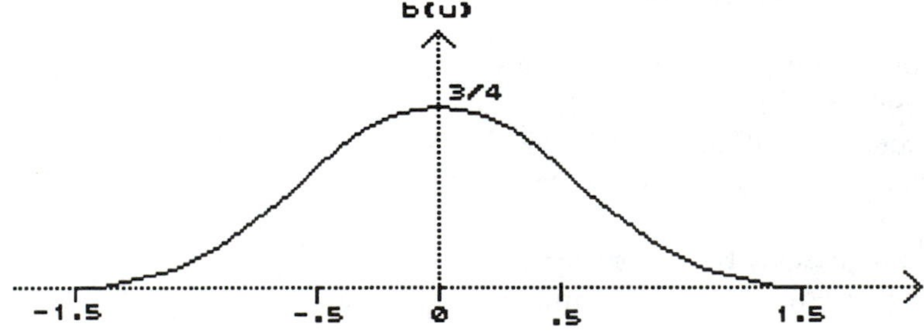


**FIGURE 7.15** Uniform quadratic B-spline.

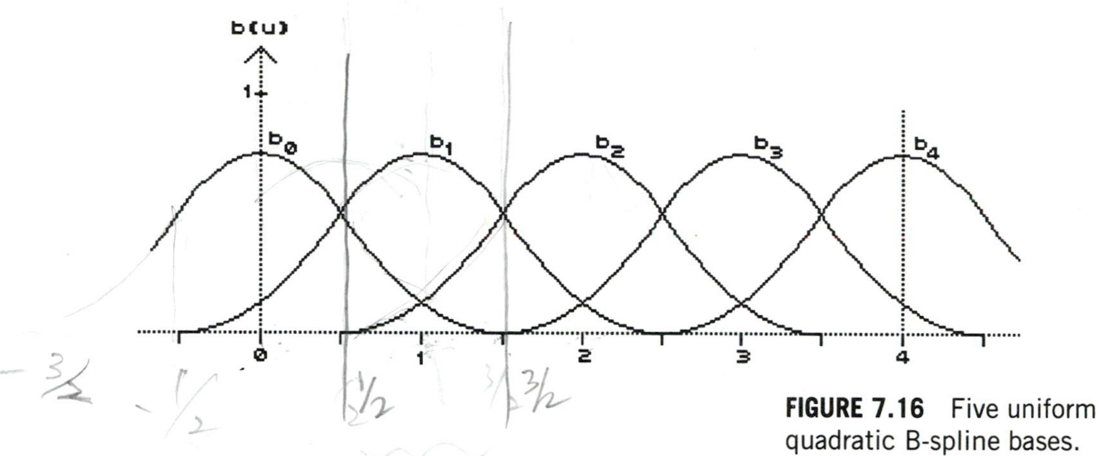


**FIGURE 7.16** Five uniform quadratic B-spline bases.

**The Uniform Quadratic B-Spline Formula** The B-splines in the above representation all have knots at 1/2, 3/2, 5/2, etc. It follows that for values of u in an interval such as $[-1/2, +1/2]$ or $[1/2, 3/2]$ etc., all three nonzero B-splines can be expressed with three equations. But we cannot do this with u going through an interval [0,1] because there would be a knot inside the interval.

| | | |
|---|---|---|
| 1: | $1/2(u^2 - 2u + 1)$ | (weighted with $p_{i-1}$) |
| 2: | $1/2(-2u^2 + 2u + 1)$ | (weighted with $p_i$) |
| 3: | $1/2(u^2)$ | (weighted with $p_{i+1}$) |

We can express the approximating curve C(u) in a subinterval between two adjacent knots, such as $-1/2$ and $+1/2$. By this we get a

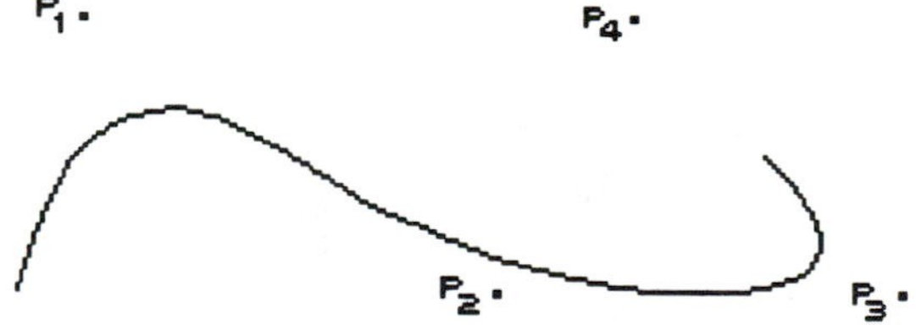


**FIGURE 7.17** Quadratic B-spline curve.

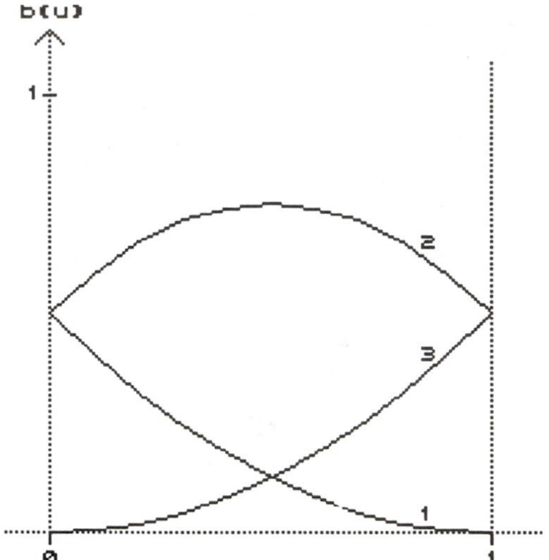


**FIGURE 7.18** The three blending functions of the uniform quadratic B-spline formula.

matrix formula in which u ranges from $-1/2$ to $+1/2$. But we would like to have a formula in which it ranges from 0 to 1 as in the cubic case. So we shift the B-splines by 1/2 to give their knots integer values. We then write the three blending functions on [0,1] (see Figure 7.18). We express C(u) as the sum of these curves, rewrite in terms of powers of u, transform into a matrix expression, and get:

$$C(u) = 1/2*(u^2,u,1)*\begin{pmatrix} 1 & -2 & 1 \\ -2 & 2 & 0 \\ 1 & 1 & 0 \end{pmatrix}*\begin{pmatrix} p_{i-1} \\ p_i \\ p_{i+1} \end{pmatrix}$$

In using this formula, we make the parameter u go in small steps from 0 to 1 for each group of three adjacent control points. We force the curve through a control point or attach it to a terminal point by specifying the point twice. The curve will have a sharp corner in such a point. Figure 7.19 shows cubic and parabolic B-spline curves with the same four control points; both are attached to the terminal points. The cubic B-spline curve is smoother than the quadratic one and stays farther away from intermediate control points.

**Hand-Drawing Rule** This rule is very simple for quadratic B-splines. We obtain the part of the curve near control point $P_i$ by drawing one line segment between $P_{i-1}$ and $P_i$ and a second line segment between $P_i$ and $P_{i+1}$. We mark the midpoints of the two segments. The piece of the curve starts at the first midpoint with the slope of the first segment and ends at the second midpoint with the slope of the second segment.

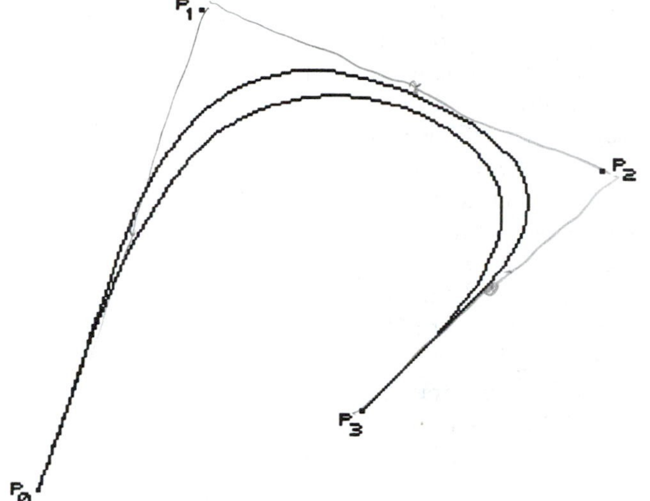


**FIGURE 7.19** Comparison of quadratic and cubic B-spline curves.

# 7.3 GENERAL B-SPLINES

So far we have restricted ourselves to uniform B-splines. These constitute a subset of the general B-splines as originally introduced by Curry and Schoenberg (CUSC47). In computer graphics, it is usually sufficient to work with uniform B-splines only. The reason, as already mentioned, is that we are more concerned with the visual appearance of the curve and rarely with its mathematical properties. The appearance of an approximating curve constructed with general B-splines differs very little from one obtained with uniform B-splines.

In most of the literature on computer graphics, only general B-splines are described. They are used extensively in computer-aided design (CAD) applications. Their formulation is as easy to use as the uniform B-spline formula. However, their theoretical development is quite difficult and is well beyond the scope of this book. Therefore we will not give an analysis of them, only the formulas.

The term "B-spline" from now on will refer to general B-splines if not otherwise stated.

The general B-splines of any degree and to any knot values $u_i$ can be defined by the Cox-de Boor recursion formula for general B-splines (DEBO78):

$$b_{i,1}(u) = 1 \text{ if } u_i \leq u < u_{i+1}$$

$$0 \text{ elsewhere}$$

$$b_{i,k}(u) = \frac{(u-u_i)b_{i,k-1}(u)}{u_{i+k-1}-u_i} + \frac{(u_{i+k}-u)b_{i+1,k-1}(u)}{u_{i+k}-u_{i+1}}$$

The Cox-de Boor formula is elegant, but not very intuitive. The two subscripts of b are i, which tells with which control point this particular B-spline is associated, and k, which is the degree + 1 of the polynomials constituting the B-spline. The knot values can be choosen at will. It is even possible to choose the same knot value several times. This will make the denominators in this formula 0. In this case the numerators are also 0; we adopt the convention that 0/0 = 0. Note that the second formula gives a recursive relation for the b's: the B-splines of degree four are defined in terms of the B-splines of degree three and these in terms of the B-splines of degree two, and so on. The first relation defines B-splines of degree 0; they are simple step functions. The sum of the B-splines of the same degree is identical to 1 everywhere.

To get an approximating curve to n + 1 control points, attached to the first and last point, we choose the following n + k + 1 knot values:

$$u_i = 0 \qquad \text{if } 0 \leq i < k$$

$$u_i = i - k + 1 \qquad \text{if } k \leq i \leq n$$

$$u_i = n - k + 2 \qquad \text{if } n < i \leq n + k$$

Usually several knot values will coincide at the ends of the parameter interval. We then construct a curve C in the following way:

$$C(u) = \sum_{i=0}^{n} b_{i,k}(u) * p_i$$

It would lead us too far astray to discuss all the aspects of general B-splines. We merely give an example for cubic B-splines, for which k = 4.

**The General Cubic B-Splines** If n + 1 control points $P_0$ to $P_n$ are given, we choose n + 5 knot values $u_0$ to $u_{n+4}$ for which:

$$u_i = 0 \qquad \text{if } 0 \leq i < 4$$

$$u_i = i - 3 \qquad \text{if } 4 \leq i \leq n$$

$$u_i = n - 2 \qquad \text{if } n < i \leq n + 4$$

This defines an interval consisting of n − 1 different knots. At each end of the interval the four terminal knots collapse into one knot, giving three subintervals of length 0 at each end. The other knots are equally spaced over the interval, thereby yielding n − 2 subintervals of length 1. (When the K + 1 knots are equispaced, the resulting B-splines are called *uniform or canonical B-splines.*) Now we can apply the recursive formula above to get the general B-splines.

The general B-splines of degree 3 to this set of knots will consist of uniform B-splines in the middle of the range of the knots but, in the subintervals closer to the terminal knots, they will consist of splines differing in properties and shapes from the others. We demonstrate with an example of nine control points $P_0$ to $P_8$.

$$u_0 = u_1 = u_2 = u_3 = 0$$

$$u_4 = 1, u_5 = 2, \ldots, u_8 = 5$$

$$u_9 = u_{10} = u_{11} = u_{12} = 6$$

Figure 7.20 shows the general cubic B-splines to these knots. There are nine B-splines. All are composed of polynomials of degree 3 inside the interval but are identical to 0 on all the rest of the real number axis outside the interval. The three middle ones are uniform and are therefore themselves natural cubic splines. The first three terminal ones are not natural cubic splines because they have discontinuities at the knot 0, either in the function value (the first or leftmost B-spline), or in the first derivative (the second one), or in the second

**FIGURE 7.20** General cubic B-splines.

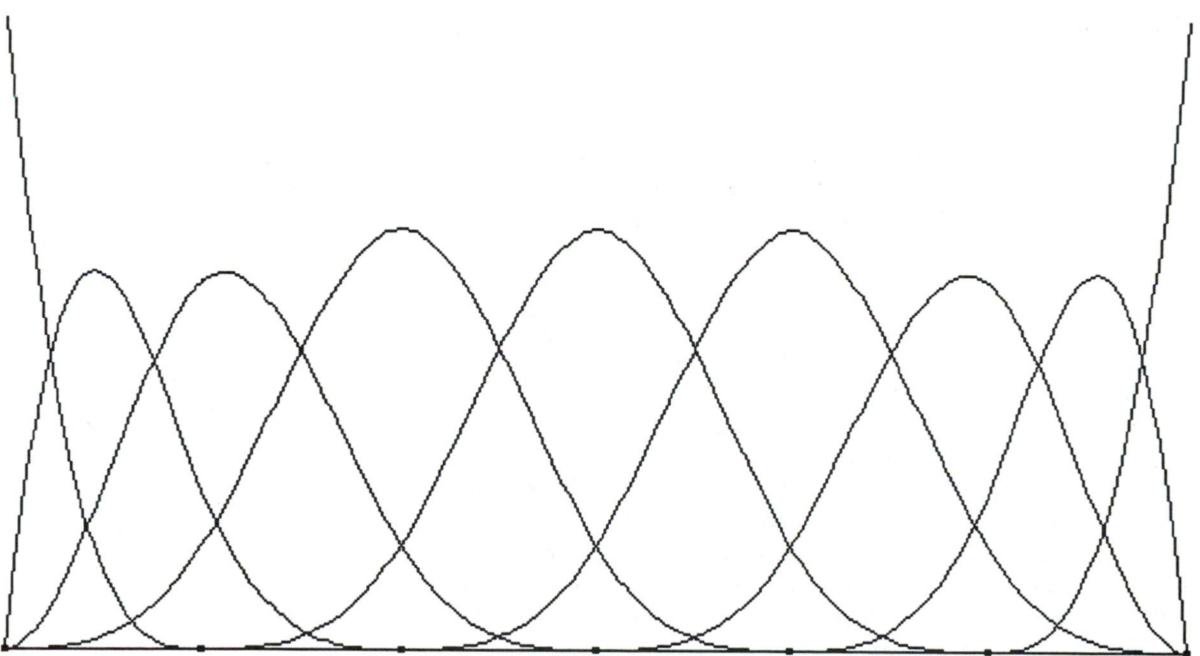

derivative (the third one). At the other end, similar things are true. There are only six subintervals as opposed to the eight that we would have if we were working with uniform B-splines. If we define C as:

$$C(u) = \sum_{i=0}^{8} b_i(u)*p_i$$

then C is an approximating curve to the control points. We see that the B-spline curve to the given nine control points is again a weighted sum of the B-splines. At the ends of the interval (at u = 0 and u = 6 in the figure) only one B-spline is nonzero and has the value 1. From this we can conclude that, at the end points of the interval, the function values C(u) depend only on the corresponding control points ($P_0$ and $P_8$ in our example). This implies that C(u) goes through the terminal points. At all other points in the interval the value of C(u) is a weighted sum of four B-splines between knots and a weighted sum of three B-splines at the knots. As described in the last section, we can force the uniform B-spline curve to go through the terminal control points. However, this curve would still differ from the general B-spline curve in the following way.

The "uniform" curve, even if we force it through the terminal control points, depends on only two control points in the terminal intervals and on three control points in the next-to-terminal intervals. In the other intervals it depends on four control points. The general B-spline curve everywhere depends on the maximum possible number of control points, which is four. Toward the ends of the curve, that is, for the first three and the last three control points, there is no such "neat" correspondence between knot and control point as we had when using the uniform B-splines; at the knot $u_i$ the value of the uniform B-spline curve was $C(u) = 1/6p_{i-1} + 2/3p_i + 1/6p_{i+1}$ for every i.

For the general B-spline curve we have at the knot next to the left end of the interval:

$$C(u) = 1/4p_1 + 7/12p_2 + 1/6p_3$$

and a similar relation for the knot next to the last. These relations hold only at the end regions of the curve. In the middle, there are only uniform B-splines and both types, uniform B-splines and general B-splines, are identical. Furthermore, the slopes of the curve at the terminal points are the same as the slopes of the straight lines from the respective terminal point to its adjacent control point.

There is no simple matrix formula for the whole range, from the first to the last control point, because the B-splines near the ends are different. For the leftmost two and the rightmost two subintervals, different matrices are needed. One way to calculate values of the curve

C is with the recursion formula that defines the general B-splines (NESP79, p.321).

**A General B-Spline Drawing Algorithm** The program that we now present generates a general B-spline curve C of any degree using recursion. The cubic uniform B-spline formula given before is restricted to the cubic case and to uniform B-splines. (Another algorithm for general B-splines that uses matrices without recursion is described later. While it will calculate a general B-spline curve, it is limited to the cubic case.) The advantage of the recursion algorithm is that it can generate B-splines of any degree, while using matrices requires different matrices for uniform B-splines of different degrees and even different matrices within the same degree for general B-splines. On the other hand, the matrix formulas are much faster and degrees other than 3 are seldom used, so each of the methods have their strengths and weaknesses.

The recursion formula that defines the general B-splines can be used directly to calculate the points on the curve C as shown below. The procedure GENBSPL calculates the value $C(u) = (c_x, c_y, c_z)$ of the B-spline curve of any degree $k-1$ for $n+1$ control points. It is to be called with values of u changing by small amounts between 0 to $n-k+1$. The control points are passed as two global arrays x[0..n], y[0..n] when working in the plane, and as three global arrays x[0..n], y[0..n], and z[0..n] when working in space. One failing of the routine is that it recalculates the values of the B-splines for certain values of u, when it could make use of the regularly repeating shapes of the uniform B-splines in the middle and of symmetries in the B-splines at the ends. Further, other methods require less computation and are numerically more stable (see, for example GORI74, DEBO72, and COXM72). In addition, some programming languages, such as BASIC, don't permit recursive formulations.

```
procedure GENBSPL (var cx,cy,cz  :  real;
                           n,k  :  integer;
                             u  :  real);
var  i  :  integer;
     b  :  real;

function knot(i: integer): integer;
begin
  if i < k
  then knot := 0
  else if i > n
       then knot := n-k+2
       else knot := i-k+1
end {function knot};
```

```
function bspline(i,k : integer;
                  u : real)  :  real;
var den  :  real;
    sum  :  real;

begin
  if k = 1
  then begin
    sum := 0;
    if (knot(i) <= u) and (u < knot(i+1))
    then sum := 1
  end {then}
  else begin
    sum := 0;
    den := knot(i+k-1)-knot(i);
    if abs(den) > 0.00001 then
      sum := (u-knot(i))*b_spline(i,k-1,u)/den;
    den := knot(i+k)-knot(i+1);
    if abs(den) > 0.00001 then
      sum := sum+(knot(i+k)-u)*b_spline(i+1,k-1,u)/den
  end {else};
  b_spline := sum
end {function bspline};

begin
  cx:= 0; cy := 0;
  for i := 0 to n do begin
    b := b_spline(i,k,u);
    cx := cx+x[i]*b;
    cy := cy+y[i]*b
  end
end {procedure GENBSPL};
```

**A Nonrecursive Drawing Algorithm** Now we show that matrix expressions can be used in a drawing algorithm for general cubic B-spline curves in much the same way as for uniform B-splines. No repetition of terminal points is necessary to attach the curve to these points as this is automatically true for these general B-spline curves. But it is certainly allowable to specify a control point two or three times, getting the same effects as with uniform B-splines. A point C(u) on the curve is calculated as:

$$C(u) = 1/12*U*M*P^T$$

where

$$U = (u^3,u^2,u,1),$$

M is one of the following matrices:

$$M1 = \begin{pmatrix} -12 & 21 & -11 & 2 \\ 36 & -54 & 18 & 0 \\ -36 & 36 & 0 & 0 \\ 12 & 0 & 0 & 0 \end{pmatrix} \qquad M2 = \begin{pmatrix} -3 & 7 & -6 & 2 \\ 9 & -15 & 6 & 0 \\ -9 & 3 & 6 & 0 \\ 3 & 7 & 2 & 0 \end{pmatrix}$$

$$M = \begin{pmatrix} -2 & 6 & -6 & 2 \\ 6 & -12 & 6 & 0 \\ -6 & 0 & 6 & 0 \\ 2 & 8 & 2 & 0 \end{pmatrix}$$

$$M3 = \begin{pmatrix} -2 & 6 & -7 & 3 \\ 6 & -12 & 6 & 0 \\ -6 & 0 & 6 & 0 \\ 2 & 8 & 2 & 0 \end{pmatrix} \qquad M4 = \begin{pmatrix} -2 & 11 & -21 & 12 \\ 6 & -15 & 9 & 0 \\ -6 & -3 & 9 & 0 \\ 2 & 7 & 3 & 0 \end{pmatrix}$$

and $P^T$ is one of the following control point vectors:

$$\begin{pmatrix} p_0 \\ p_1 \\ p_2 \\ p_3 \end{pmatrix} \begin{pmatrix} p_1 \\ p_2 \\ p_3 \\ p_4 \end{pmatrix} \quad \cdots \quad \begin{pmatrix} p_{n-4} \\ p_{n-3} \\ p_{n-2} \\ p_{n-1} \end{pmatrix} \begin{pmatrix} p_{n-3} \\ p_{n-2} \\ p_{n-1} \\ p_n \end{pmatrix}$$

We do not multiply with the same matrix in all subintervals. For the first subinterval, represented by the first control point vector, we use the matrix M1; for the second subinterval, the matrix M2; then the uniform matrix M is used until the next to last subinterval, represented by the next to last control point vector, where matrix M3 is used; and for the last, the matrix M4.

How often the uniform matrix M is used depends on the number of control points n + 1. The number n must be at least 6; in that case the uniform matrix M is used zero times. For less than seven control points there would be fewer than four subintervals and the above formula would not be applicable. For six control points, we would use three different matrices, for five control points two different matrices, and for four control points the general cubic B-spline curve is identical to a cubic Bezier curve, described later, and is calculated with a single matrix. These special situations will not be described.

You can see that the matrix formulas for general B-splines have disadvantages in that they imply complicated rules and therefore are awkward to program. Offsetting this, they are nonrecursive and fast, which is of value in certain applications. You will be correct in thinking that the matrix formulas for higher order general B-splines are even more complicated and that they need many different matrix specifications, especially if they are to be of general applicability. The recursive drawing algorithm indeed has important benefits. A nonrecursive program can be found in HARR83. There is no simple rule for drawing general B-splines by hand.

# 7.4 INTERPOLATING B-SPLINE CURVES

We mention this only because it occurs in the literature and could be somewhat confusing. Although the primary use of B-splines is the construction of an approximating curve, B-splines can also be used to construct an interpolating curve through given points in the following way.

If $n+1$ control points $P_0$ to $P_n$ are given and b is the uniform cubic B-spline defined in Section 7.2, then the $n+3$ functions:

$$b_i(u) = b(n*u-i) \qquad i = -1, \ldots n+1$$

are linearly independent and can be used as a basis for the construction of the curve. The parameter values at which the spline interpolates through the points $P_i$ are set to $u_i = i/n$, for $i = 0, \ldots n$, and constitute $n+1$ equidistant knots in [0,1]. The curve is constructed as:

$$C(u) = \sum_{i=-1}^{n+1} a_i*b_i(u)$$

in which the $a_i$ are *unknown.* (In the approximation problem we multiplied with *known* coefficients, the point coordinates.)

We have two more B-splines $b_i$ and two more coefficients $a_i$ than we need to make the curve comply solely with the $n+1$ restrictions given by the control points (that is, to make the curve merely go through the points). We can make C(u) comply with $n+3$ conditions by appropriately specifying the coefficients $a_i$. We therefore calculate the $a_i$ so that the derivatives $C''(0)$ and $C''(1)$ have the value 0 and the $C(u_i)$ assume the values $p_i$. Doing so yields a curve C(u) that interpolates through all the control points $P_i$ and has second derivatives at the terminal points equal to 0. This C(u) is identical with the cubic natural spline described in Section 7.1.1 above, yet it is obtained by a different mathematical procedure. The linear system to be solved is:

$$B*a = P$$

where

$$a = (a_{-1}, a_0, \ldots, a_{n+1})^T$$

$$P = (0, p_0, \ldots, p_n, 0)^T$$

and

$$B = \begin{pmatrix} n^2 & -2n & n^2 & 0 & . & . & 0 \\ 1/6 & 2/3 & 1/6 & 0 & . & . & 0 \\ 0 & 1/6 & 2/3 & 1/6 & 0 & . & 0 \\ . & . & & & & . & . \\ 0 & 0 & . & . & . & 0 & 0 \\ . & . & & & & . & . \\ 0 & . & 0 & 1/6 & 2/3 & 1/6 & 0 \\ 0 & . & . & 0 & 1/6 & 2/3 & 1/6 \\ 0 & . & . & 0 & n^2 & -2n & n^2 \end{pmatrix}$$

The interested reader should see GILO78 for more details and how to handle different end conditions. Also keep in mind that the curve constructed with this method is identical with an interpolating cubic spline and therefore is a global curve, not locally controlled by the interpolated points $P_i$.

# 7.5 CLOSED B-SPLINE CURVES

Up to this point we have approximated open curves only. If we want to approximate a closed curve (one that connects to itself), the construction can be done with uniform B-splines of any order and we use the uniform B-spline formula. The only difference from open curves is the way in which the control points enter the formula. The sequence of control points also must be extended on both ends in a cyclic way.

**The Cubic Case** If four control points $P_0$, $P_1$, $P_2$, $P_3$ are given, one sequence in which they could enter the formula is:

$$P_3, P_0, P_1, P_2, P_3, P_0, P_1$$

This results in an evaluation of the uniform cubic B-spline formula with the following sequence of control point vectors:

$$\begin{pmatrix} P_3 \\ P_0 \\ P_1 \\ P_2 \end{pmatrix} \begin{pmatrix} P_0 \\ P_1 \\ P_2 \\ P_3 \end{pmatrix} \begin{pmatrix} P_1 \\ P_2 \\ P_3 \\ P_0 \end{pmatrix} \begin{pmatrix} P_2 \\ P_3 \\ P_0 \\ P_1 \end{pmatrix}$$

The first evaluation draws the curve from $P_0$ to $P_1$ (the two middle control points in the set), the next from $P_1$ to $P_2$, and so on, the last evaluation closing the curve back to $P_0$.

**The Parabolic Case** If four control points $P_0$, $P_1$, $P_2$, $P_3$ are given, the sequence in which they enter the formula could be:

$$P_3, P_0, P_1, P_2, P_3, P_0.$$

Therefore the parabolic B-spline formula is evaluated with the following sequence of control point vectors:

$$\begin{pmatrix} P_3 \\ P_0 \\ P_1 \end{pmatrix} \quad \begin{pmatrix} P_0 \\ P_1 \\ P_2 \end{pmatrix} \quad \begin{pmatrix} P_1 \\ P_2 \\ P_3 \end{pmatrix} \quad \begin{pmatrix} P_2 \\ P_3 \\ P_0 \end{pmatrix}$$

The first evaluation draws the curve from in between $P_3$ and $P_0$ to in between $P_0$ and $P_1$, and so on; the last one will close it. Figure 7.21 shows a cubic and a parabolic closed curve with the same four control points. The curve that goes closer to the control points is the quadratic. The fact that some control points occur twice in the list of approximated points does not mean a stronger pull of the curve in the direction of these points. This happens only when the repeated occurrences are adjacent in the sequence; that is not true here.

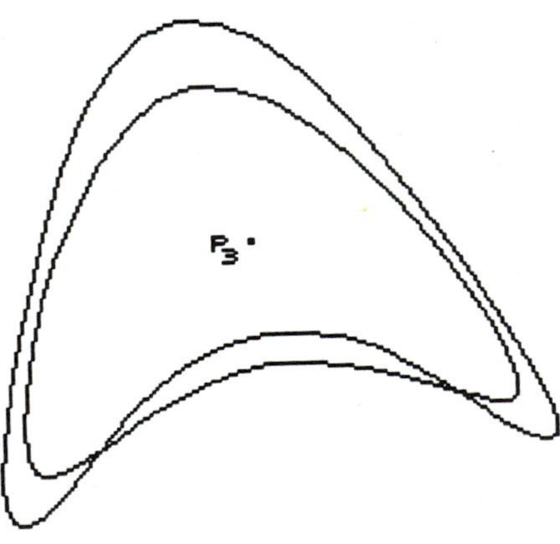


**FIGURE 7.21** Closed quadratic and cubic B-spline curves.

**The Convex Hull Property** B-splines have the so-called *convex hull property.* A closed B-spline curve will never cross the convex hull of its defining control points. Intuitively, the convex hull of points in a plane is the area defined by a rubber band stretched around all the points. (This property is actually a special case of the more general variation-diminishing property of B-spline curves, but this is not too interesting in computer graphics.) Convex hulls are important in clipping a curve against a window or a view volume. It is easiest to first test the convex hull of the points that define the curve. If the convex hull does not intersect the clipping area, then neither does the B-spline curve. Only when the convex hull intersects is it necessary to examine the curve itself for clipping.

# EXERCISES FOR CHAPTER 7

## Section 7.0 Parametric Representations

To become familiar with parametric curve representations, here are some curves for practice. They are called *hypocycloids.* You should write code that draws these curves either on the screen or on a plotter. The only graphics primitive needed is the straight line. Draw the curves by computing points along them that are connected by straight lines.

A hypocycloid is produced when a small circle with radius r rolls inside a bigger circle with radius R. Any point a on the perimeter of the small circle describes a hypocycloid. The form of the curve depends on the ratio of R to r. A generalization is obtained if the point a does not lie on the perimeter of the small circle but above or below. The point's distance from the center of the small circle is expressed by $r_0$ (see Figure 7.22).

**FIGURE 7.22**

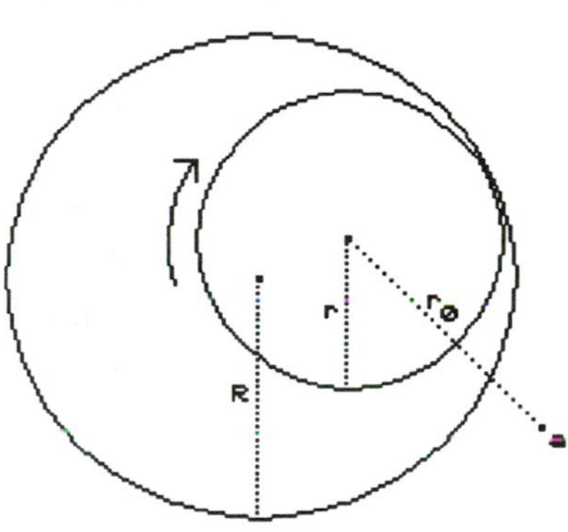


These curves serve as a good example for the usefulness of parametric representations because they are easily expressed in this way, while implicit formulas for them of the type y = f(x) are extremely complicated. The parametric form of a hypocycloid with u as parameter is:

$$x = (R-r)*\cos(u) + r_0*\cos(u(R-r)/r)$$

$$y = (R-r)*\sin(u) - r_0*\sin(u(R-r)/r)$$

Below we see some examples. In example 1 in Figure 7.23, $r_0 = r$, that is, point a lies on the perimeter of the small circle and R/r = 2.5. As this is not an integer ratio, the parameter u needs to go from 0 to $4\pi$.

**FIGURE 7.23** Example 1.

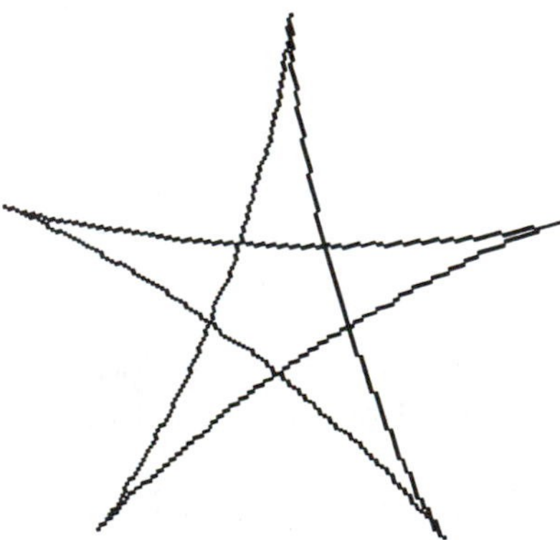

In example 2 in Figure 7.24, we have R/r = 8 and $r_0$ = 3*r. In example 3 in Figure 7.25 we again have an integer ratio: R/r = 7. $r_0$ is much bigger than r: $r_0$ = 5*r.

**FIGURE 7.24** Example 2.

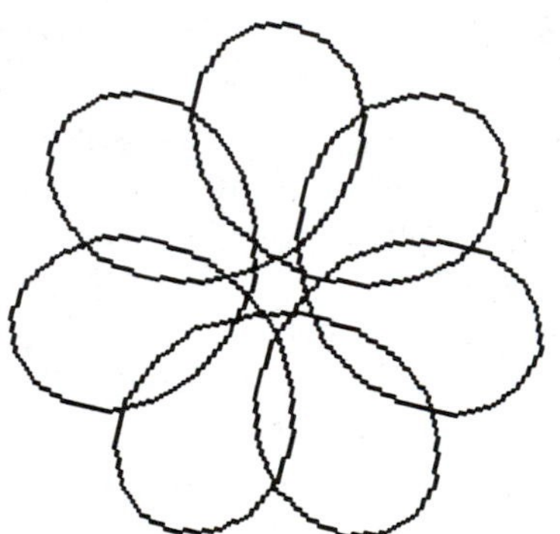

**FIGURE 7.25** Example 3.

1. Produce curves with different ratios of R/r and r = $r_0$.
2. Produce curves with different values for $r_0$. What is the characteristic feature of a curve with $r_0 > r$?
3. Find out how the curves look when r comes close to R and $r_0$ is much bigger than r. What happens when r > R? Physically this is not possible, because the bigger circle cannot roll inside the smaller one, but mathematically this might still work and might produce an interesting curve.
4. What is the characteristic feature of the hypocycloids when $r_0$ is smaller than r? What happens for $r_0 = 0$? Find out by producing several such curves.

# Section 7.2 Uniform B-Splines

5. Write a procedure

```
cub_bspl_curve(cpx,cpy : cp_vector);
```

that draws the part of a canonical cubic B-spline curve to four consecutive control points. Their coordinates are specified in the two arrays cpx and cpy. Use the type declaration:

```
type cp_vector = array[1..4] of real;
```

6. Extend the procedure cub_bspl_curve to three dimensions by adding a parameter of type cp_vector that contains the z-coordinates of four consecutive control points.
7. Define some points in 3-D space and use the three-dimensional procedure cub_bspl_curve to draw a B-spline curve in space.
   a. Draw the curve on the screen with orthographic projection by ignoring the computation of the z-values.
   b. Draw the curve on the screen with perspective projection by computing the projection for each point on the curve produced by the drawing algorithm and connecting them by straight lines.
8. This exercise is analogous to Exercise 5 except for the order of the B-spline curve. Write a procedure

```
qu_bspl_curve(cpx,cpy : cp_vector);
```

that draws the part of a uniform quadratic B-spline curve to three consecutive control points. Their coordinates are specified in the two arrays cpx and cpy. Use the type declaration:

```
type cp_vector = array[1..3] of real;
```

9. Show that a basic uniform cubic B-spline can be drawn with the uniform B-spline formula by choosing the seven control points:

   (−3,0), (−2,0), (−1,0), ( 0,1), ( 1,0), ( 2,0), and ( 3,0)

   (the y-values are all equal, except for the middle one, and the x-values are equidistant.) The points must be used in the listed order. What is the necessary sequence of control point vectors? Draw this curve on the screen.
10. What control points and what sequence of control point vectors must be chosen to draw a basic canonical quadratic B-spline? Draw this curve on the screen.

## The Hand-Drawing Rule for Uniform B-Splines

To become familiar with B-spline curves, practice drawing them by hand using the hand-drawing rule presented in the text. The exercises below give an opportunity to do this.

11. Draw by hand the open cubic B-spline curve to the control points (0,1), (1,2), (2,0), and (0.5,0.5).
12. Draw by hand the open uniform cubic B-spline curve to the five control points given in Figure 7.26.

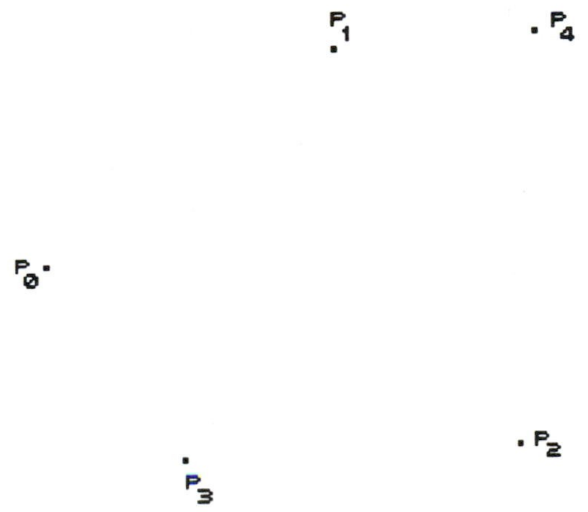

**FIGURE 7.26**

13. Draw by hand the open uniform quadratic B-spline curve to the five control points of Exercise 12.
14. If a control point is specified twice we can still use the hand-drawing rule to draw the curve. The twice-specified point is considered as two distinct points that are very close together, and so almost plays a double role. Do this until you are proficient. *Hint:* When advancing with the points we consider the twice-specified point as two points (see Figure 7.27). It shows only the part of the curve that is very close to $P_3$. The shape of the curve outside this part depends on other control points and therefore is not shown. With a little practice we can apply the drawing rule while totally collapsing the two distinct images of $P_3$.

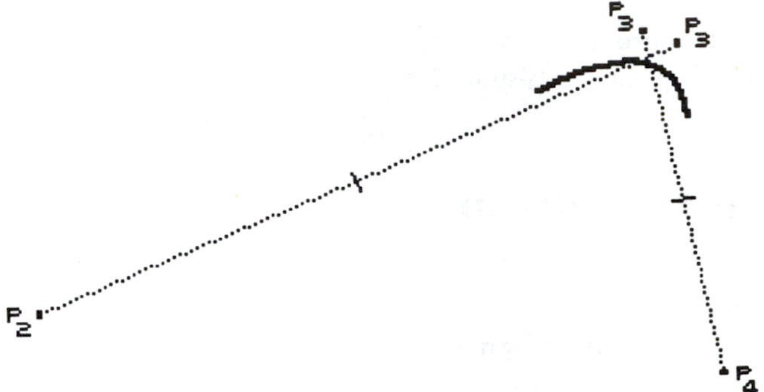


**FIGURE 7.27**

16. If a control point is specified three times, using the hand-drawing rule is easy. We draw straight lines from this point in the direction of the adjacent control points to precisely 1/6 the distance to these points. From then on we use the hand-drawing rule with no change. Do this with the points of Figure 7.28 considering $P_1$ and $P_2$ to be specified three times.

**FIGURE 7.28**

# Section 7.3 General B-Splines

General B-splines cannot be used to draw closed curves but they can be used to draw open curves attached to the end points.

17. Implement a procedure that uses the recursive Cox-de Boor formula to draw a general B-spline curve. Draw this curve to the control points $(-2,-1)$, $(-2.5,0.5)$, $(0,0)$, $(1.5,1.5)$, and $(1.5,-1)$.
18. Implement the nonrecursive drawing algorithm for general cubic B-splines as explained in the text.

# Section 7.5 Closed B-Splines

19. Draw by hand the closed cubic B-spline curve to the control points $(0,1)$, $(1,2)$, $(2,0)$, and $(0.5,0.5)$.
20. Choose four control points that form the vertices of a square, for example, $(-1,-1)$, $(1,-1)$, $(1,1)$, and $(-1,1)$. Draw the closed cubic B-spline curve to these points. It looks like a perfect circle. Is the curve in this particular case mathematically identical to a circle?
21. Draw the closed quadratic B-spline curve to the control points $(0,1)$, $(1,2)$, $(2,0)$, and $(0.5,0.5)$.
22. Draw by hand the closed cubic B-spline curve to the control points in Figure 7.29. Observe the order of the points!

**FIGURE 7.29**

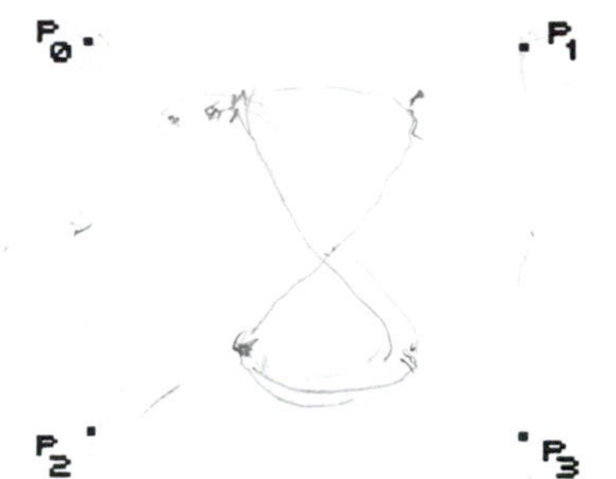


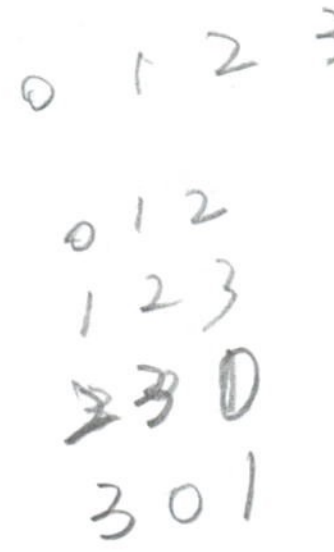

# Other Curves & Surface Patches

# 8

Chapter 8 continues the topics of the last chapter to cover some variants on splines, Bezier curves, and the application of curves to the generation of surfaces. There are nine sections.

**8.0 Introduction** outlines the topics of the chapter and their importance to computer graphics. This chapter extends your knowledge of interpolating and approximating curves.

**8.1 Catmull-Rom Curves and Splines under Tension** are built up from basic curves similarly to B-splines. They are able to interpolate by relaxing certain conditions. By generalizing them, we get the so-called "splines under tension."

**8.2 Closely Approximating Spline Curves** are locally controlled curves that, while not interpolating, can be made to come closer to the control points than B-splines.

**8.3 Bezier Curves** are another type of approximating curves useful in computer graphics.

**8.4 Parametric Surfaces** gives some groundwork for our discussion of ways to create surfaces.

**8.5 Uniform B-Spline Surfaces** result from an application of basic B-splines to three dimensions.

**8.6 General B-Spline Surfaces** are an extension of the curves of Section 7.3 to the generation of surfaces.

**8.7 Catmull-Rom Patches** permit the construction of surfaces from joined portions that interpolate through the control points.

**8.8 Bezier Surfaces** are an application of Bezier curves to determine a surface that approximates to sets of control points.

# 8.0 INTRODUCTION

The objects in the real world that we wish to picture on the screen are three-dimensional. We must be able to define their surfaces before we can project them onto a two-dimensional viewing surface. While some objects have planar surfaces that can be represented as joined polygons, this is too limiting. We need to study ways to represent curved surfaces. The two-dimensional curves of the last chapter form a basis for this important task.

Before we do this extension from two to three dimensions, however, we want to discuss some additional ways to draw planar curves, so this chapter begins by describing these additional methods for constructing 2-D curves.

As you have seen, a major difference between splines and curves based on B-splines is that the former interpolate while the latter approximate to the control points. Also, the splines lack local control. Can we somehow get the advantage of local control and the ability to interpolate?

The answer to this question is yes, but we may have to sacrifice continuity of derivatives to achieve it. Catmull-Rom curves are one way to define a locally controlled interpolating curve. A generalization of the concept behind these curves permits trading the closeness of approximation for smoothness.

The most important topic of this chapter is the generation of surfaces by extending the equations for 2-D curves into three dimensions. While the idea is straightforward, it is not as easy to visualize.

# 8.1 CATMULL-ROM CURVES AND SPLINES UNDER TENSION

*Catmull-Rom curves* interpolate through given points. While they can be constructed for any degree, only third-degree curves are important and popular in computer graphics. These we discuss below. *Splines under tension* are a generalization of the Catmull-Rom curves. They also interpolate through the control points.

The Catmull-Rom curve is built from basic functions similar to the uniform B-spline, but it lacks continuity of the second derivatives at the knots. The basic functions are obtained in a fashion similar to that described in the discussion of local control in Section 7.1.2, except we remove the requirement of second-order continuity. We get the 16 conditions needed to determine 16 constants in four cubic equations by adding three other requirements. These three new requirements are specified values for the slopes at the three middle knots; this gives a fully determined system. The choice of these specified values exerts a strong influence on the appearance of the resulting curve. If they are chosen to be ½ in the left knot, 0 in the middle knot, and −½ in the right knot, we obtain the basis of a Catmull-Rom curve. Figure 8.1 shows the result of doing this. Compare it to Figure 7.6 of Chapter 7.

We call this curve the *Catmull-Rom basis b.* To interpolate $n+1$ control points $P_0, \ldots, P_n$ we use $n+1$ bases, $b_0, \ldots, b_n$ which are obtained by shifting b by integer amounts in exactly the same way as for uniform B-splines:

$$b_i(u) = b(u-i).$$

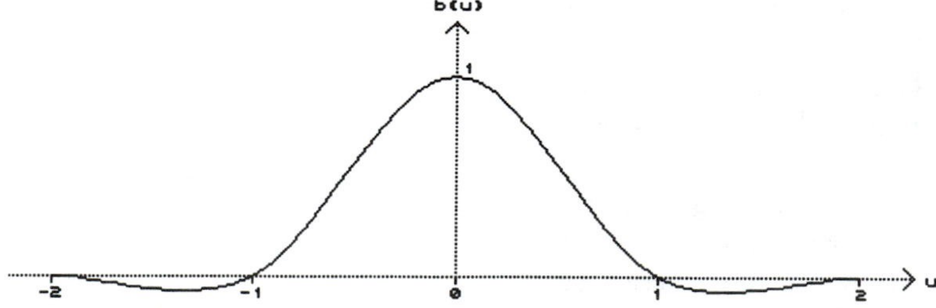


**FIGURE 8.1** Catmull-Rom basis.

The sum of these Catmull-Rom bases is equal to 1 throughout the entire interval $[1, n-1]$. The interpolating curve can therefore be defined as:

$$C(u) = \sum_{i=0}^{n} b_i(u) * p_i.$$

The resulting combined curve goes through all control points and at each control point the slope is parallel to the straight line that connects the two neighboring control points. The curve resembles a uniform cubic B-spline curve in this respect. The parts of the curve that correspond to terminal parameter intervals are again influenced by the origin. The drawing algorithm below will ignore these parts.

We can obtain a generalization of the Catmull-Rom curve by using parameters for the values of the derivatives of the basis curve at the middle three knots. At the left knot we use c, at the middle knot 0, and at the right knot $-c$. Curves obtained with their bases so defined are called *splines under tension;* the Catmull-Rom curve is just a special case. (Mathematically, these are really not splines, but the name "splines under tension" is suggestive and popular, as we explain below.)

There are other types of curves in the literature that are often referred to as splines under tension. They are not generalized Catmull-Rom curves and we will not describe them.

The appearance of the resulting combined curve from a generalized Catmull-Rom basis fits the name "splines under tension" well. When the value of c is small (less than 0.5), the resulting curve looks as if it has been pulled from its terminal points so as to be stretched out. The smaller that c is chosen, the more the curve is streched, but it still goes through the control points. This makes the curve shorter with sharper bends. (This behavior is not apparent in the graphs of the single parameter curves.) Regardless of the value of c, the tangent to the curve at the control points is always parallel to the line connecting its two adjacent neighbors. This is possible because the combined curve is, in general, not a polynomial but an algebraic function.

Figure 8.2 shows three splines under tension, all with the same control points, but different values of c. The tightest one has $c = 0.3$, the next has $c = 0.5$ (which makes it a Catmull-Rom curve), and the loosest one has $c = 1$.

For $c = 0$, the combined curve degenerates to a polygon connecting the control points. A very popular choice, $c = 0.5$, gives a Catmull-Rom curve. The Catmull-Rom curve is visually similar to a cubic B-spline curve except that it interpolates through the control points rather than approximating to them. Since it has no second-order continuity, it lacks the grace of the B-spline curve. Values of c above 1

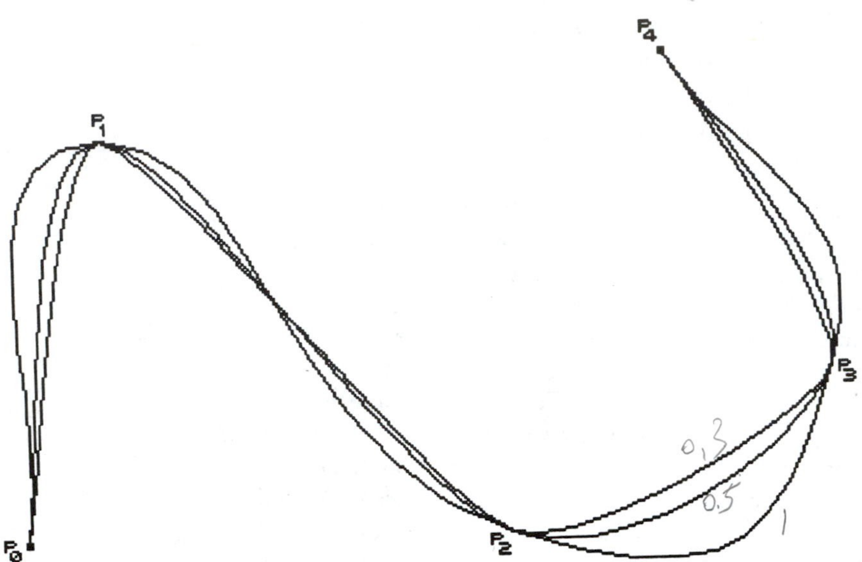


**FIGURE 8.2** Tighter and looser splines under tension.

lead to a "slack" in the curve which becomes so strong with increasing c that the curve will make loops between the control points. For c values smaller than 0 the curve makes loops at the control points. Useful c values are therefore limited to the interval [0, 1].

Catmull-Rom curves and splines under tension don't have the convex hull property and are not spline curves in a strict mathematical sense.

**A Drawing Algorithm** Using the above conditions, we develop the equations for the four different polynomials that constitute the basis of the spline under tension. If we transfer them all to the parameter interval [0, 1], collect terms, and express C(u) as a matrix formula, we obtain:

$$C(u) = (u^3, u^2, u, 1) * \begin{pmatrix} -c & 2-c & c-2 & c \\ 2c & c-3 & 3-2c & -c \\ -c & 0 & c & 0 \\ 0 & 1 & 0 & 0 \end{pmatrix} * \begin{pmatrix} p_{i-1} \\ p_i \\ p_{i+1} \\ p_{i+2} \end{pmatrix}$$

This matrix generates the part of the Catmull-Rom curve or spline under tension between the middle two points of the four in the p-vector. If we have repeated specification of control points, this curve behaves quite differently from a B-spline curve. The curve will be attached to the terminal points if we specify them twice. The tangent to the curve where it enters a terminal point will then be parallel to the line connecting the terminal point to its neighbor. A triply specified terminal point produces an *overshoot* that sticks out beyond that point. If a middle point is specified twice, the curve makes a loop there, while a triple specification will produce two overshoots. In that case, the curve will look as if two disconnected pieces cross each other at the point.

Catmull-Rom curves and splines under tension can easily be made to form closed curves if we specify the control points in a cyclic manner. Figure 8.3 shows a closed Catmull-Rom curve with four control points.

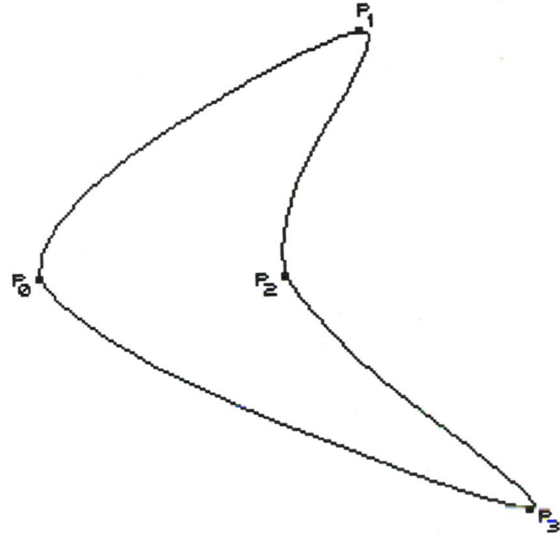


**FIGURE 8.3** Closed Catmull-Rom curve.

**Hand-Drawing Rule** The hand-drawing rule for both Catmull-Rom curves and splines under tension is very simple. We know that the curve goes through the control points. The slope of the curve at point $P_i$ is parallel to the line connecting $P_{i-1}$ with $P_{i+1}$. This is enough to draw an approximate outline of the curve.

## 8.2 CLOSELY APPROXIMATING SPLINE CURVES

It is possible to combine the properties of B-splines and Catmull-Rom curves and get a locally controlled curve that comes closer to the control points than a B-spline curve but still does not interpolate. We show it for the cubic case only. A parameter that can range from 0 to 1 controls how close the combined curve comes to the control points. A value of 0 yields a distance of 0, giving an interpolating Catmull-Rom curve. A value of 1 yields a B-spline curve. Values in between yield curves that approximate closer than a B-spline and lack second-order continuity. The transition between the extremes is a smooth one. Larger values of the parameter produce more graceful curves that stay farther away from the control points. The calculation is done with a simple matrix formula (a is the variable parameter):

$$C(u) = 1/6*(u^3,u^2,u,1)*\begin{pmatrix} 2a-3 & -6a+9 & 6a-9 & -2a+3 \\ -3a+6 & 9a-15 & -9a+12 & 3a-3 \\ -3 & 0 & 3 & 0 \\ a & 6-2a & a & 0 \end{pmatrix}*\begin{pmatrix} p_{i-1} \\ p_i \\ p_{i+1} \\ p_{i+2} \end{pmatrix}$$

This curve cannot really be attached to the terminal points for all possible values of a. Triple specification of a terminal point will produce an overshoot for a = 0 because the curve is a Catmull-Rom curve. With double specification, the curve doesn't reach that point for a = 1 because it is a cubic B-spline curve. Figure 8.4 shows a curve for a = 0.4 and one for a = 1 (a cubic B-spline). $P_0$ and $P_4$ have both been specified twice. The curve farther from the control points is the B-spline curve.

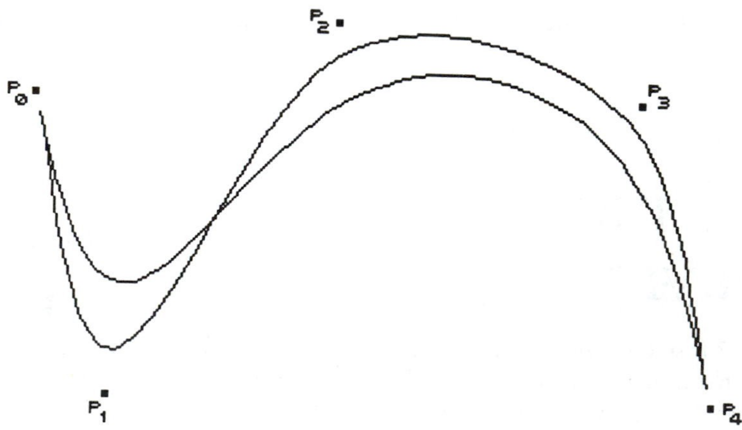


**FIGURE 8.4** Cubic B-spline curve and closely approximating spline curve.

# 8.3 BEZIER CURVES

Bezier methods can be used in a variety of ways to interpolate or to approximate to a set of control points with curves of any degree. These methods are based on the *Bernstein polynomials*. There are n+1 Bernstein polynomials of degree n, defined on the interval [0,1] by:

$$b_i(u) = C(n,i)*u^i(1-u)^{n-i} \qquad i = 0, \ldots, n$$

C(n,i) is the binomial coefficient: C(n,i) = n!/(i!(n − i)!). For example, the four Bernstein polynomials of degree three are:

$$(1-u)^3,\ 3u^1(1-u)^2\ ,\ 3u^2(1-u)^1,\ u^3.$$

These polynomials are always nonnegative within [0,1]. A combined curve to a set of control points is formed by linearly combining these polynomials weighted with the x-, y-, or z-coordinates in basically the same way as with uniform B-splines. All Bernstein polynomials have one local maximum in [0,1]. The maximum of $b_i$ is at the location i/n and at this location $b_i$ is greater than all the others. Furthermore, for u = 0 we have $b_0(u) = 1$ with all the others 0; for u = 1, $b_n(u) = 1$ with all the others 0. This can be seen in Figure 8.5, which graphs the five Bernstein polynomials of degree 4.

## 8.3.1 General Bezier Curves

With n+1 control points, $P_0$ to $P_n$, a Bezier curve is defined as:

$$C(u) = \sum_{i=0}^{n} p_i * b_i(u) \qquad \text{for } 0 \leq u \leq 1$$

From the above properties of $b_i$, it follows that C(u) goes through $P_0$ and through $P_n$. For parameter values i/n, where $b_i$ has its maximum and is larger than all the others, the control point $P_i$ will exert the strongest pull on the curve in its direction, but C(u) will in general not go through these points. Therefore the Bezier curve is an approximating curve. Its slope at a terminal point coincides with the straight line from this point to the adjacent point. A Bezier curve of degree n will be continuous in all its derivatives.

A main difference from the B-spline curve is that the Bezier curve is globally, not locally controlled by the points $P_i$. Changing one of the control points affects the course of C most strongly in the neighborhood of this point but it also affects the course of the whole curve.

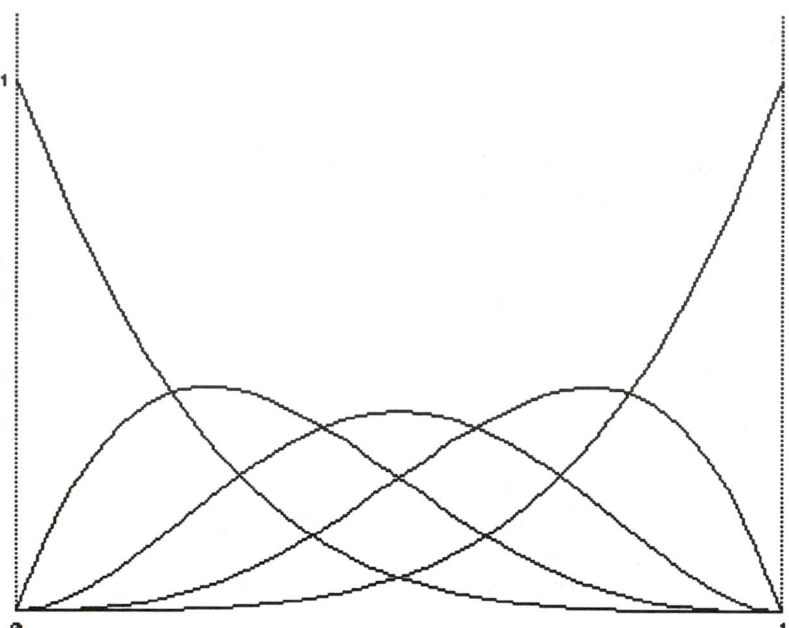


**FIGURE 8.5** Bernstein polynomials of degree 4.

**A Drawing Algorithm** The Bezier method is a special case of the general B-spline method. If n + 1 control points $P_0$ to $P_n$ are given and a general B-spline approximation of degree n is performed, then the resulting curve is identical to the Bezier curve of degree n to these points. When the degree of the general B-splines is just one lower than the number of points, the parameter interval will be [0,1] and one-half of the knots will be equal to 0 and the other half equal to 1. The B-splines will not be piecewise polynomials, as no knot values are within the parameter range; therefore the general B-spline drawing procedure can be used to draw Bezier curves as well. Nonrecursive algorithms are easy to use, but for each degree a different matrix is necessary. Matrix formulas for degrees 2, 3, 4, and 5 are shown below.

For degree 2, with three control points the formula is:

$$C(u) = (u^2, u, 1) * \begin{pmatrix} 1 & -2 & 1 \\ -2 & 2 & 0 \\ 1 & 0 & 0 \end{pmatrix} * \begin{pmatrix} p_0 \\ p_1 \\ p_2 \end{pmatrix}$$

Degree 3, four control points:

$$C(u) = (u^3,u^2,u,1) * \begin{pmatrix} -1 & 3 & -3 & 1 \\ 3 & -6 & 3 & 0 \\ -3 & 3 & 0 & 0 \\ 1 & 0 & 0 & 0 \end{pmatrix} * \begin{pmatrix} p_0 \\ p_1 \\ p_2 \\ p_3 \end{pmatrix}$$

Degree 4, five control points:

$$C(u) = (u^4,u^3,u^2,u,1) * \begin{pmatrix} 1 & -4 & 6 & -4 & 1 \\ -4 & 12 & -12 & 4 & 0 \\ 6 & -12 & 6 & 0 & 0 \\ -4 & 4 & 0 & 0 & 0 \\ 1 & 0 & 0 & 0 & 0 \end{pmatrix} * \begin{pmatrix} p_0 \\ p_1 \\ p_2 \\ p_3 \\ p_4 \end{pmatrix}$$

Degree 5, six control points:

$$C(u) = (u^5, \ldots, 1) * \begin{pmatrix} -1 & 5 & -10 & 10 & -5 & 1 \\ 5 & -20 & 30 & -20 & 5 & 0 \\ -10 & 30 & -30 & 10 & 0 & 0 \\ 10 & -20 & 10 & 0 & 0 & 0 \\ -5 & 5 & 0 & 0 & 0 & 0 \\ 1 & 0 & 0 & 0 & 0 & 0 \end{pmatrix} * \begin{pmatrix} p_0 \\ p_1 \\ p_2 \\ p_3 \\ p_4 \\ p_5 \end{pmatrix}$$

All these matrices are easily derived directly from the definition of the Bernstein polynomials. The development is essentially the same as for the uniform B-spline formula, so we do not repeat it. In all cases the parameter u must go from 0 to 1. Figure 8.6 shows a Bezier curve of degree five with six control points. It will be seen that with degree 5, the curve stays quite far from the control points; with a higher degree, this is exaggerated. As we have said, it is everywhere influenced by all the control points. Changing one of the inner control points results in only a slight change of the curve but this change will be of a nonlocal nature. These attributes nearly forbid the use of general Bezier curves with a higher number of control points when close approximation to them is important.

## 8.3.2 Piecewise Bezier Curves

There is a special case of the Bezier method that does permit close approximation of points. We accomplish this by using a sequence of Bezier curves of modest degree (2, 3, or 4). In effect we create a *piecewise Bezier curve.* The pieces can be of different degrees. If one of the pieces

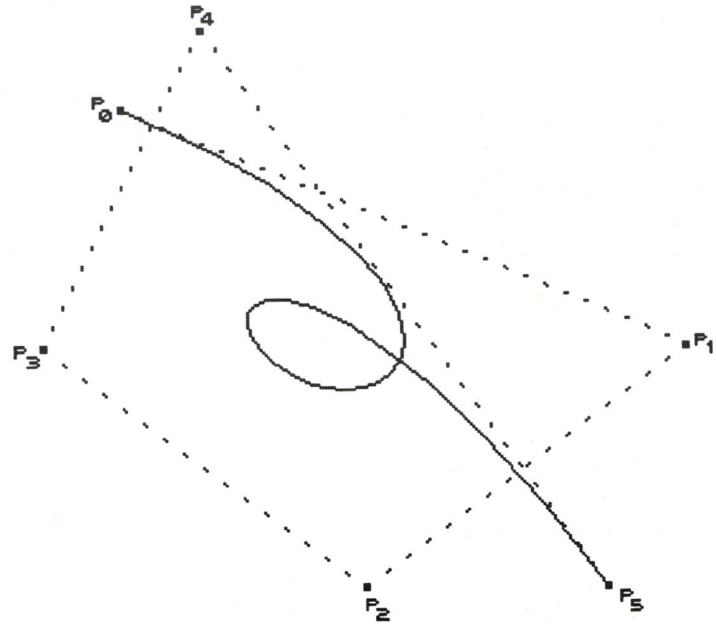


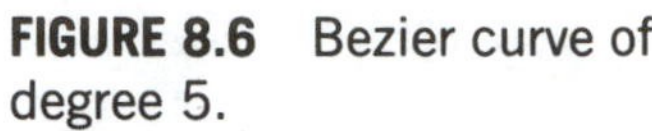
**FIGURE 8.6** Bezier curve of degree 5.

is a Bezier curve of degree 3, then it will pass through the points $P_i$ and $P_{i+3}$ but only approximate to the two control points in between. The intermediate points will define the slopes of the piece of the curve on the interval from $P_i$ to $P_{i+3}$. If we choose the in-between points of all the pieces properly, the entire curve will have a continuous first derivative. Figure 8.7 shows such a curve with seven control points.

Both pieces are cubics. The first goes from $P_0$ to $P_3$, the second from $P_3$ to $P_6$. The slopes of the first piece are controlled by $P_1$ and $P_2$, the slopes of the second piece by $P_4$ and $P_5$. Figure 8.8 shows the curve to the same control points except that $P_4$ has been changed to be collinear with $P_2$ and $P_3$. This makes the slopes of the two pieces identical where they meet in $P_3$ so the curve has a continuous first derivative. We can continue this to produce long, complicated curves with continuous first derivatives. If we use only parabolic pieces, the curve will interpolate through every second point and the points between can be used to set the slopes. We must ensure that they are collinear with their left two neighbors and collinear with their right two neighbors to avoid corners. If we use only cubic pieces, the curve will interpolate through every third point and the two inner points will control the slopes, providing more flexibility. Modeling such curves can easily be done interactively, moving the points that control the slopes to mold the curve through the other points.

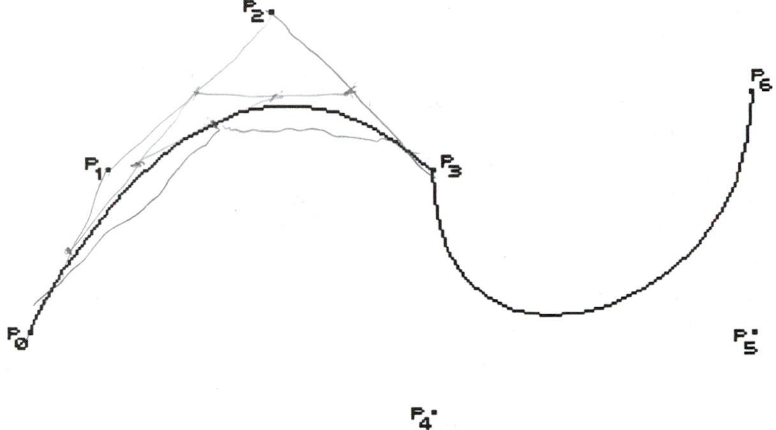


**FIGURE 8.7** Piecewise cubic Bezier curve.

The pieces are drawn using the above formulas. For example, for cubic pieces we use the cubic formula and specify the control point vectors in the following way:

$$\begin{pmatrix} p_0 \\ p_1 \\ p_2 \\ p_3 \end{pmatrix} \quad \begin{pmatrix} p_3 \\ p_4 \\ p_5 \\ p_6 \end{pmatrix} \quad \begin{pmatrix} p_6 \\ p_7 \\ p_8 \\ p_9 \end{pmatrix} \quad \text{etc.}$$

This method allows us to do the following. We specify a sequence of control points through which a curve should pass: these are the points $P_0$, $P_3$, $P_6$, ... above. We then specify auxiliary points: these are the points $P_1$, $P_2$, $P_4$, $P_5$, ... above, which serve only to control the slopes of the curve at the control points. The piecewise Bezier curve with this

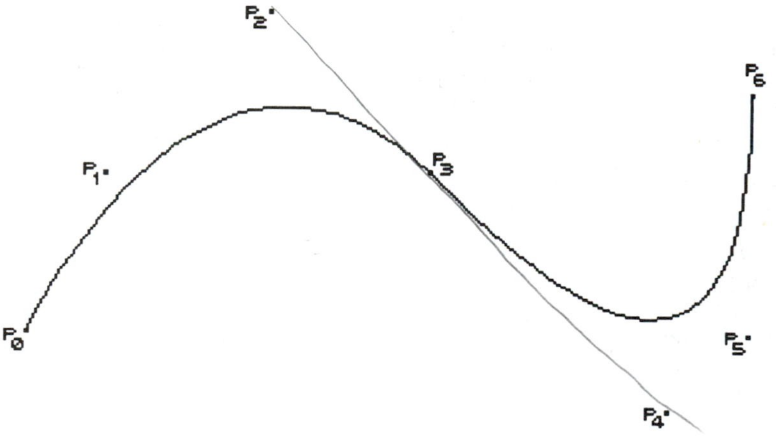


**FIGURE 8.8** Piecewise cubic Bezier curve.

set of points will then interpolate through all the control points and still be only locally controlled. If we specify auxiliary points before and after a control point that are collinear with this control point, the Bezier curve to this set of points will have a continuous first derivative; it will be attached to the first and last control points; it will look almost as smooth as a B-spline curve; and it will interpolate through all control points. The latter property can be considered an advantage over the B-spline curve in certain applications. The calculation is no more complicated than the uniform B-spline formula.

The specification of the auxiliary points is very easy if it is done interactively with a mouse or similar device that allows natural movement in an animated graphics display with visual feedback. Some of the drawing programs for Apple computers, such as Illustrator and Cricket-Draw, allow direct manipulation of Bezier curves by "dragging" points with the mouse to control the shape with the curve following the changes in real time.

General and piecewise Bezier curves can easily be made to form closed curves. To do this, we specify the control points in a cyclic manner analogous to the closed curves described above. Bezier curves have the convex hull property.

**Hand-Drawing Rule** The rule for sketching a cubic Bezier curve by hand is a little more complicated to develop than for B-splines. From the matrix formula we find that, for u = ½, the curve assumes the value:

$$C_x(1/2) = 1/8*x_{i-1} + 3/8*x_i + 3/8*x_{i+1} + 1/8*x_{i+2}$$
$$C_y(1/2) = 1/8*y_{i-1} + 3/8*y_i + 3/8*y_{i+1} + 1/8*y_{i+2}$$

This point can be found geometrically by finding the midpoint $M_1$ of the line from $P_{i-1}$ to $P_i$, the midpoint $M_2$ of the line from $P_i$ to $P_{i+1}$, and the midpoint $M_3$ of the line from $P_{i+1}$ to $P_{i+2}$. Then we find the midpoint of the line $M_1 - M_2$, $M_4$, and the midpoint of the line $M_2 - M_3$, $M_5$. Finally we take the midpoint of the line $M_4 - M_5$, M. Point M will have the coordinates $C_x(1/2)$ and $C_y(1/2)$, as you will find from substitution into the above equations.

The coordinates of $M_4$ are:
$$((x_{i-1} + 2x_i + x_{i+1})/4, (y_{i-1} + 2y_i + y_{i+1})/4)$$
The coordinates of $M_5$ are:
$$((x_i + 2x_{i+1} + x_{i+2})/4, (y_i + 2y_{i+1} + y_{i+2})/4)$$

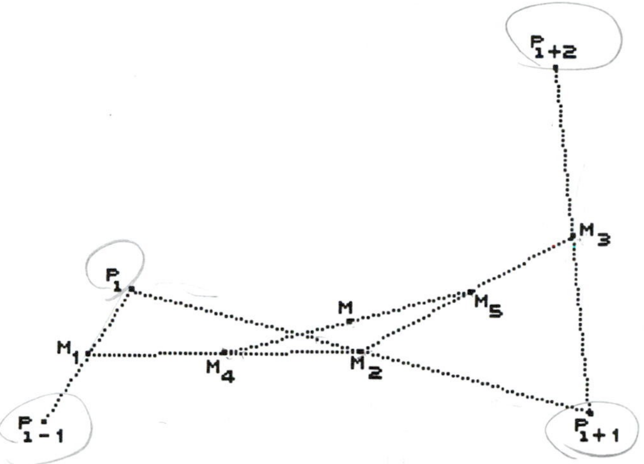


**FIGURE 8.9** Hand-drawing a Bezier curve.

From this it follows that the slope of the line connecting these two points is:

$$\frac{-y_{i-1} - y_i + y_{i+1} + y_{i+2}}{-x_{i-1} - x_i + x_{i+1} + x_{i+2}}.$$

This is also the slope of the curve at the point corresponding to u = ½, therefore the curve goes through M with the slope of this line. Figure 8.9 shows this process of finding the point M. The slope of the curve at a terminal point ($P_{i-1}$ or $P_{i+2}$) coincides with the straight line from this point to its neighbor.

So far, we have confined our discussion to curves on a plane. A curve can be a space curve, one in three-dimensional space. For these, we would have three parametric equations, adding one, $z = Z(u)$, that gives the z-coordinates in terms of the parameter u. We prefer not to treat these; instead we consider them as curves traced on a 3-D surface. They can be considered as a special case within the topic of parametric surfaces.

# 8.4 PARAMETRIC SURFACES

We now move from curves to surfaces. A plane cannot contain a surface, so we must think in 3-D space. A surface can be described by a single function that establishes a relation between three variables x, y, and z:

$$z = f(x,y)$$

Here x and y are both independent variables. For the same reason as in the plane, we prefer to use parametric representation. To describe a parametric surface in 3-D space, we use three functions, but each function has two independent variables u and v, the parameters:

$$x = x(u,v),\ y = y(u,v),\ \text{and}\ z = z(u,v).$$

If only one parameter varies and the other is kept at a constant value, say $v = c$ and u is allowed to vary, then $x(u,c)$, $y(u,c)$, $z(u,c)$ describe a curve which runs on that surface. The slope of the projection of this curve on the (x,y)-plane is:

$$dy/dx = (dy/du)/(dx/du)$$

The derivatives with respect to u are all partial. The slopes of the projections on the other planes and the symmetric cases for fixed u and variable v can be derived similarly. But the projections of such curves on any of the planes of the coordinate system are not identical with the intersections of the surface with any of these planes. For example, to get the intersection of the surface with the (x,y)-plane, we observe that all such points in the surface will have $z = 0$. We then set $z(u,v) = 0$. This is a relation between u and v. We should transform this into a parameterized relation with a single parameter of the form:

$$u = U(w) \quad \text{and} \quad v = V(w)$$

The intersection is then described as a curve in the (x,y)-plane through a single parameter, w:

$$x = x(U(w),V(w)) \quad \text{and} \quad y = y(U(w),V(w))$$

We will not go into more detail here.

In complete analogy to parametric curves in 2-D space, we can easily limit a surface to a certain region by limiting the range of the parameters to a finite two-dimensional interval, for example, the rectangular area $[0,n] \times [0,m]$.

We obtain a surface that interpolates or approximates a set of control points in much the same way as we did with curves in the plane. We construct three surfaces, one of which interpolates or approximates the x-coordinates, one the y-coordinates, and one the z-coordinates of the control points. Each of these specific surfaces is defined on a rectangular area of the two arguments u and v, which can also be called a two-dimensional interval. Let this range be the rectangle $[0,n] \times [0,m]$. The particular parameter values (u,v) that determine the approximation or interpolation will be the same in all three surfaces.

An example will make this clearer. We desire to construct a surface that contains a control point P, $(p_x,p_y,p_z)$. If we construct three surfaces with a given parameter range so that, at a particular point $(u_0,v_0)$ within this range, we have $x(u_0,v_0) = p_x$, $y(u_0,v_0) = p_y$, and $z(u_0,v_0) = p_z$, then it is evident that the surface goes through the point $(p_x,p_y,p_z)$.

The same idea can be applied to surfaces that approximate (come near to) the point. We define basic surfaces b(u,v), which are combined as a weighted sum using the coordinates of the control points as the weights. This is analogous to what we have done before in two dimensions.

# 8.5 UNIFORM B-SPLINE SURFACES

We can define a basic surface b(u,v) by multiplying the uniform cubic B-spline b(u) from Section 7.2.1 with itself, but with two different independent parameters u and v:

$$b(u,v) = b(u)*b(v)$$

The parameters u and v both range over the interval $[-2,2]$, so the parameter pair ranges over the area $[-2,2] \times [-2,2]$. We use the letter b for both the curves b(u) and b(v) and the basic B-spline surface b(u,v). This should not lead to confusion as the context will differentiate; the surface b will have two arguments instead of one. Figure 8.10 shows a 3-D view of this surface. Outside the range of definition the surface b(u,v) is identical to 0. Within its range, the surface b is pieced together from 16 different surface equations because the above definition involves the multiplication of each of the four curve pieces that comprise b(u) with each of the four pieces of the curve b(v). This surface is continuous up to its second partial derivative, as is true for each of the curves b(u) and b(v).

From the previously known values for b(u) and b(v), we have:

```
b( 0,-1) = b( 0, 1) = b(-1, 0) = b( 1, 0) = 1/9,
b(-1,-1) = b(-1, 1) = b( 1,-1) = b( 1, 1) = 1/36,
b( 0, 0) = 4/9,
etc.
```

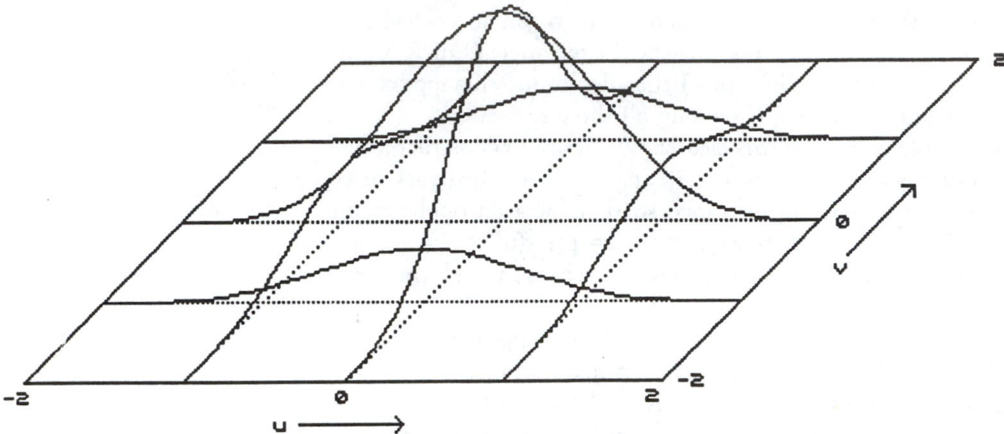


**FIGURE 8.10** Basic uniform B-spline surface.

Here we do not have knots as we had with the basic B-spline. The grid on which the basic surface is defined shows 10 lines. These lines delimit 16 subareas in which the 16 different surfaces that comprise b(u,v) are defined. These specific surfaces are connected together at the boundaries of the rectangular subregions.

In using this approach, be sure to observe the following. If we want to interpolate or approximate a set of points in space by a surface, we first define a rectangular grid for the range for the parameters. Each control point is then associated with one grid point. (This of course does not mean that the surface will be rectangular or confined somehow to a rectangular area in any of the coordinates.)

The grid only relates the parameter values to the control point coordinates. How the control points are related to each other on the final surface is totally independent of this. Figure 8.11 shows an arrangement of a grid of parameter values, where 6∗5 control points are given. In effect, we are considering points $P_{i,j}$ with i going from 0 to 5 and j from 0 to 4.

We need as many basic surfaces as there are grid points. They are obtained by simply shifting the surface b(u,v) by integer amounts to the proper grid points. This is done formally by:

$$b_{i,j}(u,v) = b(u-i, v-j) \quad \text{for } i = 0,\ldots,n \text{ and } j = 0,\ldots,m$$

These basic surfaces are considered only in the interpolation area [0,n] × [0,m]. In all inner subareas (not adjacent to the edge of [0,n] ×

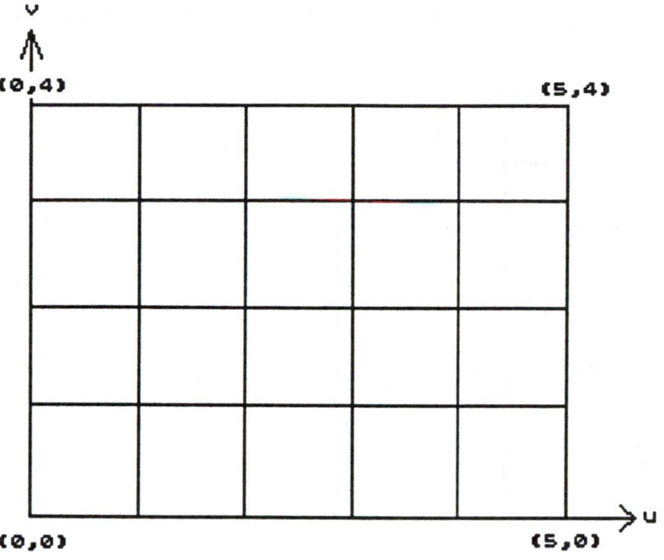


**FIGURE 8.11** Parameter grid.

[0,m]) the sum of the $b_{i,j}$ is equal to 1. At any point within an inner subregion 16 surfaces are nonzero. The restrictions of these surfaces to an inner subarea are called the 16 *blending surfaces* in this subarea. That their sum is equal to 1 follows from the fact that the sum of all $b_i(u)$ is equal to 1 in $[1,n-1]$ and the same is true for the $b_j(v)$ in $[1,m-1]$.

**Construction of a Uniform B-Spline Surface** A surface that approximates the x-coordinates of the control points is obtained by forming:

$$S_x(u,v) = \sum_{i=0}^{n} \sum_{j=0}^{m} x_{i,j} b_{i,j}(u,v)$$

The same is done again for the y-coordinates of the control points to obtain $S_y(u,v)$ and again for the z-coordinates to obtain $S_z(u,v)$. These three coordinates describe the final uniform B-spline surface in space as u and v move through their entire range.

**Properties of the B-Spline Surface** This surface normally does not go through any control point; it is an approximating surface. The value $S(u,v)$ is a weighted sum of four to 16 surrounding control points. Figure 8.12 shows which control points are involved in determining the value of the surface at a point $(u,v)$.

In an inner subarea, S always is a weighted sum using at least nine and at most 16 surrounding control points. Exactly on a grid point

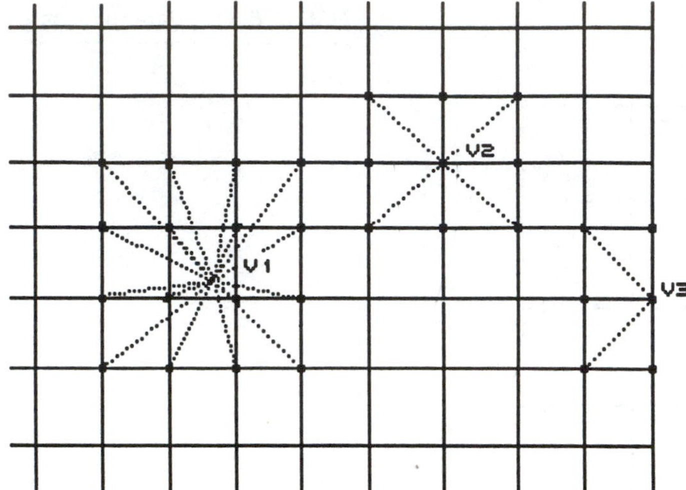


**FIGURE 8.12** Control points involved in a surface value.

(point V2), only nine basic surfaces are nonzero. At a point not on any grid line (point V1) 16 basic surfaces are nonzero.

In an outer subarea (as at point V3), S is a weighted sum of from four up to 12 surrounding control points. You should verify this for yourself. Point V1 is an inner point; its coordinates therefore are determined by 16 surrounding control points. V2 is on an intersection of two grid lines and is therefore determined by nine control points. V3 is on the edge and is therefore determined by six control points and the origin. Several other positions are possible. In the outer subareas the sum of the basic surfaces is less than 1, so the uniform B-spline surface is influenced by the origin of the coordinate system in that it is pulled toward it. This should be avoided—the drawing algorithms presented later will automatically take care of this. Not all surface points in outer subareas are used to draw the surface.

**Specifying Control Points More Than Once** In this approach for constructing surfaces, it is not possible to pull the curve closer or through a single control point by specifying this point two or three times. You can deduce from the formalism that a cubic B-spline surface is forced through a given point if this point is specified nine times in a $3 \times 3$ area, and similarly, the surface is pulled more strongly in the direction of a control point if the point is specified four times in a $2 \times 2$ area of the grid. The flexibility that we have to define curves is more restricted here because of the rectangular parameter grid with which the control points must be associated. We cannot arbitrarily respecify one point without influencing the arrangement of all the other points. Repeating a point in the interior of the grid, along a line, implies the introduction of an additional column of grid points in order to keep the grid rectangular. A similar effect is true if we repeat a point along a column in the interior of the grid. If a grid is defined with repeated control points to begin with, then we obtain the desired effect on the surface. But the repetition of points later on is more complicated than with curves.

Figure 8.13 shows a parameter grid with 6 × 6 control points, in which the control point $P_{2,2}$ is specified nine times. Only the subscripts are shown in the drawing. This leads to a parameter grid of 8 × 8 in which certain grid points have no associated control points. If more control points are created to fill in the gaps, then the surface can be drawn and it will be forced through the control point $P_{2,2}$.

We have a choice of ways to fill in the missing points. If we put the middle point into the empty spaces left and right or above and below, we introduce sharp ridges in the surface running close to the repeated points (but not going through them). Where these ridges cross, the surface will assume the value of the ninefold specified point in a sharp peak. All this is in neat analogy to curves on the plane. We can avoid the ridges by not repeating the existing neighboring points, generating new ones instead. For example, we might use the arithmetic mean of the middle point and its neighbor.

In contrast, the repetition of control points is easy to do at the boundaries of the grid. Figure 8.14 shows how this is done, analogously

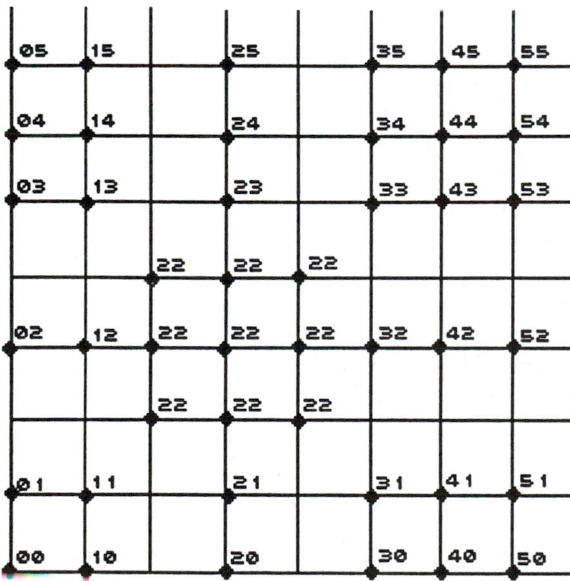


**FIGURE 8.13** Repeated specification of an inner control point.

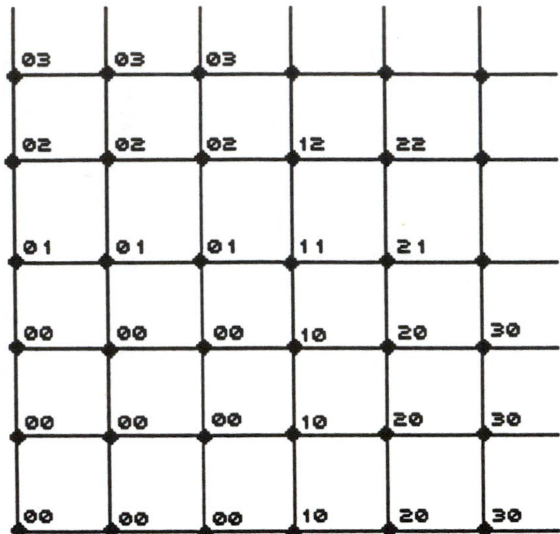


**FIGURE 8.14** Repeated specification of boundary control points.

to curves, on the lower left boundary of the parameter grid. The subscripts show which control points are repeated. With this we achieve the following. The B-spline surface is attached to the four outer control points because each are present nine times. It will not be attached to the other control points on the boundaries, but the surface will be attached to the B-spline curve that approximates the boundary control points.

**A Drawing Algorithm** In order to derive a matrix formula for the calculation of surface points in an inner subarea, we could proceed in a way similar to the uniform B-spline formula for curves. We need to multiply all 16 blending surfaces by the proper control points and sum them together. The proper control points are the four control points associated with the corner grid points of the inner subarea plus the 12 control points associated with the 12 grid points adjacent to the subarea. Figure 8.15 shows an inner subarea double-shaded and the 16 control points associated with it.

The next step would be to group the powers of u and extract the row vector $(u^3,u^2,u,1)$ on the left of the expression. Then we would group the powers of v and extract the column vector $(v^3,v^2,v,1)^T$ on the right. This gives an expression of the form:

$$S(u,v) = U * C * V^T$$

in which S(u,v) is the surface, U and V are the two above vectors, and C is a 4 × 4 matrix in which every element is a combination of all 16

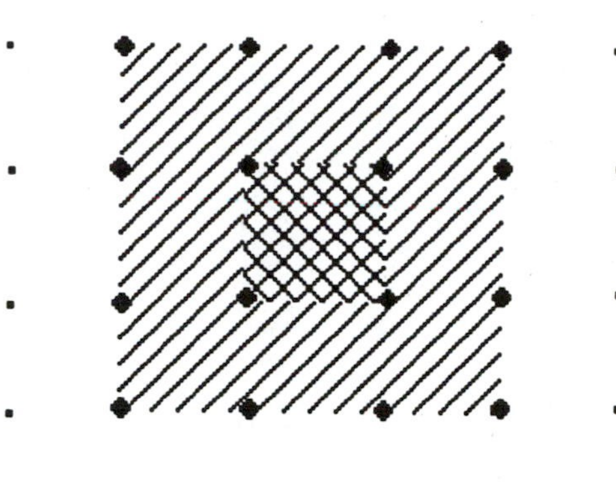

**FIGURE 8.15** Relation of patch and control points.

control points with certain numbers. C can be decomposed further into three matrices, but such a calculation is hardly feasible because it is too lengthy. We will do it another way.

We have expressed the B-spline curve in a subinterval [0,1] as:

$$C(u) = 1/6 * U * M * P$$

where U is a row vector of powers of u, M is a $4 \times 4$ matrix of coefficients, and P is the vector of the four control points determining the course of the curve in this subinterval. You will remember that there are three such expressions, one in which the control point vector P contains the x-coordinates of the control points, another the y-coordinates, and the third the z-coordinates. We apply the same logic here. The control points are actually constants, but assume that they are functions of the parameter v. For any fixed v they behave like constants. We rewrite the formula and put v as the second argument into the function C:

$$C(u,v) = 1/6 * U * M * P(v)$$

This is identical to the formulation:

$$C(u,v) = 1/6 * U * M * \begin{pmatrix} p_{i-1}(v) \\ p_i(v) \\ p_{i+1}(v) \\ p_{i+2}(v) \end{pmatrix}$$

As u goes through [0,1] repeatedly for different values of v, we get a new B-spline curve for every new value of v. Let's now assume that the control point coordinates $p_{i-1}(v)$, $p_i(v)$, $p_{i+1}(v)$, and $p_{i+2}(v)$ are functions of v defined in the interval [0,1] for v. If we multiply the u-interval and the v-interval into a $[0,1] \times [0,1]$ square, in which u moves horizontally and v moves vertically, then we can draw the different B-spline curves for different v values next to each other. Together they describe a surface over this unit square.

We now relate the points P(v) to the given 16 control points. For each v we have four points. As v goes from 0 to 1 these four points move on four curves. We require that each of these curves be a B-spline curve for four control points: $P_{i-1}(v)$ moves on the curve for the control points $P_{i-1,j-1}$, $P_{i-1,j}$, $P_{i-1,j+1}$, and $P_{i-1,j+2}$ and so on. $P_{i+2}(v)$ moves on the curve for $P_{i+2,j-1}$, $P_{i+2,j}$, $P_{i+2,j+1}$, and $P_{i+2,j+2}$. So the points P(v) actually generate curves if v is considered a variable. We will write S now instead of C to indicate that this expresses a surface:

$$S(u,v) = 1/6 * U * M * \begin{pmatrix} p_{i-1}(v) \\ p_i\ (v) \\ p_{i+1}(v) \\ p_{i+2}(v) \end{pmatrix}$$

To express the points P(v) as functions of the four control points that define their curves, we use the same matrix formula and transpose it to make the control point vector a row vector:

$$\begin{aligned} p_{i-1}(v) &= 1/6(p_{i-1,j-1}, p_{i-1,j}, p_{i-1,j+1}, p_{i-1,j+2}) * M^T * V^T \\ p_i(v) &= 1/6(p_{i,j-1}, p_{i,j}, p_{i,j+1}, p_{i,j+2}) * M^T * V^T \\ p_{i+1}(v) &= 1/6(p_{i+1,j-1}, p_{i+1,j}, p_{i+1,j+1}, p_{i+1,j+2}) * M^T * V^T \\ p_{i+2}(v) &= 1/6(p_{i+2,j-1}, p_{i+2,j}, p_{i+2,j+1}, p_{i+2,j+2}) * M^T * V^T \end{aligned}$$

Substituting these row vectors into the matrix expression above gives:

$$S(u,v) = 1/36 * U * M * P * M^T * V^T$$

with

$$U = (u^3, u^2, u, 1)$$

$$P = \begin{pmatrix} p_{i-1,j-1} & p_{i-1,j} & p_{i-1,j+1} & p_{i-1,j+2} \\ p_{i,j-1} & p_{i,j} & p_{i,j+1} & p_{i,j+2} \\ p_{i+1,j-1} & p_{i+1,j} & p_{i+1,j+1} & p_{i+1,j+2} \\ p_{i+2,j-1} & p_{i+2,j} & p_{i+2,j+1} & p_{i+2,j+2} \end{pmatrix}$$

and

$$V = (v^3, v^2, v, 1).$$

M is the matrix from the uniform cubic B-spline formula:

$$M = \begin{pmatrix} -1 & 3 & -3 & 1 \\ 3 & -6 & 3 & 0 \\ -3 & 0 & 3 & 0 \\ 1 & 4 & 1 & 0 \end{pmatrix}$$

We call this the *uniform bicubic B-spline formula.* It expresses that part of S which is closest to the middle four control points in the matrix P. This is analogous to the uniform cubic B-spline formula for curves which expresses the curve piece closest to the two middle points in the control point vector. When we calculate the value of S in such a subarea, we use the 16 control points surrounding this subarea. To display this part of S, the expression has to be evaluated for both u and v moving in small steps from 0 to 1. All this has to be done three times, once for P filled with the x-coordinates, once with the y-coordinates, and once with the z-coordinates. The surface part so obtained is called a *bicubic B-spline patch*. For this reason, the 16 control points that determine this patch are called the *patch matrix.*

To move from patch to patch, we move the 4 × 4 patch matrix in some systematic way over the whole array of control points and start u and v at 0 for every patch. The patches will join together with second-order continuity and form a smooth surface. The array of control points can be of any size (a rectangular arrangement, of course) but the patch matrix is always of size 4 × 4.

This formula cannot calculate the surface in the outer subareas because 16 surrounding control points are not available there, as seen in Figure 8.12. It is possible to attach the surface to the four corner points of the control point array and simultaneously to the B-spline curves connecting these points along the edges of the whole approximation area by specifying boundary control points three times. This implies that the corner control points are specified nine times. Figure 8.16 shows a surface consisting of two bicubic patches and the 20 control points for the two patches. The 20 control points are assumed to be arranged in a 5 × 4 control point matrix:

$$\begin{pmatrix} P_{00} & P_{01} & P_{02} & P_{03} \\ P_{10} & P_{11} & P_{12} & P_{13} \\ P_{20} & P_{21} & P_{22} & P_{23} \\ P_{30} & P_{31} & P_{32} & P_{33} \\ P_{40} & P_{41} & P_{42} & P_{43} \end{pmatrix}$$

The patch matrices are submatrices of the control point matrix. Two patch matrices are possible in this case. They are indicated by the rectangles surrounding them:

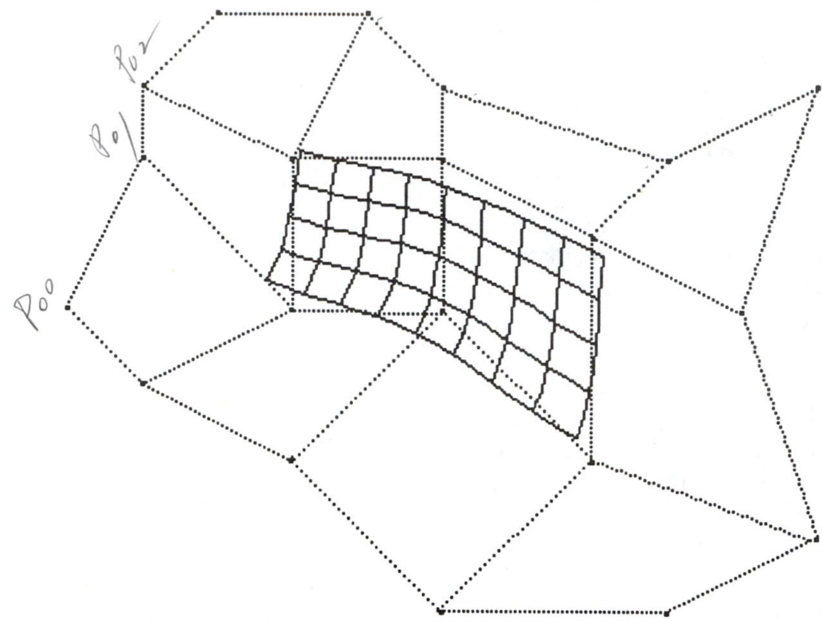

**FIGURE 8.16** Two joined B-spline patches.

$$\begin{array}{|cccc|}
\hline
P_{00} & P_{01} & P_{02} & P_{03} \\
P_{10} & P_{11} & P_{12} & P_{13} \\
P_{20} & P_{21} & P_{22} & P_{23} \\
P_{30} & P_{31} & P_{32} & P_{33} \\
\hline
\multicolumn{1}{c}{P_{40}} & \multicolumn{1}{c}{P_{41}} & \multicolumn{1}{c}{P_{42}} & \multicolumn{1}{c}{P_{43}}
\end{array}
\qquad
\begin{array}{|cccc|}
\multicolumn{1}{c}{P_{00}} & \multicolumn{1}{c}{P_{01}} & \multicolumn{1}{c}{P_{02}} & \multicolumn{1}{c}{P_{03}} \\
\hline
P_{10} & P_{11} & P_{12} & P_{13} \\
P_{20} & P_{21} & P_{22} & P_{23} \\
P_{30} & P_{31} & P_{32} & P_{33} \\
P_{40} & P_{41} & P_{42} & P_{43} \\
\hline
\end{array}$$

We can see that the patch matrices must "overlap" within the control point matrix. The above two patch matrices yield the two joining bicubic B-spline patches of Figure 8.16.

## 8.6 GENERAL B-SPLINE SURFACES

The appearance of general and uniform B-spline surfaces is not very different. The general ones are calculated in a different manner, however. Everything can be derived by analogy to the general B-spline curves and to the uniform B-spline surfaces. It is not necessary to repeatedly specify corner points and edge points in order to attach the surface to the corners and to the boundary curves because this is automatically the case with the general B-spline surface. The basic surfaces from which the approximating surface is constructed are formed as a product of two general B-splines with two independent arguments u and v:

$$b_{ij}(u,v) = b_i(u)*b_j(v)$$

Here we assume that both of the general B-splines are of the same degree and in particular that they are cubics (that is, $k = 4$). Of course the above formulation is valid for all general B-spline surfaces and allows any degree and combinations of different degrees. The control point coordinates must be associated with a rectangular parameter grid, as in the uniform case, but the grid definition is somewhat different and depends on the degree of the B-splines chosen.

If we have $n+1$ by $m+1$ control points, then we define a rectangular parameter grid with $n+k+1 \times m+k+1$ grid points. The grid points $(u_i, v_j)$ must fulfill:

$$\begin{aligned} u_i &= 0 && \text{if } 0 \leq i < k \\ u_i &= i-k+1 && \text{if } k \leq i \leq n \\ u_i &= n-k+2 && \text{if } n < i \leq n+k \end{aligned}$$

and

$$\begin{aligned} v_j &= 0 && \text{if } 0 \leq j < k \\ v_j &= j-k+1 && \text{if } k \leq j \leq m \\ v_j &= m-k+2 && \text{if } m < j \leq m+k \end{aligned}$$

Usually entire rows and columns of grid points will coincide at the edges of the parameter grid. (Remember, grid points are not control points and coinciding grid points don't mean coinciding control points!) Corresponding to this grid, the basic surfaces are defined as the product above with b(u) and b(v) both defined with the Cox-de Boor recursion formula (see Section 7.3 on general B-splines):

$$\begin{aligned} b_{i,1}(u) &= 1 \text{ if } u_i \leq u < u_{i+1} \\ &= 0 \text{ elsewhere} \end{aligned}$$

$$b_{i,k}(u) = \frac{(u-u_i)b_{i,k-1}(u)}{u_{i+k-1} - u_i} + \frac{(u_{i+k}-u)b_{i+1,k-1}(u)}{u_{i+k} - u_{i+1}}$$

and

$$\begin{aligned} b_{i,1}(v) &= 1 \text{ if } v_i \leq v < v_{i+1} \\ &= 0 \text{ elsewhere} \end{aligned}$$

$$b_{i,k}(v) = \frac{(v-v_i)b_{i,k-1}(v)}{v_{i+k-1} - v_i} + \frac{(v_{i+k}-v)b_{i+1,k-1}(v)}{v_{i+k} - v_{i+1}}$$

For bicubic surfaces, we set $b_{i,j}(u,v) = b_{i,4}(u)*b_{j,4}(v)$. The general B-spline surface is then defined as:

$$S(u,v) = \sum_{i=0}^{n} \sum_{i=0}^{m} p_{i,j} b_{i,j}(u,v)$$

No patching is done with general B-spline surfaces! The calculation of b(u) and b(v) must be done with the recursive algorithm as in Section 7.3. This calculates not just a patch but the whole surface when u goes in small steps from 0 to $n-k+2$ and v from 0 to $m-k+2$.

# 8.7 CATMULL-ROM PATCHES

What we have done with B-spline curves can also be done with Catmull-Rom curves. The Cartesian product of two Catmull-Rom curves defines a Catmull-Rom surface. This surface goes through the control points and is continuous up to its first partial derivative. We will not give a general formula; instead we present the formula for calculating one Catmull-Rom patch below. A *Catmull-Rom patch* is that part of the whole surface that is stretched between four neighboring control points. The whole Catmull-Rom surface is calculated by calculating all its patches.

$$S(u,v) = 1/4*(u^3,u^2,u,1) * M * P * M^T * (v^3,v^2,v,1)^T$$

$$\text{M is the matrix: } \begin{pmatrix} -1 & 3 & -3 & 1 \\ 2 & -5 & 4 & -1 \\ -1 & 0 & 1 & 0 \\ 0 & 2 & 0 & 0 \end{pmatrix}$$

P is the patch matrix of the 16 control points surrounding this patch:

$$P = \begin{pmatrix} p_{i-1,j-1} & p_{i-1,j} & p_{i-1,j+1} & p_{i-1,j+2} \\ p_{i,j-1} & p_{i,j} & p_{i,j+1} & p_{i,j+2} \\ p_{i+1,j-1} & p_{i+1,j} & p_{i+1,j+1} & p_{i+1,j+2} \\ p_{i+2,j-1} & p_{i+2,j} & p_{i+2,j+1} & p_{i+2,j+2} \end{pmatrix}$$

The parameters u and v are varied by small increments from 0 to 1 for every patch. The Catmull-Rom patch is attached to the four inner control points of the patch matrix. The patches must be taken "overlapping" from the control point matrix. The surface can be attached to the corner points of the control point mesh and to the Catmull-Rom curves at the boundaries by specifying the boundary points twice. This implies that the corner points will be specified four times.

The same can be done with splines under tension and with closely approximating splines. We only need to put the proper matrix into the surface formula.

# 8.8 BEZIER SURFACES

A *Bezier surface* is defined as the Cartesian product of two Bezier curves in much the same way as we defined general B-spline surfaces as the Cartesian product of two general B-spline curves. The degree of the particular Bezier curve depends on the number of control points with which a surface is constructed. Again, the number of control points must be of the form $m \times n$ for two integers m and n. These control points are associated with a rectangular grid of parameter values. With a large number of control points, we will get a Bezier surface of high degree. Such a surface does not stay very close to the control points, so the piecewise Bezier surfaces are more often used. We describe both kinds of surfaces below.

## 8.8.1 General Bezier Surfaces

To define this surface, we first define the basic elements from which it is composed. In the same way that the general Bezier curve is formed as a linear combination of Bernstein polynomials, the surface is formed from a linear combination of basic surfaces, which, by analogy to the polynomials, can be called *Bernstein surfaces.* These basic surfaces are all defined on the area $[0,1] \times [0,1]$ and are the Cartesian products of all Bernstein polynomials of some degree in these intervals. If $(n+1) \times (m+1)$ control points are used, then $n+1$ polynomials $b_i(u)$ of degree n and $m+1$ polynomials $b_j(v)$ of degree m result, as shown in Section 8.3.1. The Cartesian products of all $b_i$ with all $b_j$ yields $(n+1) \times (m+1)$ surfaces:

$$b_{i,j}(u,v) = b_i(u)*b_j(v)$$

The surface from the given control points is then defined as:

$$S(u,v) = \sum_{i=0}^{n} \sum_{j=0}^{m} p_{i,j} b_{i,j}(u,v)$$

As the parameters u and v cover the area $[0,1] \times [0,1]$ the point $S(u,v)$ covers the surface.

This is a theoretical definition that characterizes the general Bezier surface. It is attached to the four outer control points $P_{0,0}$, $P_{n,0}$, $P_{0,m}$, and $P_{n,m}$. The edges of the surface consist of Bezier curves for the control points along the edges. A formula for calculating a general Bezier surface with 5 × 4 control points is:

$$S(u,v) = (u^4,u^3,u^2,u,1) * M4 * (p_{ij}) * M3^T * (v^3,v^2,v,1)^T$$

M4 and M3 are the matrices for the appropriate degree described in Section 8.3.1 and $(p_{ij})$ is a matrix of control points in an arrangement like this:

$$\begin{pmatrix} p_{0,0} & \cdot & \cdot & \cdot p_{0,3} \\ \cdot & \cdot & \cdot & \cdot \ \cdot \\ \cdot & \cdot & \cdot & \cdot \ \cdot \\ p_{4,0} & \cdot & \cdot & \cdot p_{4,3} \end{pmatrix}$$

The parameters u and v both go in small steps through the interval [0,1].

A similar disadvantage to that of the Bezier curve is that this surface does not stay close to the control points, especially for larger numbers of points where the degree of the surface is accordingly higher. Together with the lack of local control over the surface, this inflexibility is a problem in interactive design. A solution consists in restricting to Bezier surfaces of lower degrees, accommodating larger numbers of control points by patching these surfaces together. This is described below.

## 8.8.2 Bezier Patches

As indicated above, the entire surface is not always best constructed as a single general Bezier surface. As with curves, we can piece together several patches of lower degree; usually these patches are of degree 2 or 3. Nine control points arranged in a mesh of 3 × 3 can be covered with a patch with degrees 2 × 2; 16 control points in an arrangement of 4 × 4 will be covered by a patch with degrees 3 × 3. Figure 8.17 shows a patch for 4 × 3 control points. The calculation of surface points in this patch is done with the formula presented for the general Bezier surfaces but the matrices involved are for the appropriate lower degrees (3 and 2). Figure 8.18 shows two patches joined together at the boundary indicated by the arrows. Each patch is biquadratic and determined by nine control points. The two patch matrices of nine control

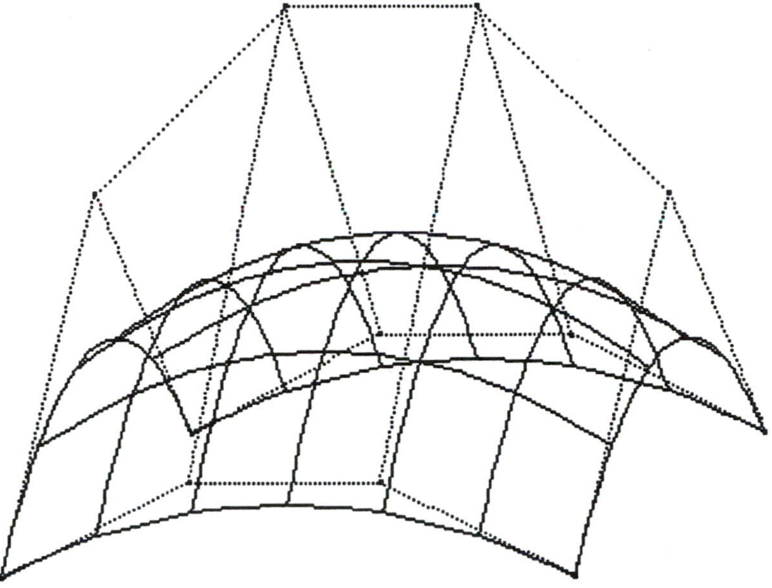

**FIGURE 8.17** Bezier patch.

points each share three points at the boundary. All 15 control points can be seen as the edges of the underlying mesh.

The patch matrices are not taken from the control point matrix as we do with B-spline or Catmull-Rom patches. They overlap only by

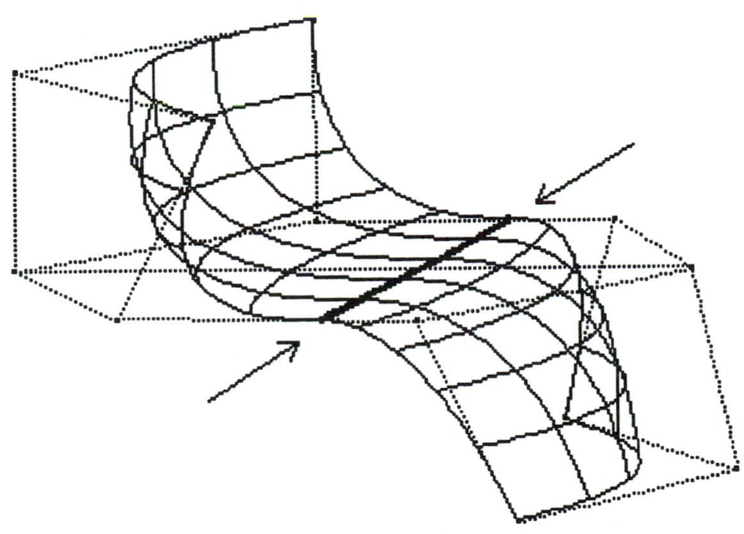

**FIGURE 8.18** Two joined Bezier patches.

one row or column of points. Therefore from 7 × 7 control points we can produce only four patches. The schematic is shown below:

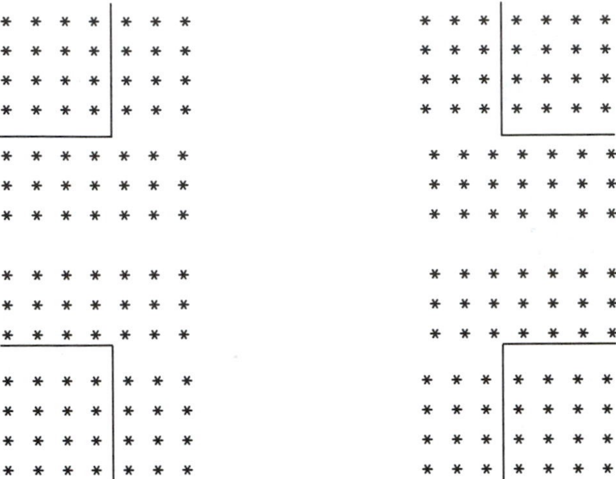

The Bezier patches are automatically attached to the outer four control points of the patch matrix. First-order continuity across the boundary between two patches is not easily accomplished if the control points are entered freehand or interactively. First, each boundary point must be collinear with the two nonboundary points adjacent to it, but this is not enough. Let us call these three collinear points a *collinear boundary triple.* If two adjacent collinear boundary triples are parallel, then the two polygons spanned by them are planar and there is no problem. But if they are not parallel, then the two polygons spanned by them are not planar; in this case the ratio of lengths of the collinear boundary triples must be constant. If this is not true, then the two patches will meet with a sharp ridge along the boundary. In an interactive environment with three-dimensional visual feedback it will not be easy to set the control points so as to satisfy these requirements. The three-dimensional coordinates of the control points must be calculated properly by a program in order to guarantee the first order-continuity.

Figure 8.19 shows a mesh of 20 control points forming two arrays of 3 × 4 control points each, sharing four points along the boundary. Each array determines a degree 2 × 3 Bezier patch, which is not shown. The boundary and the four collinear boundary triples are shown by solid lines. The three closest collinear boundary triples are parallel, the farthest is not, so those two quadrangles are not planar. The length ratios of the last two boundary triples are obviously not equal, therefore the

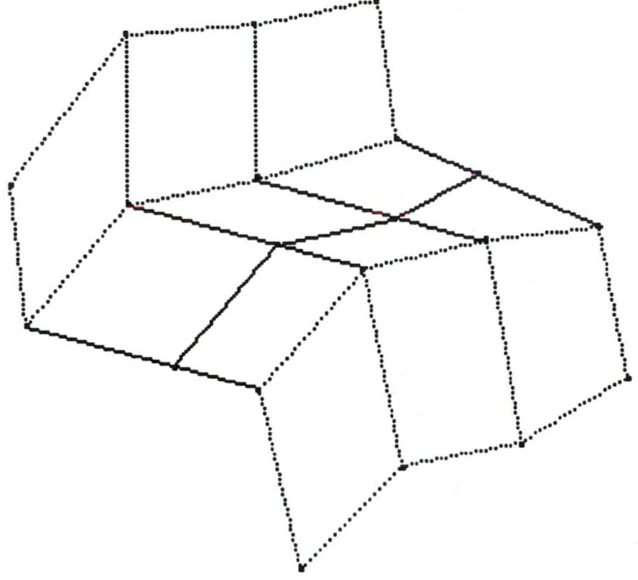

**FIGURE 8.19** Control points that would lead to a ridge.

Bezier patches form a sharp ridge where they meet along the edge between the farthest two boundary points.

# EXERCISES FOR CHAPTER 8

## Section 8.1 Catmull-Rom Curves

1. Write a procedure

   CR_curve(cpx,cpy : cp_vector; tens : real);

   that draws the part of a Catmull-Rom curve to four consecutive control points. The point coordinates are specified in the two arrays cpx and cpy. Use the type declaration:

   type cp_vector = array[1..4] of real;

   tens is the tension parameter.

2. Use the procedure CR_curve to draw an open Catmull_Rom curve to some specified control points, for example, the five points:

   (0,0) (0.5,2) (2.5, −0.5) (4,1) (6.5,0.5)

in the given order. The main loop in the driving program needs to call the procedure with control point vectors that advance by one coordinate for every piece of the curve, as explained in the text. The parameter tens is equal to 0.5.

3. Use CR_curve to draw an open Catmull-Rom curve, attached to the end points, to the above five control points.
4. Use CR_curve to draw open Catmull-Rom curves to the control points in Exercise 3 with varying parameter tens. What do you observe when tens gets close to and becomes 0? What if tens becomes negative? What if tens becomes bigger than 3?
5. Use CR_curve to draw closed Catmull-Rom curves to the above control points with varying parameters tens.
6. Extend the procedure CR_curve to three dimensions by adding a parameter of type cp_vector that contains the z-coordinates of four consecutive control points.
7. Specify control points in 3-D space and draw a Catmull-Rom curve to these points.
   a. Draw the curve on the screen with orthographic projection by ignoring the computation of the z-value.
   b. Draw the curve on the screen with perspective projection by computing the projection for each point on the curve produced by the drawing algorithm and connecting them by straight lines.
8. Use the hand drawing rule to draw an open Catmull-Rom curve to the five control points: $(-1,0)$ $(0.5,2)$ $(2.5,-0.5)$ $(4,1)$ $(3,0.5)$.

## Section 8.2 Closely Approximating Spline Curves

9. Write a procedure

```
close_curve(cpx,cpy : cp_vector; cl : real);
```

   that draws the part of a closely approximating spline curve to four consecutive control points. Their coordinates are specified in the two arrays cpx and cpy. Use the type declaration given in Exercise 1.
10. Use the procedure close_curve to draw a closely approximating open spline curve to the six control points:

   $(2,-0.5)$ $(0,0)$ $(0.5,2)$ $(2.5,-0.5)$ $(4,1)$ $(6.5,0.5)$

   The main loop in the driving program needs to call the procedure with control point vectors that advance by one coordinate for every piece of the curve, as explained in the text. Use cl = 0.5 to get a curve in between a B-spline and a Catmull-Rom curve.

11. Draw closely approximating open spline curves to the control points in Exercise 10 with parameter cl values of 0, 0.3, 0.6, and 1. What happens when cl becomes negative? When cl becomes bigger than 1?

# Section 8.3 Bezier Curves

12. Write a procedure

    Bez_curve(cpx,cpy : cp_vector);

    that draws the part of a Bezier curve to four consecutive control points. Their coordinates are specified in the two arrays cpx and cpy. Use the type declaration given in Exercise 1.

13. Use the procedure Bez_curve to draw a Bezier curve to the 10 control points below in the given order:

    (−2,2) (−1,2) (−1,1) (0, 0) (0.5,−0.5)
    (2,0) (2,1) (2,3) (3.5,1.5) (4.5,1.5)

    The main loop in the driving program needs to call the procedure with control point vectors that advance by three points for every piece of the curve, as explained in the text. Verify that the point triples with the knots in the center are collinear.

14. Use the procedure Bez_curve to draw a closed Bezier curve to the nine control points below in the given order:

    (0,0) (−1.5,0) (−2,−1) (0,−2) (1,−2.5) (3,−1) (2,0) (1,1)
    (1,0)

    Only three of these points can serve as knots. Which are they? *Hint:* watch for collinearity.

15. Extend the procedure Bez_curve to three dimensions by adding a parameter of type cp_vector that contains the *z*-coordinates of four consecutive control points.

16. Specify control points in 3-D space and draw a Bezier curve to these points.
    - **a.** Draw the curve on the screen with orthographic projection by ignoring the computation of the *z*-value.
    - **b.** Draw the curve on the screen with perspective projection by computing the projection for each point on the curve produced by the drawing algorithm and connecting them by straight lines.

17. Use the hand-drawing rule to draw a Bezier curve to the four control points: $(-1,1)$ $(0,0)$ $(2,1.5)$ $(3.5,1)$.

## Section 8.5 B-Spline Surfaces

18. Given the following control point matrix (the letter P is left out; only the two subscripts are shown):

$$\begin{bmatrix} 00 & 01 & 02 & 03 & 04 \\ 10 & 11 & 12 & 13 & 14 \\ 20 & 21 & 22 & 23 & 24 \\ 30 & 31 & 32 & 33 & 34 \\ 40 & 41 & 42 & 43 & 44 \end{bmatrix}$$

How many different cubic B-spline patches are used to produce the open uniform cubic B-spline surface to the above control point matrix? Indicate the corresponding patch matrices in the control point layout.

19. Use the same control point matrix as in Exercise 18. How many different quadratic B-spline patches are used to produce the open uniform quadratic B-spline surface to the above control point matrix? Indicate the corresponding patch matrices in the control point layout.

20. A B-spline patch is not attached to any control points but is close to the four inner control points of the patch matrix (see Figure 8.20). The patch is close to the four heavy control points and hovers above them in space as the 16 control points of the patch form a trough.

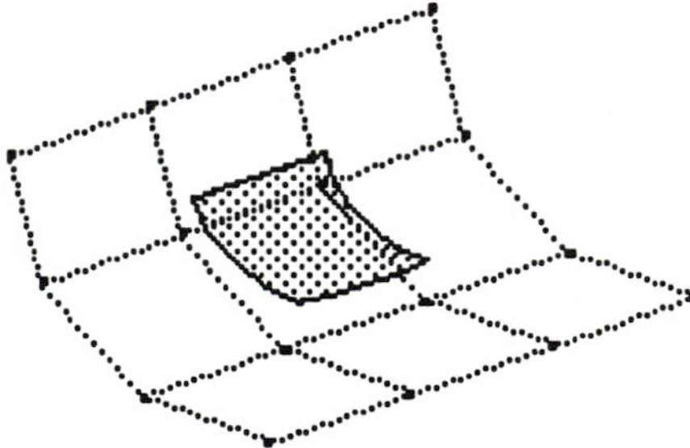

**FIGURE 8.20**

Figure 8.21 shows an arrangement of the 25 control points of Exercise 18 in space. Sketch the patches resulting from the four possible patch matrices by hand for this control point arrangement.

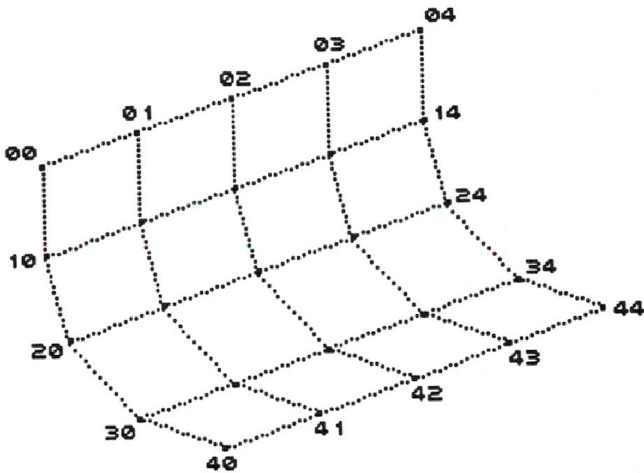


**FIGURE 8.21**

**Movement of a Surface Point** The rules for matrix multiplication help you to remember the direction of movement of a point in the parametric surface with varying parameters u and v. Envision the schematic below:

$$(u^3, u^2, u, 1) \bullet \begin{bmatrix} x & x & x & x \\ x & x & x & x \\ x & x & x & x \\ x & x & x & x \end{bmatrix} \bullet \begin{bmatrix} v^3 \\ v^2 \\ v \\ 1 \end{bmatrix}$$

The matrix indicated by x is M multiplied with the patch matrix P, multiplied with $M^T$, see the text. For now we will call this matrix P′. If u is a row vector at the left of P′ and v is a column vector at the right of P′ then u is multiplied with columns of P′ and v is multiplied with rows of P′.

This helps us remember: varying u moves down in the patch matrix, varying v moves right in the patch matrix:

```
        v
     ------->
    | x x x x
    | x x x x
  u | x x x x
    | x x x x
    v
```

If the patch matrix is:

$$\begin{bmatrix} 11 & 12 & 13 & 14 \\ 21 & 22 & 23 & 24 \\ 31 & 32 & 33 & 34 \\ 41 & 42 & 43 & 44 \end{bmatrix}$$

then varying u from 0 to 1, keeping v fixed, moves a surface point from close to control point 12 in the direction of 42 or from 13 to 43, depending on where v is kept. (These are only approximate locations, but the schematic helps us to understand the parametric patches.)

**21.** Show the curves of constant u and of constant v in the four patches sketched in Exercise 20.

**22.** Let P be the patch matrix. Show analytically that the last row of P is not involved in forming the surface when u = 0 and the first row is not involved when u = 1. What follows from this for the curves of constant u in the surface when u = 0 and when u = 1?

**23.** Let P be the patch matrix. Show analytically that the last column of P is not involved in forming the surface when v = 0 and the first column is not involved when v = 1. What follows from this for the curves of constant v in the surface when v = 0 and when v = 1?

**24.** Write a procedure

```
cub_bspl_patch(cp : p_matrix);
```

that draws a cubic B-spline patch to 16 control points given by the parameter cp. Use the type declaration:

```
type point    = record x,y,z : real
                end;
     p_matrix = array[0..3,0..3] of point;
```

Draw the patch with crosshatch lines. One set of lines is the constant u-curves, the other set the constant v-curves. Project the lines either orthographically by ignoring the computation of the z-coordinate or perspectively by computing the perspective projection of every point calculated by the drawing procedure and connecting them by straight lines.

**25.** Specify the control points and the patch matrices needed to draw the basic uniform cubic B-spline surface as shown in the text in Figure 8.10, using procedure cub_bspl_patch. *Hint:* You need 49 control points.

**26.** Define 3-D coordinates for the points in Exercise 19 so that they have approximately the positions shown in Figure 8.20. Use the procedure cub_bspl_patch to draw the four patches to these control points.

The following 20 control points are specified to form a pipelike construct and are used in Exercises 27 and 28. The control point matrix is:

$$\begin{bmatrix} 00 & 01 & 02 & 03 & 04 \\ 10 & 11 & 12 & 13 & 14 \\ 20 & 21 & 22 & 23 & 24 \\ 30 & 31 & 32 & 33 & 34 \end{bmatrix} = \begin{bmatrix} (\ 1,0,-2)(\ 1,0,-1)(\ 1,0,0)(\ 1,0,1)(\ 1,0,2) \\ (\ 0,1,-2)(\ 0,1,-1)(\ 0,1,0)(\ 0,1,1)(\ 0,1,2) \\ (-1,0,-2)(-1,0,-1)(-1,0,0)(-1,0,1)(-1,0,2) \\ (0,-1,-2)(0,-1,-1)(0,-1,0)(0,-1,1)(0,-1,2) \end{bmatrix}$$

Enter these points in a program and rotate them slightly about the x-axis and about the y-axis before you draw patches to them; this gives a more interesting display. The pipe has four points around its perimeter and five points lengthwise. With the above arrangement u goes around the pipe and v goes lengthwise.

**27.** We can have two patches lengthwise and four patches around the pipe if we specify the patch matrices in a cyclic manner. This gives us a pipelike-shaped B-spline surface that is closed around the pipe but open at the ends. What are the eight patch matrices that achieve this? *Hint:* the control point matrix is repeated cyclicly in vertical direction. Use procedure cub_bspl_patch to draw these eight patches, projecting orthographically.

**28.** We can make the pipe surface longer, that is, continue it in both directions so that it ends flush with the first and last column of control points. This is achieved by specifying the first and the last column in the control point matrix three times. This gives us 20 patch matrices. Use procedure cub_bspl_patch to draw the resulting surface projecting orthographically.

**29.** The following 16 control points lie on a torus. To draw the whole torus surface we need to draw 16 patches. Specify the 16 patch matrices that achieve this. *Hint:* repeat the control point matrix cyclicly in a vertical and a horizontal direction.

$$\begin{bmatrix} 00 & 01 & 02 & 03 \\ 10 & 11 & 12 & 13 \\ 20 & 21 & 22 & 23 \\ 30 & 31 & 32 & 33 \end{bmatrix} = \begin{bmatrix} (3,\ 0,0) & (0,\ 0,3) & (-3,\ 0,0) & (0,\ 0,-3) \\ (2,\ 1,0) & (0,\ 1,2) & (-2,\ 1,0) & (0,\ 1,-2) \\ (1,\ 0,0) & (0,\ 0,1) & (-1,\ 0,0) & (0,\ 0,-1) \\ (2,-1,0) & (0,-1,2) & (-2,-1,0) & (0,-1,-2) \end{bmatrix}$$

30. Make a hand sketch of the torus of Exercise 29 and show how the constant u-curves and the constant v-curves run on the torus surface.
31. Make a hand sketch of the torus of Exercise 29 and show the patch corresponding to the patch matrix which is identical to the control point matrix.
32. Use procedure cub_bspl_patch to draw the whole torus of Exercise 29, projecting orthographically.

# Approximating Spheres with Cubic B-Spline Patches

This is a little more tricky than for a torus because the parametric description of a sphere surface always leads to poles. But this problem can be overcome.

33. Given the following 10 control points in space (we now use a different notation to enhance the geometric meaning of the points):

$$
\begin{array}{llll}
N = (0,\ 2,\ 0) & & & \\
N_0 = (2,\ 1, -2) & N_1 = (2,\ 1, 2) & N_2 = (-2,\ 1, 2) & N_3 = (-2,\ 1, -2) \\
S_0 = (2, -1, -2) & S_1 = (2, -1, 2) & S_2 = (-2, -1, 2) & S_3 = (-2, -1, -2) \\
S = (0, -2,\ 0) & & &
\end{array}
$$

(N stands for north, S for south.)

These points form a closed polyhedron in space with 12 facets as shown in Figure 8.22. We can approximate it by a totally closed B-spline surface. The four side patches will be of normal "rectangular" form. But the top and bottom patches degenerate to triangular form because they have to be "pulled" over the poles. An example of a corresponding patch matrix is:

$$
\begin{bmatrix}
N_2 & N_3 & N_0 & N_1 \\
N & N & N & N \\
N_0 & N_1 & N_2 & N_3 \\
S_0 & S_1 & S_2 & S_3
\end{bmatrix}
$$

It corresponds to the patch close to the triangle N $N_1$ $N_2$. Follow the four paths of varying u when moving down the columns of this matrix to see how they overcross at the north pole. The same happens at the south pole. The following control point matrix allows the definition of the 12 patch matrices to produce the closed surface by repeating it cyclicly from left to right:

**FIGURE 8.22**

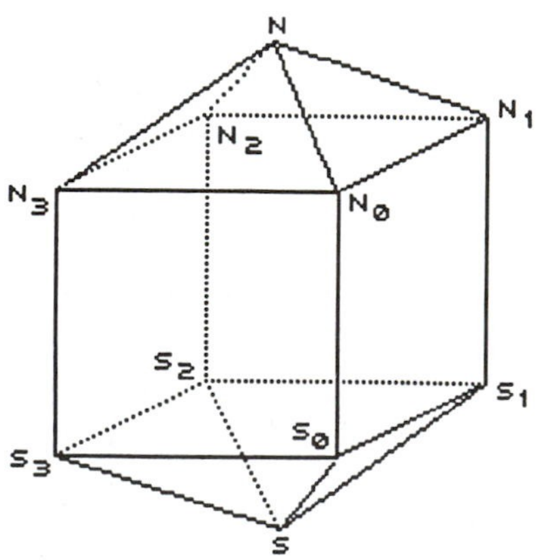

$$\begin{bmatrix} N_2 & N_3 & N_0 & N_1 \\ N & N & N & N \\ N_0 & N_1 & N_2 & N_3 \\ S_0 & S_1 & S_2 & S_3 \\ S & S & S & S \\ S_2 & S_3 & S_0 & S_1 \end{bmatrix}$$

Use procedure cub_bspl_patch to draw this surface, projecting orthographically.

34. The control point polyhedron in Figure 8.23 can be approximated by a totally closed B-spline surface. Define the control point matrix that can be cyclicly repeated from left to right and from top to bottom to yield the minimum required number of patch matrices.

**FIGURE 8.23**

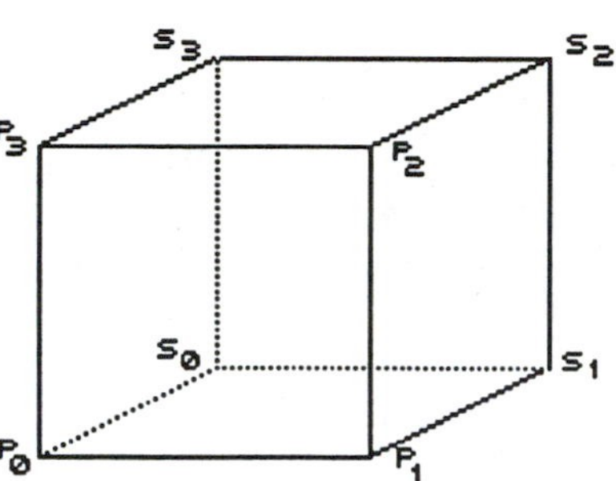


# Section 8.6 General B-Spline Surfaces

35. Implement a procedure that uses the recursive Cox-de Boor formula to draw a general B-spline surface. Define 25 control points in space—similar to the arrangement of Exercise 18 —and use the procedure to draw a general cubic B-spline surface to these points.

# Section 8.7 Catmull-Rom Patches

The exercises for Section 8.5 can all be done with Catmull-Rom patches instead of B-spline patches. The only exception is the repetition of control points. In Exercise 28 the left and right column of the control point matrix must be specified only twice in order to extend the pipe all the way to the outer control points.

36. Write a procedure

```
CR_patch(cp : p_matrix);
```

that draws a Catmull-Rom patch (tension parameter fixed at 0.5) to 16 control points specified in p_matrix, projecting orthographically. For p_matrix use the same type declaration as in Exercise 24.

# Section 8.8 Bezier Patches

General higher order Bezier curves and surfaces are not useful in computer graphics, but piecewise cubic curves and patches are very popular.

To draw a piecewise Bezier surface we must define the control points properly, meeting all the requirements specified in the text to avoid ridges. We do not have as much freedom as with uniform B-spline surfaces.

37. Write a procedure

Bez-patch(cp : p_matrix);

that draws a bicubic Bezier patch to 16 control points specified in p_matrix, projecting orthographically. For p_matrix use the same type declaration as in Exercise 24.

38. Given the following control point matrix of 48 points:

$$\begin{bmatrix}
(0,4,-2) & (0,2,-4) & (0,-2,-4) & (0,-4,-2) \\
(1,4,-2) & (2,2,-4) & (2,-2,-4) & (1,-4,-2) \\
(2,4,-1) & (4,2,-2) & (4,-2,-2) & (2,-4,-1) \\
(2,4,0) & (4,2,0) & (4,-2,0) & (2,-4,0) \\
(2,4,1) & (4,2,2) & (4,-2,2) & (2,-4,1) \\
(1,4,2) & (2,2,4) & (2,-2,4) & (1,-4,2) \\
(0,4,2) & (0,2,4) & (0,-2,4) & (0,-4,2) \\
(-1,4,2) & (-2,2,4) & (-2,-2,4) & (-1,-4,2) \\
(-2,4,1) & (-4,2,2) & (-4,-2,2) & (-2,-4,1) \\
(-2,4,0) & (-4,2,0) & (-4,-2,0) & (-2,-4,0) \\
(-2,4,-1) & (-4,2,-2) & (-4,-2,-2) & (-2,-4,-1) \\
(-1,4,-2) & (-2,2,-4) & (-2,-2,-4) & (-1,-4,-2)
\end{bmatrix}$$

This matrix can be used to define four bicubic Bezier patches. Knot points are the points in rows 1, 4, 7, and 10. If the first row is repeated as row 13 to close the fourth patch back to the first one, these four patches form a partly closed piecewise Bezier surface. Rotate these points slightly in space, then use Bez_patch to draw the surface. (This surface is similar to the one used by Martin Newell for his teapot, described in CROW87).

# Light and Color

# 9

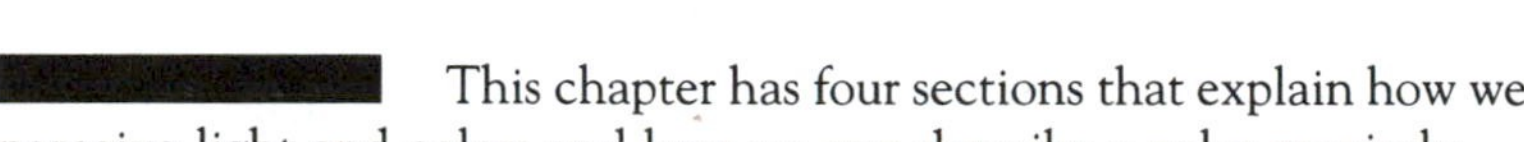

This chapter has four sections that explain how we perceive light and colors and how we can describe a color precisely.

**9.0 Introduction** points out how the use of color is important in computer graphics.

**9.1 Light** summarizes the physics of light.

**9.2 Colors** explains how we perceive colors and how color primaries or their complements can be mixed to produce other colors.

**9.3 Color Descriptions** gives detailed information on four systems for describing colors quantitatively, how these relate to color displays, and how they are interrelated.

## 9.0 INTRODUCTION

Until now, when we spoke of light, the major variable was its intensity and we imagined a monochrome display. If pixels can be only black or white, the only way to vary the intensity of light is to vary the ratio of black and white pixels in a given area. But we cannot continue to overlook color, an extremely important property of light. This brings us to a new aspect of computer graphics.

Observe how thoroughly we ignored color. In scan conversion, we just computed locations in a raster; in windowing and clipping, we transformed numbers from one coordinate system to another and computed the intersection of lines. Transformations in the plane and in space redefined the coordinates of objects. Curves and surfaces allowed us to define smooth outlines of objects independently of how they were to be displayed. In dealing with hidden line techniques, we came a little closer to the problems of producing pictures that look real. But all these things can very well be done in a black-and-white environment.

Now we are about to enter the exciting area of colors—colors that are taken from the real world around us, colors that we try to analyse and understand as a topic in themselves, colors that are governed by the laws of physics and that add another dimension to our pictures.

# 9.1 LIGHT

From physics, we learn that light is a narrow band of electromagnetic frequencies with wavelengths that range from approximately 400 to 700 nanometers. When electromagnetic energy at these wavelengths hits the retina of the eye, we have the sensation of light. The measurement of light is therefore inseparable from the physiological aspects of human sight. A wavelength of 400 nanometers (nm) is perceived as violet; increasing wavelengths are blue, cyan, green, yellow, and finally red, at 700 nm.

There are three terms used to describe the quality of a light source beyond its purely physical description as a spectrum of different wavelengths and intensities. These terms are *radiance*, *luminance*, and *brightness*. They are not independent from one another, but their interrelationship is very complex. We will look at them individually.

*Radiance* is the total amount of energy that flows from the electromagnetic (light) source. The amount can be measured with instruments and is usually expressed in watts, a standard measure of any kind of energy.

Not all energy from light sources excites the sensors in the human eye equally. Subjectively speaking, some wavelengths seem brighter to us than others although their sources radiate the same energy measured in watts. We need a different measure for the amount of energy we perceive from a given light source. This perceived energy is called *lumi-*

*nance;* its measuring unit is the lumen. It tells how much a light of a certain quality excites the sensors in the human eye. For example, a light with a wavelength of 380 nm can have considerable energy (radiance) and yet will hardly be perceived, because this light is at the higher frequency end of the band for which we have a sensation. The luminance of such a light source is almost zero.

*Brightness* is very subjective and is practically impossible to measure. The brightness of a source tells how "bright" the light looks to the viewer. We know that when we turn on a light in a dark room it first seems very bright to us. As soon as our eyes have adapted to it, it will look "normal" no matter how much light it emits "wattwise." This is because the eye-brain system adjusts to the given light environment. Now, brightness does not mean this immediate sensation before adaptation; rather, it means the subjective feeling of the brightness of a given light source after all adaptations have taken place. For example, the light of a burning candle in a dark room will look bright even after we have fully adapted; this is probably because it is much brighter than everything else in this room. The same candle will not look bright to us if we see it outside in the sunlight.

The relation between luminance and wavelength can be established experimentally. It is shown in Figure 9.1, which plots wavelength against relative sensitivity. The light in this graph always has a constant

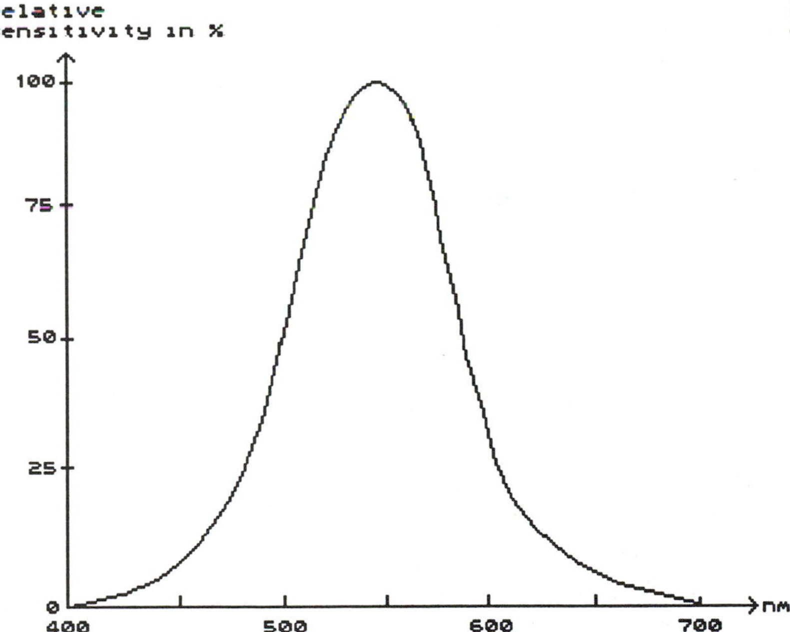


**FIGURE 9.1**

radiance of 1 watt for all wavelengths. If this watt of energy is emitted at a wavelength of 560 nm (green), the luminance is highest (680 lumens) and we take this as 100 percent sensitivity. The luminance decreases rapidly as the wavelength changes slightly. It is practically zero at 380 and 740 nm. This does not mean that a lumen of red light is less than a lumen of green light: these two lumens of light produce the same sensory response. But we need many more watts of red light energy to produce one lumen of sensation than we need to produce one lumen of sensation from green light.

**Measuring Point Light** To discuss the measurement of light, we must make some abstractions. One concept that is not very close to reality but still is very helpful is the notion of a *point light source.* This abstraction assumes that an infinitely small light source (a point) can emit light. In Chapter 14, we will work with these point light sources because more realistic sources, distributed sources, are mathematically difficult to handle.

The light emitted by a point source radiates in all directions. We can think of the point source as being surrounded by a sphere that catches all the light from the source. If the sphere is large, the light will have a low intensity per unit area when it reaches the surrounding surface. If the sphere is small, the unit intensity will be high. But the total amount of light reaching the sphere will always be the same. The *intensity* of a point source therefore has to be measured as the amount of light it produces in relation to a certain spatial angle.

The unit of an angle in the plane is a radian: the angle that intercepts an arc of length r when the vertex of the angle is at the center of a circle of radius r. The spatial analogy is the angle whose vertex is at the center of a sphere of radius r that subtends an area of $r^2$. This unit of spatial angles is called a steradian. In Figure 9.2 we see a sphere of radius r surrounding a point light source and an area of $r^2$ on its surface. The spatial angle subtended by this area is one steradian no matter the shape of the area.

The amount of light, measured in lumens, that falls on one steradian of a sphere containing the point light source is constant no matter how large the sphere is. We see that it makes sense to measure the strength of a point light in lumens per steradian. This measuring unit is called a candela. A point light source of one candela produces $4\pi$ lumens because $4\pi r^2$ is the surface of the entire sphere. It follows from this that the amount of light hitting an area of constant size decreases with the square of the distance to the light source.

**Measuring Distributed Light** The alternate to point light is light coming from a surface. All light sources of the real world (except possibly stars) are distributed sources. When we "see" a surface, what

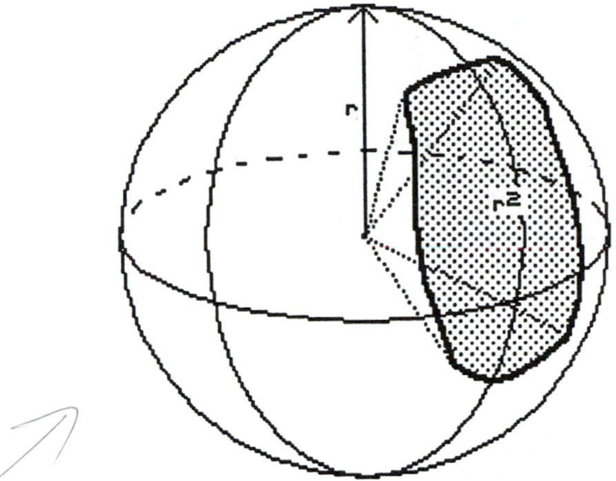


**FIGURE 9.2**

we see is light coming from every point on that surface. We can think of this as infinitely many point sources, each of which has practically zero light intensity. To compute the total amount of light from a surface, we really have to evaluate an integral, but we will not pursue this.

Luminance is defined as the amount of light coming from a luminous surface, measured as light intensity per unit of surface. The light intensity unit is the candela and the surface unit is the square meter. Candela/sq-meter ("nit") is the international unit of measurement for luminance.

With a real surface, these infinitely many very weak point light sources don't emit their light with equal strength in all directions, that is, they don't *diffuse* perfectly, so in reality the light coming from a surface depends on the angle at which we look at it. Here we make a second useful abstraction. We assume that surfaces are perfectly diffusing, a property called *lambertian.* This means that the light coming from them has the same strength no matter the angle of the viewer. In Chapter 14 we will add some more abstractions to arrive at a workable illumination model.

# 9.2 COLORS

**Color Sensation** Humans have known about colors long before we could describe them physically as certain wavelengths in the spectrum of the electromagnetic waves. Still, the knowledge of the physical nature of color really tells us only that the sensation of color is something that is contributed entirely by ourselves. There are no colors in the physical universe. Electromagnetic radiation has nothing that resembles

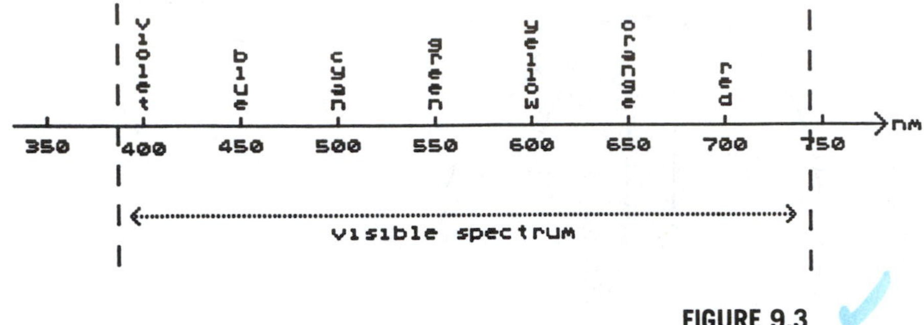


FIGURE 9.3

color—it is only our perception that creates color. Figure 9.3 shows which wavelengths are perceived as which colors. The horizontal scale is in nanometers.

Color sensation is an important element in our visual recognition process. It influences what we see and helps us recognize complicated visual information. It even influences our mood; for example, red and orange are generally viewed as "warm" colors, blue and cyan as "cold."

Two facts concerning our visual recognition system are experimentally established and widely accepted:

1. We see color through special sensors in the retina of the eye, called *cones*. These sensors are concentrated in a small area called the *fovea*, which is only 0.25 millimeter in diameter. Outside the fovea there are very few cones and therefore reduced color sensation, mainly the perception of gray scale intensities.
2. All the colors we can perceive can be obtained by mixing the hues red, green, and blue. This leads to the assumption that there are three types of cones, each responding to red, green, or blue light. The color of an object is perceived by the degree to which each of these types of cones is excited.

This is the background underlying the concept of a color monitor, which produces all colors by a mixture of red, green, and blue. The process corresponds directly to the way our visual system perceives colors.

**The Primaries** In Figure 9.3 we saw the colors corresponding to wavelengths. The color range in the spectrum of visible light is called the *rainbow colors* because a rainbow consists of these colors. But there are many colors that we cannot find in the rainbow, for example, pink, brown, black, white, ochre, and magenta. How are these generated?

The rainbow colors are those with a single pure wavelength. Light in the real world, however, will usually be a mixture of colors of different

## COLOR CRT TECHNIQUES

Almost every color CRT displays a color image with the *shadow mask technique* (defined below). All the varied colors that we see are produced by mixing the three primaries: red, green, and blue. These three colors are produced on the CRT surface by exciting three different types of phosphors, chosen to emit light of either red, green, or blue color when hit by the electron beam. The phosphors are laid down carefully in various patterns on the inner front surface of the CRT.

We now present three commonly used techniques. In one, the so-called *delta construction,* these phosphors are laid down as tiny dots of about 0.35 mm size. The pattern is such that one red, one green, and one blue dot form a delta-shaped equilateral triangle called a *triad.* Figure 9.A shows a part of such a layout in which two triads are highlighted. These triads repeat in an interlaced pattern over the whole inner surface of the tube. To produce a red dot, we just aim an electron beam precisely enough so that it will hit only the red phosphor, never a green or blue phosphor. While the principle is simple, accomplishing it is very difficult.

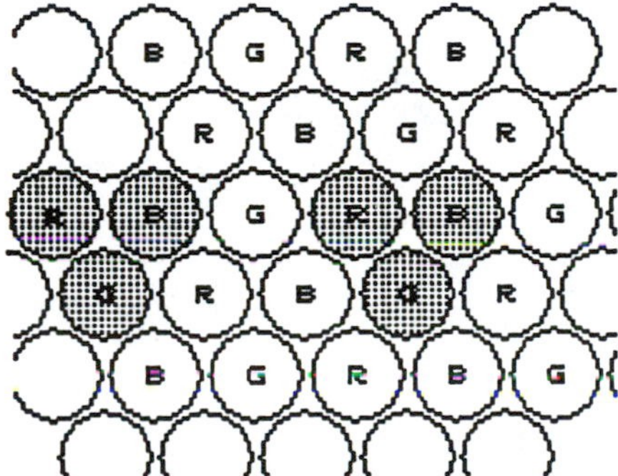

**FIGURE 9.A**

There is a good reason for laying down the phosphor dots in such a pattern. This pattern together with a shadow mask allows a subset of the electrons to strike only phosphors of the correct color without hitting phosphors of another color. The *shadow mask* is a thin metal plate with tiny apertures such that there is precisely one aperture per triad. The center-to-center spacing of the apertures is between 0.6 to 0.7 mm (this is called the *pitch* of the shadow mask). The mask is mounted inside the tube at a distance of about 13 mm from the front surface. There are also three separate electron guns mounted in a delta-shaped cluster. The beams of these three guns are deflected together in such a way that they converge and cross over at the plane of the shadow mask. The arrangement of guns, shadow mask, and triads ensures that the beam from one gun can impinge only on one of the three phosphor types and is "shadowed" from the other two. Since the beams originate at different points they pass through the apertures at different angles; this permits only electrons from one gun to strike the corresponding phosphor dot.

Figure 9.B shows how apertures and triads correspond. The apertures, shown in black, sit in the centers of their triads. This is the view we might have when looking at the shadow mask and the triads from a point in the center between the three guns (except that we would see only those parts of the triads that are now covered by the black apertures). Moving to the red gun we would see only the red phosphor dots. The same holds for green and blue.

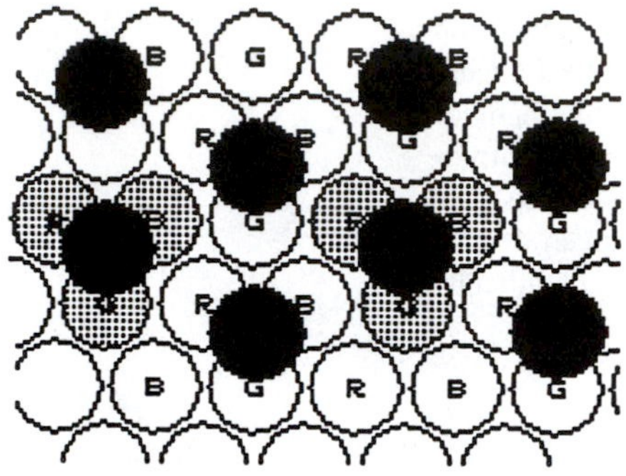


**FIGURE 9.B**

The arrangement of triads and apertures as shown in Figure 9.B is for the center portion of the screen only. In the outer portions it is not as regular in order to compensate for the slant of the electron beams. The overall arrangement is shown in Figure 9.C. You can see in the figure how the beams cross over in the plane of the shadow mask when they penetrate through an aperture. The green gun is at the top of the triangular gun arrangement, therefore its beam can strike only the green phosphor dot at the bottom of its triad. The arrangement for red and blue is similar.

The pixel data in the frame buffer contain color information, the intensities for the three primaries R, G, and B. We describe later in this chapter precisely how the pixel data, which are just numbers, are transformed into the three primary intensities.

It is essential that the three guns, although their beams are always moved together, have their intensities changed individually. For example, if only the red gun is at full intensity, with green and blue at zero, then that location will look red on the screen, because only the red phosphor dot will be hit by an electron beam.

It is important to recognize that the thickness of the combined beams from the three guns is made much wider than one aperture in the shadow mask. If it were exactly the same size, the precision required for

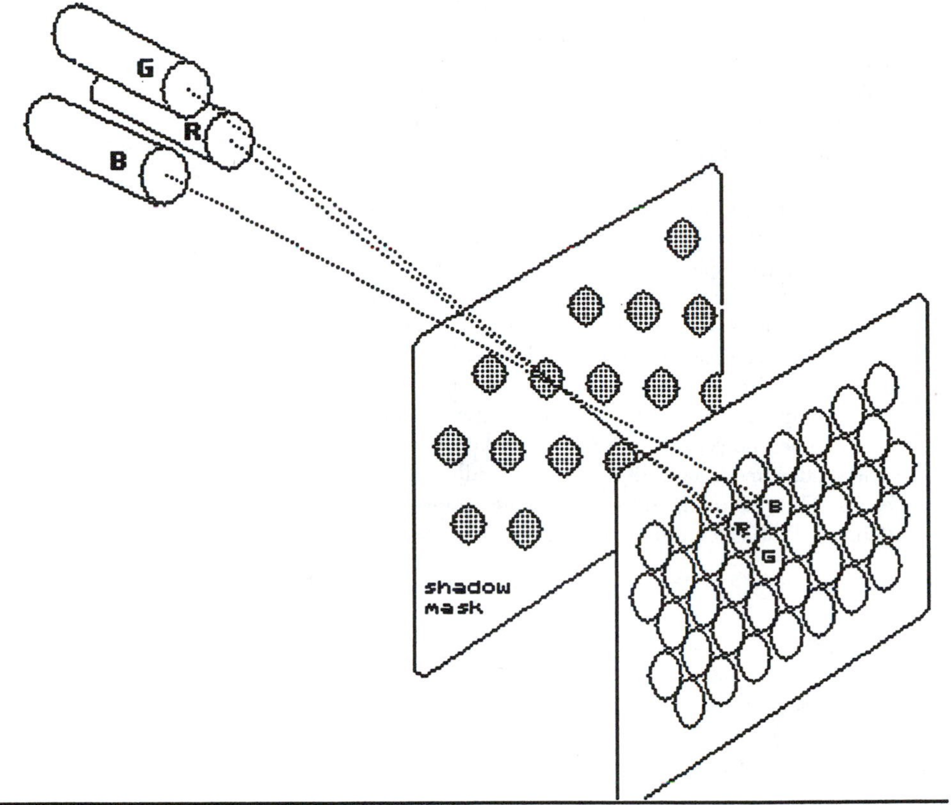


FIGURE 9.C

sending the correct color information at exactly the right instant would be almost impossible to attain. This is because the ratio between holes to metal in the shadow mask is only about 2:8. If the (combined) beam were just a little off, the screen could look much darker or totally dark even if all three intensities were full for each pixel, because the beam might be turned on when it was in between two apertures on its horizontal path. The vertical adjustment would be very difficult as well; it could happen that, for certain scan lines, the beam's horizontal path might never hit an aperture in the mask. If the positions where the beam sends pixel information "beats" with the aperture positions then strong moire patterns develop on the display. In short, a precise adjustment would not be possible.

The above difficulties can be overcome by making the combined beam thick enough to always cover at least two apertures in the mask. Therefore a single pixel extends over two to three apertures. If a single green pixel is displayed it can very well have been formed by two green phosphor dots or even two and a half, depending on its position on the screen. If you examine a color monitor or a TV display with a magnifying glass, you can confirm this.

The net result is that there is no fixed relation between the size of the frame buffer and the shadow mask pitch. This makes the resolution of a color CRT display independent of the shadow mask pitch; it is merely a function of the frame buffer size.

Another arrangement is the *inline tube*, which has its three electron guns in one horizontal line rather than triangular. This allows somewhat higher precision. The pattern of phosphor dots on the screen happens to be precisely the same as in the delta system but the individual triad consists of three dots in one horizontal line (see Figure 9.D). Sometimes the phosphor dots on the screen are not round but elongated rectangles (maybe this is so on your TV monitor). In such a case the apertures in the shadow mask are rectangles as well. This is carried to the extreme in another arrangement. The phosphors are not in triads but in vertical narrow stripes. The shadow mask looks like a very fine grill consisting of fine vertical bands. The electron guns in this case are arranged as in the inline tube. Consult RAST85 for more information on this.

**FIGURE 9.D**

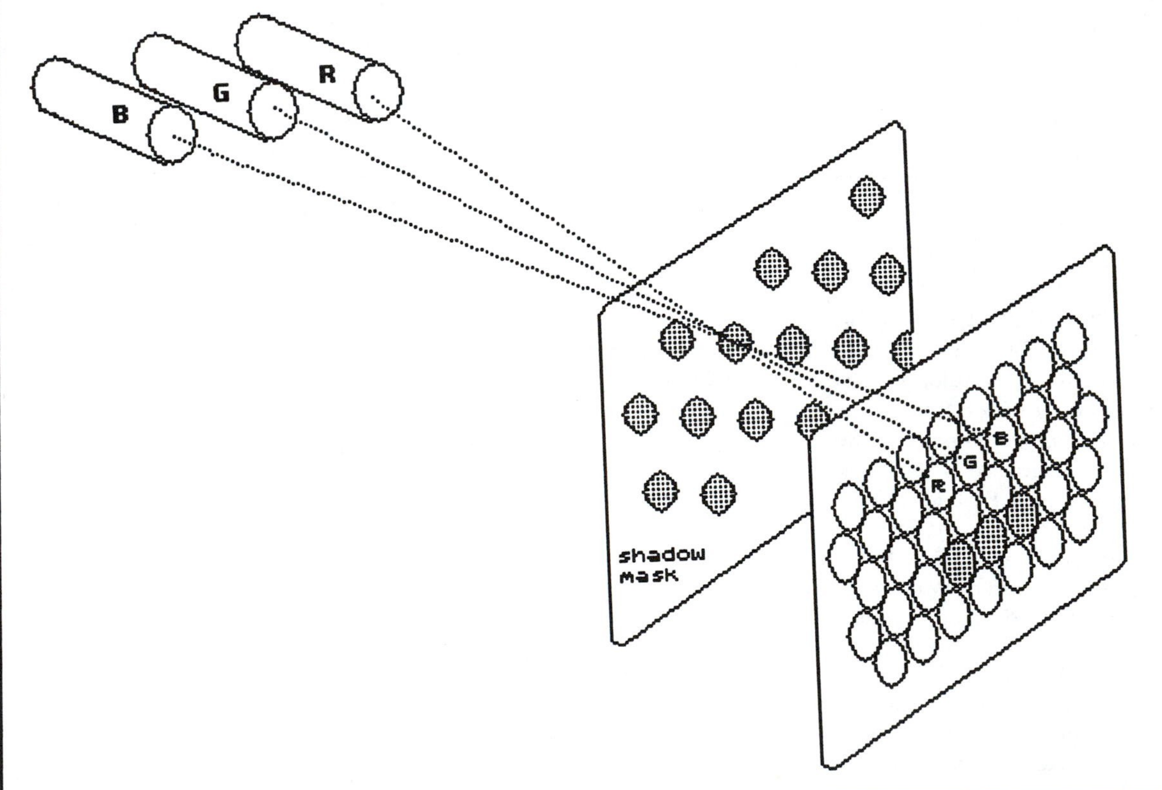

wavelengths. A true white light consists of equal radiance levels across the entire rainbow spectrum; it is a mixture of sources of all wavelengths each radiating with the same radiance. It is experimentally established that the same sensation of white light can be produced by the proper mixture of only three colors in the spectrum. We cannot take just any three colors; they must be chosen so that no two of them can produce the sensation of the third. Whenever we have a combination of three colors that achieves this we call them *primaries*.

The most widely used primaries are the colors red, green, and blue. (Other primaries are possible but have not become popular, maybe because the human eye-brain system works with something close to red, green, and blue, as we have seen.) These primaries, when mixed properly, can produce not only white but almost every other color that we can perceive. This is because they are widely separated on the spectrum. Thus the color yellow can be sensed in two different ways: as light with a wavelength of about 600 nm, or as a mixture of green and red light. In the first case the cones for green and the cones for red are excited by the yellow wavelength since it is about halfway in between these two. In the second case these two groups of cones are each excited by precisely the light for which they have their peak response. Physiologically almost the same process is involved: impulses from the red and from the green cones, combine in the brain to give the sensation of yellow (there are no cones for yellow). (Note carefully that we are mixing light. Mixing paint colors is entirely different.)

The color cyan can be produced in two ways also, analogous to the above. But the color magenta is really an artifact of the brain; it does not occur in the spectrum. The only way to produce it is by a proper mixture of red and blue. We sense this color by internally calculating the ratio between the radiances of red and blue light.

With the colors yellow, cyan, and magenta (and their shades) we have exhausted those that can be produced by a mixture of two of the primaries red, green, and blue (abbreviated RGB). But there is a huge range of color sensations—all artifacts of the brain— that are produced by a mixture of three of the primaries. The most important and easiest to remember is white. A color like pink would be a mixture similar to white but with a stronger contribution from red than from green and blue.

Gray is a white with all primaries equally strong but weaker than in full white. We can go continuously down the gray scale by diminishing all radiances equally until they are all at zero; then we have black.

A color like brown is a mixture of red, green, and blue in which the red has a radiance approximately two times as strong as the green, about four times as strong as the blue, and all primaries are at a low luminance. Figure 9.4 shows the additive color-mixing scheme. As a two-dimensional layout, it cannot show all possible combinations.

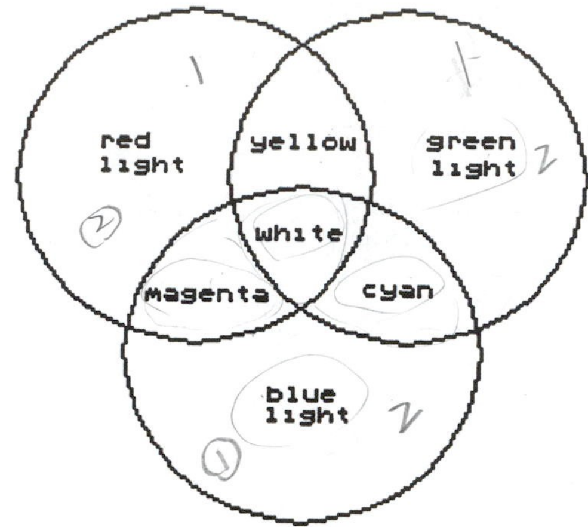


**FIGURE 9.4**

In summary, colors are produced by adding light of the primaries in the proper radiances. Therefore we call such a system *additive*. Color monitors follow an additive principle. The lights emitted by the different phosphors combine to produce the desired color sensation. The amount of light emitted by a given phosphor depends on the intensity of the electron beam hitting it. Therefore the radiance of a certain primary is often called its *intensity*.

**Complementary Colors** When we take white light and subtract one of the primaries, we get a mixture of the remaining two primaries, which will be either yellow, cyan, or magenta. We call those the three *complementary colors*. Can we produce all the other colors by adding combinations of these on a monitor? No, because whichever two we add, we will always have a mixture of all three primaries and hence a color close to white. For example, adding yellow and cyan gives R + G plus G + B, which is white with a strong green component, or a greenish white. Actually we will always end up with a tint of white when the luminances are high and with a tint of gray when they are low. There is no way we could create, for example, a pure blue.

Still, these complementary colors are not useless. On the contrary, they are extremely important, perhaps even more so than the RGB primaries. They can be viewed as primaries when we consider paints and dyes. Paints and dyes are quite different from light-emitting sources. They never produce their own light; instead, they reflect light that falls onto them or filter light that passes through them, absorbing more or less light in the process.

Let us think of cyan dye painted onto white paper. Without the dye the paper would reflect the whole of the white light falling onto it from the environment, so it would look white. With the cyan dye painted on it, the light passing through and coming back from the paper surface consists only of green and blue (and cyan) wavelengths. The red wavelengths are missing—they were absorbed while passing through the cyan dye. We can think of the cyan dye as a mass of fine particles that are able to reflect and scatter all wavelengths except for the red ones. So the light that passes through this mass is reflected and scattered from one particle to the other. When it finally manages to escape it has lost its red wavelength; it has been subtracted.

Let's go a step further and see what yellow dye does. Obviously it consists of particles that can reflect and scatter everything except the blue wavelengths, so light that passes through will contain only the wavelengths red and green (and yellow), and will therefore appear yellow to us. The blue wavelength has been subtracted.

Now, if we mix cyan and yellow dye, what color results? White light that falls on this mixture will lose the red wavelength through the cyan particles and the blue wavelength through the yellow particles. All that is left will be green light. This is something we can easily verify and every painter can tell from experience that green will be the result of such a mixture.

We call a color system that behaves this way *subtractive.* This subtractive system is more familiar to us than the additive system. But the additive system is not a natural one for us only because we are not used to it. It is physically as "real" as our practical experience with mixing paints and dyes. Figure 9.5 shows the subtractive color-mixing scheme. Whenever two colors are mixed we get the color shown in the

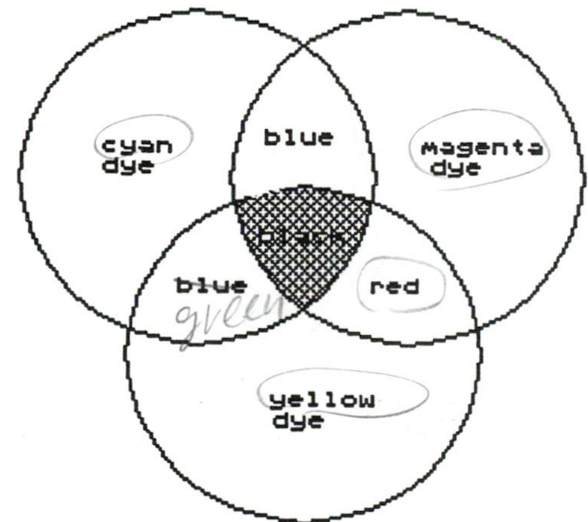


**FIGURE 9.5**

intersection. White does not show in this scheme, since white is obtained by "not mixing" any colors, in other words, not painting anything onto the originally white paper.

A very light pink can be obtained by painting only a tiny portion of magenta and of yellow onto the white surface so that much of its white will still shine through. In other words, only a little of the green light and a little of the blue light will be subtracted (by magenta and yellow). The result can be compared to a mixture of RGB, in which all three primaries are about equally strong, but the red primary is somewhat stronger than the other two. So we are eventually getting the same mixture of red, green, and blue as the one we used above to obtain pink.

If we paint onto a nonwhite background, we cannot obtain white or any light color that has white in it, like the pink of our example. Because the system is subtractive, the more dye we put onto the background, the more we subtract from it, so nothing can get lighter. Here we seem to run into difficulties. Aren't there paints that we can paint onto a black background so that it becomes this color? Yes, but in such a case the layer of paint is so thick that the light never penetrates through to the background. It is reflected (maybe minus some wavelengths) before it can ever reach it. In this case we are actually *creating* a new background or replacing the given one with one of a different color. The paints we should think of, which most closely demonstrate the subtracting effect, are watercolors. These have to be used on a white background. But even artists painting with oil colors prefer to start out with a white background.

There is another seeming contradiction. If we paint all three subtractive primaries with watercolors onto a white paper, we don't get black, but a dirty grayish brown. The explanation is that the yellow watercolor, although it subtracts the blue wavelengths, does not do so completely. Some blue light will always escape. The same is true for the other two primaries. What sounds so easy in theory is only imperfectly realized in practice. The combination lets a variety of wavelengths pass whose composition depends on a number of factors beyond our control.

Practically all the light that we see in the world around us has gone through a subtractive color-forming process. The only exceptions are the light of the sun, the stars, lamps, and the light coming from a TV screen or some color CRT display. The colors of objects, like cars, green plants, houses, practically everything that does not produce its own light, subtracts more or less of the whole spectrum. The so-called *nonemitter displays* like photographs, printed matter, and paintings belong in this group.

# 9.3 COLOR DESCRIPTIONS

We have seen that we can choose three primaries and express practically all other colors as a combination of those. The primaries we choose and how they interact depends on the type of display we use (emitter or nonemitter). In the following discussion, we will use the word *color* in a broader sense. Color means not only a primary or a color of the rainbow spectrum but everything we can perceive as a visual color sensation from the world around us: white as well as black and the millions of other strange mixtures that we can sense.

We really need some way to precisely define the colors we see. It would be convenient if this could be done by specifying the color's wavelength; then the color could be described by a single number. But several facts make this impossible. One is that only the rainbow colors can be specified by wavelength and most colors, including sunlight, are conglomerates of several rainbow colors. Another is that even a rainbow color will not be sufficiently described by its wavelength. Two objects of the same color can still appear different because of the amount of color that comes from them. One object could be a bright blue and the other a darker blue, though the color is the same blue in both cases. One possibility is to use the primaries themselves to describe a given color. What we must specify is the amount of each primary in a mixture.

## 9.3.1 The RGB System

When working in an environment that uses a color CRT as a display, we can use the RGB color system for specifying colors. RGB stands for the red, green, and blue primaries of an additive display, like a CRT. The colors that can be produced by a color monitor can easily be described by three numbers: the three luminances (adjusted by the amount of white, see below), also called the intensities, of these primaries. The color specification is very close to the physical production of the colors. The number of different intensities possible for each primary depends on the width of the color lookup table (see sidebar). These widths range at the present time from about eight intensities in small desktop computers to 256 in better graphics boards. As each intensity can combine with others to yield a different color, this gives in the first case $8^3$ = 512, and in the second $256^3$ = 16 million different colors. The monitor itself (except for its quality) has nothing to do with the number of colors that can be displayed on it.

To represent the RGB color system we need a three-dimensional model because three independent parameters describe a color. These

## THE LOOKUP TABLE TECHNIQUE

The most widely used technique to display frame buffers on color monitors is through a *lookup table*. A lookup table is a convenient way to increase the number of colors displayed on the monitor without increasing the depth of the frame buffer. There are several variations of this technique; we will explain only the most straightforward one.

A frame buffer contains only numbers. The color produced is determined by the number in the lookup table and this can be conveniently changed. We explain this technique with an example. Figure 9.E shows the circuitry schematic of a frame buffer and a lookup table. We assume a frame buffer of depth four, which is shown in the drawing as four layers. Four bits correspond to each pixel. These bits are at the same location in the frame buffer but in different layers. (These layers are often called bit planes.) The four-bit group corresponds to a specific address in the frame buffer and its content is a number between 0 and 15. The association between the number at a frame buffer address and the color of the corresponding pixel is established through the color lookup table, which is itself a RAM area addressable by the main processor, just like the frame buffer. We see it on the right in the figure.

FIGURE 9.E

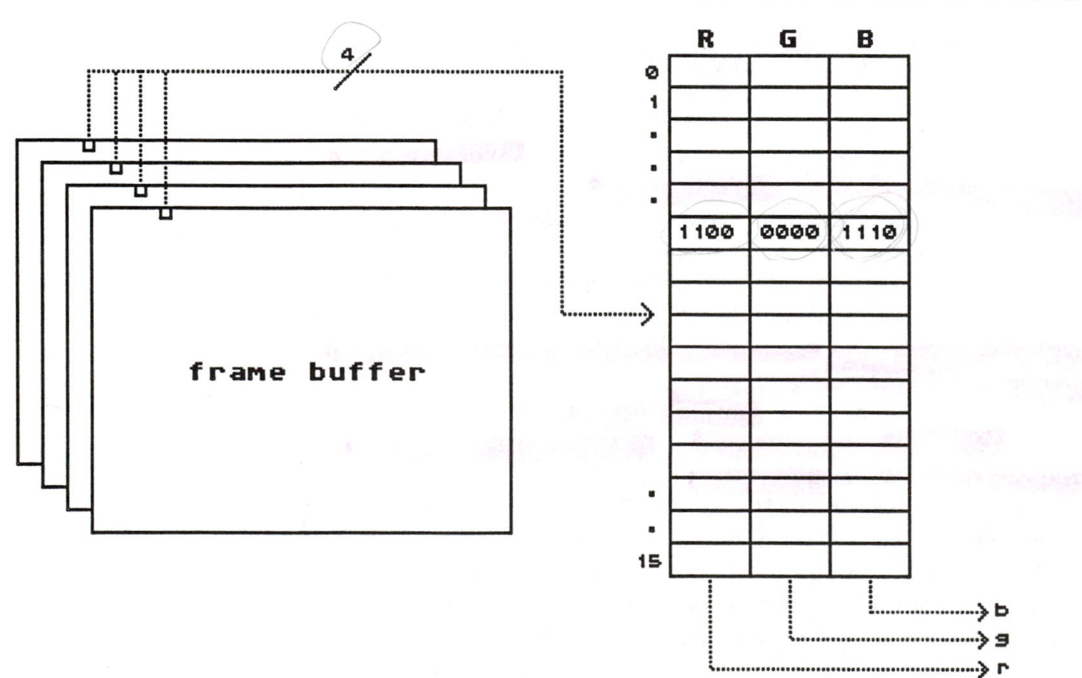

When the CRT controller produces a certain address to be displayed, the content of this address is put on the four-bit-wide data bus (in our example). This value is then used for the address into the lookup table. If the content of the frame buffer location is 5, then location 5 in the lookup table is addressed. The table contains intensities for the three primaries. In our example, the table has an overall width of 12 bits, four bits for each primary. The intensity for each primary can therefore be a number between 0 and 15. The contents of the three addressed entries in the table are read out, transformed into analog intensities and fed to the electron guns for the respective primaries. Our example gives an intensity of 12 for red, 0 for green and 14 for blue. The given pixel would therefore look magenta on the display.

The table of our example allows 16 intensities each for red, green, and blue. By writing any of these values into a table location we can produce any combination of the primaries with these intensities. This amounts to $16^3 = 4096$ different colors. Unfortunately these combinations cannot all be present at the same time in the table, because its size is only 16. Therefore only 16 different colors can be present simultaneously on the screen even with the lookup table. But these 16 colors can be chosen from an overall palette of 4096.

A frame buffer with one byte per pixel would require a lookup table of length $2^8 = 256$. The width is independent from the length. One byte per primary would result in an overall width of 24 bits—not far-fetched for a good-quality graphics board. This corresponds to a palette of $2^{24} = 16$ million colors. More than this is not very useful because the human eye can hardly distinguish among that many colors. All 256 colors of this huge palette could be present simultaneously on the screen.

Addressing a pixel, reading its content, using it as the address into the lookup table, reading out the three intensities, transforming those to analog, and feeding them to the display circuitry has to be done for each individual pixel on the screen. Imagine a screen with one million pixels, a noninterlaced display, and a refresh rate of 60 frames per second (a high-quality Tektronix monitor has something like this). The hardware has to do this 60 million times per second, which leaves about 14 to 15 nsec for each pixel (horizontal and vertical sync pauses must be included). No wonder that only the fastest RAMs can be used for lookup tables!

parameters are the luminances of the primaries. In nature, these values don't have an upper limit; the lower limit is zero but an upper limit physically does not exist. On a color monitor, the upper limit is the strongest luminance the monitor can produce for any of the primaries. So we set the lowest luminance to 0 and the highest to 1, in effect normalizing the values.

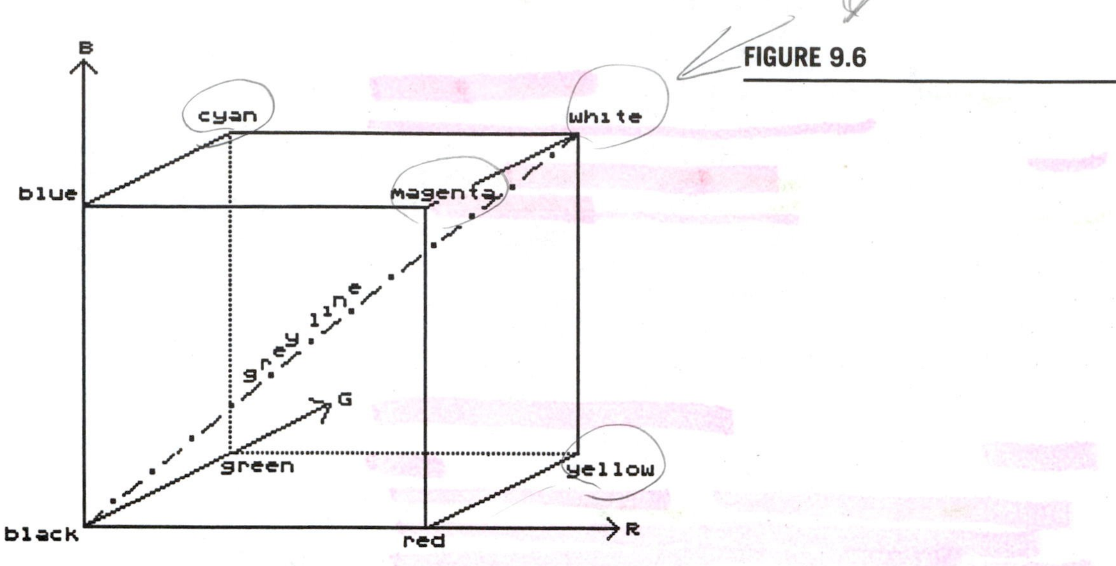


FIGURE 9.6

With these conventions we can use a Cartesian coordinate system and associate the primaries with the spatial coordinate axes, which we call R, G, and B. The origin will be luminance 0, which gradually increases to 1 along any of the axes. The set of all possible combinations is then contained in a cube whose side is equal to 1. This is called the *RGB color cube,* shown in Figure 9.6.

The gray levels lie along the diagonal from black (0,0,0) to white (1,1,1) on which points have equal amounts of all primaries. It is shown as a dot-dashed line. There are other systems, however, and we shall explore several.

## 9.3.2 The HSV System

The letters HSV stand for *hue, saturation,* and *value.* This system offers a more intuitive and user-friendly definition of colors. It can easily be derived from the RGB color cube. If we look at the cube from a point on the black-white diagonal at some distance from the white corner, the corners will surround us—the cube will look like a regular hexagon. In the middle of the hexagon we will have white and on the six corners the colors red, yellow, green, cyan, blue, and magenta (see Figure 9.7).

Figure 9.8 shows only the hexagon without any cube edges. Also, the hexagon is rotated so that we have green at the top. This hexagon shows us all colors. There are gradual transitions along the edges and the colors become more white as we move toward the center. Only black is missing.

FIGURE 9.7

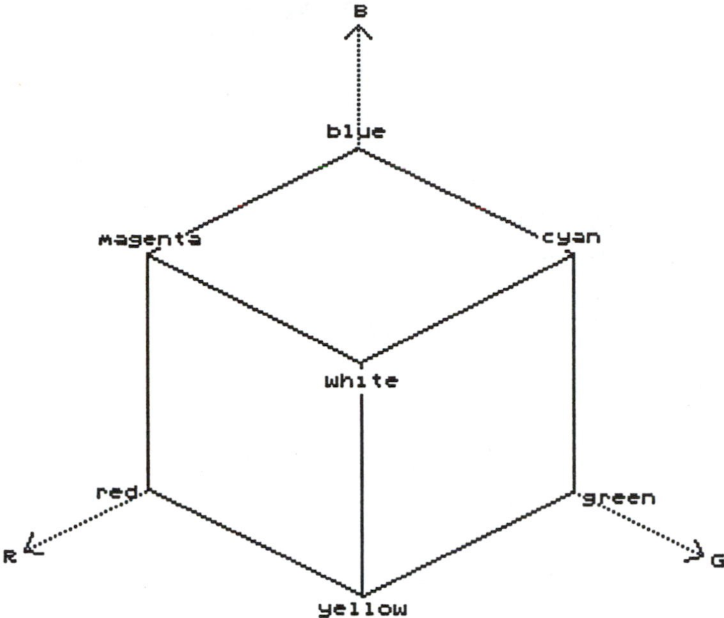


This problem is solved by adding a third dimension to the hexagon. It will be used as the base of a six-sided pyramid, with the apex above the center. After this pyramid is created it is turned so that the hexagon faces up (see Figure 9.9). The height of the hexpyramid is 1. The point at the apex represents the color black. The vector from the

FIGURE 9.8

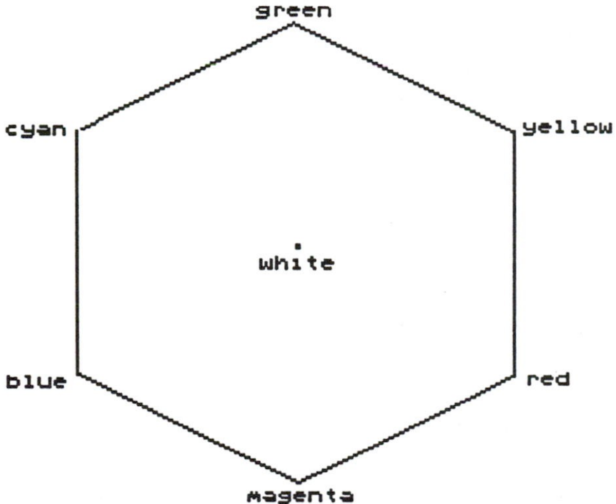

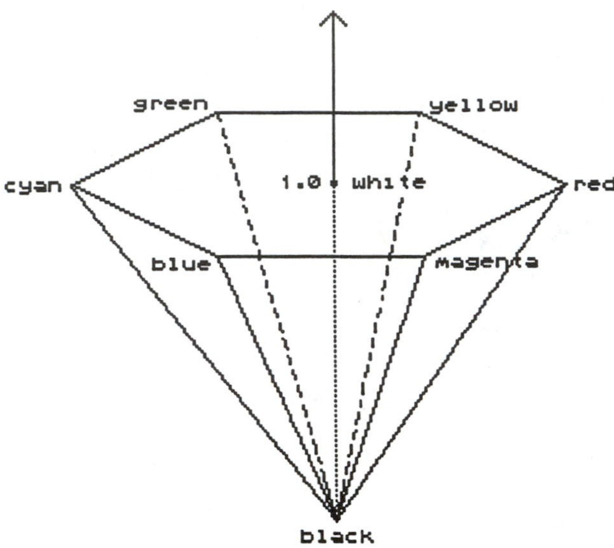


**FIGURE 9.9**

apex upward is called the value vector V. The hexagon corresponds to V-values of 1. Any color now corresponds to a point within this hexpyramid. Full-intensity colors are located in the hexagon; their V-values are 1. The further down we get, the lower the intensity and the darker the color. At V = 0 we have black. So V expresses the value (intensity) of a color.

Hue, H, is relatively easy to describe. In a sense it is the characteristic "color" of the color, which we describe by the words red, green, and so on, even if the given color in the broad sense is only a reddish or greenish white or gray. The hue will be described by a number between 0 and 360, which is the angle in a ccw sense starting at red = 0°. A certain hue angle comprises all points on the radial that emanates from the center with this angle as well as all points on a vertical half-plane intersecting the hexpyramid along this radial. A point below the hexagon represents a darker color but still, along with the same point vertically above, one of the same hue. A point further from the boundary represents a color that is less saturated (see below) than a color of a point on the same radial but closer to the boundary. We also see that complementary colors are opposites, 180° from each other.

Saturation, S, also called *purity,* is the most difficult to visualize. Look at Figure 9.10. It shows the spectral energy distribution of a certain color. Most wavelengths in the spectrum radiate with an almost equal energy, but one wavelength is much stronger. Called the *dominant wavelength,* it determines the hue of the given color. The other wavelengths that radiate about equally strongly but less than the dominant one

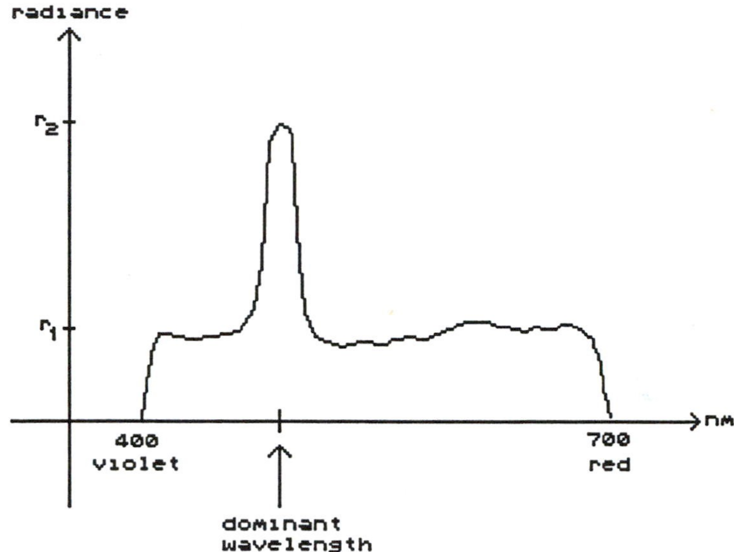


**FIGURE 9.10**

produce a lighter or darker white, which is added to and dilutes or desaturates the hue. The saturation of the color is given by the values of $r_1$ and $r_2$. An absolutely pure light has no white (gray) tones in it, so $r_1 = 0$. When $r_1 = r_2$ we have just white and the saturation is 0.

The value of the saturation is a ratio ranging from 0 on the center line (V-axis) to 1 on the boundary of the hexagon. Saturation is the distance of a point from the center line. Fully saturated colors lie on the boundary of the hexagon. The center line represents all colors with saturation of 0. Moving along this line from the white point down to the apex gives white through gray until black is reached. These colors have no hue in them because this line is always equally far away from all perimeter points.

## 9.3.3 The HLS System

Similar to the HSV system, this system is frequently used in color CRT displays, especially in Tektronix hardware. The letters HLS stand for *hue, lightness,* and *saturation.* In a broader sense, the physiological characteristics of a color are its hue (in the sense of rainbow color), its lightness (its brightness or luminance), and its saturation (the degree to which it is undiluted by white), as we have seen above. The HLS system is based on the Ostwald color system, proposed in 1931. It too

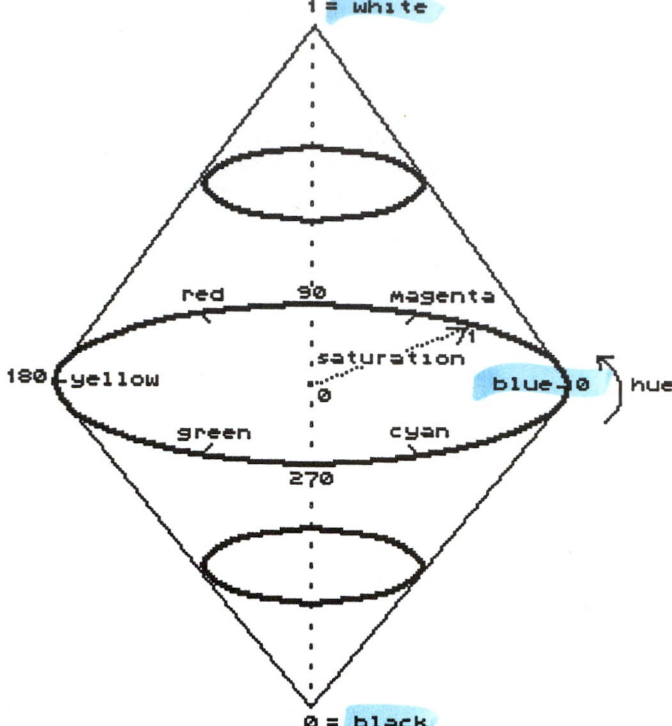


FIGURE 9.11

needs a three-dimensional representation, similar to the HSV system, called the *color double cone* (see Figure 9.11).

On the perimeter of a central disk are located the colors blue, magenta, red, yellow, green, and cyan, spaced 60° apart from each other. The upper apex of the cone is white and the lower apex is black. The colors on the perimeter blend gradually into each other. Each point on the perimeter of the disk describes a color that is a blend of the two adjacent colors, whereby the ratio of the blend is determined by the ratio of distances from the adjacent two colors. Here a blue hue is at angle 0.

A point not on the perimeter contains a blend of all colors. The greater the distance of the point from any of the perimeter colors, the less of that color in the blend. Therefore these points describe pastel colors which contain a certain amount of white. What is meant by hue and saturation is the same as with the HSV system, but here angle 0 corresponds to blue.

The lightness is the height in the double cone. It will be given as a number between 0, corresponding to the lower apex, and 1, corresponding to the upper apex. It is the intensity of the color. At the highest intensity all colors merge into white and at the lowest they merge into black.

The center of the central disk describes white of medium intensity, not full intensity as in the hexpyramid diagram. It can be understood as a mixture of all colors with equal intensity. The higher we move up in the cone the more we move toward white; the more we move down, the more we move toward black. If we start at the perimeter at the angle 0 (color blue) and move in a straight line toward the top we add more and more white, so we will go through light blue to an almost white pastel blue until finally we have the brightest white. This will happen with any color we start with. The shrinking of the diameter of the cone toward the top and the bottom expresses the idea that all colors converge to white as we move up or to black as we move down. Moving along the straight line between top and bottom gives all the gray levels from white to black.

## 9.3.4 The CIE System

CIE stands for Commission Internationale de l'Eclairage. The color system worked out by this commission in 1931 is very adaptable to color programming. To explain it we first discuss color triangles.

**Color Triangles** When we have a color system consisting of three primaries, we can represent it graphically by an equilateral triangle. As mentioned before, any three colors can be used as primaries as long as no one of them can be created by a combination of the other two.

In Figure 9.12 the primaries are at the corners of the triangle, called X, Y, and Z. Any color is a point C within this triangle. The point's position with respect to the corners expresses the relative contribution of the primaries to the color. More precisely, the contribution of X is proportional to the area of the triangle CYZ opposite to X. The same is true for the primaries Y and Z. The contribution of a primary to a point C is "full" if C is at the corner and zero if C is on the opposite edge. The areas have certain absolute sizes that depend on the size of the original triangle. The sizes can be considered as the luminances that the primaries contribute to the color.

A color can then be expressed by three numbers (the areas of the subtriangles), which are called its *chromaticity values.* The sum of the chromaticity values will always be the same no matter where C is located.

The size of the original whole triangle is still variable. If we work with primaries of high luminances we will have large triangles; otherwise, small ones. This system of expressing colors can be represented by a three-dimensional geometric model with the Cartesian coordinates

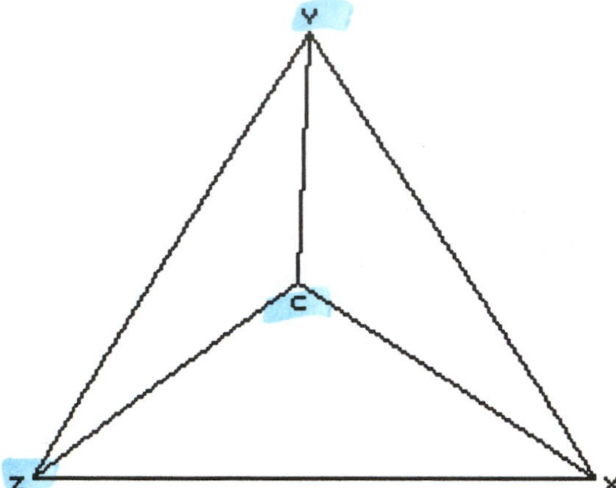


**FIGURE 9.12**

X, Y, and Z. The primaries are points on the axes whose distances from the origin depend on their luminance. With all three primary luminances equal, these three points define an equilateral triangle—the triangle we had above. The color of C in terms of hue is expressed by the vector from the origin to the point C in this triangle and the luminance of C by the length of the vector. Colors that differ only in luminance but not in hue lie on the same vector.

If we want a system that describes just the hue of a color, ignoring its luminance, we must ignore the length of the vector. The purpose of the color triangle is to develop such a system. Intuitively, luminance could be multiplied in later as a common factor. We can achieve this by dividing the chromaticity values of C by their sum:

$$x_c = \frac{X_c}{X_c + Y_c + Z_c} \qquad y_c = \frac{Y_c}{X_c + Y_c + Z_c} \qquad z_c = \frac{Z_c}{X_c + Y_c + Z_c}$$

We call these normalized chromaticity values *chromaticity coefficients.* Their sum is always equal to 1:

$$x_c + y_c + z_c = 1$$

Geometrically this corresponds to using only the triangle spanned by the points at distance 1 from the origin, shown in Figure 9.13.

Since the sum of the three values equals 1, it suffices to specify only two of them, say $x_c$ and $y_c$, $z_c$ then equals $1 - x_c - y_c$. We can express this geometrically by projecting the equilateral triangle onto the (x,y)-plane. A color is now expressed by only two parameters, x and y, in a Cartesian coordinate system, shown in Figure 9.14. The primaries we choose sit on the corners of a right triangle. We have now made a step toward understanding the CIE color system.

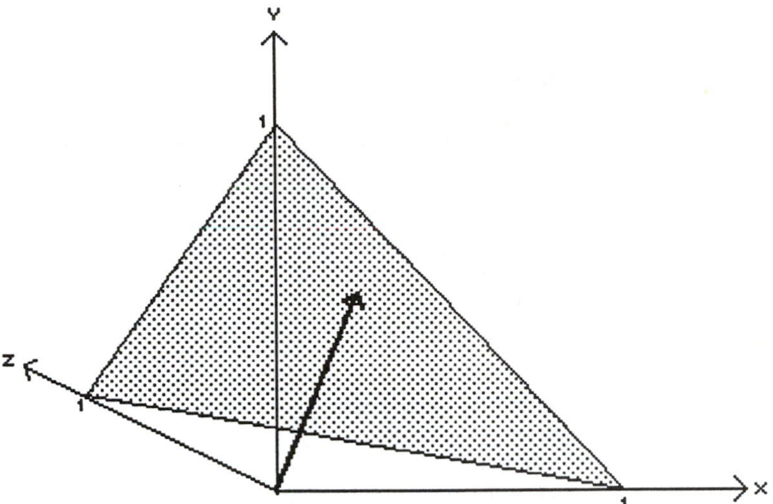


FIGURE 9.13

**Alignment to White** We have assumed that the luminances of the three primaries at the corners are equal. The consequence is that the point within the triangle where the primaries combine to white will not lie in the center. White light is composed of light of all visible wavelengths, each radiating with the same energy. The luminance values of these component lights will be far from equal as we saw in the luminance curve in Figure 9.1.

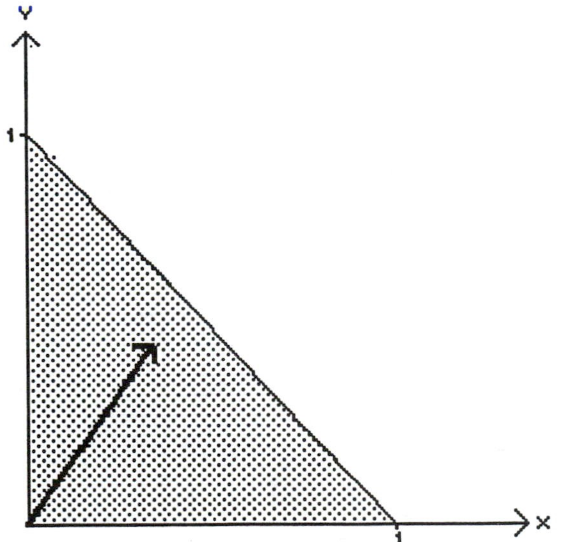


FIGURE 9.14

Also, when we compose white light from three primaries, these primaries must radiate with about equal energy. This will imply that their luminance values will not be equal. If the primaries are, for example, red, green, and blue, only small luminances of blue and red compared to a large luminance of green are required to form white. Equal luminances on the corners mean that the white point will be far from blue and red and close to green. If we mix equal luminances of red and green and blue we will not get white.

Still, we prefer to have the white point in the middle of the triangle. This can be achieved by lowering the luminances of the primaries that have too much "weight" in the mix. The factors that achieve this are called the *luminosity coefficients* of the primaries. They depend on which primaries are used and to which white they are aligned.

The problem of aligning to white is not theoretical but occurs with every color monitor. To align a color monitor the amplifier circuits for the three primaries (whatever these are) are adjusted so that equal intensity specifications for the primaries (in the lookup table) will result in the desired white and from there through the whole gray scale down to black. The luminance of full-scale blue or full-scale red will always be much lower than that of full-scale green.

**The CIE Diagram** Let us choose any three primaries, say red, green, and blue, and try to match all possible colors by combinations of these. We will always find some colors that cannot be made no matter how pure and how saturated the primaries. This will not change if we use a different set of three primaries. Some colors not achieved before might now be possible, but there will be other colors that we could match with the former set of primaries but not with the new set.

Assume we have a color, for example, some full-saturated cyan, that we cannot match with our given set of three primaries, red, green, and blue, no matter how hard we try. We will now apply a scheme that allows us at least to express which combination of our primaries could theoretically define that color. If we add a little red (r) to the cyan to be matched, then we will be able to match it in terms of green (g) and blue (b). In our example let the amount of red added to cyan be 0.05, and let this desaturated cyan be matchable by $0.4 * g + 0.4 * b$. Now we have:

$$\text{cyan} + 0.05 * r = 0.4 * g + 0.4 * b.$$

From this we deduce:

$$\text{cyan} = -0.05 * r + 0.4 * g + 0.4 * b.$$

So we have a negative weight in the combination. This theoretical match does not help us because we cannot apply negative weights. This

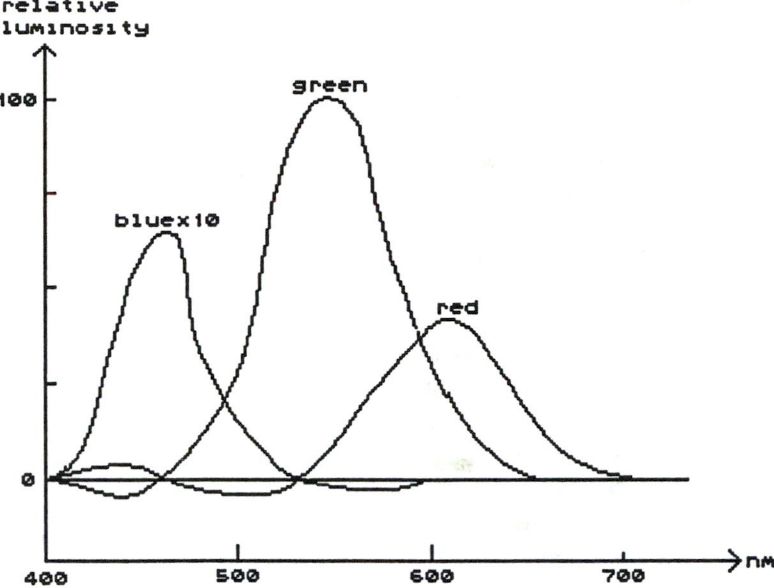


**FIGURE 9.15** Response characteristic for red, green, and blue.

scheme is demonstrated in Figure 9.15, which shows what weights of red, green, and blue are necessary to match any colors in the rainbow spectrum. For many colors we need negative weights.

The fact of negative weights suggests that our primaries were not pure enough or not saturated enough. We had to desaturate the cyan, that is, pull it more toward white by adding some of the third primary, in order to match it with the first two. If our blue and green were more saturated (farther away from white), we should be able to match the given cyan without pulling it closer to white. We should have a "bluer" blue and a "greener" green. The same applies to the third primary, red.

This thought led the CIE to introduce three supersaturated colors as primaries which don't exist in reality, X, Y, and Z. These primaries will never be used to generate colors on any real device; they will be used only to describe colors in terms of a two-dimensional Cartesian coordinate system and permit us to read some important true color relationships directly from the diagram. The system will be two-dimensional because the sum of the primary weights (the chromaticity coefficients) will always be 1 (see the color triangles above) and the weights can now always be positive. It is of course possible to describe colors that don't exist, but this is insignificant. What counts is the fact that we can describe all visible colors by positive chromaticity coefficients.

Note that here we observe the same distinction between chromaticity values and chromaticity coefficients (that add up to 1). But the coefficients don't describe the luminance of a color; that can be obtained by providing a luminance value Y. In the CIE system, then, a color can be fully described by the two coefficients (x,y) and the luminance value Y. This is again essentially a three-dimensional description, but if we ignore the luminance factor Y we have a precise two-dimensional color definition.

We can transform from chromaticity coefficients (x,y,z) to chromaticity values (X,Y,Z) not by multiplying with the luminance value Y but by scaling the coefficients with the proper factor so that y transforms into Y. The convention is that the Y chromaticity value directly expresses the luminance of the color. The factor to use is Y/y.

Figure 9.16 shows the diagram. The whites lie in the center of the area. Blue in the lower left corner and red in the lower right corner are connected by a straight line, called the purple boundary. All visible colors are now expressed as points on this two-dimensional diagram. The fully saturated rainbow colors lie on a horseshoe-shaped curve. The diagram is arranged so that the y-chromaticity coefficient has a dual function. It not only expresses the position of a color in the chart but also represents its relative luminance. What does this mean? As stated above, the CIE coefficients don't describe a color's luminance, but the relative luminance conveyed by the y coefficient has the following meaning. If two colors $A = (x_A, y_A)$ and $B = (x_B, y_B)$ are radiating with the same energy, the ratio of their absolute luminances is $y_A/y_B$. If we want these colors to shine with the same absolute luminances Y, we have to scale them with the factors $Y/y_A$ and $Y/y_B$, respectively, which are in an inverse ratio to $y_A/y_B$. In doing so we get their chromaticity values: $(X_A, Y, Z_A)$ and $(X_B, Y, Z_B)$. This tells us that the chromaticity value Y of a color expresses the absolute luminance and the chromaticity coefficient y expresses the relative luminance.

When the chromaticity values Y are identical, the colors have the same luminances, but the total chromaticities of these colors can still be different: $T_A = X_A + Y + Z_A$ and $T_B = X_B + Y + Z_B$. The total chromaticity of a color is not the same as its luminance. It is in effect the weight that this color has in mixtures.

**Color Gamuts** The description of a color in an RGB system, when ignoring luminance, can be done using color triangles. It is then essentially the same as a CIE description. Both use triangular coordinates; the only difference is that the primaries in CIE are hypothetical and in RGB the primaries are real. Transformations between RGB and CIE descriptions are expressed by simple linear equations and so can be done geometrically. The CIE chart spans an area so wide that it contains all visible colors. If we choose any three real primaries, they will lie somewhere in the CIE chart. All colors obtainable by these three primaries are contained in the triangle spanned by them. We can see that no triangle spanned by three points within the outward bent horseshoe

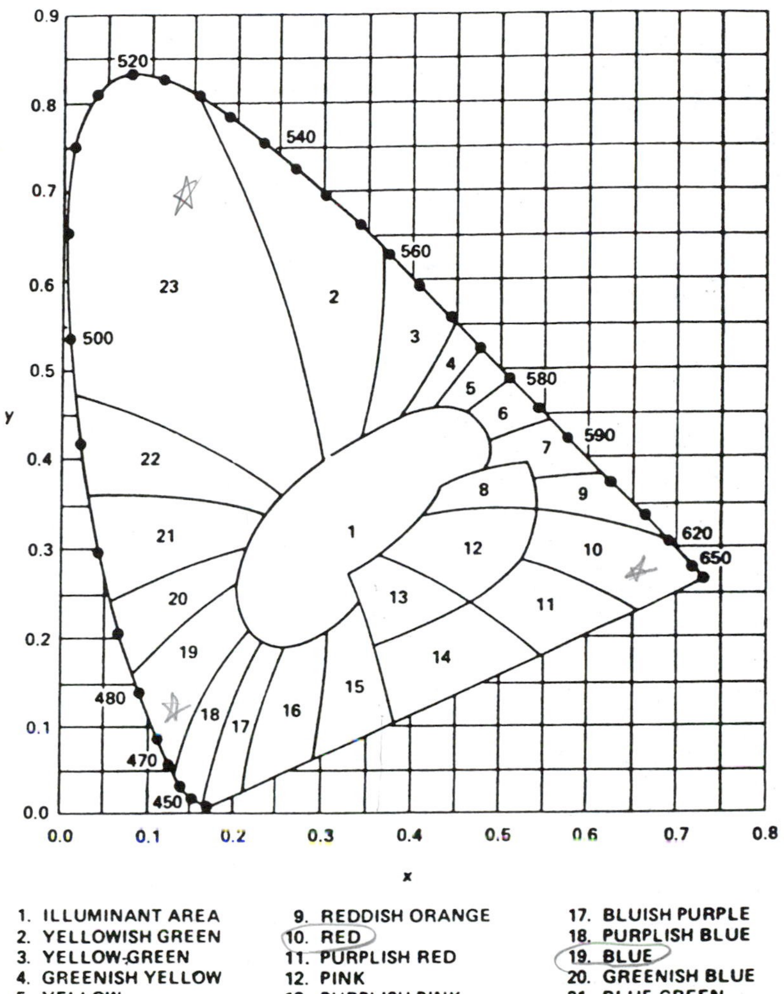

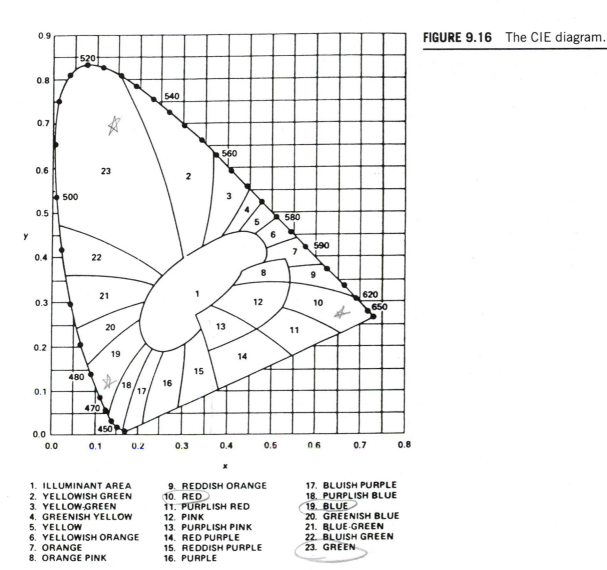

**FIGURE 9.16** The CIE diagram.

curve can cover the whole area within the curve. Choosing more than three primaries would allow us to draw a quadrilateral, pentagon, or other figure, but such polygons are still not able to cover the whole area.

Using the CIE diagram we can readily make choices of primaries and see immediately which colors we can obtain from them. The triangle spanned by the primaries within the diagram shows that range. We call such a color range a *color gamut*. Figure 9.17 shows the triangle

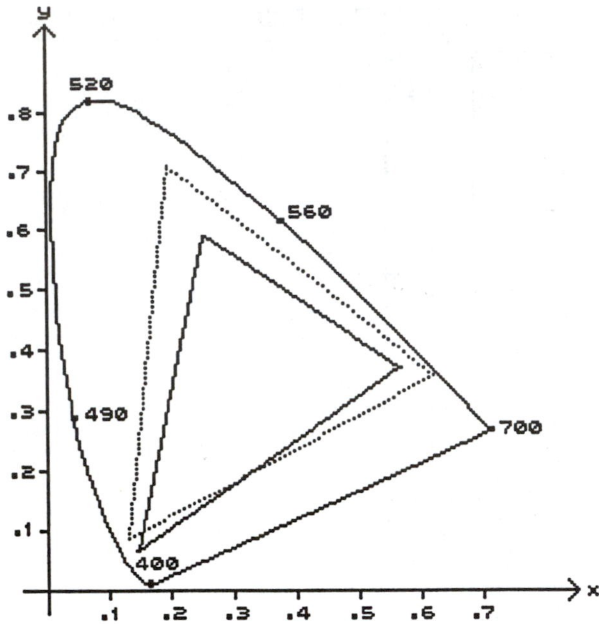


FIGURE 9.17

of the primaries chosen in 1953 by the National Television Standards Committee (NTSC) in dotted lines and the triangle of a good-quality graphics color monitor in solid lines. The diagram is very useful for comparing the color gamuts for different monitors.

The table below shows the chromaticity coefficients (x,y) for the color monitor in Figure 9.17. The z coefficient is $1-x-y$.

| | | |
|---|---|---|
| R: | 0.628 | 0.346 |
| G: | 0.268 | 0.588 |
| B: | 0.150 | 0.070 |

It is also possible to show the color gamuts for color printers and hard-copy devices in the CIE diagram. Mixing colors on a white background as done by a printer is basically a subtractive process. The difference between an additive and a subtractive process is not that different hues are produced when mixing given colors but that the product is of increased luminance in additive mixing and of decreased luminance in subtractive. As the CIE diagram is luminance independent it is also independent of the type of color mixing. But it is hard to visualize the resulting color in a subtractive case. Mixing red and green gives orange-yellow on a screen and in the diagram. Mixing it on paper gives brown, which is actually orange-yellow with a very low luminance and is therefore not shown in the diagram. To add to the problem, printers work with a fourth color, black, which has no fixed corresponding point in the diagram.

**Dominant Wavelength** The diagram allows us to obtain the *dominant wavelength* (the hue) of any given color such as A geometrically. We draw the dominant wavelength vector, which is a line connecting the point A and the white point, W. Moving away from W along this vector we will intersect the boundary of the area, say at point B. The wavelength corresponding to B is the dominant wavelength of the color (see Figure 9.18).

If we hit the purple boundary, as in Figure 9.19 at point B, we have a nonspectral color because purple hues don't occur in the rainbow spectrum. Consequently, there is no dominant wavelength. In such a case we elongate the connecting line in the opposite direction and hit the boundary there, say at point D. That color, approximately 495 nm, is said to be the *complementary dominant wavelength* of color A. The purity of the color is expressed by the ratio of the length AW to the

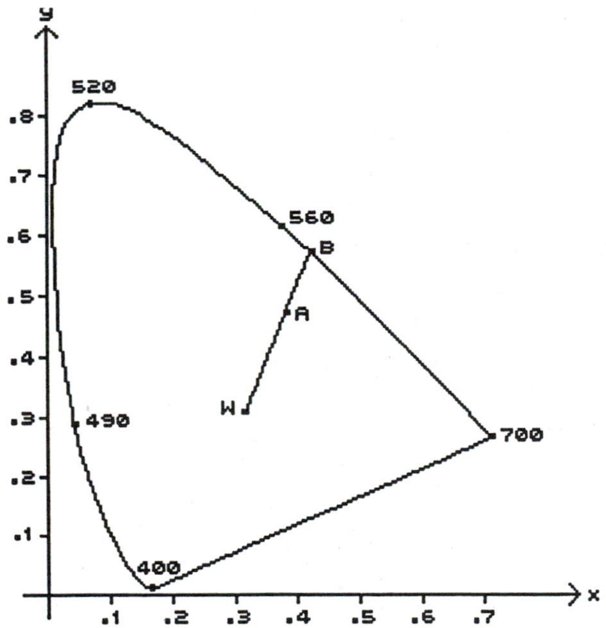


**FIGURE 9.18**

FIGURE 9.19

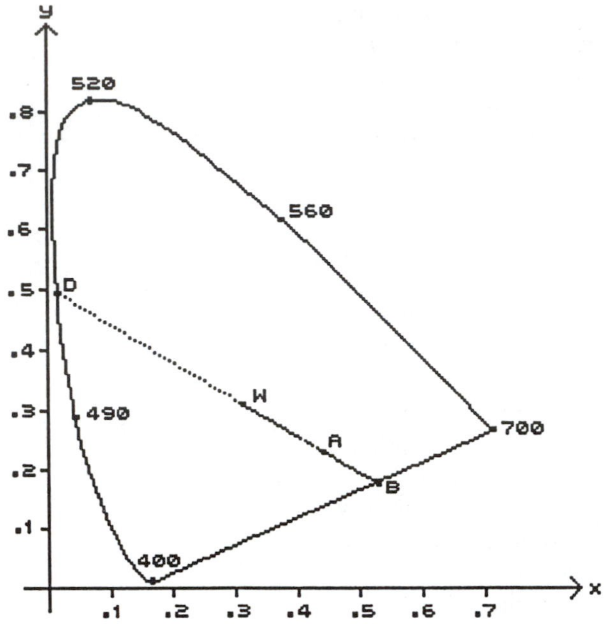


length of the whole line. We see immediately that white has a purity of 0 and colors on the boundary have a purity of 1.

**Mixing Colors** When we mix two colors A and B we plot the corresponding points in the diagram and connect them by a straight line. All colors along this line can be produced by mixing A with B in varying luminances. This is called *interpolation in color space* or *color programming* (see Figure 9.20).

There is more to it than just drawing a line. We have merely stated that we can obtain all colors on the line from A to B. But the color that results from a given mixture depends on a nontrivial relation. If precise results are not needed, we can say that, for example, mixing A with B at equal luminances will produce a color at the center of the line. This rough estimate is often inadequate. The reason is that colors have different weights. We know that to achieve white only a very small luminance of blue is required compared to somewhat more of red and a very great luminance of green. If we mix A and B with equal luminances, the resulting color in general will not lie at the center of the line. The CIE chromaticity diagram is helpful in determining the result. The y-coordinate of a color in the diagram also expresses this color's luminance in relation to the luminances of all other colors in the diagram, the so-called *relative luminance*.

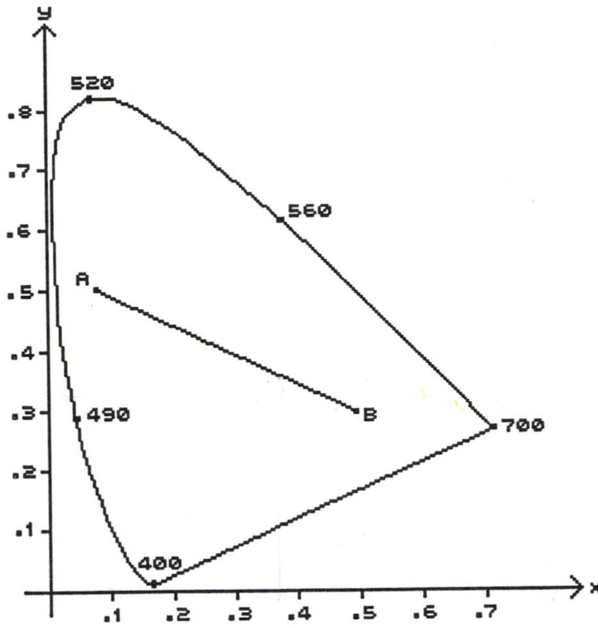

**FIGURE 9.20**

Take the line of Figure 9.20 as an example. A has the chromaticity coefficients (x,y,z) = (0.08,0.5,0.42) and B has (x,y,z) = (0.5,0.3,0.2). This means that the luminances of A and B are in a ratio of 5/3 if no other adjustments are made. In order for B to radiate with the same luminance as A, B has to radiate with 5/3 as much power as A. In this analysis we don't need any absolute luminance values because we just want to express our result on the CIE diagram. Therefore we can work with relative values even if they temporarily fall outside the diagram.

After applying the factor 5/3, B has the coefficients (0.83,0.5,0.33) compared to A, which has (0.08,0.5,0.42). Observe that we have achieved equality of the y-coefficients, which means equal luminance of A and B. Now adding the coefficients of A and B together we get (0.91,1.0,0.75), which is not in the diagram. We normalize this to 1 so we can associate a point in the CIE diagram with it and get (0.342,0.37,0.28). This point lies on the line from A to B because it is a linear combination of the A and B coordinates, but it is much closer to B than to A. In this example we have assumed only that the absolute luminances of A and B are equal; their relative values don't matter.

To program such color computations is not difficult. We need to do this when, for example, we want to see what colors we get when we merge two separate color images on the screen. In a practical application the colors A, B, and so on will be described by triples $(x_A, y_A, Y_A)$,

$(x_B, y_B, Y_B)$, and so on where Y are the luminances. In such a case the color weights are computed as:

$$T_A = \frac{Y_A}{y_A} \qquad T_B = \frac{Y_B}{y_B}$$

Then the chromaticities of the mixture are computed as:

$$x_M = \frac{x_A T_A + x_B T_B}{T_A + T_B} \qquad y_M = \frac{y_A T_A + y_B T_B}{T_A + T_B} \qquad Y_M = Y_A + Y_B$$

The main value of the CIE diagram is that we can visualize the color we are supposed to obtain when we merge colors on the screen. If the screen is badly gamma-corrected and/or badly white-aligned, the CIE diagram will be the only reliable source to visualize the result. With a perfectly gamma-corrected and white-aligned monitor we obtain correct results just by linearly interpolating color data, as for example that represented in the lookup tables. (A white-aligned monitor produces a white color from equal intensity values for the primaries in the lookup table. Adjusting potentiometers can be set to compensate for the difference in phosphor reactions to the electron beam. Gamma correction was described in Chapter 2.)

## 9.3.5 Transformations

Obviously the same color can be expressed in various ways, five of which we have covered: RGB, HSV, HLS, CIE, and the cyan/magenta/yellow subtractive system (CMY). As you should expect, it is possible to transform from one description into another. We will describe some of the more common transformations.

**RGB to CMY** This transformation is necessary when we want to make a hard copy of a CRT display on a color hard copy device (dot matrix, ink jet, or laser printer). Printers follow a subtractive model, so they usually use the CMY color system, augmented by black. Whenever a picture has been created for a CRT display using RGB color descriptions, producing a hard copy of the screen picture involves the transformations between these two different descriptions.

If we directly produce the same colors on the printer as we have on the screen, namely red, green, and blue, in the same intensities, it is easy to see that we get totally wrong results. Red + green is yellow on the screen, but brown on the printer. Red + green + blue is white on the screen, but a very dark brown on the printer. No colors at all is black on the screen but white on the printer, and so on. Mixing more and more colors together gives us an ever brighter result on a CRT display while it gives us an ever darker result on a printer.

We might imagine that we can get correct results by mixing the primaries red, green, and blue on the printer with intensities complementary to those in the CRT display: for highest on the screen use lowest on the printer, and vice versa. But if we do this we soon find out that this doesn't work either. The reason is that the primaries red, green, and blue, when used subtractively, are too subtractive. For example, a red dye is one that extinguishes all wavelengths except the red one. When mixed with a green dye, which extinguishes all wavelengths except green, the result would extinguish everything, at least in theory. In reality this results in a variety of dark brown colors.

When producing hard copies it is not possible (and not desirable) to avoid the overlapping of different colors on the paper, which is actually needed to blend the subtractions. It turns out to be best to work on the paper with primaries that each extinguish only one of the wavelengths. These are cyan, magenta, and yellow (CMY). While a certain color on the screen is produced by adding the necessary wavelengths to the original black, it is produced on the paper by subtracting the unnecessary wavelengths from the original white. This explains the transformation formulas below.

Two different formulas are often encountered. A formula for deriving the CMY intensities for any given RGB intensities is:

$$
\begin{aligned}
C &= 1 - R \\
M &= 1 - G \\
Y &= 1 - B
\end{aligned}
$$

The intensities in both systems are given in fractions with 1 as the highest intensity. This formula is purely theoretical as it assumes that full intensities of CMY together produce black, which is not the case.

For real hard copy output we need to add black (Bl) as a fourth primary, so the formulas become:

$$
\begin{aligned}
C &= \max(RGB) - R \\
M &= \max(RGB) - G \\
Y &= \max(RGB) - B \\
Bl &= 1 - \max(RGB)
\end{aligned}
$$

Again, the intensities are given as fractions with 1 as the maximum. The term max(RGB) is the maximum of any primary intensity of the RGB combination. An inverse transformation is not needed because there are no applications in which a color hard copy has to be transformed to RGB. When a color hard copy is digitized, the hardware (the video digitizer) automatically gives RGB values.

As an example, transform a dark greenish yellow on the screen to the proper CMYBl values. The dark greenish yellow is given as (RGB) = (0.4,0.5,0), which stands for low red, not so low green, no blue. Max(RGB) = 0.5, so we get:

$$\begin{aligned} C &= 0.5 - 0.4 = 0.1 \\ M &= 0.5 - 0.5 = 0.0 \\ Y &= 0.5 - 0.0 = 0.5 \\ Bl &= 1.0 - 0.5 = 0.5 \end{aligned}$$

We get mainly a mixture of yellow and black dots on the paper, resulting in dark yellow. A little bit of cyan (a few cyan dots) will be strewn in to give the dark yellow a greenish tint. There are more examples in the exercises.

**RGB and HLS** These transformations are more complex. Both systems are used to define colors for CRT displays. In these transformation formulas we assume that the RGB values are defined in a range from 0 to 1, H is defined in a range from 0 to 360 and H and S are defined in a range from 0 to 1.

In a transformation from RGB to HLS we first set M = max(RGB) and m = min(RGB) and compute (r,g,b):

$$r = \frac{M-R}{M-m} \qquad g = \frac{M-G}{M-m} \qquad b = \frac{M-B}{M-m}$$

At least one of the (r,g,b) values will be 0 depending on which RGB intensities equal the maximum, and at least one of them will be 1 depending on which RGB intensities equal the minimum.

Then we compute the intensity I: I = (M+m)/2.

Computation of the saturation S is done with one of two formulas depending on whether I is smaller or greater than 0.5:

$$\text{if } I \leq 0.5: S = \frac{M-m}{M+m}, \qquad \text{if } I > 0.5: S = \frac{M-m}{2-M-m}$$

For the computation of H we use one of three different formulas depending on which of the (r,g,b) is 0:

$$\begin{aligned} \text{if } r = 0: &\quad H = 60(2+b-g) \\ \text{if } g = 0: &\quad H = 60(4+r-b) \\ \text{if } b = 0: &\quad H = 60(6+g-r) \end{aligned}$$

If the saturation S is 0 we can assign an arbitrary value to H.

In a transformation from HLS to RGB we first compute M and m:

$$\text{if } L \leqslant 0.5: \quad M = L(1+S)$$
$$\text{if } L > 0.5: \quad M = L + S - LS$$
$$m = 2L - M$$

Then we compute R:

$$\text{if}\, H < 60: R = m + (M-m)\frac{H}{60}; \qquad \text{if}\, H < 180: R = M;$$
$$\text{if}\, H < 240: R = m + (M-m)\frac{240-H}{60} \qquad \text{if } H < 360: R = m$$

Then G:

$$\text{if}\, H < 120: G = m; \quad \text{if}\, H < 180: G = m + (M-m)\frac{H-120}{60};$$
$$\text{if}\, H < 300: G = M \quad \text{if}\, H < 360: G = m + (M-m)\frac{360-H}{60}$$

Then B:

$$\text{if}\, H < 60: B = M; \quad \text{if}\, H < 120: B = m + (M-m)\frac{120-H}{60};$$
$$\text{if}\, H < 240: B = m; \quad \text{if}\, H < 300: B = m + (M-m)\frac{H-240}{60}.$$

A system that allows the user to specify colors in HLS must be able to do a transformation to RGB because technically, at the lowest hardware level, every CRT monitor is driven with RGB primaries. So the transformation from HLS to RGB is often built into the system.

**RGB and CIE** To establish a relation between these two systems, we must know the CIE chromaticity coefficients of the given RGB primaries and of the white to which the monitor is aligned:

$$R: x_R, y_R, z_R \qquad G: x_G, y_G, z_G \qquad B: x_B, y_B, z_B \qquad W: X_W, Y_W, Y_W$$

The z-coordinates are really redundant as they can be derived from x and y. Notice that the white alignment is given in absolute chromaticity values. On a monitor the white alignment is produced by combining the primaries with unequal luminances. Primaries with a low relative luminance, like blue, need to be brought into the combination with a reduced absolute luminance, which implies a reduced total chromaticity, in order not to exert too much weight. The sum of the total chromaticities (the adjusted weights) of the three primaries gives the desired white. This can be expressed by the linear system:

$$\begin{bmatrix} x_R & x_G & x_B \\ y_R & y_G & y_B \\ z_R & z_G & z_B \end{bmatrix} \begin{bmatrix} T_R \\ T_G \\ T_B \end{bmatrix} = \begin{bmatrix} X_W \\ Y_W \\ Z_W \end{bmatrix}$$

Expressing a color that is given in one system in terms of the other is basically simple, but requires several computations. What we show now is nothing but the application of Cramer's rule to that system. We first compute the transformation determinant $k_D$:

$$k_D = \begin{vmatrix} x_R & x_G & x_B \\ y_R & y_G & y_B \\ z_R & z_G & z_B \end{vmatrix}$$

Then nine conversion factors $k_1$ through $k_9$:

$$k_1 = \frac{y_G z_B - y_B z_G}{k_D} \qquad k_2 = \frac{x_B z_G - x_G z_B}{k_D} \qquad k_3 = \frac{x_G y_B - x_B y_G}{k_D}$$

$$k_4 = \frac{y_B z_R - y_R z_B}{k_D} \qquad k_5 = \frac{x_R z_B - x_B z_R}{k_D} \qquad k_6 = \frac{x_B y_R - x_R y_B}{k_D}$$

$$k_7 = \frac{y_R z_G - y_G z_R}{k_D} \qquad k_8 = \frac{x_G z_R - x_R z_G}{k_D} \qquad k_9 = \frac{x_R y_G - x_G y_R}{k_D}$$

With these we compute the total chromaticity values $T_R$, $T_G$, and $T_B$ for the primaries:

$$T_R = k_1 X_W + k_2 Y_W + k_3 Z_W \qquad T_G = k_4 X_W + k_5 Y_W + k_6 Z_W$$
$$T_B = k_7 X_W + k_8 Y_W + k_9 Z_W$$

The k and T values are constant for a given set of primaries and white, so they can be kept as fixed constants for a given monitor and used for the conversions in both directions.

In order for the following transformations to be correct, we assume that the monitor is gamma-corrected. This means that the data-to-luminance relation is linear on this monitor.

**CIE to RGB** If a color C is given as $(x_C, y_C, Y_C)$, we first compute its chromaticity values:

$$X_C = \frac{x_C}{y_C} Y_C \qquad Y_C = Y_C \qquad Z_C = \frac{z_C}{y_C} Y_C$$

Then the RGB components of the color C:

$$R_C = \frac{k_1}{T_R}X_C + \frac{k_2}{T_R}Y_C + \frac{k_3}{T_R}Z_C$$

$$G_C = \frac{k_4}{T_G}X_C + \frac{k_5}{T_G}Y_C + \frac{k_6}{T_G}Z_C$$

$$B_C = \frac{k_7}{T_B}X_C + \frac{k_8}{T_B}Y_C + \frac{k_9}{T_B}Z_C$$

**RGB to CIE** If a color is given by its RGB values as $(R_C G_C B_C)$, we first compute its chromaticity values:

$$X_C = x_R T_R R_C + x_G T_G G_C + x_B T_B B_C$$

$$Y_C = y_R T_R R_C + y_G T_G G_C + y_B T_B B_C$$

$$Z_C = z_R T_R R_C + z_G T_G G_C + z_B T_B B_C$$

These are transformed into the chromaticity coefficients:

$$T_C = X_C + Y_C + Z_C$$

$$x_C = X_C/T_C \qquad y_C = Y_C/T_C \qquad z_C = Z_C/T_C$$

The exercises give you opportunities to practice all of these transformations.

# EXERCISES FOR CHAPTER 9

1. Assume a frame buffer with one byte per pixel. How many different colors can be displayed simultaneously on the screen?
2. Assume a frame buffer with one byte per pixel and a lookup table with length 256 and width 24 bits (eight for red, eight for green, and eight for blue). How many different colors can be displayed overall?
3. Assume a frame buffer of depth four (four bits per pixel). Specify the size of the lookup table needed to display 16 colors simultaneously from a palette of 512.
4. Approximately where in the RGB color cube (Figure 9.6) is the color brown? Remember that brown is just a dark yellow. Approximately where is it in the HSV hexpyramid (Figure 9.9)? Approximately where is it in the HLS double cone (Figure 9.11)?
5. For this exercise you need a colored CIE diagram. (If you only have a black-and-white diagram you can still practice locating a color mix.) Locate the two colors A = (0.2,0.1,0.7) and B = (0.5,0.4,0.1) in the diagram and find what color results when

mixing them with equal luminances. The resulting color lies on the straight line connecting A and B. Compute the location of this point and indicate it in the diagram.

## Transforming Color Expressions

6. Transform the RGB color (0.8,0.3,0.4) into the equivalent CMYBl expression.
7. Write a procedure for transforming RGB into CMYBl.
8. Transform the RGB color (0.5,0.1,0) into the equivalent HLS expression.
9. Write a procedure for transforming RGB into HLS.
10. Write a procedure for transforming HLS into RGB.

## COLOR PLATE 1

*This fractal landscape consists of five mountains. Each mountain is a fractally distorted surface (see 10.2). All surfaces consist of a 150 x 150 point grid. For display purposes, the four adjacent points in the surface were considered as two triangles. Dimension is created through the use of faceted shading. A one point light source was assumed and positioned on the upper right. (Created by Cornel Pokorny)*

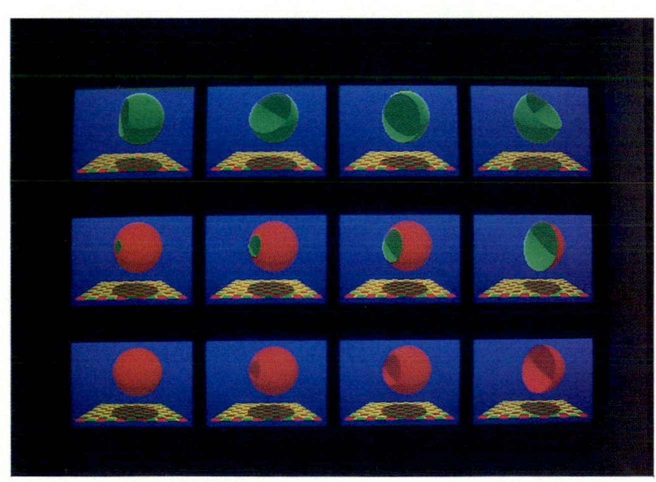

## COLOR PLATE 2

*Non-reflecting spheres in various stages of rotation. Note the shadows in the hollows and below the spheres. The technique used is Ray Tracing (see 15.4). It is frequently used in Solid Modelling. Exercises 15.21 - 15.24 focus on this technique (using the Boolean union, intersection, and difference of objects). These Boolean operations are illustrated with some examples in the subsection on Solid Modelling (17.1.4). (Created by Ahmad Motiei)*

## COLOR PLATE 3

*The technique used here is the same as in Color Plate 2 except for the addition of the reflecting surfaces. Note the complicated multiple reflections in the hollow of the big sphere. (Created by Adrian Brandt)*

## COLOR PLATE 4

*The three interlocking tori were drawn using Depth Sorting (see 11.3.2) and the Painters Algorithm (see 11.3.3). The parametric description of a torus was used to define the vertices of triangles on its surface. All triangles were defined counter-clockwise. The second and third torus were obtained by rotating and shifting the first one. Then all triangles were depth sorted and drawn together using faceted shading. (Created by Hsueh-Mei Hsu)*

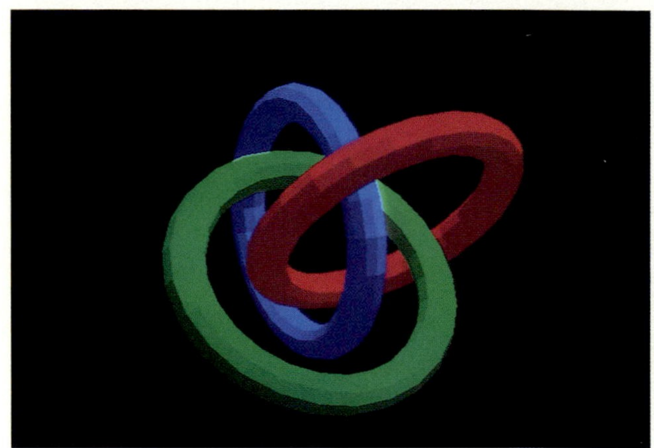

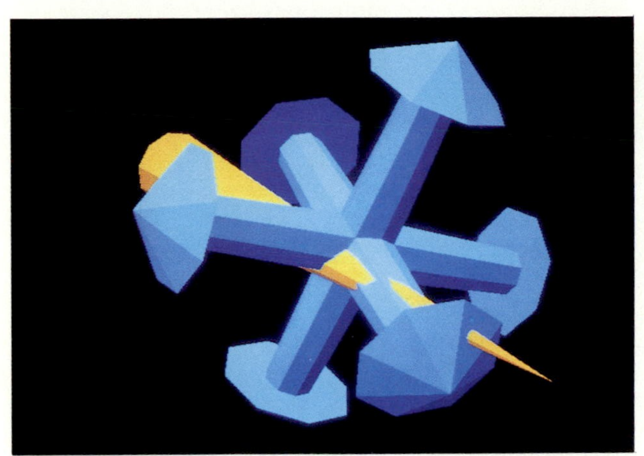

## COLOR PLATE 5

*This scene was created by using Warnock's Algorithm (see 12.10). The shaft and hood of one arrow was defined explicitly, the other five were obtained by rotating the first one around the point of origin. An eight-sided pyramid was added and rotated. All triangles were sorted into three lists. Faceted shading was done assuming two points of light. (Created by Cornel Pokorny)*

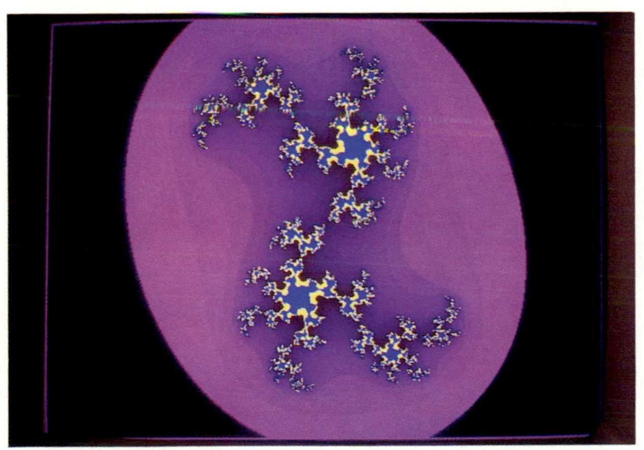

## COLOR PLATE 6

*This is a Julia Set of the function* $z^2 + (0.421, 0.30795)$ *and its immediate vicinity. The display was created by testing only for the attactor* $\infty$ *(see 10.5, Attractor Method for Basins). The color of a point is determined by its distance from the point of origin. (Created by Cornel Pokorny)*

## COLOR PLATE 7

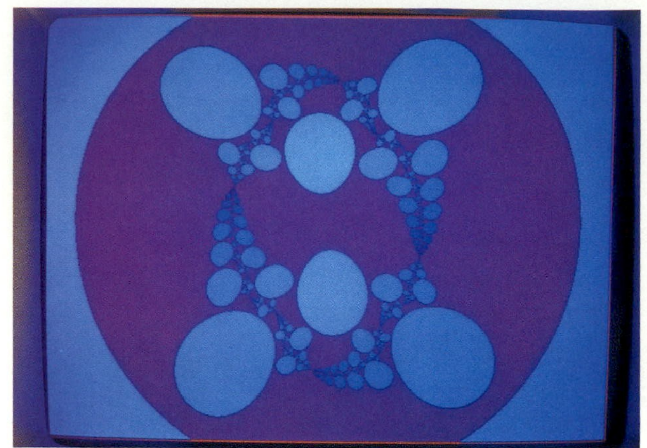

*This is a Julia Set of the function $1/(z^2+(0.5,0.1)$ and its immediate vicinity. The display was created by testing for the same attractor as in Color Plate 6. The Julia Set is inside the grapevine-shaped garland. (Created by Cornel Pokorny)*

## COLOR PLATE 8

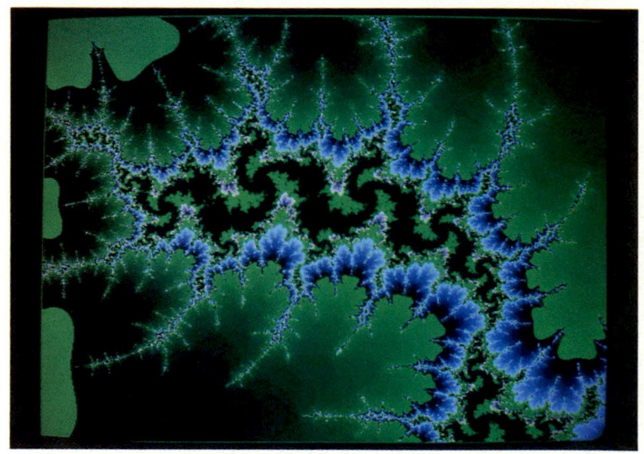

*A Mandelbrot Set close-up (see 10.5). The Mandelbrot Set has an enormous variety of differently shaped details. The structure is in the area $-1.389846 < re < -1.389814$ and $-0.010762 < im < -0.010738$. (Created by Cornel Pokorny)*

**COLOR PLATE 9**

*VersaCAD/MacIntosh edition workscreen with floor plan layout on the screen.*

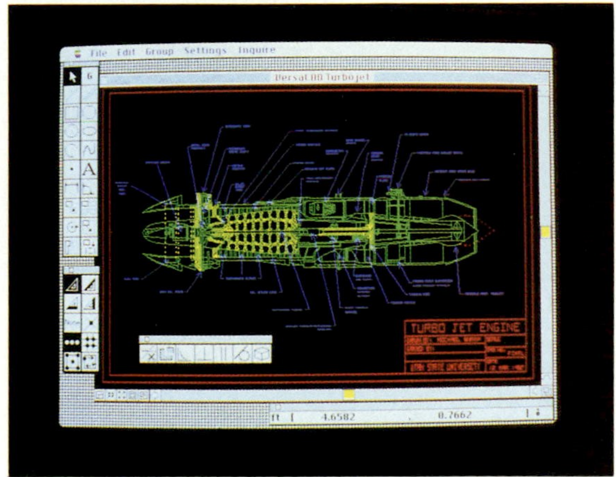


**COLOR PLATE 11**

*Turbo jet engine being designed on screen.*

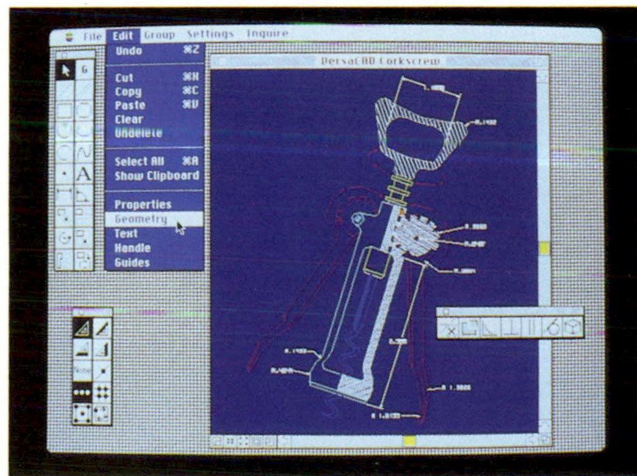


**COLOR PLATE 10**

*VersaCAD corkscrew design with Edit menu displayed.*

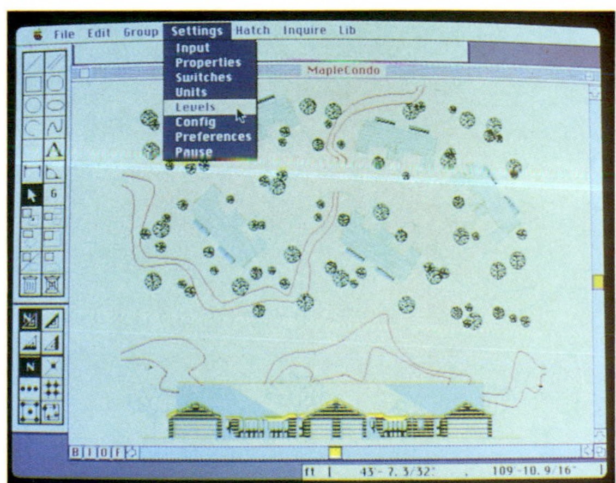


**COLOR PLATE 12**

*Viewing different elevations of a condominium complex on screen. Note the pull-down menu in upper left-hand corner.*

**(Special thanks to VersaCad for these examples of Computer-Aided Design (CAD) and for the one reproduced in Figure 17.18.)**

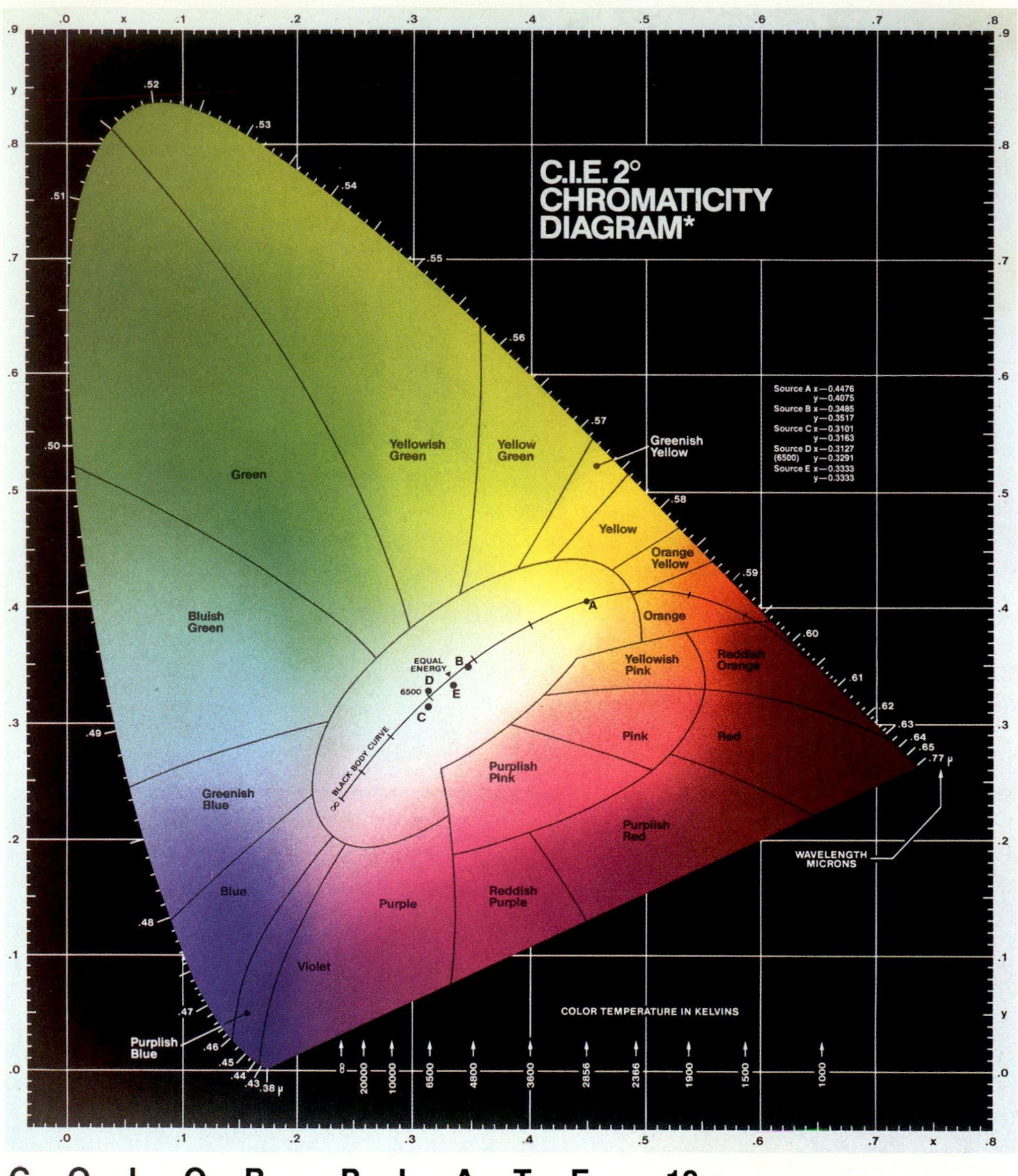


# C O L O R P L A T E 13

*The C. I. E. Chromaticity Diagram is an industry standard for describing the color reproduction capability of a color monitor. Shown here are all perceivable colors in a two-dimensional arrangement. The pure colors are located on the upper boundary of the curve. In nature most colors are mixtures of pure colors and correspond to the ones found within the boundaries of the curve. Color intensity is ignored in this diagram, that is why colors such as brown and gray are not visible. (Courtesy Photo Research)*

COLOR PLATE 14

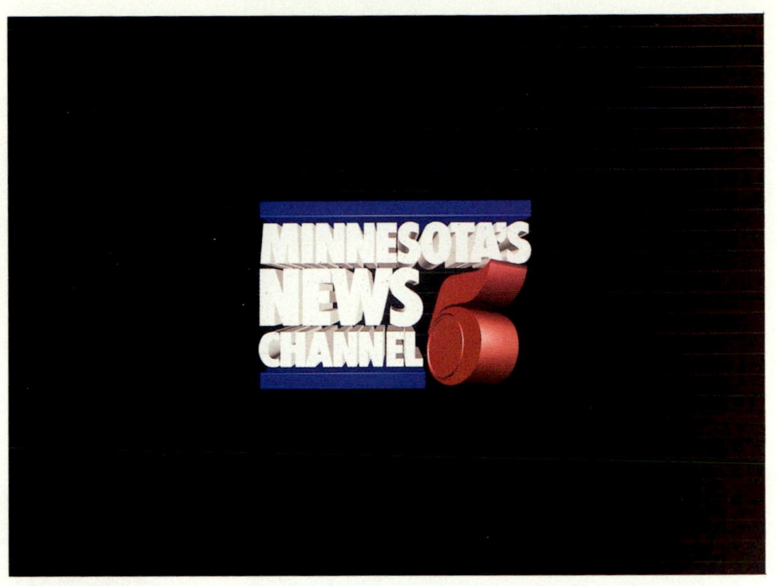


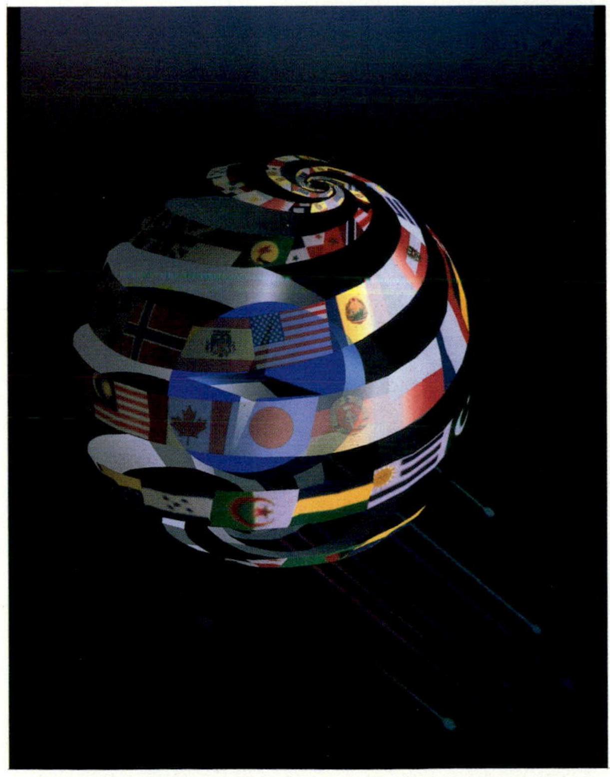

COLOR PLATE 15

*Use of computer graphics in television commercials. (Produced on Cubicomp equipment courtesy KSTP-TV and Data Motion Arts, Inc.)*

**COLOR PLATE 16**
*General driving simulation. (Courtesy Evans & Sutherland)*

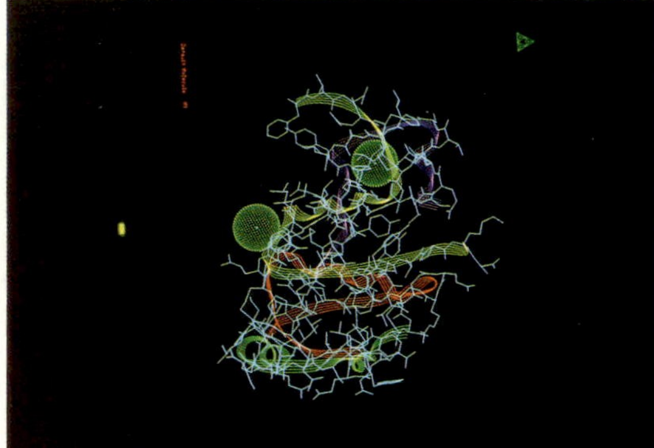

**COLOR PLATE 17**
*A model of protein insulin produced using Tripos SYBYL molecular modelling software. (Courtesy Evans & Sutherland)*

**COLOR PLATE 18**
*A raster rendering of the X-29. (Courtesy Graumman Aerospace Corporation and Evans & Sutherland)*

**COLOR PLATE 19**
*Chrylser Laser rendered using a ray tracing algorithm. (Courtesy Chrysler Motors and Evans & Sutherland)*

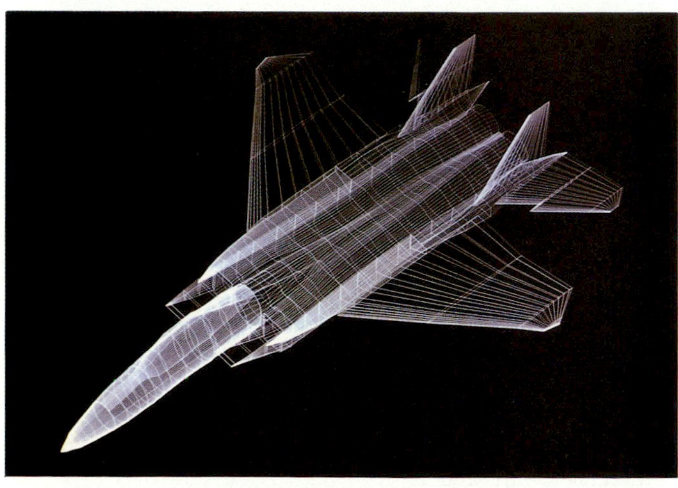

**COLOR PLATE 20**
*Wire frame rendering of an F-15. (Courtesy Evans & Sutherland)*

# Fractals

# 10

Fractals are an interesting way to produce computer-generated pictures that simulate the irregularities of natural scenes. There are six sections in the chapter.

**10.0 Introduction** explains what a fractal is and gives some background.

**10.1 An Artificial Fractal** develops the von Koch curve, a simple example of a fractal, and introduces you to some new ideas related to dimension.

**10.2 The Similarity Relation** is important for determining the dimension of a fractal.

**10.3 Fractal-Generating Algorithms** describes some production rules that are the basis for drawing fractals.

**10.4 Random Fractal Surfaces** possess statistical self-similarity and hence are closer to natural fractals. We develop the full details for producing a natural-looking surface.

**10.5 Mandelbrot and Julia Sets and Fatou Dusts** are generated using iterative processes in the complex plane. Beautiful fractal figures result from these computationally expensive procedures.

**10.6 Creating Fractals through Iterated Transformations** describes a technique which has recently become important in image processing.

# 10.0 INTRODUCTION

Until now, the objects that we have displayed have been made up of planar polygons or described by smooth curves. Suppose we want to show a natural scene, one with mountains, trees, clouds, and so on. It is hardly feasible to define the many points that would be required for the projection of that scene, especially if we want to reproduce the colors as well as the shapes and textures. We conclude that it is impractical to try to replace a camera with the computer screen. Often, though, it is not some existing natural scene that we desire, but one that we see in our imagination, one that an artist might paint. If we do this with only the methods so far described, the result will look "unnatural." A picture made up of drawn curves or polygons is different from nature in that it is too precise, too regular, too contrived.

There is a solution to this problem in a mathematical entity called a fractal. A *fractal* is a set of points with a fractional dimension.

Fractals are highly irregular shapes that have countless counterparts in the real world. Examples are coastlines, island clusters, turbulences, river networks, clouds, snowflakes, and galaxies. No natural surface, when examined closely enough, is smooth and regular; it actually contains tiny pits and irregularities. One can say that nature is always irregular. So, if we can create fractals in a computer, we have the tool to mimic nature. Since a fractal is a mathematical entity, this should be possible.

The term *fractional dimension* explains the origin of the word. Consider an infinite line or finite line segment. It is always possible to specify every point on it by a single number which can be interpreted as the distance from some reference point. This fact tells us that this line is of dimension one. This seems so trivial that we pay no attention to it. It is identical to the fact that we measure a line with a one-dimensional measure like length. No one would try to measure a line in terms of area. Such a measurement can never yield a useful result because a two-dimensional measuring unit is applied to a one-dimensional set. Intuitively, we know that the area of a line is 0 no matter how long the line is.

When we measure an area, we use a two-dimensional unit (square feet, square meters, etc.). We certainly wouldn't try to use length as the measure of an area. This makes no sense because the result is infinity: no matter how small the area, an infinitely long line can be fitted into it. Areas, then are then two-dimensional.

The volume of any line or any area always is 0 because volume is a three-dimensional unit. We can fit an infinitely long line or infinitely big area into any volume, no matter how small. An intuitive explanation of this situation might be: A one-dimensional unit is too weak for measuring a two-dimensional or three-dimensional entity. If it is applied the result will always be infinite, no matter what the real extent of the measured object. A two-dimensional unit is too strong for measuring a line and too weak for measuring a volume. In the first case the result will always be 0; in the latter case, it will always be infinite. Measuring units must be of the same dimension as the measured object!

We can reason the other way around. If we have a measuring unit that yields a proper result when applied to some object, then the object must have the same dimension as the unit. This will help us to find the dimension of fractals.

Let's look now at some fractals. The first one is the coastline of England. (This topic is part of the fascinating history of fractals.) Looking at a map we see that this is a very rugged line. How long is the coastline of England? The answer to this question reveals one of the strange properties of fractals. To get an answer, we will use a method for measuring the length of a curve.

**Measuring the Length of a Curve** The method we'll use consists of repeatedly aligning a yardstick against the curve, continuing where the end of the yardstick touches the curve, and counting how often this can be done. This method works well for many sorts of curves. Let's demonstrate it for a semicircle. We take the radius as our first measuring unit and align it against the curve. It will fit three times; 3 is our first approximation for the length of the semicircle. Since there was a piece left over, we think that we will get a better result by applying a shorter measuring unit, so we take 0.1 for our unit. This unit will fit 31 times into the curve; our new approximation is 3.1. This result is larger than the one before, but we expected that. Now, to get an even better result, we measure the curve once more with an even shorter unit, this time 0.01, and we see that this one fits into the curve 314 times. Again this result, 3.14, is larger than the one before but we see that the amount of growth is very small.

Indeed, if we perform more measurements, say, with 0.001 as the unit, then with 0.0001, the results will be 3.141 and 3.1415. The results grow but the amount of growth gets smaller, showing that the results do not grow without limit. Of course we need a mathematical proof but

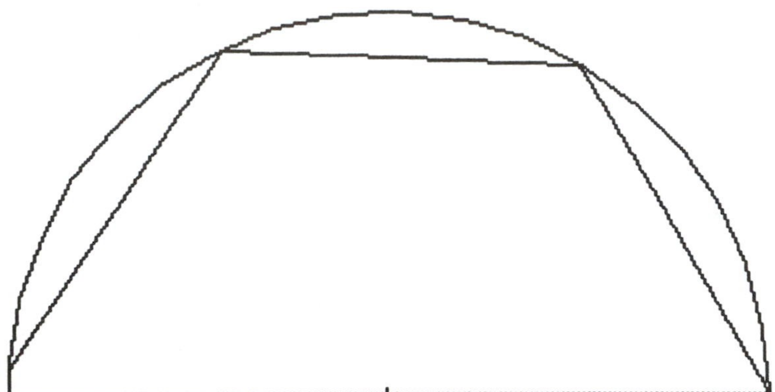

**FIGURE 10.1** Semicircle measured with the radius as unit.

the concept of this method of measuring the length of a curve can be seen clearly from the example. In the case of a semicircle, the measured lengths for ever smaller measuring units approach a limit which we consider to be the true length of the semicircle.

Suppose we use this method to measure the length of the seacoast or, more practically, some part of it. We start out with a measuring stick one sea mile long and we end up with a result of perhaps 1000 sea miles in length. We know that this is certainly a very rough approximation, so we try a second measuring process with a 100-meter measuring stick. The result we get might be (let's say) 3000 sea miles.

We certainly expected the larger result, but it is astonishing that it grew by such an amount. We still hope that we will see a tendency for the approximate lengths to settle down to a smaller growth, so we try another measurement process, this time with a 10-meter measuring stick. The result we get now really discourages us as it will be much larger than before—it might be about 8000 sea miles.

In the case of measuring a seacoast, we find no improvement when we use smaller measuring units. A man could walk right along the coast in steps one meter long. When we add together the number of steps, we see no tendency for the results to slow down in their growth. Whenever we decrease the length of the measuring stick, the measured length will continue to grow. Even if we let a mouse run along the coast and make it follow the boundary between water and land exactly, the resulting length will again be several factors larger than before. The measured length apparently grows without bound (see MAND77, RICH61). In short, it is not possible to measure the length of the coastline exactly and precisely. The reason is the "ruggedness" of the coastline. Let's look at Figures 10.2 to 10.4. That's what the coastline might look like when seen from very high above.

**FIGURE 10.2**

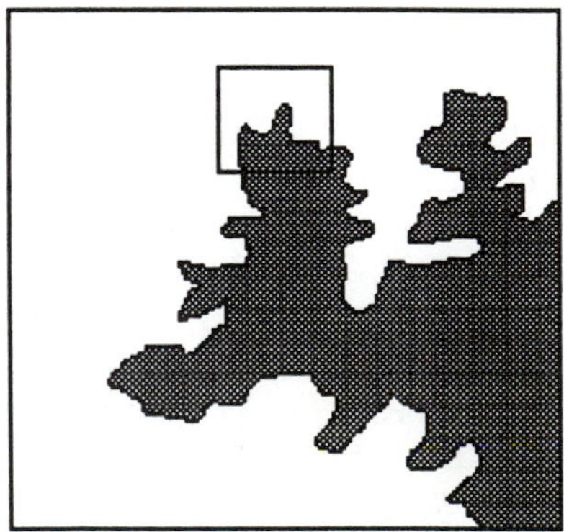

If we focus on a small part of the line, we see that the details of the line are as rugged as the whole line (see Figure 10.2). The next step of focus does not change the overall impression and this will continue no matter how close we go. We must characterize a coastline as infinitely rugged.

Certainly, we do come to a limit as we come closer to the molecular or atomic structure of matter. We also meet a limit in the macro scale in the structure of the planet and solar system. But the existence of these limits will not enable us to measure the length of the coastline exactly.

The coastline is an example of a line in which the details, no matter how small, bear a strong resemblance to the whole line (see Figure 10.4). Here it is the attribute "rugged" that seems to stick to the line endlessly, always showing up no matter how closely we look. This attribute is repeated continuously in forever smaller details of the whole.

**FIGURE 10.3**

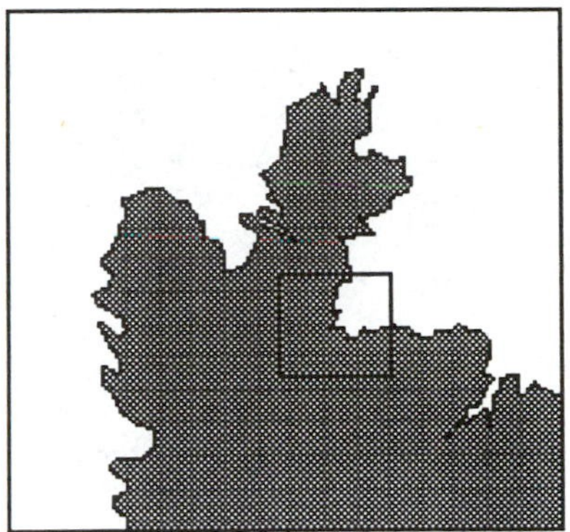

**FIGURE 10.4**

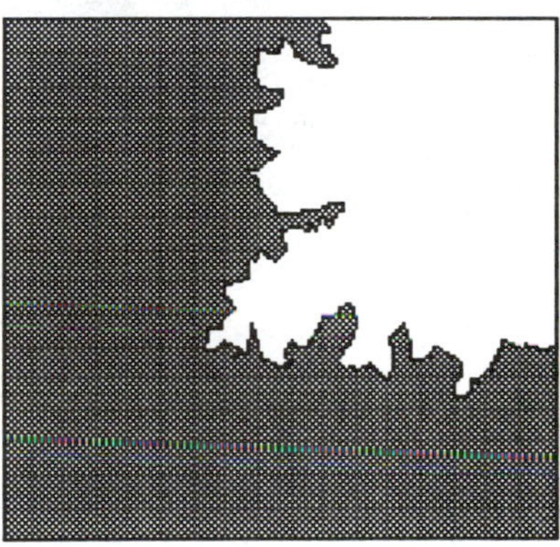

# 10.1 AN ARTIFICIAL FRACTAL

We began this chapter with the notion that fractals might help us to draw curves that mimic nature. Now we know a little about what must be done to accomplish this. Can we produce a fractal in the computer? The answer is yes, so let's look at an example. Our first artificially created fractal is the *triadic von Koch curve,* which we simply call the *Koch curve.* Its creation is easy. We start with a straight line of length one. This line we call the curve of order zero.

We create the Koch curve of order one by taking out the middle third of the straight line and replacing it with two lines of the same length, meeting at a 60 degree angle, as in Figure 10.5. The curve of order two is obtained by repeating the replacement process with each of the four line segments. The resulting curve of order two is a little more rugged, as shown in Figure 10.6.

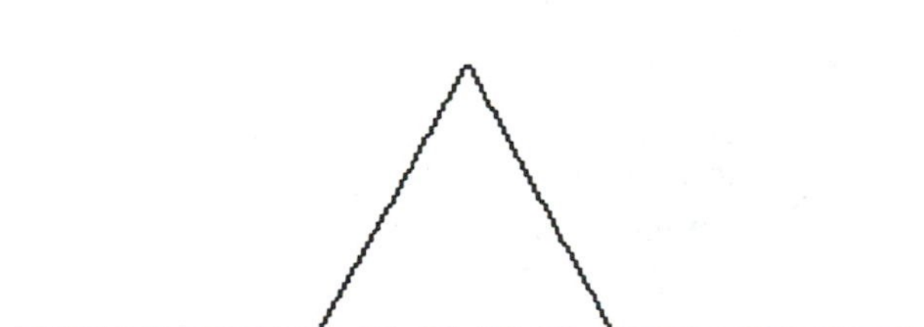

**FIGURE 10.5** Triadic Koch curve of order one.

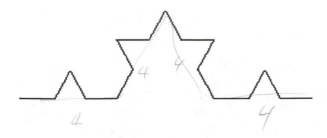

**FIGURE 10.6** Triadic Koch curve of order two.

We do the same thing with each of the 16 segments in the order two curve to get the Koch curve of order three. Assume that this process is continued ad infinitum; this gives a mathematically precise definition of a Koch curve. How long is it, we ask?

It turns out that this is impossible to measure. When we attempt to measure the length of this line, we will get the same surprise as with the coastline. Let's first apply a measuring stick of length 1/3 to the line. Due to the totally regular rule of construction of the curve, we can say definitely that this unit will fit exactly four times into the curve, and the measuring result will be 4/3. Therefore, the approximate length of the curve (ignoring all the rugged detail in it) will be 4/3, measured with this unit. Let L(m) be the length obtained with a measuring unit m. Then we have:

$$L(1/3) = 4/3.$$

The measuring unit 1/9 will fit exactly 16 times into the curve, so we get:

$$L(1/9) = 16/9$$

and generally,

$$L(1/3^k) = (4/3)^k.$$

This shows that making the measuring unit smaller will make the results approach infinity, so the true length of the Koch curve is infinite. A line of infinite length is crammed into a finite area of the plane without intersecting itself! But also every small part of the Koch curve has an infinite length, because it consists of reduced instances of the Koch curve. The answer to the question about the length of the Koch curve is: This curve cannot be measured in terms of length. So we ask: In what terms can it be measured? This is actually a question about the dimension of this curve. Let us look at the Koch curve just as a set of points in the plane and ask what dimension it has.

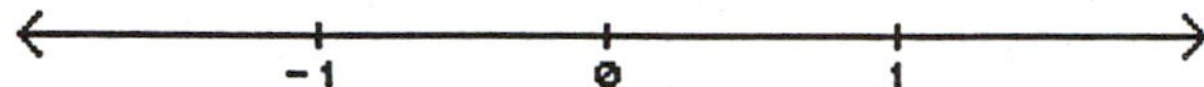

**FIGURE 10.7** Real number axis.

The problem with the Koch curve is not that it is infinitely long. A line may have infinite length and it is still possible to define every point on the line by a single number. This shows that an infinitely long line can be one-dimensional. The example in Figure 10.7 is just the real number axis that stretches from $-\infty$ to $+\infty$. Every point on this line is described by one single number that specifies its distance from the origin. We can readily indicate specific points on the Koch curve but none of these can be described by a single number specifying, let's say, its distance along the curve from the leftmost point. All these distances and all distances between single points on that line are infinite. That shows that length or distance is not a proper measure for this curve. The truth is that a one-dimensional measure is too weak for the Koch curve.

The dimension then must be more than one. Could it have a dimension of two and be measurable in terms of area? No, we cannot find any part of the curve that has a positive area. If we try to find the area of the Koch curve, we end up with an area of 0. That shows that a two-dimensional measure is too strong for the Koch curve. The solution to this dilemma lies in between. The Koch curve is a set of points with a dimension greater than one and smaller than two. It has a fractional dimension. It is a fractal.

There are actually different notions of dimension. Here we mention only two: the Hausdorff-Besicovitch dimension and the topological dimension. These can be different for the same set of points. The topological dimension of the Koch curve is one, because, in terms of topology, this set of points is a line. If a single point is taken out anywhere in the curve, then it is severed, giving two distinct and noncoherent parts. But the topological dimension does not provide any measure of the curve in the sense of length or area or whatever. To obtain that we must use the Hausdorff-Besicovitch dimension. Unfortunately, this theory is too complicated to be presented in this book and is of limited usefulness in computer graphics. It does provide a means to define a real number as the dimension of this type of object. The precise definition of the Hausdorff-Besicovitch dimension can be found in BEUR37.

There is a relatively simple method to determine the dimension of this curve and using it will let us find out a little more about fractals. This method implies the use of a similarity relation, useful in determining the dimension of many different fractals.

# 10.2 THE SIMILARITY RELATION

The first steps we take here are mostly of a suggestive nature and are so trivial that it may be difficult to see the essential point. Assume we have a set of points whose dimension we don't know; let this set be a segment of a straight line. We define the length of the whole line segment as equal to 1 and divide it into a number of equal parts, let's say three thirds (see Figure 10.8). Obviously we can compose the whole line from the three parts, all of which are similar to the whole, but scaled down to one-third in size. This scaling relation is r and we have r = 1/3. We express the whole as 3 times the *similarity relation:*

$$1 = 3*r$$

What is inconspicuous but important in this equation is that r is raised to the power 1. As the exponent 1 satisfies this equation, it follows that the dimension of our original set is one.

This reasoning will become more understandable with the example of Figure 10.9. Here we have a rectangular-shaped area, which constitutes the whole and is set equal to 1. Let's divide all its sides into three equal parts.

It is obvious that we get nine parts, which are all similar to the whole by a similarity relation of r = 1/3. (Important: It is not r =

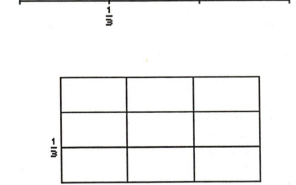

**FIGURE 10.8** Line segment consisting of three thirds.

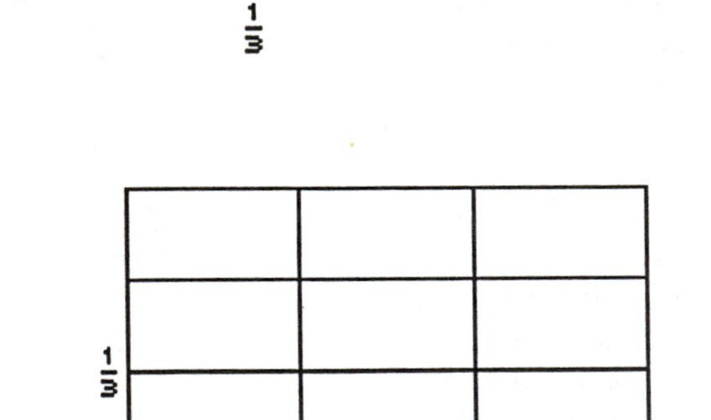


**FIGURE 10.9** Similarity relation on a rectangle.

1/9. Every part is obtained from the whole by scaling it down by 1/3.) We express the whole now as the sum of nine of its parts times the similarity relation r, which now must be raised to the power 2 in order to satisfy the equation:

$$1 = 9*r^2$$

The equation that expresses the whole as the sum of its parts, using the similarity relation, r, can be written as:

$$1 = 9*r^D.$$

The value of D to satisfy this equation is 2. It follows that our set of points is two-dimensional.

If we repeat this for any parallelepiped and choose a similarity relation of $r = 1/3$ then the whole is composed of 27 similar parts (Figure 10.10) and we get the equation $1 = 27 \cdot r^D$, which requires $D = 3$, so this is the dimension of the parallelepiped. All this is very trivial but important.

A similar object is obtained by enlarging or shrinking the original object by multiplying each of its dimensions in one-, two-, or three-dimensional space with the same number. And the similarity relation is just this number. In the case of a one-dimensional object one multiplication is necessary to achieve the scaling to a similar object, in the case of a two-dimensional object two multiplications are necessary, and so on. This operation is not trivial when we apply it to the Koch curve.

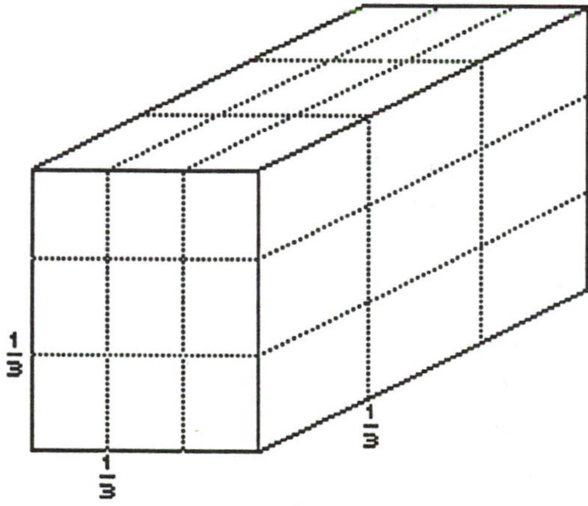


**FIGURE 10.10** Similarity relation on a parallelepiped.

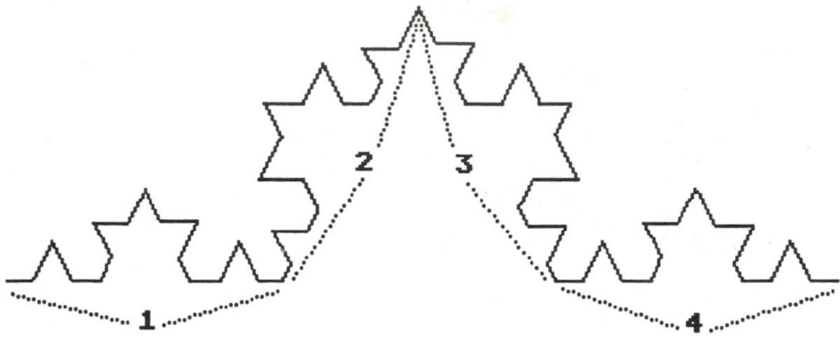


**FIGURE 10.11** Koch curve consisting of four similar parts.

We can see that the whole curve can be composed of exactly four similar parts (see Figure 10.11).

Do not forget that the parts are as "rugged" as the whole curve, because the ruggedness is infinite. So these four parts are really identical to the whole, except for their size. Furthermore, we can see that the size (perhaps as indicated by the straight line distance from one end to the other) of each of these four parts is just 1/3 of the whole, so the similarity relation is r = 1/3. Therefore, we have the equation $1 = 4 \cdot (1/3)^D$. D must be log4/log3, which is 1.2857. So the Hausdorff-Besicovitch dimension of the Koch curve is 1.2857. A Koch curve can only be measured in terms of unit Koch curves or any other unit curves that have exactly the same dimension.

Because the dimension of most sets of this type is fractional, Mandelbrot coined the term "fractal" for them (MAND82). The exact definition of a fractal, as given in MAND82, still looks pretty complicated and may not make much sense to a nonmathematically oriented reader, but you should at least see it:

> A fractal is a set of points whose fractional dimension is strictly bigger than its topological dimension.

According to this, the Koch curve is a fractal. As its dimension is greater than one, it somehow fills more of space than a simple line, which has the dimension D = 1, but it fills less than an area, which has the dimension D = 2. We will look at other fractals of higher dimension than the Koch curve and these will fill more of space than the Koch curve. The dimension can be as great as two with the Dragon curve, which is an area-filling curve, but it is still a fractal and not an area; its topological dimension is still one and therefore smaller than the fractional dimension.

# 10.3 FRACTAL-GENERATING ALGORITHMS

Now that we have seen an example of a fractal and how it can be constructed, we should see how a fractal can be generated by a computer. The generation of fractals can be done using what are called *production rules*. We will demonstrate this geometrically. For the triadic Koch curve the production rule is shown in Figure 10.12.

This rule says that the straight line on the left must be replaced by the shape on the right. Here, as in all production rules, the element to start with is a straight line. Therefore the line and the arrow can be omitted; it is enough to show just the replacement part. This is the same as in MAND82, with the exception that he sometimes starts with a square or other shape. In such a case, the production rule must be applied to all four sides of the square. Figure 10.13 shows the Koch curve after five generating steps.

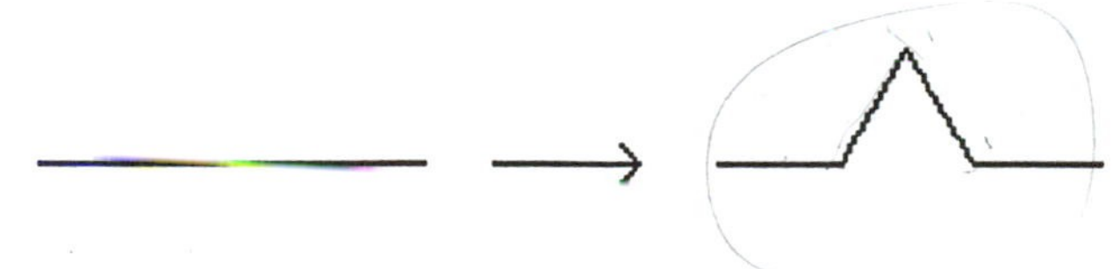

**FIGURE 10.12** Koch curve production rule.

**FIGURE 10.13**

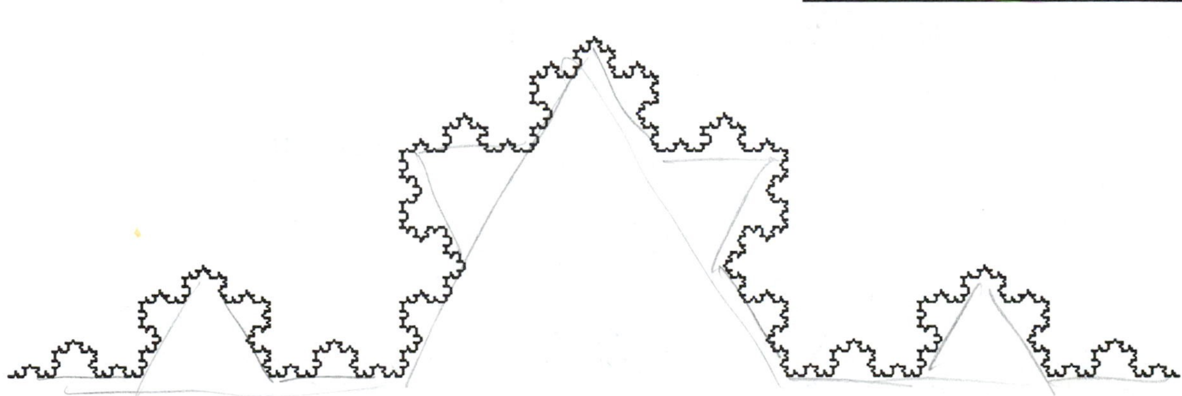

**FIGURE 10.14** Another production rule.

We will now look at some more regular fractals that show the infinite variety and beauty of these objects. Figure 10.14 shows the production rule for a Koch curve variation which produces a fractal line of higher dimension than the previous one. The three lines meet at right angles and are of the same length. From this, and with some geometric analysis, we find that the similarity relation is $r = 1/\sqrt{5}$ and that three such pieces form the whole curve; the relationship is $1 = 3* (1/\sqrt{5})^D$, which yields D = 1.365. The curve that develops from this production rule after three steps is shown in Figure 10.15.

**FIGURE 10.15**

Another Koch curve production rule and the resulting curve after two generating steps is shown in Figure 10.16. The similarity relation is r = 1/4; eight parts constitute the whole, so we get D = 1.5. The production rule for the beautiful C-curve and the curve after 12 generating steps is shown in Figure 10.17. Here it is more difficult to see from the curve what the similarity relation is, but we can derive it from the production rule: $r = 1/2*\sqrt{2}$; two parts form the whole, so we have $1 = 2*(1/2*\sqrt{2})^D$, which yields D = 2. This dimension is the same as for an area, therefore the C-curve is called an *area-filling curve.*

We mention one more curve, one that is often produced because it is eye-catching: the dragon curve. Its production rule, shown in Figure 10.18, does not start from a straight line but from two sides of a rectangular isosceles triangle. Each side is then replaced with the two sides of a rectangular isosceles triangle but the replacement has to alternate

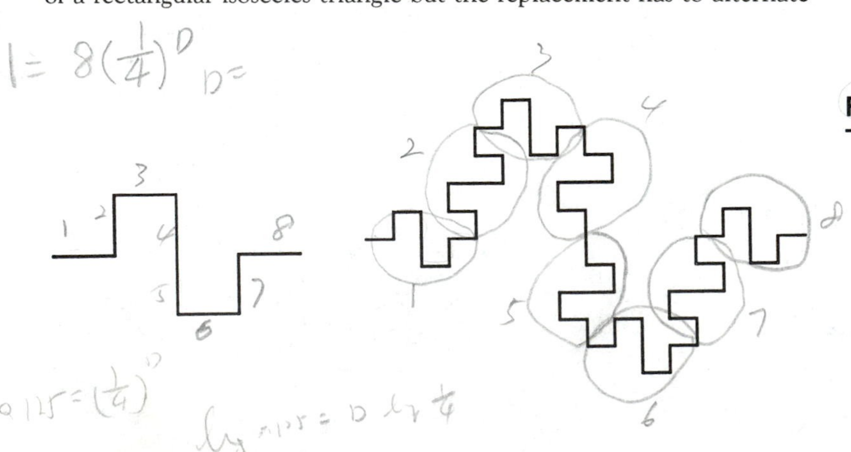

**FIGURE 10.16**

FIGURE 10.17

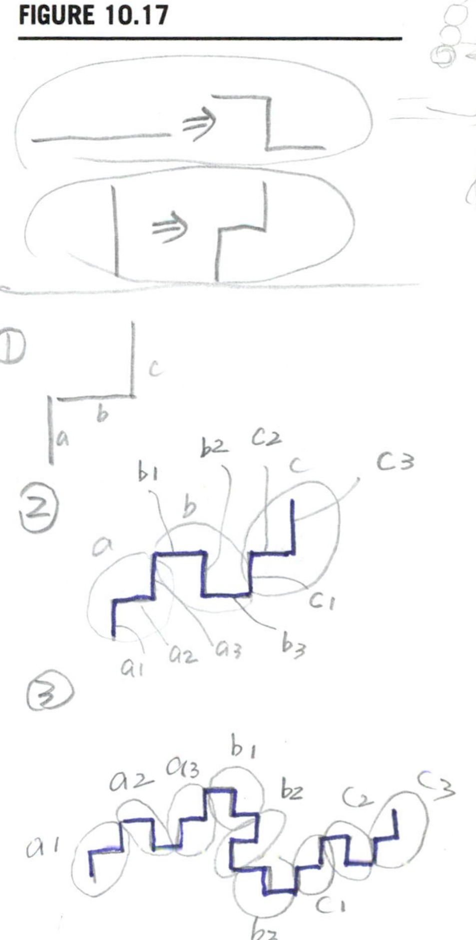

between left and right, and the alternation sequence must be strictly the same in all generation steps. In Figure 10.18 we use first left and then right. It is somewhat difficult to see from the curve itself what the similarity relation is, but we can derive it from the production rule: $r = 1/2*\sqrt{2}$. Two dragons scaled by this ratio form a whole dragon. We have $1 = 2*(1/2*\sqrt{2})^{D}$, which yields $D = 2$. The dragon curve, too, is an area-filling curve. It is shown in Figure 10.19.

All the fractal curves listed above can be drawn on a line plotter and are easy to program when using recursion. Amazing effects can be produced by changing the line color in some systematic way. Here's an example of recursion that draws a Koch curve. The variables x and y are global reals:

```
procedure koch(dir : integer; length : real);
var       dirup,dirdn  : integer;
begin
   {modulo 6 arithmetic}
   dirup := dir+1; if dirup > 5 then dirup := 0;
   dirdn := dir-1; if dirdn < 0 then dirdn := 5;
   if 0.01 < length
   then begin
      koch(dir  ,length/3);
      koch(dirup,length/3);
      koch(dirdn,length/3);
      koch(dir  ,length/3)
   end
   else begin {terminate if length ≤ 0.01}
      case dir of
         0: begin x := x+length                          end;
```

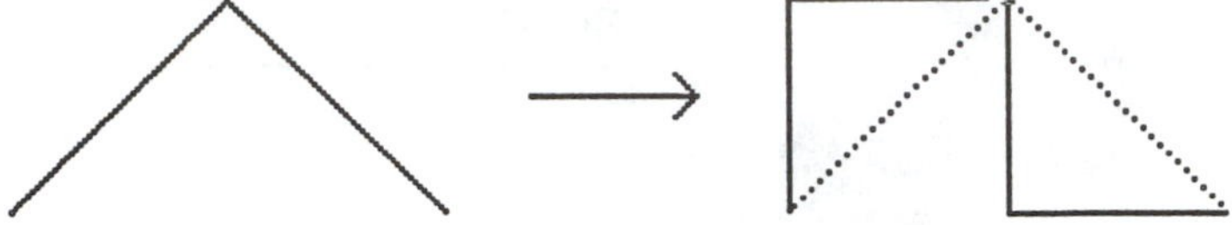

**FIGURE 10.18** Production rule of the Dragon curve.

**FIGURE 10.19** Dragon curve.

```
      1: begin x := x+length/2; y := y+0.86602*length end;
      2: begin x := x-length/2; y := y+0.86602*length end;
      3: begin x := x-length                         end;
      4: begin x := x-length/2; y := y-0.86602*length end;
      5: begin x := x+length/2; y := y-0.86602*length end
    end {case};
    draw(x,y)
  end {procedure koch};
```

This procedure draws a horizontal Koch curve (direction = 0) of length "length" if called as follows:

koch(0,length);

The modulo arithmetic at the start is explicit because the mod operator does not give the desired result for a negative operand. The six possible drawing directions rotate ccw from 0° to 300° for cases 0 to 5. The 0.86602 factor is the cosine of 60°.

# 10.4 RANDOM FRACTAL SURFACES

Objects in nature rarely exhibit *self-similarity* (the parts mimic the whole) as do the Koch curve, C-curve, dragon curve, and so on, but they possess a related property, called *statistical self-similarity*. Nature is full of such fractals. The coastline at the beginning of the chapter is a good example. The closer we look at the line, the more detail we see. A set is statistically self-similar with a ratio r if it is composed of several distinct subsets each of which is identical in all statistical respects to the set S, scaled down by r. A subset will never be congruent or identical to the scaled-down whole set S, as was the case with the Koch curve. Therefore the definition of self-similarity is more difficult to handle and to verify.

In statistics, two distributions are said to be similar if all the so-called *moments* are equal. In practice it is impossible to verify that all moments of the statistical distribution are identical. Claims of statistical self-similarity are usually based on the identity of only a few moments. But if a statistical self-similarity can be found for a certain scaling ratio r with sufficient certainty, and if the whole set S is composed of N such distinct parts, then by analogy to the artificially created regular fractals, the dimension of this fractal can be calculated as:

$$D = \log N/\log(1/r).$$

Often, though, for fractals in nature this r will be difficult to find because a part of a random fractal, such as a coastline, is often statistically self-similar to the whole scaled with any ratio r. In other words, if some part of the coastline is taken, then we can scale the whole coastline, say by three or four or five and always find statistical self-similarity with the part. In such cases the fractal dimension must be computed using a different concept, the so-called *box dimension*. We do not go into this here, but the interested reader can find an explanation in VOSS85.

Fractals that resemble such natural phenomena are generated in computer graphics. You may have seen these in television commercials. The generating algorithms differ from the production rules of Section 10.3 in that they include random numbers. The fractals that are so created are different every time. They are used to forge landscapes, mountains, surfaces, island clusters, waves, and clouds. All are of higher dimension than the ones we have looked at till now; all are higher than two. Not all random fractals are of such higher dimensions but the ones that are useful for fractal forgeries in computer graphics are. This section deals with random fractals but is limited to fractal surfaces.

*Fractal surfaces* are sets of points whose fractional dimension is between two and three. What a Koch curve or a coastline or some other fractal line is in the plane, this fractal surface is in space. Usually these are very complex surfaces with infinitely great detail. As the fractal dimension of such a surface is greater than two, it somehow fills more of the space than a mathematically exact 2-D surface, but it does not fill the whole space. Generally one can say that the greater the dimension, the more rugged the appearance. Natural landscapes normally have a fractional dimension of about 2.15; very rugged landscapes, some areas in the French Alps, for example, can have a dimension of up to 2.5, but this is about the limit. An artificially created fractal landscape like the landscape in color plate C-1 has a statistical self-similarity range that extends from arbitrarily large to arbitrarily small scales because of the properties of the statistical factors.

Such a tremendous range for the ratio is never the case with natural landscapes. The similarity ratio can be variable and extend over a range of values as mentioned above for the coastline, but the scale over which self-similarity can be observed must be finite. The lower limit is set by the regular, nonfractal, crystalline structure of sand, clay, and so forth and the upper limit by the finite strength of matter which is ultimately formed into spheres of various sizes by gravity. A fractal is a mathematical ideal and serves only as to approximate the real world. Fractal geometry, though, is the best known approximation and is superior to other geometries (Euclidian, etc.) when it comes to descriptions of the real world.

**Generating Random Fractals** A truly random fractal cannot be generated on a computer because it has an infinitely complex shape. We are limited to generating and rendering only a finite approximation to it. There are several methods for generating fractal curves and surfaces. A few of these are shear displacement, modified Markhov processes, and random midpoint displacement.

**Shear Displacement and Markhov Processes** We briefly describe and outline these two older methods because of the considerable literature on them. They find application in some situations but are not as good as newer methods.

In a *shear displacement process* (MAND75), a line is cut at a random point with a uniform distribution, then the left and right parts are displaced vertically in opposite directions for a random distance with a Gaussian distribution. This is repeated on the parts, producing finer and finer detail; we stop when the detail is fine enough. An analogous process can be done for a plane. A random point in the plane is determined from a uniform distribution and then a random angle is determined from a uniform distribution. A line through this point at this angle constitutes a shear line of the plane. The two parts are then displaced in opposite directions by random distances with a Gaussian distribution. The shear displacement method is computationally very expensive; newer methods are an improvement.

The *Markhov process* method was also developed by Mandelbrot (MAND69, MAND71). It can create fractals of dimensions between one and two, that is, fractal lines. It does not create fractal surfaces. We move in the x-direction by constant steps; y-values are created as random points at each x-value. First, n random values from a Gaussian distribution are computed. Each y-value is computed as a weighted sum of the last n values times a random variable. The sequence of (x,y)-pairs constitutes the points on a fractal curve. Such a curve exhibits persistence in that the current value is affected by values in the recent past. Although the points are random, they are still related to each other and not totally independent; it is called a Markhov process. For graphics applications this method has certain shortcomings. One is that the step size is constant and it is difficult to produce a local scale magnification of the line afterward. Another is that the line cannot be made to pass through specified points, and it tends to run away to either the positive or negative direction as it is created.

**Random Midpoint Displacement** This is a generalization of conventional subdivision methods (LCWB80). We explain it first for a line and then for a surface.

**Generation of a Fractal Line** We start with the two end points of a straight line segment, say A and B. We then displace the midpoint of the line vertically by a random amount h. Call this displaced midpoint Md. The displaced midpoint is then connected to A and B and the process is repeated with the lines A to Md and Md to B. We repeat this with all subdivisions until there is sufficient detail. The mean of the distribution of the random number h must be 0 and the mean of the displacement amount abs(h) must be proportional to the distance between the end points of the segment.

It is essential that the mean of the displacement amount be proportional to the length of the line whose midpoint is being displaced. This ensures that the roughness of the fractal is at all times independent of the scale. If we did not make the mean of the displacement proportional to the current length, we would get increased roughness as we proceed and the required statistical self-similarity would be lost. If this process is carried out to the limit, a fractal is created.

If the initial line starts at a with a height of h(a), ending at b with a height of h(b), then the height at the midpoint is (h(a) + h(b))/2. This value is displaced by a random amount proportional to b minus a. Figure 10.20 shows one displacement step.

We give a Pascal procedure (fracline) that carries out the process. We make some simplifications to ease the programming task. Up to 100 points on the final fractal line are provided for by the singly subscripted array line[ ]. Each element in the array can store the displacement (up or down) of one of the points. The procedure is passed integer values a and b that designate the subscript values corresponding to the start and end points of the initial line. The displacements at these points are given in variables line[a] and line[b] that are global to fracline. Another global parameter is rug, a floating point number that determines the ruggedness of the fractal. The procedure makes two recursive calls to itself with the current end points of the (subdivided) line. The difference between the two subscripts of the current line decreases by a factor of two each time; the recursive calls terminate when this difference is 1.

```
var line    :    array[1..100] of real;
    rug     :    real;

procedure fracline(a,b : integer);
var midpoint     :    integer;
begin
if b-a > 1 {this terminates the recursion}
  then begin
    midpoint := (a+b) div 2;
    line[midpoint] := (line[a]+line[b])/2
                    + rand*(b-a)*rug;
    fracline(a,midpoint);
    fracline(midpoint,b);
  end {if b-a > 1}
end {procedure fracline};
```

Observe that a function rand is used to provide a random number for the displacement of the midpoint. This is scaled by (b − a), which is used instead of the true length of the current segment. The displacement is also multiplied by the ruggedness factor, rug. A factor near 0 keeps the displacement small, giving a nearly straight line. We experiment with values for this factor to get the right size. If rand is a random generator that produces uniformly distributed numbers between − 1 and + 1, then a rug value of 0.15 gives a line similar to that in Figure 10.21. A rug value of 0.3 gives a line similar to that in Figure 10.22. Because

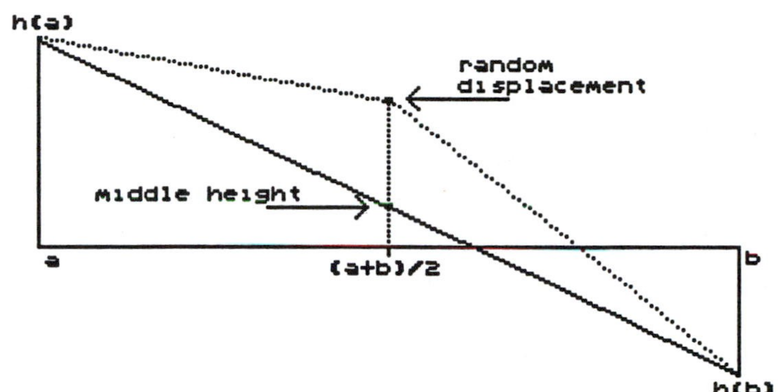


**FIGURE 10.20** Random mid-point displacement.

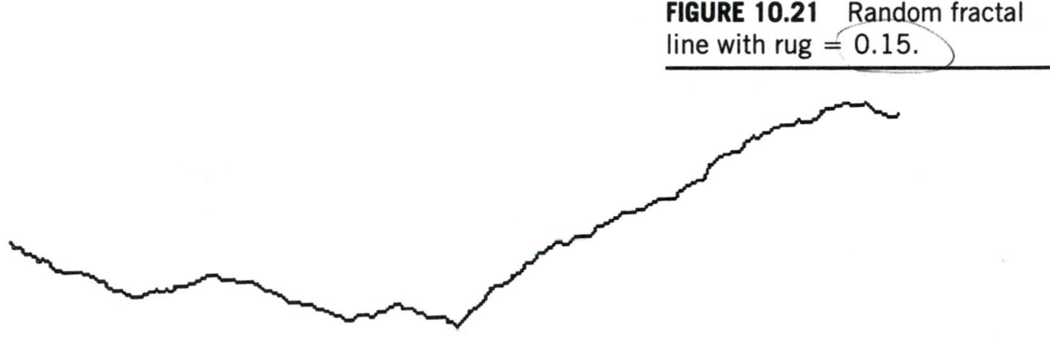

**FIGURE 10.21** Random fractal line with rug = 0.15.

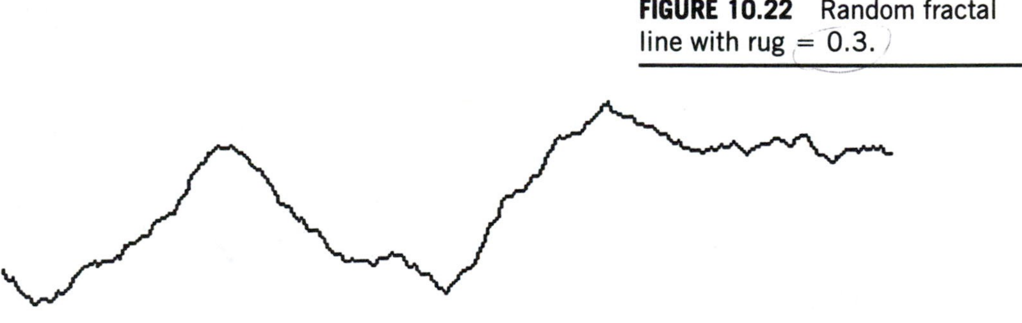

**FIGURE 10.22** Random fractal line with rug = 0.3.

of the random element, the output never looks the same, but on average the lines will have about the same ruggedness when rug is fixed. The procedure produces only the displacement points in the array line. These points are then to be connected by straight lines.

The above recursive algorithm that creates a random fractal line uses the same principle as fractal surface generation. Understanding it will help you understand that more complicated process.

**Generation of a Fractal Surface** We now extend the above to three dimensions to generate a random fractal surface. We start with a rectangular surface with the corner points a, b, c, and d. The initial heights at the corner points are h(a), h(b), h(c), and h(d). We displace the midpoint of each side just as above. At the point (a+b)/2 we get (h(a)+h(b))/2 plus a random displacement proportional to the length from a to b; we do the same for all four sides. We must also displace the height at the center point (a+b+c+d)/4 of the rectangle. We take the mean of the height values at the corners: (h(a)+h(b)+h(c)+h(d))/4 plus a random displacement proportional to the sum of the lengths of all sides. Figure 10.23 shows, at left, a surface at the start and the five displacement points; at the right is the resulting surface after this one step.

For the next step, each of the four new rectangles will have its five midpoints displaced. The resulting facets are not planar, but they can easily be converted into planar triangles by adding a diagonal line to each facet. The result of this is a fractal grid surface. Such a surface is easy to display with hidden lines removed as we will explain in Chapter 13. The procedure fracrect below performs this process without removing the hidden lines. Figure 10.24 explains how subscripts are

**FIGURE 10.23** One step of surface displacement.

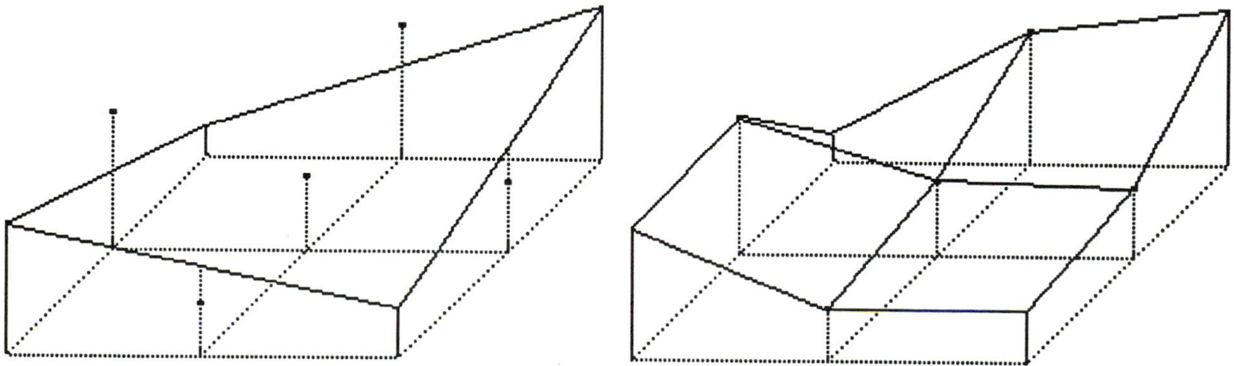

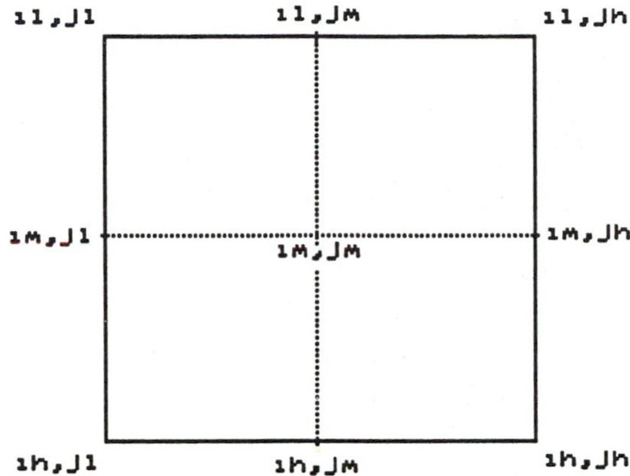

**FIGURE 10.24** Subscript layout.

assigned. The upper left corner point of the rectangle has the subscripts il and jl; the lower right corner point has ih and jh (l stands for low and h for high). (This is based on the idea that most screens define the origin at the upper left corner.) The procedure computes heights at the midpoints and then calls itself recursively for the four new rectangles.

In fracrect, the first recursive call is for the upper left rectangle; it will compute five new height values. The second recursive call is for the upper right rectangle; it must not compute a new height value on the left side of this rectangle. This has already been computed by the first call and will consequently be used in the computation of all smaller rectangles adjacent to the point by the subcalls of the first call! Changing the value would destroy the fractal property of the resulting surface and would turn it into an almost random surface. The same is true for the value at the top of the lower left rectangle and for the top of the lower right rectangle. In other words, any value in the array, once set, is not reset. This problem is solved readily by checking whether a value in the array has been set or not, and we can tell this by initializing all values to a number that will never occur in the process. The whole surface is represented by a rectangular array whose subscripts represent the grid coordinates and whose values are the heights. The declaration of rect allows for a final display up to 25 × 25.

```
var rect    :    array[1..25,1..25] of real;
    rug     :    real;

procedure fracrect(il,jl,ih,jh : integer);
{l means low, m means mid, h means high}
var im,jm   : integer;
begin
  im := (il+ih) div 2; jm := (jl+jh) div 2;
```

```
  if jm < jh then begin
    if rect[il,jm] = -10000 then
    rect[il,jm] := (rect[il,jl]+rect[il,jh])/2
                  + random*rug*(jh-jl);
    rect[ih,jm] := (rect[ih,jl]+rect[ih,jh])/2
                  + random*rug*(jh-jl)
  end {if};
  if im < ih then begin
    if rect[im,jl] = -10000 then
    rect[im,jl] := (rect[il,jl]+rect[ih,jl])/2
                  + random*rug*(ih-il);
    rect[im,jh] := (rect[il,jh]+rect[ih,jh])/2
                  + random*rug*(ih-il)
  end {if};
  if (im < ih) and (jm < jh) then
  rect[im,jm] := (rect[il,jl]+rect[ih,jl]
                + rect[il,jh]+rect[ih,jh])/4
                + random*rug*(abs(ih-il)+abs(jh-jl));
  if (im < ih) or (jm < jh) then begin
    fracrect(il,jl,im,jm);
    fracrect(il,jm,im,jh);
    fracrect(im,jl,ih,jm);
    fracrect(im,jm,ih,jh)
  end {if}
end {procedure fracrect};
```

The procedure produces only the heights at the grid points. To display the surface the heights have to be connected by straight lines or the individual facets have to be drawn as filled polygons. The factor rug has the same meaning as for the fractal line above. Figures 10.25 through 10.27 show the surfaces for three different values of rug. They are drawn without hidden line removal.

This is a useful technique for producing fractal forgeries of landscapes, especially of mountains. The grid is ordinarily much finer, 150 × 150, for example. It is not the production of the grid heights that is time consuming, rather doing the display. Obviously the factor rug has some relationship to the fractional dimension of the surface.

We should be aware that we don't fulfill the precise requirements of self-similarity when we create a line or a surface in this way. One reason is that the displacement amount is not proportional to the length of the line or to the length of the side of the facet, but it would be more costly to compute the length through a square root in every step. Another reason is that the direction of displacement is not perpendicular to the line piece or surface piece for which it is performed. This, too, is a deviation from the precise requirement. The approximations we use are

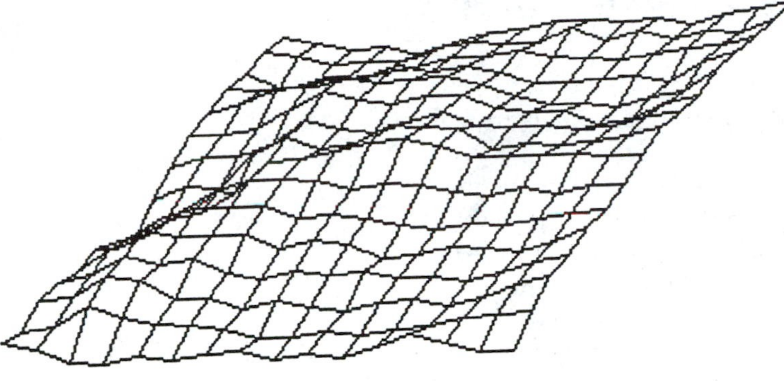

**FIGURE 10.25** Fractal grid surface with rug = 0.2.

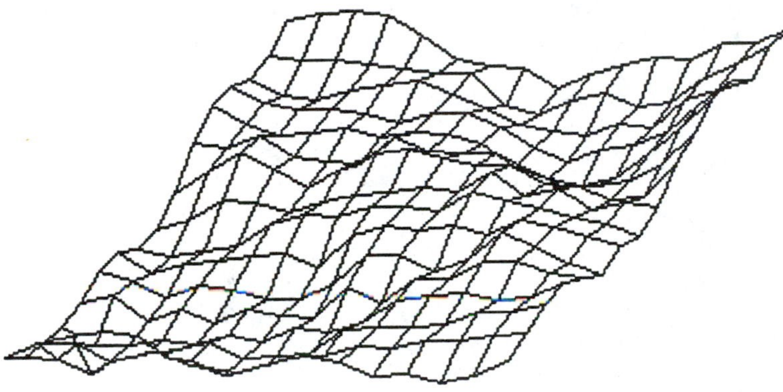

**FIGURE 10.26** Fractal grid surface with rug = 0.3.

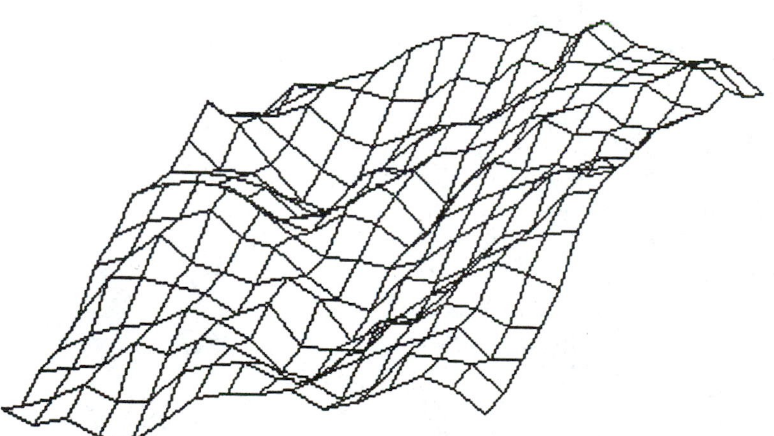

**FIGURE 10.27** Fractal grid surface with rug = 0.4.

good enough for practical purposes. A mountain landscape produced with this method is shown in color plate C-1.

**Creating Fractals through Iterated Transformations** Any geometric shape (not necessarily a fractal) that exhibits self similarity can be produced by a succession of linear transformations that fulfill certain conditions. These are called contractive affine transformations and they consist of rotations, translations, and scalings designed to produce a smaller image than the original one. An image that consists of several self similar parts can be expressed as the union of several affine transformations of itself. These parts may be scaled or rotated before being joined.

For example, we can apply a succession of matrices that represent transformations to the corner point of a rectangle, choosing the matrices either systematically or randomly from this set:

$$A_1 = \begin{bmatrix} .5 & 0 & 0 \\ 0 & .5 & 0 \\ 0 & 0 & 1 \end{bmatrix} \qquad A_2 = \begin{bmatrix} .5 & 0 & 0 \\ 0 & .5 & 0 \\ .5 & 0 & 1 \end{bmatrix}$$

$$A_3 = \begin{bmatrix} .5 & 0 & 0 \\ 0 & .5 & 0 \\ .5 & .5 & 1 \end{bmatrix} \qquad A_4 = \begin{bmatrix} .5 & 0 & 0 \\ 0 & .5 & 0 \\ 0 & .5 & 1 \end{bmatrix}$$

We continue to apply a transformation to each resulting point; the generated points eventually cover the entire rectangle. Even though the resulting points have real values as coordinates, we round them to integers before displaying so all the pixels of the display are represented in the final result.

Since the above affine transformations can generate the rectangle, they serve as a definition of it. Rather than storing the bit map of the rectangle, we can instead store the affine transformations with (in the general case at least) great economy.

A fractal image usually can be covered by affine transformations of itself. In the case of the rectangle, these are quite obvious, but that is not always true. We can find an affine transformation matrix algebraically from three points on the original and the corresponding points on the self similar part of it.

As an example of generating a well known fractal, consider the C-curve. From the generating rule, we know how to construct C-curves like that of Figure 10.17. Imagine a horizontal line of length 1 starting at the origin; the first self similar part is rotated by 45°cw starting at the origin. The second self similar part is rotated by 45° ccw starting at the point (0.5. −0.5). We use this to write code to generate a downward-looking C-curve (opposite to that of Figure 10.17):

```
for i := 1 to 100000 do begin
  case random of
  0: begin
    x1 := (x+y)*0.5;
    y  := (-x+y)*0.5;
    x  := x1
  end {0};

  1: begin
    x1 := (x-y+1)*0.5;
    y  := (x+y-1)*0.5;
    x  := x1
  end {1};
```

It is certainly more efficient to store the code than the bit map of the resulting C-curve.

See Section 10.6 for further details.

# 10.5 MANDELBROT AND JULIA SETS AND FATOU DUSTS

We conclude this chapter with a discussion of three very popular fractals: the Mandelbrot set, Julia sets, and Fatou dusts. The computational method for these is such that they cannot be drawn on a line plotter, although some of these fractals are indeed lines. They have to be produced on a raster display.

These are all defined in the complex plane, so we must use complex arithmetic to produce them. We review this now.

The complex number plane is a two-dimensional plane practically identical to the two-dimensional Cartesian drawing plane. The horizontal axis is the real axis; the vertical axis is the imaginary axis. Complex numbers can be plotted on this plane as number pairs, practically identical to Cartesian coordinate pairs. We refer to the complex number as (a,b), (c,d), and so on; the real part is given first, the imaginary part second. So (a,b) and $a+bi$ mean the same. The whole complex plane, together with $\infty$, is designated by C. The rules for adding and subtracting complex numbers and for multiplying a complex number by a real factor are identical to those for vector addition and subtraction and scalar multiplication in Cartesian coordinates. The rules for multiplication and division of complex numbers with each other are different.

Complex arithmetic rules are:

$$\alpha \cdot (a,b) = (\alpha a, \alpha b) \; (\alpha \text{ is a real number})$$
$$(a,b) + (c,d) = (a+c, b+d)$$
$$(a,b) \cdot (c,d) = (ac-bd, ad+bc)$$
$$(a,b)/(c,d) = (ac+bd, bc-ad)/(c^2+d^2)$$

Distance d between two complex numbers, (a,b) and (c,d):

$$d = \sqrt{(a-c)^2 + (b-d)^2}$$

The origin in the complex plane is (0,0).

We will often use the square root of a complex number. A complex number (a,b) can be written in exponential form: $(a,b) = re^{i\Phi}$, which is $(r \cdot \cos\Phi, r \cdot \sin\Phi)$ according to Euler's formula. (This is just the polar form of the point in the complex plane.) In this expression $r = \sqrt{a^2+b^2}$. It follows that $\sqrt{(a,b)} = \sqrt{re^{i\Phi/2}} = \pm(\sqrt{r} \cdot \cos(\Phi/2), \sqrt{r} \cdot \sin(\Phi/2))$. The trigonometric formulas for the half-angle are:

$$\cos(\Phi/2) = \sqrt{1/2(1+\cos\Phi)} \quad \text{and} \quad \sin(\Phi/2) = \sqrt{1/2(1-\cos\Phi)}.$$

Putting those into the expression for $\sqrt{(a,b)}$ and multiplying by r within the radical, we get $\pm(\sqrt{1/2(r+r \cdot \cos\Phi)}, \sqrt{1/2(r-r \cdot \cos\Phi)})$. As $a = r \cdot \cos\Phi$ we have:

$$\sqrt{(a,b)} = \pm(\sqrt{1/2(r+a)}, \sqrt{1/2(r-a)}).$$

The deficiency of this formula is that it computes the same squareroots for (a,b) and (a, −b) although they are not identical. This is corrected by taking the imaginary part negative if $b < 0$ and positive if $b \geqslant 0$.

**The Mandelbrot Set** The *Mandelbrot set* is named after B. Mandelbrot, who first studied it in the 1970s (MAND77). It is easy to create. Strictly speaking, the Mandelbrot set is not a fractal; it is a subset of the complex plane, but its boundary is a fractal. It is this boundary which reveals infinite detail of amazing variety when looked at under high magnification.

To create the Mandelbrot set we perform a simple iteration in the complex plane. We will indicate a complex number by just one letter: $z = (zr,zi)$, $c = (cr,ci)$, and so on. If $z_i$ is a complex number in the iteration process, the next number is $z_{i+1}$ and is obtained by $z_{i+1} = z_i^2 + c$ in which c is a fixed complex number chosen to be not farther than 2 away from the origin.

We choose some such number c and a starting value $z_0 = (0,0)$, then iterate $z_1$, $z_2$, $z_3$, … . After every step we check the distance of $z_i$

from the origin. As soon as it exceeds 2 we stop the iteration because this sequence will go to ∞. If so, then this number c is not in the Mandelbrot set. If the distance of $z_i$ from the origin never becomes bigger than 2, then c belongs to the Mandelbrot set. This is because the Mandelbrot set is defined as:

$$\{c \epsilon C: \lim z_i \neq \infty \text{ under } z_{i+1} = z_i^2 + c,\ z_0 = (0,0)\}.$$

We can never know with certainty that an iteration will never go to ∞ because we cannot run the iteration forever to see if this will eventually occur. But we can set a limit, say 50 iteration steps, and if $z_i$ after so many steps still is not farther than 2 from the origin, we assume that c is in the Mandelbrot set.

We can create the figure by trying all c-values from some rectangular area of the complex plane. We make the rectangular area correspond to pixel locations of the screen. If c belongs to the set, we make this pixel black; if c does not belong to the set, we set the pixel to white. Figure 10.28 shows the Mandelbrot set. There seem to be parts isolated from the main set, but this is only a deficiency of the display because the Mandelbrot set is really connected (DOHU82).

Many closeups of the Mandelbrot sets are shown in a beautiful color display. Here is the crucial thing to do in order to get such beautiful Mandelbrot pictures. If a c-value does not belong to the set, we don't just set the corresponding pixel to white but we remember how many

**FIGURE 10.28** Mandelbrot set.

iteration steps it took until $z_i$ jumped over the boundary. We set the pixel to a color according to this number of iterations. That is basically all! Figure 10.29 shows a closeup of the set, namely the area from $-0.7375$ to $-0.73125$ on the real axis and from 0.19375 to 0.2 on the imaginary axis. This area is displayed with 200 × 200 pixels and the limit for the iterations is 90.

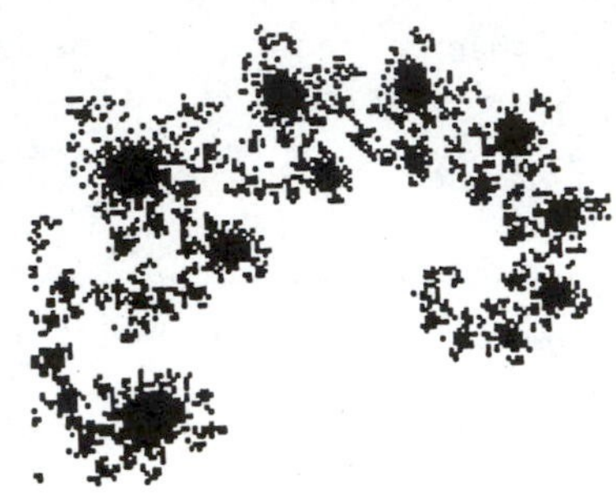

**FIGURE 10.29** Mandelbrot set closeup.

Experience is needed to find good color choices for pixels and good boundary regions for the Mandelbrot subset. If we are too far away from the set, we get just one or two plain colors; if we are too close—inside the set—we get plain black. To get good, interesting closeups, we might have to scan a very small area; it can be necessary to use double precision arithmetic. Also, the limit we set for the decision to stop iterations must be high: 700 is no exaggeration. Mandelbrot closeups are extremely computation intensive. A very fast processor or a math chip can save literally days and weeks of processor time.

**Julia Sets** (This section can be omitted without loss of continuity.) *Julia sets* are one of the most widely studied fractals but many questions concerning them remain to be solved. For example, almost nothing is known about their fractional dimension. Work on these sets was begun by G. Julia and P. Fatou about the time of the first world war (JULI18, FATO19). A Julia set is not necessarily a fractal but most Julia sets are.

Like the Mandelbrot set, Julia sets are defined in the complex plane C. Let P(z) and Q(z) be two polynomials with complex arguments without common divisors; then $R(z) = P(z)/Q(z)$ is a rational function in C. For each rational function a Julia set can be defined as explained below.

The rational function R(z) is used to iterate any given point of C: $z_{i+1} = R(z_i)$. Depending on the starting point, such an iteration sequence can behave in several different ways. Of importance now are those starting values that repeat themselves cyclically when iterated. For example, take $P(z) = z^2$ and $Q(z) = 1$; then $R(z) = z^2$. The point $e^{2i\pi}/7 = (.6234,.7818)$ iterates to $(-.2225,.9749)$, then to $(-.9009,-.4338)$, then back to $(.6243,.7818)$, and repeats this cycle forever. Denote such a periodic cycle by Γ. The above three points are called *periodic,* their periods are of length 3. Points with a period of 1 are considered periodic, too.

We have to characterize the periodic cycles further. If $z_0$ is a periodic point with period n for the function R, then it is a periodic point with period 1 for the function $R^n$, ($R^n = R°R°\ldots R$, applied n times). Iterating a point in $R^n$ is the same as iterating it in R and paying attention to every *n*th iterate only. Let $z_0, z_1, \ldots, z_{n-1}$ be the points of the cycle Γ with period n. Now consider the iteration function $R^n$

and take any of the periodic points $z_i$ from $\Gamma$. Iterating with a point $z_i$ from the cycle is not interesting because it jumps onto itself forever (the period is 1 for $R^n$!). But if we take a point very close to $z_i$ and iterate it, several different things might happen.

**a.** It can be attracted by $z_i$, that is, it comes arbitrarily close to $z_i$; we call *$z_i$ attractive.*

**b.** It can be repelled by $z_i$, that is, it is not attracted by $z_i$, but maybe it is attracted by some other point, or by $\infty$, or comes closer and withdraws again in a chaotic manner; we call $z_i$ *repelling.*

**c.** It can be neither attracted nor repelled, but circles $z_i$ on a curve forever; we call $z_i$ *indifferent.*

The above intuitive explanations have precise mathematical definitions. To find to which of the three groups an n-cycle periodic point $z_i$ of R belongs, we compute the derivative of $R^n$ at the point $z_i$, $L = (R^n)'(z_i)$. In case (a) $|L| < 1$; in case (b) $|L| > 1$; and in case (c) $|L| = 1$. It follows from the chain rule of differentiation that the value of L is the same for all $z_i$ in a cycle; therefore the whole cycle $\Gamma$ belongs to one of these groups. This allows us to categorize all periodic cycles of a function R into one of the three classes.

We want to examine the repelling periodic cycles of R. Without going into mathematical detail we state that for every rational function R(z) there are infinitely many repelling periodic cycles and therefore infinitely many repelling periodic points. Let P be the set of all repelling periodic points of R. The Julia set of R, $J_R$, is defined as the closure of P. In other words, $J_R$ is the set of all limit points of P. In this sense P more or less outlines $J_R$.

In some cases there is a more intuitive way to describe the Julia set of R. Attractive cycles don't always exist, but if there is one, $\Gamma$, consisting of the points $z_0, \ldots, z_{n-1}$, we group, for each $z_i$, all points attracted to it through iteration with $R^n$ into one set and call this set $A(z_i)$, the *basin of attraction* of $z_i$. $J_R$ is the boundary of $A(z_i)$; that is, it is the set of all limit points of $A(z_i)$, no matter which $z_i$ is taken. The union of $A(z_0), A(z_1), \ldots, A(z_{n-1})$ is the basin of attraction of this cycle, $A(\Gamma)$. $J_R$ is also the boundary of $A(\Gamma)$. This is an interesting property because there are usually several basins of attraction with totally different shapes yet with identical boundaries. From this it follows that $J_R$ must, in many cases, be fractal.

Another property of $J_R$ is that $J_R$ is identical to $J_{R^n}$. So we can display $J_{R^n}$ instead of $J_R$ if this is easier. Also, $J_R$ is invariant under R: $R(J_R) = J_R$.

Here's an example. Take $z^2 + c$ as the rational function R(z), where c is the complex constant $(-.12,.74)$. This R has an attractive three-cycle consisting of the three points a = (−.65306,.56253), b = (−.00995,0.00527), and c = (−.11993,.73990). If we iterate with R°R°R then each of these points is attractive with period 1. The point ∞ also is attractive. Each of these four points has its basin of attraction; they are shown in Figures 10.30 through 10.33 in black. As we can see, the basins are in the first three cases the union of countless many disjoint sets. Most of them are so small that they can't be seen in the display. A(a), A(b), A(c), and A(∞) are very different from each other, yet their boundaries are identical and equal $J_{R\circ R\circ R}$, therefore they are identical to $J_R$.

In Figure 10.30, the union of the black areas is the basin of attraction of the point a = (−.65306, .56253). The boundary of this set is $J_R$. The point a itself lies in the large area at the upper left. In Figure 10.31, the union of the black areas is the basin of attraction of the point b = (−.00995, 0.00527). The boundary of this set is $J_R$. The point b itself lies in the large center area. In Figure 10.32, the union of the black areas is the basin of attraction of the point c = (−.11993,.73990). The boundary of this set is $J_R$. The point c itself lies in the upper of the two big parts. The black area in Figure 10.33 is the basin of attraction of the point ∞; it extends outside the rectangle to infinity. The boundary of this set is $J_R$. The white area is the union of all the other basins of attraction. A(∞) is connected and its boundary is easier to see than in the previous three cases.

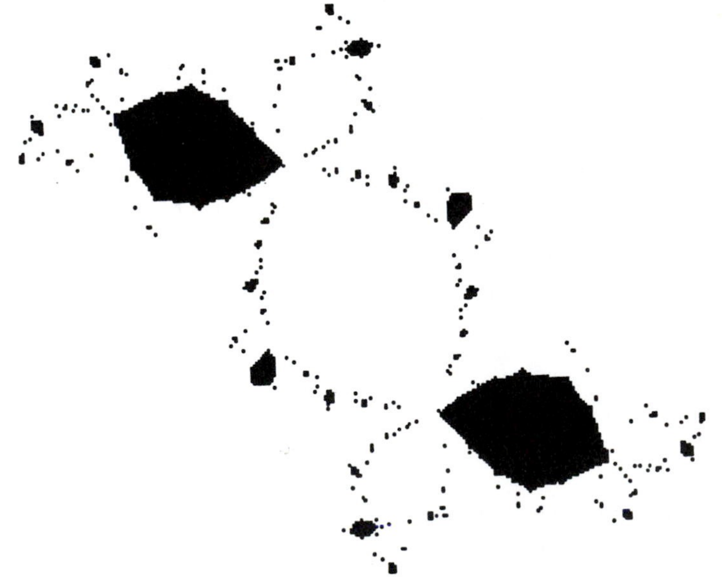

**FIGURE 10.30**

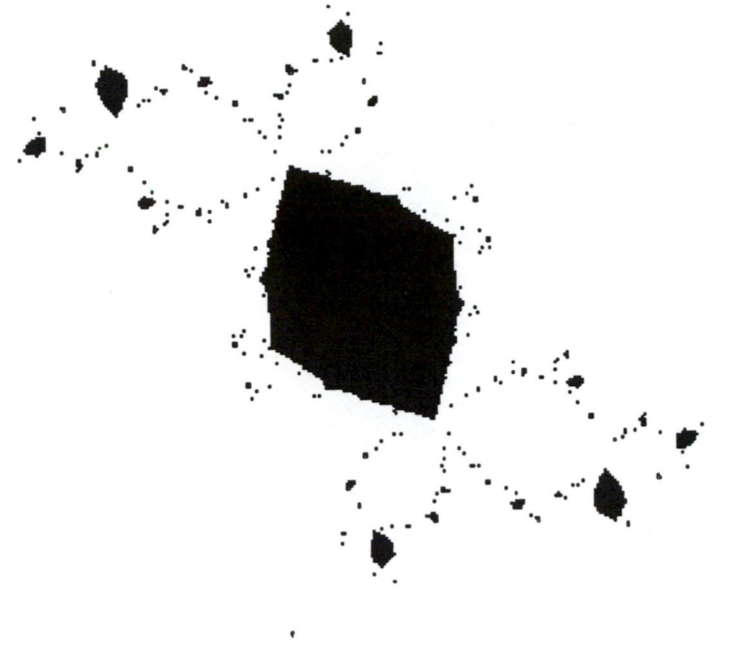

FIGURE 10.31

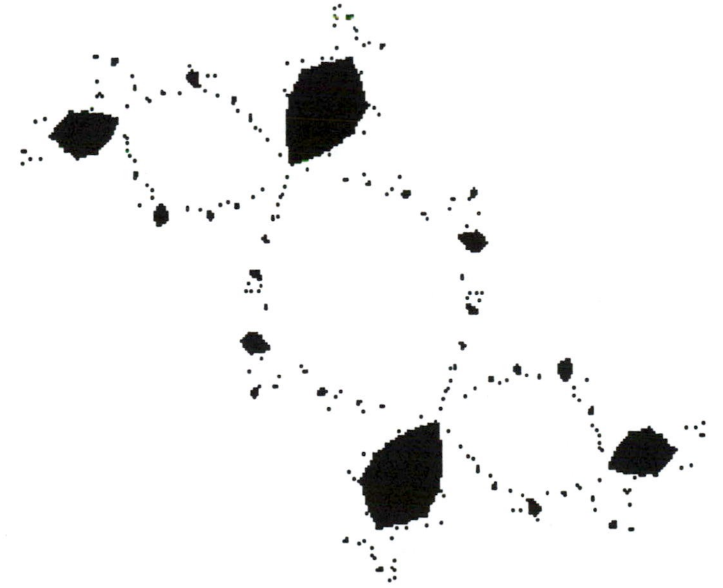

FIGURE 10.32

**FIGURE 10.33**

**Displaying a Julia Set: Pre-image Method** Julia sets are harder to display than the Mandelbrot set. Here is one method. A pre-image of a point $z_0$ is any point z such that $R(z) = z_0$. Given R and a point $z_0$, then $I(z_0) = \{z\epsilon C{:}R^k(z) = z_0 \text{ for } k = 1,2, \ldots\}$ describes the set of all pre-images of $z_0$. A Julia set $J_R$ has the property that, for every point $z_0 \epsilon J_R$, the set $I(z_0)$ is dense in $J_R$. In other words the set of all pre-images of $z_0$ pretty much outlines the Julia set. If R is not too complicated, the pre-image of a point can be expressed by a formula. For example, $R(z) = z^2+c$. The pre-image z of $z_0$ satisfies $R(z) = z_0$, so $z^2+c = z_0$; it follows that there are two pre-images $z_1 = +\sqrt{z_0-c}$ and $z_2 = -\sqrt{z_0-c}$. We will explain the pre-image method further only for $R(z) = z^2+c$. For more complicated functions, the inverse can not be expressed as a formula and the pre-images have to be found by Newton's method.

Beginning with a starting point and repeating the formula, we can compute pre-images of pre-images, continuing until we reach a preset limit n. There are always two possible pre-images of each point. It would be most complicated and require tremendous buffer space to pursue the pre-images of each solution when they double with every step. But it is not necessary to do so. We use just one of the two pre-images randomly so that they are chosen with about equal probability.

How do we find a starting point in the Julia set? Luckily we don't really need one. If we iterate inversely and choose any pre-image at random, then, for mathematical reasons beyond the scope of this book, every point from C will be pulled toward $J_R$ and once there it will jump into $J_R$ forever. So we take, for example, (1,0) as the starting point, compute the two pre-images, and choose one at random. We can still set both pixels corresponding to both solutions. It takes only a few steps until the pre-images are in the Julia set. The more points we produce, the better. How many points should we produce? For cases in which the Julia set is not very ragged we get a pretty good picture with about 2000 iterations (see Figures 10.34 and 10.35).

The shortcoming of the method quickly becomes obvious when we try to display more complicated sets. Figure 10.36 shows two such attempts for $R(z) = z^2+(-.12,.74)$. Compare these to Figure 10.33. The outline of $J_R$ is recognizable but there are still gaps in the line although both 10,000 (left) and 20,000 (right) iterations were done. In the right display, $J_R$ is outlined better. The gaps result from the fact that the pre-images seldom reach these areas. Increasing the number of iterated points does not help very much. Gaps will be visible even after 40,000 iterations.

**FIGURE 10.34** Julia set of $R(z) = z^2 + (.2,.2)$.

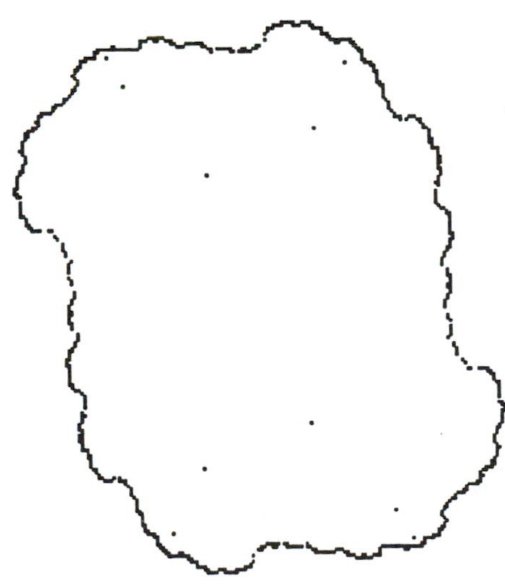

**FIGURE 10.35** Julia set of $R(z) = z^2 + (-.12,.5)$.

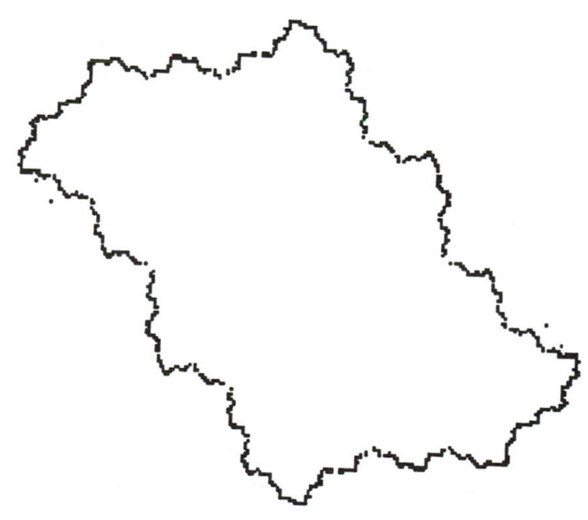

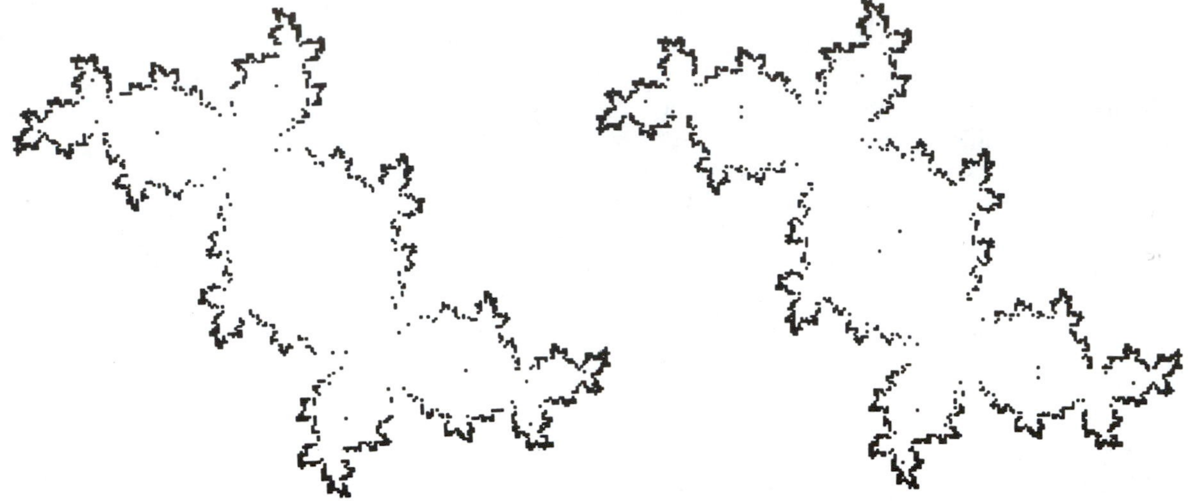

**FIGURE 10.36** Julia set of $R(z) = z^2 + (-.12,.74)$, displayed with 10,000 points (left) and 20,000 points (right).

**Attractor Method for the Julia Set** When the pre-image method does not yield good results, we can try the following. Essentially, we work with just one attractor. Call this point a (a can be $\infty$). We check a point, $x_0$, that corresponds to a pixel to see if it is attracted to a. This test is $|x_i - a| < \epsilon$ (except if $a = \infty$, it is $|x_i| > r$). If this terminating condition is not met after, say, 50 iterations, we assume that the starting point is not attracted to a. We do this testing for the four corner points of the pixel. If all four corner points are attracted, or if none of the four corner points are attracted, we know that the boundary is not within the pixel. However, if just one or two or three are attracted and the others are not, then the boundary of the Julia set is in the pixel and we set the pixel. The pixels that we set display an outline of the Julia set.

**Attractor Method for Basins** This method works under the same conditions as the attractor method above, but it does not display the Julia set, Instead it displays one or several basins of attraction. Such displays are as informative as the Julia set itself and are usually much prettier and more colorful. We need to find an attractive point (including $\infty$). To have the attractor $\infty$ is sufficient, the method is first explained for the case when $\infty$ is the attractor.

We cover the area of interest with a fine lattice such that each lattice point corresponds to one pixel. Then we iterate with each lattice point $x_0$ until $|x_i| > r$, which means that $x_0$ is attracted by $\infty$. If this condition is not met after, say, 50 steps, then we assume that $x_0$ is not attracted by $\infty$; we set the pixel corresponding to this lattice point to black, otherwise to white. This method is the easiest to program and produces a filled-in Julia set if $J_R$ is connected. Figure 10.37 shows the filled in Julia set for $z^2+(-.544,-.54)$ produced with this method. The lattice consists of $361 \times 361$ points, the area is $[-1.5,1.5] \times [-1.5,1.5]$, and the limit for iterations is 42. It would be almost impossible to display this $J_R$ using the pre-image method.

The relation between lattice points and pixels will be apparent from this example. Suppose the rectangle of interest is from $-1$ to $+1$ on the real axis and from $-0.625$ to $+0.625$ on the imaginary axis. We want to display this using the entire screen, which has $640 \times 400$ pixels with a square pixel ratio. (Since the area of interest has the same proportions as the screen, no distortions are introduced.) This is the relation that associates a pixel $x_\pi, y_\pi$ with a point (a,b) in the complex lattice plane:

$$a = (x_\pi - 320)/320, \qquad b = (y_\pi - 200)/320.$$

For Figure 10.37, we tested $\infty$ only. Suppose that we have several attractors $a_1$, $a_2$, $a_3$, . . . (one of them might be $\infty$). Then we again cover the area of interest with a fine lattice and iterate for each lattice point $x_0$, but we expand the stopping condition to include every possible attractor. The stopping condition must be: if $|x_i| > r$ or $|x_i - a_1| < \epsilon$ or $|x_i - a_2| < \epsilon$ or $|x_i - a_3| < \epsilon$ and so on, with $\epsilon$ and r as above. The iteration will always stop and meet one of the conditions (if we test for all existing attractors). We keep track of which particular OR clause was met and set the corresponding pixel to a certain color. This fills each of the basins with a different color. With more than two attractors, the boundaries between them are fractal and this makes such displays very interesting.

Figures 10.30 through 10.32 were produced with this method. The iteration function was $(R°R°R)(z)$ with $R(z) = z^2 + (-.12,.74)$; the attractors are listed with the figures. Only one attractor was checked for each display because of the black/white restriction. With a color display all four attractors can be checked in the iteration and the four basins can be produced simultaneously.

The above shows that we always need some additional information about a Julia set and have to do some preparations before we can successfully compute and display it. The Mandelbrot set is much easier to display because there is only one, so one program will do all possible closeups. But there are infinitely many different Julia sets; the function

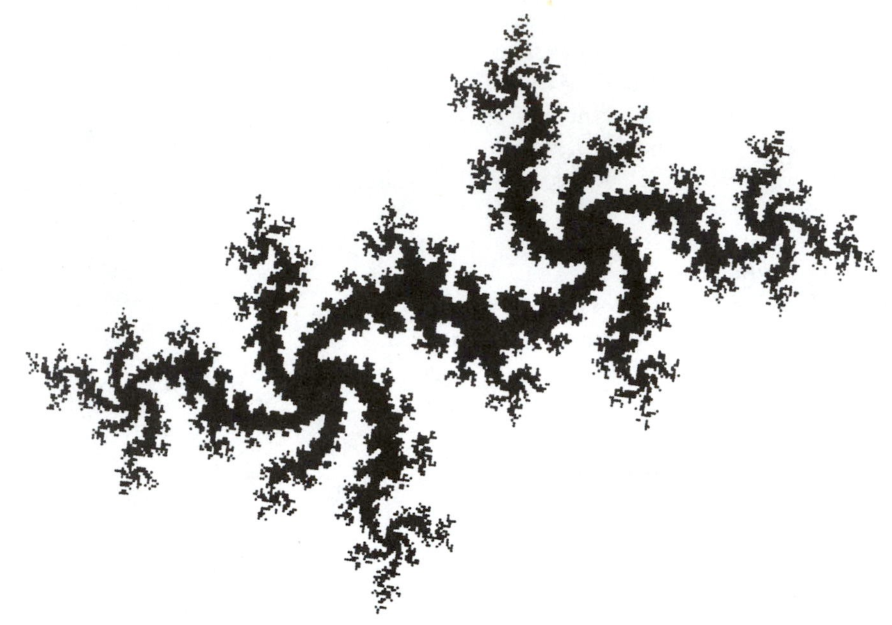

**FIGURE 10.37** Filled-in Julia set for $z^2 + (-.544, -.54)$.

$z^2 + c$ alone gives us an infinite and amazing variety of different pictures depending on c.

The same phenomenon occurs here as with the Mandelbrot set. We usually get nicer pictures if we don't go for the Julia set itself (which is just a fractally distorted line or a dust), but instead count how many iteration steps it takes before a decision is made. This number determines the color of the particular pixel. For further information on Julia sets, consult PERI86 and CUGS83.

**Fatou Dusts** Julia sets that are topologically not lines but are totally disconnected are sometimes called *Fatou dusts*. They are hard to create because the only attractive point is $\infty$. If an iteration does not start very close to the Fatou dust it will quickly drop into $A(\infty)$, so the dust points can easily escape the scanning process. We can catch the dust points easier if the iteration limit is not set high and the scanning raster is dense. Theoretically, the chance that a grid point is in the Fatou dust is 0 and the chance that it is in $A(\infty)$ is 1, so if we iterate too long we will always go to $\infty$.

# 10.6 CREATING FRACTALS THROUGH ITERATED TRANSFORMATIONS

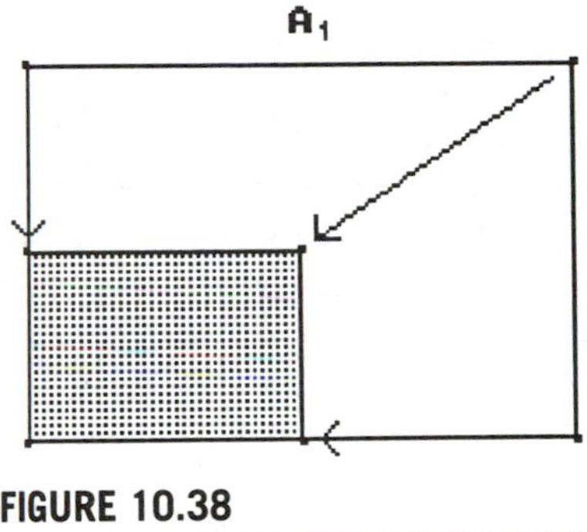

FIGURE 10.38

Any geometric shape (not necessarily a fractal) that exhibits self similarity can be produced by a succession of linear transformations that fulfill certain conditions. These are called contractive affine transformations and they consist of rotations, translations, and scalings designed to produce a smaller image than the original one. An image that consists of several self similar parts can be expressed as the union of several affine transformations of itself. These parts may be scaled or rotated before being joined. A simple but illustrative example is a rectangle. Figure 10.38 shows how the contractive affine transformation $A_1$ transforms a rectangle into a smaller one that covers 1/4 of it. Figure 10.39 shows how a rectangle can be covered with four scaled down images of itself. The scaled down images are marked with the affine transformations $A_1$ through $A_4$ that produce them. Rectangle $A_1$ is obtained by scaling the original rectangle by a factor of 0.5, rectangles $A_2$, $A_3$ and $A_4$ are obtained through scaling by the same factor and subsequent translation.

The four corresponding affine transformations $A_1$ through $A_4$ are expressed below by matrices. It is assumed that the original rectangle has its lower left corner at the origin:

$$A_1 = \begin{pmatrix} .5 & 0 & 0 \\ 0 & .5 & 0 \\ 0 & 0 & 1 \end{pmatrix} \qquad A_2 = \begin{pmatrix} .5 & 0 & 0 \\ 0 & .5 & 0 \\ .5 & 0 & 0 \end{pmatrix}$$

$$A_3 = \begin{pmatrix} .5 & 0 & 0 \\ 0 & .5 & 0 \\ .5 & .5 & 1 \end{pmatrix} \qquad A_4 = \begin{pmatrix} .5 & 0 & 0 \\ 0 & .5 & 0 \\ 0 & .5 & 1 \end{pmatrix}$$

FIGURE 10.39

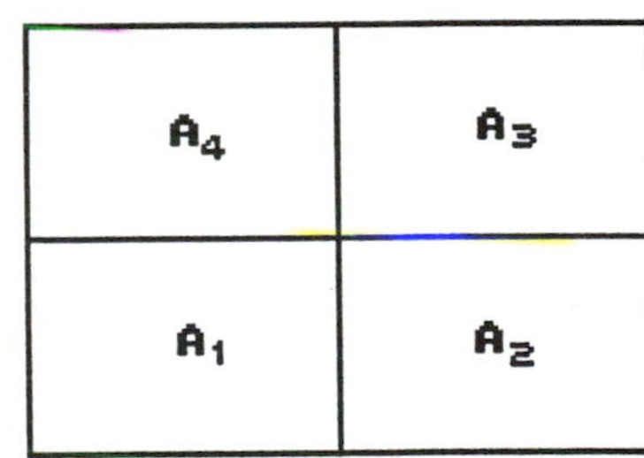


If we take the point (0,0) and compute its four images with $A_1$ through $A_4$ we get the four points shown in Figure 10.40. As (0,0) is the left lower corner of the original rectangle, the four transformations of (0,0) are the left lower corners of the four images of the rectangle. If we compute the images of these four points with the four transformations we get the 16 points shown in Figure 10.41. Each transformation produces four points in its corresponding image rectangle. Computing the images of these 16 points with all four transformations gives us 64 points as shown in Figure 10.42.

FIGURE 10.40

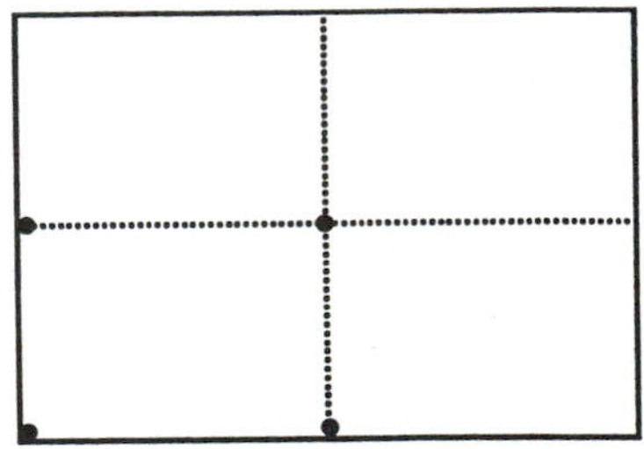

We see that by repeating this over and over again, we fill up the whole rectangular area. The number of points is increased by the factor 4 with each step and the rectangle is filled in a systematic and regular manner.

But it is not necessary to proceed in such a systematic way. If we don't apply all four transformations to the starting point but only one, chosen at random with equal probability, we get any of the four successor points with equal probability. Let us find out what happens if we iterate in this way: Again applying any of the transformations at random to the successor point we get any one of the 16 points of the second step. After the third iteration we get any one of the 64 possible points of the third step. The first iterated point, the second, and the third all lie on different grids that become finer and finer. Theoretically we will never produce a point twice with this method. But in practice it is different.

Because of the limited accuracy of the machine arithmetic there are only a finite number of points within the rectangular area that the machine can produce. Therefore we will not continue to get points on finer and finer grids. After the finest grid possible with the given machine arithmetic is reached, we will produce points on this grid only, and therefore will eventually produce points identical to former points in the iteration. This opens the possibility that all successors of all points will eventually be produced. In other words, if we continue such an iteration long enough we will finally cover the whole rectangle with points.

Since the above affine transformations can generate the rectangle, they serve as a definition of it. The rectangle can be produced by applying them with equal probability to an arbitrary starting point and iterating just long enough. This is certainly a clumsy way to define a rectangle, but it is a very good way to define a highly complex fractal image.

A fractal image usually can be covered with several transformed instances of itself. If we can specify the transformations that do this we have a description of the fractal. Let us look at a way to find these transformations if they are not so obvious as in the case with the rectangle.

An affine transformation is uniquely determined by three different points and their transformations; we show this below. We use homogeneous coordinates to describe the points and "homogeneous matrices" to describe the transformations. Let the three points be:

$$P_1 = (x_1, y_1, 1)$$
$$P_2 = (x_2, y_2, 1)$$
$$P_3 = (x_3, y_3, 1).$$

**FIGURE 10.41**

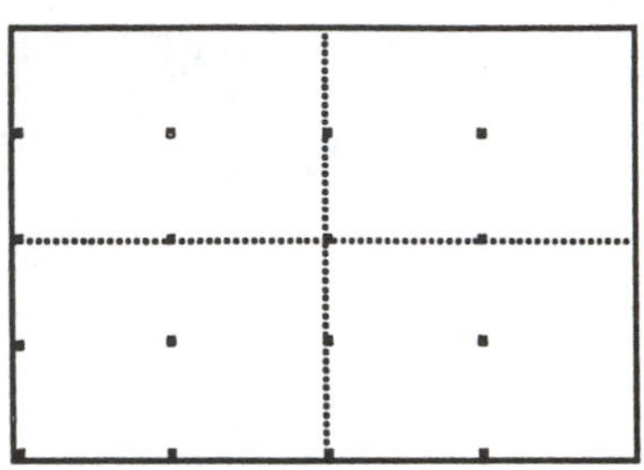

**FIGURE 10.42**

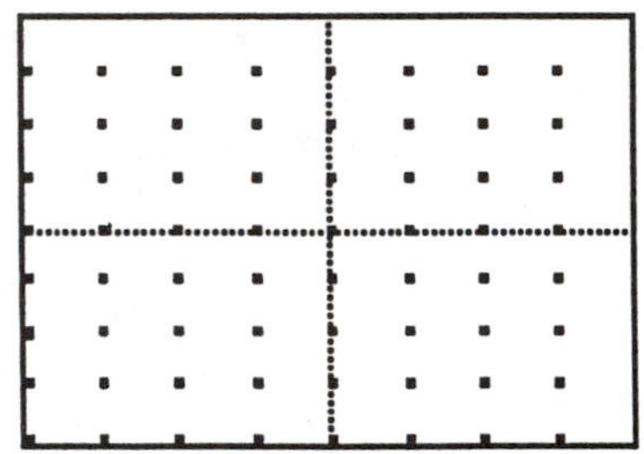

Let their transformations be:

$$\begin{aligned} Pt_1 &= (xt_1, yt_1, 1) \\ Pt_2 &= (xt_2, yt_2, 1) \\ Pt_3 &= (xt_3, yt_3, 1). \end{aligned}$$

Let the affine transformation be expressed by the matrix:

$$\begin{pmatrix} a & b & 0 \\ c & d & 0 \\ e & f & 1 \end{pmatrix}$$

then we have the equations:

$$(xt_1, yt_1, 1) = (x_1, y_1, 1)\begin{pmatrix} a & b & 0 \\ c & d & 0 \\ e & f & 1 \end{pmatrix},$$

$$(xt_2, yt_2, 1) = (x_2, y_2, 1)\begin{pmatrix} a & b & 0 \\ c & d & 0 \\ e & f & 1 \end{pmatrix},$$

$$(xt_3, yt_3, 1) = (x_3, y_3, 1)\begin{pmatrix} a & b & 0 \\ c & d & 0 \\ e & f & 1 \end{pmatrix},$$

A,b,c,d,e and f are the unknowns. This leads to 2 linear systems:

$$\begin{pmatrix} x_1 & y_1 & 1 \\ x_2 & y_2 & 1 \\ x_3 & y_3 & 1 \end{pmatrix}\begin{pmatrix} a \\ c \\ e \end{pmatrix} = \begin{pmatrix} xt_1 \\ xt_2 \\ xt_3 \end{pmatrix} \text{ and } \begin{pmatrix} x_1 & y_1 & 1 \\ x_2 & y_2 & 1 \\ x_3 & y_3 & 1 \end{pmatrix}\begin{pmatrix} b \\ d \\ f \end{pmatrix} = \begin{pmatrix} yt_1 \\ yt_2 \\ yt_3 \end{pmatrix}$$

The solutions are:

$$a = \frac{\begin{vmatrix} xt_1 & y_1 & 1 \\ xt_2 & y_2 & 1 \\ xt_3 & y_3 & 1 \end{vmatrix}}{det} \quad c = \frac{\begin{vmatrix} x_1 & xt_1 & 1 \\ x_2 & xt_2 & 1 \\ x_3 & xt_3 & 1 \end{vmatrix}}{det} \quad \frac{\begin{vmatrix} x_1 & y_1 & xt_1 \\ x_2 & y_2 & xt_2 \\ x_3 & y_3 & xt_3 \end{vmatrix}}{det}$$

$$b = \frac{\begin{vmatrix} yt_1 & y_1 & 1 \\ yt_2 & y_2 & 1 \\ yt_3 & y_3 & 1 \end{vmatrix}}{det} \quad d = \frac{\begin{vmatrix} x_1 & yt_1 & 1 \\ x_2 & yt_2 & 1 \\ x_3 & yt_3 & 1 \end{vmatrix}}{det} \quad f = \frac{\begin{vmatrix} x_1 & y_1 & yt_1 \\ x_2 & y_2 & yt_2 \\ x_3 & y_3 & yt_3 \end{vmatrix}}{det}$$

$$\text{with det} = \begin{vmatrix} x_1 & y_1 & 1 \\ x_2 & y_2 & 1 \\ x_3 & y_3 & 1 \end{vmatrix}.$$

As mentioned above we have to cover the original image with transformed instances of itself. To derive an individual affine transformation for this covering process we first identify a self similar part. Then we specify three points on the original: $P_1$, $P_2$, $P_3$, and the three corresponding points on the self similar part of it: $Pt_1$, $Pt_2$, $Pt_3$. From their coordinates we determine the transformation matrix using the above formulas.

This must be done until the whole original is covered. When all transformations are determined in this manner, we use them with equal probabilities to iterate on an arbitrary starting point. (For better probability distributions see BASL88.) Basically, the probabilities, with which the different transformations are used should be proportional to the areas of their respective images. After a few iterations any starting point will reach the original image and once there, the further iterates will randomly jump around within it, eventually reaching every point of it. This reproduces the original image more or less accurately. The better the original is covered by its transformed images and the more precisely the individual transformations are, the better the approximation. A slight inaccuracy produces only a slight deviation from the precise image, because the underlying mathematical process is basically stable.

Let us look at the fractal in Figure 10.43. There are many ways to cover it with self similar images. Of course we are looking for the simplest way. Figure 10.44 will help to identify self similar parts. One of these parts is shaded. The unshaded part is also self similar. So we can cover the whole image with just two transformations.

We could as well take the scroll to the left of the shaded one as another self similar part. The remaining unshaded part would then be smaller by one scroll but it would still be self similar. Thus we could cover the whole image with three transformations instead of two. Applying the 3 point method to find the two transformations we obtain

$$A_1 = \begin{bmatrix} .693 & .400 & 0 \\ -.400 & .693 & 0 \\ .0 & .0 & 0 \end{bmatrix} \text{ and } A_2 = \begin{bmatrix} .346 & -.200 & 0 \\ .200 & .346 & 0 \\ .693 & .400 & 1 \end{bmatrix}$$

The coefficients of $A_1$ and $A_2$ are all that is needed to store this fractal. Indeed, this technique is used to "store" pictures that consist mostly of fractal parts. What is stored are only the affine transformations necessary to recreate the picture. This requires much less storage space than a bit map; compression rates of 1 to 10000 are commonly achieved.

FIGURE 10.43

FIGURE 10.44

The finding of the original fractal image, detection of self similarities etc. is done automatically with image processing techniques.

To show that we can use this technique to create some of our well known fractals we will produce the C-curve and the dragon curve. We know from the generating rule that the C-curve consists of two instances of itself both scaled down by $\frac{1}{2}\sqrt{2}$. If we imagine the whole curve as a horizontal line of length 1 starting at the origin, then its first self similar part is rotated by 45° cw and starts at the origin. Its second self similar part is rotated by 45° ccw and starts at the point (0.5, −0.5). (This describes a downward bent C-curve.) Here we don't need to use the 3-point-method to find the transformations as we already know what they are. Below we see code that shows the two transformations and iterates an arbitrary starting point 100000 times subjecting it randomly to the first or second transformation. The result is shown in Figure 10.45.

FIGURE 10.45

```
for i := 1 to 100000 do begin
  case random of
  0: begin
    x1 := ( x+y)*0.5;
    y  := (-x+y)*0.5;
    x  := x1
  end {0};

  1: begin
    x1 := (x-y+1)*0.5;
    y  := (x+y-1)*0.5;
    x  := x1
  end {1}
  end {case};
  setpix(round(x),round(y))
end {for i};
```

The self similarity in the dragon curve is somewhat harder to detect. This curve, too, consists of two instances of itself, both scaled down by $\frac{1}{2}\sqrt{2}$. If we imagine the whole curve as a horizontal line of length 1 starting at the origin, then its first self similar part is rotated by 45° cw and starts at the origin. Its second self similar part is rotated by 135° cw and starts at the point (1,0). Below we see the code for these two transformations and in Figure 10.46 the result of 100000 iterations of a point.

```
for i := 1 to 100000 do begin
  case random of
  0: begin
    x1 := ( x+y)*0.5;
    y  := (-x+y)*0.5;
    x  := x1
  end {0}

  1: begin
    x1 := (-x+y)*0.5 + 1;
    y  := (-x-y)*0.5;
    x  := x1
  end {1};
  end {case};
  setpix(round(x),round(y))
end {for i};
```

The iterated transformation method allows you to produce fractals with short and simple codes. But the method is applicable only to raster displays. We can make the resulting fractals look more interesting and

FIGURE 10.46

prettier by setting the pixels in different colors depending on which transformation is used. See BASL88 for more information.

# EXERCISES FOR CHAPTER 10

## Complex Arithmetic and Julia Sets

1. Write a procedure for the iteration step $z \rightarrow z^2 + c$, a procedure for complex multiplication, and one for complex division. With these the Newton iteration step can be programmed (see Exercise 2.).
2. Find three-cycles of $R(z) = z^2 + c$ with $c = (-.39054, -0.58679)$. *Hint:* You have to find solutions of $(R°R°R)(z) = z$ or the zeros of $(R°R°R)(z) - z = 0$. You can do this using Newton's iteration method:

$$z_{i+1} = z_i - \frac{(R°R°R)(z_i) - z_i}{(R°R°R)'(z_i) - 1}$$

The chain rule of differentiation gives:

$$(R°R°R)'(z) = (R'°R°R)(z) \bullet (R'°R)(z) \bullet R'(z) \text{ and } R'(z) = 2z.$$

Use the procedures written in Exercise 1 to program the Newton iteration.

## Programming Generating Rules

3. Generate a C-curve. In a C-curve there are eight possible directions in which any line can be drawn. They are cyclic: 0, 1, 2, 3, 4, 5, 6, and 7 (see Figure 10.47). A C-curve in direction 0 consists of two C-curves, one in direction $(0+1) \bmod 8$ followed by one in direction $(0-1) \bmod 8$ (see Figure 10.48). Verify that this is true for all eight directions. The length of each of these two curves is $\frac{1}{2}\sqrt{2}$ of the original C-curve's length.

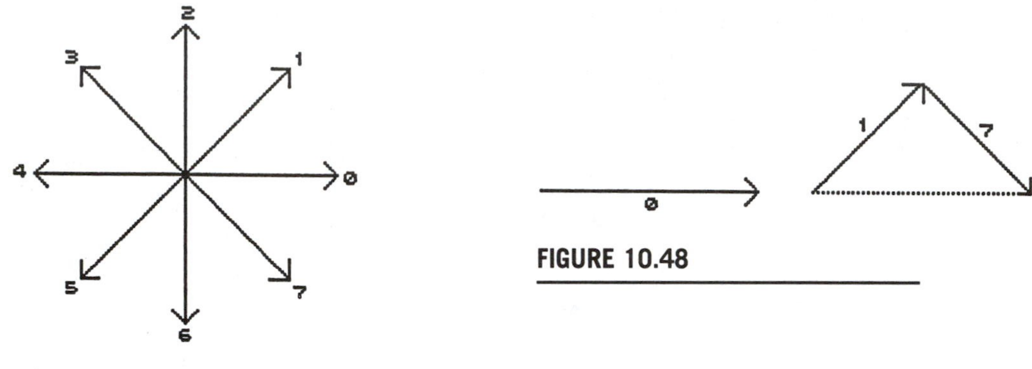


FIGURE 10.48

FIGURE 10.47

Using these simple rules, write a recursive procedure for drawing a C-curve. The procedure needs two arguments: the direction and the length of the curve. Keep track of the depth of recursion through a global depth counter and stop further calls when a certain depth is reached, for example, eight. In such a case just draw a straight line. You need a line-draw primitive that draws a straight line given one of the eight possible directions and the length.

4. In a Koch curve there are six possible drawing directions. Use reasoning similar to that in Exercise 3 to write a recursive procedure to draw a Koch curve. Demonstrate that it works correctly on all hardware you have at your disposal.
5. Show in an informal way that the Koch curve does not intersect itself.
6. Generate a dragon curve. Use reasoning similar to that in Exercise 3 to write a procedure for drawing a dragon curve. Use the generating rule given in the text.

For exercises 7 through 9, investigate a variation to the Koch curve, described by the following generating rule. Start with a straight line.

FIGURE 10.49

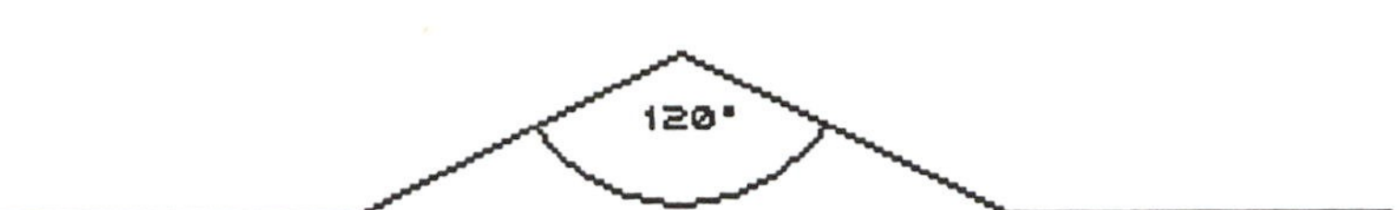


Take out the middle and replace it by an isosceles triangle with an angle of 120° at the top so that the resulting four line pieces are equally long (Figure 10.49).

7. Determine the dimension of the resulting curve with the similarity relation.
8. Show that this curve doesn't intersect itself.
9. Write a recursive procedure to draw this curve.

## Fractal Grid-Surfaces

10. Implement the procedure fracrect and generate a fractal grid surface. You can save memory by declaring the grid rectangles as type integer instead of as real. Allow the computed height values to use a large part of the available integer range in order to gain resolution. This can be done by simply multiplying all height values with a large scale factor.
11. Display the grid surface after scaling the height values and the subscript values to your display. Consider the subscripts of the array containing the grid values as the x- and z-coordinates of a grid point and the contents of the array element as the y-coordinate (after proper scaling). Computations for rotation and projection of the grid surface are done only to the individual triangle or rectangle that is to be displayed and not for the whole grid surface. Display by drawing lines without hidden line removal, using first, a slight rotation around the x-axis to tilt the surface toward the viewer and orthographic projection; second, the same as before but with perspective projection.
12. Same as exercise 11 but display the grid surface as a line display using "fake" hidden line removal. Draw the projection of each facet as a polygon filled with the background color, then draw its outline with a different color. Use rotation and perspective projection as in (11). Draw the polygons beginning with the one farthest away.

# Iterated Affine Transformations

13. Reproduce the spiral of Figure 10.50 as closely as possible. You need four different transformations: One scales the whole image by 0.8 and rotates it ccw by 20°. The other three scale it by 0.2 and translate it to the ends of the arms of the first transformed image.

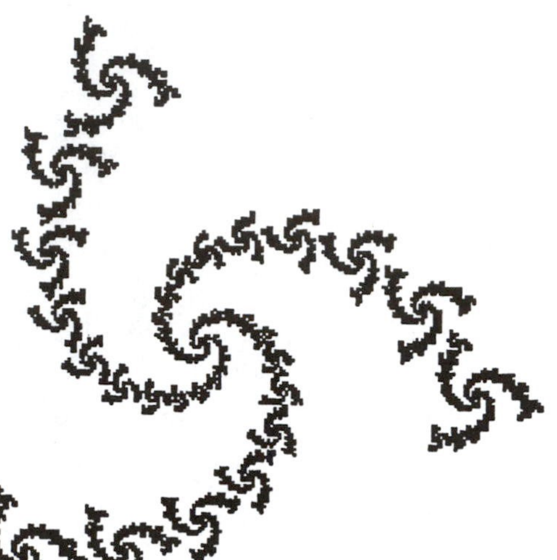

**FIGURE 10.50**

14. Reproduce the image of Figure 10.51 as closely as possible. You need five different transformations that are analogous to the ones explained in exercise 13. Just the scaling factors and the rotation angle are different.

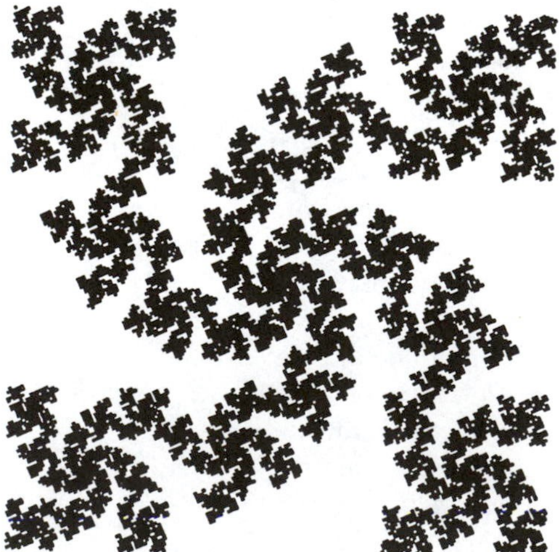

**FIGURE 10.51**

15. This example uses an image in which the self similar parts are vastly different in size, see Figure 10.52. Reproduce this image with four different transformations. It is essential that you use different probabilities here.

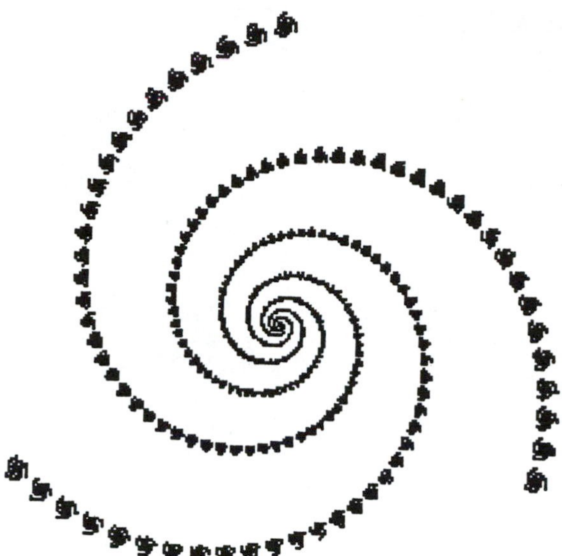

**FIGURE 10.52**

# Hidden Lines and Surfaces: Depth Sorting Methods

# 11

Chapter 11 is the first of three chapters that develop a number of methods for recognizing the parts of a scene that are behind other objects and therefore are not seen and should not be drawn. The methods of this chapter are practical only when the surfaces of objects are planar polygons.

**11.0 Introduction** shows why removal of hidden lines and surfaces is important and how curved surfaces can be represented by planar polygons.

**11.1 Polygon Meshes** considers the data structures that can represent a set of polygons making up the surface of an object.

**11.2 Backface Removal** requires that we identify those faces of a surface that point away from the viewer and are therefore not seen. A backface is "removed" simply by not drawing it. However, this doesn't handle faces that point to the viewer but are occluded by other faces of objects in the scene.

**11.3 Depth Sorting Methods** are a more general class of methods for removal of hidden surfaces that depend on finding which faces lie behind other faces. It is practical to do this only for triangular faces, so a first step is to decompose polygons into triangles.

# 11.0 INTRODUCTION

Many three-dimensional objects have surfaces that are planar polygons, for example, cubes, pyramids, prisms, and so on. More complex objects, such as houses, are often built from these. Many machine parts are formed from plates and have no curved surfaces. Even when an object has curved surfaces, it can often be well approximated by planar polyhedrons joined together; these simulate the actual surface. For example, the surface of a cylinder can be represented by many long narrow rectangles. When such an approximation is inadequate, the description of the curved surface must be done through a mathematical definition in three variables. Often, though, proper rendering of a surface composed of planar polygons can make the surface appear curved, as we will describe in Chapter 14.

If we are able to define an object or a scene using only planar surfaces, the display algorithms can take advantage of this fact and produce the display by just drawing the edges of the describing polygons or by showing the polygons as filled areas. Displaying objects that really have curved surfaces is much more complicated and is beyond our scope.

Throughout this chapter, then, our spatial objects will be considered to have plane polygonal surfaces. When such an object is displayed by drawing only the edges, the result is a *wireframe model*. This is easy to do, hence wireframe models are often used, even when the real object is opaque. However, such a wireframe representation of a solid object may appear ambiguous because it shows all edges of the object including those that should not be visible. Figure 11.1 is an example. Most of these ambiguities disappear if the hidden lines are removed. This also makes the object appear to have depth.

**FIGURE 11.1** Ambiguous wireframe model.

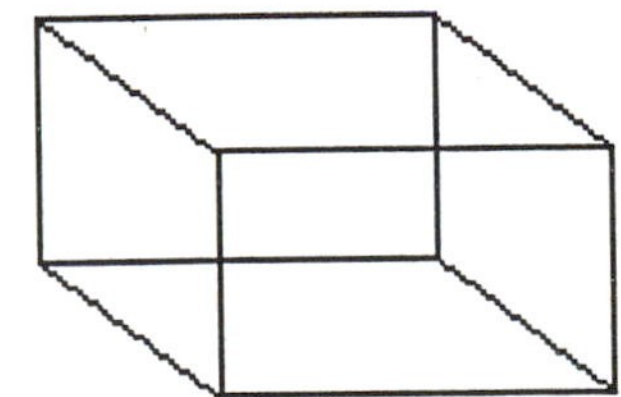

It is difficult and requires considerable computation to distinguish between visible and invisible edges of an object. It is easier to find those planar polygons that are not to be shown, rather than to find their edges. The first efforts in this area focused on techniques for removing hidden lines rather than hidden surfaces, however. The reason for this is that, initially, all displays were vector scan devices that could not display a solidly filled area, something that is easy for today's raster scan displays. When solid objects are displayed using filled areas, the display problem reduces to the easier problem of elimination of hidden surfaces.

Even so, hidden line removal algorithms deserve special attention not just because there are still some vector scan displays in operation, but because the very popular line plotters are physically vector devices and have difficulties in displaying solid surfaces. Hidden surface algorithms will not work for them.

One of the goals in computer graphics is to generate the images of real world objects as realistically as possible. Another is to produce abstract images from our imagination (computer graphic art). We may wish to model shapes through freehand sketching. A most important application is computer-aided design in which objects are fully specified. In all cases the shapes that are to be displayed are usually complex.

Theoretically, the complete description of a random 3-D shape can require an infinity of number triples to fully define its surface. At the other extreme, a sphere can be described by a single simple mathematical formula. The same is true for a torus (a shape like an inner tube) as well as for many other ideal shapes. A cylinder is a bit more complicated to describe. All of these can be approximated by plane polyhedrons to an arbitrarily fine precision, but such representations become very awkward when the number of faces is too great.

It is sometimes possible to build up a complex object from several simple ideal components; sometimes a component "subtracts" from the assemblage. The points on the surface of each component are then described by the mathematical formula for the component. Constructing the representation of a shape in this way is called *solid modeling.* Some computer-aided design graphics systems provide for solid modeling in a very user-friendly, interactive way. While not all types of real world objects are easy to construct by solid modeling, some are naturally composed of ideal shapes; for example, a roller bearing is made of spheres, cones, and cylinders.

Many shapes that we wish to display are too complex to be described by such a set of mathematical formulas. In such cases, it is common to use only a limited number of key points on their surface and then to generate surface points between these by interpolating or approximating with surfaces of appropriate properties. This method is intermediate between the simply described shapes and the worst case of many, many number triples.

Consider a classic example. If we want to represent a graceful teapot, there are no simple ideal shapes whose formulas describe the whole teapot. If we use solid modeling, we will have to build up the teapot from many different ideal shapes (cylinders, cones, spheres, toruses, etc.). Since the number of components is very large, there is no advantage to this approach. Nor is it feasible to describe the teapot by listing, say, 1000 or more number triples on its surface. The solution is to define only a few points on the surface of the object and to specify the type of surface that will correctly interpolate these points. Bicubic patches work well in this example. We get as many points as we need on the surface of the teapot by generating points on these interpolating surfaces. We discussed some ways to generate such surfaces in Chapter 8.

Another way to construct shapes is interactively. This is common for a shape that is not a literal copy of some real world object. Here we first specify a limited number of points which approximately outline the desired shape. Surfaces that interpolate or approximate to these points are then automatically computed and displayed by the graphics system. If we are not satisfied with the resulting appearance, we can change the position of some points, add points or take some away, or impose restrictions on the interpolating surface. We continue this until we obtain the desired shape.

We call it a *synthetically constructed shape* when we fit a surface to a limited number of surface points. While the resulting picture may have properties quite different from the real world object, this method makes the representation feasible. Such synthesis of shape representation is often encountered in computer-aided design.

Before we discuss the removal of hidden lines and faces, we need to describe how a 3-D object can be represented within the computer. There are two commonly used methods to describe 3-D shapes: by polygon meshes and by parametric bicubic patches. We covered bicubic patches in Chapter 8. Polygon meshes will be introduced here; not much preparation is needed.

# 11.1 POLYGON MESHES

A *polygon mesh* is one way to describe almost all three-dimensional real world objects, but this method is better adapted and easier for objects that contain many planar surfaces and straight edges. Buildings fall in this category, as do cubes or boxes. However, the polygon mesh method is not limited to objects whose surfaces are planes. An object with smooth curved surfaces can be described in this way, at least roughly. The rough polygon mesh can later be smoothed by approximating surfaces in the graphics system. Alternatively, it can be rendered in such a way that it looks smoothly curved although it is actually only a grouping of polygons. (We will discuss this in Chapter 14 when we talk about shading.) For all these reasons polygon meshes play a most important role in the representation of three-dimensional shapes.

A polygon mesh is not simply an unrelated set of polygons. The polygons that constitute a mesh have the property of *adjacency*. A polygon mesh must reflect this property as well as record the sequence of vertices or edges that compose the individual polygons (we discussed this in Chapter 2). There are several ways to represent a polygon mesh;

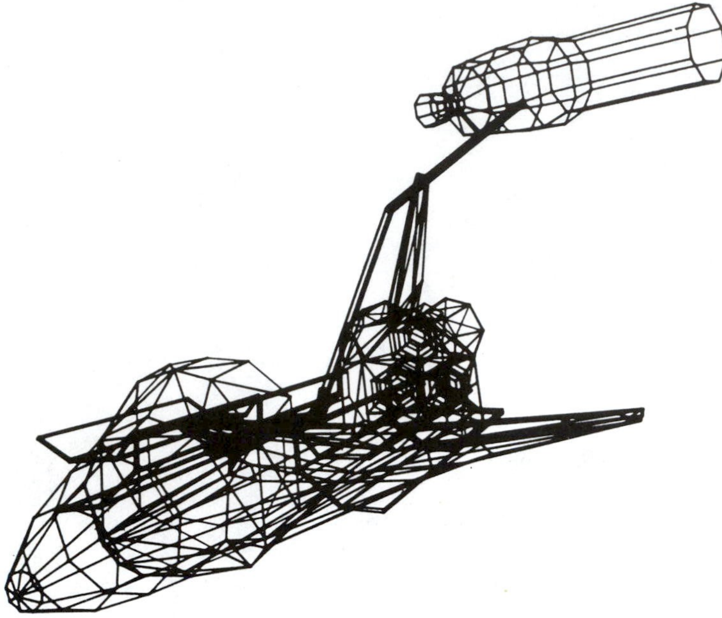

**FIGURE 11.2** Simple example of a three-dimensional wireframe object represented by polygons. (Courtesy of Evans and Sutherland.)

each has its advantages and disadvantages. We will consider two different representations. Figure 11.2 shows an example of a mesh:

A polygon mesh should permit us to do the following:

- Identify a specific polygon in the mesh.
- Identify all the edges belonging to a polygon.
- Identify those polygons that share a given edge.
- Identify the vertices (end points) of any edge.
- Change the mesh.
- Display the mesh.

Any acceptable mesh representation must provide for the above. However, the quality of the representation is determined by the ease of obtaining that information. In addition, speed and storage are important. Two different sorts of polygon meshes will be described that differ in these aspects.

## 11.1.1 Explicit Polygons Mesh

In an *explicit polygons mesh,* each vertex is stored once as a number triple in a vertex table. We then define a polygon as a sequence of such vertices. This can be realized by defining the polygons as linked lists of pointers into the vertex list. Figure 11.3 illustrates this; the corresponding data structure is shown in Figure 11.4.

This representation of a mesh has the advantage of taking up the least amount of storage. Changing the mesh is also very easy and efficient. To change one vertex, we change only this number triple in the vertex list. Deletion and addition of polygons is also quite easy.

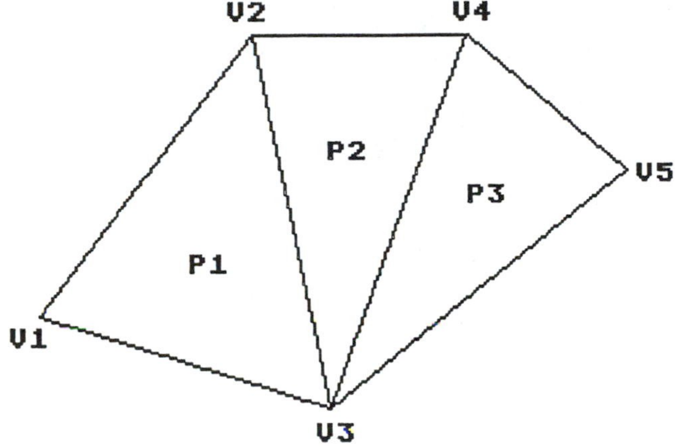


**FIGURE 11.3** Polygon mesh.

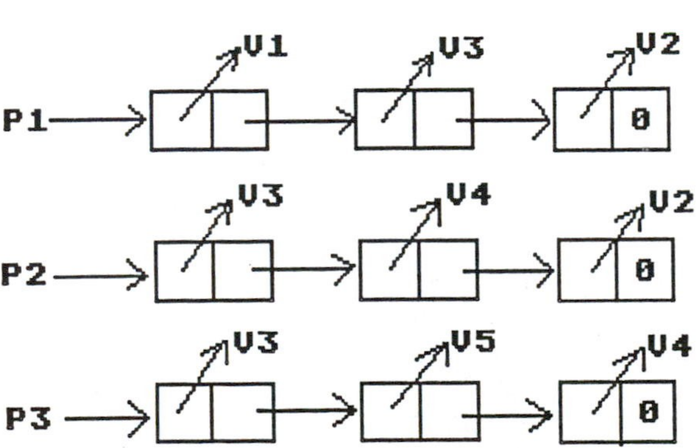


**FIGURE 11.4** Data structure.

| | X | Y | Z |
|---|---|---|---|
| V1 | 100 | 100 | 100 |
| V2 | 300 | 350 | 50 |
| V3 | 350 | 50 | 50 |
| V4 | 420 | 300 | 150 |
| V5 | 470 | 200 | 180 |

The problem with a vertex table, however, is that if the polygons sharing a specified edge are to be found, then all polygons must be checked to see whether or not they incorporate this edge. The same is true if all polygons sharing a given vertex are to be found. This is no real handicap for small meshes but becomes increasingly bad with larger ones. Furthermore, displaying the mesh requires traversing the entire list of polygons, connecting their vertices by straight lines. This displays the mesh correctly but draws every edge twice. Again, this isn't important for small meshes but, for large ones, the factor of two in speed of display can be important. This is particularly true in time critical applications, for example, in the real-time animated displays of flight simulation.

**An Implementation Example** A simple but very useful realization of this mesh structure is possible when all the polygons are triangles. When this is true, a record can be used to store information on the three vertices of each face. Instead of pointers, we can just store the subscripts from the vertex array in the record (in ccw order). More information can be included in the triangle record, depending on what is useful for the application. Examples are the coefficients of the triangle plane, the coefficients of the perspective-transformed triangle plane, color or illumination of the triangle, whether it is a backface or not, and so forth. A tradeoff is involved in deciding whether to recompute these structures when needed or to compute them in advance, which uses more memory.

Here are the type and data structure declarations for the triangle polygon mesh in Pascal:

```
constant num_vertex   =   {number of vertices};
         num_triang   =   {number of triangles};

type          point   =   record      x,y,z  :  real
                          end;

           triangle   =   record      a,b,c  :  integer;
         {plane coefficients}  pa,pb,pc,pd,
     {persp.-transf. coeff.} psa,psb,psc,psd  :  real;
                                      color  :  integer;
                                   backface  :  boolean
                          end;

var          vertex   =   array[1..num_vertex] of point;
             triang   =   array[1..num_triang] of triangle;
```

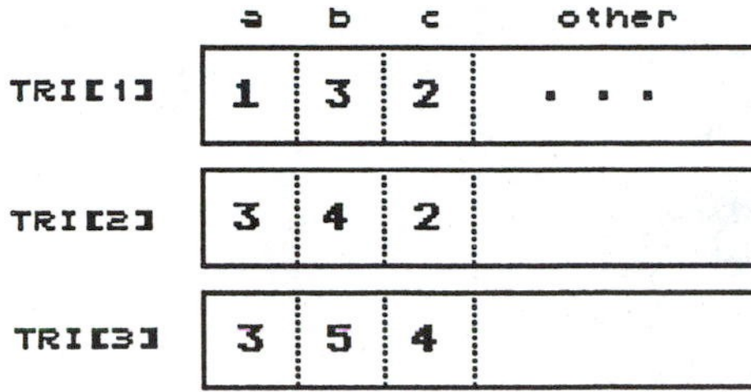


**FIGURE 11.5** Records can store the data when all polygons are triangles.

Figure 11.5 shows the array of triangle records representing the polygon mesh of Figure 11.3. A variation of this is to store the triangle data not as an array but as a linked list. It is then easy to group them into different categories and shuffle them back and forth just by changing pointers. An example of this will be presented with the Warnock algorithm in Chapter 12.

## 11.1.2 Explicit Edges Mesh

The *explicit edges mesh* is an alternate representation that overcomes practically all the disadvantages of an explicit polygons mesh. It consists of three structures and makes intensive use of pointers.

First, there is a table of all vertices in the mesh, just as in the explicit polygons mesh. Each vertex is stored once in this table as a number triple. A second structure is a linked list of all edges in the mesh. An edge is determined by the two vertices that it connects, so every record of the edge list has a pair of pointers into the vertex table. In addition, the edge record contains pointers into a polygon list (described below) and a counter. There is one pointer to each polygon that contains this edge; in normal cases, that is, solid objects without holes, enclosed all around by polygonal facets, there will be two such pointers to polygons. The example below is not such a closed solid object. The counter records the number of polygons that share this particular edge, so this counter equals the number of polygons pointed to in the edge description. (There are special applications where an edge is shared by more than two polygons. The edge description then must be altered somewhat.)

The third structure is a list of the polygons. This is a linked list of pointers into the edge list. These pointers access, in the proper order, all the edges of which the polygon is composed.

Figure 11.6 shows a polygon that we will use for an example of the explicit edges mesh.

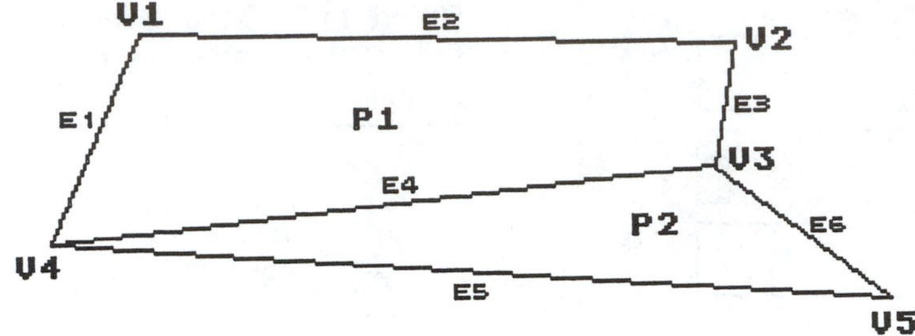


**FIGURE 11.6** Polygon for the explicit edges mesh example.

The vertex table for the polygon in Figure 11.6 is:

$$V1 = (x_1,y_1,z_1)$$
$$V2 = (x_2,y_2,z_2)$$
$$V3 = (x_3,y_3,z_3)$$
$$V4 = (x_4,y_4,z_4)$$
$$V5 = (x_5,y_5,z_5)$$

The list of edges is:

```
        ELIST = ptrE1
with
        E1 = (1,ptrV1,ptrV4,ptrP1,nil,ptrE2)
        E2 = (1,ptrV1,ptrV2,ptrP1,nil,ptrE3)
        E3 = (1,ptrV2,ptrV3,ptrP1,nil,ptrE4)
        E4 = (2,ptrV3,ptrV4,ptrP1,ptrP2,ptrE5)
        E5 = (1,ptrV4,ptrV5,ptrP2,nil,ptrE6)
        E6 = (1,ptrV3,ptrV5,ptrP2,nil,nil).
```

ELIST is a pointer to the first edge. The edges each consist of an integer counter (the number of polygons sharing this edge) and five pointers: two pointers to the vertices of this edge, two pointers to the adjacent polygons, and one pointer to the next edge. One of the two polygon pointers is nil if the edge belongs to only one polygon. The last edge ends with a nil pointer. This linkage makes it possible to traverse all edges simply from the first to the last. The list of polygons is:

```
        PLIST = (ptrP1,ptrP2,nil)
with
        P1 = (ptrE1,ptrE4,ptrE3,ptrE2,nil)
        P2 = (ptrE4,ptrE5,ptrE6,nil).
```

Here, PLIST is a list of pointers to the polygons. Because the number of polygons is variable, it ends with a nil pointer so the end of the list can be detected. Each polygon is itself a linked list of pointers to its edges; it ends with a nil pointer because the number of edges is also variable. In the description of the polygons, the edges are given in counterclockwise order. This order is essential in many applications of polygon meshes such as getting the orientation of a polygon in space for backface removal. In the edge definition, the order of the two vertices is unimportant. Figure 11.7 shows the structure for the example of Figure 11.6.

To display this mesh, we traverse the list of all edges; thus every edge is drawn only once. Polygons that share a given edge are all given in the edge description; the same is true for the two vertices of this edge. It is no problem to find all edges of a given polygon. Changing a vertex is also easy and has no side effects. Adding or deleting a vertex

**FIGURE 11.7** Linked list structure.

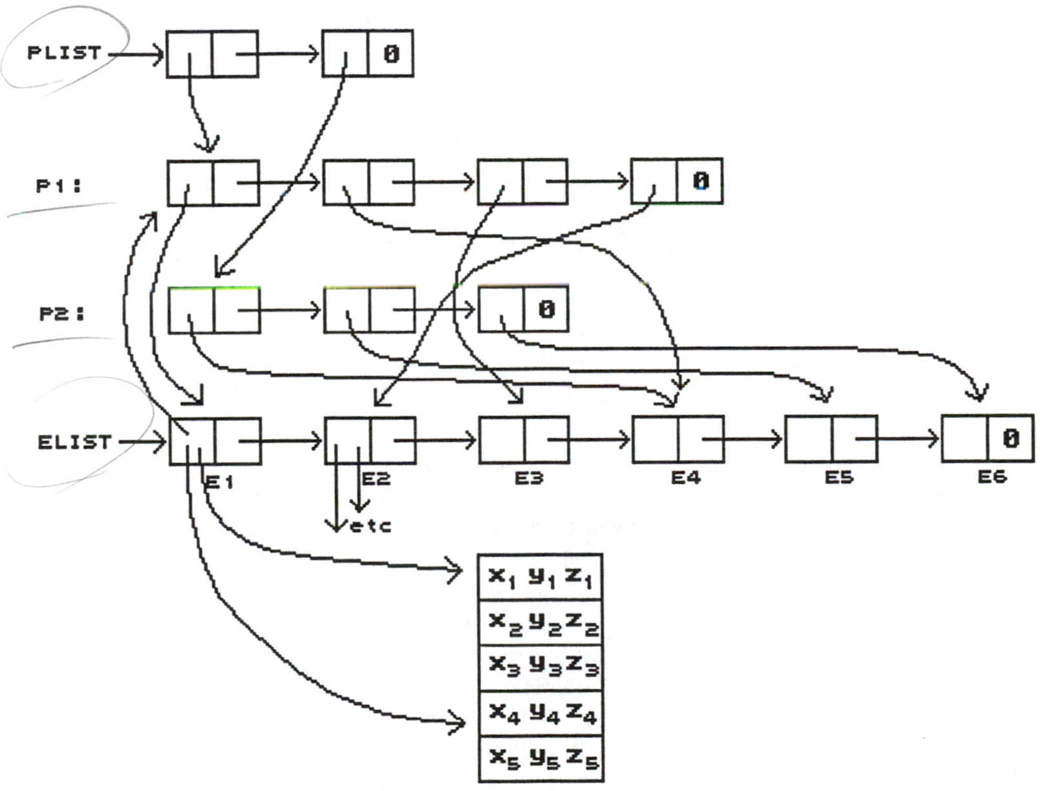

is more complicated because references to this vertex must be created or destroyed.

However, with this representation, it is not easy to find the edges incident to a given vertex; all edges of the mesh must be checked. It is possible to include more information in the mesh description to make such problems easier to solve, but the more cross-references and relations there are, the more complicated it is to generate and make changes.

Since this polygon mesh contains redundant information, it can be inconsistent. An incorrect entry may not only lead to a different mesh, but in general it will lead to a contradiction. For example, an explicit edge mesh could have an edge description that refers to a polygon as being adjacent to this edge while that polygon in reality is not. Many other inconsistencies are possible. There are algorithms that check polygon meshes to find inconsistencies. The correction of the inconsistency is quite a different problem; this cannot be done by a program.

For example, the integer counter in the above edge description serves only to check one aspect of consistency. A program could first set all counters to zero, then go through all polygon lists increasing the counter in an edge record whenever this edge is referred to. Then the program goes through all edge records checking whether the counter is equal to the number of references to polygons. If it is not equal, information is displayed telling which edge is inconsistent.

With this background on representation of shapes by polygon meshes, we can proceed to the topic of hidden surface removal.

# 11.2 BACKFACE REMOVAL

If a spatial object is composed of polygons, it is easy to identify those surfaces of the object that face away from the viewer. These surfaces are not seen and therefore will not be displayed. The technique to do this is called *backface removal.*

A short review of vectors is in order. (A fuller discussion is in the appendix.) A vector has direction in space and length; its starting point is not significant so two parallel vectors of equal length are identical. This means that we can move a vector freely as long as it stays parallel to itself. We use a number triple (x,y,z) to define the vector with its start point assumed at the origin. When the start point of the vector is the origin, its end point is the point (x,y,z). In this sense a point and a vector from the origin are identical. For mathematical formalism, it is not necessary to distinguish between these but the difference is important for clear understanding. In this book, we will use number triples to define both points and vectors and call the triple a point or a vector, whichever is appropriate.

If two vectors (A,B,C) and (x,y,z) are normal to each other in space, then their dot product is 0:

$$(A,B,C) \cdot \begin{bmatrix} x \\ y \\ z \end{bmatrix} = 0$$

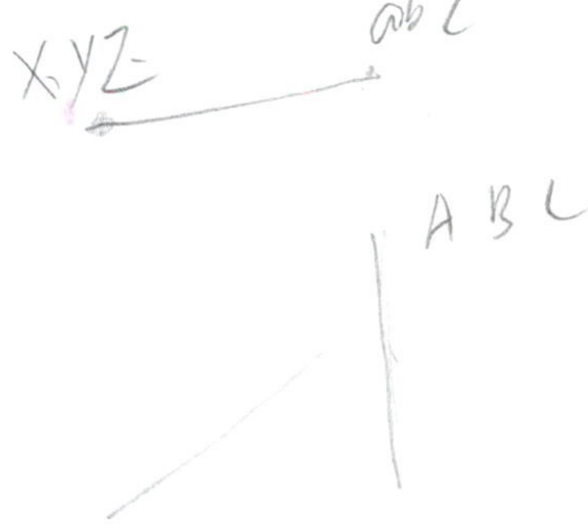

Therefore all vectors (points) (x,y,z) for which $Ax + By + Cz = 0$ lie on a plane that contains the origin; vector (A,B,C) is normal to that plane. We also say that the plane is normal to that vector. The plane has two sides. We will use the term *positive side* to designate the side that looks in the same direction as the normal vector points.

Let's go one step further. If (a,b,c) is another vector, then all points $(x-a, y-b, z-c)$ for which $A(x-a) + B(y-b) + C(z-c) = 0$ lie in another plane normal to (A,B,C). If $(x-a, y-b, z-c)$ lies in this plane, then (x,y,z) lies in a plane parallel to this one that is translated by the vector (a,b,c). Hence $A(x-a) + B(y-b) + C(z-c) = 0$ is the representation of a plane through point (a,b,c) and normal to vector (A,B,C). A shorter way to write this is $Ax + By + Cz - D = 0$ with $D = Aa + Bb + Cc$. Figure 11.8 illustrates this. The quadrilateral indicates the plane and the coordinate system is right-handed.

The vector (A,B,C) points in a certain direction. We can put its starting point into the plane by translating its starting point to the point (a,b,c), which certainly lies in the plane. The end of the vector is now the point $(A+a, B+b, C+c)$ (see Figure 11.9).

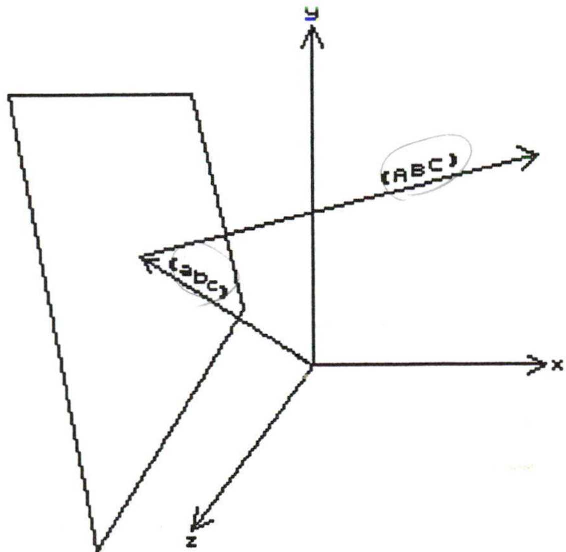


**FIGURE 11.8**

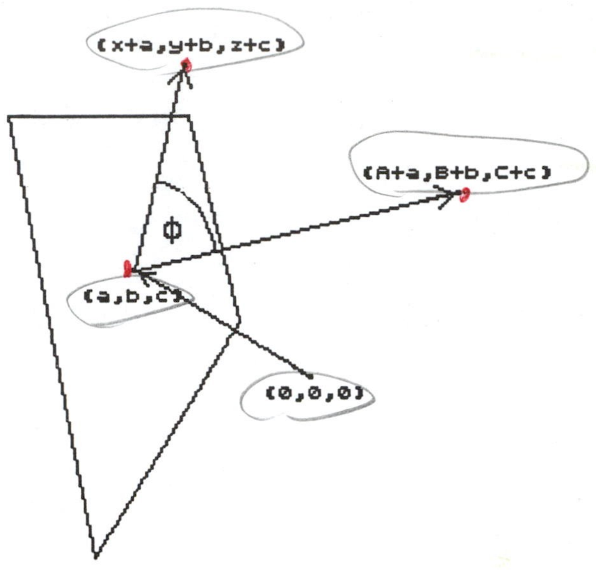


**FIGURE 11.9** The angle Φ is smaller than π/2.

If a point (x,y,z) lies on the same side of the plane (the positive side) as (A+a,B+b,C+c) then it can be expressed as (x+a,y+b,z+c) where (x,y,z) must be such that the angle Φ between the vectors (x,y,z) and (A,B,C) must be smaller than π/2. Therefore cos(Φ) > 0. It follows that:

$$(A,B,C)\cdot\begin{bmatrix}x\\y\\z\end{bmatrix} = |(A,B,C)|\cdot|(x,y,z)|\cdot\cos\Phi > 0.$$

Inserting (x+a,y+b,z+c) into the plane representation gives:

$$A(x+a)+B(y+b)+C(z+c)-D = (A,B,C)\cdot\begin{bmatrix}x\\y\\z\end{bmatrix} + D - D > 0$$

This tells us that the plane representation yields a positive result for every point on the side of the plane that looks in the direction that (A,B,C) points. Consequently it will yield a negative result for all points on the other side.

For example, suppose (A,B,C) = (5, −3,1). Let (a,b,c) = (0,2,4). Then the plane through (a,b,c) normal to (A,B,C) is:

$$Ax + By + Cz = D, \text{ with } D = (5)(0)+(-3)(2)+(1)(4) = -2.$$

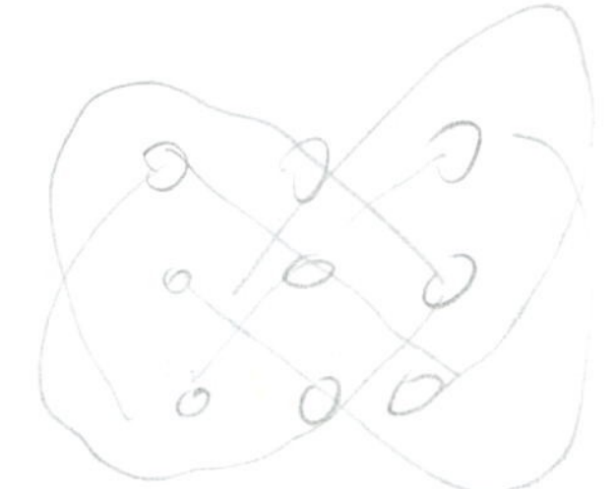

The equation of the plane is $5x - 3y + z + 2 = 0$. Is $(3,5,-6)$ on the positive side?

$$(5)(3) + (-3)(5) + (1)(-6) + 2 = 15 - 15 - 6 = -4, \text{ no.}$$

What about $(0,0,0)$?

$$(5)(0) + (-3)(0) + (1)(0) + 2 = 0 - 0 + 0 + 2 = 2, \text{ yes.}$$

What about $(A,B,C) + (a,b,c) = (5,-1,4)$?

$$(5)(5) + (-3)(-1) + (1)(4) + 2 = 34, \text{ of course.}$$

We often want the equation of a plane determined from three points in that plane. If $P_1$, $P_2$, and $P_3$ with the coordinates $(x_1,y_1,z_1)$, $(x_2,y_2,z_2)$, and $(x_3,y_3,z_3)$ are three noncollinear points, then the coefficients of the representation $Ax+By+Cz-D = 0$ for the plane through these points can be found by solving the linear system:

$$Ax_i + By_i + Cz_i - D = 0 \qquad \text{for } i = 1,2,3$$

for the unknowns A, B, C, and D. This linear system is always solvable.

These determinants give the solution:

$$A = \begin{vmatrix} 1 & y_1 & z_1 \\ 1 & y_2 & z_2 \\ 1 & y_3 & z_3 \end{vmatrix} \quad B = \begin{vmatrix} x_1 & 1 & z_1 \\ x_2 & 1 & z_2 \\ x_3 & 1 & z_3 \end{vmatrix} \quad C = \begin{vmatrix} x_1 & y_1 & 1 \\ x_2 & y_2 & 1 \\ x_3 & y_3 & 1 \end{vmatrix} \quad D = \begin{vmatrix} x_1 & y_1 & z_1 \\ x_2 & y_2 & z_2 \\ x_3 & y_3 & y_3 \end{vmatrix}$$

We can specify the three points as $P_1P_2P_3$, $P_2P_3P_1$, or $P_3P_1P_2$ (these are in the same cyclic order). However, if the cyclic order of the points is changed, the direction of the normal vector is reversed.

Assume that we specify three points in a counterclockwise sense while looking onto them from a point Z in space and that the equation of the plane through these three points is $Ax+By+Cz-D = 0$. It is a very useful property of this plane representation that it will produce a result greater than 0 for the point Z itself (in a right-handed system). This was verified in the above example. It follows that every point on the same side of the plane as Z will also yield a positive result while points on the other side of the plane will yield a negative one.

This now lets us determine whether a surface is visible from any given point in space. If a surface is defined by a polygon, this polygon lies in a plane (our polygons have to be planar). We find the representation of this plane by specifying three points in it, usually three vertices of the polygon, and we agree to the convention that the points will be specified in a counterclockwise sense as viewed from a point Z in space from which we consider the surface as visible. Then every point in space for which the plane representation yields a positive result lies on the same side of the plane as Z, so the surface is visible from such a point. If a point produces a negative result in the plane representation, then it lies on the other side of the plane and we consider the plane to be invisible from that point.

The visibility notion for a solid object is the following. We assume that a solid object is bounded by polygons. Each surface of the object has an inside and an outside. The inside is certainly invisible because it is always occluded by the mass of the object. (Outside surfaces can also be occluded but this is a different problem that we postpone.) If we determine the plane representations of all surfaces in such a way that outside points yield a positive result and inside points a negative one, we can determine the orientation of any point in space with respect to surfaces of the object.

Figure 11.10 shows a solid prism together with a point Z, first in side view and then in top view. The top view is more informative for our purpose. The three side surfaces are indicated by the letters α, β, γ, and the planes in which they lie are shown as straight lines. Z is "outside" in relation to plane α, "inside" in relation to β and "inside" in relation to γ ("inside" doesn't necessarily mean inside the object). Every point from which surface β is visible must lie on the side of plane β which is opposite to point Z. The same holds for γ. We see that inside or outside is information that only we can supply to the system because only we can see what the object is like.

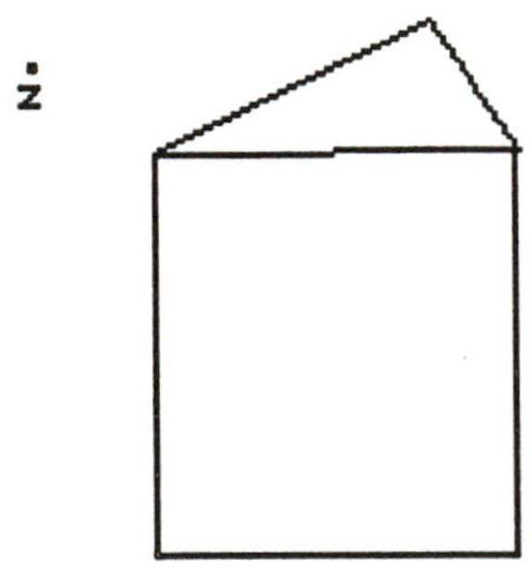

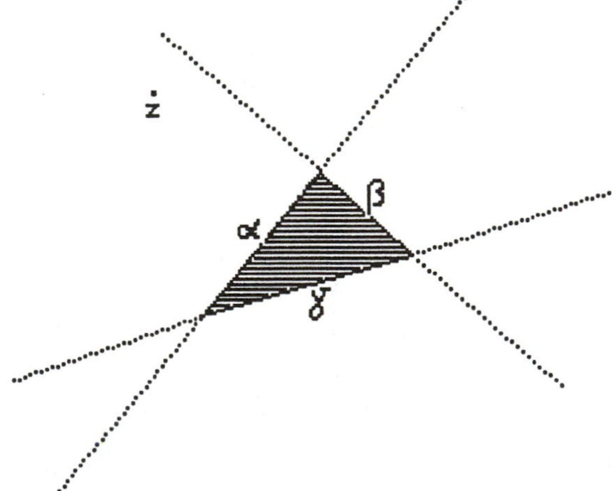


**FIGURE 11.10** Prism in side view and top view.

We supply this information when we specify the three points that define the plane that contains the surface in question. Surface $\gamma$, for example, is the one we see straight on in the side view. When specifying the plane for $\gamma$, we must specify the chosen three vertices of this rectangle in a ccw sense. The three points we specify for surface $\alpha$ also have to be in a ccw sense when we look at them from somewhere in the vicinity of Z.

Once we know the plane equations, we can readily find out whether a surface is visible from any given point. If Z were the position of the viewer, we would insert Z into the plane representations for $\alpha$, $\beta$, and $\gamma$, get the results $>0$, $<0$, and $<0$ respectively, and then display surface $\alpha$ only. The top and bottom surfaces of the prism are ignored in this example but they are handled in exactly the same way.

*Backface removal* can be performed if all polygons describing an object have been entered in such a way that the orientation of a plane can be retrieved unambiguously from the polygon information. Polygons are sometimes defined by their vertices, sometimes by their edges. In both cases we have to specify them in a ccw sense as viewed from outside the object. In some data structures the coefficients of the plane representation for each polygon are calculated once and stored. In others they are calculated upon demand. The calculation can be based on the first three vertices in the data structure that defines the polygon. (If the polygon is defined by edges, then the first two edges will point to the first three vertices.) When an object is transformed in space, the plane coefficients have to be either recalculated from the transformed vertices or transformed themselves. The second method is usually easier.

Going ccw around a convex polygon always produces a ccw order in the encountered vertices. But we have to be careful when concave polygons are involved. Figure 11.11 shows that the points $P_1$, $P_2$, $P_3$ are not oriented in a ccw sense in the left polygon even when traversing the polygon ccw. But it is always possible to renumber the vertices so that a ccw sense is achieved by the first three. This should be done when entering such polygons.

Checking for backface removal differs depending on whether the projection is perspective or orthographic. With perspective projection, the point to be checked against all plane representations is the center of projection; each plane representation must be evaluated with this point. If the result is $>0$ ($<0$) the surface is visible, otherwise it is invisible in a right (left)-handed system. In contrast, when backface removal is done with orthographic projection, the test is much simpler. The normal vector of a plane representation is (A,B,C). It points in opposite directions depending on rhs or lhs. In a rhs (lhs) a normal pointing toward (away from) the viewer indicates a front face. Therefore a positive $z$-coordinate indicates a visible face in both cases. No com-

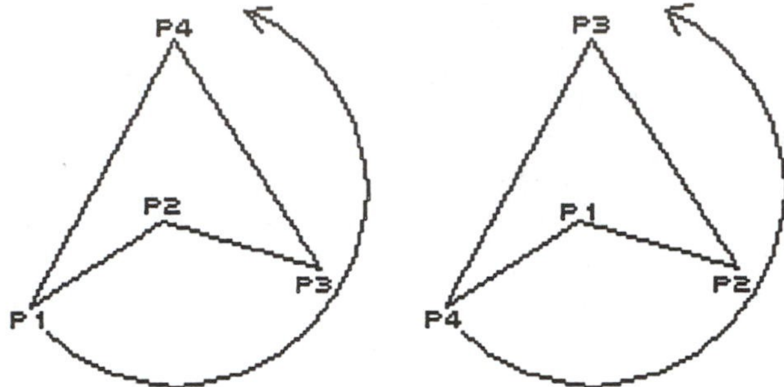


FIGURE 11.11

putation has to be performed; we only look at the sign of C. It is wise to consider a surface as a backface if the result is not 0 but still very small. This is because round-off error should be allowed for. That is, see if C > 0.0001.

Figure 11.12 shows an object for which backface removal is done, a right-handed system is assumed and the plane normals are shown. The results are different depending on the projection. With orthographic projection surfaces a, b, and c are visible, because their plane normals have a component toward the view plane. With perspective projection only surface b is visible.

**Displaying a Single Convex Object** The above methods can be used to remove hidden surfaces or hidden lines when a single convex object is displayed, no matter whether the object is to be displayed by solid filled areas or just by its edges (wireframe with hidden lines removed). On such objects no front faces can be hidden; they are all visible. Therefore backface removal is all that needs to be done. If hidden lines are to be removed, the technique is simple. The object is defined as a collection of polygons and backface removal is done. We then draw as if we were displaying polygonal surfaces, except we draw only their edges.

Figure 11.13 shows an octahedron with the vertices indicated by numbers. Edges drawn twice are shown as heavy lines, edges drawn once as normal lines and edges drawn zero times as dotted lines. From the standpoint of the viewer four surfaces are visible and four are not. This leads to the edges 21, 23, 25, and 26 being drawn twice. All other edges are drawn one or zero times.

Outlines of the object are drawn exactly once because they are the edges of only one visible polygon. If the plane of a polygon is precisely edge-on (with orthogonal projection, coefficient C of the plane representation equals 0; with perspective projection, plane representation yields 0 for the center), it is just a straight line and it is immaterial whether this line is drawn or not. There will always be another edge of a visible polygon that coincides with this line.

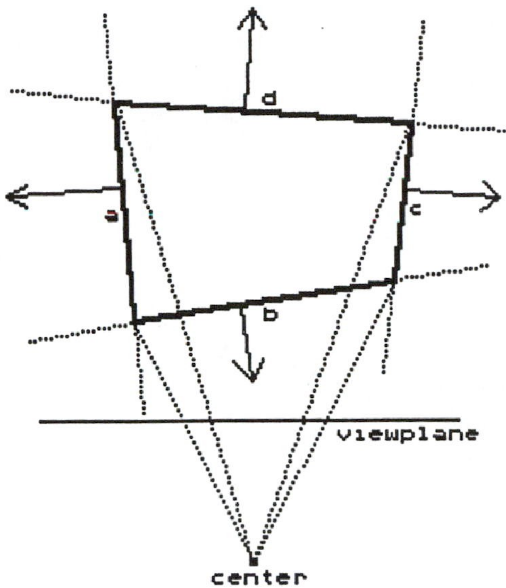


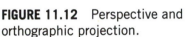

**FIGURE 11.12** Perspective and orthographic projection.

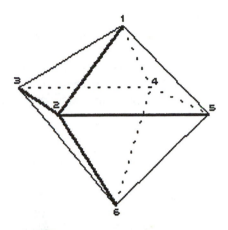

**FIGURE 11.13** Octahedron drawn by outlines.

**Concave Objects; Several Objects** If an object is concave, some front faces can be partly or totally hidden by other parts of the object. Similarly, if several objects are displayed, even if all are convex, one object can occlude parts of another. Backface removal does not solve the problem because it displays all front faces regardless of occlusion. Figure 11.14 shows a concave object in which face a, which would normally show, is partly hidden by other faces.

**FIGURE 11.14** Concave object.

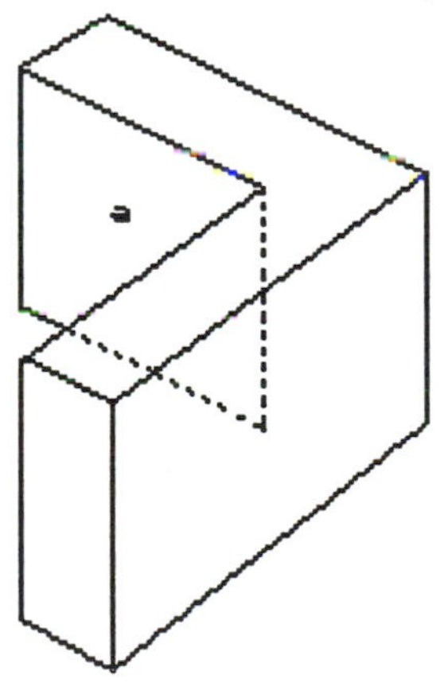


Even though it does not solve this type of problem, backface removal is useful as a preprocessor for general hidden surface or hidden line removal techniques, because it typically reduces by about 50 percent the number of the polygons to be considered by the more general and complex algorithms that we now consider.

# 11.3 DEPTH SORTING METHODS

The methods described in this section are more powerful than those described before because they are not restricted to single convex objects. We still deal only with scenes whose objects are all defined by planar polygonal surfaces, but there may be multiple objects that can be concave as well as convex. This handles the majority of cases. We impose two restrictions, however. The scenes cannot have surfaces that mutually penetrate or mutually occlude each other or themselves. Obviously, the polygons that make up the scene are stored in some data structure. Without excluding generality we make several assumptions:

a. The polygons are stored in one or more polygon meshes.
b. A view plane transformation is to be performed.
c. Perspective projection is to be performed.

To draw the scene with hidden surfaces or lines removed, we first do two things: (1) transform all the polygon vertices to the desired view plane; (2) do a perspective transformation on all polygon vertices. This puts the objects to be displayed into the desired position.

With the polygons in position, we do a backface test on each polygon in turn. If it is a backface we do not consider it further. If the polygon is not a backface, we store all its vertices in a small temporary array (because an array is easier to handle than the linked list structure).

Once the polygon's vertices are in the temporary array, we decompose it into triangles; whenever we split off a triangle from a polygon, we add its three vertices to another array, the triangle array. This will eventually contain the front faces of the whole scene in the form of triangles. (The *i*th triangle goes from position $3 \cdot i - 2$ to $3 \cdot i$ in this doubly subscripted array.) Figure 11.15 shows a polygon with four ver-

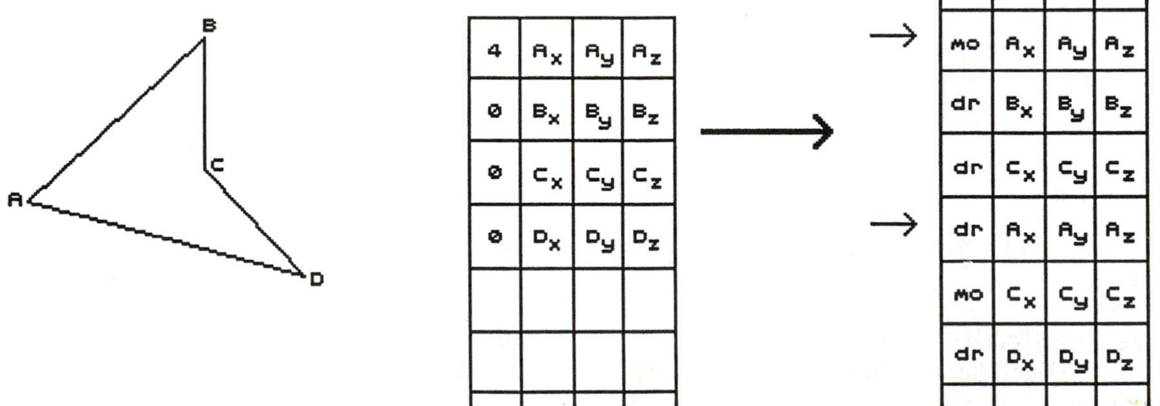


**FIGURE 11.15** Four-sided polygon, its data structure, and decomposition.

tices, its representation in the temporary array, and the two triangles in the triangle-array that result from its decomposition. The small arrows point to the start of these triangles. The entries mo and dr in the triangle array will be explained later.

The next step is to sort these nonbackface triangles into order based on their depth behind the view plane. After depth sorting, we can continue in two different ways. First, if we are to draw the scene as solid objects, we must remove occluded parts of the triangles. In this case we can draw all triangles starting with the farthest first; when we draw another triangle on top, it is automatically hidden. This method is called the *painter's algorithm.* Second, if the scene consists only of lines, then we must remove hidden lines. This is more complex because a line can be totally hidden by some triangle, cut so that only one portion remains, or cut so that two portions remain.

We will now explain algorithms for each of these steps in the order in which they are applied: decomposition into triangles, depth sorting, painter's algorithm, and hidden line removal.

## 11.3.1 Decomposition into Triangles

Deciding which of two polygons is farthest from us is easiest to accomplish if the two polygons are triangles, because triangles are the simplest form of polygons and are always convex. So we want to decompose all four or more sided polygons into triangles. This decomposition is easy if the polygon is convex. It is more complicated if the polygon is concave. We do not consider polygons that are self-intersecting because such polygons don't make sense as surfaces of solid objects.

The method we will use decomposes both concave and convex polygons. We begin with the leftmost vertex of the polygon, A, which is certainly a convex one (see Figure 11.16). It can be found by finding the smallest x-value of all polygon vertices. We take the vertices adjacent to it, B and C. A, B, and C form the leftmost triangle. A fourth vertex that does not belong to this triangle, p, is shown connected by a dotted line. This line is not necessarily an edge because p may not be adjacent to either B or C. The reason we look at p is to see if the polygon is concave; p can lie inside of ABC if it is.

If no other vertex p of the polygon lies inside our triangle, we can cut it off from the polygon. Figure 11.16 shows examples of the four basically different situations of p with respect to this triangle. We will use what is called a minimax test to eliminate some easy cases (like cases 1 and 2 in Figure 11.16). A *minimax test* consists of first finding the smallest rectangle containing the triangle and then checking to see if p is inside or outside this rectangle. Let $(x_1,y_1)$, $(x_2,y_2)$, and $(x_3,y_3)$

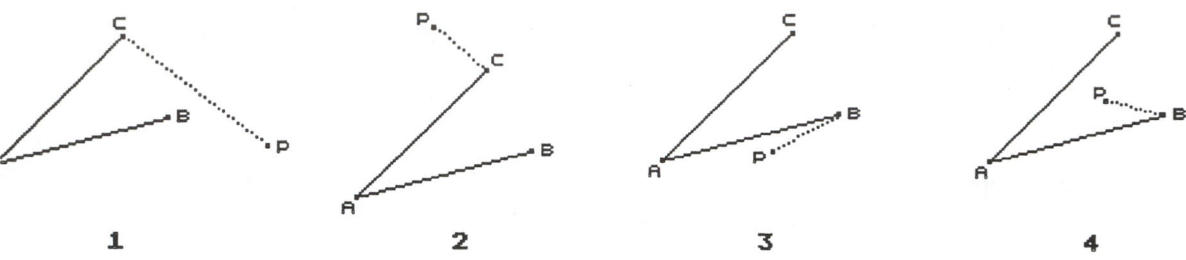


**FIGURE 11.16** Several cases of the leftmost triangle.

be the vertices of the triangle. The smallest containing rectangle is determined by its lower left corner:

$$\min(x_1,x_2,x_3),\ \min(y_1,y_2,y_3)$$

and its upper right corner:

$$\max(x_1,x_2,x_3),\ \max(y_1,y_2,y_3).$$

To check whether or not p lies inside the rectangle we make four tests (see Figure 11.17):

**FIGURE 11.17** Smallest containing rectangle.

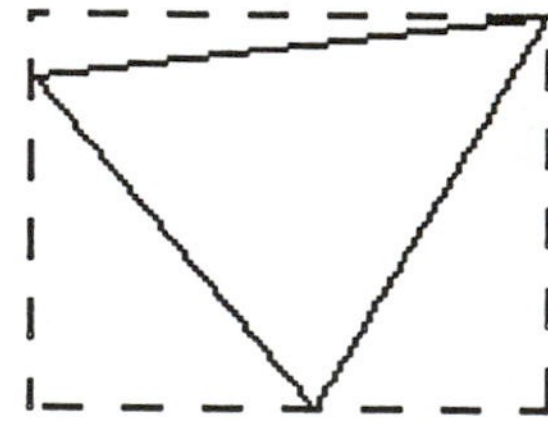

$$p_x < \min(x_1,x_2,x_3)$$
$$p_y < \min(y_1,y_2,y_3)$$
$$p_x > \max(x_1,x_2,x_3)$$
$$p_y > \max(y_1,y_2,y_3).$$

(Actually, these tests can be simplified because we know that triangle ABC is the leftmost one. All we need are three tests:

$p_x > \max(B_x,C_x)$ $\{p_y$ is insignificant$\}$
$p_y > \max(A_y,B_y,C_y)$ $\{p_x$ is insignificant$\}$
$p_y < \min(A_y,B_y,C_y)$ $\{p_x$ is insignificant$\}$

Refer to Figure 11.16. If any one of these conditions is true, then p is certainly outside the leftmost triangle's rectangle.)

The minimax test requires much less computation than the general triangle-inside test that is described below. We use it first in the hope of saving time. If it does not exclude all points p, we must go on.

**The Triangle-Inside Test** In cases 3 and 4 of Figure 11.16, the minimax test fails to eliminate p. To develop the *triangle-inside test,* we first look at a formula for a line through two points. The expression:

$$f(x,y) = (x-x_1)(y_2-y_1)-(x_2-x_1)(y-y_1)$$

determines a straight line through the points $(x_1,y_1)$ and $(x_2,y_2)$ in the following way:

$f(x,y) = 0$ for $(x,y)$ on the line
$f(x,y) < 0$ for $(x,y)$ on one side of the line
$f(x,y) > 0$ for $(x,y)$ on the other side of the line

Two arbitrary points lie on the same side of the line if the expression yields the same sign for both.

This can be used for the triangle-inside test. A point can be inside a triangle only if it lies on the same side as the vertex that is opposite the line. We must check against all three sides (see Figure 11.18). The point $p_1$ lies on the same side as A with respect to the side BC and the analog is true for the other two sides. The point $p_2$ does not lie on the same side as C with respect to the side AB, so it is outside the triangle.

The Pascal functions below implement the test and describe it formally.

```
type point = record x,y : real
             end;

function same_side(p1,p2,l1,l2 : point) : boolean;
{is true if p1 and p2 lie on the same side
  of the line through l1 and l2}
begin
  same_side :=
      ((p1.x-l1.x)*(l2.y-l1.y)-(l2.x-l1.x)*(p1.y-l1.y))
       *((p2.x-l1.x)*(l2.y-l1.y)-(l2.x-l1.x)*(p2.y-l1.y)) > 0
end {function same_side};

function inside(p,a,b,c : point) : boolean;
{is true if p lies inside the triangle a,b,c;
 false if p lies outside or on the boundary}
begin
  inside :=
      same_side(p,a,b,c)
        and same_side(p,b,a,c)
          and same_side(p,c,a,b)
end {function inside};
```

The tests must be performed for the leftmost triangle against every polygon vertex p that does not belong to this triangle and that has not

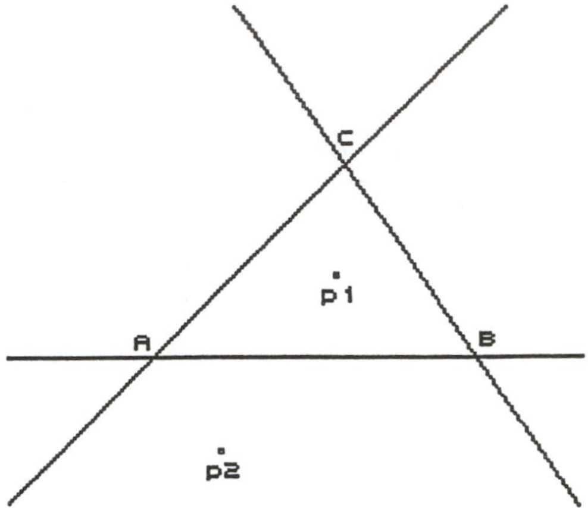


FIGURE 11.18 Points inside and outside a triangle.

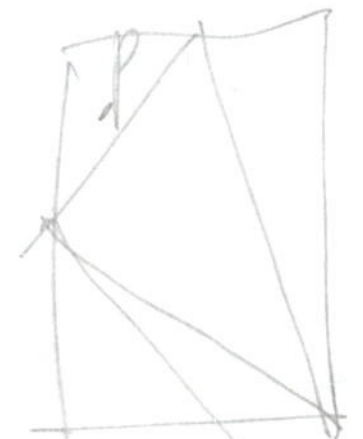

been eliminated by the minimax test. Of course, we could do only general triangle inside tests; the prior minimax test just saves time.

We show the original polygon in the temporary array and in the figures by its vertices A, B, C, D, and so on. (Keep in mind that a vertex still consists of x-, y-, and z-coordinates.) We precede each vertex by a draw (dr) command. The order of storage implies the (cyclic) order of drawing, so we draw from the first vertex to the second, from the second to the third, and so on until we draw from the last one to the first. In the triangle array, the command before a vertex means that a move (mo) or a draw (dr) has to be performed to this vertex.

Distinguishing between these two commands is not very important when solid bodies are displayed but it is essential when a hidden line algorithm is to be performed. We make this distinction now in anticipation of that operation. When a polygon is split apart, the line of the split will form a new edge with a move command to the start of both pieces. We will summarize the splitting operation with two examples.

The polygon in Figure 11.19 has five vertices. The names of the vertices do not imply their order—that is determined by the sequence of the vertices in the array. The leftmost vertex is A, its two neighbors are B and C. Let the array describing the polygon be:

drC drD drE drB drA

Note that a draw from A to C is implied.

There is no vertex inside ABC so this triangle can be split off. The split produces two new polygons from the old one. We create new sequences from the temporary array by removing some vertices and changing the dr command to a mo command for the first vertex (in

FIGURE 11.19 Cutting off a triangle; no vertex inside ABC.

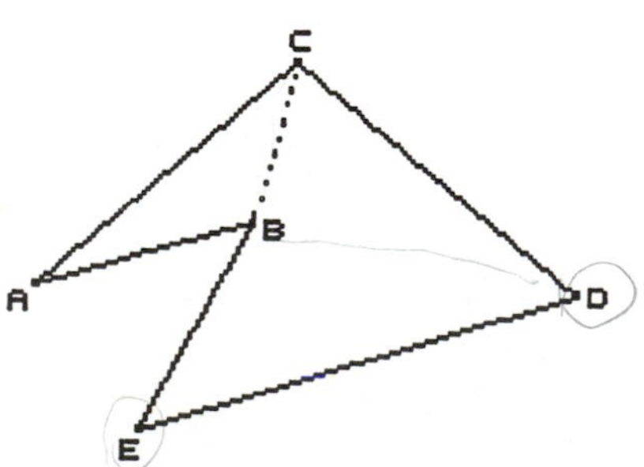

cyclic order) of those left behind. This first vertex is always known because vertices that are removed are always in cyclic sequence.

The first new polygon is the triangle. Its sequence is formed by removing everything in the polygon array except the leftmost vertex and its two neighbors (D and E are removed). The first element (vertex) in the set left after this removal is B so it is a mo. In effect, we fill the "hole" with a mo command. This sequence is added to the triangle array.

The second new polygon is formed by removing only the leftmost vertex (A is removed). The first vertex in the set after the removed A gets the mo command, so C gets a mo. If the second polygon is a triangle, it will also be added to the triangle array; otherwise it will be kept in the temporary array and splitting goes on. We illustrate with:

drC drD drE drB drA → drC moB drA and moC drD drE drB

If there are vertices inside the leftmost triangle ABC (for example, p and q in Figure 11.20) then we have to take the leftmost of those (p) and split the polygon into two smaller ones by connecting A and p. If either of these is a triangle, we add it to the triangle array (of course, neither may be a triangle). Figure 11.20 shows such a case. There are two vertices, p and q, inside ABC. The polygon can be split by connecting A with p but not by connecting A with q.

**FIGURE 11.20** Cutting off a triangle; two vertices inside ABC.

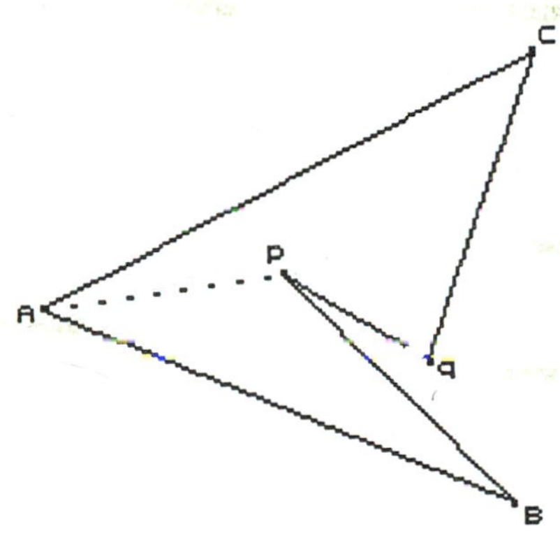


One of these polygons is obtained by removing all vertices between p and A in the cyclic ordering (this is just B); then A gets a move command. The other polygon is obtained by removing all vertices between A and p (C and q); p gets a move command. Here is the temporary array and the two results:

drC drq drp drB drA → drC drq drp moA and mop drB drA

If any of the two new polygons is a triangle (pBA is), it is added to the triangle array. If both parts have more than three vertices, we have to keep splitting them. To do this, we store one of them on a stack for later processing. Explicit stack management can be avoided by programming the splitting procedure recursively.

Eventually every polygon of the scene will be split into triangles, so the whole scene will consist only of triangles. These triangles are now *depth sorted,* a process also called *geometric sorting.*

## 11.3.2 Geometric Sorting

We can know which triangles in the scene can occlude other triangles if we put them in an *occlusion-compatible order.* This term means to arrange in a sequence such that one member can occlude (hide) the

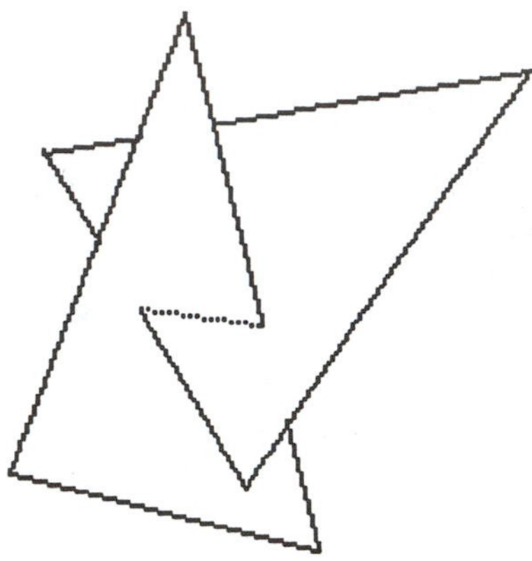

**FIGURE 11.21** Two triangles penetrating each other.

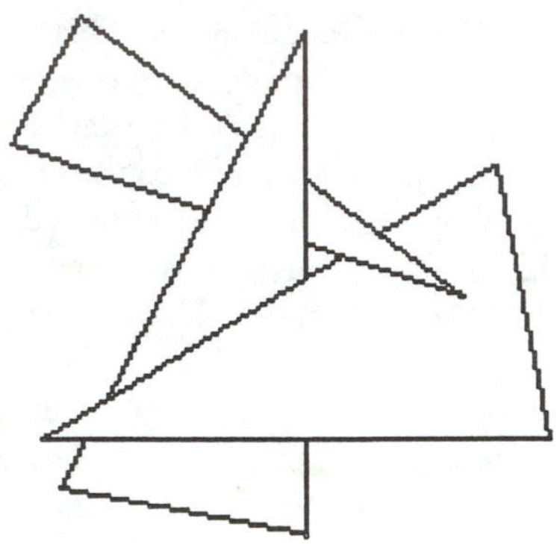

**FIGURE 11.22** Three cyclic overlapping triangles.

following members. Doing so is not a trivial matter. In the case of a mutual occlusion or penetration of triangles, as in Figures 11.21 and 11.22, such an order does not even exist. To handle such cases requires a further decomposition of the triangles into still smaller ones.

If we exclude these cases (which rarely occur in real world objects), the occlusion-compatible order can be derived by comparing the triangles pairwise. In this comparison we want to find a point in one triangle and a point in the other whose x- and y-coordinates are equal but whose z-coordinates differ. The depth order will then depend on the z-coordinates. (We must exclude mutual penetration, etc., to assure this.) Only when the two triangles overlap do we compare their z-coordinates, so we look at this topic now.

**Testing for Overlapping Triangles** In finding out whether the triangles overlap we use only the (x,y)-coordinates, so we work with the triangle's projections. The first test we perform is a minimax test for two triangles. This test can tell in some cases that two triangles do not overlap. For each triangle we compute the smallest containing rectangle and check these for overlapping. (The overlapping check for rectangles is so obvious that we will not explain it.) If the rectangles don't overlap, neither do the triangles. If they do, we need to examine them more closely (see Figure 11.23).

We apply increasingly more expensive tests to narrow down the cases that remain after minimax. To verify that two triangles $T_1$ and $T_2$ do overlap we check each edge of $T_1$ against each edge of $T_2$ for intersections. (Remember, we are working with projections now.) As soon

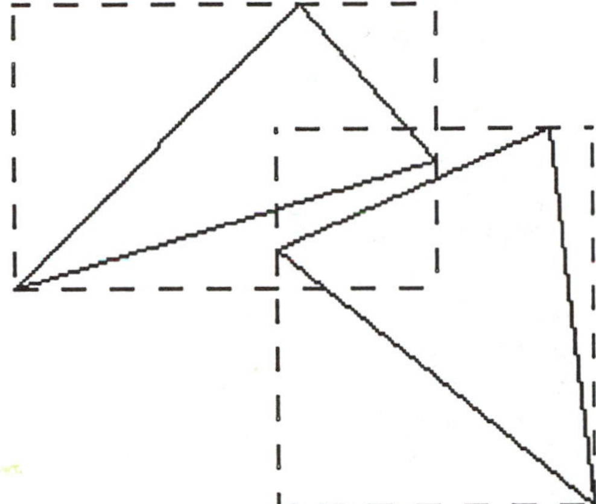

**FIGURE 11.23** The smallest containing rectangles overlap.

as we find an intersection, we can stop further testing; they overlap. We should keep in mind, however, that two triangles can overlap even if none of their edges intersect; this can occur in the case of total containment of one triangle in the other, which will be our last test.

If two lines are given by their end points, the first from $(x_1,y_1)$ to $(x_2,y_2)$ and the second from $(x_3,y_3)$ to $(x_4,y_4)$, they can be tested for intersection by first performing a minimax test:

$$\max(x_1,x_2) < \min(x_3,x_4)$$
$$\max(x_3,x_4) < \min(x_1,x_2)$$
$$\max(y_1,y_2) < \min(y_3,y_4)$$
$$\max(y_3,y_4) < \min(y_1,y_2)$$

If any of these conditions is true, the lines don't intersect. This minimax test is less expensive than the intersection test below.

If none of the above conditions is true, then we must continue as follows. First we check to see if the lines are parallel. This is true if they have the same slopes. If the slopes are equal, then $D = 0$ in:

$$D = (x_3 - x_4)(y_1 - y_2) - (x_1 - x_2)(y_3 - y_4).$$

So, if $D = 0$, there is no intersection. (It is best to check $|D| < \epsilon$ with $\epsilon$ depending on the machine arithmetic to allow for numerical precision.)

If $|D| > \epsilon$, we proceed with a second test. Compute:

$$s = [(x_3 - x_4)(y_1 - y_3) - (x_1 - x_3)(y_3 - y_4)]/D$$
$$t = [(x_1 - x_2)(y_1 - y_3) - (x_1 - x_3)(y_1 - y_2)]/D.$$

If $0 < (s,t) < 1$ then the lines have an intersection at point $(x,y)$ between their end points. The intersection point $(x,y)$ is given by:

$$x = x_1 + s(x_2 - x_1)$$

$$y = y_1 + s(y_2 - y_1).$$

(We don't usually need the coordinates of the intersection; it is enough to know that they do intersect.) This test does not consider one line just touching the other at its end point as an intersection. This means that a triangle touching another on its perimeter will not be treated as an overlap. (There is an unusual possibility because of this—see below.) We must test each edge of $T_1$ against each edge of $T_2$, a total of nine tests of pairs of edges.

If all nine tests of edge pairs of the two triangles don't show an intersection, then there are two possible cases: either one triangle is contained in the other or they don't overlap (see Figure 11.24).

After the above minimax and edge-intersection tests, our last test is for containment of one triangle within the other. Before we do a general triangle-inside test, we use minimax again with the center of one of the triangles against the containing rectangle of the other. Let $(x_1,y_1)$, $(x_2,y_2)$, and $(x_3,y_3)$ be the vertices of a triangle (ignoring the z-coordinates because we are working with projections). Its center is:

$$x_c = (x_1 + x_2 + x_3)/3 \qquad y_c = (y_1 + y_2 + y_3)/3.$$

The minimax test is straightforward. The general containment test is the triangle-inside test previously described. Based on these final tests, we have either "inside" or "outside" (see Figure 11.24).

The unusual possibility referred to above is when the two triangles overlap with two vertices of one just touching the sides of the other. We miss this case although it could be handled by one more test.

**Depth Comparison** As a result of all these tests, we now know, for each pair of triangles, if they overlap. If they don't, their relative

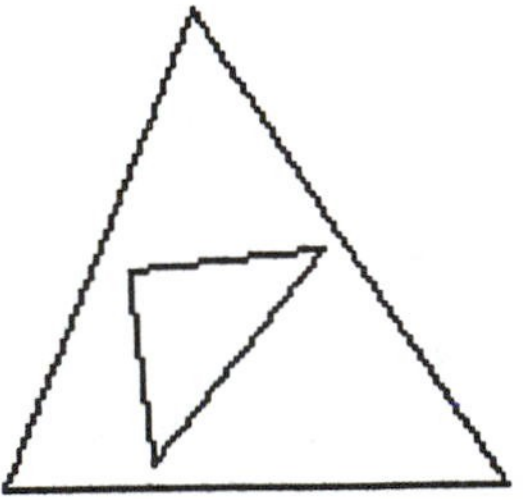

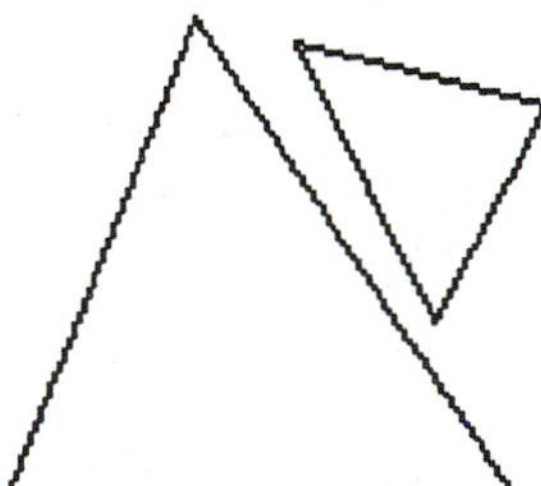

**FIGURE 11.24** No intersection between triangle edges.

depths are insignificant. If they do overlap, we have to decide which triangle is in front. Here again there are simple tests that give us results in many cases and more complicated tests that must be applied if the simpler ones fail.

A simple testing method is again the minimax test, this time applied to the z-coordinates. If all z-coordinates of one triangle are smaller than all z-coordinates of the other or vice versa, we know which triangle is in front and which in back. Figure 11.25 shows two triangles, A and B with overlapping projections, viewed from a point high up on the y-axis. The positive z-axis extends upward and the (x,y)-plane looks like a horizontal line. Keep in mind that the triangles shown in the figure are already perspective-transformed images so that an orthographic projection of them onto the (x,y)-plane is all that is left to do to get their projections onto the screen.

In Figure 11.25 the minimum z-coordinate of A is greater than the maximum z-coordinate of B. Triangle B therefore partly or totally occludes triangle A. This z-minimax test is easy to perform. For a pair of triangles A, B that overlap, we test:

min(z-coord of A) > max(z-coord of B) → A behind B
min(z-coord of B) > max(z-coord of A) → B behind A

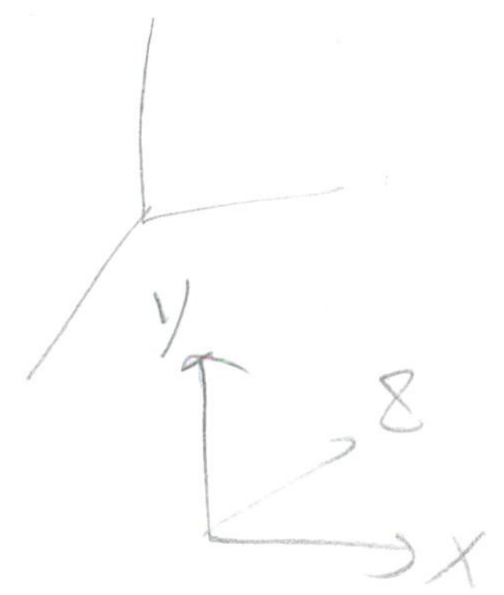

However, the depth question is not always so easily solved, A possible case is shown in Figure 11.26. None of the z-minimax conditions is true. In this case we must find a point within the projection of each triangle that has the same (x,y)-values and then compute the z-coordinates of the two points. The relation between these z-coordinates

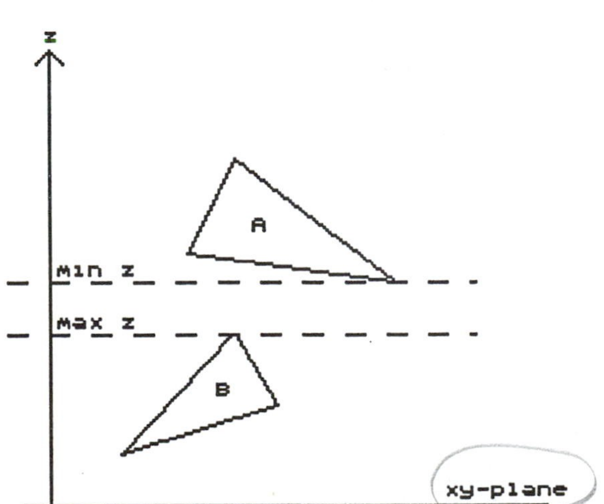


**FIGURE 11.25**

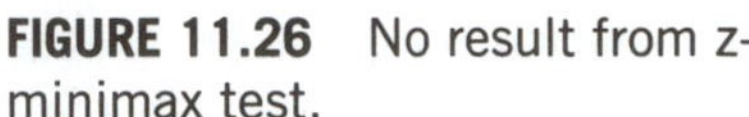

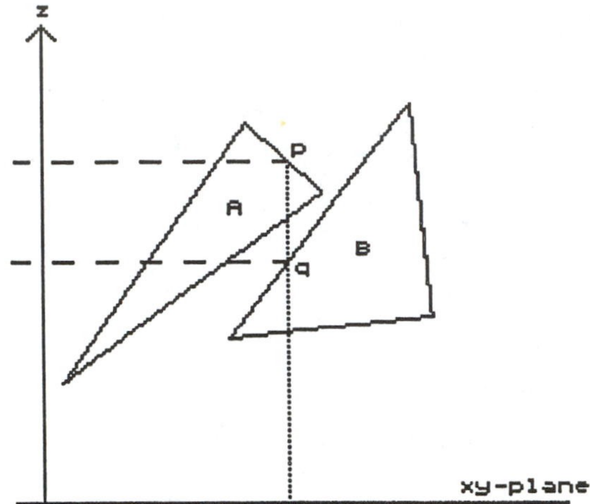


**FIGURE 11.26** No result from z-minimax test.

determines the depth relation between A and B. This depth relation may not apply between the entire triangles, but it is certainly true for their overlapping parts; that is all that concerns us.

The vertical line through q and p in Figure 11.26 indicates points with the relationship of concern. In this case they lie on the intersection of two triangle edges in the (x,y)-plane. The point on triangle A corresponding the these (x,y)-coordinates is p; the point on B is q. Since q has the smaller z-coordinate, we conclude that A is behind B.

If the z-minimax test is inconclusive, we proceed to find points with the same (x,y)-coordinates on each of the overlapping triangles. Since they overlap, there is always such a point and we already have information about it. Remember that we have already determined that either one projected edge intersects another or one triangle is totally contained in the other. (Minimax tests never prove overlapping, they just disprove it.) If we have done an edge intersection test, we know values of s and t at an intersection point; if we have done a containment test, we know a center point—each of these points lies in both of the participating triangles. When there is containment, we just check the two z-values at the center point. When we have edge intersections, we continue as follows.

When the intersection point is on an edge of triangles A and B, let $(P_1,P_2)$ and $(P_3,P_4)$ be the end points of the two edges for triangles A and B respectively. We compute, using the known values of s and t:

$$z_A = z_1 + s_1(z_2 - z_1) \text{ and } z_B = z_3 + t(z_4 - z_3).$$

$z_A$ and $z_B$ are the relative depths of the two triangles at the common point. If $z_A < z_B$ then A occludes B; if $z_A > z_B$ then B occludes A.

But what if $z_A = z_B$? Then we cannot yet decide and must do further testing. We look for additional edge intersections. It is not necessary that we find a second intersection on one of the current edges. It is enough to find just any other intersection of edges of these two triangles. Because the triangles are never coplanar (see below), we can always find a common point with differing z-coordinates.

The above equality $z_A = z_B$ must be interpreted with consideration for round-off errors. Exact equality will probably never occur, so we use the test $|z_A - z_B| < \epsilon$ with a small value for $\epsilon$ instead. If we do not do this, two triangles might touch or be very close to each other just at that one point in space but otherwise be far apart in depth. Numerical imprecision in the computer arithmetic can give us $z_A < z_B$ when it actually should be $z_A \geqslant z_B$. If we base the decision on the first, we occlude one triangle by the other in the wrong way. The value to choose for $\epsilon$ depends on the hardware.

We have said that two triangles are never exactly coplanar, but what if they test as coplanar for the given machine precision? In this case they would be almost coplanar in reality and the objects to which they belong must practically touch in space. Real world objects are solid, so the interiors of the objects are on opposite sides of the planes in question. Hence, one of the planes is a backface and has already been eliminated from consideration. In other words, this case can never occur!

To summarize, if the z-minimax test fails, we test triangle edges for intersections. If an intersection results in two numerically equal z-values, we look for a second intersection. If these z-values are more than $\epsilon$ unequal we decide, otherwise we look for a third intersection. There are two possibilities now. First, a third edge intersection exists. Here the z-values must be more than $\epsilon$ unequal, and we can decide. (We know from the above that the triangles aren't coplanar.)

Second, a third intersection does not exist. This is the case when just the tip of one triangle reaches into the other. In this case (see Figure 11.27),we have to find which vertex of one of the triangles lies inside the other. Sometimes there is only one, sometimes there are two solutions. So we do a point-triangle minimax test followed if necessary by a triangle-inside test for all combinations of vertices and triangles until this vertex is found. At that point, p, we compute the z-coordinate of the plane in which the other triangle lies. (Actually, there is a subcase for two edge intersections where we do not find a vertex inside the other triangle. This is when the vertex just touches a side of the other triangle. You will be asked to explore this situation in an exercise.)

**FIGURE 11.27** Only two edge intersections.

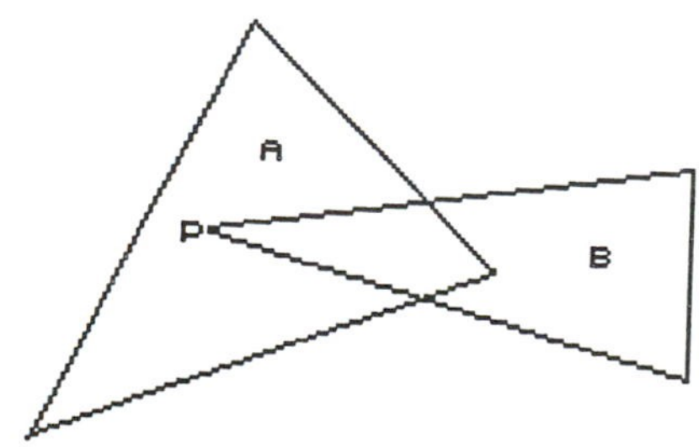


Let A be the triangle whose projection contains the point $p = (p_x, p_y)$ in Figure 11.27 and let $(x_1, y_1, z_1)$, $(x_2, y_2, z_2)$, and $(x_3, y_3, z_3)$ be its vertices. Let B be the other triangle. The depth of the point $(P_x, P_y)$ in the plane of triangle A is:

$$z_A = -a/c(p_x - x_1) - b/c(p_y - y_1) + z_1$$

with

$$a = (y_2 - y_3)(z_1 - z_3) - (z_2 - z_3)(y_1 - y_3)$$
$$b = (z_2 - z_3)(x_1 - x_3) - (x_2 - x_3)(z_1 - z_3)$$
$$c = (x_2 - x_3)(y_1 - y_3) - (y_2 - y_3)(x_1 - x_3).$$

The point $(p_x,p_y,p_z)$ lies in the plane of triangle B, so we have $z_B = p_z$. If $z_A < z_B$ then A occludes B, if $z_A > z_B$ then B occludes A.

**Establishing Depth Order** We are now able to determine for each pair of triangles whether they overlap and if so, which is nearer to us. To express this *depth order,* we create for each triangle a linked list containing pointers to those triangles that are in front of it. We also create a counter for each triangle that records how many triangles are behind it. We see an example in Figure 11.28 with the lists for the six triangles:

FIGURE 11.28

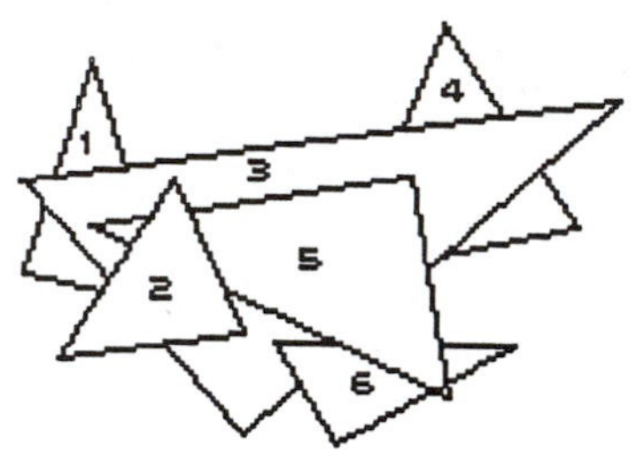


| triangle | counter | list |
|---|---|---|
| 1 | 0 | 3 5 2 |
| 2 | 3 | |
| 3 | 2 | 2 5 6 |
| 4 | 0 | 3 5 |
| 5 | 4 | 2 |
| 6 | 1 | 5 |

This ordering is easily established. Each combination of triangles is taken from the triangle array, checked for overlap, its depth order determined, and its list and counters updated accordingly. This is explained by the pseudocode:

```
for i := 1 to n-1 do
   for j := i+1 to n do begin
      if triangles i and j overlap
      then begin
         find their depth relation
         if j in front of i
         then begin
            add j to the list for i
            add 1 to counter[j]
         end
         else begin
            add i to the list for j
            add 1 to counter[i]
         end
      end {overlap case}
end {for j and i}
```

## 11.3.3 Hidden Surface Removal (Painter's Algorithm)

At this point we have removed backfaces, decomposed the remaining polygons into triangles, and sorted into depth order. We have set up the data structure just described and are ready to display the triangles as solid surfaces or as their boundary lines. For the former, we will use the *painter's algorithm*. Display of just the boundary lines requires hidden line removal, explained in the next section.

In comparison to the work already done, the painter's algorithm is no big deal. We go through the array and draw all those triangles that have a counter of 0. These are the ones with no other triangles under them. Whenever we draw such a triangle we step through the triangles in its list and decrease the counters of these triangles by 1. (The number of triangles to be drawn under them is reduced by the one we are to draw.) We mark the counter of the triangle drawn in order not to draw it again. Through this operation, new 0's will appear. We continue this process until no triangles are left.

The sequence in Figure 11.29 shows the progress of the painter's algorithm in single steps. The original data is that of Figure 11.28. Changes occur in the counters and the picture. The triangle lists are shown for reference; marked counters are expressed by an asterisk.

**FIGURE 11.29**

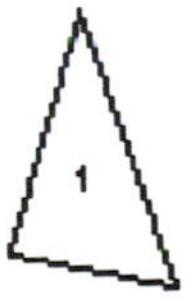

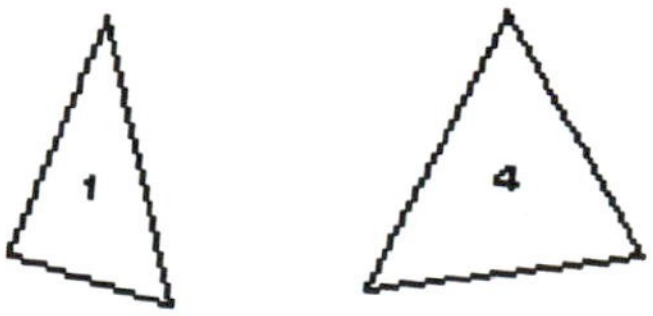

| *Triangle* | *List* | *Counters* | *Counters after* | *Picture* |
|---|---|---|---|---|
| 1 draw | 3 5 2 | 0 | * | |
| 2 | | 3 | 2 | |
| 3 | 2 5 6 | 2 | 1 | |
| 4 | 3 5 | 0 | 0 | |
| 5 | 2 | 4 | 3 | |
| 6 | 5 | 1 | 1 | |
| | | | | |
| 1 | 3 5 2 | * | * | |
| 2 | | 2 | 2 | |
| 3 | 2 5 6 | 1 | 0 | |
| 4 draw | 3 5 | 0 | * | |
| 5 | 2 | 3 | 2 | |
| 6 | 5 | 1 | 1 | |
| | | | | |
| 1 | 3 5 2 | * | * | |
| 2 | | 2 | 1 | |
| 3 draw | 2 5 6 | 0 | * | |
| 4 | 3 5 | * | * | |
| 5 | 2 | 2 | 1 | |
| 6 | 5 | 1 | 0 | |

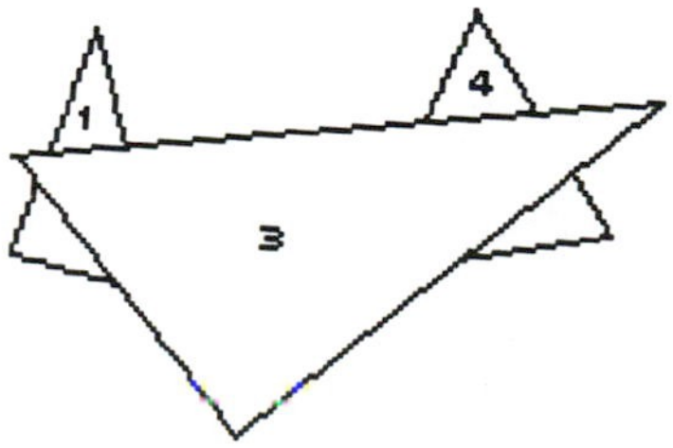

```
1          3 5 2      *           *
2                     1           1
3          2 5 6      *           *
4          3 5        *           *
5          2          1           0
6 draw     5          0           *
```

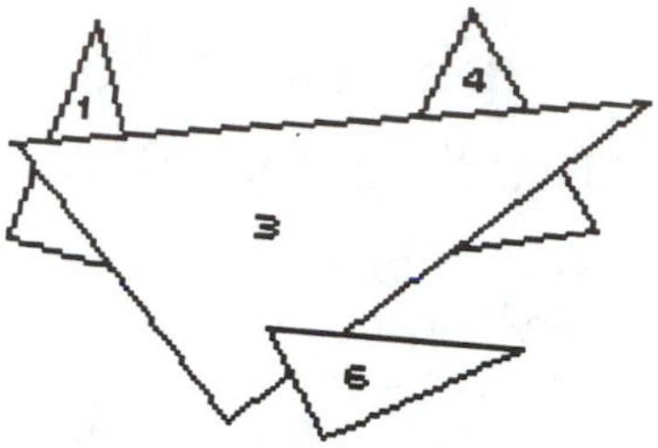

```
1          3 5 2      *           *
2                     1           0
3          2 5 6      *           *
4          3 5        *           *
5 draw     2          0           *
6          5          *           *
```

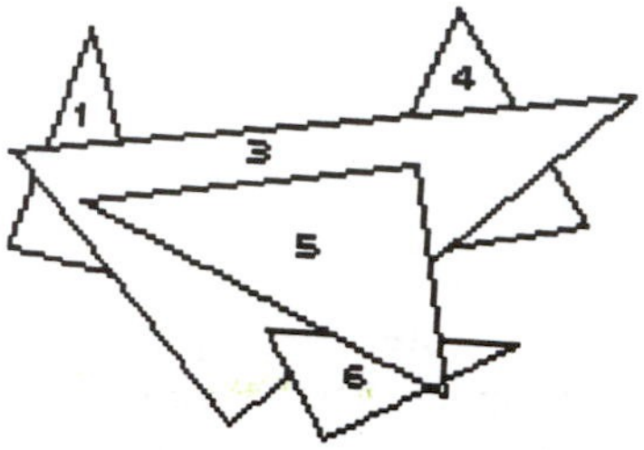

```
1          3 5 2      *           *
2 draw                0           *
3          2 5 6      *           *
4          3 5        *           *
5          2          *           *
6          5          *           *
```

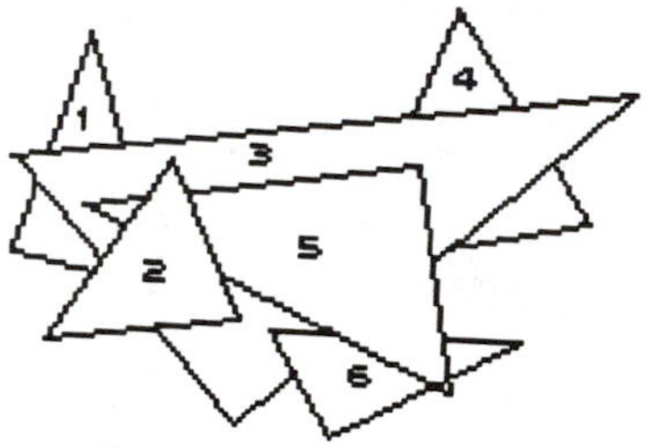

The painter's algorithm works only on raster devices and then only if solid objects are drawn by filling polygons. The essential principle that makes it work is that an area, once set to a certain color, can then be reset to a different color. (For monochrome, this is just white or black.) Every pixel's color can be repeatedly changed. What this means is that when a polygon is drawn, it superimposes itself onto whatever was there before.

**Fake Hidden Line Removal** On a raster device this algorithm can also be used to display a scene of solid objects by drawing only their edges. This is not a contradiction of what was said above. The scene still must be drawn by filling polygons. We first do a fill with the background color, then we draw its outline. The filling will erase all earlier lines that lie under the polygon. The result is as if only its edges were drawn. The sequence of filling first and drawing the outline second is very important in this operation to prevent the polygon-filling algorithm from erasing the outline of the polygon.

As we said above, a scene that consists not only of triangles but also of bigger polygons is still best represented internally by only triangles. The quadrilateral abcd in Figure 11.30 is represented as the two triangles abd and bcd. When we fill the two triangles with the same color they merge to the required shape. But when we draw outlines only we would display the dividing line as well. How can this be avoided? An easy solution is to add to each triangle vertex (internally it usually is a pointer) an operator M or D, meaning move or draw. This has to be done by hand when creating the structure. The two triangles are then DaDbMd and MbDcDd. Overlap tests, depth sorting, polygon filling, and other such procedures ignore these operators, but when we draw the outline we follow them.

**FIGURE 11.30**

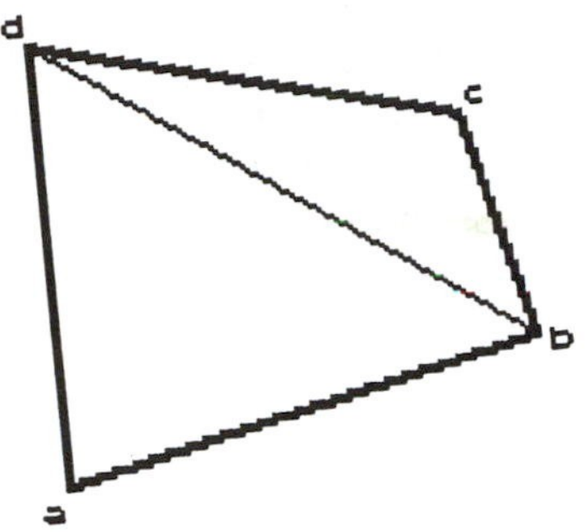


## 11.3.4 Hidden Line Removal

On vector scan CRTs it is not possible to erase a line by overdrawing it with the background color and on plotters no erase whatsoever is possible. For both devices, a line once drawn cannot be undone or removed by covering it, so the painter's algorithm cannot be used. Vector scan CRTs are still in use and plotters will remain popular for a long time. For these devices, we need a different solution to remove hidden lines and surfaces. Actually, removing hidden surfaces is not important because they are practically never used for displaying solidly filled objects (although one could do it on a line plotter). We now concentrate on how to remove hidden lines.

### VECTOR SCAN CRTs

This is a CRT tube just like the one explained in Chapter 2. It differs from the raster scan CRT in the way the electron beam is moved. Instead of moving in a fixed pattern across the screen, its movement depends on what is displayed. The display circuitry is designed to be able to move the beam in a straight line from any given point to any other given point on the screen. From this comes the term *random scan CRT*. Starting and ending positions of such a move are specified in Cartesian coordinates with repect to a fine but finite grid of addresses.

The beam's path is determined by a straight line generator in hardware that feeds the beam deflection yoke with voltages that change at a steady rate as the vector is being traced out. This makes the display circuitry more complicated than the raster scan circuitry. Consequently, the speed of the beam movement is much slower than in a raster scan, but it has the advantage over the raster scan that straight lines never exhibit staircaselike *jaggies*.

When a straight line is drawn, the beam is turned on at the start point and turned off at the end point. A picture is formed on the screen by drawing all the straight lines of which it consists. The entire picture has to be redrawn rapidly to keep it steady and to avoid flicker on the display.

Another difference from the raster scan is the way the displayed picture is stored in memory. There is no frame buffer. Instead, the picture must be described by a sequence of move and draw commands, called the *display file*. Figure 11.A shows a triangle on the vector scan display and the corresponding display file. To maintain a steady picture this file is executed by the display circuitry as if it were an infinite loop. Changing the display file changes the picture instantly.

**FIGURE 11.A**

```
start:
       draw a
       draw b
       draw c
       goto start
```

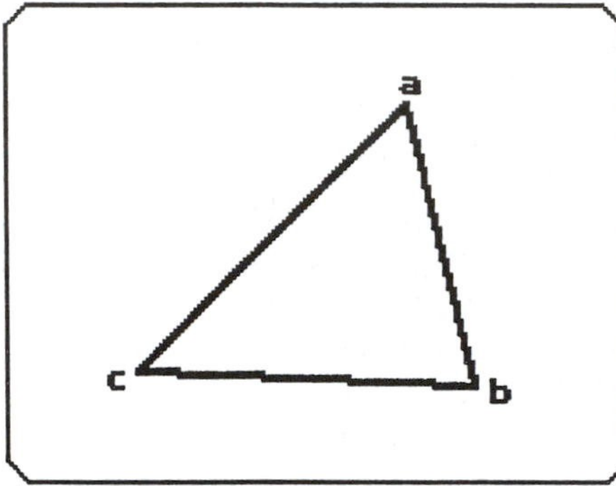


Simple pictures are refreshed faster than complex ones. To maintain a picture of 2000 lines at a refresh rate of 30 per second, the circuitry must be able to produce 60,000 lines per second. This adds the requirement of speed to the complexity. When displaying filled polygons, the number of lines to be drawn will soon exceed what can be done in the allowed time and the picture will start to flicker.

An example of a refresh vector CRT is the IBM 3251. The vector scan CRT does not allow the display of colors, except for the beam penetration tube which can produce only a very limited range and is complicated. The shadow mask technique, used to produce colors on raster scan CRTs (see Chapter 9), is not applicable to vector scan tubes. For these reasons this is a disappearing technology.

A variation of the vector scan CRT is the direct view storage tube developed by Tektronix (for example, the TEK4014). It differs from the above described technology in that it does not refresh the picture but has a fine storage grid behind the face plate that stores the traced-out picture in the form of electrostatic charges. Selective erase (erasing only one single element of the picture) is not possible. The whole picture has to be erased and redrawn minus that element. Neither can color be produced. This too is an outdated technology.

The preparation work for the painter's algorithm—decomposition into triangles and depth sorting—is a necessary requirement for hidden line removal. So we just have to add some further processing to suppress the drawing of the hidden parts of the polygon outlines.

We begin with the array of ordered triangles as in the painter's algorithm but, instead of drawing a filled polygon whenever a triangle is to be drawn, it will be "hidden-line-drawn" (we will use the abbreviation h-draw). Doing an h-draw is a lengthy process that requires considerable computation. Except for this change, everything else is identical. Whenever we find a triangle with counter 0 we h-draw it, step through its list of triangles in front, and decrease the counters of the triangles listed there by 1. We also mark the counter of this triangle in order not to h-draw it again. New 0's continue to appear as a result and we continue this process until no triangles are left.

Before we can explain the h-draw process, you must have a clear understanding of the relation between a straight line segment and a triangle. Figure 11.31 shows a line from point a to point b and a triangle. There are five possible ways in which the triangle can hide the line:

1. the line is not hidden
2. point a is hidden, point b is not
3. point b is hidden, point a is not
4. the whole line is hidden
5. a portion of the line is hidden, end points are not

To perform h-draw we need a routine that determines when a particular triangle hides a given line and computes the intersection point(s). For now, assume that we have this code so that you can get acquainted with the main idea of the algorithm.

When a triangle is to be h-drawn, we decompose it into its three sides and process each side individually. The list of triangles in front contains the triangles that can hide any of the three sides. We therefore give each of the three sides a list of triangles in front; these lists originally will be identical to the list for the triangle.

**FIGURE 11.31** Situations for a line and triangle.

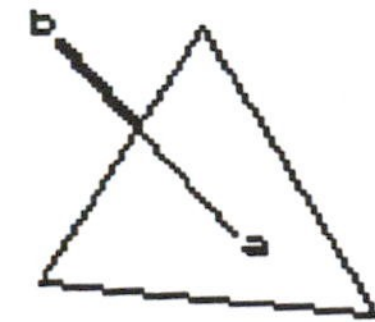

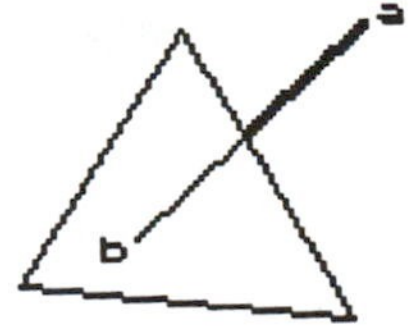

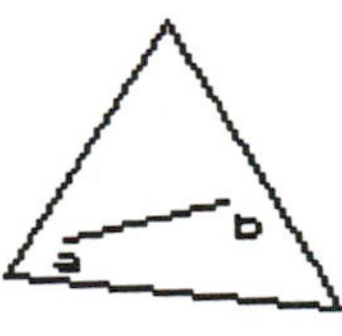

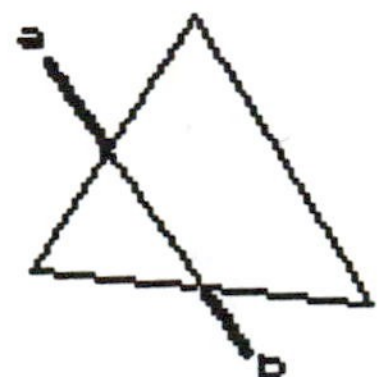

When we check a line against a triangle it is possible that we will end up with two line pieces (case 5). Each of these pieces must be checked against the remaining triangles in the list. Each check can increase the number of pieces by 1 and we have to remember them all. To do this, we use a stack on which we store all line segments that are to be checked. We initialize this stack with the three vertices of the triangle that is to be h-drawn. We also initialize a so-called "current point" with the third of the vertices (the start point of the first line segment). The line segment we are to check against the triangles in the list is one that starts at the current point and ends at the point stored on the top of the stack. Along with each point on the stack we store a move or draw command (initially all are dr) and the list of triangles that lie in front. We illustrate the stack for a triangle with vertices a,b,c and a list of triangles in front consisting of the triangles 1, 2, and 3 (the notation is as in the last section).

The stack is initialized as:

```
current point          command  point  list
     c            top:   dr       a    1 2 3
                         dr       b    1 2 3
                         dr       c    1 2 3
```

This situation means that the line from point c (current point) to point a (top of stack) is to be checked against the triangles 1, 2, and 3 before it can be drawn. (Actually, the stack will only have a pointer to the list of triangles in front but for demonstration purposes we show the whole list. The lists that are pointed to must be separate lists even though they are initially equal because the individual lists will be changed.)

We now give the h-draw algorithm in pseudocode. Some explanations are necessary: "push" means that something is put onto the top of the stack; "pop" means that the top of the stack is assigned to something and then removed from the stack; "command" and "list" always refer to the top of the stack.

H-draw first initializes the stack with the three edges of the triangle to be h-drawn. It then checks the command and the list; if the command is a move, nothing can be hidden because nothing is drawn, so the move can be performed. If the list is empty, there is no triangle in front of the line, so the command can be performed no matter what it is. Whenever a command is performed, the current point is changed to the one on the top of the stack and the top of the stack is removed.

If the command is a draw and the list is not empty, h-draw checks the line from the current point to the stack top against the first triangle in the list. It does this by calling a routine (which we will write later). Whatever the result of this check, no more checks against this triangle will be made, so this triangle is immediately removed from the list.

Now, depending on the five possible outcomes (see Figure 11.31) of the check, different actions take place.

In case 1 nothing is done. We have already removed the initial triangle from the list; the next check will be against another triangle.

In case 2 there is one intersection of the line with the triangle and the triangle hides the current point. We want a move to the intersection followed by a draw to the point currently on the top. The draw command is already on the top, so h-draw pushes a move to the intersection.

In case 3 there is one intersection and the current point is not hidden. We want to draw to the intersection and then move to the top (even though the top is hidden, we need it to process the next line segment). So h-draw changes the command to move. Ahead of this move there must be a draw to the intersection, so h-draw pushes a draw to the intersection. This draw can be hidden by the remaining triangles so it gets the same list as the former top.

In case 4 the whole line is hidden so h-draw changes the command to move in preparation for the next line check.

In case 5 there are two intersections. Instead of drawing to the top we can draw only to the intersection closer to the current point, followed by a move to the intersection farther from it, followed by a draw to the top. This last draw is already on the stack, so h-draw first pushes a move to the farther intersection and then a draw to the closer intersection. The draw still must be checked against the remaining triangles, so it gets the same list as the former top.

### Description in Pseudocode

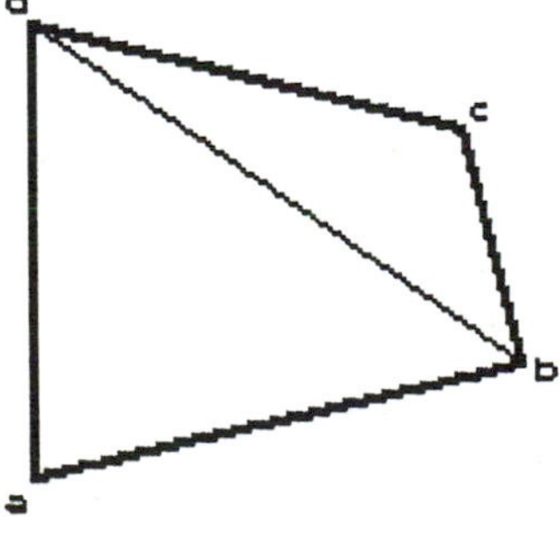


```
h-draw triangle a,b,c:
begin
   push c and list of the triangle;
   push b and list of the triangle;
   push a and list of the triangle;
   current-point := c;

   repeat
      if command = move or list empty
      then begin
         perform the command;
         current-point := pop the stack
      end {then}
      else begin
         check first triangle in list against
         line from current-point to top of stack;
         remove first triangle from list;

         case 1 {nothing hidden}
         no action;
```

```
        case 2 {startpoint hidden, endpoint not}
        push move and intersection;

        case 3 {endpoint hidden, startpoint not}
        change command to move;
        push draw and intersection and same list as top;

        case 4 {totally hidden}
        change command to move;

        case 5 {middle part hidden, endpoints not}
        push move and farther intersection;
        push draw and closer intersection
            and same list as top
      end {else}
    until stack empty
end {h-draw triangle a,b,c};
```

### THE PEN PLOTTER

There are basically two kinds of pen plotters. One is the *flatbed plotter*. In this plotter the paper lies on a flat surface. In some constructions it is held there by electrostatic force or by other means and does not move. The pen is held in a complicated mechanism that can move up-down and left-right. These plotters can deal with paper of small to medium size.

In another type of construction the paper does not remain at rest on the flatbed but can slide up and down (see Figure 11.B). This is achieved by two rollers that pinch the paper onto the flatbed and are rotated as necessary. The pen-holding mechanism moves only left and

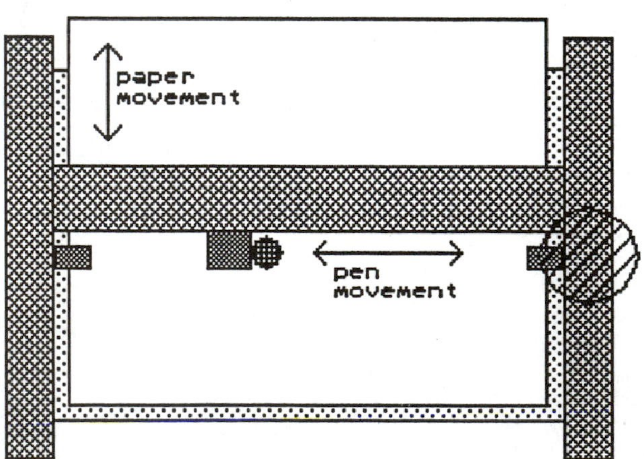


**FIGURE 11.B**

right. Each point on the paper can be reached through a combined movement of paper and pen holder. Such a mechanism is less complicated and more reliable than the first type. But these plotters can only handle papers of small size because a big sheet cannot be slid around on the flatbed very fast. The accuracy of flatbed plotters, especially the first kind, is very high. But in all constructions there is a limit to the usable paper size.

The second kind of plotter is the *drum plotter*. A long strip of paper, which can be in a roll, is fed over a drum. Turning the drum moves the paper forward or backward along its length. The pen in the holder is moved sideways across the width of the paper. Through combined movements each point on the paper can be reached, as in a flatbed plotter of the second type. The drum plotters can partly overcome the limits in paper size of the above two constructions. The drawing can be of any desired length, but the width is limited to the width of the drum. In big plotters the drum can be several feet wide. A disadvantage is that the accuracy is somewhat lower than in a flatbed plotter.

The plotters are usually equipped with a carousel containing pens of several different colors and thicknesses from which the holding mechanism can choose. The pens in the carousel can easily be exchanged by hand, so plotters have the ability to draw lines in a wide variety of colors and thicknesses. When moving to a certain point the pen is lifted, when drawing the pen is lowered.

What a pen plotter can do well and accurately is to draw straight lines—and that's it. Physically a pen plotter is a vector device as opposed to raster devices like dot matrix, ink jet, and laser printers. Curves are always approximated by short straight line segments. A plotter can fill areas with one solid color by drawing many parallel fill lines, but this is a time-consuming process. Plotters are usually equipped with software that lets them draw circles, ellipses, wedges, and rectangles and fill these either solidly or in various crosshatch patterns.

Plotters also have their own built in character generator which allows them to write text when sent the proper string in ASCII. Often the writing direction, size, and slant of the characters can be changed continuously to allow for all sorts of labeling.

The output quality of a pen plotter can be matched by a low-end laser printer with about 300 dots per inch resolution. If it were not for the ability to produce a wide variety of colors, small pen plotters would soon be replaced by laser printers. Big pen plotters have advantages over laser printers (manageable paper size) that will keep them around for a long time.

To clarify the h-draw process, we step through a specific case, shown in Figure 11.32. Triangle 1 is to be h-drawn; it has triangles 2 and 3 in front. In the descriptions, the current point (cur) is at the left, then the command, then the point, then the list. The analysis is shown. The first tableau is from initialization.

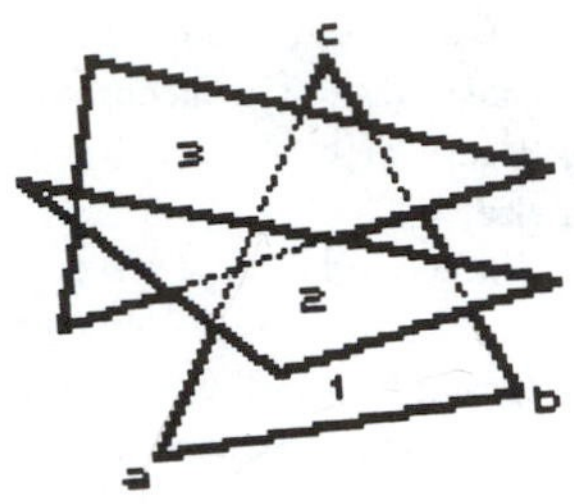


```
c dr a  2 3      command=dr, list not empty.
  dr b  2 3      check line ca against 2, remove 2.
  dr c  2 3      case 5, intersections d and e:
                 push mo e, push dr d and list.

c dr d  3        command=dr, list not empty.
  mo e           check line cd against 3, remove 3.
  dr a  3        case 3, intersection f:
  dr b  2 3      command := mo, push dr f and list.
  dr c  2 3
```

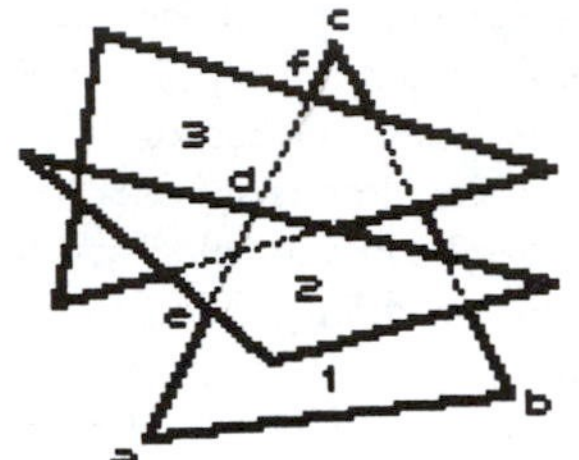


```
c dr f           list empty:
  mo d           perform draw f,
  mo e           cur := f, pop stack.
  dr a  3
  dr b  2 3
  dr c  2 3

f mo d           command=mo:
  mo e           perform move d,
  dr a  3        cur := d, pop stack.
  dr b  2 3
  dr c  2 3

d mo e           command=mo:
  dr a  3        perform move e,
  dr b  2 3      cur := e, pop stack.
  dr c  2 3

e dr a  3        command=dr, list not empty.
  dr b  2 3      check line ea against 3, remove 3.
  dr c  2 3      case 1: no action.

e dr a           list empty:
  dr b  2 3      perform draw a,
  dr c  2 3      cur := a, pop stack.

a dr b  2 3      command=dr, list not empty.
  dr c  2 3      check line ab against 2, remove 2.
                 case 1: no action.

a dr b  3        command=dr, list not empty.
  dr c  2 3      check line ab against 3, remove 3.
                 case 1: no action.
```

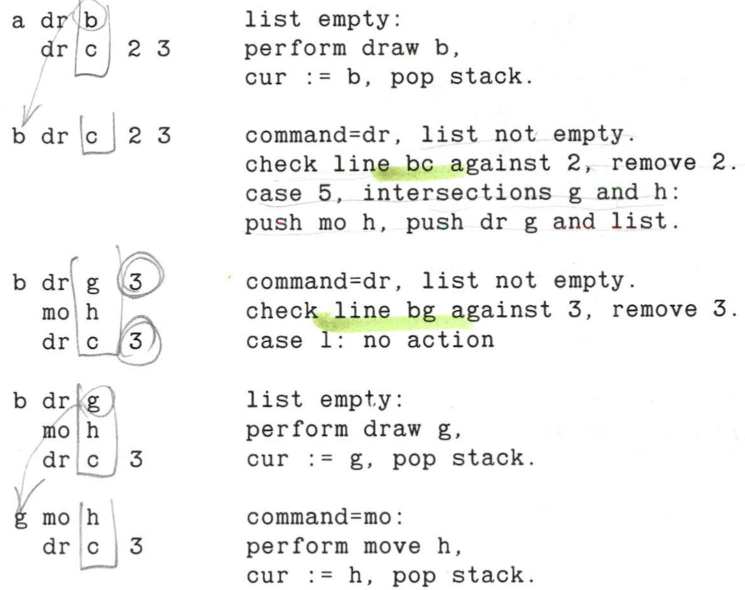

```
a dr b          list empty:
  dr c  2 3     perform draw b,
                cur := b, pop stack.

b dr c  2 3     command=dr, list not empty.
                check line bc against 2, remove 2.
                case 5, intersections g and h:
                push mo h, push dr g and list.

b dr g  3       command=dr, list not empty.
  mo h          check line bg against 3, remove 3.
  dr c  3       case 1: no action

b dr g          list empty:
  mo h          perform draw g,
  dr c  3       cur := g, pop stack.

g mo h          command=mo:
  dr c  3       perform move h,
                cur := h, pop stack.
```

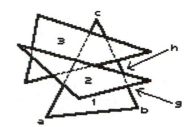

FIGURE 11.32

and so on.

We now outline a routine for finding which of the five cases applies, determining the intersections for cases 2, 3, and 5. When we decomposed polygons into triangles, we tested whether a point was within a triangle by doing a sequence of tests. First we did a point-triangle minimax test; if this test did not give the result "outside," we had to perform a true triangle-inside test. Here we do the same things. For the current point and the point on top of the stack we have to determine if they are inside or outside the triangle. We will not repeat this, but we will describe what must be done depending on the outcomes of these two tests. We also suggest a possible formulation of this routine.

The routine does not need arguments for the line and the triangle being tested because these are always the same. The coding must always test the line from the current point to the top of the stack against the first triangle in the list on the top of the stack. The routine will return three items: an integer for the case that applies and two floating point values for the intersections (if they exist). We have already seen the formulas for computing intersections.

When the two points are tested against the triangle, the following situations can arise. First, both points are inside the triangle. It follows that the whole line is inside the triangle and is totally hidden: return case 4, both intersection arguments are empty.

Second, one point is inside, the other outside: return case 2 or case 3 depending on which point is inside. Next test each triangle edge for an intersection with the line. For one of the edges an intersection will exist; this is returned in the first intersection argument.

Third, both end points are outside the triangle. To distinguish between cases 1 and 5, we test each triangle edge for an intersection with the line. If no intersections exist, the whole line is outside the triangle and not hidden: return case 1, both intersection arguments are empty. If intersections exist, there will be two of them and the line traverses the triangle: return case 5. Determine which of the two intersections is closer and which farther from the current point; return the closer one in the first argument and the farther one in the second. The closer intersection is easily determined. Let $(cur_x, cur_y)$ be the current point, $(a_x, a_y)$ and $(b_x, b_y)$ the two intersections. Then:

If $abs(cur_x - a_x) < abs(cur_x - b_x)$ or $abs(cur_y - a_y) < abs(cur_y - b_y)$,
then $(a_x, a_y)$ is closer, otherwise $(b_x, b_y)$.

This is all that is required to do hidden surface and hidden line removal. We stress that cyclic overlapping and penetrating polygons are not allowed. Such cases can be handled with depth sorting but the algorithms become conceptually much more complicated and computationally expensive. It is better to use the Z-buffer or subdivision methods (presented in Chapter 12), which can handle almost any imaginable case.

# EXERCISES FOR CHAPTER 11

1. Backface removal. Write a program that displays a cube stored in a polygon mesh and produces successive views of it with backfaces removed from positions that correspond to a viewer walking around the cube.
2. Practice polygon splitting using the polygon:

   drD drF drG drR drE drT drW drQ

   Assume that the leftmost vertex is Q and that it is connected to R. Derive the two resulting polygons from the algorithm without using any drawing.

3. Practice establishing depth order by setting up the lists and the counters manually for the triangles shown in Figure 11.33.

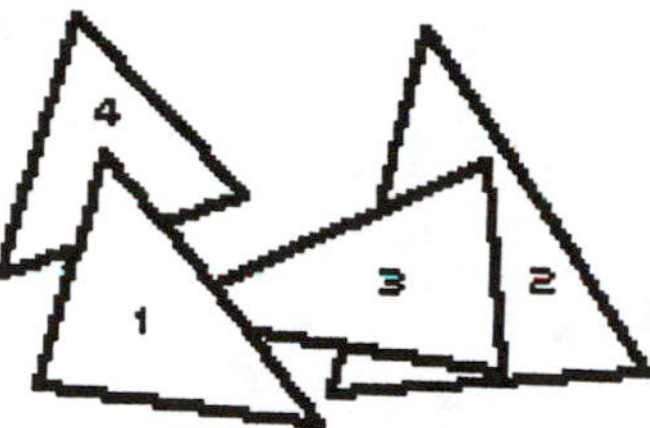


FIGURE 11.33

4. Practice the painter's algorithm as shown in the text using the lists and counters obtained in Exercise 3.
5. Practice the hidden line h-draw technique from the text using the triangles shown in Figure 11.34.

FIGURE 11.34

# Hidden Lines and Surfaces: Depth Buffer and Screen Subdivision Methods

# 12

Chapter 12 is the second of three that describe algorithms for hidden line or surface removal. This chapter covers two methods that are more general in scope and can handle cases beyond those of the last chapter.

**12.0 Introduction** tells how these methods differ from the previous ones and what limitations are imposed on them.

**12.1 Screen Subdivision Method (Warnock Algorithm)** is a "divide and conquer" technique that colors rectangular areas of the screen when it is determined that all of it should be painted identically. The method subdivides the screen systematically until this is true; at times this reduces the area to a single pixel.

**12.2 Depth Buffer Methods** are conceptually simple but computationally and/or memory-intensive methods that can handle all hidden surface problems no matter how complicated the scene.

# 12.0 INTRODUCTION

The previous chapter introduced the important topic of hidden surface removal but there are limitations to what the methods of that chapter can do. In this chapter we describe two general and powerful hidden surface methods, screen subdivision and depth buffer methods. These work only for raster displays and therefore cannot be used on vector scan devices such as pen plotters. Both take advantage of the fact that a picture can be decomposed into its atomic parts, the pixels. At that level the only graphics primitive the algorithms need is SetPix. We do not need to compute intersections of lines or polygons with other lines or polygons as in the depth sorting methods. Everything can be reduced to testing whether a given pixel is or is not within a certain polygon of the scene. If this is the case, the distance of this polygon point from the screen or from the center of projection must be determined—this is the only place where depth computation comes in. Finally, the single pixel is set with the proper color.

As we describe them, both methods require that the objects be bounded by planar polygons. (The depth-buffer method can be used to display all sorts of scenes, even with objects that are bounded by curved surfaces. In such cases it is added as a postprocess to the rendering method. See for example, the description of Catmull's rendering algorithm in Chapter 8.) We impose this restriction to stay within the intended scope of the book.

Displaying a scene by computing and displaying all its pixels is certain to work but is costly. To reduce the cost, the screen subdivision algorithm, described first, tries to avoid going that far in decomposing a picture. It does not use the line and polygon primitives, only pixel and rectangle. We have not discussed rectangles before but they are just a special case of the polygon.

The algorithm does not need to draw a general polygon but it must be able to determine whether a polygon of the scene overlaps with another rectangle or with a pixel. We must determine whether two line segments intersect but the intersection point itself is not needed. (There are versions of the algorithm that also determine and use the intersection points but they should not be classified as pure screen subdivision methods. Rather, they lie somewhere between our version and depth sorting methods. These other versions must be able to draw a filled polygon of arbitrary shape.)

The screen subdivision algorithm can be varied slightly to draw only the outlines of polygons. In this case it acts like a "fake" hidden line algorithm; that is, it still works, but only on raster displays.

Throughout this chapter, then, our spatial objects will be considered to have plane polygonal surfaces. Other than that there are no restrictions as to the complexity of the scene. Objects can penetrate or cyclicly overlap each other.

## 12.1 SCREEN SUBDIVISION METHOD (WARNOCK ALGORITHM)

The *screen subdivision method* was first presented by John Warnock (WARN68, WARN69) and is often called the *Warnock algorithm*. It can be used to display scenes in which the objects are bounded by plane polygonal surfaces. The scenes can be of any complexity. In this respect the algorithm is as powerful as the Z-buffer algorithm presented later, without needing a Z-buffer, but it is more complicated. The version of the painter's algorithm presented in Chapter 11 excluded objects that penetrate each other or overlap in a cyclic way. There are no such restrictions here.

The polygons that describe the surfaces of the objects can have any shape. However, we will consider only triangles. This is not a restriction as far as the complexity of the scene is concerned because, as you have seen, we can decompose any planar polygon into triangles. The reason for the limitation to triangles is only to systematize the data structure describing the objects. If, for some reason, we do not want to split polygons into triangles, it is possible to implement a more general rectangle-polygon overlap test within the Warnock algorithm. But this has nothing to do with the essential idea of the Warnock Algorithm.

One aspect of this method is somewhat related to the idea underlying the bufferless version of the Z-buffer algorithm, described in the next section. In that method, the decision of how to color a given area on the screen is made for the smallest possible area, a pixel. It is made individually for each area of one pixel size after computing the depth at the pixel center of all polygons that intersect this pixel.

In the Warnock algorithm, the decision of how to color a given area is not necessarily made at the pixel level. The algorithm tries to make the decision for as large an area as possible, in particular a rectangle containing many pixels. If it can determine that a whole rectangle is to be filled with one and the same color, this is done. This is less likely for bigger rectangles, more likely for smaller rectangles, and always possible for pixels.

The basic form of the algorithm draws rectangles filled with one solid color, but these can be as small as single pixels. It starts out with a rectangle equal to the whole screen and checks whether it should be filled. If the rectangle is empty or if its contents belong to only one polygon, it is filled solidly with the background color or the color for that polygon. If this is not the case, the rectangle is made smaller by subdividing it into four smaller rectangles and checks are performed on each of these. The process may continue until the test rectangle becomes as small as a single pixel. At that point, a simple decision about the display is always possible.

There are implementations of the algorithm that not only draw rectangles but also polygons of various shapes. They differ from the basic algorithm in that a rectangle might be filled when its contents belong only partly to a polygon. The rectangle is then filled partly with the background color and partly with the polygon clipped to this rectangle. The intent of this approach is to avoid subdivisions. But doing so is opposite to the main idea which is to avoid polygon clipping.

We describe the basic algorithm in detail. Later we outline a variation that contains polygon clipping and filling. This requires additional logic. The additional overhead pays off only for simple scenes; for more complicated scenes nothing is gained.

We first use pseudocode to describe the basic version without bothering to compute the intersections between rectangles and triangles. The pseudocode just finds out whether there is overlap or not. The polygons—in our case triangles—that are checked are the perspective projections of the polygons of the scene onto the screen.

For a given rectangle do:

If the rectangle is pixel size, check all triangles to see if they contain the pixel center.

If no triangle contains the pixel center, set this pixel to the background color.

If one or more triangles contain the pixel center, set the pixel to the color of the triangle closest to the screen at the pixel center.

If the rectangle is bigger than pixel size, check all triangles for overlap with the rectangle.

If no triangle of the scene overlaps, fill the rectangle with the background color.

If a triangle surrounds the rectangle and is closer in depth than all other surrounding or overlapping triangles, fill the rectangle with this triangle's color.

Otherwise subdivide the rectangle.

end.

We see that a simple depth test is made either when a rectangle becomes as small as a pixel or at the four corner points of a rectangle. We do not scan the whole screen pixelwise; whenever a rectangle is found to be of one color, then it is displayed without being further subdivided.

The algorithm needs analytic criteria to find whether a triangle overlaps with a given rectangle and, if so, whether or not the rectangle is totally contained in the triangle. To explain these we assume the following triangle and rectangle coordinates:

Triangle vertices: $P_1 = (x_1, y_1)$
$P_2 = (x_2, y_2)$
$P_3 = (x_3, y_3)$

Area boundaries: $x_l$ left boundary
$x_r$ right boundary
$y_b$ bottom boundary
$y_t$ top boundary

The minimax test can be used to determine whether a triangle is wholly outside one of the rectangle boundaries. We apply this test first because it is the least expensive. We compute:

$$xmin = \min(x_1, x_2, x_3)$$

$$xmax = \max(x_1, x_2, x_3)$$

$$ymin = \min(y_1, y_2, y_3)$$

$$ymax = \max(y_1, y_2, y_3)$$

If any of the conditions below is true, there is no overlap:

$$xmax < x_l$$

$$x_r < xmin$$

$$ymax < y_b$$

$$y_t < ymin$$

The above test will determine that a triangle like the one in Figure 12.1 is not overlapping. Triangles that are not removed by the above test can still be disjoint from the rectangle. We want to know this because if there is no overlap we can avoid further subdivision. So we have to do more testing.

The next test to apply is an edge-rectangle intersection test. This test can determine certain cases in which there is no overlap. A straight line through two triangle vertices $(x_1,y_1)$ and $(x_2,y_2)$ can be expressed as:

$$f(x,y) = (x-x_1)(y_2-y_1) - (y-y_1)(x_2-x_1)$$

We insert the four corners of the rectangle into f(x,y) and if $f(x_l,y_b)$, $f(x_l,y_t)$, $f(x_r,y_b)$, and $f(x_r,y_t)$ all have the same sign, then the edge from $(x_1,y_1)$ to $(x_2,y_2)$ does not intersect the rectangle. We have to do this test for all three edges of the triangle. If no triangle edge intersects the rectangle, then the triangle either does not overlap (see Figure 12.2), or it contains the whole rectangle (see Figure 12.3). We can distinguish between these two cases through a general triangle-inside test as described in Chapter 11. If the center of the rectangle is inside the triangle, the whole rectangle must be inside; otherwise it is outside.

If one of the edge-rectangle tests indicates an intersection, the triangle does not necessarily overlap. Figure 12.4 shows such a case. We need to perform more tests to find out whether there is overlap. These tests are more expensive. Possible cases are shown in Figure 12.5.

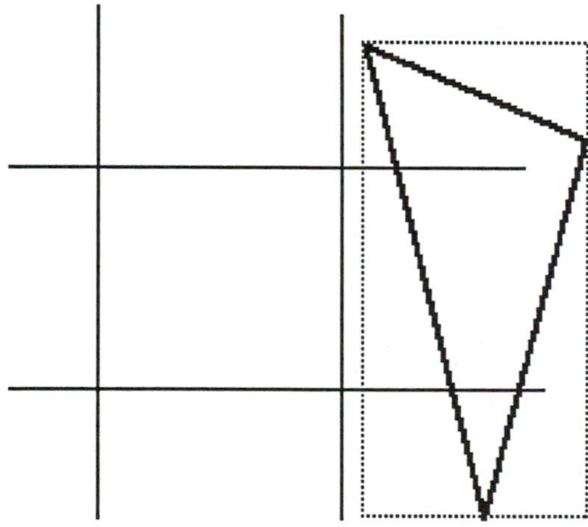

**FIGURE 12.1**

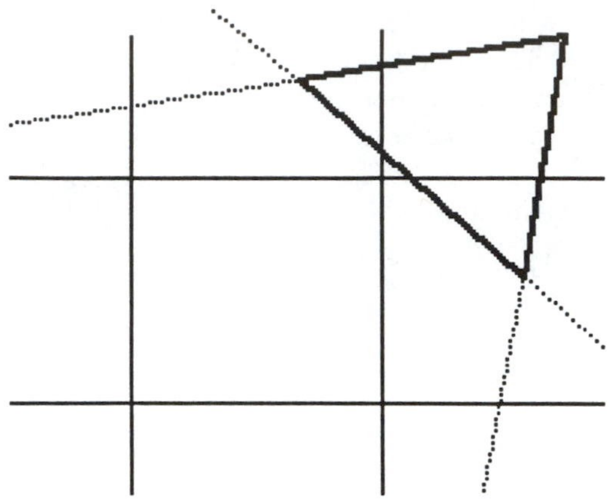

FIGURE 12.2

Cases a and b can be detected by seeing if the triangle vertices are inside the rectangle. If (x,y) is a triangle vertex, we perform the tests:

$$x_l < x$$
$$x < x_r$$
$$y_b < y$$
$$y < y_t$$

If all are true, then vertex (x,y) is inside the rectangle. We check all three vertices in this manner but we can stop as soon as we find a vertex inside. In this case there is overlap.

FIGURE 12.3

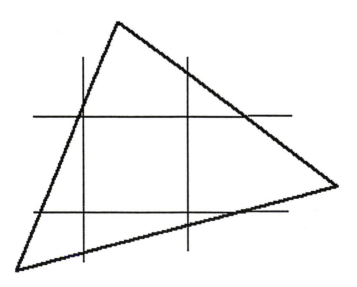

**FIGURE 12.4**

**FIGURE 12.5**

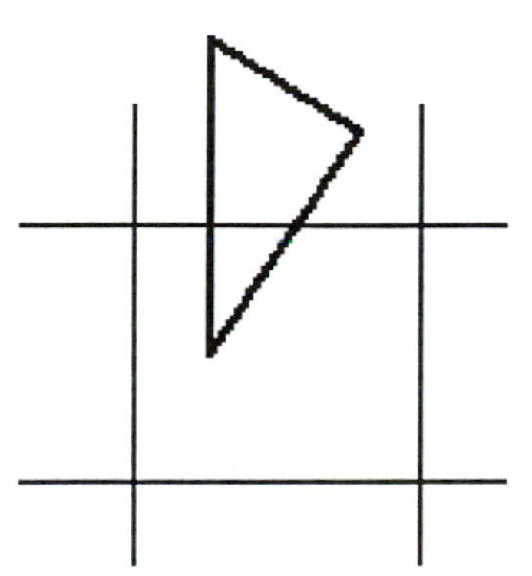

a.

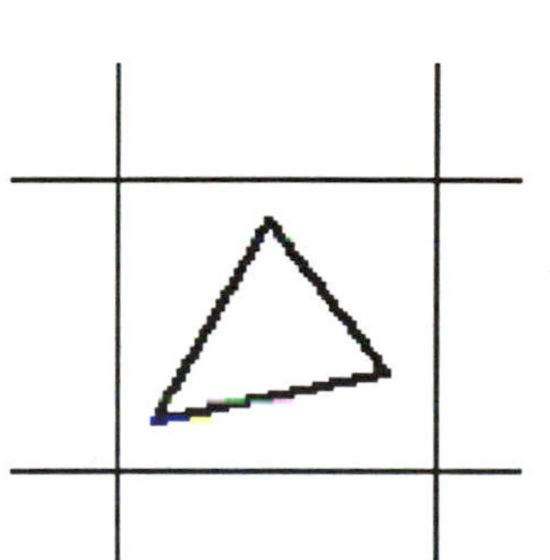

b.

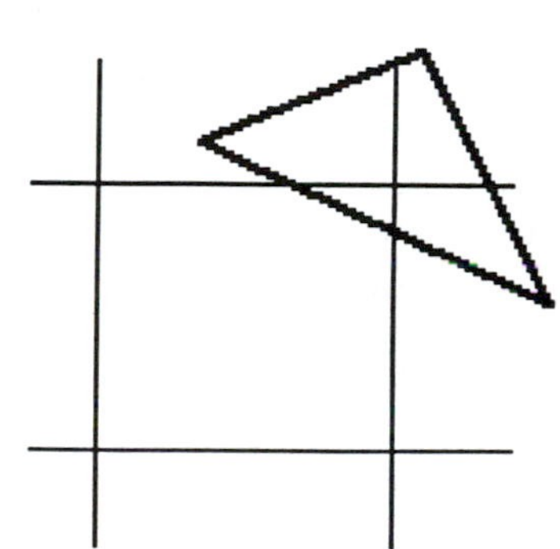

c.

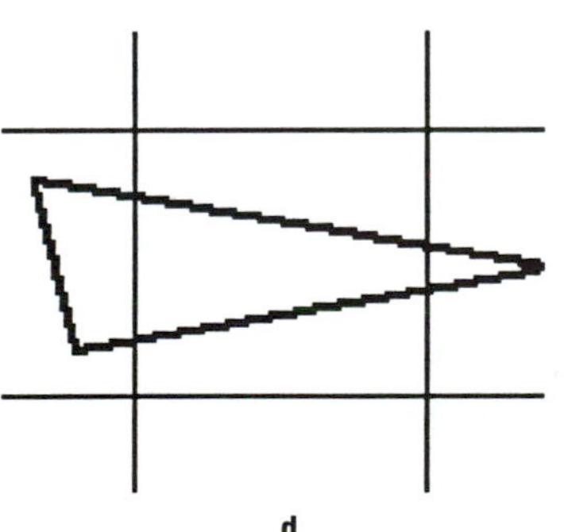

d.

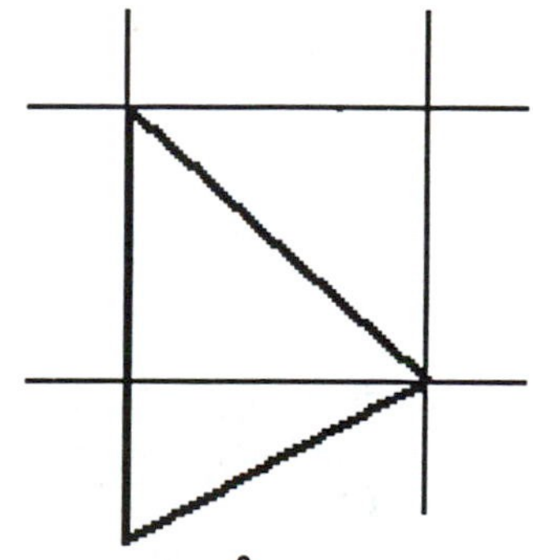

e.

Cases c, d, and e will still test negative. Case c can be detected by a general triangle inside test, but d and e will still escape. To catch d we perform an edge intersection test as described in Chapter 11 (not identical to the extended edge-intersection test above). This test would also detect cases a and c but not b. Case e is one of several "coinciding" situations in which one triangle edge coincides with a rectangle edge and another one with the diagonal of the rectangle or with another edge of the rectangle. To check for these edge-edge coinciding cases is expensive. It can be avoided altogether by performing all checks in floating point arithmetic and by distorting all triangle coordinates a little from their integer screen values. We will not treat these cases further as they do not occur very frequently.

All this version of the algorithm needs to do is determine, for a given triangle and rectangle, whether the triangle is disjoint from, surrounding, or intersecting the rectangle. The algorithm also needs to determine the depth of a triangle at a certain point. As the scene is projected perspectively, this depth must be computed as the intersection of a line parallel to the z-axis with the plane of the triangle's perspective transformation. That means that a perspective transformation of all vertices in the scene has to be done before starting the algorithm. We will always assume in the following that the vertices have been transformed. The (x,y)-values of these projected triangles are used to determine overlap with rectangles on the screen; the z-values are used for the plane and depth computations.

In order to avoid repeated transformations of projected vertices to screen coordinates, we scale all perspective-projected (x,y) pairs with proper factors. This is a simple transformation from user coordinates to screen coordinates, demonstrated below through an example. From this transformation, we can determine the size of the objects on the screen as well.

Depth values are computed using the formula explained before for depth sorting (Chapter 11) and shown again below. The record structure of each triangle should contain the coefficients of its plane equation to avoid repetition of the computations.

If $ax + by + cz - d = 0$ is the equation of a plane, the depth $z$ at a screen point $(x_s, y_s)$ is:

$$z = \frac{-ax_s - by_s + d}{c}$$

When rectangles have been reduced to pixel size, we compute the depth value for all triangles that contain this pixel. The closest triangle is the one with the smallest z-value (lhs).

When a rectangle is not of pixel size, we do the following. For each surrounding triangle we compute its depth at the four corner points of the rectangle. For each intersecting triangle, we compute the depth of its plane equation at the four corner points. If one of the surrounding triangles has depth values that are all smaller than all other depth values, this triangle is certainly closest to the screen.

This is a sufficient but not a necessary condition. In Figure 12.6 we see a screen and two triangles in heavy lines from above. The planes are shown in light lines. The depth is computed at the corners of the rectangle shown by dotted lines. We see only a two dimensional projection of the situation, but it reveals the underlying problem. The surrounding triangle is closer than the intersecting triangle but the algorithm cannot verify this because point b is closer than point a. To proceed, the rectangle is subdivided. After the subdivision, shown in Figure 12.7, the depth situation is conclusive in the left part. In the right part only one surrounding triangle exists, so both rectangles can be filled.

**Improvements to the Algorithm** We can avoid repeating overlap checks by using linked lists. In languages like C or Pascal, this is easy to program. We can reduce the number of triangles that have to be checked against each rectangle in the subdivision process by taking advantage of information acquired at a higher level of the subdivision process. If a triangle surrounds a rectangle, it will also surround all parts thereof. If a triangle is disjoint from a rectangle, it will be disjoint from all parts thereof. So, for the subdivided rectangles, this information doesn't need to be derived again by going through the set of checks. How can it be made available?

We will maintain three lists of pointers to triangles. One contains all disjoint triangles; we call it Dlist. Another contains all surrounding triangles; we call it Slist. The third contains all intersecting ones; we

FIGURE 12.6

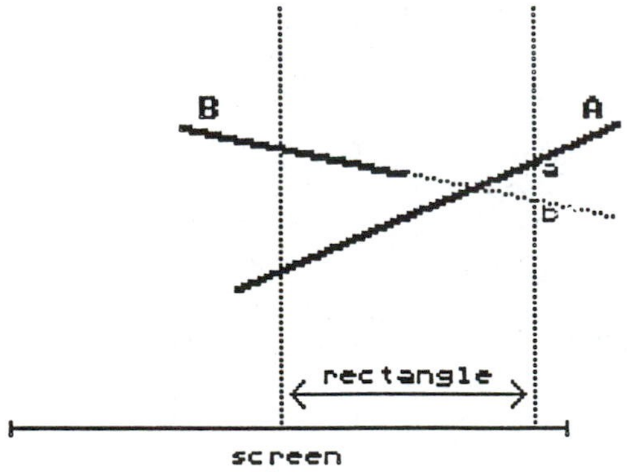

FIGURE 12.7

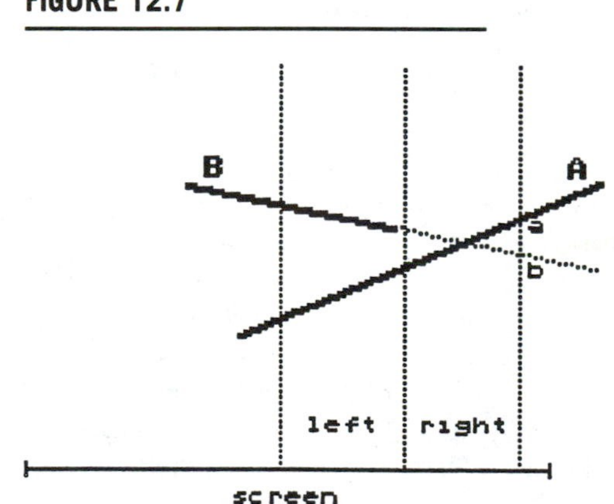

call it Ilist. These have to be updated when descending or ascending in the subdivision process. Some reflection will make it clear that Slist and Dlist can only grow and Ilist can only shrink when descending to finer subdivisions. The opposite is the case when ascending from completed subdivisions.

It makes sense to physically remove the triangles from Ilist and add them to Dlist or Slist when stepping to finer subdivisions. Because the triangles on Dlist are not checked at all, they are really out of the way. This can significantly speed up the process for complicated scenes with many triangles.

Slist and Dlist behave like first in-last out (FILO) stacks: what was put in first will be taken out last. When a rectangle is processed, we first put a certain number, d, of triangles from Ilist onto Dlist and another number, s, from Ilist onto Slist. Whenever this rectangle is filled, either directly or by further subdivisions, before stepping up in the hierarchy, the triangles to be returned to Ilist are the first s on top of Slist and the first d on top of Dlist. This allows efficient shuffling of the triangles between the lists. Only Ilist does not behave like a stack. The elements to be taken from Ilist can be anywhere within that list.

Pascal has elegant ways to handle this. Subdividing a rectangle can be done by four recursive calls. Each recursive call can have and maintain its own local variables and use these local variables to keep the count of elements that are put onto Slist and onto Dlist. Before the call finishes, we return precisely this many elements from the respective lists to Ilist. Another way, chosen here, is to use local pointers to the tops of Dlist and Slist as they appear at the start of the processing of the rectangle. Before ending the processing, all elements from the top down to but not including the one pointed to will be returned to Ilist.

At the beginning, when the whole screen is the first rectangle, the Ilist contains all triangles of the scene, the other two lists are empty. We will explain how the lists are handled for a general case somewhere down in the subdivision process.

For a given rectangle, all triangles in the Ilist are checked for overlap. Surrounding ones are moved to the Slist, disjoint ones to the Dlist. Then all triangles in the Slist and all plane equations of triangles in the Ilist are checked for their depth. If this rectangle can be filled and no further subdivisions are needed, all the triangles moved to the Dlist or Slist by this rectangle must be returned to the Ilist. This guarantees that, after processing a rectangle, the lists will be in the same state as before. Otherwise we subdivide and step down one level through a recursive call.

To explain this strategy we use the following convention. The subdivisions of a given rectangle are processed in the order 1, 2, 3, 4 as shown in Figure 12.8. The subdivisions of rectangle 2 are identified

**FIGURE 12.8**

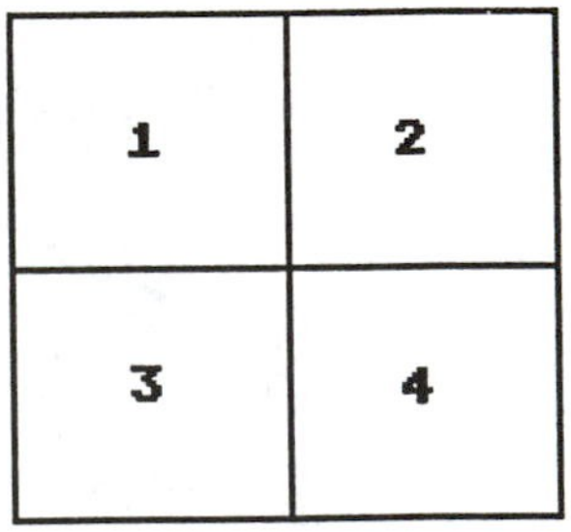

| 1 | 2 |
|---|---|
| 3 | 4 |

by 21, 22, 23, 24, so the highlighted rectangle in Figure 12.9 is 412. The original starting rectangle is identified by a space—it precedes all other identifications. The local pointers to the top of the Slist and Dlist at the start of the process are Spointer and Dpointer; we suffix the rectangle identification. So Spointer and Dpointer when processing rectangle 412 initially will be Spointer412 and Dpointer412. The lists are singly linked and terminated by nil, here indicated by a 0. New elements are inserted at the front.

FIGURE 12.9

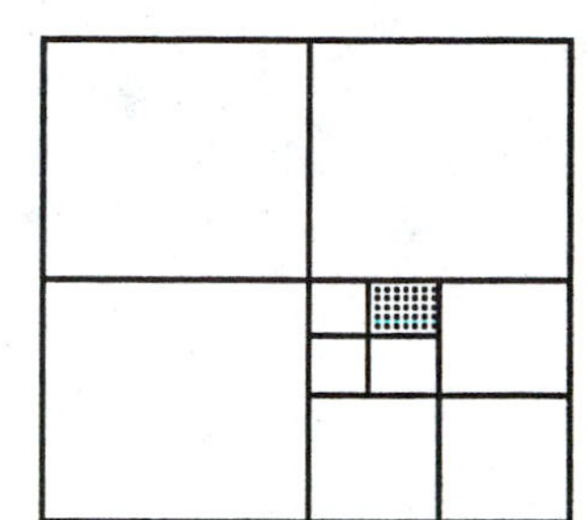

Figure 12.10 shows an example of Slist. Spointer points to its first element. After two more elements have been inserted at the front, Spointer automatically points "further down" although it is never changed. The lists actually have a header element to allow removal of elements. It is shown in Figure 12.10 but in the examples below this is ignored.

Figure 12.11 shows the screen with three triangles a, b, and c. The lists at the start will be:

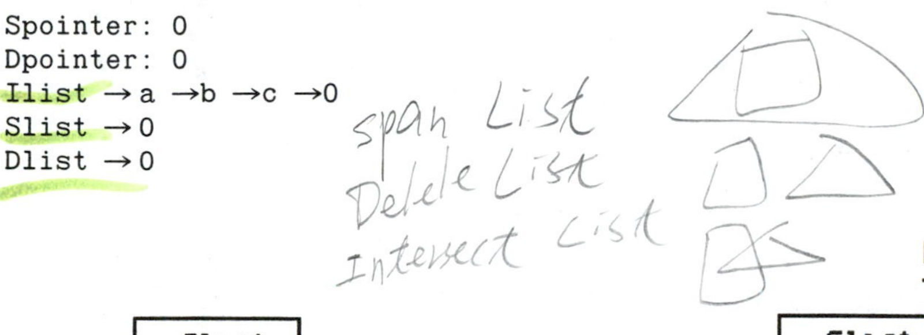

```
Spointer: 0
Dpointer: 0
Ilist →a →b →c →0
Slist →0
Dlist →0
```

FIGURE 12.10

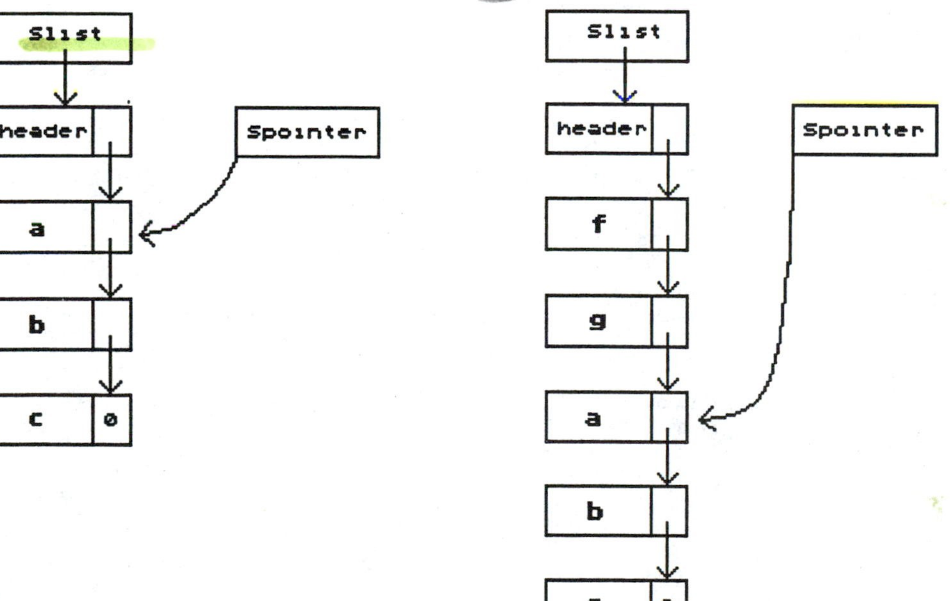

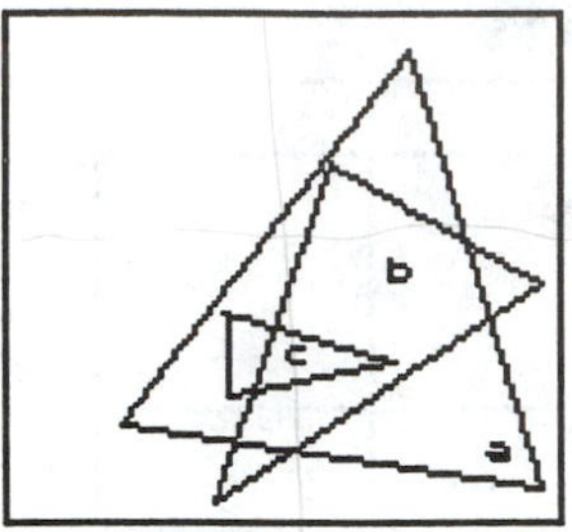


FIGURE 12.11

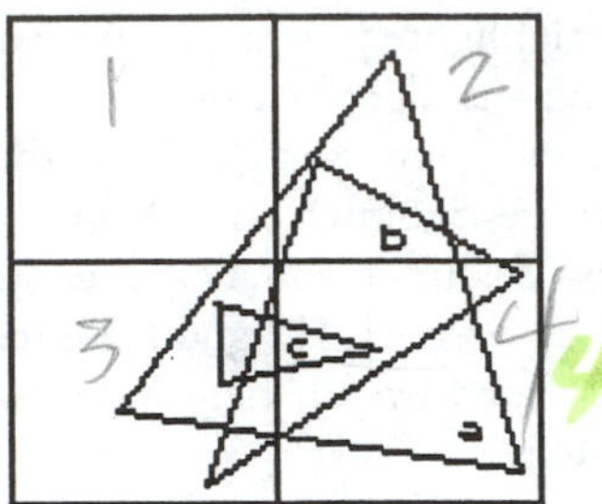


FIGURE 12.12

Processing of rectangle 1 will move triangles b and c to Dlist as these are now disjoint (see Figure 12.12).

```
Spointer1: 0
Dpointer1: 0
Ilist →a  →0
Slist →0
Dlist →b  →c  →0
```

After processing rectangle 1, the lists will again be as before because the process returns elements starting from Slist and Dlist until it meets 0. We now skip rectangles 2 and 3. Processing rectangle 4 will not change the lists, because all triangles are still intersecting (see Figure 12.13).

```
Spointer4 : 0
Dpointer4 : 0
Ilist →a →b →c →0
Slist →0
Dlist →0
```

FIGURE 12.13

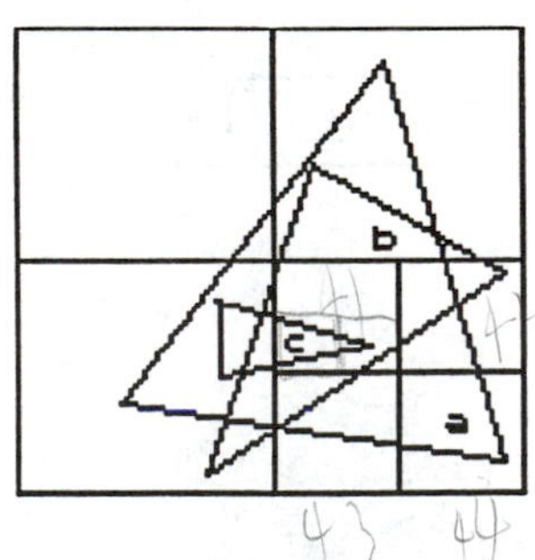


The processing of rectangle 41 will move triangle a to the Slist, as it is now surrounding (see Figure 12.13).

```
Spointer41 : 0
Dpointer41 : 0
Ilist →b →c →0
Slist →a →0
Dlist →0
```

Figure 12.14 shows rectangle 41 with its four subdivisions magnified. When 412 is processed it will move b to the Slist and c to the Dlist:

```
Spointer412 : a
Dpointer412 : 0
Ilist →0
Slist →b →a →0
Dlist →c →0
```

But rectangle 412 can be filled, so no further subdivision is needed. After filling, the triangles moved to Slist and Dlist by 412 will be returned to Ilist. Everything from the top of Slist down to but not including a and everything from the top of Dlist down to but not including 0 is moved to Ilist. So, before rectangle 413 is processed, the lists will again look like this:

```
Ilist →b →c →0
Slist →a →0
Dlist →0
```

Process 413 will use the information that a is surrounding. It moves b to Slist, then subdivides. All its subdivisions will start with the lists:

```
Ilist →c →0
Slist →b →a  →0
Dlist →0
```

Process 4131 will not change the lists, because triangle c is still intersecting. Process 41313 will add c to Slist:

```
Spointer41313 : b
Dpointer41313 : 0
Ilist →0
Slist →c →b →a →0
Dlist →0
```

It fills the rectangle, returns c to Ilist, and ascends one step in the recursion.

We have shown some of these steps in detail and have assumed that the surrounding triangles are never closer than the intersecting ones, so we could move far down in the recursion to show the list-handling strategy. It can of course happen that a rectangle is filled while another triangle intersects it; this just shortens the subdivision process.

**FIGURE 12.14**

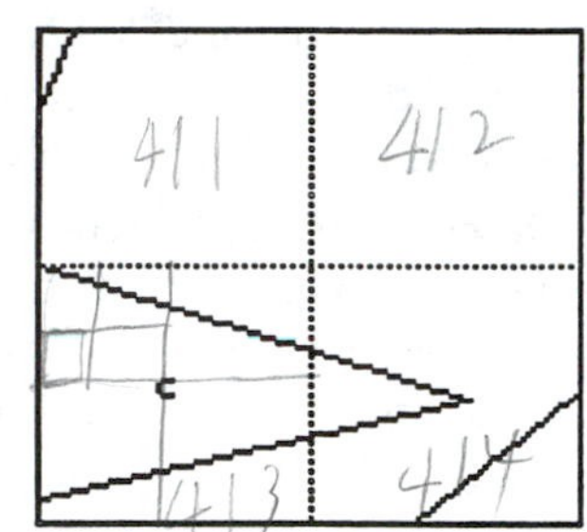


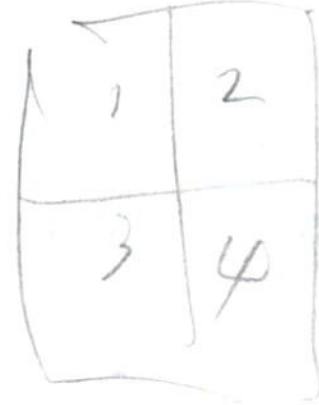

We can further decrease the number of triangles to be considered through a backface test. This is easily implemented by considering backface triangles as disjoint. When processing the very first rectangle—the entire screen—these triangles will be put onto Dlist, not to be considered again until the whole screen is filled.

**Description in Pseudocode** A description in full Pascal code would be very long. We prefer to show the essential ideas in pseudocode and give some helpful programming hints.

This version of the algorithm has all triangles originally contained in the linked list Ilist. During the processing they will be distributed among Ilist, Slist, and Dlist and shuffled back and forth as shown above. We therefore need routines for removing a single triangle or a whole group of triangles from one list and inserting it into another.

```
const   num_vertex     = {number of vertices}

type    point          = record x,y,z    :   real
                         end;

        ptriangle      = ^triangle;

        triangle       = record a,b,c    :   integer
                          pa,pb,pc,pd    :   real;
                                 next    :   ptriangle
                         end;

        t_situation    = (surround,disjoint,intersect);

var     vertex         : array[0..num_vertex] of point;

procedure drawrec(xl,xh,yl,yh,color : integer);
begin
{draws the rectangle specified by
the above screen coordinates
in the specified color}
end;

function test_rec_tri
     (r1,r2 : point; ptr : tpointer) : t_situation;
begin
{tests the rectangle given by the two corner points
 r1 and r2 against the triangle pointed to by ptr.
 Also checks for backface which it considers as
 disjoint. It returns one of 3 possible
 triangle situations:
      surround
 or   disjoint
 or  intersect}
end;
```

```
procedure  fill(xl,xh,yl,yh  : integer);
var        midx,midy         : integer;
           r1,r2             : point;
           situation         : t_situation;
           Spointer,
           Dpointer,
           ptr               : t_pointer;

procedure moveto(list,ptr : tpointer);
begin
{moves the triangle pointed to
 by ptr from Ilist to the list
 indicated by the parameter list}
end;

begin
  if (xl = xh) and (yl = yh)
  then begin {pixel size}
    {move ptr through all triangles of
     Slist and compute their depths
     at point (x1,y1),
     move ptr through all triangles of
     Ilist and check for each whether
     point (x1,y1) lies inside; if yes,
     compute the depth of the triangle
     at point (x1,y1);

     if any intersections did exist,
     set the pixel (x1,y1) to the color
     of the triangle with the minimum depth
     considering both these lists;

     if no triangles intersected,
     set pixel (x1,y1) to background color}
  end {pixel size}

  else begin {rectangle size}
     Spointer := {top element of the Slist}
     Dpointer := {top element of Dlist}
     r1.x := xl; r1.y := yl;
     r2.x := xh; r2.y := yh;
  {move the pointer ptr through all
   triangles of Ilist and for each ptr do}
   situation := test_rec_tri(r1,r2,ptr);
   case situation of
       surround  : moveto(Slist,ptr);
       disjoint  : moveto(Dlist,ptr);
       intersect : {advance ptr}
    end {case};
```

```
        {move the pointer ptr through all
         triangles of Slist and for each ptr
         compute the depth of the triangle on all
         four corner points of the rectangle xl,xh,yl,yh.

         If one triangle is closer on all corners than
         all the others then move ptr through all
         triangles of Ilist and for each triangle
         compute the depth of the plane equation
         on all four corner points as above.

         If no intersecting plane equation has
         a depth that is anywhere closer than
         the surrounding triangle:}

         drawrec(xl,xh,yl,yh,ptr^.color);

        {in all other cases:}

         xm := (xl+xh) div 2;
         ym := (yl+yh) div 2;
         if                  (ym < yh)  then fill(     xl,xm,ym+1,yh);
         if (xm < xh) and (ym < yh> then fill(xm+1,xh,ym+1,yh);
                                         fill(     xl,xm,     yl,ym);
         if (xm < xh)                 then fill(xm+1,xh,     yl,ym);

       {move all triangles from top of
        Slist down to but not including
        Spointer back to Ilist;
        move all triangles from top of
        Dlist down to but not including
        Dpointer back to Ilist}
     end {rectangle not down to pixel size}
end {procedure fill};
```

**Programming Considerations: Coordinate Transformation** In computer graphics terms, the algorithm uses *image space coordinates* (the two-dimensional screen coordinates) and *object space coordinates* (the three-dimensional user coordinates). The parameters for the fill algorithm use the corners of a rectangle on the screen, so they should be of integer type. The control of the subdividing recursive calls is then a clear and easy matter. Integers give a precise specification of the extent of the subrectangles, which is necessary to avoid handling the same pixels several times. Further subdivisions are terminated precisely when upper and lower bounds of a rectangle coincide. It would be harder to control all this if it were done in real numbers.

The comparisons of rectangles to triangles must take place in image space coordinates. As the description of objects in a scene is usually done in user coordinates, we need to transform these into the screen coordinate system for the comparison process. We should not round them to integers. Instead we treat the rectangle coordinates as real numbers during the computation. This avoids the several annoying ambiguities in inside tests and intersection tests that were pointed out above.

We can do this by looping through the vertex table and transforming all vertex values before doing a fill. A numerical example should make this clear. Suppose a scene is defined in user coordinates:

$$\begin{aligned} wxl &= -2 \\ wyl &= -1.5 \\ wxh &= 2 \\ wyh &= 1.5 \end{aligned}$$

As is often done for convenience, the origin of the user coordinate system is in the center. This window will now be displayed on the entire screen with screen coordinates 0 to 639 in x and 0 to 479 in y. The loop below does the simple transformation of all vertices:

```
for i := 1 to num_vertex do begin
   vertex[i].x := vertex[i].x•160 + 320;
   vertex[i].y := vertex[i].y•160 + 240
end;
```

(The z-values need not be transformed because they are used only for depth comparisons, not for absolute depth values. The plane equations must all be computed from these transformed coordinates. If a perspective projection is desired, the vertices must be perspective-transformed before this transformation is done. In no case can illumination parameters be derived from the transformed vertices. They have to be precomputed using the original user coordinates and stored in the triangle records, or else a set of untransformed vertices has to be kept somewhere to allow these computations.)

**Finding the Closest Surrounding Triangle** For any given rectangle in the subdivision process it is necessary to find the surrounding triangle that has smaller depth values at the four corner points than all other depth values of surrounding or intersecting triangles. This is not as trivial as it seems. We explain it below.

If Slist is not empty, it is easy to find the triangle in Slist that has the smallest depth at a particular corner point, for example, (xl,yl). We need only obtain a pointer to this triangle, ptr0.

We next do an extended check. We find the triangle in Slist *and* Ilist that has the smallest depth at a given corner point (for triangles in Ilist we check just the plane equation) and obtain a pointer to it. We do this extended test for all four corner points of the given rectangle and obtain ptr1, ptr2, ptr3, ptr4.

If these four pointers are all equal to ptr0, then ptr0 points to the closest surrounding triangle and the rectangle can be filled with this color. When there is an inequality, no further extended tests have to be done. In this case subdivision is needed.

**A Version that Avoids Some Subdivisions** We mentioned above that there are versions of the Warnock algorithm that avoid some of the successive subdivisions of the rectangular area, but they require that we fill only portions of the rectangle. In our view, this violates the spirit of the method, but here is a description of one of these in a kind of pseudocode:

- If no triangle of the scene overlaps with the rectangle, fill the rectangle with the background color.
- If a single triangle overlaps and is totally contained within the rectangle, fill the rectangle with the background color and then draw this triangle.
- If a single triangle overlaps and is partly contained in the rectangle, fill the rectangle with the background color and then draw the part of the triangle inside the rectangle.
- If a single triangle overlaps and totally surrounds the rectangle, fill the rectangle with the triangle's color.
- If one or more triangles overlap and one of them totally surrounds the rectangle and is closer in depth than all other overlapping triangles, fill the rectangle with this triangle's color.
- In all other cases subdivide the rectangle.

## 12.2 DEPTH BUFFER METHODS

*Depth buffer methods* are the most powerful and general techniques for hidden surface removal. There are many different implementations of this idea; most of them need an enormous buffer space. They can give a realistic display of even the most complex scenes no matter whether objects are bounded by curved or planar surfaces and no matter whether objects mutually penetrate or occlude each other.

These methods use both the image and object space descriptions for their calculations and checking and they compute the necessary information on a pixel by pixel basis. While these methods can handle objects with true curved surfaces, the mathematics required is beyond the level of this book, so we confine ourselves to surfaces composed of planar polygons. (Remember that we will describe shading techniques that make these appear rounded.) We will discuss two versions of depth-buffer methods. We first mention some characteristics and prerequisites that are common to them.

These methods rely heavily on a modified polygon fill algorithm. The objects to be displayed are described by specifying their bounding polygons, which is most conveniently done by defining a polygon mesh for each object. The objects can be of any shape—there is no restriction to convex objects. The surfaces can even mutually penetrate and cyclicly occlude each other.

When concave polygons occur in the scene, they should be specified so that a unique orientation can be derived from the first three points, as described in Section 11.1. If this is ignored the depth buffer method is still operational as the depth calculation does not need the orientation of a plane, but backface removal cannot be done. We assume that the polygons are either defined properly for back face removal or that the backface check has already been performed and the polygons are marked if they are backfaces.

Backface removal will cut the computing time about in half. Both versions of depth buffering will be explained for perspective projection because this is the one most commonly used in computer graphics. Applying the method to orthographic projection actually is a simplification. For both algorithms we use perspective depth transformation, which preserves depth information for every transformed point (see Section 6.1.3.)

When we look at a polygon in space, what we actually see is its projection. Its image on the screen is made visible by setting the pixels within the projection of the boundary of this polygon to certain color values. It can happen that several different polygons, even if totally disjoint in space, have overlapping projections on the screen: the same pixels are occupied by the projections of different polygons. In such a case we see only the polygon that is closer to the screen. In other words, we set the pixels to the color of the polygon that is closer at this particular point. In essence this distance calculation has to be done for every pixel in the projection of a polygon.

## 12.2.1 Z-Buffer Algorithm

The basic outline of the *Z-buffer method* is derived from the above. The projection of a polygon is scanned scan line by scan line and within each scan line pixel by pixel. For each pixel the distance from the view plane of that polygon point which projects onto this pixel is computed, and this distance is stored in the Z-buffer, also called depth buffer. The stored value will be compared to the depths of other polygon points that project onto this same pixel.

In the best case the Z-buffer has as many storage cells as there are pixels on the screen. Each storage cell must be able to hold a *depth value*, that is, a real number. It is easy to imagine that such a depth buffer will be much bigger than the whole frame buffer—a condition hardly ever met in average graphics systems. A high-resolution graphics display of 1000 × 1000 pixels requires a Z-buffer of one million real numbers where each real number requires four bytes. This is usually out of the question. However, there are versions of the algorithm that use a smaller Z-buffer.

What we want to do is to put into the Z-buffer the distance of the point of the polygon that is closest to the screen. As with all minimum-finding procedures, we initialize the whole Z-buffer with a large number, one that is certain to be larger than any distance to any point in any polygon. When a polygon projection is scanned, then, for each pixel we enter the distance of the corresponding polygon point if it is less than the number already in that Z-buffer location. At the same time, we set the frame buffer for that pixel to the color of that polygon point. When we conclude the process for all the polygons, only the depth of the one that is closest will survive in the Z-buffer and the color of this point will survive in the frame buffer. When we are through, the frame buffer will contain all visible parts of the scene correctly.

In doing the implementation we take advantage of geometric properties of straight lines, planes, and perspective projection to make the computations less extensive than they originally seem to be.

**Description of the Algorithm** We now explain the Z-buffer algorithm for a single polygon from a scene of many polygons. The actions described have to be repeated for each polygon in the scene.

Because we work with relative depth values only, the whole Z-buffer is originally filled with 1's, which is the highest relative depth in the view box.

The description of the scene in the polygon mesh(s) gives us an order in which we can go sequentially through all the polygons. A single polygon from the scene is processed as follows.

**a.** *Perspective Depth Transformation* The polygon vertices are transformed into the view box using the relations given in Section 6.1.3:

$$x_t = d \cdot x/(d+z)$$

$$y_t = d \cdot y/(d+z)$$

$$z_t = z/(d+z)$$

The polygon so obtained is still three-dimensional and is henceforth called the *transformed polygon.* If we plan to do smooth shading and illumination (discussed in Chapter 14), we need to save the untransformed vertices, so the transformed values will be put into a second table.

b. *Plane Equation* We write the coordinates of the transformed polygon again as (x,y,z). Now we find the equation of the plane in which the transformed polygon lies. This is done by taking the first three vertices, $(x_1y_1z_1)$, $(x_2y_2z_2)$, and $(x_3y_3z_3)$ and computing:

$$A = y_1(z_2 - z_3) + y_2(z_3 - z_1) + y_3(z_1 - z_2)$$

$$B = z_1(x_2 - x_3) + z_2(x_3 - x_1) + z_3(x_1 - x_2)$$

$$C = x_1(y_2 - y_3) + x_2(y_3 - y_1) + x_3(y_1 - y_2)$$

$$D = x_1(y_2z_3 - y_3z_2) + x_2(y_3z_1 - y_1z_3) + x_3(y_1z_2 - y_2z_1)$$

The four values A, B, C, and D determine the equation of the plane in which the transformed polygon lies:

$$Ax + By + Cz - D = 0$$

These coefficients are stored together with the transformed polygon.

c. *Orthographic Projection* The transformed polygon is now projected onto the view plane. This projection requires no calculation—it consists of just discarding the z coordinate of each vertex. We call the projection the *projected polygon.*

d. *Clipping* The projected polygon is still defined in real world coordinates. How much of the screen it covers and where on the screen it is located depends on the window the user specifies for the view plane. We assume this window to be (wxl,wyl,wxh,wyh). A viewport might also be specified. If it is not certain that the entire scene will fit in the window, clipping must be done, but only simple two-dimensional clipping. Scanning of the projected polygon will be restricted to its clipped part. It can happen that a projected polygon is totally clipped away so that nothing is left to be scanned.

e. *Transformation from Window to Screen Coordinates* It may be necessary to transform the real world coordinates of the projected, clipped polygon into absolute device coordinates, depending on the device on which we display. We do this without rounding to integers, because we intend in step f to use a polygon fill algorithm like the one in Chapter 2. If the polygon fill algorithm can accept the polygon vertices in real world coordinates, this step can be skipped.

f. *Scanning* This is the most complicated step in the process. For every point of the polygon that is displayed by a pixel we have to

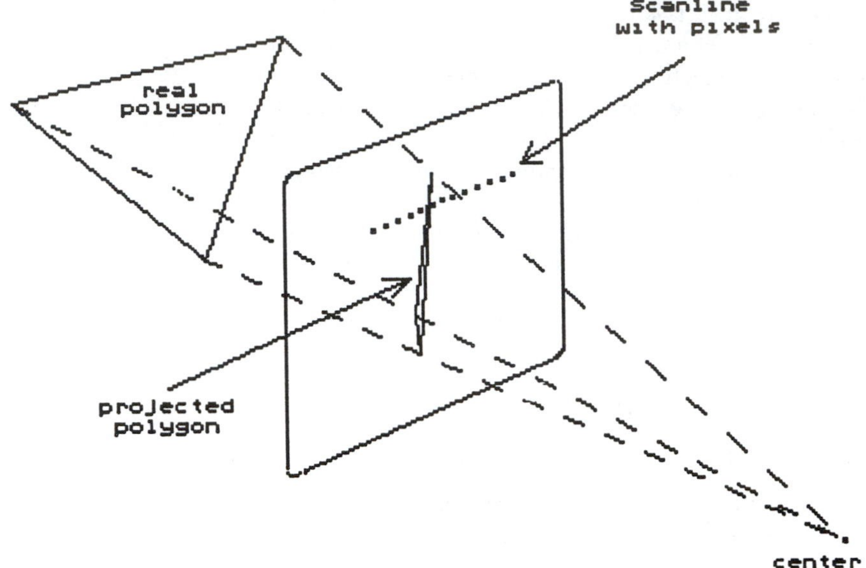


**FIGURE 12.15** Scanning the projected polygon.

find its distance from the view plane. How many points these are depends on how the displayed polygon looks on the screen. A very large polygon in real world coordinates might be projected onto a very narrow one on the screen with a width of maybe only a few pixels (see Figure 12.15).

It is for only these few pixels that we must investigate the corresponding points on the real polygon. It would be impractical to scan through the real polygon because we don't know what step size would bring us to the next pixel in the display. It is therefore the final projection of the polygon in device coordinates, clipped if necessary, which guides us through the scanning process. We will advance pixelwise on the screen (that is, in absolute screen coordinates) and for each pixel we have to find the corresponding depth. This is explained below in detail.

For a given pixel on the screen we first have to find the real world coordinates corresponding to this pixel in the viewing transformation. This is done by an inverse window-to-viewport transformation which transforms from normalized to window coordinates. To keep matters simple we assume that the viewport is the whole screen. If a different viewport is specified then the transformation must include it. Let the absolute screen coordinates go from 0 to xmax in the left-right direction and from 0 to ymax in the bottom-top direction. We need to know xmax and ymax to do the transformation from screen coordinates to normalized coordinates. Then the pixel address (x,y) on the screen will correspond to the point $(x_w, y_w)$ in real world coordinates where:

$$x_w = wxl + x\frac{wxh - wxl}{xmax} \qquad y_w = wyl + y\frac{wyh - wyl}{ymax} \tag{1}$$

We set q = (wxh − wxl)/xmax. Finding the depth of the point $(x_w, y_w)$ consists of finding the point on the transformed polygon of which $(x_w, y_w)$ is the projection. The z-coordinate of this point is the relative depth of $(x_w, y_w)$. Because the projection of the transformed polygon onto the view plane is orthographic, the z-coordinate is found by computing the intersection of the plane in which the transformed polygon lies with the straight line through $(x_w, y_w)$ and parallel to z.

The z-coordinate is obtained by substituting $x_w$ and $y_w$ for x and y respectively in the plane equation $Ax + By + Cz - D = 0$ and solving for z. We get:

$$z(x_w, y_w) = \frac{-Ax_w - By_w + D}{C} \tag{2}$$

We will call this value the depth of pixel (x,y), and write it as depth(x,y). As we step pixelwise through the projected polygon on the screen, we increase x in steps of 1. Increasing x by 1 increases $x_w$ by q. From this we get:

$$z(x_w + q, y_w) = \frac{-A(x_w + q) - By_w - D}{C} = z(x_w, y_w) - q \cdot A/C$$

We see that the depth of a certain pixel changes by a constant amount when stepping to the next pixel:

$$\text{depth}(x+1, y) = \text{depth}(x, y) - q \cdot A/C \tag{3}$$

A similar relation could be developed for the change in y when stepping to the next scan line, but this would save very little computation.

Scanning the projected polygon is done in the following way. We first compute the value q•A/C (it does not change for the entire polygon). Then we scan the projected polygon using the polygon fill algorithm of Chapter 2, but, instead of drawing a horizontal scan line from the start pixel to the end pixel, we compute the depth of the start pixel with formula (2) and perform the depth calculation on every pixel between start and end using formula (3). Every depth value will be compared with the Z-buffer value for that pixel. If the depth of the pixel is smaller than the Z-buffer value previously stored for this pixel, we replace the Z-buffer entry with the smaller value and set this pixel in the frame buffer to the color of the polygon. If we are to do smooth shading (Phong shading, for example, discussed in Chapter 14), we compute this pixel's illumination from the untransformed vertices and set the pixel accordingly. We scan the whole projected polygon in this manner.

We see that the real distance of a polygon point from the screen (the real depth) is not needed; we use the relative depth. While this is not identical to the real depth, it preserves the order and that is all we need. It is much easier to compute than the real depth. Figure 12.16 shows three polygons in real world space and three points on them that project to the same point in the view plane by a perspective projection. The perspective depth transformations of such points all lie on a line parallel to the $z$-axis. Their $z$-coordinate is their relative depth. The smallest relative depth corresponds to the smallest real world depth.

Now we go back to step 1 and process the next polygon, repeating until all polygons are processed.

This algorithm is the simplest general-purpose hidden surface algorithm. Its only disadvantage is that it requires an enormous storage capacity for the buffer. The next section explains a way of using the algorithm without taking up so much buffer space.

**FIGURE 12.16** Relative depth values.

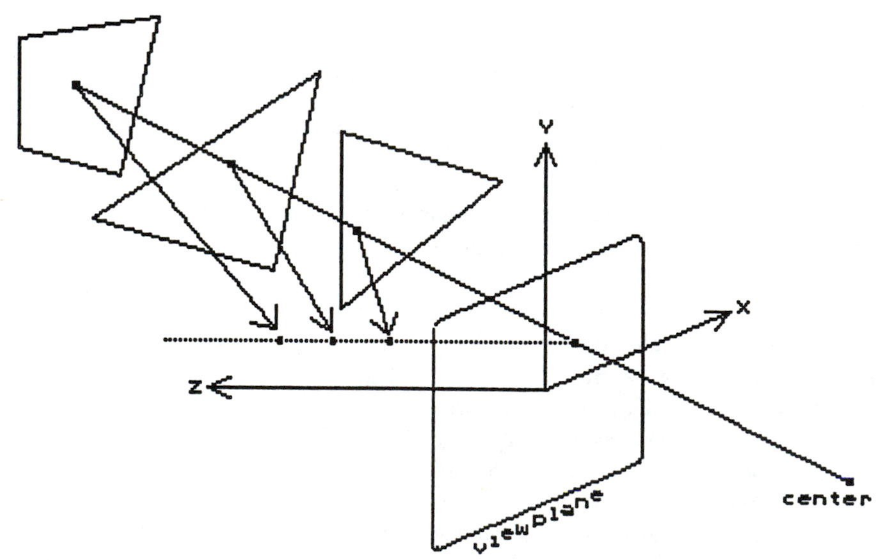

## 12.2.2 Scan Line Algorithms

The scan line algorithm can be implemented in several ways. We describe two of these. The implementation we first describe uses a Z-buffer of the size of one scan line. The second requires no depth buffer at all but is much more computation intensive. Other variations take better advantage of geometric properties of planes and coherence and therefore require less computation, but have more difficult logic, require the maintenance of more complex data structures, and are harder to program.

The name of the algorithm is probably derived from the fact that it is most convenient to proceed along scan lines when processing individual pixels.

**Scan Line Buffer Version** This version uses a Z-buffer of the size of one scan line, called a *scan line buffer.* Its logic is similar to that of the pure Z-buffer algorithm. (Also see NESP79, Section 24-4). Whatever data structure represents the polygons of a scene, it should give us a way to go sequentially through all the polygons. It helps to put the polygons in an order that will facilitate their later processing. For our present purpose, this order is on the maximum y-value that the projection of a polygon has on the screen. To obtain this order we process the polygons one at a time as described below (see Figure 12.17).

To get the polygons in the proper order, we perform five steps. Step a is the perspective depth transformation of all the vertices as described in Section 6.1.3. We then compute the plane of the transformed polygon (step b). With the coefficients of the plane equation, we don't need the depth coordinates of the vertices, so we discard them; this is equivalent to an orthographic projection onto the view plane (step c). Now we clip to the window on the view plane (step d). Next we transform all vertices of the projected, clipped polygon to screen

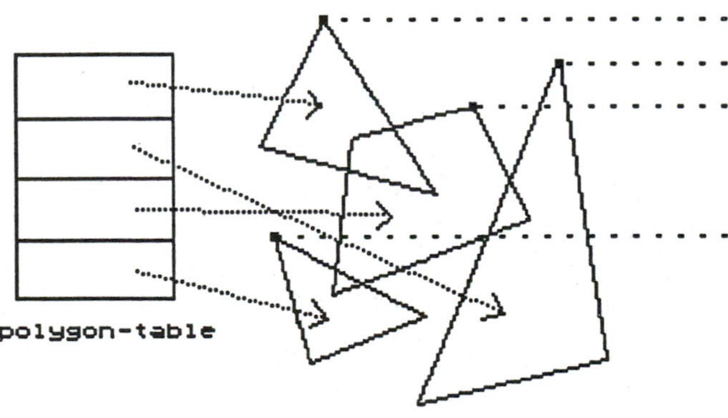


**FIGURE 12.17** Order of the polygons.

coordinates (step e), but we adjust the y-coordinates to a value halfway between two integers. After doing these five steps, we add this polygon to a separate data structure that contains the projected, clipped polygons in screen coordinates; let it be SPOL.

Now we find the largest and the smallest y-values of all the vertices of each polygon. We use the largest y-values as the key for sorting. We don't rearrange the data structure of polygons, but get pointers to them in descending order of keys. We then construct a table (we will call it the *polygon table*) that contains not only the pointer but also the largest y-value, the smallest y-value, and the coefficients of the plane equation for each polygon.

| ymax | ymin | ABCD | pointer |
|---|---|---|---|
| | | | |

Once this table is created the algorithm proceeds as follows. Two subscripts are maintained, INPOL and OUTPOL. These point into the table to the range of polygons that are intersected by the current scan line. On decreasing the scan line value by 1 (lowering the scan line), we update INPOL by looking for ymax values larger than the scan line value and we update OUTPOL by looking for ymin values larger than the scan line value. We do not have to search the entire table. Polygons that could be included are all below INPOL and polygons that could be excluded are all between INPOL and OUTPOL. The logic of keeping this table is essentially the same as described in Chapter 2, Section 2.2.2.

For each scan line, the algorithm initializes the scan line buffer to all 1's, which is the maximum relative depth. It updates the pointers INPOL and OUTPOL in the polygon table. The currently intersected polygons are those in the index range from OUTPOL through INPOL.

We look up an individual polygon in the data structure SPOL. We now do something that corresponds to processing a single scan line in the polygon fill algorithm. It is best accomplished as follows. Two consecutive vertices form an edge. We check the two y-values against the scan line. If one is larger and the other smaller, this edge intersects, so we compute the x-value of the intersection and round to the nearest integer. This x-value is sorted in ascending order into an x-table. When all edges of this polygon are processed we have an even number of entries in the x-table. In the majority of applications, there are only convex nonintersecting polygons, usually just triangles. For this case, we end up with exactly two x-values.

For all pixels from the first to the second intersection, the relative depth is computed, compared to the depth already stored in that position of the scan line buffer and, if smaller, entered into the buffer at that position. If we do this, we also set the frame buffer at the position of the scan line and the current x-value to the color derived from the currently intersected polygon. We continue until all intersection pairs for this scan line and this polygon are processed.

Then the next intersecting polygon for that same scan line is processed in the same way. When all polygons from OUTPOL through INPOL are processed, the frame buffer contains all visible parts of the scene for that scan line. This is repeated for all scan line values from the top to the bottom of the screen address range.

**Informal Description of the Scan Line Buffer Version**

```
Set whole frame buffer to background;

create SPOL which contains all polygons
perspective-transformed, projected, clipped,
transformed to screen coordinates;
create polygon_table of pointers into SPOL
sorted on ymax of the polygons' vertices;

for scan from ymax downto 0 do begin
  update INPOL and OUTPOL according
  to the new scan line value;

  set scan line buffer to all 1;

  for I from OUTPOL to INPOL do begin
    {polygon(I) has vertex(1) through vertex(K_I),
      and K_I + 1 = 1, cyclicly}
    for J from 1 to K_I do begin
      compute x-value of intersection of
      edge from vertex(J) to
      vertex(J + 1) with scan line;
      round x-value;
      sort x-value into the x_table
    end {for J};

    {we have an even number of
    intersections with edges: 2*n}
    {enter intersection of polygon(I)
    with scan line into buffer:}
    for J from 1 to n do begin
      for X from x_table[J*2-1] to x_table[J*2] do begin
```

```
            {process the Jth pair of x-values}
            compute depth(X,scan) from plane coefficients
            in the polygon_table[I];
            if depth(X,scan) is smaller than buffer_entry(X) then
               enter depth(X,scan) into this buffer position
               and set the frame buffer(X,scan) to the
               color derived from polygon(I)
         end {for X}
      end {for J}
   end {for I}
end {for scan}.
```

**Bufferless Version** The logic of this version is a little more complicated. Instead of a scan line buffer it uses a *scan line table,* which is smaller than a scan line buffer. (Also see HEBA86, pp. 264–265).

The version described here skips the clipping of step d and performs a simplified clipping during the computations for each scan line. Because of this it does not need to create the data structure SPOL.

The action also is along successive scan lines. It starts like the version above. The vertices of a polygon are perspective-transformed, its plane coefficients are computed, and a pointer to this polygon is entered into the polygon table, sorted on descending ymax values. So the polygon table contains only ymax and ymin in perspective-transformed real world coordinates. The other perspective-transformed vertices of the polygon are forgotten again.

The scan line value is transformed to real world coordinates for updating the polygon table. For a given scan line value the pointers INPOL and OUTPOL are updated, and the intersecting polygons are found through the pointers between INPOL and OUTPOL. It looks up the polygons in their original representation and computes the perspective transformations of their vertices; then it computes the x-values of the intersections of edges with the scan line and transforms them into screen coordinates. These x-values are sorted into the scan line table in ascending order. Also stored in the scan line table together with each x-value is the subscript of the current polygon in the polygon table. This subscript tells for which polygon this x-value is an intersection. It will serve as a pointer to this polygon.

Simplified clipping is performed while these entries are made. If the y-values of an edge lie on different sides of a scan line (in real world coordinates), then the x-value of the intersection is computed and rounded. If it is outside the screen range (which we assume to be 0 to 639), then, if the x-value is smaller than 0 we enter 0 into the table; if it is larger than 639 we enter 639, always together with the appropriate pointer to the current polygon. Clipping of y-values is not neccessary because scan lines never assume values that are outside the screen.

When all currently intersected polygons have been processed, the scan line table contains the intersections of the current scan line with the edges of all polygons. It will also contain pointers to the intersected polygons. An even number of these pointers will always point to the same polygon. In Figure 12.18 the scan line has the six intersections a, b, c, d, e, and f. The scan line table will contain these six x-values paired with pointers into the polygon table below:

| x-value (sorted asc.): | a | b | c | d | e | f |
|---|---|---|---|---|---|---|
| pointer to polygon: | 3 | 2 | 1 | 2 | 3 | 1 |

| | | | | | | | |
|---|---|---|---|---|---|---|---|
| active flag 1: | off | off | off | on | on | on | off |
| active flag 2: | off | off | on | on | off | off | off |
| active flag 3: | off | on | on | on | on | off | off |
| number of on flags: | 0 | 1 | 2 | 3 | 2 | 1 | 0 |

When the scan line table is ready we step through the pixels on the screen from left to right and at a height that corresponds to the current scan line value. We just march along until we reach an x-value. When we meet an x-value, we look at the corresponding pointer and set an active flag associated with this polygon to on, indicating that this polygon is active. The active flag of this polygon will be turned off when an x-value of this polygon is met a second time. It might be turned on and off again if there are more than two intersections.

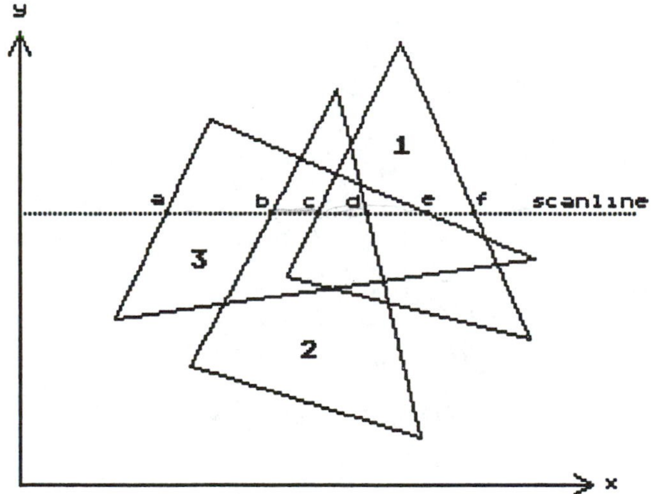


**FIGURE 12.18** Polygon and scan line intersections.

For any given pixel a certain number of active flags will be on. Three cases can be distinguished:

1. If it is zero, nothing is done to the pixel.
2. If it is one, we set this pixel to the color derived from the active polygon.
3. If it is greater than 1, we compute the relative depths of the corresponding points in all active polygons, compare them, and set the pixel to the color derived from the polygon that has the smallest relative depth.

The table above shows the status of the active flags in the intervals between crossings of intersection points in the scan line table. This is repeated for all scan lines from the top to the bottom of the screen. After the last scan line is processed the screen shows all visible parts of the scene.

### Informal Description of the Bufferless Version

```
Set whole frame buffer to background;

create polygon_table of pointers into polygons
sorted on ymax of the polygons' perspective-
transformed vertices;

for scan from high-y downto low-y do begin
  {scan, high-y, low-y are in real world coordinates}
  update INPOL and OUTPOL according
  to the new scan line value;

  for I from OUTPOL to INPOL do begin
    {polygon(I) has vertex(1) through vertex(K_I),
    and K_I+1 = 1, cyclicly}
    for J from 1 to K_I do begin
      compute x-value of intersection of
      edge from transformed vertex(J)
      to transformed vertex(J+1) with scan line
      {scan line is in real world coordinates,
      x-value is transformed to screen coordinates};
      clip x-value if necessary;
      sort x-value and I into the scan line table
    end {for J}
  end {for I};

  {set one scan line of pixels}
  set all active flags to off;
  for X from low-x to high-x do begin
```

```
    {check the scan line table}
    if an entry in the scan line table is
    equal to X then check its pointer and
    switch the corresponding active flag;
    if number of on flags = 0 then
      nothing;
    if number of on flags = 1 then
      set pixel to color of polygon
      whose active flag is on;
    if number of on flags > 1 then
      compute relative depth for all polygons
      whose active flag is on,
      using the plane coefficients
      in the polygon_table;
    set pixel to color of polygon
      whose relative depth is smallest
  end {for X}
end {for scan}.
```

Both algorithms obviously perform some actions and arithmetic many times instead of storing results in appropriate data structures for reuse. Among these inefficiencies are:

1. The perspective transformation of polygons is done at the time the polygon list is created and then as often as the polygon is intersected by the scan line.
2. Finding the intersections of edges of a polygon with the scan line is done by checking all edges instead of keeping them in a sorted table and only including new ones and excluding old ones as is done in the polygon-filling algorithm.
3. The intersections of the edges with the scan line are computed again for every new scan line value instead of just keeping them stored and adding a constant derived from the slope of that edge, as in the polygon-filling algorithm.
4. The depth values for the polygons are computed over again for every point on the polygon, although the depth values for adjacent pixels differ by a constant that could be computed just once for each polygon and added, as in the depth-buffer algorithm.

Taking advantage of all these possibilities gives the extreme in avoiding superfluous computations. But the logic becomes much more complicated and many more data structures have to be maintained and updated. Doing computations for the various types of coordinates (screen coordinates or real world coordinates) is not essential but it does reduce the amount of arithmetic.

# EXERCISES FOR CHAPTER 12

1. Outline in pseudocode the basic idea of the Warnock algorithm. The Warnock algorithm fills either pixels or rectangular areas. In Figure 12.19 you see how you can indicate this by hand. The small-size squares are pixels not to be further subdivided. The upper eight white pixels are filled as two 2 × 2 blocks, the lower eight as one 2 × 2 block and four individual pixels. Use this method in the following exercises.

**FIGURE 12.19**

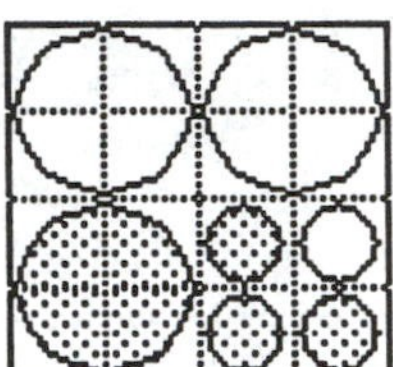

2. Given the screen and the triangle definition in Figure 12.20, assume the background to be white and the triangle to be black. Perform the Warnock algorithm by hand and indicate in either black or white the areas that are filled as a whole.

**FIGURE 12.20**

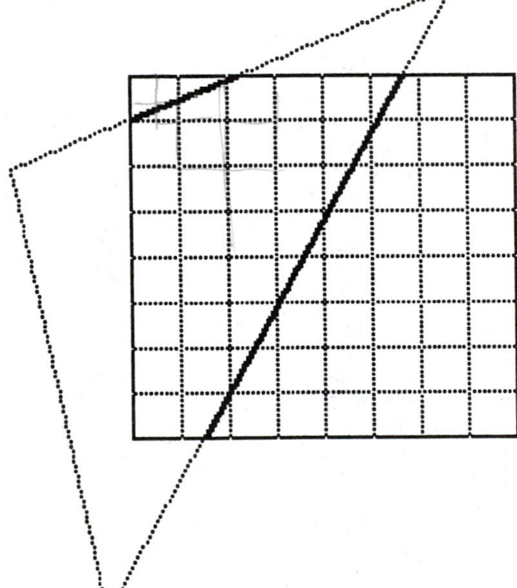

In Figure 12.21 you see not only the filled areas as in Exercise 2, but also numbers that show the order in which the algorithm fills them in.

**FIGURE 12.21**

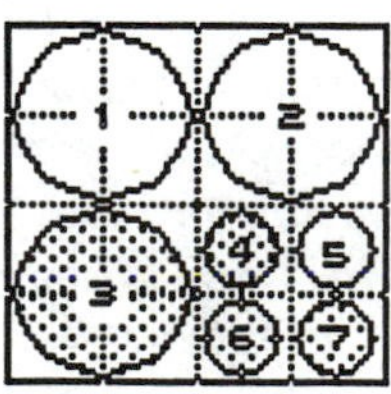


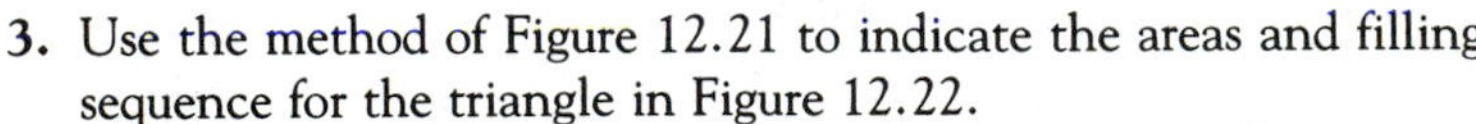

3. Use the method of Figure 12.21 to indicate the areas and filling sequence for the triangle in Figure 12.22.

FIGURE 12.22

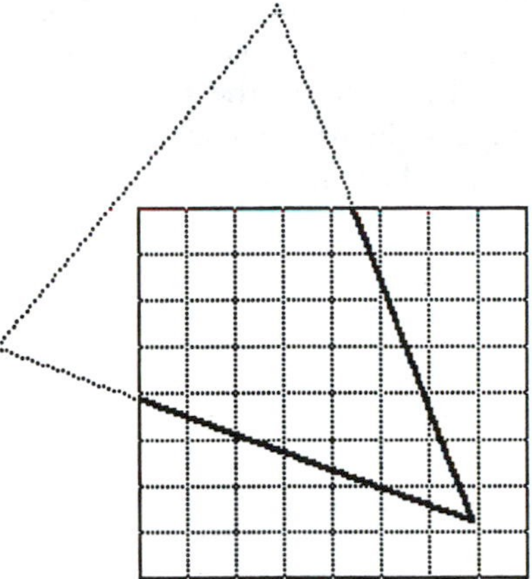

4. At the pixel level, no more handling of the Slist, Dlist, and Ilist is done (the lists are not changed), but they are still checked. Which lists are checked at this level?
5. Consider Figure 12.23. How do the lists look when the algorithm is down to pixel (4,4)? How do they look at pixel (3,3)? How do they look at pixel (2,6)? (The small figures indicate how to number the triangles.)

FIGURE 12.23

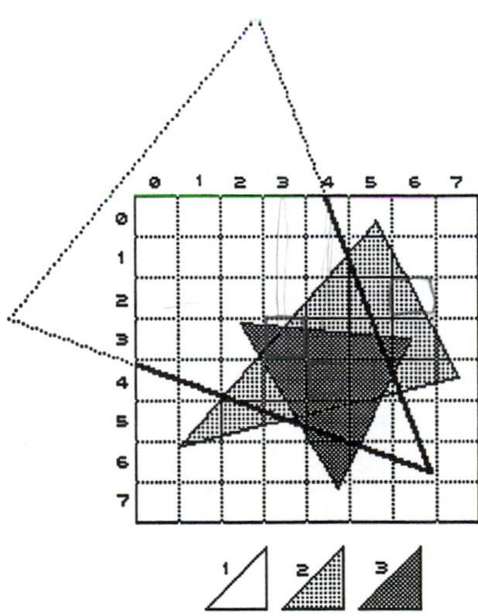

6. Given the window wxl = 1, wyl = 1, wxh = 4, wyh = 4 (observe that this is a square window) and a screen with coordinates 0 to 639 in x and 0 to 399 in y, with a square pixel ratio, describe the transformation from user to screen coordinates that puts the center of the window in the center of the screen and does not distort the objects. *Hint:* Use the whole height but not the whole width of the screen to map the window.

# Hidden Lines and Surfaces: Special Cases

# 13

In this third chapter on removing hidden lines and surfaces, we consider two special cases, both of which display mathematical functions of two independent variables. There are three sections.

**13.0 Introduction** gives some background information.

**13.1 Hidden Line Removal for Two-Dimensional Functions** explains how we can draw curves that represent a surface by drawing lines at a sequence of constant values of each independent variable. It is doing the second set of curves that is difficult.

**13.2 Hidden Surface and Hidden Line Removal for Grid Surfaces** tells about the display of functions where the surface is a linear interpolation of values at grid points that are uniformly spaced in each direction.

# 13.0 INTRODUCTION

In mathematics and engineering it is often useful to display a surface function of the form:

$$z = f(x,y).$$

In this notation the (x,y)-plane is imagined to be horizontal and the z-values are heights above the plane; z then defines a surface in space. In computer graphics, nearly all coordinate systems put the (x,y)-plane in the screen with the z-axis perpendicular to it. The form above could be in conflict with either our imagination or with this computer graphics coordinate convention, so we will switch y and z and express the function as:

$$y = f(x,z).$$

Here, the function is defined on the horizontal (x,z)-plane in a left- or right-handed coordinate system. It is essential for f to be a single-valued function of x and z, or else there will be two surfaces. Such a function can be displayed without hidden lines using the relatively simple *floating horizon algorithm.* We will explain the algorithm for raster displays.

# 13.1 HIDDEN LINE REMOVAL FOR TWO-DIMENSIONAL FUNCTIONS

We will display the function by drawing two sets of space curves. One set of curves are intersections of f(x,z) with planes of constant z-values; the other set are intersections of f(x,z) with planes of constant x-values. The effect is to display the surface as if it were crosshatched. Drawing these curves is simple; the difficulty is the necessity of suppressing hidden lines. We will develop the algorithm for this in steps.

### 13.1.1 Unidirectional Hatching

When we draw the first set of curves, suppressing the hidden parts of the curves is easy. We will assume that the first curves are the intersections of f(x,z) with planes of constant z-values. If our viewing position is from the negative z-axis in a left-handed system, the planes with smaller z-values are closer to us.

The essential ideas behind the algorithm are:

**a.** Draw the nearest curves before those farther away,
**b.** Draw only those parts of each curve that are above or below anything drawn so far.

This is shown in Figure 13.1. The curves 1 through 5 are drawn in that order. Whenever a curve dips below the upper horizon or rises above the lower horizon, it is not drawn; we do only those parts above the upper or below the lower horizon. We update the respective horizon by the part that sticks out. On the left side of the display we see the upper side of the surface; in the middle and on the right are parts of the lower side.

The curves that form the surface are of course drawn by just setting pixels on the raster display. We assume that the display has a width of w pixels and a height of h pixels. Each pixel to be set is addressed by two integers ix and iy; ix ranges from 1 to w and iy from 1 to h. The upper and lower horizons are kept in two integer arrays of length w, called up_hor and lo_hor. Up_hor will hold the greatest iy values and lo_hor the smallest iy values so far drawn.

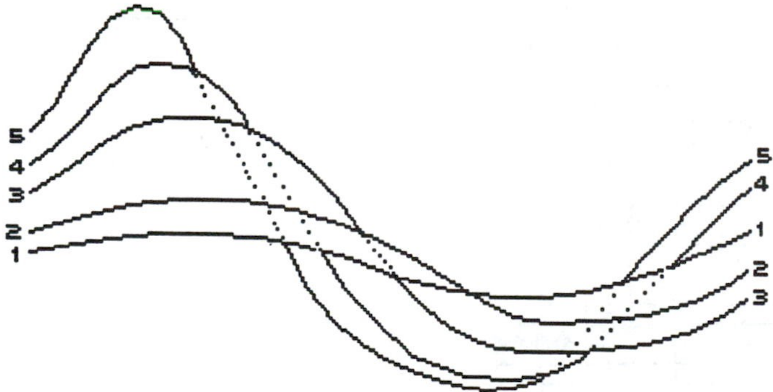


**FIGURE 13.1**

For now we restrict ourselves to drawing a curve from left to right and we will draw it in increments of (at most) one pixel horizontally. We achieve this by evaluating y = f(x,z), z = constant, with increments to x such that there is at most one pixel increment on the display. The vertical increment for one such step can be any value.

Let y be the height of the curve at the position (x,z). We first round x and y to the nearest integers: curr_x = round(x) and curr_y = round(y). Then we compare curr_y to up_hor[curr_x]. If curr_y > up_hor[curr_x], we set the pixel (curr_x,curr_y) and also update up_hor[curr_x] to curr_y. Otherwise, we compare curr_y to lo_hor[curr_x]. If curr_y < lo_hor[curr_x], we set pixel (curr_x,curr_y) and update lo_hor[curr_x] to curr_y. If neither condition is true, we do nothing.

To start the process, we must initialize the horizon arrays up and lo. One plan might be to initialize them with the first curve values. This works if the horizontal range of all later curves is the same as the first one. However, if the surface is displayed in a slanted view, later curves might extend farther to the right or left than the first. An example is shown in Figure 13.2. Curve 1 starts at the curr_x-position 8. The above initialization plan would be limited to the positions from 8 up. Curve 2 starts at curr_x-position 5 and would therefore find three uninitialized elements of up_hor and lo_hor. A similar situation occurs when drawing curve 3 and all later curves.

We need a more general initialization rule. This is simple to do. We just initialize both horizons with numbers that never occur in the process. Then, when a curve value at position curr_x is computed, we will know whether the up_hor[curr_x] and lo_hor[curr_x] values have been set. If they have not, we simply set them to this curve value; if

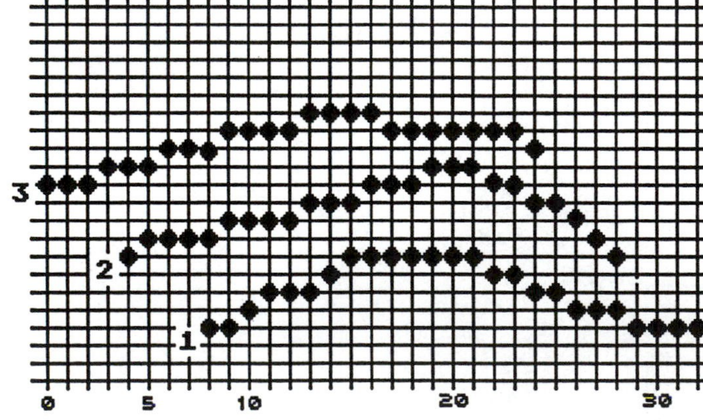


**FIGURE 13.2**

they have been set, we use them for comparisons, updating them as described above. The initialization values will be maxint for up and minint for lo. We can see that this initialization rule includes the simple one described above.

There is another problem to consider. Figure 13.3 shows a very flat and a very steep curve. The steep parts of the curve look very sparse because only one pixel is set per horizontal step. How can we remedy this?

If we were to use smaller steps in x-direction when evaluating the function, then for a very steep part of the function several x-values might be rounded to the same curr_x-position although the y-values are different. As long as the y-values increase we would set the corresponding pixels on the same curr_x-position, so the curve would look somewhat denser in its ascending part. But in the descending part, we would not set more than one pixel on the same curr_x-position because the higher horizon would suppress it. Also, having so many function evaluations is time consuming. For these reasons this is not an acceptable solution.

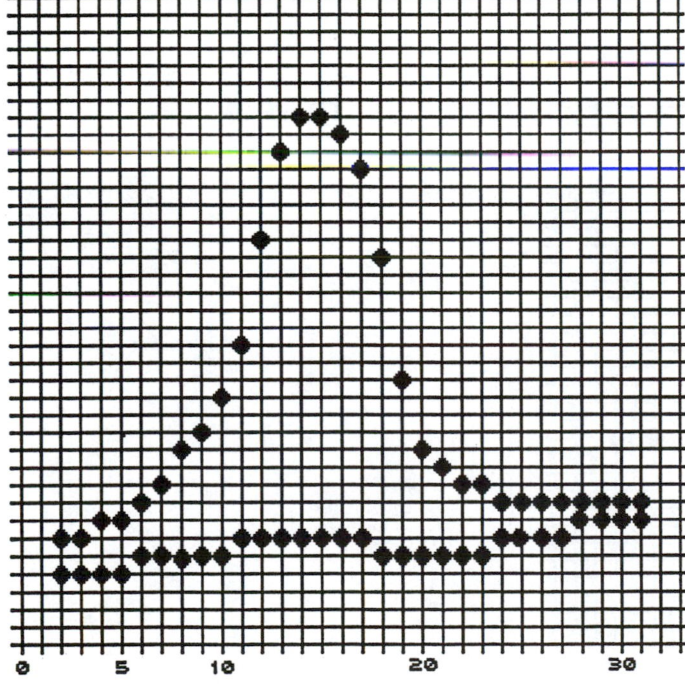


**FIGURE 13.3**

A better solution consists of both setting one pixel at every evaluated curve position and linking these positions by straight lines. We must know where to start the line, which we can achieve by remembering the curr_x-value that resulted from rounding the last x-position for which the function was evaluated. (Keep in mind that successive x-values don't necessarily lead to increasing curr_x-positions and that later we will have to evaluate the function for (x,z) pairs that can lead to decreasing curr_x-positions.)

When we know the former curr_x-position, we know the starting location of the line; if the new curr_y-value is above the upper horizon, the line must start from the upper horizon at the former curr_x-position. This is true even when the former curr_y position is below the upper horizon because parts below the horizon must not be drawn. A similar situation applies for a line drawn to a new curve point below the lower horizon, so we consider this in detail only for the upper horizon. In Figure 13.4, the upper horizon is shown by black dots. The new curve is very steep and is indicated by crosses. We refer to the crosses with the notation curr_y[i] even though curr_y is not an array in the algorithm; for example, curr_y[5] is the cross in column 5.

Assume for simplicity that the curr_x-values increase by 1 with every new function evaluation. From curr_x = 0 through 5 the curr_y-values are all below the upper horizon—what we do in this case is

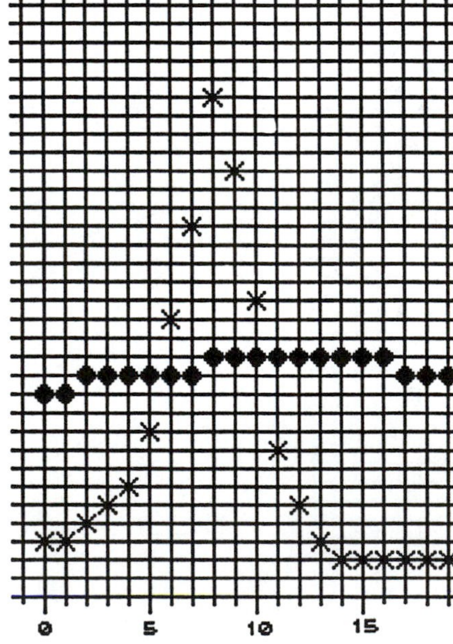


**FIGURE 13.4**

described a little later. At curr_x = 6 the curr_y-value is above the upper horizon: curr_y[6] > up_hor[6]. The former curr_x-value is 5. We can see that we have to draw a line to the point (6,curr_y[6]). The starting point of the line is not (5,curr_y[5]); it must be the point (5, up_hor[5]) in order not to draw lines below the horizon. Also, we must update the upper horizon up_hor[6] to curr_y[6]. The same situation will continue until curr_x = 10.

At curr_x = 11 there is a new situation: curr_y is below the upper horizon, curr_y[11] < up_hor[11]. We need to draw a line from (10, up_hor[10]) to (11,up_hor[11]) but not to (11,curr_y[11]) to avoid drawing below the upper horizon. This continues in our example until the right edge of the figure. Even if we should redraw the existing horizon, no harm is done. To describe this a little more formally; we let form__x be the former curr_x-value. Then we can always draw from (form_x, up_hor[form_x]) to (curr_x,up_hor[curr_x]). We apply this rule for the part of the curve from curr_x = 0 to curr_x = 5 as well. This will merely redraw the upper horizon. The result of using this method is shown in Figure 13.5.

Generalizing this to both horizons gives a simple algorithm. Here is the action for one step:

Let form_x be the former and curr_x the current horizontal position; let curr_y be the function value at position curr_x:

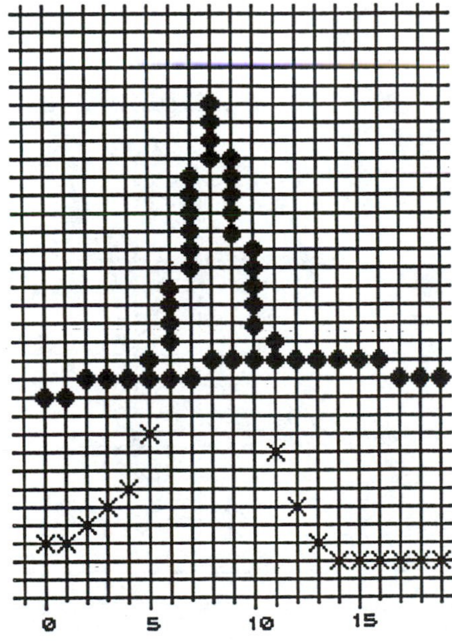


**FIGURE 13.5**

upper horizon: set up_hor[curr_x] = max(up_hor[curr_x], curr_y); draw a line from (form_x, up_hor[form_x]) to (curr_x, up_hor[curr_x]);

lower horizon: set lo_hor[curr_x] = min(lo_hor[curr_x], curr_y); draw a line from (form_x, lo_hor[form_x]) to (curr_x, lo_hor[curr_x]).

Repeating this for all function evaluations at a constant z-value with increasing x-values gives us one of the curves. Drawing all the curves for increasing constant z-values gives us the surface display, but it is only hatched in one direction.

This simple form of the algorithm is easy to program and produces a correct surface display. It has the disadvantage of redrawing both horizons at every step whether they are changed or not. This can be eliminated in part by adding more detail to the algorithm.

We can do this by remembering not only the former curr_x-value, form_x, but also the former curr_y-value, form_y. After updating the upper and lower horizons we compare form_y to up_hor[form_x] and curr_y to up_hor[curr_x]. We know that we certainly don't have to draw a line above the upper horizon if both the former and the current function values are below the upper horizon: form_y < up_hor[form_x] and curr_y < up_hor[curr_x]. In all other cases a draw may be necessary. Figures 13.6 through 13.9 show the four essential cases for the upper

**FIGURE 13.6**

form_y < up_hor[form_x];
curr_y < up_hor[curr_x].

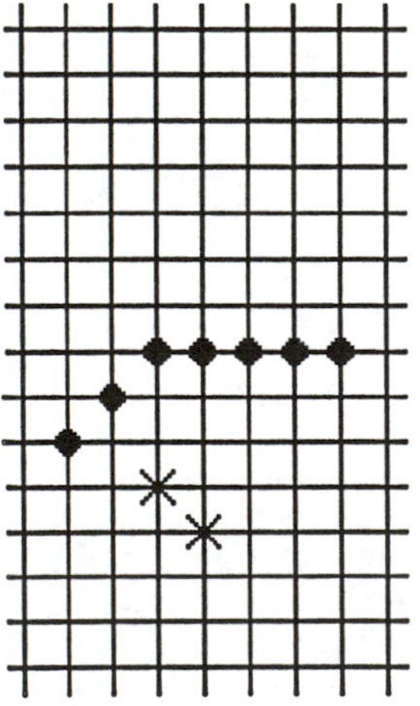

**FIGURE 13.7**

form_y < up_hor[form_x];
curr_y = up_hor[curr_x].

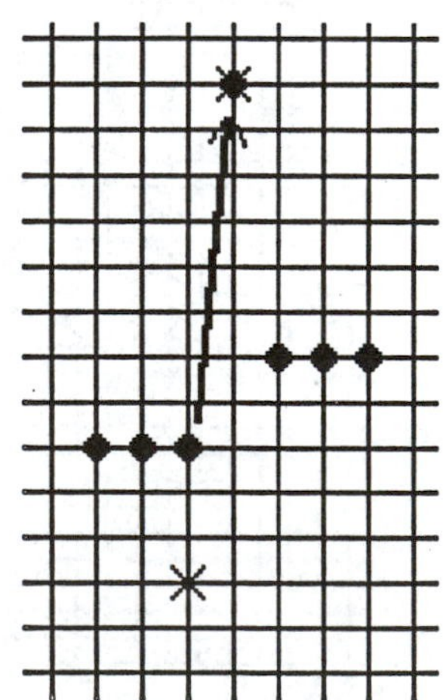

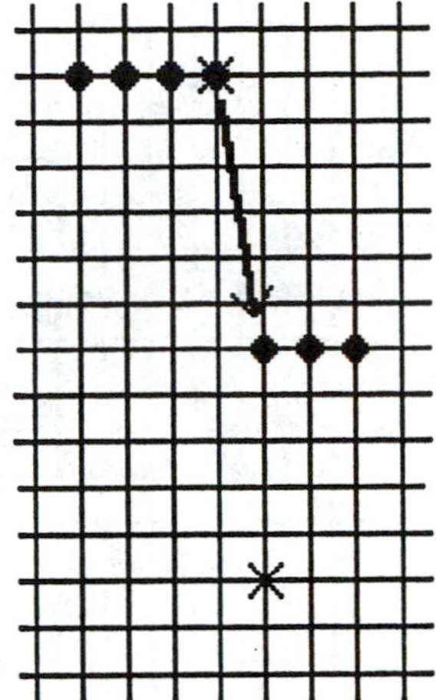

**FIGURE 13.8**

form_y = up_hor[form_x];
curr_y < up_hor[curr_x].

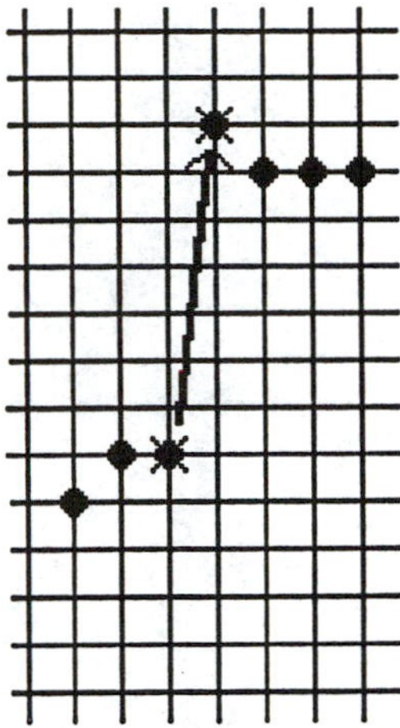

**FIGURE 13.9**

form_y = up_hor[form_x];
curr_y = up_hor[curr_x].

horizon. The drawing direction is from left to right. The horizon is indicated by dots, the values form_y and curr_y by crosses. Remember that the upper horizon is updated to curr_y before the test.

The improved algorithm is:

Let form_x be the former and curr_x the current horizontal position; let form_y be the former and curr_y the current function value:

upper horizon: set up_hor[curr_x] = max(up_hor[curr_x], curr_y); if form_y = up_hor[form_x] or curr_y = up_hor[curr_x] then draw a line from (form_x, up_hor[form_x]) to (curr_x, up_hor[curr_x]);

lower horizon: set lo_hor[curr_x] = min(lo_hor[curr_x], curr_y); if form_y = lo_hor[curr_x] or curr_y = lo_hor[curr_x] then draw a line from (form_x, lo_hor[form_x]) to (curr_x, lo_hor[curr_x]).

We need to check both horizons because there are cases in which we must draw two lines: if a curve is so steep that it jumps from above the upper to below the lower horizon or vice versa in one step. Figures 13.10 and 13.11 show these two cases. With more elaborate testing we can eliminate even more instances in which no line drawing is necessary. We will not discuss this.

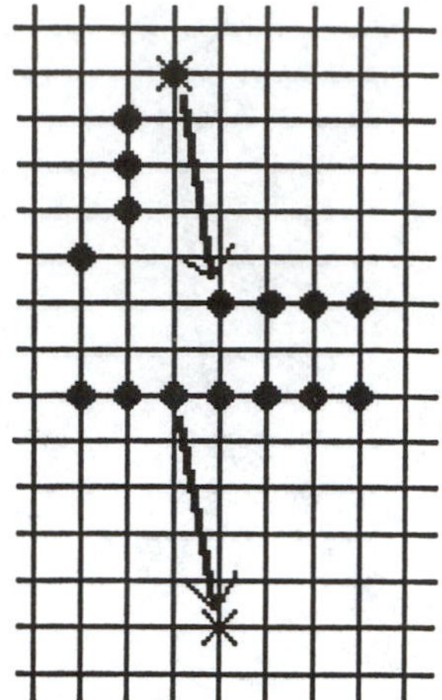

**FIGURE 13.10**

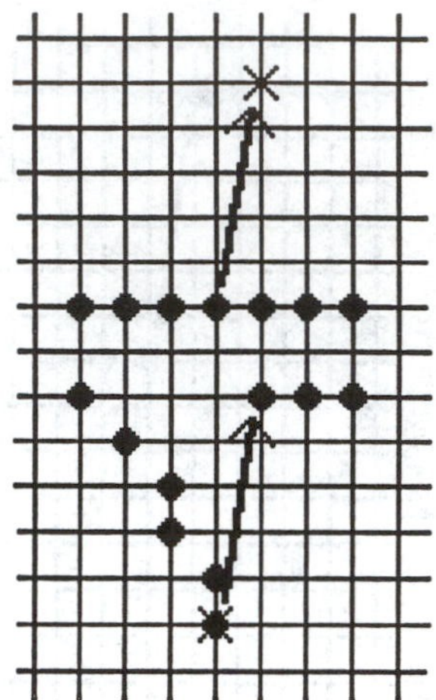

**FIGURE 13.11**

The surface is usually displayed in a slanted view. We can achieve this by performing rotations in space for every computed number triple (x,f(x,z),z) of the surface. A rotation ccw about y is done to obtain a corner-on view of the surface area and a rotation ccw about x is done to tilt the area toward the viewer. The rotated point is then projected orthogonally—the z-coordinate is discarded—and these points are used in the floating horizon algorithm. An example is shown in Figure 13.12. The function:

$$f(x,z) = 18*\sin^9(.35*(x^2+z^2))*\exp(-x^2-z^2)+\sin(x+.3)*\cos(z-.3)$$

is drawn in the area $[-\pi,\pi]$ x $[-\pi,\pi]$ using the above form of the algorithm. The function is evaluated along 41 lines of constant z-values and on each line on 380 equidistant x-values. After each evaluation the number triple (x,f(x,z),z) is rotated in space, first ccw around the y-axis by 29° and then ccw around the x-axis by 40°.

**Coded Algorithm** The algorithm is described partly in pseudocode to avoid distracting detail.

We assume a definition area of [0,1] x [0,1] for the function.

f(x,z) is the function value at (x,z).
num_crv is the number of curves in the display minus 1.
num_pix is the maximum number of pixels from left to right
    in one curve on the display.
hight is a scaling factor to determine the height of the
    curves on the display.
up_hor and lo_hor are integer arrays of sufficient range.

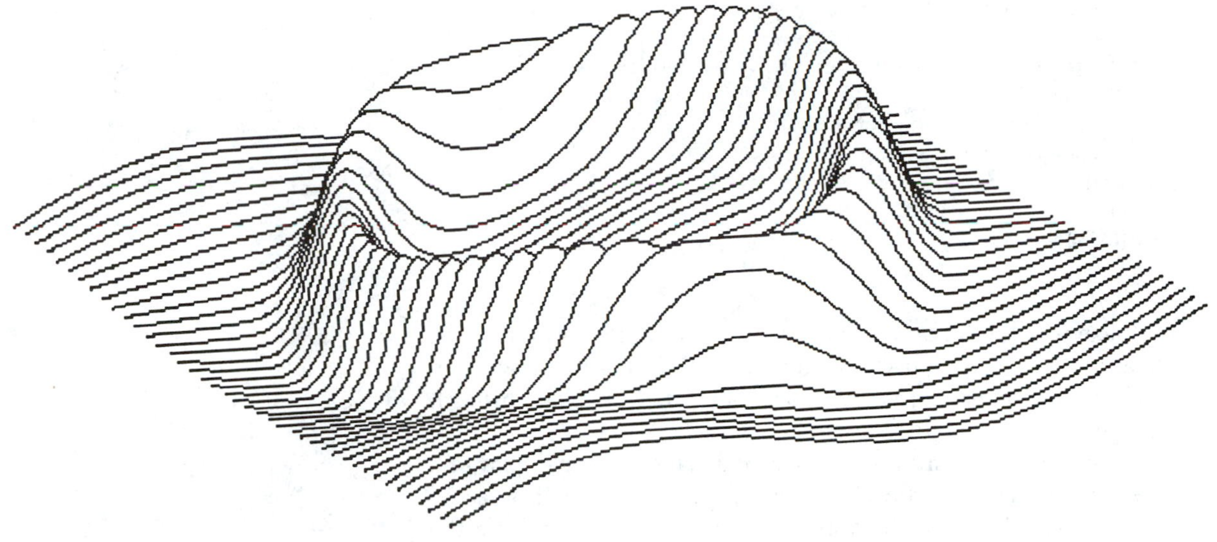

**FIGURE 13.12**

```
for z from 0 to 1 in steps of 1/num_crv do begin
   for x from 0 to 1 in steps of 1/num_pix do begin
      compute y = f(x,z);
      rotate (x,y,z) around y
            and then around x
            giving (xr,yr,zr);

      form_x := curr_x;
      form_y := curr_y;
      curr_x := xr*width;
      curr_y := yr*hight;
      if up_hor[curr_x] not initialized
      then begin {initialize up_hor and lo_hor}
         up_hor[curr_x] := curr_y;
         lo_hor[curr_x] := curr_y
      end
      else begin {update up_hor and lo_hor}
         up_hor[curr_x] := max(up_hor[curr_x],curr_y);
         lo_hor[curr_x] := min(lo_hor[curr_x],curr_y)
      end;

      {the code below is not executed for
      the very first point in a curve}
      if x > 0
      then begin
         if form_y = up_hor[form_x] or curr_y = up_hor[curr_x]
         then begin
            move(form_x,up_hor[form_x]);
```

```
            draw(curr_x,up_hor[curr_x])
          end;
          if form_y = lo_hor[form_x] or curr_y = lo_hor[curr_x]
          then begin
            move(form_x,lo_hor[form_x]);
            draw(curr_x,lo_hor[curr_x])
          end
        end
    end {for x}
end {for z};
```

A problem which has not been discussed yet and was not solved in the code above is the possibility of increasing thickness of the lines when the surface function along a curve is oversampled. We explain this with an example.

Assume that the maximum horizontal extent on the display of a curve for constant z, width, is 300 pixels. This width is before the surface is rotated around the y-axis. In this case we will sample the surface function at 300 equidistant locations in the x-direction in order to have precisely one sample per pixel.

After a rotation of 60 degrees about y, the curve will extend over $300*\cos(60°) = 150$ pixels horizontally. Sampling at 300 locations along x will give us two samples per horizontal pixel. Wherever the slant of the curve is about 45°, this can lead to a thick line by setting twice as many pixels as necessary. Reducing the number of samples to $width*\cos(\Phi)$, where $\Phi$ is the angle of rotation, allows only one sample per horizontal step thereby preventing this effect. (A rotation about x has no influence on this.) Figure 13.13 shows how an oversampled curve will look in its 45° parts.

### 13.1.2 Crosshatching

Above, we displayed the surface function by drawing the curves of intersections of f(x,z) with planes of constant z-values. We want to further develop the algorithm to display the surface in a crosshatch manner, drawing curves of intersections of f(x,z) with planes of constant x-values. But adding the second set of curves is not trivial.

It might seem that all we need do is draw both sets of curves on top of each other, but this will not suppress all hidden lines. Figures 13.14 and 13.15 show two individual sets of curves. Figure 13.16 shows the result of an overlay and Figure 13.17 the correct display that we want.

The correct result is obtained by drawing the two sets of curves alternately, using the same upper and lower horizon for both. Both sets

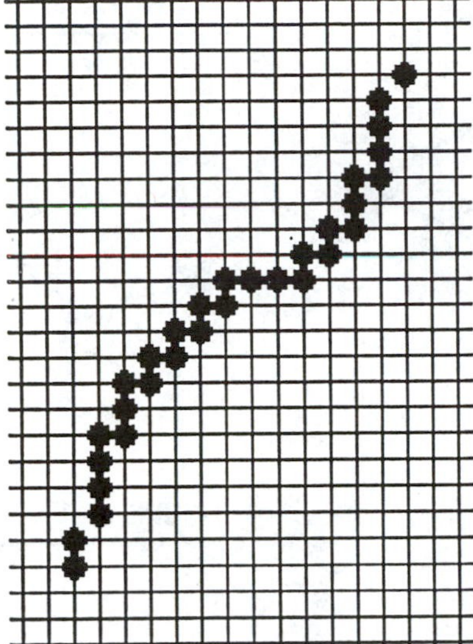

FIGURE 13.13

must be drawn in the order of increasing z-values. One possible way of doing this is first to draw a curve at constant z and then draw all pieces of the constant x-curves between the first and the next constant z-curve that we are to draw. After this, we draw the next curve for constant z. Figure 13.18 shows the order and direction in which the curve and pieces of curves are to be drawn. Another possibility is to draw a curve at constant x, then the pieces of constant z-curves between the constant x-curve and the next constant x-curve that is to be drawn. This is shown in Figure 13.19.

**FIGURE 13.14** Curves of constant z.

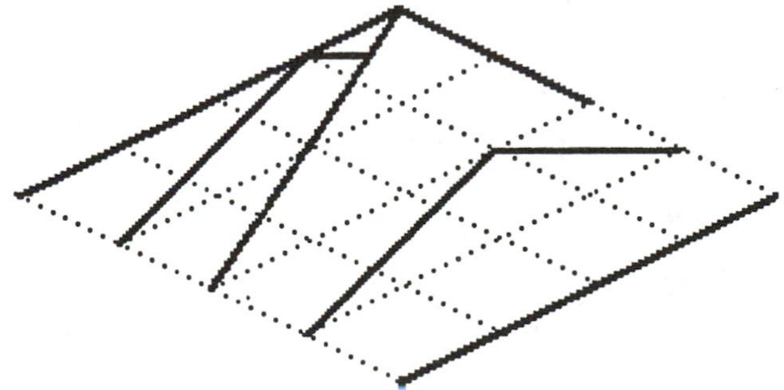

**FIGURE 13.15** Curves of constant x.

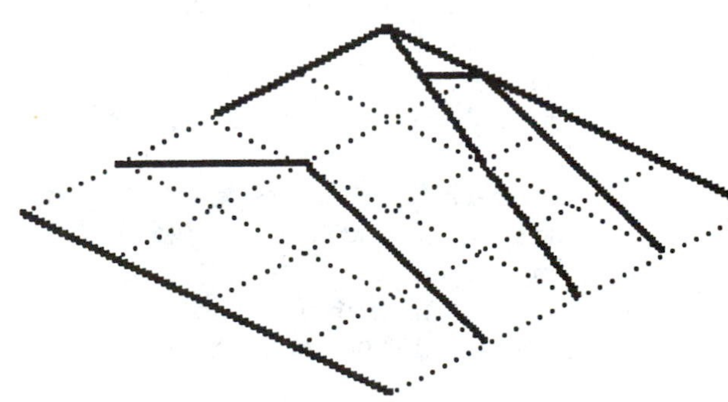

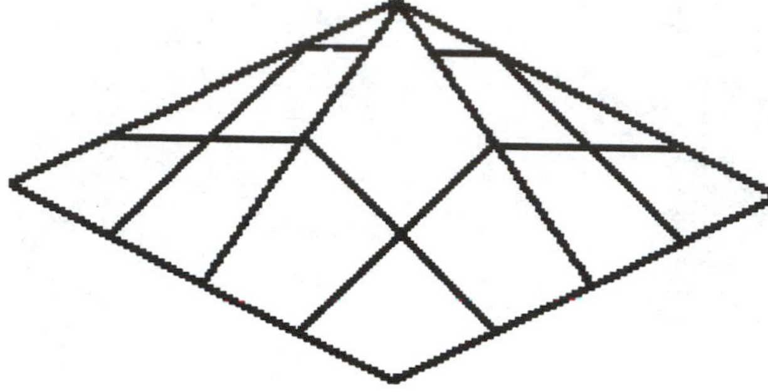

**FIGURE 13.16** Overlay.

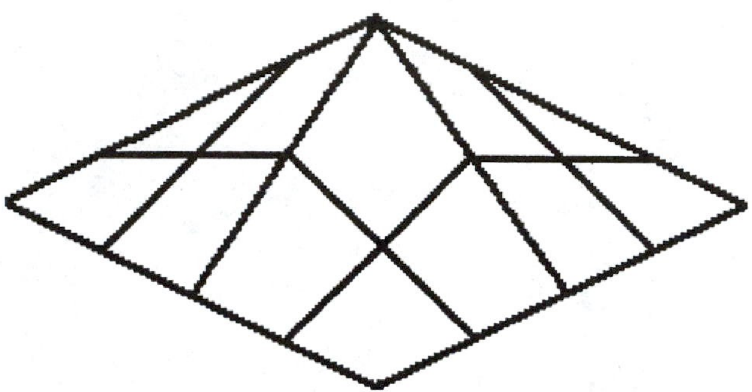

**FIGURE 13.17** Correct display.

Several problems arise when drawing a surface in this way. One is the problem of oversampling as described above. We now consider this in more detail.

No matter what angle, $\Phi$, is used for rotation about y, either the constant z-curves or the constant x-curves will be oversampled unless we reduce the number of samples accordingly. The number of pixels horizontally will be width*cos($\Phi$) for the constant z-curves and width*sin($\Phi$) for the constant x-curves. But we cannot use these values directly for the number of samples in the respective directions. For a very small $\Phi$, say 2° and a width of 300, we'd have only 11 samples for the constant x-curves, and for $\Phi = 0$ we'd have 0 samples.

We must not let this number become too small. When there is only a small horizontal extent, the curve will be steep. Even if we use a large number of samples, it will still produce a good appearance because, for a slant considerably over 45°, oversampling will hardly make the line thicker.

One more thing has to be considered. We assume again a small rotation angle $\Phi$, say 2°, as above. If we do a crosshatch with, for

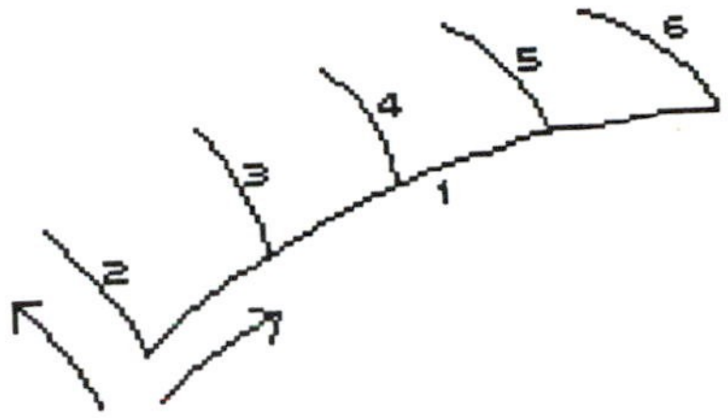

**FIGURE 13.18**

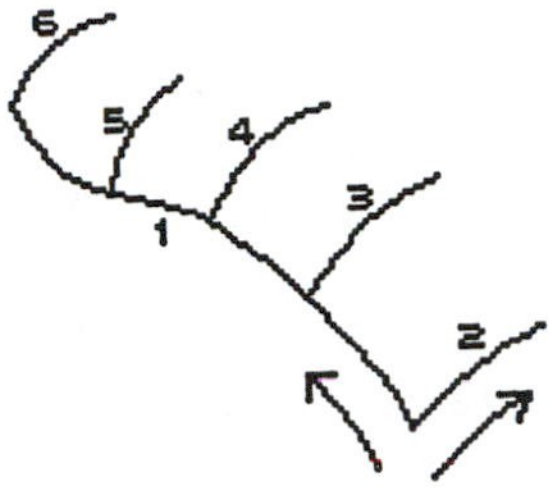

**FIGURE 13.19**

example, 25 curves in each direction, we would sample the surface function on 25 equidistant z-locations in the definition area when we draw the constant z-curves. The curves of constant x have to be drawn in 25 separate pieces. This implies that we have to sample the function at least at those z-values which were used for the constant z-curves. In our example we would use 25 equidistant z-values when drawing the constant x-curves, precisely one per curve piece. Although this makes a curve piece look like a straight line, there is no need to sample more often, because there is not even half a pixel in the horizontal direction. Even with more sampling a single piece will always look like a straight line.

If we had, for example, 35 horizontal pixels, we should sample on 50 z-locations, as this is the next multiple of 25. This would imply an oversampling of 15, but we would hit the z-values used for the constant z-curves.

We derive the following strategy from this. The number of samples should be an integer multiple of the number of crosshatch curves and greater than or equal to the number of horizontal pixels. If we apply this rule for both sets of curves, we will certainly evaluate the surface function for both sets of curves precisely at the location where they cross. If this is not observed, then, for example, pieces of the constant x-curves might not quite reach to the point where the next constant z-curve will be drawn and gaps would appear in the display.

Another problem arises when the surface is rotated ccw about y by an angle close or equal to 90°. If the rotation angle is precisely 90°, the drawing order of Figure 13.18 will suppress all constant z-curves except the first one. All constant z-curves are just vertical straight lines. The constant x-curves are still drawn correctly. The pieces of constant x-curves extend to the left precisely above the point where the next vertical line (the constant z-curve) would start. These curves will therefore never be drawn.

On the other hand, crosshatching a surface does not make much sense for rotation angles of 0° or 90° because one set of curves will degenerate to vertical lines that convey no information about the shape of the curve. They can just as well be left out.

When the rotation angle is close to 0° or 90° the appearance of the steep set of crosshatch curves can be poor. This problem is easily solved by changing the order in which the curves and curve pieces are drawn. In general we can say that the drawing order of Figure 13.18 will produce correct drawings for rotation angles from 0° up, but not near 90°, and the order of Figure 13.19 will produce correct drawings for rotation angles from 90° down, but not near 0°. There is a considerable overlap in which both orders work well. A general drawing algorithm should change the drawing order at 45°. We must avoid, however, rotating the surface about y by negative angles or by more than 90°.

**Coded Algorithm** The algorithm for crosshatching a surface function is described partly in pseudocode to avoid distracting detail. All terms and identifiers are the same as in the coded algorithm for unidirectional hatching. In addition we compute the number of samples for the two sets of curves from the rotation angles and from the number of curves to be drawn, stepx and stepz. Stepx is the smallest multiple of the number of curves that is bigger than width*cos($\Phi$) and stepz is the analog for width*sin($\Phi$). Rotating a computed surface point, updating the horizons, and drawing a line to that point is a piece of code that is needed twice in almost identical form so we put it in the procedure rotate_update_draw.

```
procedure rotate_update_draw(x,y,z : real);
begin
  rotate (x,y,z) around y
        and then around x
        giving (xr,yr,zr);

  form_x := curr_x;
  form_y := curr_y;
  curr_x := xr*width;
  curr_y := yr*hight;

  if up_hor[curr_x] not initialized
  then begin {initialize up_hor and lo_hor}
    up_hor[curr_x] := curr_y;
    lo_hor[curr_x] := curr_y
```

```
  end
  else begin {update up_hor and lo_hor}
    up_hor[curr_x] := max(up_hor[curr_x],curr_y);
    lo_hor[curr_x] := min(lo_hor[curr_x],curr_y)
  end;

  {the code below is not executed for
   the very first point in a curve}
  if x > 0
  then begin
    if form_y = up_hor[form_x] or curr_y = up_hor[curr_x]
    then begin
      move(form_x,up_hor[form_x]);
      draw(curr_x,up_hor[curr_x])
    end;
    if form_y = lo_hor[form_x] or curr_y = lo_hor[curr_x]
    then begin
      move(form_x,lo_hor[form_x]);
      draw(curr_x,lo_hor[curr_x])
    end
  end
end {procedure rotate_update_draw};

begin
  stepx := trunc((round(width*cos(angy))-0.5)/num_crv)
                *num_crv+num_crv;
  stepz := trunc((round(width*sin(angy))-0.5)/num_crv)
                *num_crv+num_crv;

  for z from 0 to 1 in steps of 1/num_crv do begin
    {draw a constant-z-curve}
    for x from 0 to 1 in steps of 1/stepx do
      rotate_update_draw(x,f(x,z),z);
    if z < 1 then
    {draw num_crv pieces of constant-x-curves}
    for x := 0 to 1 in steps of 1/num_crv do
      for zh := z to z+1/num_crv in steps of 1/stepz do
        rotate_update_draw(x,f(x,zh),zh)
  end {for z}
end.
```

The same function as before is shown in Figure 13.20 as a crosshatched surface. The rotation angles are also the same. Figure 13.21 shows the same function in a perspective in which the underside is visible. The rotations are: y-axis 20°, x-axis −20°.

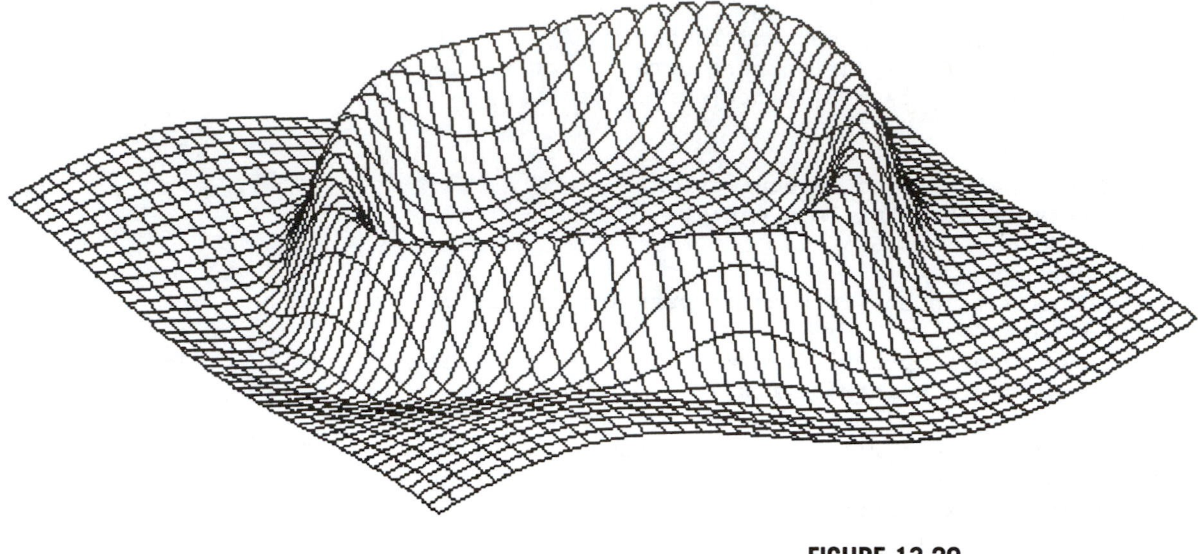

FIGURE 13.20

FIGURE 13.21

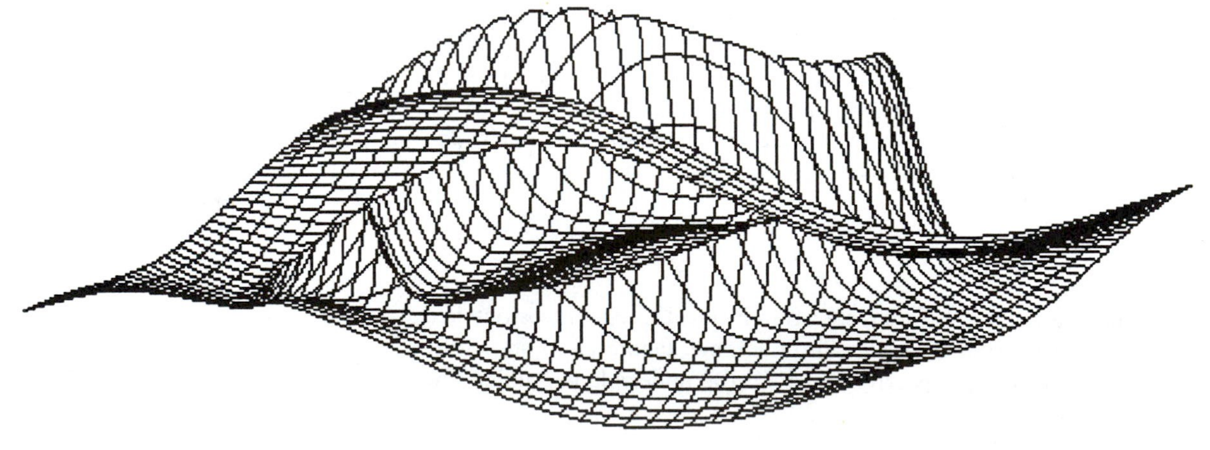

# 13.2 HIDDEN SURFACE AND HIDDEN LINE REMOVAL FOR GRID SURFACES

This section deals with another special case of a 3-D object, a grid surface. A *grid surface* is one that interpolates among values defined only at the nodes of a rectangular mesh. The algorithm for removing hidden lines from a grid surface is well described, but more tersely, in ANDE82. Grid surfaces are often used to display a function of two independent arguments that are defined on a plane, for example, the (x,z)-plane, y = f(x,z). The function value corresponding to a certain argument (x,z) is depicted as the height above the plane (the value of f(x,z)) at point (x,z). The set of all function values over the area of the (x,z)-plane in which the function is defined constitutes a surface in space. A three-dimensional figure is necessary to display such a function realistically. Relief surfaces as described in the previous section are a good example, but modeling a relief surface by calculating many values of f(x,z) is extremely expensive and time consuming.

It helps to calculate the function values only for a lesser number of grid points in the (x,z)-plane and then to connect the adjacent points in space by straight lines. This gives a grid surface. In effect, we interpolate linearly between the plotted points. This grid surface is then projected onto a two-dimensional medium (a piece of paper or a display screen). We give up three-dimensionality for the sake of an easy, fast, and inexpensive picture. In most cases this makes sense, because our visual system easily understands projections of three-dimensional objects on two-dimensional media. The main reason is that the information available to the human eye-brain system is always two-dimensional, if we ignore the slight difference in the information presented to our two eyes.

At the very least, we should remove hidden lines when projecting such a grid surface to accentuate the three-dimensional appearance. On a raster display, we could use the painter's algorithm to perform a "fake" hidden line removal, but we want to examine how hidden lines as such can be removed. The projected image of such a grid surface has geometric properties that make hidden line removal easier than in the general case.

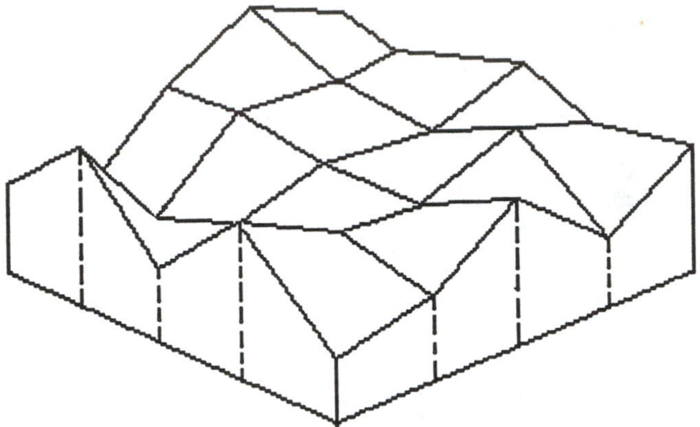

**FIGURE 13.22** A grid surface.

Figure 13.22 shows a typical grid surface. Some of its facets are partly or totally hidden. Drawing such a surface by hand is not difficult, but to do it in the computer requires the determination of whether a facet is hidden. To do this, we decompose this grid surface. It consists of the sum of all its facets, defined on a rectangular grid that is not necessarily uniformly spaced. Each facet is the upper bound of a prism with a rectangular base which is in the (x,z)-plane. Of course, in the general case, the facets of a grid surface can also extend below the x,z-plane but we start with the simpler case of all positive values for f(x,z). This is easier to visualize and we really don't lose generality.

Figure 13.23 shows two isolated prisms from the edge of the grid surface toward us, with the prism between them removed. The facets are usually not planar rectangles as indicated by the cross lines in the drawing. We now investigate the conditions under which one facet can occlude another.

Whether or not a facet can occlude another depends on the point in space from which the surface is viewed. We will start with a general approach and let the viewpoint be at a variable point above the surface but with its x- and z-coordinates within the rectangular area of defini-

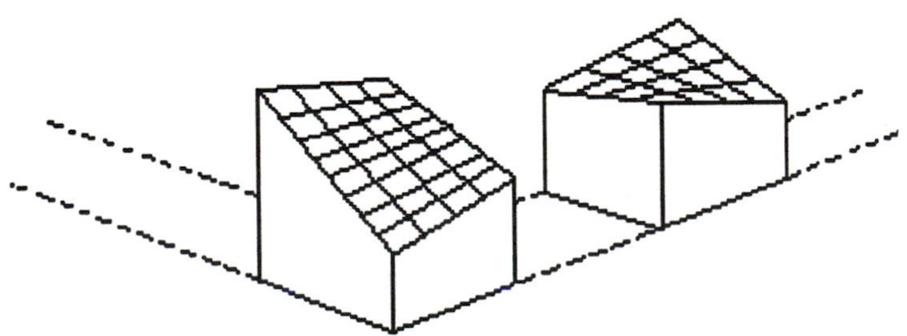

**FIGURE 13.23** Two prisms of a grid surface.

tion of the grid surface. Although this approach is general, it imposes no more difficulties than placing the viewpoint in a special position in space.

Figure 13.24 shows what we can see when viewing the two prisms of the grid surface from straight above at a point between the prisms. The dots mark the grid points in the (x,z)-plane and hidden lines are shown dashed. If the vertical edges of the prisms are extended, they all converge to a single point in the drawing, the *vanishing point*, VZ. VZ is behind the (x,y)-plane. This view is like looking down from an airplane onto a landscape of tall skyscrapers. The skyscraper notion is not only a good comparison but also extremely helpful in training our imagination. But there is a difference between our grid surface and the skyscrapers. The top facets of the prisms in the grid can be slanted and nonplanar, while the skyscrapers are usually topped by horizontal and planar facets. We have to remember this difference.

Before describing the construction of a grid surface, we must precisely define the grid surface in 3-D space. We assume that $x_0, \ldots, x_n$ and $z_0, \ldots, z_m$ are strictly increasing sequences of real numbers, not necessarily uniformly spaced. We use i to subscript the x-values and j to subscript the z-values. Points in the (x,z)-plane with coordinates $(x_i,0,z_j)$ are called *grid points*. The planes that are vertical to the (x,z)-plane and intersect it along the lines $x = x_i$ or $z = z_j$ are called *grid*

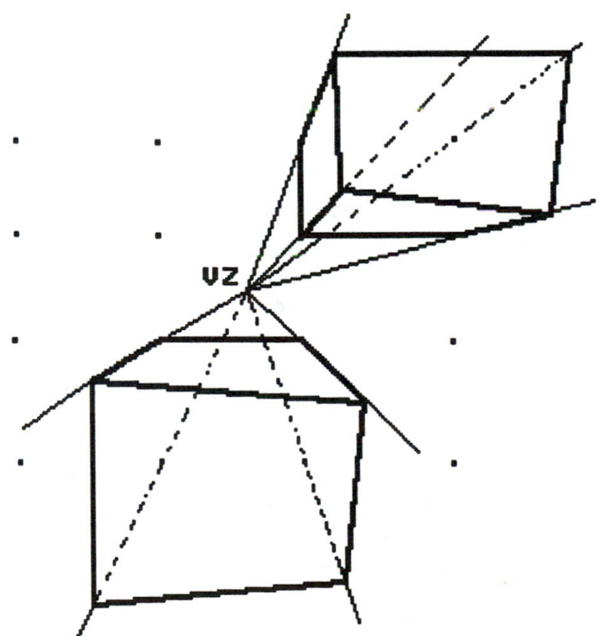


**FIGURE 13.24** Top view of two prisms.

*planes*. The rectangle in the (x,z)-plane which is bounded by the lines $x = x_i$, $x = x_{i+1}$, $z = z_j$, and $z = z_{j+1}$ is called the *grid element (i,j)*. There are exactly n*m grid elements.

The function to be displayed is usually defined for all points in the (x,z)-plane. The function value at point $(x_i,z_j)$ is $y_{i,j}$. To display the function, we get the $y_{i,j}$ values, connect those that belong to horizontally adjacent grid points by straight lines, and do the same for the vertically adjacent grid points. This gives us a connected grid of straight lines in 3-D space. It corresponds to approximating the function between the grid points by a bilinear combination of the four corner points of this grid element. For example, if $y_{i,j}$, $y_{i,j+1}$, $y_{i+1,j}$, and $y_{i+1,j+1}$ are the function values in the four grid-points surrounding grid-element(i,j), then:

$$\alpha\beta y_{i,j}+(1-\alpha)\beta y_{i,j+1}+\alpha(1-\beta)y_{i+1,j}+(1-\alpha)(1-\beta)y_{i+1,j+1},\ 0 \leq (\alpha,\beta) \leq 1$$

is the value of the grid surface on every point within the grid element. The part of the grid surface above grid element(i,j) is called *facet(i,j)*. (You will find that, for $(\alpha,\beta)$ = (0,0), (0,1), (1,0), and (1,1), the above reduces to the values of $y_{i,j}$ at the corners.)

We will project the edges of the facet and assume that this gives the projection of the facet itself, even though this is not always exactly correct. There are situations where the projection of a facet is not bounded by the projection of its boundary. But if we do not make this assumption, our algorithm will be impracticably complex. After all, the facets themselves are only an approximation of the true function value. We do get a reasonably good image of the grid surface.

To display the grid surface realistically, we must project it onto the view plane using perspective projection. It can be viewed from different points in 3-D space. As we explained in Chapter 6, the point from which we view it is called the viewpoint, with coordinates $(VP_x,VP_y,VP_z)$. To define the view unambiguously, we also have to specify the direction of our view: $(VA_x,VA_y,VA_z)$, a vector in 3-D space. In our projections the view plane is always normal to the viewing direction. If $x_0 \leq VP_x \leq x_n$ and $z_0 \leq VP_z \leq z_m$, we say that we view the grid surface *face-on* (from above). The picture we see in such a case is like that in Figure 13.25. If exactly one of these conditions holds, we view the grid-surface *edge-on* (from one side); if neither of the conditions holds, we view it *corner-on*, as in Figure 13.26. In all these cases we assume that $VP_y > 0$, that is, the viewpoint is above the (x,z)-plane. (To be completely general, we must allow $VP_y < 0$, but our considerations can all be done for the simpler case.) It is essential that $VP_y \neq 0$.

Viewing from such a point means projecting the grid surface onto the view plane (this is normal to the viewing direction). This projection transforms it into a two-dimensional image. In the view plane, we will take x-coordinates to the right and y-coordinates upward.

In Figures 13.25 and 13.26, the drawing is done as if we were looking toward the viewer (the viewer's eye is at VP) from behind the grid surface. Only the face of the grid surface toward the viewer is shown. The view plane is the screen. VP is the point from which the viewer sees the projection; it is identical to the center of projection.

When viewing the grid surface face-on, the perspective projection implies that the projections of the vertical edges of the prisms all converge to a single point in the view plane, VZ, which is the point where a line parallel to the y-axis through the viewpoint penetrates the view plane, as in Figure 13.25.

When viewing the grid surface edge-on or corner-on, again all projections of the vertical prism edges converge to a single point, which is defined precisely as above but in this case lies outside the projected grid surface, as in Figure 13.26.

**Occlusion-Compatible Order** When drawing the projection of the grid surface, we draw only the boundaries of the facets and only those which are not hidden by another facet. How is this achieved? It is done by drawing facet by facet in an *occlusion-compatible order,* that is, a facet that could be occluded by another facet is drawn only after that facet. An important characteristic of grid surfaces is that, in what-

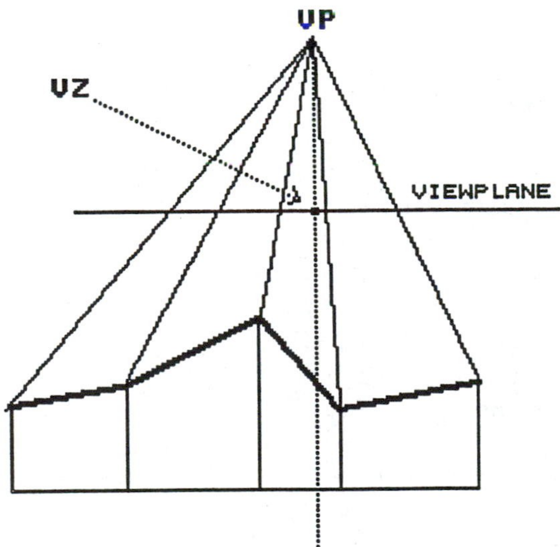


**FIGURE 13.25** Face-on view.

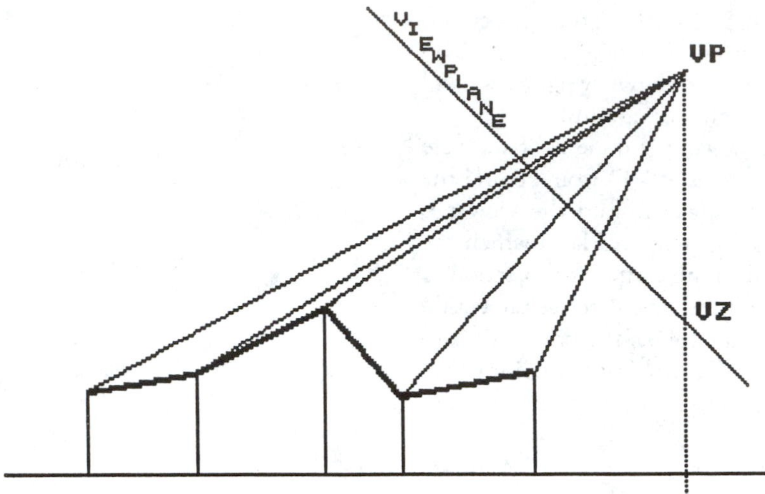


**FIGURE 13.26** Edge-on or corner-on view.

ever manner they are viewed, there is always a unique occlusion-compatible order in which the facets can be arranged. This is a consequence of the regular way that the grid elements are laid out. Grid surfaces differ in this respect from general hidden line problems where an occlusion-compatible order of facets either does not exist or is very hard to find.

It turns out that finding an occlusion-compatible order for a grid surface is easy. To explain it, we go back to the original grid surface in 3-D space and imagine ourselves sitting at the viewpoint above the grid surface, looking toward a point in some facet. The ray of our vision is shown in Figure 13.27. Only a few of the vertical edges of the prisms are indicated. Now imagine that the prisms extend upward to infinity so that our ray of vision must penetrate any prisms that are between us and the point toward which we look. In this case, it penetrates three prisms before reaching its destination point in the upper left facet. Figure 13.28 will clarify this.

Figure 13.28 shows the same situation as Figure 13.27 but in cross section. The plane of the cross section is vertical to the (x,z)-plane and contains the ray of our vision. It intersects with grid planes and possibly with facets. The vertical lines in the figure are extensions of the grid planes. They show where the ray of vision penetrates through a prism. Before the ray of vision can reach the point on the facet we are looking at, it must go through all the (extended) prisms along that ray that are closer to the viewpoint. Any of these prisms could obstruct our view of the point if the facet of its grid surface is tall enough.

In the projected image, the vanishing point VZ plays the role of

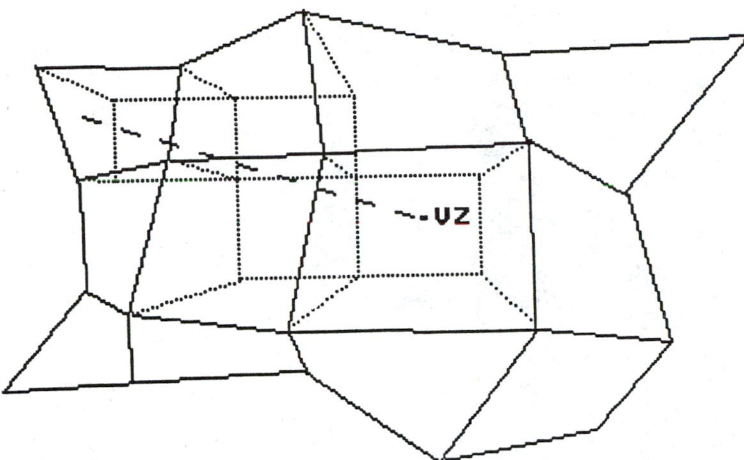


**FIGURE 13.27** The ray of vision, top view.

the viewpoint and a ray of vision is any ray emanating from VZ. If we draw a ray from VZ to any facet in the projected image, this ray will traverse the projections of several prism bases before it reaches the destination facet. This means that, in 3-D space, this ray would pass through all the corresponding prisms before reaching the destination prism. In an occlusion-compatible order the facets in these prisms must come before the facet of the destination prism. The question now is whether or not it is possible to arrange all the facets of the whole grid surface in such an order that the prisms penetrated by any ray emanating from the vanishing point will be in correct order.

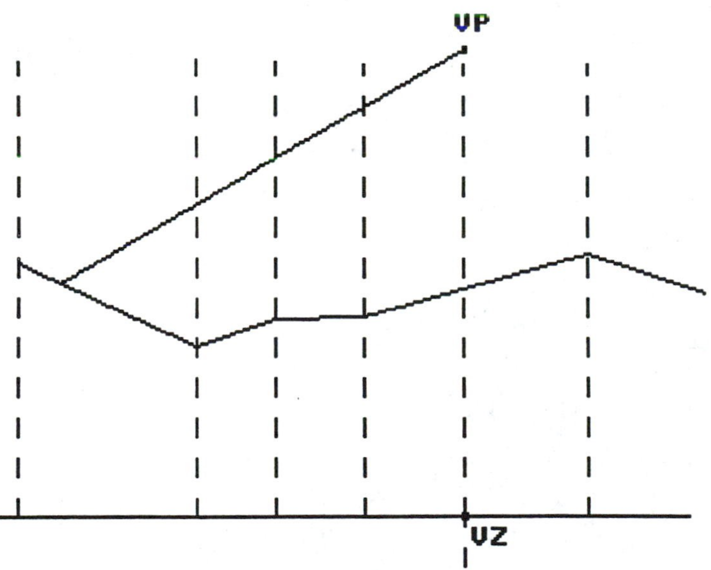


**FIGURE 13.28** The ray of vision, side view.

Of course, this order will depend on the position of the point VZ. But wherever VZ might be, such an arrangement is easy to accomplish for grid surfaces and this is an important fact behind this hidden line algorithm. For some locations of VZ, many different occlusion-compatible orders are possible.

To develop the algorithm, set the following:

$$x_{-1} = z_{-1} = -\infty \quad \text{and} \quad x_{n+1} = z_{m+1} = \infty$$

that is, to the smallest or largest numbers in the computer. Let K and L be such that $x_{K-1} \leq VZ_x < x_K$ and $z_{L-1} \leq VZ_z < z_L$, and also define the following:

$$\begin{array}{ll} K1 = \max(K,1) & KN = \min(K-1,n) \\ L1 = \max(L,1) & LM = \min(L-1,m) \end{array}$$

Then an occlusion-compatible order for any position of VZ is given by these Pascal for loops:

```
for i := K1 to n do
for j := L1 to m do facet(i,j);

for i := KN downto 1 do
for j := L1 to m do facet(i,j);

for i := K1 to n do
for j := LM downto 1 do facet(i,j);

for i := KN downto 1 do
for j := LM downto 1 do facet(i,j);
```

For some VZ positions, some loops are empty in the above scheme. The figures below indicate VZ and show the occlusion-compatible order by enumerating the projected grid elements. The projection of the grid onto the view plane can turn it in any direction, therefore the i-range and j-range are indicated.

Figure 13.29 shows the ordering of the facets for a face-on view. The formulas yield:

$$\begin{array}{ll} K = 3 & L = 2 \\ K1 = 3 & KN = 2 \\ L1 = 2 & LM = 1 \end{array}$$

No loops are empty.

Figure 13.30 shows the ordering of the facets for an edge-on view. The formulas yield:

$$\begin{array}{ll} K = 0 & L = 3 \\ K1 = 1 & KN = -1 \\ L1 = 3 & LM = 2 \end{array}$$

Two loops are empty.

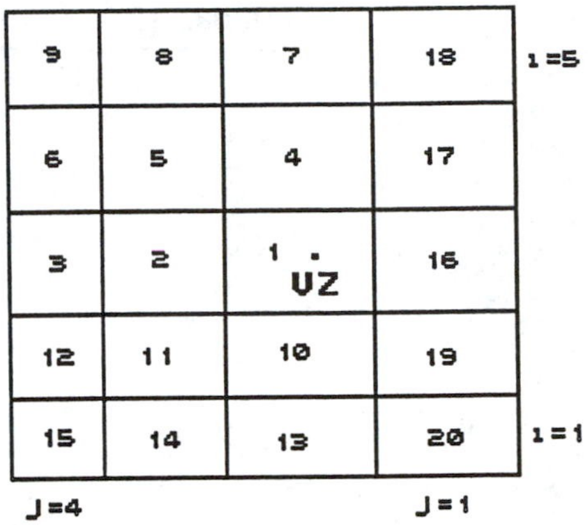

| | | | | |
|---|---|---|---|---|
| 9 | 8 | 7 | 18 | I=5 |
| 6 | 5 | 4 | 17 | |
| 3 | 2 | 1 · UZ | 16 | |
| 12 | 11 | 10 | 19 | |
| 15 | 14 | 13 | 20 | I=1 |
| J=4 | | | J=1 | |

**FIGURE 13.29**

Figure 13.31 shows the ordering of the facets for a corner-on view. The formulas yield:

$$\begin{array}{llll} K &= 6 & L &= 0 \\ K1 &= 6 & KN &= 5 \\ L1 &= 1 & LM &= -1 \end{array}$$

Three loops are empty.

The occlusion-compatible order can be characterized as a sequential order of the facets from $\text{facet}_1$ to $\text{facet}_{n \cdot m}$ with the property that if $\text{facet}_i$ can occlude $\text{facet}_j$ then $i < j$. If the projections of the facets are drawn in an occlusion-compatible order, then whenever a facet is drawn, all facets that can occlude it will have been drawn already. In drawing a facet we draw only the part not occluded by facets drawn so far.

**The Perimeter** We want to draw perspective projections of facets onto the view plane. These projections will henceforth be called

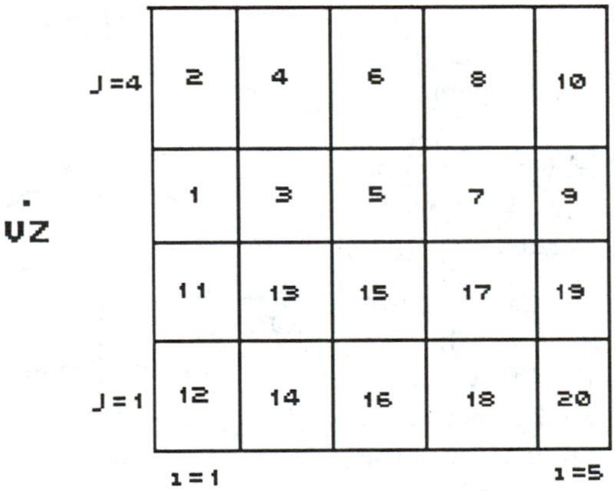

| | | | | | |
|---|---|---|---|---|---|
| J=4 | 2 | 4 | 6 | 8 | 10 |
| · UZ | 1 | 3 | 5 | 7 | 9 |
| | 11 | 13 | 15 | 17 | 19 |
| J=1 | 12 | 14 | 16 | 18 | 20 |
| | I=1 | | | | I=5 |

**FIGURE 13.30**

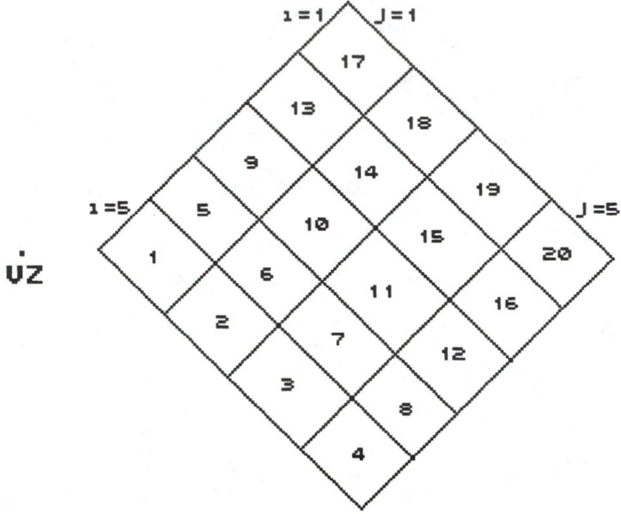

FIGURE 13.31

just "facets." The algorithm proceeds as follows. When the facets are drawn in occlusion-compatible order, those facets already drawn form a polygon that has an outside perimeter, henceforth referred to as "perimeter." Whenever a new facet is drawn the perimeter will be updated to include the new facet. The importance of the perimeter is that, when we want to draw a line to represent the edge of the facet, we never draw that part of the line that lies within the perimeter (that part of the facet is hidden). Compare this to the test against the upper and lower horizons for 2-D functions.

The initialization of the perimeter depends on the viewpoint.

a. If the grid surface is viewed face-on, the perimeter is initialized with the facet that contains VZ. Figure 13.32 shows this perimeter at the start and three facets later. The light lines indicate the portions of the perimeter not yet drawn.
b. If viewed edge-on, the perimeter is initialized with the sum of all front edges of the front facets. Figure 13.33 shows this perimeter at the start and three facets later.
c. If viewed corner-on, the perimeter is initialized with the front edges of all front facets in x- and in y-direction. Figure 13.34 shows this perimeter at the start and three facets later.

When $VP_y \neq 0$, as we have supposed, the images that are drawn have two important properties: they are always coherent and they are *star-convex* around VZ. The latter property means that if two image points lie on a ray from VZ, then all points on the ray between them also belong to the image. Star-convexity is a direct consequence of the

**FIGURE 13.32** Generating a face-on perimeter.

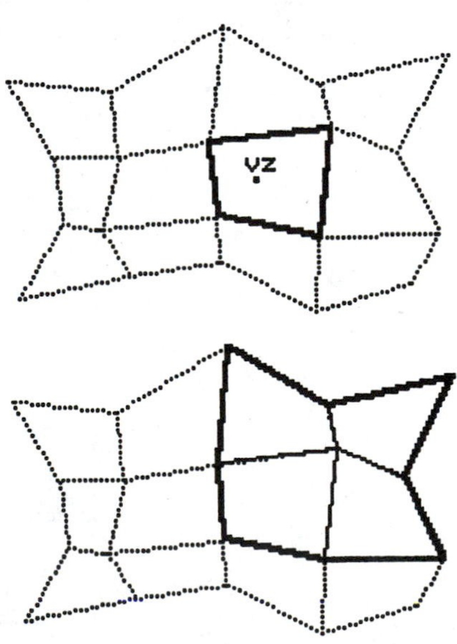

occlusion-compatible order in which the drawing is done. We only have to remember that we defined occlusion-compatibility using a ray emanating from VZ and it becomes clear that the one implies the other. At every stage of the drawing process the image has these two properties.

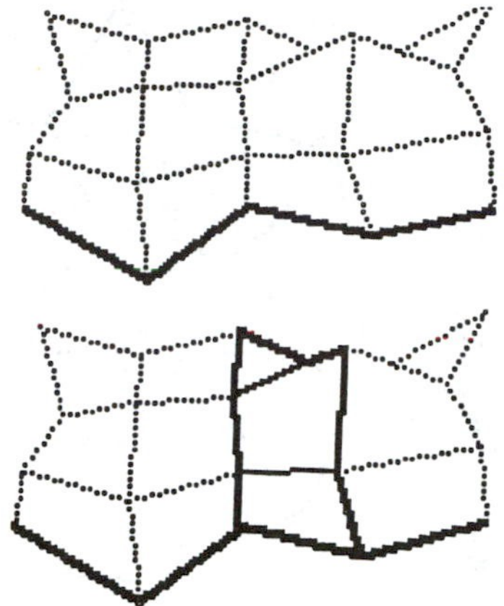

**FIGURE 13.33** Generating an edge-on perimeter.

However, there is another possible position of the viewpoint, a variation on the edge-on and the corner-on views, called *horizontal view*. The view is horizontal when $VP_x$ or $VP_z$ or both lie outside the range of the grid points but $VP_y = 0$ and the viewing direction VA is within the (x,z)-plane. The up-direction of the image in the view plane is identical with the y-coordinate of the unprojected grid surface. VZ does not exist (it is infinitely far away) and the image is not star-convex. The notion "star-convex" must be replaced with something that might be called "parallel-convex" with respect to the vertical. This means that when two image points lie on a vertical line, all points on the line between them also belong to the image. The occlusion-compatible order is either that for edge-on or for corner-on order depending on the location of VP.

The shape of the perimeter depends on the way the grid surface is viewed. The following figures show the perimeter in two different cases. A vertex of the perimeter can be determined uniquely by the angle of a line from VZ to this vertex and by its distance from VZ. This last property of the perimeter is a consequence of the star-convexity. If the vertex angles would reverse direction while traversing the perimeter vertices in consecutive order, then the vertices would always describe a non-star-convex shape. This is called the *monotonicity of the vertex angles of the perimeter.* It is valid at all times while updating the perimeter. It has strong consequences for the running time of the algorithm.

In the case of a face-on view, the perimeter looks as shown in Figure 13.35. The vanishing point VZ lies within the image. If the perimeter is traversed counterclockwise then the corresponding angles will monotonically increase. The perimeter is called the outer perimeter (there is no inner perimeter).

**FIGURE 13.34** Generating a corner-on perimeter.

In the case of an edge-on view the perimeter looks as shown in Figure 13.36. The point VZ lies outside the image. The boundary nearest to VZ is called the inner perimeter, the other boundary the outer perimeter. If the perimeter is traversed counterclockwise, the corresponding angles will monotonically increase on the outer perimeter but decrease on the inner perimeter. A corner-on perimeter looks similar to this one.

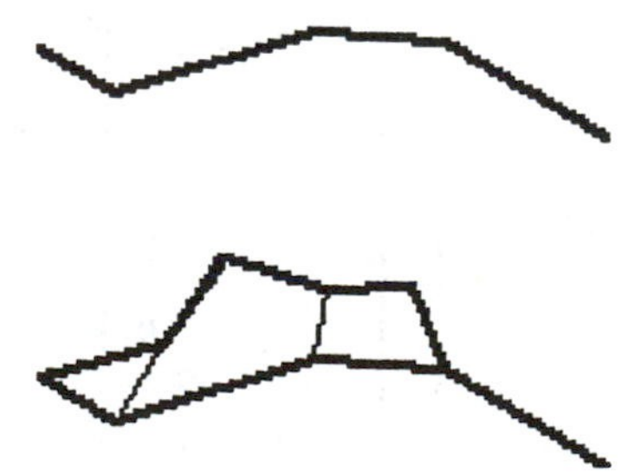

If a grid surface is viewed horizontally, the projections of the vertical edges of the prisms are parallel vertical lines (see Figure 13.37). The horizontal view comes closest to the edge-on or corner-on view because the angles around VZ in those views have a maximum and a minimum value. We can replace the "angle around VZ" by "left-right"

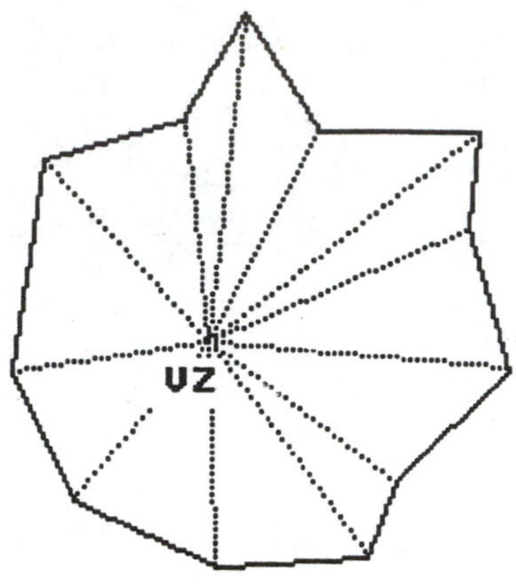


**FIGURE 13.35** Face-on perimeter.

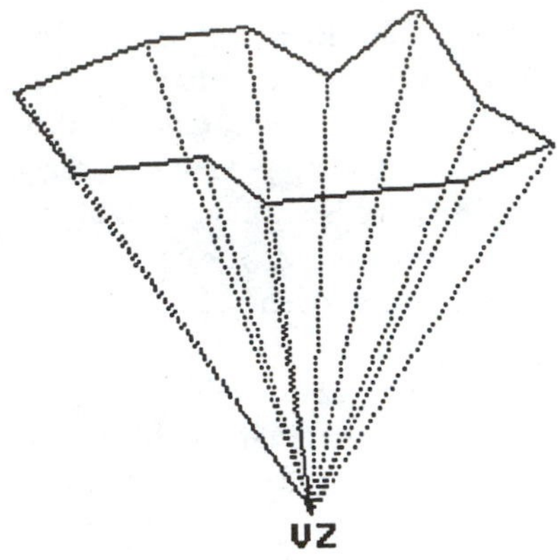


**FIGURE 13.36** Edge-on perimeter.

in the image of a horizontal view. Then the algorithms for edge-on or corner-on processing can handle this case.

In the following, "facet" means the projection of a facet onto the view plane. When the perimeter is updated by a facet, basically the angles of the leftmost and of the rightmost facet vertex are determined (in a ccw order around VZ); let's call them fmin and fmax. The "con-

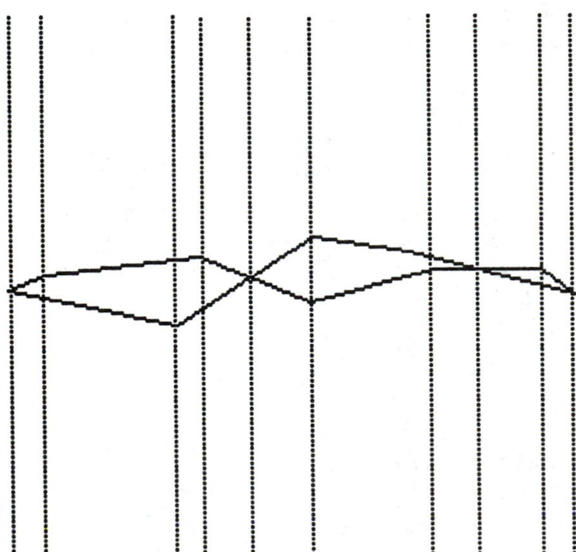

**FIGURE 13.37** Horizontal view, edge-on perimeter.

taining perimeter vertices" are the vertex Pmin, which is just smaller or equal to fmin, and Pmax which is just larger or equal to fmax. All perimeter edges that could intersect the edges of the facet can be found by starting with Pmin and following the perimeter in a ccw direction until Pmax. This is the direct consequence of the angle monotonicity. Without this property the search for perimeter edges that could intersect with the facet vertices would have to go through the entire perimeter. This would give the algorithm a running time of at least order $N_2$.

Some preprocessing of the facet can be done before the search of the perimeter vertices begins. This preprocessing reduces the number of facet vertices that can intersect. It consists of checking whether the facet is occluded by those facets that are immediately adjacent to it and closer to the viewpoint. It can happen that the facet occludes itself by being so much slanted away from the viewpoint that its upper surface cannot be seen. In this case a check against the perimeter boundary is unnecessary. If the facet partly occludes itself then some of its edges need not be checked further against the perimeter. But keep in mind that the algorithm that updates the perimeter by a facet also works without this preprocessing.

**Facet Preprocessing** If a facet is viewed edge-on then its vertices can lie in four different arrangements. The vertices are numbered according to increasing angles (see Figure 13.38). The dark edge drawn between vertices $F_1$ and $F_4$ is already present because it is the edge of a facet that precedes the current facet in occlusion-compatible order. The cases can be distinguished by calculating the z-coordinate of the cross product $(F_4 - F_1) \times (F_2 - F_1)$ and of the cross product $(F_4 - F_1) \times (F_3 - F_1)$. If $F_2$ lies to the right of the vector from $F_1$ to $F_4$ then $(F_4 - F_1) \times (F_2 - F_1)_z$ is negative. The same applies for the position of $F_3$. The table shows how these four cases are distinguished:

| case | 1 | 2 | 3 | 4 |
|---|---|---|---|---|
| $(F_4-F_1)\times(F_2-F_1)_z$ | - | + | - | + |
| $(F_4-F_1)\times(F_3-F_1)_z$ | - | + | + | - |

The edge already present is either a part of or inside the perimeter, but the other three edges can leave the perimeter. The vertices of these edges are shown in the next table (only the index of F is shown):

| case | 1 | 2 | 3 | 4 |
|---|---|---|---|---|
| edge can leave outer perimeter | 1234 | | 123 | 234 |
| edge can leave inner perimeter | | 1234 | 234 | 123 |

If a facet is viewed corner-on, there are 10 different arrangements of its vertices. The vertices are numbered so that $F_1$ has the smallest and $F_4$ the largest angle (see Figure 13.39).

The dark edges drawn between vertices $F_1$, $F_2$, and $F_4$ are already present because they are edges of the two adjacent facets that precede the current facet in occlusion-compatible order.

| case | 1 | 2 | 3 | 4 | 5 | 6 | 7 | 8 | 9 | 10 |
|---|---|---|---|---|---|---|---|---|---|---|
| $(F_4-F_1)\times(F_2-F_1)_z$ | − | − | − | − | − | + | + | + | + | + |
| $(F_2-F_1)\times(F_3-F_1)_z$ | + | − | + | − | + | − | + | − | + | − |
| $(F_4-F_2)\times(F_3-F_2)_z$ | + | − | + | + | − | − | + | − | − | + |

With only three calculations, case 1 is not distinguishable from 3 nor case 6 from 8. But this is not important as 1 is handled identically to 3 and 6 identically to 8. The edges already processed are either a part of or inside the perimeter, but the other two edges can leave the perimeter. The vertices of these edges are shown in the next table (only the index of F is shown):

| case | 1 & 3 | 2 | 4 | 5 | 6 & 8 | 7 | 9 | 10 |
|---|---|---|---|---|---|---|---|---|
| edge can leave outer perimeter | | 134 | 134 | 134 | 134 | | 34 | 13 |
| edge can leave inner perimeter | 134 | | 34 | 13 | | 134 | 134 | 134 |

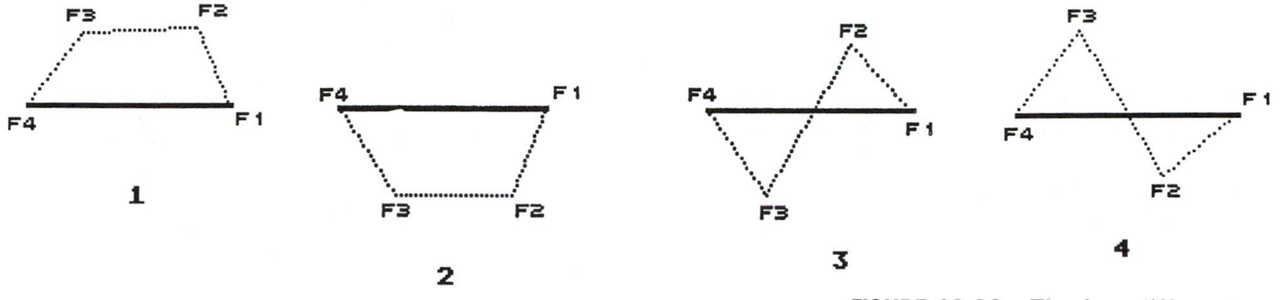


**FIGURE 13.38** The four different positions of edge-on facets.

**FIGURE 13.39** The ten different positions of corner-on facets.

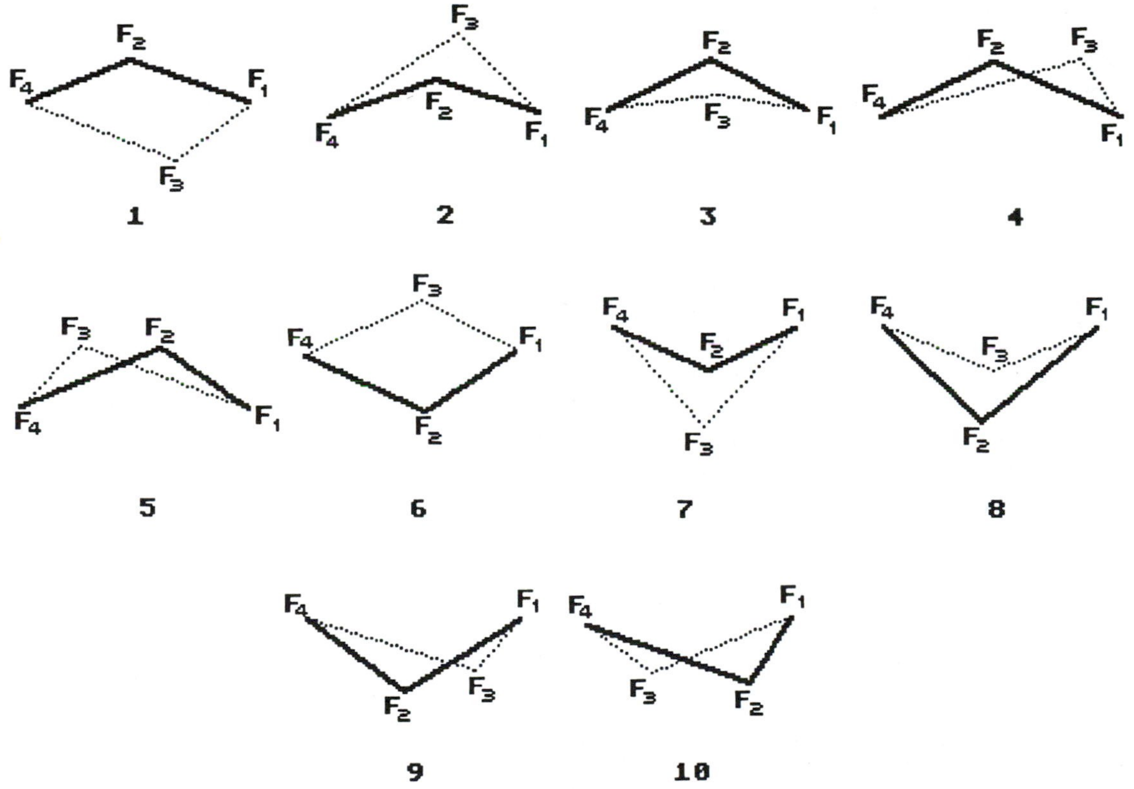

**The Pseudoangles** When searching for the two perimeter vertices that contain the current facet, we need to compare the angles formed by perimeter and facet vertices with respect to VZ. It is computationally expensive to work with real angles. This can be avoided by not using the angle and distance of a vertex from VZ as the sole definition of this vertex, keeping instead its Cartesian coordinates. Then the real value of the angle isn't needed and we can use instead a so-called *pseudoangle* as long as it maintains the angular order of all vertices with respect to VZ. It will be defined to do this; it is much easier to compute. The appropriate data structure for the perimeter is a linked list of the perimeter vertices. When traversing this list in one direction the pseudoangles will monotonically increase (or decrease). The pseudoangles will be used only to find those perimeter vertices that contain the facet. Each element of the perimeter list will contain the Cartesian coordinates and the pseudoangle of a vertex. The pseudoangle is defined as shown in Figure 13.40.

**FIGURE 13.40** Pseudoangle.

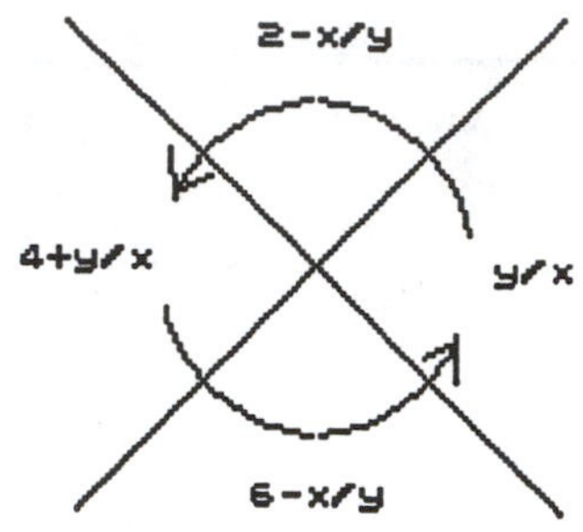


At 45° the value of the pseudoangle is 1; at 135° it is 3; at 225° it is 5; and at 315° it is −1. This discontinuity when crossing 315° must be considered when comparing the pseudoangles of vertices. Therefore the code below contains a function to perform this comparison.

**Coded Algorithm** In most practical applications (for example, terrain maps) the grid points are equally spaced in both the x- and z-directions. Such grids require the least amount of memory: a two-dimensional array g stores the whole grid surface. The x-coordinate of a grid point is expressed by the first index i of an array element and the z-coordinate by the second index j. The height at this grid point is the value of the element g(i,j).

The position of VP in relation to the grid surface determines the occlusion-compatible order and the type of perimeter we are going to use (face-on, edge-on, or corner-on). We must do a view plane transformation and a perspective projection of each grid element.

There are some rough rules of thumb for good view plane transformations. We put the view reference point R approximately in the middle of the grid surface. This makes the view plane normal automatically equal to the vector from VP to R. Let 2d be the distance from VP to R. We put the view plane (the screen) onto which we project at about the distance d from R, so it will be halfway between these two points. This yields a good perspective. We set view up to give the upward direction that we desire.

After the view plane transformation, we do a perspective projection onto the view plane with VP as the center. VP now has the coordinates (0,0, −d).

It is unnecessary to do the two transformations on all facets before we start to draw. Doing so would require a memory about twice as large as the original array that holds the grid surface data. We really only need to transform the vertices of the facet that we are about to process. However, depending on the order in which we proceed through the facets, if we store just about one row or one column of the transformed vertices we can avoid repeating the same transformation up to four times per vertex. This is not shown in the code.

The code below updates the perimeter by the facet(i,j) in the case of a face-on view of the grid surface with the facet viewed edge on: i = k or j = l (see Figure 13.29). Four different traversing orders of the facet vertices have to be distinguished depending on the position of facet(i,j) relative to facet(k,l). In the case considered here a counterclockwise order of the vertices of facet(i,j) is $F_{i+1,j}$, $F_{i+1,j+1}$, $F_{i,j+1}$, and $F_{i,j}$; in the case i > k and j = l this sequence is $F_{i,j}$, $F_{i+1,j}$, $F_{i+1,j+1}$, and $F_{i,j+1}$; and so forth. For simplicity's sake no preprocessing of the facet is done, although this could greatly reduce the number of vertices to be traversed. Nor do we do corner-on processing of facets. Our purpose is not to cover every possible case, only to illustrate the idea of the algorithm.

Finding the subscripts for the traversing order in the four different edge-on cases looks somewhat tricky in the code but it just takes advantage of the regularity in the subscript changes when circling the four vertices counterclockwise (see Figure 13.41).

This code does not do the entire job of displaying the grid surface. We make several assumptions: the perspective projection of the grid surface has been done; the projection of the surface point $(x_i, y_j, z_{i,j})$ has the coordinates fx(i,j) and fy(i,j) in the view plane; the coordinates of VZ in the view plane are (vzx,vzy); the perimeter is a circular linked list.

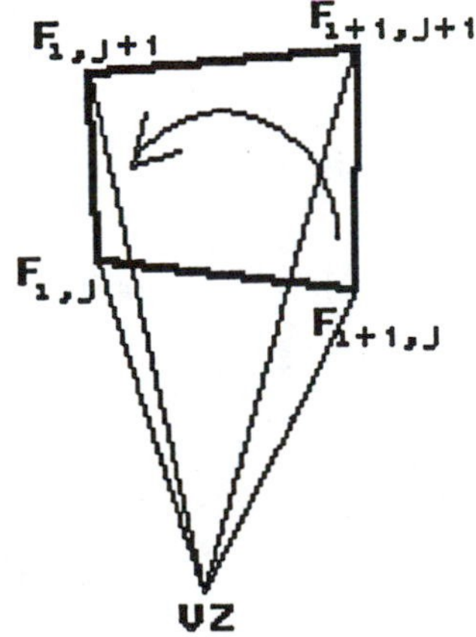


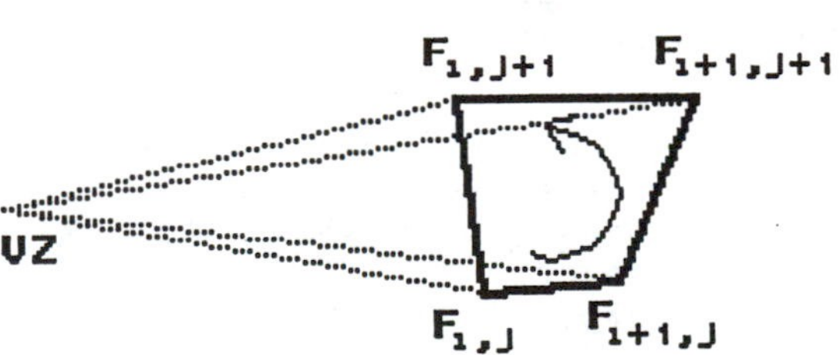


**FIGURE 13.41** Counterclockwise traversal of facet-vertices.

```
type vertex  = record x,y,a :  real;
                      p     : ^vertex
               end;

var dpx,dpy,dfx,dfy,
    cp1,cp2,cp3,cp4     :   real;
    firstp,
    facet,lastf         :  ^vertex;

procedure intersect(var ix,iy : real);
var d,s : real;
begin
  d := -dfx*dpy + dfy*dpx;
  s := (-(pl^.x-fl^.x)*dpy + (pl^.y-fl^.y)*dpx)/d;
  ix := fl^.x + s*dfx;
  iy := fl^.y + s*dfy;
end {procedure intersect};

function angle(x,y : real) : real;
begin
  x := x-vzx; y := y-vzy;
  if abs(x) ≥ abs(y)
  then if x > 0
    then angle := y/x
    else angle := 4+y/x
  else if y > 0
    then angle := 2-x/y
    else angle := 6-x/y
end {function angle};

function smaller(a1,a2 : real) : boolean;
begin {discontinuity in the third quadrant}
  if (a1 > 5) and (a2 < 1)
  then smaller := true
  else smaller := a1 < a2
end {function smaller};

procedure fill_facet_list(i,j : integer);
{enters the vertices of facet(i,j)
 into the facet-list in a ccw order}
var di,dj : integer;
    f     : ^vertex;

begin
  {distinguishing the four different cases of edge-on}}
  if i = k
  then if j > 1
    then begin di := 1; dj := 0
```

```
      end
    else begin di := 0; dj := 1
      end;
  if j = 1
  then if i > k
    then begin di := 0; dj := 0
      end
    else begin di := 1; dj := 1
      end;

  f := facet;
  repeat
    with f^ do begin
      { obtain (x,y) through view plane transformation and
        perspective projection of (i+di,g[i+di,j+dj],j+dj) }
      a := angle(x,y);
      f := p;
      if di = dj
      then di := (di+1) mod 2
      else dj := (dj+1) mod 2
    end
  until f = nil
end {procedure fill_facet_list};

begin {code for finding the intersections}
{create list for four facet-vertices; this is
 done once only outside this code, therefore
 it is shown as a comment
 new(facet);      lastf := facet;
 new(lastf^.p);   lastf := lastf^.p;
 new(lastf^.p);   lastf := lastf^.p;
 new(lastf^.p);   lastf := lastf^.p;
 lastf^.p := nil; }

{put facet(i,j) into the list}
fill_facet_list(i,j);

{find the first of the two containing
 perimeter vertices: firstp}

{set pointers to the first two perimeter-vertices}
p1 := firstp; p2 := p1^.p;

{set pointers to the first two facet-vertices}
f1 := facet; f2 := f1^.p;

repeat
  dpx := p2^.x-p1^.x;   dpy := p2^.y-p1^.y;
  dfx := f2^.x-f1^.x;   dfy := f2^.y-f1^.y;
```

```
{calculate cross products}
cp1 := dpy*(f1^.x-p1^.x) - dpx*(f1^.y-p1^.y); {(P1P2)X(P1F1)}
cp2 := dpy*(f2^.x-p1^.x) - dpx*(f2^.y-p1^.y); {(P1P2)X(P1F2)}
cp3 := dfx*(p1^.y-f1^.y) - dfy*(p1^.x-f1^.x); {(F1P1)X(F1F2)}
cp4 := dfx*(p2^.y-f1^.y) - dfy*(p2^.x-f1^.x); {(F1P2)X(F1F2)}

{if a crossing from in to out exists then compute it}
if (cp1 ≥ 0) and (cp2 < 0) and (cp3 ≥ 0) and (cp4 < 0)
then intersect(ix,iy);
{if a crossing from out to in exists then compute it}
if (cp1 < 0) and (cp2 ≥ 0) and (cp3 < 0) and (cp4 ≥ 0)
then intersect(ix,iy);

{advance pointers}
if smaller(p[2].a,f[2].a)
then begin
  p1 := p2; p2 := p2^.p
end
else begin
  f1 := f2; f2 := f2^.p
end
until f2 = nil
end {code for finding the intersections};
```

This code finds all intersections of the edges of facet(i,j) with the perimeter. Advancing to the next perimeter vertices and facet vertices is explained in the next figures. The terms larger or smaller refer to the angles of the vertices. A pair of perimeter vertices, $P_i$ and $P_{i+1}$, and a pair of facet vertices, $F_1$ and $F_2$, are involved in an intersection calculation. The first facet edge starts with $F_1$ and the first perimeter edge starts with $P_i$, so the next larger F-vertex must be taken for $F_2$ and the next larger P-vertex for $P_{i+1}$. These are the end points of the respective edges. These edges are checked against each other for a possible intersection using the cross product method. If an intersection exists it is computed. Then one of the edges must be advanced. If the biggest of the four vertices is a P-vertex then the facet edge must be advanced. Advancing the perimeter edge in this case would lead to a perimeter edge where both end points are larger than the facet edge, so no intersection is possible. Also, if $F_2 < P_{i+1}$ then the next F-vertex can be still smaller than $P_{i+1}$, so there can be another vertex edge intersecting with the current perimeter edge. The reasoning is analogous when the largest vertex is an F-vertex. In the case of equality, we advance F, leading to a proper termination of the search process. Figure 13.42 shows the rule for advancing and Figure 13.43 gives an example.

**FIGURE 13.42**

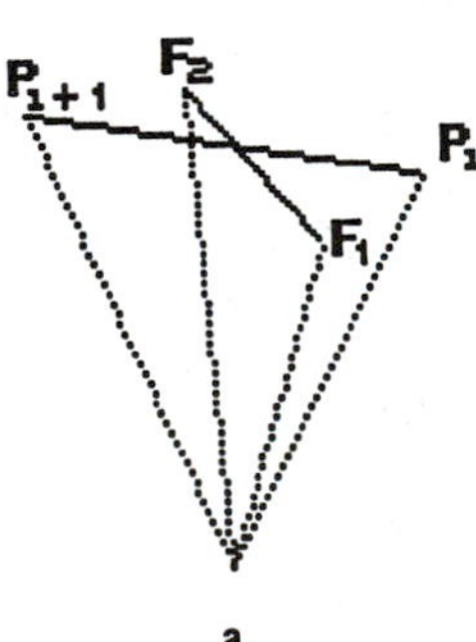


a.

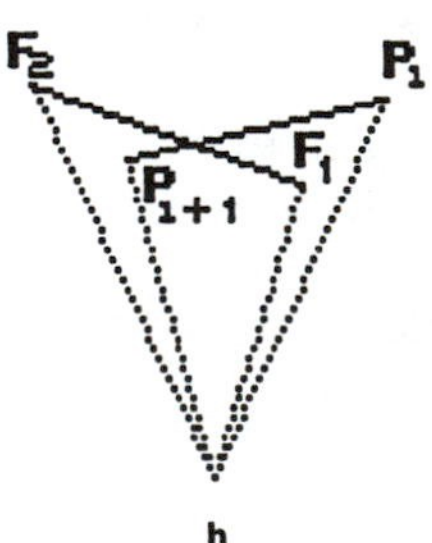


b.

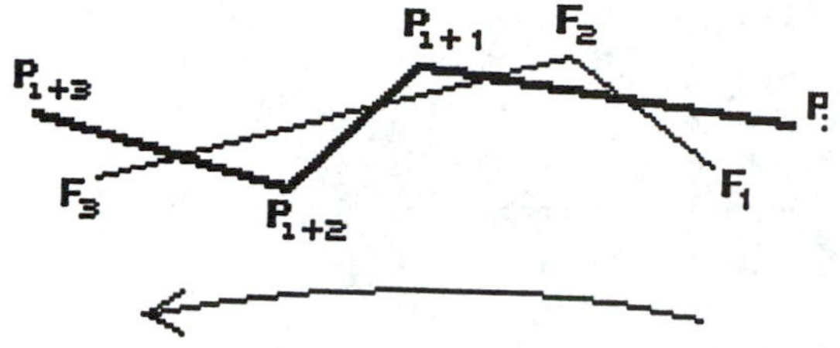


**FIGURE 13.43** Facet and perimeter intersections.

Figure 13.43 shows which edges have to be tested for intersection:

first : $P_iP_{i+1}$ and $F_1F_2$
advance F : $P_iP_{i+1}$ and $F_2F_3$
advance P : $P_{i+1}P_{i+2}$ and $F_2F_3$
advance P : $P_{i+2}P_{i+3}$ and $F_2F_3$

The algorithm requires only the first of the perimeter vertices, $P_{min}$. The search for $P_{min}$ is a straightforward traversal of the perimeter list and is not included in the code. By taking into account the order in which facets are added to the perimeter, it is not necessary to search the entire perimeter for $P_{min}$.

The code is for the case of a face-on view; in this case there is only an outer perimeter. In the other cases there is an inner and an outer perimeter and a facet must be checked against both, one at a time. There is always an even number of intersections. The first one comes from an outgoing facet edge, the second from an ingoing one, and so on in an ccw sense. All intersections are added to the perimeter. F-vertices between an outgoing and an ingoing intersection also will be added and P-vertices between those intersections will be removed. All edges between newly added vertices will be drawn. For a face-on view the grid surface drawing grows from the inside out.

**Extreme Cases** The algorithm for initializing and updating the perimeter must be changed a little in certain extreme cases. We have assumed so far that the viewpoint VP does not lie within a grid plane. But if this is the case, then VZ will lie on the projection of a line $x = x_k$ or $z = z_l$ or on both. The implication of this is that the perimeter vertices will not have monotonically increasing angles when traversed counterclockwise. But the code above requires strict angle monotonicity. An easy way to solve this problem is to divide the grid surface into two or four parts. If VP lies on the line $x = x_k$ then the grid surface is divided into the parts left and right of this line. Similarly, when VP lies on the line $z = z_l$ we have an upper and a lower part. If VP lies on a grid point, then we have two dividing lines and four parts of the grid surface. These parts cannot occlude each other, so they can be processed independently.

We then consider only the processing for one quadrant of the grid surface and within that quadrant only the processing of a facet adjacent to the boundary $x = x_k$. All other cases can be derived by symmetry. We assume that VP lies on the grid point $(x_k, z_l)$ and that we process the right upper quadrant. The perimeter is initialized with the facet(k,l) (see Figure 13.44). $P_b$ is the transformation of vertex (k,g[k,l+1],l+1). $P_a$ is the transformation of vertex (k+1,g[k+1,l],l).

The leftmost two facet vertices of a facet(k,j) with $j > l$ will lie on a ray from VZ to $P_b$. When such a facet is processed, the F-vertices to be considered are:

F1 = transformation of (k+1,g[k+1,j],j)
F2 = transformation of (k+1,g[k+1,j+1],j+1)
F3 = transformation of (k,g[k,j+1],j+1])

in this order. If the y-coordinate of F3 is greater than the y-coordinate of $P_b$, then F3 is taken as an intersection. From this we derive the following algorithm. When a facet adjacent to the ray from VZ to $P_b$ is processed we use the same loop as in the code for advancing the edges of perimeter and facet. But after terminating the loop we perform the above check and may get one more intersection. The same thing has to be done for facets adjacent to the ray from VZ to $P_a$. The strategy of including the computed intersections into the perimeter is the same as above. Figure 13.45 shows a grid surface in such a special case.

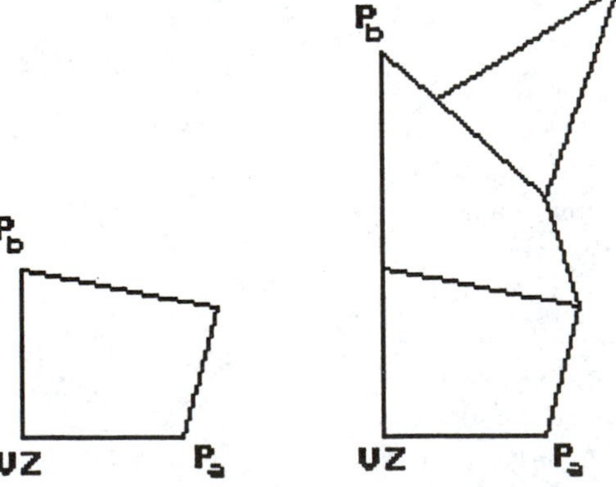


**FIGURE 13.44** Special case, perimeter at start and two facets later.

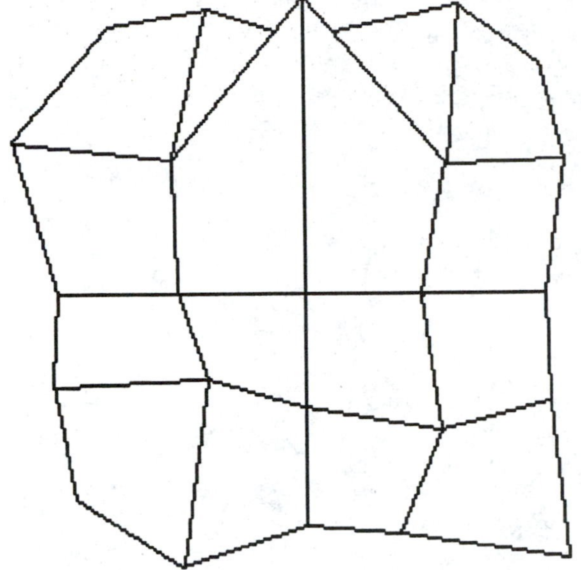

**FIGURE 13.45** Face-on view. VP is above a grid point.

# EXERCISES FOR CHAPTER 13

## Section 13.1 (Hidden Line Removal for 2-D functions)

1. Implement the floating horizon algorithm for crosshatch and draw the function y = (1/5)*sin(x)*cos(z) − (3/2)*cos(7a/4)*exp(−a), with $a = (x-\pi)^2 + (z-\pi)^2$, displayed in the area $[0,2\pi] \times [0,2\pi]$. A display of this function in unidirectional hatch can be seen in ROGE85.

## Section 13.2 (Hidden Line Removal for Grid Surfaces) Occlusion-Compatible Order

2. Use the procedure fracrect developed in the exercises for Chapter 10 to draw a fractal grid surface. Display the grid surface as a line display with hidden lines removed (fake hidden line removal).

Draw the facets in occlusion-compatible order as explained in this chapter. Draw the projection of each facet as a polygon filled with the background color, then draw its outline with a different color. Rotate all grid points before drawing and project perspectively.

## Edge-Perimeter Intersections

3. Use the cross products as done in the code to distinguish clearly between the following borderline cases. (F-vertices don't coincide with P-vertices.) Is an intersection produced or not?
   a. Start point of facet edge inside the perimeter, end point on the perimeter.
   b. Start point of facet edge on the perimeter, end point inside the perimeter.
   c. Start point of facet edge on the perimeter, end point outside the perimeter.
   d. Start point of facet edge outside the perimeter, end point on the perimeter.
   e. Start point of facet edge on the perimeter end point on the perimeter.
4. a. An outgoing F-edge intersects right through a P-vertex (see Figure 13.46). This F-edge will be checked against two P-edges. In this case only the intersection at the start point of a P-edge is considered. Why?

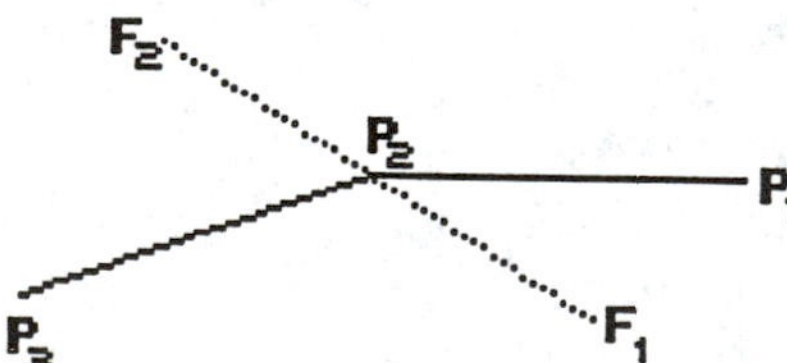


FIGURE 13.46

   b. An ingoing F-edge intersects right through a P-vertex (see Figure 13.47). This F-edge will be checked against two P-edges. In this case only the intersection at the end point of a P-edge is considered. Why?

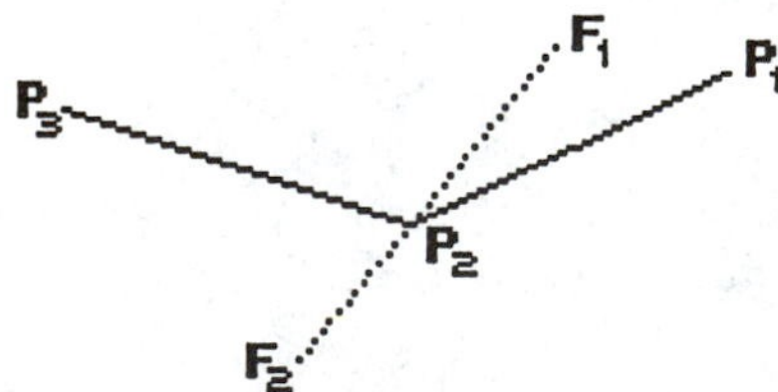


FIGURE 13.47

In Exercises 5 through 10 practice by hand (graphically) and verify with the cross products the cases illustrated in Figures 13.48 through 13.53. Indicate what intersections will be produced in each case.

5.

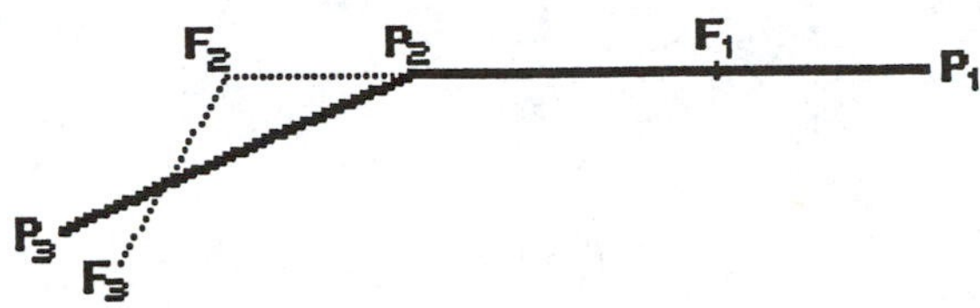


FIGURE 13.48

6.

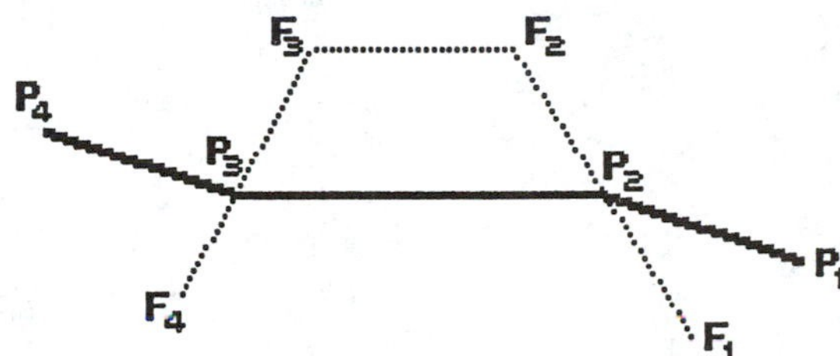


FIGURE 13.49

7.

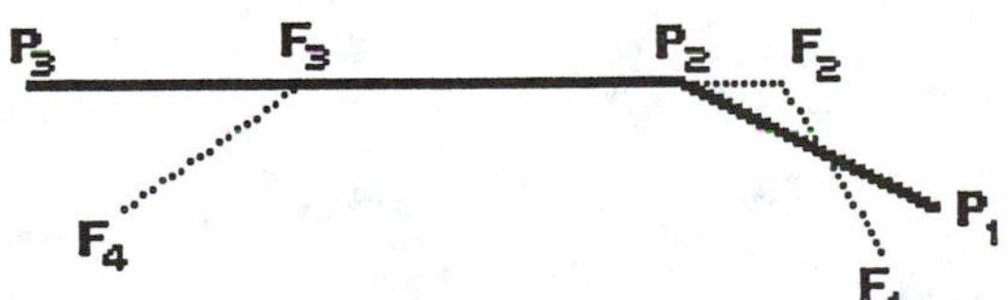


FIGURE 13.50

8.

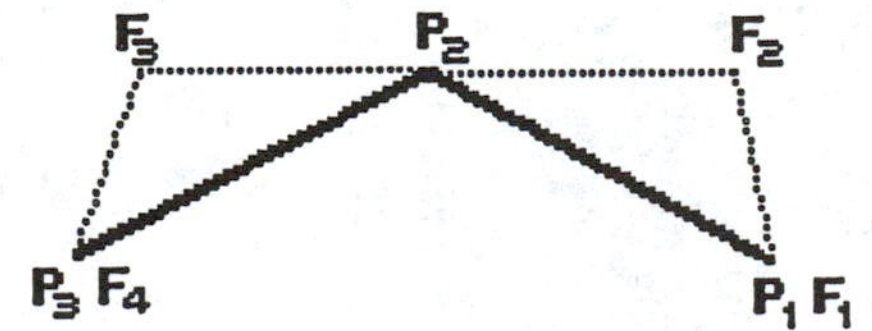


FIGURE 13.51

9.

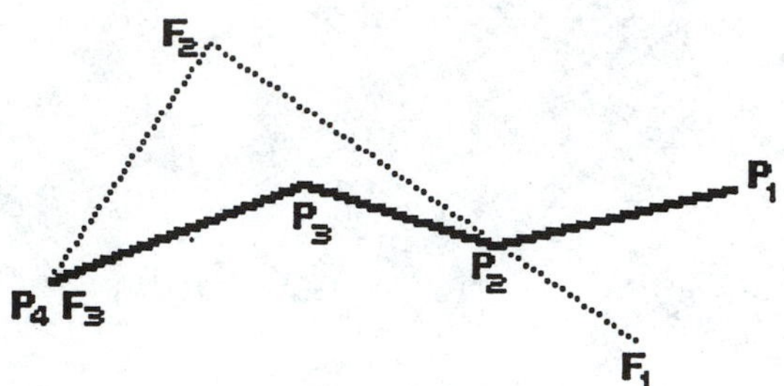


FIGURE 13.52 ________________

10.

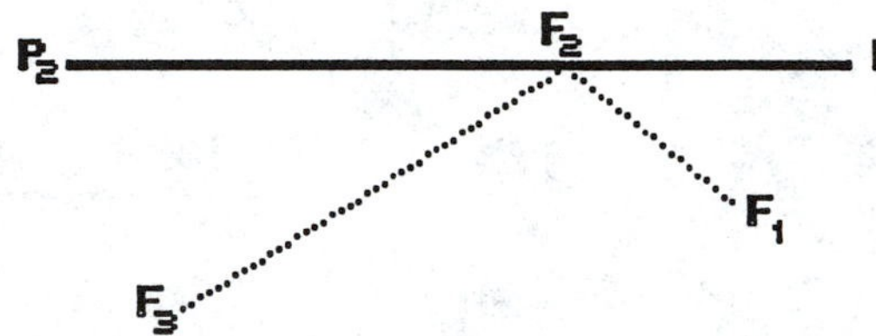


FIGURE 13.53 ________________

# Reflections and Shading

# 14

In Chapter 14 we study methods that help to make displayed objects look real by considering how light reflects or refracts from them. We look at several ways to apply shading to create the appearance of smoothness even when a surface is composed of planar polygons. The chapter has three sections.

**14.0 Introduction** outlines some factors that are important in creating realism.

**14.1 Lighting of Objects** considers both the sources of light and its interaction with the surfaces of the objects that we display on the screen.

**14.2 Shading Methods** are techniques for rendering the surfaces of displayed objects to make them appear smoothly rounded, creased, or peaked as desired.

# 14.0 INTRODUCTION

One of the major goals of computer graphics is to give an image visual realism, but producing images that look real is very difficult to achieve. The dictionary defines *rendering* as making a drawing in ways that bring out form and modeling. We want to render each part of our scenes to simulate objects of the real world. But we cannot work only with individual objects; there are interactions between the objects within a scene. Light reflects from one object onto others. Objects cast shadows. They have textures, colors, and highlights, or they may be transparent. Models must be developed for each of these phenomena. Most important in this context is the interaction between light and the surfaces of an object.

In an earlier chapter we investigated the properties of light and its colors; this chapter focuses on the interaction of light with surfaces. This interaction results in modifications of the light in several ways. One interaction modifies the qualities of light, its wavelength, composition, and intensity, another changes the direction of the light rays.

# 14.1 LIGHTING OF OBJECTS

For a realistic scene, we must render the objects of the scene in colors that closely resemble their real colors. This is not a trivial matter. What happens when we see an object in reality? We perceive it because of the light that comes from the surfaces of the object to our eyes. Visual perception is a complicated process that has been studied extensively; we will not go into detail. We mention only one aspect here.

There is a phenomenon called the *Mach band effect,* first observed by the Austrian physicist Ernst Mach, that makes smooth intensity changes look sharper than they really are. Under certain circumstances this effect influences the appearance of displayed surfaces in a most unwelcome way. The Mach band effect occurs whenever the light intensity on a surface changes abruptly.

In the next section, we will concentrate on where the light that falls on our objects comes from, its qualities, and how the object interacts with it. A model for the interaction of light with a surface is called an *illumination model.* This section will describe one such model, a simplified explanation of what occurs in the real world. Our model gives good results in the quest for visual realism.

### 14.1.1 Light Sources

Every object that we see in the real world emits light. This light has different origins. One possibility is that the object itself produces the light and emits it, for example, a lamp, the sun, or the stars (see Figure 14.1). Another more common case is that the light comes from somewhere else and is reflected by the object. In Figure 14.2 light from the sun is reflected by the gray sphere. This second case is the only one we will study in this chapter.

When we see an object, we actually see the light reflected from its surfaces. The light that is reflected originates basically from two different types of sources. One type we will call a light-emitting source. The other type we will call a light-reflecting source because the light coming from it is not produced by it.

*Light emitting sources* can be either *point sources* or *distributed sources*. If the light emitting surface is small compared to the surface onto which it shines, we have a point source, otherwise we have a distributed source. The distinction is not very sharp but that is not important because the mathematical models to handle both are only slightly different. We will call the light from the first *point light* and the other *distributed light* (see Figures 14.3 and 14.4).

*Light-reflecting sources* are all nonemitting objects in a scene, including objects that are not shown in the scene; in other words, the whole environment. When we try to produce realistic displays, we must recognize that reflected light is coming from practically all directions: the walls of the room, all illuminated objects, the sky, the landscape, whatever. It follows that a surface that is not exposed directly to a light-emitting source will still be visible because of the multitude of reflecting light sources around it. For example, something that is outside but shaded from the sun is still visible because the sky itself and many other things are light-reflecting sources. Light coming from such sources is called *ambient light* or *background light*.

In order to compute how much light is reflected from a particular surface of an object we need to consider these two types of sources. Each of them contributes something to the illumination of the particular surface. Figure 14.5 shows an example. The viewed object is a cube. Its front surface is illuminated by point light coming from the light bulb and by ambient light coming from the wall.

**FIGURE 14.1** Light emitting object.

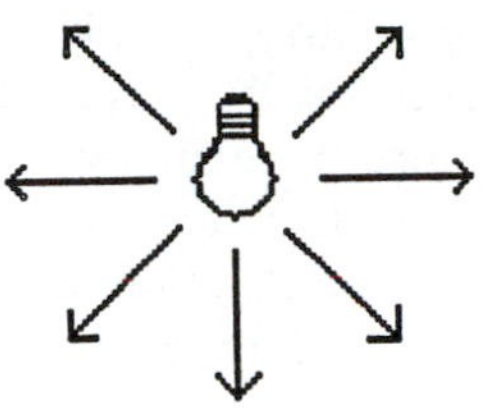

**FIGURE 14.2** Light-reflecting object.

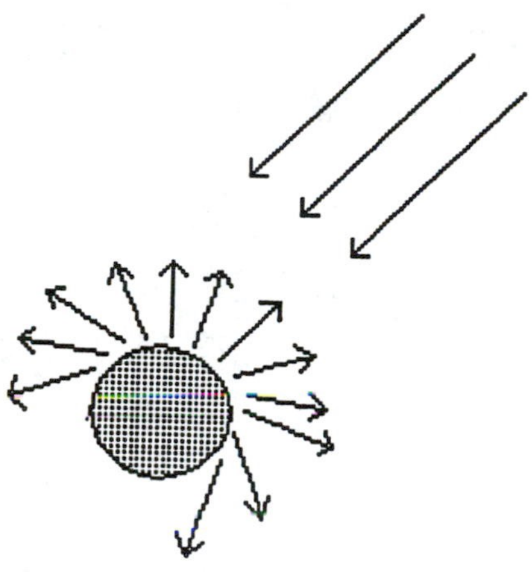

**FIGURE 14.3** The sun as a point light source.

### 14.1.2 Reflections

When light falls on a surface, it can be reflected, absorbed, or transmitted through the surface. These three effects are not exclusive; usually all of them take place. At this point, we are concerned only with reflection. It is reflected light that makes an object visible. The precise physical process of reflection is a very complicated one, well beyond the scope of this book, but a precise simulation of the physical process is unnecessary. We can get good results from simple models.

Since there are two types of light sources, we have two different types of light. There are also two types of reflection: diffuse reflection and specular reflection. The reflection model we use works with both sources. We now investigate how the two types of light sources interact with the two types of reflection.

**Diffuse Reflection** In *diffuse reflection,* incoming light is not reflected in a single direction but is scattered almost randomly in all possible directions. In addition, the incoming light is influenced by the surface. A surface will hardly reflect all the incoming light; part will be absorbed by the surface. The part that is not absorbed will be reflected randomly in all directions. Therefore, the direction from which the incoming light comes is unimportant (see Figure 14.6).

**FIGURE 14.4** A fluorescent light as a distributed light source.

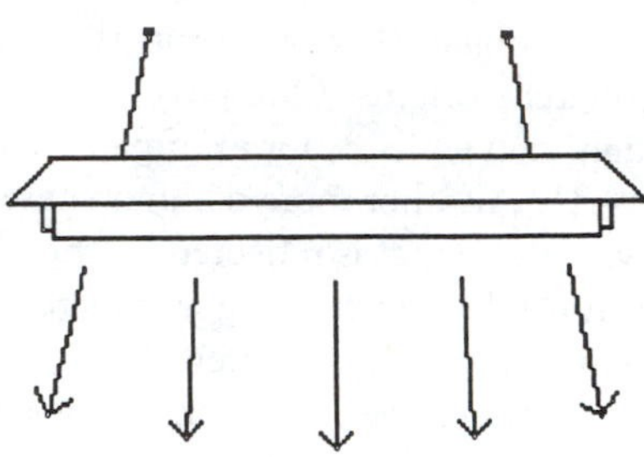

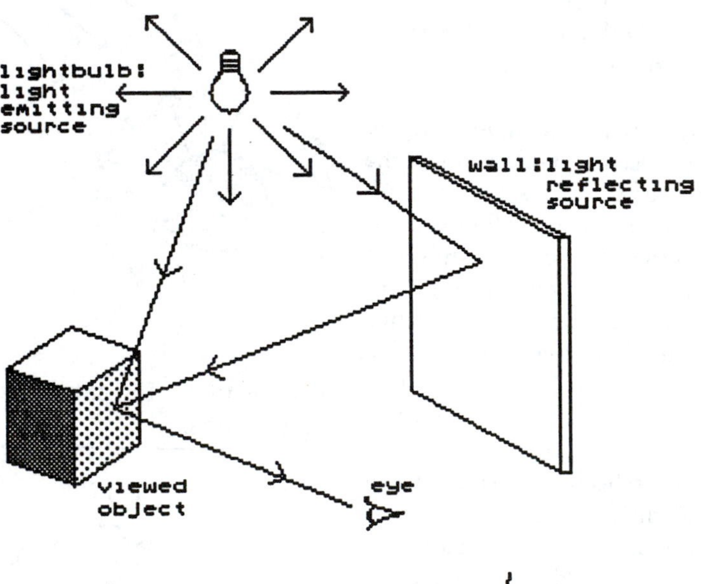


**FIGURE 14.5** Object simultaneously illuminated by two types of light sources.

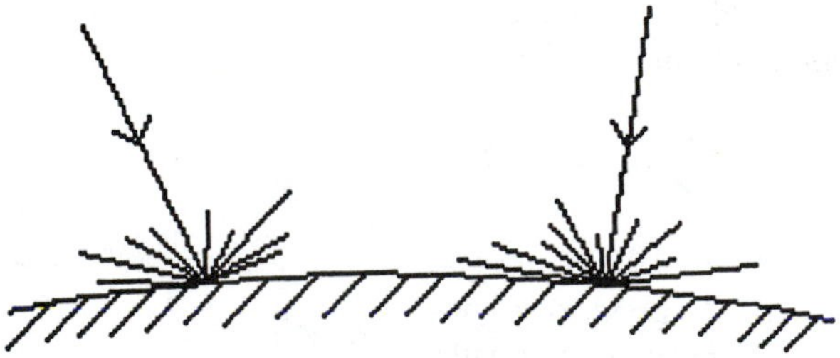

**FIGURE 14.6**

How much of the light is absorbed differs for different wavelengths of the incoming light. If a surface absorbs the red and blue wavelengths totally and green partly, it then reflects no red or blue light and only part of the green light. The surface will appear dark green.

We work in the RGB color system as explained in Chapter 9. The diffuse reflectivity of a surface is described by three parameters:

$$k_{dr} = \text{diffuse reflectivity for red}$$
$$k_{dg} = \text{diffuse reflectivity for green}$$
$$k_{db} = \text{diffuse reflectivity for blue}$$

These parameters are specified as values in the range [0,1]. The above example of a dark green surface might have a diffuse reflectivity of $(k_{dr},k_{dg},k_{db}) = (0,0.5,0)$.

The incoming light, whether ambient, point light, or diffuse light, will also consist of three components which describe its intensity in terms of red, green, and blue: $I_r$, $I_g$, $I_b$. In the real world there is no upper limit to the intensity of light but in computer graphics we have a maximum intensity for any of the three colors. These intensities are usually numbers assigned to the primaries of a particular color in the lookup table. The greatest value number depends on the hardware; the lowest intensity is always 0. We assign 1 to the highest intensity and 0 to the lowest in order to be machine independent.

Let us consider diffuse reflection of the several light sources. First we consider the diffuse reflection of ambient light. Ambient light comes randomly from all possible directions and also is reflected randomly in all possible directions. There is no single angle from which the light comes and no single angle to which it goes. We can think of it as being reflected equally in all directions. This means that the angle at which the reflecting surface is tilted in space is insignificant. The light coming from it will always be the same, producing a uniform illumination of the surface at any viewing position. The illumination will always be the same no matter whether the surface is curved or not.

The ambient light that hits the surface is described by the three components $I_{ar}$, $I_{ag}$, $I_{ab}$. Let us describe the reflected light by the three components $I_r$, $I_g$, $I_b$. We can compute the intensity of each component of the reflected light separately:

$$I_r = k_{dr} * I_{ar}$$
$$I_g = k_{dg} * I_{ag}$$
$$I_b = k_{db} * I_{ab}$$

These values for $I_r$, $I_g$, and $I_b$ describe the contribution from ambient light to the total illumination of a surface. Other light sources and other reflection mechanisms will add their share to the overall illumination.

Next we consider the diffuse reflection of point light. Point light differs from ambient light in that we must consider the angle from which it comes in our reflection model. Light from a distributed light source also comes in at an angle. We will not further distinguish between these two types of light and will treat them equally. They both constitute light that comes in at some incident angle. The *incident angle* is the angle $\Phi$ between the vector that points to the light source, L, and the surface normal at this point, N (see Figure 14.7).

**FIGURE 14.7** The incident angle.

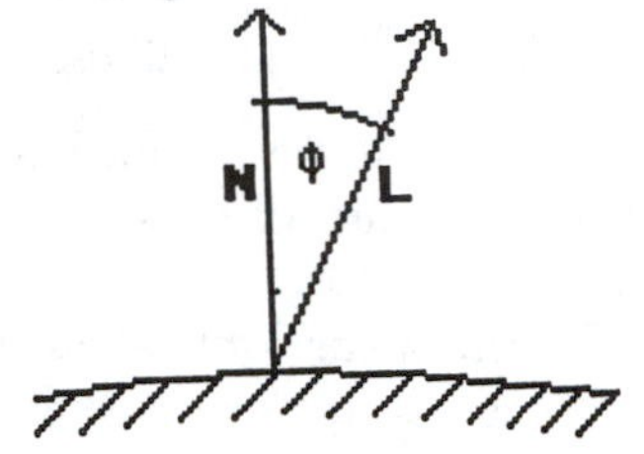


The property of the surface that produces diffuse reflection randomly scatters a part of any incoming light ray no matter from what angle the light ray comes. The rest is absorbed. But a light ray that hits a surface straight on brings more light per unit area of the surface than an equally intense light ray that hits the surface obliquely. To clarify this concept, we make a slight simplification.

We consider the incoming light rays to be parallel. This comes very close to reality for two reasons. First, the light sources are either very, very far away (like the sun) or very far compared to the size of the illuminated object. The light rays are so nearly parallel that the slight variations of the incident angles for a light source at finite distance do not make perceptible differences in intensity. Second, real "point" light sources are not really points, but areas. So, strictly speaking, the light rays hitting a certain area are never totally parallel but at different angles. The model would become unsurmountably complicated if we tried to consider all this and it would contribute little.

We account for the intensity of impinging light by the density of the light rays that come from the source. Figure 14.8 shows this. A certain number of light rays come from the left, hitting a flat surface perpendicular to the light rays. When the surface is tilted, it is hit by fewer light rays. When it is parallel to the light rays, no light at all will hit the surface. This shows that the intensity of the impinging light decreases when the surface is tilted. The intensity of the impinging light is proportional to the number of light rays that hit an area of constant size. This proportion is the cosine of the incident angle $\Phi$, $0 \leq \Phi \leq \pi/2$. We call this *Lambert's cosine law* (see Figure 14.8).

The lines in the figure represent the density of the incoming light. In case a the incident angle is 0; five light rays hit the surface. In case b the incident angle is 45°; only about four rays hit the surface although the rays are equally dense. In case c the incident angle is 90°; no light rays hit the surface.

This means that we must multiply all intensities of the incoming light by $\cos\Phi$ to get the actual intensity with which light hits the surface. It is the actual intensity at the surface that is reflected through diffuse reflection.

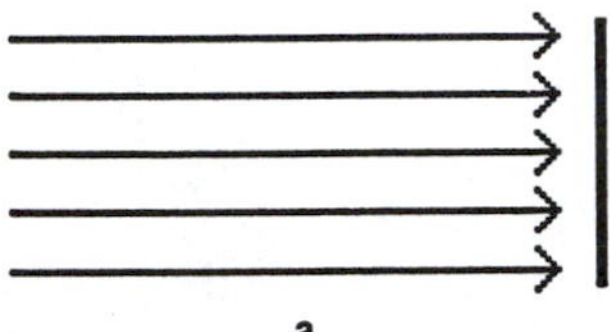


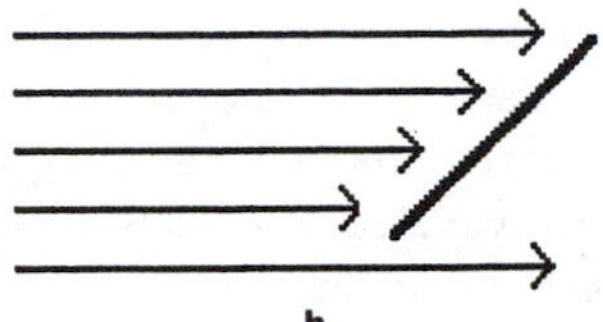


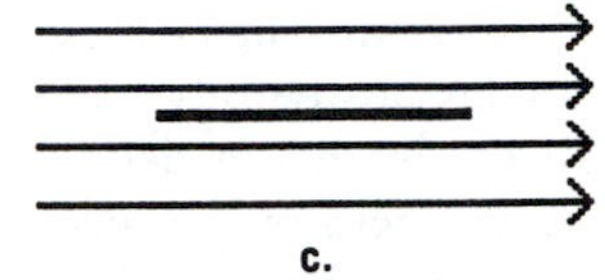


**FIGURE 14.8** Light strikes a flat surface.

Another factor that influences the density of a point light is the distance of the point light source from the surface. Usually the distances involved are so large compared to the size of the illuminated surface that the differences due to distance for different points on the surfaces of an object are negligible. In most applications, then, the distance from the point source can be ignored. In a small minority of scenes, it is important to allow for this, so the formula will include a distance parameter d.

Suppose that the intensity of light coming from a point source (or distributed source) is $I_{pr}$, $I_{pg}$, $I_{pb}$. The contribution of the point light to the overall illumination is:

$$I_r = I_{pr}*\cos\Phi*k_{dr}/d$$
$$I_g = I_{pg}*\cos\Phi*k_{dg}/d$$
$$I_b = I_{pb}*\cos\Phi*k_{db}/d$$

The cosine of the incident angle $\Phi$ can be computed as the dot product of the vector L pointing to the light source and the vector N normal to the surface: $\cos\Phi = NL$. Both vectors must be normalized for this computation. For scenes that are illuminated by the sun or by a far light source, the division by d is ignored. (Theoretically, the intensity of light coming from a point source decreases as $1/d^2$, but this is only for true point light sources, which never really exist. When a light source is an area, the decrease is less rapid. The above formula is a realistic model.)

We then have, for diffuse reflection of both ambient light and point light,

$$I_r = I_{ar*}k_{dr} + I_{pr*}k_{dr*}\cos\Phi/d$$
$$I_g = I_{ag*}k_{dg} + I_{pg*}k_{dg*}\cos\Phi/d$$
$$I_{brb} = I_{ab*}k_{db} + I_{pb*}k_{db*}\cos\Phi/d$$

**Specular Reflection** *Specular reflectivity* is the property of a surface that reflects incoming light in a nearly fixed direction and without affecting its quality. It is this reflection that produces highlights on shiny objects. We will use the empirical model of Bui-Truong Phong (PHON75) to simplify the very complex physical characteristics of specularly reflected light. In this model the specular reflection has no influence on the wavelength of the incoming light. All wavelengths (or RGB components) of the incoming light are reflected equally.

Figure 14.9 illustrates specular reflection. The vector L points in the direction of the light source. N is the surface normal at the point where the light hits. The vector R points in the direction of the reflected light. L, N, and R are always in one plane. The spatial angle between L and N is identical to the angle between N and R.

**FIGURE 14.9** Geometric reflection model.

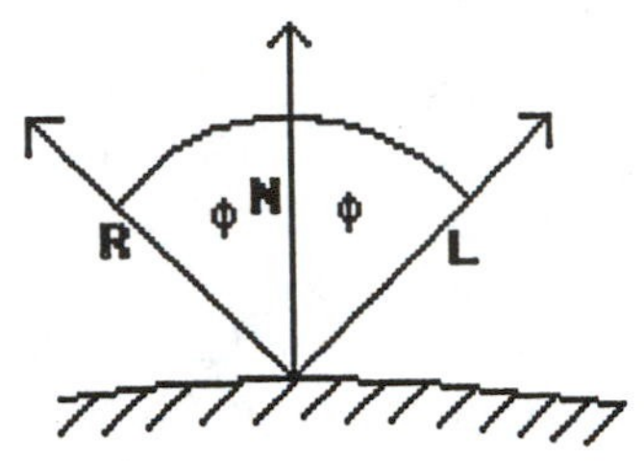


If we continue the systematic approach, we should now consider specular reflection of ambient light. Well, to be blunt, in our model there simply is no such thing. This is sensible because ambient light comes from all possible angles, so specular reflection must have the same effect on ambient light as diffuse reflection has: it reflects it in all possible directions. The only difference is that the ambient light is reflected without any change in quality. This amounts to giving the object some of the color of the ambient light in addition to its own color. The practical effects are subtle and are usually ignored.

So, the specular reflection of point light is all that has to be considered. The essential characteristic of specular reflection is that it depends on the angle of the incoming light. Only point light comes in at a prescribed angle.

There is one parameter to describe the quality of a specular reflection. It tells how the reflected light is concentrated around the reflection (mirror) direction. It is the *shininess* of the surface. A very shiny surface will reflect almost all the incoming light precisely in the direction of the reflection vector. A less shiny surface will reflect much of the incoming light along this vector but another part is scattered a little around the reflection vector. In Phong's model, the shininess of a surface is characterized by an integer n. Formally, this is done by multiplying the intensity of the incoming light by $\cos^n\Theta$. The angle $\Theta$ is the spatial angle by which the direction of reflected light deviates from the precise direction of reflection. Figure 14.10 shows a plot of $\cos^n\Theta$ for several values of n.

Assume that light with intensity I is coming from direction L. The reflection vector is R. Light that is reflected precisely in the direction of R has a deviation angle 0. It will therefore be reflected with intensity $I*\cos^n 0 = I$. Reflected light not precisely in the direction of R is at an angle $\Theta > 0$ to R. It is reflected with intensity $I*\cos^n\Theta$, a small value for large n. In other words, when n is large, little of the light is reflected in directions that deviate from R and, even for small values of $\Theta$, it will be practically 0. Very shiny surfaces, like polished

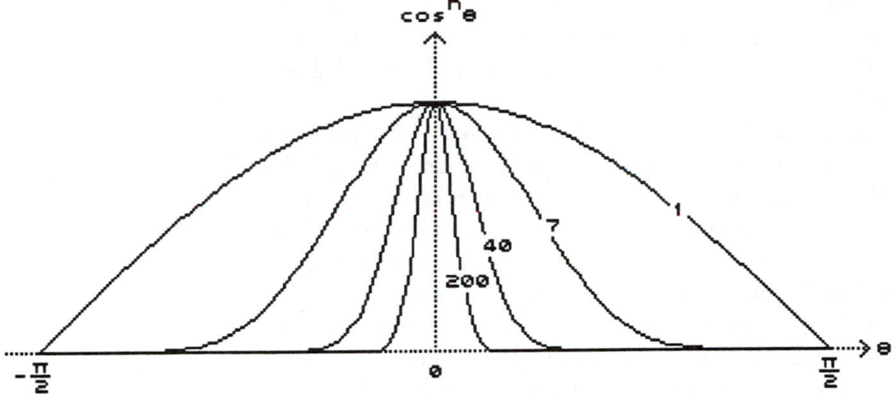


**FIGURE 14.10** Spatial distribution function for specular reflection.

silver, will have a large value of n (150 or more); less shiny surfaces have values of n as small as 1, for example, cardboard or paper.

Figure 14.11 shows how the angle Θ is involved in the intensity of the light ray coming from the incident point to the eye (the dotted line). We call this line the *line of vision.* Its direction is described by the vector V, also called the *viewing direction.* This line is not necessarily in the same plane with L, N, and R. If R and V are normalized, $\cos\Theta = R \cdot V$.

Our model simplifies the true case. Specular reflection actually is dependent on the angle of incidence and on the wavelength (see below). In general, the amount of reflected light increases as the angle of inci-

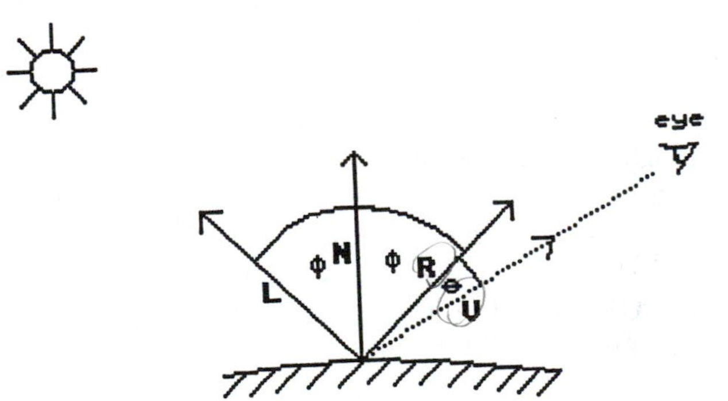


**FIGURE 14.11** Deviation of the line of vision from R.

dence grows. Light that strikes a surface at the grazing angle will be reflected totally, while light that strikes at a small incident angle may be only partially reflected. The rest is either absorbed, reflected diffusely, or transmitted.

You are familiar with this effect in glass. When we look at a sheet of glass at a low incident angle (almost face-on), we see "through" the glass because the light rays emanating from the objects behind the sheet pass through and reach our eyes. Very little is absorbed, and very little reflected. But it is hard to see objects through the glass when the glass surface is almost in line with the line of vision. The light coming from those objects strikes the surface opposite to us at a high incident angle and is therefore reflected from the surface. Only a small part of these light rays reach our eyes, making these objects almost invisible to us. To further impair our view of the objects, there will be mirror images of objects on our side of the sheet because the light emitted from them will be reflected toward us. Figure 14.12 shows such a situation. Object 1 will be clearly visible; object 2 is almost invisible. What reaches our eyes are reflected light rays from other objects on our side of the sheet.

How much is reflected depends not only on the incident angle $\Phi$ but also on the wavelength l of the incoming light. It is expressed by $w(\Phi,l)$, which is the ratio of specularly reflected light to the incident light. $W(\Phi,l)$ is called the *specular reflection coefficient* (NESP79) or *specular reflectance* (COTO82). Figure 14.13 shows the curves of $w(\Phi,l)$ for glass, gold, and silver as a function of only the incident angle. A complete description of $w(\Phi,l)$ requires a surface function or a table. The surface description of $w(\Phi,l)$ for copper can be seen in COTO82.

As $w(\Phi,l)$ is very complex, it is usually replaced by a constant $k_s$. This constant plays the same role as do the constants $k_{dr}$, $k_{dg}$, and $k_{db}$ in the diffuse reflection model, except that there is no distinction between red, green, and blue. So the formula for Phong's reflectance model is:

$$I_r = I_{pr*}k_{s*}\cos^n\Theta$$
$$I_g = I_{pg*}k_{s*}\cos^n\Theta$$
$$I_b = I_{pb*}k_{s*}\cos^n\Theta$$

Combining the results for diffuse ambient light, diffuse reflected light, and specularly reflected point light yields the model:

$$\begin{aligned} I_r &= I_{ar*}k_{dr} + I_{pr*}(k_{dr*}\cos\Phi/d + k_{s*}\cos^n\Theta) \\ I_g &= I_{ag*}k_{dg} + I_{pg*}(k_{dg*}\cos\Phi/d + k_{s*}\cos^n\Theta) \quad \ldots \quad (1) \\ I_b &= I_{ab*}k_{db} + I_{pb*}(k_{db*}\cos\Phi/d + k_{s*}\cos^n\Theta) \end{aligned}$$

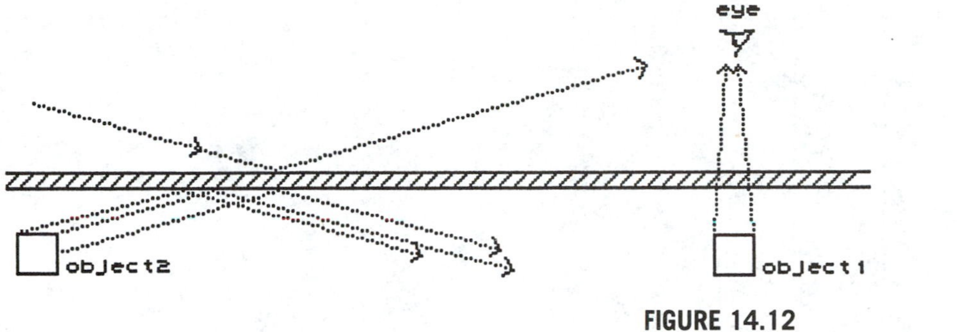


FIGURE 14.12

If there are several point light sources, their contributions are added linearly.

The above formula is not precise enough for physical reflection effects but it is usually adequate for producing realistic highlights similar to real specular reflections. This model is not adequate for materials whose reflectance changes significantly with the incident angle, like glass, for example. For such a material we should not use a constant $k_s$ but should at least approximate the curve for $w(\Phi)$. The model is fine for silver, acceptable for gold, and good for all materials with low reflectivity.

Figure 14.14 shows how a highlight is produced on a spherical shiny surface if one distant light source is present. In the figure the light source is outside the picture. The surface is of medium specular reflectivity with n = 12. At the surface points a, b, and c, the light is

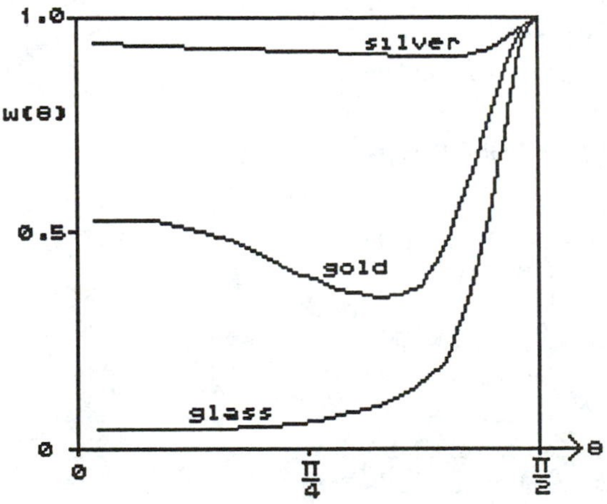


FIGURE 14.13 Specular reflection as a function of the incident angle Θ.

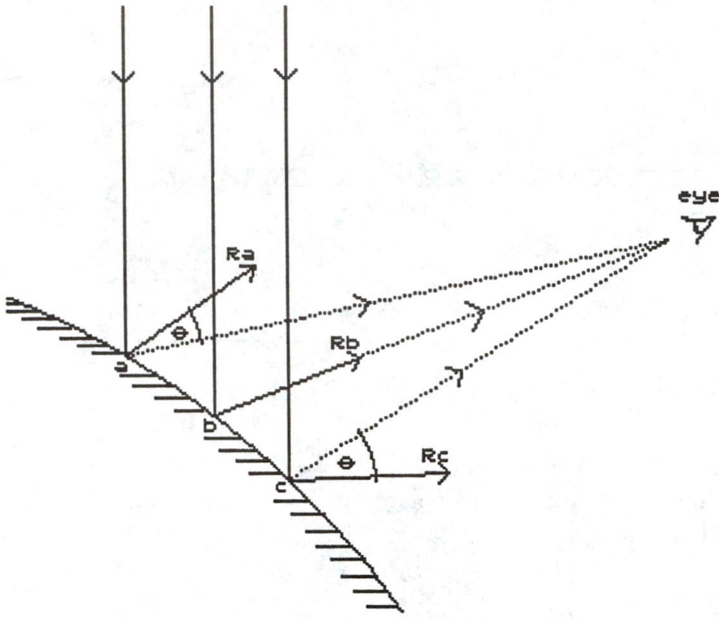


**FIGURE 14.14** Specular highlight on a spherical surface.

reflected for the most part in the directions $R_a$, $R_b$, and $R_c$. At point b, almost all the incoming light is reflected toward the eye, but much less light will reach the eye from points a and c because the ray to the eye from those points deviates considerably from $R_a$ and $R_c$. These deviation angles are about 35°, so the intensity of the light coming from a and c to the eye is $(\cos 35°)^{12} = 0.09$ times the intensity of the incoming light; only 1/11 of the incoming light goes to the eye from those points. From points still farther away from point b, practically no light will reach the eye. We will therefore see a bright spot around point b whose brightness at a and c (and all other points at that distance from b) is only 1/11 of its central brightness. Such a bright spot is called a *specular highlight.*

**Computing the Illumination** When we render an object on a CRT, we first compute its projection on the screen. As pixels are the smallest displayable units and are not further divisible, we compute the illumination for each point on the surface of the object that corresponds to a pixel on the display. Then we set the pixel to that value.

Our scene will often have one or more point light sources. To compute their contributions to the overall illumination of a given pixel, we need the following information: (1) the direction vector to the light source L (for more than one light source we have $L_1$, $L_2$, etc.), (2) the normal vector N, (3) the reflection vector R (for more than one light source we have $R_1$, $R_2$, etc.), and (4) the viewing direction V, all for the surface point that corresponds to that pixel. Usually we will assume a point light source to be far enough away to consider the rays from it as parallel; when that is not true, we compute L anew for each illumination computation.

For the following example, assume the following points in a scene:

- (x,y,z) is a point on the surface of an object which corresponds to a pixel on the screen.
- $(S_x,S_y,S_z)$ is the location of a point light source.
- $(E_x,E_y,E_z)$ is the position of the eye. This point will usually coincide with the center of perspective projection and will then have the coordinates $(0,0,-d)$ with some positive value d in a left-handed coordinate system.

We compute L: $L_x = S_x - x$, $L_y = S_y - y$, $L_z = S_z - z$ and normalize it.

We compute V: $V_x = E_x - x$, $V_y = E_y - y$, $V_z = E_z - z$ and normalize it.

The surface normal N is more complicated to compute. It depends on the type of surface we have. If we know an analytical description of the surface, the computation of the surface normal at a given point is straightforward but not always easy. For example, on a bicubic B-spline or Bezier patch, we must evaluate a biquintic expression. If the object is described by a polygon mesh or similar structure, its surfaces are planar polygons. If such an object is rendered with faceted shading, we just need one surface normal for each polygon. This surface normal is easily derived from the plane equation (see Section 11.1). If the object is rendered with smooth shading (covered below), we need the surface normals at each vertex. The surface normal at a vertex is defined as the average of the normals of the polygons surrounding the vertex. The reflection vector R is also complicated to compute. Two methods are described below.

As soon as we have L, V, N, and R we can compute $\cos\Phi = L \cdot N$ and $\cos\Theta = V \cdot R$. We must not forget that all vectors involved in the cosine computations must be normalized. Then we compute the illumination with formula (1). If we don't need precise illumination, only rough highlights, we can avoid the computation of R and work with approximations. See HEBA86, p. 280 and the explanations below.

Figure 14.15 shows the vectors and angles in an (x,y,z)-coordinate system. The vector N is along the bisector of L and R (the spatial half-angle between L and R). N, L, and R are in the (x,y)-plane. We assume

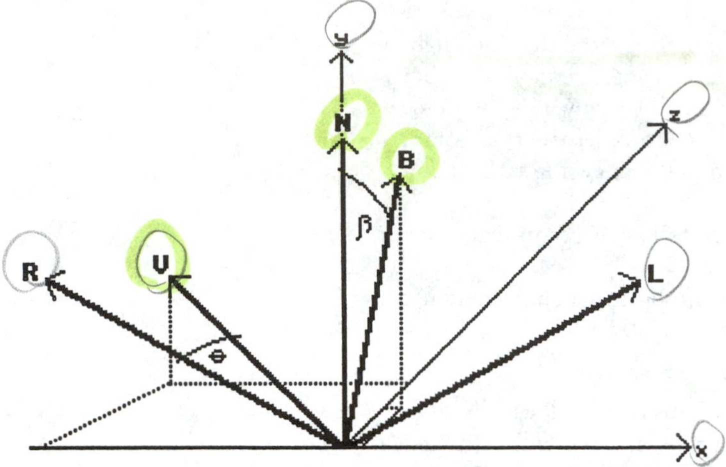


FIGURE 14.15

V close to R; in other words, we assume a small angle $\Theta$. The bisector B of V and L is easy to compute:

$$B = \frac{V+L}{|V+L|}$$

V is not necessarily in the plane of L and R, so neither is B. The angle $\Theta$ between V and R is not the same as the angle $\beta$ between B and N. If the incident angle $\Phi$ is not close to 90° and the angle $\Theta$ is small, there is a nearly linear relation between $\Theta$ and $\beta$. So we can use $B \cdot N$ as an approximation for $R \cdot V = \cos\Theta$.

If $\Phi$ approaches 90°, this approximation becomes increasingly worse even for small angles $\Theta$. Figure 14.16 shows this case. L and R are just a little above the x-axis in the (x,y)-plane. V is very close to R and just a little above the (x,z)-plane. Therefore the bisector B lies almost along the z-axis, so $N \cdot B$ is approximately 0, although $R \cdot V$ is almost 1.

**Setting the Lookup Tables** You know now that there are three contributors to the illumination of any point on a surface: ambient light, diffusely reflected point light, and specularly reflected point light. These contributions will usually vary over the surface of an object. The problem now is to adjust the contributions such that their sum will not exceed the maximum intensity settings of a particular display. If formula (1) yields a value larger than the maximum intensity for any of the primary colors, we could just reduce that value to the maximum. While this is safe to do, it will lead to a loss in variation of colors and intensities if too many of the computed illuminations have to be trimmed down. On the other hand, we can scale down all the contributions by a certain

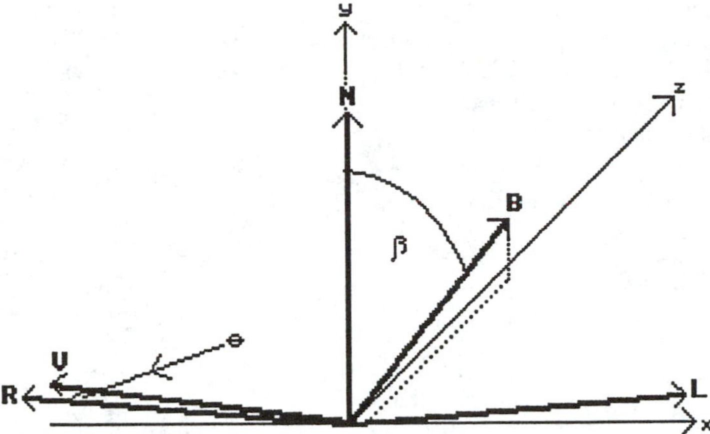


FIGURE 14.16

factor, say 0.9. This avoids illuminations that are too high for extended areas of the object but may make some areas on the object so dark that they will appear indifferently black without exhibiting any hue. The proper weighting of the contributions from the three different types of light usually has to be found by experimentation.

Another problem to consider is that we can display only a limited number of different colors. This limit is given by the depth of the frame buffer. When computing illuminations of a pixel, we could prepare the corresponding color by proper entries in the lookup table and use this color for that pixel. If the hardware allows the simultaneous display of even 256 different colors, we can soon exceed this limit.

A way to solve this problem is to prepare a certain set of colors beforehand. Depending on the color we want to give the object, we prepare a lowest and a highest intensity of that color. For example, suppose that, for our hardware, the intensities for all three primaries go from 0 to 255. We want the object to be brown. We will set the darkest brown to RGB = (150,100,50) and the lightest to (255,220,200) to allow for specular highlights (this is a yellowish white). If we want 50 different intensities of brown altogether, we will distribute the intensities from the lowest to the highest over 50 places and enter those into the lookup table. Let us put the darkest brown into table position 1 and the brightest into position 50. The positions from 2 to 49 have to be filled with the in-between values. How do we compute those?

The way the human eye perceives intensity changes is related to the ratio of the intensities. Assume we perceive a certain change in intensity between intensities $I_1$ and $I_2$. Then we will perceive the same change in intensity between $I_2$ and $I_3$ if $I_1/I_2 = I_2/I_3$. If we want the red intensities to change in equal steps from 150 to 255, we need to multiply 150 with the same factor 49 times to get 255. This factor is $f_r = (255/150)^{1/49} = 1.010888$. For the other primaries we compute the factors similarly, getting $f_g = 1.016221$ and $f_b = 1.028696$. We then multiply the values 150, 100, and 50 respectively by these factors and round to integers for the entries in the lookup table:

| position | entries | | |
|---|---|---|---|
| 1 | 150 | 100 | 50 |
| 2 | 152 | 102 | 51 |
| 3 | 153 | 103 | 53 |
| 4 | 155 | 105 | 54 |
| . | . | . | . |
| . | . | . | . |
| 49 | 252 | 216 | 194 |
| 50 | 255 | 220 | 200 |

(You should check some of these.)

Now, to get the illumination for a pixel we search the lookup table for the color closest to the computed color and use that. This gives colors that are close enough for practical purposes. If the range and number of colors to choose from is increased, we will be even closer to the correct illuminations.

There are other ways to do color computation; the above is just one technique. Note especially that the intensities used in our example may be wrong because the color brown cannot be precisely defined. Further, the above intensities will produce different colors on different monitors. Familiarity with your monitor and experimentation will bring good results.

**Computing the Reflection Vector** We will present two methods for computing the reflection vector. The first is geometric and uses vector algebra. It is probably the simplest method. The other method, while more complicated, is interesting because it uses no geometry at all; it is purely analytic. Beyond these two, there are some other methods (see ROGE85) that we will not discuss.

**Geometric Method** Light comes from a light source and hits the surface at a certain point. The vector pointing to the light source is L, the normal vector to the surface at the point is N, and the vector that points in the direction of the reflection is R. We know that the angle of reflection is equal to the angle of incidence. In other words, the angle between N and L is equal to the angle between N and R. As the vectors L, N, and R are all in one plane we can draw the reflection model as shown in Figure 14.17. The incident angle and reflection angle are both $\Phi$. The vector A is parallel to $-$L. As R and A are both at the angle

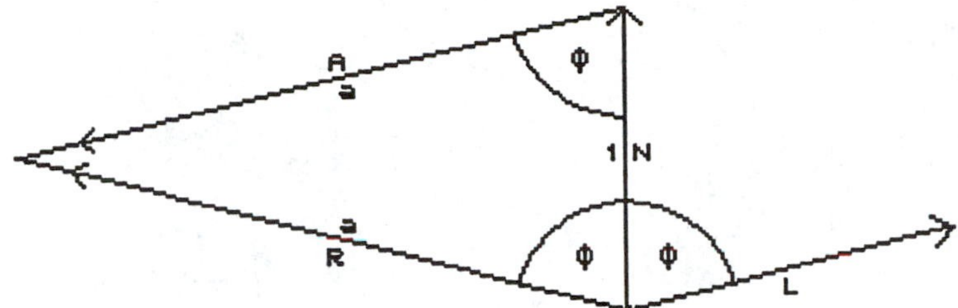


**FIGURE 14.17** Reflection model.

Φ to N they form an isosceles triangle with base N. N and L have length 1 because they are normalized; A and R have length a. Now we use the cosine theorem to express the length of A in terms of the lengths of N and R and the angle Φ: $a^2 = a^2 + 1 - 2a \cdot \cos\Phi$, from which it follows that $a = 1/(2 \cdot \cos\Phi)$. So the vector A actually equals $-L \cdot a$, which is $-L/(2 \cdot \cos\Phi)$ where $\cos\Phi = N \cdot L$. By simple vector addition we get $R = N + A$, so we have the formula:

$$R = N - L/(2N - L).$$

If cosΦ is 0 then L is normal to N and we have $R = -L$. If $\cos\Phi < 0$ then the light hits the surface from the backside of the surface normal and we must reverse the reflection vector. The code below describes the computation of R.

```
procedure reflec(nx,ny,nz,lx,ly,lz : real; var rx,ry,rz : real);
{computes the reflection vector for given
 surface normal direction and light direction}
var a  :  real;
begin
  a  := sqrt(nx*nx+ny*ny+nz*nz);
  nx := nx/a; ny := ny/a; nz := nz/a;
  a  := sqrt(lx*lx+ly*ly+lz*lz);
  lx := lx/a; ly := ly/a; lz := lz/a;
  tcphi := 2*(nx*lx+ny*ly+nz*lz);
  if tcphi > 0
  then begin
    rx := nx - lx/tcphi;
    ry := ny - ly/tcphi;
    rz := nz - lz/tcphi
  end;
  if tcphi = 0 {N and L normal}
  then begin
    rx := -lx;
    ry := -ly;
    rz := -lz
  end;
```

```
  if tcphi < 0
  then begin
    rx := -nx + lx/tcphi;
    ry := -ny + ly/tcphi;
    rz := -nz + lz/tcphi
  end;
  a := sqrt(rx*rx+ry*ry+rz*rz);
  rx := rx/a; ry := ry/a; rz := rz/a
end {procedure reflec};
```

**Analytic Method** The vectors N, L, and R have the same meaning as above and all are normalized. We assume that N and L are not collinear. If $\Phi$ is the angle between N and L then cos$\Phi$-NL. The cross product gives us the coefficients of the vector $(P_x,P_y,P_z)$ normal to N and L:

$$P_x = N_yL_z - N_zL_y$$
$$P_y = N_zL_x - N_xL_z$$
$$P_z = N_xL_y - N_yL_x$$

The point R = (x,y,z) satisfies the three equations:

$$P_xx + P_yy + P_zz = 0 \quad (2)$$
$$N_xx + N_yy + N_zz = \cos\phi \quad (3)$$
$$x^2 + y^2 + z^2 = 1 \quad (4)$$

(2) is because vector R is normal to P. (3) is because the reflection angle is equal to the incident angle. (4) is because it is normalized.

Multiplying (2) by $N_z$ and (3) by $P_z$ and subtracting (3) – (2) we get:

$$(P_zN_x - P_xN_z)x + (P_zN_y - P_yN_z)y = P_z\cos\Phi \quad (5)$$

Multiplying (2) by $N_y$ and (3) by $P_y$ and subtracting (3) – (2) we get:

$$(P_yN_x - P_xN_y)x + (P_yN_z - P_zN_y)z = P_y\cos\phi \quad (6)$$

We extract y from (5) and z from (6):

$$y = ((P_z\cos\Phi - (P_zN_x - P_xN_z)x)/(P_zN_y - P_yN_z)$$
$$z = ((P_y\cos\Phi - (P_yN_x - P_xN_y)x)/(P_yN_z - P_zN_y)$$

We put y and z into equation (4), multiply with $(P_yN_z - P_zN_y)^2$, and get:

$$x^2(P_zN_y - P_yN_z)^2 + (P_z\cos\Phi - (P_zN_x - P_xN_z)x)^2 + (P_y\cos\Phi - (P_yN_x - P_xN_y)x)^2 = (P_yN_z - P_zN_y)$$

This can be written as a quadratic equation of the form $a_xx^2 - b_xx + c_x = 0$ with

$$a_x = (P_xN_y - P_yN_x)^2 + (P_xN_z - P_zN_x)^2 + (P_yN_z - P_zN_y)^2$$
$$b_x = 2\cos\Phi P_y(P_yN_x - P_xN_y) + 2\cos\Phi P_z(P_zN_x - P_xN_z)$$
$$c_x = P_y^2(\cos^2\Phi - N_z^2) + P_z^2(\cos^2\Phi - N_y^2) + 2P_zP_yN_zN_y$$

We subscript a, b, c with x because they express the quadratic equation in x. Doing similar transformations to derive the quadratic equations in y and z we find that $a_x = a_y = a_z$, so we call this value just a. For $b_y$ and $b_z$ we get different expressions. The c-values don't matter.

The vector $(L_x, L_y, L_z)$ also satisfies equations (2), (3), and (4), therefore its coordinates are solutions of the respective quadratic equations. Knowing one solution of a quadratic equation of the above form, we obtain the other one by subtracting it from the linear coefficient of the normalized equation. For example:

$$x = b_x/a - L_x.$$

So we can find the reflection vector by computing:

$$\cos\Phi = N_xL_x + N_yL_y + N_zL_z.$$

If $|\cos\Phi| = 1$ then N and L are collinear and we have R = L. Otherwise we compute:

$$a = (P_xN_y - P_yN_x)^2 + (P_xN_z - P_zN_x)^2 + (P_yN_z - P_zN_y)^2$$
$$b_x = 2\cos\Phi P_y(P_yN_x - P_xN_y) + 2\cos\Phi P_z(P_zN_x - P_xN_z)$$
$$b_y = 2\cos\Phi P_x(P_xN_y - P_yN_x) + 2\cos\Phi P_z(P_zN_y - P_yN_z)$$
$$b_z = 2\cos\Phi P_x(P_xN_z - P_zN_x) + 2\cos\Phi P_y(P_yN_z - P_zN_y)$$
$$x = b_x/a - L_x$$
$$y = b_y/a - L_y$$
$$z = b_z/a - L_z$$

As N and L are not collinear, $a \neq 0$, so the computation can be performed. The code below describes the computation of R.

```
procedure reflec(nx,ny,nz,lx,ly,lz : real; var rx,ry,rz : real);
{computes the reflection vector for given
 surface normal direction and light direction}
var   cphi,a,
      px,py,pz    :  real;
begin {procedure reflec}
  a  := sqrt(nx*nx+ny*ny+nz*nz);
  nx := nx/a; ny := ny/a; nz := nz/a;
  a  := sqrt(lx*lx+ly*ly+lz*lz);
  lx := lx/a; ly := ly/a; lz := lz/a;
  cphi := nx*lx+ny*ly+nz*lz;
```

```
  if abs(cphi) = 1
  then begin  {N and L collinear}
    rx := lx;
    ry := ly;
    rz := lz
  end
  else begin  {N and L not collinear}
    px := ny*lz - nz*ly;
    py := nz*lx - nx*lz;
    pz := nx*ly - ny*lx;
    a  := sqr(px*ny-py*nx)
         +sqr(px*nz-pz*nx)
         +sqr(py*nz-pz*ny);
    rx := 2*cphi*(py*(py*nx-px*ny)+pz*(pz*nx-px*nz))/a-lx;
    ry := 2*cphi*(px*(px*ny-py*nx)+pz*(pz*ny-py*nz))/a-ly;
    rz := 2*cphi*(px*(px*nz-pz*nx)+py*(py*nz-pz*ny))/a-lz
  end
end {procedure reflec};
```

### 14.1.3 Refraction and Transparency

This section presents a simple model for refraction and transparency and illustrates the effects of these processes. Our purpose is to give you an overview of the problems and techniques involved in rendering realistic scenes. We will not explain how to incorporate refraction and transparency into the rendering process; that is most effectively done using ray-tracing techniques, covered in Chapter 15.

Not all light that falls onto a surface is reflected or absorbed. Some of it is transmitted through the surface into the object and continues to travel inside the object. The amount of light and how far it travels depends on the transparency and the thickness of the material. Materials like optical glass fibers have high transparency. Inside such a material the light can travel for miles without significant dimming. Other materials, such as ordinary glass, certain liquids, and even some sea creatures, have a medium transparency; light will not travel so far inside such a material. Still other materials are opaque: metal, wood, brick. Incident light will for the most part be reflected or absorbed and substantially none penetrates into the material.

**Refraction** We focus on nonopaque materials. When light falls on the surface, a certain portion of it penetrates into the material and continues to travel inside. However, the direction of light that penetrates through the surface is changed. The change in direction can be computed by a simple formula, *Snell's law of refraction:*

$$n*\sin\Theta = n'*\sin\Theta'$$

In this formula n and n′ are the refractive indices of the materials on the different sides of the surface and Θ and Θ′ are the respective angles of the light ray with the surface normal at the point of incidence. This is shown in Figure 14.18. In general we can say that the light ray is bent toward the denser material. One of the materials is that of the object, the other usually is air; for underwater scenes the other would be water. (In the appendix, we show how the refracted ray can be computed.)

You have certainly observed the effect of refraction: a straight stick partially inserted into water appears bent. Still stronger are the effects of refraction when we watch a goldfish swim in a round fishbowl. It sometimes looks enlarged, sometimes vanishes totally from our view, and sometimes is seen twice, once through the glass and once through the water surface.

Figure 14.19 illustrates the practical effects of refraction. The scene consists of a glass prism and an opaque object. The scene is projected perspectively to the screen on the left; the center of projection is outside the picture. Because of the effects of refraction, part of the opaque object will be invisible and part of the ground on which the prism and the object are standing will be visible. This is illustrated by the light rays that emanate from various points in the scene. Only those rays that converge to the center of projection come from visible points in the scene whether or not they are refracted.

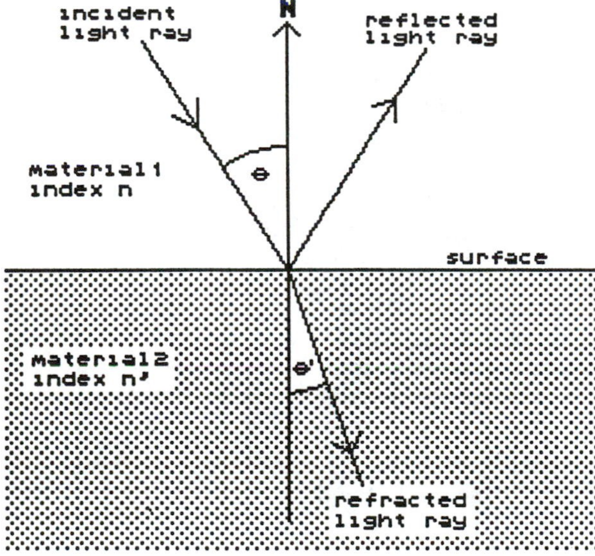


**FIGURE 14.18** Refraction model.

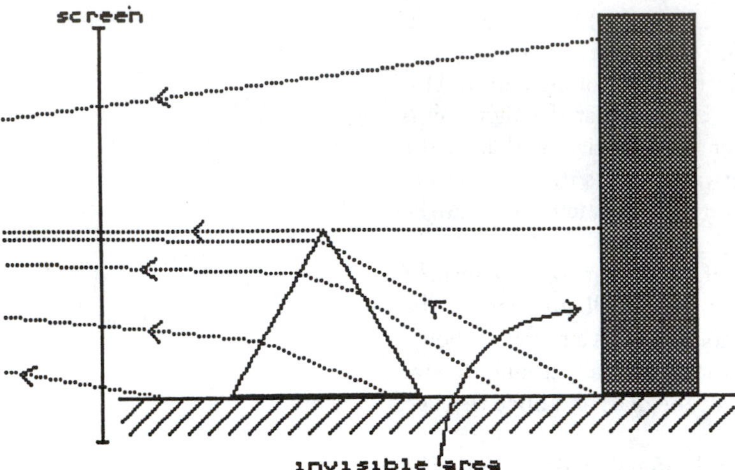


**FIGURE 14.19** Effects of refraction in a scene.

**Transparency** Once light has penetrated into a transparent object, it continues to travel inside, gradually weakening in intensity. This effect can be modeled with a transparency factor. The dimming of the light depends on the transparency factor and on the distance the light travels through the object. Properties of the light are also affected. Consider the situation where light from the surface of some opaque object goes through a transparent object before it reaches the eye. The original color and intensity of this light is changed by passing through the transparent object. This is precisely the effect of sunglasses. Imagine a scene in front of which there is a piece of pink glass. Objects behind this glass will still be visible but their colors will be tinted with some "red shift."

We look now at an early intensity model that ignores the distance traveled inside a transparent object and also the refraction effects (NNSA72). A surface that occludes another surface in the scene can be modeled to be transparent by:

$$I = tI_f + (1-t)I_b \qquad 0 \leq t \leq 1$$

In this formula $I_f$ and $I_b$ are the intensities of the front and back surfaces, t is a transparency factor for the front object, and I the resulting intensity to which the area of occlusion is set in the frame buffer. We see that this is a linear model; $t = 0$ results in a totally transparent front object, $t = 1$ in an opaque front object, and values between result in an "in-between" transparency.

The above formula must be applied for all three primaries. For example, let the front surface be plain blue with RGB = (0,0,1) and the back surface white with RGB = (1,1,1). We can verify that varying t from 0 and 1 gives I values ranging from white through whitish blue, light blue, to plain blue.

This model gives only a rough approximation. The hues of the in-between values are not always correct (see Chapter 9 on this). The model also ignores the thickness of the material and is therefore inadequate for curved transparent surfaces. More powerful and more complicated models have been developed (KAYD79, KDGD79), that take refraction into account as well.

A more complete refraction model must also deal with diffuse refraction. Incident light is not only refracted according to the refraction formula but a part of it is refracted diffusely, scattering around the refraction angle. Further, a more complete transparency model must recognize that there is also internal scattering of the light when it travels through an object.

Incorporating the effects of refraction and transparency into the rendering of a scene is most effectively done using ray-tracing techniques. These techniques offer the advantage that reflections, transparencies, perspective transformation, hidden surface removal, and surface mapping can all be handled at the same time. A purely geometric approach is almost impossible. We discuss ray-tracing in Chapter 15.

## 14.2 SHADING METHODS

The form of an object is enhanced by shading, which helps to display the object as realistically as possible. In this section we discuss some well-known methods for shading. But first we must distinguish between the internal representation of the object and the real world solid object that it is supposed to represent.

Consider objects with smooth nonplanar surfaces. As discussed in Chapter 8, unless the surface of an object has a simple mathematical description or can be assembled from such, we have to describe its surface with parametric bicubic patches or the like. Rendering them is complicated and time consuming. But there are rendering methods that make a surface appear smoothly curved even if internally it is not represented as smooth.

A typical example is illustrated in Figure 14.20. Internally, the object is just a prism with six faces. We can render this prism in such a way that it looks like a cylinder in the display, using shading methods which we will describe in this section. We will consider only solid objects that are internally represented as solids bounded by planar polygons. Note the discrepancy between the seemingly smooth mantle

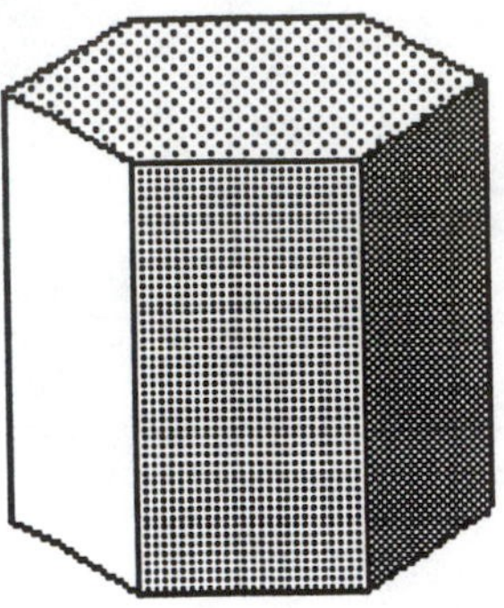
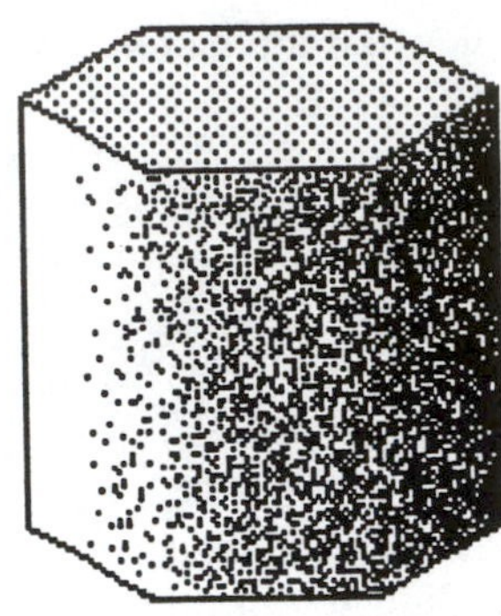

**FIGURE 14.20** Internal representation of a solid and its smoothly shaded display.

of the cylinder and the polygonal edges of the top and bottom surface. All shading methods discussed below are notorious for this effect.

In what follows we will concentrate only on shading techniques and other necessary rendering techniques such as hidden surface removal. Our objective is to make a surface composed of planar polygons appear smoothly curved.

## 14.2.1 Lambert Shading

*Lambert shading* does not achieve our goal of making the displayed object appear smooth, but studying it leads to two methods that do accomplish the goal. For each polygon that makes up the surface of the object, we compute its surface normal and apply the illumination model to compute an intensity for this surface. We then project the polygon and fill the projection with this intensity. The result will be a faceted object, that is, the object will look precisely as it is represented internally.

By increasing the number of polygons that bound the object we can get closer to a smooth appearance in the display. If the object is uncomplicated, like a cone or a cylinder, this is feasible. For more complicated objects, the number of polygons is too great. Figure 14.21 shows the prism of Figure 14.20 with an increased number of vertical facets. To make the appearance really smooth would require the polygons to be very narrow—of the order of a few pixels—which is impractical. The Lambert shading method, also called *faceted shading,* never gives a smooth-looking surface.

**FIGURE 14.21**

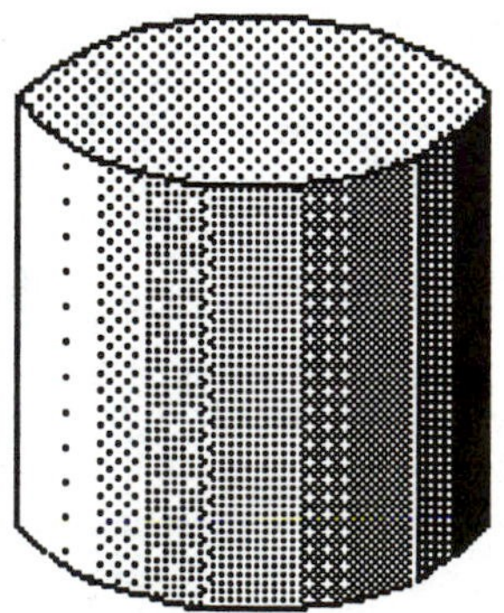

## 14.2.2 Gouraud Shading

Our first serious attempt toward a smooth display is a technique developed by Gouraud (GOUR71). The basic idea of *Gouraud shading* is to display each surface polygon of the object with an intensity that varies

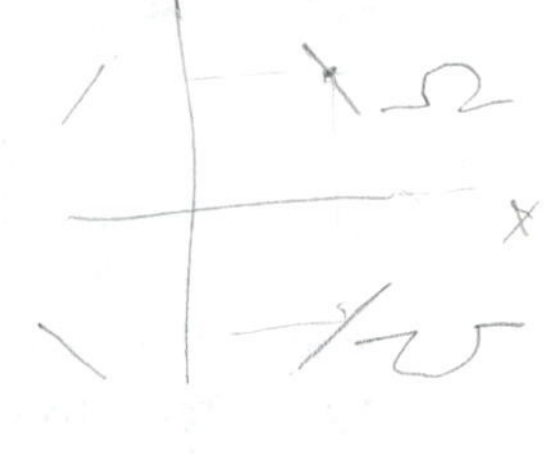

smoothly across it. We will find that this method has some major problems but it is worthwhile to study it as a preliminary to the second method.

The object is internally represented by a polygon mesh. Certain preparatory steps are required. At each vertex of the object we compute the surface normal, defined as the average of the normals of the polygons that surround this vertex. In Figure 14.22 the vertex A is surrounded by the polygons 1, 2, 3 and 4. The surface normals of the polygons are shown as light arrows and the normal at A as a heavy arrow. Figure 14.23 shows an octahedron with all normals of the visible vertices indicated. Call these the vertex normals. As soon as a vertex normal is computed we can compute an intensity at this vertex according to our illumination model. When the intensities of all vertices are known we can start to render the object.

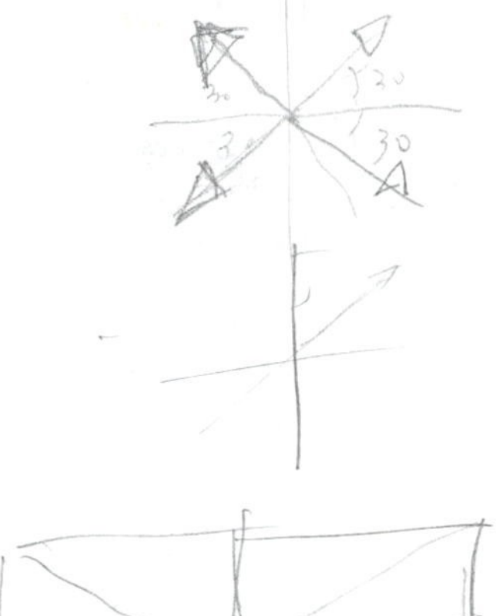

We consider now the data structure that contains the vertex normals. The example below assumes that the polygons are stored in a mesh as explicit polygons (see Section 11.1). In that data structure a polygon is represented by a linked list of pointers to its vertices. The vertices of the solid object are stored just once in the vertex table. We expand this vertex table to contain not only the (x,y,z)-coordinates of the vertex but also the vertex-normal. This is illustrated by Figures 14.24 and 14.25.

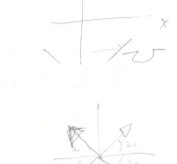

**FIGURE 14.23**

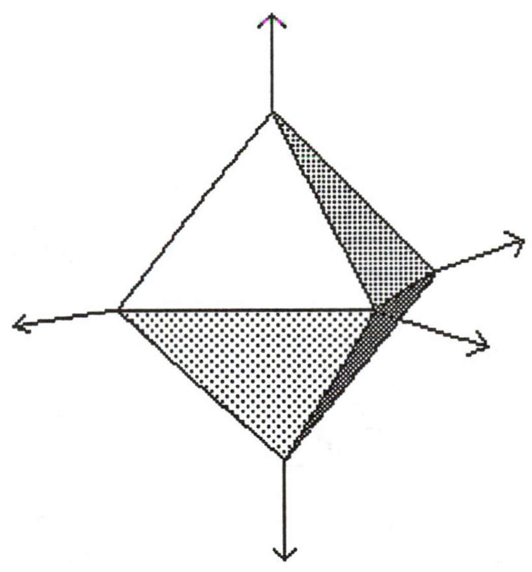

**FIGURE 14.22**

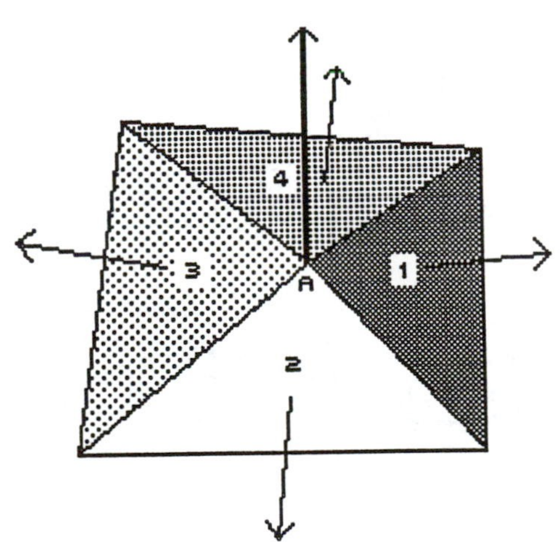

Figure 14.24 shows a part of a solid object consisting of two triangles, Figure 14.25 shows the corresponding data structure with the table of vertices and normals. The space for the normals is at the right side of the table; values are not yet entered. The computation of the vertex normals is done automatically through the vertex normal algorithm which is given below in pseudocode.

FIGURE 14.24

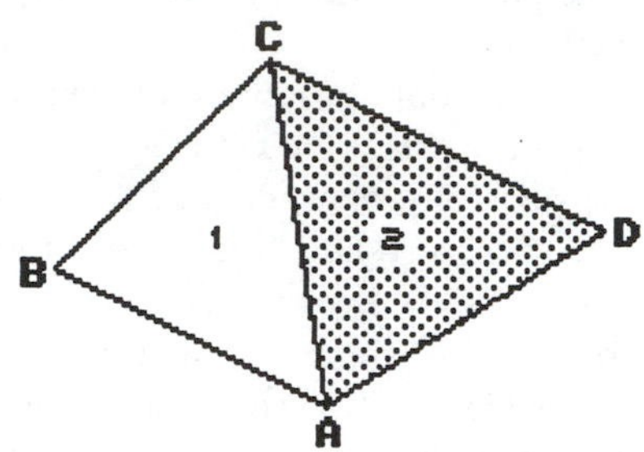


**Vertex Normal Algorithm**

```
{computes the vertex normals
 for all vertices of the solid}
For each vertex of the mesh do begin
   sum := 0;
   For all polygons of the mesh do begin
      Check if the polygon contains
      a pointer to this vertex;
      If yes, add this polygon's
      surface normal to sum
   end;
   normalize sum;
   vertex_normal := sum
end;
```

In the above, you may have noticed that we took the vertices in cw order. This produces outward-pointing normals in a left-handed system. We did not divide sum by 3 in the last statement because all we want is the direction of this vector.

The rendering process consists of filling the projections of the polygons of the surface, basically using the polygon-filling algorithm of Chapter 2 with one essential difference. We do not just fill with a single

FIGURE 14.25

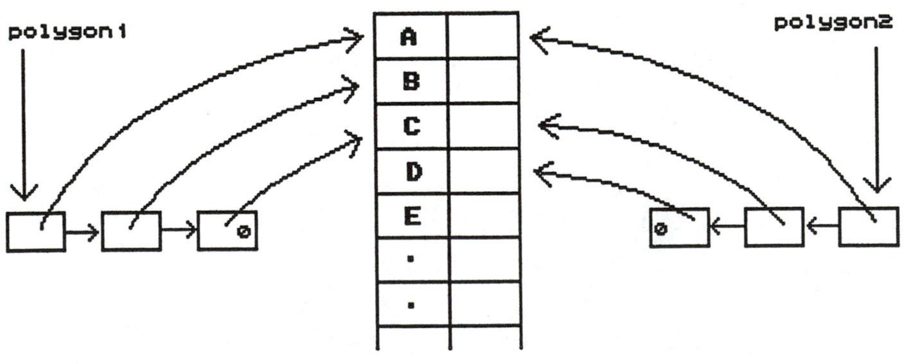

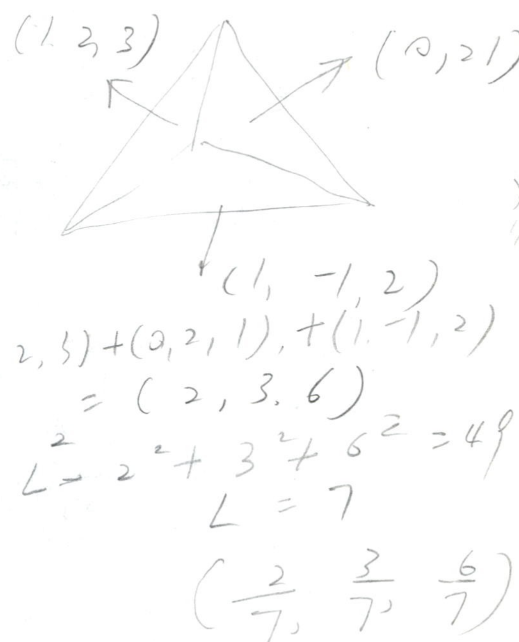

color but with an intensity that is computed as a bilinear interpolation of the intensities at the vertices. The part of the fill algorithm that actually draws a fill line needs to be replaced by a loop that individually sets each pixel along the fill line. This interpolation is explained in Figure 14.26. Let us compute the intensity of pixel P. P lies on the scan line from $P_1$ to $P_2$; $P_1$ and $P_2$ are the intersections of the scan line with the polygon edges. First we get the intensities of $P_1$ and $P_2$, which are linearly interpolated from the intensities of the two vertices spanning the respective edges:

$$I_{P1} = sI_A + (1-s)I_B, \quad s = P_1B/AB$$
$$I_{P2} = tI_C + (1-t)I_B, \quad t = P_2B/CB$$

This works because $P_1B/AB$ is the length from $P_1$ to B divided by the length of the whole edge AB; $P_2B/CB$ is the analog for the other edge. But it is not necessary to compute these lengths; we can get the same ratios by just taking the differences in the y-coordinates of these points: $s = (y_{P1} - y_B)/(y_A - y_B)$ and $t = (y_{P2} - y_B)/(y_C - y_B)$. These differences will never be 0 because the polygon fill algorithm ignores edges parallel to the scan line.

When we have the intensities at $P_1$ and $P_2$, the intensity at P is obtained as a linear interpolation:

$$I_P = u_P I_{P1} + (1-u_P)I_{P2} \qquad u_P = PP_2/P_1P_2$$

where $u_P$ can be computed as $(x_{P2} - x_P)/(x_{P2} - x_{P1})$.

But we don't really need to compute $u_P$ because the intensity computation for P can be performed incrementally for a given scan line. Let P and Q be two consecutive pixels on the scan line. Then:

$$I_P = u_P I_{P1} + (1-u_P)I_{P2} \quad \text{and} \quad I_Q = u_Q I_{P1} + (1-u_Q)I_{P2}$$

By subtraction we get:

$$I_Q = I_P + (u_Q - u_P)(I_{P1} - I_{P2}).$$

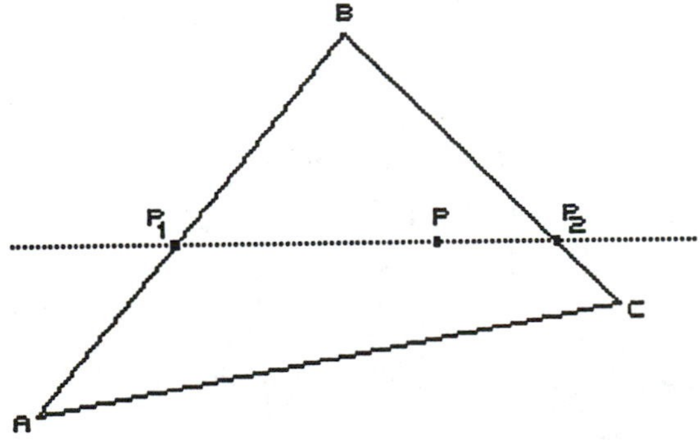


FIGURE 14.26

The term $(u_Q - u_P)(I_{P1} - I_{P2})$ is computed only once for every scan line; it then remains constant, so only one addition needs to be done for every pixel.

What Gouraud shading does is to fill the projection of the object with intensities that vary continuously across the edges of adjoining polygons. Such polygons will blend into each other, giving the appearance of a smoothly curved surface. If we interpolate the intensities of all polygons of the object into each other, the whole object will look smooth. However, we are free to defeat the interpolation wherever we want to show a sharp edge or a crease. We can do this by working with different surface normals at the vertices of edges across which we don't want smooth blending.

The cylinder of Figure 14.20 is a typical example. The intensities are smoothed between adjoining mantle polygons but not between the mantle polygons and the top polygon. This maintains the sharp edge at the top. Figure 14.27 shows a crease.

**Creases and Peaks** The technique of maintaining a crease is explained below. As an example we want to display an object that looks like the one shown in Figure 14.27 with a crease in the middle.

The polygons that are stored internally look like those shown in Figure 14.28. At the vertices A, B, E, and F we will compute surface normals averaged from the polygons to the left and to the right of the respective edges. But at the vertices C and D we must *not* work with averaged surface normals. The normals we need to compute are shown in Figure 14.29. To shade the polygon CEFD we need to work with the normals $N_{C1}$, $N_E$, $N_F$ and $N_{D1}$. To shade CDBA we need to work with $N_{C2}$, $N_{D2}$, $N_B$ and $N_A$. (The outer four normals are shown also to indicate how the outer polygons must be shaded, but they are not named, because they don't play a role in this discussion.)

The problem is how to tell the shading algorithm that at the vertices C and D there is more than one surface normal and that it has to pick just the right one. How this problem can be solved in a program depends very much on the type of data structure used for the internal representation of the object.

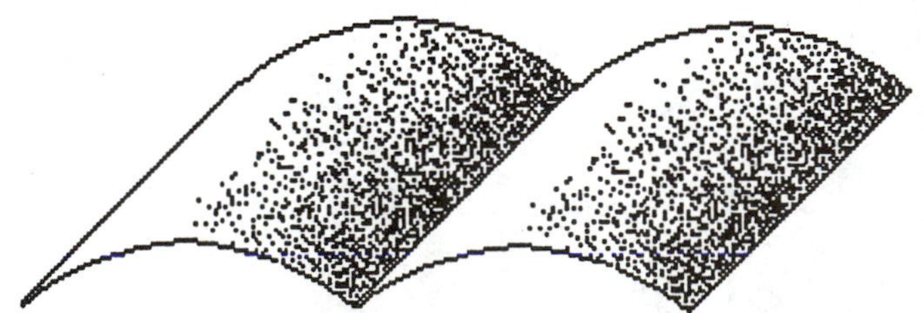

**FIGURE 14.27**

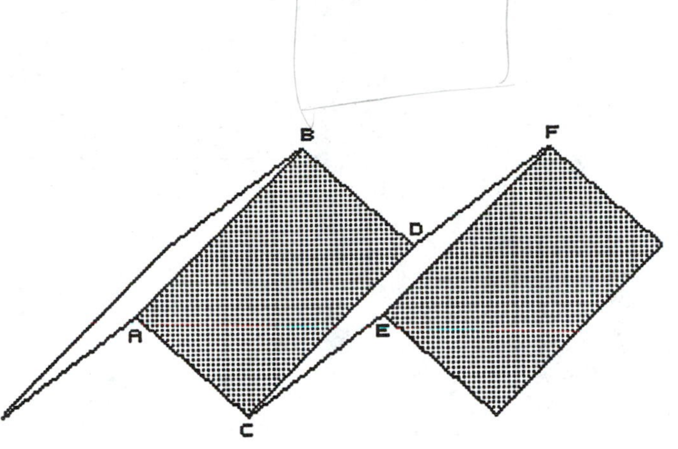


FIGURE 14.28

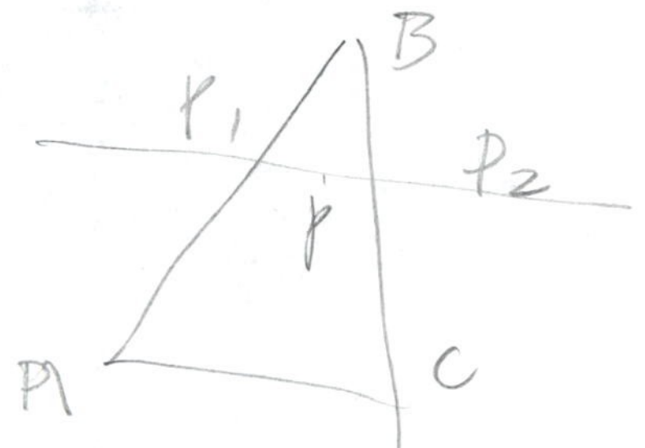

We certainly want a solution that allows us to use the above algorithm, which automatically computes all the vertex normals we need. We should avoid a solution that forces us to subject certain vertices like C and D in Figure 14.29 to special treatment.

One possible solution is presented for the explicit polygon type of polygon mesh. To obtain a crease along a certain edge between two polygons, we must avoid the computation and use of averaged vertex normals at the ends of that edge. Now, if a vertex were in just one polygon, the above algorithm will compute just the normal of that polygon as the vertex normal. The following is based on this fact.

We can easily fool the algorithm into thinking that the polygons CEFD and CDBA are not adjacent by storing the vertices C and D twice in the vertex list: $C_1$, $C_2$ and $D_1$, $D_2$. The two C's and the two D's will have the same values, so they refer to the same point in space, but there will be different pointers to them. Figure 14.30 shows a part of the vertices and normals table and the pointers of the two polygons in question. Which polygon uses which vertices is a part of the defi-

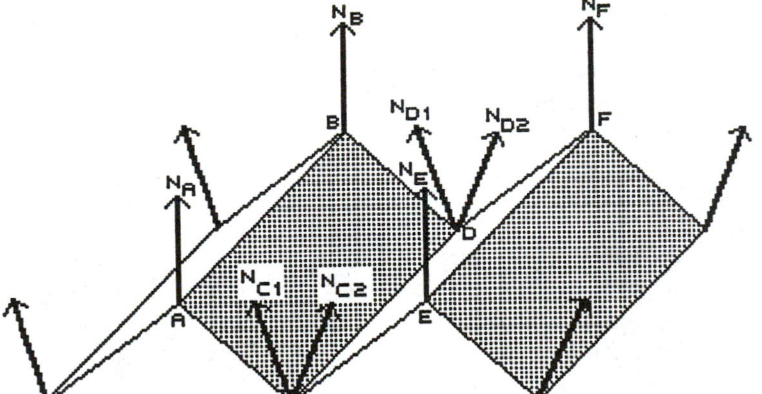


FIGURE 14.29

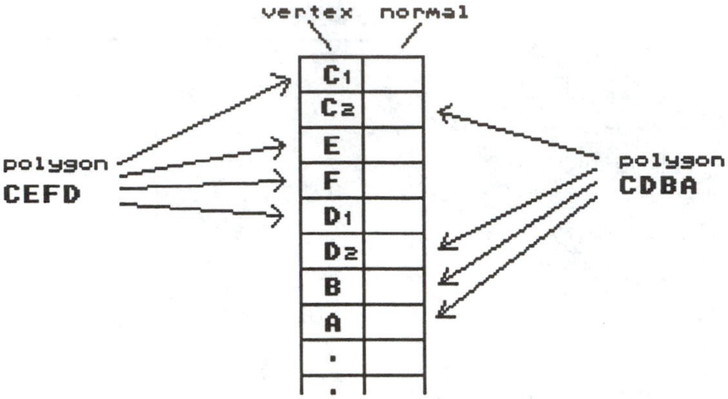

vertex normal

polygon CEFD

$C_1$ $C_2$ E F $D_1$ $D_2$ B A

polygon CDBA

FIGURE 14.30

nition process of the polygon mesh and has to be specified "by hand" when the object is constructed. The vertex normal algorithm will find $C_1$ belonging only to polygon CEFD and $C_2$ belonging only to CDBA. Therefore it will compute different surface normals for $C_1$ and $C_2$. The same will happen at $D_1$ and $D_2$. When shading is done on these polygons, no interpolation of intensities will take place at the transition and a crease will appear.

Here is another example. We want to display a cone as shown in Figure 14.31. We will discuss how we represent the cone internally and also how the vertices have to be specified to achieve smooth surfaces, creases, and peaks in just the right places. We cannot obtain a smooth bottom edge; instead, we will have a polygonal silhouette as on the cylinder in Figure 14.20.

FIGURE 14.31

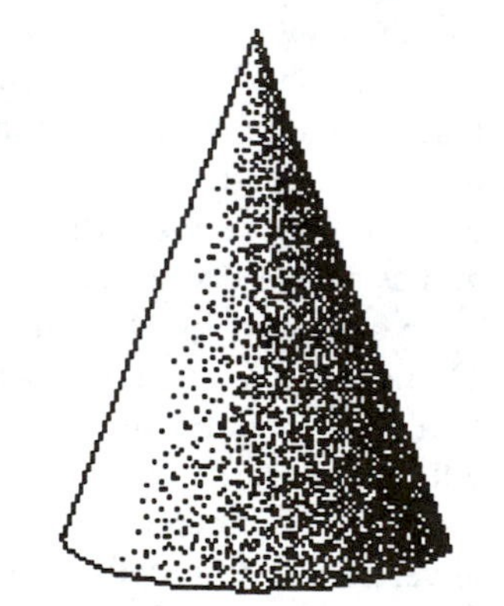

Internally we will represent the cone as a four-sided pyramid (see Figure 14.32). A three-sided pyramid could be used but the smoothed result won't be as good as with a four- or more sided pyramid. At E we want a sharp peak. The edges AE, BE, etc. should be smoothed; at the bottom edges AB, BC, etc. we want the creases. At the bottom vertices we must use vertex normals averaged from the two triangles left and right of the vertex but not including the bottom polygon ABCD. At the top, the situation is more complicated. We want to smooth across the sides AE, BE, etc. all the way from the bottom to the top, but not across the peak at E. This can be achieved by using four top points $E_1, \ldots, E_4$ which are all identical to E in their coordinates, but each will be shared only by two adjacent triangles. We realize this by representing each side triangle by four vertices as shown in Figure 14.33. The side polygons will be $ABE_2E_1$, $BCE_3E_2$, and so on.

FIGURE 14.32

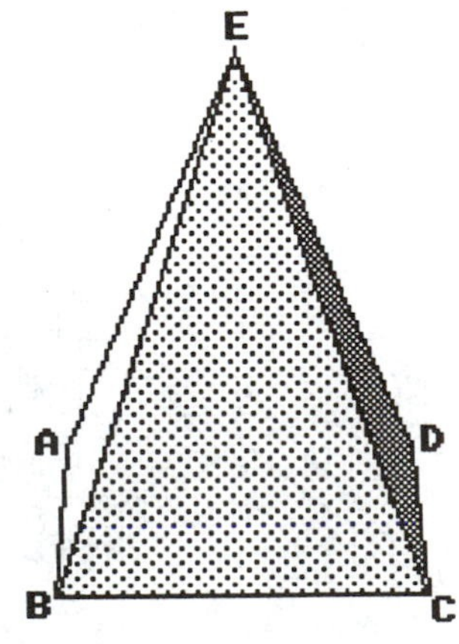


We also need a separate polygon at the bottom: $D_1C_1B_1A_1$, shown in Figure 14.34. Here $A = A_1$, $B = B_1$, $C = C_1$, $D = D_1$. Observe that the vertices are listed counterclockwise when looking at the bottom from below the pyramid. This ensures that the bottom will not be included in the computation of the vertex normals in A, B, C, and D. At the top there is no polygon $E_1E_2E_3E_4$. Figure 14.35 shows the resulting vertex normals. There are many opportunities for playing tricks with the data structure defining the object. The mantle polygons above are defined ccw such that the last two vertices have identical coordinates. This allows us to treat them either as quadrangles or as triangles, whichever is convenient. When determining vertex normals we let the algorithm go through all four vertices to find out whether a polygon is adjacent to a given vertex. When filling a mantle polygon we must work with quadrangles in order to use all four different vertex normals.

When depth sorting, we ignore the fourth vertex in the polygons in order to have triangles to work with. In that case we should also break the bottom polygon into two triangles. They will be coplanar and will be shaded as if they were one quadrangle.

This method of inducing creases and peaks is not the only one. We can also introduce a pair of additional very narrow polygons on either side of the edge where there is to be a crease. These polygons must have the same slope as the polygons originally adjacent at the edge. The whole intensity interpolation will then take place within these narrow polygons; and if they are narrower than a single pixel, the intensity interpolation is defeated. This method is a little more complicated and not pursued further.

**Problems with Gouraud Shading: Total Flattening** A typical problem arising with Gouraud shading is flattening. If we want to display a wavelike curved surface like the one shown in Figure 14.36 we would

**FIGURE 14.33**

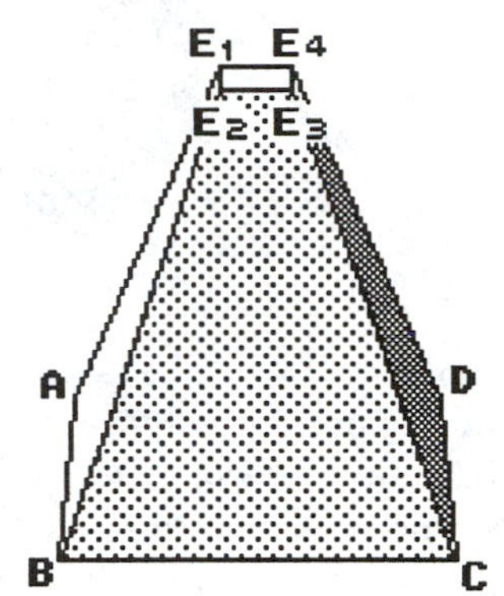


**FIGURE 14.34**

**FIGURE 14.35**

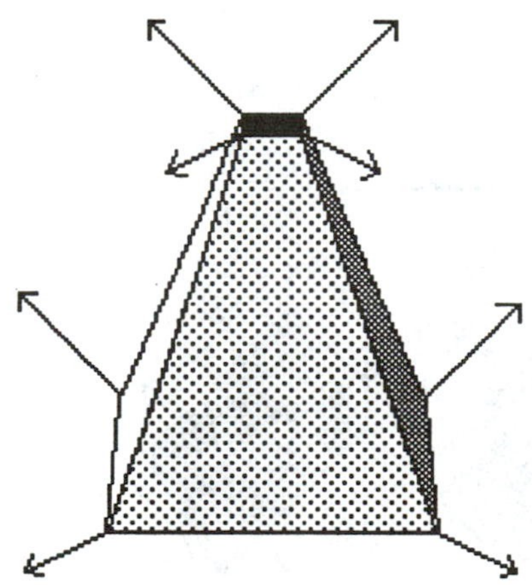

**FIGURE 14.36**

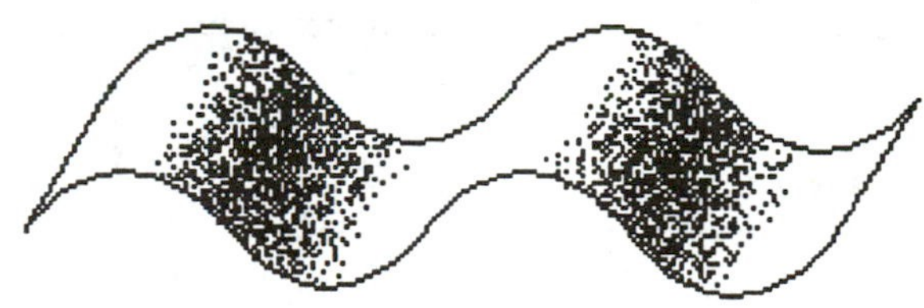

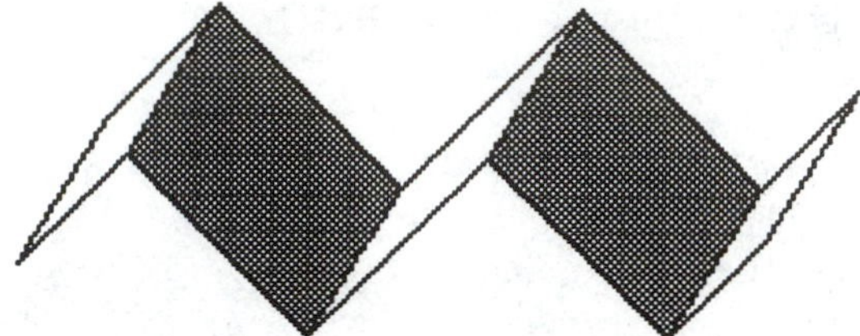

FIGURE 14.37

internally store a surface as shown in Figure 14.37. We expect that the smoothing process will give us the wavelike shape. For a very simple mathematical reason we will get a totally flat surface (except for the ends which will be bent upward or downward).

The reason is that the vertex normals on the ridges and in the valleys are all parallel, as Figure 14.38 shows. The intensities at all vertices are the same and interpolation yields a constant intensity throughout the area from the leftmost ridge to the rightmost valley. We can solve this problem by introducing additional edges in the middle between each ridge and valley. Each of the polygons 1, 2, and 3 will be divided into two polygons by an edge as shown in Figure 14.39. The vertex normals at the new vertices will be normal to the polygons 1, 2, and 3 respectively.

Shading will now give a smooth wavelike surface. It is sometimes suggested that we replace each of the problematic polygons (1, 2, and 3 in our example) by three new ones, all in the same plane as the original one. Doing this gives smooth but more pronounced ridges and valleys (see for example, ROGE85). The scheme we choose depends on the picture we want to produce.

**Poor Highlights** There is another problem with Gouraud shading for which there is no cure. It often happens that highlights from specular reflection are poorly represented. To clarify this, imagine a

FIGURE 14.38

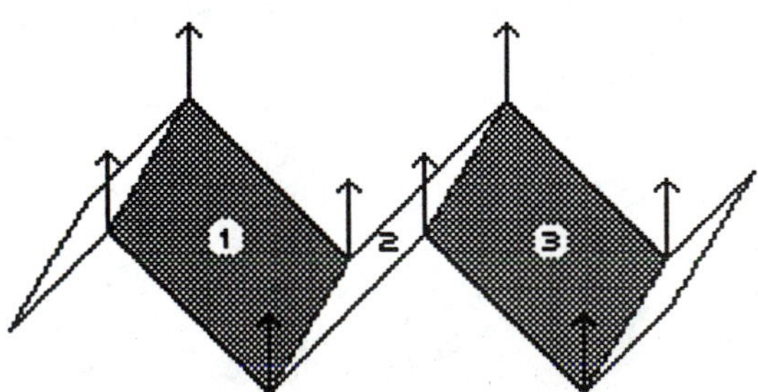


FIGURE 14.39

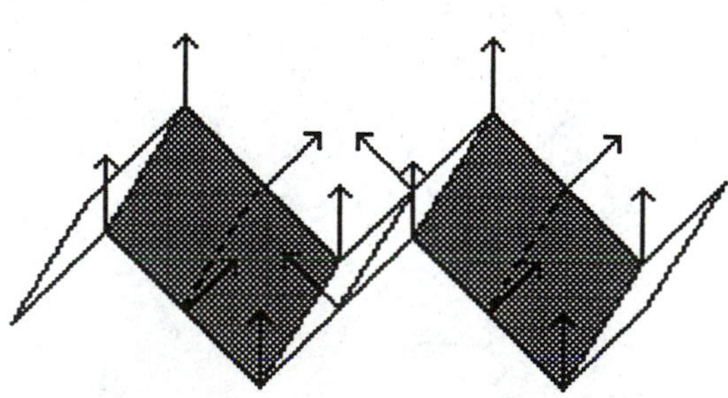

scene in which the light source, or object, or viewer slowly changes its position. As long as the viewing direction is close to the reflection direction (how close depends on the shininess of the surface), a highlight will be produced around the pyramid vertex (see Figure 14.40).

When positions change (for example, the light source moves), these two directions separate more and more and the highlight gets weaker or disappears instead of just changing its location on the surface. In Figure 14.41 the angle $\theta$ has become so big that Phong's illumination model will compute an essentially 0 specular reflection for that vertex. In both figures, 14.40 and 14.41, the object is shown as it is stored internally; the display will of course be a smooth cone. (In the figure, while we have Gouraud shading, we have used an illumination model from Phong.)

Above, we assumed the likely case that the other vertices don't have a specular reflection because their vertex normals are not in a reflecting position. The intensity interpolation therefore will not produce a highlight anywhere. This is in stark contrast to what happens on a smooth shiny object in reality. When the light source moves as shown in the figures, the specular reflection on the object also moves slightly toward the viewer.

Moving the object itself or the position of the viewpoint has the same effect as moving the light source. If a vertex should get exactly into the proper position, a highlight will appear on the smoothed object at the location corresponding to that vertex. Further position changes will cause the highlight to disappear; it might reappear at a position corresponding to a different vertex.

This weakness in handling highlights can be summarized as follows. On a Gouraud shaded object, specular highlights cannot really

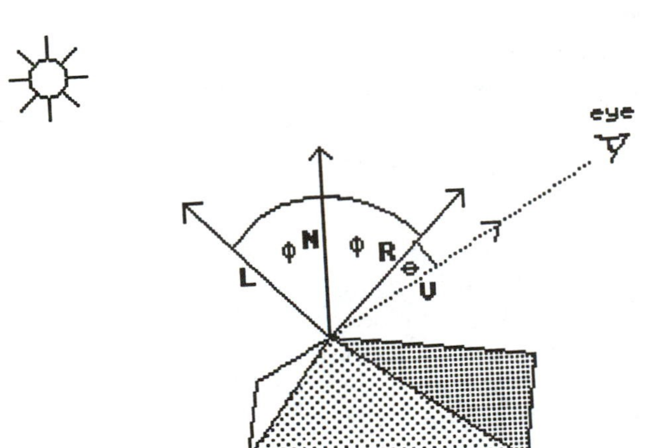


**FIGURE 14.40**

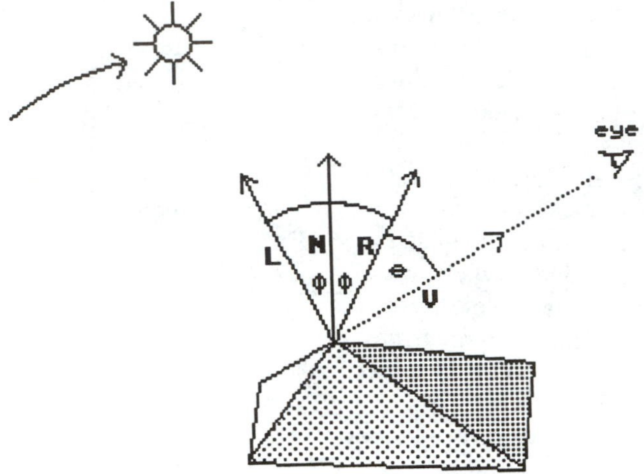


FIGURE 14.41

move; they can only disappear and reappear at a different location. This effect is especially pronounced for objects of high shininess and in animation.

When the shininess of the object is low, something faintly resembling a movement of the highlight can occur. Imagine that the changes in positions of viewer, light source, or object are such that a real highlight would move along an edge from one vertex to the next. With Gouraud shading, in such a case the highlight at the first vertex would become dimmer, then turn into a long shape corresponding to the edge, then become a dim highlight around the second vertex, and finally brighten.

The explanation for this is that with low shininess, the specular reflection at a vertex will disappear only for relatively large values of $\theta$. In this case it is possible that the highlight at one vertex is still present, although dimmer, while the highlight at another vertex starts to appear. This effect can easily include several vertices if they are not far apart. This gives an oversized and irregularly shaped highlight. The phenomenon, typical of Gouraud-shaded objects, frequently occurs when that method is used.

Another failure of highlights from Gouraud shading is that the size of the highlight doesn't vary with the shininess of the object. In reality, the highlight on a very shiny smooth object is small, bright, and pronounced. A Gouraud-shaded object with a high shininess parameter either will not have a highlight at all (when the angles aren't just right), or it will have a highlight much too big (if the angles are correct). Increasing the shininess parameter will not make the highlight smaller, it will only generate it less often.

**Irregular Shading of Concave Polygons** If a polygon is concave, Gouraud shading can yield a discontinuity in the intensities at the concave vertex. This generates the impression of something similar to a sharp protrusion where there shouldn't be one. Consider the polygon of Figure 14.42. The scan lines above D will interpolate intensities at A, B, and C only. The scan lines below D will suddenly add the intensity at D into the interpolation. If the intensity at D is quite different from the others, a sudden point-shaped change in intensity will occur at D. This problem can be avoided by using only convex polygons as the bounding surfaces for solid objects, which is easy to do. For example, the polygon ABCD should be replaced by two triangles, ABD and CBD.

## 14.2.3 Phong Shading

Another method for smoothing the display is a technique developed by Bui-Truong Phong, called *Phong shading* (PHON75). It is similar to Gouraud shading in its use of vertex normals. The essential difference is that it interpolates the vertex normals themselves rather than the intensities at the vertices. The intensity for each pixel across the facet is computed. The technique is explained below. (Again, we ignore everything except the shading operation.)

We again have an internal representation of the solid as a surface of planar polygons that is stored in a polygon mesh. Before the shading can begin, we do the same preparation step as for Gouraud shading: we compute the vertex normals. We then fill the projections of all bounding polygons of the object using basically the polygon fill algorithm of Chapter 2. The essential modification to the algorithm consists of replacing the drawing of a fill line by a loop that computes the intensity for every individual pixel within that line and sets the pixels accordingly. Using the examples and the formalism developed for Gouraud shading, the explanation becomes very easy.

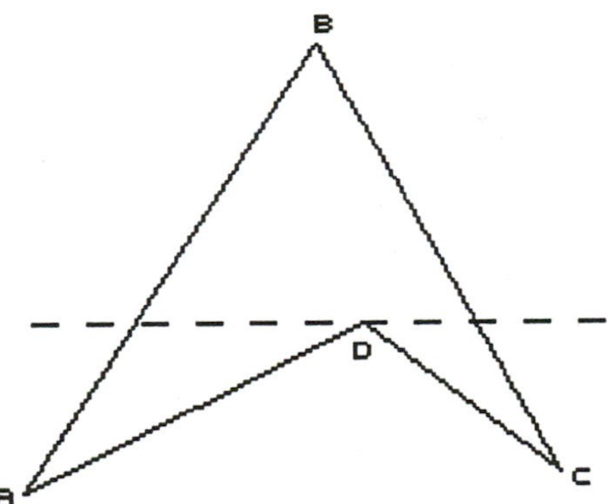


**FIGURE 14.42**

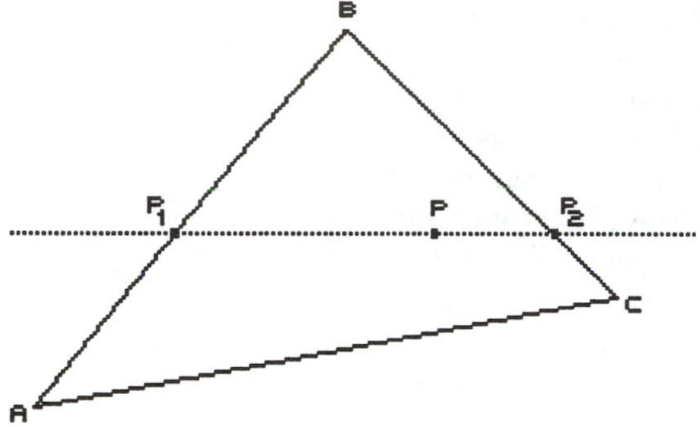


FIGURE 14.43

We assume that we have the vertex normals $N_A$, $N_B$, and $N_C$ as shown in Figure 14.43. P lies on the scan line from $P_1$ to $P_2$, which are the intersections of the scan line with the polygon edges. First we need the normals at $P_1$ and $P_2$, which are linearly interpolated from the vertex normals of the respective edges (we must not forget to normalize them before interpolating):

$$N_{P1} = sN_A + (1-s)N_B \qquad s = P_1B/AB$$
$$N_{P2} = tN_C + (1-t)N_B \qquad t = P_2B/CB$$

s and t have the same meaning as in Gouraud shading. Again we can compute them from the differences of the y-coordinates of the involved points. When we have the normals of $P_1$ and $P_2$, the normal of P is obtained as:

$$N_P = u_P N_{P1} + (1-u_P)N_{P2} \qquad u_P = PP_2/P_1P_2$$

We don't need to compute $u_P$ at all because the normal computation can be performed incrementally for a given scan line. Let P and Q be two consecutive pixels on the scan line. Then:

$$N_Q = N_P + (u_Q - u_P)(N_{P1} - N_{P2})$$

The term $(u_Q - u_P)(N_{P1} - N_{P2})$ has to be computed only once for every scan line and then remains constant.

In contrast to Gouraud shading, the intensity computation has yet to be done. As soon as we have $N_P$ we normalize it. The vectors L and V can in most cases be considered as constant. (If we really want to change them for every pixel then we must do this in object space. This involves finding the points on the 3-D polygon that are projected onto these pixels.) Using $N_P$, L, and V we compute an illumination for the pixel P using the above illumination model.

**Creases and Peaks** Creases and peaks are produced precisely as in Gouraud shading.

**Problems with Phong Shading** Phong shading does not solve all the problems of Gouraud shading. The difficulties with polygonal silhouettes, creases, and outlines still exist and cannot be overcome. The same holds for the irregular shading produced on concave polygons (but this can be overcome). The flattening of the wavelike surface is present also and must be solved in the same way as in Gouraud shading.

The major advantage of Phong shading is that it has no problems with highlights.

**Summary** To summarize, Phong shading is more expensive in terms of processor time but it yields smoothly shaded objects that look better than Gouraud-shaded ones, especially in the handling of highlights. Phong shading is the most widely used algorithm for smooth shading.

# EXERCISES FOR CHAPTER 14

## Section 14.1 (Lighting of Objects)

For the procedures d_reflec and ds_reflec below, use the type point, which can be used as a vector in space, a point in space, or an RGB intensity:

```
type point = record a,b,c : real
             end;
```

1. (Diffuse reflection) Write a procedure d_reflec that computes the intensity of a surface according to the diffuse reflection model portion of equation (1). Given are the normalized surface normal $(n_x,n_y,n_z)$ pointing *out* of the object, the ambient light intensity $(I_{ar},I_{ag},I_{ab})$, the point light intensity $(I_{pr},I_{pg},I_{pb})$, the diffuse reflectivity factors of the surface $(k_{dr},k_{dg},k_{db})$, and the normalized vector pointing to the point light source $(l_x,l_y,l_z)$. Declare the parameters norm, alight, plight, diff, lvect as of type point.

   Depending on how you compute the surface normal, you might or might not have to reverse all the signs to make it point out of the object. When computing the cosine of the incident angle, the result can be negative if the light comes from the side opposite to where the surface normal points. In that case set the cosine to 0.
2. (Computing the reflection vector) Implement the computation of the reflection vector given the surface normal and the direction to the light source.

3. (Specular reflection) Write a procedure ds_reflec that computes the intensity of a surface according to the diffuse reflection plus specular reflection model of equation (1). Given are the normalized surface normal ($n_x$,$n_y$,$n_z$), the ambient light intensity ($I_{ar}$,$I_{ag}$,$I_{ab}$), the point light intensity ($I_{pr}$,$I_{pg}$,$I_{pb}$), the diffuse reflectivity factors of the surface ($k_{dr}$,$k_{dg}$,$k_{db}$), the specular reflectivity factors ($k_{sr}$,$k_{sg}$,$k_{sb}$), the normalized vector pointing to the point light source ($l_x$,$l_y$,$l_z$), and the normalized vector pointing to the viewer's eye (the center of projection). Declare the parameters norm, alight, plight, diff, spec, lvect, and vvect as of type point.

   As in Exercise 1 you must pay attention to the direction of the surface normal. Use the computation of the reflection vector implemented above.

# Section 14.2 (Shading Methods)

4. (Lambert shading) Use the procedure fracrect implemented in the exercises for Chapter 10 to generate a fractal grid surface. Draw the facets of the grid surface in occlusion-compatible order as filled polygons. Split every quadrangle into two triangles to obtain unique surface normals. Illuminate the triangles with the Lambert shading method using the procedure d_reflec from Exercise 1.

   Gouraud and Phong shading can be implemented with an enhancement of the polygon fill algorithm of Chapter 2. Instead of filling with one solid color we compute a new color for each pixel during the filling process. So the call to hline in the fill algorithm is replaced by a loop that performs a certain computation for each pixel. But in some other ways the fill algorithm can be simplified. It is sufficient to fill only triangles and quadrangles, as polygons with more vertices are not necessary when specifying solid objects in space. Also, it is sufficient to fill only convex polygons, as both shading methods produce poor results for concave polygons—which can be avoided as well when defining a solid object.

5. Simplify the polygon fill algorithm of Chapter 2 to handle only up to four vertices and only convex polygons. The latter implies that there are always exactly two intersections of the scan line with polygon edges.
6. (Gouraud shading) Adapt the simplified fill algorithm to Gouraud shading. Extend the data structure that holds the information for the currently intersected edges to include the intensities at the

vertices of the edges. For every scan line compute the intensities at the two intersection points and then the constant term to be added to obtain the intensities of successive pixels, as shown in Section 14.2.2.

7. (Phong shading) Adapt the simplified fill algorithm to Phong shading. Extend the data structure that holds the information for the currently intersected edges to include the vertex normals at the vertices of the edges (or pointers to them). For every scan line compute the normals at the two intersection points and then the constant term to be added to obtain the normals of successive pixels, as shown in Section 14.4.3. The normals must be normalized before every computation step to insure that they go into the computations with equal weight.
8. (Phong shading) Assume that the normals at the scan line intersection are as shown in Figure 14.44. Show that adding a constant vector, as in the formula in Section 14.2.3 to obtain all in-between normals, gives normals as shown in Figure 14.44. These normals are not all of the same length and therefore must be normalized to compute the pixel illumination.

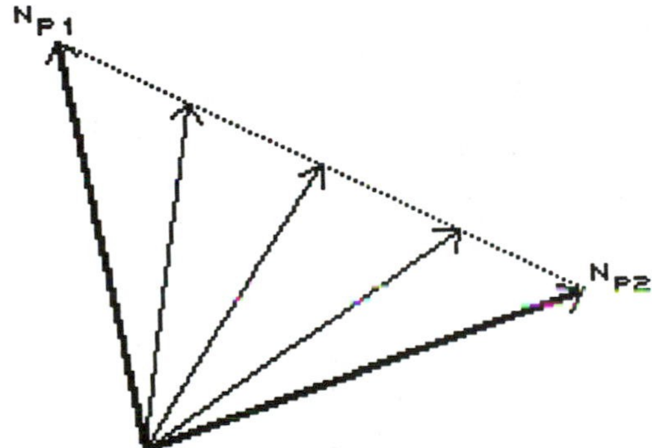


**FIGURE 14.44**

9. To prepare an object for Gouraud or Phong shading the vertex normals have to be computed. Write a procedure vert_norm that goes through an object's polygon mesh description, computes all vertex normals, normalizes them, and stores them in the vertex table together with the vertex. Assume a simple polygon mesh structure as presented in Section 11.1.2.
10. Declare an octahedron in space like the one shown in Figure 14.23, observing ccw specification of all triangle vertices. Use the simple polygon mesh structure. Allocate space in the vertex table for the vertex normals. Compute the vertex normals with the procedure vert_norm.

# Surface Mapping and Ray Tracing

# 15

This chapter extends the ideas of Chapter 14 about providing a realistic appearance to images by showing how to add patterns and textures to surfaces. There are five sections.

**15.0 Introduction** outlines what is discussed in the chapter.

**15.1 Describing a Surface Parametrically** is a review of the mathematics used to describe surfaces in this chapter.

**15.2 Pattern Mapping** is a technique for applying a predefined pattern to a smooth surface.

**15.3 Texture Mapping** extends the concept to permit a surface to exhibit the appearance of some desired texture.

**15.4 Ray Tracing** permits the graphic display to show reflections and refractions that are characteristic of shiny and transparent objects.

## 15.0 Introduction

In our quest for visual realism, surface mapping plays an important role. Real world objects are seldom uniformly colored or perfectly smooth, as we have assumed until now. Usually there is a variation of surface color and texture. There are basically three techniques that have been developed in computer graphics to achieve the impression of natural colors, texture, and appearence.

One technique is pattern mapping. It consists of the addition of a separately defined pattern to a surface and is done when a surface should not be uniform in color. It is like pasting wallpaper on a wall or painting a picture on the surface of the object. This will not change the smoothness of the surface, it will only add different colors to various areas of the surface.

The second technique is texture mapping. It consists of intentionally roughening the surface of an object to give it a more realistic appearance. This roughening or disturbing of the surface is a mathematically complicated process and is computationally intensive. In a way it is comparable to pattern mapping. We define on a separate flat area a surface with the desired texture or roughness and then "paste" it on the surface of the object.

The third technique is ray tracing, which makes images appear to be reflecting and/or transparent.

The procedures of this chapter are mathematically more demanding than the techniques described in the previous chapter, so we must make some preparation. We will deal with surfaces that are represented parametrically. We base our discussion on two examples: a sphere and a torus. The main feature of these representations is that one parametric formula (usually involving transcendental functions) describes the whole surface, in contrast to Chapter 8 where we used patches of cubic polynomials. We do this because it would be even more mathematically demanding to surface-map or ray-trace parametric bicubic patches.

When we describe ray tracing we will depart from this. We will work with both spheres and cubes that are represented implicitly rather than parametrically.

# 15.1 DESCRIBING A SURFACE PARAMETRICALLY

Pattern mapping and texture mapping make extensive use of parametric surfaces. Since the formalism relies so heavily on it, we introduce two surfaces to serve as concrete examples: a sphere surface and a torus surface. We use the word *surface* to stress the fact that the parameterization describes just the surfaces and not the whole three-dimensional volumes of these objects. Parameterizations for the latter also exist but are not used in this book.

As explained in Chapter 8, two parameters are required to represent a surface in space. We call them u and v and let each range from 0 to 1. The surface is represented by three equations in u and v:

$$x = X(u,v) \qquad y = Y(u,v) \qquad z = Z(u,v)$$

(x,y,z) is a point in a left-handed Cartesian coordinate system (lhs).

Recall that, by holding one parameter fixed and and varying the other through its range, the point (x,y,z) will describe a curve in space. Holding v fixed and varying u gives us a constant v-curve. This curve could as well be called a variable u-curve; the second term is sometimes more descriptive because it suggests that a point on the curve moves when that parameter moves. The direction in which a point on a variable u-curve moves with varying u indicates the direction of the partial derivative of the surface at this point with respect to u. The analog holds for v. We need to have a clear picture of these directions to compute quantities such as surface normals correctly. We will indicate in our figures which parameter is held constant and the particular constant value for this curve. This lets us put more information into a drawing.

**A Sphere** The surface of a sphere with radius R around the origin in an lhs is described by three equations in the parameters u and v:

$$\begin{aligned} x &= R*\cos(2\pi u)*\sin(\pi v) \\ y &= R*\cos(\pi v) \\ z &= R*\sin(2\pi u)*\sin(\pi v) \end{aligned}$$

It will help to compare this to a globe of the earth (see Figure 15.1). The variable u-curves are horizontal circles with the y-axis as their center; these are circles of latitude. For example, holding v at 0.5 will keep the corresponding sin terms in the equations for x and for z constant at 1; y will assume the value 0. Now varying u from 0 to 1 lets the point (x,y,z) travel in a full circle of radius R around the origin at a height of y=0 (the equator of the sphere). The direction of motion is ccw when looking down from the positive y-axis. Other values of v produce a y different from 0 and the variable u-curves will be smaller circles at the height of y. They will be circles of latitude between the equator and the poles. The variable v-curves are semicircles of longitude running from the north to the south pole when v varies from 0 to 1.

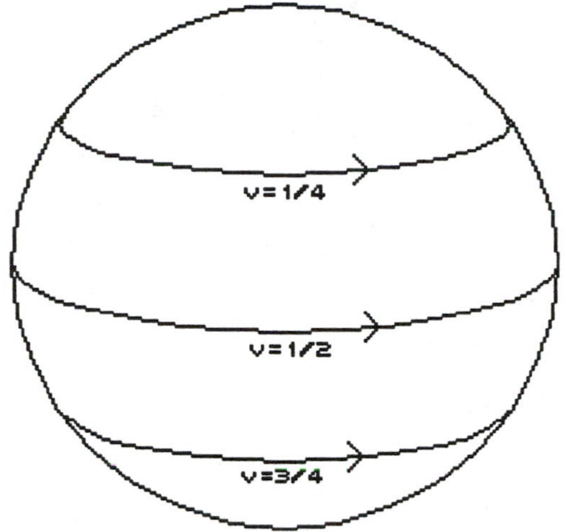


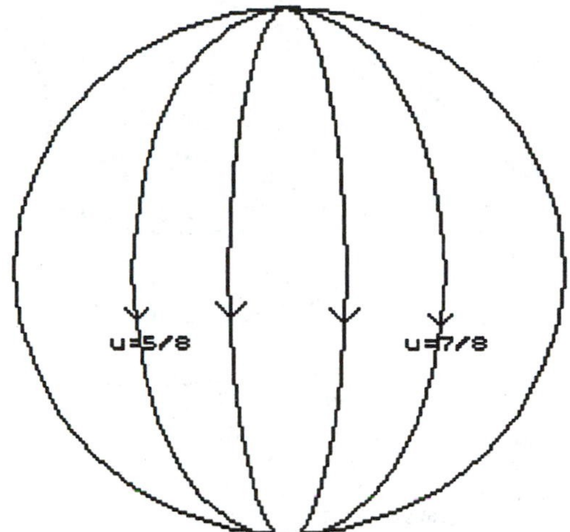


**FIGURE 15.1** Variable u-curves and variable v-curves.

**A Torus** For the description of a torus surface with the origin at the center, we need two radii as indicated in the diagrams in Figure 15.2. The parametric description of the torus surface is:

$$\begin{aligned} x &= (R+r*\cos(2\pi v))*\cos(2\pi u) \\ y &= r*\sin(2\pi v) \qquad \ldots \qquad (1) \\ z &= (R+r*\cos(2\pi v))*\sin(2\pi u) \end{aligned}$$

**FIGURE 15.2** Horizontal and vertical cross sections through a torus.

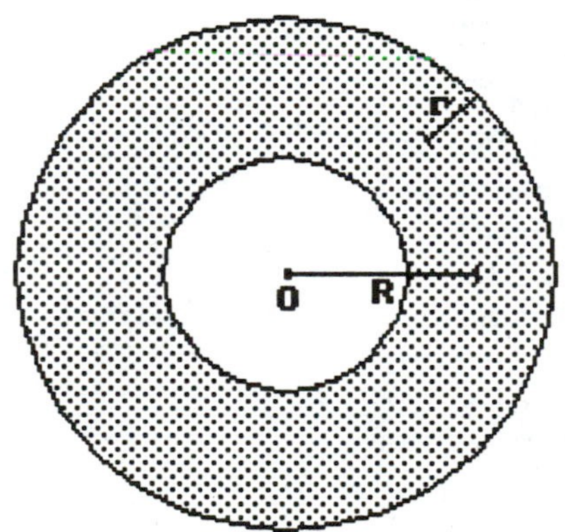


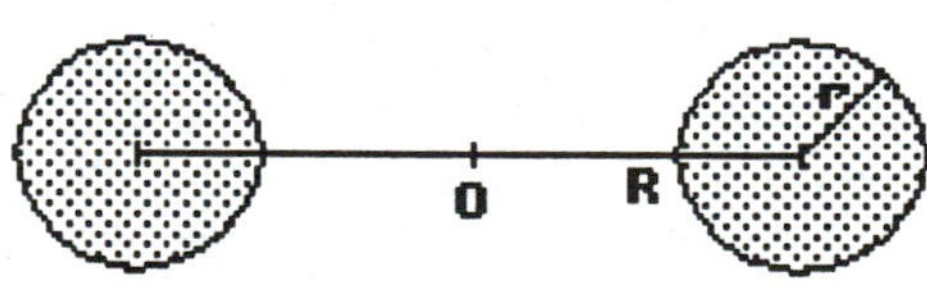

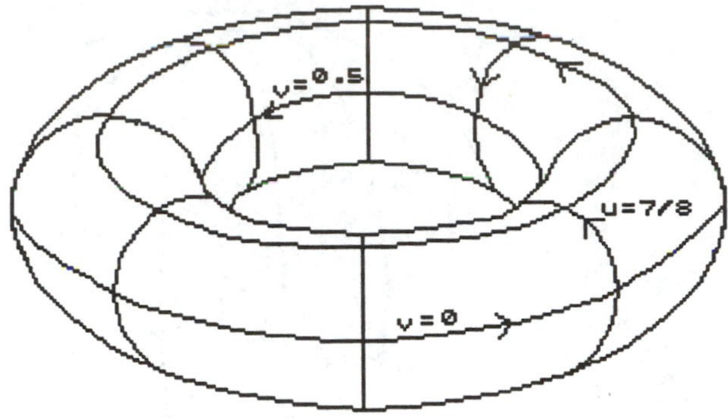


FIGURE 15.3

Figure 15.3 shows the constant parameter curves. The constant v-curves are horizontal circles, ccw around the y-axis when looking down from the positive y-axis. The constant u-curves are vertical circles. We can imagine a constant u-curve as the line of intersections of a vertical half plane bounded by the y-axis with the torus surface. The direction of movement of a point on such a curve is upward on the outside of the torus.

# 15.2 PATTERN MAPPING

We now begin the first of our surface mapping procedures—*pattern mapping*. As outlined above, the surface that we map onto is described by three functions of the two parameters u and v. Each (u,v) pair within the parameter range uniquely corresponds to a point on the surface. We define the pattern that we will map onto this surface as another function of the two variables u and v: m(u,v). A value of the mapping function, m(u,v), is usually interpreted as a color value. Each point in the definition range of the pattern corresponds to precisely one point on the surface. It is this one-to-one correspondence which is so essential to pattern (and texture) mapping and which is achieved through the parameterized representation. No matter what shape the surface has, the parameter range that describes it can always be rectangular and the pattern is also described on this same range of values.

Our first example uses the sphere discussed above. The parameter range to describe the entire spherical surface is the rectangle [0,1] × [0,1]. We will define the pattern on this same rectangle of (u,v)-values as a rectangular grid of heavy straight black lines (see Figure 15.4). Mapping this pattern onto the sphere is done by displaying the point

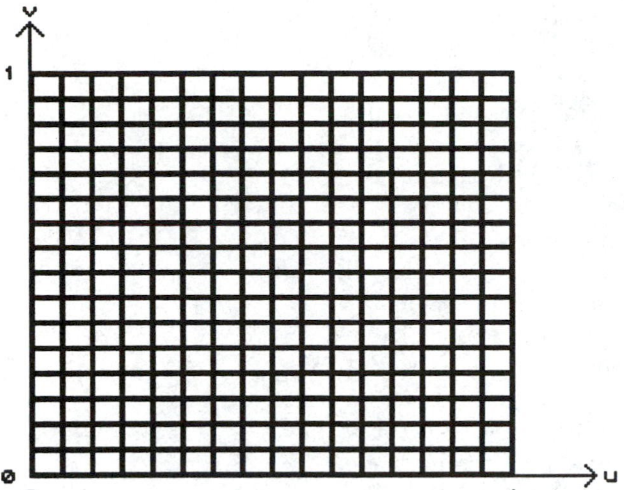


**FIGURE 15.4** The function m(u,v).

(x(u,v),y(u,v),z(u,v)) on the sphere in the color of the point (u,v) in the pattern m(u,v). The grid will be mapped onto the sphere as shown in Figure 15.5. This is not an unfamiliar pattern for a sphere. But we must be aware that actually a strong distortion takes place. The entire highest horizontal line is mapped onto one single point, the north pole of the sphere; the lowest horizontal line is mapped onto the south pole, which is invisible in this picture.

Whenever we map a rectangular area onto a whole sphere we have this or a similar sort of distortion around some "pole" of the sphere. Instead of thinking about theoretical solutions to such distortions, we

**FIGURE 15.5**

will concentrate on practical solutions that are good enough to serve our purpose: mapping something onto a surface. It helps that it is usually sufficient to map onto only a part of a surface; and if we map onto only a part of a sphere, we can avoid the influence of the poles. It also helps that many surfaces don't have poles. The torus is a good example; the mantle of a cone or of a cylinder is another. On such surfaces the problem of poles just doesn't exist.

The pattern used above was a grid of straight lines. This was a particularly simple one which could be defined easily by a mathematical formula. But a pattern doesn't have to be mathematically defined. It could be a drawing produced by hand with a paint system or a picture taken with a video camera. In any case, we must store it in a bit map. This bit map is then considered as the parameter range and values to be mapped onto the surface are taken from it. Figure 15.6 shows how the same pattern looks when mapped onto a torus. Observe that there is no "polar" distortion, because there are no poles!

How is mapping (displaying a map on a surface) done? Let's examine some possible approaches.

**First Approach** We can march through the range of parameters taking small steps in u and v. For each such (u,v) pair, get the corresponding mapping color m(u,v), compute the point (x,y,z) that corresponds to (u,v), project it onto the screen, and set the pixel there to the color m(u,v).

While this sounds reasonable, there are problems. One problem is that it is impossible to determine a correct size for the steps through u and v. If we use some arbitrary constant step size, we could select pixels that are too far apart in some areas of the parameter range, so far apart that they are not adjacent on the screen, leaving uncolored gaps. In other areas of the parameter range we could set some pixels several times, because a step in parameter space does not advance us in image

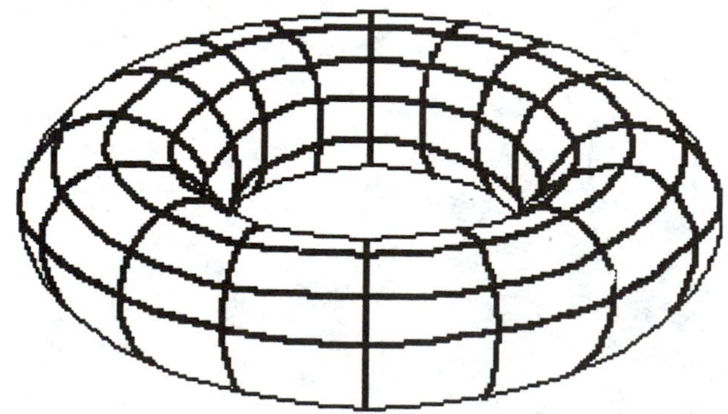

**FIGURE 15.6**

space (the screen). The first problem can be taken care of by choosing a very small step size. It is out of the question to calculate the precise size of step that would result in setting every pixel within the projection. We would have to take a very small step size in order to be safe. However, then we could not do antialiasing. With a very small step size we will set the same pixel several times in some areas. But that leaves this pixel set to the last color value. All previous values are overwritten by the last setting, although they should have an influence on the intensity of that pixel. This leads to strong aliasing in the mapped pattern.

To do *antialiasing,* we use the average of all pattern values that map onto the same pixel. With a large amount of computation and using lots of memory for storing values, this could be done, but the method would be very slow.

**Second Plan** We reverse the above approach. Go through the pixels on the screen and compute for each pixel center which point on the surface projects there. If there is such a surface point, there is a certain (u,v) pair corresponding to it. We take this (u,v) and set the pixel we started with to m(u,v). The method based on this idea is called *inverse pixel mapping.*

This is a rough idea of the scheme; it needs to be refined. In many cases, sampling the map only at points corresponding to pixel centers would not generate the desired pattern on the surface because two adjacent pixel centers can correspond to widely separated locations in the map. Intermediate regions are skipped and don't influence the intensity of that pixel; we get the same aliasing effect described above but for a different reason. What we should do is not just compute the point (u,v) corresponding to the pixel center, but the entire area in the (u,v)-range that corresponds to the area covered by the pixel. Consider a pixel to be a rectangular area in image space. This area is determined by its four corner points. For each of these corner points the corresponding (u,v) can be found. These four (u,v)-points describe a quadrilateral in the (u,v)-range (in general this will not be a rectangle). The size of this quadrilateral can vary widely.

What we want to do, in simplified terms, is to set the pixel to the average color of the quadrilateral in the (u,v)-range. Figure 15.7 shows a part of the grid of Figure 15.4 which we want to map onto the sphere and shows how the area corresponding to a pixel might look. (This is the dotted quadrilateral.) In this particular example the colors are only black and white and the value to which the pixel must be set is the average of the black and white in this area. This averaging reduces the aliasing effects that frequently occur in pattern mapping.

Sometimes the pattern to be mapped is a digitized picture or photograph. Such a pattern is not mathematically defined like the above

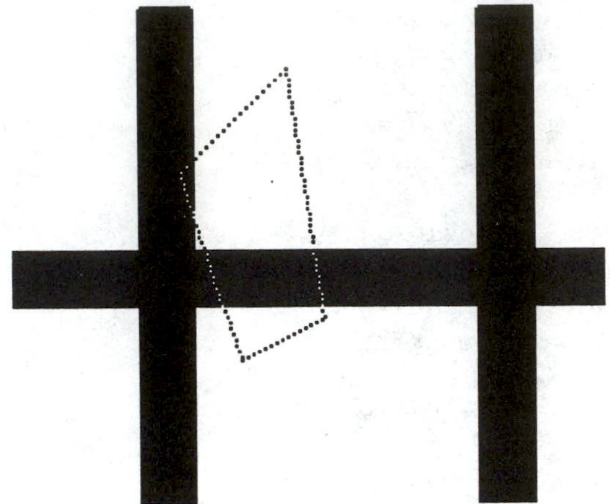

FIGURE 15.7

grid of black lines; it is a bit map. The quadrilateral corresponding to a screen pixel may then cover a number of pattern pixels or parts thereof in the (u,v)-range. Here, again, an average of the colors of the covered pattern pixels must be found (if more than one is covered) and the screen pixel must be set to this value. There are several techniques to determine this average color. They are not very complicated so we will not explain them.

On the other hand, the process of finding the (u,v)-point for a given (x,y) on the screen is not simple. It can require the solution of a system of two nonlinear equations. For simple x = X(u,v), y = Y(u,v), and z = Z(u,v) functions (a sphere, for example), the u and v can be expressed in closed form by equations and computed. But, for a general surface, such a closed form does not exist. So for each point (x,y) we may have to perform a generalized Newton-Raphson iteration. Such mathematics is done in algorithms for displaying curved surfaces (for example, in BLIN78), and in certain ray-tracing techniques (see SWBA86), but is not described in this book. GEWH88 gives a simple treatment of Newton-Raphson iteration.

As described in Chapter 8, we often define surfaces through parametric bicubic patches (Bezier curves, B-splines). In this case, a generalized Newton-Raphson iteration could be done but other techniques are available that require less computation: *surface subdivision techniques.* Based on the Oslo algorithm, they don't really divide the surface; instead they replace the original set of control points (see Chapters 7 and 8) by a finer grid of control points. The more control points there are, the closer they are to the surface they generate. The convex-hull property of these curves ensures that a surface patch will always be within the minimax box spanned by its control points. It is easy to check through which minimax-box a given straight line passes. This box can be further subdivided until the boxes are practically pixel-size. We only mention this and will not elaborate further.

As an example of inverse pixel mapping we will map the bit map shown in Figure 15.8 onto a sphere with radius R and center at (0,0,c). The boundary line is a part of the map. But we do not want to map the bit map onto the whole surface of the sphere, just onto a part of it. To do this, we must determine the corresponding subrange of (u,v) and then define the bit map within this range. In our example, the area onto which we map is in the upper octant facing us (see Figure 15.9). This area corresponds to the parameter range $0.68 \leq u \leq 0.93$ and $0.13 \leq v \leq 0.5$.

**FIGURE 15.8**

The bit map must be defined to correspond with this range, no matter what its extent in pixels. So we let u run horizontally and v vertically through the map and associate the left boundary with $u = 0.68$, the right one with $u = 0.93$, the bottom with $v = 0.5$, and the top with $v = 0.13$.

We use a perspective projection. For each point $(x_s,y_s)$ on the screen (the projection plane) we have to find the intersection of the sphere with a straight line emanating from the center of projection and going through the point $(x_s,y_s)$. We express this line in parameterized form. Let $(x_p,y_p,z_p)$ be the coordinates of the center of projection and $(x_s,y_s,z_s)$ the coordinates of the point on the screen. The general description of the line in parameterized form is:

$$
\begin{aligned}
x &= x_p + t(x_s - x_p) \\
y &= y_p + t(y_s - y_p) \\
z &= z_p + t(z_s - z_p)
\end{aligned}
$$

To simplify these expressions, we assume that the center of projection is on the z-axis with a z-value of $-d$ and the projection plane (the screen) is the plane $z = 0$. This implies that $z_s = 0$. The line equations then simplify to:

$$
\begin{aligned}
x &= t*x_s \\
y &= t*y_s \\
z &= (t-1)*d
\end{aligned}
$$

At the intersection of this line with the sphere we have:

$$
\begin{aligned}
t*x_s &= R*\cos(2\pi u)*\sin(\pi v) \\
t*y_s &= R*\cos(\pi v) \\
(t-1)*d &= R*\sin(2\pi u)*\sin(\pi v)+c
\end{aligned}
$$

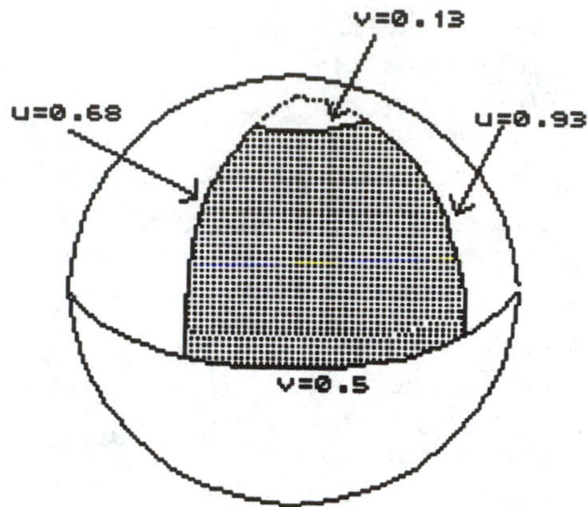


**FIGURE 15.9**

If we express v in terms of $y_s$ and t and insert this into the other two equations, we end up with a system of two transcendental equations in the two unknowns t and u for which there is no closed solution. We'd have to find a solution by a Newton-Raphson iteration. Unfortunately in such transcendental cases Newton-Raphson needs good starting values in order to converge and therefore is not easy to handle.

However, in our particular case of a sphere there is a simple implicit expression for the surface:

$$x^2 + y^2 + (z - c)^2 = R^2$$

Inserting (x,y,z) from the parameterized line representation gives us a quadratic equation in t:

$$t^2 * ({x_s}^2 + {y_s}^2 + d^2) - t * (2d^2 + 2dc) + (d + c)^2 - R^2 = 0$$

Solving for the two solutions for t gives us the two intersection points of the line with the surface; we use the one with the smaller z-coordinate. Using this value of t, we obtain:

$$x = x_s * t, \qquad y = y_s * t, \qquad z = (t - 1) * d$$

from the equation for the line. Knowing (x,y,z) on the surface of the sphere, we can compute the corresponding (u,v) in closed form:

$$v = \cos^{-1}(y/R)/\pi \qquad \text{and} \qquad u = \cos^{-1}\left(\frac{x}{R * \sin(\cos^{-1}(y/R))}\right)/(2\pi)$$

It is only because the sphere equations are simple that we get closed form solutions for u and v. In practically all other cases this will not occur because we do not have a simple implicit equation for the surface.

To display this sphere, we first tilt it by 25° toward the screen (we perform a rotation about a line parallel to the x-axis through the center of the sphere), giving a display similar to that of Figure 15.9. Then we must scale the coordinates of the sphere to absolute screen coordinates. For example, if the sphere has $R = 2$, it will extend horizontally from $-2$ to $+2$ (in its own coordinate system). If the center of the sphere is at (0,0,4) and the center of projection at (0,0,−4), making $d = 4$, the projection of the sphere will extend from approximately $-1$ to $+1$ on the projection plane (in units in which the sphere is defined).

Suppose that the sphere is to be displayed on a screen with absolute coordinates ranging from 0 to 639 left to right and from 0 to 399 bottom to top. We want the projection of the sphere to extend over 300 pixels horizontally and to have its center at the middle of the screen. If we display with these parameters, any point (x,y,z) on the sphere is transformed to absolute screen coordinates by first doing the perspective projection:

$$x_s = x*4/(z+4) \quad \text{and} \quad y_s = y*4/(z+4).$$

Then the scaling and translation below is done to arrive at the absolute screen coordinates $(x_a,y_a)$:

$$x_a = x_s*150+320 \quad \text{and} \quad y_a = y_s*150+200.$$

Let's follow the transformations that take place in bringing a point from the bit map onto the screen. Let (u,v) be the coordinates of a point in the bit map. This leads to the point $(x,y,z) = (X(u,v),Y(u,v),Z(u,v))$ on the sphere. It is rotated by 25° toward the plane $z = 0$, done by a matrix multiplication. Then it is projected perspectively onto the plane $z = 0$, giving the point $(x_s,y_s)$. The last step is the transformation to absolute screen coordinates $(x_a,y_a)$.

In inverse pixel mapping we must go backward through all this. Start out with a point $(x_a,y_a)$ and find the corresponding (u,v). To get $(x_s,y_s)$ we compute:

$$x_s = (x_a-320)/150 \quad \text{and} \quad y_s = (y_a-200)/150.$$

The step from $(x_s,y_s)$ to (x,y,z) can be done (as explained above) by solving the quadratic equation for t. However, usually there is no such simple procedure and this step is the difficult one.

What we actually should have computed is the intersection of the straight line with the sphere after it has been tilted. But, because a sphere does not change under rotations, we can compute the Cartesian coordinates of the intersection from the implicit equations and then rotate the point back to get the Cartesian coordinates of the point on the untilted sphere. With the torus above we would not have been able to do this.

This means that as soon as we have the intersection point (x,y,z) we rotate it back by 25° by applying the inverse of T which is, in homogeneous matrix notation:

$$\begin{bmatrix} 1 & 0 & 0 & 0 \\ 0 & 0.9063 & 0.4226 & 0 \\ 0 & -0.4226 & 0.9063 & 0 \\ 0 & 1.6904 & 0.3747 & 1 \end{bmatrix}$$

We can now find the corresponding (u,v) pair from the parameterized description of the untilted sphere.

To continue our example, we want to find the four points in the (u,v)-range that correspond to the four pixel corners of the pixel (427,189). If this is the screen coordinate of the lower left corner of the pixel, the four corners are:

(427,189) (427,190) (428,189) (428,190)

Table 15.1 shows the values obtained from the computation. We use only the smaller value of the two solutions of the quadratic equation for t because that one corresponds to a smaller z-coordinate and therefore to a visible point. The computation of u also gives two solutions; these are always of the form u and $1-u$. The smaller of these corresponds to a point on the back side of the sphere, so the larger one is taken.

**Table 15.1**

| $x_a$ | $y_a$ | $\sqrt{D}$ | t | x | y | z |
|---|---|---|---|---|---|---|
| 427 | 189 | 11.51463 | 1.58910 | 1.13356 | -.11653 | 2.35638 |
| 427 | 190 | 11.52435 | 1.58889 | 1.13341 | -.10593 | 2.35557 |
| 428 | 189 | 11.41461 | 1.59120 | 1.14567 | -.11669 | 2.36481 |
| 428 | 190 | 11.42442 | 1.59100 | 1.14552 | -.10607 | 2.36399 |

After rotating the points (x,y,z) backward we obtain the values shown in Table 15.2.

**Table 15.2**

| x | y | z | v | u |
|---|---|---|---|---|
| 1.13356 | .58901 | 2.46113 | .40485 | .85104 |
| 1.13341 | .59897 | 2.46487 | .40319 | .85122 |
| 1.14567 | .58530 | 2.46870 | .40546 | .85223 |
| 1.14552 | .59528 | 2.47244 | .40380 | .85241 |

The bit map is assumed to consist of 100 pixels in the u-direction and 150 pixels in the v-direction; this is to be mapped into the given parameter subrange. Let $(u_b,v_b)$ be the coordinates of the point in the bit map that corresponds to (u,v) in this mapping. Then $(u_b,v_b)$ is related to (u,v) by:

$$u_b = 400*u - 272 \qquad \text{and} \qquad v_b = 405.4*v - 52.7$$

The four points are as listed below and lie in the bit map as shown in Figure 15.10. The rectangle in this figure is the area of one bit map-pixel.

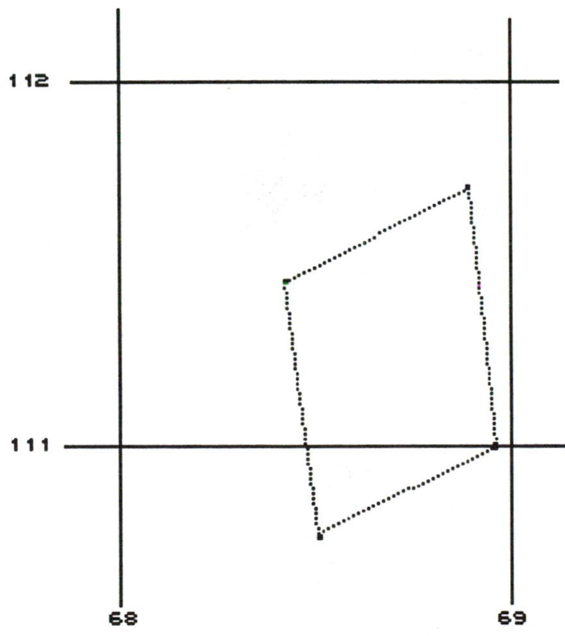


**FIGURE 15.10**

| $u_b$ | $v_b$ |
|---|---|
| 68.41 | 111.42 |
| 68.49 | 110.75 |
| 68.89 | 111.67 |
| 68.96 | 111.00 |

The result of the pattern mapping of this example is shown in Figure 15.11. Observe the narrowing of the pattern toward the pole of the sphere.

FIGURE 15.11

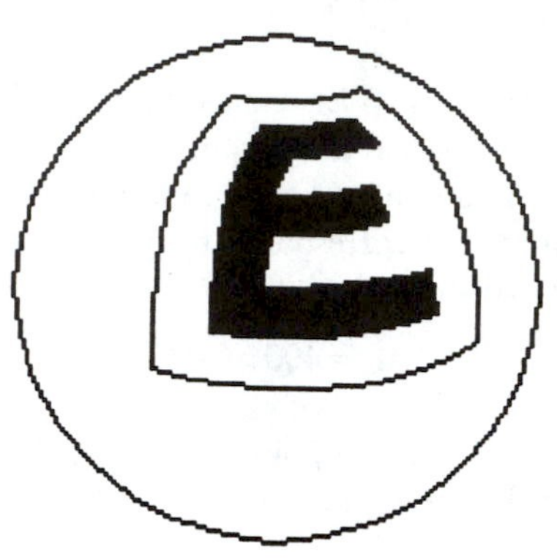

A variation of inverse pixel mapping that achieves better antialiasing was described by Blinn and Newell (BLNE76). In that variation, antialiasing is done through *filtering,* a technique of image processing. In the method we described above, the average of all the intensities in the area is taken as the pixel intensity, but Blinn and Newell sample the intensities at regularly spaced points within the area, including the point corresponding to the pixel center. The pixel intensity is then computed as a weighted average of the sample intensities, giving the pixel center the highest weight. No area computations are necessary. Consult BLNE76 for more information.

**Third Possibility** We look now at a third way to do pattern mapping as an alternative to the two schemes that we have already explored. We take subareas of the parameter range that are small enough so that the corresponding area on the screen covers just about one pixel. It helps that the parameter range is rectangular; we can take rectangular subareas also. We won't do any complicated computations in order to find a rectangular subarea of just the right size. Instead we will try out a given subarea and if its corresponding screen area has more than a single pixel center, we will make it smaller. In short, what we use is a *surface subdivision algorithm* (see CATM75). The essential algorithmic idea is:

1. The surface onto which we map is recursively subdivided into four parts until the projection of a part covers at most one pixel on the screen.
2. The intensity of this pixel is set to the average intensity of the corresponding subarea in the parameter range. The part of the surface corresponding to this subrange is then considered to be displayed.
3. The process stops when the whole surface is displayed.

The surface is subdivided into smaller parts. This is no contradiction to a subdivision of the parameter range, because a subdivision of the parameter range implies a subdivision of the surface. There is no fixed size relation between the subparts of the parameter range and the corresponding subparts of the surface parts or even between the latter and their projections on the screen. But that doesn't matter.

What we need to know is how many pixel centers are contained in the projection of a subarea onto the screen. If $[u_1,u_2] \times [v_1,v_2]$ is a subrange of the parameters, then the precise area on the screen that corresponds usually has curved edges. We approximate this area by a four-sided polygon which is easily obtained. We first compute the points on the surface that correspond to the four corners of the subrange. These we project onto the screen, giving four floating point numbers that determine the vertices of the polygon.

(If the surface consists of bicubic patches, CATM74 shows a fast way to find the corners corresponding to the subarea in the map, significantly speeding up the procedure. Evaluation of the bicubic expression at each point isn't required. See that reference for further details.)

To find out how many pixel centers lie in a polygon we must determine how many integers lie in the range of the floating point values. We can use a rough test. For example, we can find the smallest rectangle containing the polygon and if this rectangle is more than 2 wide or high, we assume that the polygon contains more than one pixel center, so we subdivide this region. To be more precise, we would do a quadrilateral inside test for the pixel center and the polygon (we describe such a test later, in Section 15.3). If the pixel center lies inside the polygon we set the pixel to the average color of the mapping function in the corresponding parameter subrange. A disadvantage of this is that we always end up with polygons that contain no pixel center. This polygon is lost—never displayed.

Figure 15.12 shows a part of a surface over a pixel grid. The lines represent the boundaries on the surface corresponding to subdivision lines in the parameter range. Some areas are further subdivided into four subareas; others contain more than one pixel center. Figure 15.13 shows an individual area enlarged with its approximating four-sided polygon. The area contains just one pixel center.

There is a variation to this algorithm that does not lose any polygons (also described in CATM74). It does not test pixel centers but rather tests the area of the obtained polygon. Further subdivision of a subregion stops when the area of the corresponding polygon is approximately the size of one pixel square. (This works if there are no weirdly shaped polygons, an occurrence of low probability.) This terminating condition also leads to polygons that contain no pixel center, but that doesn't matter, as you will see.

The reason why we stop at this size is that, on the one hand, we want the polygons as small as possible. The smaller the polygons, the

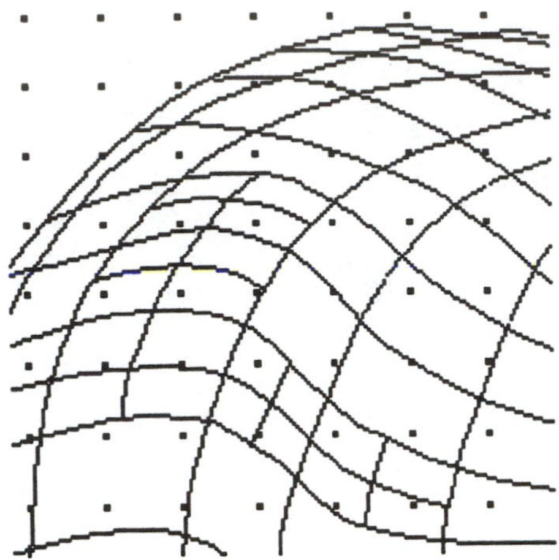

FIGURE 15.12

smaller the error. A smaller patch area has fewer curved boundaries, so it better resembles its approximating polygon. On the other hand, if we subdivided further, we would add to the complexity of figuring out the contributions to individual pixels. Since we don't gain additional benefit from subdividing the polygons further, we stop when the area of the map corresponds to a single pixel area. Note, though, that there may be more than one pixel corresponding to the polygon because the two kinds of areas overlap instead of matching exactly.

When the subdivision process ends, we compute, for each pixel square that corresponds, what percentage of the pixel area the polygon covers. The contribution to the pixel color value should be proportional. We compute this proportionality by maintaining an *accumulation cell* (a floating point value) which stores how much of the pixel value has accumulated so far. If, for example, a polygon covers 1/3 of the pixel square (x,y), the accumulation cell for (x,y) is looked up and if found to hold 1/3, this means that previous polygon(s) cover 1/3 of this pixel area and have already contributed to its illumination. This means that the illumination derived from the polygon in question will be attributed to pixel (x,y) on a 1:1 basis. The accumulation cell (x,y) will then be set to 2/3.

This is illustrated in Figure 15.14. The rectangular areas are the pixels on the screen. The heavy outlined area is a polygon at the end of the subdivision process. It covers about 75 percent of the area of pixel (220,303), 15 percent of pixel (219,303), 3 percent of pixel (219,304) and 30 percent of pixel (220,304), so the average intensity in the corresponding part of the pattern will be attributed to these pixels according to these percentages. This ensures that no area of the pattern

FIGURE 15.13

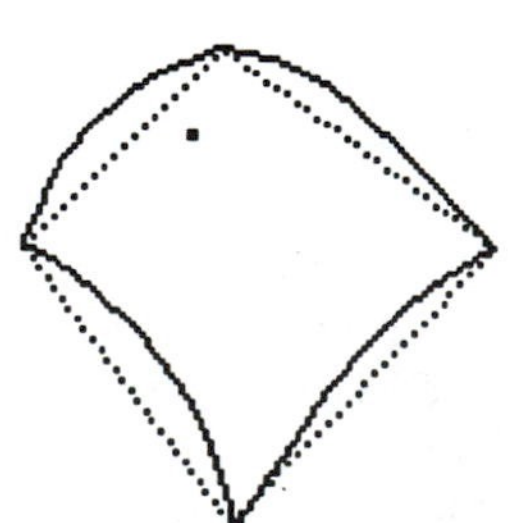

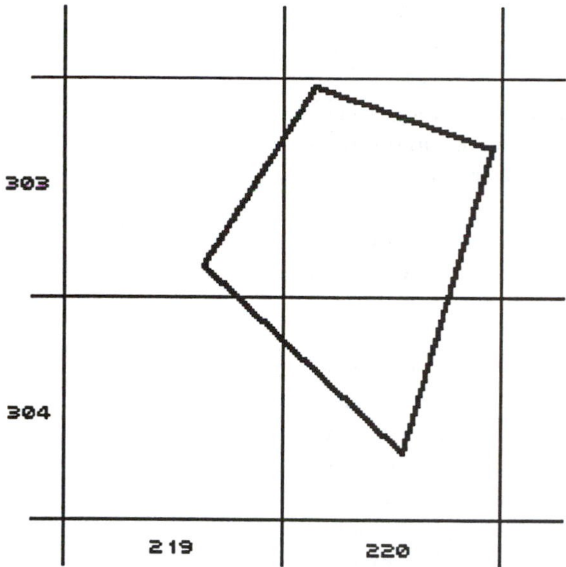

FIGURE 15.14

map is ignored. Every part is attributed to some pixel. This attribution technique very effectively mitigates aliasing effects but, as you see, it is not achieved without effort. We have to compute the intersections of the polygon with the pixel squares to figure out those percentages.

This algorithm is usually performed simultaneously with a Z-buffer test. With both Z-buffer and accumulation cell requirements, the memory used is considerable. However, it works at good speed and the results look good.

# 15.3 TEXTURE MAPPING

*Texture mapping* is another method of obtaining realism in the surface to be displayed. The procedure we will describe is Blinn's method of *surface normal perturbation* (BLIN78). The general idea is easy to grasp. It is well explained in Blinn's article.

Consider an orange. As a first approximation, you can think of an orange as a sphere. It would be more realistic to form it from bicubic patches to allow it to deviate from a perfect spherical shape. Still, it would have a perfectly smooth surface when what is wanted is a surface with many little irregular bumps. Blinn's approach consists of finding an independent function that defines a bumpy surface or, more generally, a function that describes a certain texture, regular or irregular. We then patch this function onto the surface, giving it texture. When we look for the independent function, we do not care onto what surface we will later patch it.

Assume that we can somehow define or describe an orange peel surface, or perhaps some other more rugged one. (How we can do this will be discussed later.) This function might look like the one shown in Figure 15.15.

This function is to be patched onto the smooth surface as if we were to paste on real orange peels to make it look bumpy. We first develop the mathematics to do this texture mapping; we will return later to the problem of defining the texture function. Let us call the texture function T. It will be defined as a function of the two arguments u and v: T(u,v). It is not a vector-valued but a scalar-valued function, meaning that T(u,v) just generates numbers. The surface onto which we will map it is described in parameterized form using two parameters u and v (like the sphere or the torus examples, or a composite of bicubic patches: S(u,v)). The full range of the parameters describes the whole surface and a certain part of that range describes a portion of the surface. We mention this because it is often necessary to add texture to only a part of the surface.

We could define T(u,v) only on that part of the full parameter range that corresponds to the area on the surface that is to be textured, but we could also define it over the parameter range of the whole surface. We can then use just a portion of the entire T(u,v) for the patch. We will do this in the development below.

Suppose that the range of parameters for the whole surface is $(u,v) \in [0,1] \times [0,1]$. We define T over this same range as in Figure 15.15.

**FIGURE 15.15**

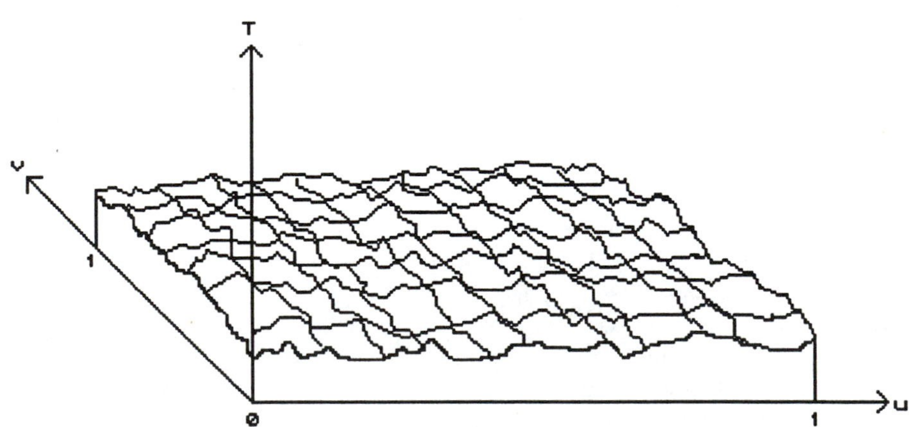

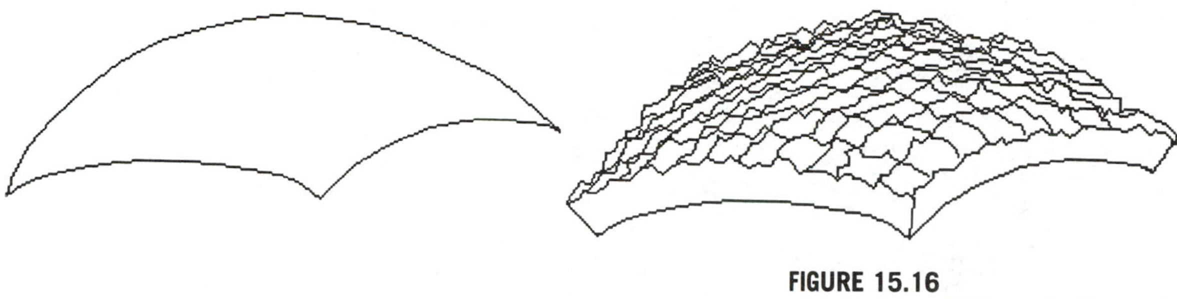

**FIGURE 15.16**

The texturing is achieved by patching T onto the corresponding part of the surface S; precisely how this is done is explained below. Figure 15.16 shows a smooth surface on the left and the same surface with added texture on the right. The important thing to realize is that the texture function T is added to the surface S in the *direction of the normal* to S. In effect, we perturb the smooth surface perpendicularly by amounts given by T(u,v). Adding T to S in this way creates a new surface S′. The mathematical formalism that describes this addition is given below. For a given parameter value (u,v), we have the surface point S(u,v) = (x(u,v),y(u,v),z(u,v)) and the value T(u,v). The normal to S at this point is the cross product of the partial derivatives $S_u(u,v)$ and $S_v(u,v)$.

$$N = S_v \times S_u$$

We scale N to the length 1 and call it n:

$$n = \frac{N}{|N|}$$

It is advisable to pay attention to the direction in which the above cross product points. The mathematics developed below is not influenced by this but later, when shading the surface, we should know the direction of the perturbed surface normal. Then we can reverse it if necessary to make it point away from the object, not into it. The variable u-curves and variable v-curves run within the surface S in certain directions with growing u and v. These directions indicate the directions of the vectors $S_u$ and $S_v$, depending on how the parameterization of S is specified. Therefore it is always easy to determine in which directions the vectors $S_u$, $S_v$ and N are pointing. In a left-handed coordinate system (which we assume throughout this explanation) the cross product vector follows the reverse corkscrew rule. In our particular examples (sphere and torus) the above surface normal n points to the outside of the object.

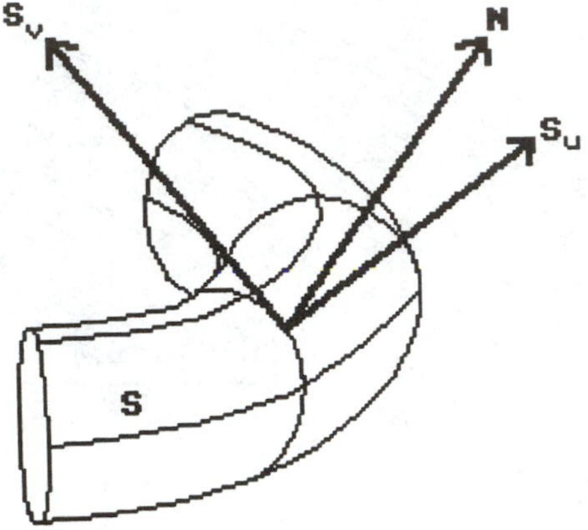


FIGURE 15.17

Figure 15.17 shows a part of the torus surface and the partial derivatives $S_u$ and $S_v$ at a certain point. They lie in a plane tangent to S at this point. Computing the cross product in the above order yields a normal vector N that points out of the surface, as shown in the figure. Adding the texture function T to the surface S in the direction of n is done by multiplying n by T(u,v) and adding this vector to the vector S(u,v). This creates the new surface that we call S′:

$$S'(u,v) = S(u,v) + T(u,v)*n \qquad \ldots \quad (2)$$

We now need to compute N′, the normal to S′, in order to render S′. This is computed as the cross product of the vectors $S'_u(u,v)$ and $S'_v(u,v)$, so we find these.

$$S'_u(u,v) = S_u(u,v) + T_u(u,v)*n + T(u,v)*n_u$$
$$S'_v(u,v) = S_v(u,v) + T_v(u,v)*n + T(u,v)*n_v \qquad \ldots \quad (3)$$

Observe that we have applied the rule for differentiating a product, as n is itself a vector-valued function of u and v. The vectors $n_u$ and $n_v$ depend on the curvature of the surface S. Normally this curvature is so small that $|n_u|$ and $|n_v|$ are negligible. We commit only a small error in discarding the terms $T(u,v)*n_u$ and $T(u,v)*n_v$.

In the continuation of the development, we don't repeat the arguments (u,v) for the vector-valued functions S, $S_u$, and $S_v$ and for the scalar valued function T. This simplification gives:

$$S'u \approx S_u + T_u*n \qquad \text{and} \qquad S'_v \approx S_v + T_v*n$$

The normal to S′ at (u,v) is now $N' \approx S'_v \times S'_u$. We compute $N' \approx S_v \times S_u + T_u*S_v \times n + T_v*n \times S_u + T_v*T_u*n \times n$.

Keep in mind that $T_u$ and $T_v$ are scalars. In the above formula they have been set out to the front of their respective terms, but we must not change the order in the cross products. First, we know that $S_v \times S_u = N$ and $n \times n = (0,0,0)$. So we have

$$N' \approx N + T_u * S_v \times n + T_v * n \times S_u \qquad \ldots \quad (4)$$

With formula (4) N′ can be computed, normalized, and then used to compute the intensity of the surface at that point.

**Geometric Explanation** A geometric view of N′ is helpful in visualizing the process of texture mapping. It is shown in Figure 15.18. N′ is obtained by perturbing the surface normal N. This is done by adding two vectors, shown in light lines, which are parallel to the derivatives $S_u$ and $S_v$. The length of these two vectors determines the perturbation of N.

We can get a geometric visualization of the method if we rewrite formula (4). Because n is normal to $S_u$ and $S_v$ and $|n| = 1$ we have:

$$n \times S_u = -S_v * \frac{|S_u|}{|S_v|}, \qquad S_v \times n = -S_u * \frac{|S_v|}{|S_u|} \text{(reverse corkscrew rule!)}$$

So we have:

$$N' \approx N - \alpha * T_u * S_u - \beta * T_v * S_v \qquad \ldots \quad (5)$$

in which

$$\alpha = \frac{|S_v|}{|S_u|} \quad \text{and} \quad \beta = \frac{|S_u|}{|S_v|}.$$

We will present the visualization only in terms of the parameter u, because for v, everything is analogous. First assume that $S_u$ and $S_v$ have the same length, 1:

$$|S_v b = |S_v b = 1.$$

Then α and β = 1 and $|N| = 1$. $T_u(u,v)$ is the derivative of T in the u-direction at the point (u,v). Figure 15.19 shows the function T(u,v) for constant $v = v_0$, which is a cross section of T in the u-direction. Suppose that at the point $(u_0,v_0)$ $T_u = -1/4$. The normal to the curve at this point is obtained by tilting a vertical of length 1 to the right by the amount 1/4 because the normal to the curve is normal to the derivative. If T were totally flat, then the normal would be the vector (0,1) but as T has the derivative −1/4, we perturb the normal vector (0,1) by adding the vector $-T_u*(1,0)$ to it. The above function

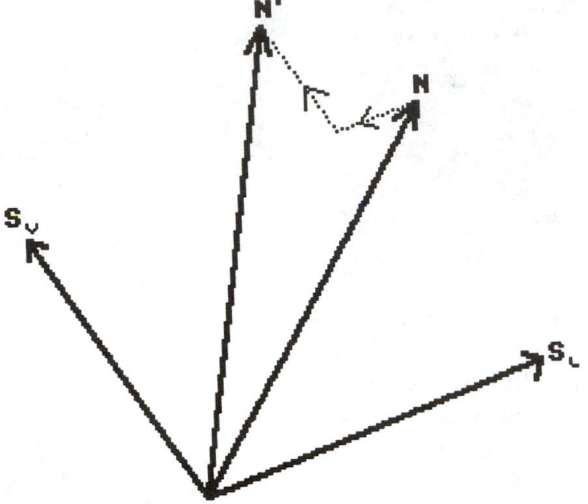


FIGURE 15.18

applies in the two-dimensional plane of the cross section along the direction of u. We move now to the surface S onto which we have mapped the function T. We will again look at a cross section of this surface, this time along the derivative $S_u$ at the point corresponding to $(u_0, v_0)$.

Figure 15.20 shows the situation. The normal N to the original surface S is perpendicular to the vector $S_u$—it plays the role of the vertical in Figure 15.19. The formula for obtaining N′ shows that we

FIGURE 15.19

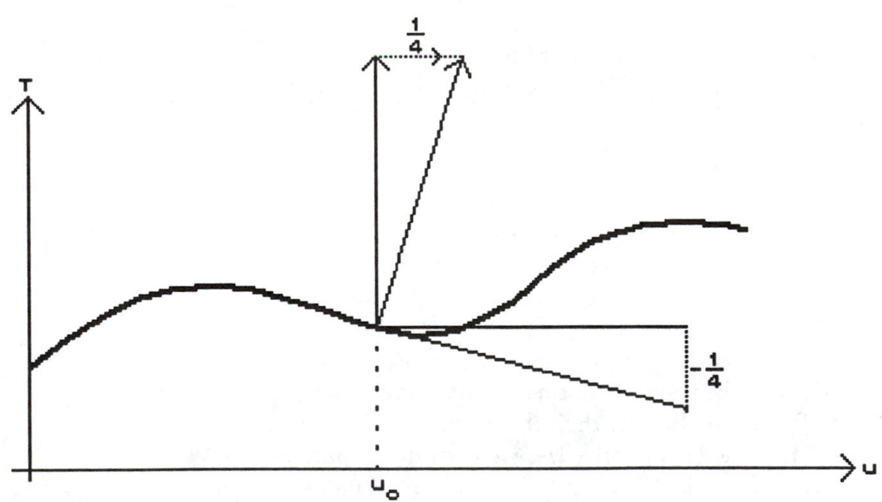

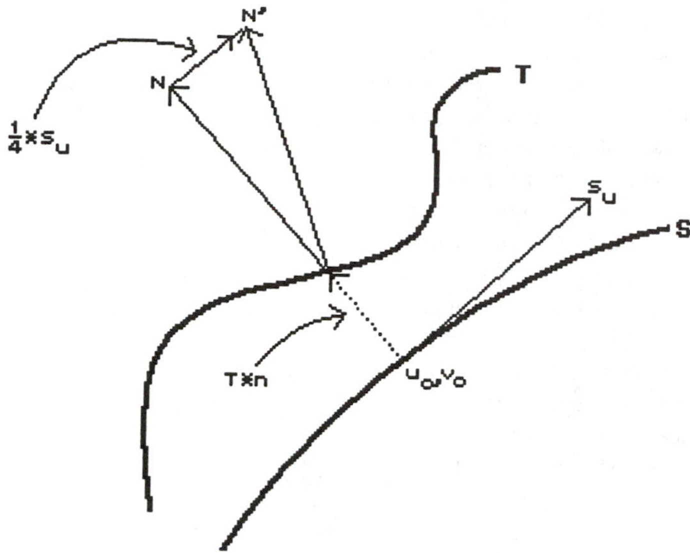


**FIGURE 15.20**

have to subtract $T_u * S_u$. With $T_u$ being $-1/4$ we do the same as we did in Figure 15.19: we tilt N in the direction of $S_u$ by 1/4. If $T_u$ were positive, we would have an ascending part of T in relation to $S_u$ and we would tilt N backward, against the direction of $S_u$. Reasoning geometrically, this is precisely what we would expect.

To obtain N′ according to formula (4) we must do another tilt of the surface normal N, this time along the direction of $S_v$. Since this is entirely analogous, we don't need to repeat it.

The perturbations we thus produce for N really give us N′, the normal to the surface S+T (speaking loosely). This is due to the fact that we assumed the lengths of $S_u$, $S_v$, and N to be 1. If $|N|$ were different from 1 then subtracting the vectors $T_u * S_u$ and $T_v * S_v$ would not produce the same tilt of N′ as is shown for the normal to the curve in Figure 15.20. For example, if N had a length much larger than 1, then adding $T_u * S_u$ and $T_v * S_v$ would result in a very slight tilt.

To continue the explanation for other cases, we now assume that $|S_u| = |S_v| = d > 1$. (We take $S_u$ and $S_v$ equal so as to develop this explanation stepwise.) The factors $\alpha$ and $\beta$ in the formula will be 1 and therefore will play no part.

Use Figure 15.20 to follow this explanation. According to the rule for the cross product, we have $|N| = d^2$. In addition to N being longer, the vector $T_u * S_u$ that we add to N also will be longer; its length will be longer by the factor d than in the former example. Still, the tilt thus produced is only 1/d of the previous tilt. Does this mean that our visual approach to the formula is incorrect?

No, this seeming inconsistency has the following explanation. When $S_u$ and $S_v$ are both larger than 1, the surface S spans a larger area as u and v go through the parameter space. When u moves along its axis in parameter space (with v constant), the corresponding point on the surface will move with d times the speed along the constant v-curve. As the surface corresponding to a certain u- and v-range is d times as large in u- and v-directions, the texture described by T(u,v) is stretched over an area d times as large (in u- and v-directions) when mapped onto this surface. This implies that all slopes of T (relative to the surface S) will be reduced by the factor 1/d through the mapping. This is precisely what happens.

D was taken greater than 1 to make the explanations more concrete and less abstract, but of course it can be any number. If it is less than 1 then the opposite effect will take place. All slopes of the texture function T will be increased by the factor d (relative to the surface S) through the mapping.

We consider now the case of $|S_u| \neq |S_v|$. Let $|S_u| = d$ and $|S_v| = 1$, which simplifies without loss of generality. It follows that $|N| = d$, $\alpha = 1/d$, and $\beta = d$. This case will demonstrate the roles of $\alpha$ and $\beta$ in formula (4).

Our assumptions imply that the surface S is scaled in the u-direction by the factor d but not scaled in the v-direction in contrast to the (u,v)-range over which T is defined. Therefore the derivatives of S′ in the u-direction must be scaled by 1/d in relation to the surface S. Figure 15.20 helps to visualize this. As N and $S_u$ are both scaled by d the tilt of $N' = N - T_u * S_u$ would be unchanged, indicating an unchanged value for $S'_u$. But now the factors $\alpha$ and $\beta$ come into play. According to formula (4), N is tilted in the u-direction by $-T_u * \alpha * S_u$. Now if $\alpha = 1/d$, the tilt in u-direction is indeed scaled by 1/d. In the v-direction, the derivatives of S′ in relation to the surface are unchanged as there is no scaling in this direction. On the other hand, as we have seen above, the surface normal N is scaled by d whereas $S_v = 1$. This would lead to a scaling of 1/d of all derivatives in the v-direction except for the factor $\beta = d$. According to formula (4), N is tilted in the v-direction by $-T_v * \beta * S_v$. So the derivatives $S'_v$ really are unscaled.

If $S_u$ and $S_v$ are both $\neq 1$ and different from each other, we simply have a combination of the scaling effect and of the effects of $\alpha$ and $\beta$.

The visualizations that we have gone through suggest that the formula represents a precise computation of the normal to the perturbed surface. But we know that formula (4) is only approximate. Where was the error committed and how can we visualize it? The error came from discarding the terms $T * n_u$ and $T * n_v$. Let us first consider a case in which no error is committed. If S is perfectly flat, then $n_u$ and $n_v$ both equal 0 and we commit no error in discarding the terms $T*n_u$ and $T*n_v$ in Equations (3). Formula (4) is exact in this case.

When S is curved, the situation is different. When we map T onto an outwardly curved piece of S, T is stretched somewhat; when we map it onto an inwardly curved piece of S, T is compressed. This is the case even when the area of S onto which we map T is of the same size as the area on which T is defined (so that no scaling of T to the size of S is involved). This stretching or compressing of T, which is due entirely to the curvature of S, implies subtle distortions in the normals. These effects are described by the terms $T*n_u$ and $T*n_v$ in (3), the only ones depending on the curvature of S. In practically all applications $n_u$ and $n_v$ are negligibly small, so we can discard the above terms without compromising the result.

Another geometrical explanation can be found in BLIN78.

**Definition of a Texture Function** We now understand the mapping of T onto S. Where do we get the texture function T? We will build up the explanation stepwise. First, we start with an overly simple example and define the texture function in a two-dimensional table, shown below in Pascal. The size of the table depends on how precisely we want to define the function. We assume that the parameters u and v range through $[0,1] \times [0,1]$ for that part of the surface onto which the texture should be mapped. We also define the texture function over that area.

```
var tab : array[0..63,0..63] of real;

function t(u,v : real) : real;
var nu,nv  :  integer;
begin
  nu := trunc(u*64);
  nv := trunc(v*64);
  t  := tab[nu,nv]
end {function t};
```

This describes a two-dimensional step function on $[0,1] \times [0,1]$ consisting of constant valued squares of sides equal to 1/64 whose values are in the two-way table tab[ ]. It is not adequate for mapping because, for that application, we need the derivatives $T_u$ and $T_v$, each of which are 0 within the squares and undefined on the boundaries. But it shows how a table can be used for this purpose and is the first step in defining a useful texture function.

The next step consists of creating a continuous function in which the table values apply only at the grid points (i/64,j/64). At argument values between the grid points, the function value is derived by bilinear interpolation from the values from the table.

```
function t(u,v : real) : real;
var  nu,nv             : integer;
     alf,bet,
     t00,t01,t10,t11,
     tu0,tu1           : real;

begin
  nu  := trunc(u*64);
  nv  := trunc(v*64);
  alf := u*64 - nu;      { 0 ≤ alf < 1 }
  bet := v*64 - nv;      { 0 ≤ bet < 1 }
  t00 := tab[nu,nv];
  t01 := tab[nu,nv+1];
  t10 := tab[nu+1,nv];
  t11 := tab[nu+1,nv+1];
  tu0 := t00+alf*(t10-t00);
  tu1 := t01+alf*(t11-t01);
  t   := tu0+bet*(tu1-tu0)
end {function t};
```

This function is actually a grid surface (see Chapter 13). It consists of nonplanar quadrilaterals separated by sharp ridges. Its derivatives in the u- and v-directions are constants within each square (whose sides are 1/64 long). They are undefined on the boundaries. Mapping it onto the surface would give a recognizable texture, but the texture would not be smooth bumps because the derivatives are discontinuous. Figure 15.21 shows a bumpy texture with randomly spaced bumps; this is an interim state as all bumps are equally high and not smooth. It was defined on a $16 * 16$ table using a random number generator. We could make the grid finer, change the density of the bumps, or give the bumps a random height.

We could get a smooth appearing texture function by using the table values to generate bicubic B-spline patches. The resulting surface would give us smoothly changing derivatives in all directions. There is a much less expensive way to get smoothly changing derivatives. We approximate the derivatives of T by finite differences along u or v with an increment equal to the distance between grid points, that is, 1/64. What we get are the partial derivatives of quite a different function.

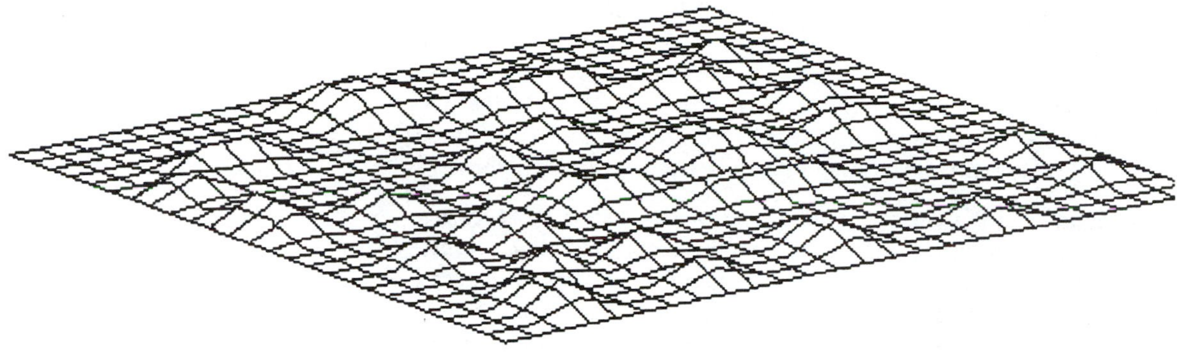

**FIGURE 15.21**

But we really don't care what this function is, for we only need the derivatives $T_u$ and $T_v$. The following Pascal functions return values of the two partial derivatives. (The appendix explains the approximation of derivatives by finite differences.)

```
function tu(u,v : real) : real;
var       d              : real;
begin
  d  := 1/64;
  tu := (t(u+d,v)-t(u-d,v))/(2*d)
end {function tu};

function tv(u,v : real) : real;
var       d              : real;
begin
  d  := 1/64;
  tv := (t(u,v+d)-t(u,v-d))/(2*d)
end {function tv};
```

Above, we have used central differences to define the derivatives. However, as it stands, the subscripts of t can range from $-1$ to 65 and cause subscript under- or overflow. One easy way to avoid this is to overspecify the table to contain entries for these subscripts: array[$-1..65, -1..65$] of real. Another, more useful way is to perform a modulo operation on all subscripts in order to redirect under- or overflow in a cyclic manner to the other end of the table. This can be used to repeat the texture defined in the table over a larger area of the surface. The last two functions would generate a texture consisting of smooth bumps.

A very effective way to create bump textures is to draw a sample of the bump texture by hand and then repeat it cyclicly as suggested above. When we draw with a black-and-white paint system, we are actually filling a frame buffer with bits. Hence our drawing fills some area of the frame buffer with a design of our choice. We can consider this area as the table defining the bump texture. The 1-bits are the high values and the 0-bits are the low (or vice versa). We interpolate these table entries bilinearly and compute the derivatives as shown above.

**Mapping the Texture** The texture can be mapped by applying an inverse pixel-mapping method as described for pattern mapping. We must, however, proceed in a somewhat different way. You will recall that we found the area in the parameter range that corresponds to one pixel area on the screen and averaged the intensities of that area to obtain the intensity of the pixel. In mapping a texture, we cannot just average the bump texture over a subarea because that would result in smoothing out the bumps. An obvious solution would be to compute intensities at a higher resolution within this pixel area and then average those to the pixel intensity, but this would be costly.

Rather than do this, we will sample the texture function only at the pixel centers, perturb the surface normal, and compute the intensity with Phong's illumination model. This can lead to the same aliasing effects as described for pattern mapping. If the effects are severe, we can reduce them by filtering the texture function. Roughly stated, filtering implies that we sample the texture function at the point corresponding to the pixel center and at some points spaced around it in some regular way. The $T_u$ and $T_v$ values from the samples are combined as weighted sums which are used in the perturbation and intensity calculation for that pixel.

When mapping onto a sphere, there is the possibility of compressing the texture too much near a pole. This is sometimes desired, sometimes not. How can it be avoided? The location of a pole depends on the parametric representation we select for the sphere. A sphere can be expressed by many different parametric representations, each of which can have poles at different locations. If we map a single texture onto an entire sphere, we cannot avoid the poles. But mapping is usually done by repeating the process of mapping a small texture onto a small area of the sphere. Therefore, when we get close to a pole, we can change the parametric representation to another one that doesn't have a pole in the neighborhood of the mapped area.

Another method would be to map a texture only onto an area that is not close to a pole and then display other areas of the sphere by rotating this area around the center of the sphere to put it into the right position (of course this can be done only with spheres!). Care must be taken that the texture boundaries match somewhat where they are pieced together. This can be handled by careful definition of the texture function. Actually, this procedure creates overlapping parts of the sphere surface onto which we map twice. If the textures in the overlapping parts match, for example if they are both flat, there will be no problem. The overlapping areas will be small if the patches are themselves small.

# 15.4 RAY TRACING

We now look at an easy and very efficient technique that is especially good for creating pictures that consist of objects with shiny surfaces in which other objects of the scene are reflected. Even more complicated scenes with objects that refract as well as reflect can be rendered with this method. Of course it can display simple scenes with dull objects as well. It is the most versatile rendering technique in computer graphics and is used frequently in solid modeling.

Every visual impression we get from the world around us is conveyed to us through light rays that emanate from whatever we see. As explained in Chapter 14, visible objects emit light, which they either produce themselves or receive from elsewhere and reflect or refract toward us. Whenever a light ray reaches our eyes, we see the thing that originally generated that ray, whether or not the ray has been reflected and changed in direction several times on its way to us.

When several objects are in a scene, especially shiny ones, light emanating from some point often reaches our eyes in several ways. Consider the light from the light bulb in Figure 14.5 (Chapter 14).

Figure 15.22 shows a more conspicuous and well-known case: a ball reflected in a mirror. Light rays coming from areas of the ball can reach our eyes from two different directions. One point in such an area is shown in the figure. There is also a portion of the ball from which the light rays reach us directly and still a third portion from which they reach us only by reflection in the mirror. All this adds up to give us the impression of two balls, the real one and its mirror image, seemingly behind the mirror.

Now think of a scene with more than one mirror and perhaps objects with curved mirrorlike surfaces; together they provide many paths for the light rays that reach our eyes. We will see not just one but several mirror images of objects, mirror images of mirror images, and so on.

It would be very hard to duplicate precisely what nature does. We'd have to send out light rays from all point sources in the scene in all directions, follow and reflect them whenever they hit a shiny surface, and continue to follow each of the reflected rays. If a ray hits a nonshiny

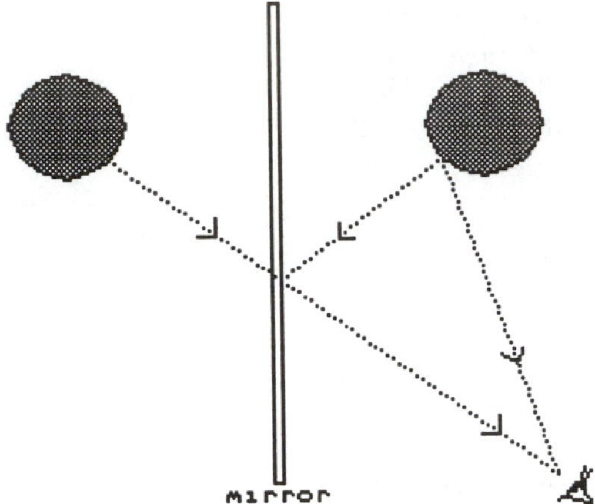


FIGURE 15.22

but somewhat diffusely reflecting surface, we'd have to spread it out into countless weaker rays emanating from this point and follow each of those. Each ray will eventually fly off into space or end up in the dull surface of a nonreflecting object, or (and these are the rays we see) end up in our eyes.

Whenever a ray hits our eyes we see its intensity, that is, simply stated, its color. This color is what is left of the original intensity of the ray when it came from its source, say the sun. At the source it was composed of many different wavelengths mixed together. Follow a possible history of this ray on its way to our eyes. Whenever it hit a shiny surface it was changed in its direction and very little in its properties (specular reflection, Section 14.1.2). Whenever it hit a diffusely reflecting surface, some of its wavelengths were partly or totally consumed by this surface. Only the remaining wavelengths managed to escape, scattered in many different directions. One of those escapees—the one we finally see—might have struck still another diffusely reflecting object, which took other light rays out of its spectrum. One of the escapees of this second scattering finally happened to reach our eyes with only some wavelengths remaining.

Each ray that reaches us has a history that formed its intensity. Most rays in a scene never reach our eyes.

It is impractical to figure out the direction for a ray from a given point so that, after reflections, etc., it will end up at the eye of a person who looks at this scene. But it is not difficult to trace backward the path a ray has traveled in reaching the eye. We can do this by positioning the onlooker at the center of projection; only rays that reach this point contribute to the perceived picture. The contribution of such a ray to the picture is the intensity it has when reaching the eye, which is the intensity with which it passes the screen plane.

Now the smallest element of a picture on a raster display is a pixel. We can set such a pixel to the intensity of the ray that goes through it on its way from wherever in the scene to the center of projection. Theoretically, we could imagine a bunch of rays going through a pixel passing through several distinct points within the pixel area and average their intensities to obtain the pixel intensity. If we have enough computing power and enough time nothing keeps us from doing that, and we will probably get a picture that is somewhat better, probably with less alias effects, and so on. But the principle used in such an approach is the same as when we follow only one ray through the center of the pixel and set it to the intensity of that ray.

This is what we describe below as the ray-tracing technique. We shall not be very elaborate; it will be just a sketch with examples.

**Considering Reflection Only** As the term ray-tracing suggests, we trace the path that a light ray travels before it reaches our eyes. This tracing is done backward and done once for each pixel on the screen. An example will serve to clarify (see Figure 15.23). We assume a scene consisting of two totally shiny spheres hovering over a flat black-and-white checkerboard ground. The background—the space—is dark blue.

The figure shows three cases. The ray through pixel a bounces off sphere 2, then off sphere 1 before hitting the checkerboard in a black area, so pixel a will be black. The ray through b bounces off sphere 1

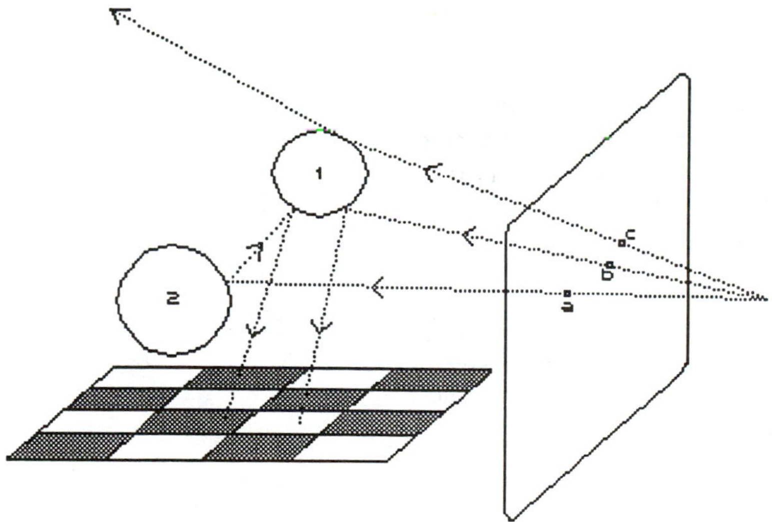


**FIGURE 15.23**

and hits the checkerboard in a white area, so pixel b will be white. The ray through c bounces off sphere 1 into space. Pixel c will be blue.

The ray is a straight line in parameterized form, originating at the center of projection $(0,0,-d)$, and going through the center of a pixel with the address $(x_s,y_s)$. If a pixel address is given in absolute screen coordinates, it must be transformed into the same coordinate system in which the scene is described, object space coordinates, so $(x_s,y_s)$ is assumed to be in object space coordinates. Since there are reflecting objects, a ray may eventually go in any direction. Consider the line given by:

$$x = x_s * u$$
$$y = y_s * u$$
$$z = d * u - d$$

Will this ray strike a sphere, and if so, which sphere? It is easy to find out.

The equations of the spheres are given implicitly:

$$(x-x_{c1})^2 + (y-y_{c1})^2 + (z-z_{c1})^2 - r_1^2 = 0$$
$$(x-x_{c2})^2 + (y-y_{c2})^2 + (z-z_{c2})^2 - r_2^2 = 0$$

$(x_{c1},y_{c1},z_{c1})$ is the center and $r_1$ the radius of sphere 1; the same for sphere 2. Everything is mathematically very similar to the pattern-mapping example in Section 15.2.4, except that the sphere has an arbitrary center.

We solve for u from the quadratic equation:

$$u^2(x_s^2+y_s^2+d^2)\text{-}2u(x_s x_{c1}+y_s y_{c1}+d^2+dz_{c1}) \\ +x_{c1}^2+y_{c1}^2+(d+z_{c1})^2-r_1^2 = 0$$

We also solve the quadratic equation for the second sphere. If there are no real solutions, there is no intersection with the spheres. In that case we try every other object in the scene, including the plane equation for the checkerboard (see below for this). If there are real solutions for the values we assume for the pixel point $(x_s,y_s)$, we take the smallest value for u because it corresponds to the entry point of the ray into the closest sphere and so to a visible point. We call this point on the spherical surface $(x_j,y_j,z_j)$. We assume the intersection is with sphere 1. We know that the sphere is totally shiny, so we have to reflect the ray on the sphere and continue to follow it. So for this point we compute the surface normal, N, which is trivial for a sphere:

$$N = (x_j-x_{c1},y_j-y_{c1},z_j-z_{c1})$$

Then we normalize N and compute the reflection vector, $(x_r, y_r, z_r)$. The reflected ray travels with the parameterized expression:

$$x = x_j + u * x_r$$
$$y = y_j + u * y_r$$
$$z = z_j + u * z_r$$

The point (x,y,z) travels away from the sphere as a reflected ray as u increases.

We now check to see if this reflected ray hits another object. We try for an intersection with the second sphere, again by solving a quadratic equation for u in the same manner as above. If there are intersections with the second sphere we take the smaller value for u because we need only the entry point into the sphere. As the second sphere is totally shiny, we again have to compute a reflection vector, and continue as we did before. We can theoretically strike the first sphere again, reflect back, and so on. But this probability becomes smaller with every reflection. Still, we should provide for an end of such cases by limiting them to, say, six reflections.

There are other possibilities. We might not strike sphere 1 at all, nor sphere 2, and not even the checkerboard base. In this case the ray goes off into space, so we set the corresponding pixel to dark blue and the tracing process terminates. If after striking sphere 1 we don't hit any other object (including the checkerboard), then the ray also goes off into space and the pixel is set to dark blue. We know that the ray goes off into space when every test for intersection, including every object in the scene in the testing, is negative.

If a ray hits the checkerboard ground—either immediately or after being reflected by the spheres—the pixel is set to either black or white depending on what square the ray hit because we assume the checkerboard is nonreflective.

It is not necessary to go through all these possibilities in order to summarize the algorithmic idea in pseudocode. The direction we follow is actually the reverse of the real ray direction, but we still call it the direction of the ray.

**a.** For a given pixel $(x_s, y_s)$ follow the ray from the center of projection through this pixel.
**b.** Check all objects in the scene to see if they intersect with this ray. If there are intersections, take the one that is closest when traveling along the ray. This intersection corresponds to the "hit" object. If there are no intersections, the "hit" object is the background (or space).

c. If the "hit" object is opaque (for example the checkerboard), set $(x_s, y_s)$ to the color of the object at this point (here one can include the production of shadows, see below). Take the next pixel; go to a.

d. If the "hit" object is shiny, compute the reflection vector and follow the ray from the "hit" point along this vector; go to b. Emergency brake: If there are too many reflections in succession, set pixel to background; take next pixel; go to a.

**Shadows** It is possible to include shadows in the picture. When we intersect an opaque object, instead of simply setting the pixel to its lighted color, we check to see if there is a shadow there. This is done by starting a ray from the intersection point parallel to the light source vector L, checking for an intersection against all objects in the scene. We don't need to know the point of intersection, just whether there is an intersection. If so, we set the pixel to the color of the opaque object but reduced somewhat in its intensity.

We see that spheres are easy to deal with in ray tracing; only a single equation has to be checked for the intersections and the surface normal is easily obtained. Even spheres that penetrate each other pose no problem for this algorithm. Therefore, ray-traced pictures are almost exclusively composed of spheres and objects composed of spheres.

If an object is composed of planar surfaces, a cube for example, we must change the method some. There are two techniques that we can use. In the first we compute the intersections of the parameterized ray with those planes that correspond to front faces of the cube with relation to the point where the ray starts. We assume that a backface test has removed the other planes from consideration.

Once an intersection with a frontface is found, we check if this point also lies on the cube, that is, within the area of the plane that is part of the cube surface. For this we need to design an inside test for a point and a square, similar in spirit to the general triangle-inside test described in Section 11.3. This test must be done in either the (x,y)- or the (x,z)- or the (y,z)-plane, so all five points to be tested must be projected onto one of these planes before the test can be carried out. This projection cannot be done without thought because in some cases the five projected points will lie in one line. However, there is always at least one plane in which the projected points are not collinear.

For a convex object like a cube there can be at most one plane intersection that also lies on a front face of the cube, so as soon as such a point is found we can stop further testing. In Figure 15.24 we look down from above at a ray and four planes of a cube. Planes 1 and 3 are backfaces, so no intersections need be computed, but intersections with planes 2 and 4 must be computed and also go through an inside test.

**FIGURE 15.24**

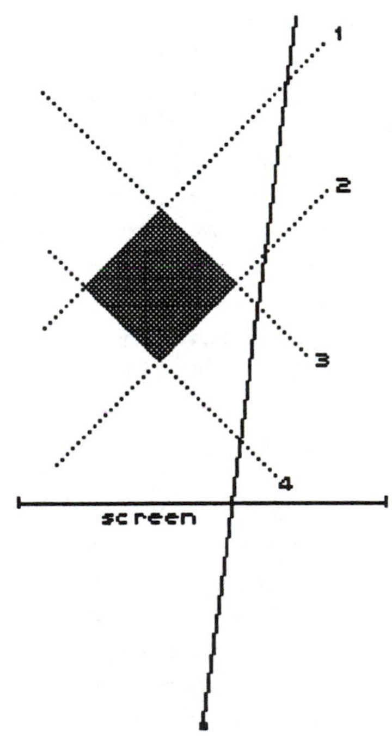

One or both of the top and bottom planes will be a backface, so one more set of tests may have to be done. If two or more cubes are present or if there are concave objects, we have to check all frontfaces for intersection with this ray. If several frontface intersections on the cubes or objects are found, we have to choose the one with the lowest positive u value. This is the point where the ray is reflected; then we start the whole process again.

The second method is to consider the cube as an intersection of six half-spaces. A half-space is a plane together with the space on one side of it. It is the simplest solid primitive and is often used in solid modeling (see Chapter 17). A half-space can be expressed by its plane equation:

$$Ax + By + Cz - D = 0$$

We adopt the convention that the surface normal (A,B,C) points into the half-space. If the cube is composed of half-spaces, all surface normals will point into the cube. For a given ray we compute the u-values where it intersects with the six planes, $u_1, \ldots, u_6$. The general parameterized description of a ray is:

$$x = s_x + u*d_x$$
$$y = s_y + u*d_y$$
$$z = s_z + u*d_z$$

The ray intersects the plane $Ax + By + Cz - D = 0$ at the u-value:

$$u = \frac{D - Ad_x - Bs_y - Cs_z}{Ad_x + Bd_y + Cd_z}$$

To avoid division by 0 we initially make sure that $|Ad_x + Bd_y + Cd_z| > 0.0001$. When the ray intersects, it can either enter or leave the half-space. We know which from the angle between the direction cosines and the surface normal; if it is less than 90° the ray enters. We determine this for every plane by computing the sign of the dot product of $(d_x,d_y,d_z)$ and (A,B,C). A positive result means it enters the half-space.

If $Ad_x + Bd_y + Cd_z$ is close to 0, the ray is numerically parallel to the half-space and we set u = maxint. We now can know if the ray is traveling inside or outside the cube. We insert the starting point $(s_x,s_y,s_z)$ into the plane equation and check the resulting sign. If positive, the ray is inside and we classify u as an exit value; otherwise u is an entry value.

We determine the biggest entry u-value $u_{in}$ and the smallest exit u-value $u_{ex}$. If $u_{in} < u_{ex}$ the ray hits the cube at this u-value and on the corresponding face.

Applying this strategy to the drawing of Figure 15.24 we obtain two entry u-values at planes 2 and 4 of which the former is the larger. We obtain two exit u-values at the planes 1 and 3 of which the latter is the smaller. (We should also test the top and bottom planes but we will ignore this.) The smallest exit u-value, $u_{ex}$, is at plane 3, the largest entry u-value, $u_{in}$, is at plane 2. As $u_{in} > u_{ex}$ this ray has missed the cube.

We can see that objects bounded by planes pose more problems than spheres. The problems become even greater when we ray trace objects composed of free-form bicubic patches (see SWBA86).

**Including Refraction** When the objects in a scene are not only shiny but also transparent, light rays hitting them are not only reflected but can also penetrate through them, whereby their direction is altered and their intensity changed. Refraction adds additional paths for rays to reach our eyes. Figure 15.25 shows a sphere of solid glass that reflects and refracts light rays. It shows three different paths for rays from point P to point C (our eyes): direct, reflected, and refracted.

Ray tracing can handle refraction as well as reflection. As we go backward along the rays the basic process will be different from what might be suggested in Figure 15.25. In this figure light from P reaches C along different paths and therefore passes through different pixels on the screen.

We must restate the problem to make it tractable for ray tracing. The fact that light rays have several ways to reach a certain point implies that rays coming from different areas can arrive at the same point with identical directions. Figure 15.26 will help to clarify this. Again we have a solid glass sphere. Light rays 1 and 2 both reach the point C from P, 1 by reflection and 2 by refraction. Both go through the same

**FIGURE 15.25**

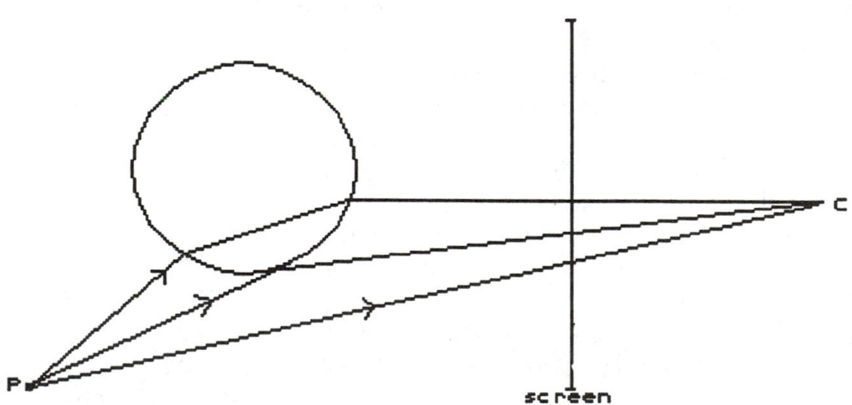

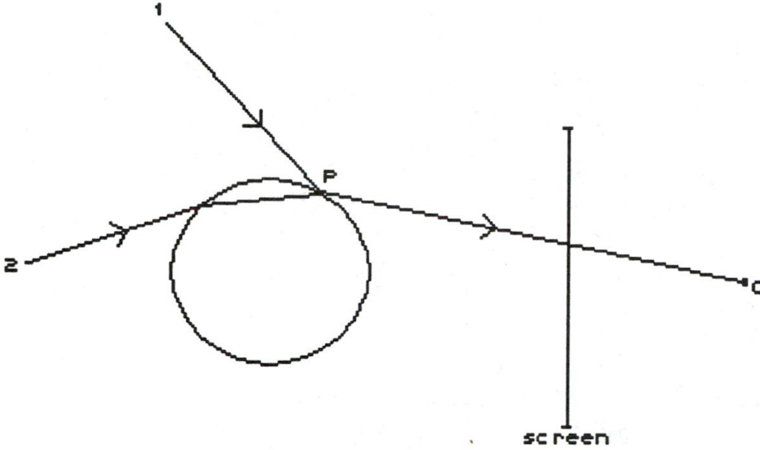


FIGURE 15.26

pixel and contribute their intensities to it. As ray tracing works one pixel at a time, we only need to know about all the rays that pass through the pixel in order to find this pixel's intensity. The essential algorithmic idea is that, for a given pixel, when we trace backward along the ray, we may have to split the path into two at a point where it hits a refracting object.

To do this, we produce a ray from the center of projection through a pixel and find the point where it strikes the sphere. There we split it in two and follow both branches. One branch is the reflected ray and the other the refracted ray. When other objects in the scene are struck by a branched ray, the ray might again be split in two if the object both reflects and refracts. If the object is only reflecting, no splitting of the ray is done and only the reflected ray will be followed; if the object is dull, that branch of the ray ends here. Also if the ray strikes no more objects but escapes into space, the branch ends.

Theoretically a multitude of reflections and refractions can occur in the scene, but it is customary to stop after about five splittings. This will limit the maximum number of branches to follow to 32. In reality each reflection and refraction decreases a light ray's intensity, which prevents endless reflections, so we are not too far from the real physical process in setting such a limit.

When all branches of a ray have come to an end we have to sum up all their contributions to obtain the intensity of the pixel that was traversed by that ray.

**Description in Pseudocode** In order to simplify the pseudocode and for clarity, we assume not only data types that are allowed in a Pascal program but also some assignments and operations that are impossible.

We assume that there is a type ray which is not merely a three-component vector, but a data structure consisting of six components: a point in 3-D space from which the ray emanates and a vector that defines its direction. The function intens has such a ray as argument and returns the intensity of this ray.

In dealing with intensities, we assume a type rgb consisting of three integers holding RGB values. This is the type of the function intens. The global variables are lsou (intensity of the light source), back (intensity of the background), and ambi (intensity of the ambient light).

The intensity of ray r is composed of three contributions: the contribution of the reflected branch, caused by specular reflection and assigned to spec by a recursive call; the contribution of the refracted branch, caused by refraction and assigned to refr by a recursive call; and the contribution of the nonreflecting, dull surface, assigned to dull and formed by point light from the light source and by ambient light. The three local variables spec, refr, and dull are also of type rgb.

We assume further that we can do an assignment of an rgb type to a variable of rgb type, and also a scalar multiplication of a number with an rgb type.

L is the vector pointing to the light source; N is the surface normal. We assume there are n objects, object[j], j = 1..n. For each of the objects there is a specular reflectivity factor ks[j], a refractivity factor kr[j], and a diffuse reflectivity factor kd[j]. They bear a complicated relation to each other. To make our model less complicated, we limit ourselves to two types of objects: transparent ones and opaque ones. We do this to avoid the case of all three factors being nonzero which would be complicated.

If an object is opaque, light does not pass through and we express this by setting kr = 0 (no refracted light). The other two factors ks and kd can then be whatever is desired. They are not related in any simple manner.

If the object is transparent, light from a point source will not be consumed by the object and we express this by setting kd = 0 for all three primaries (the object itself has no color). The other two factors ks and kr will sum to 1 expressing that point light will partly pass through and partly be reflected, more of the one and less of the other.

```
global var          depth  :  integer;
          back, lsou, ambi :  rgb;

function intens(r  :  ray)  :  rgb;
var spec, refr, dull  :  rgb;
```

```
begin
  depth := depth + 1;
  if depth > 6
  then intens := back
  else begin
    check ray r for intersection
    with all objects of the scene;
    if no intersections
    then
      if r parallel to L
      then intens := lsou
      else intens := back
    else begin
      take closest of intersections,
      which is with object[j];
      compute normal N;
      if ks[j] > 0
      then begin
        compute reflection ray flec;
        spec := ks[j]*intens(flec)
      end
      else spec := 0;
      if kr[j] > 0
      then begin
        compute refraction ray frac, see below;
        refr := kr[j]*intens(frac)
      end
      else refr := 0;
      check for shadow;
      if shadow
      then dull := kd[j]*ambi
      else dull := kd[j]*(lsou*NL + ambi);
      intens := spec + refr + dull
    end;
  depth := depth - 1
end {function intens};
```

Computing the refraction ray frac is more difficult, because it does not start out at the intersection point (see Figure 15.27). We first compute the refraction ray that goes into the object. Then we follow that and find the point where it exits the object; this is the first intersection with that same object. We then compute a refraction ray at the exit using inverted refractive indices because the ray is leaving the object. The exit point together with the new direction gives the refraction ray frac. Computation of a refraction vector is shown in the appendix.

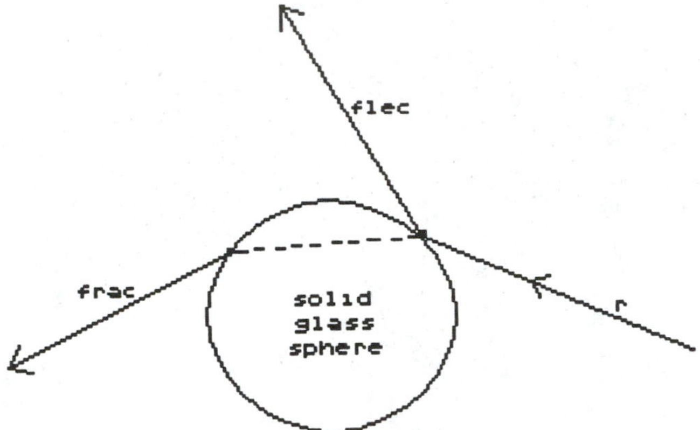


FIGURE 15.27

# EXERCISES FOR CHAPTER 15

## Section 15.1

1. Write a program that displays a wireframe torus using the parametric description presented in the text. It displays the torus by drawing curves of constant u and constant v. The numbers of curves are given by two variables nu and nv. Compute points on these curves by stepping the nonconstant parameter in little steps through its range. Display the torus by:
   a. rotating every computed point individually
   b. projecting each rotated point orthographically
   c. transforming the projection to screen coordinates
   d. connecting the projections by straight lines
2. Repeat Exercise 1 but project perspectively. The parametric equations specify a torus with center at (0,0,0). Therefore a part of the torus will, so to speak, stick out in front of the screen. This would produce an exaggerated perspective distortion. Therefore, display a torus with center behind the screen in the positive z-axis area. The description of a torus with center at $(0,0,c_z)$ is:

$$x = R*\cos(2\pi u)*\sin(\pi v)$$
$$y = R*\cos(\pi v)$$
$$z = R*\sin(2\pi u)*\sin(\pi v) + c_z$$

   Remember that every computed point must be translated by $-c_z$ before the rotation and by $c_z$ afterwards.

3. Repeat Exercise 2 but display a sphere. Here, too, rotation makes sense, because, although the object's shape in space does not change, we can see different positions of the poles. Mathematically, the perspective projections of the constant u- or constant v-curves are not ellipses anymore, although the difference is not perceptible.

# Sections 15.2 (Pattern mapping)

4. Implement the inverse pixel mapping method described in the text. Assume a sphere described parametrically by

$$x = R*\cos(2\pi u)*\sin(\pi v)$$
$$y = R*\cos(\pi v)$$
$$z = R*\sin(2\pi u)*\sin(\pi v)$$

Define a bit map pattern, for example the letter A. Use the range $0.68 \leq u \leq 0.93$, $0.13 \leq v \leq 0.5$ and map it onto the sphere. Display the sphere after rotating by 30° about the x-axis toward the viewer.

# Section 15.3 (Texture mapping)

5. Use inverse pixel mapping to map a texture onto a sphere. Define a simple texture function somewhat like the one shown in the text (see Definition of a Texture Function in Section 15.3). Map this texture onto the same area of the sphere as used in Exercise 4. Sample the texture function only at the center of pixels. Don't rotate the sphere toward the user. Assume a light source behind you and to the left at an elevation of about 45°.

Exercise 5 is already very close to ray tracing. A difference is that with pattern mapping and texture mapping we need to reconstruct the (u,v)-pair that corresponds to the point on the sphere that is hit by the straight line through the screen (the "sampling ray"). Only then can we find out what the pattern or normal perturbation at this point is. In ray tracing we don't need to do this.

# Section 15.4 (Ray tracing)

Exercises 6 through 9 are a series in which a scene is made successively more complicated.

6. Implement the ray-tracing algorithm for one sphere as described in Section 15.4. Assume the sphere to be totally shiny ($k_s = 1$), to have no color of its own ($k_d = 0$), and no refraction ($k_r = 0$). When a ray misses the sphere, it ends in space and the associated pixel is set to blue. (So far this sphere is invisible, because all rays eventually end in space. The whole screen will be blue.)
7. Put a light source in the scene by defining a vector lvec that points to it. For every ray check its angle with lvec by computing the dot product of the ray with lvec. If it is close to 1, then the angle is small and the pixel is set to white. The sphere should now have one highlight.
8. If a ray goes off into space, set the pixel not to a uniform blue but compute the angle at which the ray goes into space. Then set the pixel to darker blue for high angles (upward pointing rays) and light blue for lower angles (more horizontal rays). This produces a more natural-looking sky and makes the shiny sphere more visible. Experiment with other color settings.
9. Put a nonreflecting object in the scene, for example, a horizontal checkerboard below the sphere. Define it by a plane equation. For every ray check its intersection with that plane using the parameterized line representation for the ray. Let the ray be:

$$x = x_s + u*x_d$$
$$y = y_s + u*y_d$$
$$z = z_s + u*z_d$$

where $(x_s,y_s,z_s)$ is the starting point and $(x_d,y_d,z_d)$ the direction. Let $Ax + By + Cz - D = 0$ be the plane equation. An intersection can be obtained by computing:

$$u = \frac{D - Ax_s - By_s - Cz_s}{Ax_d + By_d + Cz_d}.$$

If u is positive then there is an intersection (negative u-values represent intersections in the reverse ray direction). Avoid divisions by zero—parallel case! A positive u-value is inserted into the ray representation and yields the ray-plane intersection. Check whether this point is within the boundaries of the checkerboard. For a horizontal plane this is easy; for nonhorizontal planes see Exercise 10. If the point is within the checkerboard boundaries repeat the checks to find within what square the intersection lies, then set the pixel to black or white.
10. In ray-tracing we often have to compute the intersection of a ray with a plane. When such an intersection point is found we have to check whether this point lies within certain boundaries. If we were to ray trace a pyramid with triangular surfaces, then the

boundaries are triangles; if we ray trace a cube, the boundaries are rectangles. The inside test is easier to perform when done in a two-dimensional plane. So we project the vertices of the polygon in space and the intersection point onto, for example, the (x,y)-plane—by just ignoring the z-coordinates—and then perform the test. But this is not always a good choice. If the surface normal of the polygons plane is parallel to the (x,y)-plane, we have to project onto a different plane. In short, we cannot project onto the plane that is parallel to the surface normal.

Let $(n_x,n_y,n_z)$ be the surface normal. Then,

if $n_x = 0$, $(n_x,n_y,n_z)$ is parallel to the (y,z)-plane;
if $n_y = 0$, $(n_x,n_y,n_z)$ is parallel to the (x,z)-plane;
if $n_z = 0$, $(n_x,n_y,n_z)$ is parallel to the (x,y)-plane.

As not all components can be simultaneously zero there is always a way to project properly. Write code that determines the projection.

Exercises 11 through 18 add additional features to the scenes of Exercises 7 through 9.

11. Check for shadows in the scene. Whenever a ray hits a dull (or partly dull) object the color of the pixel is finally computed. But with shadows we first start a ray from this point in the direction of the light source vector lvec (from Exercise 5) and check this ray for intersection with all objects in the scene (except the object where the ray starts). When an intersection is found, no further objects have to be checked. If no intersection exists, the color of that pixel is computed normally. If an intersection exists, the color is computed as above and then somewhat reduced in intensity.
12. Before we insert more spheres into the scene we design a mapping from screen to user coordinates so that only a small portion of the screen is ray traced. With this method we can produce a coarse preview of the final picture in a much shorter time. Find the transformation that ray traces the scene onto pixels $0 - 90$ in x and $0 - 90$ in y.
13. Insert several spheres in the scene and position them all above the checkerboard. Make them all totally shiny. The spheres can touch or penetrate each other. Check all spheres for intersection. If several intersections exist, take the one with the smallest u-value. Otherwise check for intersection with the checkerboard plane.
14. Make some of the spheres nonreflecting and give them color: $k_s = 0$, $k_d = (k_{dr},k_{dg},k_{db})$ (some nonzero values). In this case you need to set some ambient light $(I_{ar},I_{ag},I_{ab})$ and specify the inten-

sity of the light source ($I_{pr}$,$I_{pg}$,$I_{pb}$). Use the diffuse reflection model of Chapter 14.

15. Make some of the spheres touch or penetrate the checkerboard. In this case the plane equation always has to be checked for intersection. This intersection point must be compared to all sphere intersections, because it could be closer than a sphere intersection.
16. Define a totally reflecting tetrahedron in space and write code to ray trace it. You can eliminate the planes of backfaces from further consideration. Check all other planes for intersection and perform an inside test for the intersection point (see Exercise 5). Once an intersection is found, the other planes can be ignored, because no two frontfaces can be intersected simultaneously. Implement the computation of the reflection vector.
17. Include the tetrahedron into the scene with the spheres.
18. Make some of the objects (spheres or the tetrahedron) partly reflecting and partly dull with their own color by setting ks = 0.5 and ($k_{dr}$,$k_{dg}$,$k_{db}$) to some value greater than 0. Compute the illumination with the model of Chapter 14, but the reflected ray needs to be further pursued until it comes to an end. See the recursive programming technique presented in the code for Section 15.4.
19. Write a procedure that computes the refraction ray for a ray that hits a solid glass sphere. Two refraction rays must be computed: one that enters and one that leaves the sphere. The second one is the final refraction ray to be considered in further computations. See Section 14.1.3 and the appendix. Assume refractive indices of $n_{air} = 1$, $n_{glass} = 1.4$.

    *Hint:* Let l be a vector of magnitude 1 pointing to the light source, n the unit surface normal, $R_{fr}$ the refraction vector. $R_{fr}$ can be obtained through this sequence of computations:

    compute $\cos a = n*l$,
    compute $\sin a = (1-\cos^2 a)^{1/2}$,
    compute $\sin a' = n_{air}/n_{glass}*\sin a$,
    compute $\cos a' = (1-\sin^2 a')^{1/2}$.
    compute $\sin(a-a') = \sin a * \cos a' - \cos a * \sin a'$,
    compute $d = \sin a / \sin(a-a')$,
    compute $R_{fr} = -n - d*l$.

# Animation

# 16

Chapter 16 explains how conventional animated pictures are made, how the computer can assist in this, and how computer-produced pictures can be animated.

**16.0 Introduction** defines what is meant by animation and how computers relate to it, and explains the physiology that makes a sequence of still pictures appear as smooth motion.

**16.1 Devices for Producing Animation** shows the different processes for exhibiting animated pictures on movie screens and CRTs.

**16.2 Computer-Assisted Animation** tells how the laborious procedures needed for conventional animation can be simplified by generating "in-between" pictures with a computer.

**16.3 Real Time Animation** describes ways for adding animation to computer graphics; sprites and lookup table changes are two such procedures. Animation for flight simulation is an important application that requires sophisticated hardware.

**16.4 Frame by Frame Animation** can produce complex moving pictures on simple computers but these cannot be done in real time. The individual pictures are displayed by a device other than the computer.

# 16.0 INTRODUCTION

Animation, long associated with cartoons and sometimes rising to higher art forms, seems quite the opposite of mathematics and logic. At first glance, it seems to be something that depends on intuition and feelings. The computer can play an important role in these productions but there has been much reluctance to accept it. This attitude has slowed the development of computer support of animation. However, the computer can be an immensely helpful tool, as we shall see.

Our study of animation in relation to computer graphics must begin with a look at conventional animation methods. We first define animation, investigate why animation is possible at all, go on to look at some ways the computer assists the animator, and finally see how we can add animation to computer graphics.

*Animation* essentially means to make something "come alive." The term also means the technique of producing pictures that move. Animation is not necessarily just movement, although "movement is the essence of animation" (HALA74). It can also consist of a change of shape or color. What role can computer graphics or, more generally, the computer, play in the animation of pictures? How can we add animation to computer graphics? In other words, how can we use a computer to produce pictures that move in addition to those that just stand still?

The reason why animation works lies within human physiology. All of the technical developments in animation take advantage of this fact so this is where we begin.

When we see a video movie on a TV screen or a conventional movie in the theater, we perceive smooth and continuous motion. You already know that this movement is really an illusion that is achieved by rapidly displaying a sequence of still pictures that differ only slightly from one to the next.

A real object moving through our field of vision excites a sequence of light-sensitive cells in the eye. These cells lie on the path of its projection onto the retina. Strictly speaking, in terms of the excited cells, there is a jerky change—a digitization—because there are only a finite number of discrete cells; we are not really provided with a continuously moving impulse. It is the visual processes in the brain that create the sensation of continuous motion.

Our optical perception system has developed the ability to cope with a lot of jerkiness in the impulses. Each blink of the eye interrupts the optical impulses for a short time without disturbing our vision. Obstacles between the moving object and our eyes, changing light levels, shadows passing over the moving object, all contribute to the discontinuities but we "see around" these things through an ability to integrate jerky optical signals into a perception of smooth motion.

This ability is so fully developed that we cannot see jerkiness under a certain threshold even if we try. Nobody is able to see the flickering of a neon lamp, although it does so 60 times per second. The integration effect implies that we cannot see a picture that does not last long enough, even if it is totally different from the images before and after. It is integrated out of existence by the overwhelming presence of the images that come before and after.

This integration capability explains why we can provide discrete, jerky impulses to the eye and still the optical perception system will give us the sensation of smooth motion, so long as we don't overdo it. What is the limit in jerkiness?

We can create continuous motion by producing still pictures that "snapshot" an object at time intervals of about 1/30 of a second. This can be done with hand-drawn pictures of the object or with photographs taken in a rapid sequence. Experience shows that presenting this sequence of still pictures, allowing only 1/30 of a second for each, results in a perception of smooth motion. Actually, we can slow the rate of presenting the pictures to 20 per second, where we begin to perceive a beginning of jerkiness.

It is interesting to observe that the smoothing or integrating effect does not take place with equal facility for impulses received on different areas of the retina. You might have observed that you can see the flicker of a CRT screen displaying a still picture when you don't look straight at it but from the corner of your eye.

## 16.1 DEVICES FOR PRODUCING ANIMATION

There are mainly two very different kinds of devices that produce moving pictures based on this fact. These are CRT screens whose pixels are rapidly changed and conventional movie projectors. (Recently small liquid crystal displays have appeared on the market that are fast enough to serve as TV displays but these will not be considered here.) We will look at the film projector technique first.

A *film projector* produces images by shining a white light beam through a transparent medium on which the picture is painted with transparent dyes. By passing through the dyes the light is robbed of certain wavelengths—a subtractive process—and the remaining colors hit the screen, producing the picture that is then reflected to our eyes. The projector holds each picture frame for a while and then exchanges it quickly for the next one; during the change the light is temporarily blocked off. About 100,000 individual pictures are stored on the film for an hour-long movie. Creating these many individual pictures takes much, much longer than the time needed to display them.

A video movie uses a *CRT*. The CRT is used both for television and for computer graphics; technically there is no difference between a graphics monitor and a TV monitor, so you already know how images are produced on this device. To produce animation on a CRT screen, then, we have to produce a sequence of different images rapidly, at least 20 per second. While the display tubes are the same, there is a basic difference between TV and computer graphics in the way the information is provided to the display circuitry.

If the CRT is used as a *graphics monitor,* the image is always held in a frame buffer. This buffer provides the information to the circuitry about what color to put into each pixel of the hundreds of thousands that compose the screen. So to change the picture, we must change the contents of the frame buffer. This proves to be a speed bottleneck in the process. The frame buffer is comparable to one frame of movie film and the display circuitry to the film projector. Animation on a graphics CRT monitor actually means producing new frame buffer contents at very high speed, comparable to the task of producing (not merely projecting) film frames with such a speed. Of course, for film, this would be impossible considering the chemical processes of development.

Several techniques have been developed to overcome the bottleneck in changing the frame buffer. A common one is to work with more than one frame buffer. While one is being displayed, the graphics system fills the other with a new picture. Then the memory area to be scanned by the circuitry is changed to the other frame buffer by simply changing a base address in the CRT controller or something similar. To change the base address takes essentially no time so the displayed picture changes at once. The viewer is never aware of the changing of the frame buffer.

Another technique uses additional memory areas besides the frame buffer to hold parts of the image. As the frame buffer is scanned, the scan jumps to the other area, then back again to the frame buffer. This method is used to display cursors, sprites, and related objects.

Even so, it is still a major problem to create or change frame buffer contents fast enough for animation. It can be done for very simple pictures with conventional hardware and for more complicated pictures with extremely fast hardware, such as that used for flight simulation. But, as a general statement, we have to say that a computer graphics system is not well adapted to produce animation.

If the CRT is used as a *TV monitor* there is no counterpart to a frame buffer that holds the picture information. The process starts at the video camera that transforms the scene into an electronic signal. The receiver portion of the TV set gets the signal continuously from the air, transforms it through hardware into RGB intensities and synchronization pulses, and feeds these to the display circuitry. There is no fixed relation between the picture information and a particular pixel location on the screen, except indirectly through horizontal and vertical synchronization. The major difference is that the TV signal is analog while the graphics information is digital. The signals for a whole line of the display are one continuous stream. No memory has to be scanned, created, or changed to make the display. Therefore there is no speed bottleneck. The signal can easily carry the information for 30 different pictures per second. (There are details of interlacing, phase alternation, and so on that we omit.)

Still, the essential point is that even a TV monitor creates only still pictures, although in rapid sequence. No picture ever moves in and of itself.

The *video recorder* can record TV information. It stores individual pictures on a magnetic tape. The signals for one *field*—between two vertical sync signals—are recorded as they come from the air onto the tape as one *track*—a slanted path of magnetization across the tape. The frames for a video recorder can also be produced directly by a video camera.

Thirty frames per second can easily be recorded and a tape of reasonable length can contain the information for several hours of animation. When playing back a videotape the TV set reads the signal off the tape, transforms it, and feeds it to the display circuitry, just as if it received the signal from the air.

Producing a videotape with a video camera is a much faster process than producing a film. It is becoming increasingly popular because no chemical development is involved. However, the quality is still not equal to film. So film plus film projector and video camera plus CRT are the two major devices for the production of animation for movies and television. Where does computer graphics come in?

# 16.2 COMPUTER-ASSISTED ANIMATION

When we speak of animated movies we mean animation with drawn pictures, not movies staged with actors in real world scenes. For several decades, Walt Disney movies have been a prototype. Today there are countless animated cartoons on TV and many animated TV commercials. The techniques involved have evolved rapidly, using the most up-to-date equipment to make their production fast and economic. The newest tool in this area is the computer with its graphic capabilities.

**Conventional Animation** Such movies are created by first writing a script for the story. From the script a series of pictures is hand-drawn that show important moments in the story. This series of pictures is called the *storyboard.* For a TV commercial it might have about 15 different pictures, more for the others.

After the storyboard is created the actual animation process begins. It consists of producing hundreds or thousands of individual pictures, called *frames,* which then have to be individually filmed or recorded on videotape. The process of producing all these frames can be mechanized in different ways; computer graphics is the most recent. Computers have a potential here that is far from complete realization.

However, no matter how much we mechanize, the intervention of the human artist, the animator, will always be a considerable and very costly part of the animation. What is done first is the same as it was several decades ago. With the help of the storyboard the most experienced and skilled animators draw *key frames.* These are frames selected for their key role in the motion, because of their importance as *anchors,* as extreme positions in the movement, as certain characteristic postures and expressions of the character, or for special visual effects. The key frames are spread timewise throughout the development of motion between pictures in the storyboard. They are not close enough together to be used as the actual animation frames.

The final animation is achieved by filling the gaps between adjacent key frames with *in-between frames.* How many need to be drawn to fill the gap depends on how far apart the key frames are in time. In-between frames are easier to produce than key frames and in conventional animation they were drawn by the less skilled and less expensive apprentice animators. Today they can be drawn by the computer! Figures 16.1 through 16.4 represent a sequence of animation frames.

**Computer Generated In-Between Frames** It will help you to understand how this process can be mechanized by first looking at some

**FIGURE 16.1**

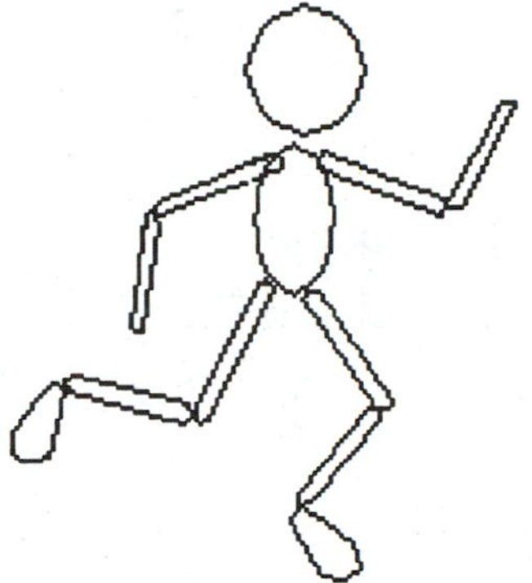

**FIGURE 16.2**

**FIGURE 16.3**

**FIGURE 16.4**

conventional techniques used to facilitate it. A common technique is to decompose an animation picture into several parts that can move more or less independently. These parts are drawn individually on a clear plastic material and are called *cels* (short for cellulose). The individual cels can be overlaid to produce the whole picture and then filmed or video recorded as one frame. When the animation character tilts its head or lifts an arm, for example, the change can be produced by appropriately moving the individual cels that show the head and the arm. Consecutive in-between frames differ only slightly from each other so often several in-between frames can be created this way. Figure 16.5 shows eight cels containing moveable parts of the cartoon character above.

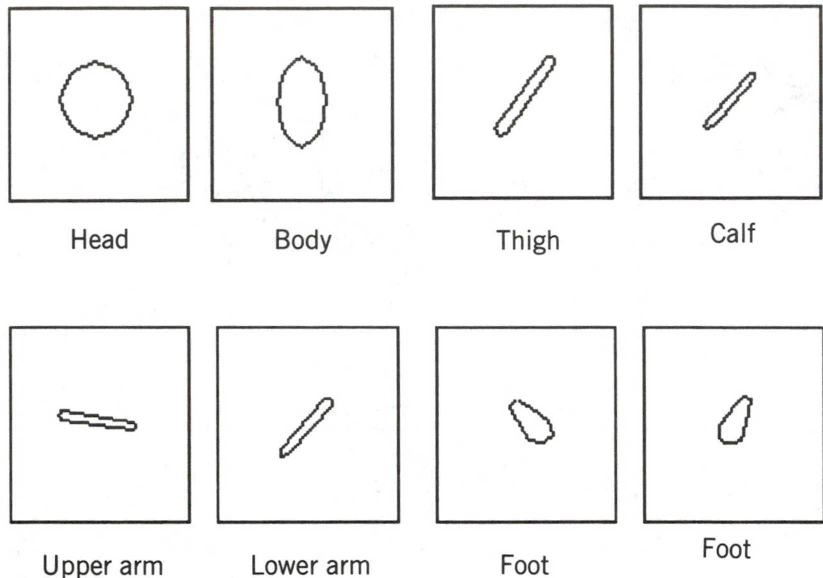


FIGURE 16.5

There are always parts in the picture that have to be drawn anew in each in-between frame, such as facial expressions, but the amount of hand drawing can be drastically reduced with this method. It takes advantage of the fact that not everything in a picture changes from one in-between frame to the next. If the character is talking, it may be enough to have just mouth and hand movements, making no change to the rest of the picture. This greatly increases the speed of production.

It is now possible to enter a key frame into a computer by using an animation paint system, a specialized version of those we will discuss in the next chapter. A graphics tablet allows us to just trace the key frame. The animation paint system composes the picture as sequences of *strokes.* A stroke is a straight or curved line portion of the drawing. While the stroke is being displayed, the system creates a sequence of number pairs and stores them internally. These number pairs are the coordinates of the points through which the stroke goes. Strokes stored in this manner can be handled mathematically by the computer; they can be translated, rotated, or changed in size.

The key frame is entered by drawing all strokes of which it consists. Actually the entire key frame does not have to be entered. Something resembling the above cel technique is possible, letting the animator work "celwise" and later overlay the cels. The animator then enters the key frame in the same manner. It is important that it be with the same strokes, which now, of course, are all somewhat different.

The graphics system must know how the strokes in the two frames correspond.

Some systems allow the user more freedom; the number of strokes can be different in the two frames. In such a case the system will divide strokes into shorter ones to match them up.

If the animator tells the computer how many in-between frames to produce, the computer will do an interpolation to gradually turn all the strokes of the first frame into the strokes of the second frame. It will choose an interpolation step size to produce the desired number of in-between frames.

To gradually transform one stroke into another, the computer must progressively transform the points of one stroke into those of the next. To do this, it is necessary that both strokes consist of the same number of points. But the user cannot determine the number of points in the stroke. The number of points in corresponding strokes may differ even if the strokes outwardly look identical.

This problem can be solved by the system. It determines which stroke has fewer points and then adds to them to make the numbers equal. Figure 16.6 will help to explain this. On the left we see a stroke in the first cel and on the right the corresponding stroke in the second cel. The first stroke consists of 11 points, the second of only seven. The system finds that it has to add four points to the second stroke. There are six intervals in the second stroke, more than the points to be added. Special techniques are used to distribute the added points within the intervals. The inserted points are shown as light dots.

If there were more points to be inserted than intervals, the system would insert two per interval at positions 1/3 and 2/3 among the original points until the excess points are accommodated, and then only one point per interval. This is not difficult because the portions between the points are always straight lines. Without going into too much detail, you can see that the system tries to insert the additional points as equally distributed as possible. More about this in, for example, THAL86.

Once the number of points in two corresponding strokes are equal, the points can be interpolated. The simplest form of this, *linear inter-*

**FIGURE 16.6**

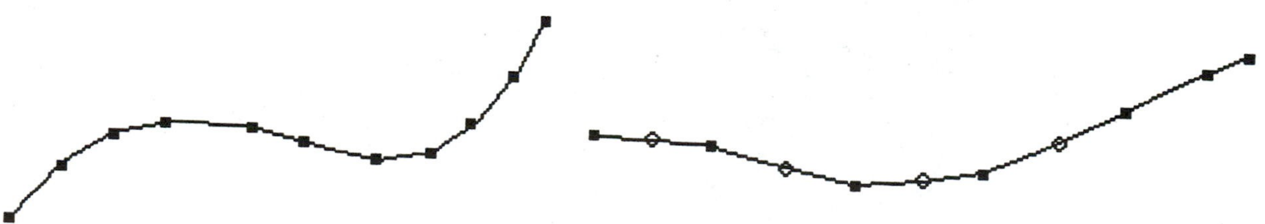

*polation,* may result in motion between key frames that is jerky and unnatural. *Curvilinear interpolation,* if done properly, will give smooth motion. One possibility is to define two Bezier curves, one for each end of the stroke. In a user-friendly system these are easy to specify interactively with a mouse or its equivalent. These curves connect the corresponding end points of the two strokes and thereby specify the paths these end points take from one key frame to the next. The computer will compute intermediate end points between the first stroke and the next stroke. For the other points on the strokes the system will compute in-between curves along which they will be interpolated. The mathematics is simplified by having the user define the curves through their end points and the slopes at the ends instead of the four control points. Figure 16.7 shows this.

The two user-defined curves are curve 1 and curve 2. The strokes each have four points. We can see that the slopes at the inner points of the stroke change gradually. The closer a point is to an end point, the more its slope resembles that of the end point. The situation is somewhat exaggerated in the figure to make the concept clear. As the slopes are in-between, the curves will also be in-between. For each in-between frame four new stroke points will be computed at intervals along these curves and connected by straight lines. So the first stroke gradually changes into the second stroke.

To determine the interpolated slope at an intermediate point, the system has to compute its distance from the end points. Slopes can be

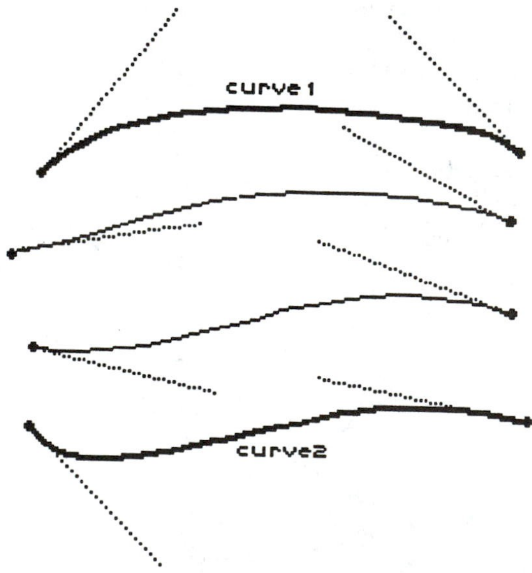


**FIGURE 16.7**

interpolated by treating them as normalized vectors, using a variant on the mathematics we presented for Bezier curves to represent them in terms of slopes at their ends.

There is another problem in addition to getting smooth curves for the in-between points. We must avoid jerkiness in time. It is easy to specify how fast the motion is to be. To make it slow we just ask for many in-between frames, to make it fast we will request only a few. Still, there can be sudden changes in speed, jerkiness in time, at the key frames.

If we want to have the motion gradually speed up or slow down, or if we just want to have better control over the speed, we must be able to specify where along the in-between path an in-between frame should be created. This can be done when using curvilinear interpolation. We know from Chapter 7 that the path along a curve can be described through a parameter moving from 0 to 1 and that the points corresponding to equidistant parameter values are not necessarily equally spaced on the curve.

Figure 16.8 shows a Bezier curve shaped by manually "pulling" the slopes attached to the end points as indicated by the dotted lines (more about this in Chapter 17). The points on the curve correspond to parameter steps of 0.1. We see that as long as the Bezier curve is smooth and not extreme in any way those points are almost equidistant. If we force the curve into sharper turns, for example, by pulling the slopes very hard, the points will be crowded together in the areas of sharp curvature even though these correspond to equidistant parameter values (see Figure 16.9). Usually such sharp turns are not desired. If they are present, the motion will be slower there.

In Figure 16.10 we see the same curve as in Figure 16.8, but the points that correspond to successive parameter values are at decreasing distances. It is easy to specify and implement this through a *bias number* that can crowd the points to either the left or right. In short, it is possible to give the user control over the speed of the motion between two key frames. We could even provide for specifying the distance ratios interactively by clicking on a scale.

In another technique (REEV81), which uses moving point constraints, the user doesn't specify Bezier curves for the paths of motion but can explicitly specify each point along the path.

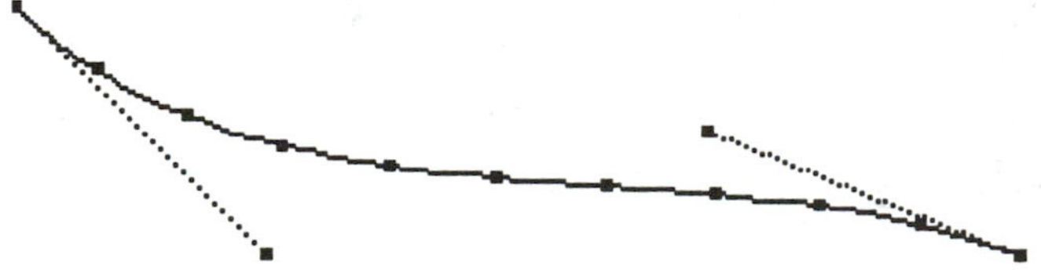

**FIGURE 16.8**

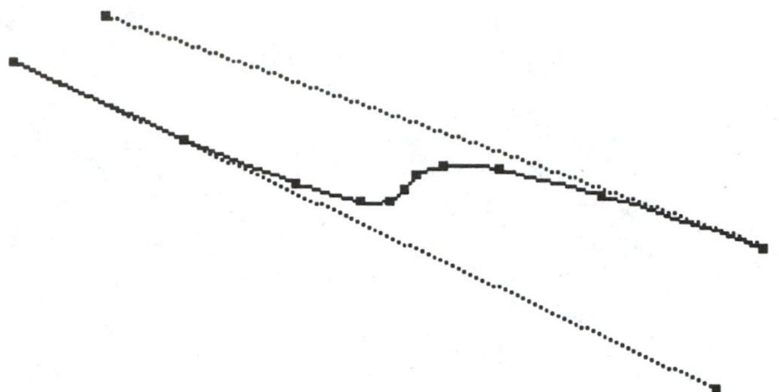

**FIGURE 16.9**

Look at Figure 16.11. The two heavy lines are the corresponding strokes of two key frames. The end points of the strokes are connected by a sequence of points, the same number for each sequence. These are the "moving points." The system will figure out transformations (translations, rotations, and scaling) that gradually transform the stroke of key frame 1 into that of key frame 2, so that the end points move along these "moving points" and the inner points move along paths implied by these transformations. With this technique the user has even more control over the time intervals.

In a color movie the frames all have to be colored in. This was another very time-consuming task in traditional animation but it can be done by the computer. Filling an area outlined by a boundary, for example by solid lines, uses a *seed fill* (see Chapter 17). It is very useful in paint systems. All the computer needs to know is a start point within the area to be filled, the seed point. If the animator provides the corresponding seeds in both key frames, the in-between seed points will always be inside the in-between areas, so the system can automatically color all in-between frames.

The animator always has the option of manually inserting or deleting lines or making small changes and touch-ups in the in-between frames to accommodate details that cannot easily be done by the automation.

In animation systems, user friendliness, ease of entry, and speed are critical. With experience, natural-looking animations can be pro-

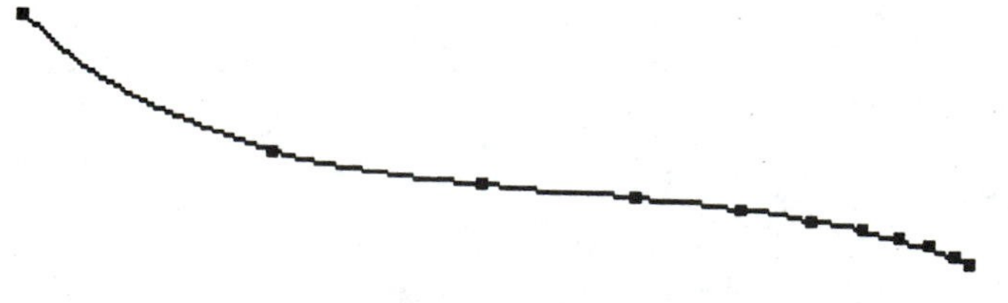

**FIGURE 16.10**

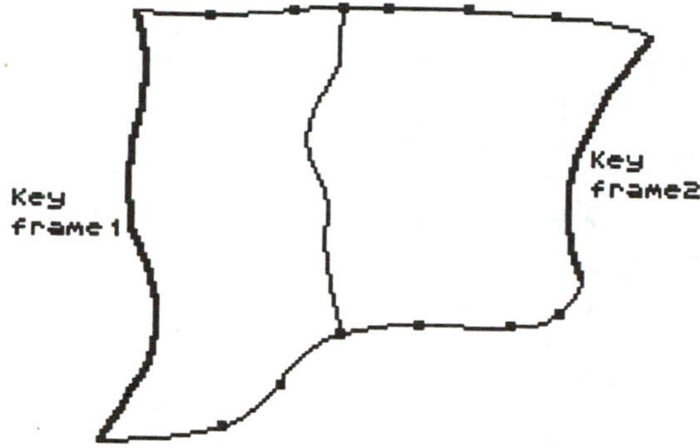


FIGURE 16.11

duced in a fraction of the time and with much less manpower than that needed for conventional animation.

**Drawbacks** This kind of animation is strictly two-dimensional, therefore there are some things the system cannot do. All objects and characters are flat, not spatial. They don't have a front and back. It is not possible to turn an object around gradually, because new lines, formerly invisible, will appear and others disappear. A pairwise correspondence between lines in adjacent key frames doesn't exist. The animator can overcome the problem by doing more touch-ups.

## 16.3 REAL TIME ANIMATION

The previous section showed how computer graphics is used in assisting handmade animation. There is a wide range of applications in which all frames of an animation sequence are exclusively created by the computer. One type is *real time animation.*

Real time animation may be the ultimate in computer graphics. It is the production of pictures that move directly on the screen, comparable to a moving TV picture. The best-known applications are for flight simulation and computer games.

Consider computer games. The growing capacity and speed of computer chips allows real time animation in software for games that have a simple pictorial environment and background. We see an increasing number of games that are done only in software with "off the shelf" hardware. Special-purpose hardware, sprites, for example, allow the creation of games with more sophisticated pictorial environments and backgrounds.

**Computer Games in Software** Consider a software version of a well-known computer game: PacMan. The pictorial content is simple: a stationary maze and five moving objects. Whenever a picture is as simple as this, real time animation is no problem. PacMan can be run on a desktop computer like the Macintosh in black and white. The Motorola 68000 processor can update the picture in the frame buffer fast enough so that the motion appears smooth. We refer to a specific machine only to make the example more concrete; the explanation below applies to any hardware.

To achieve speed, we employ at least two frame buffers; we'll call them A and B. The technique is sometimes called page flipping or ping-ponging. We assume that A is currently being displayed and B is being drawn in response to the user's input. Both frame buffers contain a copy of the stationary maze. The four ghosts and the pacman are in constant motion. We will omit programming details like keeping track of the current positions of the five objects, reading the mouse or joystick input, producing the proper sounds, and so on.

Redrawing B consists of first erasing all five figures by overdrawing them with little rectangles in the background color. Then all five objects are redrawn into the frame buffer at their new positions, done by copying templates. The smallest amount of motion is only one or two pixels and depends on the object and the situation. We know that the ghosts have to be able to move faster than the pacman in order to produce excitement, so we must have the option to move by different amounts from frame to frame.

Drawing a template into the frame buffer can be time consuming if the template has to be shifted by just a few pixels, because some parts of the template would cross word or byte boundaries. Therefore a great number of templates is provided depending on the position in relation to the word or byte boundaries; these are called offset templates. If the four ghosts are all different, we might need up to 16 $\times$ 4 different ghost templates, but we always can copy them starting at word boundaries and save time.

For the pacman we might need even more templates because its mouth points in one of four possible directions, the direction in which it moves. For each of these we need a different template and a set that is offset from word (or byte) boundaries. The opening and closing of the mouth itself is not really an additional burden because the offset templates can be prepared with different mouth apertures. For vertical movements we don't need offset templates so here we only need to have different templates to achieve the mouth movement. Figure 16.12 shows two pacman templates. In the right one the pacman is shifted by two pixels in relation to the byte boundaries and the mouth is a little more closed.

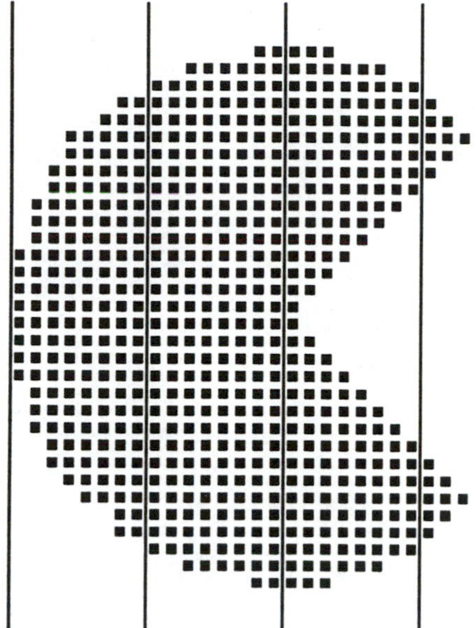

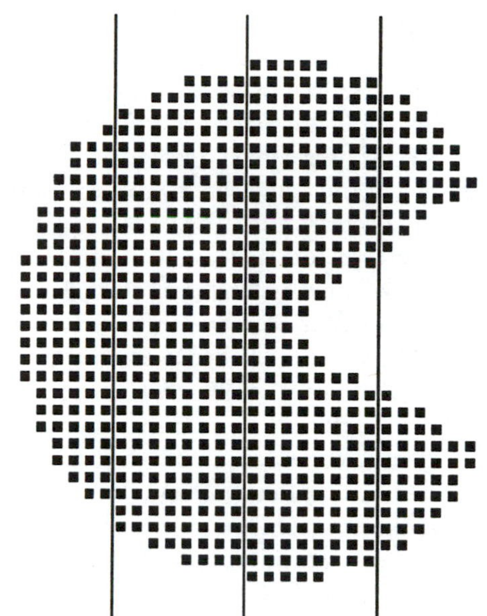

**FIGURE 16.12** Two pacman templates.

As soon as the copying is completed the display is switched from A to B. After the switch the new situation is redrawn in the A buffer. We could wait for a vertical blanking before switching the display, but this would cause a delay. So we switch on the fly whenever a new picture is ready. Sometimes this can produce a little jerk in an object when the switch occurs exactly at the time when the beam is halfway through drawing this object but the gain in speed is worth this tradeoff.

Such a program should be written in assembly language because a lot of low-level bit manipulation is involved. Most game programs for desktop computers are written in assembly.

**Graphic Computer Games in Hardware** The hardware versions of these games work with chips that support one or several sprites, for example, the Video Display Processors TMS9118, TMS9228, etc. from Texas Instruments, the 6566/6567 chip used in the Commodore 64, or the "Denise" chip used in the Amiga.

A *sprite* is a little object whose pattern is positioned relative to a set of Cartesian (x,y)-coordinates. The position can be controlled to a resolution of one pixel and the sprite is moved by changing only positional information. For this reason the graphics information defining the sprite can remain in fixed RAM locations. This considerably reduces the software needed for this sort of animated graphics.

It is essential to note that the sprite appears on the screen without being stored in the frame buffer. When the sprite appears on the screen, it covers whatever would otherwise be displayed there but does not destroy it in the frame buffer, so when the sprite moves, the background appears automatically. The frame buffer often contains only a static background picture that doesn't need to be changed. To fully understand this you must understand the principle of bit-mapped graphics display. We explained this in Chapter 2 but we will repeat it briefly.

When a frame buffer is scanned to put its picture onto the CRT display, hardware produces each of the addresses of all memory cells of the frame buffer for every display cycle. This hardware also produces the signals for horizontal and vertical synchronization that keep the monitor circuitry in alignment. The different chips that do this may be an intelligent graphics coprocessor, a CRT controller, or a sprite supporting chip. We will call it a VDP, or video display processor.

We will assume a somewhat simplified system that is not like any specific hardware although our description will be closest to the sprite handling done in the Commodore 64 (see COMM82). Assume that the frame buffer consists of 320 × 200 pixels. (In the Commodore there is actually characterwise display management even in bit-mapped mode, but we ignore that.)

The VDP has two internal registers that hold the x- and y-addresses of a certain location on the screen expressed as an (x,y)-coordinate pair. This address is the starting location on the screen for a sprite. We call it the sprite x- and the sprite y-address. After producing the addresses of one horizontal scan line the VDP always checks the sprite y-address. If this y-address equals that of the next scan line, the first raster line of the sprite is contained in the scan line. In this case the VDP checks a certain location in RAM, usually at the end of the video memory, that contains the starting address of the sprite description, a sprite pointer. Where this address points is the sprite description in a bit map, like the bit map for a character, but usually larger in size. The 6566/6567 chip from Commodore works with descriptions that are 63 bytes long, corresponding to bit maps of 24 × 21 bits. Commodore's name for a sprite is a movable object (MOB).

When there is equality of the scan line y-value with the sprite y-address, certain internal counters and comparisons start working. In principle, this is what is done. At some place during the scan line there will be equality of the current x-position of the frame buffer scan with the sprite x-address. At that point, instead of producing the frame buffer address corresponding to pixel (x,y), the VDP will produce the sprite starting address that it found when checking the RAM at the end of the video memory. That sprite starting address is updated appropriately (3 is added in the case of the Commodore because the sprite is 3 bytes = 24 bits wide). The net result is that the contents of the sprite description rather than the frame buffer are sent to the display circuitry.

Figure 16.13 shows this schematically. On the left is RAM memory, partly used as frame buffer and partly as sprite pointers and sprite descriptions. On the right are some registers of a sprite-supporting chip. This holds the sprite addresses that define locations in the frame buffer (that is, on the screen) along with color registers. The essential idea of the technique is that the chip scans either the frame buffer or the sprite description.

The content of the sprite description is also checked before being sent to the display circuitry. When a bit in this description is 1, the specified sprite color is sent out; when the bit is 0, the frame buffer information corresponding to this location is sent out. This makes the sprite transparent where it is uncolored. The sprite color is held in a separate register. In order to have several sprites the chip has to provide for more of these register pairs, color registers, and the associated checks.

The starting address of the sprite description, the sprite description itself, and the sprite color can be defined by the programmer. Where the programmer puts the sprite description is up to him or her.

**FIGURE 16.13**

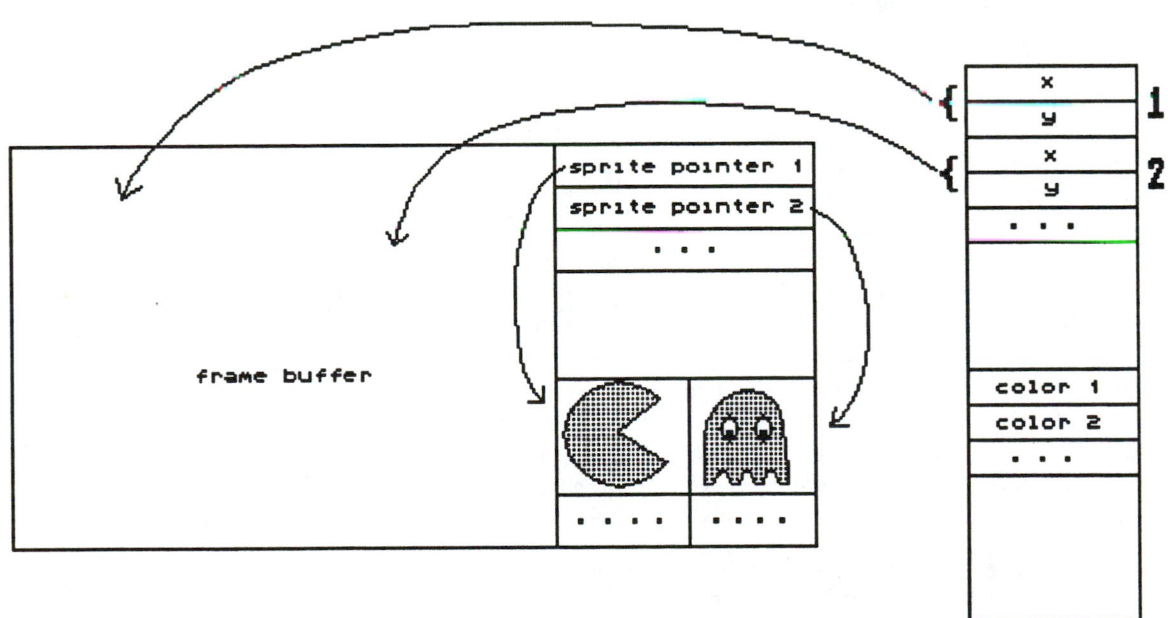

Creating a sprite consists of writing bit maps into the RAM areas pointed to by the sprite pointers. The 6566/6567 checks up to eight sprite pointers per scan line and therefore can have the parts of eight different sprites on one scan line. To move the sprites, we write into the register pairs that contain their screen positions, changing them during vertical blanking, that is, between two frames. When the next frame is displayed, the sprites will be at those positions.

The 6566/6567 is also a hardware device that handles collision detection between sprite and sprite and between sprite and objects specified in the foreground color. The chips of the TMS9118 family also do this. A collision occurs whenever two nontransparent bits of two or more different sprites happen to be displayed at the same position. The chip then produces an interrupt which the programmer can use.

These chips also allow for the definition of priorities for the sprites. These specify which of several different sprite colors will be displayed if they overlap. Changing the shape of a sprite can be done by writing into its RAM area description or by using different sprite descriptions (see below). In the 6566/6567 chip a sprite is basically one solid color, but different sprites can be of different colors. In certain display modes an individual sprite can have up to three different colors (plus transparent), but we will not go into these details.

This permits all sorts of sophisticated programming. For example, changing the sprite pointer between frames and having several slightly different sprite descriptions allows changing the sprite itself in addition to just moving it. Changing the sprite (x,y)-address at the time of a horizontal scan line interrupt allows more than eight sprites on the screen simultaneously, but only at different vertical positions.

Remember that the above description only gives the basic principle of displaying an object that is actually not in the frame buffer. The precise process is more complicated and differs for different hardware. A full understanding requires familiarity with the specific hardware. The interested reader should consult, for example, the product descriptions for the TMS9118 chip family, as COMM82 does not really contain a chip description.

The current direction is to produce chips that expand on the principle to an even greater extent. Graphics display chips will soon be available and architectures are being designed that will operate without frame buffers, collecting the information for the display from various distributed sources including video cameras. This will provide for displays that show a TV-like picture, intermixing moving objects and traditional graphics that are now produced with frame buffers.

**Lookup Table Animation** A totally different sort of animation is *lookup table animation.* We have learned how a lookup table is used to relate colors to the numbers in the frame buffer. By changing the lookup table values, we can get animation. For example, we assume a frame buffer of depth four, that is, four bits per pixel; this means that the value in a frame buffer location can be a number between 0 and 15. We assume a lookup table of 12 bits overall width, four bits for each primary and a length of 16, corresponding to the range of values possible in the frame buffer. Each primary can be specified in 16 different intensities and we can have at most 16 different colors on the screen at the same time. Figure 16.14 shows a schematic for our example.

When the CRT controller produces a frame buffer address to be displayed, the content of this address is used as an address into the lookup table. If the content of the frame buffer location is 6, then location 6 in the lookup table is addressed. The table contains intensities for the three primaries. Suppose these are 14 for red, 13 for green, and 1 for blue. The contents of the three addressed entries in the table are read out, transformed into analog intensities, and fed to the electron guns for the respective primaries. The given pixel would therefore look yellow on the display.

It is possible to change the color of that pixel without making a change in the frame buffer. The main processor can, for example, write 0 into location 6 of the red table. Our pixel will immediately become

**FIGURE 16.14**

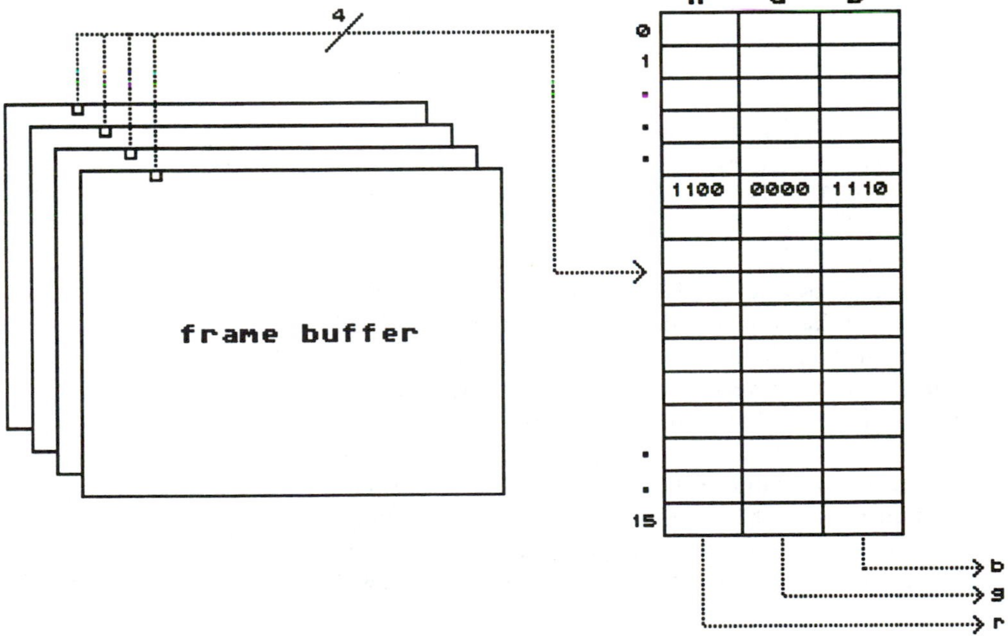

green. At the same time, all other pixels with a 6 in their frame buffer locations would immediately turn green because they all get their color from location 6 in the table!

Now we can see how the lookup table technique can produce animation. We use a very simple example: moving a blue ball across the screen from left to right. To achieve this we draw 10 instances of the ball on the screen, all in different colors. Actually we should say we draw them in different numbers; what color these numbers represent is determined later. Figure 16.15 shows this.

In the frame buffer, the background pixels all consist of 0's and the balls are drawn as filled polygons with buffer values of 1 through 10. The colors of the balls depend on the lookup table entries but that is not important because we will change them. First we make the background and all balls look black. This is done by filling the lookup table positions 0 to 10 with 0's. Nothing will be seen on the screen. In order to make the first ball appear on the screen with a blue color, we enter the intensities (0,0,15) into position 1 of the table. Now we want to make ball 1 black and ball 2 blue. To do this we make two changes to the lookup table: (0,0,0) into position 1 and (0,0,15) into position 2. This is repeated for all consecutive balls and a single ball appears to move across the screen. Below is a Pascal code segment that does this. It makes the balls appear in blue one after the other and finally leaves the last one as blue on the screen. The procedure setlook(r,g,b,pos) enters the specified intensities into the table at the position pos.

```
for i := 0 to 10 do  {makes everything black}
  setlook(0,0,0,i);
setlook(0,0,15,1);   {displays first ball}
for i := 2 to 10 do begin
  setlook(0,0,0,i-1); {resets one ball and}
  setlook(0,0,15,i)   {displays the next}
end;
```

By writing the proper loops we can make the ball bounce back and forth endlessly. The speed of this animation depends solely on the speed with which entries in the lookup table are made. If one entry were made per vertical blanking then the above 10 positions can be produced in one-third of a second. If the motion is too fast we have to insert pauses between the lookup table changes.

The object can be of arbitrary complexity. Fifteen is the maximum number of different positions that can be animated by this technique with a lookup table adequate for 16 simultaneous colors, because one color has to be saved for the background. But if we have a system with

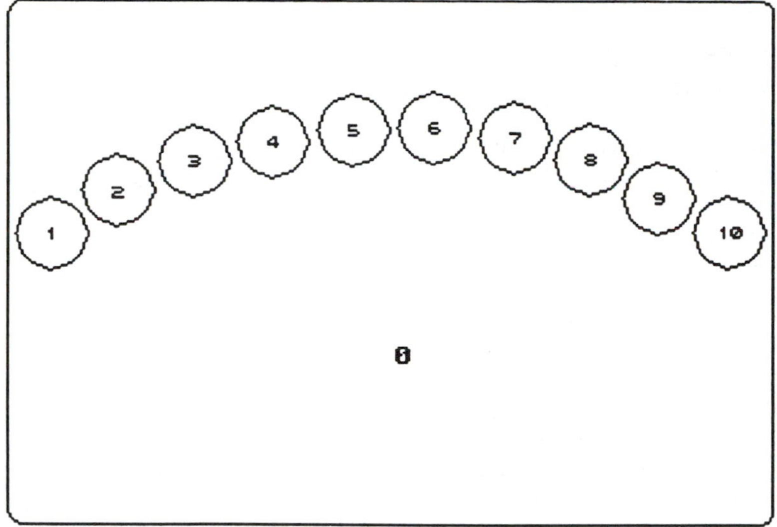


FIGURE 16.15

a larger lookup table—256 is common—we have much more potential and we can move several objects of different colors individually.

The above motion would not appear very smooth because the steps between the individual frames are much too great. To smooth it requires smaller steps but then the different ball positions can overlap and the problem becomes more complicated.

Lookup table animation is very popular. Practically all desktop computers with color screens have a demonstration portfolio of impressive pictures. Many of them are animated with this technique. The Neochrome paint system running on the Atari ST lets the user define colors directly in the lookup table by clicking the mouse. You can produce lookup table animation automatically by specifying a range through which the colors will cycle.

**Flight Simulation** This is an important application of animated computer graphics. We will give a short sketch, although computer graphics is only one aspect of it. Fast computers can simulate the response of an aircraft to the movements the pilot makes at the controls for acceleration, deceleration, change of direction, and so on. These reactions were formerly displayed to the pilot in a mock cockpit packed with meters and gauges. Later the display of a filmed landscape was added to simulate what would be seen through the cockpit windows, but this was not very satisfactory.

Today it is possible to display a landscape that changes according to the movements of the aircraft. Typically the cockpit windows can be

## DISPLAYING COLORS BEYOND THE FRAME BUFFER LIMIT

The lookup table technique allows the creation of a huge palette of colors, but only a fraction of these can be displayed at the same time on the screen. This number is given by the length of the lookup table. If the depth of the frame buffer is n, this number is $2^n$.

But you may have seen demonstration programs and color paint systems that show more colors on the screen at one time than are possible based on the depth of the frame buffer. How is this achieved? It is done by fast changes in the lookup table during the display. In this respect it is related to lookup table animation.

Assume a frame buffer of size 320 × 200 and of depth four and accordingly a lookup table of length 16. With nine bits width we can display 16 colors from a palette of 512. Here is a way to get more than 16 colors onto the screen simultaneously—maybe even all 512. The example does not try to produce a certain picture; it shows only the principle.

We fill the frame buffer so that we have all numbers from 0 to 15 in 10 adjacent scan lines. Normally these lines will display all 16 colors that we have encoded into the lookup table. We assume further that the horizontal sync pulse of the CRT controller or some other signal that indicates the end of one scan line generates an interrupt. As soon as this interrupt occurs we have about 15 microseconds to change some entries in the lookup table. This action is time critical; it has to be finished before the end of the horizontal blanking, a time when the lookup table is not accessed. If the interrupt routine manages to change at least one entry in this time, we will have a new color in the next scan line, because the phosphors in the scan line above are still "glowing" and will do so for the duration of a complete frame. This gives us a total of 17 colors. If we continue like this we can produce 25 different colors on these scan lines.

Usually there will be enough time to change more than one entry and the numbers in the frame buffer and lookup table will be carefully prepared to produce a certain picture. Of course, the interrupt routine has to know which scan line is being displayed to produce the correct change in the table. At the end of the frame the lookup table must be reset to the original values so that the process can be repeated in the next frame. But the vertical retrace lasts long enough so that this is no problem.

## "EXTRA" COLORS ON THE AMIGA

The Commodore Amiga uses another interesting technique to display all colors of its palette on the screen at the same time. We will only sketch the principle. For full technical details, consult the Amiga ROM Kernel Reference Manual.

The frame buffer has a variable depth that can be set by the programmer in order to save memory for other purposes when a large color range or high resolution is not needed. The greatest depth is five bit planes; correspondingly, the color lookup table has a length of 32. Its width is 12 bits, four for each primary. This results in a palette of 4096 colors of which 32 can be on the screen simultaneously.

However, the machine can be set to a specific mode, the hold and modify (HAM) mode. In this mode it uses memory equivalent to a 320 × 200 resolution with six bits per pixel. Of these six bits only four are used to define a color. The remaining two are called HAM bits and can have the following settings: 00, 01, 10, and 11. These are interpreted as follows:

- 00: Use the 4 color bits to address the lookup table.
- 01: Hold the color setting from the last pixel and use the color bits to modify the red component.
- 10: Hold the color setting from the last pixel and use the color bits to modify the green component.
- 11: Hold the color setting from the last pixel and use the color bits to modify the blue component.

The last used intensities of the primaries are held in a register. When a HAM-00 pixel is displayed, the register is filled from the lookup table. In the other cases, the four color bits replace either the red, the green, or the blue component in the register and these define the pixel color. In this way, the Amiga can achieve a color change from one pixel to the next (from left to right) by any amount as long as this change is limited to one primary. It is possible to change to any possible color of the palette within the space of three pixels. There is no difficulty in having all 4096 colors on the screen simultaneously. Abrupt changes are not possible but with careful setting, the "smears" are very inconspicuous and fine, gradual color changes can be displayed.

Software has recently been developed that fills the frame buffer in HAM mode with a digitized color picture and sets the HAM pixel values automatically.

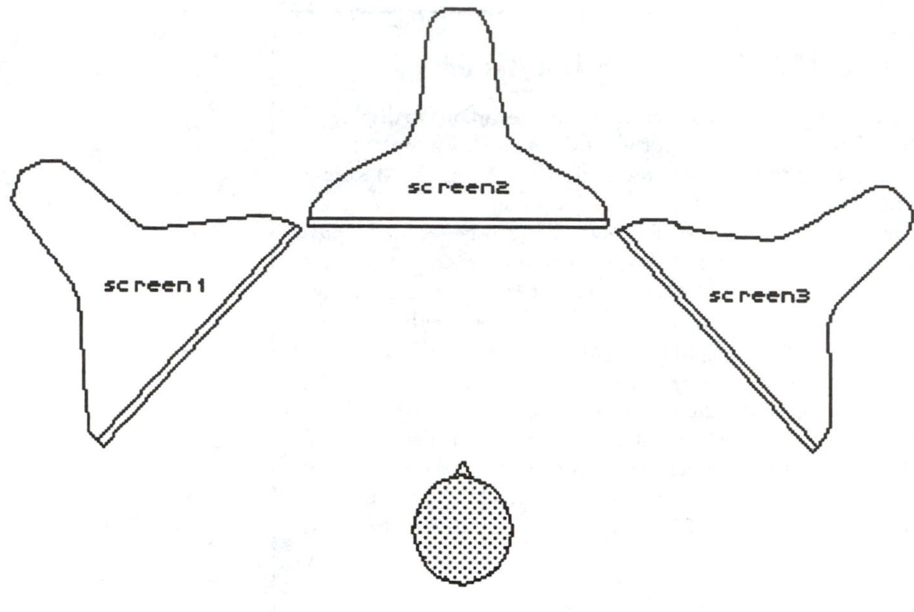


FIGURE 16.16

simulated by three or four CRT displays, each of which displays a part of the landscape so as to give the impression of one continuous picture. In Figure 16.16 we are looking down at a typical arrangement of three CRT displays and the pilot. The display is derived from a terrain map that is stored in a database and contains the topology of the terrain over which the training and testing flights take place. This consists of such structures as mountains, valleys, lakes, rivers, roads, building clusters, and the airport.

The graphics display processors used for this are usually custom made. They can do the necessary three-dimensional transformations of data points, the projections of the display, the filling of polygons, and so forth very fast in hardware. Today silicon technology has improved so much that even mass-produced general graphics processors can do polygon fill for convex polygons in hardware.

With all this speed it is possible to display pictures composed of a reasonable number of filled polygons rapidly enough to achieve real time animation. The picture, of course, has to correspond to what the pilot would see from the window of the real aircraft. This depends on the location, tilt, angle, and speed of the aircraft.

The reaction of the aircraft to control movements depends on many parameters: its shape, design of the fins and wings, position of the fins, current speed, inertia, thrust from the engines, and so on. The simulation involved is so complicated that it can only be solved numerically. Only the fastest array processors that have as much parallelism as possible are able to do this simulation in real time.

This is all very costly, but the benefits make it worthwhile. We can carry out many tests of a new airplane that exists only on the drawing board by entering all these parameters into the simulator. The optical display that simulates a real flight over a real landscape makes it a very valuable testing and training tool.

Let us look at the graphics component a little closer. We assume that the display consists of three screens, simulating three cockpit windows. To achieve a "connected" real time display the main simulator that knows about the position of the aircraft has to convey it to the three graphics processors. Each processor knows the direction of its window and will use whatever data of the terrain map it needs to produce its correct display. The three processors can work in parallel. The landscape displays must be programmed so that a variable amount of detail from the database is used depending on the distance from certain objects. This means that more detail is used as the distance decreases but the width of field also decreases. Otherwise this could become a display speed bottleneck. The proper organization of the database plays a role. Figure 16.17 shows three such screens as they would look to the pilot. The scene shows a horizon, some hills, a street, fields, and a farm building. The aircraft is moving in a curve to the right with a corresponding tilt of the wing.

**FIGURE 16.17**

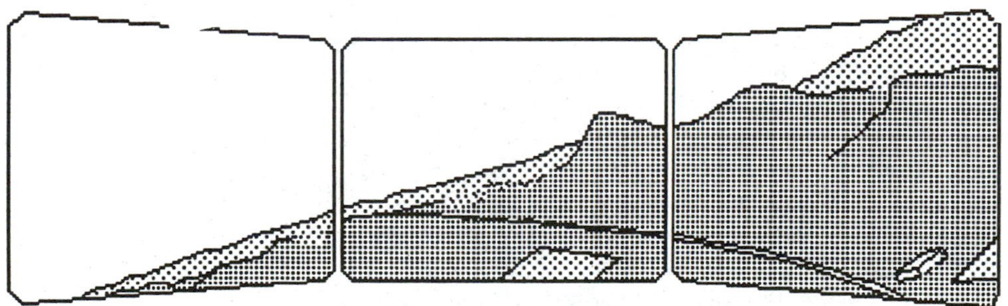

# 16.4 FRAME BY FRAME ANIMATION

Another type of animation is *frame by frame animation.* This sort of animation can be created with modest graphics hardware, even with a desktop computer. Additionally we need a video tape recorder or a movie camera with single-frame exposure and a darkroom.

Actually, whenever very sophisticated computer graphics is to be animated we must resort to this type of animation. We know that even on fast hardware the production of smoothly shaded surfaces, depth sorting, drawing of texture- and pattern-mapped objects, ray-traced scenes with reflections, and the like takes time. The generation of a single frame in the buffer is so complex that real time animation is not possible. Still, we have seen such animated pictures on graphics monitors and on TV. With our current knowledge we can generate a single frame containing such a picture. It is just a general computer graphics task, but how can we get animation? This is considered below.

**Recording on Film or Video Tape** Whenever a single picture is finished in the frame buffer it can be displayed and then filmed or videotaped as a single frame. Even though this might take days, in time the entire sequence of frames can be produced. Then we display them in rapid succession. This sort of animation is used primarily for the production of TV commercials and increasingly for movies.

There are problems to this approach. In filming, there is the interim production of an optical picture, with a possibility of additional noise or disturbance. Over longer periods of time the brightness of the monitor can undergo slight changes as can the light level of the room. Such changes can be aggravated by the filming itself so they may be perceivable when it is played back. It is necessary to have a room with stable light conditions.

We could totally avoid the production of an interim optical picture by recording the content of the frame buffer directly as one magnetic track on videotape. But here too we are confronted with difficulties.

The signal stored on a videotape is identical to the color TV broadcast signal. This is a complicated composition of several different kinds of information: luminance, hue, saturation, horizontal sync pulses, color reference burst, vertical blanking, and reference black level. It is called the *NTSC composite video signal.* One TV frame is composed of two interlaced fields. Each field consists of 262.5 horizontal scan lines and the whole TV frame consists of 525 interlaced scan lines. (However, only about 500 are displayed on the screen to allow time for vertical retrace.) The composite TV signal carries 60 fields per second, which corresponds to 30 frames. (The precise field rate is 59.94 Hz.)

Today's video tape recorders are of the helical type. The magnetic reading and writing heads are located on a spinning cylinder around which the magnetic tape is pulled in a slanted track. The rotation speed of the cylinder and the tape speed depend on the type of machine. The majority of today's video recorders record one field per video track. The read and write head-carrying cylinder rotates at 60 rpm (older types rotate faster). The tape is wound more or less completely around the cylinder, depending on the type of recorder (see Figure 16.18).

While the cylinder rotates, the tape is pulled over it in a slanted path and a video track is read or written that goes in a slanted path across the tape, as in Figure 16.19. The audio signals are recorded on a special audio track by other heads. A pulse for each frame is also recorded. Some devices can later add and read a binary time code for each field. This time code is added in the video track and does not affect the signal. This is important in videotape editing for finding and identifying individual fields. For more on this subject see, for example, ANDE84.

The best quality video recording is achieved with recorders of the C type in which the tape is wound almost all the way around the cylinder, as shown in Figure 16.18. These recorders use one-inch-wide tape. Recording on a video cassette recorder (in which the tape is not operated on an open reel but is enclosed in a cassette and is only 3/4 inch or 1/2 inch wide) usually implies lower picture quality.

In our application, we want to record a single frame stored in the frame buffer of a graphics system. The normal output from the frame

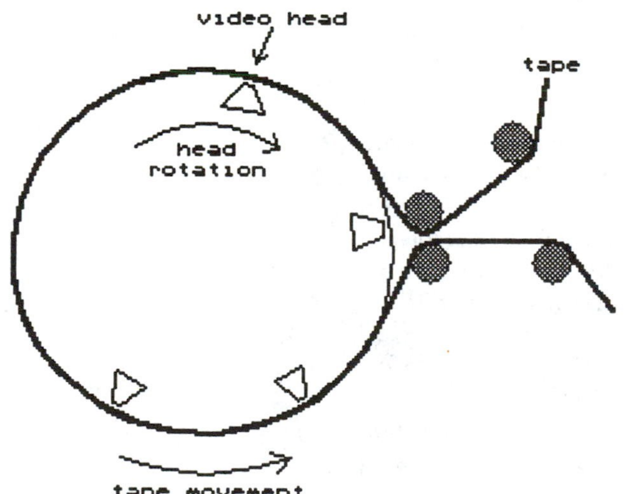


**FIGURE 16.18**

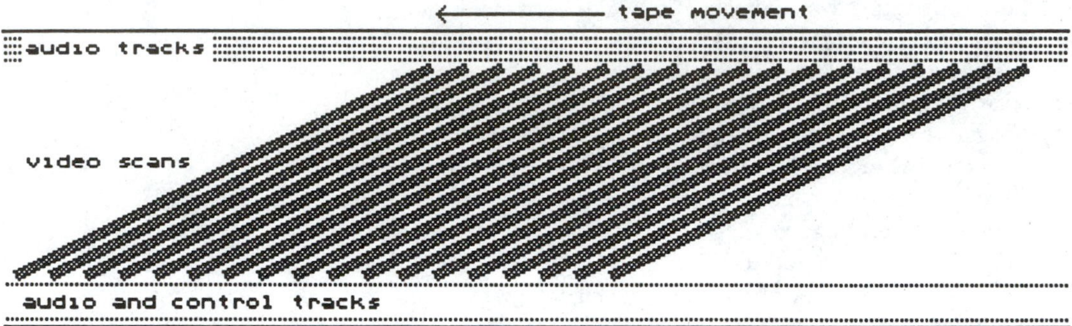


FIGURE 16.19

buffer to the monitor can be in a variety of ways. If it is just an RGB signal, consisting of three separate signals for red, green, and blue with sync pulses on the green, then it has to be transformed into the NTSC standard to be recordable on videotape. Graphics boards in the middle price range can produce an NTSC composite video output. A so-called genlock feature is needed that ties the scan rate of the frame buffer to the recording rate. Another item that has to be taken care of by the circuitry is that a frame buffer can have a various number of scan lines, while the NTSC frame always has 525.

It is very likely that we will soon see devices that record the video information digitally. A step in this direction are RGB video cameras that store the information in RGB code rather than NTSC composite. Red, green, and blue intensities and the horizontal sync signals are stored for each scan line. To play back such a tape requires either an RGB monitor or a converter to produce the NTSC signal for an ordinary TV screen. At present, video recording is mostly analog; only the time code is digital.

**Storing Frames in Memory** We can see complicated animated scenes on computer graphics screens for low-priced desktop computers. One example is the "Juggling Robot" on the Amiga computer. In this particular case the individual frame is a fairly complicated scene generated by ray tracing. The robot consists of many spheres that are partially overlapping but not reflecting. It is juggling three spheres that are totally reflecting. All the spheres cast shadows on the ground. Although scenes consisting of spheres are the simplest case of ray tracing it is absolutely impossible to produce this picture in 1/20 of a second.

The animation in this case actually is frame by frame animation. It consists of 20 or so frames, which gives about one second of viewing.

These frames are displayed in cyclic order by changing the starting address of the area to be scanned during the vertical blanking time; the display then repeats. It is like page flipping only more than two frame buffers are used. On computers with a large enough memory, several frames can be pregenerated and stored. With a resolution of 320 × 200 in color mode, one frame requires 32K bytes. The whole animation can be stored in 640K bytes.

**Interactiveness in Drawing Systems** In a paint or drawing system or CAD/CAM system there is also some real time animation on the screen. Examples are rubber-band lines, growing rectangles, ellipses that change in shape with the movement of the input device, and so on. This really is animated graphics. The animation in these cases is achieved by rapidly drawing, erasing, and then redrawing the graphics primitive in question. Here animation is not the primary objective. It is merely a requirement for giving the fast response desired to keep the shape of the graphics primitive in synchronization with the action of the user. Paint and drawing systems are described in Chapter 17.

# EXERCISES FOR CHAPTER 16

1. Write a program that produces lookup table animation. The animation consists of a sphere that moves across the screen from left to right and back, repeating this in an endless loop. Draw individual spheres in consecutive colors such that the spheres just touch each other, see Figure 16.20.

**FIGURE 16.20**

2. Produce the same animation as in Exercise 1 but achieve a smoother motion by overlapping the individual spheres by half the diameter (see Figure 16.21).

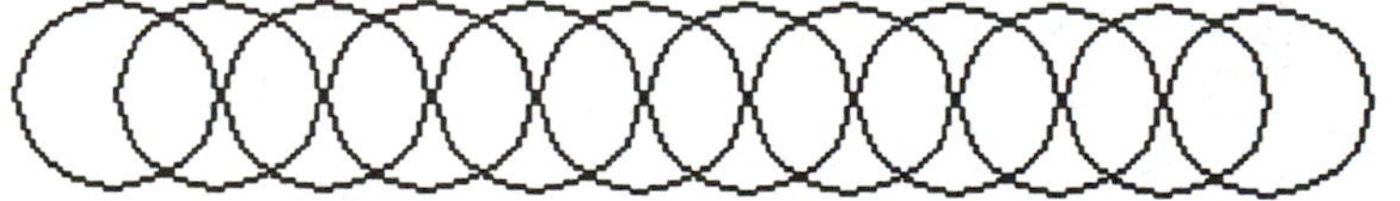

**FIGURE 16.21**

This can be achieved using only the two shapes shown in Figure 16.22.

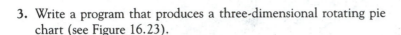

FIGURE 16.22

3. Write a program that produces a three-dimensional rotating pie chart (see Figure 16.23).

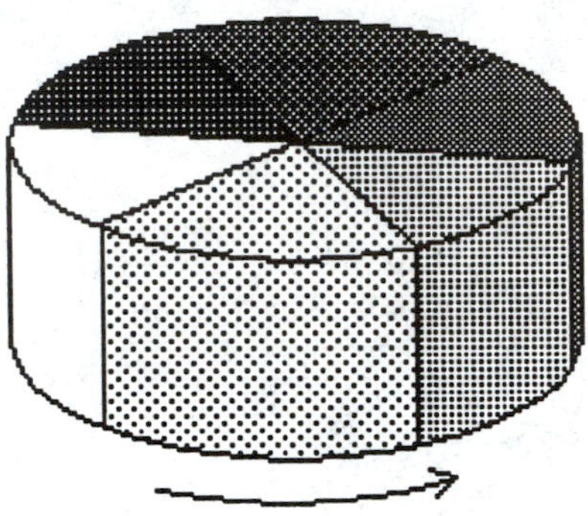

FIGURE 16.23

*Hint:* A three-dimensional pie chart that seems to rotate around its center can be drawn by computing points on the circumference of an ellipse, then drawing straight lines from the center of the ellipse to the points on the circumference, each line in a different color.

If you do not have enough colors, draw groups of consecutive lines in the same color. From the end points of lines drawn within the front half of the pie, draw vertical lines of constant length with the same color as the line (see Figure 16.24).

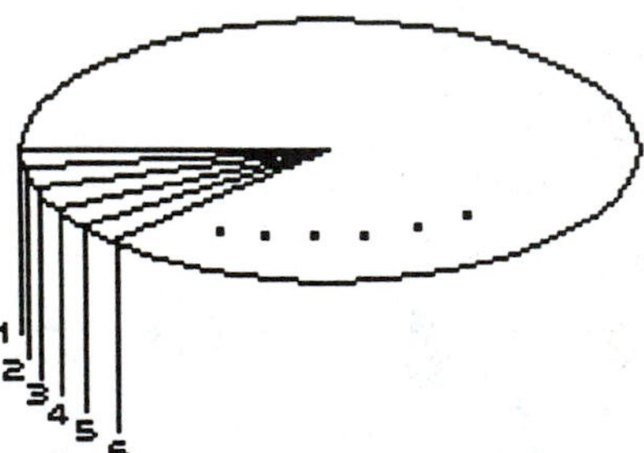


FIGURE 16.24

Motion is achieved by setting a group of consecutive lines to the same color, adding lines in the succeeding direction to the group, and removing lines from the group at the other end. The motion is smoother if your system allows many different colors.

# Graphics and the User

# 17

This chapter focuses on the user of the graphics system. After all, the purpose of computing is to fill the needs of persons who will use or benefit from operating the machine with its associated software. At the same time, Chapter 17 is written to provide you with the opportunity to test what you have learned in this book.

**17.0 Introduction** points out the importance of considering the user's needs in system development and examines what some of those needs are.

**17.1 User-Oriented Software** covers a number of applications in which the user's interface with the system is facilitated by graphics or which are inherently graphics based, including access to operating systems features, paint systems, computer-aided design, solid modeling, and desktop publishing.

**17.2 Implementing User Interaction** imposes a number of requirements on the interface that are implemented through polling or, preferably, interrupt mechanisms.

**17.3 Segmentation** is necessary for a graphics display to let the user decompose it into parts or to group it into larger units. This has great significance for the underlying data structures.

**17.4 Standards for Graphics** are of great importance to the user.

**17.5 Uses and Techniques of Printers** describes the most important hard-copy devices in computer graphics together with some common raster-printing techniques.

# 17.0 INTRODUCTION

Most of this book has dealt with algorithms and programming considerations for creating graphics on the screen or in hard copy. At the same time, it is equally important that, as the builder of a package that incorporates graphics, you will be especially aware of the user's needs. The person who will actually sit at the terminal and use the package that you create is the most important component of the whole system.

This chapter starts by asking why a graphics interface is of value to the user in the first place, considers how the operating system can be accessed more flexibly through graphics, describes a number of graphics applications that are examples of user-computer interaction, moves into some topics that underlie the user-machine interface, and then discusses standards for graphics and their importance to both programmer and user. We end the chapter with a consideration of how the user can obtain a hard copy of the graphics display.

Too often, the designers of systems have overlooked the problems users face, particularly new users. Program developers have a tendency to use terse, nonmnemonic abbreviations in their command structures. While a short version of a command saves a lot of typing, it does prolong the learning curve and contributes to users having to relearn much if they access the package infrequently. Graphics can change this. Pictures can supplement or even replace words, producing significantly better recognition of what the command is supposed to do. Often the operation is speedier when the user can point to an object on the screen rather than typing in its name. For example, moving a picture or a block of text is simpler when a pointing device is used to define the item and to designate the new location. When the results of the move are immediately shown on the screen after dragging an object with the pointer, the user is more in control and feels a part of the system, not just a passive participant. This instant feedback is also important to let users know immediately when they have asked for something they didn't really want. (This implies the necessity of having an UNDO function whenever the results could be catastrophic.)

Experienced users also benefit from a graphics interface to the system. The mouse becomes almost part of your hand if the actions are intuitive and natural. Visual feedback is a welcome reassurance that the action being performed is what one really wanted. A change in the shape of the cursor can give instant knowledge of mode changes that would otherwise be more difficult to remember. Even the words and icons used to describe elements of modern systems are more descriptive: *folders* that hold a group of related files, *wastebaskets* to indicate a trashing operation, disk units represented visually, and so on. At the same time, a totally graphics/mouse-oriented interface is sometimes counterproductive. For example, it is upsetting to have to take your hand from the keyboard during word processing if an action can only be done by clicking on a menu pulled down with the mouse. This is why good software has keyboard equivalents for at least the most used commands.

As we describe some typical software packages that are strongly graphics dependent, we hope that you will take note of and emulate the good features, those things that make learning and using the product easier. We also hope that you will continually review in your mind those elements of computer graphics you have learned that are employed to implement each feature.

## 17.1 USER-ORIENTED SOFTWARE

The user's needs are an integral part of any design, whether software or hardware. There are so many development details to keep track of that being constantly aware of the effect of every little design decision on the ultimate user may be difficult. But we stress the necessity of doing it! This is especially important in interactive systems.

Our plea applies not just to the graphics portion of the product. Every action, whether or not it is graphics related, should be, in the familiar and over-worked terminology, user-friendly. In this chapter we try to show how this goal can be attained when graphics is an integral part of the software project. As you read this, you should be aware of what graphics operations and data structures are needed to provide this feature. At times, we will suggest that providing some "goodie" may require an extension to the topics presented in previous chapters. Then we will summarize and explain these new aspects of computer graphics.

## 17.1.1 Interfacing with the Operating System

The functions of an operating system are many and varied but the major purpose is to isolate the user from the many details of making the hardware carry out requests. A large part of this relates to file handling: retrieving, storing, copying, deleting, and rearranging files on secondary storage media. Other parts are dedicated to accepting user requests from a number of input devices and providing a data stream to an assortment of output devices. Systems more sophisticated than a simple single-user microcomputer operating system must keep track of multiple functions for multiple users who are all using the system at the same time. We will not discuss most of this because we want to concentrate on the user/machine interface and the role that graphics can play in the interaction.

In the beginning of computers, the user talked to the system through cards with a job-control language (JCL). Those of us that lived with computers in the early days knew that learning to use JCL effectively was harder than learning a programming language. Part of the trouble was the way the manuals were written; they certainly didn't have the naive user in mind! The fact that commands were cryptic and not very mnemonic made memorizing the commands very arduous. To make matters worse, every machine's JCL was different; moving to a new computer was a major undertaking. After the demise (thank goodness) of card input, the heritage of JCL continued. But not for long. Newer computer systems adopted better ways for the user to communicate; more often than not, the leaders in this were microbased personal computers.

One of the first steps in this direction of getting around cryptic command languages was to avoid them altogether. Many of the early micros came up in BASIC; since there was so little application software, the presumption was that one would always want to write a simple program to carry out the task. This was also the case in many dedicated word processor systems—the machine came up in WP mode when it was turned on. Of course, this was too restrictive and could not last for long.

CP/M (Control Program/Micro) was an early success in crossing the line between machines from different manufacturers. Here there was a real attempt to make the commands easy to remember: DIR to display a directory, COPY to duplicate a disk (also used to format a new disk, but at least there was a dialog screen to get the proper selection), and similar commands that were user oriented. However, there were still many details that required rote memorization: Using * and ? in commands as wild cards, the severe limitations on file name lengths and valid characters; abbreviations that were control characters or strange combinations like PIP, DDT, XSUB, and SYSGEN. The mess was almost as bad as the old JCL system when various options were appended to the basic command via single-letter combinations. When IBM entered the personal computer market, the DOS (Disk Operating System) that the PC used showed no improvement. Because it added many new commands to do more (admittedly useful) things, the poor user was back to studying obtuse manuals and memorizing hard ways to do things.

And then there was the Macintosh! This caused a real revolution in the way the user issued commands: by pointing to pictures instead of typing a command line.

**The Macintosh Interface** Actually it wasn't the Macintosh computer that started the trend to the pictorial interface. Some years earlier at Xerox's PARC research center, experimental graphics terminals and graphics-oriented operating systems interfaces showed that a mouse was a versatile pointing device and that pictures ("icons") were more descriptive than words and letters on the screen. Apple Computer obviously borrowed heavily from the concept that was pioneered by a competitor. You may wonder why Xerox doesn't receive more credit for leading the way. Well, so do we. Much of the reason is the lack of commercial success of the systems, due largely to the high price. Desktop publishing is another Xerox innovation that will probably never receive proper acknowledgement. We hope you will forgive us if we too say that something is a Macintosh feature when the credit really lies elsewhere. Certainly Apple should receive applause for popularizing the "desktop" metaphor.

Even within Apple, it was not the Macintosh computer that first made a graphics interface available to the general public. Their Lisa line, never popular due to a high price and lack of software, was the first system marketed widely in the new style. But "Mac" was the system that most people associate with the concept of pictures rather than words, mouse rather than keys, "desktop" rather than screen, and related ideas. From the time it is first turned on, there is an impressive assortment of clever ideas that are intuitive rather than learned. For example, if you turn on your Mac without a disk, a picture of a diskette appears with a question mark superimposed. As soon as the system disk is inserted, the question mark changes to a smiling face. What a clever way to communicate, you say, not realizing that this hides the fact that the system files are so large that they must be kept on a disk and that the disk action is not terribly speedy.

We hardly have time or space to give you a guided tour through the Macintosh (though Apple provides a program and voice cassette that does this, another nice touch). We just want to point out some things that graphics can do to make the interface with the operating system more intuitive.

Figure 17.1 shows a typical Macintosh screen. The concept that one is working at a desk is suggested by a gray pattern on the screen that resembles a desk blotter. The Trash (looking like a garbage can) is at the lower right. Icons that represent each drive on the system are displayed at the right side with labeled pictures of the floppy disks they contain. At the top are headings to pull-down menus that appear as if on a roller shade when touched with the mouse with the button depressed. Holding the button down while moving the mouse down ("dragging") highlights each selection on the menu in turn. Releasing the button activates the highlighted selection and the menu disappears, being replaced with whatever was on that part of the desktop.

A directory for the disk is brought to the screen by clicking on the icon for the disk to select it—its icon is highlighted to show this—and then selecting OPEN from the File menu. This double action displays the directory in a window on the screen. But doing two things is slow, so the more experienced user knows that double clicking on the disk icon brings up the directory more quickly. The same technique is used to open a file. First click on its icon to select it from the directory listing and then select OPEN from the File menu. Again, a double click

**FIGURE 17.1** Typical Macintosh screen.

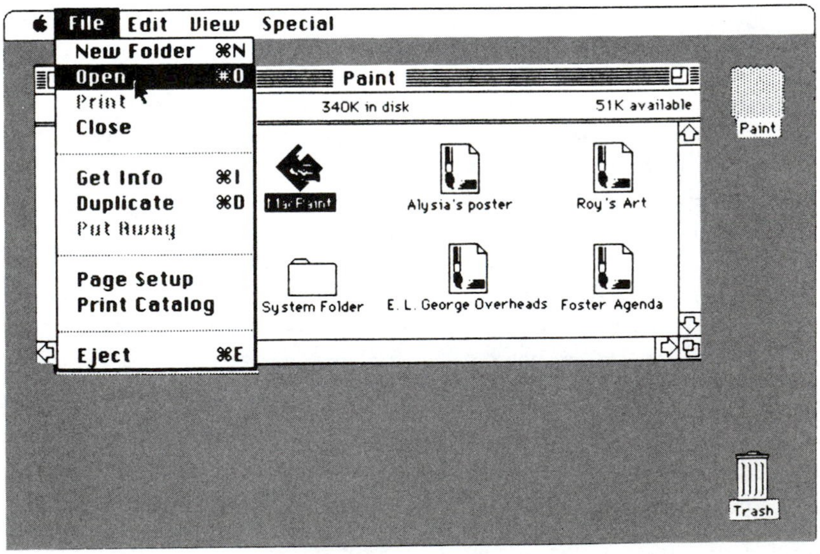

on the icon is faster. Files are shown normally as icons (labeled pictures) but alternatively as a more readable list of file names.

Windows on the screen can be moved by dragging them with their title bar. (Windows in this sense are different from the coordinates spaces of Chapter 4. These are really rectangular "display sheets" for icons and other information.) They can be enlarged or shrunk by dragging the double square at the lower right. If there are too many file icons to fit in the window, you can scroll vertically or horizontally by dragging the "slider box" within the right or bottom border. Alternatively, a line-by-line scroll results from clicking on arrows at the ends of the borders.

Files are copied by dragging their icon to the destination; this may be another disk or a folder. (A folder is just another name for a subdirectory but is perhaps more descriptive to an office worker who has had little experience with computers.) Entire disks are copied similarly by dragging their icon. Files are deleted by "throwing them away" into the trash can (as they are dragged, the icon follows the mouse). In the Macintosh system, a discarded file can be retrieved by opening the Trash and spilling its contents onto the desk, just as one might dig into the waste basket to get a discarded paper.

There is much more to it, of course, but we only want to give you the flavor of a graphics-oriented interface. What are the programming techniques behind such actions that we have not yet discussed? We need to go into how the system knows that a mouse has been moved and a button pressed. If there are two or three buttons, as is the case on some mice, which one was pressed? How does it detect a double click? Is displaying a menu and then removing it a routine kind of picture? How is highlighting accomplished? How are icons stored and how can they be edited?

There is one additional and very important point to make about the Macintosh system. Apple insists that all developers of software abide by a common set of principles; for example, windows should almost always have a title bar, a double box for sizing, borders with sliders and arrows for scrolling, everything standardized. Menus are always to act in the same fashion. Every application is supposed to do things in the same way as regards opening and closing files, deleting or changing text, and so on. This is certainly in the user's interest. One real advantage to standardized software is that the transition to a new piece of software is much easier than when the interfaces are different and similar activities involve different commands. We will discuss graphics standards later in this chapter.

To make it easier for developers of Macintosh software to conform to the standardized approach, there is, first of all, extensive documentation. *Inside Macintosh* describes the operating system in 1200-plus pages and *Macintosh Revealed* tells how to program a Mac in 1100 more. This is not just verbosity—system calls, through which almost everything that shows on the screen is implemented, are cryptic and numerous and must be invoked in the correct sequence. A program begins with several initializing steps: setting up variables specific to the application, updating desk accessories (memory-resident utilities that can be called upon within the application), and defining the appearance of the cursor (the shape of the cursor on the screen can signal different things). After this preparation, standard systems routines are called to handle "events." This is where the user's interactions are accepted, analyzed, and responded to. Standard data structures in the form of records are used to get and pass information between small modules that consist mostly of system calls. Their names (as implemented in Borland's Turbo Pascal) are quite descriptive: DoMouseDown, DoKeyPress, DragWindow, ClearWindow, HideCursor, and hundreds more.

A special graphics package (QuickDraw) is also part of the Macintosh system. It provides routines (again from Turbo Pascal) to do things like: GetPen, MoveTo, EraseRect, FillOval, and so forth.

The hard part of learning to write an application for the Macintosh is learning what these many routines do, how to set things up to use them, and the order in which to make the calls. The tools are there but there is an apprenticeship to serve.

Of course, providing a toolbox for the developer is not unique to the Macintosh. Similar kinds of routines are available in GEM (Graphics Environment Manager) which runs on IBM PC's and many other computers. There is also Windows, another developer's package and, more recently, OS/2 for IBM's newer system, the PS/2.

**The X-Window System** A very recent and popular graphics user interface is the X-Window System, an emerging standard windowing system. It is currently supported by a broad range of hardware and software manufacturers.

We should not consider it as a general graphics standard. Its intent is to standardize user interaction with the computer in a user-friendly way. The particular application can be of any type, but the mode of interaction is as graphic as possible. The main input device is the mouse. The output depends on the type of application, but is always organized in a hierarchy of windows. Any number of windows can be displayed simultaneously on the screen. The user determines their number, their sizes and locations, and their priorities, that is, which ones lie on top.

The user can control several processes that run in parallel. For example, an application that outputs text interacts through a terminal emulator window while a graphics application draws in a graphics window at the same time .

There are some significant differences from other windowing systems. One is that X-Windows is a public domain system—everyone is free to use it. For that reason, it has been quickly adopted by many manufacturers. Another major difference is that X-Windows is network compatible. It allows programs executing on one machine in a network to display their output and take their input from other machines in the network, completely transparent to the application. X-Windows is fully programmable and provides high-level tools as well as being network compatible. It can be considered the state of the art in window systems.

## 17.1.2 Presentation Graphics

But, after accessing the system, the user wants to use the computer. One use is to create charts and the like. Perhaps nowhere is the contrast in effectiveness between a picture and a "thousand words" more dramatic than in presenting data with a punch in the business world. Whether it be for analysis by the individual, for making a point to associates, for impressing a potential client, or for catching the public's attention through an advertisement, *presentation graphics* is an important adjunct to managing, marketing, and sales. There are many ways that computer-generated graphics assists the process, though there is more to it than just acquiring a good computer and associated software. No program by itself can provide the artistic touch that good presentation graphics requires.

Many types of charts and graphs are used. These include the familiar pie and bar charts and line graphs. Specialized versions—high-low-close charts for stock prices, Gantt charts for project planning, connected boxes for organization charts—are common.

The graphics concerned is not sophisticated. You already know the procedures that can produce any of these. But the average business-person needs a simple-to-use package. Since the graphics is not complex, a standard personal computer is adequate to generate a chart as a display on the CRT. Putting the output into final form, usually as a slide, is another matter—more on this below.

The variants on the basic styles are many. A pie chart may have one slice moved out from the center ("exploded"). Bar charts can be stacked, aligned horizontally or vertically, presented in perspective, shaded to provide a three-dimensional appearance, and so forth. Line graphs can use various styles for the data points or can hide the points. Several graphs that are drawn together can be distinguished by line type or color and can be shaded to look three-dimensional. Any of these charts and graphs are more dramatic in color, and a proper choice of colors can add impact to the message being conveyed. The correct scaling is important. Captions and legends contribute as well, and good graphics packages permit a choice of type styles, sizes, and fonts.

There are three phases to the production of a business graphic. First is the accumulation of data to be displayed, next is the design and production of the graphic, and third is putting it into final form for presentation. Most of the time a spreadsheet program is the source of data, but many packages can accept ASCII files in a variety of formats.

One option for the second step is to use a spreadsheet program with built-in graphics capabilities. Most spreadsheet programs include this feature, but the flexibility is usually poorer than with an independent program. Most independent programs can interface to standard spreadsheets as well as use data from standard files. Often they provide a library of prepared images ("clip art") that can be added to the final output. A liberal set of colors is available, but these depend on the graphics hardware. Most presentation graphics programs can utilize any of the standard graphics boards and monitors.

The third step in producing presentation graphics is hardware related. A color slide is the output form that is normally desired. The simplest way to get this is to photograph the CRT directly. Specialized camera arrangements let you avoid having to jury-rig the setup. A more professional product results from special film recorders that use the computer's bit map or, better still, accept commands to duplicate the picture in higher resolution. While a standard 35mm slide cannot really utilize a resolution better than about 2000 lines vertically, some film recorders produce images with up to 10,000 vertical lines. (These are of value in getting sharp images on larger format film.) Film recorders, especially those that give high resolution, are expensive and may have to be operated by trained technicians, so a frequent alternative is to employ a service bureau that specializes in producing slides from the data.

An alternative to the production of slides is to display the graphic directly on a CRT, either one similar to the normal computer screen, though usually larger than those commonly used with the computer, or on TV screens. (Here a change in the output signal may be required to give the NTSC signal, as explained in Chapter 16.) One advantage of this kind of output is the ease with which animation can be included. Sound can also be combined to add a verbal message to the image.

Have you noticed anything here that we have not already explained? What about a slice of a pie chart that moves in and out of the pie while changing its color? Can that be done through the animation techniques we discussed in the last chapter? Would the techniques for drawing curves that we presented in Chapter 7 and 8 have application in doing effective line graphs? Could you do a perspective projection of a vertical bar chart with hidden surfaces removed based on what you learned in Chapters 6 and 11?

Suppose you were hired to develop a package that makes it easy for users to create presentation graphics without knowing how graphics is done. Could you let them choose the scale, the orientation of axes, the color of the display, and so forth? Would you give them a menu of options from which to choose? Would these choices require keyboard input or selection with a mouse? How would you go about determining the list of features that should be included? There is much more than just knowing how to create graphic images yourself.

### 17.1.3 Paint Systems

A *paint system* is a software package that facilitates "artistic" creations in computer graphics. The original graphics project that showed the world the power of computers to draw images, Sutherland's Sketchpad, was probably the first of these. The MacPaint program that Apple included with their Macintosh computers demonstrated the utility of this kind of program. That was limited to black and white; newer programs run on color systems. The basic operation in a paint program is to draw curves, lines, and various shapes on the screen in response to commands and movement of a pointing device, typically a mouse.

Having the user enter drawing commands through a mouse is not the only way to interface, however. A noninteractive style is possible by using a sequence of drawing commands in a kind of graphics language. It is important that you see the difference between interactive and noninteractive systems. The latter are much easier to implement. For example, suppose you want to draw the outline of a house as in Figure 17.2. With just a little training, you might write the following program (we present it as a Pascal segment):

```
begin
   move (a);
   draw (b);
   draw (c);
   draw (d);
   draw (e);
   draw (a);
end.
```

**FIGURE 17.2**

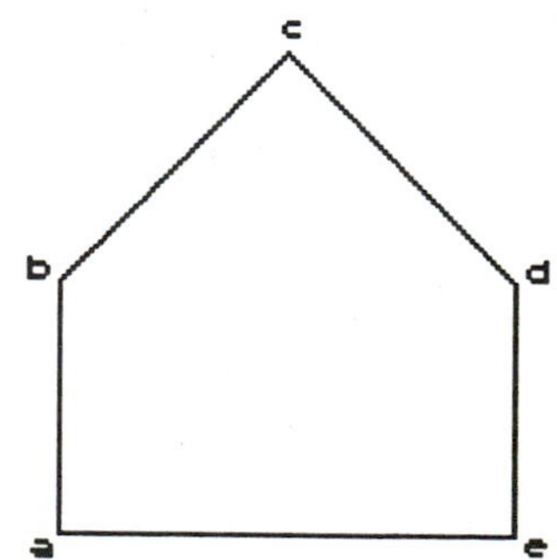


We have used letters to represent the coordinates of the points. It would be more user friendly if these points were relative to some origin and had a scale selected by the user rather than being absolute screen coordinates. All you would need to provide in creating such a noninteractive system is a set of graphics primitives. These primitives would be procedures called by the program statements. Of course, you would probably provide a fuller set of primitives than move and draw, and giving a good selection of colors would be nice. The user would have to compile the program before it could be executed, but once that was done, almost any desired drawing could be produced. Until recently, this was the only style of user-oriented graphics.

Contrast this style of user-oriented graphics program with the interactive one that we describe below. Most people will prefer the interactive style, but you should recognize the advantages of having the user write a program to do the graphics.

Degas Elite, an advanced paint program for the Atari ST computer, is representative of today's interactive style. It takes advantage of the power and reasonably good graphics in 16 colors that the Atari system provides at a remarkably low price. The Degas program can also operate in the other higher resolution modes of the ST but these do not provide a full range of colors. This system is representative of a good paint program.

The program is largely mouse driven although many of the commands have keyboard equivalents. Figure 17.3 shows the main menu screen. At the very top of the screen is a menu bar with five selections for pull-down menus; these are really a part of the Atari operating system but are customized for Degas. Below this is a palette of 16 boxes that offer color choices (there are fewer than 16 in higher resolution modes). Pointing to one of these and clicking the left mouse button selects the current drawing color; a check mark indicates this. (These colors represent the current settings of the lookup table; there are ways to modify it. Our black-and-white representation doesn't do justice to the actual colors.) The leftmost color is the background and the rightmost shows the cursor.

The lookup table can be changed in several ways. By dragging one color box onto another, we change that table entry to match the first. Double clicking on a color brings up a dialog screen that lets you adjust its RGB intensities. Still another option is to select from a display that shows all 512 possible colors. You can even match an existing color from within a picture. A novel feature is the automatic definition of intermediate colors ranging between two that are simultaneously selected. The original default color table can be restored by a special command. A color that is once set can be selectively changed later either by a change to the color box or using the special CHANGE command from the main menu, which allows you to point to a pixel of the color to be changed. CYCLE, can create multicolored lines as the cursor is moved.

Below the color panel are 15 brush shapes that are selected in the same way as a color. The box for the current selection is highlighted. The leftmost box is a cross hair that shows the precise pixel where the cursor is located. Any one of the 15 brushes can be redefined by the

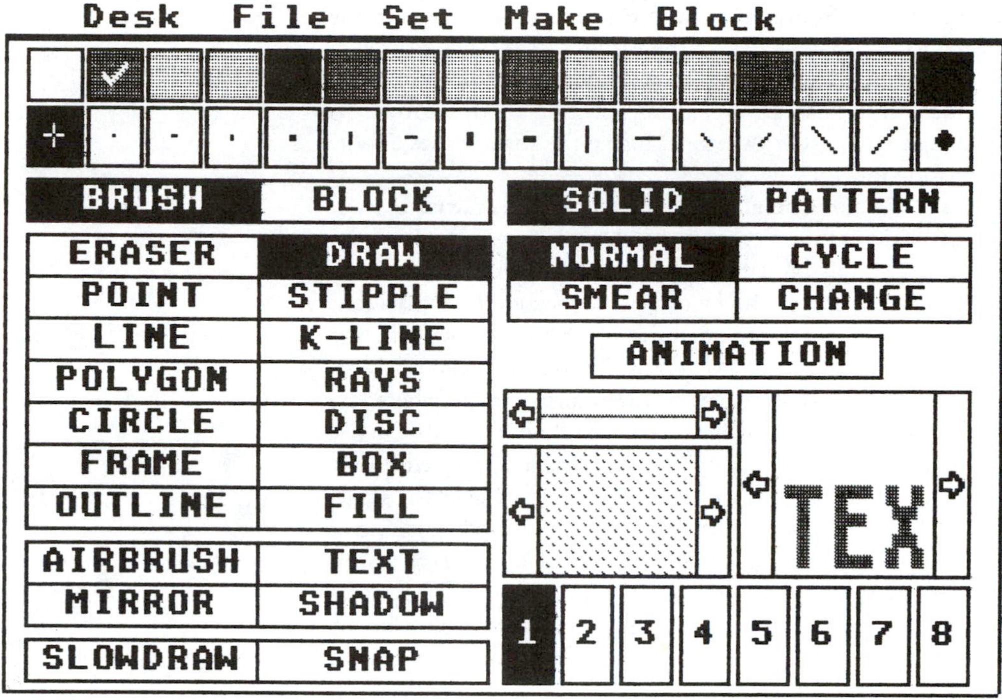


**FIGURE 17.3** Main menu of Degas Elite.

user into a new shape with one of the options in the MAKE menu. This allows a customized monocolor brush pattern within an $8 \times 8$ matrix. In addition to the redefined brush and default brushes, you can define a rectangular block from a picture and use it as if it were a brush. In that way a multicolored brush of any size from one pixel up is available. A custom brush or a block may be saved for later use.

At the lower right in the main menu are eight boxes that represent the eight possible workscreens. One workscreen can be copied into another and portions of the picture on one screen can be copied to another screen by cutting and pasting. Saved pictures can be loaded into any of the workscreens and a screen can be saved individually.

Above the workscreen panel are boxes that show the current line type, the fill pattern, and the text size and font. These boxes reflect the colors in effect for these items. The line type can be changed to an assortment of pixel arrangements within a 16-pixel repeated segment defined with a second MAKE option or by clicking on arrows to cycle through a set of predefined types. The fill pattern can also be changed through a third MAKE option or cycled by clicking on arrows. A fill pattern can be changed from opaque (where it covers everything already on the screen) to transparent (where the earlier picture shows through those pixels that are in background color). A variety of text styles and sizes is provided which can be cycled for selection by the arrows. In addition, you can create your own font, load a file that defines a font, or edit an existing font.

The rest of the main menu allows selection of the drawing action. BRUSH or BLOCK permit freehand sketching by movements of the mouse. A dialog screen, brought up by double clicking on BLOCK, permits a choice of whether the block will be opaque or transparent ("X-ray" mode) and controls whether the block can extend past the screen boundaries. Once either BRUSH or BLOCK has been selected, clicking the right mouse button enters the drawing mode where the main menu is replaced by a drawing screen. By holding down the left button and dragging, you leave a trail on the screen as defined by the brush pattern or block. A click of the left button deposits a single instance of the brush or block, but the use of POINT mode guarantees that only a single copy is deposited. At any time, the most recent action can be removed by the UNDO key. Another press of UNDO restores it. You can return to the menu to change the current selection by pressing the right button, so this acts as a toggle between the main menu and the drawing screen.

Other drawing actions from the main menu are self-explanatory. Selecting ERASER permits the deletion of a portion of the drawing with a default eraser size. (You can also erase by drawing or depositing a brush stroke or block that has background color.) LINE draws a line from the point where the left button is clicked to the point where it is clicked again; a rubber band is drawn as the mouse is moved. K-LINE draws continuous lines with new segments connecting each button click. This is terminated with the right button. RAYS are a set of lines that all start from a common center and end where the left button is clicked. They too are terminated by the right mouse button. POLYGON normally draws a filled polygon but can be made to draw only the outline. The special feature of POLYGON is that the figure is closed by forcing the last side to end at the initial point.

CIRCLE draws the outline of a circle or ellipse that grows from its center as you drag the mouse across the screen until the button is released. A second click on the left button is required to fix the circle in position; it can be moved anywhere on the screen until this is done. FRAME is similar to CIRCLE except it creates a rectangular outline. A BOX is a filled FRAME and a DISC is a filled CIRCLE. A FRAME or BOX can be created with rounded or square corners. The filling is either a solid color or the fill pattern depending on whether you selected SOLID or PATTERN. The current fill pattern is used with that option.

An object that is outlined can be filled with a different color or pattern by FILL. OUTLINE adds an outline around a block of a different color.

These objects can be aligned more accurately by setting SNAP. This creates an invisible grid (you can set the spacing) and objects are aligned on the nearest grid point.

AIRBRUSH gives the result indicated by its name. A circular pattern of randomly placed pixels "sprays" onto the screen while you depress the mouse button and a desired density of "paint" is deposited by controlled movement of the mouse. STIPPLE is similar except its pattern is that of the current brush.

SMEAR is a special effect. It randomizes the colors at the junction of two colors as the object is drawn. SHADOW adds a shadow in the color, width, and direction of choice as an object is drawn. By using MIRROR, each drawing action creates two objects, one the mirror image of the other. The reflections can be across a horizontal or vertical axis.

Adding text to a picture is easy. After choosing TEXT from the main menu and a size and color for the characters, upon returning to the drawing mode any keystrokes appear on the screen. When a desired message has been entered, it is moved into correct position with the mouse before a click fixes it in place. These can be rotated to lie along an axis.

A BLOCK is much more than a special brush type. It is a portion of a picture that is copied into a special buffer. A block is defined by first pressing the ESC key, then dragging the mouse to outline the block and releasing the button. Blocks do not have to be rectangular; a general polygon can enclose a block. Once defined, they can be copied, moved, saved, loaded, inverted, stretched, distorted, or rotated. The rotation capability lets you rotate any part of a picture with a precision of one degree.

Usually, there is a need to touch up the picture before it is finished. Modifications to soften outlines, add shading and highlights, or make other small changes are necessary. Beginning with the early paint programs, most programs permitted you to enlarge a portion of the image and work on it pixel by pixel. In MacPaint, this was termed the "fat bits" feature, wherein an area of the screen was shown with a magnification sufficient to display the pixels individually. Using the mouse, you point to a pixel and click. This causes it to change in color. Of course, on the Macintosh, this only turned the color off or on.

In Degas Elite, there are several degrees of magnification, from three times to 12 times, invoked through the function keys on the keyboard. The magnified portion is displayed on one side of the screen while the original is on the other side. As you work within the magnified part, the original copy reflects the changes as they occur. The color that is set to selected pixels is the current color. You can also draw in the magnified image just as on the ordinary screen. You can pan across the image to obtain a magnified copy of any part of it.

Another nice thing in Degas is the ability to SLOW DRAW. This mode gives a much smaller change on the screen for a given amount of mouse movement. This allows you to be more precise in drawing curves freehand, such as when a line parallel to a previous one is needed or when a freehand curve is to touch an object at a certain point.

Degas implements crude animation through lookup table modification. If a range of colors is designated, ANIMATION will automatically cycle through the range of colors. The color choices in the picture must be correct to give the moving picture effect, and with only 16 colors available, objects are not able to move very realistically. Still, rather dramatic effects are possible. The best of these seem to be nature scenes, such as waterfalls where the color cycling among shades of blue and white produces the appearance of flowing, splashing water.

Since there are many different paint programs, the question of exchanging pictures among them is important. Degas can save pictures in a number of ways and utility programs have been written that convert from one format to another. A format developed for the Commodore Amiga called Interchange File Format (IFF) may become a standard for personal computer artwork.

Built into Degas is the ability to load a picture created in a different resolution. This involves a type of color change to cope with the different bit planes in the three resolutions for the Atari ST. You can also ask for a compressed picture file to reduce the file space that otherwise would be needed if the bit map were saved without modification.

Printing a picture without a color printer is another interesting problem. Degas can do this, but the conversion from colors to black-and-white shading is not that well developed, though color differences are suggested. Figure 17.4 shows examples of pictures created in Degas Elite. The originals were in color but the hard copy lacks this because it was done with a regular dot matrix printer. Many of the illustrations in this book were created in Degas, although few use the full range of features provided by the program. There are significant differences among the various paint programs. We will mention only two.

Degas draws the graphics primitives—lines, rectangles, circles, and so on—into the frame buffer using XOR against the pixels already there. This becomes apparent when, for example, a moving rubber-band line crosses through a black portion on the screen. Inside this portion it will look white while outside it is black. Only when the user releases the mouse button to fix it is the graphics primitive drawn by directly setting the frame buffer pixels; then even the part of the rubber-band line within the black area will appear black. A primitive drawn

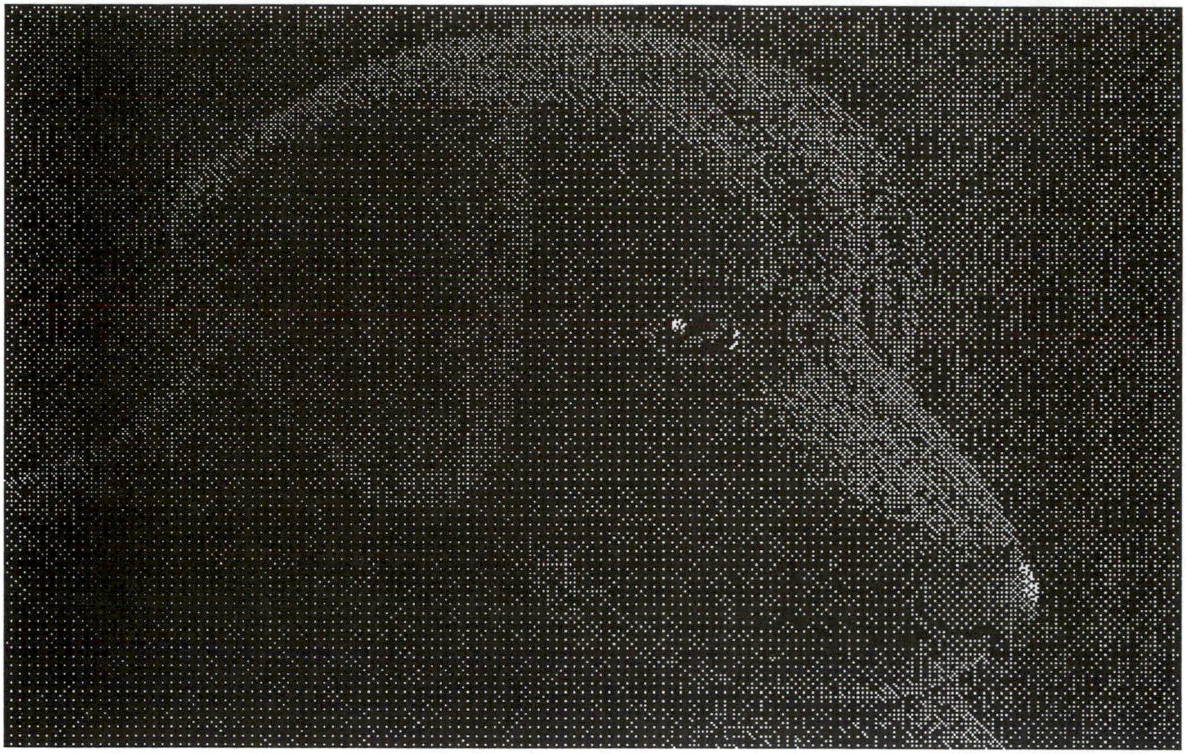

**FIGURE 17.4a**
''Puppy'', a demo picture by Tom Hudson, author of Degas.

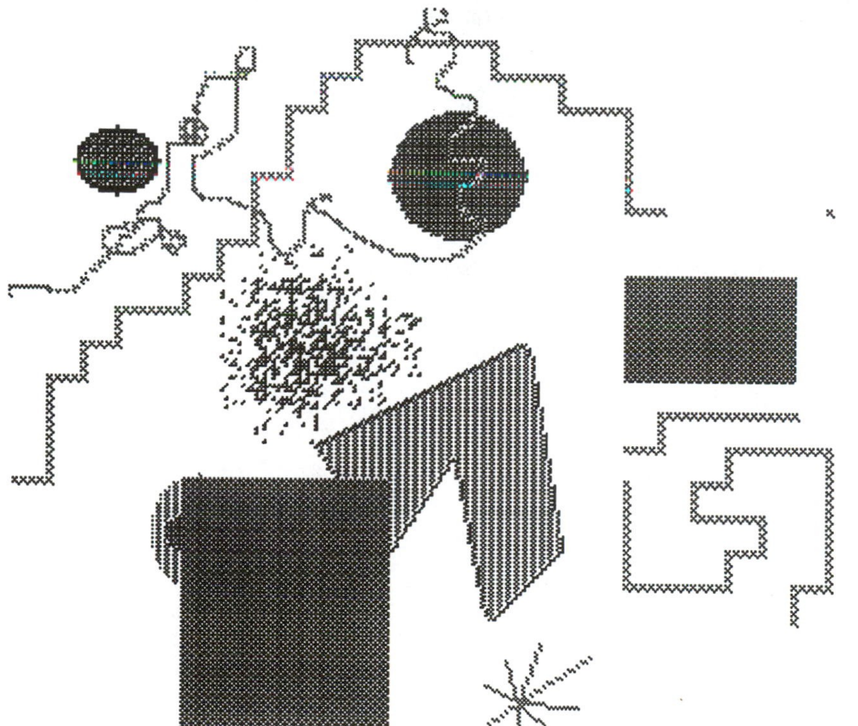

**FIGURE 17.4b**
Some doodling in Degas (original had 9 colors).

in XOR can easily be removed from the frame buffer by drawing it again in XOR mode a second time at the same location.

In contrast, when a primitive is being constructed, MacPaint copies the frame buffer into a working area. The graphics primitive is drawn there on top of the other objects and this area is displayed. While this is being done, another copy of the frame buffer without the primitive is prepared. The display then switches to this area and the graphics primitive is drawn into that area. Only when the user fixes the primitive by releasing the mouse button is it drawn into the frame buffer. As a consequence a rubber-band line or other primitive drawn through a black portion will always appear black. With fast switching between multiple buffers a smooth display can be achieved.

Degas creates only a bit map of the picture, while other paint programs (Cricket Draw and Illustrator on the Macintosh) also store the coordinates of objects internally so as to create a vectorized description. These coordinates allow the transformation of drawn objects by scaling, shearing, rotating, or translating.

Before we go on to the next topic, you should reflect on whether any of the features of a paint program require graphics operations that we haven't discussed. Could you do a rubber-band line? What about rays from a common center? What type of data structure could be used to keep track of the successive edges of a polygon? Would filling an irregular object be difficult when the fill is to proceed from a designated starting point and expand over all adjacent pixels of the same color (seed fill)? How would you implement an eraser, AIRBRUSH, SMEAR, MIRROR, or BLOCKs?

Isn't a user-written graphics program superior in some ways? Certainly it would take less space to store the program than to store the bit map of a Degas picture. Editing with a text editor rather than redoing some part of the picture could be simpler. While Degas permits segmenting the picture into blocks that can be saved individually, having small modules in the program is an extremely easy and natural way to accomplish the same thing. The programming approach ought to be more machine independent.

## 17.1.4 Computer-Aided Design

We mentioned in Chapter 1 that computer-aided design (CAD) is a most important application of computer graphics. Basically, a CAD system facilitates the making of engineering drawings in both two- and three-dimensional views. You might want to use the features of such a program if, for example, you were planning to rearrange your furniture, do some landscaping, or add a covered patio to your residence. These are simple drafting projects that are not hard for an experienced draftsman but are not so easy for the rest of us. The computer makes the output look professional even if the user is not.

For those whose business is the design and layout of complex projects, computer-based design and drafting systems are ways to cut costs, obtain results more rapidly, utilize libraries of previously created parts, and optimize the design. Alternative designs can be tested and compared. It is easy to modify previous versions of drawings or items from the library. Customer presentations are facilitated. Designs and their specifications can be stored more compactly as magnetic files rather than on bulky paper with better organization of information and faster retrieval times. However, the major advantage is probably not cost saving but improved designs.

Advanced systems do much more than act as a replacement for the draftsman. Once an object has been specified, the program can compute its properties, such as areas, volumes, cross sections, and so forth. Color output can discriminate between portions of the design that have different functions, such as showing fire protection lines distinct from ordinary water lines, the hot water system distinguished from cold, and so on. The different portions of a complex wiring diagram in a control system can be set apart by color or each can be drawn on a separate layer with the various layers overlaid to produce the whole.

Fields of application include aerospace (airplanes and space vehicles), automotive (bodies, drive train, control systems, springs, brakes, other components), mechanical (machines, parts, plastic objects, molds and fixtures), civil (roads, bridges, dams, structures), electronic and electrical (circuit boards, integrated circuits, wiring diagrams, motors, electrical supply systems), architecture (buildings, landscaping, room layout)—the list goes on and on. Some idea of the importance of the field in a commercial sense comes from the names of companies active as vendors of hardware and software: IBM, GE/Calma, Hewlett-Packard, Lockheed, Boeing, Digital Equipment, and more specialized firms such as Computervision and Applicon.

Perhaps the greatest economic advantages come not just from CAD itself but its integration with other steps in the manufacturing process. For example, the production of the masks that are used in the manufacture of integrated circuits is now largely automated with CAD. Another example is CAD/CAM, an acronym for CAD plus computer-aided manufacturing. The concept is to use the design specifications and dimensions created in the design phase for input to automated manufacturing. Modern production tools can be controlled through computerization to produce mechanical parts with little intervention by humans and with greater precision than ever before. Such NC (numerically controlled) machines can get their input from the CAD system, with the hope of eventually realizing the dream of paperless manufacture where hard-copy drawings are never required.

Another extension of CAD with great potential is called CAE (computer-assisted engineering). The computation of properties of an object (areas, volumes) referred to above is only the beginning. One application is to create the intermediate cross sections of an airplane wing from a few key sections made by the engineer, similar to the in-betweening described in Chapter 16. Another important instance of CAE is to use the finite element method (FEM) to calculate the behavior of a part while still in the design stage (even before a sample has been manufactured).

In using FEM, a complex object is decomposed into smaller, simpler elements and the governing laws and mathematical equations are applied to these subelements. Computer graphics comes into play in designating the nodes (vertices) that the elements share and that actually define the boundaries of the elements. After making a model of the object on the screen, the engineer uses a mouse or other pointing device to indicate the location of these nodes within the object. The system automatically verifies that the nodes are consistent with the requirements of the procedure and builds a database of the coordinates of the nodes associated with the elements that they define. A mathematical program then takes over to compute the solution to the mathematical equations that model the behavior. Graphics is again employed to show the results. For example, if temperatures within the engine block of an automobile are being computed, colored regions could show the portions at similar temperatures.

The first CAD systems were used in the aerospace industry on powerful mainframe computers. A number of graphics terminals shared the large computing facility. Many systems were developed that used dedicated minicomputers; some of these computers had specialized components to facilitate the graphics operations. More recently desktop computers have been utilized but the ordinary personal computer has hardly enough power; a math coprocessor is almost mandatory. While these less costly installations provide many of the features of the larger ones, they may operate with exasperating slowness.

These are the kinds of things that an advanced CAD system lets the user do:

- Draw lines with specified type, thickness, and end styles, that are perpendicular, parallel, or tangent to other graphic objects. Trim the lines to size or terminate them at an intersection.
- Draw polygons, circles, ellipses, arcs, splines, Bezier curves, boxes with sharp or rounded corners. Fill these solid or with variable patterns of a chosen color. Inscribe or circumscribe them in various combinations. Produce chamfers and fillets. Do cross hatching.

- Break an object into its components or group a set of objects into a single entity. Classify a portion of the design as a "layer" that can be overlaid on other portions. Assign names to groups or overlays for easier reference.
- Set a grid with variable spacing and cause lines and graphic objects to "snap" to the grid points, then erase the grid. Define how close the pointer must be when selecting a group, an object, part of an object, a corner, an intersection.
- Copy, move, rotate, make mirror images, shrink, grow, or stretch individual objects and groups.
- Provide for user input either from the keyboard or via menus.
- Add, delete, modify, move, size, or rotate text. Change size and style of letters and select from different fonts. On rotation, preserve the reading of text from left to right or bottom to top.
- Store the information in a variety of formats (such as IGES or DXF) to allow interchange with other programs. Load, copy, delete, plot files that describe the design. Provide interfaces to other software packages, such as linking a desktop version to a mainframe system.
- Create a 3-D image from 2-D drawings or the reverse. Do shading and rendering.
- Produce a bill of materials and pricing information automatically.
- Display the drawing on one screen while displaying messages on a second.

As you read through this list of CAD features, did you ask yourself, "Do I know how that could be done?" There are many similarities to paint systems. Of course, the orientation is different because CAD is directed to a different set of users. One important feature is present that we have not discussed before—the ability to put a set of objects into a group or to explode a group into its component parts. We will have more to say about this type of operation later in this chapter.

We will describe two typical CAD systems. First we discuss a typical mainframe system, the CADAM system marketed by IBM and based on the original software developments of Lockheed. The other end of the spectrum is represented by VersaCAD, a program that runs on IBM PCs and the Apple Macintosh.

**CADAM** The system comprises a graphics workstation, the mainframe computer, and production support (tape decks and plotters). The workstation consists of a graphics terminal, keyboard, pointing device, and auxiliary function-key panel. Initially a vector display was used but more recently the graphics display is on a raster scan CRT that provides selective erase, color, and freedom from flicker. The pointing device can be a light pen or digitizing tablet.

Figure 17.5 shows the CRT screen after the user has signed onto the system. Messages are displayed at the top and bottom of the screen while the central portion is used to create the drawing. The messages at the top include the type of function being performed, an identifier for the "view" (the overlay being worked on), window parameters, prompts to the user, error messages, and numeric data. At the bottom of the screen is a menu of options from which the user selects with the light pen or other pointer and an echo of keyboard input. The origin for coordinates is indicated by a set of (x,y)-axes. This can be moved or rotated.

In addition to selecting from the menu, the user inputs numeric and character data through a keyboard that resembles a typewriter with

**FIGURE 17.5** CADAM workscreen.

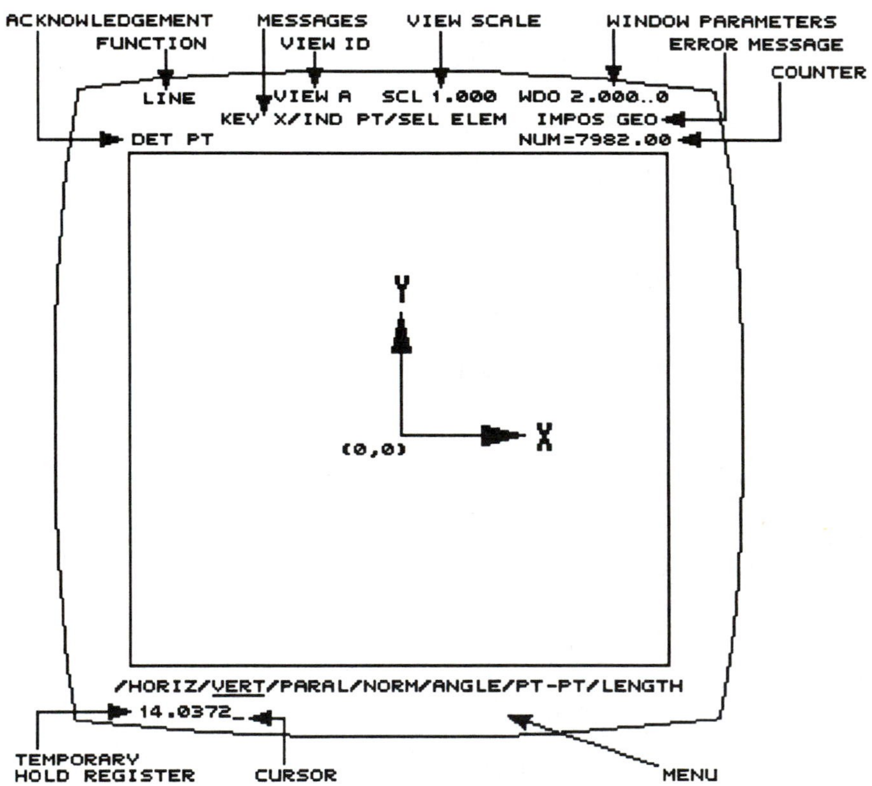

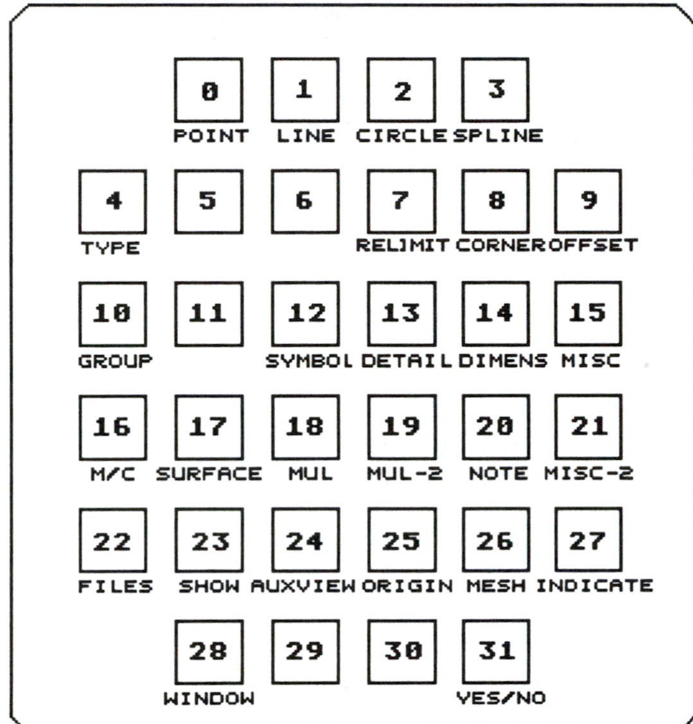


**FIGURE 17.6** CADAM function keys.

special keys. The function-key panel, shown in Figure 17.6, is a separate auxiliary set of keys that are lighted to show which keys are currently active. A template normally overlays the keyboard because the function keys can be programmed to have different actions.

Sometimes an overlay on a digitizer tablet is used to select from another menu of options but usually moving the stylus on the digitizer just moves the cursor around on the screen, similar to using a mouse. An alternate and more normal pointer is the light pen (desribed later in this chapter). When a point is selected, its coordinates are displayed. A selected object is highlighted. Input of coordinate values from the keyboard can also be made to designate a point more accurately. By combining menu selections with pressing the proper function key, the user can ask for a wide variety of actions that include most of those listed above.

CADAM is capable of both 2-D and 3-D designs. A wide variety of computational actions can be performed on the objects the user creates. Drawing elements can be stored and recalled from libraries and these are maintained in a hierarchical data structure. Stock libraries are

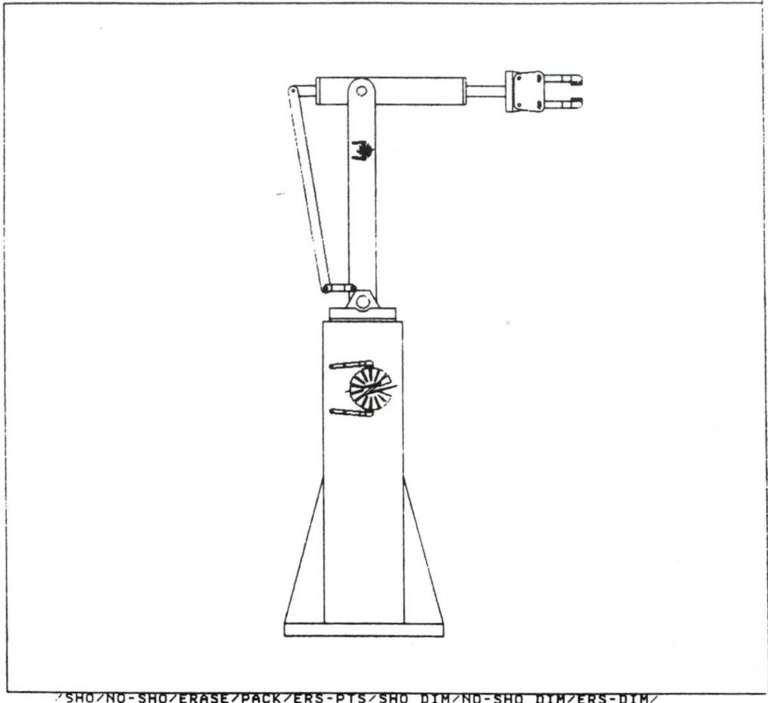


**FIGURE 17.7**

available to avoid the need for each user to create his or her own. Figure 17.7 is representative of the kind of drawing that can be created.

The reasons for basing this giant software system on a mainframe computer are, in part, the size of the program and the complexity of the computations it does. The design criteria include a response time of less than one second to any command. However, if the system is overloaded by many users performing complex tasks at the same time, this is not attained. Having a shared system is also helpful when a team of engineers is working simultaneously on the design.

We will walk through the creation of a double-line floor plan for an apartment unit in a planned apartment complex. After setting up to start a new drawing, including setting the scale for the drawing, the architect creates a grid on which to work. He or she then chains a sequence of lines to give the outline of the walls, creates and adds door and window details (these might come from the library), and adds details for fixtures such as toilet, shower, and wash basin. A special module changes the single-line walls to double-line mode with the requested thickness and orientation. Different types of crosshatching between the wall lines indicates the kind of construction. Once the typical apartment unit has been created, it can be copied to give the layout for adjacent units, with some units reflected into mirror images. The basic design is then modified to customize and add special features to individual units.

So many options are provided in CADAM that learning to use it is no easy matter. There are many training aids provided but still it is a lengthy process to become expert in the use of its multitude of features. The system is correspondingly expensive, not just because of the relatively powerful computer, but also because of the elaborate and specialized workstations and the software license. Even with a shared system, the cost is on the order of $100,000 per station.

**Solid Modeling** Before we describe a second computer-aided design system we will talk a little about solid modeling and describe its essential features. *Solid modeling* is the action of designing, constructing, and modifying a three-dimensional model of an object using a solid modeling package, a *solid modeler.* The display of the constructed solid object on a raster CRT through computer graphics is only one aspect. In addition the package can compute the center of mass, cross-sections, weight, strength, and so forth for the object. A fully featured solid modeler allows the user to construct solid objects interactively and directly on the screen without having to program the object definitions or the rendering procedures. We often work without an initial drawing. A good description of the technical aspects of solid modeling can be found in MUUS87.

**FIGURE 17.8**

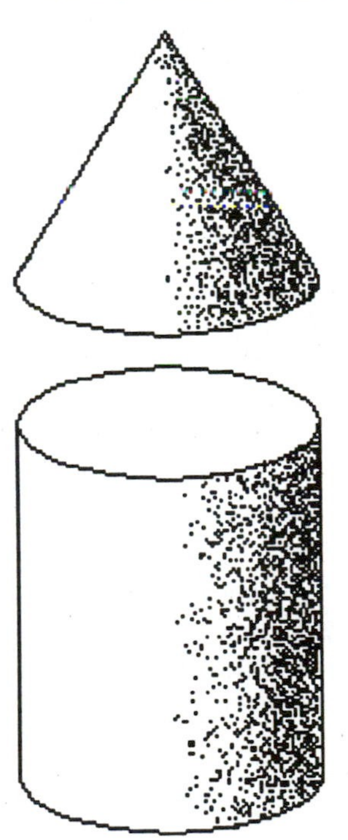

**Combining Solid Primitives** Several ways to do solid modeling have been developed. One approach is called *combinatorial solid geometry* (CSG). The system provides solid, three-dimensional primitives to the user like half-spaces, ellipsoids (of which spheres are a special case), truncated cones (of which cylinders are a special case), blocks, pyramids, and prisms. The user specifies individual solid primitives and how they are to be combined. The composition of a more complicated object from solid primitives can be accomplished by set operations. Set operations include the union, intersection, and difference of sets. The choice of the primitive solids available varies from system to system.

To explain this let us take two solid primitives: a cone and a cylinder. In choosing them we specify their diameters and heights. We can have the system display the primitives as shaded solid objects or just as wireframes—as ghost pictures—which is much faster. Figure 17.8 shows the two objects as solids just to enhance the spatial impression. We want to compose the two primitives into a compound object, therefore it would be a waste of time to display them as solid objects. This will be done only when the final object is constructed. Now we have to position them properly in space. Depending on the particular solid modeler we are working with there are several ways to do this. Typically we have to enter their positional parameters in numerical form: their orientation and location coordinates.

It would be nice if we could always drag the ghost pictures with stylus or mouse to put them into their proper locations. But some motions can't be done with a mouse, like rotating a solid around an axis. Nor can pointing to the screen give a precise location. Perhaps future devices and software will be developed that will allow these actions, but it can't be done yet.

After positioning the cone on top of the cylinder we do a union operation. In a CSG type solid modeler the cone is considered as one set and the cylinder as another. To make the combined object be the union of the two sets, the data structure that describes it must be updated. Mathematically the union is the set of all those points in space that belong to either one of the primitives at their current positions. The union of the two sets will constitute a rocket shaped object shown in Figure 17.9. The combined object is internally represented by a graph like the one we will describe later in Section 17.4.3. This graph is in general not a tree. In addition to the geometric parameters and a transformation matrix, the data structure contains the Boolean operation that combines them.

The other two set operations will also be demonstrated with these same two primitives. We put the cone somewhat into the cylinder as shown in Figure 17.10. If we define the combinied object to be the intersection of the two we get the object shown in Figure 17.11. Mathematically the intersection is the set of all points in space that belong to both primitives simultaneously. This is the overlap volume of the two primitives.

The difference operation is demonstrated with the next two figures. We position cone and cylinder so that they penetrate, as shown in Figure 17.12. If we specify the combined object as the difference "cone minus cylinder," we get what is shown in Figure 17.13. The resulting object is the cone after the part penetrated by the cylinder has been cut out. Mathematically this is the set of those points in space that belong to the cone and at the same time don't belong to the cylinder.

The object can be constructed to arbitrary complexity. Resulting objects can be combined with primitives or other objects. During the design and construction phase it is sufficient to work with ghost pictures (wireframe models). A solid, shaded display has to be produced only from time to time and at the end of the composition process. The solid modeling packages differ considerably in terms of user interaction. It takes some learning time to become really familiar with a particular solid modeler so that one can effectively use it.

**FIGURE 17.9**

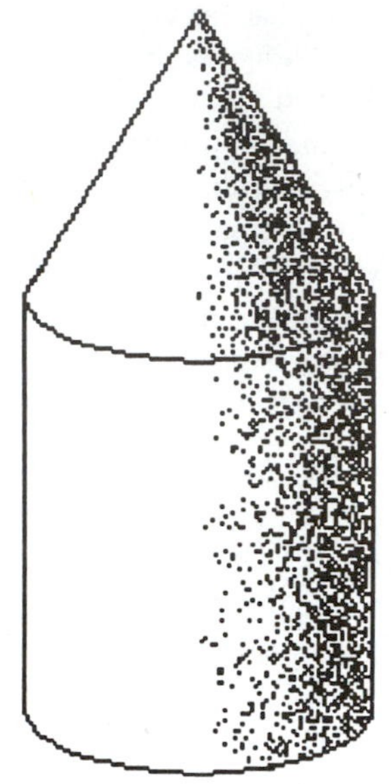

**FIGURE 17.10**

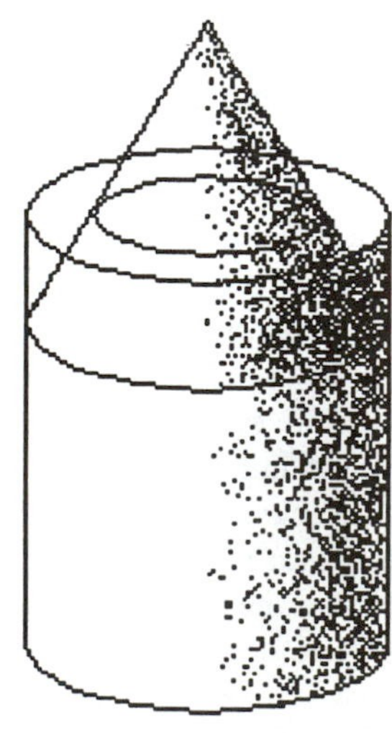

**Rendering the Combined Solid** An actual internal computation or construction of the combined object as the union, intersection, or difference of several primitives is not done. The final object only is rendered. The preferred rendering technique is ray tracing that we described in Section 15.4. Here is a short summary of the underlying idea.

We know from the previous discussion of ray tracing that displaying the union of objects in space is easily achieved at no additional cost. Mutual penetrations and the like pose no problems.

Displaying the intersection of two solids can be done as follows. When a ray hits the first object it continues and is followed until it hits a second object (if any). Only then is a "hit" assumed and the pixel's color set.

Displaying the object "primitive A minus primitive B" can be done as follows. If primitive A is first hit by the ray, a hit is assumed and the ray ends. If primitive B is hit first, the ray continues on within B. If A is hit now before the ray has left B, no hit is assumed. But, if the ray leaves B while still inside A, a hit is assumed. The properties of the surface of primitive B at the penetration point are assumed.

We have to extend these ideas to render more complex Boolean combinations of primitives. It is not very complicated logically, but the more complicated an object we construct the longer will it finally take to display it as a solid.

**FIGURE 17.11**

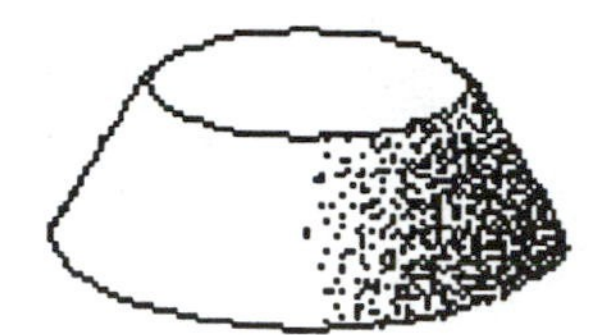

**FIGURE 17.12**

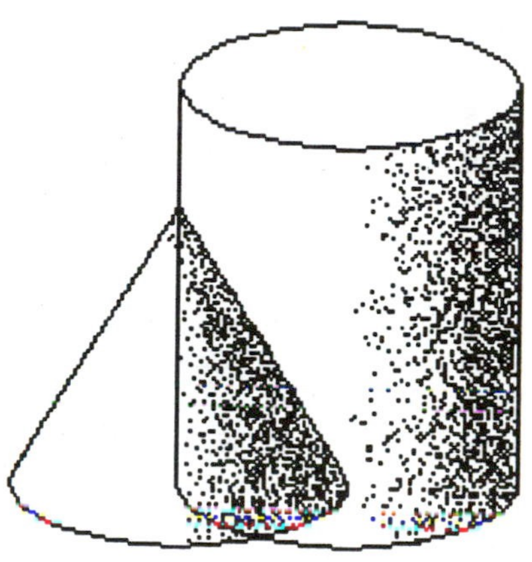

**Specifying Bounding Surfaces** Another approach to solid modeling is called *boundary representation.* Here solids are constructed from surfaces. In such a system the user specifies the types and positions of the surfaces that are to form the boundary of the solid object. These surfaces can be planes, spherical surfaces (surface of a sphere), cylindrical surfaces (mantle of a cylinder), conical surfaces (mantle of a cone), sweep representations (see below), or bicubic patches (Bezier, B-spline). We call such a definition an implicit boundary representation.

**Sweep Representations** The user can define a bounding surface through specifying a flat object and a path along which the object is swept through space. The path is usually a straight line or a circle.

A cylinder with a bore along its axis can be defined by specifying the cross section as a flat object and sweeping it along a straight line perpendicular to it (see Figure 17.14).

As an example for a circular sweep representation we define a torus—compare the torus description in Chapter 15. When a flat disk is rotated around an axis that lies in the same plane as the disk, we get a torus (this is often used as the mathematical definition of a torus). Figure 17.15 shows on the left a flat disk in the (x,y)-plane. This disk is rotated around the y-axis, producing the horizontal torus on the right.

**FIGURE 17.13**

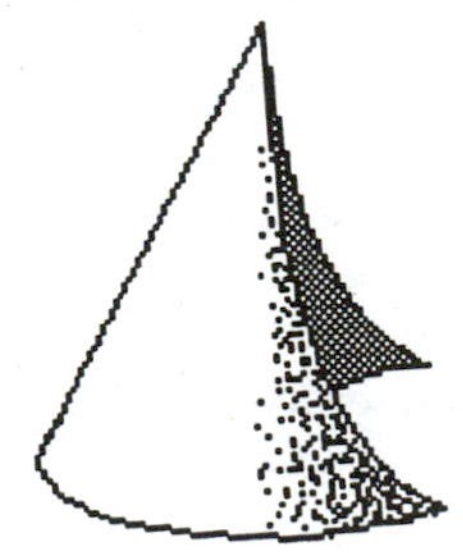

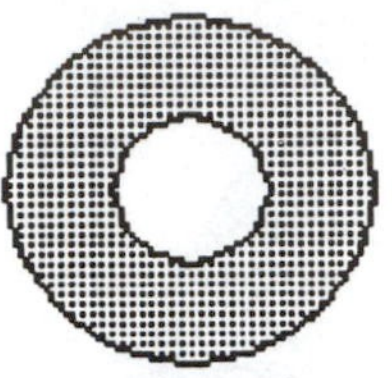

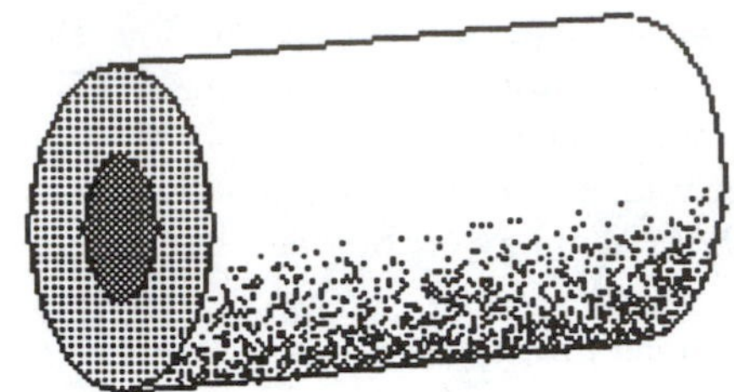

FIGURE 17.14

In addition to the above methods, solids can be modeled explicitly. Here the user specifies as many points as possible on the surface of the object. These are considered as vertices of planar facets. The object that is described by these polyhedrons is rendered smoothly (Phong shading) or faceted (Lambert shading or by ray tracing).

FIGURE 17.15

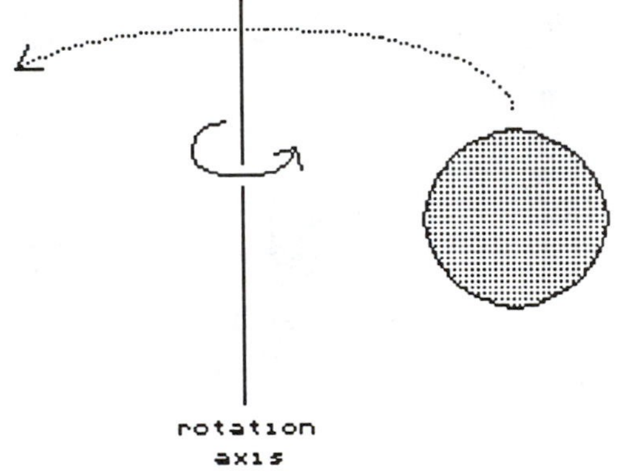


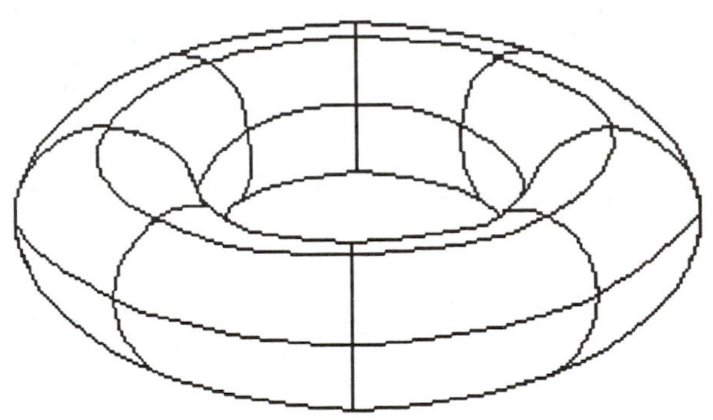

**VersaCAD** Our second example of CAD is a personal computer-based CAD system that is typical of those available at a more reasonable cost than mainframe-based systems. A typical single-user installation will cost less than $10,000. It represents one of the more complete software packages; other programs at even lower cost are available but do not include so many features.

VersaCAD was initially developed for IBM PCs (enhanced with graphics boards, special monitors, and mouse or tablet) but more recently has been ported to the Apple Macintosh, which is more "graphics ready" in its basic configuration. It performs both two- and three-dimensional drafting. A hard disk is required because of the size of the program. The built-in bill of materials generator and linkage to mainframe CAD systems is unique.

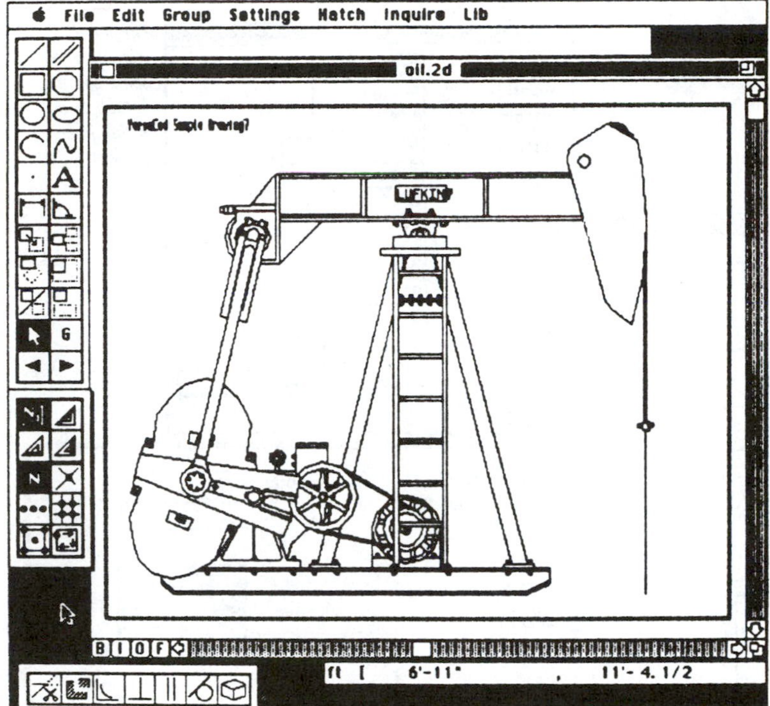


**FIGURE 17.16** VersaCAD workscreen.

We will describe the Macintosh version; the PC version has the same capabilities with somewhat different techniques for invoking them. Figure 17.16 illustrates the workscreen, with a menu of drawing options (the "tool menu") displayed in a column at the left. Lines, boxes, circles, arcs, and so forth are graphics primitives that are selected from the tool menu. The parallel lines feature is a convenience not often found in small CAD systems. At the bottom of the screen is a submenu of variants on the drawing options together with echoes of keyboard input and a display of coordinates of a selected point. At the top is the usual Macintosh set of pull-down menus for file operations plus menus of additional options for grouping, library access, setting user choices, and so on. Some of the menu choices lead to lower level menus and dialog boxes for user/machine communication.

Some of the menus that provide options to the user are illustrated by the set in Figure 17.17. Some choices not apparent in these figures are zooming and panning. A typical drawing that can be produced is shown in Figure 17.18. VersaCAD provides automatic dimensioning in a choice of units. A variety of snap options are available. Constraints can be placed to define how close the pointer must be for selecting an

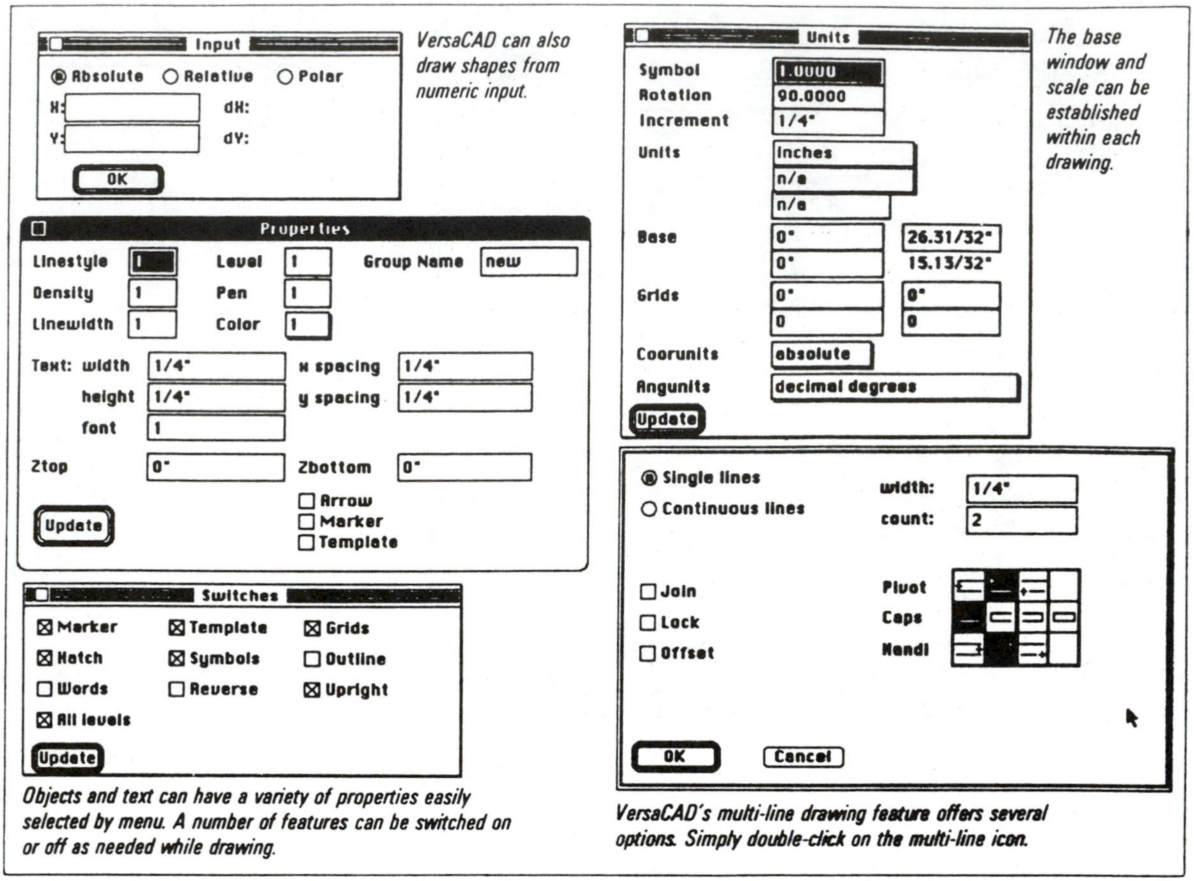

*VersaCAD can also draw shapes from numeric input.*

*The base window and scale can be established within each drawing.*

*Objects and text can have a variety of properties easily selected by menu. A number of features can be switched on or off as needed while drawing.*

*VersaCAD's multi-line drawing feature offers several options. Simply double-click on the multi-line icon.*

**FIGURE 17.17** VersaCAD menus.

object, a group, a line, a point (corner, intersection, etc.). A portion of the screen can be selected for printing and multiple windows can be active at the same time. Overlays can be opaque or transparent. With a color CRT (available for the newer Macintosh models), these overlays can be of varied colors. Most of the features listed above as desirable in a CAD system are provided by VersaCAD.

In the 3-D area, VersaCAD can draw spheres, cylinders, cones, and polyhedrons. These can be manipulated in various ways. A 2-D area can be "extruded," rotated, or swept along a curve to generate a 3-D object. Shading and shadows from several light sources that can be placed at will and with selected colors is included. Output can be to film recorders and laser printers.

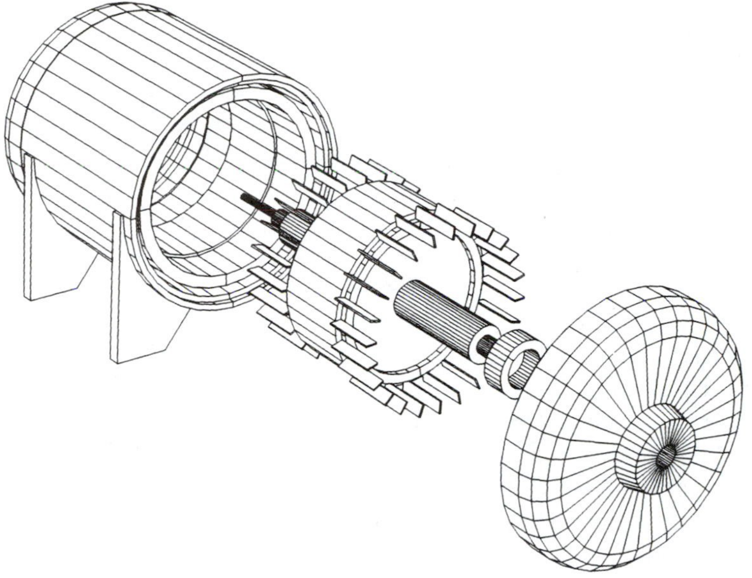

**FIGURE 17.18** Typical VersaCAD drawing.

There are some problems, though, not with the software but with the capabilities of the computer itself. This is true for all CAD systems that run on desktop computers. For example, in doing 3-D drawings, an IBM PS/2 model 60 (one of the more advanced desktop computers) took 21 minutes to remove the hidden lines from a typical demonstration drawing and 24 minutes to generate and display it with shading from a new light position. These times suggest that a complex task should be done by the computer overnight.

A 3-D CAD program can be used for many applications. For example, chemists and physicists need to see three-dimensional models of molecules with the individual atoms shown as colored spheres. This is not difficult and shading and highlights are readily provided, as we discussed in Chapter 14. For such specialized areas, the full range of CAD features is not required, so scientists often use simplified versions.

## 17.1.5 Desktop Publishing

A very popular buzzword in the computer world is "desktop publishing." It is mostly a phenomenon of personal computers and everyone seems to know what the term means: to compose a professional-looking publication without taking the conventional paths to making books and brochures. To do this, the hardware must have the ability to merge text and images, to use a variety of fonts and type styles, to arrange the material properly into pages, and to print the product with essentially commercial quality or at least provide camera-ready copy for commercial printing. Ordinarily, one would like to see the entire page on the screen or, better yet, several pages side by side. The software should permit easy use of the keyboard and pointing device to put a simulation of the finished product on the screen and then send it to a very high resolution printing device. The hardware to do all this is now available and there is software to do it but the costs are high.

As we discuss this last example of graphics-oriented applications, we will find several points of interest. We should inquire whether seeing an entire page or more at one time, with mixed pictures and text in a variety of typefaces, requires more than the kind of graphics system that we have already discussed. What kind of printer can give "commercial quality" and how do we interface with it? Are there special topics in commercial printing that the ordinary person is unaware of? We hope to answer these questions at some point in this chapter. For now, let's explore the question of what desktop publishing really involves.

The idea of doing much of the publishing operation on a computer isn't new. Commercial publishers use computers, often specially designed systems, in many phases of their work. Nearly all printing today involves making a master transparency for the printed pages with a computer. The system drives a scanning device with extremely fine resolution to produce the transparency, using the equivalent of dot matrix descriptions of the individual characters. Usually, pictures are added separately by hand, stripped onto the transparency. These transparencies are used to make the actual printing plates.

Outside of the commercial field, composition on computers has been practiced for many years. The UNIX operating system has modules expressly made to do much of the job of preparing manuscripts ready for typesetting. But this and similar systems such as Knuth's TEX system just put special codes into the text that are used by commercial typesetting machines. We have already mentioned that Xerox made significant advances in this area in the early 70s, but again it is the promotional campaigns of Apple for their Macintosh that have captured the popular imagination. They have capitalized on the excellent graphics of that machine to acquire a leading position in this new application for small computers. But good graphics on the computer is not enough; we must be able to put the output into hard copy.

The one thing needed to make desktop publishing a reality is the laser printer. Here is where Apple did make a contribution by marketing, in early 1985, an affordable laser printer. It was more than just moderately priced; it included a raster image processor (RIP) that generated characters in the professionally designed fonts that have been the hallmark of difference between computer printing of all types and commercial printing. Even more significant is that the foremost professional typesetting company offered an interface to its products.

What is really involved in desktop publishing? Several experts have published lists of critera. Here is a composite from their articles:

- The text should at least approach commercial typeset quality in that it uses well-designed typefaces with proportional spacing. It should do good justifications and that requires correct hyphenation, and the system should do it automatically. This means not just adjustable spacing between words but between characters as well. Kerning, the overlapping of some characters (such as having the bar of a capital T overhang some following letters), is desirable.
- The choice of type sizes and styles should be broad and use accepted fonts and with a range of characters far beyond that normally found on typewriters or even most computer word processors.
- Facilities should be present for setting tables and columns, with justification within these as desired.
- The system should be much more advanced than earlier efforts at computer composition. Instead of inserting codes within the text that are to be used by the commercial typesetting machine, the user should see essentially the final product on the screen (WYSIWYG = What You See Is What You Get).
- Pointing devices are essential, none of the old command languages.
- Inclusion of graphics within the text is important, and one should be able to create the graphics in a variety of ways, including importing from spreadsheets, paint programs, even CAD. One should be able to manipulate the graphics by cropping, rotating, editing, etc. Text ought to flow around illustrations with little effort by the user.
- The editing facilities should be extensive, giving all the facilities of a good word processor but with instant display of the changes. One should be able to see and work with a full page on the screen. The system must have the ability to compose and rearrange the material on the pages.
- The output device must have high resolution, with 300 dots per inch as a reasonable minimum. Since this is as much as five times less than commercial typesetting equipment, there must be an interface to these as well as to the local printing device.

We can add a few items to the list to make a really complete product: automatic index preparation (already a part of many word processors) and spelling dictionaries; footnotes that move appropriately to the bottom of the correct page; leading (the insertion of extra space between lines of type), though this might be difficult to show on the screen.

Except for the greater complexity of data structures, the only new concept in the graphics component of desktop publishing is the laser printer (see later in this chapter). Certainly presenting and manipulating graphic objects on the screen, whether these objects are characters or pictures, can be done entirely through changes to a bit map.

# 17.2 Implementing User Interaction

In this section we will consider what happens when the user makes a request of the system. We will need to consider a variety of input devices that may be connected.

## 17.2.1 Polling

One proven method of getting input from any external device, mouse, keyboard, auxiliary function keys, and so on is to have the system loop continually through a sequence of tests to see if an input signal has been sent. The input device normally sets a flag (a bit in some register) when it has data available. The system determines from the bit which device wants to send input and then queries a data register, often incorporated in the device rather than in the computer, for the data being transmitted. The problem with polling is that the system is normally committed to do only polling so other useful tasks must wait. (One could do the polling intermittently with some risk of missing an input request.) Another problem is that inputs can be missed if there are many devices and the time period when the data is valid is short.

## 17.2.2 Interrupts

A method that avoids the problems of polling is to use interrupts. This is a hardware-based technique in which the device sends a signal when it wants to send data. The central processor of the computer is designed so that, when this signal is on the interrupt line, its current activity immediately stops; it is interrupted (actually any instruction in progress is completed). The system then knows precisely when an external device needs to be serviced and, after saving the current state of the machine, it proceeds to carry out the servicing task. There can be additional interrupts received during the time of this servicing; if the new request is of higher priority, the current action stops and the new servicing is undertaken. When that is finished, the system handles the first interrupt, then finally returns to the original task. You can see that successive interrupts can be stacked up along with the data they are sending. Many keyboards operate with interrupts, not just pointing devices. We will not pursue further this important topic of interrupts and service routines except to say that there can be several levels of interrupts and an ability to disable (ignore) interrupts that are below a certain level. Handling a number of requests simultaneously usually involves establishing queues of requests and data.

## 17.2.3 Handling User Inputs

Most of the user input that we have been considering has supposed that the device was a mouse with one or more buttons. While the mouse has become ubiquitous and more or less the standard input device (other than the keyboard), there are many other items of hardware that can do the same job. We have already mentioned the light pen. Both the mouse and the light pen can signal to the system two different things: (1) that the user is making a request and (2) some information such as the coordinates of a point on the screen or which of several objects that are currently displayed is being pointed at.

A side bar describes how a mouse operates. In brief, the movement of the mouse rotates a ball that changes two internal elements (most often optical encoders but they could be potentiometers). This information about changes in horizontal and vertical position is transmitted to the system.

A number of other devices can also send the system information that is translated to the movement of a cursor on the screen. A *track ball* is something like a mouse upside down: a large ball is rotated directly by the hand. *Joysticks* are widely used in computer games. Here, a pair of potentiometers is activated by moving the joystick. An early device was two thumb wheels that changed two potentiometers. In this case, the cursor was two cross hairs that intersected at the point.

A *digitizer tablet* (also called a digitizer board) works somewhat differently. The position of a stylus relative to the edges of the tablet generates signals that reflect its x- and y-coordinates. There are many alternative techniques to generate these signals, including sensing the voltage difference between embedded wires in a matrix arrangement, interrupting optical rays that cross at the stylus position, and acoustical methods. A special advantage of a digitizing tablet is that you can trace a drawing that overlays the tablet, or pick key points from it. A digitizer-

## THE MOUSE

This is a small input device that fits into one hand and has one or more push buttons. There is a mechanical and an optical mouse. The mechanical mouse has a rubber-coated steel ball inside that slightly protrudes at the bottom. By pushing the mouse around on the table surface, the steel ball is rotated. The movement of the ball rotates two little capstan wheels whose axes are at 90° to each other (see Figure 17.A).

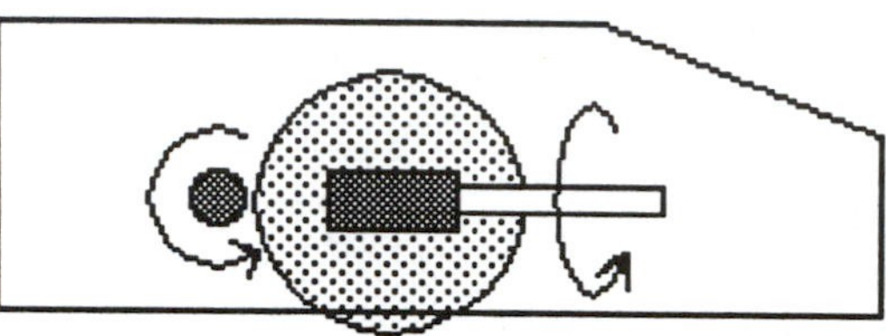

FIGURE 17.A

On the axes of the capstan wheels are small disks with openings. Their rotation causes an infrared light beam to be interrupted. This sends signals to the computer. The capstan wheels are arranged so that one of them is rotated by a vertical mouse movement and the other by a horizontal movement. Other directions rotate both wheels. The schematic is shown in Figure 17.B.

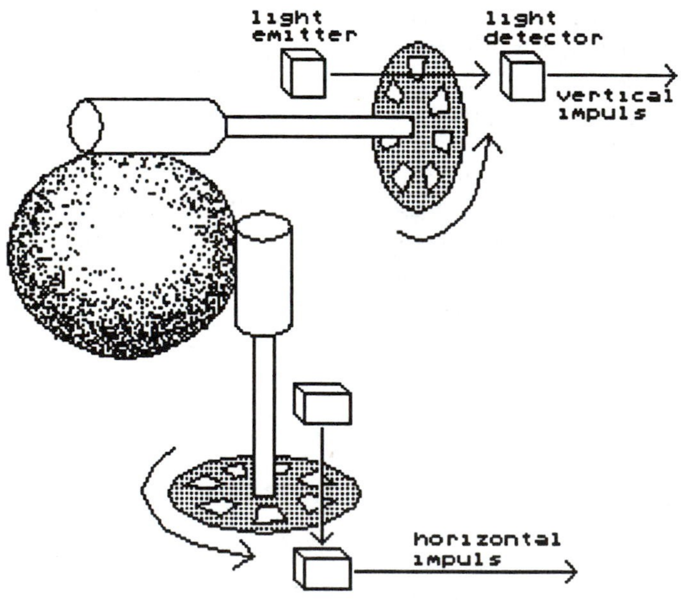


FIGURE 17.B

The mouse sends separate signals for horizontal and vertical movement, but also some other signals that help the computer determine which direction the movement is going and signals indicating depression and release of the mouse buttons. For further details you should study IMAC85 and the appropriate chip descriptions.

The optical mouse can be moved on any smooth surface that has some light-dark pattern, for example, on a paper with fine raster lines. A light source inside the mouse shines onto the surface and makes the light-dark pattern recognizable. The movement of the mouse makes the pattern move under some light-sensitive cells, producing signals that are sent to the computer. The optical mouse has no moving parts and so is not subject to mechanical wear.

Each signal sent to the computer is received by an I/O chip, for example, a Zilog Z8530 Serial Communications Controller or a Synertek SY6522 Versatile Interface Adapter, which are very common in microcomputers. The chip transforms this signal to an interrupt for the processor. The processor can get interrupts for vertical and horizontal movement (also for mouse buttons). All the processor does when getting such an interrupt is find out where the movement went by checking the status of the I/O chip and increasing or decreasing a counter for that movement.

In addition, the processor checks these counters once per vertical retrace—that is, 60 times per second—resets them to zero and computes the new position of the cursor on the display. Basically we have a combination of interrupt and polled operation. The cursor must be removed from its old position and displayed at its new one. This can, of course, trigger all sorts of other actions, like displaying a drop-down menu, drawing a rubber-band line or other graphics primitive at the new location, starting a program or an I/O operation, anything imaginable in a graphics-oriented user interface.

The mouse is very ingenious, amazingly simple, user friendly, and versatile. Still, it is a relative-motion device. It does not report its absolute location, like a stylus on a graphics tablet, only how far and in which direction it is moving. Even the direction is relative to the mouse. If it is accidentally held upside down, an up movement on the table results in a down movement of the cursor; left/right is also reversed. The mouse is not as accurate as a stylus. It is very difficult, if not impossible, to trace out a given drawing or curve with the mouse in order to enter it into the computer, for this would require holding the mouse perfectly parallel to itself during the whole tracing process. On the other hand, you can master normal mouse operations with little practice, just a matter of a few minutes. This, together with its low price, makes it one of the most popular input devices in graphics applications.

type device can be made a part of the bezel around the computer screen. If this works by interrupting optical or acoustical rays, it can be activated by pointing with a finger. There are three-dimensional versions that use the same techniques as a tablet.

A light pen (see side bar) has a different way of indicating the position on the screen where it points. The precise time when the pixels under the light pen are struck by electrons and hence are illuminated is passed back to the system and this indicates a screen position.

Another way for the user to indicate a position on the screen is to use keys on the keyboard. *Arrow keys* can be programmed to move the cursor a certain distance in the direction of the arrow. This is never as convenient or as quick as the other devices.

As you can see, any of these devices can send signals to the system to indicate a position on the screen. With this background, you should be able to understand how the cursor can be moved to follow the movement of a mouse or other pointing device. The system is continually informed of movements of the mouse. When this occurs, it blanks out the old cursor display before exhibiting the new one. If this updating is done only at every vertical blanking signal, the motion on the screen will still be a good animation since the redrawing occurs 60 times per second. (If you move the mouse rapidly enough, you can observe the cursor in discontinuous positions.)

It follows that the cursor location can trigger various responses. If the cursor touches a menu header, the system can query the button state and drop down the appropriate menu window. It can follow the motion of the mouse to highlight menu selections and branch to a routine for whatever selection has been highlighted if the button is released. All kinds of variations and extensions are possible, such as changing the action if the shift key is pressed. Objects on the screen can be selected in a similar way, except that every selectable object must be associated with a particular area of the screen.

It should also be clear how snapping to a grid can be accomplished. If the command is to set a point (display a pixel) and snap is on, the system can determine the location of the nearest grid point and set that pixel rather than the one actually under the cursor. The action is similar for snapping a line, an object, or a block of text to the grid.

# 17.3 SEGMENTATION

It is time now to consider how individual parts of an image can be put into groups or split into separate elements.

In order to explain segmentation we have to talk about some essential properties of pictorial information: how pictures can be stored,

## THE LIGHT PEN

A light pen is a pen-shaped device used for pointing at objects displayed on a CRT screen. On its tip it has a light-sensitive cell which is activated by pressing the tip to the screen or by pressing a button on the pen. We know that the picture on a CRT display flickers at a rate too fast to be perceived but this flicker is what makes a light pen possible. The phosphor emits the strongest light output at precisely the moment when it is hit by the electron beam. When the light pen senses this pulse it sends a signal to the display processor or CRT controller.

The following actions depend on the type of CRT display in use. They are essentially different on vector and on raster scan CRTs.

On a vector scan CRT the pulse is used to interrupt the display processor, which scans the display file in an infinite loop, thereby refreshing the picture. The interrupt triggers a routine that records the current position in the display file. This allows the system to find out which graphics primitive the user was pointing at when the interrupt occurred. Further actions depend on how the user interface is designed. For example, the system can highlight this primitive to tell the user that the proper element in the drawing was chosen and then await further input. The user might want to copy this element to a different place, delete it, or use it to produce similar elements.

On a raster scan CRT the pulse is used to record the beam position at the time of the pulse. For example, in the Motorola 6845 CRT controller this pulse is called the *light pen strobe*. When it arrives the CRT controller latches the current display address, which of course corresponds to the current position of the electron beam sweeping the screen. The light pen strobe will also be used to interrupt the main processor. This interrupt routine has to find out which graphics primitive the light pen was pointing at. This is not as easy as on vector displays. The speed of the electron beam on the screen surface can be as high as 20 miles per second! The latched beam position will be off the light pen position by a certain amount that is typical for a given display setup. This amount will be considered in the computation of the light pen position.

Usually the light pen is pointed at some straight line of the displayed picture. The system can find out which one it is if there is a vectorized description of the picture, a so-called pseudodisplay file. The frame buffer contents alone would not allow this. The system has to compute the distance of the light pen position from every straight line listed in the display file. This can be done when the two end point coordinates $(x_1,y_1)$, $(x_2,y_2)$ and the light pen coordinates $(x_3,y_3)$ are known:

$$d = \frac{|(y_1 - y_2)x_3 + (x_1 - x_2)y_3 + y_1x_2 - x_1y_2|}{((x_1 - x_2)^2 + (y_1 - y_2)^2)^{1/2}}$$

If for a certain line the distance d is below a tolerance number, the system assumes that this line is the one pointed at by the light pen. It can highlight the line to confirm correctness and await further user interaction. We can see that the whole process is more complicated than on a vector scan CRT. The computation of the light pen position can not always be done very accurately. Light pens don't work very well on raster scan displays.

A light pen can work only if there is something displayed on the screen that emits light. But sometimes the light pen is used to indicate a certain area or location on the screen where nothing is displayed. This is useful for establishing the end points of lines to be drawn, to indicate to the system whether a chosen area is inside or outside a displayed polygon, and the like. To achieve this, the system displays a screenful of little elements (like individual pixels or dots) in a quick flash and this permits an impulse from the light pen to be received. Again, the location on the screen usually cannot be determined very accurately.

organized, changed, and so forth. As humans we process pictorial information all the time, but subconsciously; we don't "know" what we are doing. But to make the computer deal with anything, we have to precisely define and formalize what it is we are doing and what we want the computer to do.

Pictorial information that we are given by our visual system consists of shapes, colors, depth order, motion, and probably more. It is not easy to distinguish pictorial information from the other types of information conveyed to us at the same time through our eyes.

Pictorial information is what we perceive through the power of our visual system alone, excluding all other information that we derive from supplemental higher level processes. For example, a page full of Chinese characters has the same pictorial information for a European and for an Eskimo and for a Chinese, but for the latter it conveys a lot more information because he or she can read the characters while the first two persons cannot. This additional information derived from reading the characters is not pictorial; it comes from mental processing of a different nature.

When we perceive pictorial information from the real world it is grouped into a hierarchical structure in the mind. This structure is not inherent but is added to the picture by the mind through a complicated process. The complexity of this process is demonstrated by the almost unsurmountable difficulties in realizing computer vision.

For example, when we see a person, we can make out parts of the body: head, arms, legs, torso. At the same time, these are not the smallest entities we perceive. We tend to think of an arm as composed of upper arm, lower arm, hand. A hand contains a lot of detail. We have individual names for all its parts: palm, fingers, knuckles, nails.

The same applies to what we call the head. We easily and automatically create a hierarchical structure of considerable depth from a picture.

Humans have many ways to record pictorial information: paintings, drawings, photographs, floor plans, technical drawings (the last two contain more than just the pictorial information). A good photograph of a landscape gives us basically the same pictorial information as the real thing (except for depth). A computer, too, can store pictorial information in such a way. The landscape in the photograph can be digitized and stored as an ordered set of points with certain color values in a frame buffer or on a nonvolatile medium.

Admittedly, some amount of information is lost through the digitizing process but the amount of loss is just a question of technology. It is possible to apply such fine digitization and such a huge color range that the digitized picture will contain the same information as the photograph or the painting. (Photos and paintings do not have complete exactness of detail.)

There is a distinctly different way to store information about a scene that applies only to computers and particularly for graphics. This is to store the information in what is called *vectorized form,* extracting the basic ideas. This storage method is closely related to the interpretation the human mind gives to a picture. To put pictorial information into vectorized form cannot be done without a human. A human being has to define every single individual part; it cannot be created by an automaton like a camera or a digitizing device.

Putting something into vectorized form requires that we simplify it. For example, we can simplify the front view of a house to a pentagon. In other words, we can reduce the front view to the "essence" of a front view, one that is not further reducible. Only five Cartesian coordinates are needed to define this pentagon. Its sides are ideal straight lines (see Figure 17.19).

In reality the edge of the wall or the roof, both of which we represent by straight lines, is far from being precisely straight. We idealize the elements. In so doing, there is a loss of information by the vectorization much greater than the loss if we had digitized it. But this loss is unimportant because the abstraction through vectorization retains the information that is most important to us. What is important depends on the particular application. You see what a complicated process is involved with every vectorization.

If we need more than just the pentagon-shape description of the front view, we can add rectangles to describe the windows and the door. We can go further and add lines to describe the door frame, window frames, and window bars. If we want, we can add even more detail. The windows may not be all alike; then their descriptions will be different. Eventually we will end up with a huge number of coordinates that describe lines which in turn describe the house.

**FIGURE 17.19** Idealized front view of a house.

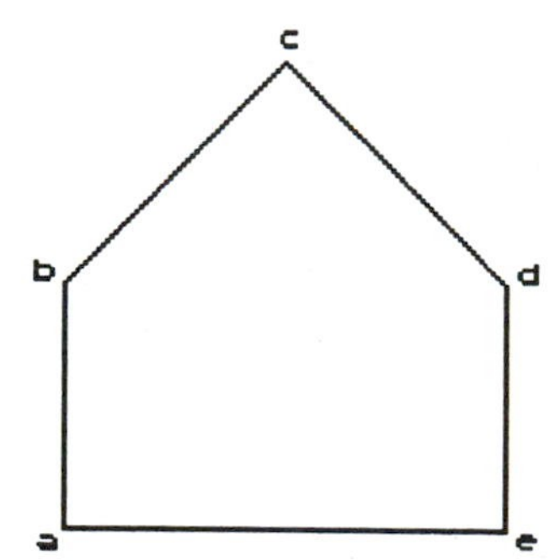

Even though a vector is represented as a straight line, do not get the impression that vectorization means that everything must consist of straight lines. Our understanding of visual information includes curved lines, polygons, and colors. (One could imagine more complex primitives but there is no real advantage to this because those can always be decomposed into the more primitive ones.) Even though our pictorial information contains other than straight lines, we still consider it as vectorized. The description requires the same kind of visual processing and idealization as the straight line examples.

Figure 17.20 shows a sequence of draw commands that eventually lead to a picture of a house but in an order that is contrary to our usual thinking and that would be difficult to do by hand. The fact that it is difficult for us to draw a house or any object in an out-of-order sequence shows that our inner perception and understanding of pictorial information is an abstract, hierarchical one. For the computer it is no problem to draw something in such a way because all the coordinates, straight lines, circles, and other basic graphical elements that describe a picture have no inherent meaning to the computer.

It contradicts our hierarchical understanding of a picture to have the graphics primitives of which it is composed in an unordered pile. It would make it hard for us to create, change, or update such a picture. We will see that it is beneficial for the manipulation and processing of pictorial information if we always put it into the same hierarchical order in which our minds put it or at least into some reasonable hierarchical order.

This grouping of the graphics primitives of a picture into a hierarchy is called *segmentation.* In the case of a house like that in Figure

**FIGURE 17.20**

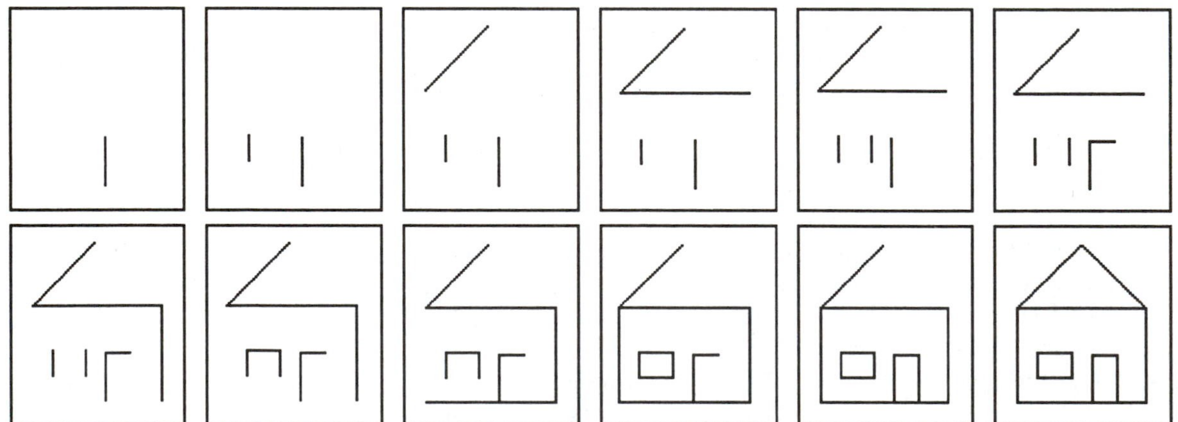

17.21, a natural segmentation would be to have all lines, polygons, and colors that describe the first window together in one segment; the lines, polygons and color for the second window in another segment; those for the door in another one, for the wall and roof in another, and so on. We can extend this to a deeper hierarchy by imagining subsegments within segments and subsegments within these. The house in the figure is too simple to be a good example; a scene consisting of several houses would be better.

The objective in segmentation is always a vectorized picture, that is, a picture abstracted and described in terms of a very limited set of graphics primitives. Segments that we describe in this chapter impose a hierarchical order on such vectorized pictorial information.

**FIGURE 17.21**

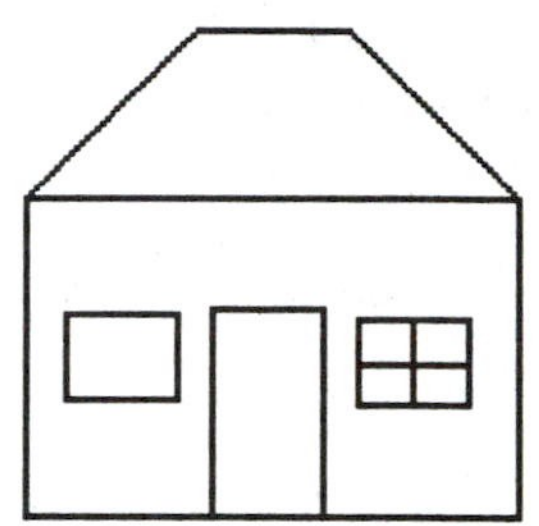

## 17.3.1 Reasons for Segmentation

When we manipulate a picture that describes a scene, the most likely manipulation will be to change parts that are units within the hierarchical structure. On the house above we might want to reposition one window a little to the side or make the door larger. When we move the window we want every part of it to move together; it would be nonsense to move just the window frame and leave the window bars behind. With segmentation it is possible to organize the software to specify a particular segment as the object of a move command. This makes dealing with the picture much easier. You can see how this relates to grouping of picture elements.

Still, organization into segments does not forbid moving the window bars alone and not the rest of the window. This might be necessary if the window bars are not properly located within the window. When we segment a picture into a hierarchy that corresponds to the natural structure of the scene, practically every change that we want to perform will refer to a specific segment or subsegment. A transformation of a segment applies to all subsegments within it down to the lowest level, but not the reverse; if you move your arm, your hand and fingers all move with it, but moving your finger does not imply moving your arm. A segmented picture description is useful when it is so organized that on the deepest level all transformations pertaining to it and to higher segments in the hierarchy are cumulative.

For example, suppose we want to animate the display of a helicopter. We can do this by displaying it many times and each time translating it a little. But we also want to show both rotors of the helicopter spinning slowly. If the rotors are described as subsegments of the helicopter, a translation of the helicopter will translate the rotors as well. Thus for the rotor subsegments we can specify rotations only.

They will be accumulated on top of their translation along with the helicopter. Without this principle, we would need to specify rotation and translation for the rotors. For situations more complex than this you can see that segmentation allows an easy and natural manipulation of the whole as well as the parts. Thus, a *segment* is a set of graphics primitives that are arranged together in an appropriate data structure. The programming language and the design of the graphics system determines what types of data structures can be used to realize a segment.

## 17.3.2 Interactive Use of Segmentation

When a picture is created interactively, segmentation is the only way to give the picture a hierarchical structure. It is a good idea to investigate the potential of segmentation in an interactive environment and later see what use can be made of it in noninteractive systems.

In the following we assume that the system provides a menu from which we select an action, a mouse or stylus-driven cursor, and the ability to see our choice of points on the screen; in short, a very friendly system. In order to define the same house as in Figure 17.19 and to indicate that these five lines belong in one segment, we might use the following sequence:

| | | |
|---|---|---|
| | user chooses: | open-segment |
| | user types: | 1 |
| | user chooses: | move |
| | user specifies: | <point a> |
| | user chooses: | draw |
| | user specifies: | <point b> |
| | . . . | |
| | . . . | |
| | . . . | |
| finally: | user chooses: | close-segment |

In this way the user creates segment 1 that contains the commands to draw the house. There are many ways to do this kind of thing. The lines that make up the house could be drawn in rubber-band mode. The "close segment" action usually closes the currently open segment by default so no number needs to be specified. Most systems disallow opening a new segment until the current segment is closed, precluding the creation of nested segments, that is, of higher hierarchies. Even with this limitation a grouping of the graphics primitives is achieved. If a system allows the creation of nested segments, hierarchical structures of arbitrary depth can be defined. Even when nested segments are not possible, the user can create as many segments as desired.

Here are some useful operations on segments that are commonly provided, although not every system gives them all. A user would like to be able to do all of these things with each segment independently:

make visible or invisible
transform (scale, translate, rotate)
copy
select
delete

The usefulness of segmentation would be further increased if the user has the option of assigning certain attributes to a segment, such as visibility, priority, highlighting, transformations, and color. Exactly how we do the assignments differs with the implementation. We will first see how these attributes are useful. We discuss them below for the most general case in which a nested hierarchical structure is possible because this applies without difficulty to simpler systems that have only one level.

The *visibility* attribute is pretty obvious. Normally a segment is visible, but it can be set to be invisible, in which case it will not be displayed, nor will any of its subsegments. An invisible segment still exists in the data structure and can be made visible at any time. Invisibility extends to all subsegments even if they are set to be visible; the setting for the higher level overrides. (The visibility attributes of a segment and the higher segments of which it is a part behave as if ANDed together, so a segment or subsegment is visible only if its visibility and all higher segment visibilities are true.) A change of visibilities results in turning on or off the display of certain segments. It is useful for design applications in which the effects of individual segments are to be tested.

The *priority* of a segment determines the order, relative to the other segments of the same hierarchical level, in which this segment will be displayed. Lowest order segments will be displayed first, highest order segments will be displayed last. On raster scan devices the effect is that a lower order segment will be overpainted by a higher order segment where they overlap. Priorities are meaningless for segments of different hierarchical levels. If segment A has lower priority than segment B, all subsegments of A also have lower priority than all subsegments of B. It very much depends on the implementation; usually priority settings are possible only in environments in which no subsegments are allowed. Priority settings can be useful for setting of background and foreground segments in connection with transformations that give animation.

The *highlighting* attribute is used to distinguish a segment from the others by displaying it in a more pronounced way. How this is done depends on the type of display. On vector scan CRTs, a line can be made brighter to highlight it. On raster scan devices a line can be displayed in a different color or it can be made to blink on and off. When a segment is highlighted, all its subsegments are highlighted, too. The highlighting attributes of a segment and its higher segments act together as if ORed together. You can see that this is valuable to indicate when an object that is drawn as a segment has been selected.

The *transformation* of a segment applies a linear transformation (rotation, scaling, translation) to the segment before display. It also applies to all subsegments of the segment. If an additional transformation was specified for a subsegment, this is added to the transformation it receives as a part of the higher segment. In this way the user can translate, scale, or rotate whole segments or even do composite transformations such as rotation about an arbitrary point. The transformations of subsegments are performed relative to the transformed higher segment. To demonstrate this, let's use the helicopter example (see Figure 17.22). For the main segment a translation is specified. For the subsegments rotor #1 and rotor #2 rotations around their hubs are specified. Therefore the rotors will be both translated and rotated.*

A *color* attribute would normally be applied a little differently in that the color of a subsegment would always be the same as the including segment, but if displayed by itself, it would have its own color.

As the user defines segments and specifies attributes interactively, internal data structures must be created and updated with every new command so that the latest version will be written to an external file whenever the user quits. The graphics primitives are included in these data structures. In this way, when the user wants to continue to work on the picture at a later session, he or she can add to the previously created segments.

At the present time it is hard to find a system that gives all the above options although this sort of software is under active development in many places. The standard known as PHIGS (discussed in Section 17.4.3) proposes hierarchical structures that can be edited interactively. Older software gives few of the above features. For example, in many packages a segment once closed cannot be reopened to make a change. To make any change requires that the segment first be deleted and then

---

*To make the rotation of the main rotor look real, the rotor has to be specified in 3-D coordinates. The rotation must be done in 3-D, which is then projected.

**FIGURE 17.22** Individual transformations for subsegments.

entirely recreated. On the other hand, some systems give options that are not particularly useful, such as the ability to rename a segment.

## 17.3.3 Implementing Segments

In this section, you will learn how segmentation can help to make the system more powerful and friendly. Implementation of segments requires a certain type of data structure; the type of display hardware used influences this. For vector scan devices, the data structure is a *display file* that must be scanned in real time by the display hardware and only simple structures can be used. In raster scan displays there is no such limitation and a hierarchical ordering of picture elements can be implemented. We will distinguish between these two cases.

**Implementation on Raster Scan CRTs** We consider raster scan first because it imposes no limitations on the type of hierarchical structure that can be implemented. Therefore a very general data structure can be developed and implemented. First let us see how graphics primitives can be grouped together within the data structure that holds the commands for the primitives.

**Description of the Data Structure** The most powerful data structure is a linked list because it is fully dynamic. In an interactive environment in which we do not know beforehand how many segments there will be, how many primitives a segment will contain, how many subsegments, how deeply nested, and so on, a truly dynamic data structure is the best choice.

We will start a new linked list whenever the user opens a segment. Whenever the user specifies a graphics primitive, a list element containing the command for that primitive and any necessary parameters is appended to the list. Whenever the user opens a segment within a segment, the system starts a sublist within this list that receives the primitives of that subsegment.

We can express a hierarchy of arbitrary refinement and depth in this way. Every segment or subsegment is expressed as a linked list. Every segment starts with a list header that contains three elements.

The first is a link to the next segment at the same hierarchical level, the second is a pointer to the first subsegment of this segment, and the third is a pointer to the first graphics primitive of this segment. Any one of these elements can be nil. This diagram illustrates it:

```
List header:
```

| Link to next list on same level | Link to first list on sublevel | Link to first graphics primitive |
|---|---|---|
| 1 | 2 | 3 |

Through element 1, all segments of the same level in the hierarchy are linked; the last of these pointers is nil. Exactly one of the elements 2 and 3 is nil. If a segment has subsegments, link 2 points to the header of the first subsegment, which in turn points to the next header until this list ends with nil. In such a case link 3 is nil. If a segment has no subsegments, link 2 is nil and link 3 points to the first graphics primitive, which in turn points to the next one until this list ends with nil.

To show the flexibility of this data structure we assume an example picture consisting of three segments: house1, house2, and some other object. House1 consists of four subsegments: outline, window1, window2, door. Window1 has no subsegments while window2 consists of two subsegments: frame and bars. Door has no subsegments, house2 has no subsegments, and the other object has no subsegments. Figure 17.23 illustrates this.

The corresponding linked list structure is shown in Figure 17.24. On the highest level there is only one pointer that points to the header of the first segment in the picture, house1. To see what a list of graphics primitives looks like, consider Figure 17.25 which shows just the outline of house2 and the corresponding linked list. Each letter represents a number pair (or a number triple) in Cartesian coordinates.

**FIGURE 17.23**

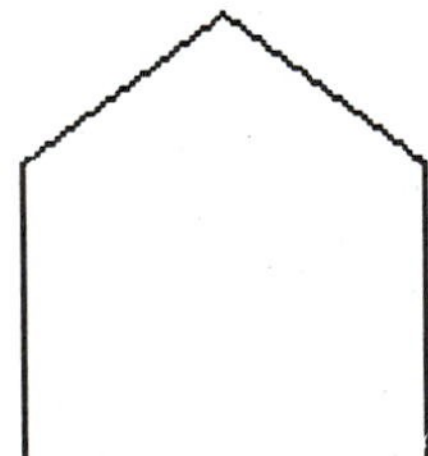

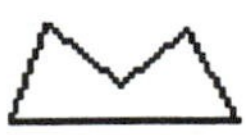

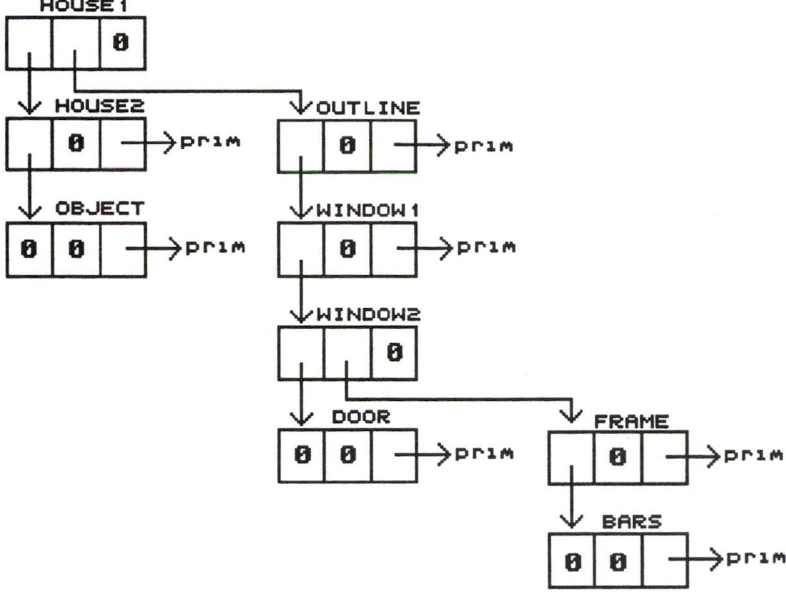


**FIGURE 17.24** Hierarchical linked list structure.

The linked list structure of Figure 17.24 represents just the bare hierarchical structure. Segmentation really becomes useful through the addition of segment attributes. These are added to the data structure by including them in the header element of the list. For this we need to enlarge the header element to include one bit for visibility, a real number for the priority, one bit for highlighting, values for the color, and a matrix for the transformation. The size of the matrix depends on the dimension in which the system is working. When a list or sublist is first created the transformation matrix is initialized as an identity matrix.

**FIGURE 17.25** Graphic object and its list of graphics primitives.

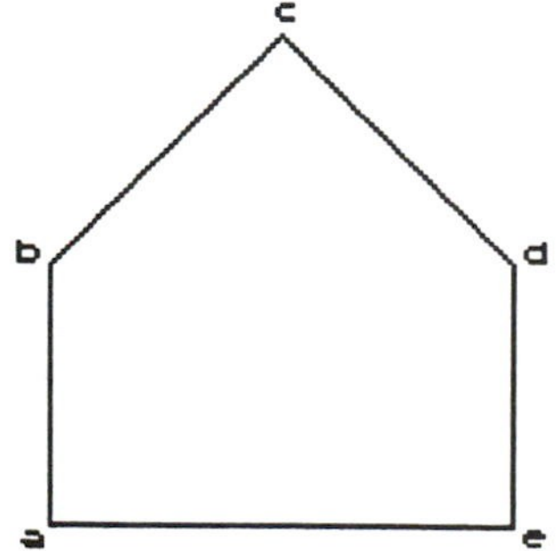


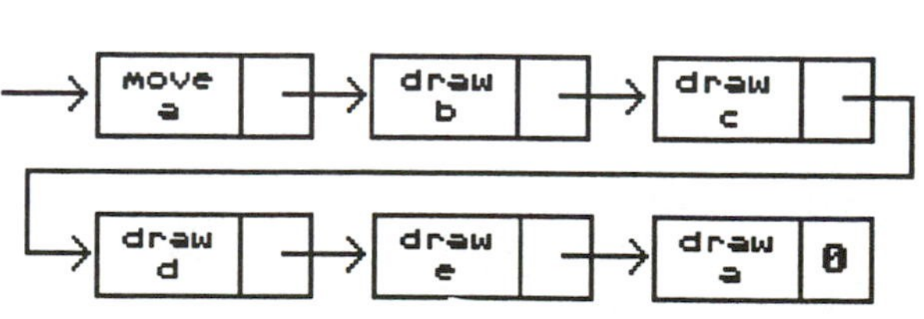

**Displaying the Data Structure** We show below type declarations and a procedure (partly in pseudocode) for traversing and displaying a fully hierarchical segment structure with accumulating transformations. Visibilities, priorities, and highlighting are not present in the example. To display the whole picture, the procedure is called with the pointer to the highest segment in the hierarchy.

Recursion makes it easy to program the traversal through the hierarchical structure. We will walk through the procedure. It is essential to provide a transformation matrix (locmat) local to the particular recursive call; this is assigned the value of the global matrix upon entry into that recursion. The global matrix (globmat) is updated to represent the accumulated transformations by multiplying it with the transformation matrix for the segment to be displayed (mat). Then comes the recursive call for displaying the subsegments followed by the loop for displaying the graphics primitives (either the subsegments call is empty or the loop for the graphics primitives is empty). After returning from displaying the subsegments or from displaying the list of graphics primitives, the global matrix is reset to its value upon entry and the next segment on the same level is displayed. When these are exhausted the procedure returns.

We assume a two-dimensional environment, a matrix assignment statement, and a matrix multiplication statement.

```
type element    =    record op      :  integer;
                            x,y     :  real;
                            prim    :  ^element
                     end;

     header     =    record head,sub :  ^header;
                            prim     :  ^element;
                            mat      :  array[0..2,0..2] of real;
                     end;

     headpt     =    ^header;

var globmat   :   array[0..2,0..2] of real;

procedure disp_segment(p   : headpt);
var locmat  :  array[0..2,0..2] of real;

begin
  locmat := globmat;
  while p <> nil do with p^ do begin
    globmat := globmat*mat;
    disp_segment(sub);
    display the graphics primitives
```

```
    starting with prim until nil,
    using globmat for transformation;
    globmat := locmat;
    p := head;
  end {while p <> nil with p^}
end {procedure disp_seg};
```

The above implementation is only one of many possibilities but it is very versatile and powerful. Most of the other implementations will be simplifications of this. If the display is a raster scan CRT, the structure is traversed only once in order to scan convert the graphics primitives into the frame buffer; the display hardware scans only the frame buffer, not the data structure.

**Interactive Creation of the Data Structure** The user probably employs a sketch that indicates what should be in each segment and subsegment as a guide in creating a hierarchically structured picture. The system should allow the user to create the required data structure interactively and not have to specify unique names for every segment and subsegment. The input of graphics primitives should be possible by typing coordinates or pointing with the mouse or stylus-driven cursor relative to the user's coordinate scale. (Other features such as color, line styles, etc. could be added.) The basic principle of the interaction can be described as follows.

The commands open segment and close segment are either typed or chosen from the menu. No number or name has to be specified. An open command that follows an open command opens a subsegment within the current segment. An open command that follows a close command opens a segment at the same hierarchic level as the last closed segment. A close command closes the most recently opened segment that has not yet been closed. (Open and close induce something comparable to a parenthesis structure.)

As an example, we show how the structure of Figure 17.23 can be created interactively. O stands for an open command and C for a close command. The actions enclosed by < > represent the user actions with the pointing device. Comments are enclosed in { }. The sequence of interactions has indentation to indicate the hierarchical structure:

O {start house1}<br>
  O <draw outline><br>
  C<br>
  O <draw window1><br>
  C<br>
  O {start window2}<br>
    O <draw frame>

```
                C
                O <draw bars>
                C
            C {end window2}
            O <draw door>
            C
        C {end house1}
        O <draw house2>
        C
        O <draw object>
        C
```

At every point during the creation process, the user must be able to find out where he or she is in the structure. This could be provided by highlighting all primitives or segments on the same hierarchical level as the current one whenever the user requests it and moving up in the hierarchy with every consecutive request. This is basically the same process as the interactive selection of picture elements below.

**Interactive Selection of Segments or Primitives** The user may want to select a certain segment or graphics primitive to change, delete, or otherwise modify. This should follow the style of the packages described earlier where selection is by clicking on the primitive. The system should respond by highlighting the primitive, for example, by displaying it in a different color. If the user wants to select not the primitive but the segment containing it, he or she clicks once more on the primitive. This will indicate to the system to move up one level in the hierarchy and this should be signaled by highlighting all the primitives belonging to this (sub)segment. Additional clicks continue moving upward in the structure to select any segment or subsegment in the picture. Any change in an attribute that is specified will be stored at the level of the chosen (sub)segment.

This works unless the user has made a segment invisible. A less user-friendly way to solve this problem is to assign unique names or numbers to each segment; then a segment can be specified by typing its name or number. This places a burden on the user, who still cannot reach individual graphics primitives. A method more in keeping with interaction and more user-friendly is to supply a command just for this purpose that overrides any invisibilities and displays everything in the picture. There should be a way to undo this and restore the visibility attributes as they were.

The sequence of Figure 17.26 shows such a selection process. The whole scene is the one defined in the data structure of Figure 17.24. After clicking on the horizontal window bar the user gets picture a in which this bar is highlighted. After clicking one more time the second

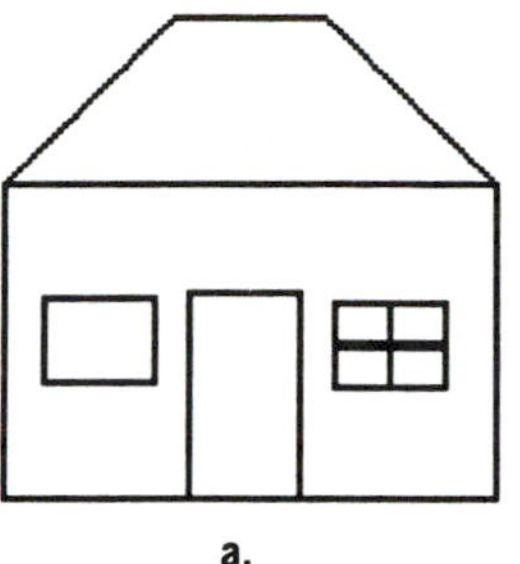

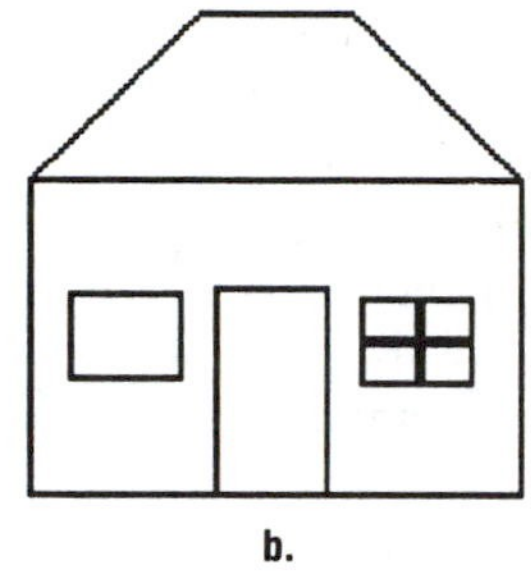

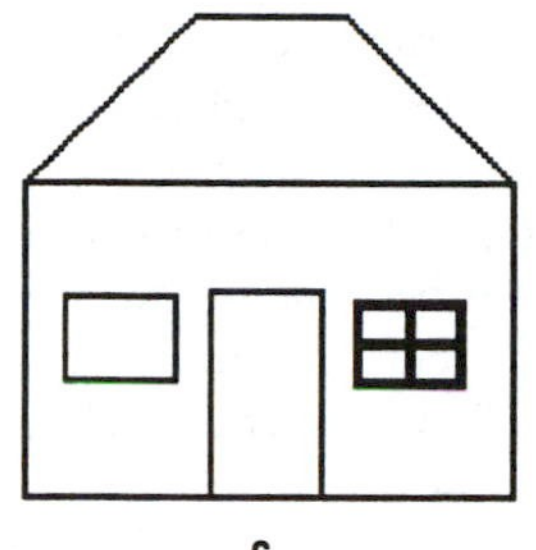

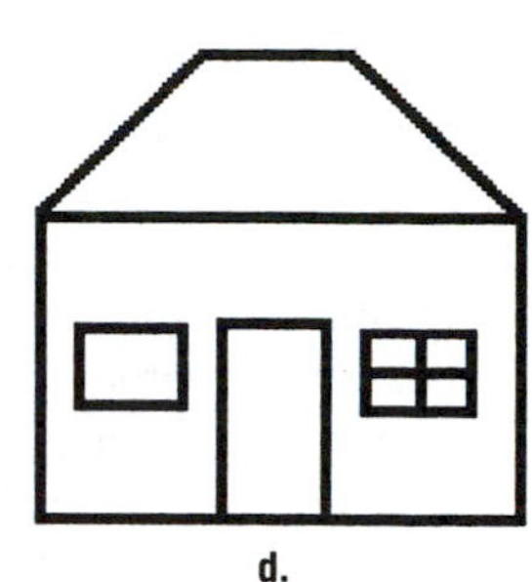


**FIGURE 17.26** Hierarchical selection sequence.

bar will be highlighted because these two bars form the next higher segment, picture b. After the next click the whole of window2 will be highlighted, picture c. If the user wants to move window2, he or she will specify a translation. With one more click, all of house1 will be highlighted, picture d. Now the whole house could be moved. Another click would highlight the whole scene.

**Implementation on Vector Scan CRTs** In refresh vector scan CRTs, the display circuitry must traverse the data structure itself in order to display the picture; the list of graphics primitives is repeatedly scanned and executed. This list of graphics primitives is called the *display file*. It must be a simpler structure than above because the refresh must be done with such a speed that flickering is avoided (at least 30 redrawings of the picture per second). It is usually a one-dimensional array occupying contiguous memory locations. Segmentation is then realized by setting up a segment directory that contains, for each segment, its number, starting location in the array, length, and visibility:

| name | address | length | visib. |
|---|---|---|---|
| 1 | add1 | l1 | 0 |
| 2 | add2 | l2 | 1 |
| 3 | add3 | l3 | 1 |
| . | . | . | . |
| . | . | . | . |

The picture is displayed by going through the directory, starting with the first segment. Each segment is first checked for visibility. If visible, its starting location and length are taken from the table and the corresponding commands in the display file are executed.

With this display file technique, segment transformations cannot be performed in the manner described above for raster scan devices. When a segment is changed, all its entries in the display file would have to be changed according to the transformation. This is one reason why vector scan technology is becoming outdated and little new software is being produced for it. Further, the traversal speed of the data structure can be a bottleneck, which effectively prevents nested segments and hierarchical structures.

The segment directory table can also contain entries for highlighting and for priority, but an entry for a transformation matrix would be useless, as we have observed. The handling of highlighting and the generation of a copy of a segment are straightforward processes, but priority handling will slow down the display. Deleting a segment is done by physically removing its reference from the directory and its graphics primitives from the array. The hole that is left behind should be closed by compacting the array.

You will find information on several other types of display files and segmentation structures in connection with vector scan devices in FOLE84, p. 157, and HEBA86, p. 147.

## 17.3.4 Noninteractive Use of Segmentation

In a noninteractive graphics system, the user writes a program of instructions (commands) to the system for creating graphics. Here, segmentation is not a necessity but it can make certain parts of the programming task easier. On the other hand, writing the program to include segmentation is itself an added burden. Let us examine the value of segmentation when the system is not interactive.

The display hardware on which the user program runs, whether raster scan or vector scan, plays a significant role. This could be hidden from the user but to make the difference clear, we use a small example. The user writes a program body that consists of two calls of graphics primitives to display a straight line (see Figure 17.27):

```
begin
move(a)
draw(b)
end.
```

We will consider the execution of these primitives first for a vector scan display, then for raster scan.

FIGURE 17.27

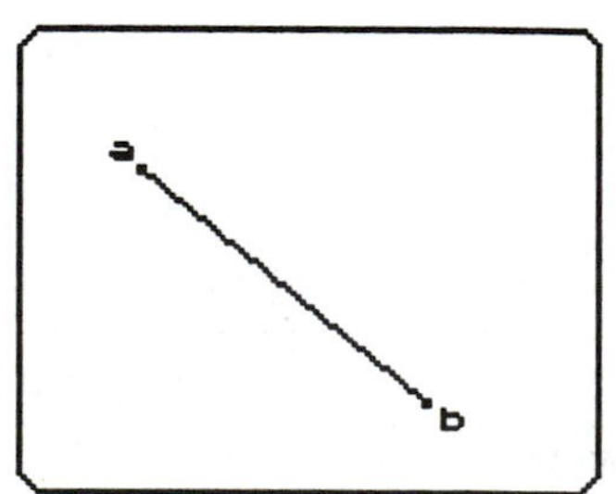

a. Refresh vector scan. A display file that is external to the program is produced. Each routine updates this display file by adding the respective command. The display file will be:

```
start:   move a
         draw b
         goto start
```

The display hardware constantly scans the display file to make the electron beam redraw the picture in rapid succession. Creation of the display file will immediately produce the picture on the vector scan CRT.

b. Refresh raster scan. The move routine updates the current cursor position and the draw routine applies a DDA algorithm that sets those locations in the frame buffer corresponding to the pixels on the straight line from a to b. The display hardware constantly scans the frame buffer, so this line will appear on the screen. This setup is by far the most common.

When the user writes a program to do graphics, it represents a noninteractive, predetermined picture. A given program will always produce the same picture. The graphics programmer can provide for some modest changes, such as for color, size, and position, but a truly different picture can never be created while the program is executing.

Hierarchical segmentation can be included in a user program as shown below. This is a program for producing the scene of Figure 17.23. Each segment is represented by a different procedure with one argument for transformation, m, and one for highlighting, high. If a segment has subsegments, the procedure for this segment must have a local transformation matrix. This matrix will be assigned the transformation to be performed on a subsegment before this subsegment's procedure is called. The procedure call for the subsegment is done with the product of the local matrix and the matrix with which the higher level procedure itself is called; this is the parameter m.

A two-dimensional environment is assumed, so transformation matrices are of size $3 * 3$ (homogeneous). Cartesian coordinates that are parameters of move and draw commands are expressed by a single letter. Matrix multiplications are indicated by multiplication symbols; this is also true for the multiplication of Cartesian coordinates with a matrix. We use pseudocode to set up the transformation matrix. The color used for highlighting is called high.

```
program picture;
type tmat = array[0..2,0..2] of real
            {transformation matrix};
var locmat   : tmat;
```

```
procedure house1(   m       :    tmat;
                   high     :    boolean);
var locmat    :    tmat;

procedure outline(    m      :    tmat;
                     high    :    boolean);
  begin
    if high then color(highlight);
    move(a*m);
    draw(b*m);
    draw(c*m);
    draw(d*m);
    draw(e*m);
    draw(a*m)
  end {procedure outline};

  procedure window1(   m      :    tmat;
                      high    :    boolean);
  begin
    if high then color(highlight);
    {primitives for window1}
  end {procedure window1};

  procedure window2(   m      :    tmat;
                      high    :    boolean);
    var locmat    :    tmat;
    procedure frame(   m      :    tmat;
                      high    :    boolean);
    begin
      if high then color(highlight);
      {primitives for frame}
    end {procedure frame};

    procedure bars(   m      :    tmat;
                     high    :    boolean);
    begin
      if high then color(highlight);
      {primitives for bars}
    end {procedure bars};

  begin {procedure window2}
    locmat := {transformation for frame};
    frame(locmat*m,high);
    locmat := {transformation for bars};
    bars(locmat*m,high);
  end {procedure window2};

  procedure door(   m      :    tmat;
                   high    :    boolean);
```

```
   begin
      if high then color(highlight);
      {primitives for door}
   end {procedure door};

begin {procedure house1}
   locmat := {transformation for outline};
   outline(locmat*m,high);
   locmat := {transformation for window1};
   window1(locmat*m,high);
   locmat := {transformation for window2};
   window2(locmat*m,high);
   locmat := {transformation for door};
   door(locmat*m,high)
end {procedure house1};

procedure house2...
procedure object...

begin {picture}
   locmat := {identity};
   house1(locmat,true);
   locmat := {translation};
   house2(locmat,false)
end {picture}.
```

The main program calls the procedures; in the example, house1 is drawn highlighted, house2 is drawn normal and translated, and the object is not drawn at all. Simple changes in the main program allow the user to change the scene, transform some parts, highlight others, display or not display segments, and so on. When a transformation is set for a segment, it will apply to all subsegments. Transformations are cumulative. Transformations to subsegments must be specified prior to their calls in the respective procedure bodies and will be relative to the including segment. Highlighting a segment affects all its subsegments, but the user can easily override highlighting in the subprocedures.

Certain segment attributes and commands, though useful in an interactive application, are useless here. What they do must now be done by editing the program. The above code shows that a parameter for visibility is superfluous—an invisible segment will just not be called. The same holds for commands to open and close segments. A segment is defined by programming the part of the program that represents it, so adding or deleting a primitive from a segment is done at the program-editing level by adding or deleting calls to routines or to primitives. Also, deleting a segment is not done by a command but by deleting it from the program. Priority among segments is handled by the order in which they are called in the program.

Actually, segmentation in a noninteractive system is nothing but using a modular programming technique. The above can be considered as an exercise in a disciplined, clear programming style. To formulate segments as procedures is only one of many ways to implement the idea. Often segmentation techniques are less sophisticated than the above.

One of these simpler methods is to represent the whole picture in a so-called *pseudodisplay file,* which stores all graphics primitives that make up the picture in a linear order. It is called "pseudo" because it is not external to the program and is not scanned by the display hardware. The pseudodisplay file is automatically created as a side effect by the routines that produce the graphics primitives. Alternatively, the routines for the graphics primitives can create the pseudodisplay file only and not activate such things as DDAs. That is, the graphics primitives are not immediately executed. The actual display of the primitives is done by an additional routine that scans the pseudodisplay file and is called toward the end of the program body (see HARR83). This is done to simulate a setup complying with the Core standard (see Section 17.4.1).

Using this technique, a segment table much like the one in Section 17.3.3 together with the routines open-segment, close-segment, and similar ones, can be implemented. This serves as a simulation of the refresh vector scan display technique. You can find more information in HARR83, p. 122 ff. and HEBA86, p. 143 ff.

# 17.4 STANDARDS FOR GRAPHICS

Every aspect of computers, both software and hardware, can benefit if there are *standards.* When standards exist and are adhered to, users of systems are assured that components work well together and can move more easily from one installation or application to another. Users also have a better way to compare performance and features of competing products. Unfortunately, standards are very hard to agree on and often have a short useful life. Graphics standards are no exception.

One of the basic goals of standardization is to acknowledge time-proven developments while weeding out things of temporary value. Another goal is to unify the diverse efforts of workers in the field and to increase their effectiveness by providing a common language. Usually this results in simplification. The user's interface to graphics systems is especially affected by the presence of standards.

Unfortunately, standardization in computer graphics so far has not been very successful. A major reason is that the field is developing rapidly. It is impossible to standardize something that is not a stable entity; the pace of development of new hardware and software is such as to defy significant efforts for standardization. Still, it is important to examine some of the attempts.

## 17.4.1 The Core System

The Core standard was developed in 1975-1977. At that time, vector scan CRTs and line-drawing devices such as line plotters were the main graphics output devices. Raster graphics did not play a major role and was not expected to become important. Graphics applications were mostly driven by large mainframe computers designed for number crunching. Because of this environment, a three-dimensional concept was incorporated in Core from the very beginning. Drawing wireframe models of objects that could be rotated in space and displayed through different types of projections was the principal focus of the Core routines. Core consequently developed sophisticated 3-D viewing functions. It also defined many interactive input functions.

The increasing importance of raster devices, while not considered in the original concept, was acknowledged later. Some raster graphics capabilities, such as the display of colors and solid filled areas, were added as additional functions, but colors and solid filled areas are only a fraction of the capabilities of raster displays, so even with these added features Core lacks the definition of certain tools necessary to use raster graphics to its full extent.

We will not list and describe all the graphics procedures that Core includes; there are more than 100. We will only give an overview of its main characteristics.

**Segments** Core allows the creation of segments. In Core's view a segment is a group of graphics primitives that can be manipulated together as a unit. It does not expand on this idea to allow the creation of hierarchically nested segments.

Segments can really just be opened and closed. Whatever graphics primitive is defined between the opening and closing becomes a member of this segment. A segment can be transformed interactively by scaling, translation, and rotation, which must be done in this order. Attributes of segments include highlighting, visibility, and transformation.

**Viewing Functions** Core allows the user to define 2-D and 3-D windows and viewports. A unified link to particular display devices is provided by specifying viewports in normalized device coordinates (NDC). Transforming from those to absolute device coordinates is an easy task. Core uses the window-to-viewport transformation or its inverse to transform between user and NDC space. Clipping in 2-D and 3-D is provided.

In doing view plane transformation as described in Chapter 6, Core provides routines for setting the view reference point, the view distance, the view plane normal, and the view-up direction. The system is designed to compute what would be projected onto the film of a camera pointed from the viewing point toward the object. The type of projection (parallel or perspective) used in these computations can be specified.

These concepts have proven to be useful and attractive. The extensions to another standard, GKS, to accommodate 3-D will likely adopt most of these features.

**Input Devices** Core attempts to achieve generality and device independence through the concept of logical input devices. Input devices are classified into six groups. Although all are logical, their choice stems from the hardware environment of the seventies when light pens, thumbwheels, and digitizer boards were very common:

| | |
|---|---|
| locator | inputs an (x,y) position |
| stroke | inputs a sequence of (x,y) positions |
| valuator | inputs a value |
| button | inputs which of several buttons is pressed |
| keyboard | inputs a character |
| pick | identifies a displayed object |

There are many input procedures that utilize these. For example, READ LOCATOR reads the current NDC values from the specified locator, which could be a keyboard-driven cursor on the display.

**Graphics Primitives** There are six graphics primitives in Core. We will give only a brief description. How the parameters are specified in a particular implementation depends on the language binding; we will show the parameters. The arguments are 3-D points. When a primitive is to be displayed, the projection of the point is considered.

- marker(x,y,z) displays the current marker symbol at the specified location.
- polymarker(n,xpts,ypts,zpts) displays the current marker symbol at the n locations specified in the three arrays.
- line(x,y,z) creates a line from the current to the specified position in space and displays it.
- polyline(n,xpts,ypts,zpts) creates n-1 lines connecting in the given order the n points specified in the three arrays and displays them.
- text(string) writes a text string starting at the current position.

- polygon(n,xpts,ypts,zpts) draws a filled polygon whose n vertices are given through the above three arrays. The polygon is automatically closed back to point 1 from point n.

Attributes can be assigned to the primitives: for lines, the color and style; for text, the writing direction (left, right, up, down), the size, spacing, and color of the characters, the font, e.g., Roman, Gothic, Italic; for polygons, the color of the boundary and the interior.

The display mode of a picture can be set to:

| | |
|---|---|
| fast: | draw only the outlines of polygons; this results in a wireframe display |
| fill: | fill the polygons but do not perform hidden surface removal |
| hidden-line: | remove hidden lines from the wireframe representation |
| hidden-surface: | remove hidden surfaces |

**Metafiles** Core provides for a device-independent display-record format for archiving images as files. The files that contain such information are called *metafiles.* They serve as storage for graphics images. They also serve to allow transfer between sites, as image descriptions for intelligent terminals that can display them on their own, as a source for making hard-copy images, or as the basis for an eventual graphics interface standard.

A graphics system based on the Core standard is not well adapted to deal effectively with modern raster graphics. Core's main strength is in the area of high-performance mainframe-driven 3-D vector graphics such as those in some CAD/CAM installations. With the disappearance of these, Core is also disappearing. Some of the good features of Core have been included in newer standards and may survive, such as the synthetic camera model (the view plane transformation).

### 17.4.2 The Graphical Kernel System (GKS)

This effort to develop a standard was started roughly at the same time as Core. Hence, like Core, it is characterized by an underrepresentation of raster graphics features. This is reflected by the fact that raster graphics was only patched into GKS and consequently references to it are sparse in the GKS description (see HDGS83). Although GKS pays more attention to raster graphics than Core, it still does not allow full use of its capabilities.

GKS specifies a set of graphics procedures—more than 100—that permit the description of virtually any pictorial information in a unique manner. Almost 50 percent of the names of procedures start with SET, which makes them hard to remember. These procedures were designed to be called from within a system that allows a user to create graphics interactively. Of course the routines can also be used in a noninteractive user program. GKS also provides some routines that deal with the archiving of pictures on external files.

**Logical Workstations** GKS introduced the concept of the logical workstation. Graphical input and output devices have their own capabilities which can be very different from one another. GKS tries to treat them all similarly. Workstations are classified into nine different types; a graphical input and output device will always fit into one of these categories. Every device of the same type can then be handled in the same way. This requires the particular installation to add individual device drivers that interpret the GKS commands.

For example, the type of a line might be interpreted on a plotter as a certain pen, on a color CRT as a certain color, and on a vector scan CRT as white or as a certan dot-dash line pattern. This is determined by the individual device driver, but GKS can always generate the same command.

GKS can also assign attributes to an individual workstation, for example, a particular viewport setting. An image sent to that workstation will be displayed there at a different location than when sent to another workstation. GKS provides many routines to exploit this idea in terms of windows, viewports, line types, fill types for polygons, and so forth.

**Language Binding** GKS itself is defined independently of a specific programming language, but any GKS-conforming implementation of a graphics system must be written in some programming language. For example, it might be convenient for a given procedure to return a parameter as boolean. If the language in which the system is implemented does not have the type boolean, the required information must be returned differently, perhaps as 0 for false and 1 for true. For another example, decisions must be made as to how a procedure should convey the four possible directions of text alignment: up, down, left, right. What numbers are to be associated with which direction?

Because it would be beneficial for all implementers to follow the conventions, the GKS description contains *language binding*, which sets these guidelines for FORTRAN. Recently de facto language bindings have been developed by software producers for the C language.

**Graphics Primitives** GKS has reduced the six primitives of Core to four main primitives that can do the equivalent things:

1. polyline(n,xpts,ypts)
2. polymarker(n,xpts,ypts)
3. fill area(n,xpts.ypts)
4. text(x,y,string)

In addition, two other primitives have been added that apply to raster devices and other hardware advances. These are:

5. cell array(xl,yl,xh,yh,n,m,ca)
6. generalized drawing primitive(n,px,py,id,il,ia)

Associated with each primitive is a set of parameters (in parentheses), which define particular instances of the primitive. In the first three primitives, xpts and ypts are arrays giving the n points (xpts[1],ypts[1]) to (xpts[n],ypts[n]). Observe that these are two-dimensional Cartesian coordinates, as opposed to the Core primitives, which are three-dimensional.

Polyline draws n − 1 line segments joining adjacent points starting with the first and ending with the last. The type or color of the line can be set by calling another procedure before calling polyline.

Polymarker draws a marker at each of the n point positions. The type of the marker is given by a separate call. Line segments between the markers are not drawn.

Fill area draws a filled polygon whose vertices are given by n points. The polygon is automatically closed back to point 1 from point n. The fill pattern for the interior is set by a separate call.

The text primitive accepts a string of arbitrary length and the start position (x,y) of the string as arguments. This string is written as text into the picture. Many different attributes of the text, like writing direction or size of the characters, can be specified by a separate call.

The cell array primitive accepts two points in world coordinates (xl,yl) and (xh,yh) that specify the lower left and top right corners of a rectangular area into which the bit map, ca, of size n ∗ m is to be mapped. Consult HDGS83 for a precise description.

The generalized drawing primitive (GDP) is the mechanism that GKS provides to make use of the hardware capabilities of certain special workstations. These include drawing circles, ellipses, and even spline curves. The id parameter specifies the type of GDP to be performed. It is used by the individual device driver that invokes one of the built-in general primitives. px and py are arrays of points to specify a set of screen positions that can be used by the GDP. Here again see HDGS83 for further reference.

**Logical Input Devices** GKS has essentially the same logical devices as the Core system; some names are changed. Keyboard is now string, as strings are always input by a keyboard, and button is now choice as it basically chooses one of several buttons.

| | |
|---|---|
| locator | inputs an (x,y) position |
| pick | identifies a displayed object |
| choice | selects from a set of alternatives |
| valuator | inputs a value |
| string | inputs a string of characters |
| stroke | inputs a sequence of (x,y) positions |

We give examples for some physical devices typical of the late '70s that realize the above logical devices. Often one logical device can be simulated by another as one physical device can simulate another. The examples below are not the only possibilities.

- The locator can be realized by a stylus on a tablet, by a keyboard-driven cursor, or by a thumbwheel-driven cursor.
- The pick can be realized on a vector scan CRT by a light pen and on a raster CRT by a light pen (with less reliability), but better by a screen cursor driven by a stylus or the keyboard.
- The choice can be realized by checking the status of several buttons.
- The valuator can be realized by thumbwheels.
- The string can be realized by a keyboard.
- The stroke can be most effectively realized by a stylus on a tablet.

GKS purposely does not specify the relation between a physical device and the logical device. Any physical device that can input an (x,y) position can be a locator. The language binding and the drivers of the specific implementation take care of associating the physical device with the logical device.

There are new physical devices now. The mouse did not exist when Core or GKS were defined, but it falls readily into either locator or stroke and, as we will see, can be used for pick and choice. The digitizer board is still a valuable input device. Three of the device classes would suffice today: locator, string, and stroke. Light pens are disappearing—they don't work very well with raster displays. Thumbwheels were frequently used as locators or valuators but they are harder to operate than a mouse or stylus and can be so easily simulated by these that there is now little justification for them. The classes pick and choice are similarly handled.

In the spirit of GKS, it is the type of application (not just the hardware) of an input device that puts it into one of the six classes. But as choosing, picking, and valuating can all be done with a locator, why not have only a locator and achieve greater simplification? The system software can achieve the same goals with only the one.

**Modes of Interaction** All logical devices can be used via three modes: REQUEST, SAMPLE, and EVENT.

In REQUEST mode a device is read only upon some action by the user. Assume that a stylus is used as a locator on a particular workstation. When the graphics system software executes the procedure REQUEST LOCATOR(WS,DV,NT,X,Y), it will go into a wait state until the user has pressed the stylus button. Only then is the position of the stylus read and conveyed to the parameters X and Y of the procedure call. WS specifies the workstation at which the request is to be executed. (We do not discuss the other parameters.) The software can now use the values obtained by the call, for example, to draw a line to the point (X,Y).

Another example: REQUEST PICK(WS,DV,ST,SEG,PICKID), which determines that a graphic element is being selected. When this is executed, the program will again wait for user action and then read the device. On a raster scan workstation this might be the position of a stylus even though there is no position parameter in the call. (On a vector scan workstation the internal action will be totally different, but this is transparent to the user.) After obtaining the position, the system checks all vectors in the picture to find the one that is closest to that position (see Figure 17.28 below). SEG will be assigned the number of the segment to which this vector belongs. If this vector has a pick identifier associated with it, PICKID will be assigned this value. This provides for an even closer identification within the segment. The actions of the other combinations of REQUEST are similar.

In SAMPLE mode a device is read immediately without waiting for a trigger. A typical example is to put SAMPLE LOCATOR (WS,DV,NT,X,Y) in an infinite loop. For variety, assume that the locator is a mouse. Every time the procedure is executed the current position of the mouse is put into variables X and Y and the software goes on. The example below shows a while loop in Pascal that draws a rubber-band line in XOR mode on the screen to wherever the cursor is until the mouse button is released. The loop is terminated by the boolean function mouse_button_release, which is achieved through an EVENT, explained below.

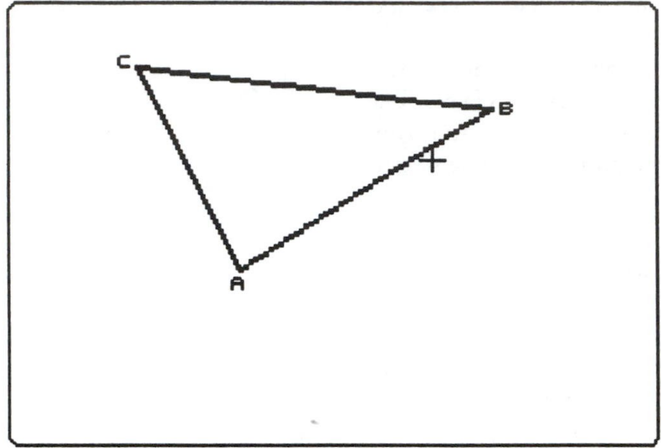


FIGURE 17.28

```
while not mouse_button_release do begin
  drawxor(x1,y1);
  sample_locator(ws,dv,nt,x,y);
  drawxor(x,y);
  x1 := x; y1 := y
end;
```

The third type is the EVENT mode. If a device is in this mode, any inputs from it are put in a queue. There is only one queue for all classes. The procedure AWAIT EVENT(TIMEOUT,WS,CLASS,DV) checks the queue. If it is not empty, it removes the first event from the queue and returns information concerning it to the current event report. It also sets the parameter CLASS to the device type that produced this input. If the queue is empty, the program waits at most TIMEOUT seconds and then goes on; CLASS is assigned NONE. It is critical that the program not be suspended indefinitely as in REQUEST mode when no input comes.

After EVENT, subsequent statements in the program check the parameter CLASS to find which input device produced the event. If it is the desired one, the information is obtained by GET LOCATOR(...), for example. If it is from another device it is either ignored or some other action is performed. The user can really have several input devices under control at the same time, provided the graphics system uses these procedures in a proper manner. As an example, consider the implementation of the function mouse_button_release which we have used above. The mouse button can be considered as of type choice. In this application it is not the same as the movement mechanism, which is of type locator. We assume that on the particular workstation the routines that start rubber-band line drawing put the mouse button into EVENT mode and make sure that no other device of this class is in EVENT mode. Then all that must be checked after an event is whether the class is choice or not. We set the timeout to 0 so that no waiting takes place. As long as the class is none or different from choice the function returns the value false.

```
function mouse_button_release : boolean;
var class      :      integer;
begin
   await_event(0,ws,class,dv);
   if class = choice
   then mouse_button_release := true
   else mouse_button_release := false
end;
```

Figure 17.28 shows three lines in a raster display and a mouse-driven cross-hair cursor, a locator. The software always knows where the cursor is and can easily determine the distance of the cursor from each of the three lines. As it is close enough to line AB, the locator will pick this line. Formerly, on vector scan displays, such picks were done by light pens.

Figure 17.29 shows the mouse-driven cursor (locator) on the word "yellow," choosing from a menu. On the left side of the screen we see a bar representing numbers between 0 and 100 that could indicate the intensity of the chosen color. By touching this with the cursor, we can prompt the display of the corresponding number on the screen. The

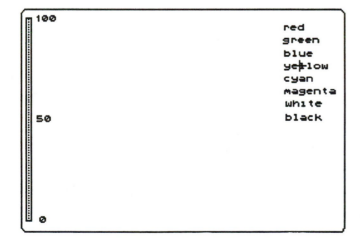


**FIGURE 17.29**

number changes with the movement of the cursor and the user clicks the button when the desired number is indicated.

In choosing a word from the menu, the mouse-locator acts as a pick or as a choice. Such choices were formerly done with light pens from the screen or by pressing certain buttons. When used on the number bar, the mouse-locator acts as a valuator, for which thumbwheels were formerly used. The class choice could still be used for various button inputs but valuator and pick could all fall into one with locator. As far as input devices go, the classification is somewhat outdated.

Output devices are not classified in GKS. Vector scan CRTs play too big a role within GKS considering the fact that they are disappearing, being supplanted by raster scan displays. In hard-copy output, the line plotter acts as a vector device. Large line plotters will certainly be around for quite a while but small ones are being supplanted by raster printers—dot matrix, ink jet, and laser printers. These are not dealt with sufficiently by GKS.

**Segmentation in GKS** Graphics primitives can be grouped together in segments. Software can be designed so that the segments can be opened, defined, and closed interactively, using only GKS routines. Such segments can be handled as explained in Section 17.3. They can be given attributes and can be assigned to particular workstations so that certain attributes are in effect only at those workstations. But segments cannot be nested and they cannot be edited. Once a segment is closed a change to it can be made only by deleting and recreating it.

**Metafiles** GKS provides for saving drawings that have been interactively created on external files, as explained before. These files are also called metafiles in the GKS description. The concept and the ideas are similar to those presented in the metafile description of Core. For further reference see EKPF84.

Much firmware and hardware has been created according to the concepts of Core and GKS. A whole generation of Tektronix terminals, including high-quality raster displays, has been designed to be driven by a mainframe, responding to commands to create, transform, and close segments, to select or deselect views and surfaces, to change color lookup tables, and so on. These terminals usually have high resolution, noninterlaced display, built-in 2-D transformation firmware, and lookup table management to produce excellent single bit plane displays, as well as many more features. Still, they have only a limited range of colors and do not contain features that make use of gradual color changes; the standards didn't consider these.

One shortcoming of GKS is that it is conceptually only two-dimensional, though an extension to 3-D is underway that will likely include most of Core's 3-D viewing functions. Another shortcoming is that it does not allow a hierarchy of segments. This is a consequence of the hardware situation at the time of its development. A display file that has to be scanned continuously in real time allows only a limited complexity to avoid flicker on a vector scan display. A further shortcoming is that the original concept, like that of Core, does not include a means for evoking the full capabilities of raster displays. Bit maps can be described through the cell array, but aside from describing a bit map, nothing is provided that permits the processing possible for raster graphics like smoothly shaded solid objects or surfaces with patterns and texture.

## 17.4.3 Programmer's Hierarchical Interactive Graphics System (PHIGS)

The PHIGS standard is a more modern approach that has been developed under the regulations of the American National Standards Institute. It tries to overcome the shortcomings of older device-independent graphics systems—poor utilization of advanced hardware and inefficient data structures. Many of the Core and GKS concepts are repeated in PHIGS. PHIGS has the same graphics primitives and logical devices as GKS. It works with the same three modes of interaction: REQUEST, SAMPLE, and EVENT. It also has the concept of logical workstations. These are concepts that have proven useful, even though device classification is somewhat outdated.

The main ways that PHIGS differs from GKS are its three-dimensional graphics primitives and its more sophisticated data structures. The polyline, for example, can be specified with number triples as well as with number pairs, which enables the description of spatial objects. Language bindings for PHIGS are specified in FORTRAN, C, and Ada.

We will focus on the data structures of PHIGS, which are called structures. PHIGS structures are essentially the same as the nested segments explained in Section 17.3.3 but go beyond them. In Section 17.3.3, the nested segments were treelike graphs; PHIGS allows the creation of segments that are not treelike. A structure contains *structure elements* which can be graphics primitives, attributes, a view selection, a transformation matrix, or a pointer to another structure—these last are called *execute elements.* When a structure has such pointers it is called a *structure network.* Structures are fully editable. Elements may be inserted interactively or deleted from structures. This is one of the main differences from GKS.

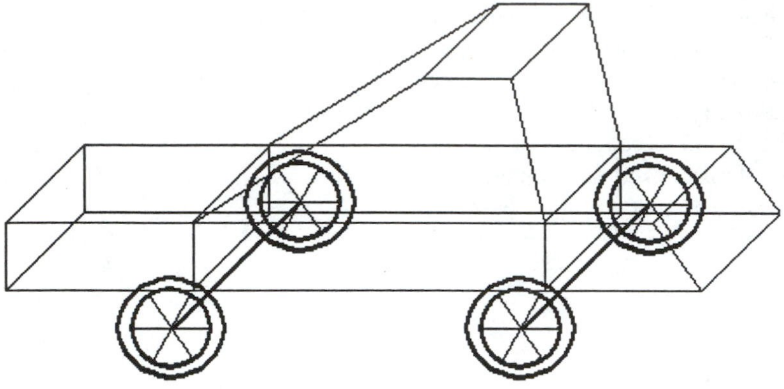

**FIGURE 17.30**

The example below explains the structure concept; it is taken (with some simplifications) from the excellent article ABBU86. This article describes a PHIGS implementation in Pascal. The car in Figure 17.30 is a three-dimensional object. It consists of a frame and four wheels. Both are substructures of the main structure CAR pointed to by execute elements.

In Figure 17.31 we see the corresponding structure network. CAR consists of FRAME and WHEELS. FRAME consists of the chassis drawn in normal color and the two axles that are drawn in black. Instead of black we could certainly have another color when displaying on a color device. The structure WHEEL is defined only once but is referenced four times, therefore the structure network is not a tree. It appears at four different positions during display because the four execute elements are preceded by translation matrices that are accumulated during the structure traversal.

WHEEL refers to CIRCLE two times. Between the first and second of the calls to CIRCLE there is a scaling transformation that makes the second circle smaller than the first. We can also see that attributes like color, when encountered during traversal, stay in force until changed again.

An object defined in a structure is displayed by traversing the structure in a manner demonstrated by the code in Section 17.3.3. The traversing code needs a global transformation matrix, like GLOBMAT, into which all matrices encountered during traversal are accumulated as well as a local one, like LOCMAT. Whenever a graphics primitive is encountered, it is transformed with GLOBMAT and displayed. When an execute element is encountered, the current value of GLOBMAT is saved in LOCMAT and then the execute element is traversed by a recursive call to the display procedure. Upon returning from the child structure, GLOBMAT is reset to its value at the time of the call, using

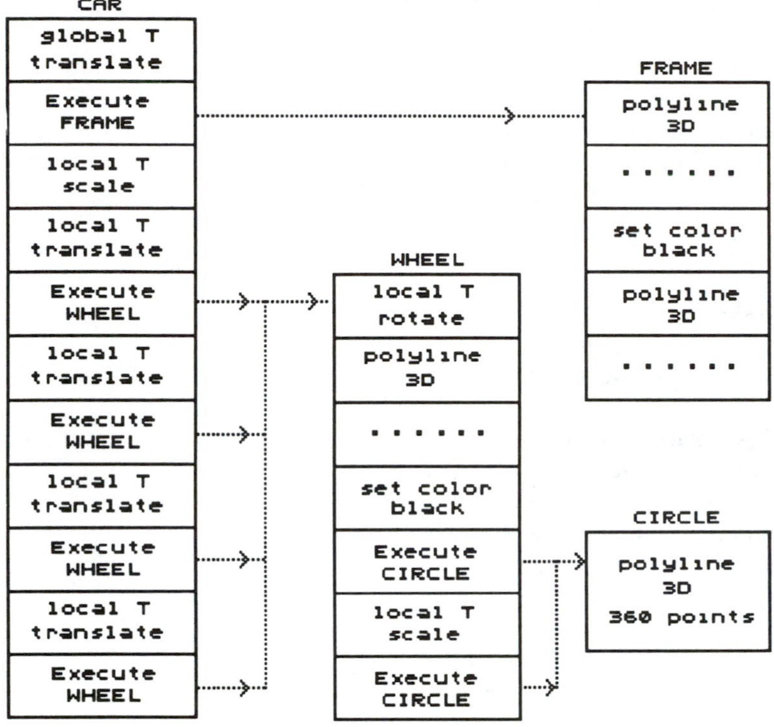


**FIGURE 17.31**

the values in LOCMAT. This reflects the principle that the transformations encountered in traversing a child structure are not accumulated into the transformations of the higher structure.

A redisplay of the object and consequently a traversal of the structure is necessary every time the object is edited. Editing could include changing a transformation matrix. A real time rotation of an object is achieved by changing its transformation matrix gradually through an interactive editing operation. We should not have to go into more detail on how the data structures are programmed, how interactive editing is done, and so on because the basic characteristics of PHIGS are apparent from the above example. Its main strength is the flexible and powerful data structure which can precisely reflect the hierarchy of elements in a picture.

The most crucial difference from GKS is that the currently developed PHIGS extension, PHIGS+, is approaching the problem of full raster graphics utilization. These extensions to PHIGS allow us to define parametric curves and parametric curved surfaces. The realization is through B-splines and other cubic curves and patches. Through these it is possible to render smooth shapes like airplane wings, car bodies, and many smooth mechanical parts. The rendering uses the techniques of Gouraud and Phong shading. It includes shading, lighting, depth cuing, and direct color specifications. All these features depend on the capabilities of the display to produce fine, gradual color changes.

There are of course graphics systems in place that can do all this. But the point here is that a standardization effort incorporating all aspects of such rather complicated software is now being manifested. PHIGS+ could become the universal graphics standard.

### 17.4.4 Other Standards

We now mention some other standards whose fuller description would go beyond the scope of the book.

IGES (Initial Graphics Exchange Specification) is a graphic-image storage and transfer standard of specific interest to users of CAD/CAM systems. Its main objective is to allow a complete description of annotated drawings and engineering information on parts and assemblies. It differs considerably from Core and GKS in that it includes about 50 more graphics primitives such as conic arcs, surfaces of revolution, several types of finite elements, B-spline curves, and B-spline surfaces.

VDM (Virtual Device Metafile) is a proposed graphical-image storage and transfer standard that is designed for maximum compatibility with both Core and GKS.

VDI (Virtual Device Interface) is intended as a companion document for the VDM standard.

NAPLPS (North American Presentation Level Protocol Syntax) is a graphics device interface standard with a special focus on videotex and teletext terminals.

## 17.5 Use and Techniques of Printers

Printers, especially raster printers, constitute the most important user interface in terms of hard-copy output in computer graphics. To stress the essential technological characteristics of raster printers we will first have a brief look at nonraster printers, also called *formed character printers*. Many basic construction principles are still the same. These printers are not particularly useful in computer graphics. But even outside computer graphics they are gradually being supplanted by raster printers as the increasing quality of the raster printers allows high-quality printout. Formed character printers are slowly disappearing.

## 17.5.1 Formed Character Printers

Daisy wheel printers work on the same principle as a typewriter. Typewriters have a hard rubber platen over which the paper rolls. A character is printed on the paper by having a metal type strike against an inked ribbon, forcing the transfer of ink to the paper, leaving the shape of the type on the paper in quite good quality. We can drive the mechanics of a typewriter with a motor and control the stream of letters to be typed with a computer—then we have a letter font printer.

A daisy wheel printer is so called because the type characters are arranged at the ends of radials of a very lightweight plastic wheel that looks like a daisy flower. The wheel is rotated to bring the desired letter into printing position and then is knocked onto the ribbon and paper by a little hammer. The types can be arranged in different ways: on a rotating chain, on a golf ball-size print head, or on variations of the daisy arrangement.

Formed character printers produce good-looking letters but a disadvantage is that they need a separate type for every possible character. This becomes an insurmountable task when printout in a complicated writing system is required, such as Chinese or Japanese. Nor can good graphics be produced with such a printer.

**FIGURE 17.32** First strike.

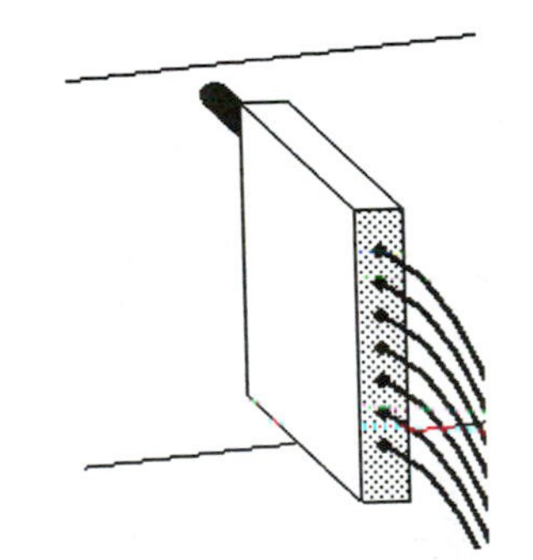

## 17.5.2 Dot Matrix Printers

This type of printer also has a platen but has only a single print head consisting of a vertical column of pins. By striking a pin against the ribbon onto the paper, a single dot is produced. Letters are formed as dot matrices defined in a character generator. While the head moves across the paper the pins strike at just the right times to form every possible dot matrix. Figures 17.32 through 17.36 show how a print head with seven pins produces a T. In text mode, the computer sends ASCII codes to the printer, which has its own character generators. The character generators consist of a ROM area in which the bit matrices for several different fonts of characters are stored. Many of the newer dot matrix printers also have a RAM area in which the user can store other bit maps and can direct the printer to use these instead of the ROM area. When in text mode, the printer advances the paper to the next line after one line is completed.

**FIGURE 17.33** Second strike.

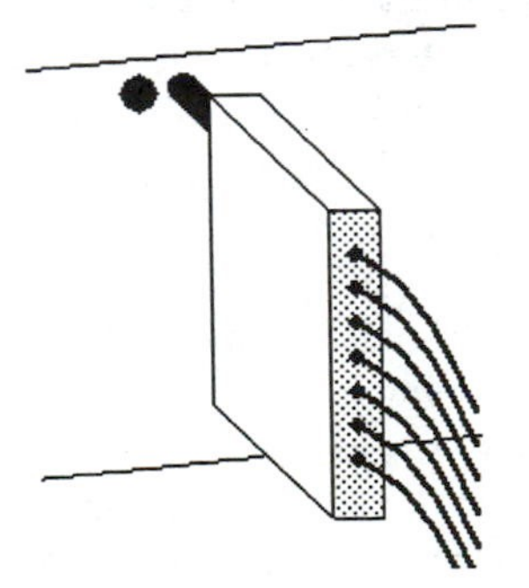

Practically all the newer dot matrix printers can be switched to graphics mode. In this mode the basic operation of the printer is much different. The codes sent to it from the computer are not interpreted as ASCII codes but directly as bit patterns. A common technique is to set the transmission protocol so that the computer sends and the printer receives eight-bit bytes.

A second difference in graphics mode is that the bit pattern is not used to address the character generator but to directly set the configuration of the pins for a particular strike. The printers usually have more than seven pins; less expensive ones have eight or nine. In the latter case only the upper eight pins would be used in graphics mode. Each byte accounts for one column of dots. The printer stores all the bytes for one line in a buffer before it prints so that it can sweep across the page at a fixed speed.

The third difference is that the printer automatically sets the paper advance so that the uppermost dot in one line is adjacent to the lowest dot in the previous line. The printer can thus cover the whole paper area with a raster of dots.

The ratio of the horizontal to vertical distance between raster dots is not necessarily 1:1. There are wide differences between competing products. Many printers can be set to have larger or smaller horizontal dot spacing by changing the number of horizontal microsteps between two consecutive pin pulses. The vertical distance between pins cannot be changed. Some printers can be set to advance the paper by only half a vertical dot distance, which gives a very dense raster that helps in the production of graphics.

Essentially any rasterized picture can be produced on these printers. The computer just has to slice the picture into eight-bit long columns and send the resulting bit patterns row by row. The usual application for a dot matrix output is to dump the contents of a frame buffer onto the paper. If the frame buffer stores just a black-and-white picture with 1 bit per pixel, we have a 1:1 relationship between pixels and dots. All a screen dump program has to do is to read the bits out of the frame buffer in the proper order and send these 8-bit patterns to the printer. The printers usually have a resolution of about 600 dots across the width of the paper, which can often be increased through several resolution steps to 1200. An average-size frame buffer can easily be dumped to the dot matrix printer as long as it is strictly black and white without gray levels.

The task of dumping a picture becomes more demanding if the frame buffer stores it with gray levels. A dot matrix printer is a bilevel display; it can only strike or not strike a pin. It has little capacity to produce dots of different gray levels. When the picture is stored as gray levels, representing one pixel by one dot on the printer can still be

**FIGURE 17.34** Third strike.

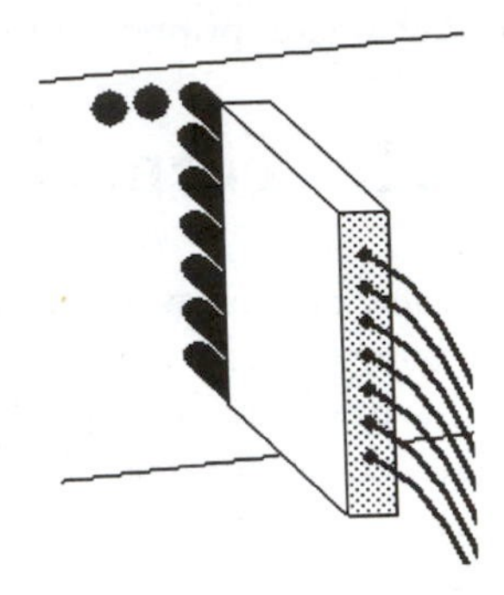

**FIGURE 17.35** Fourth strike.

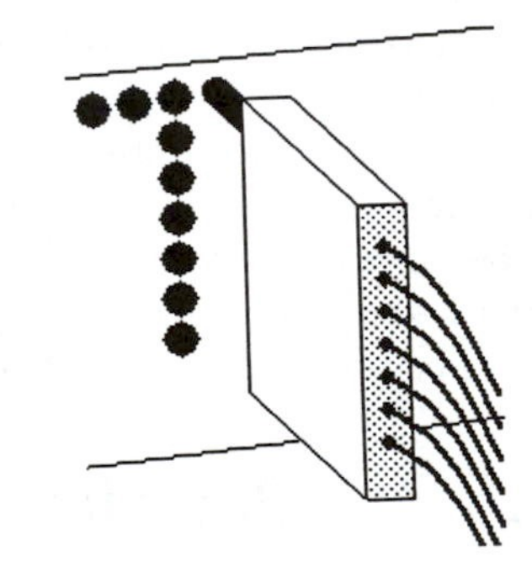

**FIGURE 17.36** Fifth strike.

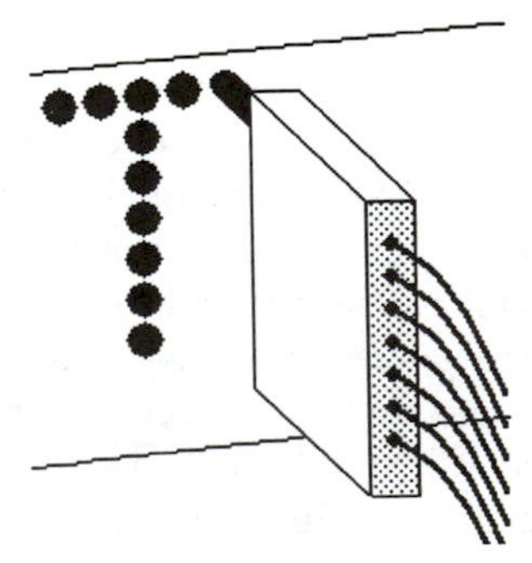

done by setting a threshold number below which a pixel is considered as black and otherwise as white. There are many strategies for determining such thresholds, all belonging in the area of image processing. In any case, such strategies lead to a loss of information through the loss of gray levels.

Suppose we want to represent a continuous tone, also called *halftone image,* on a bilevel display. We will illustrate this and indicate a way to solve it through an example. We assume that the picture is stored with four bits per pixel, resulting in 16 grey levels, the frame buffer size is 320 × 200. The printer can produce 640 dots across the paper with a raster ratio of approximately 1:1. One technique to produce a halftone printout is called *dithering.* In our example we represent each pixel by a matrix of 2 × 2 dots on the printer, called a *dither matrix.* Five dither matrices are used, shown in Figure 17.37.

This leads to a variable density for the population of dots on the paper, resulting in apparent gray levels through the merging effects of our perception. The picture requires twice as many dots in both directions. It becomes twice as large, but will still fit on the paper as the printer can produce 640 dots horizontally. Only five gray levels are preserved with these dither matrices. We have to print several different gray levels on the display with the same dither matrix. For example, we could apply this grouping:

| | |
|---|---|
| grey level 0 – 3 | matrix 4 |
| grey level 4 – 7 | matrix 3 |
| grey level 8 – 10 | matrix 2 |
| grey level 11 – 13 | matrix 1 |
| grey level 14 – 15 | matrix 0 |

Lowest gray levels correspond to black and highest to white on the display. The sizes of the groups of gray levels should not be equal. Experimenting is needed; you may find that the difference in apparent grayness on paper is large between matrices 3 and 4 but small between matrices 0 and 1. To make the difference correspond to the appearance on the screen takes trial and error. It is not possible to predict what grouping will be best.

To preserve all 16 gray levels we have to use 4 * 4 dither matrices that actually allow for 17 grey levels. Figure 17.38 shows the first five of these.

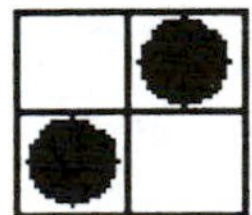

**FIGURE 17.37**

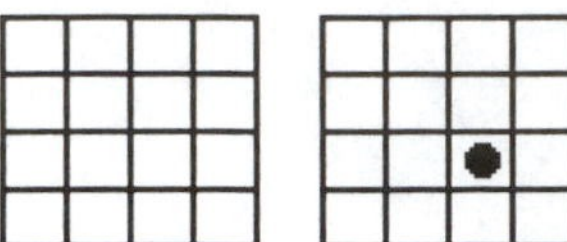 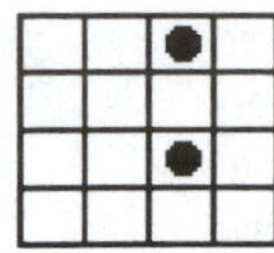 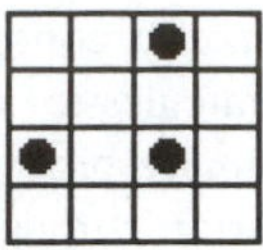 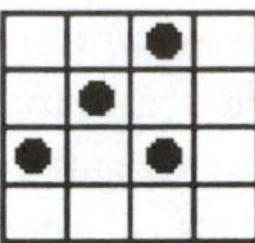

FIGURE 17.38

The others are obtained by executing the generating pattern:

$$\begin{bmatrix} 16 & 8 & 2 & 10 \\ 12 & 4 & 14 & 6 \\ 3 & 11 & 1 & 9 \\ 15 & 7 & 13 & 5 \end{bmatrix}$$

The numbers indicate the positions in which new dots are added to the matrix, so the matrix 3 has dots on positions 1, 2, and 3. As we have one matrix too many we will not use one of them, for example, matrix 15. Now the picture will require 1280 points horizontally. It probably will not fit onto the paper unless the printer can be set to produce 1280 points in one row. If the vertical paper feed can be set to 1/2 dot distance, as mentioned above, we again have a square dot ratio and can fit the image on the paper.

The individual dither matrices contain the dots in a very unordered and nonsymmetric layout. This is on purpose. The dot layout must be designed so that in areas of identical intensity no conspicuous patterns appear on the printout. If the four-dot dither matrix were designed as shown in Figure 17.39, an area of this intensity would show horizontal lines.

FIGURE 17.39

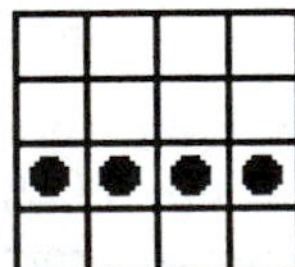

Printing each pixel as a dither matrix will soon lead to a problem. Assume that the frame buffer is of the size 640 × 400 with a depth of four and we want to preserve all 16 gray levels. We would need to print 2560 dots across the page. Printers can't do this. However, there is a solution. The basic idea is that we do not print each pixel but each array of 2 × 2 pixels as a 4 × 4 dither matrix. Internally we compute the average gray level of the four pixels of a 2 × 2 array by adding all gray levels and dividing by 4. This will give us a real number between 0 and 15. After rounding to the nearest integer we have the average gray level of this 2 × 2 pixel array. This array is now printed by the corresponding dither matrix (see Figure 17.40).

FIGURE 17.40

15 13
11 12
12.75

4

Printing with 16 gray levels gives reasonably smooth-looking output. If the original picture in the frame buffer has even more gray levels, we can preserve them in the printing by using larger dither matrices. A 6 × 6 matrix allow 37 different levels and can be used if 32 gray levels are stored in the frame buffer. Of course, we are trading resolution for gray levels. Up to a certain extent more gray levels make the output look better to the human eye even with decreased resolution. The human visual system can derive much information from changing intensity levels and can easily reconstruct outlines and shapes that are somewhat blurred, so this tradeoff gives an increase in printout quality. This ends when the dither matrices become so big that they are individually recognizable as squares. Matrices of 8 × 8 are usually too large. For more about dither matrices see FOLE84.

### 17.5.3 Ink Jet Printers

Ink jet technology uses an ink jet head that has a number of vertically or otherwise arranged nozzles. This head sweeps across the paper much like the dot matrix print head, but instead of striking pins against a ribbon onto the paper, little ink droplets are shot out from the nozzles against the paper. Each nozzle is connected by a tiny channel to a separate ink chamber, which is surrounded by piezocrystals. Those give a little jerk when an electric impulse of about 80 volts is applied. This pulsing shoots out the ink drop.

Another technique, developed recently by Hewlett-Packard, is free of any mechanically moving parts. Each ink channel is surrounded close to its nozzle by a material with high electric resistance. When a very short but extremely high pulse of current is applied to this area, the heat causes the ink to boil into a gas bubble. The sudden pressure is sufficient to push out one droplet through the nozzle. The bubble disappears within a fraction of a millisecond and capillary forces form another meniscus of ink on the nozzle surface, thereby pulling more ink toward the nozzle. These ink jet heads have the nozzles arranged in a circle around the main ink feeder channel.

No ribbon is necessary in ink jet printers and the speed is about the same as for a dot matrix printer. Letters, numbers, and other shapes are again formed in a raster of dots.

One of the important advantages of these printers is their quietness compared to the noisy dot matrix printers—a very valuable quality in offices. Another advantage is that there is practically no wear on the head. Still, the technological trend seems to go in the direction of throwaway jet heads once the ink supply is exhausted. High-quality heads have more than 30 nozzles over a vertical distance of 3 to 4 mm and can produce printout that is indistinguishable by eye from formed characters.

There are problems with this technology which are gradually being overcome. A very notorious one was the sensitivity of the jet heads. The nozzles easily became clogged when the printer was not in use. Replacing the main ink feeder tank could be a messy job. Another disadvantage is that most types still require special paper.

Another promising new development is thermo jet technology. It works with a special ink called plastic or solid ink. This is not ink in the common sense but a material that is liquid only at a certain high temperature and solid at room temperature. During operation, the material in the ink jet heads and reservoirs is heated to this high point and droplets can be ejected toward the paper where they immediately solidify. This solves the most notorious problem of ink jet printers, namely ink drying in the nozzles, thereby clogging them.

Ink jet technology is still a strong competitor to other raster printer technologies even if the quality of the latter is increasing, because it offers certain advantages. For example, there is a certain minimum size of the dots produced by the impacting pins in a dot matrix printer, as a pin can not be made arbitrarily thin, but the dots formed from individual ink drops can be much smaller. The mechanical parts of both dot matrix and ink jet printers, like paper transport, rubber platen, and so on are certainly much simpler than those of laser printers.

## 17.5.4 Laser Printers

These printers are becoming more and more popular as the technology advances and their prices come down. We only sketch the technical background and in simplified terms.

Inside the printer is a cylindrical drum whose width is about the width of the paper. This drum is coated with a photoelectric substance, a material that develops a positive or negative charge when hit by light. A laser beam is directed at the drum. Wherever this beam hits the drum it will charge it with electrons, thus drawing an electrostatic latent image on the drum.

After this image is drawn, the drum passes over a reservoir of black powder which is attracted by the electrostatic charge. This so-called toner sticks to the drum surface only where the surface is charged. The drum now carries the picture in the form of black particles. The paper is charged with a very high potential and brought into contact with the drum, causing the powder to jump onto the paper. The powder is then fused to the paper by feeding it over heated rollers. This part of the process is identical to that in a copying machine.

The basic difference between a copying machine and a laser printer is the way the electrostatic latent image is formed on the drum. A laser

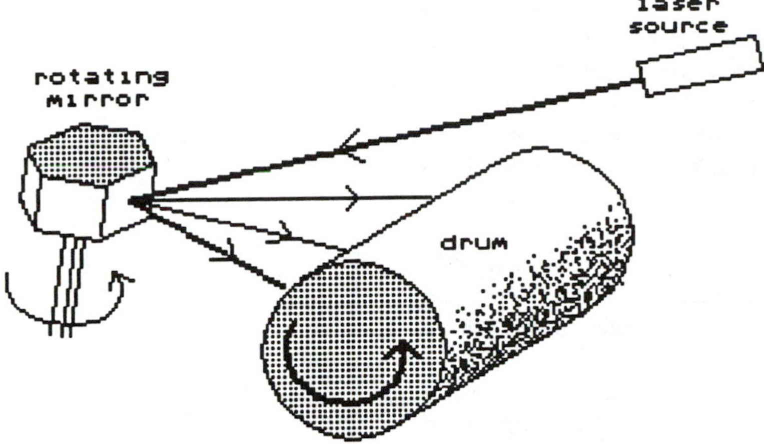


FIGURE 17.41

source emits a laser beam in a fixed direction but with varying intensity. This beam is deflected by a rotating mirror (see Figure 17.41). The mirror usually has eight or 16 facets; in the drawing it is simplified.

The rotating mirror sweeps the beam across the width of the drum in horizontal scan lines. At the same time the drum slowly rotates in small steps so that the scan lines are parallel across its entire surface. Thus the beam can draw a rasterized picture by being turned on and off at the proper moments. The beam movement is independent of the picture and is always the same.

Laser printers usually have their own processor and memory. The cheaper ones usually print with a resolution of 300 dots per inch. They have internal character generators in ROM which they scan in much the same way as a CRT controller scans the character generator in text mode to put the characters onto the screen. In such a mode the printer can be driven by receiving only ASCII codes from the computer and the printing speed can be several pages per minute. If they have little intelligence and memory, the output of graphics can be very time consuming. The computer must drive them the same way it drives a dot matrix printer, that is, by sending the whole picture as a bit map. With such a high resolution, this requires a lot of data and creating a printout in this way can easily take hours.

The more advanced printers have an internal memory of one to two megabytes in which they can store the image for an 8 × 11-inch page. They also have internal software that enables them to use different character fonts, load characters from the computer, enlarge or shrink them, and so on, according to commands from the driving computer. A PostScript interpreter is often used to execute these commands. The memory is comparable to a frame buffer in which pictures and text are created by internal software. These printers have a full set of graphics primitives. They can execute commands sent to them by the computer, scale, skew, or rotate characters, draw lines, polygons, even curves and shapes, and fill them solid or with patterns. They can also do dot dithering to simulate halftoning. When their internal buffer has been filled, it is scanned and printed out. All this is independent of the resolution.

Higher resolutions (600 dots per inch) require a steep increase in internal memory. In more recent developments, the laser beam can create dots of varying size, thereby increasing the ability of the printer to create halftones.

Low-end laser printers are still about ten times as expensive as dot matrix printers, but we can expect a significant price drop within the next decade, making them more affordable.

## 17.5.5 Color Printers

Dot matrix, ink jet, and laser printers can be made to print in color. This is achieved by repeating a basic black-and-white printing process four times on the same paper with the four colors cyan, magenta, yellow, and black. All colors can be produced by a proper mixture of these three subtractive primaries plus black (see Section 9.3.5).

A *color dot matrix printer* is equipped with a ribbon that consists of four parallel strips in the four colors. The driver program sends the print head over the same line of print four times while activating a different color each time. The task consists of decoding a given pixel or an array of pixels into its color components, transforming from RGB into CMYB, choosing the proper dither matrices, and sending the proper bit patterns columnwise to the printer. This is called *color dithering.*

We will explain it with an example. Assume a display of 640 × 400 pixels represented in a frame buffer of the same size and a depth of eight bits per pixel. The colors on the display are determined through a lookup table with eight bits per RGB primary. We assume that the printer is able to produce 640 dots across the paper width. If we print with 4 × 4 dither matrices, we can preserve 17 intensity levels on the printout. We group the pixels into 4 × 4 blocks and print each block as four dither matrices, one for each printer primary. Assuming a print head of eight pins, it is advantageous to prepare a memory area large enough to hold the result of the analysis of a strip of 640 × 8 pixels. Such a strip contains 160 × 2 of these pixel blocks.

The first problem is to analyze the colors. Sometimes a lookup table can only be written to but not read from by the main processor.

If this is the case, then whenever a lookup table entry is made, the processor must also write a copy to an array. We look up the intensities of all three RGB primaries of each $4 \times 4$ pixel block and average and round to obtain the average RGB values of this group: (r,g,b). We transform those into normalized values between 0 and 1 and then into CMYB values using the formula:

$$
\begin{aligned}
c &= \max(rgb) - r \\
m &= \max(rgb) - g \\
y &= \max(rgb) - b \\
b &= 1 - \max(rgb)
\end{aligned}
$$

We store the cmyb values for each of the $160 \times 2$ pixel blocks in order not to have to read the pixels and lookup table several times. Then we determine through tables which dither matrices to use for the different printer primaries.

Let's look at the cyan primary only; all the others are analogous. The cyan table TC will be an array of 18 numbers, something like this:

```
TC[0]     0.0000
TC[1]     0.1200
TC[2]     0.2280
TC[3]     0.3252
           ...
TC[16]    0.9777
TC[17]    1.0000
```

If TC[i] < c < TC[i + 1], we use dither matrix [16 − i]. Observe that the numbers are not equally spaced. The length of the subintervals decreases by a factor of 0.9 from one to the next in this example. This is an attempt to compensate for the fact that there is only a small intensity difference between dither matrices 15 and 16 but a larger one between dither matrices 0 and 1. This 0.9 factor may not be the best choice—some experimenting is needed to find a good distribution, and the distributions for different primaries might not be the same. We take this into account by having separate tables for the primaries.

We need to complete a whole row of printout for each primary, so we take the c-values of block (1,1) and (2,1), determine their dither matrices, and print out the leftmost column of each, which gives the first eight-pin column for cyan on the printer. Then we do the same for the second column, and so forth. After the entire cyan row is printed we repeat the same process for magenta, then yellow, and finally black, without moving the paper. This gives one row of color printout. We repeat the above process for the remaining rows of the picture.

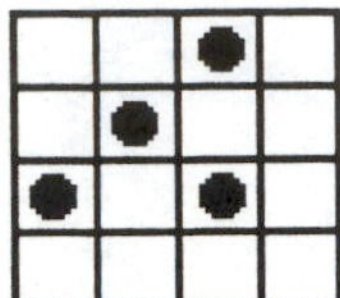
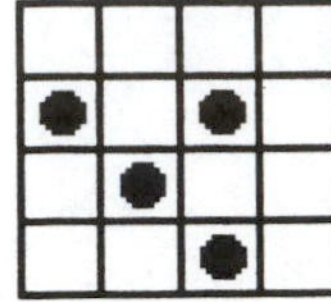
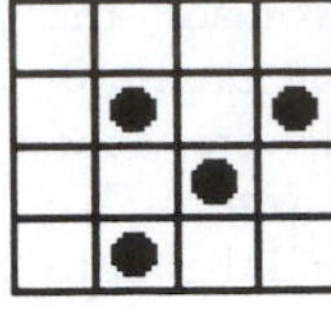
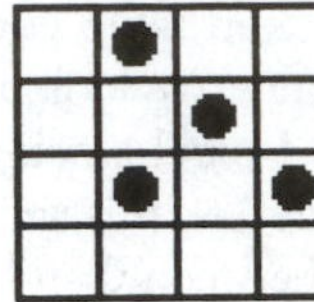

**FIGURE 17.42**

Experiments suggest that it is advantageous not to use the same dither matrices for different primaries. This increases the likelihood that color dots are more randomly spread around and makes the formation of patterns of any sort less probable. There are many ways to define a particular dither matrix. Figure 17.42 shows four different dither matrices with four dots obtained by rotating the original one by 90 degrees.

*Color ink jet printers* basically follow the same principle of dithering to achieve halftones, except that different ink jet heads are needed for the different primaries.

The Hewlett-Packard ink jet printer we described above works with the thermo jet principle; it is a color ink jet printer. So is the Pixelmaster printer, operating with solid ink technology. Both basically have four jet heads, one for each of the primaries cyan, magenta, yellow and black. The Pixelmaster has eight nozzles on each print head and produces a resolution of 240 dots per inch.

*Color laser printers* work on the same basic principle as black-and-white laser printers. The paper is imprinted four times, halftones are achieved through dithering and, in newer developments, also through varying dot size. Color laser printers are still very expensive and the production of a single A4 format print can take up to five minutes.

**A Look to the Future** It is hard to be definitive about printing hardware developments. Dot matrix printers will certainly continue to be very common for a long time because they are a time-proven and mature technology.

Although laser printers seem very promising, there are other technologies that could take the lead. Instead of using a laser beam to create the electrostatic latent image, there could be a dense array of light-emitting diodes across the whole width of the drum, which could be switched on and off at the proper moments while the drum slowly rotates.

It is possible to use ion beams rather than light. With these, the drum surface doesn't have to be light sensitive. It can be of a less fragile material in order to withstand more pressure. This allows the toner powder that has been deposited on the paper to simply be pressed in under high pressure; no heat is needed. These last two technologies have the definite advantage of fewer moving parts.

# EXERCISES FOR CHAPTER 17

## Paint and Drawing Systems

The polygon fill algorithm of Chapter 2 fills an area within a polygonal outline that is defined by its vertices. In paint and drawing systems, region-filling algorithms are often used. Such algorithms differ from the polygon fill algorithm in that the areas—regions—to be filled are defined in bit-maps by the color values of the pixels. This means that these fill algorithms must be able to read pixels in the bit-map as well as set them. The purpose of these region-filling algorithms is to fill the given regions with a certain color or pattern.

We consider two types of regions and of region-filling algorithms. One type of region is called *boundary defined.* The defining boundary is an eight- or four-connected sequence of pixels all of the same color that surrounds pixels which have a color different from the boundary color. The pixels inside the boundary comprise the region. An algorithm that fills such a region is called a boundary-fill algorithm. Figure 7.43 shows a region surrounded by a boundary of black pixels. In this example the boundary is eight-connected. If the boundary had to be four-connected, the boundary would be open and the region would extend over the whole pixel array. The interior consists of pixels of three different colors.

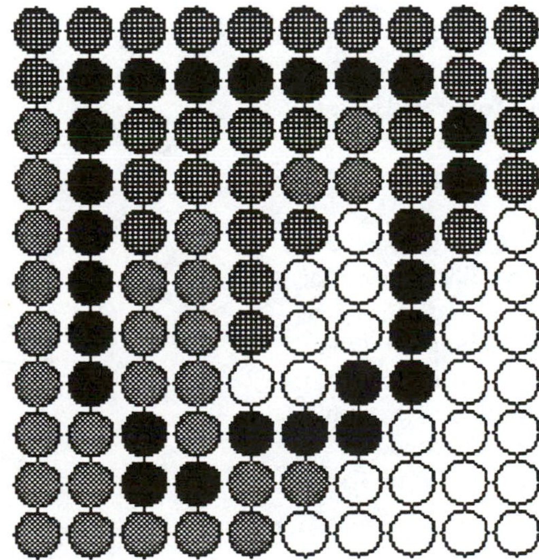

**FIGURE 17.43**

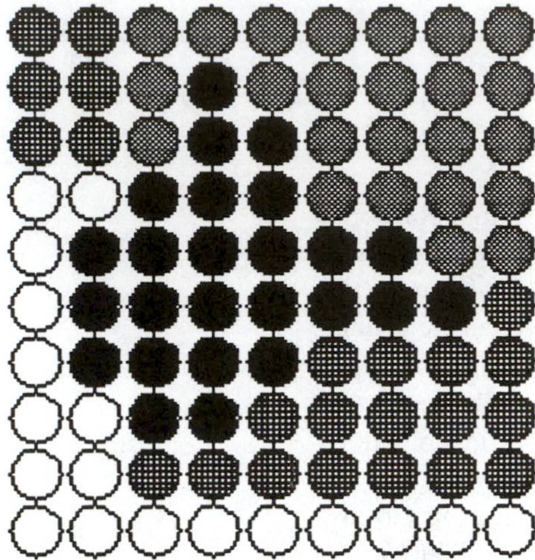

FIGURE 17.44

The second type of region is called *interior defined.* The interior is an eight- or four-connected set of pixels all of the same color. This interior defines the region. The boundary of the region consists of all pixels adjacent to the interior and of a different color. An algorithm that fills such a region is called a flood-fill algorithm. Figure 17.44 shows a four-connected region in black. The boundary consists of pixels of three different colors.

(We defined the term eight-connected in Chapter 2. Four-connected means that adjacent pixels must only be above or below, or to the right or left of each other.) Algorithms for eight-connected regions also work for four-connected ones, but the converse is not true. Below are simple pseudocodes for both algorithms and a four-connected region. In developing these algorithms we used this fact: the boundary of an eight-connected region is four-connected and the boundary of a four-connected region is eight-connected.

The two types of algorithms that are described are called *boundary fill* and *flood fill* respectively. Both algorithms start the filling process at an arbitrary pixel (x,y) inside the region. In a paint and drawing system the user will move the cursor inside the region with the mouse and then press the button to initialize the filling process. The starting position for the fill is the cursor position. (This is called a *seed fill* of the region.)

You are to do a number of exercises based on the pseudocodes. You will need the graphics primitive SetPix and a function ReadPix(x,y) that returns this pixels color.

```
procedure boundary_fill(        x,y,
                     boundary_color,
                        fill_color     :     integer);
begin
   check color of pixel(x,y);
   if it is not boundary-color
   and not fill_color
   then begin
      set it to fill_color,
      fill the regions starting
      at the pixels above
                    below
                    left
                    right
      of the just filled pixel
      by 4 recursive calls
   end
end {procedure boundary_fill};

procedure flood_fill(        x,y,
                 region_color,
                   fill_color     :     integer;
begin
   check color of pixel(x,y);
   if it is region_color
   then begin
      set it to fill_color,
      fill the regions starting
      at the pixels above
                    below
                    right
                    left
      of the just filled pixel
      by 4 recursive calls
   end
end {procedure flood_fill};
```

1. Implement the boundary fill algorithm.
2. Implement the flood fill algorithm.
3. What is the sequence in which the flood-fill algorithm sets the pixels when filling a given region? Draw a diagram that illustrates this.

**Rubberbanding** This is a very popular and user friendly way to draw straight lines in paint and drawing systems. In the following exercises, you will develop a rubberband drawing routine stepwise. The exercises assume a black-and-white display. You will need the graphics primitive SetPix and a function ReadPix(x,y) that returns this pixels color. You will be XORing pixels in the frame buffer. XORing a pixel consists of inverting this pixels value: If it is 0, set it to 1; if it is 1, set it to 0.

If a system doesn't have a mouse for moving the cursor on the screen, it can be accomplished through keystrokes. The exercises ask you to simulate the mouse and its buttons through the keyboard.

4. Write a procedure

   XORCURSOR(x,y_ : integer);

   that draws a crosshair cursor in the frame buffer in XOR mode such that the center is at location (x,y). The size of the cursor is nine pixels horizontally and nine pixels vertically.

5. Write a procedure

   XORLINE(x,y : integer);

   that draws a straight line in the frame buffer in XOR mode using the simple straight line DDA.

6. Write a procedure MOVECURSOR that moves the crosshair cursor according to keys that are read by the program from the keyboard. The arrow keys move the cursor five pixels in the arrow's direction and four other keys also move the cursor: E (moves one pixel upward), D (one to the right), S (one to the left), and X (one downward). The movement of the cursor is done by drawing the cursor at its old position with XORCURSOR to remove it, then updating the variables that hold the current cursor position, and finally drawing the cursor at the new position with XORCURSOR. If the cursor is too close to one of the display boundaries, draw the corresponding cursor arm shorter. The cursor should not ever move off the screen.

7. Implement interactive drawing of a rubberband line. Use the letter R to start the rubberband line as well as to end it. When an R is hit, the rubberband mode is switched on and the current cursor position $(x_0,y_0)$ is remembered. Then, whenever the cursor is moved, a straight line is drawn with XORLINE from $(x_0,y_0)$ to the new cursor position (in addition to moving the cursor). Whenever the cursor is moved, the line is first XORed away and is then redrawn from $(x_0,y_0)$ to the new cursor position (both with XORLINE). When R is hit a second time, the rubberband mode is switched off. Now, after the cursor is moved, a straight line is drawn in SET (not

in XOR!) in the frame buffer from $(x_0, y_0)$ to the position the cursor had when rubberband mode was switched off. You should draw the line only after the cursor has been moved away. (If you draw the line before the cursor is moved, you could wipe out a part of the drawn line. Why does this happen, and under what circumstances?)

# Mathematical Appendix

This appendix develops the mathematics useful in computer graphics more fully than the summary in Chapter 1. The order of topics is the same as in that chapter.

## Coordinate Systems

The position of a point in a plane or in space is given by its coordinates. In a Cartesian system these are the distances from two perpendicular axes (from three mutually perpendicular axes in space). Figures A.1 and A.2 show some examples:

In Figure A.1, point P is at x = 3, y = 2. We represent P as the number pair (3,2); by convention, the x-coordinate is given first. Similarly, Q = (−2,1) and, in Figure A.2, R = (30, −4). Observe that the scale factors (units/distance) can be varied and they need not be the same along the different axes. The origin O is the point (0,0) in two dimensions (2-D).

In three dimensions (3-D), while Cartesian axes are always perpendicular to each other, there are two possible orientations. If the x-axis is to the right and the y-axis is upward, the *z*-axis can point away from the viewer, giving a left-handed system (LHS), or toward the viewer in a right-handed system (RHS). These terms come from the fact that one can orient the thumb, forefinger, and middle finger of the left hand along the positive x-axis, the positive y-axis, and the positive *z*-axis respectively if it is an LHS. If it is an RHS, only the right hand allows a corresponding alignment of the fingers (see Figure A.3). We will use an LHS most often in this book.

A point in 3-D is given by the number triple (x,y,*z*) where these are the distances from the respective axes. The origin in 3-D is (0,0,0).

FIGURE A.1

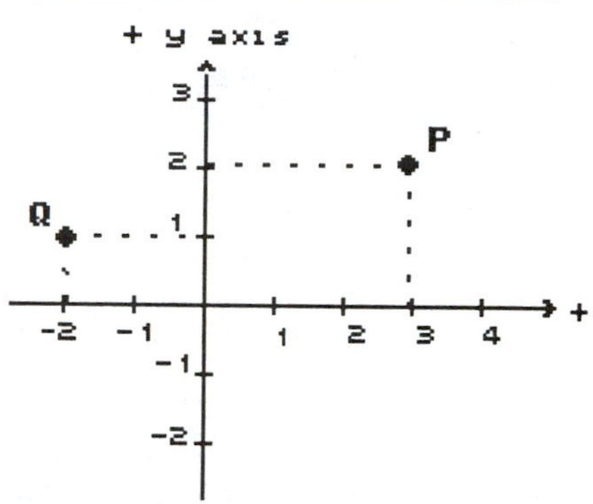


FIGURE A.2

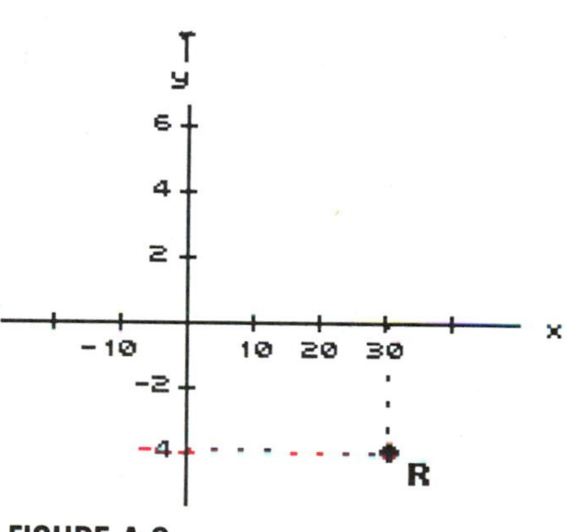


FIGURE A.3

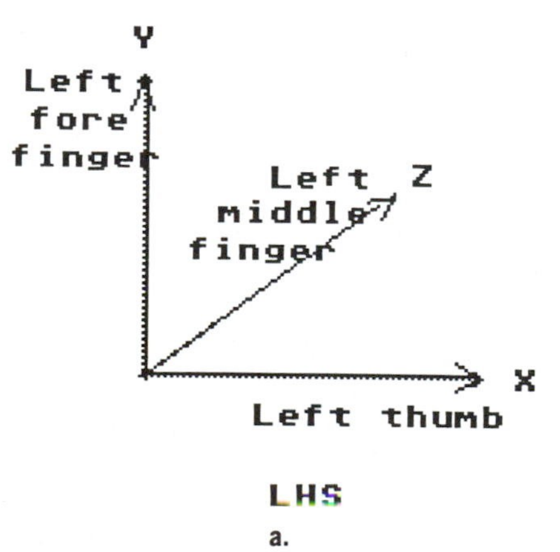

a.

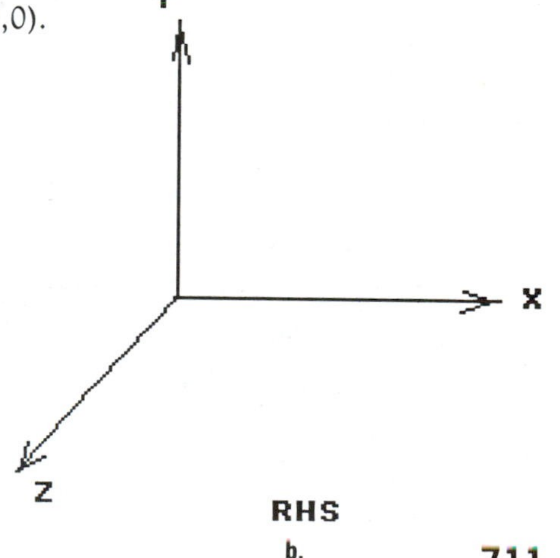

b.

By using the Pythagorean theorem, it is easy to compute the distance from $P_1 = (x_1,y_1)$ to $P_2 = (x_2,y_2)$:

$$\text{Dist} = ((x_2-x_1)^2 + (y_2-y_1)^2)^{1/2}.$$

In Figure A.1, the distance from P to Q is $(5^2 + 1^2)^{1/2} = 5.09902$. In 3-D, $(z_2-z_1)^2$ is added to the sum in parentheses.

Many other coordinate systems are possible. We will sometimes use polar coordinates where the position is specified as (r,i) with r being the distance from a chosen origin and i the counterclockwise (ccw) angle from a chosen reference line (see Figure A.4).

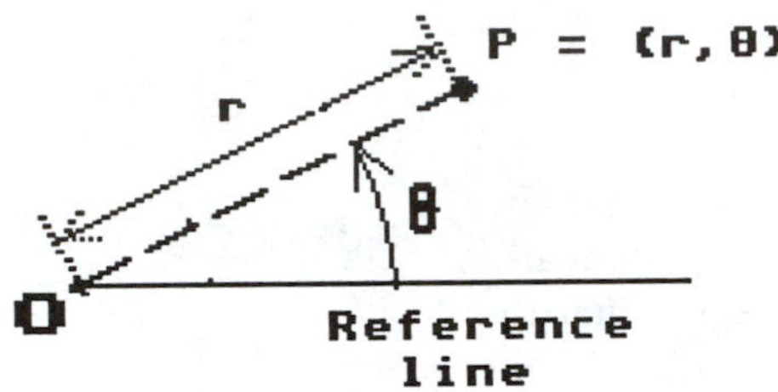


**FIGURE A.4**

In 3-D, r and two angles from two reference planes give the polar coordinates.

Rotating a point by a given angle is a common operation. Rotating a point by ϑ (measured ccw) is equivalent to rotating the axes by ϑ in a clockwise (cw) direction. The formulas are easier to derive from the latter. We will use Figure A.5 to derive them.

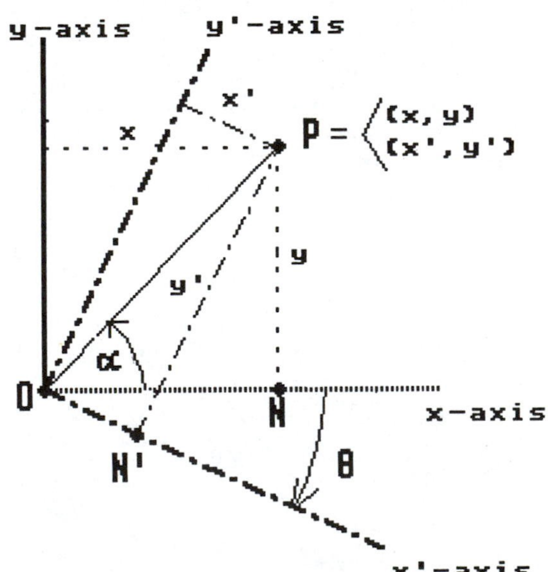


**FIGURE A.5**

From Figure A.5, it is apparent that:

$$x = ON = OP\cos\alpha$$
$$y = NP = OP\sin\alpha$$
$$x' = ON' = OP\cos(\alpha+\vartheta)$$
$$y' = N'P = OP\sin(\alpha+\vartheta)$$

Since:

$$\cos(\alpha+\vartheta) = \cos\alpha\cos\vartheta - \sin\alpha\sin\vartheta$$
$$\sin(\alpha+\vartheta) = \sin\alpha\cos\vartheta + \cos\alpha\sin\vartheta$$

it follows that:

$$x' = x\cos\vartheta - y\sin\vartheta$$
$$y' = y\cos\vartheta + x\sin\vartheta$$

# Analytical Geometry

Analytical geometry is the representation of geometric figures through algebraic equations. We are most interested in straight lines, planes, and simple curves given by conic sections, especially circles and ellipses.

The equation of a straight line is a relation between y and x that gives the y-coordinate when an x-coordinate is specified (or the reverse). There are several forms, three of which involve the slope of the line, or the increase in y-value due to a corresponding change in x-value. The slope is constant for a line so any two points $P_1$ and $P_2$ define the slope:

$$\text{Slope} = \frac{\Delta y}{\Delta x} = \frac{y_2 - y_1}{x_2 - x_1}.$$

The delta symbol is a widely used notation for the difference between two values. We then have these forms:

$$\text{Two point: } \frac{y - y_1}{x - x_1} = \frac{y_2 - y_1}{x_2 - x_1},\ x_2 \neq x_1.$$

$$\text{Point-slope: } \frac{y_2 - y_1}{x_2 - x_1} = m,\ x_2 \neq x_1, \text{ where } m = \text{slope}.$$

Slope-intercept: $y = mx + b$, where b is value of y at $x = 0$.

The slope is also the tangent of the angle between the x-axis and the line. Two parallel lines have the same slope because both make the same angle with the x-axis. For two perpendicular lines, $m_1 = -1/m_2$ as Figure A.6 demonstrates:

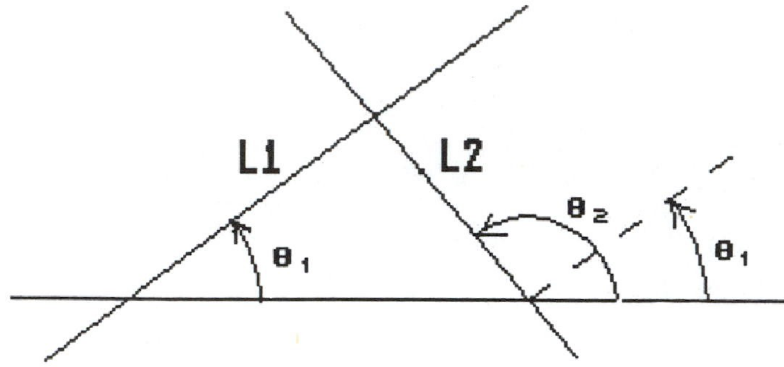


FIGURE A.6

It is clear that $\vartheta_2 = \vartheta_1 + 90°$, so:

$$m_2 = \tan \vartheta_2 = \tan(\vartheta_1 + 90°) = -\cot \vartheta_1 = -1/(\tan \vartheta_1) = -1/m_1.$$

(If one of the lines is vertical so that the slope is undefined, the development requires taking limits.)

In addition to the above forms, there is the general form for a straight line:

$$Ax + By + C = 0, \text{ with A and B not both zero.}$$

For $B \neq 0$, the slope $m = -A/B$ and the intercept $b = -C/B$. An equation with only first powers of the variables is called a linear equation and extends to linear equations in more than two variables.

$Ax + By + Cz + D = 0$ defines a plane. If $D = 0$, the plane goes through the origin. If $-D = Ax_1 + By_1 + Cz_1$, the plane contains $P_1 = (x_1, y_1, z_1)$.

We will use Figure A.7 to develop the equation for the distance of a point from a line. $P_1 = (x_1, y_1)$ is a point not on the line $L = Ax + By + C = 0$ and $P_2 = (x_2, y_2)$ is the intersection of L with L′, a line that is perpendicular to L through $P_1$. The equation for L′ is $Bx - Ay + C' = 0$ from previous relationships.

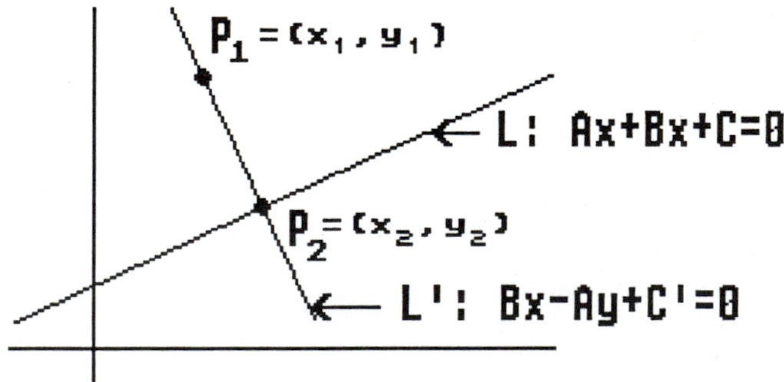


FIGURE A.7

Since $P_2$ is on both L and L', its coordinates satisfy both line equations:

$$\begin{aligned} L:&\quad Ax_2 + By_2 + C = 0 \\ L':&\quad Bx_2 - Ay_2 + C' = 0 \end{aligned}$$

Eliminating $y_2$ gives $(A^2+B^2)x_2 + AC + BC' = 0$, or:

$$x_2 = -\frac{AC + BC'}{A^2 + B^2}.$$

Eliminating $x_2$ gives:

$$y_2 = \frac{AC' - BC}{A^2 + B^2}.$$

$P_1$ is also on L', so $C' = Ay_1 - Bx_1$. Substituting for C' in the above equations for $x_2$ and $y_2$, we have:

$$x_2 = -\frac{AC + B(Ay_1 - Bx_1)}{A^2 + B^2}$$

$$y_2 = \frac{A(Ay_1 - Bx_1) - BC}{A^2 + B^2}$$

This gives:

$$\begin{aligned} x_1 - x_2 &= \frac{x_1(A^2+B^2) + AC + B(Ay_1 - Bx_1)}{A^2 + B^2} \\ &= \frac{A(Ax_1 + By_1 + C)}{A^2 + B^2} = A(W) \end{aligned}$$

and

$$\begin{aligned} y_1 - y_2 &= \frac{y_1(A^2+B^2) - A(Ay_1 - Bx_1) + BC}{A^2 + B^2} \\ &= \frac{B(Ax_1 + By_1 + C)}{A^2 + B^2} = B(W) \end{aligned}$$

where (W) represents the common factor.

The distance of $P_1$ from the line is then:

$$(A^2W^2 + B^2W^2)^{1/2} = |W|\,(A^2+B^2)^{1/2} = \frac{|Ax_1 + By_1 + C|}{(A^2+B^2)^{1/2}}$$

The distance from the point $P_1 = (x_1, y_1, z_1)$ to a plane defined by $Ax + By + Cz + D = 0$ is given by a similar formula:

$$\text{Dist} = \frac{|Ax_1 + By_1 + Cz + D|}{(A^2 + B^2 + C^2)^{1/2}}.$$

This formula is more readily developed by using vectors (see texts on vector algebra).

Formulas for curves can also be expressed by parametric equations. If $y = f(x)$, there is a lack of symmetry because we must think of y as dependent on the independent variable x. While we may be able to invert this to give x as a function of y, it is often preferable to rewrite the function as two functions of a separate independent variable u that we call the parameter: $x = X(u)$ and $y = Y(u)$. Now, as u varies, both x and y assume new values and trace out the curve. For a straight line between $(x_1,y_1)$ and $(x_2,y_2)$, if

$$x = x_1 + u\,(x_2 - x_1) \text{ and } y = y_1 + u(y_2 - y_1),$$

then, as u varies from 0 to 1, points on the line are generated between the two ends. $u = 0$ gives the point $(x_1,y_1)$; $u = 1$ gives $(x_2,y_2)$; and intermediate values give other points at distances from the beginning that are equal to the fraction u times the length of the line. Points outside the line segment are generated by values of u outside the range [0,1].

The three parametric equations $x = X(u)$, $y = Y(u)$, and $z = Z(u)$ generate points on a space curve.

Conic sections are curves formed by the intersection of a plane and a cone and have equations that are quadratic in x and y. The general second-order equation:

$$Ax^2 + Bxy + Cy^2 + Dx + Ey + F = 0$$

describes any of the conics; which one depends on the value of $B^2 - 4AC$, called the discriminant. If:

DISC $= 0$, the curve is a parabola
DISC $< 0$, the curve is an ellipse
DISC $> 0$, the curve is a hyperbola

Rotating the points of a conic about the origin does not change the value of the discriminant, nor does the sum of A and B change.

A circle is described parametrically by the equations

$$x = r \cos \vartheta,\ y = r \sin \vartheta, \text{ where } \vartheta \text{ is the parameter.}$$

Using different values for r in the two equations generates an ellipse.

# Algebra

The solution of a quadratic equation in one variable $(Ax^2 + Bx + C = 0)$ is conveniently found through the quadratic formula:

$$x = \frac{-B \pm (B^2 - 4AC)^{1/2}}{2A}.$$

Nonlinear equations of the form f(x) = 0 can be solved by Newton's method. This is a technique for successively improving the accuracy of estimates of the solution using the formula:

$$x_{n+1} = x_n - \frac{f(x_n)}{f'(x_n)}, \text{ where } f' \text{ is the derivative of f.}$$

Example

$$\text{Suppose } f(x) = x^2 - 2\sin x = 0$$
$$f'(x) = 2x + 2\cos x.$$

A sketch of f(x) indicates a solution near x = 1.3. When $x_0 = 1.3$, f(1.3) = −0.23712, f′(x) = 3.13500, and $x_1 = 1.37564$. Continuing, $x_2 = 1.39783$, $x_3 = 1.40300$, and so on.

A system of linear equations can be solved simultaneously by elimination or, equivalently, through the ratios of determinants, known as Cramer's rule. For two equations:

$$\begin{matrix} a_1x + b_1y = c_1 \\ a_2x + b_2y = c_2 \end{matrix}, \quad x = \frac{\begin{vmatrix} c_1 & b_1 \\ c_2 & b_2 \end{vmatrix}}{\begin{vmatrix} a_1 & b_1 \\ a_2 & b_2 \end{vmatrix}}, \quad y = \frac{\begin{vmatrix} a_1 & c_1 \\ a_2 & c_2 \end{vmatrix}}{\begin{vmatrix} a_1 & b_1 \\ a_2 & b_2 \end{vmatrix}}.$$

The vertical bars represent determinants. A similar arrangement solves a set of n equations. Computing the determinant is explained below under matrices.

**FIGURE A.8**

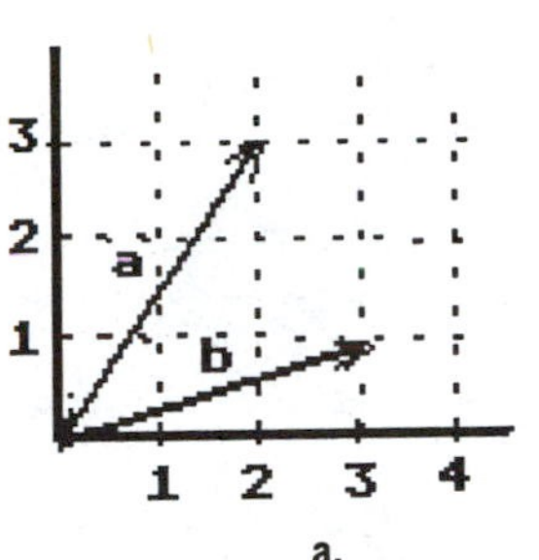


a.

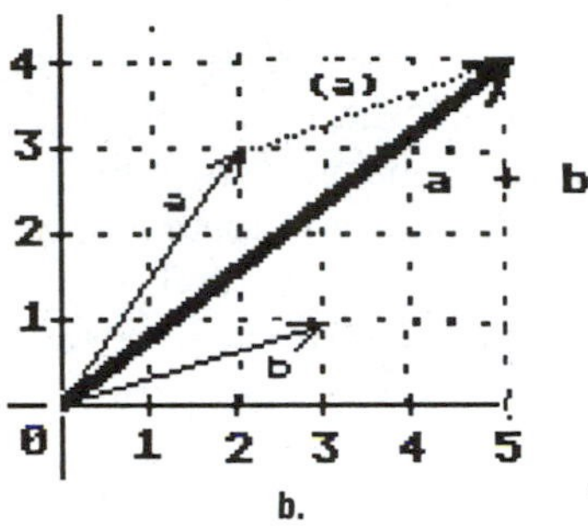


b.

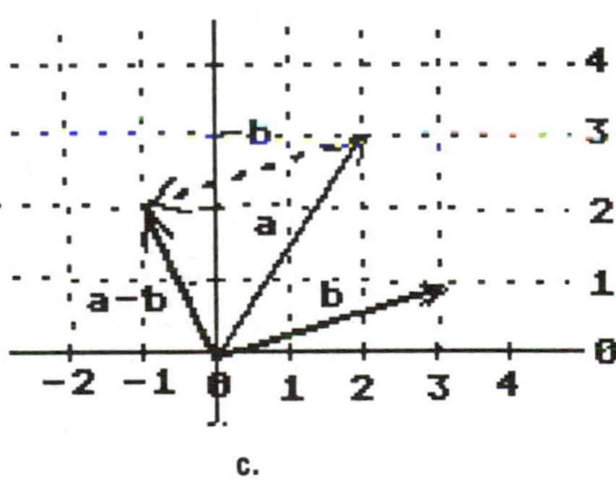


c.

# Vectors

A vector is a compound quantity; it has both magnitude and direction. This means that it can be pictured as a directed line segment whose length represents the magnitude and whose orientation (an arrow is placed on the far end) represents the direction. Two vectors with the same magnitude and direction are equal. Normally a vector is considered to be a free vector that can be moved parallel to itself so equal vectors can be superimposed. Vectors are also represented as a number pair where the values are the x- and y-coordinates of the end point when the start point is at the origin of Cartesian axes. These numbers are called the components of the vector.

Two vectors are added graphically by drawing the second vector starting at the end point of the first. One vector is subtracted from a second by adding its negative, which is the vector in the opposite direction with the same length. See Figure A.8 for examples.

$$a = (2,3) \quad b = (3,1) \quad a+b = (5,4) \quad a-b = (-1,2)$$

Vectors are often written using boldface lowercase letters as we have done in the figure.

An alternate (and preferred) way to add or subtract vectors is to add or subtract the components:

$$\text{If } \mathbf{v}_1 = (x_1,y_1) \text{ and } \mathbf{v}_2 = (x_2,y_2), \text{ then:}$$
$$\mathbf{v}_1 + \mathbf{v}_2 = (x_1+x_2, y_1+y_2),\ \mathbf{v}_1 - \mathbf{v}_2 = (x_1-x_2, y_1-y_2).$$

The length or magnitude of a vector is written with bars: $|\mathbf{v}|$, and $|\mathbf{v}| = (x^2 + y^2)^{1/2}$ when $\mathbf{v} = (x,y)$. This is exactly the length of the vector when drawn in the Cartesian plane. Normalizing a vector means making its length unity without changing its direction. To normalize vector $\mathbf{v}$, divide each component by $|\mathbf{v}|$.

When working with vectors, ordinary numbers are called scalars to distinguish them. Multiplying a vector by a scalar multiplies its length. In terms of components, if $\mathbf{v} = (x,y)$, $c\mathbf{v} = (cx,cy)$.

Any vector in space can be expressed as a weighted sum of basis vectors. Unit vectors parallel to the three coordinate axes are often used as the basis, and these are frequently designated as **i, j,** and **k**. Hence we can write $\mathbf{v} = v_1\mathbf{i} + v_2\mathbf{j} + v_3\mathbf{k}$ with suitable choice of the three coefficients.

Two vectors can be multiplied together and there are two kinds of products. The dot product is a scalar, also called the scalar product. Another name is the inner product. It is computed by adding the products of the corresponding components:

$$\mathbf{v}_1\,\mathbf{v}_2 = (x_1x_2 + y_1y_2) \text{ but this is equivalent:}$$
$$\mathbf{v}_1\,\mathbf{v}_2 = |\mathbf{v}_1||\mathbf{v}_2|\cos\vartheta \ (\vartheta \text{ is the angle between } \mathbf{v}_1 \text{ and } \mathbf{v}_2).$$

The second kind of vector product is the cross product, also called the vector product or the outer product. It is a vector and is computed by:

$$\mathbf{v}_1 \times \mathbf{v}_2 = \mathbf{n}\,|\mathbf{v}_1|\,|\mathbf{v}_2| \sin\vartheta \ (\vartheta \text{ is the angle between } \mathbf{v}_1 \text{ and } \mathbf{v}_2).$$

The vector **n** in the cross product is a unit vector (length = 1) that is perpendicular to the plane containing $\mathbf{v}_1$ and $\mathbf{v}_2$. The direction of **n** is such that $\mathbf{v}_1$, $\mathbf{v}_2$, and **n** form a RHS when taken in that order. A vector that is perpendicular to a plane is said to be normal to the plane.

When two vectors are perpendicular, their dot product is zero (because $\cos 90° = 0$). Two parallel vectors have a cross product of zero (because $\sin 0° = 0$). These conditions are used to test for perpendicular or parallel vectors.

In three dimensions, a vector is defined by three components. The dot product is $(x_1x_2 + y_1y_2 + z_1z_2)$. The cross product is defined exactly as above.

A plane can be defined by three noncollinear points or by two nonparallel vectors. A plane has two sides. If two vectors are drawn to connect the three points in ccw order, the cross product of the vectors points from the positive side. Figure A.9 illustrates this.

FIGURE A.9

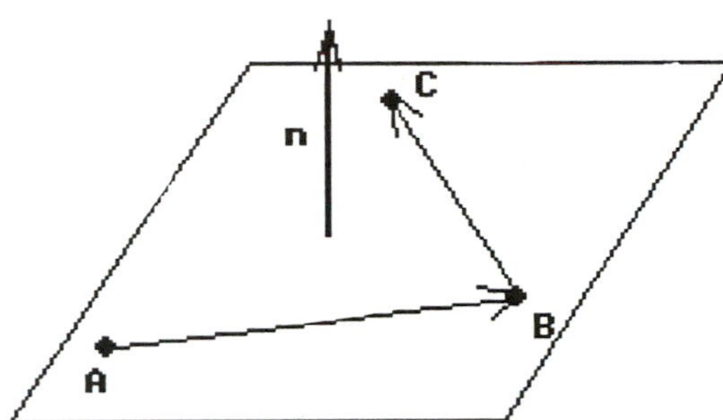


As an example of vector arithmetic, consider this problem. When light enters a transparent object, it is refracted (its direction is changed) when the indices of refraction are not the same. The change of direction is given by the relation:

$$\sin \alpha' = (\mu/\mu') \sin \alpha,$$

where $\alpha$ and $\alpha'$ are the angles between the vector normal to the surface and the entering and leaving rays, and $\mu$ and $\mu'$ are the refractive indices (see Figure A.10).

FIGURE A.10

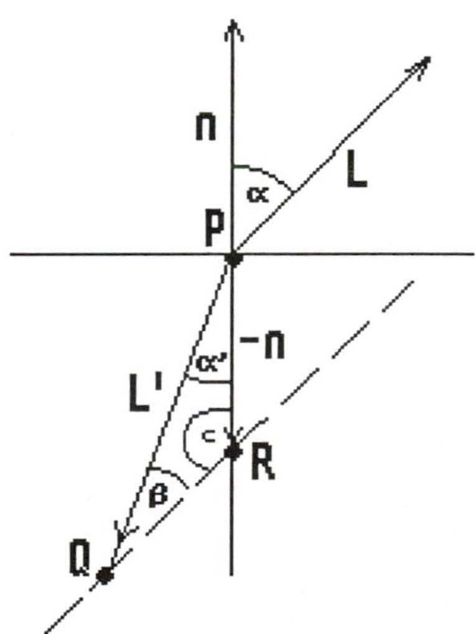


We wish to determine the components of **L**′, given **L** (a unit vector pointing to the light source), **n** (a unit vector normal to the surface), and the values of $\mu$ and $\mu'$. We draw the line from Q to R parallel to **L** and through the end point of $-$**n**. It is clear that angle c $= 180° - \alpha$, and, because they are the internal angles of triangle PQR, that $\alpha' + \beta + c = 180°$. From these relations, angle $\beta = \alpha - \alpha'$. From the law of sines we have:

$$d/1 = (\sin \alpha')/(\sin(\alpha - \alpha')) \text{ where } d = \text{length of QR}.$$

We then get **L**′ by vector addition: **L**′ $= -$**n** $-$ d**L**. Ordinarily we would normalize **L**′ by dividing by its length.

# Matrices

A matrix is another compound quantity composed of components or elements arranged as a rectangular array, so it has rows and columns. A matrix of r rows and c columns is said to be r x c in size. A matrix is often represented as an uppercase letter in boldface while its components are represented as the same lowercase letter with two subscripts, the first indicating the row and the second the column where it appears. The matrix is also represented as the general element enclosed in square brackets:

$$A = \begin{pmatrix} a_{11} & a_{12} & a_{13} \\ a_{21} & a_{22} & a_{23} \\ a_{31} & a_{32} & a_{33} \end{pmatrix} = [a_{ij}].$$

In the above, **A** is 3 × 3. A matrix is square if the number of rows equals the number of columns. Matrices do not have to be square, but most matrices used in computer graphics are square.

Two matrices of the same size can be added or subtracted:

$$\mathbf{C} = \mathbf{A} + \mathbf{B} = [a_{ij} + b_{ij}] = [c_{ij}]$$

$$\mathbf{D} = \mathbf{A} - \mathbf{B} = [a_{ij} - b_{ij}] = [d_{ij}]$$

If a matrix is multiplied by a scalar, each of its elements is multiplied by the scalar: $c\mathbf{A} = [ca_{ij}]$.

Two matrices can be multiplied if they are conformable for multiplication, meaning that the number of columns of the first equals the number of rows of the second. When **A** is r × c and **B** is c × t, the product **E** = **A B** is r × t. Its elements are:

$$e_{ij} = \sum_{k=1}^{c} a_{ik} b_{kj},\ i = 1..r,\ j = 1..t,$$

which is the sum of products of elements in row i of **A** times those in column j of **B** taken in pairs as we move across the rows and down the columns. The order of the factors (**A** and **B**) cannot be interchanged in matrix multiplication.

**Example**

$$\text{Let } \mathbf{A} = \begin{pmatrix} 3 & 2 & 4 \\ -1 & 1 & 0 \\ 3 & 0 & 1 \end{pmatrix} \quad \text{and } \mathbf{B} = \begin{pmatrix} 1 & 3 & 1 \\ 2 & 2 & 0 \\ -2 & 0 & 2 \end{pmatrix}$$

$$3\mathbf{A} = \begin{pmatrix} 9 & 6 & 12 \\ -3 & 3 & 0 \\ 9 & 0 & 3 \end{pmatrix}$$

$$\mathbf{A} + \mathbf{B} = \begin{pmatrix} 4 & 6 & 5 \\ 1 & 3 & 0 \\ 1 & 0 & 2 \end{pmatrix} \quad \mathbf{A} - \mathbf{B} = \begin{pmatrix} 2 & -2 & 3 \\ -3 & -1 & 0 \\ 5 & 0 & -1 \end{pmatrix}$$

For **E** = **A B**, here are some typical elements:

$$e_{31} = a_{31}b_{11} + a_{32}b_{21} + a_{33}b_{31}$$

$$(3)(1) + (0)(2) + (1)(-2) = 3 + 0 - 2 = 1,$$

$$e_{23} = (-1)(1) + (1)(0) + (0)(2) = -1 + 0 + 0 = -1,$$

$$e_{33} = (3)(1) + (0)(0) + (1)(2) = 3 + 0 + 2 = 5.$$

Completing for all rows and columns gives:

$$\mathbf{E} = \begin{pmatrix} -1 & 16 & 11 \\ 1 & -2 & -1 \\ 1 & 12 & 5 \end{pmatrix}$$

If the components of a vector are written in a row, the vector can be thought of as a special case of a matrix, one with only one row. Similarly, writing the elements in a column makes the vector another special case of a matrix. When vectors are so written, they are called row vectors or column vectors. These two forms can make the vector conformable for multiplication, so multiplication of vectors and matrices is defined. Curly brackets are sometimes used to designate a column vector, so if the components of **v** are 3, −1, and 4:

$$\mathbf{v} = (3 \quad -1 \quad 4) \text{ and } \{\mathbf{v}\} = \begin{pmatrix} 3 \\ -1 \\ 4 \end{pmatrix}.$$

**Example**

Using **A** and **v** as defined above,

$$\mathbf{A}\{\mathbf{v}\} = \begin{pmatrix} 23 \\ -4 \\ 13 \end{pmatrix}, \quad \mathbf{v}\mathbf{A} = (22 \quad 5 \quad 26).$$

This means that **v** {**v**} forms the dot product of **v** with itself, according to the rules for matrix multiplication.

Since the rows of a matrix are, in effect, row vectors, we can think of a matrix as a column of row vectors or, conversely, as a row of column vectors.

A system of linear equations can be written in matrix form. For example, this set of three equations:

$$\begin{aligned} 4x_1 - 3x_2 + 2x_3 &= -1 \\ x_1 + 2x_2 - x_3 &= 7 \\ 2x_1 + x_2 + x_3 &= 2 \end{aligned}$$

is the same as **A**{x} = {b}, where

$$\mathbf{A} = \begin{pmatrix} 4 & -3 & 2 \\ 1 & 2 & -1 \\ 2 & 1 & 1 \end{pmatrix}, \quad \{x\} = \begin{pmatrix} x_1 \\ x_2 \\ x_3 \end{pmatrix}, \quad \{b\} = \begin{pmatrix} -1 \\ 7 \\ 2 \end{pmatrix}$$

Solving a system of n equations by elimination can be accomplished by augmenting **A** with {**b**} (appending the elements of {**b**} as an additional column of **A**), and then performing elementary row transformations until the **A** matrix is upper triangular. Elementary row operations are (1) multiplying all the elements of one row by a nonzero constant, (2) adding the elements of one row to the corresponding elements of another row, and (3) interchanging the elements in two rows. A matrix is upper triangular when all elements below the main diagonal are zero. The main diagonal of an $n \times n$ matrix is the diagonal row from $a_{11}$ to $a_{nn}$.

**Example**

Solve the system of equations given above.

$$\begin{pmatrix} 4 & -3 & 2 & -1 \\ 1 & 2 & -1 & 7 \\ 2 & 1 & 1 & 2 \end{pmatrix} \overset{(1)}{\rightarrow}$$

$$\begin{pmatrix} 4 & -3 & 2 & -1 \\ 0 & 2.75 & -1.5 & 7.25 \\ 0 & 2.5 & 0 & 2.5 \end{pmatrix} \overset{(2)}{\rightarrow}$$

$$\begin{pmatrix} 4 & -3 & 2 & -1 \\ 0 & 2.75 & -1.5 & 7.25 \\ 0 & 0 & 1.3636 & -4.0909 \end{pmatrix}$$

In step (1) we subtracted 1/4 times the first row from the second and 2/4 times the first row from the third. In step (2) we subtracted 2.5/2.75 times the new second row from the new third row. This made the **A** part of the augmented matrix upper triangular. Now we are ready to get the solution by back substitution. Interpreting the array after step (2) as a set of equations, we see that both $x_1$ and $x_2$ have been eliminated from the third equation, so we get $x_3 = -4.0909/1.3636 = -3$. Now we put that value into an equation (2) to get $x_2 = (7.25-(-1.5)(-3))/2.75 = 1$. Similarly, from equation (1), $x_1 = (-1-(2)(-3)-(-3)(1))/4 = 2$.

There are variations on this basic scheme that can minimize errors caused by rounding off in the successive computations. See numerical analysis books such as GEWH84.

The matrices that we use in this book are always square. A square matrix has some important properties. When all elements on the main diagonal are unity and all others are zero, the matrix is called the identity matrix and the symbol **I** is used. In this case, when **A** is the same size,

$$\mathbf{I\,A} = \mathbf{A\,I} = \mathbf{A},$$

which is an exception to the rule that matrix multiplication is noncommutative.

Except for certain pathological cases, a square matrix has an inverse, written $\mathbf{A}^{-1}$, and:

$$\mathbf{A}\,\mathbf{A}^{-1} = \mathbf{A}^{-1}\,\mathbf{A} = \mathbf{I},$$

another exception to the noncommutative rule. The inverse of matrix **A** can be found by augmenting **A** with the identity matrix, performing elementary row operations to transform **A** into the identity matrix, which transforms **I** into $\mathbf{A}^{-1}$. Multiplying with the inverse can solve a system of equations:

$$\mathbf{A}^{-1}\mathbf{A}\,\{x\} = \mathbf{A}^{-1}\{b\} = \mathbf{I}\,\{x\} = \{x\},\ \text{so}\ \{x\} = \mathbf{A}^{-1}\{b\}.$$

Unless $\mathbf{A}^{-1}$ is needed for some other reason, this is not the most efficient way to solve a system of equations.

A square matrix has a determinant, a scalar quantity that is often represented by magnitude bars. The best way to evaluate the determinant is to expand in terms of minors until we have reduced to $2 \times 2$ determinants that are equal to the difference in products of the elements on the two diagonals. The minor is the determinant formed by striking out one row and column. This example will clarify, where **A** is the same matrix as before:

$$\det(\mathbf{A}) = \begin{vmatrix} 4 & -3 & 2 \\ 1 & 2 & -1 \\ 2 & 1 & 1 \end{vmatrix} = (4)\begin{vmatrix} 2 & -1 \\ 1 & 1 \end{vmatrix} - (-3)\begin{vmatrix} 1 & -1 \\ 2 & 1 \end{vmatrix} + (2)\begin{vmatrix} 1 & 2 \\ 2 & 1 \end{vmatrix}$$

$$= (4)\,(2-(-1)) + (3)\,(1-(-2)) + (2)\,(1-4) = 15.$$

For a diagonal matrix, the determinant is the product of the elements on the main diagonal. Triangularization does not change the value of the determinant except that a row interchange will change its sign. We can verify this by computing det(A) after the triangularization we did above:

$$\begin{vmatrix} 4 & -3 & 2 \\ 0 & 2.75 & -1.5 \\ 0 & 0 & 1.3636 \end{vmatrix} = (4)\,(2.75)\,(1.3636) = 15.$$

# Derivatives

The need for calculus is relatively modest in computer graphics; we use only formulas for derivatives. The important standard formulas are just tabulated. These assume that u is the independent variable and use the notation $x' = dx/du$, $y' = dy/du$:

$$du/du = 1,\ dx/dx = 1,\ dy/dy = 1$$
$$d(x+y)/du = x' + y'$$

$$dy/dx = (dy/du)(du/dx) = y'/x'$$
$$dx^n = n(x^{n-1})x'$$
$$d(\sin x) = -(\cos x)x'$$
$$d(\cos x) = (\sin x)x'$$

We can approximate the derivative through finite difference ratios. The definition of the derivative is:

$$\frac{dx}{du} = \lim_{\Delta u \to 0} \frac{\Delta x}{\Delta u},$$

where the delta symbol represents the difference in two values. Hence, if $\Delta u$ is quite small, the ratio will be nearly equal to the derivative.

A table of values for a function at equispaced values of the independent variable permits the computation of a column of differences; from that column another set of differences can be calculated and still other columns of differences in succession. If f(u) is a linear function, the first differences will be constant. If f(u) is an nth degree polynomial, the nth column of differences will be constant.

**Example**

Suppose $f(u) = u^2 - 2u + 1$ (a quadratic). Begin at $u_0 = 1.5$ and take $\Delta u = 0.5$. We use subscripts to designate the successive entries ($u_0 = 1.5$, $u_1 = 2.0$, . . ., $f_0 = 0.25$, $f_1 = 1.0$, . . .). We compute each ${}^1f_n = f_{n+1} - f_n$ and ${}^2f_n = {}^1f_{n+1} - {}^1f_n$ to get the following table:

| u | f | ${}^1f$ | ${}^2f$ |
|---|---|---|---|
| $u_0 = 1.5$ | $f_0 = 0.25$ | | |
| | | 0.75 | |
| $u_1 = 2.0$ | $f_1 = 1.0$ | | 0.5 |
| | | 1.25 | |
| $u_2 = 2.5$ | $f_2 = 2.25$ | | 0.5 |
| | | 1.75 | |
| $u_3 = 3.0$ | $f_3 = 4.0$ | | 0.5 |
| | | 2.25 | |
| $u_4 = 3.5$ | $f_4 = 6.25$ | | 0.5 |
| | | 2.75 | |
| $u_5 = 4.0$ | $f_5 = 9.0$ | | |

Obviously the third differences will all be 0. We can use this fact to extend the table for values of f. For example, the next entry in the ${}^1f$ column will be 3.25 (2.75 + 0.5) and f(4.5) will be 12.25 (9.0 + 3.25). In fact, from two computed values of f(u), if we know the constant value for ${}^2f$, we can construct the entire table of f-values. We illustrate this below, where parentheses indicate values obtained in this way:

| u | f | ${}^1f$ | (${}^2f = 0.5$) |
|---|---|---|---|
| 1.5 | 0.25 | | |
| | | 0.75 | |
| 2.0 | 1.0 | | |
| | | (1.25) | |
| 2.5 | (2.25) | | |

| | | |
|---|---|---|
| 3.0 | (4.0) | (1.75) |
| 3.5 | (6.25) | (2.25) |
| 4.0 | (9.0) | (2.75) |
| etc. | etc. | etc. |

This can be used with polynomials of any degree with a significant saving of computation time. Speed is important in computer graphics when curves are to be displayed in real time. The method requires the preliminary computation of n values of the function to find the value of $^{n-1}f$. We also need $^{n}f$, but this is easy to get because, when f is an nth degree polynomial,

$$^{n}f = a_0\, n!\, u^n \text{ where } a_0 \text{ is the coefficient of } x^n.$$

Applying this to the above quadratic, we get $^{2}f = (1)(2!)(0.5)^2 = 0.5$. (See GEWH84 for proof of this and additional information on difference tables.)

The finite difference defined above is called the forward difference because it uses a value beyond the current point in its computation. If a value at the previous point is used, we form the backward difference: $\Delta f_n = f_n - f_{n-1}$. Neither the forward nor backward difference divided by the difference in u values gives as accurate an estimate of the derivative as a central difference formula. The central difference, often represented as $\delta f$, is computed by:

$$\delta f_n = \frac{f_{n+1} - f_{n-1}}{2u}$$

# Complex Numbers

Complex numbers are another type of compound quantity, being composed of a real part and an imaginary part. They occur quite naturally in solving quadratic equations where $(b^2 - 4ac)^{1/2}$ requires taking the square root of a negative quantity. If we represent $(-1)^{1/2} = i$, a complex number can be written as a + ib. This can be plotted on the complex plane, known as an Argand diagram, where the real axis is drawn horizontally and the imaginary axis vertically. This indicates that a complex number can also be represented by the number pair (a,b). A vector from the origin to the point (a,b) is essentially equivalent, so a polar form is also used to represent the complex value.

The operations of addition and subtraction are exactly equivalent to the same operations with vectors. However, multiplication and division are defined differently.

Let $z = (a,b) = a + ib$.

$cz = (ca,cb)$ where c is a scalar.

$$(z_1)(z_2) = (a_1 + ib_1)(a_2 + ib_2) = (a_1a_2 - b_1b_2) + i(a_1b_2 + a_2b_1),$$

$$(z_1)/(z_2) = \frac{(a_1a_2 + b_1b_2) - i(a_1b_2 - a_2b_1)}{(a_2{}^2 + b_2{}^2)}.$$

These formulas come directly from multiplying out and remembering that $i^2 = -1$.

The magnitude of a complex number is obtained exactly as with a two-component vector:

$$|z| = (a^2 + b^2)^{1/2}.$$

# Binary Numbers

Computers basically store all values as binary numbers. These use 2 as a base and are composed of bits that may be either 0 or 1. (Actually, the values are one of two voltage states that we interpret as 0 or 1.) The bits in a binary number have a place value just as the digits in our usual base 10 numbers do, but in a binary quantity each bit to the left represents the next power of 2 rather than a power of 10. For example, 1101 is:

| | | | | | |
|---|---|---|---|---|---|
| bits: | 1 | 1 | 0 | 1 | |
| weight: | $2^3$ | $2^2$ | $2^1$ | $2^0$ | |
| value: | 8 | + 4 | + 0 | + 1 | = 13 as a base 10 number. |

Shifting to the right (losing the rightmost bit in the process) divides the number by 2 while a left shift (filling in at the right with 0) doubles it:

Right shift: $1101_2 \rightarrow 110_2 = 6_{10}$
Left shift: $1101_2 \rightarrow 11010_2 = 26_{10}$

(When numbers of different bases are used together, it is customary to show the base as a subscript.) The division above is integer division so the fractional part is lost. Since the computer's registers can do shifts on their contents quite readily, doubling or halving is a fast operation.

Two binary numbers are added by adding each corresponding bit. The addition table is simple: $0+0 = 0$, $1+0 = 1$, $1+1 = 10$, with the 1 here carried over to the next set of bits, so we also need $1+1+1 = 11$. Here is an example:

```
       1 1 1   1  ← carries
       1 1 0 1 0 0 1
     + 1 0 1 1 0 0 1
     ---------------
sum  1 1 0 0 0 0 1 0
```

The other operations of subtraction, multiplication, and division are similar to those in base 10 arithmetic, but we will not use them in the book. We will need the logical operations of AND, OR, and XOR. These tables show the results:

| AND | 0 | 1 |
|---|---|---|
| 0 | 0 | 0 |
| 1 | 0 | 1 |

| OR | 0 | 1 |
|---|---|---|
| 0 | 0 | 1 |
| 1 | 1 | 1 |

| XOR | 0 | 1 |
|---|---|---|
| 0 | 0 | 1 |
| 1 | 1 | 0 |

With AND, both bits must be 1 for the result to be a 1; with OR, the result is 1 if either or both bits are 1; with XOR, the result is a 1 if either is a 1 but not both. With multiple bit quantities, the operations are performed on each pair of corresponding bits.

## Random Numbers

A true random number is a value that cannot be predicted or computed in advance. We might get a random number by drawing values from a mixed pool of numbers or by throwing dice. In a computer, pseudorandom numbers are computed by an algorithm that gives results resembling true random numbers and pass one or more tests for randomness. A simple scheme is to multiply a seed number by another (carefully chosen) value and taking several digits from the middle of the product. Often this value is used as the seed for getting the next one.

There are other techniques but the method is less important than the concept.

## Data Structures

While it is not strictly mathematics, we include a brief discussion of data structures of importance in computer graphics. A data structure is a method for storing a set of related values in the computer.

Pascal, the programming language that we use to illustrate the algorithms in the book, permits arrays, records, and linked lists. In an array, a number of variables of the same type are formed into a list. All are referred to by the same identifier, being distinguished by a subscript that shows the order within the list. An array resembles a vector in this respect. The elements of an array may themselves be arrays, so a table of values is possible; a doubly subscripted array resembles a matrix. Arrays can have more than two subscripts.

Records are groupings of items that may be of different types. A typical illustration is to combine Check_number, Date, Payee, Amount, and Transaction_code into a record. Records differ from arrays in that each part of the record (called a field) has a name separate from the name of the record itself. Fixed records permit only fields that are identical in each invocation while variant records allow the fields within the records to vary depending on a field called the tag field.

A sequence of records can be linked together into a linked list. To create such a linked list, a record structure is declared that contains, in addition to the data, a field that is a pointer to another record of the same structure. An example illustrative of the use of a linked list to implement a polygon mesh is:

```
{ Declare the record structure }

type vertex = record
                  x,y,z : real;
                  pvtx : ^vertex { points to another record }
              end;
var
        start, current : ^vertex; { also pointers }
```

We create the first instance of a record of type vertex by the call new(start). By the statement current := start, we also point current to this same record. Another record in the list is created by the call new(current^.pvtx). With this argument in the call, space is allocated for the second record of the list and the pointer within the first record is set to point to the second. Fields within a record that is pointed to by the variable current are referenced by current^.x, current^.y, and so on. Setting current := current^.pvtx points current to the last created record. The variable start still points to the head of the list. We can continue in this way to create as many records as we desire; all are linked together in a chain. Normally new records are created only as they are needed.

Figure A.11 is an illustration of a linked list of records with a structure as declared above. Start points to the beginning and is called a head pointer. The end of the list is indicated by setting its pointer to nil, denoted by 0 in the figure.

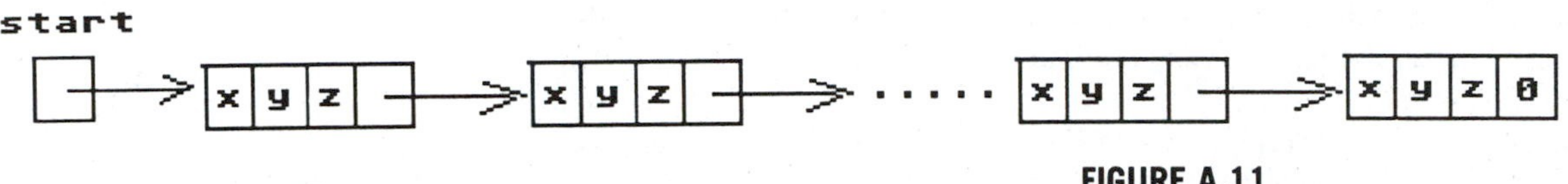


FIGURE A.11

There are many variants of linked lists. A tree structure can be constructed if each record has pointers to more than one other record. A binary tree has two pointers to other records within each record, as shown in Figure A.12.

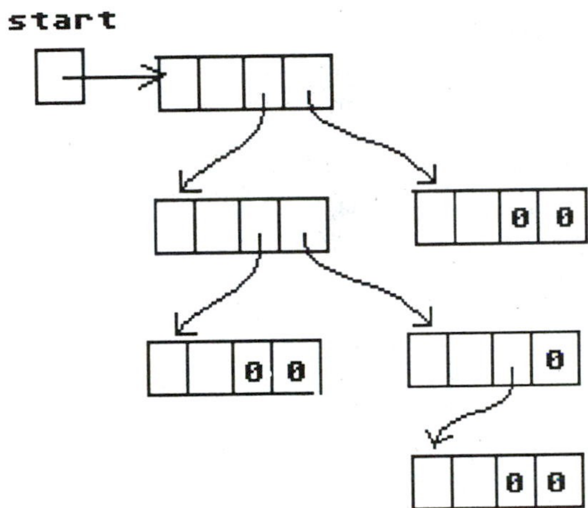


FIGURE A.12

# BIBLIOGRAPHY

ANDE82 Anderson DP: "Hidden Line Elimination in Projecyed Grid Surfaces." MRC Technical Summary report #2447. Madison: Mathematics Research Center, University of Wisconsin, December 1982.

ANDE84 Anderson GH: *Video Editing and Post Production: A Professional Guide.* White Plains, NY: Knowledge Industry Publications, 1984.

BASL88 Barnsley MF, Sloan AD: "A Better Way to Compress Images". *Byte* (January 1988).

BEUR37 Besicovitch AS, Ursell HD: "Sets of Fractional Dimensions (V): On Dimensional Members of Some Continuous Curves." *Journal of the London Mathematical Society* 12 (1937): 18–25.

BLNE76 Blinn JF, Newell ME: "Texture and Reflection in Computer Generated Images." *Communications of the* ACM 19, 10 (1976): 542–547.

BLIN78 Blinn JF: "Simulation of Wrinkled Surfaces." *Computer Graphics* 12, (1978): 286–292.

BRES77 Bresenham JE: "A Linear Algorithm for Incremental Digital Display of Circular Arcs." *Communications of the* ACM 20, 2 (February 1977): 100–106.

BRON74 Brons R: "Linguistic Methods for the Description of a Straight Line on a Grid." *Comp. Graph. Image Processing* 3 (1974): 48–62.

BRON85 Brons R: "Theoretical and Linguistic Methods for Describing Straight Lines." In *Fundamental Algorithms for Computer Graphics*, Nato ASI Series, Vol. F17. New York: Springer Verlag, 1985.

CAD184 CADAM: *The CADAM System Training Handbook and Procedure Guide.* CADAM, 1984.

CAD284 CADAM: *CADAM 3-D Handbook.* CADAM, 1984.

CATM74 Catmull E: "A Subdivision Algorithm for Computer Display of Curved Surfaces." Technical Report. Computer Science Department, University of Utah, December 1974.

CATM75 Catmull E: "Computer Display of Curved Surfaces." In *Computer Graphics Pattern Recognition Data Struct.*, Proc. IEEE Conf. May 1975, p. 11.

CLAR80 Clark JH: "A VLSI Geometry Processor for Graphics." *Computer* 12, 7 (July 1980).

COHE69 Cohen D: "On Linear Difference Curves." *Computer Display Review* Watertown, Mass.: Keydata Corporation, 1969. (This review is now published periodically by GML Associates, 594 Marrett Rd., Lexington, Mass. Articles on graphics techniques are contained in volume 4.)

COMM82 Commodore Business Machines: *Commodore 64 Programmer's Reference Guide.* Commodore Business Machines and Howard W. Sams, 1982.

COTO82 Cook RL, Torrance KE: "A Reflectance Model for Computer Graphics." ACM *Transactions on Graphics* (January 1982): 7–24.

CAPI85 Castle CMA, Pitteway MLV: "An Application of Euclid's Algorithm to Drawing Straight Lines." In *Fundamental Algorithms for Computer Graphics.* Nato ASI Series, Vol. F17. New York: Springer Verlag, 1985.

CLAR80 Clark JH: "A VLSI Geometry Processor for Graphics." *Computer* 12,7 (July 1980).

COXM72 Cox MG: "The numerical evaluation of B-splines." *J. Inst. Maths. Applics.* 10 (1972): 130–149.

CROW87 Crow F: "Displays on Display. The Origins of the Teapot." *IEEE CG&A* (1987): 8.

CUGS83 Curry J, Garnett L, Sullivan D: "On the Iteration of Rational Functions: Computer Experiments with Newton's Method." *Commun. Math. Phys.* 91 (1983): 267–277.

CUSC47 Curry HB, Schoenberg IJ: "On Spline Distributions and their Limits: the Polya Distribution Functions." *Bull. Amer. Math. Soc.* 53, Abstract 380t (1947): 109.

DEBO72 deBoor C: "On Calculating with B-Splines." *J. Approx. Theory* 6 (1972): 50–62.

DEBO78 deBoor C: *A Practical Guide to Splines.* New York: Springer Verlag, 1978.

DOHU82 Douady A, Hubbard JH: "Iteration de Polynomes Quadratic Complexes." *CRAS* (Paris) 294 (1982): 123–126.

EKPF84 Enderle 6, Kansy K, Pfaff G: *Computer Graphics Programming, GKS—the Graphics Standard.* New York: Springer Verlag, 1984.

FATO19 Fatou P: "Sur les Equations Fonctionelles." *Bull. Soc. Math. Fr.* 47 (1919): 161–271; 48; 33–94, 208–314.

FIMO87 Fichter W, Morf M, eds.: *VLSI CAD Tools and Applications.* Kluwer Academic Publishers, 1987.

FOLE84 Foley JD, Van Dam A: *Fundamentals of Interactive Computer Graphics.* Reading, MA: Addison Wesley, 1982.

FREE70 Freeman H: "Boundary Encoding and Processing." In BS Lipkin and A Rosenfeld, eds., *Picture Processing and Psychopictorics.* New York: Academic Press, 1970: 241–266.

GEWH84 Gerald CF, Wheatley PO: *Applied Numerical Analysis.* Reading, MA: Addison Wesley, 1984.

GILO78 Giloi WK: *Interactive Computer Graphics.* Englewood Cliffs, New Jersey: Prentice-Hall, 1978.

GORI74 Gordon WJ, Riesenfeld RF: "B-Spline Curves and Surfaces." In RE Barnhill and RF Riesenfeld, eds., *Computer-Aided Geometric Design.* New York: Academic Press, 1974.

GOUR71 Gouraud H: "Continuous Shading of Curved Surfaces." *IEEE Trans. on Computers* (June 1971): 623–629.

HARR83 Harrington S: *Computer Graphics, A Programming Approach.* New York: McGraw-Hill, New York 1983.

HDGS83 Hopgood FRA, Duce DA, Gallop JR, Sutcliffe DC: *Introduction to the Graphical Kernel System (GKS).* London: Academic Press, 1983.

HEBA86 Hearn D, Baker P: *Computer Graphics.* Englewood Cliffs, New Jersey: Prentice-Hall, 1986.

HORN76 Horn BKP: "Circle Generators for Display Devices." *Computer Graphics and Image Processing* 5 (1976): 280–288.

HUKA84 Hung SHY, Kasvand T: "On the Chord Property and its Equivalences." Proceedings 7th Int. Conf. on Pattern Recognition, Montreal, 1984: 116–119.

IMAC85 *Inside Macintosh, Volume III.* Reading, MA: Addison Wesley, 1985.

JOLH73 Jordan BW, Lennon WJ, Holm BC: "An Improved Algorithm for the Generation of Non-parametric Curves." *IEEE Trans.*, C-22, 12 (December 1973): 1052–1060.

JULI18 Julia G: "Sur l'Iteration de Fonctions Rationnelles." *Journal de Math. Pure et Appl.* 8 (1918): 47–245.

KAPP85 Kappel MR: "An Ellipse-Drawing Algorithm for Raster Displays." In *Fundamental Algorithms for Computer Graphics.* Nato ASI Series, Vol. F17. New York: Springer Verlag, 1985.

KAYD79 Kay DG: "Transparency, Refraction and Ray Tracing for Computer-Synthesized Images." Master's thesis, Cornell University, 1979.

KDGD79 Kay DG, Greenberg D: "Transparency for Computer Synthesized Images." *Computer Graphics* 13 (1979): 158–164.

KUBO85 Kubo S: "Continuous Color Presentation Using a Low-cost Ink Jet Printer." In Kunii TL, ed., *Frontiers in Computer Graphics.* Tokio: Springer-Verlag, 1985: 344–353.

LCWB80 Lane JM, Carpenter LC, Whitted T, Blinn JF: "Scan Line Methods for Displaying Parametrically Defined Surfaces." *Communications of the* ACM 23 (Jan. 1980): 23–34.

LIBA84 Liang YD, Barsky BA: "A New Concept and Method for Line Clipping." ACM *Transactions on Graphics* 3, 1 (Jan. 1984): 1–22.

MAND69 Mandelbrot BB: "Computer Experiments with Fractional Gaussian Noises." *Water Resources Research* 5 (1969): 228.

MAND71 Mandelbrot, BB: "A Fast Fractional Gaussian Noise Generator." *Water Resources Research* 7 (1971): 543–553.

MAND75 Mandelbrot BB: "Stochastic Models for the Earth's Relief, the Shape and the Fractal Dimension of the Coastlines, and the Number-Area Rule for Islands." *Proc. Nat. Acad. Sci. USA* 72 (1975): 3825–3828.

MAND77 Mandelbrot BB: *Fractals: Form, Chance, and Dimension.* San Francisco: W. H. Freeman, 1977.

MAND82 Mandelbrot BB, *The Fractal Geometry of Nature.* New York: W. H. Freeman, 1982.

MARO82 Maron MJ: *Numerical Analysis: A Practical Approach.* New York: Macmillan, 1982.

MUUS87 Muuss MJ: "Understanding the Preparation and Analysis of Solid Models." In Rogers DF and Earnshaw RA, eds., *Techniques for Computer Graphics.* New York: Springer Verlag, 1987.

NESP79 Newman WM, Sproull RF: *Principles of Interactive Computer Graphics.* New York: McGraw-Hill, 1979.

NNSA72 Newell NE, Newell RG, Sancha TL: "A Solution to the Hidden Surface Problem." Proc. ACM Annual Conf. Boston (August 1972): 443–450.

PERI86 Peitgen HO, Richter PH: The beauty of fractals. Springer Verlag, Berlin Heidelberg New York, 1986.

PHON75 Phong Bui-Tuong: "Illumination for Computer Generated Images." *Communications of the* ACM 18, 6 (June, 1975): 311–317.

PITT67 Pitteway MLV: "Algorithm for Drawing Ellipses or Hyperbolae with a Digital Plotter." *Comput. J.* 10, 3 (November 1967): 282–289.

RAST85 Conrac Corporation: *Raster Graphics Handbook.* New York: Van Nostrand Reinhold, 1985.

REEV81 Reeves WT: "In-betweening for Computer Animation Utilizing Moving Point Constraints." Proc. ACM SIGGRAPH (1981): 263–269.

RICH61 Richardson LF: "The Problem of Contiguity: An Appendix of Statistics of Deadly Quarrels." *General Systems Yearbook* 6 (1961): 134–187.

ROGE85 Rogers DF: *Procedural Elements for Computer Graphics.* New York: McGraw-Hill, 1985.

SCHO67 Schoenberg IJ: "On Spline Functions." In Shisha O. ed., *Inequalities.* New York: Academic Press, 1967, pp. 114, 157, 255–291.

SCHO73 Schoeberg IJ: "Cardinal Spline Interpolation," *CBMS* 12, SIAM Philadelphia (1973).

SPSU68 Sproull RF, Sutherland IE: "A Clipping Divider," AFIPS Conf. Proc. 33 (1968): FJCC, p. 765.

SUTH63 Sutherland IE: "Sketchpad: A Man-Machine Graphical Communication System." SJCC 1963. Baltimore, MD: Spartan Books: p. 329

SWBA86 Sweeney AJ, Bartels RH: "Ray Tracing Free-Form B-Spline Surfaces." *IEEE Computer Graphics and Applications,* 6 (Feb 1986): 41–49.

TARA80 Taramon SK, ed., *Meeting Today's Productivity Challenge.* Society of Manufacturing Engineers, 1980.

TEXA86 *TMS34010 User's Guide.* Texas Instruments, 1986.

THAL86 Thalmann D, Magnenat-Thalmann N: *Computer Animation, Theory and Practice.* New York: Springer Verlag, 1986.

VOSS85 Voss RF: "Random Fractal Forgeries." Course notes 15 of the twelfth annual ACM SIGGRAPH conference. San Francisco, 1985.

WARN68 Warnock JE: A Hidden Line Algorithm for Halftone Picture Representation. University of Utah Computer Science Dept. Rep., TR 4–5 (May 1968): NTIS AD 761 995.

WARN69 Warnock JE: A Hidden Surface Algorithm for Computer-Generated Halftone Pictures, University of Utah Computer Science Dept. Rep., TR 4–15 (June 1969): NTIS AD 753 671.

# Index

References to thorough explanations or definitions of a subject (main references) are printed in bold. Simple references and brief explanations are printed in regular type.

Grantham

886-5855